# Precalculus:
# A Problems-Oriented Approach

## CUSTOM EDITION PREPARED EXCLUSIVELY
## FOR UNIVERSITY CALIFORNIA, DAVIS

David Cohen I Theodore B. Lee I David Sklar

CENGAGE
Learning™

Australia • Brazil • Japan • Korea • Mexico • Singapore • Spain • United Kingdom • United States

# CENGAGE
## Learning™

**Precalculus: A Problems-Oriented Approach: Custom Edition Prepared Exclusively for University California, Davis**

David Cohen | Theodore B. Lee | David Sklar

Executive Editor:
Michele Baird

Maureen Staudt

Michael Stranz

Project Development Editor:
Linda de Stefano

Senior Marketing Coordinators:
Sara Mercurio

Lindsay Shapiro

Production/Manufacturing Manager:
Donna M. Brown

PreMedia Services Supervisor:
Rebecca A. Walker

Rights & Permissions Specialist:
Kalina Hintz

Cover Image:
Getty Images*

ISBN-13: 978-0-495-07840-1

ISBN-10: 0-495-07840-9

**Cengage Learning**
5191 Natorp Boulevard
Mason, Ohio 45040
USA

Cengage Learning is a leading provider of customized learning solutions with office locations around the globe, including Singapore, the United Kingdom, Australia, Mexico, Brazil, and Japan. Locate your local office at:
**international.cengage.com/region**

Cengage Learning products are represented in Canada by Nelson Education, Ltd.

For your lifelong learning solutions, visit **custom.cengage.com**

Visit our corporate website at **cengage.com**

Printed in the United States of America

# Custom Table of Contents

To our parents:
Ruth and Ernest Cohen
Lorraine and Robert Lee
Helen and Rubin Sklar

# Tribute to David Cohen

Because he loved the part in "The Myth of Sisyphus," where Camus re-envisions Sisyphus eternally condemned to the task of pushing a giant boulder to the summit of a mountain only to watch it roll back down again—descending the hill and smiling, I like to remember my dad in similar moments of inbetweenness. When the unknown and hope would combine to make anything seem attainable. When becoming conscious of a situation did not necessarily signify limitation by it, but instead, liberation from it.

And so I imagine my dad, after hours of working at the computer, between a thoughtful sip of coffee and suddenly realizing the clearest way to word a problem. After years of early morning commutes to avoid 405 traffic, solitary interludes that began with waking to a still-dark sky and still-dreaming family, and ended with walking, transformed into a professor, into a UCLA lecture hall. After a lifetime of doing his best for those he cared about, intervals of good and poor health simply challenged him to give a little more. My dad endured his task bravely, from his decision 15 years ago to fight leukemia until last May, when the illness reminded us that even fathers and teachers are mortal, regardless of scheduled office hours or books left unwritten.

A couple months ago, my dad told me the five most important things in life to him; teaching and writing these math books were both on that list. I was never a "registered" student of his, but to anyone using this book, especially students, I pass on what I know he would have told me: Your best is always good enough. Enjoy.

*Emily Cohen*

• • •

My dad was gifted at teaching. He had an innate ability to explain things simply and relevantly. He excelled at combining his explanations with a patient ear and his self-defined nerdy sense of humor.

I remember when my dad taught me to read. I had become upset one night while we were out to dinner because I couldn't read the menu. Frustrated, I expressed my dismay from my booster chair. My dad responded with the first of my reading lessons. He began by pointing out something I already knew, the letter "a." He carefully explained that this letter was actually a word . . . every day after that he would write new words on one of his ubiquitous lined yellow notepads and teach them to me. Eventually we began to form simple sentences. He always kept my attention because he made up sentences that made me laugh. The frogs go jog, the cat loves the dog, so on and so forth. My dad's sense of humor was quite captivating.

I was lucky in high school to have someone to assist me with all of my mathematical questions. My math teachers seemed to have a special aptitude for making formulas, theories, and problems both complicated and boring. My dad was good at simplifying these matters for me. He was so good at explaining math to me that I would often remark afterward, with the hindsight of an enlightened one, "Oh, that's all? Why didn't they just say that in the first place?" I took comfort in knowing that math didn't have to be complicated when it was explained well.

Hemingway said that the key to immortality was to write a book. I feel lucky because my dad left behind several. Try reading one—you might find that you actually like it!

*Jennifer Cohen*

•  •  •

I first met Dave Cohen in spring 1981, when I signed up for an algebra course he was teaching as part of my graduate studies at UCLA. I quickly took a liking to his conversational style of teaching and the clear explanations he would use to illustrate an idea. Dave and I began an informal, weekly meeting to discuss solutions to various problems he would pose. Usually he would buy me a cup of coffee and present me with some new trigonometric identity he had discovered, or some archaic conic section property he had come across in an old 1886 algebra book. We would discuss the problem ("Did it have a solution? Was it really an identity? Could we prove it?"), then go about our business.

In summer 1981, I had the opportunity to TA a course called Precalculus, which used Dave's notes (sometimes written by hand), rather than a traditional textbook. I had no idea what the term "precalculus" meant, and soon learned that these notes Dave had prepared were beginning to define, or at the least greatly expand, the subject. It was the beginning of a textbook.

Two years later, after graduating UCLA, I was pleased to receive a copy of *Precalculus,* by David Cohen. Dave had scribbled a note to me saying: "Thanks for the great coffee breaks." I was pleased to see that some of our weekly problems appeared in that book (others showed up years later). More importantly, that book, and every other text Dave has ever written, talked to you. Even now, when I read this book, I can hear Dave talking, and sometimes even listening. Lecturing was never a part of Dave Cohen's vocabulary.

Since that time Dave has written books entitled *College Algebra, Trigonometry,* and *Algebra and Trigonometry.* Most have gone on to multiple editions, including this one. In each edition Dave has sought the better explanation, the "cooler" problem, the more interesting data set. I've had the honor of working with him on all of these books, and we had developed a mathematical friendship. Perhaps some of you reading this have a great study partner; one who intuitively knows what the other is thinking. That was the relationship Dave and I had.

I last saw Dave in November 2001, when we met at UCLA to (naturally) have a cup of coffee and discuss this textbook. He was excited about the quality of problems and interesting data sets he had found to use in this book. He felt this was going to be the best book he had ever written.

In May 2002, just after completing much of this manuscript, Dave Cohen passed away from complications caused by his leukemia. His legacy of fine textbooks (and this is, perhaps, his finest) and great teaching has influenced a generation of students and teachers. Everyone who had contact with Dave feels a bit richer from the experience. His total lack of ego, curiosity about the world, and respect for what others think, made him one of the finest human beings I have ever met.

*Ross Rueger*

# About the Co-Authors

David Sklar was a longtime friend of David Cohen, whom he met while they were both attending graduate school at San Francisco State University. Because of his relationship with the author, he has followed the progress of this book since work started on the first edition. He brings a unique blend of teaching and professional experience to the table, having taught at San Francisco State University, Sonoma State University, Menlo College, and City College of San Francisco. At the same time, David is a researcher and consultant in the field of optics—you'll notice that interest in some of the new group projects in the text. David is an active member of the American Mathematical Society, Mathematical Association of America, is past chairman of the Northern California section of the MAA, and serves on the mathematics department advisory board at San Francisco State University.

David is joined by Theodore Lee, professor of mathematics at City College of San Francisco. Ted is a highly respected teacher who brings nearly 30 years of teaching experience to this project and provides a valuable perspective on teaching precalculus mathematics. On three separate occasions he has been honored with distinguished teaching awards from his colleagues at CCSF. Ted has also been honored by Alpha Sigma Gamma, CCSF's student honor society, as a favorite teacher. A fourth-generation Californian, Ted received his bachelor's degree from the University of California, Berkeley, and his master's degree from the University of California, Los Angeles.

Both David and Ted understand the factors that make the book so special to the people who use it—the clear writing, the conversational style, the variety of problems (including many challenging ones), and the thoughtful use of technology. They have made every effort to maintain the standard and quality of David Cohen's work.

# Fundamentals

Real numbers, equations, graphs—these topics set the stage for our work in precalculus. How much from previous courses should you remember about solving equations? Section 1.3 provides a review of the fundamentals. The rest of the chapter reviews and begins to extend what you've learned in previous courses about graphs and graphing. For example, we use graphs to visualize trends in

- Spending by the television networks to broadcast the Olympic Games (Exercise 21, page 27)
- Internet usage (Exercise 23, pages 27–28)
- Carbon dioxide levels in the atmosphere (Example 5, page 25)
- U.S. population growth (Exercises 7 and 8 on page 53)

## 1.1 SETS OF REAL NUMBERS

Here, as in your previous mathematics courses, most of the numbers we deal with are real numbers. These are the numbers used in everyday life, in the sciences, in industry, and in business. Perhaps the simplest way to define a real number is this: A **real number** is any number that can be expressed in decimal form. Some examples of real numbers are

$$7 \, (= 7.000 \ldots)$$
$$\sqrt{2} \, (= 1.4142 \ldots)$$
$$-2/3 \, (= -0.\overline{6})$$

(Recall that the bar above the 6 in the decimal $-0.\overline{6}$ indicates that the 6 repeats indefinitely.)

Certain sets of real numbers are referred to often enough to be given special names. These are summarized in the box that follows.

As you've seen in previous courses, the real numbers can be represented as points on a *number line,* as shown in Figure 1. As indicated in Figure 1, the point associated with the number zero is referred to as the **origin.**

The fundamental fact here is that there is a **one-to-one correspondence** between the set of real numbers and the set of points on the line. This means that each real number is identified with exactly one point on the line; conversely, with each point on the line we identify exactly one real number. The real number associated with a given point is called the **coordinate** of the point. As a practical matter, we're

*Natural numbers have been used since time immemorial; fractions were employed by the ancient Egyptians as early as 1700 B.C.; and the Pythagoreans, in ancient Greece, about 400 B.C., discovered numbers, like $\sqrt{2}$, which cannot be fractions.* —Stefan Drobot in *Real Numbers* (Englewood Cliffs, N.J.: Prentice-Hall, Inc., 1964)

*What secrets lie hidden in decimals?* —Stephan P. Richards in *A Number for Your Thoughts* (New Providence, N.J.: S. P. Richards, 1982)

**Figure 1**

Origin

$-4 \quad -3 \quad -2 \quad -1 \quad 0 \quad 1 \quad 2 \quad 3 \quad 4$

## PROPERTY SUMMARY    Sets of Real Numbers

| Name | Definition and Comments | Examples |
|---|---|---|
| Natural numbers | These are the ordinary counting numbers: 1, 2, 3, and so on. | 1, 4, 29, 1066 |
| Integers | These are the natural numbers along with their negatives and zero. | $-26, 0, 1, 1776$ |
| Rational numbers | As the name suggests, these are the real numbers that are *ratios* of two integers (with nonzero denominators). It can be proved that a real number is rational if and only if its decimal expansion *terminates* (e.g., 3.15) or *repeats* (e.g., $2.\overline{43}$). | $4 (= \frac{4}{1}), -\frac{2}{3},$ $1.7 (= \frac{17}{10}), 4.\overline{3},$ $4.1\overline{73}$ |
| Irrational numbers | These are the real numbers that are not rational. Section A.3 of the Appendix contains a proof of the fact that the number $\sqrt{2}$ is irrational. The proof that $\pi$ is irrational is more difficult. The first person to prove that $\pi$ is irrational was the Swiss mathematician J. H. Lambert (1728–1777). | $\sqrt{2}, 3 + \sqrt{2},$ $3\sqrt{2}, \pi, 4 + \pi,$ $4\pi$ |

**Figure 2**

usually more interested in relative locations than precise locations on a number line. For instance, since $\pi$ is approximately 3.1, we show $\pi$ slightly to the right of 3 in Figure 2. Similarly, since $\sqrt{2}$ is approximately 1.4, we show $\sqrt{2}$ slightly less than halfway from 1 to 2 in Figure 2.

It is often convenient to use number lines that show reference points other than the integers used in Figure 2. For instance, Figure 3(a) displays a number line with reference points that are multiples of $\pi$. In this case it is the integers that we then locate approximately. For example, in Figure 3(b) we show the approximate location of the number 1 on such a line.

**Figure 3**        (a)                                    (b)

Two of the most basic relations for real numbers are **less than** and **greater than,** symbolized by $<$ and $>$, respectively. For ease of reference, we review these and two related symbols in the box on page 3.

In general, relationships involving real numbers and any of the four symbols $<$, $\leq$, $>$, and $\geq$ are called **inequalities.** One of the simplest uses of inequalities is in defining certain sets of real numbers called *intervals*. Roughly speaking, any uninterrupted portion of the number line is referred to as an **interval.** In the definitions that follow, you'll see notations such as $a < x < b$. This means that *both* of the inequalities $a < x$ and $x < b$ hold; in other words, the number $x$ is between $a$ and $b$.

(a) The open interval $(a, b)$ contains all real numbers from $a$ to $b$, excluding $a$ and $b$.

(b) The closed interval $[a, b]$ contains all real numbers from $a$ to $b$, including $a$ and $b$.

**Figure 4**

---

**DEFINITION**  |  **Open Intervals and Closed Intervals**

---

The **open interval** $(a, b)$ consists of all real numbers $x$ such that $a < x < b$. See Figure 4(a).

The **closed interval** $[a, b]$ consists of all real numbers $x$ such that $a \leq x \leq b$. See Figure 4(b).

---

## PROPERTY SUMMARY   Notation for Less Than and Greater Than

| Notation | Definition | Examples |
|----------|------------|----------|
| $a < b$ | $a$ is less than $b$. On a number line, oriented as in Figure 1, 2, or 3, the point $a$ lies to the left of $b$. | $2 < 3; -4 < 1$ |
| $a \leq b$ | $a$ is less than or equal to $b$. | $2 \leq 3; 3 \leq 3$ |
| $b > a$ | $b$ is greater than $a$. On a number line oriented as in Figure 1, 2, or 3, the point $b$ lies to the right of $a$. ($b > a$ is equivalent to $a < b$.) | $3 > 2; 0 > -1$ |
| $b \geq a$ | $b$ is greater than or equal to $a$. | $3 \geq 2; 3 \geq 3$ |

Note that the brackets in Figure 4(b) are used to indicate that the numbers $a$ and $b$ are included in the interval $[a, b]$, whereas the parentheses in Figure 4(a) indicate that $a$ and $b$ are excluded from the interval $(a, b)$. At times you'll see notation such as $[a, b)$. This stands for the set of all real numbers $x$ such that $a \leq x < b$. Similarly, $(a, b]$ denotes the set of all numbers $x$ such that $a < x \leq b$.

| EXAMPLE | 1 | Understanding interval notation |

Show each interval on a number line, and specify inequalities describing the numbers $x$ in each interval.

$$[-1, 2] \quad (-1, 2) \quad (-1, 2] \quad [-1, 2)$$

**SOLUTION**
See Figure 5.

| $[-1, 2]$ | $(-1, 2)$ | $(-1, 2]$ | $[-1, 2)$ |
| $-1 \leq x \leq 2$ | $-1 < x < 2$ | $-1 < x \leq 2$ | $-1 \leq x < 2$ |

Figure 5

In addition to the four types of intervals shown in Figure 5, we can also consider **unbounded intervals.** These are intervals that extend indefinitely in one direction or the other, as shown, for example, in Figure 6. We also have a convenient notation for unbounded intervals; for example, we indicate the unbounded interval in Figure 6 with the notation $(2, \infty)$.

Figure 6

COMMENT AND CAUTION   The symbol $\infty$ is read *infinity*. It is not a real number, and its use in the context $(2, \infty)$ is only to indicate that the interval has no right-hand boundary. In the box that follows we define the five types of unbounded intervals. Note that the last interval, $(-\infty, \infty)$, is actually the entire real-number line.

## ▌PROPERTY SUMMARY   Unbounded Intervals

For a real number $a$ the notations for unbounded intervals are:

| Notation | Defining Inequality | Example |
|---|---|---|
| $(a, \infty)$ | $x > a$ | $(2, \infty)$ <br> ⟶ at 2 |
| $[a, \infty)$ | $x \geq a$ | $[2, \infty)$ <br> ⟶ at 2 |
| $(-\infty, a)$ | $x < a$ | $(-\infty, 2)$ <br> ⟵ at 2 |
| $(-\infty, a]$ | $x \leq a$ | $(-\infty, 2]$ <br> ⟵ at 2 |
| $(-\infty, \infty)$ |  | $(-\infty, \infty)$ <br> ⟵⟶ at 2 |

## EXAMPLE   2   Understanding notation for unbounded intervals

Indicate each set of real numbers on a number line:
**(a)** $(-\infty, 4]$;       **(b)** $(-3, \infty)$.

**Figure 7**

**SOLUTION**
**(a)** The interval $(-\infty, 4]$ consists of all real numbers that are less than or equal to 4. See Figure 7.
**(b)** The interval $(-3, \infty)$ consists of all real numbers that are greater than $-3$. See Figure 8.

**Figure 8**

We conclude this section by mentioning that our treatment of the real-number system has been rather informal, and we have not derived any of the rules of arithmetic and algebra using the most basic properties of the real numbers. However, we do list those basic properties and derive some of their consequences in Section A.2 of the Appendix.

## ▌EXERCISE SET 1.1

### A

*In Exercises 1–10, determine whether the number is a natural number, an integer, a rational number, or an irrational number. (Some numbers fit in more than one category.) The following facts will be helpful in some cases: Any number of the form $\sqrt{n}$, where n is a natural number that is not a perfect square, is irrational. Also, the sum, difference, product, and quotient of an irrational number and a nonzero rational are all irrational. (For example, the following four numbers are irrational: $\sqrt{6}$, $\sqrt{10} - 2, 3\sqrt{15}, and -5\sqrt{3}/2$.)*

**1. (a)** $-203$
   **(b)** $203/2$

**2. (a)** $27/4$
   **(b)** $\sqrt{27/4}$

**3. (a)** $10^6$
   **(b)** $10^6/10^7$

**4. (a)** $8.7$
   **(b)** $8.\overline{7}$

**5. (a)** $8.74$
   **(b)** $8.\overline{74}$

**6. (a)** $\sqrt{99}$
   **(b)** $\sqrt{99} + 1$

**7.** $3\sqrt{101} + 1$          **8.** $(3 - \sqrt{2}) + (3 + \sqrt{2})$
**9.** $(\sqrt{5} + 1)/4$          **10.** $(0.1234)/(0.5677)$

*In each of Exercises 11–20, draw a number line similar to the one shown in Figure 1. Then indicate the approximate location of the given number. Where necessary, make use of the approximations $\sqrt{2} \approx 1.4$ and $\sqrt{3} \approx 1.7$. (The symbol $\approx$ means is approximately equal to.)*

**11.** $11/4$         **12.** $-7/8$        **13.** $1 + \sqrt{2}$
**14.** $1 - \sqrt{2}$      **15.** $\sqrt{2} - 1$     **16.** $-\sqrt{2} - 1$
**17.** $\sqrt{2} + \sqrt{3}$    **18.** $\sqrt{2} - \sqrt{3}$   **19.** $(1 + \sqrt{2})/2$
**20.** $(2\sqrt{3} + 1)/2$

*In Exercises 21–30, draw a number line similar to the one shown in Figure 3(a). Then indicate the approximate location of the given number.*

**21.** $\pi/2$       **22.** $3\pi/2$       **23.** $\pi/6$       **24.** $7\pi/4$
**25.** $-1$        **26.** $3$          **27.** $\pi/3$       **28.** $3/2$
**29.** $2\pi + 1$                   **30.** $2\pi - 1$

*In Exercises 31–40, say whether the statement is* TRUE *or* FALSE. *(In Exercises 37–40, do not use a calculator or table; use instead the approximations $\sqrt{2} \approx 1.4$ and $\pi \approx 3.1$.)*

**31.** $-5 < -50$     **32.** $0 < -1$       **33.** $-2 \leq -2$
**34.** $\sqrt{7} - 2 \geq 0$   **35.** $\frac{13}{14} > \frac{15}{16}$   **36.** $0.\overline{7} > 0.7$
**37.** $2\pi < 6$      **38.** $2 \leq (\pi + 1)/2$   **39.** $2\sqrt{2} \geq 2$
**40.** $\pi^2 < 12$

*In Exercises 41–54, express each interval using inequality notation and show the given interval on a number line.*

**41.** $(2, 5)$      **42.** $(-2, 2)$      **43.** $[1, 4]$
**44.** $[-\frac{3}{2}, \frac{1}{2}]$    **45.** $[0, 3)$       **46.** $(-4, 0]$
**47.** $(-3, \infty)$    **48.** $(\sqrt{2}, \infty)$    **49.** $[-1, \infty)$
**50.** $[0, \infty)$     **51.** $(-\infty, 1)$    **52.** $(-\infty, -2)$
**53.** $(-\infty, \pi]$    **54.** $(-\infty, \infty)$

## B

**55.** The value of the irrational number $\pi$, correct to ten decimal places (without rounding off), is 3.1415926535. By using a calculator, determine to how many decimal places each of the following quantities agrees with $\pi$.

   **(a)** $(4/3)^4$: This is the value used for $\pi$ in the Rhind papyrus, an ancient Babylonian text written about 1650 B.C.

   **(b)** 22/7: Archimedes (287–212 B.C.) showed that $223/71 < \pi < 22/7$. The use of the approximation 22/7 for $\pi$ was introduced to the Western world through the writings of Boethius (ca. 480–520), a Roman philosopher, mathematician, and statesman. Among all fractions with numerators and denomina-

tors less than 100, the fraction 22/7 is the best approximation to $\pi$.

   **(c)** 355/113: This approximation of $\pi$ was obtained in fifth-century China by Zu Chong-Zhi (430–501) and his son. According to David Wells in *The Penguin Dictionary of Curious and Interesting Numbers* (Harmondsworth, Middlesex, England: Viking Penguin, Ltd., 1986), "This is the best approximation of any fraction below 103993/33102."

   **(d)** $\frac{63}{25}\left(\frac{17 + 15\sqrt{5}}{7 + 15\sqrt{5}}\right)$: This approximation for $\pi$ was obtained by the Indian mathematician Scrinivasa Ramanujan (1887–1920).

*Remark:* A simple approximation that agrees with $\pi$ through the first 14 decimal places is $\frac{355}{113}\left(1 - \frac{0.0003}{3533}\right)$. This approximation was also discovered by Ramanujan. For a fascinating account of the history of $\pi$, see the book by Petr Beckmann, *A History of $\pi$*, 16th ed. (New York: Barnes & Noble Books, 1989), and for a more modern look at $\pi$, see Richard Preston's article, "The Mountains of Pi," in *The New Yorker* (March 2, 1992, pp. 36–67).

## C

*In Exercises 56–58, give an example of irrational numbers a and b such that the indicated expression is* **(a)** *rational and* **(b)** *irrational.*

**56.** $a + b$        **57.** $ab$         **58.** $a/b$

**59. (a)** Give an example in which the result of raising a rational number to a rational power is an irrational number.

   **(b)** Give an example in which the result of raising an irrational number to a rational power is a rational number.

**60.** Can an irrational number raised to an irrational power yield an answer that is rational? This problem shows that the answer is "yes." (However, if you study the following solution very carefully, you'll see that even though we've answered the question in the affirmative, we've not pinpointed the specific case in which an irrational number raised to an irrational power is rational.)

   **(a)** Let $A = (\sqrt{2})^{\sqrt{2}}$. Now, either $A$ is rational or $A$ is irrational. If $A$ is rational, we are done. Why?

   **(b)** If $A$ is irrational, we are done. Why?
   *Hint:* Consider $A^{\sqrt{2}}$.

*Remark:* For more about this problem and related questions, see the article "Irrational Numbers," by J. P. Jones and S. Toporowski in *American Mathematical Monthly*, vol. 80 (1973), pp. 423–424.

# 1.2 ABSOLUTE VALUE

*There has been a real need in analysis for a convenient symbolism for "absolute value" . . . and the two vertical bars introduced in 1841 by Weierstrass, as in $|z|$, have met with wide adoption; . . .*—Florian Cajori in *A History of Mathematical Notations*, vol. 1 (La Salle, Ill.: The Open Court Publishing Co., 1928)

As an aid in measuring distances on the number line, we review the concept of *absolute value*. We begin with a definition of absolute value that is geometric in nature. Then, after you have developed some familiarity with the concept, we explain a more algebraic approach that is often useful in analytical work.

---

**DEFINITION** | Absolute Value (geometric version)

---

The **absolute value** of a real number $x$, denoted by $|x|$, is the distance from $x$ to the origin.

---

For instance, because the numbers 5 and $-5$ are both five units from the origin, we have $|5| = 5$ and $|-5| = 5$. Here are three more examples:

$$|17| = 17 \qquad |-2/3| = 2/3 \qquad |0| = 0$$

---

**EXAMPLE** 1 **Evaluating expressions containing absolute values**

Evaluate each expression:
**(a)** $5 - |6 - 7|$;  **(b)** $||-2| - |-3||$.

**SOLUTION**

**(a)** $5 - |6 - 7| = 5 - |-1|$  **(b)** $||-2| - |-3|| = |2 - 3|$
$\qquad\qquad\qquad = 5 - 1 = 4$  $\qquad\qquad\qquad\qquad = |-1| = 1$

---

As we said at the beginning of this section, there is an equivalent, more algebraic way to define absolute value. According to this equivalent definition, the value of $|x|$ is $x$ itself when $x \geq 0$, and the value of $|x|$ is $-x$ when $x < 0$. We can write this symbolically as follows:

---

**DEFINITION** | Absolute Value (algebraic version)

---

$$|x| = \begin{cases} x & \text{when } x \geq 0 \\ -x & \text{when } x < 0 \end{cases}$$

EXAMPLE
$|-7| = -(-7) = 7$

---

By looking at examples with specific numbers, you should be able to convince yourself that both definitions yield the same result. We use the algebraic definition of absolute value in Examples 2 and 3.

---

**EXAMPLE** 2 **Rewriting expressions to eliminate absolute value**

Rewrite each expression in a form that does not contain absolute values:
**(a)** $|\pi - 4| + 1$;  **(b)** $|x - 5|$, given that $x \geq 5$;  **(c)** $|t - 5|$, given that $t < 5$.

**SOLUTION**

**(a)** The quantity $\pi - 4$ is negative (since $\pi \approx 3.14$), and therefore its absolute value is equal to $-(\pi - 4)$. In view of this, we have

$$|\pi - 4| + 1 = -(\pi - 4) + 1 = -\pi + 5$$

**(b)** Since $x \geq 5$, the quantity $x - 5$ is nonnegative, and therefore its absolute value is equal to $x - 5$ itself. Thus we have

$$|x - 5| = x - 5 \qquad \text{when } x \geq 5$$

**(c)** Since $t < 5$, the quantity $t - 5$ is negative. Therefore its absolute value is equal to $-(t - 5)$, which in turn is equal to $5 - t$. In view of this, we have

$$|t - 5| = 5 - t \qquad \text{when } t < 5$$

**EXAMPLE** **3** **Simplifying an expression containing absolute values**

Simplify the expression $|x - 1| + |x - 2|$, given that $x$ is in the open interval $(1, 2)$.

**SOLUTION**
Since $x$ is greater than 1, the quantity $x - 1$ is positive, and consequently,

$$|x - 1| = x - 1$$

On the other hand, we are also given that $x$ is less than 2. Therefore the quantity $x - 2$ is negative, and we have

$$|x - 2| = -(x - 2) = -x + 2$$

Putting things together now, we can write

$$|x - 1| + |x - 2| = (x - 1) + (-x + 2)$$
$$= -1 + 2 = 1$$

In the box that follows, we list several basic properties of the absolute value. Each of these properties can be derived from the definitions. (With the exception of the *triangle inequality,* we shall omit the derivations. For a proof of the triangle inequality, see Exercise 67.)

**PROPERTY SUMMARY** **Properties of Absolute Value**

1. For all real numbers $x$, we have
   (a) $|x| \geq 0$;
   (b) $x \leq |x|$ and $-x \leq |x|$.
   (c) $|x|^2 = x^2$.

2. For all real numbers $a$ and $b$, we have
   (a) $|ab| = |a||b|$ and $|a/b| = |a|/|b|$ $(b \neq 0)$;
   (b) $|a + b| \leq |a| + |b|$ (the triangle inequality).

| EXAMPLE | 4 | Rewriting an expression to eliminate absolute value |

Write the expression $|-2 - x^2|$ in an equivalent form that does not contain absolute values.

**SOLUTION**
Note that $x^2$ is nonnegative for any real number $x$, so $2 + x^2$ is positive. Then $-2 - x^2 = -(2 + x^2)$ is negative. Thus

$$|-2 - x^2| = -(-2 - x^2) \quad \text{using the algebraic definition of absolute value}$$
$$= 2 + x^2$$

Alternatively,

$$|-2 - x^2| = |-1(2 + x^2)|$$
$$= |-1||2 + x^2| \quad \text{using Property 2(a)}$$
$$= 2 + x^2$$

Distance $= |5 - 7| = |7 - 5| = 2$

3  4  5  6  7  8

**Figure 1**

If we think of the real numbers as points on a number line, the distance between two numbers $a$ and $b$ is given by the absolute value of their difference. For instance, as indicated in Figure 1, the distance between 5 and 7, namely, 2, is given by either $|5 - 7|$ or $|7 - 5|$. For reference, we summarize this simple but important fact as follows.

**PROPERTY SUMMARY** Distance on a Number Line

For real numbers $a$ and $b$, the **distance** between $a$ and $b$ is $|a - b| = |b - a|$.

| EXAMPLE | 5 | Using absolute value to rewrite statements regarding distance |

Rewrite each of the following statements using absolute value notation:
**(a)** The distance between 12 and $-5$ is 17.
**(b)** The distance between $x$ and 2 is 4.
**(c)** The distance between $x$ and 2 is less than 4.
**(d)** The number $t$ is more than five units from the origin.

**SOLUTION**
**(a)** $|12 - (-5)| = 17$ or $|-5 - 12| = 17$
**(b)** $|x - 2| = 4$ or $|2 - x| = 4$
**(c)** $|x - 2| < 4$ or $|2 - x| < 4$
**(d)** $|t| > 5$

| EXAMPLE | 6 | Displaying intervals defined by absolute value inequalities |

In each case, the set of real numbers satisfying the given inequality is one or more intervals on the number line. Show the interval(s) on a number line.
**(a)** $|x| < 2$  **(b)** $|x| > 2$  **(c)** $|x - 3| < 1$  **(d)** $|x - 3| \geq 1$

**Figure 2**
$|x| < 2$

**Figure 3**
$|x| > 2$

**Figure 4**
$|x - 3| < 1$

**Figure 5**
$|x - 3| \geq 1$

**SOLUTION**

**(a)** The given inequality tells us that the distance from $x$ to the origin is less than two units. So, as indicated in Figure 2, the number $x$ must lie in the open interval $(-2, 2)$.

**(b)** The condition $|x| > 2$ means that $x$ is more than two units from the origin. Thus, as indicated in Figure 3, the number $x$ lies either to the right of 2 or to the left of $-2$.

**(c)** The given inequality tells us that $x$ must be less than one unit away from 3 on the number line. Looking one unit to either side of 3, then, we see that $x$ must lie between 2 and 4 and $x$ cannot equal 2 or 4. See Figure 4.

**(d)** The inequality $|x - 3| \geq 1$ says that $x$ is at least one unit away from 3 on the number line. This means that either $x \geq 4$ or $x \leq 2$, as shown in Figure 5. [Here's an alternative way of thinking about this: The numbers satisfying the given inequality are precisely those numbers that do *not* satisfy the inequality in part (c). So for part (d), we need to shade that portion of the number line that was not shaded in part (c).]

# EXERCISE SET 1.2

## A

*In Exercises 1–16, evaluate each expression.*

1. $|3|$
2. $3 + |-3|$
3. $|-6|$
4. $-6 - |-6|$
5. $|-1 + 3|$
6. $|-6 + 3|$
7. $\left|-\frac{4}{5}\right| - \frac{4}{5}$
8. $\left|\frac{4}{5}\right| - \frac{4}{5}$
9. $|-6 + 2| - |4|$
10. $|-3 - 4| - |-4|$
11. $||-8| + |-9||$
12. $||-8| - |-9||$
13. $\left|\frac{27 - 5}{5 - 27}\right|$
14. $\frac{|27 - 5|}{|5 - 27|}$
15. $|7(-8)| - |7| \cdot |-8|$
16. $|(-7)^2| + |-7|^2 - (-|-3|)^3$

*In Exercises 17–24, evaluate each expression, given that $a = -2$, $b = 3$, and $c = -4$.*

17. $|a - b|^2$
18. $a^2 - |bc|$
19. $|c| - |b| - |a|$
20. $|b + c| - |b| - |c|$
21. $|a + b|^2 - |b + c|^2$
22. $\frac{|a| + |b| + |c|}{|a + b + c|}$
23. $\frac{a + b + |a - b|}{2}$
24. $\frac{a + b - |a - b|}{2}$

*In Exercises 25–38, rewrite each expression without using absolute value notation.*

25. $|\sqrt{2} - 1| - 1$
26. $|1 - \sqrt{2}| + 1$
27. $|x - 3|$ given that $x \geq 3$
28. $|x - 3|$ given that $x < 3$
29. $|t^2 + 1|$
30. $|x^4 + 1|$
31. $|-\sqrt{3} - 4|$
32. $|-\sqrt{3} - \sqrt{5}|$
33. $|x - 3| + |x - 4|$ given that $x < 3$

34. $|x - 3| + |x - 4|$ given that $x > 4$
35. $|x - 3| + |x - 4|$ given that $3 < x < 4$
36. $|x - 3| + |x - 4|$ given that $x = 4$
37. $|x + 1| + 4|x + 3|$ given that $-\frac{5}{2} < x < -\frac{3}{2}$
38. $|x + 1| + 4|x + 3|$ given that $x < -3$

*In Exercises 39–48, rewrite each statement using absolute value notation, as in Example 5.*

39. The distance between $x$ and 1 is $1/2$.
40. The distance between $x$ and 1 is less than $1/2$.
41. The distance between $x$ and 1 is at least $1/2$.
42. The distance between $x$ and 1 exceeds $1/2$.
43. The distance between $y$ and $-4$ is less than 1.
44. The distance between $x^3$ and $-1$ is at most 0.001.
45. The number $y$ is less than three units from the origin.
46. The number $y$ is less than one unit from the number $t$.
47. The distance between $x^2$ and $a^2$ is less than $M$.
48. The sum of the distances of $a$ and $b$ from the origin is greater than or equal to the distance of $a + b$ from the origin.

*In Exercises 49–60, the set of real numbers satisfying the given inequality is one or more intervals on the number line. Show the interval(s) on a number line.*

49. $|x| < 4$
50. $|x| < 2$
51. $|x| > 1$
52. $|x| > 0$
53. $|x - 5| < 3$
54. $|x - 4| < 4$
55. $|x - 3| \leq 4$
56. $|x - 1| \leq \frac{1}{2}$
57. $|x + \frac{1}{3}| < \frac{3}{2}$
58. $|x + \frac{\pi}{2}| > 1$
59. $|x - 5| \geq 2$
60. $|x + 5| \geq 2$

## B

**61.** In parts (a) and (b), sketch the interval or intervals corresponding to the given inequality:

(a) $|x - 2| < 1$;

(b) $0 < |x - 2| < 1$.

(c) In what way do your answers in (a) and (b) differ? (The distinction is important in the study of *limits* in calculus.)

**62.** Show that for all real numbers $a$ and $b$, we have

$$|a| - |b| \le |a - b|$$

*Hint*: Beginning with the identity $a = (a - b) + b$, take the absolute value of each side and then use the triangle inequality.

**63.** Show that

$$|a + b + c| \le |a| + |b| + |c|$$

for all real numbers $a$, $b$, and $c$. *Hint*: The left-hand side can be written $|a + (b + c)|$. Now use the triangle inequality.

**64.** Explain why there are no real numbers that satisfy the equation $|x^2 + 4x| = -12$.

## C

**65.** (As background for this exercise, you might want to work Exercise 23.) Prove that

$$\max(a, b) = \frac{a + b + |a - b|}{2}$$

*Hint*: Consider three separate cases: $a = b$; $a > b$; and $b > a$.

**66.** (As background for this exercise, you might want to work Exercise 24.) Prove that

$$\min(a, b) = \frac{a + b - |a - b|}{2}$$

**67.** Complete the following steps to prove the triangle inequality.

(a) Let $a$ and $b$ be real numbers. Which property in the summary box on page 7 tells us that $a \le |a|$ and $b \le |b|$?

(b) Add the two inequalities in part (a) to obtain $a + b \le |a| + |b|$.

(c) In a similar fashion, add the two inequalities $-a \le |a|$ and $-b \le |b|$ and deduce that $-(a + b) \le |a| + |b|$.

(d) Why do the results in parts (b) and (c) imply that $|a + b| \le |a| + |b|$?

# 1.3   SOLVING EQUATIONS (REVIEW AND PREVIEW)

*I learned algebra fortunately by not learning it at school, and knowing that the whole idea was to find out what x was, and it didn't make any difference how you did it.* —Physicist Richard Feynman (1918–1988) in Jagdish Mehra's *The Beat of a Different Drum* (New York: Oxford University Press, 1994)

*The title of al-Khwarizmi's second and most important book,* Hisab al-jabr w'al muqabala [830] . . . *has given us the word* algebra. Al-jabr *means transposing a quantity from one side of an equation to the other, while* muqabala *signifies the simplification of the resulting equation.* —Stuart Hollingdale in *Makers of Mathematics* (Harmondsworth, Middlesex, England: Penguin Books, Ltd., 1989)

*"Algebra is a merry science," Uncle Jakob would say. "We go hunting for a little animal whose name we don't know, so we call it x. When we bag our game we pounce on it and give it its right name."* —Physicist Albert Einstein (1879–1955)

Consider the familiar expression for the area of a circle of radius $r$, namely, $\pi r^2$. Here $\pi$ is a constant; its value never changes throughout the discussion. On the other hand, $r$ is a variable; we can substitute any positive number for $r$ to obtain the area of a particular circle. More generally, by a **constant** we mean either a particular number (such as $\pi$, or $-17$, or $\sqrt{2}$) or a letter with a value that remains fixed (although perhaps unspecified) throughout a given discussion. In contrast, a **variable** is a letter for which we can substitute any number selected from a given set of numbers. The given set of numbers is called the **domain** of the variable.

Some expressions will make sense only for certain values of the variable. For instance, $1/(x - 3)$ will be undefined when $x$ is 3 (for then the denominator is zero). So in this case we would agree that the domain of the variable $x$ consists of all real numbers except $x = 3$. Similarly, throughout this chapter we adopt the following convention.

## The Domain Convention

The domain of a variable in a given expression is the set of all real-number values of the variable for which the expression is defined.

It's customary to use the letters near the end of the alphabet for variables; letters from the beginning of the alphabet are used for constants. For example, in the expression $ax + b$, the letter $x$ is the variable and $a$ and $b$ are constants.

---

**EXAMPLE  1  Specifying variables, constants, and the domain in an expression**

Specify the variable, the constants, and the domain of the variable for each of the following expressions:

**(a)** $3x + 4$;  **(b)** $\dfrac{1}{(t - 1)(t + 3)}$;  **(c)** $ay^2 + by + c$;  **(d)** $4x + 3x^{-1}$.

**SOLUTION**

|  | VARIABLE | CONSTANTS | DOMAIN |
|---|---|---|---|
| **(a)** $3x + 4$ | $x$ | $3, 4$ | The set of all real numbers. |
| **(b)** $\dfrac{1}{(t - 1)(t + 3)}$ | $t$ | $1, -1, 3$ | The set of all real numbers except $t = 1$ and $t = -3$. |
| **(c)** $ay^2 + by + c$ | $y$ | $a, b, c$ | The set of all real numbers. |
| **(d)** $4x + 3x^{-1}$ | $x$ | $4, 3$ | The set of all real numbers except $x = 0$. |

*Note:* The number 2 that appears in part (c) above is an exponent; $y^2$ is shorthand notation for the product $y \times y$. Similarly, in part (d) $x^{-1}$ is shorthand notation for $1/x$.

---

Now let's review the terminology and skills used in solving two basic types of equations: *linear equations* and *quadratic equations*.

---

**DEFINITION  |  Linear Equation in One Variable**

A **linear** or **first-degree equation in one variable** is an equation that can be written in the form

$$ax + b = 0 \qquad \text{with } a \text{ and } b \text{ real numbers and } a \neq 0$$

---

Here are three examples of linear equations in one variable:

$$2x = 10, \qquad 3m + 1 = 2, \qquad \text{and} \qquad \frac{y}{2} = \frac{y}{3} + 1$$

As with any equation involving a variable, each of these equations is neither true nor false *until* we replace the variable with a number. By a **solution** or a **root** of an equation in one variable, we mean a value for the variable that makes the equation a true statement. For example, the value $x = 5$ is a solution of the equation $2x = 10$, since, with $x = 5$, the equation becomes $2(5) = 10$, which is certainly true. We also say in this case that the value $x = 5$ **satisfies** the equation. To check an equation means to verify that the original equation with the solution substituted for the variable is a true statement.

Equations that become true statements for *all* values in the domain of the variable are called **identities.** Two examples of identities are

$$x^2 - 9 = (x - 3)(x + 3) \qquad \text{and} \qquad \frac{4x^2}{x} = 4x$$

The first is true for all real numbers; the second is true for all real numbers except 0. In contrast to this, a **conditional equation** is true only for some (or perhaps none) of the values of the variable. Two examples of conditional equations are $2x = 10$ and $x = x + 1$. The first of these is true only when $x = 5$. The second equation has no solution (because, intuitively at least, no number can be one more than itself).

We say that two equations are **equivalent** when they have exactly the same solutions. In this section, and throughout the text, the basic method for solving an equation in one variable involves writing a sequence of equivalent equations until we finally reach an equivalent equation of the form

$$\text{variable} = \text{a number}$$

which explicitly displays a solution of the original equation. In generating equivalent equations, we rely on the following three principles. (These can be justified by using the properties of real numbers discussed in Appendix A.2.)

---

## Procedures That Yield Equivalent Equations

1. Adding or subtracting the same quantity on both sides of an equation produces an equivalent equation.
2. Multiplying or dividing both sides of an equation by the same nonzero quantity produces an equivalent equation.
3. Simplifying an expression on either side of an equation produces an equivalent equation.

---

The examples that follow show how these principles are applied in solving various equations. *Note:* Beginning in Example 2, we use some basic factoring techniques from elementary or intermediate algebra. If you find that you need a quick reference for factoring formulas, see the inside back cover of this book. For a detailed review (with many examples and practice exercises) see Appendix B.4.

---

| EXAMPLE | 2 | Solving equations equivalent to linear equations |
|---|---|---|

**(a)** Solve: $3[1 - 2(x + 1)] = 2 - x$.

**(b)** Solve: $ax + b = c$; where $a, b,$ and $c$ are constants, $a \neq 0$.

**(c)** Solve: $\dfrac{1}{x + 5} = \dfrac{2}{x - 3} + \dfrac{2x + 2}{x^2 + 2x - 15}$.

**SOLUTION**

**(a)** $3[1 - 2(x + 1)] = 2 - x$

$$3[1 - 2x - 2)] = 2 - x \qquad \text{simplifying the left-hand side}$$
$$3(-1 - 2x) = 2 - x$$
$$-3 - 6x = 2 - x$$
$$-3 - 5x = 2 \qquad \text{adding } x \text{ to both sides}$$
$$-5x = 5 \qquad \text{adding 3 to both sides}$$
$$x = -1 \qquad \text{dividing both sides by } -5$$

CHECK   Replacing $x$ with $-1$ in the original equation yields

$$3[1 - 2(0)] \stackrel{?}{=} 2 - (-1)$$
$$3(1) \stackrel{?}{=} 2 + 1 \qquad \text{True}$$

**(b)** $ax + b = c$

$$ax = c - b \qquad \text{subtracting } b \text{ from both sides}$$
$$x = \frac{c - b}{a} \qquad \text{dividing both sides by } a \text{ (recall that } a \neq 0)$$

CHECK   Replacing $x$ with $\dfrac{c - b}{a}$ in the original equation yields

$$a\left(\frac{c - b}{a}\right) + b \stackrel{?}{=} c$$
$$c - b + b \stackrel{?}{=} c$$
$$c \stackrel{?}{=} c \qquad \text{True}$$

**(c)** A common strategy in solving equations with fractions is to multiply through by the least common denominator. This eliminates the need to work with fractions. By factoring the denominator $x^2 + 2x - 15$, we obtain

$$\frac{1}{x + 5} = \frac{2}{x - 3} + \frac{2x + 2}{(x + 5)(x - 3)}$$

From this we see that the least common denominator for the three fractions is $(x + 5)(x - 3)$. Now, multiplying both sides by this least common denominator, we have

$$\frac{(x + 5)(x - 3)}{x + 5} = \frac{2(x + 5)(x - 3)}{x - 3} + \frac{(2x + 2)(x + 5)(x - 3)}{(x + 5)(x - 3)}$$
$$x - 3 = 2(x + 5) + 2x + 2$$
$$x - 3 = 2x + 10 + 2x + 2 \qquad \text{simplifying}$$
$$x - 3 = 4x + 12 \qquad \text{simplifying}$$
$$-3x - 3 = 12 \qquad \text{subtracting } 4x \text{ from both sides}$$
$$-3x = 15 \qquad \text{adding 3 to both sides}$$
$$x = -5 \qquad \text{dividing both sides by } -3$$

CHECK   The preceding steps show that *if* the equation has a solution, then the solution is $x = -5$. With $x = -5$, however, the left-hand side of the original equation becomes $1/(-5 + 5)$, or $1/0$, which is undefined. We conclude therefore that the given equation has no solution.

In Example 2(c) the value $x = -5$, which does not check in the original equation, is called an **extraneous root** or **extraneous solution.** How is it that an extraneous solution was generated in Example 2(c)? We multiplied both sides by $(x + 5)(x - 3)$. Since we didn't know at that stage whether the quantity $(x + 5)(x - 3)$ was nonzero, we could not be certain that the resulting equation was actually an equivalent equation. [Indeed, as it turns out with $x = -5$, the quantity $(x + 5)(x - 3)$ *is* equal to zero.] For this reason, it is always necessary to check in the original equation any solutions you obtain as a result of multiplying both sides of an equation by an expression involving the variable. We restate this advice in the box that follows.

## PROPERTY SUMMARY    Extraneous Solutions

Multiplying both sides of an equation by an expression involving the variable may introduce extraneous solutions that do not check in the original equation. Therefore, it is always necessary to check any candidates for solutions that you obtain in this manner.

---

**EXAMPLE** 3 | Solving equations where the unknown is the denominator

Solve the given equation for $x$:

$$y = \frac{ax + b}{cx + d} \qquad \text{where } cx + d \neq 0, \; yc - a \neq 0$$

**SOLUTION**
Multiplying both sides of the given equation by the nonzero quantity $cx + d$ yields

$$\begin{aligned}
y(cx + d) &= ax + b \\
ycx + yd &= ax + b && \text{simplifying} \\
ycx - ax &= b - yd && \text{gathering terms involving } x \\
x(yc - a) &= b - yd && \text{factoring} \\
x &= \frac{b - yd}{yc - a} && \text{dividing both sides by } yc - a \neq 0
\end{aligned}$$

You should check for yourself that the expression for $x$ on the right-hand side of this last equation indeed satisfies the original equation.

---

In the example just concluded, we used a basic factoring technique from elementary algebra to solve the equations. Factoring is also useful in solving *quadratic equations.*

---

**DEFINITION** | Quadratic Equation

A **quadratic equation** is an equation in one variable that can be written in the form

$$ax^2 + bx + c = 0 \qquad \text{with } a, b, \text{ and } c \text{ real numbers and } a \neq 0$$

To solve a quadratic equation by factoring, we rely on the following familiar and important property of the real-number system.

## PROPERTY SUMMARY
### Zero-Product Property of Real Numbers

$$pq = 0 \quad \text{if and only if} \quad p = 0 \text{ or } q = 0 \quad \text{(or both)}$$

| **EXAMPLE** | **4** | **Applying the zero-product property to solve quadratic equations** |
|---|---|---|

Solve:

**(a)** $8x^2 - 3 = 10x$;      **(b)** $4x^2 - 9 = 0$.

**SOLUTION**

**(a)** In preparation for using the zero-product property, we first rewrite the equation so the right-hand side is zero. Then we have

$$8x^2 - 10x - 3 = 0$$
$$(2x - 3)(4x + 1) = 0 \qquad \text{Check the factoring.}$$

$$\begin{array}{c|c} 2x - 3 = 0 & 4x + 1 = 0 \\ x = \dfrac{3}{2} & x = -\dfrac{1}{4} \end{array}$$

You can check that the values $x = 3/2$ and $x = -1/4$ both satisfy the given equation.

**(b)** Using difference-of-squares factoring, we have

$$(2x - 3)(2x + 3) = 0$$

$$\begin{array}{c|c} 2x - 3 = 0 & 2x + 3 = 0 \\ x = \dfrac{3}{2} & x = -\dfrac{3}{2} \end{array}$$

You can check that the values $x = 3/2$ and $x = -3/2$ both satisfy the given equation.

Here's another perspective on Example 4(b). Instead of using factoring to solve the equation $4x^2 - 9 = 0$, we can instead rewrite it as $x^2 = 9/4$. Taking the principal square root of both sides then yields

$$\sqrt{x^2} = \sqrt{9/4}$$

and therefore

$$|x| = \frac{3}{2} \quad \text{(Why?)}$$

By looking at this last equation, we can see that there are two solutions, $x = 3/2$ and $x = -3/2$. (Those are the only two numbers with absolute values of $3/2$.) We abbreviate these two solutions by writing $x = \pm 3/2$. In practice, we usually omit showing the step involving the absolute value. For example, to solve the equation $9x^2 - 2 = 0$, just rewrite it as $x^2 = 2/9$. Then "taking square roots" immediately yields the two solutions $x = \pm\sqrt{2/9} = \pm\sqrt{2}/3$.

Not all quadratic equations can be solved by factoring. Consider, for example, the equation $x^2 - 2x - 4 = 0$. The only three possible factorizations with integer coefficients are

$$(x - 4)(x + 1) \qquad (x + 4)(x - 1) \qquad (x - 2)(x + 2)$$

but none yields the appropriate middle term, $-2x$, when multiplied out. In cases such as these, we can use the *quadratic formula,* given in the box that follows. (In Section 2.1, we'll derive this formula and look at some of its implications. For now, though, the focus is simply on using this formula to calculate solutions.)

### The Quadratic Formula

The solutions of the quadratic equation $ax^2 + bx + c = 0$, where $a \neq 0$, are given by

$$x = \frac{-b \pm \sqrt{b^2 - 4ac}}{2a}$$

  **EXAMPLE 5** | Using the quadratic formula to solve a quadratic equation

Use the quadratic formula to solve the equation $2x^2 = 3 - 4x$.

**SOLUTION**
We first rewrite the given equation as $2x^2 + 4x - 3 = 0$, so that it has the form $ax^2 + bx + c = 0$. By comparing these last two equations, we see that $a = 2$, $b = 4$, and $c = -3$. Therefore

$$x = \frac{-b \pm \sqrt{b^2 - 4ac}}{2a} = \frac{-4 \pm \sqrt{4^2 - 4(2)(-3)}}{2(2)}$$

$$= \frac{-4 \pm \sqrt{40}}{4} = \frac{-4 \pm 2\sqrt{10}}{4} = \frac{-2 \pm \sqrt{10}}{2}$$

Thus, the two solutions are $\dfrac{-2 + \sqrt{10}}{2}$ and $\dfrac{-2 - \sqrt{10}}{2}$.

The techniques that we've reviewed in this section for solving linear and quadratic equations will be used throughout this book; you'll see applications in analyzing graphs and functions and in solving many types of applied problems. Linear and quadratic equations both fall under the general heading of *polynomial equations.*

### DEFINITION | Polynomial Equation

A **polynomial equation** in one variable is an equation of the form

$$a_n x^n + a_{n-1} x^{n-1} + \cdots + a_1 x + a_0 = 0$$

where the subscripted letter $a$'s represent constants and the exponents on the variable are nonnegative integers.

**EXAMPLES**

(a) $4x^2 - 5x - 1 = 0$

(b) $x^3 - 2x^2 - 3x = 0$

(c) $2x^4 - \frac{4}{3}x^3 + x^2 - 3x + \sqrt{2} = 0$

If $a_n$ is not zero, the **degree** of the polynomial equation is the largest exponent of the variable that appears in the equation. For example, the degrees of equations (a), (b), and (c) in the box above are 2, 3, and 4, respectively.

As we've seen in this section, polynomial equations of degree 1 (linear equations) and polynomial equations of degree 2 (quadratic equations) can be solved by using fairly basic algebra. So too can some higher-degree equations. For instance, we can use factoring and the zero-product property to solve equation (b) in the box above. We have

$$x^3 - 2x^2 - 3x = 0$$
$$x(x^2 - 2x - 3) = 0 \qquad \text{factoring out the common factor } x$$
$$x(x - 3)(x + 1) = 0 \qquad \text{factoring the quadratic}$$

Therefore

$$x = 0 \quad \text{or} \quad x - 3 = 0 \quad \text{or} \quad x + 1 = 0 \qquad \text{using the zero-product property}$$

From these last three equations we conclude that the solutions of the third-degree polynomial equation $x^3 - 2x^2 - 3x = 0$ are $x = 0, 3,$ and $-1$. (You should check for yourself that each of these numbers indeed satisfies the equation.)

Unfortunately, not all polynomial equations are as easy to solve as this last one.

Chapter 12 contains a more complete discussion of polynomial equations and an answer to the following question: Is there a general formula, similar to the quadratic formula, for solving *any* polynomial equation?

# EXERCISE SET 1.3

## A

*In Exercises 1–5, determine whether the given value is a solution of the equation.*

**1.** $4x - 5 = -13; x = -2$ 

**2.** $\dfrac{1}{x} = \dfrac{3}{x} - 1; x = 2$

**3.** $\dfrac{2}{y - 1} - \dfrac{3}{y} = \dfrac{7}{y^2 - y}; y = -3$

**4.** $(y - 1)(y + 5) = 0; y = 5$

**5.** $m^2 + m - \frac{5}{16} = 0; m = \frac{1}{4}$

**6.** Verify that the numbers $1 + \sqrt{5}$ and $1 - \sqrt{5}$ both satisfy the equation $x^2 - 2x - 4 = 0$.

*Solve each equation in Exercises 7–19.*

**7.** $2x - 3 = -5$

**8.** $2m - 1 + 3m + 5 = 6m - 8$

**9.** $1 - (2m + 5) = -3m$

**10.** $(x + 2)(x + 1) = x^2 + 11$

**11.** $t - \{4 - [t - (4 + t)]\} = 6$

**12.** $\dfrac{x}{3} + \dfrac{2x}{5} = \dfrac{-11}{5}$

**13.** $1 - \dfrac{y}{3} = 6$

**14.** $\dfrac{x - 1}{4} + \dfrac{2x + 3}{-1} = 0$

**15.** $\dfrac{1}{x} = \dfrac{4}{x} - 1$

**16.** $\dfrac{1}{y} + 1 = \dfrac{3}{y} - \dfrac{1}{2y}$

**17.** $\dfrac{1}{x - 3} - \dfrac{2}{x + 3} = \dfrac{1}{x^2 - 9}$

**18.** $\dfrac{1}{x - 5} + \dfrac{1}{x + 5} = \dfrac{2x + 1}{x^2 - 25}$

**19.** $\dfrac{4}{x + 2} + \dfrac{1}{x - 2} = \dfrac{4}{x^2 - 4}$

**20.** $\dfrac{3}{2x + 1} - \dfrac{4}{x + 1} = \dfrac{2}{2x^2 + 3x + 1}$

**21.** $\dfrac{5}{x - 4} - \dfrac{3}{2x^2 - 5x - 12} = \dfrac{1}{2x + 3}$

**22. (a)** $\dfrac{2}{3x} = \dfrac{3}{x}$

**(b)** $\dfrac{2}{3x} = \dfrac{3}{x + 1}$

**(c)** $\dfrac{2}{3x} = \dfrac{3}{x} + 1$

**23. (a)** $\dfrac{3}{x - 2} = \dfrac{5}{9x}$

**(b)** $\dfrac{3}{x - 2} = \dfrac{5}{9x - 2}$

**(c)** $\dfrac{3}{x - 2} = \dfrac{5}{\frac{5}{3}x - 2}$

*In Exercises 24–33, solve each equation by factoring.*

**24.** $x^2 - 5x - 6 = 0$

**25.** $x^2 - 5x = -6$

**26.** $10z^2 - 13z - 3 = 0$

**27.** $3t^2 - t - 4 = 0$

**28.** $(x + 1)^2 - 4 = 0$

**29.** $x^2 + 3x - 40 = 0$

**30.** $x(2x - 13) = -6$

**31.** $x(3x - 23) = 8$

**32.** $x(x + 1) = 156$

**33.** $x^2 + (2\sqrt{5})x + 5 = 0$

*In Exercises 34–41, use the quadratic formula to solve each equation. In Exercises 34–39, give two forms for each solution: an expression containing a radical and a calculator approximation rounded off to two decimal places.*

**34.** $2x^2 + 3x - 4 = 0$

**35.** $4x^2 - 3x - 9 = 0$

**36.** $x(x + 6) = -2$

**37.** $x(3x + 8) = -2$

**38.** $2x^2 - 10 = -\sqrt{2}x$

**39.** $\sqrt{3}x^2 + \sqrt{3} = 6x$

**40.** $12x^2 - 25x = -12$

**41.** $24x^2 + 23x = -5$

*In Exercises 42–47, solve the equations using any method you choose.*

**42.** $x^2 = 24$

**43.** $2y^2 - 50 = 0$

**44.** $\frac{1}{8} - t^2 = 0$

**45.** $x^2 - \sqrt{5} = 0$

**46. (a)** $u(u + 18) = -81$

**(b)** $u(u + 18) = 81$

**47. (a)** $x^2 + 156x + 5963 = 0$

**(b)** $144y^2 - 54y = 13$

**48.** Solve each of the following equations for $x$.   *Hint*: As in the text, begin by factoring out a common factor.

**(a)** $x^3 - 13x^2 + 42x = 0$

**(b)** $x^3 - 6x^2 + x = 0$

*For Exercises 49–58, solve each equation for x in terms of the other letters.*

**49.** $3ax - 2b = b + 3$

**50.** $ax + b = bx - a$

**51.** $ax + b = bx + a$

**52.** $\frac{x}{a} + \frac{x}{b} = 1$

**53.** $\frac{1}{x} = a + b$

**54.** $\frac{1}{ax} = \frac{1}{bx} - \frac{1}{c}$

**55.** $\frac{1}{a} - \frac{1}{x} = \frac{1}{x} - \frac{1}{b}$

**56. (a)** $y = mx + b$, where $m \neq 0$

**(b)** $y - y_1 = m(x - x_1)$, where $m \neq 0$

**(c)** $\frac{x}{a} + \frac{y}{b} = 1$

**(d)** $Ax + By + C = 0$, where $A \neq 0$

**57.** $(ax + b)^2 - (bx + a)^2 = 0$, where $a \neq \pm b$

**58.** $(x - p)^2 + (x - q)^2 = p^2 + q^2$

## B

*In Exercises 59–64, solve each equation for x in terms of the other letters.*

**59.** $a^2(a - x) = b^2(b + x) - 2abx$, where $a \neq b$

**60.** $\frac{b}{ax - 1} - \frac{a}{bx - 1} = 0$, where $a \neq b$

**61.** $\frac{a - x}{a - b} - 2 = \frac{c - x}{b - c}$

**62.** $\frac{x + 2p}{2q - x} + \frac{x - 2p}{2q + x} - \frac{4pq}{4q^2 - x^2} = 0$

**63.** $\frac{x - a}{x - b} = \frac{b - x}{a - x}$, where $a \neq b$

**64.** $1 - \frac{a}{b}\left(1 - \frac{a}{x}\right) - \frac{b}{a}\left(1 - \frac{b}{x}\right) = 0$

*In Exercises 65–68, solve each equation for the indicated variable.*

**65.** $S = 2\pi r^2 + 2\pi rh$; for $h$

**66.** $\frac{x_1 x}{a^2} + \frac{y_1 y}{b^2} = 1$; for $y$

**67.** $d = \frac{r}{1 + rt}$; for $r$

**68.** $S = \frac{rl - a}{r - 1}$; for $r$

*Solve the equations in Exercises 69–74. (In these exercises, you'll need to multiply both sides of the equations by expressions involving the variable. Remember to check your answers in these cases.)*

**69.** $\frac{3}{x + 5} + \frac{4}{x} = 2$

**70.** $\frac{5}{x + 2} - \frac{2x - 1}{5} = 0$

**71.** $1 - x - \frac{2}{6x + 1} = 0$

**72.** $\frac{x^2 - 3x}{x + 1} = \frac{4}{x + 1}$

**73.** $\frac{x}{x - 2} + \frac{x}{x + 2} = \frac{8}{x^2 - 4}$

**74.** $\frac{2x}{x^2 - 1} - \frac{1}{x + 3} = 0$

**75.** Given the equation $\frac{1}{x} = \frac{1}{a} + \frac{1}{b}$:

**(a)** Solve to show $x = \frac{ab}{a + b}$, provided $a + b \neq 0$.

**(b)** Check the solution.

**Figure 1**

---

## ▍1.4   RECTANGULAR COORDINATES. VISUALIZING DATA

*The name coordinate does not appear in the work of Descartes. This term is due to Leibniz and so are* abscissa *and* ordinate *(1692).* —David M. Burton in *The History of Mathematics: An Introduction,* 2nd ed. (Dubuque, Iowa: Wm. C. Brown Publishers, 1991)

In previous courses you learned to work with a rectangular coordinate system such as that shown in Figure 1. In this section we review some of the most basic formulas and techniques that are useful here.

The point of intersection of the two perpendicular number lines, or **axes**, is called the **origin** and is denoted by the letter $O$. The horizontal and vertical axes are often labeled the **x-axis** and the **y-axis**, respectively, but any other variables will

(a)  A graph of the formula $s = 16t^2$ in a $t$-$s$ coordinate system. [The formula relates the distance $s$ (in feet) and the time $t$ (in seconds) for an object falling in a vacuum.]

(b)  A graph of the equation $F = \frac{9}{5}C + 32$ in a $C$-$F$ coordinate system. (The equation gives the relationship between the temperature $C$ on the Celsius scale and $F$ on the Fahrenheit scale.)

**Figure 2**

do just as well for labeling the axes. See Figure 2 for examples of this. (We'll discuss curves or graphs like the ones in Figure 2 in later sections.)

Note that in Figures 1 and 2 the axes divide the plane into four regions, or **quadrants,** labeled I through IV, as shown in Figure 1. Unless indicated otherwise, we assume that the same unit of length is used on both axes. In Figure 1, the same scales are used on both axes; not so in Figure 2.

Now look at the point $P$ in Figure 3(a). Starting from the origin $O$, one way to reach $P$ is to move three units in the positive $x$-direction and then two units in the positive $y$-direction. That is, the location of $P$ relative to the origin and the axes is "right 3, up 2." We say that the **coordinates** of $P$ are $(3, 2)$. The first number within the parentheses conveys the information "right 3," and the second number conveys the information "up 2." We say that the **$x$-coordinate** of $P$ is 3 and the **$y$-coordinate** of $P$ is 2. Likewise, the coordinates of point $Q$ in Figure 3(a) are $(-2, 4)$. With this coordinate notation in mind, observe in Figure 3(b) that $(3, 2)$ and $(2, 3)$ represent different points; that is, the order in which the two numbers appear within the parentheses affects the location of the point. Figure 3(c) displays various points with given coordinates; you should check for yourself that the coordinates correspond correctly to the location of each point.

Some terminology and notation: The $x$-$y$ coordinate system that we have described is often called a **Cartesian coordinate system.** The term *Cartesian* is used in honor of René Descartes, the seventeenth-century French philosopher and mathematician. The coordinates $(x, y)$ of a point $P$ are referred to as an **ordered pair.**

(a)

(b)

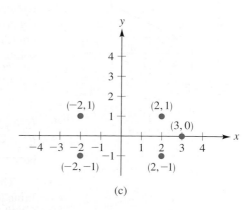

(c)

**Figure 3**

Recall, for example, that $(3, 2)$ and $(2, 3)$ represent different points; that is, the order of the numbers matters. The $x$-coordinate of a point is sometimes referred to as the **abscissa** of the point; the $y$-coordinate is the **ordinate**. The notation $P(x, y)$ means that $P$ is a point that has coordinates $(x, y)$. At times, we abbreviate the phrase *the point whose coordinates are* $(x, y)$ to simply *the point* $(x, y)$.

The next part of our work in this section depends on a key result from elementary geometry, the Pythagorean theorem. For reference, we state this theorem and its converse in the box that follows. (For proofs of the Pythagorean theorem, see Exercises 32 and 33 at the end of this section or Exercise 100 in the Chapter Review Exercises.)

### The Pythagorean Theorem and Its Converse

1. Pythagorean Theorem
   (See Figure 4.) In a right triangle the lengths of the sides are related by the equation

   $$a^2 + b^2 = c^2$$

   where $a$ and $b$ are the lengths of the sides forming the right angle and $c$ is the length of the hypotenuse (the side opposite the right angle).
2. Converse
   If the lengths $a$, $b$, and $c$ of the sides of a triangle are related by an equation of the form $a^2 + b^2 = c^2$, then the triangle is a right triangle, and $c$ is the length of the hypotenuse.

**Figure 4**

### EXAMPLE    1    Using the Pythagorean theorem to find a distance

Use the Pythagorean theorem to calculate the distance $d$ between the points $(2, 1)$ and $(6, 3)$.

### SOLUTION
We plot the two given points and draw a line connecting them, as shown in Figure 5. Then we draw the broken lines as shown, parallel to the axes, and apply the Pythagorean theorem to the right triangle that is formed. The base of the triangle is four units long. You can see this by simply counting spaces or by using absolute value, as discussed in Section 1.2: $|6 - 2| = 4$. The height of the triangle is found to be two units, either by counting spaces or by computing the absolute value: $|3 - 1| = 2$. Thus we have

$$d^2 = 4^2 + 2^2 = 20$$
$$d = \sqrt{20} = \sqrt{4}\sqrt{5} = 2\sqrt{5}$$

*Note*: Since $d$ is a distance, we disregard the solution $-\sqrt{20}$ of the equation $d^2 = 20$.

**Figure 5**

The method we used in Example 1 can be applied to derive a general formula for the distance $d$ between any two points $(x_1, y_1)$ and $(x_2, y_2)$ (see Figure 6).

**Figure 6**

Just as before, we draw in the right triangle and apply the Pythagorean theorem. We have

$$d^2 = |x_2 - x_1|^2 + |y_2 - y_1|^2$$
$$= (x_2 - x_1)^2 + (y_2 - y_1)^2 \quad \text{(Why?)}$$

and therefore

$$d = \sqrt{(x_2 - x_1)^2 + (y_2 - y_1)^2}$$

This last equation is referred to as the **distance formula.** For reference, we restate it in the box that follows.

---

**The Distance Formula**

The distance $d$ between the points $(x_1, y_1)$ and $(x_2, y_2)$ is given by

$$d = \sqrt{(x_2 - x_1)^2 + (y_2 - y_1)^2}$$

---

Examples 2–4 demonstrate some simple calculations involving the distance formula.

NOTE   In computing the distance between two given points, it does not matter which one you treat as $(x_1, y_1)$ and which as $(x_2, y_2)$, because quantities such as $x_2 - x_1$ and $x_1 - x_2$ are negatives of each other and so have equal squares.

**EXAMPLE** **2**   **Using the distance formula**

Calculate the distance between the points $(2, -6)$ and $(5, 3)$.

**SOLUTION**
Substituting $(2, -6)$ for $(x_1, y_1)$ and $(5, 3)$ for $(x_2, y_2)$ in the distance formula, we have

$$d = \sqrt{(5 - 2)^2 + [3 - (-6)]^2}$$
$$= \sqrt{3^2 + 9^2} = \sqrt{90}$$
$$= \sqrt{9}\sqrt{10} = 3\sqrt{10}$$

You should check for yourself that the same answer is obtained using $(2, -6)$ as $(x_2, y_2)$ and $(5, 3)$ as $(x_1, y_1)$. ∎

**EXAMPLE** **3**   **Using the distance formula and the converse of the Pythagorean theorem**

Is the triangle with vertices $D(-2, -1)$, $E(4, 1)$, and $F(3, 4)$ a right triangle?

**SOLUTION**
First we sketch the triangle in question (see Figure 7). From the sketch it appears that angle $E$ could be a right angle, but certainly this is not a proof. We

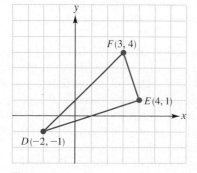

**Figure 7**

need to use the distance formula to calculate the lengths of the three sides and then check whether any relation of the form $a^2 + b^2 = c^2$ holds. The calculations are as follows:

$$DE = \sqrt{[4 - (-2)]^2 + [1 - (-1)]^2} = \sqrt{36 + 4} = \sqrt{40}$$
$$EF = \sqrt{(4 - 3)^2 + (1 - 4)^2} = \sqrt{1 + 9} = \sqrt{10}$$
$$DF = \sqrt{[3 - (-2)]^2 + [4 - (-1)]^2} = \sqrt{25 + 25} = \sqrt{50}$$

Because $(\sqrt{40})^2 + (\sqrt{10})^2 = (\sqrt{50})^2$, $D$, $E$, and $F$ are vertices of a right triangle with hypotenuse $\overline{DF}$ and right angle at vertex $E$, and so $\triangle DEF$ is a right triangle. (In Section 1.6 you'll see that this result can be obtained more easily by using the concept of slope.)

## EXAMPLE 4 Using the distance formula to find a radius

(a) Find the radius $r$ of the circle in Figure 8. (Assume that the center of the circle is located at the origin.)

(b) Compute the area and the circumference of the circle. For each answer, give exact expressions and also calculator approximations rounded to one decimal place.

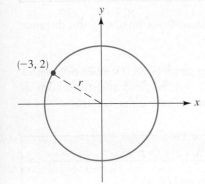

Figure 8

### SOLUTION

(a) The radius $r$ is the distance from center $(0, 0)$ to the given point $(-3, 2)$ on the circle. Using the distance formula, we have

$$r = \sqrt{(-3 - 0)^2 + (2 - 0)^2}$$
$$= \sqrt{9 + 4} = \sqrt{13} \text{ units}$$

(b) Recall the formulas for the area $A$ and the circumference $C$ of a circle of radius $r$: $A = \pi r^2$ and $C = 2\pi r$. Using the value for $r$ from part (a), we have

$$A = \pi r^2 = \pi(\sqrt{13})^2 \qquad\qquad C = 2\pi r = 2\pi\sqrt{13} \text{ units}$$
$$= 13\pi \text{ square units} \qquad\qquad\qquad \approx 22.7 \text{ units}$$
$$\approx 40.8 \text{ square units}$$

One of the important applications of rectangular coordinates is in displaying quantitative data. You see instances of this every day in newspapers, in magazines, and in textbooks as diverse as astronomy to zoology. We show some examples in the figures and discussion that follow.

Table 1 provides world population data for the period 1965–1995. In Figure 9(a) the familiar *bar graph* (or *column chart*) format is used to display the data from the table. In Figure 9(b) we've plotted the data in a rectangular coordinate system. On the horizontal axis the variable $t$ represents years; the variable $P$ represents population in units of one billion. The data in the first row of the table (which state that the population in 1965 was 3.345 billion) are plotted in Figure 9(b) as the point $(1965, 3.345)$. Likewise, the second row of data in the table gives us the point $(1975, 4.086)$, and so on. Sometimes it is more convenient to work with smaller numbers on the horizontal axis than those used in Figure 9(b). One very common way to do this is indicated in Figure 9(c), where we are now letting the variable $t$

**TABLE 1   World Population 1965–1995**

| Year | Population (billions) |
|------|----------------------|
| 1965 | 3.345 |
| 1975 | 4.086 |
| 1985 | 4.850 |
| 1995 | 5.687 |

Source: U.S. Census Bureau (International Data Base)

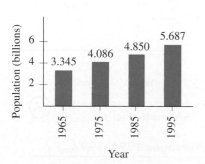

(a)  Bar graph or column chart

(b)  Rectangular coordinates with the variable $t$ representing the year

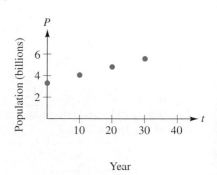

(c)  Rectangular coordinates with the variable $t$ representing the number of years since 1965

**Figure 9**
World population 1965–1995

represent *years since 1965*. In other words, the year 1965 is $t = 0$, 1966 is $t = 1$, 1967 is $t = 2$, and so on. The data in the first row of Table 1 are then plotted in Figure 9(c) as the point $(0, 3.345)$, rather than $(1965, 3.345)$. Likewise, the second row of data in Table 1 is plotted in Figure 9(c) as $(10, 4.086)$, and so on.

Both the bar graph and the rectangular plots in Figure 9 make it immediately clear that the world population is increasing. Is it increasing at a steady rate? Is it increasing rapidly? In fact, one needs to exercise caution in using graphs to draw conclusions about *how fast* the quantity being graphed (in this case, population) is increasing or decreasing. For instance, Figure 10 shows another graph of world population, this time covering the period 1800–1995. Figure 9(b) and Figure 10 may lead to different interpretations about the nature of world population growth. [In Figure 10, the four blue dots are the data points that appear in Figure 9(b).]

As another example about the need for caution in interpreting graphs, look at Figure 11, which shows two very different interpretations of the data for SAT

**Figure 10**
World population 1800–1995
Source: U.S. Census Bureau

**Figure 11**
Two visualizations and interpretations of the data in Table 2

(a) SAT math scores climbing! 😊

(b) Little improvement shown in SAT math scores! 😞

**TABLE 2 SAT Math Scores: National Averages 1994–1997**

| Year | SAT math score |
|------|----------------|
| 0 (1994) | 504 |
| 1 (1995) | 506 |
| 2 (1996) | 508 |
| 3 (1997) | 511 |

Source: The College Board

mathematics scores in Table 2. The bottom line is that graphs are useful, even indispensable, in giving us an easy way to see general trends in data, but we must exercise care in drawing further conclusions, especially regarding rates of increase or decrease. A complete analysis of how fast a quantity is increasing or decreasing may require topics from calculus or the field of statistics. For straight-line graphs, however, the concept of *slope* (reviewed in Section 1.6) tells us definitively about rates of increase or decrease. Also, when we study functions in Chapter 3, we'll make a first step toward answering general questions about rates of change.

In Example 5 we make use of a simple result that you may recall from previous courses: the *midpoint formula*. This result is summarized in the box that follows. (For a proof of the formula, see Exercise 31 at the end of this section.)

**THE MIDPOINT FORMULA**

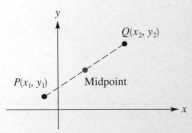

The midpoint of the line segment joining the points $P(x_1, y_1)$ and $Q(x_2, y_2)$ is

$$\left( \frac{x_1 + x_2}{2}, \frac{y_1 + y_2}{2} \right)$$

**Example**

The midpoint of the line segment joining $(2, -15)$ and $(4, 5)$ is

$$\left( \frac{2 + 4}{2}, \frac{-15 + 5}{2} \right) = (3, -5)$$

| EXAMPLE | 5 | An application of the midpoint formula |
|---|---|---|

Data concerning the amount of carbon dioxide in the atmosphere (measured in *parts per million* or *ppm*) is used by environmental scientists in the study of global warming. Table 3 provides some figures for the period 1990–1996.

**TABLE 3   Atmospheric Carbon Dioxide**

| Year | Carbon dioxide in atmosphere (ppm) |
|---|---|
| 1990 | 354.0 |
| 1992 | 356.3 |
| 1994 | 358.9 |
| 1996 | 362.6 |

Source: C. D. Keeling and T. P. Whorf, Scripps Institution of Oceanography

**(a)** Plot the data in a rectangular coordinate system. Use the variable $t$ on the horizontal axis, with $t = 0$ corresponding to the year 1990. Use the variable $c$ (to denote carbon dioxide levels, in ppm) on the vertical axis.

**(b)** Use the midpoint formula and the data for 1992 and 1994 to estimate the amount of carbon dioxide for the year 1993.

**(c)** Compute the *percentage error* in the estimation in part (b), given that the actual 1993 value is 357.0 ppm. The general formula for percentage error in an estimation or approximation is

$$\text{percentage error} = \frac{|(\text{actual value}) - (\text{approximate value})|}{\text{actual value}} \times 100$$

**SOLUTION**

**(a)** See Figure 12. Note that if $t = 0$ corresponds to 1990, then $t = 2$ corresponds to 1992, $t = 4$ corresponds to 1994, and $t = 6$ corresponds to 1996.

**Figure 12**

**(b)** The midpoint of the line segment joining the points $(2, 356.3)$ and $(4, 358.9)$ is

$$\left( \frac{2 + 4}{2}, \frac{356.3 + 358.9}{2} \right)$$

which, as you can verify, works out to

$$(3, 357.6)$$

Thus, our approximation for the carbon dioxide level in 1993 ($t = 3$) is 357.6 ppm.

**(c)** We have

$$\text{percentage error} = \frac{|(\text{actual value}) - (\text{approximate value})|}{\text{actual value}} \times 100$$

$$= \frac{|357.0 - 357.6|}{357.0} \times 100$$

$$\approx 0.2\% \qquad \text{using a calculator and rounding to one decimal place}$$

In Figure 13 we show the given data for 1992 and 1994 along with the estimated and the actual value for 1993.

**Figure 13**
The midpoint of the line segment is close to the actual data point.

CAUTION Do not assume on the basis of this one example that the midpoint approximation always works as well as it does here. In this regard, be sure to work Exercise 23 at the end of this section.

# EXERCISE SET 1.4

**A**

1. Plot the points $(5, 2), (-4, 5), (-4, 0), (-1, -1)$, and $(5, -2)$.
2. Draw the square $ABCD$ with vertices (corners) $A(1, 0)$, $B(0, 1)$, $C(-1, 0)$, and $D(0, -1)$.
3. **(a)** Draw the right triangle $PQR$ with vertices $P(1, 0)$, $Q(5, 0)$, and $R(5, 3)$.
   **(b)** Use the formula for the area of a triangle, $A = \frac{1}{2}bh$, to find the area of triangle $PQR$ in part (a).
4. **(a)** Draw the trapezoid $ABCD$ with vertices $A(0, 0)$, $B(7, 0)$, $C(6, 4)$, and $D(4, 4)$.
   **(b)** Compute the area of the trapezoid. (See the inside front cover of this book for the appropriate formula.)

*In Exercises 5–10, calculate the distance between the given points.*

5. **(a)** $(0, 0)$ and $(-3, 4)$
   **(b)** $(2, 1)$ and $(7, 13)$
6. **(a)** $(-1, -3)$ and $(-5, 4)$
   **(b)** $(6, -2)$ and $(-1, 1)$
7. **(a)** $(-5, 0)$ and $(5, 0)$
   **(b)** $(0, -8)$ and $(0, 1)$
8. **(a)** $(-5, -3)$ and $(-9, -6)$
   **(b)** $(\frac{9}{2}, 3)$ and $(-2\frac{1}{2}, -1)$
9. $(1, \sqrt{3})$ and $(-1, -\sqrt{3})$
10. $(-3, 1)$ and $(374, -335)$
11. Which point is farther from the origin?
    **(a)** $(3, -2)$ or $(4, \frac{1}{2})$
    **(b)** $(-6, 7)$ or $(9, 0)$

**12.** Use the distance formula to show that, in each case, the triangle with given vertices is an isosceles triangle.
   **(a)** $(0, 2), (7, 4), (2, -5)$
   **(b)** $(-1, -8), (0, -1), (-4, -4)$
   **(c)** $(-7, 4), (-3, 10), (1, 3)$
**13.** In each case, determine whether the triangle with the given vertices is a right triangle.
   **(a)** $(7, -1), (-3, 5), (-12, -10)$
   **(b)** $(4, 5), (-3, 9), (1, 3)$
   **(c)** $(-8, -2), (1, -1), (10, 19)$
**14. (a)** Two of the three triangles specified in Exercise 13 are right triangles. Find their areas.
   **(b)** Calculate the area of the remaining triangle in Exercise 13 by using the following formula for the area $A$ of a triangle with vertices $(x_1, y_1), (x_2, y_2)$, and $(x_3, y_3)$:

$$A = \tfrac{1}{2}|x_1y_2 - x_2y_1 + x_2y_3 - x_3y_2 + x_3y_1 - x_1y_3|$$

The derivation of this formula is given in Exercise 34.
   **(c)** Use the formula given in part (b) to check your answers in part (a).
**15.** Use the formula given in Exercise 14(b) to calculate the area of the triangle with vertices $(1, -4), (5, 3)$, and $(13, 17)$. What do you conclude?
**16.** The coordinates of points $A$, $B$, and $C$ are $A(-4, 6)$, $B(-1, 2)$, and $C(2, -2)$.
   **(a)** Show that $AB = BC$ by using the distance formula.
   **(b)** Show that $AB + BC = AC$ by using the distance formula.
   **(c)** What can you conclude from parts (a) and (b)?

*In Exercises 17 and 18, find the midpoint of the line segment joining points P and Q.*
**17. (a)** $P(3, 2)$ and $Q(9, 8)$
   **(b)** $P(-4, 0)$ and $Q(5, -3)$
   **(c)** $P(3, -6)$ and $Q(-1, -2)$
**18. (a)** $P(12, 0)$ and $Q(12, 8)$
   **(b)** $P(\tfrac{3}{5}, -\tfrac{2}{3})$ and $Q(0, 0)$
   **(c)** $P(1, \pi)$ and $Q(3, 3\pi)$

*In Exercises 19 and 20, the given points P and Q are the endpoints of a diameter of a circle. Find **(a)** the center of the circle; **(b)** the radius of the circle.*
**19.** $P(-4, -2)$ and $Q(6, 4)$
**20.** $P(1, -3)$ and $Q(-5, -5)$
**21. (a)** Using a coordinate system similar to the one shown in the following figure (or a photocopy), plot the two points from Table A corresponding to the data for the years 1984 and 1992. Ignore the information about the name of the network.
   **(b)** Use the midpoint formula with the two points that you plotted in part (a) to obtain an approximation for the dollar amount paid per TV hour for 1988. (Round the answer to one decimal place.)

**(c)** Compute the percentage error in the approximation in part (b). The actual 1988 value is given in the table.

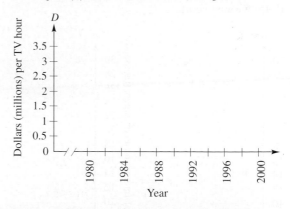

**TABLE A   How Much the Networks Paid (per TV hour) to Televise the Winter Olympics, 1980–1998**

| Year (network) | 1980 (ABC) | 1984 (ABC) | 1988 (ABC) | 1992 (CBS) | 1994 (CBS) | 1998 (CBS) |
|---|---|---|---|---|---|---|
| Millions of dollars per TV hour | 0.3 | 1.5 | 3.3 | 2.1 | 2.5 | 2.9 |

Source: World Features Syndicate

**22. (a)** Set up a coordinate system with the horizontal $t$-axis (running from 0 to at least 6) representing years after 1990 and the vertical $P$-axis (running from 14 to at least 27) representing percentage of sales due to imports; then use it to plot the data in Table B below. *Note:* you should use a broken vertical axis as in Figures 11 through 13.
   **(b)** What are the coordinates of the point in your graph that corresponds to the data for 1990? For 1992?
   **(c)** Use the midpoint formula with the two points that you listed in part (b) to estimate the percentage of import sales for the year 1991. (Round the answer to one decimal place.)
   **(d)** Compute the percentage error in the estimate in part (c), given that the actual 1991 value is 24.9%. [The formula for percentage error is given in Example 5(c).]

**TABLE B   Percentage of Retail New Car Sales in United States due to Imports, 1990–1996**

| Year | 1990 | 1992 | 1994 | 1996 |
|---|---|---|---|---|
| Percentage due to imports | 25.8 | 23.6 | 19.3 | 14.9 |

Source: American Automobile Manufacturers Assn.

**23.** Over the past two decades the Internet has grown very rapidly. Figures A and B provide estimates for the number *n* of Internet host computers, worldwide, for the years *t* = 1995–1997 and 1985–1987. Source: *Network Wizards* (http//www.nw.com)

**Figure A**          **Figure B**

**(a)** Use Figure A to complete the following table. Round the values of *n* to the nearest two million. Then use the midpoint formula and the numbers in your table to estimate the global number of Internet host computers for the year 1996.

| *t* | 1995 | 1997 |
|---|---|---|
| *n* | | |

**(b)** Use Figure B to complete the following table. Round the values of *n* to the nearest two thousand. Then use the midpoint formula and the numbers in your table to estimate the global number of Internet host computers for the year 1986.

| *t* | 1985 | 1987 |
|---|---|---|
| *n* | | |

**(c)** Compute the percentage errors to determine which estimate, the one for 1986 or the one for 1996, is more accurate. Use the following data from *Network Wizards* (http//www.nw.com) in computing the percentage errors: The number of host computers for 1986 and 1996 were 5089 and 21,819,000, respectively. (Round each answer to the nearest one percent.)

*Note*: You'll find out in part (c) that one estimate is very good, the other is way off. The point here is that without more initial information, it's hard to say whether the midpoint formula will produce a useful estimate. In subsequent chapters, we'll use *functions* and larger data sets to obtain more reliable estimates.

**24.** Have you or a friend ever run in a 10K (10,000 meter) race? When the author polled his precalculus class at UCLA in Fall 1997, he found that there were five students in the class (of 160) who said they had run a 10K in under 50 minutes. Of those five, two (one male, one female) said they had run a 10K in under 40 minutes. The world record for this event is well under 30 minutes. In this exercise you'll look at some of the world records in this event over the past decade.

**(a)** The table that follows lists the world records in the (men's) 10,000 meter race as of the end of the years 1993, 1995, and 1997. After converting the times into seconds, plot the three points corresponding to these records in a coordinate system similar to the one shown.

| Year | Time | Runner |
|---|---|---|
| 1993 | 26:58.38 | Yobes Ondieki (Kenya) |
| 1995 | 26:43.53 | Haile Gebrselassie (Kenya) |
| 1997 | 26:27.85 | Paul Tergat (Kenya) |

**(b)** Use the midpoint formula and the data for 1993 and 1995 to compute an estimate for what the world record might have been by the end of 1994. Then compute the percentage error (rounded to two decimal places), given that the record at the end of 1994 was 26:52.23 (set by William Seigei of Kenya). Was your estimate too high or too low?

**(c)** Use the midpoint formula and the data for 1995 and 1997 to compute an estimate for what the world record might have been by the end of 1996. Then compute the percentage error given that the record at the end of 1996 was 26:38.08 (set by Salah Hissou of Morocco). Was your estimate too high or too low? Is the percentage error more or less than that obtained in part (b)?

**(d)** Using a coordinate system similar to the one shown in part (a), or using a photocopy, plot the points corresponding to the (actual, not estimated) world records for the years 1993, 1994, 1995, 1996, 1997, and 1998. Except for 1998, all the records have been given above. The world record at the end of 1998 was 26:22.75 (set by Haile Gebrselassie of Kenya). Use the picture you obtain to say whether or not the record times seem to be leveling off.

**25. (a)** Sketch the parallelogram with vertices $A(-7, -1)$, $B(4, 3)$, $C(7, 8)$, and $D(-4, 4)$.
**(b)** Compute the midpoints of the diagonals $\overline{AC}$ and $\overline{BD}$.
**(c)** What conclusion can you draw from part (b)?

**26.** The vertices of $\triangle ABC$ are $A(1, 1)$, $B(9, 3)$, and $C(3, 5)$.
**(a)** Find the perimeter of $\triangle ABC$.
**(b)** Find the perimeter of the triangle that is formed by joining the midpoints of the three sides of $\triangle ABC$.
**(c)** Compute the ratio of the perimeter in part (a) to the perimeter in part (b).
**(d)** What theorem from geometry provides the answer for part (c) without using the results in (a) and (b)?

**27.** Use the Pythagorean theorem to find the length $a$ in the figure. Then find $b, c, d, e, f$, and $g$.

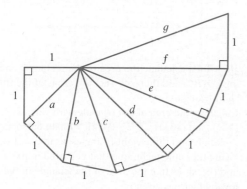

*Note:* This figure provides a geometric construction for the irrational numbers $\sqrt{2}, \sqrt{3}, \ldots, \sqrt{n}$, where $n$ is a nonsquare natural number. According to Boyer's *A History of Mathematics,* 2nd ed. (New York: John Wiley & Sons, Inc., 1991), "Plato . . . says that his teacher Theodorus of Cyrene . . . was the first to prove the irrationality of the square roots of the nonsquare integers from 3 to 17, inclusive. It is not known how he did this, nor why he stopped with $\sqrt{17}$." One plausible reason for Theodorus's stopping with $\sqrt{17}$ may have to do with the figure shown here. Theodorus may have known that the figure begins to overlap itself at the stage where $\sqrt{18}$ would be constructed.

**28.** (A numerologist's delight) Using the Pythagorean theorem and your calculator, compute the area of a right triangle in which the lengths of the hypotenuse and one leg are 2045 and 693, respectively.

**B**

**29.** The diagonals of a parallelogram bisect each other. Steps (a), (b), and (c) outline a proof of this theorem. (See Exercise 25 for a particular instance of this theorem.)
**(a)** In the parallelogram $OABC$ shown in the figure, check that the coordinates of $B$ must be $(a + b, c)$.
**(b)** Use the midpoint formula to calculate the midpoints of diagonals $\overline{OB}$ and $\overline{AC}$.
**(c)** The two answers in part (b) are identical. This shows that the two diagonals do indeed bisect each other, as we wished to prove.

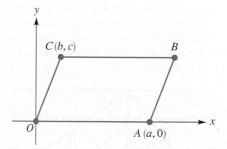

**30.** Prove that in a parallelogram, the sum of the squares of the lengths of the diagonals equals the sum of the squares of the lengths of the four sides. (Use the figure in Exercise 29.)

**31.** Suppose that the coordinates of points $P, Q$, and $M$ are

$$P(x_1, y_1) \qquad Q(x_2, y_2)$$
$$M\left(\frac{x_1 + x_2}{2}, \frac{y_1 + y_2}{2}\right)$$

Follow steps (a) and (b) to prove that $M$ is the midpoint of the line segment from $P$ to $Q$.
**(a)** By computing both of the distances $PM$ and $MQ$, show that $PM = MQ$. (This shows that $M$ lies on the perpendicular bisector of line segment $\overline{PQ}$, but it does not show that $M$ actually lies on $\overline{PQ}$.)
**(b)** Show that $PM + MQ = PQ$. (This shows that $M$ does lie on $\overline{PQ}$.)

**32.** This problem outlines one of the shortest proofs of the Pythagorean theorem. The proof was discovered by the Hindu mathematician Bhāskara (1114–ca. 1185). (For other proofs, see the next exercise and also Exercise 100 on page 83.) In the figure we are given a right triangle $ACB$ with the right angle at $C$, and we want to prove that $a^2 + b^2 = c^2$. In the figure, $\overline{CD}$ is drawn perpendicular to $\overline{AB}$.
**(a)** Check that $\angle CAD = \angle DCB$ and that $\triangle BCD$ and $\triangle BAC$ are similar.
**(b)** Use the result in part (a) to obtain the equation $a/y = c/a$, and conclude that $a^2 = cy$.
**(c)** Show that $\triangle ACD$ is similar to $\triangle ABC$, and use this to deduce that $b^2 = c^2 - cy$.

**(d)** Combine the two equations deduced in parts (b) and (c) to arrive at $a^2 + b^2 = c^2$.

**33.** One of the oldest and simplest proofs of the Pythagorean theorem is found in the ancient Chinese text *Chou Pei Suan Ching*. This text was written during the Han period (206 B.C.–A.D. 222), but portions of it may date back to 600 B.C. The proof in *Chou Pei Suan Ching* is based on this diagram from the text. In this exercise we explain the details of the proof.

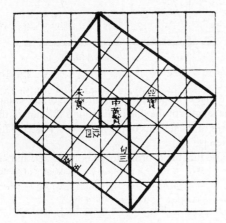

A diagram accompanying a proof of the "Pythagorean" theorem in the ancient Chinese text *Chou Pei Suan Ching* [from *Science and Civilisation in China*, vol. 3, by Joseph Needham (Cambridge, England: Cambridge University Press, 1959)].

**(a)** Starting with the right triangle in Figure A, we make four replicas of this triangle and arrange them to form the pattern shown in Figure B. Explain why the outer quadrilateral in Figure B is a square.

**Figure A        Figure B**

**(b)** The unshaded region in the center of Figure B is a square. What is the length of each side?

**(c)** The area of the outer square in Figure B is (side)$^2 = c^2$. This area can also be computed by adding up the areas of the four right triangles and the inner square. Compute the area in this fashion. After simplifying, you should obtain $a^2 + b^2$. Now conclude that $a^2 + b^2 = c^2$, since both expressions represent the same area.

## C

**34.** This problem indicates a method for calculating the area of a triangle when the coordinates of the three vertices are given.

**(a)** Calculate the area of $\triangle ABC$ in the figure.

*Hint:* First calculate the area of the rectangle enclosing $\triangle ABC$, and then subtract the areas of the three right triangles.

**(b)** Calculate the area of the triangle with vertices $(1, 3)$, $(4, 1)$, and $(10, 4)$.    *Hint:* Work with an enclosing rectangle and three right triangles, as in part (a).

**(c)** Using the same technique that you used in parts (a) and (b), show that the area of the triangle in the following figure is given by

$$A = \tfrac{1}{2}(x_1 y_2 - x_2 y_1 + x_2 y_3 - x_3 y_2 + x_3 y_1 - x_1 y_3)$$

*Remark:* If we use absolute value signs instead of the parentheses, then the formula will hold regardless of the relative positions or quadrants of the three vertices. Thus the area of a triangle with vertices $(x_1, y_1)$, $(x_2, y_2)$, $(x_3, y_3)$ is given by

$$A = \tfrac{1}{2}|x_1 y_2 - x_2 y_1 + x_2 y_3 - x_3 y_2 + x_3 y_1 - x_1 y_3|$$

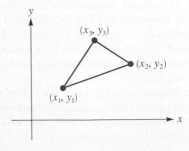

# MINI PROJECT

## DISCUSS, COMPUTE, REASSESS

As background for this discussion you should review Example 5. In that example, we used the midpoint formula to estimate the amount of carbon dioxide in the atmosphere for the year 1993 using data from the surrounding years 1992 and 1994. Consider now the following three figures (independent of Example 5). Each figure shows four data points, and there is a question mark regarding the location of a fifth. Note that the data points in each figure appear to be rising in a straight-line or near straight-line fashion.

**(a)** In your opinion, which of the following scenarios might lead to the most reliable estimate for the actual location of the fifth data point? The least reliable? What are the reasons or intuitions behind your replies?

   **(i)** Figure A: Using the midpoint formula and the data for 1994 and 1996 to obtain a possible value for the global average temperature in 1995;

   **(ii)** Figure B: Using the midpoint formula with the points (10, 50) and (30, 86) to obtain a possible value for the Fahrenheit temperature corresponding to 20 degrees on the Celsius scale;

   **(iii)** Figure C: Using the midpoint formula and the data for 1965 and 1985 to obtain a possible value for the percentage of the earth's population living in urban areas in 1975.

**(b)** Carry out the three calculations described in part (a). Then use the following information to compute the percentage error for each of your estimates: **(i)** The average global temperature for 1995 was 57.9°F; **(ii)** The temperature 20°C corresponds to 68°F; **(iii)** In 1975, 37.8% of the world's population lived in urban areas.

**(c)** Use the percentage errors you've computed as a check on your part (a) answers. Were you correct about which estimate was the most reliable and which was the least? If you missed either one, how might you adjust the reasons or intuitions that you expressed in part (a)?

**Figure A**
Global average temperature at Earth's surface

Source: Adapted from data compiled by Worldwatch Institute from Goddard Institute for Space Studies

**Figure B**
Some correspondences between temperatures on the Celsius and Fahrenheit scales. [For example, the rightmost point (40, 104) indicates that a temperature of 40 degrees on the Celsius scale corresponds to 104 degrees on the Fahrenheit scale.]

**Figure C**
Percentage of Earth's human population living in urban areas

Source: Compiled by Worldwatch Institute from United Nations, World Population Prospects: The 1996 Revision

## 1.5 GRAPHS AND GRAPHING UTILITIES

In this section we look at the connection between two basic skills that you've worked on in previous courses:

- graphing equations
- solving equations

We also look at these topics in terms of *graphing utilities*. By a **graphing utility** we mean either a graphing calculator or a computer with software for graphing and analyzing equations. Whether we are working "by hand" or with technology, the following definition underlies all.

---

| **DEFINITION** | The Graph of an Equation |
|---|---|

---

The **graph** of an equation in two variables is the set of all points with coordinates satisfying the equation.

---

| **TABLE 1** $y = 3x - 2$ | |
|---|---|
| **x** | **y** |
| 0 | −2 |
| 1 | 1 |
| 2 | 4 |
| 3 | 7 |
| −1 | −5 |
| −2 | −8 |

Suppose, for example, that we want to graph the equation $y = 3x - 2$. We begin by noting that the domain of the variable $x$ in the expression $3x - 2$ is the set of all real numbers. Now we choose values for $x$ and in each case compute the corresponding $y$-value from the equation $y = 3x - 2$. For example, if $x$ is zero, then $y = 3(0) - 2 = -2$. Table 1 summarizes the results of some of these calculations. The first line in Table 1 tells us that the point with coordinates $(0, -2)$ is on the graph of $y = 3x - 2$. Reading down the table, we see that some other points on the graph are $(1, 1)$, $(2, 4)$, $(3, 7)$, $(-1, -5)$, and $(-2, -8)$.

We now plot (locate) the points we have determined and we note, in this example, that they all appear to lie on a straight line. We draw the line indicated; this is the graph of $y = 3x - 2$ (see Figure 1). In Example 1 we ask a simple question that will test your understanding of the process we've just described and of graphing in general.

---

| **EXAMPLE** | **1** | Applying the definition of the "graph of an equation" |
|---|---|---|

Does the point $(1\frac{2}{3}, 2\frac{2}{3})$ lie on the graph of $y = 3x - 2$?

**SOLUTION**

Looking at the graph in Figure 1, we certainly see that the point $(1\frac{2}{3}, 2\frac{2}{3})$ is very close to the line, but from this visual inspection alone, we cannot be certain that this point actually lies on the line. To settle the question, then, we check to see whether the values $x = 1\frac{2}{3} = \frac{5}{3}$ and $y = 2\frac{2}{3} = \frac{8}{3}$ together satisfy the equation $y = 3x - 2$. We have

$$\frac{8}{3} \overset{?}{=} 3\left(\frac{5}{3}\right) - 2$$

$$\frac{8}{3} \overset{?}{=} 3 \qquad \text{No}$$

**Figure 1**
$y = 3x - 2$

Since the coordinates $(1\frac{2}{3}, 2\frac{2}{3})$ evidently do not satisfy the equation $y = 3x - 2$, we conclude that the point $(1\frac{2}{3}, 2\frac{2}{3})$ is not on the graph. [The calculation further tells us that the point $(1\frac{2}{3}, 3)$ *is* on the graph.]

A graphing utility produces graphs of equations in essentially the same way that we did in Table 1 and Figure 1. The graphing utility uses the given equation to compute pairs of points $(x, y)$, and it plots these points one at a time on the viewing screen. Of course, the machine is able to quickly compute and plot many more points than we used in Table 1—that's an advantage. On the other hand, the graphing utility is not "smart." For example, it does not know ahead of time that the equation $y = 3x - 2$ will be a straight line. (*You'll* know this by the end of the next section, or maybe you already remember from a previous course that the graph of any equation of the form $y = mx + b$ is always a straight line.) Later in this section and in the exercises we'll say more about some of the limitations of a graphing utility and how some thought or experimentation on your part is often necessary.

**GRAPHICAL PERSPECTIVE**

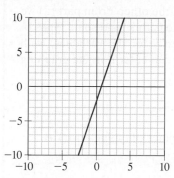

**Figure 2**
A graph of $y = 3x - 2$

In Figure 2 we show a graph of the equation $y = 3x - 2$ obtained with a graphing utility. Actually, since there are so many different types of graphing utilities, the picture we've chosen to show in this text is a kind of amalgam containing features from several types of utilities. If you have a graphing utility, you should now produce a graph of $y = 3x - 2$ for yourself and compare it to Figure 2. (If necessary refer to the user's manual that came with your calculator or software.) In this text, the label GRAPHICAL PERSPECTIVE (as you see above Figure 2) is a signal for those students with graphing utilities: Use your graphing utility, making adjustments as necessary, to obtain a view that is similar to the one shown here in the textbook. For many graphing utilities, the default view or **standard viewing rectangle** is $-10 \leq x \leq 10$ and $-10 \leq y \leq 10$. This is the view shown in Figure 2. In the next example we graph an equation first by hand, then with a graphing utility. In the graphing utility portion, you'll see a case in which the standard viewing rectangle is inappropriate and needs to be modified.

  **EXAMPLE** **2** | **An application of linear equations and graphs to temperature scales**

The equation $5F - 9C = 160$ relates temperature $F$ on the Fahrenheit scale to temperature $C$ on the Celsius scale.

**(a)** Solve the given equation for $F$ in terms of $C$. Then set up a table and graph the equation in a $C$-$F$ coordinate system ($C$ on the horizontal axis, $F$ on the vertical).

**(b)** Use a graphing utility to obtain a graph of $5F - 9C = 160$.

**SOLUTION**
**(a)** We have

$$5F - 9C = 160$$
$$5F = 9C + 160 \qquad \text{adding } 9C \text{ to both sides}$$
$$F = \frac{9}{5}C + 32 \qquad \text{dividing both sides by 5} \qquad (1)$$

Using equation (1) now, we pick values for $C$ and compute the corresponding values for $F$. To avoid working with fractions, we take values for $C$ that

**TABLE 2**    $F = \frac{9}{5}C + 32$

| $C$ | $F$ |
|-----|-----|
| 0 | 32 |
| 5 | 41 |
| 10 | 50 |
| 15 | 59 |
| −5 | 23 |
| −10 | 14 |

are multiples of 5, as indicated in Table 2. (Check for yourself that the entries in the right-hand column of the table are correct.)

In view of the data in Table 2, we'll mark off the axes as indicated in Figure 3(a), with tick marks five units apart on the $C$-axis and ten units apart on the $F$-axis. (Other markings are feasible. For example, it would be reasonable to use markings of 20 instead of 10 on the vertical axis, but it would be very clumsy to use markings at one-unit intervals.) In Figure 3(b) we've plotted the data pairs $(C, F)$ given by Table 2. These points appear to lie on a straight line, and we've drawn the line in Figure 3(c). This is the required graph.

*Note*: In elementary graphing, there is the question of how many points must be plotted before the essential features of a graph are clear. As you'll see throughout this text, there are a number of techniques and concepts that make it unnecessary to plot a large number of points. For instance, if you knew ahead of time that the graph of $F = \frac{9}{5}C + 32$ were a straight line, then you would need to plot only two points in order to draw the line.

**(b)** With a graphing utility, just as in graphing by hand, we first need to solve the given equation for one variable in terms of the other. From part (a) we have $F = \frac{9}{5}C + 32$. Because most graphing calculators (and some types of computer software) require that we use $x$ and $y$ for the variables, we'll rewrite the equation as $y = \frac{9}{5}x + 32$. Then we can enter it in the graphing utility as

$$y = \left(\frac{9}{5}\right) * x + 32 \qquad \text{The symbol * denotes multiplication.}$$

or better yet (with fewer keystrokes and less chance of typing error) as

$$y = \frac{9x}{5} + 32 \tag{2}$$

Figure 4(a) shows the "graph" of equation (2) in the standard viewing rectangle. Yes, nothing's there; evidently, no point of the required graph passes through the standard viewing rectangle. We need to find a more appropriate viewing rectangle. After some experimenting with the dimensions of the viewing rectangle, we obtain the views shown in Figure 4(b), then Figure 4(c). Figure 4(c) is an appropriate viewing rectangle; the essential features of the graph are clear, and there is not a lot of wasted space in the viewing screen, as there is in Figure 4(b).

(a)  Scales on axes are chosen to accommodate the range of numbers in Table 2.

(b)  Plot of data points $(C, F)$ from Table 2.

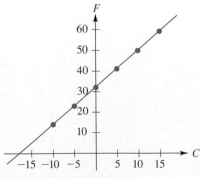

(c)  Graph of $F = \frac{9}{5}C + 32$ (or $5F - 9C = 160$)

**Figure 3**

## GRAPHICAL PERSPECTIVE

(a) The graph of $y = \frac{9}{5}x + 32$ does not pass through the standard viewing rectangle.

(b) Better, but still not an appropriate viewing rectangle.

(c) An appropriate viewing rectangle. The essential features of the graph are clear.

**Figure 4**

Finding an appropriate viewing rectangle for $y = \frac{9}{5}x + 32$ (or $F = \frac{9}{5}C + 32$)

We can use Figure 4 to introduce some common notation that is often used in describing viewing rectangles. (Even if you are not working with a graphing utility, you are apt to see this notation in other math books or on a friend's math paper.) In Figure 4(a), $x$ runs from $-10$ to $10$ in increments of $5$. A notation for this is

$$\text{Xmin} = -10 \qquad \text{Xmax} = 10 \qquad \text{Xscl} = 5$$

In the rightmost equation, "Xscl" refers to the *scale* on the $x$-axis, and the equation Xscl = 5 tells you that it is five units between adjacent tick marks or grid lines. In Figure 4(a), $y$ also runs from $-10$ to $10$ in increments of $5$, so we write Ymin = -10, Ymax = 10, and Yscl = 5. As another example of this notation, for Figure 4(c) we have (as you should check)

$$\text{Xmin} = -30 \qquad\qquad \text{Ymin} = -20$$
$$\text{Xmax} = 30 \qquad \text{and} \qquad \text{Ymax} = 80$$
$$\text{Xscl} = 10 \qquad\qquad \text{Yscl} = 20$$

Another type of shorthand that you'll see is based on the closed interval notation $[a, b]$ described in Section 1.1. With this notation we specify the size of the viewing rectangle in Figure 4(c) as

$$[-30, 30] \text{ by } [-20, 80]$$   In this notation the $x$-interval precedes the $y$-interval.

The only drawback to this notation is that the scale or number of units between tick marks is not specified. We remedy this by inserting a third number, denoting scale, in each bracket. The viewing rectangle in Figure 4(c) is then completely specified by writing

$$[-30, 30, 10] \text{ by } [-20, 80, 20]$$

---

**EXAMPLE** **3** **Specifying viewing rectangles on a graphing utility**

Figure 5 shows two views of the graph of the equation $y = 2x^3 - x^2$. Describe each viewing rectangle using the two types of notation discussed above (that is, the min-max-scl equations and the bracket notation).

(a)

(b)

**Figure 5**
Two views of $y = 2x^3 - x^2$

**SOLUTION**
For Figure 5(a) we have

$$\begin{array}{lll} \texttt{Xmin = -4} & & \texttt{Ymin = -40} \\ \texttt{Xmax = 4} & \text{and} & \texttt{Ymax = 60} \\ \texttt{Xscl = 2} & & \texttt{Yscl = 20} \end{array}$$

The bracket notation describing the viewing rectangle in Figure 5(a) is

$$[-4, 4, 2] \text{ by } [-40, 60, 20]$$

For Figure 5(b) we have

$$\begin{array}{lll} \texttt{Xmin = -0.2} & & \texttt{Ymin = -0.06} \\ \texttt{Xmax = 0.6} & \text{and} & \texttt{Ymax = 0.02} \\ \texttt{Xscl = 0.2} & & \texttt{Yscl = 0.02} \end{array}$$

The bracket notation describing the viewing rectangle in Figure 5(b) is

$$[-0.2, 0.6, 0.2] \text{ by } [-0.06, 0.02, 0.02]$$

When we graph an equation, it's helpful to know where the curve intersects the $x$- or $y$-axis. By an **$x$-intercept** of a graph we mean the $x$-coordinate of a point where the graph intersects the $x$-axis. For instance, in Figure 6 there are two $x$-intercepts: $-2$ and 4. We define $y$-intercepts in a similar manner: A **$y$-intercept** of a graph is the $y$-coordinate of a point where the graph intersects the $y$-axis. Thus, the $y$-intercept of the graph in Figure 6 is 1.

**Figure 6**
$x$-intercepts: $-2$ and 4
$y$-intercept: 1

---

**EXAMPLE**   4   **Computing x- and y-intercepts**

Figure 7 shows the graph of the equation $3x + 5y = 15$. Find the $x$- and $y$-intercepts.

**SOLUTION**
At the point where the graph crosses the $x$-axis, the $y$-coordinate is zero. So, to find the $x$-intercept, we set $y = 0$ in the given equation $3x + 5y = 15$ and solve for $x$:

$$3x + 5(0) = 15$$
$$3x = 15$$
$$x = 5$$

**Figure 7**

Thus, the $x$-intercept is 5. Similarly, to find the $y$-intercept, we set $x = 0$ in the given equation $3x + 5y = 15$ and solve for $y$:

$$3(0) + 5y = 15$$
$$5y = 15$$
$$y = 3$$

The $y$-intercept is 3.

■

In the next example we show two different ways to determine $x$-intercepts. First we use a graphing utility to obtain approximate values for the intercepts; then we use algebra to find exact values.

**EXAMPLE 5** **Finding approximate and exact values for x-intercepts**

**GRAPHICAL PERSPECTIVE**

**Figure 8**
$y = x^3 - 2x^2 - 2x$
viewing rectangle: $[-4, 4, 2]$
by $[-6, 4, 2]$

Figure 8 shows a graph of the equation $y = x^3 - 2x^2 - 2x$ obtained with a graphing utility.
**(a)** Use a graphing utility to estimate (to one decimal place) the $x$-intercepts of the graph.
**(b)** Use algebra to determine the exact values for the $x$-intercepts. Then use a calculator to check that the answers are consistent with the estimates obtained in part (a).

**SOLUTION**
**(a)** According to Figure 8, there appear to be three $x$-intercepts: one between $-1$ and 0, one that is either zero or very close to zero, and one between 2 and 3. To estimate the intercept that is between $-1$ and 0 as well as the intercept near (or possibly at) zero, we'll change the viewing rectangle shown in Figure 8 so that $x$ runs from $-1$ to 1.1 in increments of 0.1. After some experimenting with the $y$-values, we obtain the graph in Figure 9(a), which shows that the leftmost intercept is between $-0.8$ and $-0.7$. Is it closer to $-0.8$ or $-0.7$? On a graphing calculator screen (as opposed to a larger picture on a computer monitor) it may not be clear that the intercept is closer to $-0.7$ than to $-0.8$. In Figure 9(b) we've adjusted the viewing rectangle for a closer view, which shows that the intercept is indeed closer to $-0.7$ than to $-0.8$. So to one decimal place, we can say that the leftmost intercept is

**GRAPHICAL PERSPECTIVE**

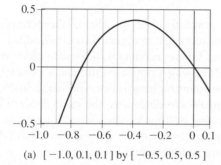

(a) $[-1.0, 0.1, 0.1]$ by $[-0.5, 0.5, 0.5]$

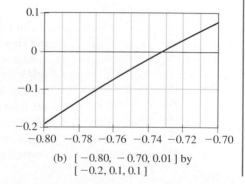

(b) $[-0.80, -0.70, 0.01]$ by $[-0.2, 0.1, 0.1]$

**Figure 9**
Adjusting the viewing rectangle to estimate an $x$-intercept for $y = x^3 - 2x^2 - 2x$

−0.7. [Actually, Figure 9(b) tells us more than this. The intercept is between −0.74 and −0.73.]

Regarding the intercept that appears in Figure 8 to be at or near zero, Figure 9(a) tells us that to one decimal place, the intercept is 0.0. In part (b) we'll show that this intercept is indeed exactly zero. (You cannot conclude this fact from Figure 9(a); see Exercise 35 for an example along these lines.)

There is one more $x$-intercept to estimate, the one in Figure 8 that is between 2 and 3. Exercise 36 asks you to use the methods we've just demonstrated to show that this rightmost $x$-intercept is approximately 2.7.

**(b)** To compute the exact values for the $x$-intercepts of the graph, we set $y$ equal to zero in the given equation $y = x^3 - 2x^2 - 2x$ to obtain $0 = x^3 - 2x^2 - 2x$. We then have

$$x^3 - 2x^2 - 2x = 0 \tag{3}$$
$$x(x^2 - 2x - 2) = 0 \qquad \text{factoring out the common factor } x$$

The zero product property from Section 1.3 now tells us that $x = 0$ or $x^2 - 2x - 2 = 0$. We can use the quadratic formula (from Section 1.3) to solve the equation $x^2 - 2x - 2 = 0$:

$$
\begin{aligned}
x &= \frac{-b \pm \sqrt{b^2 - 4ac}}{2a} \\
&= \frac{-(-2) \pm \sqrt{(-2)^2 - 4(1)(-2)}}{2(1)} \qquad \text{using } a = 1, b = -2, c = -2 \\
&= \frac{2 \pm \sqrt{12}}{2} \\
&= \frac{2 \pm 2\sqrt{3}}{2} = \frac{2(1 \pm \sqrt{3})}{2} = 1 \pm \sqrt{3} \qquad \text{See Appendix B.2 if you need to review working with radicals.}
\end{aligned}
$$

Putting things together now, we have found three roots for equation (3): 0, $1 - \sqrt{3}$, and $1 + \sqrt{3}$. The largest (and the only positive root) of these three is $1 + \sqrt{3}$; that is the rightmost $x$-intercept for the graph in Figure 8. The smallest (and the only negative root) is $1 - \sqrt{3}$; that is the leftmost $x$-intercept for the graph in Figure 8. Finally, the root $x = 0$ tells us that the middle $x$-intercept is indeed exactly zero. As you should check for yourself using a calculator, we have $1 - \sqrt{3} \approx -0.73$ and $1 + \sqrt{3} \approx 2.73$. Note that these values are indeed consistent with the estimates obtained in part (a).

In the graphing utility portion of the example just concluded, we started with the viewing rectangle in Figure 8 and then adjusted it to obtain a closer look at the $x$-intercepts. Most graphing utilities also allow you to obtain a closer look in another way, by using a ZOOM feature and a TRACE feature. For details, see the user's manual for your graphing utility. Another technology note: In part (b) of Example 5 we used algebra to determine the exact roots of the equation $x^3 - 2x^2 - 2x = 0$. Most graphing utilities have a SOLVE feature that can be used to obtain roots that, while only approximate, are accurate to several decimal places. Again, for details consult your user's manual.

As was mentioned previously in this section, when we first graph a given equation (either by hand or with a graphing utility), we try to present a view that shows all the essential features of the graph. The next example deals with one aspect of this issue.

Figure 10
Does the graph ever cross
the y-axis?

**EXAMPLE** 6 | **Obtaining information about a graph through its equation**

Figure 10 shows a graph of the equation $x^2y - x^3 + 3 = 0$.
**(a)** From the portion of the graph shown in Figure 10, it appears that there is no $y$-intercept. Use the given equation to show that this is indeed the case.
**(b)** As is indicated in Figure 10, there is an $x$-intercept between 1 and 2. Find this intercept. Give two forms for the answer: an exact expression and a calculator approximation rounded to two decimal places.

**SOLUTION**
**(a)** If there were a $y$-intercept (perhaps somewhere below the portion of the graph displayed in Figure 10), we could find it by setting $x$ equal to zero in the given equation. But with $x = 0$, the given equation becomes $3 = 0$, which is clearly impossible. We thus conclude that there is no $y$-intercept; the graph never crosses the $y$-axis.
**(b)** The $x$-intercept of the graph is determined by setting $y$ equal to zero in the given equation. That gives us $x^2(0) - x^3 + 3 = 0$, and therefore $x^3 = 3$. To solve this equation for $x$, just take the cube root of both sides to obtain

$$x = \sqrt[3]{3}$$
$$\approx 1.44 \qquad \text{using a calculator}$$

As you can see, the value $x = 1.44$ is consistent with the graph shown in Figure 10. Also, see the Graphical Perspective in Figure 11. Note that in the caption for Figure 11 we've solved the given equation for $y$ in terms of $x$. Most graphing utilities require that you enter the equation in this form.

**GRAPHICAL PERSPECTIVE**

Figure 11
To graph $x^2y - x^3 + 3 = 0$, first
solve for $y$:
$$x^2y = x^3 - 3$$
$$y = \frac{x^3 - 3}{x^2}$$

**(a)** Zoom-in view of $y = (x^3 - 3)/x^2$ shows that the graph has an $x$-intercept between 1.4 and 1.5.

**(b)** Further magnification shows that the $x$-intercept is between 1.44 and 1.45 (closer to 1.44 than 1.45).

## EXERCISE SET 1.5

### A

*In Exercises 1–6, determine whether the given point lies on the graph of the equation, as in Example 1.    Note: You are not asked to draw the graph.*

1. $(8, 6)$; $y = \frac{1}{2}x + 3$
2. $(\frac{3}{5}, -\frac{17}{5})$; $y = -\frac{2}{3}x - 3$
3. $(4, 3)$; $3x^2 + y^2 = 52$
4. $(4, -2)$; $3x^2 + y^2 = 52$
5. $(a, 4a)$; $y = 4x$
6. $(a - 1, a + 1)$; $y = x + 2$
7. **(a)** Solve the equation $2x - 3y = -3$ for $y$ and then complete the following table.

| x | −6 | −3 | 0 | 3 | 6 |
|---|---|---|---|---|---|
| y | | | | | |

   **(b)** Use your table from part (a) to graph the equation $2x - 3y = -3$.
8. **(a)** Solve the equation $3x + 2y = 6$ for $y$ and then complete the following table.

| x | −4 | −2 | 0 | 2 | 4 |
|---|---|---|---|---|---|
| y | | | | | |

   **(b)** Use your table from part (a) to graph the equation $3x + 2y = 6$.

*In Exercises 9–14, the graph of each equation is a straight line. Graph the equation after finding the x- and the y-intercepts. (Since you are given that the graph is a line, you need only plot two points before drawing the line.)*

9. $3x + 4y = 12$
10. $3x - 4y = 12$
11. $y = 2x - 4$
12. $x = 2y - 4$
13. $x + y = 1$
14. $2x - 3y = 6$

*For Exercises 15 and 16: As in Example 5, describe each viewing rectangle using the two types of notation discussed in the text (i.e., the min-max-scl equations and the bracket notation).*

15. Two views of $y = x^5 - x^4$

**(a)**

**(b)**

16. Two views of $y = \sqrt{1 - x^2}$

**(a)**

**(b)**

*In Exercises 17–20, determine any x- or y-intercepts for the graph of the equation.    Note: You're not asked to draw the graph.*

17. **(a)** $y = x^2 + 3x + 2$
    **(b)** $y = x^2 + 2x + 3$
18. **(a)** $y = x^2 - 4x - 12$
    **(b)** $y = x^2 - 4x + 12$
19. **(a)** $y = x^2 + x - 1$
    **(b)** $y = x^2 + x + 1$
20. **(a)** $y = 6x^3 + 9x^2 + x$
    **(b)** $y = 9x^3 + 6x^2 + x$

*In Exercises 21–24, each figure shows the graph of an equation. Find the x- and y-intercepts of the graph. If an intercept involves a radical, give both the radical form of the answer and a calculator approximation rounded to two decimal places. (Check to see that your answer is consistent with the given figure.)*

**21.**

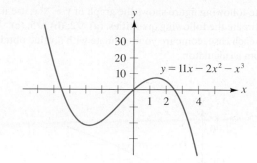

$$y = 11x - 2x^2 - x^3$$

**22.**

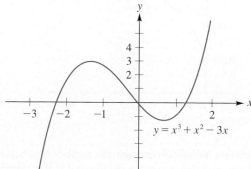

$$y = x^3 + x^2 - 3x$$

**23.**

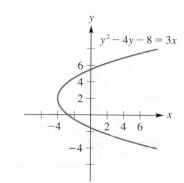

$$y^2 - 4y - 8 = 3x$$

**24.**

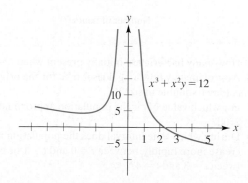

$$x^3 + x^2 y = 12$$

*For Exercises 25–30:*
Ⓖ **(a)** *Use a graphing utility to graph the equation.*
Ⓖ **(b)** *Use a graphing utility, as in Example 5, to estimate to one decimal place the x-intercepts.*

**(c)** *Use algebra to determine the exact values for the x-intercepts. Then use a calculator to check that the answers are consistent with the estimates obtained in part (b).*

**25.**  $y = x^2 - 2x - 2$

**26.**  $y = 2x^2 + x - 5$

**27.**  $y = 2x^3 - 5x$

**28.**  $y = 3x^3 + 5x^2 + x$

**29.**  $2xy - x^3 - 5 = 0$

 *Hint*: See Example 6(b) and the caption for Figure 11.

**30.**  $xy - 12y = x^2 - x - 1$

 *Hint for part (a)*: To solve the equation for y, first factor out the common term y on the left-hand side. Regarding the essential features of the graph, you should find that there are are two distinct pieces. You may have to adjust the viewing rectangle.

Ⓖ *In Exercises 31–34, use a graphing utility to graph the equations and to approximate the x-intercepts. In approximating the x-intercepts, use a "solve" key or a sufficiently magnified view to ensure that the values you give are correct in the first three decimal places.   Remark: None of the x-intercepts for these four equations can be obtained using factoring techniques.)*

**31.**  $y = x^3 - 3x + 1$

**32.**  $y = 8x^3 - 6x - 1$

**33.**  $y = x^5 - 6x^4 + 3$

**34.**  $y = 2x^5 - 5x^4 + 5$

Ⓖ **35. (a)** Graph the equation $y = x^3 + 10x + 2$ in the standard viewing rectangle. On the basis of this view, what can you say about the location of any x-intercepts?

 **(b)** The following viewing rectangle shows that $y = x^3 + 10x + 2$ has an x-intercept either at $-0.2$ or very close to $-0.2$.

 **(c)** Find a viewing rectangle to demonstrate that $-0.2$ is *not* an x-intercept.

 **(d)** Looking at the picture in part (b) and your result in part (c), what would you say is the moral of the story?

Ⓖ **36.** This exercise refers to Example 5 and Figure 8.

 **(a)** According to Figure 8, the graph of $y = x^3 - 2x^2 - 2x$ has an x-intercept between 2 and 3, slightly closer to 3 than to 2. Graph the equation in the viewing rectangle $[2.5, 3, 0.1]$ by $[-2, 3, 1]$ to see that the intercept is between 2.7 and 2.8, closer to 2.7 than to 2.8. Thus, to one decimal place, the intercept is 2.7, as stated in Example 5.

(b) Estimate the x-intercept to three decimal places by finding a suitable viewing rectangle.

## B

*For Exercises 37 and 38, refer to Figure 4(c) on page 39, which shows a graph of the equation $F = \frac{9}{5}C + 32$. The equation relates temperature C on the Celsius scale to temperature F on the Fahrenheit scale. [In Figure 4(c), C is the variable for the horizontal axis and F is the variable for the vertical axis.]*

37. (a) Use Figure 4(c) to estimate (to the nearest 5 degrees) the Celsius temperature corresponding to 0 degrees on the Fahrenheit scale. When you do this, which intercept are you looking at, the C-intercept or the F-intercept?

(b) Use the equation $F = \frac{9}{5}C + 32$ to give the exact temperature on the Celsius scale corresponding to 0 degrees on the Fahrenheit scale.

38. (a) Use Figure 4(c) to estimate (to the nearest 10 degrees) the temperature on the Fahrenheit scale corresponding to 0 degrees on the Celsius scale. When you do this, which intercept are you looking at, the C-intercept or the F-intercept?

(b) Use the equation $F = \frac{9}{5}C + 32$ to give the exact temperature on the Fahrenheit scale corresponding to 0 degrees on the Celsius scale.

39. The following figure shows the graph of $y = \sqrt{x}$. Use this graph to estimate the following quantities (to one decimal place).

(a) $\sqrt{2}$

(b) $\sqrt{3}$

(c) $\sqrt{6}$

*Hint:* $\sqrt{ab} = \sqrt{a}\sqrt{b}$

40. The following figure shows the graph of $y = \sqrt[3]{x}$; use it to estimate the following quantities. (a) $\sqrt[3]{2}$; (b) $\sqrt[3]{5}$; (c) $\sqrt[3]{6.5}$. In each case, compare your estimate with a value obtained from a calculator.

41. In a certain biology experiment, the number N of bacteria increases with time t in hours as indicated in the following figure.

Number of hours (t)

(a) How many bacteria are initially present when t = 0?

(b) Approximately how long does it take for the original colony to double in size?

(c) For which value of t is the population approximately 2500?

(d) During which time interval does the population increase more rapidly, between t = 0 and t = 1 or between t = 3 and t = 4?

*In Exercises 42 and 43, determine the x-coordinates of the points A and B. (Each dashed line is parallel to a coordinate axis.)*

**42.**

**43.**

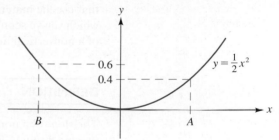

---

## MINI PROJECT | DRAWING CONCLUSIONS FROM VISUAL EVIDENCE

This discussion concerns $x$-intercepts and requires that at least one person in the group have a graphing utility. How much graphical evidence do you feel is necessary before you are "reasonably certain" about the exact value of an $x$-intercept? Or would graphical evidence alone never leave you reasonably certain? To focus the discussion, begin by considering the two views of the graph of the equation $y = x^3 + 550x + 11$ in Figures A and B.

**Figure A**
Close-up view of $y = x^3 + 550x + 11$ near an $x$-intercept. The intercept is either $-0.02$ or something very close to that.

**Figure B**
Still closer view of the $x$-intercept in Figure A (zooming in by a factor of 2). Would you say now that it is quite likely that the intercept is exactly $-0.02$?

---

## 1.6   EQUATIONS OF LINES

*He* [Pierre de Fermat (1601–1665)] *introduced perpendicular axes and found the general equations of straight lines and circles and the simplest equations of parabolas, ellipses, and hyperbolas; and he further showed in a fairly complete and systematic way that every first- or second-degree equation can be reduced to one of these types.* — George F. Simmons in *Calculus Gems, Brief Lives and Memorable Moments* (New York: McGraw-Hill Book Company, 1992)

For sufficiently short periods of time, the graphs of many real-world quantities can be closely approximated by a straight-line graph. In this section we take a systematic look at equations of lines and their graphs. (In Section 4.1 we'll see applications that use the material developed here.) We begin by recalling the concept of *slope*, which you've seen in previous courses. As defined in the box that follows, the slope of a nonvertical line is a number that measures the slant or direction of the line.

---

| **DEFINITION** | **Slope** |
| --- | --- |

The slope of a nonvertical line passing through the two points $(x_1, y_1)$ and $(x_2, y_2)$ is the number $m$ defined by

$$m = \frac{y_2 - y_1}{x_2 - x_1}$$

EXAMPLE

Calculating $m$ using $(-2, 2)$ and $(4, 5)$:

$$m = \frac{5 - 2}{4 - (-2)} = \frac{3}{4 + 2} = \frac{3}{6} = \frac{1}{2}$$

---

The two quantities $x_2 - x_1$ and $y_2 - y_1$ that appear in the definition of slope can be interpreted geometrically. As indicated in Figure 1, $x_2 - x_1$ is the amount by which $x$ changes as we move from $(x_1, y_1)$ to $(x_2, y_2)$ along the line. We denote this change in $x$ by $\Delta x$ (read: *delta x*). Thus $\Delta x = x_2 - x_1$. Similarly, $\Delta y$ is defined to mean the change in $y$: $\Delta y = y_2 - y_1$. Using this notation, we can rewrite our definition of slope as $m = \Delta y / \Delta x$.

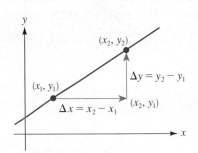

**Figure 1**
The delta notation

| **EXAMPLE** | **1** | **Using the delta notation in computing slope** |
| --- | --- | --- |

Suppose a cardiologist asks a patient to walk on a treadmill at a slow steady pace and Table 1 lists some of the data collected. In Table 1, $x$ represents time, in seconds, with $x = 0$ corresponding to the instant that the patient starts walking. The variable $y$ stands for the total distance covered by the patient after $x$ seconds. Figure 2 shows a graph obtained from these data. Compute $\Delta x$, $\Delta y$, and the slope $m$ for each of the following intervals:
**(a)** from $x = 5$ seconds to $x = 10$ seconds;
**(b)** from $x = 10$ seconds to $x = 30$ seconds.

**TABLE 1**

| $x$ (time in seconds) | 0 | 5 | 10 | 15 | 20 | 25 | 30 |
| --- | --- | --- | --- | --- | --- | --- | --- |
| $y$ (distance in feet) | 0 | 15 | 30 | 45 | 60 | 75 | 90 |

**Figure 2**

**SOLUTION**

**(a)** From $x = 5$ seconds to $x = 10$ seconds:

$$\Delta x = x_2 - x_1 = 10 \text{ sec} - 5 \text{ sec} = 5 \text{ sec}$$
$$\Delta y = y_2 - y_1 = 30 \text{ ft} - 15 \text{ ft} = 15 \text{ ft}$$
$$\frac{\Delta y}{\Delta x} = \frac{15 \text{ ft}}{5 \text{ sec}} = 3 \text{ ft/sec}$$

**(b)** From $x = 10$ seconds to $x = 30$ seconds:

$$\Delta x = x_2 - x_1 = 30 \text{ sec} - 10 \text{ sec} = 20 \text{ sec}$$
$$\Delta y = y_2 - y_1 = 90 \text{ ft} - 30 \text{ ft} = 60 \text{ ft}$$
$$\frac{\Delta y}{\Delta x} = \frac{60 \text{ ft}}{20 \text{ sec}} = 3 \text{ ft/sec}$$

Note that both parts of this exercise lead to the same value for slope. Exercises 5 and 6 ask you to check other instances of this, and in the next paragraph we prove that for a given line, the same value is obtained for slope no matter which pair of points on the line is used. Another point to observe: Slope is a rate of change. In this example, it is the rate of change of distance with respect to time, or *velocity*. We'll talk more about slope as a rate of change in Section 4.1.

Figure 3

To see why slope of a line does not depend on which two particular points on the line are used in the calculation, consider Figure 3. The two right triangles are similar (because the corresponding angles are equal). This implies that the corresponding sides of the two triangles are proportional, and so we have

$$\frac{a}{d} = \frac{b}{c}$$

Now notice that the left-hand side of this equation represents the slope $\Delta y/\Delta x$ calculated using the points $A$ and $D$, and the right-hand side represents the slope calculated using the points $B$ and $C$. Thus the values we obtain for the slope are indeed equal.

**EXAMPLE 2   Comparing slopes**

Compute and compare the slopes of the three lines shown in Figure 4.

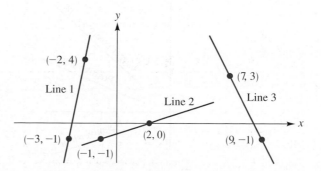

Figure 4

**SOLUTION**
First, we will calculate the slope of line 1, using the formula $m = \dfrac{y_2 - y_1}{x_2 - x_1}$. Which point should we use as $(x_1, y_1)$ and which as $(x_2, y_2)$? In fact, it doesn't matter how we label our points. Using $(-3, -1)$ for $(x_1, y_1)$ and $(-2, 4)$ for $(x_2, y_2)$, we have

$$m = \frac{y_2 - y_1}{x_2 - x_1} = \frac{4 - (-1)}{-2 - (-3)} = 5$$

So the slope of line 1 is 5. If, instead, we had used $(-2, 4)$ for $(x_1, y_1)$ and $(-3, -1)$ for $(x_2, y_2)$, then we'd have $m = (-1 - 4)/(-3 + 2) = 5$, the same result. This is not accidental because, in general,

$$\frac{y_2 - y_1}{x_2 - x_1} = \frac{y_1 - y_2}{x_1 - x_2}$$

(Exercise 55 asks you to verify this identity.) Next, we calculate the slopes of lines 2 and 3.

Slope of line 2:    $\dfrac{0 - (-1)}{2 - (-1)} = \dfrac{1}{3}$    Slope of line 3:    $\dfrac{3 - (-1)}{7 - 9} = -2$

Lines 1 and 2 both have positive slopes and slant upward to the right. Note that line 1 is steeper than line 2 and correspondingly has the larger slope, 5. Line 3 has a negative slope, $-2$, and slants downward to the right.

■

The observations made in Example 2 are true in general. Lines with a positive slope slant upward to the right, the steeper line having the larger slope. Likewise, lines with a negative slope slant downward to the right. See Figure 5.

We have yet to mention slopes for horizontal or vertical lines. In Figure 6 line 1 is horizontal; it passes through the points $(a, b)$ and $(c, b)$. Note that the two $y$-coordinates must be the same for the line to be horizontal. Line 2 in Figure 6 is vertical; it passes through $(d, e)$ and $(d, f)$. Note that the two $x$-coordinates must be the same for the line to be vertical. For the slope of line 1 we have $m = \dfrac{b - b}{c - a} = \dfrac{0}{c - a} = 0$ (provided that $a \neq c$). Thus the slope of line 1, a horizontal line, is zero. For the vertical line in Figure 6 the calculation of slope begins with

Figure 5                                  Figure 6

Figure 7

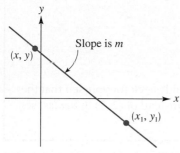

Figure 8

writing $\dfrac{e - f}{d - d}$, but the denominator is zero, and since division by zero is undefined, we conclude that slope is undefined for vertical lines. We summarize these results in the box that follows. Figure 7 shows for comparison some values of $m$ for various lines.

---

### Horizontal and Vertical Lines

1. The slope of a horizontal line is zero.
2. Slope is not defined for vertical lines.

---

We can use the concept of slope to find the equation of a line. Suppose we have a line with slope $m$ and passing through the point $(x_1, y_1)$, as shown in Figure 8. Let $(x, y)$ be any other point on the line, as in Figure 8. Then the slope of the line is given by $m = (y - y_1)/(x - x_1)$, and therefore, $y - y_1 = m(x - x_1)$. Note that the given point $(x_1, y_1)$ also satisfies this last equation, because in that case we have $y_1 - y_1 = m(x_1 - x_1)$, or $0 = 0$. The equation $y - y_1 = m(x - x_1)$ is called the **point–slope formula.** We have shown that any point on the line satisfies this equation. (Conversely, it can be shown that if a point satisfies this equation, then the point does lie on the given line.)

---

### The Point–Slope Formula

An equation of the line with slope $m$ passing through the point $(x_1, y_1)$ is

$$y - y_1 = m(x - x_1)$$

---

**EXAMPLE  3  Using the point–slope formula**

Write an equation of the line passing through $(-3, 1)$ with a slope of $-2$. Sketch a graph of the line.

**SOLUTION**
Since the slope and a point are given, we use the point–slope formula:

$$\begin{aligned} y - y_1 &= m(x - x_1) \\ y - 1 &= -2[x - (-3)] \\ y - 1 &= -2x - 6 \\ y &= -2x - 5 \end{aligned}$$

This is the desired equation. Since two points determine a line, we need to find one more point on the line. For example, for $x = 0$, $y = -5$. So the $y$-intercept is $-5$. A table and graph are displayed in Figure 9.

■

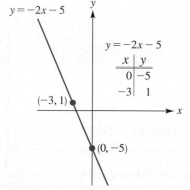

Figure 9
$y = -2x - 5$

There is another way to go about graphing the line $y = -2x - 5$ in Example 3. Since slope is (change in $y$)/(change in $x$), a slope of $-2$ (or $-2/1$) can be interpreted as telling us that if we start at $(-3, 1)$ and let $x$ *increase* by one unit, then $y$ must *decrease* by two units to bring us back to the line. Following this path in

$y = -2x - 5$

$\Delta x = 1$

$(-3, 1)$

$\Delta y = -2$

$(-2, -1)$

**Figure 10**

**Figure 11**

$(a, b)$

$y = b$

**Figure 12**

$x = a$

$(a, b)$

**Figure 13**

Figure 10 takes us from $(-3, 1)$ to $(-2, -1)$. We now draw the line through these two points, as shown in Figure 10.

**EXAMPLE 4** Finding the equation of a line through two points

Find an equation of the line passing through the points $(-2, -3)$ and $(2, 5)$.

**SOLUTION**
The slope of the line is

$$m = \frac{y_2 - y_1}{x_2 - x_1} = \frac{5 - (-3)}{2 - (-2)} = \frac{8}{4} = 2$$

Knowing the slope, we can apply the point–slope formula, making use of either $(-2, -3)$ or $(2, 5)$. Using the point $(2, 5)$ as $(x_1, y_1)$, we have

$$y - y_1 = m(x - x_1)$$
$$y - 5 = 2(x - 2)$$
$$y - 5 = 2x - 4$$
$$y = 2x + 1$$

Thus the required equation is $y = 2x + 1$. You should check for yourself that the same answer is obtained using the point $(-2, -3)$ instead of $(2, 5)$ in the last set of calculations.

**EXAMPLE 5** Finding the equation of a horizontal line

Find an equation of the horizontal line passing through the point $(4, -2)$. See Figure 11.

**SOLUTION**
Since the slope of a horizontal line is zero, we have

$$y - y_1 = m(x - x_1)$$
$$y - (-2) = 0(x - 4)$$
$$y = -2$$

Thus the equation of the horizontal line passing through $(4, -2)$ is $y = -2$.

By using the point–slope formula exactly as we did in Example 5, we can show more generally that the equation of the horizontal line in Figure 12 is $y = b$. What about the equation of the vertical line in Figure 13 passing through the point $(a, b)$? Because slope is not defined for vertical lines, the point–slope formula does not apply. However, note that as we move along the vertical line, the $x$-coordinate is always $a$, since only the $y$-coordinate varies. The equation $x = a$ expresses exactly these two facts; it says that $x$ must always be $a$, and it places no restrictions on $y$.

In the box that follows, we summarize our results concerning horizontal and vertical lines.

### Equations of Horizontal and Vertical Lines

1. The equation of a horizontal line through the point $(a, b)$ is $y = b$. (See Fig. 12.)
2. The equation of a vertical line through the point $(a, b)$ is $x = a$. (See Fig. 13.)

Another basic form for the equation of a line is the *slope–intercept form*. We are given the slope $m$ and the $y$-intercept $b$, as shown in Figure 14, and we want to find an equation of the line. To say that the line has a $y$-intercept of $b$ is the same as saying that the line passes through $(0, b)$. The point–slope formula is applicable now, using the slope $m$ and the point $(0, b)$. We have

$$y - y_1 = m(x - x_1)$$
$$y - b = m(x - 0)$$
$$y = mx + b$$

This last equation is called the **slope–intercept formula.**

**Figure 14**

### The Slope–Intercept Formula

An equation of the line with slope $m$ and $y$-intercept $b$ is

$$y = mx + b$$

---

**EXAMPLE** **6**   **Using the slope–intercept formula**

Write an equation of the line with slope 4 and $y$-intercept 1. Graph the line.

**SOLUTION**
Substituting $m = 4$ and $b = 1$ in the equation $y = mx + b$ yields

$$y - 4x + 1$$

This is the required equation. We could draw the graph by first setting up a simple table, but for purposes of emphasis and review we proceed as we did just after Example 3. Starting from the point $(0, 1)$, we interpret the slope of 4 as saying that if $x$ increases by 1, then $y$ increases by 4. This takes us from $(0, 1)$ to the point $(1, 5)$, and the line can now be sketched as in Figure 15.

**Figure 15**

---

**EXAMPLE** **7**   **Determining the slope and $y$-intercept**

Find the slope and $y$-intercept of the line $3x - 5y = 15$.

**SOLUTION**
First we solve for $y$ to write the equation in the form $y = mx + b$:

$$3x - 5y = 15$$
$$-5y = -3x + 15$$

and therefore

$$y = \frac{3}{5}x - 3$$

The slope $m$ and the $y$-intercept $b$ can now be read directly from the equation: $m = 3/5$ and $b = -3$.

As a consequence of our work up to this point, we can say that the graph of any **linear equation** $Ax + By + C = 0$, where $A$ and $B$ are not both zero, is a line, since an equation of this type can always be rewritten in one of the following three forms: $y = mx + b$, $x = a$, or $y = b$. In the box that follows, we summarize our basic results on equations of lines.

## PROPERTY SUMMARY   Equations of Lines

| Equation | Comment |
|---|---|
| $y - y_1 = m(x - x_1)$ (the point–slope formula) | This is an equation of the line with slope $m$, passing through the point $(x_1, y_1)$. |
| $y = mx + b$ (the slope–intercept formula) | This is an equation of the line with slope $m$ and $y$-intercept $b$. |
| $Ax + By + C = 0$ | The graph of any equation of this form (where $A$ and $B$ are not both zero) is a line. Special cases: If $A = 0$, then the equation can be written $y = -C/B$, which is the equation of the horizontal line with $y$-intercept $-C/B$. If $B = 0$, then the equation can be written $x = -C/A$, which represents the vertical line with $x$-intercept $-C/A$. |

**GRAPHICAL PERSPECTIVE**

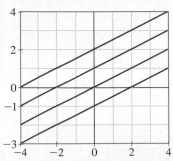

**Figure 16**
Parallel lines have the same slope. Each line here has a slope of 0.5. The equations of the lines, from top to bottom, are $y = 0.5x + 2$, $y = 0.5x + 1$, $y = 0.5x$, and $y = 0.5x - 1$.

We conclude this section by discussing two useful relationships regarding the slopes of parallel lines and the slopes of perpendicular lines. First, nonvertical parallel lines have the same slope. (See Figure 16.) This should seem reasonable if you recall that slope is a number indicating the direction or slant of a line. The relationship concerning slopes of perpendicular lines is not so obvious. The slopes of two nonvertical perpendicular lines are negative reciprocals of each other. That is, if $m_1$ and $m_2$ denote the slopes of the two perpendicular lines, then $m_1 = -1/m_2$ or, equivalently, $m_1 m_2 = -1$. For example, if a line has a slope of $2/3$, then any line perpendicular to it must have a slope of $-3/2$. For reference we summarize these facts in the box that follows. (Proofs of these facts are outlined in detail in Exercises 53 and 54.)

---

### Parallel and Perpendicular Lines

Let $m_1$ and $m_2$ denote the slopes of two distinct nonvertical lines. Then:
1. The lines are parallel if and only if $m_1 = m_2$;
2. The lines are perpendicular if and only if $m_1 = -1/m_2$.

---

EXAMPLE 8 Determining whether two lines are parallel

Determine whether the two lines $3x - 6y - 8 = 0$ and $2y = x + 1$ are parallel.

SOLUTION

By solving each equation for $y$, we can see what the slopes are:

$$3x - 6y - 8 = 0$$
$$-6y = -3x + 8$$
$$y = \frac{-3}{-6}x + \frac{8}{-6}$$
$$y = \frac{1}{2}x - \frac{4}{3}$$

$$2y = x + 1$$
$$y = \frac{1}{2}x + \frac{1}{2}$$

From this we see that both lines have the same slope ($m = 1/2$) and different $y$-intercepts. It follows therefore that the lines are parallel.

NOTE In the solution to part (b) of Example 9 we discuss how to get your graphing utility to show true proportions so that when you display the graphs of two perpendicular lines they actually look perpendicular on the display screen.

EXAMPLE 9 Finding parallel lines and perpendicular lines

In each case, find an equation for the line satisfying the given conditions, and then use a graphing utility to check that the result appears reasonable.
(a) The line passes through the point $(2, 0)$ and is parallel to the line $5x + 6y = 30$.
(b) The line passes through the point $(2, 0)$ and is perpendicular to $5x + 6y = 30$.

SOLUTION

(a) The line we are looking for is parallel to $5x + 6y = 30$ and therefore has the same slope. To find that slope, we solve the equation $5x + 6y = 30$ for $y$ as follows:

$$6y = -5x + 30$$
$$y = -\frac{5}{6}x + 5$$

The slope is the $x$-coefficient in this last equation, so $m = -5/6$. Knowing now that the slope of the required line is $-5/6$ and that it passes through the given point $(2, 0)$, we can use the point–slope formula $y - y_1 = m(x - x_1)$ to obtain $y - 0 = -\frac{5}{6}(x - 2)$, and consequently,

$$y = -\frac{5}{6}x + \frac{5}{3}$$

This is the required equation of the line passing through the point $(2, 0)$ and parallel to $5x + 6y = 30$. See the graphical perspective in Figure 17.

GRAPHICAL PERSPECTIVE

Figure 17
The line $y = -\frac{5}{6}x + \frac{5}{3}$ (in red) passes through the point $(2, 0)$ and is parallel to $5x + 6y = 30$ (in black).

**(b)** In part (a) we found that the slope of the line $5x + 6y = 30$ is $-5/6$. The slope of a perpendicular line is the opposite reciprocal of this, which is $6/5$. Knowing now that the slope of the required line is $6/5$ and that it passes through the point $(2, 0)$, we use the point–slope formula to obtain

$$y - 0 = \frac{6}{5}(x - 2)$$

$$y = \frac{6}{5}x - \frac{12}{5}$$

This is an equation of the line that passes through the point $(2, 0)$ and that is perpendicular to $5x + 6y = 30$. For a quick visual check to see whether our result is reasonable, we've used a graphing utility in Figure 18(a) to plot the given line $5x + 6y = 30$ (entering it as $y = -\frac{5}{6}x + 5$) and the perpendicular through $(2, 0)$ that we found to be $y = \frac{6}{5}x - \frac{12}{5}$. The latter line, shown in red in Figure 18(a), does appear to pass through $(2, 0)$. It does not, however, appear to be perpendicular to $5x + 6y = 30$. Assuming that our graphing utility work is correct, does this mean we've made an error in our algebra? The answer is "No, not necessarily." The problem with the graph in Figure 18(a) is that it does not show true proportions. The actual length (or number of pixels) for one unit on the $x$-axis is not the same as that on the $y$-axis. In Figure 18(b) we show a view using true proportions, and the two lines do indeed appear to be perpendicular. (If you need help obtaining a view showing true proportions, see the user's manual that came with your graphing utility. Example: On the Texas Instruments graphing calculators, the zoom choice "ZSquare" yields a viewing screen showing true proportions, albeit often with awkward numbers for Xmin and Xmax.)

**GRAPHICAL PERSPECTIVE**

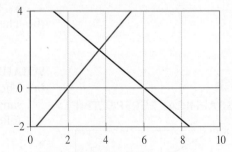

**Figure 18**
Two views of the lines $y = \frac{6}{5}x - \frac{12}{5}$ (in red) and $y = -\frac{5}{6}x + 5$ (in black)

(a) This view does not show true proportions.

(b) A *true proportions* command was used to generate this view. The two lines do appear to be perpendicular.

# EXERCISE SET 1.6

## A

*In Exercises 1–3, compute the slope of the line passing through the two given points. In Exercise 3, include a sketch with your answers.*

**1. (a)** $(-3, 2), (1, -6)$
**(b)** $(2, -5), (4, 1)$
**(c)** $(-2, 7), (1, 0)$
**(d)** $(4, 5), (5, 8)$

**2. (a)** $(-3, 0), (4, 9)$
**(b)** $(-1, 2), (3, 0)$
**(c)** $\left(\frac{1}{2}, -\frac{3}{5}\right), \left(\frac{3}{2}, \frac{3}{4}\right)$
**(d)** $\left(\frac{17}{3}, -\frac{1}{2}\right), \left(-\frac{1}{2}, \frac{17}{3}\right)$

**3. (a)** $(1, 1), (-1, -1)$
  **(b)** $(0, 5), (-8, 5)$
**4.** Compute the slope of the line in the following figure using each pair of points indicated.
  **(a)** $A$ and $B$    **(b)** $B$ and $C$    **(c)** $A$ and $C$
  The principle involved here is that no matter which pair of points you choose, the slope is the same.

*For Exercises 5 and 6, refer to Figure 2 on page 44 and find $\Delta x$, $\Delta y$, and $m = \Delta y/\Delta x$ for each of the indicated intervals. (Be sure to include units with your answers.)*
**5. (a)** $x = 10$ sec to $x = 15$ sec
  **(b)** $x = 10$ sec to $x = 25$ sec
  **(c)** $x = 5$ sec to $x = 30$ sec
**6. (a)** $x = 0$ sec to $x = 5$ sec
  **(b)** $x = 0$ sec to $x = 30$ sec

*For Exercises 7 and 8, refer to Figure A, which follows. At the beginning of this section it was mentioned that for sufficiently short periods of time, the graphs of many real-world quantities can be approximated quite accurately by a straight line. For instance, the following graph provides a close approximation to U.S. population data for the years 1970–1990.*

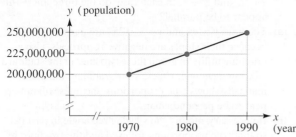

**Figure A**
U.S. population (as of July 1) for years 1970–1990

Adapted from U.S. Bureau of the Census data

**7.** Specify $\Delta x$ and $\Delta y$ for each of the following intervals.
  **(a)** $x = 1970$ to $x = 1980$    **(c)** $x = 1980$ to $x = 1990$
  **(b)** $x = 1970$ to $x = 1990$
**8.** What is the slope of the population graph in Figure A? (Be sure to include units with your answer.)

**9.** The following straight-line graph summarizes the data for world cigarette production over the years 1990–1993. Specify $\Delta t$ and $\Delta N$ for the period 1990–1993. (Include units with each answer.)

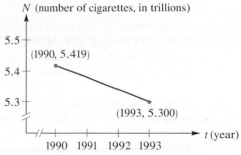

World cigarette production, 1990–1993.

Adapted from data compiled in *Vital Signs, 1998,* Lester R. Brown et al. (New York: W. W. Norton & Company, 1998)

**10.** Compute the slope $\dfrac{\Delta N}{\Delta t}$ for the straight-line graph shown in Exercise 9. (Be sure to include units as part of your answer.)
**11.** The slopes of four lines are indicated in the figure. List the slopes $m_1, m_2, m_3,$ and $m_4$ in order of increasing value.

**12.** Refer to the accompanying figure.
  **(a)** List the slopes $m_1, m_2,$ and $m_3$ in order of increasing size.
  **(b)** List the numbers $b_1, b_2,$ and $b_3$ in order of increasing size.

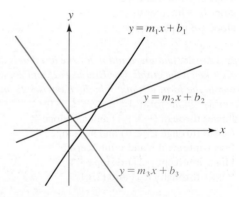

*In Exercises 13 and 14(a), three points A, B, and C are specified. Determine whether A, B, and C are **collinear** (lie on the same line) by checking to see whether the slope of $\overline{AB}$ equals the slope of $\overline{BC}$.*

**13.** $A(-8, -2); B(2, \frac{1}{2}); C(11, -1)$

**14. (a)** $A(0, -5); B(3, 4); C(-1, -8)$

    **(b)** If the area of the "triangle" formed by three points is zero, then the points must in fact be collinear. Use this observation, along with the formula in Exercise 14(b) of Exercise Set 1.4, to rework part (a).

*In Exercises 15 and 16, find an equation for the line having the given slope and passing through the given point. Write your answers in the form $y = mx + b$.*

**15. (a)** $m = -5$; through $(-2, 1)$

    **(b)** $m = \frac{1}{3}$; through $(-6, -\frac{2}{3})$

**16. (a)** $m = 22$; through $(0, 0)$

    **(b)** $m = -222$; through $(0, 0)$

*In Exercises 17 and 18, find an equation for the line passing through the two given points. Write your answer in the form $y = mx + b$.*

**17. (a)** $(4, 8)$ and $(-3, -6)$

    **(b)** $(-2, 0)$ and $(3, -10)$

    **(c)** $(-3, -2)$ and $(4, -1)$

**18. (a)** $(7, 9)$ and $(-11, 9)$

    **(b)** $(5/4, 2)$ and $(3/4, 3)$

    **(c)** $(12, 13)$ and $(13, 12)$

*In Exercises 19 and 20, write an equation of:*
**(a)** *a vertical line passing through the given point;*
**(b)** *a horizontal line passing through the given point.*

**19.** $(-3, 4)$            **20.** $(5, 8)$

**21.** Is the graph of the line $x = 0$ the $x$-axis or the $y$-axis?

**22.** Is the graph of the line $y = 0$ the $x$-axis or the $y$-axis?

*In Exercises 23 and 24, find an equation of the line with the given slope and y-intercept.*

**23. (a)** slope $-4$; $y$-intercept 7

    **(b)** slope 2; $y$-intercept $3/2$

**24. (a)** slope 0; $y$-intercept 14

    **(b)** slope 14; $y$-intercept 0

*In Exercises 25–28, find an equation for the line that is described, and sketch the graph. For Exercises 25 and 26, write the final answer in the form $y = mx + b$; for Exercises 27 and 28, write the answer in the form $Ax + By + C = 0$.*

**25. (a)** Passes through $(-3, -1)$ and has slope 4

    **(b)** Passes through $(5/2, 0)$ and has slope $1/2$

    **(c)** Has $x$-intercept 6 and $y$-intercept 5

    **(d)** Has $x$-intercept $-2$ and slope $3/4$

    **(e)** Passes through $(1, 2)$ and $(2, 6)$

**26. (a)** Passes through $(-7, -2)$ and $(0, 0)$

    **(b)** Passes through $(6, -3)$ and has $y$-intercept 8

    **(c)** Passes through $(0, -1)$ and has the same slope as the line $3x + 4y = 12$

    **(d)** Passes through $(6, 2)$ and has the same $x$-intercept as the line $-2x + y = 1$

    **(e)** Has $x$-intercept $-6$ and $y$-intercept $\sqrt{2}$

**27.** Passes through $(-3, 4)$ and is parallel to the $x$-axis

**28.** Passes through $(-3, 4)$ and is parallel to the $y$-axis

*In Exercises 29 and 30, find the x- and y-intercepts of the line, and find the area and the perimeter of the triangle formed by the line and the axes.*

**29. (a)** $3x + 5y = 15$     **30. (a)** $5x + 4y = 40$

    **(b)** $3x - 5y = 15$          **(b)** $2x + 4y = \sqrt{2}$

**31.** Determine whether each pair of lines is parallel, perpendicular, or neither.

    **(a)** $3x - 4y = 12$; $4x - 3y = 12$

    **(b)** $y = 5x - 16$; $y = 5x + 2$

    **(c)** $5x - 6y = 25$; $6x + 5y = 0$

    **(d)** $y = -\frac{2}{3}x - 1$; $y = \frac{3}{2}x - 1$

**32.** Are the lines $y = x + 1$ and $y = 1 - x$ parallel, perpendicular, or neither?

*In Exercises 33–36, find an equation for the line that is described. Write the answer in the two forms $y = mx + b$ and $Ax + By + C = 0$.*

**33.** Is parallel to $2x - 5y = 10$ and passes through $(-1, 2)$

**34.** Is parallel to $4x + 5y = 20$ and passes through $(0, 0)$

**35.** Is perpendicular to $4y - 3x = 1$ and passes through $(4, 0)$

**36.** Is perpendicular to $x - y + 2 = 0$ and passes through $(3, 1)$

Ⓖ **37. (a)** Use a graphing utility to graph the following three parallel lines in the standard viewing rectangle: $y + 4 = -0.5(x - 2)$; $y - 3 = -0.5(x + 2)$; $y = -0.5x$.

    **(b)** Experiment with different settings for Xmin, Xmax, Ymin, and Ymax. In each case, do the three lines still appear to be parallel?

Ⓖ **38. (a)** The lines $y = 4x$ and $y = -0.25x$ are perpendicular because their slopes are negative reciprocals. Use a graphing utility to graph these two lines in the standard viewing rectangle. Unless your graphing utility automatically shows true proportions, the lines will not appear to be perpendicular.

    **(b)** If necessary, modify the viewing rectangle in part (a) so that true proportions are used and the two lines indeed appear perpendicular.

**39. (a)** Find an equation of the line that passes through the origin and is perpendicular to the line $3x + 4y = 12$.

Ⓖ     **(b)** Use a graphing utility to check that your answer in part (a) is reasonable. (That is, graph the two lines using true proportions; the line you found should appear to pass through the origin and be perpendicular to $3x + 4y = 12$.)

Ⓖ **40.** In each of parts (a) through (d), first solve the equation for $y$ so that you can enter it in your graphing utility. Then use the graphing utility to graph the equation in an appropriate viewing rectangle. In each case, the graph is a line. Given that the $x$- and $y$-intercepts are (in every case here) integers, read their values off the screen and write them down for easy reference when you get to part (e).

**(a)** $\dfrac{x}{2} + \dfrac{y}{3} = 1$    **(c)** $\dfrac{x}{6} + \dfrac{y}{5} = 1$

**(b)** $\dfrac{x}{-2} + \dfrac{y}{-3} = 1$    **(d)** $\dfrac{x}{-6} + \dfrac{y}{-5} = 1$

**(e)** On the basis of your results in parts (a) through (d), describe, in general, the graph of the equation

$$\dfrac{x}{a} + \dfrac{y}{b} = 1,$$ where $a$ and $b$ are nonzero constants.

**B**

**41.** After analyzing sales figures for a particular model of CD player, the accountant for College Sound Company has produced the following graph relating the selling price $P$ (in dollars) and the number $y$ of units that can be sold each month at that price. For instance, as the graph shows, setting the selling price at \$225 yields sales of 260 units per month.

**(a)** Find an equation of the line. (Remember to use the letter $P$ instead of the usual $x$.)

**(b)** Use the equation that you found in part (a) to determine how many units can be sold in a month when the price is \$303 per unit.

**(c)** What should the price be to sell 288 units per month?

**42.** Imagine that you own a grove of orange trees, and suppose that from past experience you know that when 100 trees are planted, each tree will yield approximately 240 oranges per year. Furthermore, you've noticed that when additional trees are planted in the grove, the yield per tree decreases. Specifically, you have noted that the yield per tree decreases by about 20 oranges for each additional tree planted.

**(a)** Let $y$ denote the yield per tree when $x$ trees are planted. Find a linear equation relating $x$ and $y$. *Hint:* You are given that the point $(100, 240)$ is on the line. What is given about $\Delta y/\Delta x$?

**(b)** Use the equation in part (a) to determine how many trees should be planted to obtain a yield of 400 oranges per tree.

**(c)** If the grove contains 95 trees, what yield can you expect from each tree?

**43.** Show that the slope of the line passing through the two points $(a, a^2)$ and $(x, x^2)$ is $x + a$.   *Hint:* You'll need to use difference of squares factoring from intermediate algebra. If you need a review, see Appendix B.4.

**44.** Show that the slope of the line passing through the two points $(3, 9)$ and $(3 + h, (3 + h)^2)$ is $6 + h$.

**45.** Show that the slope of the line passing through the two points $(a, a^3)$ and $(x, x^3)$ is $x^2 + ax + a^2$.   *Hint:* You'll need to use difference of cubes factoring from intermediate algebra. If you need a review, see Appendix B.4.

**46.** Write down, and then simplify as much as possible, an expression for the slope of the line passing through the two points $(a, 1/a)$ and $(x, 1/x)$.

**47.** A line with a slope of $-5$ passes through the point $(3, 6)$. Find the area of the triangle in the first quadrant formed by this line and the coordinate axes.

**48.** The $y$-intercept of the line in the figure is 6. Find the slope of the line if the area of the shaded triangle is 72 square units.

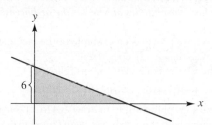

**49. (a)** Sketch the line $y = \frac{1}{2}x - 5$ and the point $P(1, 3)$. Follow parts (b)–(d) to calculate the perpendicular distance from point $P(1, 3)$ to the line.

**(b)** Find an equation of the line that passes through $P(1, 3)$ and is perpendicular to the line $y = \frac{1}{2}x - 5$.

**(c)** Find the coordinates of the point where these two lines intersect.   *Hint:* From intermediate algebra, to find where two lines $y = mx + b$ and $y = Mx + B$ intersect, set the expressions $mx + b$ and $Mx + B$ equal to each other, and solve for $x$.

**(d)** Use the distance formula to find the perpendicular distance from $P(1, 3)$ to the line $y = \frac{1}{2}x - 5$.

**50.** The following figure shows a circle centered at the origin and a line that is tangent to the circle at the point $(3, -4)$.

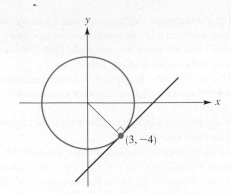

(a) Find an equation of the tangent line. *Hint:* Make use of the theorem from elementary geometry stating that the tangent line is perpendicular to the radius drawn to the point of contact.

(b) Find the intercepts of the tangent line.

(c) Find the length of the portion of the tangent line in quadrant IV.

*For Exercises 51 and 52, you'll need to recall the following definitions and results from elementary geometry. In a triangle, a line segment drawn from a vertex to the midpoint of the opposite side is called a **median**. The three medians of a triangle are **concurrent**; that is, they intersect in a single point. This point of intersection is called the **centroid** of the triangle. A line segment drawn from a vertex perpendicular to the opposite side is an **altitude**. The three altitudes of a triangle are concurrent; the point where the altitudes intersect is the **orthocenter** of the triangle.*

Ⓖ **51.** This exercise provides an example of the fact that the medians of a triangle are concurrent.

(a) The vertices of $\triangle ABC$ are as follows:

$$A(-4, 0) \qquad B(2, 0) \qquad C(0, 6)$$

Use a graphing utility to draw $\triangle ABC$. (Since $\overline{AB}$ coincides with the x-axis, you won't need to draw a line segment for this side.) *Note:* If the graphing utility you use does not have a provision for drawing line segments, you will need to determine an equation for the line in each case and then graph the line.

(b) Find the coordinates of the midpoint of each side of the triangle, then include the three medians in your picture from part (a). Note that the three medians do appear to intersect in a single point. Use the graphing utility to estimate the coordinates of the centroid.

(c) Using paper and pencil, find the equation of the medians from $A$ to $\overline{BC}$ and from $B$ to $\overline{AC}$. Then (using simultaneous equations from intermediate algebra), determine the exact coordinates of the centroid. How do these numbers compare with your estimates in part (b)?

Ⓖ **52.** This exercise illustrates the fact that the altitudes of a triangle are concurrent. Again, we'll be using $\triangle ABC$ with vertices $A(-4, 0)$, $B(2, 0)$, and $C(0, 6)$. Note that one of

the altitudes of this triangle is just the portion of the y-axis extending from $y = 0$ to $y = 6$; thus, you won't need to graph this altitude; it will already be in the picture.

(a) Using paper and pencil, find the equations for the three altitudes. (Actually, you are finding equations for the lines that coincide with the altitude segments.)

(b) Use a graphing utility to draw $\triangle ABC$ along with the three altitude lines that you determined in part (a). Note that the altitudes appear to intersect in a single point. Use the graphing utility to estimate the coordinates of this point.

(c) Using simultaneous equations (from intermediate algebra), find the exact coordinates of the orthocenter. Are your estimates in part (b) close to these values?

**53.** This exercise outlines a proof of the fact that two non-vertical lines are parallel if and only if their slopes are equal. The proof relies on the following observation for the given figure: The lines $y = m_1x + b_1$ and $y = m_2x + b_2$ will be parallel if and only if the two vertical distances $AB$ and $CD$ are equal. (In the figure, the points $C$ and $D$ both have x-coordinate 1.)

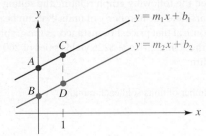

(a) Verify that the coordinates of $A$, $B$, $C$, and $D$ are

$$A(0, b_1) \quad B(0, b_2) \quad C(1, m_1 + b_1) \quad D(1, m_2 + b_2)$$

(b) Using the coordinates in part (a), check that

$$AB = b_1 - b_2 \quad \text{and} \quad CD = (m_1 + b_1) - (m_2 + b_2)$$

(c) Use part (b) to show that the equation $AB = CD$ is equivalent to $m_1 = m_2$.

**54.** This exercise outlines a proof of the fact that two nonvertical lines with slopes $m_1$ and $m_2$ are perpendicular if and only if $m_1m_2 = -1$. In the following figure, we've assumed that our two nonvertical lines $y = m_1x$ and $y = m_2x$ intersect at the origin. [If they did not intersect there, we could just as well work with lines parallel to these that do intersect at $(0, 0)$, recalling that parallel lines have the same slope.] The proof relies on the following geometric fact:

$$\overline{OA} \perp \overline{OB} \quad \text{if and only if} \quad (OA)^2 + (OB)^2 = (AB)^2$$

(a) Verify that the coordinates of $A$ and $B$ are $A(1, m_1)$ and $B(1, m_2)$.

(b) Show that

$$OA^2 = 1 + m_1^2$$
$$OB^2 = 1 + m_2^2$$
$$AB^2 = m_1^2 - 2m_1m_2 + m_2^2$$

**(c)** Use part (b) to show that the equation

$$OA^2 + OB^2 = AB^2$$

is equivalent to $m_1m_2 = -1$.

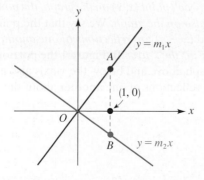

**55.** Verify the identity

$$(y_2 - y_1)/(x_2 - x_1) = (y_1 - y_2)/(x_1 - x_2)$$

What does this identity tell you about calculating slope?

## C

**56.** Find the slope $m$ of the line in the following figure.

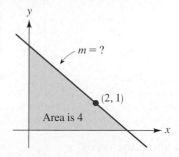

## MINI PROJECT | THINKING ABOUT SLOPE

Working within a group or with the class at large, carry out the two activities indicated below. Then, on your own, write a summary of what you have learned.

**1.** What if the definition of slope that we gave in this section had instead been

$$m = \frac{y_2 + y_1}{x_2 + x_1}?$$ Try reworking Example 1 using this version of slope and describe what happens. Why is this unsatisfactory?

**2.** Why, where, and when did the use of the letter $m$ for slope originate? See what you can find out by reading comments from mathematicians and math historians at the following Internet website:

http://mathforum.org/epigone/math-history-list

On the right-hand side of that web page, click on "search this discussion," and type in the word *slope*. As with many historical issues in many fields, don't expect one simple definitive answer. Summarize what you find out.

## ▌1.7  SYMMETRY AND GRAPHS. CIRCLES

*Symmetry is a working concept. If all the object is symmetrical, then the parts must be halves (or some other rational fraction) and the amount of information necessary to describe the object is halved (etc.).* —Alan L. Macay, Department of Crystallography, University of London

As you will see throughout this text, there are some basic techniques that help us to understand the essential features of a graph. In the box that follows, we introduce three types of *symmetry* that are useful in analyzing graphs.

## THREE TYPES OF SYMMETRY

| Type of Symmetry | Example | Definition |
|---|---|---|
| 1. Symmetry about the *x*-axis | <br>Figure 1<br>Symmetry about the *x*-axis | *For each point (x, y) on the graph, the point (x, −y) is also on the graph.* We say that the points (x, y) and (x, −y) are *reflections of one another about* (or *in*) *the x-axis.* In Figure 1 the portions of the graph above and below the *x*-axis also are said to be reflections of one another about the *x*-axis. |
| 2. Symmetry about the *y*-axis | <br>Figure 2<br>Symmetry about the *y*-axis | *For each point (x, y) on the graph, the point (−x, y) is also on the graph.* We say that the points (x, y) and (−x, y) are *reflections of one another about* (or *in*) *the y-axis.* In Figure 2 the portions of the graph to the right and left of the *y*-axis also are said to be reflections of one another about the *y*-axis. |
| 3. Symmetry about the origin | <br>Figure 3<br>Symmetry about the origin | *For each point (x, y) on the graph, the point (−x, −y) is also on the graph.* We say that the points (x, y) and (−x, −y) are *reflections of one another about the origin.* In Figure 3 the first- and third-quadrant portions of the curve also are said to be reflections of one another about the origin. In terms of the two previous symmetries, the point (−x, −y) can be obtained from (x, y) as follows: First reflect (x, y) about the *y*-axis to obtain (−x, y), then reflect (−x, y) about the *x*-axis to obtain (−x, −y). |

---

**EXAMPLE 1 Sketching reflections**

A line segment $\mathcal{L}$ has endpoints $(1, 2)$ and $(5, 3)$. Sketch the reflection of $\mathcal{L}$ about: **(a)** the *x*-axis; **(b)** the *y*-axis; and **(c)** the origin.

**SOLUTION**

**(a)** First reflect the endpoints $(1, 2)$ and $(5, 3)$ about the *x*-axis to obtain the new endpoints $(1, -2)$ and $(5, -3)$, respectively. Then join these two points as indicated in Figure 4(a), in quadrant IV.

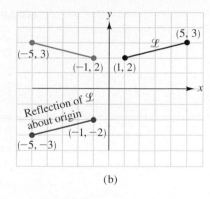

Figure 4              (a)                                    (b)

**(b)** Reflect the given endpoints about the $y$-axis to obtain the new endpoints $(-1, 2)$ and $(-5, 3)$; then join these two points as shown in Figure 4(a), in quadrant II.

**(c)** As described in the box preceding this example, reflection about the origin can be carried out in two steps: First reflect about the $y$-axis, then reflect about the $x$-axis. In part (b) we obtained the reflection of $\mathcal{L}$ in the $y$-axis, so now we need only reflect the line segment obtained in part (b) about the $x$-axis. See Figure 4(b).

In the box that follows, we list three rules for testing whether the graph of an equation possesses any of the types of symmetry we've been discussing. (The validity of each rule follows directly from the definitions of symmetry.)

---

### Three Tests for Symmetry

1. The graph of an equation is symmetric about the $y$-axis if replacing $x$ with $-x$ yields an equivalent equation.
2. The graph of an equation is symmetric about the $x$-axis if replacing $y$ with $-y$ yields an equivalent equation.
3. The graph of an equation is symmetric about the origin if replacing $x$ and $y$ with $-x$ and $-y$, respectively, yields an equivalent equation.

---

**EXAMPLE   2   Testing for symmetry about the x-axis and the y-axis**

**(a)** In Figure 5(a), obtained with a graphing utility, the graph of $y = x^4 - 3x^2 + 1$ appears to be symmetric about the $y$-axis. Use an appropriate symmetry test to find out whether the graph indeed possesses this type of symmetry.

**(b)** In Figure 5(b), obtained with a graphing utility, the graph of $x = y^2 - \frac{1}{10}y - 15$ appears to be symmetric about the $x$-axis. Use an appropriate symmetry test to find out whether the graph indeed possesses this type of symmetry. *Remark*: Most graphing utilities require that you solve the equation for $y$ before you enter it. See Exercise 61 for details.

## GRAPHICAL PERSPECTIVE

(a) $y = x^4 - 3x^2 + 1$
$[-4, 4, 2]$ by $[-4, 10, 2]$

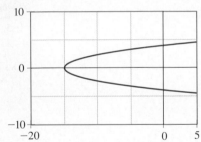

(b) $x = y^2 - \frac{1}{10}y - 15$
$[-20, 5, 5]$ by $[-10, 10, 5]$

**Figure 5**

### SOLUTION

**(a)** To test for symmetry about the $y$-axis, we replace $x$ with $-x$ in the given equation, to obtain

$$y = (-x)^4 - 3(-x)^2 + 1 \qquad \text{or} \qquad y = x^4 - 3x^2 + 1$$

Since this last equation is the same as the original equation, we conclude that the graph is indeed symmetric about the $y$-axis.

**(b)** To test for symmetry about the $x$-axis, we replace $y$ with $-y$ in the given equation, to obtain

$$x = (-y)^2 - \frac{1}{10}(-y) - 15 \qquad \text{or} \qquad x = y^2 + \frac{1}{10}y - 15$$

This last equation is not equivalent to the given equation. This tells us that the graph is not symmetric about the $x$-axis. (Exercise 61(c), a graphing utility exercise, asks for a viewing rectangle that clearly shows this lack of symmetry.)

---

**EXAMPLE  3  Testing for symmetry about the origin**

In Figure 6 it appears that the graph of $y = 2x^3 - 3x$ is symmetric about the origin. Use a symmetry test to find out whether this is indeed the case.

### GRAPHICAL PERSPECTIVE

**Figure 6**
$y = 2x^3 - 3x$,
$[-2, 2, 1]$ by $[-10, 10, 5]$
The graph appears to be symmetric about the origin.
Is this really the case?

**SOLUTION**

Replacing $x$ and $y$ with $-x$ and $-y$, respectively, gives us

$$-y = 2(-x)^3 - 3(-x) = -2x^3 + 3x$$
$$y = 2x^3 - 3x \qquad \text{multiplying through by } -1$$

This last equation is identical to the given equation, and we conclude that in this case appearances are not deceiving; the graph is indeed symmetric about the origin.

In the next two examples we use the notions of symmetry and intercepts as guides for drawing graphs. True, the graphs could be obtained more quickly using a graphing utility. The idea here, however, is to *understand* why the graphs look as they do.

**EXAMPLE 4  Using symmetry and intercepts as aids in graphing**

Graph the equation $y = -x^2 + 5$.

**SOLUTION**

The domain of the variable $x$ in the expression $-x^2 + 5$ is the set of all real numbers. However, since the graph must be symmetric about the $y$-axis (why?), we need only sketch the graph to the right of the $y$-axis; the portion to the left will then be the mirror image of this (with the $y$-axis as the mirror). The $x$- and $y$-intercepts (if any) are computed as follows:

| $x$-INTERCEPTS | $y$-INTERCEPTS |
|---|---|
| $-x^2 + 5 = 0$ | $y = -(0)^2 + 5$ |
| $x^2 = 5$ | $y = 5$ |
| $x = \pm\sqrt{5} \; (\approx \pm 2.2)$ | |

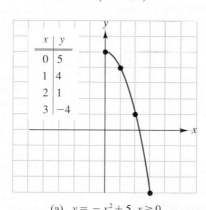

(a)  $y = -x^2 + 5, \; x \geq 0$

(b)  The graph of $y = -x^2 + 5$ is symmetric about the $y$-axis.

**Figure 7**

In Figure 7(a) we've set up a short table of values and sketched the graph for $x \geq 0$. The complete graph is then obtained by reflection about the $y$-axis, as shown in Figure 7(b). [The curve in Figure 7(b) is a *parabola*. This type of curve will be considered in detail in later chapters.]

**EXAMPLE** **5** **Using symmetry and domain as aids in graphing**

Graph: $y = -4/x$.

**SOLUTION**
Before doing any calculations, note that the domain of the variable $x$ consists of all real numbers other than zero. So, however the resulting graph might look, it cannot contain a point with an $x$-coordinate of zero. In other words, the graph cannot cross the $y$-axis. (Check for yourself that the graph cannot cross the $x$-axis either.) Now, since the graph is symmetric about the origin (why?), we need only sketch the graph for $x > 0$; the portion corresponding to $x < 0$ can then be obtained by reflection about the origin. In Figure 8(a) we've set up a table of values and sketched the graph for $x > 0$. (Note the fractional $x$-values at the end of the table: since $y$ is undefined when $x$ is zero, it's informative to pick $x$-values near zero and look at the corresponding $y$-values.) In Figure 8(b) we have reflected the fourth-quadrant portion of the graph first about the $y$-axis and then about the $x$-axis to obtain the required reflection about the origin. Figure 9 shows our final graph of $y = -4/x$.

| $x$ | 1 | 2 | 3 | 4 | 5 | 6 | 7 | 8 | $\frac{1}{2}$ | $\frac{1}{3}$ |
|---|---|---|---|---|---|---|---|---|---|---|
| $y$ | $-4$ | $-2$ | $-\frac{4}{3}$ | $-1$ | $-\frac{4}{5}$ | $-\frac{2}{3}$ | $-\frac{4}{7}$ | $-\frac{1}{2}$ | $-8$ | $-12$ |

(a) $y = -4/x$, $x > 0$

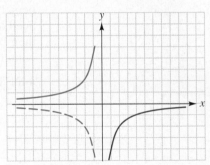

(b) Reflections about the $y$-axis and then the $x$-axis yield a reflection about the origin.

**Figure 8**

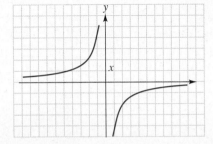

**Figure 9**
The graph of $y = -4/x$ is symmetric about the origin.

We can use the graph in Figure 8(a) to introduce the idea of an *asymptote*. A line is an **asymptote** for a curve if the distance between the line and the curve approaches zero as we move farther and farther out along the line. So for the curve in Figure 8(a) both the $x$-axis and the $y$-axis are asymptotes. (We'll return to this idea several times later in the text. For other pictures of asymptotes, see Figure 1 in Section 4.7.)

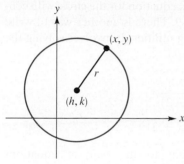

**Figure 10**

Since we've been discussing symmetry in this section, it seems appropriate to conclude with a discussion of the circle, because in some sense, this is the most symmetric curve. We can use the distance formula to obtain *the equation of a circle*. Figure 10 shows a circle with center $(h, k)$ and radius $r$. By definition, a point $(x, y)$ is on this circle if and only if the distance from $(x, y)$ to $(h, k)$ is $r$. Thus we have

$$\sqrt{(x - h)^2 + (y - k)^2} = r$$

or, equivalently,

$$(x - h)^2 + (y - k)^2 = r^2 \qquad (1)$$

(These last two equations are equivalent because two nonnegative quantities are equal if and only if their squares are equal.)

The work in the previous paragraph tells us two things. First, if a point $(x, y)$ lies on the circle in Figure 10, then $x$ and $y$ together satisfy equation (1). Second, if a pair of numbers $x$ and $y$ satisfies equation (1), then the point $(x, y)$ lies on the circle in Figure 10. (Does it sound to you as if the previous two sentences say the same thing? They don't! Think about it.) Equation (1) is called the **standard form for the equation of a circle** or the **standard equation of a circle**. For reference, we record the result in the box that follows.

### The Equation of a Circle in Standard Form

The standard equation of the circle with center $(h, k)$ and radius $r$ is

$$(x - h)^2 + (y - k)^2 = r^2$$

---

 **EXAMPLE** 6    **Finding the equation of a circle**

**(a)** Write the equation of the circle with center $(-2, 1)$ and radius 3.
**(b)** Does the point $(-4, 3)$ lie on this circle?

**SOLUTION**
**(a)** In the equation $(x - h)^2 + (y - k)^2 = r^2$, we substitute the given values $h = -2$, $k = 1$, and $r = 3$. This yields

$$[x - (-2)]^2 + (y - 1)^2 = 3^2$$

or

$$(x + 2)^2 + (y - 1)^2 = 9 \qquad (2)$$

This is the standard form for the equation of the given circle.
**(b)** To find out whether the point $(-4, 3)$ lies on the circle, we check to see if the coordinates $x = -4$ and $y = 3$ satisfy equation (2). We have

$$(-4 + 2)^2 + (3 - 1)^2 \stackrel{?}{=} 9$$
$$(-2)^2 + 2^2 \stackrel{?}{=} 9$$
$$8 \stackrel{?}{=} 9 \qquad \text{False}$$

This shows that the values $x = -4$ and $y = 3$ do not satisfy equation (2). Consequently, the point $(-4, 3)$ does not lie on the circle.

In the example just concluded we found that an equation for the circle with center $(-2, 1)$ and radius 3 is $(x + 2)^2 + (y - 1)^2 = 9$. There is another way to write this equation that is useful for work with graphing utilities. It involves solving the equation for $y$ in terms of $x$, as follows:

$$(y - 1)^2 = 9 - (x + 2)^2$$
$$y - 1 = \pm\sqrt{9 - (x + 2)^2}$$
$$y = 1 \pm \sqrt{9 - (x + 2)^2}$$

Thus the equation of the circle is equivalent to the *pair* of equations $y = 1 + \sqrt{9 - (x + 2)^2}$ and $y = 1 - \sqrt{9 - (x + 2)^2}$. In working with a graphics calculator or a computer, both of these equations are graphed to yield the required circle. See Figure 11 and the GRAPHICAL PERSPECTIVE in Figure 12. In Figure 11, note that the equation with the positive square root represents the upper semicircle, while the equation with the negative square root represents the lower semicircle.

**Figure 11**    (a) $y = 1 + \sqrt{9 - (x + 2)^2}$        (b) $y = 1 - \sqrt{9 - (x + 2)^2}$        (c) $(x + 2)^2 + (y - 1)^2 = 9$

**GRAPHICAL PERSPECTIVE**

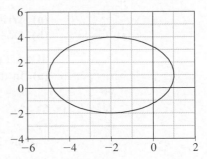

**Figure 12**
A distorted view of the circle
$(x + 2)^2 + (y - 1)^2 = 9$ results
when a *true proportions* option is
not selected on the graphing utility.

Again, let us go back to the equation obtained in Example 6 for the circle with center $(-2, 1)$ and radius 3: $(x + 2)^2 + (y - 1)^2 = 9$. An alternative form for this equation is found by carrying out the indicated algebra:

$$(x + 2)^2 + (y - 1)^2 = 9$$
$$x^2 + 4x + 4 + y^2 - 2y + 1 = 9$$
$$x^2 + 4x + y^2 - 2y - 4 = 0 \qquad (3)$$

The disadvantage of this last equation is that the center and radius are no longer readily apparent. For this reason it is useful to have a systematic procedure for converting equations such as equation (3) back into standard form. The algebraic technique from intermediate algebra known as *completing the square* allows us to accomplish this. We'll review (or reintroduce) this technique for you with two examples. (We'll have several other uses for completing the square later in this text. It's also useful at times in calculus.)

As a first example in completing the square, we convert the equation $x^2 + y^2 + 10x - 6y - 4 = 0$ into the standard form for a circle. We begin by grouping the x-terms, grouping the y-terms, and moving the constant to the other side (that is, adding 4 to both sides):

$$(x^2 + 10x \quad\quad) + (y^2 - 6y \quad\quad) = 4 \tag{4}$$

We've left the extra space within each set of parentheses because we are going to add something there. (You'll see in a moment why we want to do this.) To determine the number that we want to add in the first set of parentheses, we follow the completing-the-square procedure:

*Take half of the coefficient of x and square it.*

From equation (4), the coefficient of x is 10. Taking half of 10 and then squaring it gives us $5^2$, or 25. That's the number we want to add in the first set of parentheses. Of course, to keep the equation in balance, we have to add 25 on the other side too. So equation (4) becomes

$$(x^2 + 10x + 25) + (y^2 - 6y \quad\quad) = 4 + 25 \tag{5}$$

In the same way now, to determine the number that we want to add in the second set of parentheses, we

*Take half of the coefficient of y and square it.*

From equation (5), the coefficient of y is $-6$. Taking half of $-6$ and squaring gives us $(-3)^2$, or 9. That's the number we want to add in the second set of parentheses. To keep the equation in balance, we also add 1 to the right side to obtain

$$(x^2 + 10x + 25) + (y^2 - 6y + 9) = 4 + 25 + 9 = 38 \tag{6}$$

The whole point in completing the square is that the expressions within the parentheses are now perfect squares, and we can rewrite equation (6) as

$$(x + 5)^2 + (y - 3)^2 = 38 \quad\quad \text{Verify this factoring for yourself.}$$

This last equation is the standard form for the equation of a circle. From the equation we see that the center of the circle is $(-5, 3)$. What about the radius? In standard form, the right side of the equation is $r^2$. So we have $r^2 = 38$, and consequently $r = \sqrt{38}$.

The process that we've just described for completing the square requires that the coefficients of $x^2$ and $y^2$ both be 1. If this is not the case at the start, then you need to divide both sides of the equation by an appropriate constant, as indicated in the next example. We will modify this technique in Chapter 11 when we discuss equations in which the $x^2$ and $y^2$ terms have different coefficients.

**EXAMPLE** 7 **Completing the square and determining x-intercepts**

Refer to Figure 13, which shows a graph of the circle

$$4x^2 + 4y^2 - 24x - 12y + 29 = 0$$

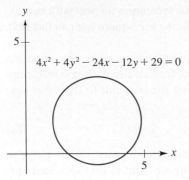

$4x^2 + 4y^2 - 24x - 12y + 29 = 0$

**Figure 13**

(a) Find the center and radius of the circle.

(b) Use a graphing utility to estimate (to two decimal places) the $x$-intercepts of the circle.

(c) Use algebra to find exact values for the $x$-intercepts.

**SOLUTION**

(a) To obtain coefficients of 1 in front of both $x^2$ and $y^2$, we divide both sides of the equation by 4:

$$x^2 + y^2 - 6x - 3y + \frac{29}{4} = 0$$

Next, we group the $x$-terms, group the $y$-terms, and subtract the constant 29/4 from both sides. This gives us

$$(x^2 - 6x \quad ) + (y^2 - 3y \quad ) = -\frac{29}{4}$$

To complete the square within the first set of parentheses we need to add $(\frac{-6}{2})^2$, which is 9. Likewise in the second set of parentheses, we want to add $(\frac{-3}{2})^2$ or $\frac{9}{4}$. So we obtain

$$(x^2 - 6x + 9) + \left( y^2 - 3y + \frac{9}{4} \right) = -\frac{29}{4} + 9 + \frac{9}{4}$$

or, equivalently,

$$(x - 3)^2 + \left( y - \frac{3}{2} \right)^2 = 4 \qquad \text{Check the arithmetic.} \tag{7}$$

Looking at this last equation, we see that the center of the circle is $(3, \frac{3}{2})$ and the radius is 2.

(b) To use a graphing utility to graph the circle, we solve equation (7) for $y$ in terms of $x$ as follows.

$$\left( y - \frac{3}{2} \right)^2 = 4 - (x - 3)^2$$

$$y - \frac{3}{2} = \pm\sqrt{4 - (x - 3)^2}$$

$$y = \frac{3}{2} + \sqrt{4 - (x - 3)^2} \qquad \text{or} \qquad y = \frac{3}{2} - \sqrt{4 - (x - 3)^2}$$

Figure 14(a) shows a graph of this pair of equations (using true proportions). The view in Figure 14(a) indicates that the smaller $x$-intercept is

**GRAPHICAL PERSPECTIVE**

(a) [0, 6, 1] by [−1, 4, 1]
True proportions

(b) [1.670, 1.680, 0.005 ] by
[ − 0.005, 0.005, 0.005]

**Figure 14**
A graph of the circle
$(x - 3)^2 + (y - \frac{3}{2})^2 = 4$ along with
a magnified view near the smaller
of the two $x$-intercepts

between 1 and 2, closer to 2 than to 1; the larger $x$-intercept is between 4 and 5, closer to 4 than to 5. Figure 14(b) shows a close-up view of the smaller $x$-intercept. Evidently, it is closer to 1.680 than to 1.670, and so our estimate to two decimal places is 1.68. Exercise 62 asks you to use a graphing utility in a similar manner to show that the larger $x$-intercept is approximately 4.32.

**(c)** The easiest way to find exact expressions for the $x$-intercepts is to use equation (7). Setting $y = 0$ in equation (7) yields

$$(x - 3)^2 + \frac{9}{4} = 4$$

$$(x - 3)^2 = \frac{7}{4} \qquad \text{Check the arithmetic.}$$

$$x - 3 = \pm\sqrt{\frac{7}{4}} = \pm\frac{\sqrt{7}}{2}$$

$$x = 3 \pm \frac{\sqrt{7}}{2}$$

In summary, the two $x$-intercepts are $3 - \sqrt{7}/2$ and $3 + \sqrt{7}/2$. As you can check for yourself with a calculator, these last two expressions are approximately 1.68 and 4.32, respectively. These values are consistent with the numbers that we obtained graphically in part (b).

# EXERCISE SET 1.7

## A

*In Exercises 1–6, the endpoints of a line segment $\overline{AB}$ are given. Sketch the reflection of $\overline{AB}$ about* **(a)** *the x-axis;* **(b)** *the y-axis; and* **(c)** *the origin.*

1. $A(1, 4)$ and $B(3, 1)$
2. $A(-1, -2)$ and $B(-5, -2)$
3. $A(-2, -3)$ and $B(2, -1)$
4. $A(-3, -3)$ and $B(-3, -1)$
5. $A(0, 1)$ and $B(3, 1)$
6. $A(-2, -2)$ and $B(0, 0)$

*In Exercises 7–24, graph the equation after determining the x- and y-intercepts and whether the graph possesses any of the three types of symmetry described on page 58.*

7. $y = 4 - x^2$
8. $y = -x^3$
9. $y = -1/x$
10. $x = y^2 - 1$
11. $y = -x^2$
12. $y = 1/x^2$
13. $y = -1/x^3$
14. $y = |x| - 2$
15. $y = \sqrt{x^2}$
16. $y = x + 1$
17. $y = x^2 - 2x + 1$
18. $x = y^3 - 1$
19. $y^2 = 2x - 4$
20. $|y| = 2x - 4$
21. $y = 2x^2 + x - 4$
22. $y = 2x^2$
23. **(a)** $x + y = 2$
    **(b)** $|x| + y = 2$
24. **(a)** $x + |y| = 2$
    **(b)** $|x + y| = 2$

Ⓖ *In Exercises 25–38:*
   **(a)** *Use a graphing utility to graph each equation in the standard viewing rectangle.*
   **(b)** *Does the graph in part (a) appear to possess any of the three types of symmetry defined on page 58?*
   **(c)** *In cases in which your answer to part (b) is Yes, adjust your viewing rectangle for a second, more careful inspection. (In Exercises 25–31, suggestions for the second look are provided.)*
   **(d)** *In cases in which, after the second look, it still appears that the graph possesses symmetry, use an appropriate symmetry test from page 59 to settle the matter.*

25. $y = x^2 - 3x$ (second view: $x$ from $-2$ to 5; $y$ from $-4$ to 10)
26. $y = x^3 - 3x$ (second view: $x$ from $-3$ to 3; $y$ unchanged)
27. $y = 2^x$ (second view: $x$ from $-3$ to 3; $y$ from 0 to 8)
28. $y = 2^{|x|}$ (second view: $x$ from $-3$ to 3; $y$ from 0 to 8)
29. $y = 1/(x^2 - x)$ (second view: $x$ from $-2$ to 2; $y$ unchanged)
30. $y = 1/(x^3 - x)$ (second view: $x$ from $-2$ to 2; $y$ unchanged)
31. $y = x^2 - 0.2x - 15$   *Hint:* Look closely at the $x$-intercepts.
32. $y = x^2 - 2x^3$     33. $y = \sqrt{|x|}$     34. $y = \sqrt{|x|^3}$
35. $y = 2x - x^3 - x^5 + x^7$      36. $y = |2x - x^3 - x^5 + x^7|$
37. $y = x^4 - 10x^2 + \frac{1}{4}x$   *Suggestion:* For the second view, try zooming out in the $y$-direction.
38. $y = x^4 - 10x^2 + \frac{1}{4}$

*In Exercises 39–42, specify the center and radius of each circle. Also, determine whether the given point lies on the circle.*

**39.** $(x - 1)^2 + (y - 5)^2 = 169; (6, -7)$

**40.** $(x + 4)^2 + (y + 2)^2 = 20; (0, 1)$

**41.** $(x + 8)^2 + (y - 5)^2 = 13; (-5, 2)$

**42.** $x^2 + y^2 = 1; (1/2, \sqrt{3}/2)$

*In Exercises 43–48, determine the center and the radius for the circle. Also, find the y-coordinates of the points (if any) where the circle intersects the y-axis.*

**43.** $x^2 + y^2 = \sqrt{2}$

**44.** $x^2 + y^2 - 10x + 2y + 17 = 0$

**45.** $x^2 + y^2 + 8x - 6y = -24$

**46.** $4x^2 - 4x + 4y^2 - 63 = 0$

**47.** $9x^2 + 54x + 9y^2 - 6y + 64 = 0$

**48.** $3x^2 + 3y^2 + 5x - 4y = 1$

*In Exercises 49 and 50, use the techniques shown in Example 7 to carry out the following procedures.*

**(a)** *Find the center and radius of the circle.*

Ⓖ **(b)** *Use a graphing utility to graph the circle and to estimate (to two decimal places) the x-intercepts.*

**(c)** *Use algebra to find exact values for the x-intercepts, and then use a calculator to check that the results are consistent with the estimates in part (b).*

**49.** $16x^2 - 64x + 16y^2 + 48y - 69 = 0$

**50.** $3x^2 + x + 3y^2 + 3y - 1 = 0$

Ⓖ **51.** In the text we said that a line is an *asymptote* for a curve if the distance between the line and the curve approaches zero as we move farther and farther out along the line. In terms of graphing, this means that as we zoom out, the curve and the line eventually appear indistinguishable. In this exercise, we'll demonstrate this using the curve $y = -4/x$ (which we graphed in Figure 9). As indicated in the text, both the x- and y-axes are asymptotes for this curve. First, graph $y = -4/x$ using a viewing rectangle that extends from $-5$ to $5$ in both the x- and the y-directions. Then take a second look using a viewing rectangle that extends from $-30$ to $30$ in both the x- and y-directions. At this scale, you'll see that the curve is virtually indistinguishable from an asymptote when either $|x| > 8$ or $|y| > 8$.

Ⓖ **52. (a)** Graph the equation $y = 20/x$ using a standard viewing rectangle.

**(b)** Although both the x- and the y-axes are asymptotes for this curve, the graph in part (a) does not show this clearly. Take a second look, using a viewing rectangle that extends from $-100$ to $100$ in both the x- and the y-directions. Note that the curve indeed appears indistinguishable from an asymptote when either $|x|$ or $|y|$ is sufficiently large.

**B**

**53.** The center of a circle is the point $(3, 2)$. If the point $(-2, -10)$ lies on this circle, find the standard equation for the circle.

**54.** Find the standard equation of the circle tangent to the x-axis and with center $(3, 5)$.   *Hint*: First draw a sketch.

**55.** Find the standard equation of the circle tangent to the y-axis and with center $(3, 5)$.

**56.** Find the standard equation of the circle passing through the origin and with center $(3, 5)$.

**57.** The points $A(-1, 6)$ and $B(3, -2)$ are the endpoints of a diameter of a circle, as indicated in the accompanying figure. Find the y-intercepts of the circle.   *Hint*: Could you do the problem if you had the equation of the circle?

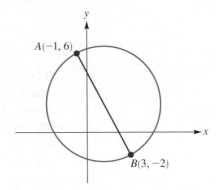

**58. (a)** Verify that the point $(3, 7)$ is on the circle
$$x^2 + y^2 - 2x - 6y - 10 = 0$$

**(b)** Find the equation of the line tangent to this circle at the point $(3, 7)$.   *Hint*: A result from elementary geometry says that the tangent to a circle is perpendicular to the radius drawn to the point of contact.

**59.** The accompanying figure shows the graphs of $y = \frac{3}{4}x - 2$ and $y = |\frac{3}{4}x - 2|$.

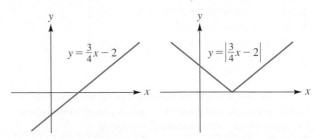

**(a)** Determine the x- and y-intercepts for each graph.

**(b)** Which portions of the two graphs are identical? (Give your answer in terms of an interval along the x-axis.)

**(c)** Explain how the graph of $y = |\frac{3}{4}x - 2|$ can be obtained from that of $y = \frac{3}{4}x - 2$ by means of reflection.

**60.** The accompanying figure shows the graphs of the two equations $y = x^2 - 6x + 8$ and $y = |x^2 - 6x + 8|$.

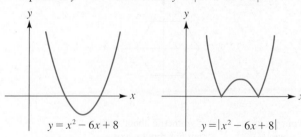

$y = x^2 - 6x + 8$          $y = |x^2 - 6x + 8|$

**(a)** Determine the $x$- and $y$-intercepts for each graph.
**(b)** Which portions of the two graphs are identical? (Give your answer in terms of intervals along the $x$-axis.)
**(c)** Explain how the graph of $y = |x^2 - 6x + 8|$ can be obtained from that of $y = x^2 - 6x + 8$ by means of reflection.

Ⓖ **61.** This exercise relates to Figure 5(b) on page 60. That figure shows a graph of the equation $x = y^2 - 0.1y - 15$. Note that this equation is solved for $x$ rather than $y$. In the standard Cartesian graphing mode, however, most graphing utilities require that the equation be solved for $y$. This exercise shows one method for obtaining the graph. (A remark at the end of this exercise mentions a second method.)

**(a)** Rewrite the equation as

$$y^2 - 0.1y - (15 + x) = 0$$

Then solve for $y$ in terms of $x$ by using the quadratic formula with $a = 1$, $b = -0.1$, and $c = -(15 + x)$. After simplifying, you should obtain

$$y = \frac{0.1 \pm \sqrt{60.01 + 4x}}{2}$$

**(b)** Enter and graph the pair of equations

$$y = \frac{0.1 - \sqrt{60.01 + 4x}}{2} \quad \text{and} \quad y = \frac{0.1 + \sqrt{60.01 + 4x}}{2}$$

using the viewing rectangle $[-20, 5, 5]$ by $[-10, 10, 5]$. Check that your graph agrees with that shown in Figure 5(b).

**(c)** Experiment to find a viewing rectangle in which it is clear that the graph of the equation $x = y^2 - 0.1y - 15$ is *not* symmetric about the $x$-axis.

*Remark:* A second method for graphing $x = y^2 - 0.1y - 15$ requires the *parametric mode* on your graphing utility. Consult the user's manual for your graphing utility to see how to access and operate this mode. Entering the following pair of equations in the parametric mode will yield the graph (or a portion of the graph): $x = t^2 - 0.1t - 15$; $y = t$.

Ⓖ **62.** Use a graphing utility and the method shown in the solution of Example 7(b) to show that the larger of the two $x$-intercepts of the circle $4x^2 + 4y^2 - 24x - 12y + 29 = 0$ is (to two decimal places) 4.32.

## C

**63.** Suppose that the circle $x^2 + 2Ax + y^2 + 2By = C$ has two $x$-intercepts, $x_1$ and $x_2$, and two $y$-intercepts, $y_1$ and $y_2$. Prove each statement.
**(a)** $\dfrac{x_1 + x_2}{y_1 + y_2} = \dfrac{A}{B}$
**(b)** $x_1 x_2 - y_1 y_2 = 0$
**(c)** $x_1 x_2 + y_1 y_2 = -2C$

---

## MINI PROJECT     |     THINKING ABOUT SYMMETRY

This mini project works well in the context of a small group discussion but, of course, it can also be carried out by individuals. Begin by studying and/or discussing the following example involving a regular hexagon. Then work on the exercise that follows. For each part of the exercise, label each figure that you create (e.g., "symmetric about the $y$- but not the $x$-axis").

Example: The following figure shows a regular hexagon.

The next four figures show some of the (infinitely many) ways to locate the regular hexagon with respect to an $x$-$y$ coordinate system.

(a) Symmetric about $y$-axis, but not about $x$-axis

(b) Symmetric about $x$-axis, but not about $y$-axis

(c) Symmetric about origin and about both axes

(d) Symmetric about origin and not about either axis

In each case below, you are given a geometric figure. Try to find a way to draw the figure with an $x$-$y$ coordinate system so that the figure is

**(a)** symmetric about the $y$-axis, but not about the $x$-axis;
**(b)** symmetric about the $x$-axis, but not about the $y$-axis;
**(c)** symmetric about the origin and both axes;
**(d)** symmetric about the origin but not about either axis.
(In some cases there are many ways, in others none.)

1. equilateral triangle:

2. rectangle:

3. regular pentagon:

4. semicircle:

5. connected semicircles:

# Chapter 1 | Summary of Principal Terms and Formulas

| Terms or notation | Page reference | Comments |
|---|---|---|
| **1.** Natural numbers, integers, rational numbers, and irrational numbers | 2 | The box on page 2 provides both definitions and examples. Also note the theorem in the box, which explains how to distinguish between rationals and irrationals in terms of their decimal representations. |
| **2.** $a < b$<br>$b > a$ | 3 | $a$ is less than $b$.<br>$b$ is greater than $a$. |
| **3.** $(a, b)$<br>$[a, b]$ | 2 | The open interval $(a, b)$ consists of all real numbers between $a$ and $b$, excluding $a$ and $b$. The closed interval $[a, b]$ consists of all real numbers between $a$ and $b$, including $a$ and $b$. |
| **4.** $(a, \infty)$ | 4 | The unbounded interval $(a, \infty)$ consists of all real numbers $x$ such that $x > a$. The infinity symbol, $\infty$, does not denote a real number. It is used in the context $(a, \infty)$ to indicate that the interval has no right-hand boundary. For the definitions of the other types of unbounded intervals, see the box on page 4. |
| **5.** $|x|$ | 6 | The absolute value of a real number $x$ is the distance from $x$ to the origin. This is equivalent to the following algebraic definition: $$|x| = \begin{cases} x & \text{if } x \geq 0 \\ -x & \text{if } x < 0 \end{cases}$$ |
| **6.** Constant, variable, and the domain convention | 10 | By a constant we mean either a particular number (such as $-8$ or $\pi$) or a letter that remains fixed (although perhaps unspecified) throughout a given discussion. In contrast, a variable is a letter for which we can substitute any number from a given set of numbers. The given set is called the domain of the variable. According to the domain convention, the domain of a variable in a given expression consists of all real numbers for which the expression is defined. |
| **7.** Linear (or first-degree) equation in one variable | 11 | These are equations that can be written in the form $ax + b = 0$, where $a$ and $b$ are constants with $a \neq 0$. |
| **8.** Solution (or root) of an equation | 11 | A solution or root is a number that, when substituted for the variable in an equation, yields a true statement. |
| **9.** Equivalent equations | 12 | Two equations are equivalent if they have the same set of solutions. |
| **10.** Extraneous solution (or extraneous root) | 14 | In solving equations, certain processes can lead to answers that do not check in the original equation. These numbers are called extraneous solutions (or extraneous roots). |

| Terms or notation | Page reference | Comments |
|---|---|---|
| **11.** Quadratic (or second-degree) equation | 14 | A quadratic equation is one that can be written in the form $ax^2 + bx + c = 0$, where $a$, $b$, and $c$ are constants with $a \neq 0$. |
| **12.** Zero-product property of real numbers | 15 | If $pq = 0$ then $p = 0$ or $q = 0$; conversely, if $p = 0$ or $q = 0$, then $pq = 0$. (We used this property in solving quadratic equations by factoring.) |
| **13.** Quadratic formula $$x = \frac{-b \pm \sqrt{b^2 - 4ac}}{2a}$$ | 16 | This is the quadratic formula; it provides the solutions of the quadratic equation $ax^2 + bx + c = 0$, where $a \neq 0$. The formula is derived in Section 2.1. |
| **14.** Polynomial equation in one variable | 16 | A polynomial equation is an equation of the form $$a_n x^n + a_{n-1} x^{n-1} + \cdots + a_1 x + a_0 = 0$$ where the subscripted letter $a$'s represent constants and the exponents on the variable are nonnegative integers. The degree of the polynomial equation is the largest exponent of the variable that appears in the equation. |
| **15.** Pythagorean theorem $a^2 + b^2 = c^2$ | 20 | In a right triangle, the lengths of the sides are related by this equation, where $c$ is the length of the hypotenuse. Conversely, if the lengths of the sides of a triangle are related by an equation of the form $a^2 + b^2 = c^2$, then the triangle is a right triangle, and $c$ is the length of the hypotenuse. |
| **16.** Distance formula $d = \sqrt{(x_2 - x_1)^2 + (y_2 - y_1)^2}$ | 21 | $d$ is the distance between the points $(x_1, y_1)$ and $(x_2, y_2)$. |
| **17.** Midpoint formula $\left( \dfrac{x_1 + x_2}{2}, \dfrac{y_1 + y_2}{2} \right)$ | 24 | This is the midpoint of the line segment joining $(x_1, y_1)$ and $(x_2, y_2)$. |
| **18.** Graph of an equation | 32 | The graph of an equation in the variables $x$ and $y$ is the set of all points $(x, y)$ with coordinates that satisfy the equation. |
| **19.** Graphing utility and standard viewing rectangle | 33 | By a graphing utility we mean either a graphing calculator or a computer with software for graphing and analyzing equations or data. The standard viewing rectangle on a graphing utility is the default view screen and coordinate system for graphing. For many graphing utilities, the standard viewing rectangle extends from $-10$ to $10$ in both the $x$- and $y$-directions. |
| **20.** $x$-intercept and $y$-intercept | 36 | An $x$-intercept of a graph is the $x$-coordinate of a point where the graph intersects the $x$-axis. Similarly, a $y$-intercept is the $y$-coordinate of a point where the graph intersects the $y$-axis. |

| Terms or notation | Page reference | Comments |
|---|---|---|
| **21.** Slope $$m = \frac{y_2 - y_1}{x_2 - x_1}$$ | 44 | $m$ is the slope of a nonvertical line passing through the points $(x_1, y_1)$ and $(x_2, y_2)$. |
| **22.** $\Delta x, \Delta y$ | 44 | If the value of a variable $x$ changes from $x_1$ to $x_2$, then $\Delta x$ denotes the amount by which $x$ changes: $\Delta x = x_2 - x_1$. Similarly, if $y$ changes from $y_1$ to $y_2$ then $\Delta y = y_2 - y_1$. With this notation, the slope formula becomes $m = \Delta y / \Delta x$. |
| **23.** Point–slope formula $y - y_1 = m(x - x_1)$ | 47 | This is the point–slope form for the equation of the line passing through the point $(x_1, y_1)$ with slope $m$. |
| **24.** Slope–intercept formula $y = mx + b$ | 49 | This is the slope–intercept form for the equation of the line with slope $m$ and $y$-intercept $b$. |
| **25.** Parallel lines $m_1 = m_2$ | 50 | Nonvertical parallel lines have the same slope. |
| **26.** Perpendicular lines $m_1 = -1/m_2$ | 50 | Two nonvertical lines are perpendicular if and only if the slopes are negative reciprocals of one another. |
| **27.** Symmetry about the $x$-axis | 58 | A graph is symmetric about the $x$-axis if, for each point $(x, y)$ on the graph, the point $(x, -y)$ is also on the graph. The points $(x, y)$ and $(x, -y)$ are *reflections* of each other about (or in) the $x$-axis. |
| **28.** Symmetry about the $y$-axis | 58 | A graph is symmetric about the $y$-axis if, for each point $(x, y)$ on the graph, the point $(-x, y)$ is also on the graph. The points $(x, y)$ and $(-x, y)$ are *reflections* of each other about (or in) the $y$-axis. |
| **29.** Symmetry about the origin | 58 | A graph is symmetric about the origin if, for each point $(x, y)$ on the graph, the point $(-x, -y)$ is also on the graph. The points $(x, y)$ and $(-x, -y)$ are *reflections* of each other about the origin. |
| **30.** Symmetry tests | 59 | (i) The graph of an equation is symmetric about the $y$-axis if replacing $x$ with $-x$ yields an equivalent equation. <br> (ii) The graph of an equation is symmetric about the $x$-axis if replacing $y$ with $-y$ yields an equivalent equation. <br> (iii) The graph of an equation is symmetric about the origin if replacing $x$ and $y$ with $-x$ and $-y$, respectively, yields an equivalent equation. |
| **31.** Equation of a circle $(x - h)^2 + (y - k)^2 = r^2$ | 63 | This is the standard form for the equation of the circle with center $(h, k)$ and radius $r$. |

## Writing Mathematics

1. The following geometric method for solving quadratic equations of the form $x^2 - ax + b = 0$ is due to the British writer Thomas Carlyle (1795–1881):

   > To solve the equation $x^2 - ax + b = 0$, plot the points $A(0, 1)$ and $B(a, b)$. Then draw the circle with $\overline{AB}$ as diameter. The $x$-intercepts of this circle are the roots of the equation.

   Use the techniques of this chapter to verify for yourself that this method indeed yields the roots for the equation $x^2 - 6x + 5 = 0$. (You need to find the equation of the circle, determine the $x$-intercepts, and then check that the numbers you obtain are the roots of the given equation.) After you have done this, carefully write out your verification in detail (using complete sentences), as if you were explaining the method to a classmate. Be sure to make explicit reference to any formulas or equations that you use from the chapter.

2. In Section 1.6 we developed the point–slope formula, $y - y_1 = m(x - x_1)$, and the slope–intercept formula, $y = mx + b$. Although these two formulas look quite different from one another, both are merely restatements of the definition of slope. Write a paragraph (or two, at the most) to explain this last sentence. Make use of the following two figures.

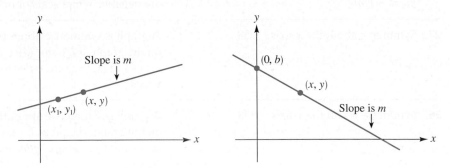

# Chapter 1 Review Exercises

*For Exercises 1–6 rewrite the statements using absolute values and inequalities or equalities.*

1. The distance between $x$ and 6 is 2.
2. The distance between $x$ and $a$ is less than 1/2.
3. The distance between $a$ and $b$ is 3.
4. The distance between $x$ and $-1$ is 5.
5. The distance between $x$ and 0 exceeds 10.
6. What can you say about $x$ if $|x - 5| = 0$?

*Rewrite each of the expressions in Exercises 7–12 in a form that does not contain absolute values.*

7. $|\sqrt{6} - 2|$
8. $|2 - \sqrt{6}|$
9. $|x^4 + x^2 + 1|$
10. (a) $|x - 3|$, if $x < 3$
    (b) $|x - 3|$, if $x > 3$
11. $|x - 2| + |x - 3|$, if:
    (a) $x < 2$
    (b) $2 < x < 3$
    (c) $x > 3$
12. $|x + 2| + |x - 1|$, if:
    (a) $x < -2$
    (b) $-2 < x < 1$
    (c) $x > 1$

*In Exercises 13–18, express each interval in inequality notation and sketch the interval on a number line.*

13. $(3, 5)$
14. $(3, 5]$

**15.** The set of all negative real numbers that are in the interval $[-5, 2]$

**16.** $(-\infty, 4)$                **17.** $[-1, \infty)$

**18.** The set of real numbers that belongs to either of the intervals $(0, \sqrt{2}]$ or $(\sqrt{2}, 2]$

*In Exercises 19–23, sketch the intervals described by the given inequalities.*

**19.** $|x - 6| < 3$                **20.** $|x - \frac{1}{2}| < 1$

**21.** $|x + 1| \geq 1$                **22.** $|x| \geq 5$

**23. (a)** $0 < |x - 4| < 5$        **(b)** $|x - 4| < 5$

**24.** Determine whether each of the following is true or false. (You should be able to do these without a calculator.)

  **(a)** $\pi \leq \sqrt{3}$                **(b)** $\frac{1}{5} > -\sqrt{2}$

*In Exercises 25–40, find all the real solutions of each equation.*

**25.** $5 - 9x = 2$                **26.** $\dfrac{x}{3} - \dfrac{3x}{5} = \dfrac{x}{6} - 13$

**27.** $(t - 4)(t + 3) = (t + 5)^2$

**28.** $\dfrac{1 - x}{1 + x} = 1$                **29.** $\dfrac{2t - 1}{t + 2} = 5$

**30.** $\dfrac{1}{1 + \dfrac{1}{x + 1}} = \dfrac{5}{6}$                **31.** $\dfrac{2y - 5}{4y + 1} = \dfrac{y - 1}{2y + 5}$

**32.** $\dfrac{2x - 3}{x - 2} = \dfrac{1}{x - 2}$                **33.** $12x^2 + 2x - 2 = 0$

**34.** $4y^2 - 21y - 18$                **35.** $\frac{1}{2}x^2 + x - 12 = 0$

**36.** $x^2 + \frac{13}{2}x + 10 = 0$                **37.** $\dfrac{x}{5 - x} - \dfrac{-2}{11 - x}$

**38.** $4x^2 + x - 2 = 0$                **39.** $t^2 + t - \frac{1}{2} = 0$

**40.** $x^3 - 8x^2 - 9x = 0$

*In Exercises 41–57, find an equation for the line satisfying the given conditions. For Exercises 41–49, write the answer in the form $y = mx + b$; in Exercises 50–57, write the answer in the form $Ax + By + C = 0$.*

**41.** Passes through $(-4, 2)$ and $(-6, 6)$

**42.** $m = -2$; $y$-intercept 5

**43.** $m = 1/4$; passes through $(-2, -3)$

**44.** $m = 1/3$; $x$-intercept $-1$

**45.** $x$-intercept $-4$; $y$-intercept 8

**46.** $m = -10$; $y$-intercept 0

**47.** $y$-intercept $-2$; parallel to the $x$-axis

**48.** Passes through $(0, 0)$ and is parallel to $6x - 3y = 5$

**49.** Passes through $(1, 2)$ and is perpendicular to the line $x + y + 1 = 0$

**50.** Passes through $(1, 1)$ and through the center of the circle $(x - 2)^2 + (y - 4)^2 = 20$

**51.** Passes through the centers of the circles $(x + 2)^2 + (y + 1)^2 = 5$ and $(x - 2)^2 + (y - 8)^2 = 68$

**52.** $m = 3$ and has the same $x$-intercept as the line $3x - 8y = 12$

**53.** Passes through the origin and the midpoint of the line segment joining the points $(-2, -3)$ and $(6, -5)$

**54.** Is tangent to the circle $x^2 + y^2 = 20$ at the point $(-2, 4)$

**55.** Is tangent to the circle $(x - 3)^2 + (y + 4)^2 = 25$ at the point $(0, 0)$

*Hint*: In Exercises 56 and 57 you might try the intercept form of the equation for a line: $\dfrac{x}{a} + \dfrac{y}{b} = 1$, where $a$ and where $a$ and $b$ are the $x$ and $y$ intercepts. See Exercise 40 in Section 1.6.

**56.** Passes through $(2, 4)$; the $y$-intercept is twice the $x$-intercept

**57.** Passes through $(2, -1)$; the sum of the $x$- and $y$-intercepts is 2. (There are two answers.)

**58. (a)** Find the perimeter of the triangle with vertices $A(3, 1)$, $B(7, 4)$, and $C(-2, 13)$.

  **(b)** Find the perimeter of the triangle formed by joining the midpoints of the sides of the triangle in part (a).

*In Exercises 59–62, test each equation for symmetry about the x-axis, the y-axis, and the origin.*

**59.** $y = x^4 - 2x^2$                **60.** $y = x^3 + 5x + 1$

**61.** $y = 2^x + 2^{-x}$                **62.** $y = 2^x - 2^{-x}$

*For Exercises 63–68, tell whether each graph appears to be symmetric about the x-axis, the y-axis, or the origin.*

**63.**                **64.**

**65.**                **66.**

**67.**

**68.**

*Graph the equations in Exercises 69–74.*

**69.** $x = 9 - y^2$

**70.** $(x + 2)^2 + y^2 = 1$

**71.** $y = 1 - |x|$

**72.** $y = |x - 2| + 2$

**73.** $(4x - y + 4)(4x + y - 4) = 0$

    *Hint:* Use the zero-product property.

**74.** $(y - x)(y - x + 2)(y - x - 2) = 0$

*You know from the text that the graph of the equation $x^2 + y^2 = 9$ is a circle with center (0, 0) and radius 3. In Exercises 75–81, use a graphing utility to investigate what happens when the equation is changed slightly. (As in graphing circles, you'll first need to solve the given equations for y.)*

**75. (a)** $x^2 + 2y^2 = 9$ (The resulting curve is an *ellipse*. We'll study this curve in a later chapter.)

   **(b)** On the same set of axes, graph the ellipse $x^2 + 2y^2 = 9$ and the circle $x^2 + y^2 = 9$. At which points do the two curves appear to intersect?

   **(c)** Carry out the calculations to verify that the points indicated in part (b) are indeed the exact intersection points.

**76.** $2x^2 + y^2 = 9$

**77. (a)** $x^2 - y^2 = 9$ (The resulting curve is a *hyperbola*. We'll study this curve in a later chapter.)

   **(b)** $x^2 - y^2 = 0$

   **(c)** On the same set of axes, graph the equations given in parts (a) and (b). Are there any intersection points?

**78.** $x^2 - y^3 = 9$

**79.** $x^3 - y^2 = 9$

**80. (a)** $x^3 + y^3 = 9$

   **(b)** $x^5 + y^5 = 9$

   **(c)** On the same set of axes, graph the equations given in parts (a) and (b). On the basis of the pattern you see, what do you think the graph of the equation $x^7 + y^7 = 9$ will look like? Draw a sketch (by hand) to show your prediction. Then use a graphing utility to see how accurate your prediction is.

**81. (a)** $x^4 + y^4 = 9$

   **(b)** $x^6 + y^6 = 9$

   **(c)** On the same set of axes, graph the equations given in parts (a) and (b). Based on the pattern you see, what do you think the graph of the equation $x^8 + y^8 = 9$ will look like? Draw a sketch (by hand) to show your prediction. Then use a graphing utility to see how accurate your prediction is.

**82.** Find a value for $t$ such that the slope of the line passing through (2, 1) and (5, $t$) is 6.

**83.** The vertices of a right triangle are $A(0, 0)$, $B(0, 2b)$, and $C(2c, 0)$. Let $M$ be the midpoint of the hypotenuse. Compute the three distances $MA$, $MB$, and $MC$. What do you observe?

**84.** The vertices of parallelogram $ABCD$ are $A(-4, -1)$, $B(2, 1)$, $C(3, 3)$, and $D(-3, 1)$.

   **(a)** Compute the sum of the squares of the two diagonals.

   **(b)** Compute the sum of the squares of the four sides. What do you observe?

*In Exercises 85 and 86, two points are given. In each case compute **(a)** the distance between the two points, **(b)** the slope of the line segment joining the two points, and **(c)** the midpoint of the line segment joining the two points.*

**85.** (2, 5) and (5, −6)

**86.** ($\sqrt{3}/2$, 1/2) and ($-\sqrt{3}/2$, −1/2)

**87.** A line passes through the points (1, 2) and (4, 1). Find the area of the triangle bounded by this line and the coordinate axes.

**88.** Let $P_1(x_1, y_1)$ and $P_2(x_2, y_2)$ be two given points. Let $Q$ be the point $(\frac{1}{3}x_1 + \frac{2}{3}x_2, \frac{1}{3}y_1 + \frac{2}{3}y_2)$.

   **(a)** Show that the points $P_1$, $Q$, and $P_2$ are collinear. *Hint:* Compute the slope of $\overline{P_1Q}$ and the slope of $\overline{QP_2}$.

   **(b)** Show that $P_1Q = \frac{2}{3}P_1P_2$. (In other words, $Q$ is on the line segment $\overline{P_1P_2}$ and two-thirds of the way from $P_1$ to $P_2$.)

**89. (a)** Let the vertices of $\triangle ABC$ be $A(-5, 3)$, $B(7, 7)$, and $C(3, 1)$. Find the point on each median that is two-thirds of the way from the vertex to the midpoint of the opposite side. (Recall that a median of a triangle is a line segment drawn from a vertex to the midpoint of the opposite side.) What do you observe? *Hint:* Use the result in Exercise 88.

   **(b)** Follow part (a) but take the vertices to be $A(0, 0)$, $B(2a, 0)$, and $C(2b, 2c)$. What do you observe? What does this prove?

**90.** In the following figure, points $P$ and $Q$ trisect the hypotenuse in $\triangle ABC$. Prove that the square of the hypotenuse is equal to 9/5 the sum of the squares of the distances from the trisection points to the vertex $A$ of the right angle.

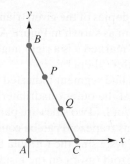

*Hint*: Let the coordinates of $B$ and $C$ be $(0, 3b)$ and $(3c, 0)$, respectively. Then the coordinates of $P$ and $Q$ are $(c, 2b)$ and $(2c, b)$, respectively.

**91.** Figure A shows a triangle with sides of lengths $s$, $t$, and $u$ and a median of length $m$. Prove that

$$m^2 = \frac{1}{2}(s^2 + t^2) - \frac{1}{4}u^2$$

*Hint*: Set up a coordinate system as indicated in Figure B. Then each of the quantities $m^2$, $s^2$, $t^2$, and $u^2$ can be computed in terms of $a$, $b$, and $c$.

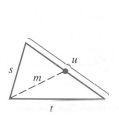

Figure A                Figure B

*In Exercises 92 and 93, the endpoints of a line segment $\overline{AB}$ are given. Sketch the reflection of $\overline{AB}$ about* **(a)** *the origin;* **(b)** *the x-axis; and* **(c)** *the y-axis.*

**92.** $A(-2, -3)$ and $B(0, 2)$

**93.** $A(3, 1)$ and $B(3, -2)$

**94.** In this exercise you'll derive a useful formula for the (perpendicular) distance $d$ from the point $(x_0, y_0)$ to the line $y = mx + b$. The formula is

$$d = \frac{|y_0 - mx_0 - b|}{\sqrt{1 + m^2}}$$

**(a)** Refer to the figure. Use similar triangles to show that

$$\frac{d}{AB} = \frac{1}{\sqrt{1 + m^2}}$$

Therefore, $d = AB/\sqrt{1 + m^2}$.

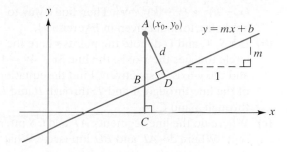

**(b)** Check that $AB = AC - BC = y_0 - mx_0 - b$.

**(c)** Conclude from parts (a) and (b) that

$$d = \frac{y_0 - mx_0 - b}{\sqrt{1 + m^2}}$$

For the general case (in which the point and line may not be situated as in our figure), we need to use the absolute value of the quantity in the numerator to ensure that $AB$ and $d$ are nonnegative.

**95.** Use the formula given in Exercise 94 to find the distance from the point $(1, 2)$ to the line $y = \frac{1}{2}x - 5$.

**96.** Use the formula given in Exercise 94 to demonstrate that the distance from the point $(x_0, y_0)$ to the line $Ax + By + C = 0$ is

$$d = \frac{|Ax_0 + By_0 + C|}{\sqrt{A^2 + B^2}}$$

**97.** Use the formula given in Exercise 96 to find the distance from the point $(-1, -3)$ to the line $2x + 3y - 6 = 0$.

**98.** Find the equation of the circle that has center $(2, 3)$ and is tangent to the line $x + y - 1 = 0$.
*Hint*: Use the formula given in Exercise 96 to find the radius.

**99.** In the figure, the circle is tangent to the $x$-axis, to the $y$-axis, and to the line $3x + 4y = 12$.

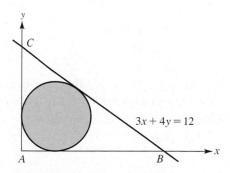

**(a)** Find the equation of the circle.
*Suggestion*: First decide what the relationships must be between $h$, $k$, and $r$ in the equation

$(x - h)^2 + (y - k)^2 = r^2$. Then find a way to apply the formula given in Exercise 94.

**(b)** Let $S$, $T$, and $U$ denote the points where the circle touches the $x$-axis, the line $3x + 4y = 12$, and the $y$-axis, respectively. Find the equation of the line through $A$ and $T$; through $B$ and $U$; through $S$ and $C$.

**(c)** Where do the line segments $\overline{AT}$ and $\overline{CS}$ intersect? Where do $\overline{AT}$ and $\overline{BU}$ intersect? What do you observe? *Remark*: The point determined here is called the *Gergonne point* of triangle $ABC$, so named in honor of its discoverer, French mathematician Joseph Diaz Gergonne (1771–1859).

**100.** This exercise outlines a proof of the Pythagorean theorem that was discovered by James A. Garfield, the twentieth President of the United States. Garfield published the proof in 1876, when he was the Republican leader in the House of Representatives. We start with a right triangle with legs of length $a$ and $b$ and hypotenuse of length $c$. We want to prove that $a^2 + b^2 = c^2$.

**(a)** Take two copies of the given triangle and arrange them as shown in Figure A. Explain why the angle marked $\theta$ is a right angle. ($\theta$ is the Greek letter "theta.")

**(b)** Draw the line segment indicated in Figure B. Notice that the outer quadrilateral in Figure B is a trapezoid. (Two sides are parallel.) The area of this trapezoid can be computed in two distinct ways: using the formula for the area of a trapezoid (given on the inside front cover of this book) or adding the areas of the three right triangles in Figure B. Compute the area of the trapezoid in each of these two ways. When you equate the two answers and simplify, you should obtain $a^2 + b^2 = c^2$.

Figure A          Figure B

---

# Chapter 1          Test

**1.** Simplify $|x - 6| + |x - 7|$, where $6 < x < 7$.

**2.** Specify the intervals that are described by the inequalities.

   **(a)** $|x - 4| < \frac{1}{10}$       **(b)** $x \geq 2$

*In Problems 3–5, find all the real solutions of each equation.*

**3.** $\dfrac{2}{x + 4} - \dfrac{1}{x - 4} = \dfrac{-7}{x^2 - 16}$

**4.** $\dfrac{1}{1 - x} + \dfrac{4}{2 - x} = \dfrac{11}{6}$

**5.** **(a)** $x^2 + 4x = 5$      **(b)** $x^2 + 4x = 1$

**6.** Solve the following equation for $x$ in terms of the other letters:

$$\frac{ax + b}{cx + d} = e \qquad \text{where } a \neq ce$$

**7.** Refer to the following graph. As indicated in the graph, the number $N$ of U.S. radio stations on the air increased in (approximately) a straight-line fashion from 1990 to 1994. Source of data: *The Universal Almanac 1997,* John W. Wright (ed.) (Kansas City: Andrews and McMeel, 1997)

**(a)** As $t$ increases from 0 to 4, we have $\Delta t = 4$ years. What is the corresponding value of $\Delta N$?

**(b)** Find the slope $\Delta N/\Delta t$ for the line. Round the answer to the nearest integer. (Include units with your answer.)

**(c)** Use your result in part (b) to answer the following question. If the number of radio stations had continued to grow in a straight-line fashion, how many stations would there have been in 1995?

**8.** The following data are from a classic experiment in biology that measured the average height of a group of sunflower plants at seven-day intervals.

**Growth in (Mean) Height of Sunflower Plants**

| Day t | Mean height h (cm) |
|-------|--------------------|
| 7     | 17.93              |
| 21    | 67.76              |

Source: H. S. Reed and R. H. Holland in *Proceedings of the National Academy of Sciences,* vol. 5 (1919), p. 140.

**(a)** Plot the two data points in the following coordinate system.

**(b)** Use the midpoint formula and the data for $t = 7$ days and $t = 21$ days to estimate what the average height of the sunflowers might have been at $t = 14$ days. (Round the answer to one decimal place.)

**(c)** Compute the percentage error in the estimation in part (b), given that the actual average height

at $t = 14$ days was 36.36 cm. Round the answer to the nearest whole percent. *Check:* You should obtain a substantial percentage error. In Chapter 5 we'll study some types of equations that do a much better job than the midpoint formula in modeling biological growth.)

*In Problems 9 and 10, find an equation for the line satisfying the given conditions. Write the answer in the form $y = mx + b$.*

**9.** Passes through $(1, -2)$ and the $y$-intercept is 6

**10.** Passes through $(2, -1)$ and is perpendicular to the line $5x + 6y = 30$

**11.** Which point is farther from the origin, $(3, 9)$ or $(5, 8)$?

**12.** Test each equation for symmetry about the $x$-axis, the $y$-axis, and the origin:
   **(a)** $y = x^3 + 5x$
   **(b)** $y = 3^x + 3^{-x}$
   **(c)** $y^2 = 5x^2 + x$

*In Problems 13 and 14, graph the equations and specify all x- and y-intercepts.*

**13.** $3x - 5y = 15$

**14.** $(x - 1)^2 + (y + 2)^2 = 9$

Ⓖ **15. (a)** Use a graphing utility to graph the equation $y = x^3 - 2x^2 - 9x$ in an appropriate viewing rectangle.

Ⓖ   **(b)** Use a graphing utility to estimate to one decimal place the $x$-intercepts of the graph.

   **(c)** Use algebra to find exact values for the $x$-intercepts.

**16.** Does the point $(-1/2, 5)$ lie on the graph of the equation $y = 4x^2 - 8x$?

**17.** The endpoints of line segment $\overline{AB}$ are $A(3, -1)$ and $B(-1, 2)$. Sketch the reflection of $\overline{AB}$ about **(a)** the $x$-axis; **(b)** the $y$-axis; and **(c)** the origin.

**18.** A line passes through the points $(6, 2)$ and $(1, 4)$. Find the area of the triangle bounded by this line and the $x$- and $y$-axes.

# 2

# Equations and Inequalities

We continue the work begun in Section 1.3 on solving equations, and then we adapt those skills in solving inequalities. Some of the applications that you'll see in this chapter are:

- Tracking population growth in the United States (Example 1 in Section 2.1)
- Predicting world records for the men's and women's 10,000-meter race (Exercises 21 and 22 in Section 2.1)
- Predicting sulfur dioxide emissions for the United States and Asia (Exercises 42 and 43 in Section 2.3) (Sulfur dioxide emissions are the main contributor to acid rain.)

*By 1900 B.C. the Babylonians had a well-established algebra. They could solve quadratic equations (positive coefficients and positive solutions only) and some types of higher degree equations as well.* —Stuart Hollingdale in *Makers of Mathematics* (London: Penguin Books, 1989)

['Abd-al-Hamid ibn-Turk, a ninth-century Persian mathematician] *. . . gives geometric figures to prove if the discriminant is negative, a quadratic equation has no [real] solution.* —Carl B. Boyer in *A History of Mathematics,* 2nd ed. (Uta C. Merzbach, revision editor) (New York: John Wiley & Sons, 1991)

## ▌2.1  QUADRATIC EQUATIONS: THEORY AND EXAMPLES

*A wealth of quadratic equations applied to genetic problems can be found in . . .* [the textbook by Albert Jacquard, *The Genetic Structure of Populations*]. —Edward Batschelet, *Introduction to Mathematics for Life Scientists,* 3rd ed. (New York: Springer-Verlag, 1979)

Recall (from Section 1.3, or from a previous course) that a **quadratic equation** is an equation that can be written in the form $ax^2 + bx + c = 0$, where $a$, $b$, and $c$ are real numbers and $a$ is not zero. In Section 1.3 we solved quadratic equations in two ways: by factoring and by the quadratic formula. The factoring method is the simpler of the two, but it can't be used in every instance. (Example: Try solving $x^2 - 2x - 4 = 0$ by factoring.) The quadratic formula, on the other hand, can be used to solve *any* quadratic equation. In this section we take a more careful look at the quadratic formula: We derive the formula and we use it, not only to solve equations, but also to *analyze* them. The technique that we'll use to derive the quadratic formula is completing the square (introduced in Section 1.7).

We'll review the technique of completing the square by solving the equation $x^2 - 2x - 4 = 0$. First, we rewrite the equation in the form

$$x^2 - 2x = 4 \tag{1}$$

with the $x$-terms isolated on the left-hand side of the equation. To complete the square, we follow these two steps:

**Step 1**  Take half of the coefficient of $x$ and square it.
**Step 2**  Add the number obtained in Step 1 to both sides of the equation.

For equation (1), the coefficient of $x$ is $-2$. Taking half of $-2$ and then squaring it gives us $(-1)^2$, or 1. Now, as directed in Step 2, we add 1 to both sides of equation (1). This yields

$$x^2 - 2x + 1 = 4 + 1$$
$$(x - 1)^2 = 5$$
$$x - 1 = \pm\sqrt{5}$$
$$x = 1 \pm \sqrt{5}$$

We have now obtained the two solutions, $1 + \sqrt{5}$ and $1 - \sqrt{5}$. Let's check that these numbers are indeed solutions of $x^2 - 2x - 4 = 0$. (We'll show the work for $x = 1 + \sqrt{5}$; you should carry out the calculations for $1 - \sqrt{5}$ on your own.) We have

$$(1 + \sqrt{5})^2 - 2(1 + \sqrt{5}) - 4 = (1 + 2\sqrt{5} + 5) - 2 - 2\sqrt{5} - 4$$
$$= 6 - 2 - 4$$
$$= 0 \qquad \text{as required}$$

In the box that follows, we summarize the process of completing the square and we indicate how it got its name.

---

**Algebraic Procedure for Completing the Square in the Expression $x^2 + bx$**

Add the square of half of the $x$-coefficient:

$$(x^2 + bx) + \left(\frac{b}{2}\right)^2 = \left(x + \frac{b}{2}\right)^2$$

**Geometric Interpretation of Completing the Square for $x^2 + bx$**

The blue region in the figure represents the quantity $x^2 + bx$, since the area is

$$x^2 + \left(\frac{b}{2}\right)x + \left(\frac{b}{2}\right)x$$

By adding the red square to the blue region, we fill out or "complete" the larger square. The area of the red region that completes the square is

$$\frac{b}{2} \cdot \frac{b}{2} = \frac{b^2}{4}$$

---

The technique of completing the square can be used to derive the quadratic formula. We start with the general quadratic equation $ax^2 + bx + c = 0$ $(a \neq 0)$ and divide both sides by $a$ (so that the coefficient of $x^2$ will be 1, as in the box above). This yields

$$x^2 + \frac{b}{a}x + \frac{c}{a} = 0$$

Subtracting $c/a$ from both sides yields

$$x^2 + \frac{b}{a}x = -\frac{c}{a}$$

Now, to complete the square, we add $[\frac{1}{2}(b/a)]^2$, or $b^2/4a^2$, to both sides. That gives us

$$x^2 + \frac{b}{a}x + \frac{b^2}{4a^2} = \frac{b^2}{4a^2} - \frac{c}{a}$$

$$\left(x + \frac{b}{2a}\right)^2 = \frac{b^2 - 4ac}{4a^2}$$

$$x + \frac{b}{2a} = \pm\sqrt{\frac{b^2 - 4ac}{4a^2}} = \pm\frac{\sqrt{b^2 - 4ac}}{2|a|}$$

$$= \pm\frac{\sqrt{b^2 - 4ac}}{2a}$$

This last equality follows from the fact that for any real number $a \neq 0$, the expressions $\pm 2|a|$ and $\pm 2a$ both represent the same two numbers. We now conclude that the solutions are

$$x = -\frac{b}{2a} + \frac{\sqrt{b^2 - 4ac}}{2a} \qquad \text{and} \qquad x = -\frac{b}{2a} - \frac{\sqrt{b^2 - 4ac}}{2a}$$

For reference, we summarize our work in the box that follows.

---

**The Quadratic Formula**

The solutions of the equation $ax^2 + bx + c = 0$ ($a \neq 0$) are given by

$$x = \frac{-b \pm \sqrt{b^2 - 4ac}}{2a}$$

---

COMMENT    The quadratic formula yields the solutions of a quadratic equation in *all* cases. However, when $b^2 - 4ac$ is negative, the solutions are *not* real numbers. See page 87 for a discussion of the discriminant.

---

**EXAMPLE**    **1**    **Using the quadratic formula**

For the years 1850 through 1990, the population of the United States can be closely approximated using the equation

$$y = 0.006609x^2 - 23.771x + 21{,}382 \qquad (2)$$

where $y$ is the population in millions, and $x$ is the year.

**(a)** To get a feeling for working with equation (2), use the equation to estimate the U.S. population in 1900. (Round the answer to one decimal place.)

**(b)** Use equation (2) and the quadratic formula to estimate the year in which the U.S. population reached 200 million.

**SOLUTION**

**(a)** Substituting $x = 1900$ in equation (2) yields

$$y = 0.006609(1900)^2 - 23.771(1900) + 21{,}382$$
$$= 75.6 \text{ million} \qquad \text{using a calculator and rounding}$$
$$\text{to one decimal place}$$

Thus our estimate for the U.S. population in 1900 is 76.6 million. *Remark*: This estimate is very good, for according to the U.S. Bureau of the Census, the population in 1900 was approximately 76.2 million.

**(b)** Using equation (2), we want to find the year $x$ in which the population $y$ reached 200 million. Substituting $y = 200$ in equation (2) yields

$$0.006609x^2 - 23.771x + 21{,}382 = 200$$

This is a quadratic equation, and to put it in the form $ax^2 + bx + c = 0$ (so that the quadratic formula can be used), we subtract 200 from both sides to obtain

$$0.006609x^2 - 23.771x + 21{,}182 = 0$$

From this last equation we see that

$$a = 0.006609 \qquad b = -23.771 \qquad c = 21{,}182$$

and, consequently,

$$x = \frac{-b \pm \sqrt{b^2 - 4ac}}{2a}$$

$$= \frac{-(-23.771) \pm \sqrt{(-23.771)^2 - 4(0.006609)(21{,}182)}}{2(0.006609)}$$

Using a calculator now and rounding to the nearest integer, we obtain the two values $x \approx 1969$ and $x \approx 1628$. We choose the value in the required range between 1850 and 1990. Thus our estimate is that 1969 was the year in which the U.S. population reached 200 million. *Remark*: This is a reasonable estimate, for according to Census Bureau data, the 1960 population was approximately 179 million, whereas the 1970 population was approximately 203 million.

COMMENT   The range of validity of the approximation formula (2) covers the years from 1850 through 1990. The year 1628 is so far outside of this range that we do not expect to get a reasonable approximation from equation (2), and we don't.

## EXAMPLE 2   Using the quadratic formula

Consider the quadratic equation $x^2 = 5 - 3x$.
**(a)** Use the quadratic formula to find the roots of the equation.
**(b)** Compute the product of the roots.
**(c)** Compute the sum of the roots.

**SOLUTION**
**(a)** Just as we did in the previous example, we first write the equation in the form $ax^2 + bx + c = 0$:

$$x^2 + 3x - 5 = 0$$

From this last equation we see that $a = 1$, $b = 3$, and $c = -5$. The quadratic formula then yields

$$x = \frac{-b \pm \sqrt{b^2 - 4ac}}{2a} = \frac{-3 \pm \sqrt{3^2 - 4(1)(-5)}}{2(1)}$$

$$= \frac{-3 \pm \sqrt{9 + 20}}{2} = \frac{-3 \pm \sqrt{29}}{2}$$

**(b)** Computing the product of the roots, we have

$$\left(\frac{-3 + \sqrt{29}}{2}\right)\left(\frac{-3 - \sqrt{29}}{2}\right) = \frac{9 - 29}{4} = \frac{-20}{4} = -5$$

So the product of the two roots is $-5$.

**(c)** For the sum of the roots we have

$$\frac{-3 + \sqrt{29}}{2} + \frac{-3 - \sqrt{29}}{2} = \frac{-3 + \sqrt{29} + (-3) - \sqrt{29}}{2}$$

$$= \frac{-6}{2} = -3$$

Therefore the sum of the roots is $-3$.

If you look over the results in Example 2, you'll see that there appears to be something of a coincidence. We found that the product of the roots of the equation $x^2 + 3x - 5 = 0$ is $-5$, which happens to be the "$c$" term in the equation. Furthermore, the sum of the roots is $-3$, which happens to be the negative of the "$b$" term in the equation. In fact, however, these are not coincidences. Rather, they are examples of the following general result.

---

**THEOREM   The Product and the Sum of the Roots of $x^2 + bx + c = 0$**

Let $r_1$ and $r_2$ be the roots of the quadratic equation $x^2 + bx + c = 0$. Then

$$r_1 r_2 = c \qquad \text{and} \qquad r_1 + r_2 = -b$$

In words: The product of the roots of $x^2 + bx + c = 0$ is the constant term in the equation, and the sum of the roots is the negative of the coefficient of the $x$-term.

---

The proof of this theorem follows exactly the same steps that we used in Example 2. For the equation $x^2 + bx + c = 0$, we have $a = 1$, and therefore the quadratic formula gives us

$$x = \frac{-b \pm \sqrt{b^2 - 4(1)c}}{2(1)} = \frac{-b \pm \sqrt{b^2 - 4c}}{2}$$

So the two roots are $r_1 = \dfrac{-b + \sqrt{b^2 - 4c}}{2}$ and $r_2 = \dfrac{-b - \sqrt{b^2 - 4c}}{2}$. Then, for the product $r_1 r_2$ we have

$$r_1 r_2 = \frac{-b + \sqrt{b^2 - 4c}}{2} \cdot \frac{-b - \sqrt{b^2 - 4c}}{2}$$

$$= \frac{b^2 - (b^2 - 4c)}{4} = \frac{4c}{4} = c \qquad \text{as required}$$

For the sum of the roots we have

$$r_1 + r_2 = \frac{-b + \sqrt{b^2 - 4c}}{2} + \frac{-b - \sqrt{b^2 - 4c}}{2}$$

$$= \frac{-b + \sqrt{b^2 - 4c} + (-b) - \sqrt{b^2 - 4c}}{2} = \frac{-2b}{2} = -b$$

as we wished to show. The next two examples show how these results are applied.

**EXAMPLE** **3** Finding the product and sum of the roots of a quadratic equation

Find the product and the sum of the roots of the quadratic equation $2x^2 + 6x - 7 = 0$.

**SOLUTION**
To apply the theorem on the product and sum of roots, the coefficient of $x^2$ in the equation must be 1. To arrange this, we divide both sides of the given equation by 2. This yields the equivalent equation

$$x^2 + 3x - \frac{7}{2} = 0$$

In this equation we have $b = 3$ and $c = -7/2$. Therefore

$$r_1 r_2 = c = -\frac{7}{2}$$

and

$$r_1 + r_2 = -b = -3$$

That is, the product of the roots is $-7/3$ and the sum of the roots is $-3$.

**EXAMPLE** **4** Finding a quadratic equation with given roots

Find a quadratic equation with roots

$$r_1 = \frac{1 + \sqrt{5}}{4} \quad \text{and} \quad r_2 = \frac{1 - \sqrt{5}}{4}$$

Write the equation in a form involving integer coefficients only.

**SOLUTION**
If $r_1$ and $r_2$ are the roots of the equation $x^2 + bx + c = 0$, we have

$$c = r_1 r_2 = \frac{1 + \sqrt{5}}{4} \cdot \frac{1 - \sqrt{5}}{4} = \frac{1 - 5}{16} = -\frac{1}{4}$$

and

$$b = -(r_1 + r_2) = -\left(\frac{1 + \sqrt{5}}{4} + \frac{1 - \sqrt{5}}{4}\right) = -\frac{2}{4} = \frac{1}{2}$$

With these values for $b$ and $c$ the quadratic equation is $x^2 - \frac{1}{2}x - \frac{1}{4} = 0$. To obtain an equation with integer coefficients (but still the same roots), we multiply both sides of this last equation by 4 to obtain

$$4x^2 - 2x - 1 = 0$$

This is the equation with the required roots and with integer coefficients.

*Suggestion*: For practice in using the quadratic formula, solve this last equation to verify that the roots are indeed $(1 \pm \sqrt{5})/4$.

In Examples 1 and 2 we found that each quadratic equation had two real roots (although in Example 1 we were interested only in one root). As the next example indicates, however, it is also possible for quadratic equations to have only one real root, or even no real roots.

**EXAMPLE** 5   **Using the quadratic formula**

Use the quadratic formula to solve each equation:
**(a)** $4x^2 - 12x + 9 = 0$;   **(b)** $x^2 + x + 2 = 0$.

**SOLUTION**
**(a)** Here $a = 4$, $b = -12$, and $c = 9$, so

$$x = \frac{12 \pm \sqrt{(-12)^2 - 4(4)(9)}}{2(4)} = \frac{12 \pm \sqrt{144 - 144}}{8}$$
$$= \frac{12 \pm 0}{8} = \frac{12}{8} = \frac{3}{2}$$

In this case our only solution is $3/2$. We refer to $3/2$ as a **double root.** *Note*: We've used the quadratic formula here only for an illustration; in this case we can solve the original equation more efficiently by factoring.
**(b)** Since $a = 1$, $b = 1$, and $c = 2$, we have

$$x = \frac{-1 \pm \sqrt{(1)^2 - 4(1)(2)}}{2(1)} = \frac{-1 \pm \sqrt{-7}}{2}$$

From this we conclude that the given equation has no real-number solutions because the expression $\sqrt{-7}$ is undefined within the real-number system. [However, if we take a broader point of view and work within the *complex-number system*, then there are indeed two solutions, albeit not real-number solutions. As you'll see in Section 12.1, or as you perhaps already know from a previous course, these two complex-number solutions can be written $(-1 \pm i\sqrt{7})/2$.]

The results in Example 5 can be interpreted in terms of graphs. For as we know from Section 1.5, the $x$-intercepts of the graph of $y = ax^2 + bx + c$ are found by solving the equation $ax^2 + bx + c = 0$. As indicated in Figure 1(a), the graph of

## GRAPHICAL PERSPECTIVE

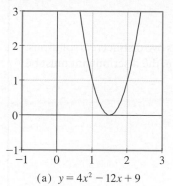

(a) $y = 4x^2 - 12x + 9$

(b) $y = x^2 + x + 2$

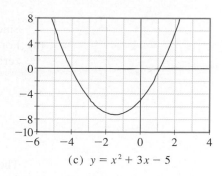

(c) $y = x^2 + 3x - 5$

**Figure 1**

In Figure 1(a) the graph of $y = 4x^2 - 12x + 9$ has only one $x$-intercept; the equation $4x^2 - 12x + 9 = 0$ has only one root. In Figure 1(b) the graph of $y = x^2 + x + 2$ has no $x$-intercepts; the equation $x^2 + x + 2 = 0$ has no real roots. In Figure 1(c) the graph of $y = x^2 + 3x - 5$ has two $x$-intercepts; the equation $x^2 + 3x - 5 = 0$ has two real roots.

$y = 4x^2 - 12x + 9$ has only one $x$-intercept; this intercept is the root of the equation $4x^2 - 12x + 9 = 0$ that we solved in Example 5(a). Figure 1(b) shows that the graph of $y = x^2 + x + 2$ has no $x$-intercepts; this reflects the fact that the equation $x^2 + x + 2 = 0$ has no real solutions. For completeness, we've also shown a graph [Figure 1(c)] that has two $x$-intercepts. We computed these two $x$-intercepts in Example 2(a) when we solved the equation $x^2 + 3x - 5 = 0$.

The quantity $b^2 - 4ac$ that appears under the radical sign in the quadratic formula is called the *discriminant*. (The term "discriminant" was coined by the nineteenth-century British mathematician James Joseph Sylvester.) If you look back at Example 2(a), you'll see that the discriminant is positive and that this leads to two real solutions. In Example 5(a), the discriminant is zero, which leads to only one real solution. Finally, in Example 5(b), the discriminant is negative and, consequently, there are no real solutions. These observations are generalized in the box that follows.

---

### The Discriminant $b^2 - 4ac$

Consider the quadratic equation $ax^2 + bx + c = 0$, where $a$, $b$, and $c$ are real numbers and $a \neq 0$. The expression $b^2 - 4ac$ is called the **discriminant.**

1. If $b^2 - 4ac > 0$, then the equation has two distinct real roots.
2. If $b^2 - 4ac = 0$, then the equation has exactly one real root, referred to as a **double root** or a root of **multiplicity two.**
3. If $b^2 - 4ac < 0$, then the equation has no real root. [There are two (nonreal) complex-number roots. This is discussed in Chapter 12.]

---

### EXAMPLE 6 Using the discriminant

(a) Compute the discriminant to determine how many real solutions there are for the equation $x^2 + x - 1 = 0$.
(b) Find a value for $k$ such that the quadratic equation $x^2 + \sqrt{2}x + k = 0$ has exactly one real solution.

**SOLUTION**

**(a)** Here $a = 1$, $b = 1$, and $c = -1$. Therefore,

$$b^2 - 4ac = 1^2 - 4(1)(-1) = 5$$

Since the discriminant is positive, the equation has two distinct real solutions.

**(b)** For the equation to have exactly one real solution, the discriminant must be zero; that is,

$$b^2 - 4ac = 0$$
$$(\sqrt{2})^2 - 4(1)(k) = 0$$
$$2 - 4k = 0$$
$$k = \frac{1}{2}$$

The required value for $k$ is $1/2$.

# EXERCISE SET 2.1

**A**

*In Exercises 1–18, solve the quadratic equations. If an equation has no real roots, state this. In cases where the solutions involve radicals, give both the radical form of the answer and a calculator approximation rounded to two decimal places.*

**1.** $x^2 + 8x - 2 = 0$
**2.** $x^2 - 6x - 2 = 0$
**3.** $x^2 + 4x + 1 = 0$
**4.** $x^2 + 12x + 18 = 0$
**5.** $2y^2 - 5y - 2 = 0$
**6.** $3y^2 - 3y - 4 = 0$
**7.** $4y^2 + 8y + 5 = 0$
**8.** $y^2 + y + 1 = 0$
**9.** $4s^2 - 20s + 25 = 0$
**10.** $16s^2 + 8s + 1 = 0$
**11.** $x^2 = 8x - 6$
**12.** $x^2 = 8x + 9$
**13.** $-3x^2 + x = -3$
**14.** $(x - 5)(x + 3) = 1$
**15.** $-y^2 - 8y = 1$
**16.** $5y(y - 2) = 2$
**17.** $t^2 = -3t - 4$
**18.** $t^2 = -3t + 4$

**19. (a)** Use the formula given in Example 1 to estimate the year that the U.S. population reached 100 million.
   **(b)** Use the following U.S. Census Bureau data to say whether your estimate in part (a) is reasonable. In 1910 the population was approximately 92.2 million; in 1920 it was approximately 106.0 million.

**20. (a)** Use the formula given in Example 1 to estimate the year that the U.S. population reached 225 million.
   **(b)** According to the U.S. Census Bureau, the U.S. population in 1980 was 226.5 million. Is your estimate in part (a) reasonable?

**21.** The chart that follows shows the world records for the men's 10,000 meter run in the years 1972 and 1998.

| Year | Time (minutes and seconds) | Runner |
|------|---------------------------|--------|
| 1972 | 27:38.4 | Lasse Viren (Finland) |
| 1998 | 26:22.75 | Haile Gebrselassie (Ethiopia) |

For the years between 1972 and 1998, the world record can be approximated by the equation

$$y = -0.09781t^2 + 385.8336t - 378,850.4046$$
$$(1972 \le t \le 1998)$$

where $y$ is the world-record time (in seconds) in the year $t$.

**(a)** Use the given equation, the quadratic formula, and your calculator to estimate the year in which the record might have been 27 minutes ($= 1620$ seconds). (You'll get two solutions for the quadratic; be sure to pick the appropriate one.) Then say by how many years your prediction is off, given the following information: On July 5, 1993, Richard Chelimo of Kenya ran a record time of 27:07.91; five days after that, Yobes Ondieki, also of Kenya, ran 26:58.38.

**(b)** Estimate the year in which the record might have been 26:30 ($= 1590$ seconds). Then say by how many years your prediction is off, given the following information: On July 4, 1997, Haile Gebrselassie ran a record time of 27:07.91; eighteen days later, Paul Tergat of Kenya ran 26:27.85.

**22.** The chart below shows the world records for the women's 10,000 meter run in the years 1970 and 1993.

| Year | Time (minutes and seconds) | Runner |
|------|---------------------------|--------|
| 1970 | 35:30.5 | Paola Pigni (Italy) |
| 1993 | 29:31.78 | Wang Junxia (China) |

For the years between 1970 and 1993, the world record can be approximated by the equation

$$y = 0.37553t^2 - 1503.7154t + 1,507,042.699$$
$$(1970 \le t \le 1993)$$

where $y$ is the world-record time (in seconds) in the year $t$. Use the given equation, the quadratic formula, and your calculator to estimate the year in which the record might have been 32 minutes ($= 1920$ seconds).

(As in Exercise 21, you'll get two solutions for the quadratic; pick the appropriate one.) Then say by how many years your prediction is off, given the following information: On September 19, 1981, Yekena Sipatova of the former Soviet Union ran a record time of 32:17.2; in the following year on July 16, Mary Decker of the United States ran 31:35.3.

(G) *In each of Exercises 23–28, you are given an equation of the form* $y = ax^2 + bx + c$. **(a)** *Use a graphing utility to graph the equation and to estimate the x-intercepts. (Use a zoom-in process to obtain the estimates; keep zooming in until the first three decimal places of the estimate remain the same as you progress to the next step.)* **(b)** *Determine the exact values of the intercepts by using the quadratic formula. Then use a calculator to evaluate the expressions that you obtain. Round off the results to four decimal places. [Check to see that your results are consistent with the estimates in part (a).]*

**23.** $y = x^2 - 4x + 1$  **24.** $y = x^2 - 10x + 15$
**25.** $y = 0.5x^2 + 8x - 3$  **26.** $y = 2x^2 + 2x - 1$
**27.** $y = 2x^2 + 2\sqrt{26}x + 13$  **28.** $y = 3x^2 - 12\sqrt{3}x + 36$

*In Exercises 29–32, find the sum and the product of the roots of each quadratic equation.*

**29.** $x^2 + 8x - 20 = 0$  **30.** $x^2 - 3x + 12 = 0$
**31.** $4y^2 - 28y + 9 = 0$  **32.** $\frac{1}{2}y^2 = 4y - 5$

*In Exercises 33–38, find a quadratic equation with the given roots* $r_1$ *and* $r_2$. *Write each answer in the form* $ax^2 + bx + c = 0$, *where a, b, and c are integers and* $a > 0$.

**33.** $r_1 = 3$ and $r_2 = 11$  **34.** $r_1 = -4$ and $r_2 = -9$
**35.** $r_1 = 1 - \sqrt{2}$ and $r_2 = 1 + \sqrt{2}$
**36.** $r_1 = 2 - \sqrt{5}$ and $r_2 = 2 + \sqrt{5}$
**37.** $r_1 = \frac{1}{2}(2 + \sqrt{5})$ and $r_2 = \frac{1}{2}(2 - \sqrt{5})$
**38.** $r_1 = \frac{1}{3}(4 - \sqrt{5})$ and $r_2 = \frac{1}{3}(4 + \sqrt{5})$

*In Exercises 39 and 40, solve the equations.* *Hint: Look before you leap.*

**39.** $x^2 - (\sqrt{2} + \sqrt{5})x + \sqrt{10} = 0$
**40.** $x^2 + (\sqrt{2} - 1)x = \sqrt{2}$
**41.** A ball is thrown straight upward. Suppose that the height of the ball at time $t$ is given by the formula $h = -16t^2 + 96t$, where $h$ is in feet and $t$ is in seconds, with $t = 0$ corresponding to the instant that the ball is first tossed.
   **(a)** How long does it take before the ball lands?
   **(b)** At what time is the height 80 ft? Why does this question have two answers?
**42.** During a flu epidemic in a small town, a public health official finds that the total number of people $P$ who have caught the flu after $t$ days is closely approximated by the formula $P = -t^2 + 26t + 106$, where $1 \le t \le 13$.
   **(a)** How many have caught the flu after 10 days?
   **(b)** After approximately how many days will 250 people have caught the flu?

*In Exercises 43–50, use the discriminant to determine how many real roots each equation has.*

**43.** $x^2 - 12x + 16 = 0$  **44.** $2x^2 - 6x + 5 = 0$
**45.** $4x^2 - 5x - \frac{1}{2} = 0$  **46.** $4x^2 - 28x + 49 = 0$
**47.** $x^2 + \sqrt{3}x + \frac{3}{4} = 0$  **48.** $\sqrt{2}x^2 + \sqrt{3}x + 1 = 0$
**49.** $y^2 - \sqrt{5}y = -1$  **50.** $\frac{m^2}{4} - \frac{4m}{3} + \frac{16}{9} = 0$

*In each of Exercises 51–54, find the value(s) of k such that the equation has exactly one real root.*

**51.** $x^2 + 12x + k = 0$  **52.** $3x^2 + (\sqrt{2k})x + 6 = 0$
**53.** $x^2 + kx + 5 = 0$  **54.** $kx^2 + kx + 1 = 0$

# B

*In Exercises 55–58, solve for the indicated letter.*

**55.** $2\pi r^2 + 2\pi rh = 20\pi$; for $r$
   *Hint:* Rewrite the equation as $(2\pi)r^2 + (2\pi h)r - 20\pi = 0$ and use the quadratic formula with $a = 2\pi$, $b = 2\pi h$, and $c = -20\pi$.
**56.** $2\pi y^2 + \pi yx = 12$; for $y$
**57.** $-16t^2 + v_0 t = 0$; for $t$
**58.** $-\frac{1}{2}gt^2 + v_0 t + h_0 = 0$; for $t$
(G) **59. (a)** On the same set of axes, graph the equations
   $$y = x^2 + 8x + 16 \text{ and } y = x^2 - 8x + 16.$$
   **(b)** Use the graphs to estimate the roots of the two equations $x^2 + 8x + 16 = 0$ and $x^2 - 8x + 16 = 0$. How do the roots appear to be related?
   **(c)** Solve the two equations in part (b) to determine the exact values of the roots. Do your results support the response you gave to the question at the end of part (b)?
(G) **60. (a)** Figure 1(c) in the text shows a graph of the equation $y = x^2 + 3x - 5$. Use a graphing utility to reproduce the graph. [Use the same viewing rectangle that is used in Figure 1(c).]
   **(b)** Add the graph of the equation $y = x^2 - 3x - 5$ to the picture that you obtained in part (a). (This new equation is the same as the one in part (a) except that the sign of the coefficient of $x$ has been reversed.) Note that the $x$-intercepts of the two graphs appear to be negatives of one another.
   **(c)** Use the quadratic formula to determine exact expressions for the roots of the two equations $x^2 + 3x - 5 = 0$ and $x^2 - 3x - 5 = 0$. You'll find that the roots of one equation are the opposites of the roots of the other equation. [In general, the graphs of the two equations $y = ax^2 + bx + c$ and $y = ax^2 - bx + c$ are symmetric about the $y$-axis. Thus, the $x$-intercepts (when they exist) will always be opposites of one another.]
**61. (a)** Use the quadratic formula to show that the roots of the equation $x^2 + 3x + 1 = 0$ are $\frac{1}{2}(-3 \pm \sqrt{5})$.
   **(b)** Show that $\frac{1}{2}(-3 + \sqrt{5}) = 1/[\frac{1}{2}(-3 - \sqrt{5})]$.
   *Hint:* Rationalize the denominator on the right-hand side of the equation.

**(c)** The result in part (b) shows that the roots of the equation $x^2 + 3x + 1 = 0$ are reciprocals. Can you find another, much simpler way to establish this fact?

**62.** If $r_1$ and $r_2$ are the roots of the quadratic equation $ax^2 + bx + c = 0$, show that $r_1 + r_2 = -b/a$ and $r_1 r_2 = c/a$.

**63.** Show that the quadratic equation

$$ax^2 + bx - a = 0 \qquad (a \neq 0)$$

has two distinct real roots.

**64.** Show that the quadratic equation

$$(x - p)(x - q) = r^2 \qquad (p \neq q)$$

has two distinct real roots.

*In Exercises 65 and 66, determine the value(s) of the constant k for which the equation has equal roots (that is, only one distinct root).*

**65.** $x^2 = 2x(3k + 1) - 7(2k + 3)$

**66.** $x^2 + 2(k + 1)x + k^2 = 0$

**67.** Here is an outline for a slightly different derivation of the quadratic formula. The advantage of this method is that fractions are avoided until the very last step. Fill in the details.

**(a)** Beginning with $ax^2 + bx = -c$, multiply both sides by $4a$. Then add $b^2$ to both sides.

**(b)** Now factor the resulting left-hand side and take square roots.

**68.** In this section and in Section 1.3, we solved quadratic equations by factoring and by using the quadratic formula. This exercise shows how to solve a quadratic equation by the **method of substitution.** As an example, we use the equation

$$x^2 + x - 1 = 0 \tag{1}$$

**(a)** In equation (1), make the substitution $x = y + k$. Show that the resulting equation can be written

$$y^2 + (2k + 1)y = 1 - k - k^2 \tag{2}$$

**(b)** Find a value for $k$ so that the coefficient of $y$ in equation (2) is 0. Then, using this value of $k$, show that equation (2) becomes $y^2 = 5/4$.

**(c)** Solve the equation $y^2 = 5/4$. Then use the equation $x = y + k$ to obtain the solutions of equation (1).

**69.** Use the substitution method (explained in Exercise 68) to solve the quadratic equation $2x^2 - 3x + 1 = 0$.

**70.** Assume that $a$ and $b$ are the roots of the equation $x^2 + px + q = 0$.

**(a)** Find the value of $a^2 b + ab^2$ in terms of $p$ and $q$.
*Hint:* Factor the expression $a^2 b + ab^2$.

**(b)** Find the value of $a^3 b + ab^3$ in terms of $p$ and $q$.
*Hint:* Factor. Then use the fact that $a^2 + b^2 = (a + b)^2 - 2ab$.

Ⓖ **71.** In this exercise we investigate the effect of the constant $c$ upon the roots of the quadratic equation $x^2 - 6x + c = 0$. We do this by looking at the $x$-intercepts of the graphs of the corresponding equations $y = x^2 - 6x + c$.

**(a)** Set a viewing rectangle that extends from 0 to 5 in the $x$-direction and from $-2$ to 3 in the $y$-direction. Then (on the same set of axes) graph the equations $y = x^2 - 6x + c$ with $c$ running from 8 to 10 at increments of 0.25. In other words, graph the equations $y = x^2 - 6x + 8, y = x^2 - 6x + 8.25, y = x^2 - 6x + 8.50$, and so on, up through $y = x^2 - 6x + 10$.

**(b)** Note from the graphs in part (a) that, initially, as $c$ increases, the $x$-intercepts draw closer and closer together. For which value of $c$ do the two $x$-intercepts seem to merge into one?

**(c)** Use algebra as follows to check your observation in part (b). Using that value of $c$ for which there appears to be only one intercept, solve the quadratic equation $x^2 - 6x + c = 0$. How many roots do you obtain?

**(d)** Some of the graphs in part (a) have no $x$-intercepts. What are the corresponding values of $c$ in these cases? Pick any one of these values of $c$ and use the quadratic formula to solve the equation $x^2 - 6x + c = 0$. What happens?

**C**

**72.** Find nonzero real numbers $A$ and $B$ so that the roots of the equation $x^2 + Ax + B = 0$ are $A$ and $B$.

---

# PROJECT | PUT THE QUADRATIC EQUATION IN ITS PLACE!

*This is easier as a group project (divide and conquer) but, of course, is open to individuals too.*

Despite the critical influence of science and mathematics in today's culture, many high school history books tell very little about the history of these fields. In mathematics, for example, it's easy to develop the false impression that mathematics is strictly a "Western" achievement, developed rather exclusively in

Greece (Pythagoras and Euclid), France (René Descartes), and England (Isaac Newton). A mere glance, however, at the following list of a few mathematicians (from the period 0 to A.D. 1400) will tell you otherwise. (All right, one Greek name does appear in the list!) The common element linking the names is that, among other mathematical achievements, each person solved quadratic equations. By checking math history books or encyclopedias in your college library, locate these names on the time line that follows. The World Wide Web is also a useful source here. *Some hints*: The listing here is in no particular order. In some cases, you'll find that only very approximate dates are known. Also, be prepared to see numerous alternate spellings.

| | |
|---|---|
| Omar Khayyam | Abraham bar Hiyya (or Chiya) |
| Mahāvira | Jia Xian |
| Bhāskara | Muhammad al-Khwārizmi |
| Diophantus | Āryabhata |
| Brahmagupta | Joranus de Nemore |

## 2.2  OTHER TYPES OF EQUATIONS

*In this chapter we propose to consider some miscellaneous equations; it will be seen that many of these can be solved by the ordinary rules for quadratic equations. . . .* —H. S. Hall and S. R. Knight, *Higher Algebra* [London: Macmillan and Co., 1946 (first edition published in 1887)]

In Sections 1.3 and 2.1 we developed techniques for solving linear and quadratic equations. In this section we consider some other types of equations that can be solved by applying those techniques. As in the previous section, we will consider only solutions that are real numbers. (Solutions involving the complex-number system are discussed in Chapter 12.) We begin with two examples involving absolute values.

| EXAMPLE | 1 | Solving an equation where the variable is inside absolute value signs |
|---|---|---|

Solve: $|2x - 1| = 7$.

**SOLUTION**
There are two cases to consider.

| If $2x - 1 \geq 0$, the equation becomes | If $2x - 1 < 0$, the equation becomes |
|---|---|
| $2x - 1 = 7$ | $-(2x - 1) = 7$ |
| $2x = 8$ | $-2x + 1 = 7$ |
| $x = 4$ | $-2x = 6$ |
| | $x = -3$ |

We've now obtained the values $x = 4$ and $x = -3$. You should check for yourself that both of these numbers indeed satisfy the original equation.

The solution in Example 1 proceeds by considering two separate cases. There is another way to solve the equation in Example 1 that avoids this two-case technique. This alternate method relies on the following basic property of the absolute value (from Section 1.2):

For any real number $a$, we have $|a|^2 = a^2$.

To apply this property in solving the equation $|2x - 1| = 7$, we square both sides of the equation to obtain

$$|2x - 1|^2 = (2x - 1)^2 = 49$$
$$4x^2 - 4x - 48 = 0$$
$$x^2 - x - 12 = 0$$

This last equation is a quadratic equation that can be solved by factoring (as in Section 1.3). We have

$$(x - 4)(x + 3) = 0$$

| $x - 4 = 0$ | $x + 3 = 0$ |
|---|---|
| $x = 4$ | $x = -3$ |

This yields the two roots $x = 4$ and $x = -3$, in agreement with the result in Example 1.

CAUTION  We obtained these two roots by squaring both sides of the original equation. However, it is not always the case that squaring both sides yields roots that check in the original equation. Consider, for example, the equation $|x| = -1$. This equation has no solution (why?) yet squaring both sides yields $x^2 = 1$, with roots $x = \pm 1$. However, neither 1 nor $-1$ checks in the original equation $|x| = -1$. The roots 1 and $-1$ are extraneous roots. We'll return to this point again, later in this section.

The solutions in Example 1 can be checked graphically. One way to do this is first to rewrite the given equation $|2x - 1| = 7$ in the equivalent form $|2x - 1| - 7 = 0$. Then, as we saw in previous sections, the roots of this last equation are the $x$-intercepts of the graph of

$$y = |2x - 1| - 7$$

As indicated in Figure 1(a), the $x$-intercepts of the graph appear to be $-3$ and 4, which are indeed the two roots obtained in Example 1. A different way to check the solutions of the equation $|2x - 1| = 7$ involves graphing the *two* equations $y = |2x - 1|$ and $y = 7$ on the same set of axes. As indicated in Figure 1(b), the graphs intersect in two points. The $x$-coordinates of those two points appear to be $-3$ and 4, which again are the two roots determined in Example 1.

## GRAPHICAL PERSPECTIVE

**Figure 1**
Two ways to check the solutions in Example 1. In Figure 1(a) the $x$-intercepts of the graph of $y = |2x - 1| - 7$ are the solutions of the equation $|2x - 1| = 7$. In Figure 1(b) the $x$-coordinates of the intersection points of the two graphs $y = |2x - 1|$ and $y = 7$ are the solutions of the equation $|2x - 1| = 7$.

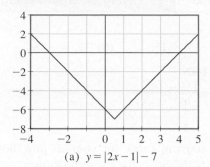

(a)  $y = |2x - 1| - 7$          (b)  $y = |2x - 1|$ and $y = 7$

**CAUTION**   Some care needs to be taken in drawing conclusions from a graph, even a graph obtained with a computer or graphing calculator. For instance, taken in isolation, the graphs in Figure 1 do not *prove* that the roots we are looking for are $-3$ and 4. Indeed, the only honest conclusion from the graphs themselves is that the two roots we are looking for must be very close to $-3$ and 4. The only way to tell whether the roots are exactly $-3$ and 4 is to use an algebraic method, as in Example 1, or to substitute each purported root in the given equation to see whether it checks. Figure 2 serves to emphasize this point. In Figure 2(a) we are looking at a portion of the curve $y = x^2 - 2.2x$ and the line $y = 0.8$ in order to find a root of the equation $x^2 - 2.2x = 0.8$. On the basis of the evidence in Figure 2(a), it appears that $x = 2.5$ may be a root. But, if you replace $x$ with 2.5 in the equation $x^2 - 2.2x = 0.8$, you'll see that it does *not* check; 2.5 is not a root. Indeed, as is indicated in the magnified view in Figure 2(b), the graphs of $y = x^2 - 2.2x$ and $y = 0.8$ do not intersect at $x = 2.5$. That is, 2.5 is not a root. *Note*: Figure 2(b) does more than just tell us that 2.5 is not a root. It tells us that the root lies in the open interval (2.5, 2.55), so certainly the digit in the first decimal place of the root is a 5. More zooming in with a graphing calculator or a computer would yield additional decimal places.

When $n$ is a natural number, equations of the form $x^n = a$ are solved simply by rewriting the equation in terms of the appropriate $n$th root or roots. For example, if $x^3 = 34$, then $x = \sqrt[3]{34}$. If the exponent $n$ is even, however, we have to remember that there are *two* real $n$th roots for each positive number. For instance, if $x^4 = 81$, then $x = \pm\sqrt[4]{81} = \pm 3$. *Note*: If you feel that you need to review the subject of $n$th roots from intermediate algebra, see Appendix B.2 at the back of this book.

## GRAPHICAL PERSPECTIVE

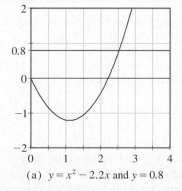

**Figure 2**
Looking for a root of the equation $x^2 - 2.2x = 0.8$

(a)  $y = x^2 - 2.2x$ and $y = 0.8$

(b)  Zoom-in view of $y = x^2 - 2.2x$ and $y = 0.8$

| EXAMPLE | 2 | Solving equations using $n$th roots |

Solve:

**(a)** $(x - 1)^4 = 15$; **(b)** $3x^4 = -48$; **(c)** $3x^5 = -48$.

**SOLUTION**

**(a)** $(x - 1)^4 = 15$

$$x - 1 = \pm\sqrt[4]{15}$$
$$x = 1 \pm \sqrt[4]{15}$$

As you can check for yourself now, both of the values, $1 + \sqrt[4]{15}$ and $1 - \sqrt[4]{15}$, satisfy the given equation.

*Remark*: We can estimate these values without a calculator. For instance, for $x = 1 + \sqrt[4]{15}$ we have

$$1 + \sqrt[4]{15} \approx 1 + \sqrt[4]{16} = 1 + 2 = 3$$

Therefore, $1 + \sqrt[4]{15}$ is a little less than 3. (In fact, a calculator shows that $1 + \sqrt[4]{15} \approx 2.97$.)

**(b)** For any real number $x$, the quantity $x^4$ is nonnegative. Therefore, the left-hand side of the equation is nonnegative, whereas the right-hand side is negative. Consequently, there are no real numbers satisfying the given equation.

**(c)** Dividing both sides of the given equation by 3 yields $x^5 = -16$, and therefore

$$x = \sqrt[5]{-16} \qquad \text{or, equivalently,} \qquad x = -\sqrt[5]{16}$$

*Calculator note*: To approximate $-\sqrt[5]{16}$ using a calculator, first recall that $\sqrt[5]{16}$ can be rewritten in the equivalent form $16^{1/5}$. (See Appendix B.3 if you need a review of rational exponents.) We then have

$$x = -\sqrt[5]{16} = -16^{1/5} \approx -1.74 \qquad \begin{array}{l}\text{using a calculator and rounding} \\ \text{to two decimal places}\end{array}$$

In Example 3 we solve two equations by factoring. As with quadratic equations, the factoring method is justified by the zero-product property of real numbers (from Section 1.3).

| EXAMPLE | 3 | Using factoring to solve equations |

Find the real-number solutions for each equation:

**(a)** $3x^3 - 12x^2 - 15x = 0$; **(b)** $x^4 + x^2 - 6 = 0$.

**SOLUTION**

**(a)** First we factor the left-hand side

$$3x^3 - 12x^2 - 15x = 0$$
$$3x(x^2 - 4x - 5) = 0$$
$$3x(x - 5)(x + 1) = 0$$

Now, by setting each factor equal to zero, we obtain the three values $x = 0$, $x = 5$, and $x = -1$. As you can check, each of these numbers indeed satisfies the original equation. So we have three solutions: 0, 5, and $-1$.

*Note*: If initially we had divided both sides of the given equation by $3x$ to obtain $x^2 - 4x - 5 = 0$, then the solution $x = 0$ would have been overlooked.

**(b)** Again we factor the left-hand side

$$x^4 + x^2 - 6 = 0$$
$$(x^2 - 2)(x^2 + 3) = 0$$

| | |
|---|---|
| $x^2 - 2 = 0$ | $x^2 + 3 = 0$ |
| $x^2 = 2$ | $x^2 = -3$ |
| $x = \pm\sqrt{2}$ | |

By setting the first factor equal to zero, we've obtained the two values $x = \pm\sqrt{2}$. As you can check, these values do satisfy the given equation. When we set the second factor equal to zero, however, we obtained $x^2 = -3$, which has no real solutions (because the square of a real number must be nonnegative). We conclude therefore that the given equation in this case has only two real solutions, $\sqrt{2}$ and $-\sqrt{2}$.

The equation $x^4 + x^2 - 6 = 0$ that we considered in Example 3(b) is called **an equation of quadratic type.** This means that with a suitable substitution, the resulting equation becomes quadratic. In particular here, suppose that we let

$$x^2 = t \qquad \text{and therefore} \qquad x^4 = t^2$$

Then the equation $x^4 + x^2 - 6 = 0$ becomes $t^2 + t - 6 = 0$, which is "quadratic in $t$." Solving for $t$, we obtain $t = -3$ or $2$. Then substituting $x^2$ for $t$, we obtain $x^2 = -3$ or $x^2 = 2$ as before. This idea is exploited in the next three examples.

**EXAMPLE 4    Solving an equation of quadratic type**

As shown in Figure 3, the graph of $y = x^4 - 6x^2 + 4$ has four $x$-intercepts. Determine these $x$-intercepts. Give two forms for each answer: an exact expression involving radicals and a calculator approximation rounded to two decimal places.

**SOLUTION**
As explained in Section 1.5, the $x$-intercepts are obtained by setting $y$ equal to zero in the given equation and then solving for $x$. So we need to solve the equation

$$x^4 - 6x^2 + 4 = 0 \tag{1}$$

This equation cannot readily be solved by factoring; however, it is of quadratic type. We let $x^2 = t$; then $x^4 = t^2$, and the equation becomes

$$t^2 - 6t + 4 = 0$$

The quadratic formula then yields

$$t = \frac{6 \pm \sqrt{36 - 4(4)}}{2} = \frac{6 \pm \sqrt{20}}{2}$$

$$= \frac{6 \pm 2\sqrt{5}}{2} = 3 \pm \sqrt{5}$$

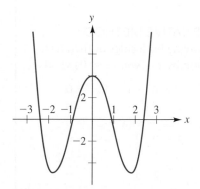

**Figure 3**
$y = x^4 - 6x^2 + 4$

Consequently, we have (in view of the definition of $t$)

$$x^2 = 3 \pm \sqrt{5}$$

and therefore

$$x = \pm\sqrt{3 \pm \sqrt{5}}$$

We've now found four values for $x$:

$$\sqrt{3 + \sqrt{5}} \qquad -\sqrt{3 + \sqrt{5}} \qquad \sqrt{3 - \sqrt{5}} \qquad -\sqrt{3 - \sqrt{5}}$$

These are the required $x$-intercepts for the graph in Figure 3. [Exercise 87 asks you to check that these values indeed satisfy equation (1).] Which is which, though? Without using a calculator, but with a little thought, you should be able to list these four quantities in order of increasing size and thereby assign them to the appropriate locations in Figure 3. (Try it before reading on!) Using a calculator now, and referring to Figure 3, we obtain the following results.

the $x$-intercept between $-3$ and $-2$:    $-\sqrt{3 + \sqrt{5}} \approx -2.29$
the $x$-intercept between $-1$ and $0$:    $-\sqrt{3 - \sqrt{5}} \approx -0.87$
the $x$-intercept between $0$ and $1$:    $\sqrt{3 - \sqrt{5}} \approx 0.87$
the $x$-intercept between $2$ and $3$:    $\sqrt{3 + \sqrt{5}} \approx 2.29.$

### EXAMPLE 5    Solving an equation of quadratic type

Solve: $6x^{-2} - x^{-1} - 2 = 0$.

**SOLUTION**
We'll show two methods. The first method depends on recognizing the equation as one of quadratic type.

FIRST METHOD
Let $x^{-1} = t$. Then $x^{-2} = t^2$ and the equation becomes

$$6t^2 - t - 2 = 0$$
$$(3t - 2)(2t + 1) = 0$$

$3t - 2 = 0 \qquad\big|\qquad 2t + 1 = 0$

$t = \dfrac{2}{3} \qquad\big|\qquad t = -\dfrac{1}{2}$

If $t = 2/3$, then $x^{-1} = 2/3$. Therefore $\dfrac{1}{x} = \dfrac{2}{3}$, and consequently, $x = 3/2$.
On the other hand, if $t = -1/2$, then $\dfrac{1}{x} = -\dfrac{1}{2}$, and consequently, $x = -2$.
In summary, the two solutions are $3/2$ and $-2$.

ALTERNATIVE METHOD
Multiplying both sides of the given equation by $x^2$ (*Note*: $x \neq 0$) yields

$$6 - x - 2x^2 = 0$$
$$2x^2 + x - 6 = 0$$
$$(2x - 3)(x + 2) = 0$$

$2x - 3 = 0 \qquad\big|\qquad x + 2 = 0$

$x = \dfrac{3}{2} \qquad\big|\qquad x = -2$

Thus we have $x = 3/2$ or $x = -2$, as we obtained using the first method.

In the next example we first use a graphing utility to approximate the solutions of an equation, then we use algebra to determine the solutions exactly. Note, however, that even in the graphing utility portion of the problem, algebra is useful. It turns out that the graph is symmetric about the $y$-axis, and that cuts the work in half.

---

### EXAMPLE 6   Solving an equation with fractional exponents

Consider the equation $2x^{4/3} - x^{2/3} - 6 = 0$.
**(a)** Use a graphing utility to approximate the roots to the nearest hundredth.
**(b)** Use algebra to determine the exact solutions. Then check that the answers are consistent with the approximations obtained in part (a).

### SOLUTION
**(a)** The roots of the given equation are the $x$-intercepts of the graph of $y = 2x^{4/3} - x^{2/3} - 6$. After experimenting with different viewing rectangles, we find that the standard viewing rectangle in Figure 4(a) does show the essential features of the graph.

### GRAPHICAL PERSPECTIVE

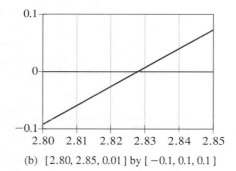

**Figure 4**
Two views of $y = 2x^{4/3} - x^{2/3} - 6$

(a)  $[-10, 10, 2]$ by $[-10, 10, 5]$   (b)  $[2.80, 2.85, 0.01]$ by $[-0.1, 0.1, 0.1]$

In looking at Figure 4(a), it appears that there are two roots: one between 2 and 4, the other between $-2$ and $-4$. It also appears that the graph may be symmetric about the $y$-axis. If so, once we find the first root between 2 and 4, then we'll automatically know the second root: It will just be the opposite of the first. To show that the graph is indeed symmetric about the $y$-axis, we can rewrite the equation $y = 2x^{4/3} - x^{2/3} - 6$ as $y = 2(x^4)^{1/3} - (x^2)^{1/3} - 6$. In this form, because of the even integer exponents on $x$, replacing $x$ with $-x$ will make no difference. So, according to the first symmetry test on page 59, the graph is symmetric about the $y$-axis. In Figure 4(b) we've zoomed in on the positive root. Since we are supposed to approximate the root to the nearest hundredth, we've zoomed in far enough to allow us to mark off the $x$-scale in units of 0.01. Figure 4(b) shows that the positive root is 2.83, to the nearest hundredth. By symmetry, the other root then is $-2.83$, also to the nearest hundredth. (We note in passing that many graphing utilities also have "solve" keys for approximating roots of equations. For details, consult your user's manual.)

**(b)** In the given equation $2x^{4/3} - x^{2/3} - 6 = 0$, we let $x^{2/3} = t$. Then $x^{4/3} = t^2$, and the equation becomes

$$2t^2 - t - 6 = 0$$
$$(2t + 3)(t - 2) = 0$$

$$2t + 3 = 0 \qquad\bigg|\qquad t - 2 = 0$$
$$t = -\frac{3}{2} \qquad\bigg|\qquad t = 2$$

We now have two cases to consider: $t = -3/2$ and $t = 2$. With $t = -3/2$, we have (in view of the definition of $t$)

$$x^{2/3} = -\frac{3}{2} \qquad \text{or, equivalently,} \qquad (x^{1/3})^2 = -\frac{3}{2}$$

This last equation has no real-number solutions, because the square of a real number is never negative. Turning our attention then to the other case where $t = 2$, we have

$$x^{2/3} = 2$$
$$(x^{2/3})^3 = 2^3 \qquad\qquad \text{Two real numbers are equal if}$$
$$\qquad\qquad\qquad\qquad \text{and only if their cubes are equal.}$$
$$x^2 = 8$$
$$x = \pm\sqrt{8} = \pm 2\sqrt{2}$$

As Exercise 88 asks you to verify, each of the values $2\sqrt{2}$ and $-2\sqrt{2}$ satisfies the original equation. These are the required roots. As you can check now by picking up a calculator, we have $2\sqrt{2} \approx 2.828$, which is indeed consistent with the approximations in part (a).

---

Some equations can be solved by raising both sides to the same power. In fact, if you review the solution given for Example 6, you'll see that we've already made use of this idea in cubing both sides of one of the equations there. As another example, consider the equation

$$\sqrt{x - 3} = 5$$

By squaring both sides of this equation we obtain $x - 3 = 25$ and, consequently, $x = 28$. As you can easily check, the value $x = 28$ does satisfy the original equation.

There is a complication, however, that can arise in raising both sides of an equation to the same power. Consider, for example, the equation

$$x - 2 = \sqrt{x}$$

By squaring both sides, we obtain

$$x^2 - 4x + 4 = x$$
$$x^2 - 5x + 4 = 0$$
$$(x - 4)(x - 1) = 0$$

Therefore

$$x = 4 \qquad \text{or} \qquad x = 1$$

The value $x = 4$ checks in the original equation, but the value $x = 1$ does not. (Verify this.) Therefore $x = 1$ is an extraneous solution, and the only solution of the given equation is $x = 4$.

The extraneous solution in this case arises from the fact that if $a^2 = b^2$, then it need not be true that $a = b$. For instance, $(-3)^2 = 3^2$, but certainly $-3 \neq 3$. In the box that follows, we summarize this remark about extraneous solutions. For reference, we also include the results from Section 1.3.

---

**┃ PROPERTY SUMMARY   Extraneous Solutions**

1. Squaring both sides of an equation (or raising both sides to an even integral power) may introduce extraneous solutions that do not check in the original equation.
2. Multiplying sides of an equation by an expression involving the variable may introduce extraneous solutions.

Therefore it is always necessary to check any candidates for solutions that you obtain in either of these ways.

---

In the next example we solve equations involving radicals. In each case, notice that *before* squaring, we first isolate one of the radicals on one side of the equation. Otherwise things become more complicated, rather than less. For instance, in Example 7(a) we're given the equation $2 + \sqrt{10 - x} = -x$. If we square both sides without first isolating the radical, we obtain

$$(2 + \sqrt{10 - x})^2 = (-x)^2$$

and, consequently,

$$4 + 4\sqrt{10 - x} + 10 - x = x^2 \quad \text{or} \quad 14 + 4\sqrt{10 - x} - x = x^2$$

As you can see, this last equation is indeed more complicated than the original.

**EXAMPLE  7    Solving equations with radicals**

Find all real-number solutions of each equation.
**(a)** $2 + \sqrt{10 - x} = -x$          **(b)** $\sqrt{2x + 3} - 2\sqrt{x - 2} = 1$

**SOLUTION**
**(a)** First isolate the radical by rewriting the given equation as

$$\sqrt{10 - x} = -x - 2$$

Squaring both sides now yields

$$(\sqrt{10 - x})^2 = (-x - 2)^2$$
$$10 - x = x^2 + 4x + 4$$
$$0 = x^2 + 5x - 6$$
$$0 = (x + 6)(x - 1)$$

$$
\begin{array}{c|c}
x + 6 = 0 & x - 1 = 0 \\
x = -6 & x = 1
\end{array}
$$

*Check for extraneous roots:* With $x = -6$ the *original* equation becomes

$$2 + \sqrt{10 - (-6)} \stackrel{?}{=} -(-6)$$
$$2 + 4 \stackrel{?}{=} 6 \qquad \text{True}$$

With $x = 1$ the original equation becomes

$$2 + \sqrt{10 - 1} \stackrel{?}{=} -1$$
$$2 + 3 \stackrel{?}{=} -1 \qquad \text{False}$$

In summary, the given equation has but one root: $x = -6$.

**(b)** The given equation contains two radicals, so initially the best that we can do is to isolate one of them before squaring. (It does not matter which.) Rewriting the given equation as $\sqrt{2x + 3} = 2\sqrt{x - 2} + 1$ and then squaring yields

$$(\sqrt{2x + 3})^2 = (2\sqrt{x - 2} + 1)^2$$
$$2x + 3 = 4(x - 2) + 4\sqrt{x - 2} + 1$$

You should check now for yourself that if we combine like terms in this last equation, then it can be rewritten as

$$-2x + 10 = 4\sqrt{x - 2}$$

Next, don't square both sides quite yet! It won't be wrong, but you can work with smaller numbers if you first divide both sides by 2 to obtain

$$-x + 5 = 2\sqrt{x - 2}$$

Now square both sides:

$$(-x + 5)^2 = (2\sqrt{x - 2})^2$$
$$x^2 - 10x + 25 = 4x - 8$$
$$x^2 - 14x + 33 = 0$$
$$(x - 3)(x - 11) = 0$$

From this last equation we conclude that $x = 3$ or $x = 11$.
*Check for extraneous roots:* With $x = 3$ the *original* equation becomes

$$\sqrt{2(3) + 3} - 2\sqrt{3 - 2} \stackrel{?}{=} 1$$
$$3 - 2 \stackrel{?}{=} 1 \qquad \text{True}$$

Next, with $x = 11$ the original equation becomes

$$\sqrt{2(11) + 3} - 2\sqrt{11 - 2} \stackrel{?}{=} 1$$
$$5 - 2(3) \stackrel{?}{=} 1 \qquad \text{False}$$

So the only solution of the given equation is $x = 3$. For a graphical perspective, see Figure 5.

## GRAPHICAL PERSPECTIVE

**Figure 5**
The curve $y = \sqrt{2x + 3} - 2\sqrt{x - 3}$ meets the horizontal line $y = 1$ at $x = 3$. That is, $x = 3$ is a solution of the equation $\sqrt{2x + 3} - 2\sqrt{x - 3} = 1$.

---

# EXERCISE SET 2.2

**A**

*In Exercises 1–6, solve each equation.*

1. $|x - 5| = 1$
2. $|x - 4| - 5 = 2$
3. $|x + 6| = 1/2$
4. $|x + 6| + 1/2 = 0$
5. $|6x - 5| = 25$
6. $|5 - 6x| = 0$

*In Exercises 7–10, solve each equation by using the squaring technique that is discussed following Example 1 in the text.*

7. $|x + 3| = 2x - 2$
8. $4|x - 2| = 3x - 4$
9. $|2x - 1| = 1 - \frac{1}{2}x$
10. $|x + 1| - |3x - 2| = 0$

Ⓖ **11.** **(a)** On the same set of axes, graph the equations $y = x^2 - 2.2x$ and $y = 0.8$. Use the same viewing rectangle that is shown in Figure 2(a) in the text. Check that your graphs are consistent with those drawn in Figure 2(a). The graphs show that the line $y = 0.8$ intersects the curve $y = x^2 - 2.2x$ at a point with an $x$-coordinate very close to 2.5. In other words, one of the roots of the equation $x^2 - 2.2x = 0.8$ is approximately 2.5.

**(b)** Take a closer look at the intersection point using the same viewing rectangle that is shown in Figure 2(b) in the text. As is pointed out in the text, this view shows that the root we are looking for is actually slightly larger than 2.5; it lies in the open interval (2.5, 2.55). Thus, the first decimal place of the root must indeed be 5, and the second decimal place must be a digit between 0 and 4, inclusive. Continue to zoom in on this intersection point until you are sure of the first three decimal places of the root.

**(c)** Use the quadratic formula to find an expression for the exact value of the root in part (b). Then evaluate the expression and round to four decimal places. Check that your answer is consistent with the result obtained graphically in part (b).

Ⓖ **12. (a)** Graph the equation $y = 3x^3 - 12x^2 - 15x$.
  **(b)** On the basis of the graph, how many roots are there for the equation $3x^3 - 12x^2 - 15x = 0$? Use the graph to estimate these roots. Then compare your estimates to the actual values obtained in Example 3(a).

Ⓖ **13. (a)** Graph the equation $y = x^4 + x^2 - 6$.
  **(b)** On the basis of the graph, how many roots are there for the equation $x^4 + x^2 - 6 = 0$? Use the graph to estimate these roots. Zoom in until you are sure about the first three decimal places of each root. Then compare your estimates to the actual values obtained in Example 3(b).

Ⓖ **14. (a)** Using a viewing rectangle that extends from $-5$ to $5$ in both the $x$- and $y$-directions, graph the equation $y = 6x^{-2} - x^{-1} - 2$. Use the graph to estimate the roots of the equation $6x^{-2} - x^{-1} - 2 = 0$. How do your estimates compare to the actual values determined in Example 5?
  **(b)** Using the viewing rectangle specified in part (a), graph the equation $y = 6x^{-2} - x^{-1} + 2$. On the basis of the graph, make a statement about the roots of the equation $6x^{-2} - x^{-1} + 2 = 0$. Then solve the equation algebraically to confirm your statement.

*In Exercises 15–58, find all real solutions of each equation. For Exercises 31–36, give two forms for each answer: an exact answer (involving a radical) and a calculator approximation rounded to two decimal places.*

**15.** $3x^2 - 48x = 0$
**16.** $3x^3 - 48x = 0$
**17.** $t^3 - 125 = 0$
**18.** $t - t^3 = 0$
**19.** $7x^4 - 28x^2 = 0$
**20.** $y^4 - 81 = 0$
**21.** $t^4 + 2t^3 - 3t^2 = 0$
**22.** $2t^5 + 5t^4 - 12t^3 = 0$
**23.** $6x = 23x^2 + 4x^3$
**24.** $x^5 = 36x$
**25.** $x^4 - x^2 = 6$
**26.** $x^4 - 5x^2 = -6$
**27.** $4y^2 = 5 - y^4$
**28.** $6y^2 = -5 - y^4$
**29.** $3t^2 + 2 = 9t^4$
**30.** $5t^2 - 1 = 4t^4$

**31.** $(x - 2)^3 - 5 = 0$
**32.** $(x + 4)^3 + 2 = 0$
**33.** $(x + 4)^5 + 16 = 0$
**34.** $(1 - x)^5 - 40 = 0$
**35. (a)** $(x - 3)^4 - 30 = 0$
  **(b)** $(x - 3)^4 + 30 = 0$
**36. (a)** $(x^2 - 1)^4 - 81 = 0$
  **(b)** $(x^2 - 1)^4 + 81 = 0$
**37.** $x^6 - 10x^4 + 24x^2 = 0$
**38.** $2x^5 - 15x^3 - 27x = 0$
**39.** $x^4 + x^2 - 1 = 0$
**40.** $x^4 - x^2 + 1 = 0$
**41.** $x^4 + 3x^2 - 2 = 0$
**42.** $2x^4 + x^2 + 2 = 0$
**43.** $x^6 + 7x^3 = 8$
**44.** $x^6 + 27 = -28x^3$
**45.** $t^{-2} - 7t^{-1} + 12 = 0$
**46.** $8t^{-2} - 17t^{-1} + 2 = 0$
**47.** $12y^{-2} - 23y^{-1} = -5$
**48.** $y^{-2} - y^{-1} = 0$
**49.** $4x^{-4} - 33x^{-2} - 27 = 0$
**50.** $x^{-4} + x^{-2} + 1 = 0$
**51.** $t^{2/3} = 9$
**52.** $t^{3/2} = 8$
**53.** $(y - 1)^3 = 7$
**54.** $(2y + 3)^4 = 5$
**55.** $(t + 1)^5 = -243$
**56.** $(t + 3)^4 = 625$
**57.** $9x^{4/3} - 10x^{2/3} + 1 = 0$
**58.** $x^{4/3} + 3x^{2/3} - 28 = 0$

*In Exercises 59 and 60, find the x-intercepts of the graphs. Round each answer to two decimal places. Check to see that your answers are consistent with the graphs.*

**59.**

$y = x^4 - 2x^2 - 1$

**60.**

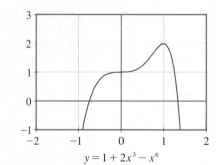

$y = 1 + 2x^3 - x^6$

*In Exercises 61–76, determine all of the real-number solutions for each equation. (Remember to check for extraneous solutions.)*

**61.** $\sqrt{1 - 3x} = 2$
**62.** $\sqrt{x^2 + 5x - 2} = 2$
**63.** $\sqrt{x + 6} = x$
**64.** $x - \sqrt{x} = 20$
**65.** $x - \sqrt{3 - x} = -3$
**66.** $\sqrt{2 - x} - 10 = x$
**67.** $4x + \sqrt{2x + 5} = 0$
**68.** $\sqrt{7 - 3x} - 6(x + 1) = 1$
**69.** $\sqrt{x^4 - 13x^2 + 37} = 1$
**70.** $\sqrt{y + 2} = y - 4$
**71.** $\sqrt{1 - 2x} + \sqrt{x + 5} = 4$
**72.** $\sqrt{x - 5} - \sqrt{x + 4} + 1 = 0$

**73.** $\sqrt{3 + 2t} + \sqrt{-1 + 4t} = 1$

**74.** $\sqrt{2t + 5} - \sqrt{8t + 25} + \sqrt{2t + 8} = 0$

**75.** $\sqrt{2y - 3} - \sqrt{3y + 3} + \sqrt{3y - 2} = 0$

**76.** $\sqrt{a - x} + \sqrt{b - x} = \sqrt{a + b - 2x}$, where $b > a > 0$

Ⓖ *In Exercises 77–86, (a) use zoom-in techniques to estimate the roots of each equation to the nearest hundredth, as in Example 6; and (b) use algebraic techniques to determine an exact expression for each root, then evaluate the expression and round to four decimal places. Check to see that your answers are consistent with the graphical results obtained in part (a).*

**77.** **(a)** $x^4 - 5x^2 = -6.2$
   **(b)** $x^4 - 5x^2 = -6.3$

**78.** **(a)** $x^4 - 5x^2 = -25/4$
   **(b)** $x^4 - 5x^2 = -13/2$

**79.** $x - 5\sqrt{x} = -3$

**80.** $x^{-2} - 5x^{-1} = -3$

**81.** $\sqrt{2x - 1} - \sqrt{x - 2} = 2$

**82.** $\sqrt{2x - 1} - \sqrt{x - 2} = 1$

**83.** $\dfrac{\sqrt{x} - 4}{\sqrt{x} + 3} + \dfrac{1}{2} = 0$

**84.** $\dfrac{\sqrt[4]{x} - 4}{\sqrt[4]{x} + 3} + \dfrac{1}{2} = 0$

**85.** $x^{2/3} - x^{1/3} = 1$

**86.** $x^{-2/3} - x^{-1/3} = 1$

**87.** Verify that the four solutions obtained in Example 4 indeed satisfy the original equation.

**88.** Verify that the values $x = \pm 2\sqrt{2}$ obtained in Example 6(b) satisfy the equation $2x^{4/3} - x^{2/3} - 6 = 0$.

**B**

*In Exercises 89–92, solve each equation.*

**89.** $\sqrt{\sqrt{x} + \sqrt{a}} + \sqrt{\sqrt{x} - \sqrt{a}} = \sqrt{2\sqrt{x} + 2\sqrt{b}}$

**90.** $\sqrt{x^2 - x - 1} - \dfrac{2}{\sqrt{x^2 - x - 1}} = 1$

   *Hint:* Let $t = x^2 - x - 1$.

**91.** $\sqrt{\dfrac{x - a}{x}} + 4\sqrt{\dfrac{x}{x - a}} = 5$, where $a \neq 0$

   *Hint:* Let $t = \dfrac{x - a}{x}$; then $\dfrac{1}{t} = \dfrac{x}{x - a}$.

**92.** $\sqrt{x^2 + 3x - 4} - \sqrt{x^2 - 5x + 4} = x - 1$, where $x > 4$

   *Hint:* Factor the expressions beneath the radicals. Then note that $\sqrt{x - 1}$ is a factor of both sides of the equation.

---

## MINI PROJECT ▌ FLYING THE FLAG

According to Clint Brookhart in his book *Go Figure!* (Lincolnwood, Ill.: Contemporary Books, 1998),

> *A flag the area of A in square feet, furled in a wind with a velocity of v in miles per hour, exerts a force of F in pounds on the flagpole equal to:* $F = 0.0003Av^{1.9}$.

**(a)** Solve the given equation for the velocity $v$ in terms of the force $F$.

**(b)** According to the *Encyclopedia Americana*, "A 5-foot by 6-foot 9-inch U.S. flag flown in bad weather [at a U.S. military post] is known as a storm flag." Suppose that the flagpole for a storm flag can withstand a force of 40 pounds before it breaks away from the wall to which it is attached. Use the result in part (a) to determine the wind speed that produces a 40-pound force on the flagpole. Round your answer to the nearest integer. (Actually, in a more realistic model, the length of the flagpole, not just the force on it, would have to be taken into account.)

---

## PROJECT ▌ SPECIFIC OR GENERAL? WHATEVER WORKS!

Sometimes in math and science, when we're stuck on a problem, we can make progress by turning from the specific to the general. This approach sometimes surprises students because of a mistaken belief that the general or more abstract case is always tougher than the specific. The specific equation that you'll work to solve in this project is

$$\sqrt{4 - \sqrt{4 + x}} - x = 0 \qquad (1)$$

**(a)** Use a graphing utility to graph the equation $y = \sqrt{4 - \sqrt{4 + x}} - x$. Then, by zooming in on the $x$-intercept, approximate the root of equation (1) to the nearest hundredth.

**(b)** Now let's try to find the exact value for the root. By using the process of isolating the radical and then squaring, show that equation (1) eventually becomes

$$x^4 - 8x^2 - x + 12 = 0$$

**(c)** At this point we are stuck; the equation obtained in part (b) can't be solved by using any of the elementary factoring techniques from intermediate algebra. Here is where we shift our focus to a slightly more general problem. Instead of equation (1), we consider

$$\sqrt{k - \sqrt{k + x}} - x = 0 \qquad (2)$$

where $k$ is a constant. Use the process of isolating the radical and then squaring to show that equation (2) eventually becomes

$$x^4 - 2kx^2 - x + k^2 - k = 0 \qquad (3)$$

**(d)** Although equation (3) is a fourth-degree equation in $x$, it is only a quadratic equation in $k$. That is, equation (3) can be written

$$k^2 - (2x^2 + 1)k + (x^4 - x) = 0 \qquad \text{Verify that this is equivalent to equation (3).}$$

Use the quadratic formula to solve this last equation for $k$ in terms of $x$. You should obtain (after simplifying) two solutions:

$$k = x^2 + x + 1 \qquad \text{or} \qquad k = x^2 - 1$$

**(e)** Finally now, in both of the equations obtained in part (d), replace $k$ with 4 [that's what it is in equation (1)], and solve each equation for $x$.

**(f)** Three of the four values that you obtain in part (e) are extraneous solutions for equation (1). Use your approximation in part (a) and a calculator to decide which value is the actual root of equation (1).

# 2.3  INEQUALITIES

*The fundamental results of mathematics are often inequalities rather than equalities.*—E. Beckenbach and R. Bellman in *An Introduction to Inequalities* (New York: Random House, 1961)

If we replace the equal sign in an equation with any one of the four symbols $<$, $\leq$, $>$, or $\geq$, we obtain an **inequality.** As with equations in one variable, a real number is a **solution** of an inequality if we obtain a true statement when the variable is replaced by the real number. For example, the value $x = 5$ is a solution of the inequality $2x - 3 < 8$, because when $x = 5$ we have

$$2(5) - 3 < 8$$

$$7 < 8 \qquad \text{which is true}$$

We also say in this case that the value $x = 5$ **satisfies** the inequality. To **solve** an inequality means to find all of the solutions. The set of all solutions of an inequality is called (naturally enough) the **solution set.**

Recall that two equations are said to be equivalent if they have exactly the same solutions. Similarly, two inequalities are **equivalent** if they have the same solution set. Most of the procedures used for solving inequalities are similar to those for equalities. For example, adding or subtracting the same number on both sides of an inequality produces an equivalent inequality. We need to be careful, however, in multiplying or dividing both sides of an inequality by the same nonzero number. For instance, suppose that we start with the inequality $2 < 3$ and multiply both sides by 5. That yields $10 < 15$, which is certainly true. But if we multiply both sides of the inequality $2 < 3$ by $-5$, we obtain $-10 < -15$, which is false. Multiplying both sides of an inequality by the same *positive* number preserves the inequality, whereas multiplying by a *negative* number reverses the inequality. In the following box, we list some of the principal properties of inequalities. In general, whenever we use Property 1 or 2 in solving an inequality, we obtain an equivalent inequality. Also, note that each property can be rewritten to reflect the fact that $a < b$ is equivalent to $b > a$. For example, Property 3 can just as well be written this way: If $b > a$ and $c > b$, then $c > a$.

## ▌ PROPERTY SUMMARY   Properties of Inequalities

For real numbers $a$, $b$, and $c$:

**Property**

1. If $a < b$, then $a + c < b + c$ and $a - c < b - c$.

2. (a) If $a < b$ and $c$ is positive, then $ac < bc$ and $\dfrac{a}{c} < \dfrac{b}{c}$.

   (b) If $a < b$ and $c$ is negative, then $ac > bc$ and $\dfrac{a}{c} > \dfrac{b}{c}$.

3. The transitive property: If $a < b$ and $b < c$, then $a < c$.

**Example**

If $x - 3 < 0$, then $(x - 3) + 3 < 0 + 3$ and, consequently, $x < 3$.

If $\dfrac{1}{2}x < 4$, then $2\left(\dfrac{1}{2}x\right) < 2(4)$ and, consequently, $x < 8$.

If $-\dfrac{x}{5} < 6$, then $(-5)\left(-\dfrac{x}{5}\right) > (-5)(6)$ and, consequently, $x > -30$.

If $a < x$ and $x < 2$, then $a < 2$.

   **EXAMPLE  1   Solving two simple inequalities**

Solve each of the following inequalities, state the solution in interval notation, and graph the solution set:
**(a)** $2x - 3 < 5$;    **(b)** $5t + 8 \le 7(1 + t)$.

**SOLUTION**
**(a)** Our work follows the same pattern that we would use to solve the equation $2x - 3 = 5$. We have

$$2x - 3 < 5$$
$$2x < 8 \qquad \text{adding 3 to both sides}$$
$$x < 4 \qquad \text{dividing both sides by 2}$$

The solution set is therefore $(-\infty, 4)$; see Figure 1.

**Figure 1**

**(b)** Again, we follow the pattern that we would use to solve the corresponding equation.

$$5t + 8 \leq 7 + 7t$$
$$-2t \leq -1 \qquad \text{subtracting } 7t \text{ and } 8 \text{ from both sides}$$
$$t \geq \frac{1}{2} \qquad \begin{array}{l}\text{dividing both sides by } -2, \text{ which}\\ \text{reverses the inequality}\end{array}$$

The solution set is therefore $[1/2, \infty)$; see Figure 2.

**Figure 2**

In Section 1.5 we saw that there is a close connection between solving equations and graphing. (Example: The roots of the equation $x^2 - 4 = 0$ are the $x$-intercepts of the graph of $y = x^2 - 4$.) It's also true that solving inequalities and graphing are closely related. Consider, for instance, the inequality $2x - 3 < 5$ that we solved in Example 1(a). To interpret this inequality geometrically, we graph the two equations $y = 2x - 3$ and $y = 5$. Then, as indicated in Figure 3(a), the graph of $y = 2x - 3$ is below the line $y = 5$ as long as $x$ is to the left of 4. The previous sentence translates algebraically into

$$2x - 3 < 5 \qquad \text{provided that} \qquad x < 4$$

This confirms the result in Example 1(a).

Similarly, for a geometric interpretation of the inequality in Example 1(b), we graph the two lines $y = 5t + 8$ and $y = 7(1 + t)$ in a $t$-$y$ coordinate system. As indicated in Figure 3(b), the line $y = 5t + 8$ is below the line $y = 7(1 + t)$ provided that $t$ is to the right of $1/2$. Furthermore, at $t = 1/2$, the lines intersect. That is, for $t = 1/2$, the quantities $5t + 8$ and $7(1 + t)$ are equal. Algebraically, we can restate this information by saying

$$5t + 8 \leq 7(1 + t) \qquad \text{provided that} \qquad t \geq \frac{1}{2}$$

This confirms the result in Example 1(b).

In the next example, we solve the inequality

$$-\frac{1}{2} < \frac{3 - x}{-4} < \frac{1}{2}$$

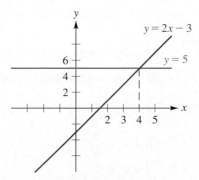

(a) To the left of $x = 4$, the line $y = 2x - 3$ is below the line $y = 5$.

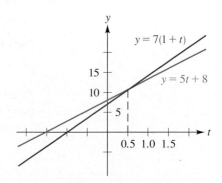

(b) The graph indicates that if $t \geq 1/2$ then $5t + 8 \leq 7(1 + t)$.

**Figure 3**

By definition, this is equivalent to the pair of inequalities

$$-\frac{1}{2} < \frac{3-x}{-4} \quad \text{and} \quad \frac{3-x}{-4} < \frac{1}{2}$$

One way to proceed here would be first to determine the solution set for each inequality. Then the set of real numbers common to both solution sets would be the solution set for the original inequality. However, the method shown in Example 2 is more efficient.

### EXAMPLE 2    Solving a compound inequality

Solve: $-\frac{1}{2} < \frac{3-x}{-4} < \frac{1}{2}$.

**SOLUTION**

We begin by multiplying through by $-4$. Remember that this will reverse the inequalities:

$$2 > 3 - x > -2$$

Next, with a view toward isolating $x$, we first subtract 3 to obtain

$$-1 > -x > -5$$

Finally, multiplying through by $-1$, we have

$$1 < x < 5$$

The solution set is therefore the open interval $(1, 5)$.

The next example refers to the Celsius ($C$) and Fahrenheit ($F$) scales for measuring temperature.* The formula relating the temperature readings on the two scales is

$$F = \frac{9}{5}C + 32$$

### EXAMPLE 3    Converting a Fahrenheit temperature range into Celsius

Over the temperature range $32° \le F \le 39.2°$ on the Fahrenheit scale, water contracts (rather than expands) with increasing temperature. What is the corresponding temperature range on the Celsius scale?

**SOLUTION**

| | |
|---|---|
| $32 \le F \le 39.2$ | given |
| $32 \le \frac{9}{5}C + 32 \le 39.2$ | substituting $\frac{9}{5}C + 32$ for $F$ |
| $0 \le \frac{9}{5}C \le 7.2$ | subtracting 32 |
| $0 \le C \le \frac{5}{9}(7.2)$ | multiplying by $\frac{5}{9}$ |
| $0 \le C \le 4$ | |

---

*The Celsius scale was devised in 1742 by the Swedish astronomer Anders Celsius. The Fahrenheit scale was first used by the German physicist Gabriel Fahrenheit in 1724.

Thus a range of 32°F to 39.2°F on the Fahrenheit scale corresponds to 0°C to 4°C on the Celsius scale.

In the next three examples we solve inequalities that involve absolute values. The following theorem is very useful in this context.

---

**THEOREM  Absolute Value and Inequalities**

If $a > 0$, then

$$|u| < a \quad \text{if and only if} \quad -a < u < a$$

and

$$|u| > a \quad \text{if and only if} \quad u < -a \quad \text{or} \quad u > a$$

---

You can see why this theorem is valid if you think in terms of distance and position on a number line. The condition $-a < u < a$ means that $u$ lies between $-a$ and $a$, as indicated in Figure 4. But this is the same as saying that the distance from $u$ to zero is less than $a$, which in turn can be written $|u| < a$. (The second part of the theorem can be justified in a similar manner.)

$-a < u < a$

**Figure 4**

---

**EXAMPLE 4  Solving inequalities containing absolute values**

Solve:
**(a)** $|x| < 1$;  **(b)** $|x| \geq 1$.

**SOLUTION**
**(a)** By the theorem we just discussed, the condition $|x| < 1$ is equivalent to

$$-1 < x < 1$$

The solution set is therefore the open interval $(-1, 1)$; see Figure 5(a).
**(b)** In view of the second part of the theorem, the inequality $|x| \geq 1$ is satisfied when $x$ satisfies either of the inequalities

$$x \leq -1 \quad \text{or} \quad x \geq 1$$

So the inequality is satisfied if $x$ is in either of the intervals $(-\infty, -1]$ or $[1, \infty)$; see Figure 5(b).

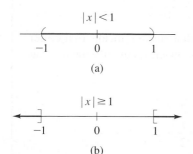
$|x| < 1$
(a)

$|x| \geq 1$
(b)

**Figure 5**

In Example 4(b) we found that the solution set consisted of two intervals on the number line. We have a convenient notation for describing such sets. Given any two sets $A$ and $B$, we define the set $A \cup B$ (read **A union B**) to be the set of all elements that are in $A$ or in $B$ (or in both). For example, if $A = \{1, 2, 3\}$ and $B = \{4, 5\}$, then $A \cup B = \{1, 2, 3, 4, 5\}$. As another example, the union of the two closed intervals $[3, 5]$ and $[4, 7]$ is given by

$$[3, 5] \cup [4, 7] = [3, 7]$$

because the numbers in the interval [3, 7] are precisely those numbers that are in [3, 5] or [4, 7] (or in both). Using this notation, we can write the solution set for Example 4(b) as

$$(-\infty, -1] \cup [1, \infty)$$

| EXAMPLE | 5 | Two different methods for solving an inequality containing absolute values |
|---|---|---|

Solve: $|x - 3| < 1$.

**SOLUTION**
We'll show two methods.

FIRST METHOD
We use the theorem preceding Example 4. With $u = x - 3$ and $a = 1$, the theorem tells us that the given inequality is equivalent to

$$-1 < x - 3 < 1$$

or (by adding 3)

$$2 < x < 4$$

The solution set is therefore the open interval (2, 4).

ALTERNATIVE METHOD
The given inequality tells us that $x$ must be less than one unit away from 3 on the number line. Looking one unit to either side of 3, then, we see that $x$ must lie strictly between 2 and 4. The solution set is therefore (2, 4), as obtained using the first method.

| EXAMPLE | 6 | Another inequality with absolute values |
|---|---|---|

Solve: $\left|1 - \dfrac{t}{2}\right| > 5$.

**SOLUTION**
Referring again to the theorem, we use the fact that $|u| > a$ means that either $u < -a$ or $u > a$. So, in the present example, the given inequality means that either

$$1 - \frac{t}{2} < -5 \qquad \text{or} \qquad 1 - \frac{t}{2} > 5$$

$$-\frac{t}{2} < -6 \qquad\qquad -\frac{t}{2} > 4$$

$$t > 12 \qquad\qquad\qquad t < -8$$

This tells us that the given inequality is satisfied when $t$ is in either of the intervals $(12, \infty)$ or $(-\infty, -8)$. Thus the solution set is $(-\infty, -8) \cup (12, \infty)$.

Earlier in this section we saw that there is a close connection between inequalities and graphs. The next example emphasizes this point again.

EXAMPLE | 7 | A graphical approach to solving an inequality

GRAPHICAL PERSPECTIVE

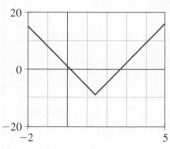

**Figure 6**
$y = |7x - 10| - 9$
$[-2, 5, 1]$ by $[-20, 20, 10]$

As is indicated in Figure 6, the graph of the equation $y = |7x - 10| - 9$ has two $x$-intercepts. Let $a$ denote the $x$-intercept between 0 and 1, and let $b$ denote the $x$-intercept between 2 and 3.

**(a)** Use the graph in Figure 6 to specify the general form of the solution set for the inequality

$$|7x - 10| - 9 \le 0$$

Use interval notation. (You can assume that Figure 6 shows all of the essential features of the graph.)

**(b)** Use a graphing utility and the ZOOM feature to estimate to the nearest hundredth the $x$-intercepts $a$ and $b$. Then state the corresponding estimate for the solution set of the inequality $|7x - 10| - 9 \le 0$.

**(c)** Use algebra to solve the inequality $|7x - 10| - 9 \le 0$. Check that the solution is consistent with the graphical results in parts (a) and (b).

**SOLUTION**

**(a)** The graph has two $x$-intercepts, which we are calling $a$ and $b$ (with $a < b$). At each of these $x$-intercepts, the quantity $|7x - 10| - 9$ is zero, while for $x$ between $a$ and $b$, the quantity $|7x - 10| - 9$ is negative (because the graph is *below* the $x$-axis). In other words, the inequality $|7x - 10| - 9 \le 0$ is satisfied by all values of $x$ in the closed interval $[a, b]$. Furthermore, the graph shows that these are the only values of $x$ satisfying the required inequality (because the graph is *above* the $x$-axis when $x$ is outside of this closed interval). In summary then, the solution set for the inequality $|7x - 10| - 9 \le 0$ has the form

$$[a, b] \qquad \text{where } a \text{ is between 0 and 1 and } b \text{ is between 2 and 3}$$

**(b)** After some experimenting with viewing rectangles of various sizes, we obtain the views displayed in Figure 7. Figure 7(a) shows that the smaller of the two intercepts is between 0.14 and 0.15, closer to 0.14 than to 0.15, so $a \approx 0.14$ to the nearest hundredth. Similarly, for the larger intercept $b$, Figure 7(b) indicates that $b \approx 2.71$, to the nearest hundredth. Our corresponding estimate for the solution set of the given inequality is then the closed interval $[0.14, 2.71]$.

GRAPHICAL PERSPECTIVE

**Figure 7**
Zoom-in views of the $x$-intercepts
for $y = |7x - 10| - 9$

(a) $[0.140, 0.150, 0.005]$ by
$[-0.05, 0.05, 0.05]$

(b) $[2.710, 2.720, 0.005]$ by
$[-0.05, 0.05, 0.05]$

**(c)** So that we can apply the theorem on page 133, we first rewrite the given inequality in the equivalent form $|7x - 10| \leq 9$. Then we have

$$-9 \leq 7x - 10 \leq 9 \qquad \text{using the first part of the theorem on page 107}$$

$$1 \leq 7x \leq 19 \qquad \text{adding 10}$$

$$\frac{1}{7} \leq x \leq \frac{19}{7} \qquad \text{dividing by 7}$$

The solution set is therefore the closed interval $[\frac{1}{7}, \frac{19}{7}.]$ The fact that it's a closed interval agrees with our graphical work in part (a). Furthermore, if you now use a calculator, you'll find that $\frac{1}{7} \approx 0.143$ and $\frac{19}{7} \approx 2.714$, values that are indeed consistent with the estimates obtained in part (b).

# EXERCISE SET 2.3

## A

*In Exercises 1–30, solve the inequality and specify the answer using interval notation.*

**1.** $2x - 7 < 11$

**2.** $6 - 4x \leq 22$

**3.** $4x + 6 < 3(x - 1) - x$

**4.** $1 - 2(t + 3) - t \leq 1 - 2t$

**5.** $\dfrac{3x}{5} - \dfrac{x - 1}{3} < 1$

**6.** $\dfrac{x - 1}{4} - \dfrac{2x + 3}{5} \leq x$

**7.** $\dfrac{2x + 1}{2} - \dfrac{x - 1}{3} < x + \dfrac{1}{2}$

**8.** $-3 \leq 2x + 1 \leq 5$

**9.** $-1 \leq \dfrac{1 - 4t}{3} \leq 1$

**10.** $\dfrac{2}{3} \leq \dfrac{5 - 3t}{-2} \leq \dfrac{3}{4}$

**11.** $0.99 < \dfrac{x}{2} - 1 < 0.999$

**12.** $\dfrac{9}{10} < \dfrac{3x - 1}{-2} < \dfrac{91}{100}$

*Hint: In Exercises 13 and 14 treat the compound inequality as two separate inequalities.*

**13.** $x - 5 \leq 2x + 3 < 10 - 3x$

**14.** $x - 3 < 3x + 1 < 17 - x$

**15. (a)** $|x| \leq \frac{1}{2}$

   **(b)** $|x| > \frac{1}{2}$

**16. (a)** $|x| > 2$

   **(b)** $|x| \leq 2$

**17. (a)** $|x| > 0$

   **(b)** $|x| < 0$

**18. (a)** $|t| \geq 0$

   **(b)** $|t| \leq 0$

**19. (a)** $x - 2 < 1$

   **(b)** $|x - 2| < 1$

   **(c)** $|x - 2| > 1$

**20. (a)** $x - 4 \geq 4$

   **(b)** $|x - 4| \geq 4$

   **(c)** $|x - 4| \leq 4$

**21. (a)** $1 - x \leq 5$

   **(b)** $|1 - x| \leq 5$

   **(c)** $|1 - x| > 5$

**22. (a)** $3x + 5 < 17$

   **(b)** $|3x + 5| < 17$

   **(c)** $|3x + 5| > 17$

**23. (a)** $a - x < c$

   **(b)** $|a - x| < c$

   **(c)** $|a - x| \geq c$

**24.** (Assume $b < c$ throughout this exercise.)

   **(a)** $|x - a| + b < c$

   **(c)** $|x + a| + b < c$

   **(b)** $|x + a| + b > c$

**25.** $\left| \dfrac{x - 2}{3} \right| < 4$

**26.** $\left| \dfrac{4 - 5x}{2} \right| > 1$

**27.** $\left| \dfrac{x + 1}{2} - \dfrac{x - 1}{3} \right| < 1$   *Hint: Combine the fractions.*

**28.** $\left| \dfrac{3(x - 2)}{4} + \dfrac{4(x - 1)}{3} \right| \leq 2$

**29. (a)** $|(x + h)^2 - x^2| < 3h^2$, where $h > 0$

   **(b)** $|(x + h)^2 - x^2| < 3h^2$, where $h < 0$

**30. (a)** $|3(x + 2)^2 - 3x^2| < \frac{1}{10}$

   **(b)** $|3(x + 2)^2 - 3x^2| < \varepsilon$, where $\varepsilon > 0$

*For Exercises 31–34:*

**(G) (a)** *Use a graph [as in Example 7(a)] to determine which of the following general forms describes the solution set of the given inequality:*

   $[a, b] \qquad (-\infty, a) \cup (b, \infty) \qquad [a, \infty) \qquad (a, \infty)$

**(G) (b)** *Use a graphing utility [as in Example 7(b)] to estimate to the nearest hundredth the value of a, and where appropriate, b.*

**(c)** *Solve the inequality algebraically and write the solution set using interval notation. Check that your answers are consistent with the graphical results in parts (a) and (b).*

**31.** $7x - 2 \geq 0$

**32.** $6 - 13x < 0$

**33.** $|8x - 3| - 2 \leq 0$

**34.** $1 - |15x - 3| < 0$

**35.** Data from the *Apollo 11* moon mission in July 1969 showed temperature readings on the lunar surface varying over the interval $-183° \leq C \leq 112°$ on the Celsius scale. What is the corresponding interval on the Fahrenheit scale? (Round the numbers you obtain to the nearest integers.)

**36.** The temperature of the variable star Delta Cephei varies over the interval $5100° \leq C \leq 6500°$ on the Celsius scale. What is the corresponding range on the Fahrenheit scale? (Round the numbers in your answer to the nearest 100°F.)

**37.** Data from the *Mariner 10* spacecraft (launched November 3, 1973) indicate that the surface temperature on the planet Mercury varies over the interval $-170° \leq C \leq 430°$

on the Celsius scale. What is the corresponding interval on the Fahrenheit scale? (Round the values that you obtain to the nearest 10°F.)

## B

**38.** Solve the inequality $|x - 1| + |x - 2| < 3$.
*Hint*: Begin by considering three cases: $x < 1$; $1 \le x < 2$; $x \ge 2$.

**39.** Solve the inequality $6 - |x + 3| - |x - 2| < 0$.
*Hint*: Adapt the hint in Exercise 38.

**40.** Given two positive numbers $a$ and $b$, we define the **geometric mean** (G.M.) and the **arithmetic mean** (A.M.) as follows:

$$\text{G.M.} = \sqrt{ab} \qquad \text{A.M.} = \frac{a + b}{2}$$

**(a)** Complete the table, using a calculator as necessary so that the entries in the third and fourth columns are in decimal form.

| $a$ | $b$ | $\sqrt{ab}$ (G.M.) | $(a + b)/2$ (A.M.) | Which is larger, G.M. or A.M.? |
|-----|-----|-----|-----|-----|
| 1 | 2 | | | |
| 1 | 3 | | | |
| 1 | 4 | | | |
| 2 | 3 | | | |
| 3 | 4 | | | |
| 5 | 10 | | | |
| 9 | 10 | | | |
| 99 | 100 | | | |
| 999 | 1000 | | | |

**(b)** Prove that for all nonnegative numbers $a$ and $b$ we have

$$\sqrt{ab} \le \frac{a + b}{2} \qquad (1)$$

*Hint*: Use the following property of inequalities: If $x$ and $y$ are nonnegative, then the inequality $x \le y$ is equivalent to $x^2 \le y^2$.

**(c)** Assuming that $a = b$ (and that $a$ and $b$ are nonnegative), show that inequality (1) becomes an equality.

**(d)** Assuming that $a$ and $b$ are nonnegative and that $\sqrt{ab} = \dfrac{a + b}{2}$, show that $a = b$.

*Remark*: Parts (b) through (d) can be summarized as follows. For all nonnegative numbers $a$ and $b$, we have $\sqrt{ab} \le \dfrac{a + b}{2}$, with equality holding if and only if $a = b$. This result is known as the *arithmetic-geometric mean inequality* for two numbers. The mini project at the end of this section shows an application of this result.

**41.** Use the result in Exercise 40(b) to prove each of the following inequalities. Assume that $p, q, r$, and $s$ all are nonnegative.

**(a)** $\sqrt{pqr} \le (pq + r)/2$    **(b)** $\sqrt{pqrs} \le (pq + rs)/2$

*Exercises 42 and 43 concern the environmental problem known as **acid rain**. The principal source contributing to acid rain is sulfur dioxide, emitted into the atmosphere through the burning of fossil fuels. Once in the clouds, the sulfur dioxide combines with water vapor to form one of the nasty ingredients of acid rain—sulfuric acid.*

**42.** In the United States over the years 1980–2000, sulfur dioxide emissions due to the burning of fossil fuels can be approximated by the equation

$$y = -0.4743t + 24.086$$

where $y$ represents the sulfur dioxide emissions (in millions of tons) for the year $t$, with $t = 0$ corresponding to 1980.
*Source*: This equation (and the equation in Exercise 48) were computed using data from the book *Vital Signs 1999*, Lester Brown et al. (New York: W. W. Norton & Co., 1999).

**(a)** Use a graphing utility to graph the equation $y = -0.4743t + 24.086$ in the viewing rectangle $[0, 25, 5]$ by $[0, 30, 5]$. According to the graph, sulfur dioxide emissions are decreasing. What piece of information in the equation $y = -0.4743t + 24.086$ tells you this even before looking at the graph?

**(b)** Assuming this equation remains valid, estimate the year in which sulfur dioxide emissions in the United States might fall below 10 million tons per year. (You need to solve the inequality $-0.4743t + 24.086 \le 10$.)

**43.** In Asia over the years 1980–2000, sulfur dioxide emissions due to the burning of fossil fuels can be approximated by the equation

$$y = 1.84t + 14.8$$

where $y$ represents the sulfur dioxide emissions (in millions of tons) for the year $t$, with $t = 0$ corresponding to 1980.

**(a)** Use a graphing utility to graph the equation $y = 1.84t + 14.8$ in the viewing rectangle $[0, 25, 5]$ by $[0, 60, 20]$. According to the graph, sulfur dioxide emissions are increasing. What piece of information in the equation $y = 1.84t + 14.8$ tells you this even before looking at the graph?

**(b)** Assuming that this equation remains valid, estimate the year in which sulfur dioxide emissions in Asia might exceed 65 million tons per year.

## C

**44.** Let $a, b$, and $c$ be nonnegative numbers. Follow steps (a) through (e) to show that

$$\sqrt[3]{abc} \le \frac{a + b + c}{3}$$

with equality holding if and only if $a = b = c$.

This result is known as the *arithmetic-geometric mean inequality* for three numbers. (Applications are developed in the projects at the ends of Sections 4.6 and 4.7.)

**(a)** By multiplying out the right-hand side, show that the following equation holds for all real numbers $A$, $B$, and $C$.

$$3ABC = A^3 + B^3 + C^3 - \frac{1}{2}(A + B + C) \\ \times [(A - B)^2 + (B - C)^2 + (C - A)^2] \quad (1)$$

**(b)** Now assume for the remainder of this exercise that $A$, $B$, and $C$ are nonnegative numbers. Use equation (1) to explain why

$$3ABC \leq A^3 + B^3 + C^3 \quad (2)$$

**(c)** Make the following substitutions in inequality (2): $A^3 = a$, $B^3 = b$, and $C^3 = c$. Show that the result can be written

$$\sqrt[3]{abc} \leq \frac{a + b + c}{3} \quad (3)$$

**(d)** Assuming that $a = b = c$, show that inequality (3) becomes an equality.

**(e)** Assuming $\sqrt[3]{abc} = \frac{a + b + c}{3}$, show that $a = b = c$.

*Hint:* In terms of $A$, $B$, and $C$, the assumption becomes $ABC = \frac{A^3 + B^3 + C^3}{3}$. Use this to substitute for $ABC$ on the left-hand side of equation (1). Then use the resulting equation to deduce that $A = B = C$, and consequently $a = b = c$.

# MINI PROJECT | AN INEQUALITY FOR THE GARDEN

Part of a landscape architect's plans call for a rectangular garden with a perimeter of 150 ft. The architect wants to find the width $w$ and length $l$ that maximize the area $A$ of the garden. Two preliminary sketches are shown in the figure that follows. (In both cases, note that the perimeter is 150 ft, as required.) Of the two sketches, the one on the right yields the larger area. In this project you'll use the inequality given in Exercise 40(b) to find exactly which combination of $w$ and $l$ yields the largest possible area.

**(a)** As background, first review or rework Exercise 40(b). If you are working in a group, assign one person to do this and then present the result to the others.

$A = 25 \text{ ft} \times 50 \text{ ft} = 1250 \text{ ft}^2$

$A = 30 \text{ ft} \times 45 \text{ ft} = 1350 \text{ ft}^2$

**(b)** Letting $w$ denote the width of the rectangular garden, and assuming that the perimeter is 150 ft, show or explain why the area $A$ is given by $A = w(75 - w)$.

**(c)** Use the inequality in Exercise 40(b) to show that $A \leq 5625/4 = 1406.25$. In words: Given a perimeter of 150 ft, no matter how we pick $w$ and $l$, the area can never exceed 1406.25 ft². *Hint:* Apply the inequality to the product $w(75 - w)$.

Ⓖ **(d)** From part (c) we know that the area can't exceed 1406.25 ft², so now the job is to find a combination of $w$ and $l$ yielding that area. To accomplish this,

take the equation obtained in part (b), replace $A$ with 1406.25, and then use a graphing utility to solve for $w$.
**(e)** As a check on the work with the graphing utility (and to stay in shape with the algebra), use the quadratic formula to solve the same equation.
**(f)** Now that you know $w$, find $l$ and describe the proportions of the required rectangle.

# 2.4 MORE ON INEQUALITIES

*The symbols of inequality $>$ and $<$ were introduced by* [Thomas] *Harriot* [1560–1621]. *The signs $\geq$ and $\leq$ were first used about a century later by the Parisian hydrographer Pierre Bouguer.* —Florian Cajori in *A History of Mathematics,* 4th ed. (New York: Chelsea Publishing Co., 1985)

*It is rather surprising to think that the man who surveyed and mapped Virginia was one of the founders of algebra as we know the subject today. Such however is the case, for Thomas Harriot was sent by Sir Walter Raleigh to accompany Sir Richard Grenville (1585) to the New World, where he made the survey of that portion of American territory.* —David Eugene Smith in *History of Mathematics,* vol. I (New York: Ginn and Co., 1923)

The last example in Section 2.3 emphasized the connection between inequalities and graphs. This is our starting point for the present section. We begin with an example in which polynomial inequalities are solved by relying on a graph. Then we'll use the ideas there to explain a method for solving inequalities even when a graph is not given.

| EXAMPLE | 1 | A graphical approach to solving inequalities |

Figure 1 shows the graph of the equation $y = x^2 - 4x + 3$. Use the graph to solve each of the following inequalities:
**(a)** $x^2 - 4x + 3 < 0$; **(b)** $x^2 - 4x + 3 \geq 0$.

**SOLUTION**
**(a)** As indicated in Figure 1, the graph of $y = x^2 - 4x + 3$ is below the $x$-axis when (and only when) the $x$-values are in the open interval $(1, 3)$. This is the same as saying that the quantity $x^2 - 4x + 3$ is negative when (and only when) the $x$-values are in the open interval $(1, 3)$. Or, rewording once more, the solution set for the inequality $x^2 - 4x + 3 < 0$ is the open interval $(1, 3)$.
**(b)** The graph in Figure 1 is above the $x$-axis when (and only when) the $x$-values are in either of the two intervals $(-\infty, 1)$ or $(3, \infty)$. This is the same as saying that the quantity $x^2 - 4x + 3$ is positive when (and only when) the $x$-values are in the set $(-\infty, 1) \cup (3, \infty)$. Furthermore, the graph shows that the quantity $x^2 - 4x + 3$ is equal to 0 when $x = 1$ and when $x = 3$. In summary, the solution set for the inequality $x^2 - 4x + 3 \geq 0$ is the set $(-\infty, 1] \cup [3, \infty)$.

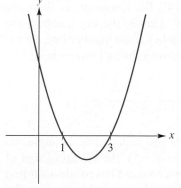

**Figure 1**
$y = x^2 - 4x + 3$

We can summarize the essential features of our work in Example 1 as follows. The $x$-intercepts of the graph in Figure 1 divide the number line into three intervals: $(-\infty, 1)$, $(1, 3)$, and $(3, \infty)$. Within each of these intervals, the algebraic sign of $x^2 - 4x + 3$ stays the same. (For example, to the left of $x = 1$, that is, on the interval $(-\infty, 1)$, the quantity $x^2 - 4x + 3$ is always positive.) More generally, it can be shown (using calculus) that this same type of behavior, regarding *persistence of sign*, occurs with all polynomials and, indeed, with quotients of polynomials as well. This important fact, along with the definition of a *key number*, is presented in the box that follows.

## PROPERTY SUMMARY    Key Numbers and Persistence of Sign

Let $P$ and $Q$ be polynomials with no common factors (other than, possibly, constants), and consider the following four inequalities:

$$\frac{P}{Q} < 0 \qquad \frac{P}{Q} \leq 0 \qquad \frac{P}{Q} > 0 \qquad \frac{P}{Q} \geq 0$$

The **key numbers** for each of these inequalities are the real numbers for which $P = 0$ or $Q = 0$. (Geometrically speaking, the key numbers are the $x$-intercepts for the graphs of the equations $y = P$ and $y = Q$.) It can be proved (using calculus) that the algebraic sign of $P/Q$ does not change within each of the intervals determined by the key numbers.

EXAMPLES
1. The key numbers for the inequality $(x - 7)/(x - 8) \geq 0$ are 7 and 8.
2. The key numbers for the inequality $(x - 3)(x + 3) < 0$ are $\pm 3$. (In this case, the polynomial $Q$ is the constant 1.)

We'll show how this result is applied by solving the polynomial inequality

$$x^3 - 2x^2 - 3x > 0$$

First, using factoring techniques from basic algebra, we rewrite the inequality in the equivalent form

$$x(x + 1)(x - 3) > 0$$

(If you need a review of factoring, see Appendix B.4.) The key numbers, then, are the solutions of the equation $x(x + 1)(x - 3) = 0$. That is, the key numbers are $x = 0$, $x = -1$, and $x = 3$. Next, we locate these numbers on a number line. As indicated in Figure 2, this divides the number line into four distinct intervals.

Figure 2

Now, according to the result stated in the box just before this example, no matter what $x$-value we choose in the interval $(-\infty, -1)$, the resulting sign of $x^3 - 2x^2 - 3x \ [= x(x + 1)(x - 3)]$ will always be the same. Thus to see what that sign is, we first choose any convenient *test number* in the interval $(-\infty, -1)$, for example, $x = -2$. Then, using $x = -2$, we determine the sign of $x(x + 1)(x - 3)$ simply by considering the sign of each factor, as indicated in Table 1.

Looking at Table 1, we conclude that the values of $x^3 - 2x^2 - 3x$ are negative *throughout* the interval $(-\infty, -1)$ and, consequently, no number in this interval satisfies the given inequality. Next, we carry out similar analyses for the remaining

**TABLE 1**

| Interval | Test number | x | x + 1 | x − 3 | x(x + 1)(x − 3) |
|---|---|---|---|---|---|
| $(-\infty, -1)$ | −2 | neg. | neg. | neg. | neg. |

On the interval $(-\infty, -1)$, the sign of $x^3 - 2x^2 - 3x \; [= x(x + 1)(x - 3)]$ is negative because it is the product of three negative factors.

**TABLE 2**

| Interval | Test number | x | x + 1 | x − 3 | x(x + 1)(x − 3) |
|---|---|---|---|---|---|
| $(-1, 0)$ | $-\frac{1}{2}$ | neg. | pos. | neg. | pos. |
| $(0, 3)$ | 1 | pos. | pos. | neg. | neg. |
| $(3, \infty)$ | 4 | pos. | pos. | pos. | pos. |

On the interval $(-1, 0)$, the product $x(x + 1)(x - 3)$ is positive because it has two negative factors and one positive factor. On $(0, 3)$, the product is negative because it has two positive factors and one negative factor. And on $(3, \infty)$, the product is positive because all the factors are positive.

three intervals, as shown in Table 2. (You should verify for yourself that the entries in the table are correct.)

Looking at the two tables now, we conclude that the sign of $x(x + 1)(x - 3)$ is positive throughout both of the intervals $(-1, 0)$ and $(3, \infty)$ and, consequently, all the numbers in these intervals satisfy the given inequality. Moreover, our work also shows that the other two intervals that we considered are not part of the solution set. As you can readily check, the key numbers themselves do not satisfy the given inequality for this example. In summary, then, the solution set for the inequality $x^3 - 2x^2 - 3x > 0$ is $(-1, 0) \cup (3, \infty)$. Furthermore, it is important to note that the work we just carried out also provides us with three additional pieces of information.

The solution set for $x^3 - 2x^2 - 3x \geq 0$ is $[-1, 0] \cup [3, \infty)$.

The solution set for $x^3 - 2x^2 - 3x < 0$ is $(-\infty, -1) \cup (0, 3)$.

The solution set for $x^3 - 2x^2 - 3x \leq 0$ is $(-\infty, -1] \cup [0, 3]$.

In the box that follows, we summarize the steps for solving polynomial inequalities.

## Steps for Solving Polynomial Inequalities

1. If necessary, rewrite the inequality so that the polynomial is on the left-hand side and zero is on the right-hand side.
2. Find the key numbers for the inequality and locate them on a number line.
3. List the intervals determined by the key numbers.
4. From each interval, choose a convenient test number. Then use the test number to determine the sign of the polynomial throughout the interval.
5. Use the information obtained in the previous step to specify the required solution set. [Don't forget to take into account whether the original inequality is strict ($<$ or $>$) or nonstrict ($\leq$ or $\geq$).]

**EXAMPLE** 2 | **Using factoring and key numbers to solve an inequality**

Solve: $x^4 \le 14x^3 - 48x^2$.

**SOLUTION**

First we rewrite the inequality so that zero is on the right-hand side. Then we factor the left-hand side as follows:

$$x^4 - 14x^3 + 48x^2 \le 0$$
$$x^2(x^2 - 14x + 48) \le 0$$
$$x^2(x - 6)(x - 8) \le 0$$

From this last line, we see that the key numbers are $x = 0, 6$, and 8. As indicated in Figure 3, these numbers divide the number line into four distinct intervals.

$(-\infty, 0)$   $(0, 6)$   $(6, 8)$   $(8, \infty)$

**Figure 3**

We need to choose a test number from each interval and see whether the polynomial is positive or negative on the interval. This work is carried out in the following table.

| Interval | Test number | $x^2$ | $x - 6$ | $x - 8$ | $x^2(x - 6)(x - 8)$ |
|----------|-------------|-------|---------|---------|---------------------|
| $(-\infty, 0)$ | $-1$ | pos. | neg. | neg. | pos. |
| $(0, 6)$ | $1$ | pos. | neg. | neg. | pos. |
| $(6, 8)$ | $7$ | pos. | pos. | neg. | neg. |
| $(8, \infty)$ | $9$ | pos. | pos. | pos. | pos. |

The table shows that the quantity $x^2(x - 6)(x - 8)$ is negative only for $x$-values in the interval $(6, 8)$. Also, as noted at the start, the quantity is equal to zero when $x = 0, 6$, or 8. Thus the solution set consists of the numbers in the closed interval $[6, 8]$, along with the number 0. We can write this set

$$[6, 8] \cup \{0\}$$

where $\{0\}$ denotes the set that has zero as its only member.

■

**EXAMPLE** 3 | **An inequality with no key numbers**

Solve:
**(a)** $x^2 - 4x + 5 > 0$;      **(b)** $x^2 - 4x + 5 < 0$.

**SOLUTION**

**(a)** The equation $x^2 - 4x + 5 = 0$ has no real solution (because the discriminant of the quadratic is $-4$, which is negative), so there is no key number. Consequently, the polynomial $x^2 - 4x + 5$ never changes sign. To see what that sign is, choose a convenient test number, for example, $x = 0$, and evaluate the polynomial: $0^2 - 4(0) + 5 > 0$. So the polynomial is positive for every value of $x$, and the solution set is $(-\infty, \infty)$, the set of all real numbers.

## GRAPHICAL PERSPECTIVE

**Figure 4**
The graph of $y = x^2 - 4x + 5$ lies entirely above the $x$-axis. Algebraically this means that the quantity $x^2 - 4x + 5$ is positive for all values of $x$. Consequently, the solution set for $x^2 - 4x + 5 > 0$ is the set of all real numbers. Equivalently, there are no real numbers satisfying $x^2 - 4x + 5 < 0$.

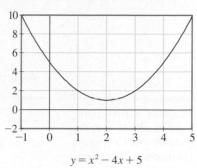

$y = x^2 - 4x + 5$

**(b)** Our work in part (a) shows that no real number satisfies the inequality $x^2 - 4x + 5 < 0$. See Figure 4 for a graphical perspective on this and on the result in part (a).

The technique used in the previous examples can also be used to solve inequalities involving quotients of polynomials. For these cases recall that the definition of a key number includes the $x$-values for which the denominator is zero. For example, the key numbers for the inequality $\dfrac{x + 3}{x - 4} \geq 0$ are $-3$ and $4$.

**EXAMPLE  4   An inequality involving a quotient of polynomials**

Solve: $\dfrac{x + 3}{x - 4} \geq 0$.

**SOLUTION**
The key numbers are $-3$ and $4$. As indicated in Figure 5, these numbers divide the number line into three intervals. In the table that follows, we've chosen a test number from each interval and determined the sign of the quotient $(x + 3)/(x - 4)$ for each interval.

**Figure 5**

| Interval | Test number | $x + 3$ | $x - 4$ | $\dfrac{x + 3}{x - 4}$ |
|---|---|---|---|---|
| $(-\infty, -3)$ | $-4$ | neg. | neg. | pos. |
| $(-3, 4)$ | $0$ | pos. | neg. | neg. |
| $(4, \infty)$ | $5$ | pos. | pos. | pos. |

From these results, we conclude that the solution set for $\dfrac{x + 3}{x - 4} \geq 0$ contains the two intervals $(-\infty, -3)$ and $(4, \infty)$. However, we still need to consider the two endpoints, $-3$ and $4$. As you can easily check, the value $x = -3$ does satisfy the given inequality, but $x = 4$ does not. In summary, then, the solution set is $(-\infty, -3] \cup (4, \infty)$. See Figure 6 for a graphical interpretation of this result. [In

**GRAPHICAL PERSPECTIVE**

**Figure 6**
The graph of $y = (x + 3)/(x - 4)$ is above the $x$-axis when $x$ is to the left of $-3$ and also when $x$ is to the right of 4. Furthermore, the graph intersects the $x$-axis (where $y = 0$) when $x = -3$. Consequently, the solution set for the inequality $(x + 3)/(x - 4) \geq 0$ is the set $(-\infty, -3] \cup (4, \infty)$.

Figure 6 the graph of the equation $y = (x + 3)/(x - 4)$ has two distinct pieces, or *branches,* separated by the vertical line $x = 4$. The points on the vertical line itself are not a part of the graph of $y = (x + 3)/(x - 4)$. We'll study graphs like this in Section 4.7, *Rational Functions.*]

---

**EXAMPLE   5   Another inequality involving quotients of polynomials**

Solve: $\dfrac{2x + 1}{x - 1} - \dfrac{2}{x - 3} < 1.$

**SOLUTION**
Our first inclination here might be to multiply through by $(x - 1)(x - 3)$ to eliminate fractions. This strategy is faulty, however, since we don't know whether the quantity $(x - 1)(x - 3)$ is positive or negative. Thus, we begin by rewriting the inequality in an equivalent form, with zero on the right-hand side and a single fraction on the left-hand side.

$$\frac{2x + 1}{x - 1} - \frac{2}{x - 3} - 1 < 0$$

$$\frac{(2x + 1)(x - 3) - 2(x - 1) - 1(x - 1)(x - 3)}{(x - 1)(x - 3)} < 0$$

$$\frac{x^2 - 3x - 4}{(x - 1)(x - 3)} < 0 \qquad \text{Check the algebra!} \tag{1}$$

$$\frac{(x + 1)(x - 4)}{(x - 1)(x - 3)} < 0$$

The key numbers are those $x$-values for which the denominator or the numerator is zero. By inspection, then, we see that these numbers are $-1, 4, 1,$ and $3$. As Figure 7 indicates, these numbers divide the number line into five distinct intervals.

**Figure 7**

Now, just as in the previous examples, we choose a test number from each interval and determine the sign of the quotient for that interval. (You should check each entry in the following table for yourself.)

| Interval | Test number | $(x + 1)(x - 4)$ | $(x - 1)(x - 3)$ | $\dfrac{(x + 1)(x - 4)}{(x - 1)(x - 3)}$ |
|---|---|---|---|---|
| $(-\infty, -1)$ | $-2$ | pos. | pos. | pos. |
| $(-1, 1)$ | $0$ | neg. | pos. | neg. |
| $(1, 3)$ | $2$ | neg. | neg. | pos. |
| $(3, 4)$ | $7/2$ | neg. | pos. | neg. |
| $(4, \infty)$ | $5$ | pos. | pos. | pos. |

From these results we can see that the quotient on the left-hand side of inequality (1) is negative (as required) on the two intervals $(-1, 1)$ and $(3, 4)$. Now we need to check the endpoints of these intervals. When $x = -1$ or $x = 4$, the quotient is zero, and so, in view of the original inequality, we exclude these two $x$-values from the solution set. Furthermore, the quotient is undefined when $x = 1$ or $x = 3$, so we must also exclude those two values from the solution set. In summary, then, the solution set is $(-1, 1) \cup (3, 4)$.

# EXERCISE SET 2.4

## A

*In Exercises 1–6, use the graph to solve each inequality. (Assume that each figure shows all of the essential features of the graph of the equation; that is, that there are no surprises "out of camera range.")*

**1. (a)** $x^2 - 3x - 4 \geq 0$
   **(b)** $x^2 - 3x - 4 \leq 0$

$y = x^2 - 3x - 4$

**2. (a)** $-\frac{1}{2}x^2 - \frac{7}{2}x - 5 > 0$
   **(b)** $-\frac{1}{2}x^2 - \frac{7}{2}x - 5 < 0$

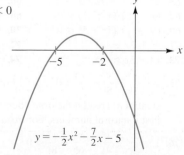

$y = -\frac{1}{2}x^2 - \frac{7}{2}x - 5$

**3. (a)** $x^4 - 4x^3 + 6x^2 - 4x + 2 < 0$
   **(b)** $x^4 - 4x^3 + 6x^2 - 4x + 2 > 0$

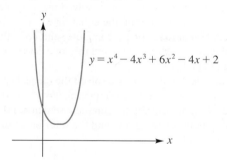

$y = x^4 - 4x^3 + 6x^2 - 4x + 2$

**4. (a)** $-3(x + 3)^2 \leq 0$
   **(b)** $-3(x + 3)^2 < 0$

$y = -3(x + 3)^2$

**5. (a)** $x^3 - 3x^2 - x + 3 \geq 0$
   **(b)** $x^3 - 3x^2 - x + 3 < 0$

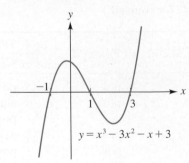

$y = x^3 - 3x^2 - x + 3$

**6. (a)** $-x^3 + 6x^2 - 12x + 9 < 0$
   **(b)** $-x^3 + 6x^2 - 12x + 9 \geq 0$

$y = -x^3 + 6x^2 - 12x + 9$

Ⓖ **7.** In the text (pages 114–115) we solved the inequality $x^3 - 2x^2 - 3x > 0$. Graph the equation $y = x^3 - 2x^2 - 3x$ and explain or describe (in complete sentences) the relationship between the graph and the solution set of the given inequality.

Ⓖ **8.** In Example 2 in the text, we solved the inequality $x^4 \leq 14x^3 - 48x^2$. Graph the equation $y = x^4 - 14x^3 + 48x^2$ and explain or describe (in complete sentences) the relationship between the graph and the solution set of the given inequality.

*Solve the inequalities in Exercises 9–60. Suggestion: A calculator may be useful for approximating key numbers.*

**9.** $x^2 + x - 6 < 0$
**10.** $x^2 + 4x - 32 < 0$
**11.** $x^2 - 11x + 18 > 0$
**12.** $2x^2 + 7x + 5 > 0$
**13.** $9x - x^2 \leq 20$
**14.** $3x^2 + x \leq 4$
**15.** $x^2 - 16 \geq 0$
**16.** $24 - x^2 \geq 0$
**17.** $16x^2 + 24x < -9$
**18.** $x^4 - 16 < 0$
**19.** $x^3 + 13x^2 + 42x > 0$
**20.** $2x^3 - 9x^2 + 4x \geq 0$
**21.** $2x^2 + 1 \geq 0$
**22.** $1 + x^2 < 0$
**23.** $12x^3 + 17x^2 + 6x < 0$
**24.** $8x^4 < x^2 - 2x^3$
**25.** $x^2 + x - 1 > 0$
**26.** $2x^2 + 9x - 1 > 0$
**27.** $x^2 - 8x + 2 \leq 0$
**28.** $3x^2 - x + 5 \leq 0$
**29.** $(x - 1)(x + 3)(x + 4) \geq 0$
**30.** $x^4(x - 2)(x - 16) \geq 0$

**31.** $(x + 4)(x + 5)(x + 6) < 0$
**32.** $(x - \frac{1}{2})(x + \frac{1}{2})(x + \frac{3}{2}) < 0$
**33.** $(x - 2)^2(3x + 1)^3(3x - 1) > 0$
**34.** $(2x - 1)^3(2x - 3)^5(2x - 5) > 0$
**35.** $(x - 3)^2(x + 1)^4(2x + 1)^4(3x + 2) \leq 0$
**36.** $x^4 - 25x^2 + 144 \leq 0$
**37.** $20 \geq x^2(9 - x^2)$
**38.** $x^2(3x^2 + 11) \geq 4$
**39.** $9(x - 4) - x^2(x - 4) < 0$
**40.** $(x + 1)^2 - 5(x + 1) > 14$
**41.** $4(x^2 - 9) - (x^2 - 9)^2 > -5$
**42.** $x(1 - x^2)^4 + (x + 3)(1 - x^2)^4 \geq 0$
**43.** $\dfrac{x - 1}{x + 1} \leq 0$
**44.** $\dfrac{x + 4}{2x - 5} \leq 0$
**45.** $\dfrac{2 - x}{3 - 2x} \geq 0$
**46.** $\dfrac{x^2 - 1}{x^2 + 8x + 15} \geq 0$
**47.** $\dfrac{x^2 - 8x - 9}{x} < 0$
**48.** $\dfrac{x^2 - 3x + 1}{1 - x} < 0$
**49.** $\dfrac{2x^3 + 5x^2 - 7x}{3x^2 + 7x + 4} > 0$
**50.** $\dfrac{x^2 - x - 1}{x^2 + x - 1} > 0$
**51.** $\dfrac{x}{x + 1} > 1$
**52.** $\dfrac{2x}{x - 2} < 3$
**53.** $\dfrac{1}{x} \leq \dfrac{1}{x + 1}$
**54.** $\dfrac{2}{x} < \dfrac{x}{2}$
**55.** $\dfrac{1}{x - 2} - \dfrac{1}{x - 1} \geq \dfrac{1}{6}$
**56.** $\dfrac{2x}{x + 5} + \dfrac{x - 1}{x - 5} < \dfrac{1}{5}$
**57.** $\dfrac{1 + x}{1 - x} - \dfrac{1 - x}{1 + x} < -1$
**58.** $\dfrac{x + 1}{x + 2} > \dfrac{x - 3}{x + 4}$
**59.** $\dfrac{x^2 - x - 2}{x^2 - 3x + 2} > 0$
**60.** $\dfrac{x^2 + 3x}{x^2 + 8x + 15} < 0$

*For Exercises 61–76:*
Ⓖ **(a)** *Use a graph to estimate the solution set for each inequality. Zoom in far enough so that you can estimate the relevant endpoints to the nearest thousandth.*

**(b)** *Exercises 61–70 can be solved algebraically using the techniques presented in this section. Carry out the algebra to obtain exact expressions for the endpoints that you estimated in part (a). Then use a calculator to check that your results are consistent with the previous estimates.*

**61.** $x^2 - 5x + 3 \leq 0$
**62.** $x^2 + x - 4 \leq 0$
**63.** $0.25x^2 - 6x - 2 < 0$
**64.** $0.25x^3 - 6x^2 - 2x < 0$
**65.** $x^4 - 2x^2 - 1 > 0$
**66.** $x^4 - 2x^2 + 1 > 0$
**67.** $(x^2 - 5)/(x^2 + 1) \leq 0$
**68.** $(x^3 - 5)/(x^2 + 1) \leq 0$
**69.** $(x^2 + 1)/(x^2 - 5) \leq 0$
**70.** $(x^2 + 1)/(x^3 - 5) \leq 0$
**71.** $x^3 + 2x \geq -1$
**72.** $x^3 - 2x \geq -1$
**73.** $x^4 - 2x > -1$
**74.** $x^5 - 2x > -1$

**75.** $x - \dfrac{x^3}{3!} + \dfrac{x^5}{5!} - \dfrac{x^7}{7!} < 0$   *Note: For natural numbers $n$, the symbol $n!$ (read $n$ factorial) denotes the product of the first $n$ natural numbers. For instance, $3! = 1 \times 2 \times 3 = 6$.*

**76.** $1 - \dfrac{x^2}{2!} + \dfrac{x^4}{4!} - \dfrac{x^6}{6!} + \dfrac{x^8}{8!} < 0$

**B**

Ⓖ **77.** Suppose that after studying a corporation's records, a business analyst predicts that the corporation's monthly revenues $R$ for the near future can be closely approximated by the equation

$$R = -0.0217x^5 + 0.626x^4 - 6.071x^3 + 25.216x^2$$
$$-57.703x + 159.955 \qquad (1 \le x \le 12)$$

where $R$ is the revenue (in thousands of dollars) for the month $x$, with $x = 1$ denoting January, $x = 2$ denoting February, and so on.

(a) According to this model, for which months will the monthly revenue be no more than \$80,000?
*Hint*: You need to solve the inequality $R \le 80$. Round each key number to the nearest integer. (Why?)

(b) For which months, if any, will the monthly revenue be at least \$120,000?

Ⓖ **78.** (Continuation of Exercise 77)

(a) Solve the inequality $R > 165$ to determine the months, if any, that the revenue will exceed \$165,000.

(b) Are there any months when the revenue will fall below \$45,000?

**79.** For which values of $b$ will the equation $x^2 + bx + 1 = 0$ have real solutions?

**80.** The sum of the first $n$ natural numbers is given by

$$1 + 2 + 3 + \cdots + n = \frac{n(n + 1)}{2}$$

For which values of $n$ will the sum be less than 1225?

**81.** For which values of $a$ is $x = 1$ a solution of the following inequality?

$$\frac{2a + x}{x - 2a} < 1$$

**82.** Solve $\dfrac{ax + b}{\sqrt{x}} > 2\sqrt{ab}$, where $a$ and $b$ are positive constants.

**83.** The two shorter sides in a right triangle have lengths $x$ and $1 - x$, where $x > 0$. For which values of $x$ will the hypotenuse be less than $\sqrt{17}/5$?

**84.** A piece of wire 12 cm long is cut into two pieces. Denote the lengths of the two pieces by $x$ and $12 - x$. Both pieces are then bent into squares. For which values of $x$ will the combined areas of the squares exceed 5 cm²?

**C**

**85.** Find a nonzero value for $c$ so that the solution set for the inequality

$$x^2 + 2cx - 6c < 0$$

is the open interval $(-3c, c)$.

**86.** Solve $(x - a)^2 - (x - b)^2 > (a - b)^2/4$, where $a$ and $b$ are constants and $a > b$.

## PROJECT | WIND POWER

*The relatively recent* [in terms of human history] *transition to coal that began in Europe in the seventeenth century marked a major shift to dependence on a finite stock of fossilized fuels whose remaining energy is now equivalent to less than 11 days of sunshine. From a millennial perspective, today's hydrocarbon-based civilization is but a brief interlude in human history.* — Christopher Flavin and Seth Dunn, "Reinventing the Energy System" in *Vital Signs, 1999,* Lester R. Brown et al. (New York: W. W. Norton & Co., 1999)

As the world's nonrenewable energy resources such as oil and coal start to become more scarce, alternative sources such wind and solar become increasingly important. In this project you'll calculate some estimates concerning wind power, an industry and technology that has grown rapidly over the past two decades. (Later, in Chapter 5, after studying exponential and logarithmic functions, we'll be able to make some rough estimates for possible depletion dates regarding resources such as oil and coal.) In working this project, you'll be reviewing math from the following sections of this book:

- 1.3 Solving Equations
- 1.6 Equations of Lines
- 2.3 Inequalities
- 2.4 More on Inequalities

*(continues)*

Wind turbines in Altamont, California. (Photo by Glen Allison, PhotoDisc.)

Year ($t = 0$ corresponds to 1985)

World wind-energy generating capacity, 1985 ($t = 0$) and 1998 ($t = 13$).

Source: Data from *BTM Consult*, published in *Vital Signs, 1999*, p. 53, Lester R. Brown et al. (New York: W. W. Norton & Co., 1999)

**(a)** The two data points in the above figure show world wind-energy generating capacity for the years 1985 and 1998. What is the slope of the line joining the two points? What are the units for the slope?

**(b)** Find the equation of the line joining the two given points. Write the answer in the form $y = mt + b$.

**(c)** Use the result in part (b) to estimate the years in which world wind-energy generating capacity was between 3000 megawatts and 7500 megawatts (inclusive). *Hint:* You need to solve the inequality $3000 \le y \le 7500$; round the answers to the nearest integers.

**(d)** Your estimates in part (c) are based on the assumption that world wind-energy generating capacity increased in a straight-line fashion from 1985 to 1998. By using techniques from statistics (and more detailed data), it can be shown that a more accurate summary of world wind-energy generating capacity over these years is given by the equation

$$y = 6.977t^3 - 64.786t^2 + 325.4t + 1012$$

where again, $t = 0$ corresponds to 1985. Using this expression for $y$, estimate the years in which world wind-energy generating capacity was between 3000 megawatts and 7500 megawatts (inclusive). (Round the key numbers to the nearest integers.) Compare your results to those in part (c).

**(e)** Although increasing rapidly, wind-energy generation is currently but a small portion of the world energy picture. For instance, whereas world wind-energy generating capacity in 1998 was 9600 megawatts, the corresponding figure for nuclear energy in 1998 was 343,000 megawatts. When might wind-energy reach this level? Use the equation in part (d) to obtain one possible answer to this question. Round your answer to the nearest five years. *Hint:* In an appropriate viewing rectangle, you want to look for the point where the curve $y = 6.977t^3 - 64.786t^2 + 325.4t + 1012$ meets the horizontal line $y = 343,000$.

**(f)** Rework part (e), but instead of using the cubic equation from part (d), use the straight-line equation obtained in part (b). Compare the results; which scenario do you think is more realistic?

# Chapter 2

## Summary of Principal Terms and Formulas

| Terms or notation | Page reference | Comments |
|---|---|---|
| **1.** Quadratic equation | 80 | A quadratic equation is an equation that can be written in the form $ax^2 + bx + c = 0$, where $a$, $b$, and $c$ are constants with $a \neq 0$. |
| **2.** Quadratic formula $$x = \frac{-b \pm \sqrt{b^2 - 4ac}}{2a}$$ | 82 | This is the quadratic formula; it provides the solutions of the quadratic equation $ax^2 + bx + c = 0$. The formula is derived on pages 81–82 by means of the useful technique of completing the square. |
| **3.** Product-and-sum-of-roots theorem | 84 | The product and the sum of the roots of the quadratic equation $x^2 + bx + c = 0$ are $c$ and $-b$, respectively. |
| **4.** Discriminant | 87 | The discriminant of the quadratic equation $ax^2 + bx + c = 0$ is the number $b^2 - 4ac$. As indicated in the box on page 87, the discriminant provides information about the roots of the equation. |
| **5.** Extraneous solution (or extraneous root) | 99 | In solving equations, certain processes (such as squaring both sides) can lead to answers that do not check in the original equation. These numbers are called extraneous solutions (or extraneous roots). |
| **6.** Solution set of an inequality | 103 | This is the set of numbers that satisfy the inequality. |
| **7.** $A \cup B$ | 107 | The set $A \cup B$ consists of all elements that are in the set $A$ or the set $B$ (or both). |
| **8.** Key numbers of an inequality | 114 | Let $P$ and $Q$ denote polynomials, with no common factors (except possibly constants), and consider the following four inequalities: $$\frac{P}{Q} < 0 \qquad \frac{P}{Q} \leq 0 \qquad \frac{P}{Q} > 0 \qquad \frac{P}{Q} \geq 0$$ The key numbers for each of these inequalities are those real numbers for which $P = 0$ or $Q = 0$. It can be proved that the algebraic sign of $P/Q$ is constant within each of the intervals determined by these key numbers. |

## Writing Mathematics

1. More than 3000 years ago, the ancient Babylonian mathematicians solved quadratic equations. A method they used is demonstrated (using modern notation) in the following example.

   To find the positive root of $x^2 + 8x = 84$:

   Rewrite the equation as $x(x + 8) = 84$, and let $y = x + 8$. Then the equation to be solved becomes $xy = 84$. Now take half of the coefficient of $x$ in the original equation, which is 4, and define another variable $t$ by $t = x + 4$. Then we have $x = t - 4$ and $y = t + 4$. Therefore

   $$(t - 4)(t + 4) = 84$$
   $$t^2 = 100$$
   $$t = 10$$

   With $t = 10$ we get $x = 10 - 4 = 6$, the required positive root.

   On your own or with a group of classmates, work through the above example, filling in any missing details if necessary. Then (strictly on your own), use the Babylonian method to find the positive root of each of the following equations. Write out your solutions in detail, as if you were explaining the method to another student who had not seen it before. This will involve a combination of English composition and algebra. Also, in part (b), check your answer by using the quadratic formula.

   **(a)** $x^2 + 14x = 72$         **(b)** $x^2 + 2Ax = B$, where $B > 0$

2. The ancient Greek mathematicians (2500 years ago) used geometric methods to solve quadratic equations or, rather, to construct line segments whose lengths were the roots of the equations. According to historian Howard Eves in *An Introduction to the History of Mathematics,* 6th ed. (Philadelphia: Saunders College Publishing, 1990):

   *Imbued with the representation of a number by a length and completely lacking any adequate algebraic notation, the early Greeks devised ingenious geometrical processes for carrying out algebraic operations.*

   One of the methods used by the ancient Greeks to solve a quadratic equation is described in the following example (using modern algebraic notation).
       To construct a line segment whose length is equal to the (positive) root of the equation $x^2 + 8x = 84$:

   Begin with a line segment $\overline{AB}$ of length 8. At $B$, construct a line segment $\overline{BC} \perp \overline{AB}$ such that the length of $\overline{BC}$ is $\sqrt{84}$. Next, let $M$ be the midpoint of $\overline{AB}$. With $M$ as center, draw a circular arc of radius $\overline{MC}$ intersecting $\overline{AB}$ (extended) at $P$. Then the length of $\overline{AP}$ is the required root.

   On your own or with a group of classmates, work through the preceding construction. That is, sketch the appropriate figure and verify that the construction indeed yields the positive root of the equation. Then, on your own, use the Greek method to determine the positive root of each of the following equations. Write out your work in detail, as if you were explaining it to a student who had not seen it before. Be sure to include the appropriate geometric figures and an explanation of why the method works.

**(a)** $x^2 + 14x = 72$     **(b)** $x^2 + 2cx = d$   $(c, d > 0)$

3. The example in Exercise 1 demonstrates a Babylonian method for solving a quadratic equation. According to Professor Victor J. Katz in *A History of Mathematics* (New York: HarperCollins College Publishers, 1993), "... whatever the ultimate origin of this method, a close reading of the wording of the [ancient clay] tablets seems to indicate that the scribe had in mind a geometric procedure [completing-the-square]. ...."

One of the earliest *explicit* uses of the completing-the-square technique to solve a quadratic is due to the ninth-century Persian mathematician and astronomer Muhammed al-Khwārizmī. The following example demonstrates al-Khwārizmī's use of completing the square to solve the equation $x^2 + 8x = 84$:

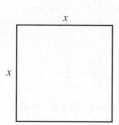

Figure A

To find the positive root of $x^2 + 8x = 84$:

Begin with a square of side $x$, as in Figure A. Take half of the coefficient of $x$: this is one-half of 8, or 4. Now form two rectangles, each with dimensions 4 by $x$, and adjoin them to the square, as indicated in Figure B. Then, as in Figure C, draw the dashed lines to complete the (outer) square.

In Figure B, the combined area of the square and the two rectangles is $x^2 + 8x$. But from the equation we wish to solve, $x^2 + 8x$ is equal to 84. In Figure C the area of the small square in the lower right-hand corner is 16. Thus the area of the entire outer square is $16 + 84$, or 100. But the area of the outer square is also $(x + 4)^2$. Therefore

Figure B

$$(x + 4)^2 = 100 \qquad \text{and, consequently,} \qquad x + 4 = 10$$

The positive root we are looking for is therefore $x = 6$.

On your own or with a group of classmates, work through the preceding example, filling in the missing details as necessary. Then, on your own, use this completing-the-square process to find the positive root of each of the following equations. Write out your solutions in detail, as if you were explaining the method to another student who had not seen it before. Be sure to include the appropriate geometric figures.

Figure C

**(a)** $x^2 + 14x = 72$     **(b)** $x^2 + 2Ax = B$, where $B > 0$

# Chapter 2    Review Exercises

*In Exercises 1–12, answer* TRUE *if the statement is true without exception. Otherwise, answer* FALSE.

1. If $x < 3$, then $x + 7 < 10$.
2. If $x < y$, then $x^2 < y^2$.
3. If $x \geq -4$, then $x \leq 4$.

4. If $-x > y$, then $x < -y$.
5. If $x < 2$, then $1/x < 1/2$.   6. $x \leq x^2$
7. If $\sqrt{x + 1} = 3$, then $x + 1 = 9$.
8. If $0 < x < 1$, then $1/x > x$.
9. If $x < 2$ and $y < 3$, then $x < y$.

**10.** If $x < 2$ and $y > 3$, then $x < y$.
**11.** If $a - b \le a^2 - b^2$, then $1 \le a + b$.
**12.** If $0 < a - b \le a^2 - b^2$, then $1 \le a + b$.

*In Exercises 13–32, find all of the real solutions of each equation.*

**13.** $12x^2 + 2x - 2 = 0$
**14.** $4y^2 - 21y = 18$
**15.** $\frac{1}{2}x^2 + x - 12 = 0$
**16.** $x^2 + \frac{13}{2}x + 10 = 0$
**17.** $\frac{x}{5 - x} = \frac{-2}{11 - x}$
**18.** $\frac{x^2}{(x - 1)(x + 1)} = \frac{4}{x + 1} + \frac{4}{(x - 1)(x + 1)}$
**19.** $\frac{1}{3x - 7} - \frac{2}{5x - 5} - \frac{3}{3x + 1} = 0$
**20.** $4x^2 + x - 2 = 0$
**21.** $t^2 + t - \frac{1}{2} = 0$
**22.** $x^3 - 6x^2 + 7x = 0$
**23.** $1 + 14x^{-1} + 48x^{-2} = 0$
**24.** $x^{-2} - x^{-1} - 1 = 0$
**25.** $x^{1/2} - 13x^{1/4} + 36 = 0$
**26.** $y^{2/3} - 21y^{1/3} + 80 = 0$
**27.** $\sqrt{4x + 3} = \sqrt{11 - 8x} - 1$
**28.** $2 - \sqrt{3\sqrt{2x - 1}} + x = 0$
**29.** $\frac{2}{\sqrt{x^2 - 36}} + \frac{1}{\sqrt{x + 6}} - \frac{1}{\sqrt{x - 6}} = 0$
**30.** $\sqrt{x - \sqrt{1 - x}} + \sqrt{x} - 1 = 0$
**31.** $\sqrt{x + 7} - \sqrt{x + 2} = \sqrt{x - 1} - \sqrt{x - 2}$
**32.** $\frac{\sqrt{x} - 4}{\sqrt{x} - 18} = 3$

*In Exercises 33–38, solve each equation for x in terms of the other letters.*

**33.** $4x^2y^2 - 4xy = -1$, where $y \ne 0$
**34.** $4x^4y^4 + 2x^2y^2 + \frac{1}{4} = 0$, where $y \ne 0$
**35.** $x + \frac{1}{a} - \frac{1}{b} = \frac{2}{a^2x} + \frac{2}{abx}$
**36.** $\frac{a}{x - b} + \frac{b}{x - a} = \frac{x - a}{b} + \frac{x - b}{a}$, where $a \ne -b$

*Suggestion:* Before clearing fractions, carry out the indicated additions on each side of the equation.

**37.** $\frac{1}{x + a + b} = \frac{1}{x} + \frac{1}{a} + \frac{1}{b}$, where $a + b \ne 0$
**38.** $\frac{1}{x} + \frac{1}{a - x} + \frac{1}{x + 3a} = 0$, where $a \ne 0$

*Solve the inequalities in Exercises 39–55.*

**39.** $-1 < \frac{1 - 2(1 + x)}{3} < 1$
**40.** $3 < \frac{x - 1}{-2} < 4$
**41.** $|x| \le 1/2$
**42.** $|3 - 5x| < 2$
**43.** $|2x - 1| \ge 5$

**44.** $x^2 - 21x + 108 \le 0$
**45.** $x^2 + 3x - 40 < 0$
**46.** $x^2 \ge 15x$
**47.** $x^2 - 6x - 1 < 0$
**48.** $(x + 12)(x - 1)(x - 8) < 0$
**49.** $x^4 - 34x^2 + 225 < 0$
**50.** $\frac{x + 12}{x - 5} > 0$
**51.** $\frac{(x - 7)^2}{(x + 2)^3} \ge 0$
**52.** $\frac{(x - 6)^2(x - 8)(x + 3)}{(x - 3)^2} \le 0$
**53.** $\frac{3x + 1}{x - 4} < 1$
**54.** $\frac{1 - 2x}{1 + 2x} \le \frac{1}{2}$
**55.** $x^2 + \frac{1}{x^2} > 3$   *Suggestion:* Use a calculator to evaluate the key numbers.

*For Exercises 56 and 57, find the values of k for which the roots of the equations are real numbers.*

**56.** $kx^2 - 6x + 5 = 0$
**57.** $x^2 + (k + 1)x + 2k = 0$

*In Exercises 58 and 59, find a quadratic equation that has integer coefficients and the given values as roots.*

**58.** $r_1 = (1 + \sqrt{5})/3$, $r_2 = (1 - \sqrt{5})/3$
**59.** $r_1 = -3$, $r_2 = -4$
**60.** Solve for $x$:

$$5\sqrt[3]{b^2 - x^2} = \sqrt[3]{(b + x)^2} + 4\sqrt[3]{(b - x)^2},$$

where $b \ne 0$.
*Hint:* Divide through by $\sqrt[3]{(b - x)^2}$. The resulting equation can be solved by using the substitution
$$t = \sqrt[3]{\frac{b + x}{b - x}}.$$

**61.** The sum of the cubes of two numbers is 2071, while the sum of the two numbers themselves is 19. Find the two numbers.
**62.** The sum of the digits in a certain two-digit number is 11. If the order of the digits is reversed, the number is increased by 27. Find the original number.
**63.** The four corners of a square $ABCD$ have been cut off to form a regular octagon, as shown in the figure. If each side of the square is 1 cm long, how long is each side of the octagon?

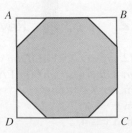

**64.** Determine $p$ if the larger root of the equation $x^2 + px - 2 = 0$ is $p$.

**65.** A piece of wire $x$ cm long is bent into a square. For which values of $x$ will the area be (numerically) greater than the perimeter?

**66.** A piece of wire $6x$ cm long is bent into an equilateral triangle. For which values of $x$ will the area be (numerically) less than the perimeter?

**67.** Find three consecutive positive integers such that the sum of their squares is 1454.

**68.** The length of a rectangular piece of tin exceeds the width by 8 cm. A 1 cm square is cut from each corner of the piece of tin, and then the resulting flaps are turned up to form a box with no top. What are the dimensions of the box if its volume is 48 cm³?

**69.** The length and width of a rectangular flower garden are $a$ and $b$, respectively. The garden is bordered on all four sides by a gravel path of uniform width. Find the width of the path, given that the area of the garden equals the area of the path.

*If an object is thrown vertically upward from a height of $h_0$ ft with an initial speed of $v_0$ ft/sec, then its height $h$ (in feet) after $t$ seconds is given by*

$$h = -16t^2 + v_0 t + h_0$$

*Make use of this formula in working Exercises 70–72.*

**70.** A ball is thrown vertically upward from ground level with an initial speed of 64 ft/sec.
  **(a)** At what time will the height of the ball be 15 ft? (Two answers.)
  **(b)** For how long an interval of time will the height exceed 63 ft?

**71.** One ball is thrown vertically upward from a height of 50 ft with an initial speed of 40 ft/sec. At the same instant, another ball is thrown vertically upward from a height of 100 ft with an initial speed of 5 ft/sec. Which ball hits the ground first?

**72.** An object is projected vertically upward. Suppose that its height is $H$ ft at $t_1$ sec and again at $t_2$ sec. Express the initial speed in terms of $t_1$ and $t_2$.
  *Answer:* $16(t_1 + t_2)$

**73.** A rectangle is inscribed in a semicircle of radius 1 cm, as shown. For which value of $x$ is the area of the rectangle 1 cm²? *Note:* $x$ is defined in the figure.

**74.** The height of an isosceles triangle is $a + b$ units, where $a > b > 0$, and the area does not exceed $a^2 - b^2$ square units. What is the range of possible values for the base of the triangle?

**75.** A circle is inscribed in a quadrant of a larger circle of radius $r$ (as shown in the figure). Find the radius of the inscribed circle.

# Chapter 2    Test

*In Problems 1–4, find all of the real solutions of each equation.*

**1. (a)** $x^2 + 4x = 5$
   **(b)** $x^2 + 4x = 1$
**2.** $x^2(x^2 - 7) + 12 = 0$
**3.** $1 + \sqrt{2 - x} - \sqrt{5 - 2x} = 0$
**4.** $|3x - 1| = 2$
**5.** Find the sum of the roots of the equation $2x^2 + 8x - 9 = 0$.

**6.** Find a quadratic equation with integer coefficients and with roots $r_1 = 2 + 3\sqrt{7}$ and $r_2 = 2 - 3\sqrt{7}$.

**7.** As indicated in the following figure, the graph of $y = x^4 - 3x^2 - 1$ has two $x$-intercepts, one between 1.5 and 2 and one between $-1.5$ and $-2$. Find exact expressions (containing radicals) for these intercepts and also calculator approximations rounded to three decimal places. Check that your calculator values are consistent with the graph.

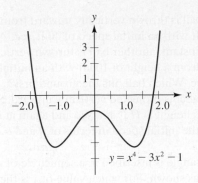

$$y = x^4 - 3x^2 - 1$$

8. Consider the equation $2x^{4/3} - x^{2/3} - 6 = 0$.
   (a) Use a graphing utility to approximate the roots to the nearest hundredth.
   (b) Use algebra to determine the exact solutions. Then check that the answers are consistent with the approximations obtained in part (a).

In Problems 9–13, solve the inequalities. Write the answers using interval notation.

9. $4(1 + x) - 3(2x - 1) \geq 1$

10. $\dfrac{3}{5} < \dfrac{3 - 2x}{-4} < \dfrac{4}{5}$

11. $|3x - 8| \leq 1$

12. $(x - 4)^2(x + 8)^3 \geq 0$

13. $\dfrac{1}{x} + \dfrac{1}{x + 1} + \dfrac{1}{x + 2} \geq 0$

14. Find the values of $k$ for which the roots of the equation $x^2 + 3x + k^2 = 0$ are real numbers.

15. The point $(a, b)$ lies in the third quadrant on the graph of the line $y = 2x + 1$. Find $a$ and $b$ given that the distance from $(a, b)$ to the origin is $\sqrt{65}$.

16. After solving the equation $1 + \sqrt{3x + 7} = x$, give an example of what is meant by an extraneous root, and explain (in complete sentences) how, in this case, the extraneous root was generated.

**CHAPTER**

# 3

# Functions

*To make a start out of particulars and make them general . . .* —William Carlos Williams (1883–1963) in his poem *Paterson*

The concept of a function is one of the most useful and broad-ranging ideas in all of mathematics. After introducing the definition of a function and function notation in Section 3.1, we use graphs in the next three sections to understand and to analyze functions. In Sections 3.5 and 3.6 we find that two functions can be combined to produce new functions. One of these ways of combining two functions is known as *composition of functions.* As you'll see, this is the unifying theme between Sections 3.5 and 3.6. In this chapter we use functions to

- Estimate how many units of a particular item a store can expect to sell at a given price (Example 7 in Section 3.1)
- Compute the average rate of increase or decrease of a patient's temperature over given time periods (Example 3 in Section 3.3)
- Analyze and compare changing patterns of consumption of red meat in China and in the United States (Exercises 19 and 20 in Section 3.3)
- Determine the rate of spread of an oil spill (Example 5 in Section 3.5)

## 3.1 THE DEFINITION OF A FUNCTION

*The word "function" was introduced into mathematics by Leibniz, who used the term primarily to refer to certain kinds of mathematical formulas. It was later realized that Leibniz's idea of function was much too limited in scope, and the meaning of the word has since undergone many steps of generalization.* —Tom M. Apostol in *Calculus,* 2nd ed. (New York: John Wiley & Sons, 1967)

There are numerous instances in mathematics, business, and the sciences in which one quantity corresponds to or depends on another according to some definite *rule.* Consider, for example, the equation $y = 2x + 1$. Each time we select an $x$-value, a corresponding unique $y$-value is determined, in this case according to the rule *multiply by 2, then add 1.* In this sense, the equation $y = 2x + 1$ represents a *function.* It is a rule specifying a $y$-value corresponding to each $x$-value. It is useful to think of the $x$-values as inputs and the corresponding $y$-values as outputs. The function or rule then tells us what output results from a given input, as indicated schematically in Figure 1.

In general, a function can be represented in one or more of the following forms:

- Algebraic, using an equation or formula (as in the previous paragraph)
- Verbal (also as in the previous paragraph)
- Tabular, using a two-column table
- Graphical, using a coordinate system and graph

After looking at some examples of these ways of representing functions, we'll give an "official" definition of the term *function* on page 132.

**129**

Input

Function or rule

Output

**Figure 1**

**Algebraic.** Many of the familiar formulas from geometry represent functions. The area $A$ of a circle depends on the radius $r$ according to the formula $A = \pi r^2$. For each value of $r$, a corresponding value for $A$ is determined by this formula or rule. The values for $r$ are the inputs, and the corresponding values for $A$ are the outputs. The field of statistics provides another rich source of examples of functions. For instance, over the years 1850–1900, the population of the United States can be closely approximated by using the equation

$$y = 0.006609x^2 - 23.771x + 21{,}382$$

where $y$ is the population in millions and $x$ is the year. (We worked with this equation in Example 1 in Section 2.1.) For this rule or function, the inputs are the numbers 1850, 1851, . . . 1900, and the corresponding outputs are the population estimates (in millions).

**Verbal.** If you count the number of times that a cricket chirps in one minute, you can estimate the air temperature (Fahrenheit) using the following rule or function: *Divide the number of chirps by 4, then add 40*; the answer will be a good estimate for the air temperature. (We're assuming here that at a given temperature, all crickets chirp at the same rate.) For instance, suppose that you count 80 chirps in one minute. This is our input. Applying the rule, we divide 80 by 4, which is 20, and then add 40 to obtain 60. Our estimate for the air temperature is 60°F; that's the output corresponding to an input of 80 chirps/min.

The terminology of proportion and variation introduced in intermediate algebra is sometimes used in the sciences to represent functions verbally. Here's an example from physics. If you drop a ball off the roof of a building, then before it hits the ground (and neglecting air resistance), *the distance the ball falls is directly proportional to the square of the elapsed time*. The equivalent algebraic representation for this verbal rule or function is

$$d = kt^2$$

where $d$ is the distance that the ball falls in time $t$, and $k$ is a constant. (If the distance $d$ is measured in feet and the time $t$ in seconds, then the numerical value for $k$ turns out to be 16, and the algebraic form of the rule or function becomes $d = 16t^2$.)

**Tabular.** In many applications a function is specified by means of a two-column table. Unless stated otherwise, we usually think of the entries in the left-hand column as the inputs and the entries in the right-hand column as the outputs. In Table 1, for example, the input 1975 yields the output $2.00. The inputs and outputs for a function needn't always be numbers. Notice that in Table 2, the inputs aren't

| TABLE 1 Federal Minimum Wage | |
|---|---|
| Year | Minimum wage (dollars) |
| 1975 | 2.00 |
| 1980 | 3.10 |
| 1985 | 3.35 |
| 1990 | 3.80 |
| 1995 | 4.25 |
| 2000 | 5.15 |

Source: U.S. Bureau of Labor Statistics

| TABLE 2 Number of Moons Each Planet in the Solar System Is Known to Have as of 2000 | |
|---|---|
| Planet | Number of moons |
| Mercury | 0 |
| Venus | 0 |
| Earth | 1 |
| Mars | 2 |
| Jupiter | 16 |
| Saturn | 18 |
| Uranus | 18 |
| Neptune | 8 |
| Pluto | 1 |

| TABLE 3 Original Names of Some Movie Stars | |
|---|---|
| Movie star | Original name |
| Kate Capshaw | Kathleen Sue Nail |
| Tom Cruise | Thomas Cruise Mapother, IV |
| Demi Moore | Demetria Guynes |
| Kevin Spacey | Kevin Fowler |
| Arnold Schwarzenegger | Arnold Schwarzenegger |

numbers, but rather names of the planets in our solar system. In Table 3, neither the inputs nor the outputs are numbers. Another item to note: As indicated in the last row of Table 3, it is possible for an input and output to be the same item. For an algebraic example of this, consider the rule defined by $y = x^2$. For the input $x = 1$, the corresponding output is $y = 1^2 = 1$. That is, the input and output are both 1.

**Graphical.** In newspapers, business, and the sciences, functions are often presented graphically. Sometimes, but certainly not always, this is in conjunction with an explicit table of values or an equation. For example, consider the minimum wage information given in Table 1. Each row of the table gives us an ordered pair of numbers that we can plot in a coordinate system. Looking at Table 1, we see that the first row gives us the point with coordinates (1975, 2.00), the second row gives us the point (1980, 3.10), and so on. The resulting graph is shown in Figure 2.

**Figure 2**
Federal minimum wage. A graphical presentation of the input/output pairs in Table 1.

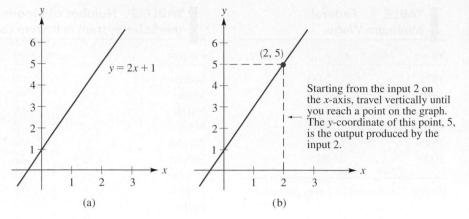

**Figure 3**
The graph of $y = 2x + 1$ represents a function.

In the first paragraph of this section we used the equation $y = 2x + 1$ as an example of a function represented algebraically. A graphical representation of this function is shown in Figure 3(a). (We've used the techniques of Section 1.6 to graph the equation $y = 2x + 1$.) Given this graphical representation of the function (and ignoring, for the moment, the fact that we have the equation $y = 2x + 1$), what is the underlying rule here for obtaining the output $y$ from a given input $x$? One way to state the rule is this:

> Given an input on the $x$-axis, for example $x = 2$ as in Figure 3(b), travel vertically until you reach a point on the graph. The $y$-coordinate of this point is the required output. According to Figure 3(b), the input $x = 2$ produces the output $y = 5$.

A less dynamic but more succinct (and more general) way to describe the relationship between the graph of a function and the "input-output" point of view is this:

> Suppose we have a graph of a function in an $x$-$y$ coordinate system. Then a point $(x, y)$ is on the graph if and only if the function assigns the output $y$ to the input $x$.

(Actually, when we take a more careful look at graphs of functions in Section 3.2, we'll adapt this last version for the very definition of the graph of a function.)

Now that we've looked at a few introductory examples, it's time to state the definition of the term *function* as it is used in mathematics. We need this definition before we can answer the following two questions, which may have already occurred to you:

Does every rule or table represent a function?
Does every graph represent a function?

As you'll see later in this section, the answer to the first question is *no*. For the second question, the answer is also negative, but we postpone that discussion until the next section. The following definition of the term *function* is broad enough to encompass all of the examples that we've looked at.

---

**DEFINITION** | **Function**

---

Let $A$ and $B$ be two nonempty sets. A function from $A$ to $B$ is a rule of correspondence that assigns to each element in set $A$ exactly one element in $B$.

---

The set $A$ in the definition just given is called the **domain** of the function. Think of the domain as the set of all inputs. For each input, the function gives us an output (from the set $B$ mentioned in the definition). The set of all outputs is called the **range** of the function. For example, for the minimum wage function represented in Table 1 (on page 131), the domain is the set {1975, 1980, 1985, 1990, 1995, 2000}, and the range is {$2.00, $3.10, $3.35, $3.80, $4.25, $5.15}.

In a moment we'll talk more about domain and range, but first reread the definition of function in the box above and note the use of the word "exactly." The inclusion of that word implies that some rules will *not* qualify as functions. For example, the rule represented in Table 4(a) doesn't qualify as a function; for the input year 1981 there are two outputs (namely, 18¢ and 20¢), whereas the definition of a function requires exactly one output. Table 4(b) remedies this problem; the rule in Table 4(b) does represent a function.

**TABLE 4(a)  Price of U.S. First-Class Stamp and the Year the Price Went into Effect**

| Year (inputs) | 1975 | 1978 | 1981 | 1981 | 1985 | 1988 | 1991 | 1995 | 1999 |
|---|---|---|---|---|---|---|---|---|---|
| Price in cents (outputs) | 13 | 15 | 18 | 20 | 22 | 25 | 29 | 32 | 33 |

**TABLE 4(b)  Price of U.S. First-Class Stamp and the Date the Price Went into Effect**

| Date (inputs) | 12/31/75 | 5/29/78 | 3/22/81 | 11/1/81 | 2/17/85 | 4/3/88 | 2/3/91 | 1/1/95 | 1/10/99 |
|---|---|---|---|---|---|---|---|---|---|
| Price in cents (outputs) | 13 | 15 | 18 | 20 | 22 | 25 | 29 | 32 | 33 |

For an algebraic example of this same issue, consider square roots and the symbol $\sqrt{\phantom{x}}$. (*Note:* The following discussion is intended to be self-contained. If after you read it, however, things don't seem clear, you should refer to the detailed review of roots in Appendix B.2 at the back of this book.) Recall from basic algebra that each positive number has two square roots. For instance, the square roots of 16 are 4 and $-4$. Thus the rule in Table 5(a) does not represent a function because for each input there are two outputs. To remedy this, the symbol $\sqrt{\phantom{x}}$ is defined in algebra to mean the *positive* square root only. Thus $\sqrt{16} = 4$, and if you are thinking of the other root, you write $-\sqrt{16} = -4$. Consequently, the correspondences in Table 5(b) do represent a function; for each input there is exactly one output.

**TABLE 5(a)  Not a Function**

| $x$ | Square roots of $x$ |
|---|---|
| 4 | 2, $-2$ |
| 9 | 3, $-3$ |
| 16 | 4, $-4$ |

**TABLE 5(b)  A Function**

| $x$ | $\sqrt{x}$ |
|---|---|
| 4 | 2 |
| 9 | 3 |
| 16 | 4 |

**EXAMPLE** **1** **Using the definition of a function**

Let $A = \{b, g\}$ and $B = \{s, t, u, z\}$. Which of the four correspondences in Figure 4 represent functions from $A$ to $B$? For those correspondences that do represent functions, specify the range in each case.

  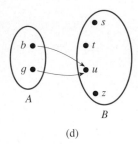

(a)　　　　　　(b)　　　　　　(c)　　　　　　(d)

**Figure 4**

**SOLUTION**
**(a)** This is not a function. The definition requires that *each* element in $A$ be assigned an element in $B$. The element $g$ in this case has no assignment.
**(b)** This is not a function. The definition requires *exactly one* output for a given input. In this case there are two outputs for the input $g$.
**(c)** and **(d)** Both of these rules qualify as functions from $A$ to $B$. For each input there is exactly one output. (Regarding the function in (d) in particular, notice that nothing in the definition of a function prohibits two different inputs from producing the same output.) For the function in (c), the outputs are $s$ and $z$, and so the range is the set $\{s, z\}$. For the function in (d), the only output is $u$; consequently, the range is the set $\{u\}$.

For functions defined by equations, we'll agree on the following convention regarding the domain: Unless otherwise indicated, the domain is assumed to be the set of all real numbers that lead to unique real-number outputs. (This is essentially the domain convention described in Section 1.3.) Thus, the domain of the function defined by $y = 3x - 2$ is the set of all real numbers, whereas the domain of the function defined by $y = 1/(x - 5)$ is the set of all real numbers except 5 (since, $1/(x - 5)$ is undefined when the denominator is zero, namely, when $x = 5$). In general, the letter representing elements from the domain (that is, the inputs) is called the **independent variable.** For example, in the equation $y = 3x - 2$, the independent variable is $x$. The letter representing elements from the range (that is, the outputs) is called the **dependent variable.** In the equation $y = 3x - 2$, the dependent variable is $y$; its value *depends* on $x$. This is also expressed by saying that $y$ *is a function of* $x$.

**EXAMPLE** **2** **Determining the domain of a function**

Find the domain of the function defined by each equation:
**(a)** $y = \sqrt{2x + 6}$;　　**(b)** $s = 1/(t^2 - 6t - 7)$.

**SOLUTION**
**(a)** The quantity under the radical sign must be nonnegative, so we have

$$2x + 6 \geq 0$$
$$2x \geq -6$$
$$x \geq -3$$

The domain is therefore the interval $[-3, \infty)$.

**(b)** Since division by zero is undefined, the domain of this function consists of all real numbers $t$ except those for which the denominator is zero. Thus to find out which values of $t$ to exclude, we solve the equation $t^2 - 6t - 7 = 0$. We have

$$t^2 - 6t - 7 = 0$$
$$(t - 7)(t + 1) = 0$$

$$t - 7 = 0 \quad | \quad t + 1 = 0$$
$$t = 7 \quad | \quad t = -1$$

It follows now that the domain of the function defined by $s = 1/(t^2 - 6t - 7)$ is the set of all real numbers except $t = 7$ and $t = -1$.

---

**EXAMPLE** | **3** | **Determining the domain of a function**

Find the domain of the function defined by each equation:

**(a)** $y = \sqrt{\dfrac{x + 3}{x - 4}};$      **(b)** $y = \sqrt[3]{\dfrac{x + 3}{x - 4}}.$

**SOLUTION**

**(a)** The quantity underneath the square root sign must be nonnegative, so we require

$$\frac{x + 3}{x - 4} \geq 0$$

This inequality can be solved by using the techniques of Section 2.4. In fact, we did solve exactly this inequality in Example 4 of Section 2.4. As you can check (preferably on your own, without looking back), the solution set is $(-\infty, -3] \cup (4, \infty)$. This is the domain of the given function.

**(b)** In contrast to the situation with square roots, cube roots are defined for all real numbers. Thus the only trouble spot for $y = \sqrt[3]{(x + 3)/(x - 4)}$ occurs when the denominator is zero, that is, when $x$ is 4. Consequently, the domain of the given function consists of all real numbers except $x = 4$. Using interval notation, this set can be written $(-\infty, 4) \cup (4, \infty)$.

---

  **EXAMPLE** | **4** | **Determining the range of a function**

Find the range of the function defined by $y = \dfrac{x + 2}{x - 3}.$

**SOLUTION**

Since the range of a function depends on the domain, we first find the domain. The domain of the given function is the set of all real numbers except 3. The range of this function is the set of all outputs $y$. One way to see what restrictions the given equation imposes on $y$ is to solve the equation for $x$ as follows: $y$ is in the range of this function if there is an $x$ in the domain such that

$$y = \frac{x + 2}{x - 3}$$

$$y(x - 3) = x + 2 \qquad \text{multiplying by } x - 3 \text{ (for } x \neq 3\text{)}$$

$$xy - 3y = x + 2$$

$$xy - x = 3y + 2$$

$$x(y - 1) = 3y + 2$$

$$x = \frac{3y + 2}{y - 1}$$

From this last equation we see that given a value for $y$, there will be an $x$ in the domain provided that $y$ is not equal to 1. (The denominator is zero when $y = 1$.) The range therefore consists of all real numbers except $y = 1$. Using interval notation, this is the set $(-\infty, 1) \cup (1, \infty)$.

We often use single letters to name functions. If $f$ is a function and $x$ is an input for the function, then the resulting output is denoted by $f(x)$. This is read $f$ *of* $x$ or *the value of f at x*. As an example of this notation, suppose that $f$ is the function defined by

$$f(x) = x^2 - 3x + 1 \qquad\qquad (1)$$

Then $f(-2)$ denotes the output that results when the input is $-2$. To calculate this output, replace $x$ with $-2$ throughout equation (1). This yields

$$f(-2) = (-2)^2 - 3(-2) + 1$$

$$= 4 + 6 + 1 = 11$$

That is, $f(-2) = 11$. Figure 5 summarizes this result and the notation.

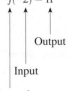

$f(-2) = 11$

Output

Input

Name of function

**Figure 5**

---

**EXAMPLE 5    Using function notation**

Let $g$ denote the minimum wage function defined by Table 1 (on page 131).
**(a)** Find $g(1975)$.
**(b)** Find $g(1990) - g(1980)$ and interpret the result.

**SOLUTION**
**(a)** The notation $g(1975)$ stands for the output corresponding to the input 1975. According to Table 1, that output is $2.00, and so $g(1975) = \$2.00$.
**(b)** We have

$$g(1990) - g(1980) = \$3.80 - \$3.10$$

$$= \$0.70$$

This represents the increase in the minimum wage from 1980 to 1990.

> ## EXAMPLE 6 Using function notation
>
> Let $f(x) = \dfrac{x}{x - 4}$.
>
> **(a)** Compute each of the following: $f(2)$, $f(t)$, and $f(a^2)$.
> **(b)** Find an input $x$ such that $f(x) = 3$.
>
> **SOLUTION**
> **(a)** For $f(2)$, replace each occurrence of $x$ in the given equation by 2 to obtain
>
> $$f(2) = \frac{2}{2 - 4} = -1$$
>
> Similarly, for $f(t)$ and for $f(a^2)$ we have
>
> $$f(t) = \frac{t}{t - 4} \quad \text{and} \quad f(a^2) = \frac{a^2}{a^2 - 4}$$
>
> **(b)** To solve the equation $f(x) = 3$, replace $f(x)$ by the given expression $x/(x - 4)$. This yields
>
> $$\frac{x}{x - 4} = 3$$
> $$x = 3(x - 4) \qquad \text{multiplying both sides}$$
> $$\text{by the quantity } x - 4 \text{ (for } x \neq 4\text{)}$$
> $$x = 3x - 12$$
> $$-2x = -12$$
> $$x = 6$$
>
> CHECK   Using the input $x = 6$, we have
>
> $$f(6) = \frac{6}{6 - 4} = 3 \quad \text{as required}$$
>
> So $x = 6$ is indeed the input that we were looking for.

As background for the next example (and for work in later sections), we introduce the concept of a *demand function* from the field of economics. As you well know, the price of an item that you're interested in has a strong influence on whether or not you actually buy that item. A function relating the selling price of an item to the number of units sold at that price is called a **demand function.** Such a function might be obtained after analyzing either a company's sales records or the results of a marketing survey. As a simple example, suppose that an auto manufacturer invites 12 people to participate in a focus group. At some point in the session, the manufacturer shows them pictures and specifications for a proposed new model. Then each of the 12 people fills out a questionnaire asking whether he or she would purchase the car at various price levels. The results, shown in Table 6, represent a demand function. Figure 6 provides a graphical representation of this same function.

**TABLE 6** Tabular Representation of a Demand Function

| Price (1000s of dollars) | Number of cars that can be sold |
|---|---|
| 12 | 12 |
| 14 | 10 |
| 16 | 6 |
| 18 | 5 |
| 20 | 2 |
| 22 | 1 |

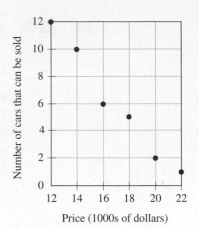

**Figure 6**
Graphical representation of the demand function

The demand function represented in Table 6 and Figure 6 involves only six data points, whereas an actual marketing survey might well produce 600 or even 6000 points. To detect patterns in the data or to make predictions, it's useful to have an equation with a relatively simple graph that somehow "fits" or summarizes the data. In Figure 7(a), for instance, you can see that the blue line does seem to fit the data points from Figure 6 quite well.

Assuming that we are using $x$ on the horizontal axis for price and $y$ on the vertical axis for the number of cars, the equation for the line in Figure 7(a) is $y = -1.143x + 25.43$. The equation was obtained by using statistical techniques that are built into many types of graphing utilities and spreadsheets. (More about that in Section 4.1.) The line is known variously as a *trend line, regression line,* or *least squares line.* We say in this case that the function defined by $y = -1.143x + 25.43$ is a *mathematical model* for the demand data displayed in Table 6 and in Figure 6.

(a) Linear model
$y = -1.143x + 25.43$

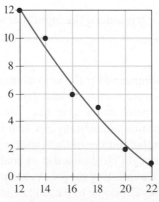

(b) Quadratic model
$y = 0.04x^2 - 2.51x + 36.57$

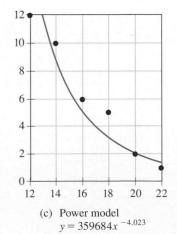

(c) Power model
$y = 359684x^{-4.023}$

**Figure 7**
Three models for the demand data in Table 6

More generally, any function used to describe or summarize a real-world situation is called a **mathematical model,** and the process of creating or developing that function is called **mathematical modeling.** In Figures 7(b) and 7(c) we show two other functions that can be used to model the demand data. We'll study these and other types of functions used in mathematical modeling in subsequent chapters.

For the demand function represented in Figure 6, prices are represented on the horizontal axis, and the numbers of items sold are on the vertical axis. However, this is not a standard convention. Economists sometimes put prices on the vertical axis and numbers of items on the horizontal axis. Example 7 shows one instance of this.

---

**EXAMPLE** 7   **Using a demand function and function notation**

Suppose that an economist for a factory outlet store determines that the demand function $p$ for a certain type of tee shirt is given by

$$p(n) = -0.012n + 20.49 \qquad (100 \le n \le 1500)$$

where $n$ is the number of tee shirts that can be sold per month at a price of $p(n)$ dollars per shirt. Solve the equation $p(n) = 16$ and interpret the result.

**SOLUTION**
Substituting the given expression for $p(n)$ into the equation $p(n) = 16$ yields

$$-0.012n + 20.49 = 16$$
$$-0.012n = 16 - 20.49$$
$$n = \frac{16 - 20.49}{-0.012} = 374.166\ldots \qquad \text{using a calculator}$$

Now since $n$ represents the number of tee shirts, we round to the nearest integer to obtain $n = 374$. Interpretation: When the price is set at \$16 per shirt, the store can expect to sell 374 tee shirts per month.

---

Before going on to the next example, we offer a word of caution to help you avoid a common error in using function notation.

NOTE OF CAUTION REGARDING FUNCTION NOTATION   It is not in general true that $f(a + b) = f(a) + f(b)$.

As an example, suppose we take $f$ to be the function defined by $f(x) = x^2$ and use the two inputs $a = 1$ and $b = 2$. Then we have

$$f(1 + 2) = (1 + 2)^2 = 3^2 = 9$$

whereas

$$f(1) = 1^2 = 1, f(2) = 2^2 = 4 \qquad \text{and, consequently,} \qquad f(1) + f(2) = 1 + 4 = 5$$

In summary, we have $f(1 + 2) = 9$ and $f(1) + f(2) = 5$, so certainly,

$$f(1 + 2) \ne f(1) + f(2)$$

> **EXAMPLE** | **8** | **Using function notation**
>
> Compute $g(x + 1)$ for the function $g$ defined by $g(x) = 1 - x - x^2$.
>
> **SOLUTION**
> We're given $g(x)$. To find $g(x + 1)$, we go to the given equation $g(x) = 1 - x - x^2$ and replace each occurrence of $x$ with the quantity $x + 1$. This yields
>
> $$\begin{aligned} g(x + 1) &= 1 - (x + 1) - (x + 1)^2 \\ &= 1 - x - 1 - (x^2 + 2x + 1) \\ &= -x^2 - 3x - 1 \qquad \text{(Check the algebra.)} \end{aligned}$$

Here's a slightly different perspective that we can apply in Example 8 and in similar situations. Instead of writing $g(x) = 1 - x - x^2$, we can write

$$g(\ \ ) = 1 - (\ \ ) - (\ \ )^2 \tag{1}$$

with the understanding that whatever quantity goes into the parentheses on the left-hand side of equation (1) must also be placed into each set of parentheses on the right-hand side. In particular then, placing the quantity $x + 1$ into all three sets of parentheses in equation (1) yields $g(x + 1) = 1 - (x + 1) - (x + 1)^2$. From here on, the algebra is the same as in Example 8.

---

# EXERCISE SET 3.1

**A**

1. As in Example 5, let $g$ denote the minimum wage function represented in Table 1.
   (a) Find $g(1975)$.
   (b) Find $g(1995) - g(1975)$ and interpret the result.
2. Let $f$ denote the function represented in Table 3.
   (a) Find $f$(Kate Capshaw).
   (b) For which input $x$ are $x$ and $f(x)$ identical?
3. Let $h$ denote the function represented in Table 2.
   (a) Is it the domain or the range of $h$ that consists of real numbers?
   (b) Find $h$(Mars).
   (c) Which is larger: $h$(Neptune) or $h$(Pluto)? Interpret the result (using a complete sentence).
4. Again let $h$ denote the function represented in Table 2.
   (a) List those inputs $x$ for which $h(x) = 1$.
   (b) For which real number $t$ will it be true that $h$(Jupiter) $+ t = h$(Saturn)?

*For Exercises 5 and 6, two sets A and B are defined as follows: A = {x, y, z}; B = {1, 2, 3}.*
(a) *Which of the rules displayed in the figures represent functions from A to B?*

(b) *For each rule that does represent a function, specify the range.*

5.

**6.**

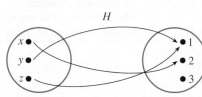

*For Exercises 7 and 8, two sets D and C are defined as follows:*
$D = \{a, b\}$; $C = \{i, j, k\}$.

**(a)** *Which of the rules displayed in the figures represent functions from D to C?*

**(b)** *For each rule that represents a function, specify the range.*

**7.**

**8.**

*In Exercises 9–16, determine the domain of each function.*

**9. (a)** $y = -5x + 1$
　**(b)** $y = 1/(-5x + 1)$
　**(c)** $y = \sqrt{-5x + 1}$
　**(d)** $y = \sqrt[3]{-5x + 1}$

**10. (a)** $s = 3t + 12$
　**(b)** $s = 1/(3t + 12)$
　**(c)** $s = \sqrt{3t + 12}$
　**(d)** $s = \sqrt[3]{3t + 12}$

**11. (a)** $f(x) = x^2 - 9$
　**(b)** $g(x) = 1/(x^2 - 9)$
　**(c)** $h(x) = \sqrt{x^2 - 9}$
　**(d)** $k(x) = \sqrt[3]{x^2 - 9}$

**12. (a)** $F(t) = t^2 + 4t$
　**(b)** $G(t) = 1/(t^2 + 4t)$
　**(c)** $H(t) = \sqrt{t^2 + 4t}$
　**(d)** $K(t) = \sqrt[3]{t^2 + 4t}$

**13. (a)** $f(t) = t^2 - 8t + 15$
　**(b)** $g(t) = 1/(t^2 - 8t + 15)$
　**(c)** $h(t) = \sqrt{t^2 - 8t + 15}$
　**(d)** $k(t) = \sqrt[3]{t^2 - 8t + 15}$

**14. (a)** $F(x) = 2x^2 + x - 6$
　**(b)** $G(x) = 1/(2x^2 + x - 6)$
　**(c)** $H(x) = \sqrt{2x^2 + x - 6}$
　**(d)** $K(x) = \sqrt[3]{2x^2 + x - 6}$

**15. (a)** $f(x) = (x - 2)/(2x + 6)$
　**(b)** $g(x) = \sqrt{(x - 2)/(2x + 6)}$
　**(c)** $h(x) = \sqrt[3]{(x - 2)/(2x + 6)}$

**16. (a)** $F(t) = (3t - 4)/(7 - 2t)$
　**(b)** $G(t) = \sqrt{(3t - 4)/(7 - 2t)}$
　**(c)** $H(t) = \sqrt[3]{(3t - 4)/(7 - 2t)}$

*In Exercises 17–26, determine the domain and the range of each function.*

**17.** $y = 4x - 5$
**18.** $y = 125 - 12x$
**19.** $y = 4x^3 - 5$
**20.** $y = 125 - 12x^3$
**21.** $g(x) = \dfrac{4x - 20}{3x - 18}$
**22.** $f(x) = \dfrac{1 - x}{x}$

**23. (a)** $f(x) = \dfrac{x + 3}{x - 5}$
**24. (a)** $g(x) = \dfrac{2x - 7}{3x + 24}$

　**(b)** $F(x) = \dfrac{x^3 + 3}{x^3 - 5}$
　**(b)** $G(x) = \dfrac{2x^3 - 7}{3x^3 + 24}$

**25.** $s = t^2 + 4$
**26.** $s = 2t^2 - 10$

**27.** Each of the following rules defines a function with domain the set of all real numbers. Express each rule in the form of an equation.

EXAMPLE

The rule *For each real number, compute its square* can be written $y = x^2$.

**(a)** For each real number, subtract 3 and then square the result.
**(b)** For each real number, compute its square and then subtract 3 from the result.
**(c)** For each real number, multiply it by 3 and then square the result.
**(d)** For each real number, compute its square and then multiply the result by 3.

**28.** Each of the following rules defines a function with domain equal to the set of all real numbers. Express each rule in words.

**(a)** $y = 2x^3 + 1$
**(c)** $y = (2x + 1)^3$
**(b)** $y = 2(x + 1)^3$
**(d)** $y = (2x)^3 + 1$

**29.** Let $f(x) = x^2 - 3x + 1$. Compute the following.

(a) $f(1)$     (e) $f(z)$     (i) $|f(1)|$

(b) $f(0)$     (f) $f(x + 1)$     (j) $f(\sqrt{3})$

(c) $f(-1)$     (g) $f(a + 1)$     (k) $f(1 + \sqrt{2})$

(d) $f(3/2)$     (h) $f(-x)$     (l) $|1 - f(2)|$

**30.** Let $H(x) = 1 - x + x^2 - x^3$.

(a) Which number is larger, $H(0)$ or $H(1)$?

(b) Find $H(\frac{1}{2})$. Does $H(\frac{1}{2}) + H(\frac{1}{2}) = H(1)$?

**31.** Let $f(x) = 3x^2$. Find the following.

(a) $f(2x)$     (c) $f(x^2)$     (e) $f(x/2)$

(b) $2f(x)$     (d) $[f(x)]^2$     (f) $f(x)/2$

*For checking*: No two answers are the same.

**32.** Let $f(x) = 4 - 3x$. Find the following.

(a) $f(2)$     (f) $2f(x)$     (k) $1/f(x)$

(b) $f(-3)$     (g) $f(x^2)$     (l) $f(-x)$

(c) $f(2) + f(-3)$     (h) $f(1/x)$     (m) $-f(x)$

(d) $f(2 + 3)$     (i) $f[f(x)]$     (n) $-f(-x)$

(e) $f(2x)$     (j) $x^2f(x)$

**33.** Let $H(x) = 1 - 2x^2$. Find the following.

(a) $H(\sqrt{2})$     (c) $H(x + 1)$

(b) $H(5/6)$     (d) $H(x + h)$

**34.** (a) If $f(x) = 2x + 1$, does $f(3 + 1) = f(3) + f(1)$?

(b) If $f(x) = 2x$, does $f(3 + 1) = f(3) + f(1)$?

(c) If $f(x) = \sqrt{x}$, does $f(3 + 1) = f(3) + f(1)$?

**35.** Let $g(x) = 2$, for all $x$. Find each output.

(a) $g(0)$     (b) $g(5)$     (c) $g(x + h)$

**36.** Let $g(t) = |t - 4|$. Find $g(3)$. Find $g(x + 4)$.

**37.** Let $f(x) = x^2 - 6x$. In each case, find all real numbers $x$ (if any) that satisfy the given equation.

(a) $f(x) = 16$     (b) $f(x) = -10$     (c) $f(x) = -9$

**38.** Let $g(t) = (4t - 6)/(t - 4)$. In each case, find all the real number solutions (if any) for the given equation.

(a) $g(t) = 14$     (b) $g(t) = 4$     (c) $g(t) = 0$

*For Exercises 39 and 40, refer to the demand function given in Example 7. In each case, solve the indicated equation for n. Round each answer to the nearest integer and interpret the result.*

**39.** $p(n) = 8$           **40.** $p(n) = 18$

*In Exercises 41 and 42, p refers to the demand function given in Example 7. Now assume that a second economist proposes an alternative model f for the demand function:*

$$f(n) = 4 + \frac{3000}{n + 100} \quad (100 \le n \le 1500)$$

*where n is the number of tee shirts that can be sold per month at a price of f(n) dollars per shirt.*

**41.** At a price level of $19 per shirt, compare the predictions for monthly sales obtained using each model. *Hint*: You need to solve each of the equations $p(n) = 19$ and $f(n) = 19$ and interpret the results.

**42.** Show that at a price level of $10 per shirt, the model $p$ predicts more than twice as many sales per month as does the model $f$. *Hint*: Solve each of the equations $p(n) = 10$ and $f(n) = 10$, and interpret the results.

*In Exercises 43 and 44, let $T(x) = 2x^2 - 3x$. Find (and simplify) each expression.*

**43.** (a) $T(x + 2)$       **44.** (a) $T(x + h)$

(b) $T(x - 2)$               (b) $T(x - h)$

(c) $T(x + 2) - T(x - 2)$    (c) $T(x + h) - T(x - h)$

*In Exercises 45–48, refer to the following table. The left-hand column of the table lists four errors to avoid in working with function notation. In each case, use the function $f(x) = x^2 - 1$ and give a numerical example showing that the expressions on each side of the equation are not equal.*

| Errors to avoid | Numerical example showing that the equation is not, in general, valid |
|---|---|
| **45.** $f(a + b) = f(a) + f(b)$ | |
| **46.** $f(ab) = f(a) \cdot f(b)$ | |
| **47.** $f\left(\dfrac{1}{a}\right) = \dfrac{1}{f(a)}$ | |
| **48.** $\dfrac{f(a)}{f(b)} = \dfrac{a}{b}$ | |

## B

**49.** Let $f(x) = (x - a)/(x + a)$.

(a) Find $f(a), f(2a)$, and $f(3a)$. Is it true that
$$f(3a) = f(a) + f(2a)?$$

(b) Show that $f(5a) = 2f(2a)$.

**50.** Let $k(x) = 5x^3 + \dfrac{5}{x^3} - x - \dfrac{1}{x}$. Show that $k(x) = k(1/x)$.

**51.** Let $f(x) = 2x + 3$. Find values for $a$ and $b$ such that the equation $f(ax + b) = x$ is true for all values of $x$. *Hint*: Use the fact that if two polynomials (in the variable $x$) are equal for all values of $x$, then the corresponding coefficients are equal.

**52.** Let $f(t) = (t - x)/(t + y)$. Show that

$$f(x + y) + f(x - y) = \frac{-2y^2}{x^2 + 2xy}$$

**53.** Let $f(z) = \dfrac{3z - 4}{5z - 3}$. Find $f\left(\dfrac{3z - 4}{5z - 3}\right)$.

**54.** Let $F(x) = \dfrac{ax + b}{cx - a}$. Show that $F\left(\dfrac{ax + b}{cx - a}\right) = x$, where $a^2 + bc \ne 0$.

**55.** If $f(x) = -2x^2 + 6x + k$ and $f(0) = -1$, find $k$.

**56.** If $g(x) = x^2 - 3xk - 4$ and $g(1) = -2$, find $k$.

**57.** Let $h(x) = x^2 - 4x - c$. Find a nonzero value for $c$ such that $h(c) = c$.

**58.** Let the function $L$ be defined by the following rule: $L(x)$ is *the exponent to which 2 must be raised to yield x*. (For the moment, we won't concern ourselves with the domain and range.) Then $L(8) = 3$, for example, since the exponent to which 2 must be raised to yield 8 is 3 (that is, $8 = 2^3$). Find the following outputs.

(a) $L(1)$  (e) $L(1/2)$
(b) $L(2)$  (f) $L(1/4)$
(c) $L(4)$  (g) $L(1/64)$
(d) $L(64)$  (h) $L(\sqrt{2})$

The function $L$ is called a *logarithmic function*. The usual notation for $L(x)$ in this example is $\log_2 x$. Logarithmic functions will be studied in Chapter 5.

**59.** Let $q(x) = ax^2 + bx + c$. Evaluate

$$q\left(\frac{-b + \sqrt{b^2 - 4ac}}{2a}\right)$$

**60.** By definition, a **fixed point** for the function $f$ is a number $x_0$ such that $f(x_0) = x_0$. For instance, to find any fixed points for the function $f(x) = 3x - 2$, we write $3x_0 - 2 = x_0$. On solving this last equation, we find that $x_0 = 1$. Thus, 1 is a fixed point for $f$. Calculate the fixed points (if any) for each function.

(a) $f(x) = 6x + 10$  (c) $S(t) = t^2$
(b) $g(x) = x^2 - 2x - 4$  (d) $R(z) = (z+1)/(z-1)$

**61.** Consider the following two rules, $F$ and $G$, where $F$ is the rule that assigns to each person his or her birth-mother and $G$ is the rule that assigns to each person his or her aunt. Explain why $F$ is a function but $G$ is not.

*In Exercises 62–64, use this definition: A **prime number** is a positive whole number with no factors other than itself and 1. For example, 2, 13, and 37 are primes, but 24 and 39 are not. By convention 1 is not considered prime, so the list of the first few primes is as follows:*

$$2, 3, 5, 7, 11, 13, 17, 19, 23, 29, \ldots$$

**62.** Let $G$ be the rule that assigns to each positive integer the nearest prime. For example, $G(8) = 7$, since 7 is the prime nearest 8. Explain why $G$ is not a function. How could you alter the definition of $G$ to make it a function? *Note*: There is more than one way to do this.

**63.** Let $f$ be the function that assigns to each natural number $x$ the number of primes that are less than or equal to $x$. For example, $f(12) = 5$ because, as you can easily check, five primes are less than or equal to 12. Similarly, $f(3) = 2$, because two primes are less than or equal to 3. Find $f(8)$, $f(10)$, and $f(50)$.

**64. (a)** If $P(x) = x^2 - x + 17$, find $P(1)$, $P(2)$, $P(3)$, and $P(4)$. Can you find a natural number $x$ for which $P(x)$ is not prime?

**(b)** If $Q(x) = x^2 - x + 41$, find $Q(1)$, $Q(2)$, $Q(3)$, and $Q(4)$. Can you find a natural number $x$ for which $Q(x)$ is not prime?

**65.** $\pi = 3.141592653589793 \ldots$ *and so on!*

For each natural number $n$, let $G(n)$ be the digit in the $n$th decimal place of $\pi$. For instance, according to the expression for $\pi$ given above, we have $G(1) = 1$, $G(2) = 4$, and $G(5) = 9$.

**(a)** Use the expression for $\pi$ given above to evaluate $G(10)$ and $G(14)$.

**(b)** Use the Internet to help you evaluate $G(100)$, $G(750)$, and $G(1000)$. *Suggestions*: Using any of the common search engines on the World Wide Web, under the categories of mathematics or science, search for "pi." Here, for example, are two sites that contain the information you need. (They were accessible at the time of this writing, March 2004.)

(University of Exeter)
http://www.ex.ac.uk/cimt/general/pi10000.htm

(The Pi-Search Page)
http://www.angio.net/pi/piquery

**C**

**66.** If $f(x) = mx + b$, show that $\dfrac{f(x_1) + f(x_2)}{2} = f\left(\dfrac{x_1 + x_2}{2}\right)$.

**67.** Let $f(x) = ax^2 + bx + c$, where $a < 0$. Show that $\dfrac{f(x_1) + f(x_2)}{2} \leq f\left(\dfrac{x_1 + x_2}{2}\right)$.

# PROJECT | A PRIME FUNCTION

*Primes fuel cryptography, the technological field behind the secret coding of computer communication as well as communication between governments.* — The Oregonian, June 26, 1999

*. . . the security of large international data networks nowadays relies on the inability of mathematicians to find an efficient method of factoring large numbers (while at the same time being able to produce large primes with ease).* —Keith Devlin, *Mathematics: The New Golden Age* (New York: Columbia University Press, 1999)

*. . . why does a large supercomputer manufacturer like Cray Research invest so much money . . .* [in searching for huge prime numbers]? *The answer is that the computation required . . . is a heavy one, stretching over days or weeks, and so it provides an excellent way to test the efficiency and accuracy of a new computer system.* —Keith Devlin, *op. cit.*

As indicated by the quotes above, prime numbers do have real-world applications. (For the definition of a prime number, see the instructions preceding Exercise 62 on page 143. For a readable explanation of how prime numbers are used in secret codes, refer to Chapter 2 in the book by Keith Devlin cited above.)

In this project you'll work with a function $F$ involving prime numbers: *For each natural number n, let F(n) be the nth prime number.* For instance, since the first, second, third, and fourth primes are 2, 3, 5, and 7, respectively, we have

$$F(1) = 2 \qquad F(2) = 3 \qquad F(3) = 5 \qquad F(4) = 7$$

At the outset, we remark that there is no simple algebraic formula for $F$.

**(a)** After creating a list of the first 40 prime numbers, complete the following table. (Though certainly not conceptually difficult, creating the list takes some time, and each error may throw off your ordering. Therefore, this is a good small-group project; some people should work as checkers.)

| $n$ | 5 | 10 | 20 | 30 | 40 |
|------|---|----|----|----|----|
| $F(n)$ | | | | | |

**(b)** Make use of the Internet or a library to complete the following table.

| $n$ | 100 | 250 | 500 | 750 | 1000 |
|------|-----|-----|-----|-----|------|
| $F(n)$ | | | | | |

*Suggestion*: Using any of the common search engines on the World Wide Web and typing *prime numbers* can lead to websites that have the information you need here. Here are two that were accessible at the time of this writing, March 2004:

> http://www.utm.edu/research/primes
> (University of Tennessee at Martin website)

and

> http://www.svobodat.com/primes

An advantage to the latter site is that a list of primes is available in spreadsheet format, in which it's immediately clear which is the *n*th prime.

**(c)** Although there is no simple algebraic formula for $F$, there are simple functions that do a good job of approximating $F$ along relatively small portions of its domain. For example, look at the graphs in Figures A and B. Figure A shows the graph of $F$ plotted from actual prime number data. Figure B shows the graph of a function $g$ used to model these data:

$$g(n) = 0.0014n^2 + 6.712n - 141.85$$

As you can see, at this scale at least, it's hard to discern any difference between the two functions.

**Figure A**
$F(n) = n$th prime, $1 \leq n \leq 1000$

**Figure B**
$g(n) = 0.0014n^2 + 6.7121n - 141.85,$
$1 \leq n \leq 1000$

Complete the following table to see some examples of how well the function $g$ approximates the $n$th prime. Round the values for $g(n)$ to the nearest integer. Round the percentage error to one decimal place. Recall that percentage error is defined by

$$\left| \frac{(\text{actual value}) - (\text{approximate value})}{\text{actual value}} \right| \times 100$$

| $n$ | 100 | 250 | 500 | 750 | 1000 |
|---|---|---|---|---|---|
| $g(n)$ | | | | | |
| Percentage error in approximation $g(n) \approx F(n)$ | | | | | |

# 3.2   THE GRAPH OF A FUNCTION

*In my own case, I got along fine without knowing the name of the distributive law until my sophomore year in college; meanwhile I had drawn lots of graphs.* —Professor Donald E. Knuth (one of the world's preeminent computer scientists) in *Mathematical People* (Boston: Birkhäuser, 1985)

When the domain and range of a function are sets of real numbers, we can graph the function in the same way that we graphed equations in Chapters 1 and 2. In graphing functions, the usual practice is to reserve the horizontal axis for the independent variable (the inputs) and the vertical axis for the dependent variable (the outputs). In terms of the familiar $x$-$y$ coordinate system, for each $x$-coordinate or input in the domain of the function, the function or rule tells you the corresponding $y$-coordinate or output in the range of the function. These ideas are summarized in the following definition.

---

**DEFINITION** | **Graph of a Function**

The graph of a function $f$ in the $x$-$y$ plane consists of those points $(x, y)$ such that $x$ is in the domain of $f$ and $y = f(x)$. See Figure 1.

**Figure 1**

---

**EXAMPLE** | **1** | **Using the definition of the graph of a function**

In Figures 2(a) and 2(b), specify the $y$-coordinates of the points $P$ and $Q$, respectively. In each case, give an exact expression and also a calculator approximation rounded to two decimal places. (We'll look at the graphs of these two functions in more detail later in this section.)

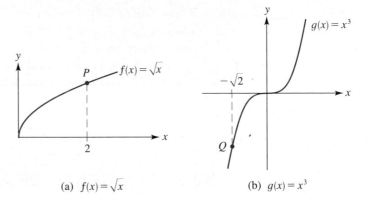

**Figure 2**

What are the $y$-coordinates of the points $P$ and $Q$?

(a) $f(x) = \sqrt{x}$        (b) $g(x) = x^3$

**SOLUTION**

In Figure 2(a), which shows a graph of the function $f$ defined by $f(x) = \sqrt{x}$, the $x$-coordinate of $P$ is 2. The $y$-coordinate is therefore $f(2) = \sqrt{2}$. Using a calculator, we find $\sqrt{2} \approx 1.41$. In Figure 2(b), which shows a graph of the function $g$ defined by $g(x) = x^3$, the $x$-coordinate of $Q$ is $-\sqrt{2}$. The $y$-coordinate is therefore

$$g(-\sqrt{2}) = (-\sqrt{2})^3 = (-\sqrt{2})^2(-\sqrt{2})^1$$
$$= 2(-\sqrt{2}) = -2\sqrt{2}$$
$$\approx -2.82 \qquad \text{using a calculator}$$

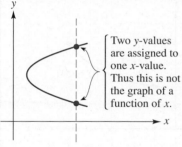

Figure 3

All of the graphs that we looked at in Section 3.1 are graphs of functions. So too are most of the graphs in Chapter 1. However, it's important to understand that not every graph represents a function. Consider, for example, the graph in Figure 3 (the red curve). Figure 3 shows a vertical line intersecting the graph in two distinct points. The specific coordinates of the two points are unimportant. What the vertical line helps us to see is that two different $y$-values (outputs) have been assigned to the same $x$-value (an input), and therefore the graph does not represent a function of $x$. These remarks are generalized in the box that follows.

## Vertical Line Test

A graph in the $x$-$y$ plane represents a function of $x$ provided that any vertical line intersects the graph in at most one point.

---

**EXAMPLE** **2** **Applying the vertical line test**

The vertical line test implies that the graph in Figure 4(a) represents a function and that the graph in Figure 4(b) does not.

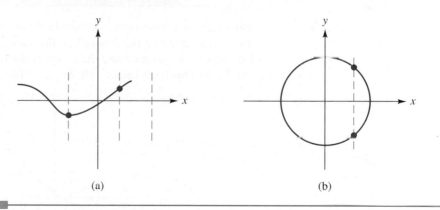

Figure 4        (a)             (b)

In Examples 2 through 4 in the previous section we used algebra to determine the domain and range of functions. If the graph of a function is given, however, we can read off that information directly. The next two examples show instances of this.

---

**EXAMPLE** **3** **Determining the domain and range of a function from its graph**

Specify the domain and the range of the function $g$ graphed in Figure 5(a).

**SOLUTION**
The domain of $g$ is just that portion of the $x$-axis (the inputs) utilized in graphing $g$. As Figure 5(b) indicates, this amounts to all real numbers $x$ from 1 to 5, inclusive: $1 \leq x \leq 5$. In interval notation, this set of numbers is denoted by $[1, 5]$. To find the range of $g$, we need to check which part of the $y$-axis is utilized in graphing $g$. As Figure 5(b) indicates, this is the set of all real numbers $y$

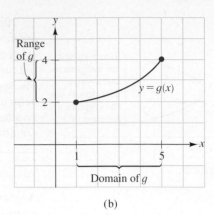

**Figure 5**          (a)                    (b)

between 2 and 4, inclusive: $2 \le y \le 4$. Interval notation for this set of numbers is $[2, 4]$.

**EXAMPLE** **4** **Determining domain, range, and function values from a graph**

The graph of a function $h$ is shown in Figure 6. The open circle in the figure is used to indicate that the point $(3, 3)$ does not belong to the graph of $h$.

**(a)** Specify the domain and the range of the function $h$.

**(b)** Determine each value: **(i)** $h(-2)$; **(ii)** $h(3)$; **(iii)** $|h(-4)|$.

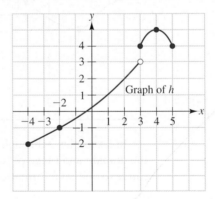

**Figure 6**

**SOLUTION**

**(a)** The domain of $h$ is the interval $[-4, 5]$. The range is the set $[-2, 3) \cup [4, 5]$.

**(b) (i)** The function notation $h(-2)$ stands for the $y$-coordinate of that point on the graph of $h$ whose $x$-coordinate is $-2$. Since the point $(-2, -1)$ is on the graph of $h$, we conclude that $h(-2) = -1$.

**(ii)** We have $h(3) = 4$ because the point $(3, 4)$ lies on the graph of $h$. Note that $h$ would not be considered a function if the point $(3, 3)$ were also part of the graph. (Why?)

**(iii)** Since the point $(-4, -2)$ lies on the graph of $h$, we write $h(-4) = -2$. Thus $|h(-4)| = |-2| = 2$.

Given a function represented by an equation $y = f(x)$, how do we obtain the graph? From Chapter 1 (or from previous courses) we have these three options:

1. Set up a table, plot points, and then draw the line or curve that the points seem to describe.
2. If the equation has the form $y = mx + b$, the graph is a line (as explained in Section 1.6), and we can draw the graph using slope-intercept information.
3. Use a graphing utility.

As a practical matter, option 1 above has a drawback. How many points must we plot before we're sure about the essential features of the graph? In later sections of this text you'll see that there are a number of techniques and concepts that make it unnecessary to plot a large number of points. For now, however, we point out that some functions arise frequently enough to make it worth memorizing the basic shapes and features of their graphs. True, you can always reach for a graphing calculator, but sometimes it helps to be able to think on your feet, so to speak. Also, if you've memorized the graph of a function, then you automatically know the domain and the range. Figure 7 displays the graphs of six basic functions. Exercises 21

(a) The absolute value function
$y = |x|$
Domain: $(-\infty, \infty)$
Range: $[0, \infty)$

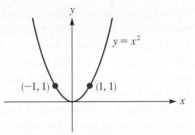

(b) The squaring function
$y = x^2$
Domain: $(-\infty, \infty)$
Range: $[0, \infty)$

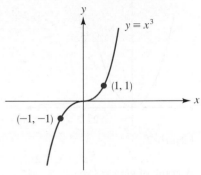

(c) The cubing function
$y = x^3$
Domain: $(-\infty, \infty)$
Range: $(-\infty, \infty)$

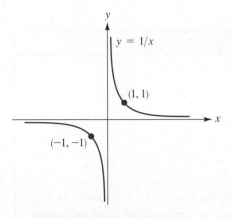

(d) The reciprocal function
$y = 1/x$
Domain: $(-\infty, 0) \cup (0, \infty)$
Range: $(-\infty, 0) \cup (0, \infty)$

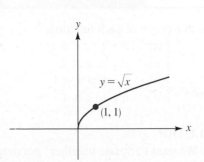

(e) The square root function
$y = \sqrt{x}$
Domain: $[0, \infty)$
Range: $[0, \infty)$

(f) The semicircle function
$y = \sqrt{1 - x^2}$
Domain: $[-1, 1]$
Range: $[0, 1]$

**Figure 7**
The graphs of six basic functions

and 22 at the end of this section ask you to set up tables and verify for yourself that the graphs in Figure 7 are indeed correct. From now on (with the exception of Exercises 21 and 22), if you need to sketch by hand a graph of one of these basic six functions, you should do so from memory.

All the graphs in Figure 7 represent functions defined by rather simple equations. In some instances, however, functions may be defined by different equations on different parts of the domain. This is illustrated in the next two examples, in which we graph *piecewise-defined functions*.

---

**EXAMPLE** | **5** | **Graphing a piecewise-defined function**

A function g is defined by $g(x) = \begin{cases} x^2 & \text{if } x < 2 \\ 1/x & \text{if } x \geq 2 \end{cases}$.

**(a)** Find $g(3/2)$, $g(2)$, and $g(3)$.
**(b)** Sketch the graph of the function g.

**SOLUTION**

**(a)** To find $g(3/2)$, which of the two equation do we use: $g(x) = x^2$ or $g(x) = 1/x$? According to the given inequalities, we should use $g(x) = x^2$ whenever the x-values are less than 2. So for $x = 3/2$ (which is surely less than 2), we have $g(3/2) = (3/2)^2 = 9/4$. On the other hand, the inequalities tell us to use the equation $g(x) = 1/x$ whenever the x-values are greater than or equal to 2. Thus we have $g(2) = 1/2$ and $g(3) = 1/3$.

**(b)** For the graph, we look back at Figures 7(b) and (d) and choose the appropriate portion of each. The result is displayed in Figure 8. The open circle in the figure is used to indicate that the point $(2, 4)$ does not belong to the graph. The filled-in circle, on the other hand, is used to indicate that the point $(2, 1/2)$ does belong to the graph.

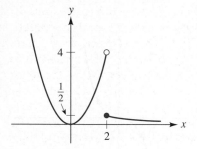

**Figure 8**

A graph of $g(x) = \begin{cases} x^2, & x < 2 \\ \dfrac{1}{x}, & x \geq 2 \end{cases}$

---

**EXAMPLE** | **6**

Sketch a graph of each function:

**(a)** $y = \begin{cases} |x| & \text{if } -1 \leq x \leq 1 \\ \sqrt{x} & \text{if } 1 \leq x \leq 4 \end{cases}$

**(b)** $y = \begin{cases} |x| & \text{if } -1 \leq x < 1 \\ \sqrt{x} & \text{if } 1 < x \leq 4 \end{cases}$

**SOLUTION**

**(a)** We want to "paste together" portions of the graphs of $y = |x|$ and $y = \sqrt{x}$. The appropriate portions of each graph are indicated in color in Figures 9(a) and 9(b). Using Figures 9(a) and 9(b) as a guide, we sketch the required graph in Figure 9(c).

**(b)** Comparing the given equations and inequalities with those in part (a), we see that there is only one difference: in part (b), the number 1 is excluded from the domain of the variable x. To graph the equations in part (b), we

(a) $y = |x|,\ -1 \le x \le 1$    (b) $y = \sqrt{x},\ 1 \le x \le 4$    (c) $y = \begin{cases} |x| & \text{if } -1 \le x \le 1 \\ \sqrt{x} & \text{if } 1 \le x \le 4 \end{cases}$

**Figure 9**

$$y = \begin{cases} |x|, & \text{if } -1 \le x < 1 \\ \sqrt{x}, & \text{if } 1 < x \le 4 \end{cases}$$

**Figure 10**

need only take the graph obtained in Figure 9(c) and delete the point that corresponds to $x = 1$. That is, we delete the point $(1, 1)$; see Figure 10.

It is useful to compare the graphs in Figures 8, 9(c), and 10. Each graph was obtained by combining portions of the basic graphs in Figure 7. In Figures 8 and 10 the graphs have a break or gap in them. We say that the graph (or more precisely, the *function*) in Figure 8 is *discontinuous* when $x - 2$. (The two pieces do not meet at $x = 2$.) The function in Figure 10 is discontinuous when $x = 1$. (There is a gap or missing point when $x = 1$.) In Figure 9(c), however, the two portions of the graph form a graph with no break or gap. We say that the function in Figure 9(c) is *continuous* when $x = 1$. A rigorous definition of continuity is properly a subject for calculus. However, even at the intuitive level at which we've presented the idea here, you'll find that the concept is useful in helping you to organize your thoughts about graphs.

The graph of a piecewise-defined function can also be obtained using a graphing utility. For details, consult the owner's manual that accompanies your calculator or software. We will, however, point out one problem to watch for. In Figure 11(a), we've used a graphing utility to graph the function $g$ from Example 5. Note the extraneous vertical line segment that was generated, connecting what should be two disjoint curves. Not all graphing utilities make this error; but if yours does, it can be corrected by switching the curve-drawing mode from *connected* to *dotted*. See Figure 11(b).

## GRAPHICAL PERSPECTIVE

**Figure 11**

$$g(x) = \begin{cases} x^2 & \text{if } x < 2 \\ 1/x & \text{if } x \ge 2 \end{cases}$$

On a TI-83 graphing calculator, for example, this function $g$ can be entered with the keystrokes $(x < 2)(x^2) + (x \ge 2)(x^{-1})$.

(a) Graphing utility produces an extraneous vertical segment in the graph of $g$.

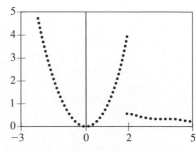

(b) Switching to dot mode eliminates the extraneous segment.

We began this section with a definition of what is meant by the *graph of a function*. The next example uses one of the six basic functions along with the line $y = x$ to help you develop some additional insight into that definition.

---

**EXAMPLE** | **7** | **Applying the definition of the graph of a function**

Figure 12 shows portions of the graphs of the functions $f(x) = \sqrt{x}$ and $y = x$. What are the coordinates of the points $P$, $Q$, and $R$ in Figure 12? (Each dashed line is parallel to one of the coordinate axes.) For those coordinates involving radicals, also supply a calculator approximation rounded to two decimal places.

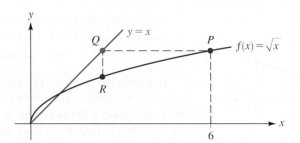

**Figure 12**
What are the coordinates of $P$, $Q$, and $R$?

**SOLUTION**
In Figure 12 the point $P$ lies on the graph of $f(x) = \sqrt{x}$. Since the $x$-coordinate of $P$ is 6, the $y$-coordinate is $f(6)$, which, according to the rule for $f$, is $\sqrt{6}$. Thus the coordinates of $P$ are $(6, \sqrt{6})$. Next, we want the coordinates of $Q$. Figure 12 shows that the points $P$ and $Q$ have the same $y$-coordinate, so the $y$-coordinate of $Q$ must also be $\sqrt{6}$. What about the $x$-coordinate of $Q$? Since $Q$ lies on the graph of $y = x$, the $x$-coordinate of $Q$ must be the same as its $y$-coordinate, namely, $\sqrt{6}$. Thus, the coordinates of $Q$ are $(\sqrt{6}, \sqrt{6})$.

Finally, let us determine the coordinates of the point $R$. According to Figure 12, the $x$-coordinate of $R$ is the same as that of $Q$, which we know to be $\sqrt{6}$. The $y$-coordinate of $R$ is then found by taking the square root of this $x$-coordinate, to obtain $\sqrt{\sqrt{6}}$. (We've used the fact that $R$ lies on the graph of $f(x) = \sqrt{x}$.)

Summarizing now, the required coordinates are as follows. (You should check for yourself that the calculator values given are correct.)

$P$:    $(6, \sqrt{6}) \approx (6, 2.45)$

$Q$:    $(\sqrt{6}, \sqrt{6}) \approx (2.45, 2.45)$

$R$:    $(\sqrt{6}, \sqrt{\sqrt{6}}) \approx (2.45, 1.57)$

# EXERCISE SET 3.2

**A**

*In Exercises 1–4, specify the y-coordinate of the point P on the graph of the given function. In each case, give an exact expression and a calculator approximation rounded to three decimal places.*

**1.**

**2.**

**3.**

**4.**

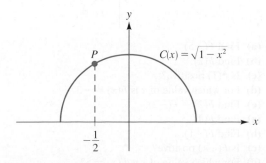

*In Exercises 5 and 6, use the vertical line test to determine whether each graph represents a function of x.*

**5.**

(a)          (b)

(c)          (d)

**6.**

(a)          (b)

(c)          (d)

*In Exercises 7–14, the graph of a function is given. In each case, specify the domain and the range of the function. (The axes are marked off in one-unit intervals.)*

**7.**

**8.**

**9.**

**10.**

**11.**

**12.**

**13.**

**14.**

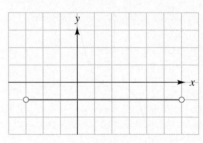

*In Exercises 15 and 16, refer to the graph of the function F in the figure. (Assume that the axes are marked off in one-unit intervals.)*

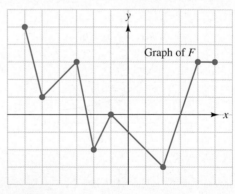

Graph of $F$

**15. (a)** Find $F(-5)$
   **(b)** Find $F(2)$.
   **(c)** Is $F(1)$ positive?
   **(d)** For which value of $x$ is $F(x) = -3$?
   **(e)** Find $F(2) - F(-2)$.
**16. (a)** Find $F(4)$.
   **(b)** Find $F(-1)$.
   **(c)** Is $F(-4)$ positive?
   **(d)** For which value of $x$ is $F(x) = 5$?
   **(e)** Find $F(5) - F(-3)$.

**17.** The following figure displays the graph of a function $f$.

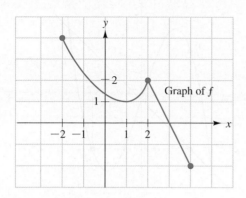

Graph of $f$

**(a)** Is $f(0)$ positive or negative?

**(b)** Find $f(-2), f(1), f(2),$ and $f(3)$.

**(c)** Which is larger, $f(2)$ or $f(4)$?

**(d)** Find $f(4) - f(1)$.

**(e)** Find $|f(4) - f(1)|$.

**(f)** Write the domain and range of $f$ using the interval notation $[a, b]$.

**18.** The following figure shows the graph of a function $h$.

**(a)** Find $h(a), h(b), h(c),$ and $h(d)$.

**(b)** Is $h(0)$ positive or negative?

**(c)** For which values of $x$ does $h(x) = 0$?

**(d)** Which is larger, $h(b)$ or $h(0)$?

**(e)** As $x$ increases from $c$ to $d$, do the corresponding values of $h(x)$ increase or decrease?

**(f)** As $x$ increases from $a$ to $b$, do the corresponding values of $h(x)$ increase or decrease?

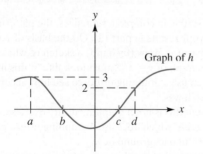

Graph of $h$

*In Exercises 19 and 20, refer to the graphs of the functions $f$ and $g$ in the figure. Assume that the domain of each function is $[-3, 3]$ and that the axes are marked off in one-unit intervals.*

**19. (a)** Which is larger, $f(-2)$ or $g(-2)$?

**(b)** Compute $f(0) - g(0)$.

**(c)** Which among the following three quantities is the smallest?

$$f(1) - g(1) \qquad f(2) - g(2) \qquad f(3) - g(3)$$

**(d)** For which value(s) of $x$ does $g(x) = f(1)$?

**(e)** Is the number 4 in the range of $f$ or in the range of $g$?

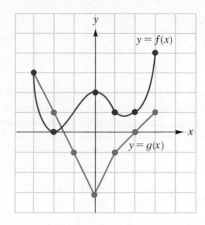

$y = f(x)$

$y = g(x)$

**20. (a)** For the interval $[0, 3]$, is the quantity $g(x) - f(x)$ positive or negative?

**(b)** For the interval $(-3, -2)$, is the quantity $g(x) - f(x)$ positive or negative?

*In Exercises 21 and 22, set up a table and graph each function. [In Exercises 22(b) and 22(c), use a calculator to compute the square roots.]*

**21. (a)** $y = |x|$

**(b)** $y = x^2$

**(c)** $y = x^3$

**22. (a)** $y = 1/x$

**(b)** $y = \sqrt{x}$

**(c)** $y = \sqrt{1 - x^2}$

*In Exercises 23–30, sketch the graphs, as in Examples 5 and 6.*

**23.** $A(x) = \begin{cases} x^3 & \text{if } -2 \le x \le -1 \\ x^2 & \text{if } x > -1 \end{cases}$

**24.** $B(x) = \begin{cases} \sqrt{1 - x^2} & \text{if } -1 \le x < 1 \\ 1/x & \text{if } x \ge 1 \end{cases}$

**25.** $C(x) = \begin{cases} x^3 & \text{if } x < 1 \\ \sqrt{x} & \text{if } x > 1 \end{cases}$

**26.** $y = \begin{cases} |x| & \text{if } x \le 0 \\ x^2 & \text{if } x > 0 \end{cases}$

**27. (a)** $y = \begin{cases} \sqrt{x} & \text{if } 0 \le x \le 1 \\ 1/x & \text{if } 1 < x < 2 \end{cases}$

**(b)** $y = \begin{cases} \sqrt{x} & \text{if } 0 \le x < 1 \\ 1/x & \text{if } 1 < x < 2 \end{cases}$

**28. (a)** $y = \begin{cases} x^3 & \text{if } x \le 0 \\ |x| & \text{if } x > 0 \end{cases}$

**(b)** $y = \begin{cases} |x| & \text{if } x \le 0 \\ x^3 & \text{if } x > 0 \end{cases}$

**29. (a)** $y = \begin{cases} \sqrt{1 - x^2} & \text{if } -1 \le x \le 0 \\ x^2 & \text{if } 0 < x \le 2 \end{cases}$

**(b)** $y = \begin{cases} \sqrt{1 - x^2} & \text{if } -1 \le x < 0 \\ x^2 & \text{if } 0 < x \le 2 \end{cases}$

30. $y = \begin{cases} x^3 & \text{if } -1 \leq x < 0 \\ \sqrt{x} & \text{if } 0 \leq x < 1 \\ 1/x & \text{if } 1 \leq x \leq 3 \end{cases}$

Ⓖ In Exercises 31 and 32, use a graphing utility to obtain the graphs of the piecewise-defined functions. If there are cases in which the graphing utility generates extraneous segments, use the dot mode to correct the situation.

31. (a) $f(x) = \begin{cases} x^3 - x & \text{if } -1 \leq x < 0 \\ x^3 + x & \text{if } 0 \leq x \leq 1 \end{cases}$

(b) $g(x) = \begin{cases} x^3 - x & \text{if } -1 \leq x < 0 \\ x^3 + x + 1 & \text{if } 0 \leq x \leq 1 \end{cases}$

32. (a) $h(x) = \begin{cases} \sqrt{1 - x^6} & \text{if } -1 \leq x < 1 \\ \sqrt{1 - (x - 2)^6} & \text{if } 1 \leq x \leq 3 \end{cases}$

(b) $k(x) = \begin{cases} \sqrt{1 - x^6} & \text{if } -1 \leq x < 1 \\ \sqrt{1 - (x - 2)^6} + 3 & \text{if } 1 \leq x \leq 3 \end{cases}$

In Exercises 33–36, determine the coordinates of the points P, Q, and R in each figure; give an exact expression and also a calculator approximation rounded to three decimal places. Assume that each dashed line is parallel to one of the coordinate axes. (In Exercise 36, note that the line is $y = x/2$ rather than $y = x$.)

33.

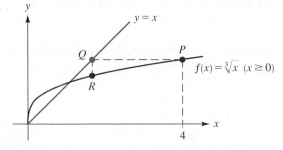

$y = x$

$f(x) = \sqrt[3]{x}$ $(x \geq 0)$

34.

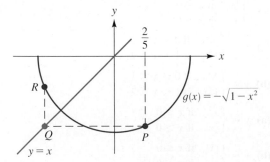

$g(x) = -\sqrt{1 - x^2}$

$y = x$

35.

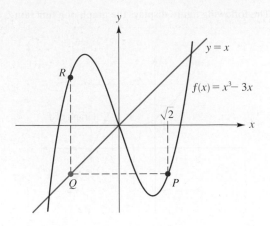

$y = x$

$f(x) = x^3 - 3x$

36.

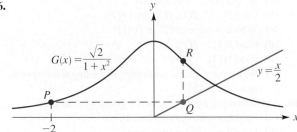

$G(x) = \dfrac{\sqrt{2}}{1 + x^2}$

$y = \dfrac{x}{2}$

**B**

Ⓖ 37. (a) Graph each of the following functions on the same screen, using the viewing rectangle $[0, 1, 0.2] \times [0, 1, 0.2]$.

$y = x$ $\quad y = x^2$ $\quad y = x^3$ $\quad y = x^4$ $\quad y = x^5$

(b) Describe, in complete sentences, the pattern you see in your results in part (a). On the basis of your results in part (a), draw (by hand) a sketch of what you think the graph of $y = x^{100}$ must look like in this interval. Then use a graphing utility to see how accurate your sketch was.

38. (Although this is not a graphing utility exercise, the previous exercise, which does use a graphing utility, provides some useful background here.)

(a) Suppose that the thickness of the line drawn by your pencil or pen is 0.05 cm, and suppose that the common unit of length marked off along both axes is 1 cm. Under these drawing conditions, where is the graph of $y = x^2$ indistinguishable from the x-axis? That is, for which x-values will the corresponding y-values be less than 0.05?

(b) Follow part (a), using $y = x^4$ instead of $y = x^2$.

# PROJECT

## IMPLICIT FUNCTIONS: BATTERIES REQUIRED?

From Chapter 1 we know that the graph of the equation $x^2 + y^2 = 1$ is a circle, as shown in Figure A. From our work in this section, we know the graph does not represent a function. However, certain pieces of the graph do represent functions. In particular, solving the equation for $y$ yields $y = \pm\sqrt{1 - x^2}$. Figures B and C show the graphs of $y = \sqrt{1 - x^2}$ and $y = -\sqrt{1 - x^2}$, respectively. Note that the graphs in Figures B and C indeed represent functions. We say that the initial equation $x^2 + y^2 = 1$ defines these functions *implicitly,* whereas each of the equations $y = \sqrt{1 - x^2}$ and $y = -\sqrt{1 - x^2}$ defines a function *explicitly.*

**Figure A**
$x^2 + y^2 = 1$

**Figure B**
$y = \sqrt{1 - x^2}$

**Figure C**
$y = -\sqrt{1 - x^2}$

Here's another example of this terminology. One of the basic functions in Figure 7 on page 149 is defined by the equation $y = 1/x$. In this form, the function is defined explicitly. If the equation is given in the equivalent form $xy = 1$, then the function is defined implicitly.

The reason we ask "Batteries Required?" in the title of this project is that a graphing calculator or a computer is often the option of choice in graphing implicitly defined functions. In some cases, it's the only option (assuming the tools of calculus are not at our disposal). As examples, consider the two equations graphed in Figures D and E. We'll talk about how these graphs were obtained.

**Figure D**
$x^2 + xy + y^2 = 1$
$[-2, 2, 2]$ by $[-2, 2, 2]$

**Figure E**
$x^2 + xy^3 + y^2 = 1$
$[-3, 3, 3]$ by $[-3, 3, 3]$

For Figure D we can rewrite the equation in the form $y^2 + xy + (x^2 - 1) = 0$. In this form, the quadratic formula can be used to solve for $y$ in terms of $x$. As you should check for yourself (using $a = 1$, $b = x$, and $c = x^2 - 1$), the result is $y = \frac{1}{2}(-x \pm \sqrt{4 - 3x^2})$. The graph of $x^2 + xy + y^2 = 1$ is now obtained by using a graphing utility to graph the *two* explicit functions,

$$y_1 = \frac{-x + \sqrt{4 - 3x^2}}{2} \quad \text{and} \quad y_1 = \frac{-x - \sqrt{4 - 3x^2}}{2}$$

In Figure E the equation cannot be solved for $y$ in terms of $x$ by elementary means. (Try it!) Furthermore, as of this writing, most graphing calculators require that functions be entered in explicit rather than implicit form. The graph in Figure E was obtained by using a computer with commercial software that doesn't necessarily require the function to be in explicit form. (Three examples of such software are *Maple*, *Mathematica*, and *LiveMath Maker*.)

## EXERCISES

*For Exercises 1–10, each equation defines one or more functions implicitly. Solve the equation for $y$ to determine explicit equations for the functions. Then use a graphing calculator or a computer to obtain the graph of the original equation.*

*For Exercises 11–14, if you have access to a computer with appropriate software, graph the given equation. Otherwise, you can look up the general form of the graph at the University of St. Andrews MacTutor website:*

http://www-groups.dcs.st-and.ac.uk/~history/Curves/Curves.html

*(Actually, in Exercises 11–13, the equations can be solved for $y$ explicitly, using elementary means, and then a graphing calculator could be used. But we are not asking for that here.)*

1. $xy = 0.1x^3 - 2x^2 - 3x - 4$   (*trident of Newton*)
2. $x^4 - 10(x^2 - y^2) = 0$   (*figure eight curve*)
3. $x^2 y + 4y - 36x = 0$   (*serpentine*)
4. $9x^2 + 16y^2 = 144$   (*ellipse*)
5. $y^2(x^2 + y^2) = 9x^2$   (*kappa curve*)
6. $9y^2 = x^3(6 - x)$   (*pear-shaped quartic*)
7. $3y^2 = x(x - 1)^2$   (*Tschirnhaus' cubic*)
8. $(x - 3)^2(x^2 + y^2) = 8x^2$   (*conchoid*)
9. $4y^2 = x(x^2 - 2x - 10)$   (*Newton's diverging parabolas*)
10. $y^2(7 - x) = x^3$   (*cissoid of Diocles*)
11. $y^2(1 - x^2) = (x^2 + 2y - 1)^2$   (*bicorn*)
12. $(x^2 + y^2 - 2x)^2 = x^2 + y^2$   (*limaçon of Pascal*)
13. $(x^2 + y^2)^2 - 8x(x^2 - 3y^2) + 18(x^2 + y^2) = 27$   (*deltoid*)
14. $x^3 + y^3 = 3xy$   (*folium of Descartes*)

# 3.3 SHAPES OF GRAPHS. AVERAGE RATE OF CHANGE

In many applications, one of the most basic questions regarding a function is this: What are the highest and lowest points (if any) on the graph? We'll use the graph of the function $G$ in Figure 1 to introduce some terminology that is useful here.

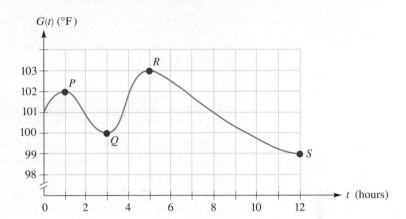

**Figure 1**
The graph of the function $G$ is a fever graph: $G(t)$ is a patient's temperature $t$ hours after midnight, where $0 \leq t \leq 12$.

In the figure, each of the points, $P$, $Q$, and $R$ is called a *turning point*. At a **turning point,** a graph changes from rising to falling, or vice versa. In Figure 1, the point $R$, with coordinates $(5, 103)$, is the highest point on the graph of the function $G$. We say that the *maximum value* of the function $G$ is 103, and this maximum occurs at $t = 5$. In terms of the temperature interpretation (described in the caption for Figure 1), the patient's temperature reaches a maximum of 103°F, and this maximum occurs 5 hours after midnight. More generally, we say that a number $f(x_0)$ is the **maximum value** of a function $f$ if the inequality $f(x_0) \geq f(x)$ holds for every $x$ in the domain of $f$. Minimum values are defined similarly: $f(x_0)$ is the **minimum value** for a function $f$ if the inequality $f(x_0) \leq f(x)$ holds for every $x$ in the domain of $f$. Assuming that the domain of the function in Figure 1 is $[0, 12]$, the minimum value of the function $G$ is 99 and it occurs at $t = 12$. (How would you express this in terms of the temperature interpretation?) *Caution:* Not every function has a maximum or minimum value. See Figure 2 for an example.

Returning to Figure 1, there are two time intervals when the patient's temperature is rising: from midnight to 1 A.M. and from 3 A.M. to 5 A.M. We say that the function $G$ is *increasing* on each of the intervals $[0, 1]$ and $[3, 5]$. Similarly (again looking at the graph), the patient's temperature is falling from 1 A.M. to 3 A.M. and again from 5 A.M. to 12 noon. We say that the function $G$ is *decreasing* on each of the intervals $[1, 3]$ and $[5, 12]$. For another example of this terminology, look at the graph of $f(x) = x^2$ in Figure 2. The function is decreasing on the interval $(-\infty, 0]$ and increasing on the interval $[0, \infty)$. For analytical work involving functions, the terms increasing and decreasing are defined in terms of inequalities. A function $f$ is **increasing** on an interval provided the following condition holds: For all pairs of numbers $a$ and $b$ in the interval, if $a < b$, then $f(a) < f(b)$. Similarly, a function $f$ is **decreasing** on an interval if the following condition holds: For all pairs of numbers $a$ and $b$ in the interval, if $a < b$, then $f(a) > f(b)$.

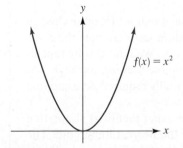

**Figure 2**
There is no maximum value for the function $f$ defined by $f(x) = x^2$, assuming that the domain is $(-\infty, \infty)$. The minimum value of the function is 0, and it occurs at $x = 0$.

In general, for functions defined by equations, the techniques of calculus are required to compute exact coordinates for turning points, maximum or minimum values, and intervals where the function is increasing or decreasing. However, these quantities can be easily approximated by using a graphing utility to zoom in on the turning points. We do this in Example 1. *Technology note*: On a graphing calculator, the TRACE key can be used in conjunction with a ZOOM key to facilitate this process. Alternatively, graphing calculators have MIN and MAX operations that produce very accurate approximations for the minimum or maximum value of a function within any interval that the user requests. For details refer to the owner's manual that came with your calculator. *Algebra note*: In Sections 4.2 and 4.5 you'll see that in certain cases we can use the methods of algebra to compute *exact* maximum and minimum values.

---

**EXAMPLE** | **1** | **Approximating the coordinates of a turning point**

In Figure 3 a graphing utility was used to generate a graph of the function $f$ defined by $f(x) = x^4 - 6x$. Assume that the chosen viewing rectangle shows all the essential features of the graph. Use a graphing utility to estimate to the nearest hundredth the coordinates of the turning point. What are the corresponding estimates for the minimum value of the function and the intervals where the function is increasing or decreasing?

**GRAPHICAL PERSPECTIVE**

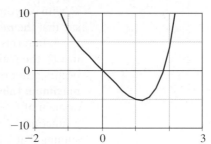

**Figure 3**
$f(x) = x^4 - 6x$
$[-2, 3, 1]$ by $[-10, 10, 5]$

**SOLUTION**
According to Figure 3, the turning point is located in quadrant IV, quite close to the point $(1, -5)$. Our goal is to obtain views that allow us to estimate the coordinates of the turning point to the nearest hundredth. We'll do this by repeatedly zooming in and, when appropriate, fine-tuning the viewing rectangle. At the outset, we remark that some trial and error is usually required here and that many different approaches are possible.

The view obtained in Figure 4(a) (after some experimenting) shows that the $y$-coordinate of the turning point is $-5.15$, to the nearest hundredth. The $x$-coordinate appears to be something between 1.14 and 1.15, but evidently we need a closer look to say whether it's nearer to 1.14 or 1.15. With that in mind, we try adjusting the $x$-specifications of the viewing rectangle so that $x$ runs from 1.140 to 1.150.

As indicated in Figure 4(b), however, adjusting only the $x$-specifications isn't very helpful; much more magnification in the $y$-direction is required. [Are you

## GRAPHICAL PERSPECTIVE

(a) [1.10, 1.20, 0.01] by
[−5.16, −5.12, 0.01]

(b) [1.140, 1.150, 0.002] by
[−5.16, −5.12, 0.01]

(c) [1.142, 1.148, 0.005] by
[−5.15125, −5.15115, 0.00005]

**Figure 4**
Three views of $f(x) = x^4 - 6x$

surprised by the seemingly horizontal line obtained in Figure 4(b)? We'll say more about it after this example.] In Figure 4(c), after more zooming and then fine-tuning of the viewing rectangle, we finally are able to see that the $x$-coordinate of the turning point is closer to 1.14 than to 1.15 (because it is to the *left* of 1.145).

In summary now, to the nearest hundredth, the coordinates of the turning point are (1.14, −5.15). Thus our *estimates* for the minimum value and intervals of increase or decrease are as follows:

$$\text{minimum value of } f: \quad -5.15$$
$$f \text{ is decreasing on:} \quad (-\infty, 1.14]$$
$$f \text{ is increasing on:} \quad [1.14, \infty)$$

**AFTERWORD ON ZOOMING FOR TURNING POINTS**   In the process of try-ing to estimate the coordinates of the turning point in Example 1, we produced the view in Figure 4(b), which seems to show a horizontal line segment rather than a curve. This is actually a common occurrence when zooming in on turning points. There are two factors at work here, one having to do with the actual shape of the graph, the other with the limitations of the display screen and technology. For many types of functions, including those defined by polynomial expressions (as in Ex-ample 1), the graph does very closely resemble a horizontal line in the immediate vicinity of a turning point. We say "resemble" here because the "true" graph, as opposed to the approximation displayed on your calculator or computer screen, is slightly curved. Remember that the calculator display or the computer screen has only a finite number of dots or *pixels* with which to display a graph. Thus, in general, the display on the screen must necessarily be an approximation, because the true graph contains infinitely many points (one point for each $x$-value in the domain). In Figure 4(b), the calculator display shows a horizontal segment because, evidently, the actual curve differs from the horizontal segment by less than one pixel.

We can use the temperature graph in Figure 1 (on page 159) to introduce an-other important concept relating to functions. According to Figure 1, the patient's temperature is increasing from midnight to 1 A.M. and again from 3 A.M. to 5 A.M. During which of these two time intervals is the temperature increasing faster? That is, how can we measure the *rate* at which the temperature is rising during a given time interval? Similarly, how can we measure and thereby compare the rates at which the temperature is falling during the time intervals from 1 A.M. to 3 A.M. and from 5 A.M. to 12 noon? One way to measure this is to use the *average rate of change,* which we define in the box that follows. (In Example 3 we'll answer the questions raised in this paragraph regarding the temperature graph.)

---

**DEFINITION** | **The Average Rate of Change of a Function**

Refer to Figure 5. The **average rate of change** of a function $f$ on the interval $[a, b]$ is the slope of the line joining the two points $(a, f(a))$ and $(b, f(b))$. If $y = f(x)$, the average rate of change is denoted by $\Delta y/\Delta x$ or $\Delta f/\Delta x$ and we have

$$\frac{\Delta y}{\Delta x} = \frac{f(b) - f(a)}{b - a}$$

**Figure 5**

---

**EXAMPLE** **2** **Computing and comparing average rates of change**

Compute and compare the average rates of change for the function $f(x) = x^2$ on the following intervals:
**(a)** $[-2, 0]$;     **(b)** $[0, 1]$;     **(c)** $[1, 2]$.

**SOLUTION**

**(a)** On $[-2, 0]$:    $\dfrac{\Delta f}{\Delta x} = \dfrac{f(0) - f(-2)}{0 - (-2)} = \dfrac{0^2 - (-2)^2}{2} = -2$

**(b)** On $[0, 1]$:    $\dfrac{\Delta f}{\Delta x} = \dfrac{f(1) - f(0)}{1 - 0} = \dfrac{1^2 - 0^2}{1} = 1$

**(c)** On $[1, 2]$:    $\dfrac{\Delta f}{\Delta x} = \dfrac{f(2) - f(1)}{2 - 1} = \dfrac{2^2 - 1^2}{1} = 3$

(Refer to Figure 6.) On the interval $[-2, 0]$ the function is decreasing, and the average rate of change is negative. On both of the intervals $[0, 1]$ and $[1, 2]$ the function is increasing, and the average rates of change are positive. The graph rises more steeply on the interval $[1, 2]$ than on $[0, 1]$, and correspondingly, the average rate of change is greater for the interval $[1, 2]$ than for $[0, 1]$.

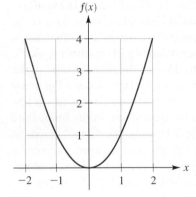

**Figure 6**
$f(x) = x^2$

A WORD OF CAUTION   Like other types of averages occurring in arithmetic and statistics, the average rate of change can mask or hide some details. For instance, the fact that the average rate of change is positive on an interval does not guarantee that the function is increasing throughout that interval. For example, look back at Figure 5; for the function shown there, the average rate of change on $[a, b]$ is positive (because the slope of the solid blue line is positive). The function, however, is increasing only on a portion of $[a, b]$, not throughout the entire interval.

| EXAMPLE | 3 | Computing and interpreting average rates of change |
| --- | --- | --- |

Compute and compare the average rates of change for the patient's temperature function $G$ in Figure 1 (page 159) on each of the following pairs of intervals. Keep track of the units in the computations.

**(a)** $t = 0$ to $t = 1$ hr and $t = 3$ to $t = 5$ hr
**(b)** $t = 1$ to $t = 3$ hr and $t = 5$ to $t = 12$ hr

**SOLUTION**
**(a)** On the interval $t = 0$ to $t = 1$ hr:

$$\frac{\Delta G}{\Delta t} = \frac{G(1) - G(0)}{1 - 0}$$

$$= \frac{102° - 101°}{1 \text{ hr}} \qquad \text{reading the coordinates from the graph in Figure 1}$$

$$= \frac{1°}{1 \text{ hr}} = 1 \text{ degree/hr}$$

Similarly, on the interval $t = 3$ to $t = 5$ hr, we have

$$\frac{\Delta G}{\Delta t} = \frac{G(5) - G(3)}{5 - 3}$$

$$= \frac{103° - 100°}{2 \text{ hr}} = \frac{3°}{2 \text{ hr}} = 1.5 \text{ degrees/hr}$$

The calculations we've just made show that, on average, the temperature is increasing slightly faster from 3 A.M. to 5 A.M. than it is from midnight to 1 A.M. This is consistent with the graph in Figure 1: The curve looks slightly steeper from 3 A.M. to 5 A.M. than from midnight to 1 A.M.

**(b)** Before computing, let us note that both answers will be negative here because the graph shows the function is decreasing throughout each of the given intervals.

On the interval $t = 1$ to $t = 3$ hr:

$$\frac{\Delta G}{\Delta t} = \frac{G(3) - G(1)}{3 - 1}$$

$$= \frac{100° - 102°}{2 \text{ hr}} = \frac{-2°}{2 \text{ hr}} = -1 \text{ degree/hr}$$

On the interval $t = 5$ to $t = 12$ hr:

$$\frac{\Delta G}{\Delta t} = \frac{G(12) - G(5)}{12 - 5}$$

$$= \frac{99° - 103°}{7 \text{ hr}} = \frac{-4°}{7 \text{ hr}} = -\frac{4}{7} \text{ degree/hr} \approx -0.6 \text{ degree/hr}$$

These answers tell us that, on average, the patient's temperature is dropping faster between 1 A.M. and 3 A.M. than it is between 5 A.M. and noon. Again, this is consistent with what we see in Figure 1: The portion of the curve between points $P$ and $Q$ appears to be steeper, in general, than that between $R$ and $S$.

**Figure 7**

For an example using the average rate of change in a different context, consider the function $s$ represented in Figure 7, with defining equation $s(t) = 16t^2$, and $t \geq 0$. This function relates the distance $s(t)$ and the time $t$ for an object falling in a vacuum. Here $t$ is measured in seconds, $s(t)$ is in feet, and $t = 0$ corresponds to the instant that the object begins to fall. For instance, after 1 sec, the object falls a distance of $s(1) = 16(1)^2 = 16$ ft. After 2 sec, the total distance will be $s(2) = 16(2)^2 = 64$ ft. Let's calculate the average rate of change of this function from, say, $t = 1$ to $t = 3$ sec. As in the temperature example, we'll keep track of the units. We have

$$\frac{\Delta s}{\Delta t} = \frac{s(3) - s(1)}{3 - 1}$$

$$= \frac{16(3)^2 \text{ ft} - 16(1)^2 \text{ ft}}{2 \text{ sec}} = \frac{128 \text{ ft}}{2 \text{ sec}} = 64 \text{ ft/sec}$$

Notice that the units here have the form *distance per unit time*. So in this case $\Delta s/\Delta t$ gives us the *average velocity* of the object. More generally, whenever we have a function expressing distance $s(t)$ in terms of time $t$, the **average velocity** over an interval is defined to be the average rate of change $\Delta s/\Delta t$ over that interval. We'll return to this idea in Example 6 at the end of this section.

Let's talk for a moment about notation. We defined the average rate of change of a function $f$ on the interval $[a, b]$ to be the quantity

$$\frac{f(b) - f(a)}{b - a} \qquad (1)$$

If, instead of $[a, b]$, we have the interval $[a, x]$, then, by definition, the average rate of change is

$$\frac{f(x) - f(a)}{x - a} \qquad (2)$$

**Figure 8**
The closed interval $[x, x + h]$

Finally, if the interval is $[x, x + h]$ as displayed in Figure 8, then the average rate of change is $\dfrac{f(x + h) - f(x)}{(x + h) - x}$, which simplifies to

$$\frac{f(x + h) - f(x)}{h} \qquad (3)$$

Each of the algebraic expressions given in (1), (2), or (3) is known as a **difference quotient.** (But whatever the name, remember, it represents an average rate of change.) Our last three examples for this section show how difference quotients can be simplified once a specific function is given. (This skill is required in calculus when studying rates of change.)

---

**EXAMPLE 4** Simplifying difference quotients of the form $\dfrac{f(x) - f(a)}{x - a}$

**(a)** If $f(x) = x^2$, find $\dfrac{f(x) - f(5)}{x - 5}$.

**(b)** If $g(x) = x^2 + 3x$, find $\dfrac{g(x) - g(a)}{x - a}$.

**SOLUTION**

**PRELIMINARY NOTE**    The solutions that follow make use of factoring techniques from intermediate algebra. If you find that you need a review of this topic, either now or in working the exercises, refer to Appendix B.4 at the back of this book.

**(a)** $\dfrac{f(x) - f(5)}{x - 5} = \dfrac{x^2 - 5^2}{x - 5}$

$\qquad\qquad = \dfrac{(x - 5)(x + 5)}{x - 5}$    using difference of squares factoring

$\qquad\qquad = x + 5$    simplifying

**(b)** Since $g(x) = x^2 + 3x$ and $g(a) = a^2 + 3a$, we have

$\dfrac{g(x) - g(a)}{x - a} = \dfrac{(x^2 + 3x) - (a^2 + 3a)}{x - a} = \dfrac{x^2 + 3x - a^2 - 3a}{x - a}$

$\qquad\qquad = \dfrac{x^2 - a^2 + 3x - 3a}{x - a}$    rearranging

$\qquad\qquad = \dfrac{(x - a)(x + a) + 3(x - a)}{x - a}$

$\qquad\qquad = \dfrac{(x - a)[(x + a) + 3]}{x - a}$    factoring by grouping

$\qquad\qquad = x + a + 3$    simplifying

---

**EXAMPLE    5**    **Simplifying a difference quotient of the form**
$$\dfrac{f(x + h) - f(x)}{h}$$

---

Let $f(x) = 2/x$. Find $\dfrac{f(x + h) - f(x)}{h}$.

**SOLUTION**

We have $\dfrac{f(x + h) - f(x)}{h} = \dfrac{\dfrac{2}{x + h} - \dfrac{2}{x}}{h}$. This last expression needs to be simplified because the numerator itself contains fractions. An easy way to simplify here is to multiply by $\dfrac{x(x + h)}{x(x + h)}$, which equals 1. This yields

$\dfrac{f(x + h) - f(x)}{h} = \dfrac{x(x + h)}{x(x + h)} \cdot \dfrac{\dfrac{2}{x + h} - \dfrac{2}{x}}{h}$

$\qquad\qquad = \dfrac{2x - 2(x + h)}{xh(x + h)}$

$\qquad\qquad = \dfrac{2x - 2x - 2h}{xh(x + h)} = \dfrac{-2h}{xh(x + h)}$

$\qquad\qquad = \dfrac{-2}{x(x + h)}$

| EXAMPLE | 6 | Computing average velocity |

Refer to the distance function $s$ in Figure 7, $s = 16t^2$.
**(a)** Find a general expression for the average velocity $\Delta s/\Delta t$ over the interval $[1, 1 + h]$.
**(b)** Use the result in part (a) to complete the following table.

| $h$ (seconds) | Average velocity $\Delta s/\Delta t$ on the interval $[1, 1 + h]$ (feet/second) |
|---|---|
| 1.0 | |
| 0.5 | |
| 0.1 | |

**SOLUTION**
**(a)** On the interval $[1, 1 + h]$ we have

$$\frac{\Delta s}{\Delta t} = \frac{16(1 + h)^2 - 16(1)^2}{(1 + h) - 1}$$

$$= \frac{16 + 32h + 16h^2 - 16}{h} = \frac{32h + 16h^2}{h}$$

$$= \frac{16h(2 + h)}{h} = 16(2 + h) = 32 + 16h$$

**(b)** From part (a) we have $\Delta s/\Delta t = 32 + 16h$. Using this result, we complete the required table as follows.

| $h$ (seconds) | Average velocity $\Delta s/\Delta t$ on the interval $[1, 1 + h]$ (feet/second) |
|---|---|
| 1.0 | $32 + 16(1) = 48$ |
| 0.5 | $32 + 16(0.5) = 40$ |
| 0.1 | $32 + 16(0.1) = 33.6$ |

**NOTE**   Exercise 36 asks you to carry out these calculations several steps further, using shorter and shorter time intervals. In calculus, this procedure leads to the concept of *instantaneous* (as opposed to *average*) *velocity*.

# EXERCISE SET 3.3

**A**

1. Using the functions in Figure 7 on page 149 for example, explain what is meant by each of the following. Your answers should be in complete sentences.
   (a) turning point
   (b) maximum value
   (c) minimum value
   (d) $f$ is increasing on an interval.
   (e) $f$ is decreasing on an interval.
2. What is the definition of the average rate of change of a function $g$ on an interval $[c, d]$? What does this have to do with slope?

*In Exercises 3–6, you are given functions with domain* [0, 4].
*Specify:*
**(a)** *the range of each function;*
**(b)** *the maximum value of the function;*
**(c)** *the minimum value of the function;*
**(d)** *interval(s) where the function is increasing; and*
**(e)** *interval(s) where the function is decreasing.*

**3.**

**4.**

**5.**

**6.**

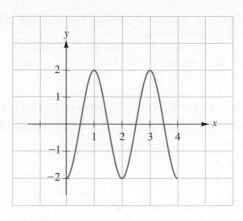

Ⓖ **7.** Assume that the accompanying viewing rectangle shows the essential features of the graph of $f(x) = x^3 - 4x - 2$. Use a graphing utility to estimate to the nearest hundredth the coordinates of the turning points. What are the corresponding estimates for the intervals where the function is increasing or decreasing?

$$f(x) = x^3 - 4x - 2$$
$$[-4, 4, 2] \text{ by } [-12, 12, 6]$$

**8.** Assume that the accompanying viewing rectangle shows the essential features of the graph of $f(x) = -x^4 + 3x + 5$. Use a graphing utility to estimate to the nearest hundredth the coordinates of the turning point. What is the corresponding estimate for the maximum value of the function? Estimate the intervals where the function is increasing or decreasing.

$$f(x) = -x^4 + 3x + 5$$
$$[-3, 3, 3] \text{ by } [-10, 10, 5]$$

*In Exercises 9–14, compute the average rate of change of the function on the given interval.*

**9.** $f(x) = x^2 + 2x$ on $[3, 5]$    **10.** $f(x) = \sqrt{x}$ on $[4, 9]$

**11.** $g(x) = 2x^2 - 4x$ on $[-1, 3]$   **12.** $g(x) = x^3 - x$ on $[1, 2]$

**13.** $h(t) = 2t - 6$ on $[5, 12]$

**14.** $h(t) = 16 - 7t$ on $[-\sqrt{2}, 2\sqrt{2}]$

**15.** The following graph shows the temperature $G(t)$ of a solution during the first 8 minutes of a chemistry experiment.

Compute the average rate of change of temperature, $\Delta G/\Delta t$, over the following intervals. (Be sure to specify the units as part of each answer.)

**(a)** $t = 0$ min to $t = 3$ min

**(b)** $t = 3$ min to $t = 6$ min

**(c)** $t = 6$ min to $t = 8$ min

**16.** Iodine-131 is a radioactive substance. The accompanying graph shows how an initial one-gram sample decays over a 32-day period; $f(t)$ represents the number of grams present after $t$ days.

**(a)** Compute $\Delta f/\Delta t$ over each of the following intervals: $t = 0$ days to $t = 8$ days; $t = 8$ days to $t = 16$ days; $t = 16$ days to $t = 24$ days; $t = 24$ days to $t = 32$ days. (Be sure to specify the units with each answer.)

**(b)** Find the average of the four answers in part (a).

**(c)** Compute $\Delta f/\Delta t$ over the interval from $t = 0$ to $t = 32$. Is the answer the same as that obtained in part (b)?

*For Exercises 17 and 18, let $y = P(t)$ denote the percentage of U.S. households in the year $t$ with at least one VCR (video cassette recorder). The following figure shows a graph of this function $P$ over the period $1978 \le t \le 1997$.*

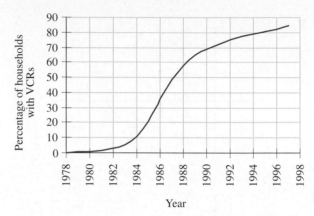

Year

*Source of data used to create graph:* A. C. Nielsen and Nielsen Media Research

**17. (a)** According to the graph, is $\Delta P/\Delta t$ greater over the period 1978–1984 or over the period 1984–1990? After answering, use rough numerical values obtained from the graph to calculate estimates for these two rates of change. Include units with answers.

**(b)** Using the following data, compute $\Delta P/\Delta t$ for the periods mentioned in part (a). Round the answers to one decimal place. $P(1978) = 0.3\%$; $P(1984) = 10.6\%$; $P(1990) = 68.6\%$.

**18. (a)** In the given graph (or in a photocopy), use a ruler to draw two line segments, one connecting the two points $(1978, P(1978))$ and $(1988, P(1988))$, the other connecting the two points $(1984, P(1984))$ and $(1997, P(1997))$. You'll find that the two line segments appear to be parallel (or nearly so). Now complete the following sentence (concerning $\Delta P/\Delta t$ on the two intervals $1978 \le t \le 1988$ and $1984 \le t \le 1997$). Because parallel lines have equal slopes, we can estimate that _____.

**(b)** Using the following data, compute $\Delta P/\Delta t$ for each of the two periods mentioned in part (a). Round the answers to one decimal place. Do your answers support the estimate you made in part (a)?

$P(1978) = 0.3\%$;      $P(1988) = 58.0\%$;
$P(1984) = 10.6\%$;    $P(1997) = 84.2\%$

*For Exercises 19 and 20, refer to the following figure, which shows consumption of red meat in the United States and in China over the period 1980–1996. Let $y = f(t)$ denote the consumption function for the United States, and let $y = g(t)$ denote the consumption function for China.*

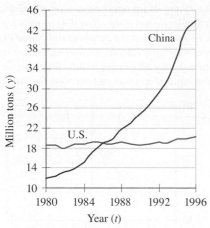

Consumption of red meat in United States and in China, 1980–1996

*Source of data used to create graph:* World-watch Institute

**19.** **(a)** Using values that you estimate from the graph, calculate $\Delta f/\Delta t$, the average rate of change of red meat consumption in the United States over the period 1980–1996. Express the answer as a fraction and as a decimal rounded to the nearest tenth.

  **(b)** Use the data in the following table to obtain a more accurate value for $\Delta f/\Delta t$ over the period 1980–1996. Round the answer to two decimal places.

| Year (t) | 1980 | 1996 |
|---|---|---|
| Consumption (y) In U.S. (million tons) | 18.68 | 20.32 |

**20.** **(a)** Using values that you estimate from the graph, calculate $\Delta g/\Delta t$, the average rate of change of red meat consumption in China over the period 1980–1996.

  **(b)** Use the data in the following table to obtain a more accurate value for $\Delta g/\Delta t$ over the period 1980–1996. Round the answer to two decimal places.

| Year (t) | 1980 | 1996 |
|---|---|---|
| Consumption (y) in China (million tons) | 11.90 | 43.83 |

**21.** Let $f(x) = 2x^2$.
  **(a)** Find $\dfrac{f(x) - f(3)}{x - 3}$.
  **(b)** Find $\dfrac{f(x) - f(a)}{x - a}$.

**22.** Let $f(x) = 4x^2$.
  **(a)** Find $\dfrac{f(x) - f(-2)}{x + 2}$.
  **(b)** Find $\dfrac{f(x) - f(a)}{x - a}$.

*For Exercises 23 and 24, let $f(x) = x^2$. Find and simplify the indicated difference quotient.*

**23.** **(a)** $\dfrac{f(2 + h) - f(2)}{h}$

  **(b)** $\dfrac{f(x + h) - f(x)}{h}$

**24.** **(a)** $\dfrac{f(1 + h) - f(1)}{h}$

  **(b)** $\dfrac{f(t + h) - f(t)}{h}$

*In Exercises 25–32:*
**(a)** *Find the difference quotient* $\dfrac{f(x) - f(a)}{x - a}$ *for each function, as in Example 4.*

**(b)** *Find the difference quotient* $\dfrac{f(x + h) - f(x)}{h}$ *for each function, as in Example 5.*

**25.** $f(x) = 8x - 3$  **26.** $f(x) = -2x + 5$
**27.** $f(x) = x^2 - 2x + 4$  **28.** $f(x) = 2x^2 - x + 1$
**29.** $f(x) = 1/x$  **30.** $f(x) = -3/x^2$
**31.** $f(x) = 2x^3$  **32.** $f(x) = 1 - x^3$

*Hint:* For Exercises 31 and 32, you'll need to use difference-of-cubes factoring from intermediate algebra. See the inside back cover for the relevant formula. For a more detailed review of the topic, refer to Appendix B.4.

*For Exercises 33–36, use the distance function $s(t) = 16t^2$ discussed on page 164 and in Example 6. Recall that this function relates the distance $s(t)$ and the time $t$ for a freely falling object (neglecting air resistance). The time $t$ is measured in seconds, with $t = 0$ corresponding to the instant that the object begins to fall; the distance $s(t)$ is in feet.*

**33.** Find the average velocity $\Delta s/\Delta t$ over the time interval $1 \le t \le 2$.

**34.** **(a)** Find the average velocity over each of the following time intervals: $[2, 3]$, $[3, 4]$, and $[2, 4]$.

  **(b)** Let $a$, $b$, and $c$ denote the three average velocities that you computed in part (a), in the order given. Is it true that the arithmetical average of $a$ and $b$ is $c$?

**35.** **(a)** Follow the method of Example 6(a) to find a general expression for the average velocity $\Delta s/\Delta t$ over the interval $[2, 2 + h]$.

  **(b)** Complete a table similar to the one shown in the solution of Example 6(b); for the $h$-values in the left-hand column use 0.1, 0.01, 0.001, 0.0001, and 0.00001.

  **(c)** Looking at your results in part (b), answer the following question. As $h$ approaches zero, what value does the average velocity in the right-hand column seem to be approaching? This target value or limit is the *instantaneous* (as opposed to average) *velocity* of the object when $t = 2$ sec.

**36.** **(a)** After rereading Example 6, extend the results in part (b) of the example by completing the following table. Don't round your answers.

| h (seconds) | 0.01 | 0.001 | 0.0001 | 0.00001 |
|---|---|---|---|---|
| Average velocity $\Delta s/\Delta t$ on interval [1, 1 + h] (ft/second) | | | | |

  **(b)** As $h$ approaches zero, what value does the average velocity $\Delta s/\Delta t$ seem to be approaching? This target value or limit is called the *instantaneous velocity* of the object when $t = 1$ sec.

**37.** Suppose that the demand function for a certain item is given by $p(x) = \dfrac{24}{2^{x/100}}$, where $x$ is the number of items that can be sold when the price of each item is $p(x)$ dollars. Compute $\Delta p/\Delta x$ over each of the intervals $0 \le x \le 100$ and $300 \le x \le 400$. Include units in your answers. Why does it make sense (economically) that the answers are negative?

**38.** Suppose that during the first few hours of a laboratory experiment, the temperature of a certain substance is closely approximated by the function $f(t) = t^3 - 6t^2 + 9t$, where $t$ is measured in hours, with $t = 0$ corresponding to the instant the experiment begins, and $f(t)$ is the temperature (°F) of the substance after $t$ hours.

(a) Find an expression for $\Delta f/\Delta t$. What are the units for $\Delta f/\Delta t$?

(b) Use the result in part (a) to complete the following table. Round the answers to four decimal places.

| Interval | [0, 0.1] | [0, 0.01] | [0, 0.001] | [0, 0.0001] |
|----------|----------|-----------|------------|-------------|
| $\Delta f/\Delta t$ | | | | |

(c) In part (b), as the right-hand endpoint gets closer and closer to 0, what value does $\Delta f/\Delta t$ seem to be approaching? This target value tells us the rate at which the temperature is changing at the *instant* the experiment begins.

**39.** Complete the following table.

| Function | $|x|$ | $x^2$ | $x^3$ |
|----------|-------|-------|-------|
| Domain | | | |
| Range | | | |
| Turning point | | | |
| Maximum value | | | |
| Minimum value | | | |
| Interval(s) where increasing | | | |
| Interval(s) where decreasing | | | |

**40.** Set up and complete a table like the one in Exercise 39 for the three functions $1/x$, $\sqrt{x}$, and $\sqrt{1 - x^2}$.

**B**

**41.** Let $f(x) = 1/x$. Find a number $b$ so that the average rate of change of $f$ on the interval $[1, b]$ is $-1/5$.

**42.** Let $f(x) = \sqrt{x}$. Find a number $b$ so that the average rate of change of $f$ on the interval $[1, b]$ is $1/7$.

**43.** Let $f(x) = ax^2 + bx + c$. Show that
$$\frac{f(x + h) - f(x)}{h} = 2ax + ah + b.$$

**44.** Find a number $a$ between 0 and 1 so that the average rate of change of $f(x) = x^2$ on the interval $[a, 1/a]$ is $10a$.

---

Ⓖ *In Exercises 45 and 46 (as opposed to Exercises 7 and 8), the viewing rectangles do not show all of the essential features of the graphs. In each case, use a graphing utility and experiment with different viewing rectangles to determine approximate x- and y-coordinates for all turning points. What are the corresponding intervals of increase and decrease for the function?*

**45.**

$f(x) = 4x^4 + x^3$
$[-4, 4, 2]$ by $[-10, 10, 5]$

**46.**

$g(x) = x^4 + 12x^3 + x^2$
$[-4, 4, 2]$ by $[-10, 10, 5]$

**47.** Let $h(x) = \sqrt{x}$. Two functions $f$ and $g$ are defined in terms of $h$ as follows:

$$f(x) = \frac{h(x) - h(2)}{x - 2} \qquad g(x) = \frac{1}{h(x) + h(2)}$$

Ⓖ (a) Using a graphing utility, graph the two functions $f$ and $g$ in the same viewing screen. What do you observe?

(b) Use algebra to explain the result in part (a). That is, either derive or verify the identity $f(x) = g(x)$. Are there any positive values of $x$ for which this equation does not hold?

**48.** Consider the function $f$ defined by

$$f(x) = x^2 + \frac{2}{x^2} \qquad (x > 0)$$

(a) Complete the table. (Round the results to four decimal places.)

| $x$ | 1 | 1.05 | 1.10 | 1.15 | 1.20 | 1.25 |
|-----|---|------|------|------|------|------|
| $f(x)$ | | | | | | |

**(b)** Which $f(x)$-value in the table is the smallest? What is the corresponding input?

**(c)** Use a graphing utility to graph the function $f$. Then use the ZOOM and/or TRACE features to find an output $f(x)$ that is less than the output you indicated in part (b).

**(d)** It can be shown using calculus that the input $x$ yielding the minimum value for the function $f$ is $\sqrt[4]{2}$. Compute $f(\sqrt[4]{2})$. Which value of $f(x)$ in the table is closest to $f(\sqrt[4]{2})$? To how many decimal places does your estimate in part (c) agree with $f(\sqrt[4]{2})$?

# 3.4 TECHNIQUES IN GRAPHING

*...geometrical figures are graphic formulas.*—David Hilbert (1862–1943)

The simple geometric concepts of reflection and translation can be used to great advantage in graphing. We discussed the idea of reflection in the $x$-axis and in the $y$-axis in Section 1.7. By a **translation** of a graph, we mean a shift in its location such that every point of the graph is moved the same distance in the same direction. The size and the shape of a graph are unchanged by a translation.

**EXAMPLE 1    Sketching combinations of translations and reflections**

The graph of a function $G$ is the quarter-circle shown in Figure 1. In each case, sketch the resulting graph after the following operations are carried out on the graph of $G$:

**(a)** a translation of four units to the right followed by a translation of one unit vertically downward;

**(b)** a translation of three units to the right followed by a reflection in the $y$-axis;

**(c)** a reflection in the $y$-axis followed by a translation of three units to the right. [Note that these are the same two operations used in part (b), but here the order is reversed.]

Figure 1

**SOLUTION**

**(a)** Figure 2 shows the result of translating the graph of $G$ four units to the right and then one unit down. (As you can check by drawing a sketch, the same end result is obtained if we first translate one unit down and then four units to the right.) *Fact:* If several translations are to be carried out in succession, the end result will be the same, no matter in what order the individual translations are carried out.

Figure 2
The red curve is the end result when the graph of $G$ is translated four units to the right and then one unit down.

Translation of the graph of $G$ by 4 units to the right

Translation by 4 units to the right followed by a translation of 1 unit down

**(b)** Figure 3(a) shows the graph of $G$ after a translation of three units to the right. When this is followed by a reflection in the $y$-axis, we obtain the result shown in Figure 3(b).

**Figure 3**
Figure (a) shows the result of translating the graph of $G$ three units to the right. When this is followed by a reflection in the $y$-axis, we obtain the red curve in Figure (b).

(a)

(b)

(c)   Figure 4 shows what happens to the graph of $G$ if we use the same two operations that were used in part (b) but reverse the order in which they are carried out. Note that the end result is quite different from that obtained in part (b).

**Figure 4**
The reflection of the graph of $G$ in the $y$-axis followed by a translation of three units to the right.

Given the graph of a function $f$, it is useful to know how to sketch efficiently the graphs of the following closely related functions. (In the following equations, $c$ denotes a positive constant.)

$$y = f(x) + c \qquad y = f(x + c) \qquad y = -f(x)$$
$$y = f(x) - c \qquad y = f(x - c) \qquad y = f(-x)$$

Each of these can be graphed by translating or reflecting the graph of $y = f(x)$. In the box that follows, we summarize the techniques that are involved. (Exercises 47–50 will help you to see why these techniques are valid, and Section 11.2 will explain these techniques from a more general point of view.)

## PROPERTY SUMMARY   Translations and Reflections

(In Items 1–4, the letter $c$ denotes a positive constant.)

| Equation | How to Obtain the Graph from That of $y = f(x)$ |
|---|---|
| 1. $y = f(x) + c$ | Translate $c$ units vertically upward |
| 2. $y = f(x) - c$ | Translate $c$ units vertically downward |
| 3. $y = f(x + c)$ | Translate $c$ units to the left |
| 4. $y = f(x - c)$ | Translate $c$ units to the right |
| 5. $y = -f(x)$ | Reflect in the $x$-axis |
| 6. $y = f(-x)$ | Reflect in the $y$-axis |

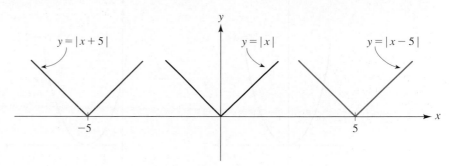

(a)  To graph $y = |x| + 2$, translate $y = |x|$ up 2 units. To graph $y = |x| - 2$, translate $y = |x|$ down 2 units.

(b)  To graph $y = |x + 5|$, translate $y = |x|$ to the left 5 units. To graph $y = |x - 5|$, translate $y = |x|$ to the right 5 units.

**Figure 5**

(a)  To graph $y = -\sqrt{x}$, reflect $y = \sqrt{x}$ in the $x$-axis. More generally, to graph $y = -f(x)$, reflect the graph of $y = f(x)$ in the $x$-axis.

(b)  To graph $y = \sqrt{-x}$, reflect $y = \sqrt{x}$ in the $y$-axis. More generally, to graph $y = f(-x)$, reflect the graph of $y = f(x)$ in the $y$-axis.

**Figure 6**

In Figure 5 we show examples of the first four techniques in the box, the techniques involving translation. Figure 6 displays examples of the remaining two techniques, the ones involving reflection. You should look over these figures carefully before going on to Examples 2 through 4, in which the various graphing techniques are combined.

**EXAMPLE  2   Using translations of $y = x^2$**

Graph: $y = (x - 2)^2 + 1$.

**SOLUTION**
Begin with the graph of $y = x^2$ in Figure 7(a). Move the curve two units to the right to obtain the graph of $y = (x - 2)^2$; see Figure 7(b). Then move the curve in Figure 7(b) up one unit to obtain the graph of $y = (x - 2)^2 + 1$; see Figure 7(c).

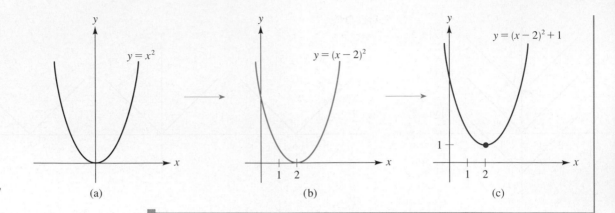

Figure 7        (a)                 (b)                 (c)

**EXAMPLE** 3 **Using translations of $y = 1/x$**

Graph the functions $y = \dfrac{1}{x - 1}$ and $y = \dfrac{1}{x - 1} + 1$.

**SOLUTION**

Begin with the graph of $y = 1/x$ in Figure 8(a). The $x$- and $y$-axes are asymptotes for this graph. Moving this graph to the right one unit yields the graph of $y = \dfrac{1}{x - 1}$, shown in Figure 8(b). Note that the vertical asymptote moves one unit to the right also, but the horizontal asymptote is unchanged. Next, we move the graph in Figure 8(b) up one unit (why?) to obtain the graph of $y = \dfrac{1}{x - 1} + 1$, as shown in Figure 8(c). (You should verify for yourself that the $y$-intercepts in Figures 8(b) and 8(c) are $-1$ and $0$, respectively.)

       (a)                 (b)                 (c)

Figure 8

**EXAMPLE** 4 **Applying reflection and translations to $y = |x|$**

Graph each equation:
**(a)** $y = -|x|$;        **(b)** $y = -|x - 2| + 3$.

**SOLUTION**
See Figure 9.

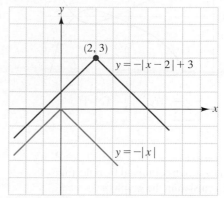

(a)  Reflecting the graph of $y = |x|$ about the $x$-axis yields the graph of $y = -|x|$. Note that both the $x$- and $y$-intercepts are zero.

(b)  Translating the graph of $y = -|x|$ two units to the right and three units up yields the graph of $y = -|x - 2| + 3$. To get the $y$-intercept: $x = 0$ implies that $y = -|0 - 2| + 3 = 1$. To get the $x$-intercept: $y = 0$ implies that
$$-|x - 2| + 3 = 0 \quad \text{so} \quad |x - 2| = 3$$
$$x - 2 = 3 \quad \text{or} \quad -(x - 2) = 3$$
$$x = 5 \quad \text{or} \quad -1$$

**Figure 9**

**EXAMPLE    5    Using algebra to determine how two graphs are related**

Figure 10 shows a graph of the function $k$ defined by $k(x) = x^4 - 3x + 1$. In each case, say how the graph of the given function can be obtained from the graph of $k$. Then use a graphing utility to verify your statement:

**(a)**  $f(x) = -x^4 + 3x - 1$;    **(b)**  $g(x) = x^4 + 3x + 1$;    **(c)**  $h(x) = x^4 - 3x + 3$.

**GRAPHICAL PERSPECTIVE**

$k(x) = x^4 - 3x + 1$
$[-2, 2, 1]$ by $[-8, 8, 4]$

**Figure 10**

**SOLUTION**
**(a)**  Note that the given expression for $f(x)$ is just the negative of $k(x)$. That is,

$$f(x) = -x^4 + 3x - 1 = -(x^4 - 3x + 1) = -k(x)$$

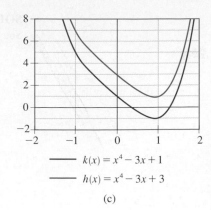

——— $k(x) = x^4 - 3x + 1$

——— $f(x) = -x^4 + 3x - 1$

(a)

——— $k(x) = x^4 - 3x + 1$

——— $g(x) = x^4 + 3x + 1$

(b)

——— $k(x) = x^4 - 3x + 1$

——— $h(x) = x^4 - 3x + 3$

(c)

**Figure 11**

Some graphs obtained by reflecting or translating the graph of $k(x) = x^4 - 3x + 1$

Therefore the graph of $f$ can be obtained by reflecting the graph of $k$ in the $x$-axis. See Figure 11(a).

**(b)** The expressions for $g(x)$ and $k(x)$ are the same except for the sign in front of the $3x$-term. After some thought (or perhaps some trial and error) we find that

$$k(-x) = (-x)^4 - 3(-x) + 1$$
$$= x^4 + 3x + 1$$
$$= g(x)$$

That is, we have $k(-x) = g(x)$, and therefore the graph of $g$ can be obtained by reflecting the graph of $k$ in the $y$-axis. See Figure 11(b).

**(c)** Comparing the two equations $k(x) = x^4 - 3x + 1$ and $h(x) = x^4 - 3x + 3$, we see that

$$h(x) = k(x) + 2$$

Thus the graph of $h$ is obtained by translating the graph of $k$ up two units in the $y$-direction. See Figure 11(c).

  **EXAMPLE 6** | **A case where the translation rule for $y = f(x + c)$ is not directly applicable**

**(a)** Graph: $y = \sqrt{-x} + 2$.     **(b)** Graph: $y = |1 - x|$.

**SOLUTION**

**(a)** Our translation rule for $y = f(x + c)$ is not directly applicable here because in the generic equation $y = f(x + c)$, the sign of the $x$-term is positive; the rule provides no information about $y = f(-x + c)$. Rather than introducing yet another rule, we'll explain how to proceed using what you've already learned. To graph $y = \sqrt{-x} + 2$, first ignore the negative sign and graph the simpler equation $y = \sqrt{x} + 2$, as shown in Figure 12(a). Then for the graph of $y = \sqrt{-x} + 2$, just reflect the graph of $y = \sqrt{x} + 2$ in the $y$-axis, as shown in Figure 12(b). (We are using the fact that replacing $x$ with $-x$ throughout an equation reflects the graph in the $y$-axis.)

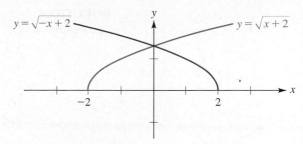

(a) Translate the graph of $y = \sqrt{x}$ to the left 2 units to obtain the graph of $y = \sqrt{x + 2}$.

(b) Reflect the graph of $y = \sqrt{x + 2}$ in the $y$-axis to obtain the graph of $y = \sqrt{-x + 2}$.

**Figure 12**
Steps in graphing $y = \sqrt{-x + 2}$:
First graph $y = \sqrt{x + 2}$; then reflect
in the $y$-axis to obtain the graph of
$y = \sqrt{-x + 2}$.

**(b)** Write the given equation in the equivalent but somewhat more familiar form $y = |-x + 1|$. Now apply the strategy explained in part (a). That is, first graph $y = |x + 1|$, and then reflect in the $y$-axis to obtain the graph of $y = |-x + 1|$. See Figure 13.

NOTE   We can use one of the properties of absolute value to obtain the graph in a different way and thus check the result in Figure 13. We have

$$y = |-x + 1| = |-1(x - 1)| = |-1||x - 1|$$
$$= |x - 1|$$

This shows that the required graph can be obtained by graphing $y = |x - 1|$ —that is, by translating $y = |x|$ one unit to the right. As you can see, this agrees with the end result in Figure 13.

**Figure 13**
Steps in graphing $y = |-x + 1|$:
First graph $y = |x + 1|$, then reflect
in the $y$-axis.

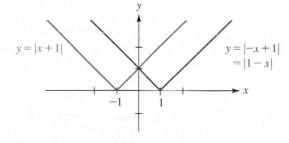

The following example makes use of all the graphing techniques presented in this section. When you reach the point where you can work each part of this example on your own, then you know the material in this section.

**EXAMPLE 7   A comprehensive example**

The graph of a function $f$ is a line segment joining the points $(-3, 1)$ and $(2, 4)$. Graph each of the following functions:

**(a)** $y = f(-x)$;     **(b)** $y = -f(x)$;     **(c)** $y = -f(-x)$;
**(d)** $y = f(x + 1)$;     **(e)** $y = -f(x + 1)$;     **(f)** $y = f(1 - x)$.

**SOLUTION**
See Figure 14.

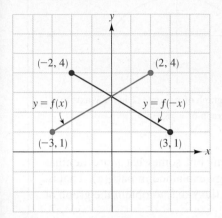

(a) Reflect the graph of $y = f(x)$ in the $y$-axis to obtain the graph of $y = f(-x)$.

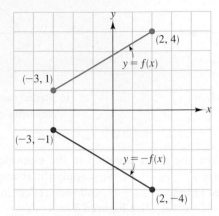

(b) Reflect the graph of $y = f(x)$ in the $x$-axis to obtain the graph of $y = -f(x)$.

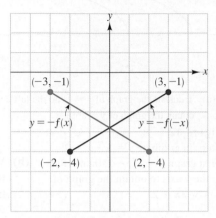

(c) Reflect the graph of $y = -f(x)$ in the $y$-axis to obtain the graph of $y = -f(-x)$. [Or reflect the graph of $y = f(-x)$ in the $x$-axis.]

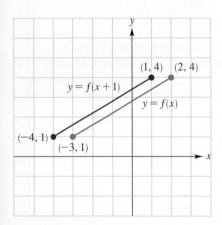

(d) Translate the graph of $y = f(x)$ one unit to the left to obtain the graph of $y = f(x + 1)$.

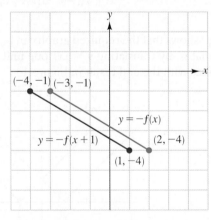

(e) Translate the graph of $y = -f(x)$ one unit to the left to obtain the graph of $y = -f(x + 1)$. [Or reflect the graph of $y = f(x + 1)$ in the $x$-axis.]

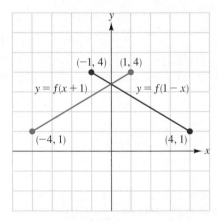

(f) Reflect the graph of $y = f(x + 1)$ in Figure 14(d) in the $y$-axis to obtain the graph of $y = f(1 - x)$. [Reason: Replacing $x$ with $-x$ in $y = f(x + 1)$ yields $y = f(1 - x)$.]

**Figure 14**

---

# ▌EXERCISE SET 3.4

**A**

*In Exercises 1 and 2, the right-hand column contains instructions for translating and/or reflecting the graph of $y = f(x)$. Match each equation in the left-hand column with an appropriate set of instructions in the right-hand column.*

**1. (a)** $y = f(x - 1)$
 **(b)** $y = f(x) - 1$

 **(c)** $y = f(x) + 1$
 **(d)** $y = f(x + 1)$

**(A)** Translate left 1 unit.
**(B)** Reflect in the $x$-axis, then translate left 1 unit.
**(C)** Translate right 1 unit.
**(D)** Reflect in the $x$-axis, then translate up 1 unit.

(e) $y = f(-x) + 1$  (E) Reflect in the $x$-axis, then translate down 1 unit.

(f) $y = f(-x) - 1$  (F) Translate down 1 unit.

(g) $y = -f(x) + 1$  (G) Reflect in the $x$-axis, reflect in the $y$-axis, then translate up 1 unit.

(h) $y = -f(x + 1)$  (H) Translate left 1 unit, then reflect in the $y$-axis, then translate up 1 unit.

(i) $y = -f(x) - 1$  (I) Translate up 1 unit.

(j) $y = f(1 - x) + 1$  (J) Reflect in the $y$-axis, then translate up 1 unit.

Hint: See Example 6.

(k) $y = -f(-x) + 1$  (K) Reflect in the $y$-axis, then translate down 1 unit.

2. (a) $y = f(x + 2) + 3$  (A) Translate left 2 units, then translate down 3 units.

(b) $y = f(x + 3) + 2$  (B) Translate left 3 units, then translate up 2 units.

(c) $y = f(x - 2) + 3$  (C) Translate right 3 units, then translate up 2 units.

(d) $y - f(x - 2)$   3  (D) Translate left 3 units, then translate down 2 units.

(e) $y = f(x + 2) - 3$  (E) Translate right 3 units and down 2 units.

(f) $y = f(x - 3) + 2$  (F) Reflect in the $y$-axis, then translate up 2 units.

(g) $y = f(x - 3) - 2$  (G) Reflect in the $x$-axis, then translate right 2 units.

(h) $y = f(x + 3) - 2$  (H) Reflect in the $x$-axis, then translate left 2 units.

(i) $y = -f(x + 2)$  (I) Translate left 2 units, then reflect in the $y$-axis.

(j) $y = -f(x - 2)$  (J) Translate right 2 units, then translate up 3 units.

(k) $y = f(2 - x)$  (K) Translate left 2 units, then translate up 3 units.

(l) $y = f(-x) + 2$  (L) Translate right 2 units and down 3 units.

*In Exercises 3–24, sketch the graph of the function.*   Hint: Start with the basic graphs in Figure 7 on page 149.

3. $y = x^3 - 3$  4. $y = x^2 + 3$

5. $y = (x + 4)^2$  6. $y = (x + 4)^2 - 3$

7. $y = (x - 4)^2$  8. $y = (x - 4)^2 + 1$

9. $y = -x^2$  10. $y = -x^2 - 3$

11. $y = -(x - 3)^2$  12. $y = -(x - 3)^2 - 3$

13. $y = \sqrt{x - 3}$  14. $y = \sqrt{x - 3} + 1$

15. $y = \sqrt{-x + 3}$  16. $y = \sqrt{-x + 3} + 2$

17. $y = \dfrac{1}{x + 2} + 2$  18. $y = \dfrac{1}{x - 3} - 1$

19. $y = (x - 2)^3$  20. $y = (x - 2)^3 + 1$

21. $y = -x^3 + 4$  22. $y = -(x - 1)^3 + 4$

23. (a) $y = |x + 4|$  24. (a) $y = \sqrt{x + 2}$
    (b) $y = |4 - x|$      (b) $y = \sqrt{2 - x}$
    (c) $y = -|4 - x| + 1$   (c) $y = -\sqrt{2 - x}$

*In Exercises 25–40, sketch the graph of the function, given that f, F, and g are defined as follows. (Hint: Start with the basic graphs in Figure 7 on page 149.)*

$$f(x) = |x| \qquad F(x) = 1/x \qquad g(x) = \sqrt{1 - x^2}$$

25. $y = f(x - 5)$  26. $y = -f(x - 5)$

27. $y = f(5 - x)$  28. $y = -f(5 - x)$

29. $y = 1 - f(x - 5)$  30. $y = f(-x)$

31. $y = F(x + 3)$  32. $y = F(x) + 3$

33. $y = -F(x + 3)$  34. $y = F(-x) + 3$

35. $y = g(x - 2)$  36. $y = -g(x - 2)$

37. $y = 1 - g(x - 2)$  38. $y = g(-x)$

39. $y = g(2 - x)$  40. $y = -g(2 - x)$

Ⓖ *As background for Exercises 41–46, you should review Example 5. In Exercises 41–46, a function f is given. Say how the graph of each of the related functions can be obtained from the graph of f, and then use a graphing utility to verify your statement (as in Figure 11).*

41. $f(x) = 3x - 2$  42. $f(x) = 4 - x^2$
    (a) $y = -3x - 2$      (a) $y - x^2 - 4$
    (b) $y = -3x + 2$      (b) $y = 1 - x^2$

43. $f(x) = x^2 + 4x + 2$  44. $f(x) = x^3 + 3x^2 - 4$
    (a) $y = x^2 - 4x + 2$      (a) $y = -x^3 + 3x^2 - 4$
    (b) $y = x^2 + 4x$      (b) $y = -x^3 + 3x^2 + 1$

45. $f(x) = x^4 - 3x + 3$  46. $f(x) = -x^3 + 3x^2 - 3x + 1$
    (a) $y = x^4 + 3x + 3$      (a) $y = -x^3 + 3x^2 - 3x - 1$
    (b) $y = -x^4 + 3x - 3$      (b) $y = x^3 + 3x^2 + 3x + 1$
    (c) $y = -x^4 + 3x$      (c) $y = x^3 - 3x^2 + 3x - 1$

47. (a) Complete the following table.

| $x$ | $x^2$ | $x^2 - 1$ | $x^2 + 1$ |
|-----|-------|-----------|-----------|
| 0 | | | |
| $\pm 1$ | | | |
| $\pm 2$ | | | |
| $\pm 3$ | | | |

(b) Using the results in the table, graph the functions $y = x^2$, $y = x^2 - 1$, and $y = x^2 + 1$ on the same set of axes. How are the graphs related?

48. (a) Complete the given table.

| $x$ | $x^2$ | $(x - 1)^2$ | $(x + 1)^2$ |
|-----|-------|-------------|-------------|
| 0 | | | |
| 1 | | | |
| 2 | | | |
| 3 | | | |
| $-1$ | | | |
| $-2$ | | | |
| $-3$ | | | |

(b) Using the results in the table, graph the functions $y = x^2$, $y = (x - 1)^2$, and $y = (x + 1)^2$ on the same set of axes. How are the graphs related?

**49. (a)** Complete the following table. (Use a calculator where necessary.)

| $x$ | $\sqrt{x}$ | $-\sqrt{x}$ |
|-----|------------|-------------|
| 0   |            |             |
| 1   |            |             |
| 2   |            |             |
| 3   |            |             |
| 4   |            |             |
| 5   |            |             |

**(b)** Using the results in the table, graph the functions $y = \sqrt{x}$ and $y = -\sqrt{x}$ on the same set of axes. How are the two graphs related?

**50. (a)** Complete the given tables. (Use a calculator where necessary.)

| $x$ | 0 | 1 | 2 | 3 | 4 | 5 |
|-----|---|---|---|---|---|---|
| $\sqrt{x}$ | | | | | | |

| $x$ | 0 | $-1$ | $-2$ | $-3$ | $-4$ | $-5$ |
|-----|---|------|------|------|------|------|
| $\sqrt{-x}$ | | | | | | |

**(b)** Using the tables, graph the functions $y = \sqrt{x}$ and $y = \sqrt{-x}$ on the same set of axes. How are the graphs related?

*In Exercises 51–53 you'll use a graphing utility to provide examples of the six graphing techniques listed in the box on page 172.*

Ⓖ **51. (a)** Graph the two functions $f(x) = \sqrt{1 + x^2}$ and $g(x) = \sqrt{1 + x^2} + 3$. Observe that the graph of $g$ is obtained by translating the graph of $f$ *up* three units. This illustrates Property 1 on page 172.

**(b)** Graph the two functions $f(x) = \sqrt{1 + x^2}$ and $h(x) = \sqrt{1 + x^2} - 3$. Observe that the graph of $h$ is obtained by translating the graph of $f$ *down* three units. This illustrates Property 2 on page 172.

Ⓖ **52.** Using the viewing rectangle $[-5, 3]$ by $[0, 5]$, graph the three functions

$$F(x) = \sqrt{1 - x^3}$$
$$L(x) = \sqrt{1 - (x + 2)^3}$$
$$R(x) = \sqrt{1 - (x - 2)^3}$$

Observe that the graph of $L$ is obtained by translating the graph of $F$ to the *left* 2 units. Also, the graph of $R$ is obtained by translating the graph of $F$ to the *right* 2 units. This illustrates Properties 3 and 4 on page 172.

Ⓖ **53.** For this exercise, use the viewing rectangle $[-4, 4]$ by $[-4, 4]$.

**(a)** On the same set of axes, graph the two functions $f(x) = 2^x$ and $g(x) = -2^x$. [*Algebra reminder*: $-2^x$

means $-(2^x)$, not $(-2)^x$]. Observe that the graph of $g$ is obtained by reflecting the graph of $f$ in the $x$-axis. This illustrates Property 5 on page 172.

**(b)** On the same set of axes graph the two functions $f(x) = 2^x$ and $h(x) = 2^{-x}$. Observe that the graph of $h$ is obtained by reflecting the graph of $f$ in the $y$-axis. This illustrates Property 6 on page 172.

**B**

**54.** Reflect the graph of $y = \sqrt{x}$ in the $y$-axis and then translate that two units to the left. What is the equation of the resulting graph? *Hint*: The answer is not $y = \sqrt{-x + 2}$.

**55.** Let $P$ be a point with coordinates $(a, b)$, and assume that $c$ and $d$ are positive numbers. (The condition that $c$ and $d$ are positive isn't really necessary in this problem, but it will help you to visualize things.)

**(a)** Translate the point $P$ by $c$ units in the $x$-direction to obtain a point $Q$, then translate $Q$ by $d$ units in the $y$-direction to obtain a point $R$. What are the coordinates of the point $R$?

**(b)** Translate the point $P$ by $d$ units in the $y$-direction to obtain a point $S$, then translate $S$ by $c$ units in the $x$-direction to obtain a point $T$. What are the coordinates of the point $T$?

**(c)** Compare your answers for parts (a) and (b). What have you demonstrated? (Answer in complete sentences.)

**56.** Let $P$ be a point with coordinates $(a, b)$.

**(a)** Reflect $P$ in the $x$-axis to obtain a point $Q$, then reflect $Q$ in the $y$-axis to obtain a point $R$. What are the coordinates of the point $R$?

**(b)** Reflect $P$ in the $y$-axis to obtain a point $S$, then reflect $S$ in the $x$-axis to obtain a point $T$. What are the coordinates of the point $T$?

**(c)** Compare your answers for parts (a) and (b). What have you demonstrated? (Answer in complete sentences.)

Ⓖ **57. (a)** Use a graphing utility to graph the function $y = x/(x - 1)$.

**(b)** From the screen display, it appears that the graph may be a translation of the basic $y = 1/x$ graph. Prove that this is indeed the case by using algebra to show that

$$\frac{x}{x - 1} = \frac{1}{x - 1} + 1. \quad \text{\textit{Hint}: Combine the quantities}$$

on the right side of the equation.

**(c)** Beginning with the graph of $y = 1/x$, what are the translations used to obtain the graph of $y = x/(x - 1)$?

*For Exercises 58 and 59, assume that $(a, b)$ is a point on the graph of $y = f(x)$, and specify the corresponding point on the graph of each equation. [For example, the point that corresponds to $(a, b)$ on the graph of $y = f(x - 1)$ is $(a + 1, b)$.]*

**58. (a)** $y = f(x - 3)$      **(c)** $y = f(x - 3) - 3$

    **(b)** $y = f(x) - 3$      **(d)** $y = -f(x)$

**(e)** $y = f(-x)$

**(f)** $y = -f(-x)$

**59. (a)** $y = f(-x) + 2$

**(b)** $y = -f(-x) + 2$

**(c)** $y = -f(x - 3)$

**(g)** $y = f(3 - x)$

**(h)** $y = -f(3 - x) + 1$

**(d)** $y = 1 - f(x + 1)$

**(e)** $y = f(1 - x)$

**(f)** $y = -f(1 - x) + 1$

**60. (a)** A function $f$ is said to be **even** if the equation $f(-x) = f(x)$ is satisfied by all values of $x$ in the domain of $f$. Explain why the graph of an even function must be symmetric about the $y$-axis.

**(b)** Show that each function is even by computing $f(-x)$ and then noting that $f(x)$ and $f(-x)$ are equal.

**(i)** $f(x) = x^2$

**(ii)** $f(x) = 2x^4 - 6$

**(iii)** $f(x) = 3x^6 - \dfrac{4}{x^2} + 1$

**61. (a)** A function $f$ is said to be **odd** if the equation $f(-x) = -f(x)$ is satisfied by all values of $x$ in the domain of $f$. Show that if $(x, y)$ is a point on the graph of an odd function $f$, then the point $(-x, -y)$ is also

on the graph. (This implies that the graph of an odd function must be symmetric about the origin.)

**(b)** Show that each function is odd by computing $f(-x)$ as well as $-f(x)$ and then noting that the two expressions obtained are equal.

**(i)** $f(x) = x^3$

**(ii)** $f(x) = -2x^5 + 4x^3 - x$

**(iii)** $f(x) = |x| / (x + x^7)$

**62.** Is each function odd, even, or neither? (See Exercises 60 and 61 for definitions.)

**(a)** $f(x) = \dfrac{1 - x^2}{2 + x^2}$

**(b)** $g(x) = \dfrac{x - x^3}{2x + x^3}$

**(c)** $h(x) = x^2 + x$

**(d)** $F(x) = (x^2 + x)^2$

**(e)** $G(x) = \begin{cases} 1 & \text{if } x > 0 \\ 0 & \text{if } x = 0 \\ -1 & \text{if } x < 0 \end{cases}$

*Suggestion for part (e):*
Look at the graph.

# MINI PROJECT | CORRECTING A GRAPHING UTILITY DISPLAY

As background for this discussion, you need to recall the definitions from intermediate algebra for expressions of the form $\sqrt[n]{x}$ and $x^{1/n}$, where $n$ is a positive integer. See Appendices B.2 and B.3 if you need a reminder, or have someone in the group consult the appendix and present the definitions and relevant examples to the group at large.

Some graphing utilities produce incomplete graphs for root functions $y = \sqrt[n]{x}$ when $n$ is an odd integer. To find out how your graphing utility operates in this respect, try the function $y = \sqrt[3]{x}$ on your graphing utility, and compare your result to Figures A and B. (You might need to enter the function in the form $y = x^{1/3}$.)

The reason for the incomplete graph in Figure A is that the graphing utility used requires nonnegative inputs in computing roots, even cube roots. Suppose for this discussion that you have this type of graphing utility. Find a way to use the techniques in this section to produce a correct graph, one similar to that shown in Figure B.

Figure A
An incomplete graph of $y = \sqrt[3]{x}$

Figure B
A complete graph of $y = \sqrt[3]{x}$

# 3.5 METHODS OF COMBINING FUNCTIONS. ITERATION

*The notation φx to indicate a function of x was introduced by . . . [John Bernoulli] in 1718, . . . but the general adoption of symbols like f, F, φ, and ψ . . . to represent functions, seems to be mainly due to Euler and Lagrange.* —W. W. Rouse Ball in *A Short Account of the History of Mathematics* (New York: Dover Publications, 1960)

*The composition of functions is basic to the study of iteration and chaos.* —Hartmut Jürgens et al., *Fractals for the Classroom: Strategic Activities,* vol. 2 (New York: Springer-Verlag, 1992)

Two given numbers $a$ and $b$ can be combined in various ways to produce a third number. For instance, we can form the sum $a + b$ or the difference $a - b$ or the product $ab$. Also, if $b \neq 0$, we can form the quotient $a/b$. Similarly, two functions can be combined in various ways to produce a third function. Suppose, for example, that we start with the two functions $y = x^2$ and $y = x^3$. It seems natural to define their sum, difference, product, and quotient as follows:

$$\text{sum:} \quad y = x^2 + x^3$$
$$\text{difference:} \quad y = x^2 - x^3$$
$$\text{product:} \quad y = x^2 x^3 = x^5$$
$$\text{quotient:} \quad y = \frac{x^2}{x^3} = \frac{1}{x} \quad (\text{if } x \neq 0)$$

Indeed, this is the idea behind the formal definitions we now give.

---

**DEFINITION** | **Arithmetical Operations with Functions**

Let $f$ and $g$ be two functions. Then the **sum** $f + g$, the **difference** $f - g$, the **product** $fg$, and the **quotient** $f/g$ are functions defined by the following equations:

$$(f + g)(x) = f(x) + g(x) \tag{1}$$
$$(f - g)(x) = f(x) - g(x) \tag{2}$$
$$(fg)(x) = f(x) \cdot g(x) \tag{3}$$
$$(f/g)(x) = f(x)/g(x) \qquad \text{provided that } g(x) \neq 0 \tag{4}$$

For the functions defined by equations (1), (2), and (3), the domain is the set of all inputs $x$ belonging to both the domain of $f$ and the domain of $g$. For the quotient function in equation (4), we impose the additional restriction that the domain exclude all inputs $x$ for which $g(x) = 0$.

---

**EXAMPLE** | **1** | **Combining functions arithmetically**

Let $f(x) = 3x + 1$ and $g(x) = x - 1$. Compute each of the following:
**(a)** $(f + g)(x)$; **(b)** $(f - g)(x)$; **(c)** $(fg)(x)$; **(d)** $(f/g)(x)$.

**SOLUTION**
**(a)** $(f + g)(x) = f(x) + g(x) = (3x + 1) + (x - 1) = 4x$, for all real $x$
**(b)** $(f - g)(x) = f(x) - g(x) = (3x + 1) - (x - 1) = 2x + 2$, for all real $x$
**(c)** $(fg)(x) = [f(x)][g(x)] = (3x + 1)(x - 1) = 3x^2 - 2x - 1$, for all real $x$
**(d)** $(f/g)(x) = \dfrac{f(x)}{g(x)} = \dfrac{3x + 1}{x - 1}$, for all real $x$ *except* $x = 1$

For the remainder of this section, we are going to discuss a method of combining functions known as **composition of functions.** As you will see, this method is based on the familiar algebraic process of substitution. Suppose, for example, that $f$ and $g$ are two functions defined by

$$f(x) = x^2 \qquad g(x) = 3x + 1$$

Choose any number in the domain of $g$, for example, $x = -2$. We can compute $g(-2)$:

$$g(-2) = 3(-2) + 1 = -5$$

Now let's use the output $-5$ that $g$ has produced as an *input* for $f$. We obtain

$$f(-5) = (-5)^2 = 25$$

Consequently,

$$f[g(-2)] = 25$$

So, beginning with the input $-2$, we've successively applied $g$ and then $f$ to obtain the output 25. Similarly, we could carry out this same procedure for any other number in the domain of $g$, provided that its output is in the domain of $f$. Here is a summary of the procedure:

1. Start with an input $x$ and calculate $g(x)$.
2. Use $g(x)$ as an input for $f$; that is, calculate $f[g(x)]$.

We use the notation $f \circ g$ to denote the function, or rule, that tells us to assign the output $f[g(x)]$ to the initial input $x$. In other words, $f \circ g$ denotes the rule consisting of two steps: *First apply g; then apply f*. We read the notation $f \circ g$ as *f circle g* or *f composed with g*. In Figure 1, we summarize these ideas.

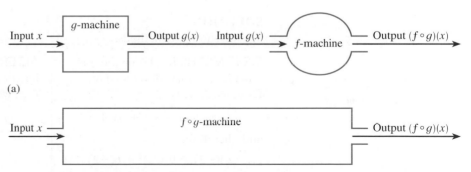

(a)

(b) Figure 1(b) indicates that, by incorporating the two steps in part (a), we can think of the composite function as one machine.

**Figure 1**
Diagram for the function $f \circ g$

When we write $g(x)$, we assume that $x$ is in the domain of the function $g$. Likewise, for the notation $f[g(x)]$ to make sense, the outputs $g(x)$ must themselves be acceptable inputs for the function $f$. Our formal definition, then, for the composite function $f \circ g$ is as follows.

---

**DEFINITION** | **Composition of Functions: $f \circ g$**

---

Given two functions $f$ and $g$, the function $f \circ g$ is defined by

$$(f \circ g)(x) = f[g(x)]$$

The domain of $f \circ g$ consists of those inputs $x$ (in the domain of $g$) for which $g(x)$ is in the domain of $f$.

**EXAMPLE** 2 **Comparing $f \circ g$ to $g \circ f$**

Let $f(x) = x^2$ and $g(x) = 3x + 1$. Compute $(f \circ g)(x)$ and $(g \circ f)(x)$.

**SOLUTION**

$$
\begin{aligned}
(f \circ g)(x) &= f[g(x)] && \text{definition of } f \circ g \\
&= f(3x + 1) && \text{definition of } g \\
&= (3x + 1)^2 && \text{definition of } f \\
&= 9x^2 + 6x + 1
\end{aligned}
$$

$$
\begin{aligned}
(g \circ f)(x) &= g[f(x)] && \text{definition of } g \circ f \\
&= g(x^2) && \text{definition of } f \\
&= 3(x^2) + 1 && \text{definition of } g \\
&= 3x^2 + 1
\end{aligned}
$$

Notice that the two results obtained in Example 2 are not the same. This shows that, in general, $f \circ g$ and $g \circ f$ represent different functions.

**EXAMPLE** 3 **Two ways to compute a composite value**

Let $f$ and $g$ be defined as in Example 2: $f(x) = x^2$ and $g(x) = 3x + 1$. Compute $(f \circ g)(-2)$.

**SOLUTION**
We will show two methods.

**FIRST METHOD**   Using the formula for $(f \circ g)(x)$ developed in Example 2, we have

$$(f \circ g)(x) = 9x^2 + 6x + 1$$

and, therefore,

$$
\begin{aligned}
(f \circ g)(-2) &= 9(-2)^2 + 6(-2) + 1 \\
&= 36 - 12 + 1 \\
&= 25
\end{aligned}
$$

**ALTERNATIVE METHOD**   Working directly from the definition of $f \circ g$, we have

$$
\begin{aligned}
(f \circ g)(-2) &= f[g(-2)] \\
&= f[3(-2) + 1] \\
&= f(-5) \\
&= (-5)^2 \\
&= 25
\end{aligned}
$$

In Examples 2 and 3 the domain of both $f$ and $g$ is the set of all real numbers. And as you can easily check, the domain of both $f \circ g$ and $g \circ f$ is also the set of all real numbers. In Example 4, however, some care needs to be taken in describing the domain of the composite function.

**EXAMPLE** 4 **Finding the domain of a composite function**

Let $f$ and $g$ be defined as follows:

$$f(x) = x^2 + 1 \qquad g(x) = \sqrt{x}$$

Compute $(f \circ g)(x)$. Find the domain of $f \circ g$ and sketch its graph.

**SOLUTION**

$$(f \circ g)(x) = f[g(x)]$$
$$= f(\sqrt{x}) = (\sqrt{x})^2 + 1 = x + 1$$

So we have $(f \circ g)(x) = x + 1$. Now, what about the domain of $f \circ g$? Our first inclination might be to say (incorrectly!) that the domain is the set of all real numbers, since any real number can be used as an input in the expression $x + 1$. However, the definition of $f \circ g$ on page 183 tells us that the inputs for $f \circ g$ must first of all be acceptable inputs for $g$. Given the definition of $g$, then, we must require that $x$ be nonnegative. On the other hand, for any nonnegative input $x$, the number $g(x)$ will be an acceptable input for $f$. (Why?) In summary, then, the domain of $f \circ g$ is the interval $[0, \infty)$. The graph of $f \circ g$ is shown in Figure 2.

**Figure 2**
The graph of the function $f \circ g$ in Example 4

---

**EXAMPLE  5   An application of composition of functions**

Suppose that an offshore oil rig is leaking and that the oil forms a circular region whose radius $r$ increases over the first 12 hours according to the function

$$r = f(t) = \frac{t}{2t + 4} \qquad 0 \le t \le 12$$

where $r$ is measured in miles, $t$ is in hours, and $t = 0$ corresponds to the instant that the leak begins.

**(a)** Using function notation, the area of a circle of radius $r$ is given by $A(r) = \pi r^2$. Find $(A \circ f)(t)$ and interpret the result.

**(b)** Compute the rate of change of the function $A \circ f$ over the interval $0 \le t \le 6$.

**SOLUTION**

**(a)** $(A \circ f)(t) = A[f(t)] = A\left(\dfrac{t}{2t + 4}\right)$

$$= \pi\left(\frac{t}{2t + 4}\right)^2$$

After squaring the fraction in this last expression, we obtain

$$(A \circ f)(t) = \frac{\pi t^2}{4t^2 + 16t + 16} \tag{1}$$

Since $f(t)$ expresses the radius in terms of time, our result in equation (1) gives the area of the oil spill in terms of time.

**(b)** By definition (from Section 3.3) the average rate of change of the function $A \circ f$ on the interval $[0, 6]$ is given by

$$\frac{\Delta(A \circ f)}{\Delta t} = \frac{(A \circ f)(6) - (A \circ f)(0)}{6 - 0} \tag{2}$$

To evaluate the difference quotient on the right side of equation (2), we need to find $(A \circ f)(6)$ and $(A \circ f)(0)$. Exercise 33 asks you to use equation (1) to check that $(A \circ f)(6) = 9\pi/64$ and $(A \circ f)(0) = 0$. Assuming these results, equation (2) becomes

$$\frac{\Delta(A \circ f)}{\Delta t} = \frac{9\pi/64}{6}$$

$$= 3\pi/128 \qquad\qquad \text{Check the arithmetic.}$$

$$\approx 0.07 \text{ (sq. miles)/hour}$$

That is, on average over the first six hours, the area of the oil spill is increasing at approximately 0.07 (sq. miles)/hour. (Exercise 34 asks you to compute the rate of change of the area over the next six-hour period and to compare it to this result for the first six hours.)

AFTERWORD ON THE SOLUTION TO EXAMPLE 5(b)   A graphing utility can also be used for the computations. For instance, with a TI-83 graphing calculator, in the $\boxed{Y=}$ screen, one enters the three functions

$$Y_1 = \frac{x}{2x + 4} \qquad Y_2 = \pi x^2 \qquad Y_3 = Y_1(Y_2)$$

Then, in the home screen, the required rate of change is obtained by evaluating the expression $\dfrac{Y_3(6) - Y_3(0)}{6 - 0}$ or, more simply, $\dfrac{Y_3(6)}{6}$, since in this example $Y_3(0) = 0$. For other types of graphing utilities, consult your user's manual.

One reason for studying the composition of functions is that it lets us express a given function in terms of simpler functions. This procedure is often useful in calculus. Suppose, for example, that we wish to express the function $C$ defined by

$$C(x) = (2x^3 - 5)^2$$

as a composition of simpler functions. That is, we want to come up with two functions $f$ and $g$ so that the equation

$$C(x) = (f \circ g)(x)$$

holds for every $x$ in the domain of $C$.

We begin by thinking what we would do to compute $(2x^3 - 5)^2$ for a given value of $x$. First, we would compute the quantity $2x^3 - 5$, then we would square the result. Therefore, recalling that the rule $f \circ g$ tells us to do $g$ *first*, we let $g(x) = 2x^3 - 5$. Then, since the next step is squaring, we let $f(x) = x^2$. Now let's see whether these choices for $f$ and $g$ are correct; that is, let us calculate $(f \circ g)(x)$ and see whether it really is the same as $C(x)$.

Using $f(x) = x^2$ and $g(x) = 2x^3 - 5$, we have

$$(f \circ g)(x) = f[g(x)] = f(2x^3 - 5) = (2x^3 - 5)^2 = C(x)$$

This equation shows that our choices for $f$ and $g$ were indeed correct, and we have expressed $C$ as a composition of two simpler functions.*

Note that in expressing $C$ as $f \circ g$, we chose $g$ to be the "inner" function, that is, the quantity inside the parentheses: $g(x) = 2x^3 - 5$. This observation is used in Example 6.

---

*Other answers are possible, too. For instance, if $F(x) = (x - 5)^2$ and $G(x) = 2x^3$, then (as you should verify for yourself) $C(x) = F[G(x)]$.

**EXAMPLE** 6 **Expressing a function in terms of two simpler functions**

Let $s(x) = \sqrt{1 + x^4}$. Express the function $s$ as a composition of two simpler functions $f$ and $g$.

**SOLUTION**

Let $g$ be the "inner" function; that is, let $g(x)$ be the quantity inside the radical:

$$g(x) = 1 + x^4$$

and let's take $f$ to be the square root function:

$$f(x) = \sqrt{x}$$

Now we need to verify that these are the appropriate choices for $f$ and $g$; that is, we need to check that the equation $(f \circ g)(x) = s(x)$ is true for every $x$ in the domain of $s$. We have

$$(f \circ g)(x) = f[g(x)] = f(1 + x^4) = \sqrt{1 + x^4} = s(x)$$

Thus $(f \circ g)(x) = s(x)$, as required. (What is the domain of $s(x)$?)

We conclude this section by describing the process of *iteration* for a function. This simple process is of fundamental importance in modern mathematics and science in the study of fractals and chaos.* The process of iteration is sequential; it proceeds step by step. We begin with a function $f$ and an initial input $x_0$. In the first step, we compute the output $f(x_0)$. For the second step, we use the number $f(x_0)$ as an *input* for $f$ and compute $f(f(x_0))$. The process then continues in this way: At each step, we use the output from the previous step as the new input.

For example, suppose that we start with the function $f(x) = x/2$ and the input $x_0 = 6$. Then, for the first three steps in the iteration process, we have

$$f(6) = \frac{6}{2} = 3$$

$$f(3) = \frac{3}{2} = 1.5$$

$$f(1.5) = \frac{1.5}{2} = 0.75$$

After this a calculator becomes convenient. Check for yourself that the iterations run as follows:

$$6 \to 3 \to 1.5 \to 0.75 \to 0.375 \to 0.1875 \to 0.09375 \to 0.046875 \to \cdots$$

This list of numbers is called the *orbit* of 6 under the function $f$. In the list or orbit, the number 3 is the *first iterate* of 6, the number 1.5 is the *second iterate* of 6, and so on. In the box that follows, we summarize these ideas and introduce a useful notation for the iterates.

---

*See, for example, pp. 314–363 in *The Nature and Power of Mathematics* by Donald M. Davis (Princeton, N.J.: Princeton University Press, 1993). For a wider view, see the book by James Gleick: *Chaos: Making a New Science* (New York: Penguin Books, 1988).

| **DEFINITION** | Iterates |
| --- | --- |

Given a function $f$ and an input $x_0$, the **iterates** of $x_0$ are the numbers $f(x_0), f(f(x_0))$, $f(f(f(x_0)))$, and so on. The number $f(x_0)$ is called the **first iterate,** the number $f(f(x_0))$ is called the **second iterate,** and so on. Subscript notation is used to denote the iterates as follows.

$$x_1 = f(x_0) \qquad \text{the first iterate}$$
$$x_2 = f(f(x_0)) \qquad \text{the second iterate}$$
$$x_3 = f(f(f(x_0))) \qquad \text{the third iterate}$$
$$\vdots$$

The **orbit** of $x_0$ under the function $f$ is the list of numbers $x_0, x_1, x_2, x_3, \dots$.

Notice that the subscripts in this notation tell you how many times to apply the function $f$. For example, $x_1$ indicates that $f$ is applied once to obtain $f(x_0)$, and $x_2$ indicates that the function is applied twice to obtain $f(f(x_0))$.

| **EXAMPLE** | 7 | **Computing iterates** |
| --- | --- | --- |

Compute the first four iterates in each case. Use a calculator as necessary. In part (b), round the final answers to three decimal places.

**(a)** $f(x) = x^2, x_0 = -2$ **(b)** $g(x) = \sqrt{x}, x_0 = 0.1$

**SOLUTION**

**(a)** $x_1 = (-2)^2 = 4$
$x_2 = (4)^2 = 16$
$x_3 = (16)^2 = 256$
$x_4 = (256)^2 = 65{,}536$

**(b)** We use the square root key (or keys) on the calculator repeatedly. As you should check for yourself, this yields

$$x_1 = \sqrt{0.1} = 0.316227\dots$$
$$x_2 = \sqrt{0.316227\dots} = 0.562341\dots$$
$$x_3 = \sqrt{0.562341\dots} = 0.749894\dots$$
$$x_4 = \sqrt{0.749989\dots} = 0.865964\dots \approx 0.866 \qquad \text{rounding to three decimal places}$$

**Figure 3**
The $y$-coordinates of the points $P$, $Q$, and $R$ are, respectively, the first three iterates of $x_0$ under the function $f$.

The process of iterating a function can be visualized in an $x$-$y$ coordinate system. We sketch the function $y = f(x)$ along with the line $y = x$, as in Figure 3. Then, starting with the initial input $x_0$ on the $x$-axis, we follow the horizontal and vertical segments to determine points $P$, $Q$, and $R$ on the graph of $f$. As the next paragraph explains, the $y$-coordinates of the points $P$, $Q$, and $R$ are the first, second, and third iterates, respectively, of $x_0$. Additional iterates are obtained by continuing this pattern. In Figure 4 we show how this looks in a specific case. The $y$-coordinates of the five points $P$, $Q$, $R$, $S$, and $T$ are the first five iterates of $x_0 = 0.1$ under the function $g(x) = -4x^2 + 4x$. Although Figure 4 at first appears more complicated than Fig-

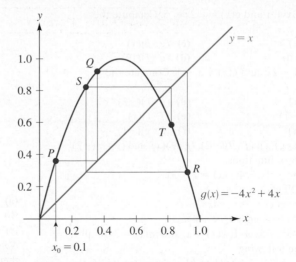

**Figure 4**
Graphical iteration of
$g(x) = -4x^2 + 4x$ with initial
input $x_0 = 0.1$. The $y$-coordinates
of the five points $P$, $Q$, $R$, $S$, and
$T$ are, respectively, the first five
iterates of $x_0$.

ure 3, it is important to understand that the pattern is formed in exactly the same way. We start with the initial input on the $x$-axis and travel vertically to determine the point $P$ on the curve. After that, each successive point on the curve is generated in the same way: Go horizontally to the line $y = x$ and then vertically to the curve.

As we've said, this paragraph explains why the $y$-coordinates of the three points $P$, $Q$, and $R$ in Figure 3 are, respectively, the first three iterates of $x_0$ under the function $f$. In Figure 3 the $x$-coordinate of $P$ is given to be $x_0$. So (according to the definition of the graph of a function), the $y$-coordinate of $P$ is $f(x_0)$. In other words, the $y$-coordinate of $P$ is the first iterate of $x_0$. Next in Figure 3, we move horizontally from the point $P$ to the point $A$. Because the movement is horizontal, the $y$-coordinate doesn't change; it's the $y$-coordinate of $P$, or $f(x_0)$. Now, what about the $x$-coordinate of $A$? Since the point $A$ lies on the line $y = x$, the $x$- and $y$-coordinates of $A$ must be identical. Consequently, the $x$-coordinate of $A$ must be the number $f(x_0)$. Finally, we move vertically in Figure 3 from $A$ to $Q$. The point $Q$ has the same $x$-coordinate as the point $A$, namely, $f(x_0)$. Now, since $Q$ lies on the graph of the function $f$, we conclude that the $y$-coordinate of $Q$ is $f(f(x_0))$. That is, the $y$-coordinate of $Q$ is indeed the second iterate of $x_0$. The reasoning to show that the $y$-coordinate of $R$ is the third iterate of $x_0$ is entirely similar, so we omit giving the details here.

# EXERCISE SET 3.5

## A

*In Exercises 1–8, compute each expression, given that the functions f, g, h, k, and m are defined as follows:*

$$f(x) = 2x - 1 \qquad k(x) = 2, \quad \text{for all } x$$
$$g(x) = x^2 - 3x - 6 \qquad m(x) = x^2 - 9$$
$$h(x) = x^3$$

**1. (a)** $(f + g)(x)$
   **(b)** $(f - g)(x)$
   **(c)** $(f - g)(0)$

**2. (a)** $(fh)(x)$
   **(b)** $(h/f)(x)$
   **(c)** $(f/h)(1)$

**3. (a)** $(m - f)(x)$
   **(b)** $(f - m)(x)$

**4. (a)** $(fg)(x)$
   **(b)** $(fg)(1/2)$

**5. (a)** $(fk)(x)$
   **(b)** $(kf)(x)$
   **(c)** $(fk)(1) - (kf)(2)$

**6. (a)** $(g + m)(x)$
   **(b)** $(g + m)(x) - (g - m)(x)$

**7. (a)** $(f/m)(x) - (m/f)(x)$
   **(b)** $(f/m)(0) - (m/f)(0)$

**8. (a)** $[h \cdot (f + m)](x)$   *Note: h and (f + m) are two functions; the notation $h \cdot (f + m)$ denotes the product function.*
   **(b)** $(hf)(x) + (hm)(x)$

**9.** Let $f(x) = 3x + 1$ and $g(x) = -2x - 5$. Compute the following.

(a) $(f \circ g)(x)$          (c) $(g \circ f)(x)$
(b) $(f \circ g)(10)$         (d) $(g \circ f)(10)$

**10.** Let $f(x) = 1 - 2x^2$ and $g(x) = x + 1$. Compute the following.

(a) $(f \circ g)(x)$          (d) $(g \circ f)(-1)$
(b) $(f \circ g)(-1)$         (e) $(f \circ f)(x)$
(c) $(g \circ f)(x)$          (f) $(g \circ g)(-1)$

**11.** Compute $(f \circ g)(x)$, $(f \circ g)(-2)$, $(g \circ f)(x)$, and $(g \circ f)(-2)$ for each pair of functions.

(a) $f(x) = x^2 - 3x - 4$; $g(x) = 2 - 3x$
(b) $f(x) = 2^x$; $g(x) = x^2 + 1$
(c) $f(x) = x$; $g(x) = 3x^5 - 4x^2$
(d) $f(x) = 3x - 4$; $g(x) = (x + 4)/3$

**12.** Let $h(x) = 4x^2 - 5x + 1$, $k(x) = x$, and $m(x) = 7$ for all $x$. Compute the following.

(a) $h[k(x)]$          (c) $h[m(x)]$          (e) $k[m(x)]$
(b) $k[h(x)]$          (d) $m[h(x)]$          (f) $m[k(x)]$

**13.** Let $F(x) = \dfrac{3x - 4}{3x + 3}$ and $G(x) = \dfrac{x + 1}{x - 1}$. Compute the following.

(a) $(F \circ G)(x)$          (c) $(F \circ G)(2)$          (e) $G[F(y)]$
(b) $F[G(t)]$                 (d) $(G \circ F)(x)$          (f) $(G \circ F)(2)$

**14.** Let $f(x) = (1/x^2) + 1$ and $g(x) = 1/(x - 1)$

(a) Compute $(f \circ g)(x)$.
(b) What is the domain of $f \circ g$?
(c) Graph the function $f \circ g$.

**15.** Let $M(x) = (2x - 1)/(x - 2)$.

(a) Compute $M(7)$ and then $M[M(7)]$.
(b) Compute $(M \circ M)(x)$.
(c) Compute $(M \circ M)(7)$, using the formula you obtained in part (b). Check that your answer agrees with that obtained in part (a).

**16.** Let $F(x) = (x + 1)^5$, $f(x) = x^5$, and $g(x) = x + 1$. Which of the following is true for all $x$?

$$(f \circ g)(x) = F(x) \quad \text{or} \quad (g \circ f)(x) = F(x)$$

**17.** Refer to the graphs of the functions $f$, $g$, and $h$ to compute the required quantities. Assume that all the axes are marked off in one-unit intervals

(a)

(b)

(c)

(a) $f[g(3)]$          (d) $(h \circ g)(2)$
(b) $g[f(3)]$          (e) $h\{f[g(3)]\}$
(c) $f[h(3)]$          (f) $(g \circ f \circ h \circ f)(2)$

*Note:* The notation in part (f) means first do $f$, then $h$, then $f$, then $g$.

**18.** (a) Let $T(x) = 4x^3 - 3x^2 + 6x - 1$ and $I(x) = x$. Find $(T \circ I)(x)$ and $(I \circ T)(x)$.
(b) Let $G(x) = ax^2 + bx + c$ and $I(x) = x$. Find $(G \circ I)(x)$ and $(I \circ G)(x)$.
(c) What general conclusion do you arrive at from the results of parts (a) and (b)?

**19.** The domain of a function $f$ consists of the numbers $-1, 0, 1, 2$, and $3$. The following table shows the output that $f$ assigns to each input.

| x    | −1 | 0 | 1 | 2 | 3 |
|------|----|---|---|---|---|
| f(x) | 2  | 2 | 0 | 3 | 1 |

The domain of a function $g$ consists of the numbers $0, 1, 2, 3$, and $4$. The following table shows the output that $g$ assigns to each input.

| x    | 0 | 1 | 2 | 3 | 4  |
|------|---|---|---|---|----|
| g(x) | 3 | 2 | 0 | 4 | −1 |

Use this information to complete the following tables for $f \circ g$ and $g \circ f$. *Note:* Two of the entries will be undefined.

| x             | 0 | 1 | 2 | 3 | 4 |
|---------------|---|---|---|---|---|
| (f ∘ g)(x)    |   |   |   |   |   |

| x             | −1 | 0 | 1 | 2 | 3 | 4 |
|---------------|----|---|---|---|---|---|
| (g ∘ f)(x)    |    |   |   |   |   |   |

**20.** The following two tables show certain pairs of inputs and outputs for functions $f$ and $g$.

| x | 0 | $\pi/6$ | $\pi/4$ | $\pi/3$ | $\pi/2$ |
|---|---|---|---|---|---|
| f(x) | 0 | 1/2 | $\sqrt{2}/2$ | $\sqrt{3}/2$ | 1 |

| y | 0 | 1/4 | $\sqrt{2}/4$ | 1/2 | $\sqrt{2}/2$ | 3/4 | $\sqrt{3}/2$ | 1 |
|---|---|---|---|---|---|---|---|---|
| g(y) | $\pi/2$ | $\pi$ | 0 | $\pi/3$ | $\pi/4$ | 0 | $\pi/6$ | 0 |

Use this information to complete the following table of values for $(g \circ f)(x)$.

| x | 0 | $\pi/6$ | $\pi/4$ | $\pi/3$ | $\pi/2$ |
|---|---|---|---|---|---|
| $(g \circ f)(x)$ | | | | | |

**21.** Let $f(x) = x^3 - 2x$ and $g(x) = x + 4$.
   **(a)** What is the relationship between the graphs of the two functions $f$ and $f \circ g$? (The idea here is to answer without looking at the graphs; use a concept from Section 3.4.)
   **(b)** Use a graphing utility to check your answer in part (a).

**22.** Let $f(x) = \sqrt{x^3 + 2x + 17}$ and $g(x) = x + 6$.
   **(a)** What is the relationship between the graphs of the two functions $f$ and $f \circ g$? (As in Exercise 21, the idea here is to answer without looking at the graphs.)
   **(b)** Use a graphing utility to check your answer in part (a).

**23.** Let $g(x) = \sqrt{x} - 3$ and $f(x) = x - 1$.
   **(a)** Sketch a graph of $g$. Specify the domain and range.
   **(b)** Sketch a graph of $f$. Specify the domain and range.
   **(c)** Compute $(f \circ g)(x)$. Graph the function $f \circ g$ and specify its domain and range.
   **(d)** Find a formula for $g[f(x)]$. Which values of $x$ are acceptable inputs here? That is, what is the domain of $g \circ f$?
   **(e)** Use the results of part (d) to sketch a graph of the function $g \circ f$.

**24.** Let $F(x) = -x^2$ and $G(x) = \sqrt{x}$. Determine the domains of $F \circ G$ and $G \circ F$.

**25.** Suppose that an oil spill in a lake covers a circular area and that the radius of the circle is increasing according to the formula $r = f(t) = 15 + t^{1.65}$, where $t$ represents the number of hours since the spill was first observed and the radius $r$ is measured in meters. (Thus when the spill was first discovered, $t = 0$ hr, and the initial radius was $r = f(0) = 15 + 0^{1.65} = 15$ m.)
   **(a)** Let $A(r) = \pi r^2$, as in Example 5. Compute a table of values for the composite function $A \circ f$ with $t$ running from 0 to 5 in increments of 0.5. (Round each output to the nearest integer.) Then use the table to answer the questions that follow in parts (b) through (d).
   **(b)** After one hour, what is the area of the spill (rounded to the nearest 10 m²)?

**(c)** Initially, what was the area of the spill (when $t = 0$)? Approximately how many hours does it take for this area to double?
**(d)** Compute the average rate of change of the area of the spill from $t = 0$ to $t = 2.5$ and from $t = 2.5$ to $t = 5$. Over which of the two intervals is the area increasing faster?

**26.** A spherical weather balloon is being inflated in such a way that the radius is given by

$$r = g(t) = \frac{1}{2}t + 2$$

Assume that $r$ is in meters and $t$ is in seconds, with $t = 0$ corresponding to the time that inflation begins. If the volume of a sphere of radius $r$ is given by

$$V(r) = \frac{4}{3}\pi r^3$$

compute $V[g(t)]$ and use this to find the time at which the volume of the balloon is $36\pi$ m³.

**27.** Suppose that a manufacturer knows that the daily production cost to build $x$ bicycles is given by the function $C$, where

$$C(x) = 100 + 90x - x^2 \qquad (0 \le x \le 40)$$

That is, $C(x)$ represents the cost in dollars of building $x$ bicycles. Furthermore, suppose that the number of bicycles that can be built in $t$ hr is given by the function $f$, where

$$x = f(t) = 5t \qquad (0 \le t \le 8)$$

   **(a)** Compute $(C \circ f)(t)$.
   **(b)** Compute the production cost on a day that the factory operates for $t = 3$ hr.
   **(c)** If the factory runs for 6 hr instead of 3 hr, is the cost twice as much?

**28.** Suppose that in a certain biology lab experiment, the number of bacteria is related to the temperature $T$ of the environment by the function

$$N(T) = -2T^2 + 240T - 5400 \qquad (40 \le T \le 90)$$

Here, $N(T)$ represents the number of bacteria present when the temperature is $T$ degrees Fahrenheit. Also, suppose that $t$ hr after the experiment begins, the temperature is given by

$$T(t) = 10t + 40 \qquad (0 \le t \le 5)$$

   **(a)** Compute $N[T(t)]$.
   **(b)** How many bacteria are present when $t = 0$ hr? When $t = 2$ hr? When $t = 5$ hr?

**29.** Express each function as a composition of two functions.
   **(a)** $F(x) = \sqrt[3]{3x + 4}$      **(c)** $H(x) = (ax + b)^5$
   **(b)** $G(x) = |2x - 3|$      **(d)** $T(x) = 1/\sqrt{x}$

**30.** Let $a(x) = x^2$, $b(x) = |x|$, and $c(x) = 3x - 1$. Express each of the following functions as a composition of two of the given functions.
   **(a)** $f(x) = (3x - 1)^2$      **(c)** $h(x) = 3x^2 - 1$
   **(b)** $g(x) = |3x - 1|$

**31.** Let $a(x) = 1/x$, $b(x) = \sqrt[3]{x}$, $c(x) = 2x + 1$, and $d(x) = x^2$. Express each of the following functions as a composition of two of the given functions.

(a) $f(x) = \sqrt[3]{2x + 1}$

(b) $g(x) = 1/x^2$

(c) $h(x) = 2x^2 + 1$

(d) $K(x) = 2\sqrt[3]{x} + 1$

(e) $l(x) = \dfrac{2}{x} + 1$

(f) $m(x) = \dfrac{1}{2x + 1}$

**32.** Express $n(x) = x^{2/3}$ as a composition of two of the functions given at the begining of Exercise 31. (If you don't recall the definition for fractional exponents, see Appendix B.3 at the back of this book.)

**33.** For this exercise, refer to equation (1) in Example 5.

(a) Show that $(A \circ f)(0) = 0$ and that $(A \circ f)(6) = 9\pi/64$.

Ⓖ (b) Use a graphing utility to graph the average-rate-of-change function $y = (A \circ f)(t)$. Note that the graph appears to pass through the point $(0, 0)$, which supports the first result in part (a).

Ⓖ (c) By zooming in, estimate the $y$-coordinate of the point on the graph corresponding to $t = 6$. What does this have to do with part (a) of this exercise?

**34.** Refer to Example 5(b).

(a) Compute the average rate of change of $A \circ f$ over the time interval from $t = 6$ to $t = 12$ hours. On average, was the area of the oil leak increasing faster over the first six hours or the second six hours?

Ⓖ (b) Graph the average-rate-of-change function $y = (A \circ f)(t)$ in the viewing rectangle $[0, 12]$ by $[0, 0.8]$. Then draw two line segments, one connecting the two points on the graph corresponding to $t = 0$ and $t = 6$, the other connecting the two points corresponding to $t = 6$ and $t = 12$. (If your graphing utility does not have a draw feature, use hard copy and draw using a ruler.) Explain in complete sentences how the picture supports your answer to the question in part (a).

*In Exercises 35–40, use the given function and compute the first six iterates of each initial input $x_0$. In cases in which a calculator answer contains four or more decimal places, round the final answer to three decimal places. (However, during the calculations, work with all of the decimal places that your calculator affords.)*

**35.** $f(x) = 2x$
(a) $x_0 = 1$
(b) $x_0 = 0$
(c) $x_0 = -1$

**36.** $f(x) = \frac{1}{4}x$
(a) $x_0 = 16$
(b) $x_0 = 0$
(c) $x_0 = -16$

**37.** $g(x) = 2x + 1$
(a) $x_0 = -2$
(b) $x_0 = -1$
(c) $x_0 = 1$

**38.** $g(x) = \frac{1}{4}x + 3$
(a) $x_0 = 3$
(b) $x_0 = 4$
(c) $x_0 = 5$

**39.** $F(x) = x^2$
(a) $x_0 = 0.9$
(b) $x_0 = 1$
(c) $x_0 = 1.1$

**40.** $G(x) = x^2 + 0.25$
(a) $x_0 = 0.4$
(b) $x_0 = 0.5$
(c) $x_0 = 0.6$

**41.** The accompanying figure shows a portion of the iteration process for $f(x) = \sqrt{x}$ with initial input $x_0 = 0.1$. Use the figure to estimate (to within 0.05) the first four iterates of $x_0 = 0.1$. Then, use a calculator to compute the four iterates. (Round to three decimal places, where appropriate.) Check that your calculator results are consistent with the estimates obtained from the graph.

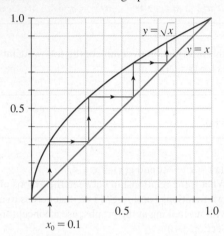

**42.** The following figure shows a portion of the iteration process for $f(x) = 3.6(x - x^2)$ with initial input $x_0 = 0.3$. Use the figure to estimate (to within 0.1, or closer if it seems appropriate) the first seven iterates of $x_0 = 0.3$. Then, use a calculator to compute the seven iterates. (Round the final answers to three decimal places.) Check that your calculator results are consistent with the estimates obtained from the graph.

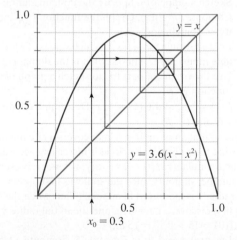

**B**

**43.** *The $3x + 1$ conjecture* Define a function $f$, with domain the positive integers, as follows:

$$f(x) = \begin{cases} 3x + 1 & \text{if } x \text{ is odd} \\ x/2 & \text{if } x \text{ is even} \end{cases}$$

(a) Compute $f(1), f(2), f(3), f(4), f(5)$, and $f(6)$.

(b) Compute the first three iterates of $x_0 = 1$.

(c) Compute the iterates of $x_0 = 3$ until you obtain the value 1. [After this, the iterates will recycle through the simple pattern obtained in part (b).]

(d) *The $3x + 1$ conjecture* asserts that for any positive integer $x_0$, the iterates eventually return to the value 1. Verify that this conjecture is valid for each of the following values of $x_0$: 2, 4, 5, 6, and 7.

*Remark*: At present, the $3x + 1$ conjecture is indeed a conjecture, not a theorem. No one yet has found a proof that the assertion is valid for *every* positive integer. Computer checks, however, have verified the conjecture on a case-by-case basis for very large values of $x_0$. As of April 2000, the conjecture had been verified for all values of $x_0$ up to approximately $1.8 \times 10^{16}$.

**44.** *The $3x + 1$ conjecture* (continued from Exercise 43) If you have access to the Internet, use Alfred Wassermann's $3x + 1$ on-line calculator located at

http://did.mat.uni-bayreuth.de/personen/wassermann/fun/3np1.html

to answer the following questions. For which $n$ does $x_n$ first reach 1 if $x_0 = 100$? If $x_0 = 1000$? If $x_0 = 10^4$? (The Web address above was accessible at the time of this writing, March 2004.)

**45.** Let $g(x) = 4x - 1$. Find $f(x)$, given that the equation $(g \circ f)(x) = x + 5$ is true for all values of $x$.

**46.** Let $g(x) = 2x + 1$. Find $f(x)$, given that $(g \circ f)(x) = 10x - 7$.

**47.** Let $f(x) = -2x + 1$ and $g(x) = ax + b$. Find $a$ and $b$ so the equation $f[g(x)] = x$ holds for all values of $x$.

**48.** Let $f(x) = (3x - 4)/(x - 3)$.

(a) Compute $(f \circ f)(x)$.

(b) Find $f[f(113/355)]$. (Try not to do it the hard way.)

**49.** Let $f(x) = x^2$ and $g(x) = 2x - 1$.

(a) Compute $\dfrac{f[g(x)] - f[g(a)]}{g(x) - g(a)}$.

(b) Compute $\dfrac{f[g(x)] - f[g(a)]}{x - a}$.

*Exercises 50 and 51 indicate how iteration is used in finding roots of numbers and roots of equations. (The functions that are given in each exercise were determined using Newton's method, a process studied in calculus.)*

**50.** Let $f(x) = 0.5\left(x + \dfrac{3}{x}\right)$.

(a) Compute the first ten iterates of $x_0 = 1$ under the function $f$. What do you observe?

(b) Use your calculator to evaluate $\sqrt{3}$ and compare the answer to your results in part (a). What do you observe?

(c) It can be shown that for any positive number $x_0$, the iterates of $x_0$ under the function $f(x) = 0.5(x + 3/x)$ always approach the number $\sqrt{3}$. (You'll see the reasons for this in Section 4.3.) Looking at your results in parts (a) and (b), which is the first iterate that agrees with $\sqrt{3}$ through the first three decimal places? Through the first eight decimal places?

(d) Compute the first ten iterates of $x_0 = 50$ under the function $f$, then answer the questions presented in part (c).

**51.** Let $f(x) = \dfrac{2x^3 + 7}{3x^2}$.

(a) Compute the first ten iterates of $x_0 = 1$ under the function $f$. What do you observe?

(b) Evaluate the expression $\sqrt[3]{7}$ and compare the answer to your results in part (a). What do you observe?

(c) It can be shown that for any positive number $x_0$, the iterates of $x_0$ under the function $f(x) = \dfrac{2x^3 + 7}{3x^2}$ always approach the number $\sqrt[3]{7}$. Looking at your results in parts (a) and (b), which is the first iterate that agrees with $\sqrt[3]{7}$ through the first three decimal places? Through the first eight decimal places?

## C

**52.** Let $f(x) = \dfrac{x - 3}{x + c}$, where $c$ denotes a constant.

(a) If $c = -1$, show that $f(f(x)) = x$.

(b) Use a graphing utility to support the result in part (a). That is, enter the function $f(x) = \dfrac{x - 3}{x - 1}$, and then have the machine graph the two functions $y = x$ and $y = f(f(x))$ in the same picture.

(c) What does the result in part (a) tell you about the iteration process for the function $y = (x - 3)/(x - 1)$? That is, what pattern emerges in the iterates? Answer in complete sentences.

(d) Now assume $c = 1$, instead of $-1$. Show that $f(f(f(x))) = x$.

(e) Use a graphing utility to support the result in part (d).

(f) What does the result in part (d) tell you about the iteration process for the function $y = (x - 3)/(x + 1)$? That is, what pattern emerges in the iterates? Answer in complete sentences.

# MINI PROJECT | A GRAPHICAL APPROACH TO COMPOSITION OF FUNCTIONS

As we saw in this section, the iteration process can be carried out either algebraically or graphically. Composition of functions can also be represented graphically. The accompanying figure shows the graphs of two functions $f$ and $g$, the line $y = x$, and an input $a$. Use the figure and the ideas of this section to discover and then explain how to find the point $(a, g[f(a)])$ on the graph of the composite function $g \circ f$.

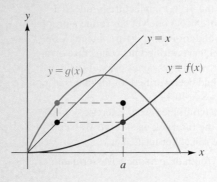

# 3.6 INVERSE FUNCTIONS

*If anybody ever told me why the graph of $y = x^{1/2}$ is the reflection of the graph of $y = x^2$ in a 45° line, it didn't sink in. To this day, there are textbooks that expect students to think that it is so obvious as to need no explanation. This is a pity, if only because [in calculus] it is such a common practice to define the natural logarithm first and then define the exponential function as its inverse.* —Professor Ralph P. Boas, recalling his student days in the article "Inverse Functions" in *The College Mathematics Journal,* vol. 16 (1985), p. 42.

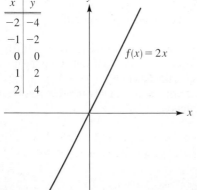

**PROBLEM SOLUTION**

We shall introduce the idea of inverse functions through an easy example. Consider the function $f$ defined by $f(x) = 2x$. A short table of values for $f$ and the graph of $f$ are displayed in Figure 1.

Now we ask this question: What happens if we take the table for $f$ (in Figure 1) and interchange the entries in the $x$ and $y$ columns to obtain a new table that looks like the following?

| $x$ | $y$ |
|---|---|
| −4 | −2 |
| −2 | −1 |
| 0 | 0 |
| 2 | 1 |
| 4 | 2 |

← New table formed by interchanging the inputs and outputs for $f$

Several observations are in order. Our new table does itself represent a function (in this case): for each input $x$ there is exactly one output $y$. Let's call this new function $g$. Note that each output is one-half of the corresponding input. So the

| $x$ | $y$ |
|---|---|
| −2 | −4 |
| −1 | −2 |
| 0 | 0 |
| 1 | 2 |
| 2 | 4 |

$f(x) = 2x$

**Figure 1**

function $g$ can be described by the formula $g(x) = x/2$. In summary, we began with the "doubling function," $f(x) = 2x$; then, by interchanging the inputs with the outputs, we obtained the "halving function," $g(x) = x/2$.

The doubling function $f$ and the halving function $g$ are in a certain sense opposites; each reverses, or undoes, the effect of the other. That is, if you begin with $x$ and then calculate $g[f(x)]$, you get $x$ again; similarly, $f[g(x)]$ is also equal to $x$. (Verify these last two statements for yourself.)

The two functions $f$ and $g$ that we've been discussing are an example of a pair of *inverse functions*. The general definition for inverse functions is given in the box that follows.

---

**DEFINITION** | **Inverse Functions**

---

Two functions $f$ and $g$ are **inverses** of one another provided that

$$f[g(x)] = x \qquad \text{for each } x \text{ in the domain of } g$$

and

$$g[f(x)] = x \qquad \text{for each } x \text{ in the domain of } f$$

---

**EXAMPLE 1  Applying the definition of inverse functions**

Suppose that $f$ and $g$ are a pair of inverse functions.
**(a)** If 13 is in the domain of $g$, find $f[g(13)]$.
**(b)** If $\sqrt{5}$ is in the domain of $f$, find $g[f(\sqrt{5})]$.

**SOLUTION**
**(a)** By the definition of inverse functions, the equation $f[g(x)] = x$ is true for each $x$ in the domain of $g$. In particular then, using $x = 13$, we have $f[g(13)] = 13$.
**(b)** Since $\sqrt{5}$ is in the domain of $f$, the definition of inverse functions gives us $g[f(\sqrt{5})] = \sqrt{5}$.

---

**EXAMPLE 2  Applying the definition of inverse functions**

Verify that the functions $f$ and $g$ are inverses, where

$$f(x) = \frac{1}{3}x + 2 \qquad \text{and} \qquad g(x) = 3x - 6$$

**SOLUTION**
In view of the definition, since both $f$ and $g$ have domain all real numbers, we must check that $f[g(x)] = x$ and $g[f(x)] = x$, for all real numbers $x$. We have

$$f[g(x)] = f(3x - 6)$$
$$= \frac{1}{3}(3x - 6) + 2 = x \qquad \text{(Check the algebra.)}$$

Thus, $f[g(x)] = x$. Now we still need to check that $g[f(x)] = x$. We have

$$g[f(x)] = g\left(\frac{1}{3}x + 2\right)$$

$$= 3\left(\frac{1}{3}x + 2\right) - 6 = x \qquad \text{Again, check the algebra.}$$

Having shown that $f[g(x)] = x$ and $g[f(x)] = x$, we conclude that $f$ and $g$ are indeed inverse functions.

---

**EXAMPLE 3    Two perspectives on inverse functions**

Suppose that $f$ and $g$ are a pair of inverse functions. If $f(2) = 3$, what is $g(3)$?

**SOLUTION**
We can use either of two methods.

**FIRST METHOD**    The quantities 3 and $f(2)$ are declared to be equal. Thus whether we use 3 or $f(2)$ as an input for $g$, the result must be the same. We then have

$$3 = f(2)$$
$$g(3) = g[f(2)]$$
$$g(3) = 2 \qquad \text{using the fact that}$$
$$g[f(x)] = x \text{ for any}$$
$$x \text{ in the domain of } f$$

Thus $g(3) = 2$.

**ALTERNATIVE METHOD**    Think of a table of values for the function $f$. Since $f(2) = 3$, one entry in the table must look like this:

| $x$ | | | 2 | |
|---|---|---|---|---|
| $y$ | | | 3 | |

Now, $g$ reverses the roles of $x$ and $y$, so in the table for $g$, one entry must look like this:

| $x$ | | | 3 | |
|---|---|---|---|---|
| $y$ | | | 2 | |

Thus $g(3) = 2$, as obtained previously.

---

It is customary to use the notation $f^{-1}$ (read $f$ *inverse*) for the function that is the inverse of $f$. So in Example 2, for instance, we have

$$f(x) = \frac{1}{3}x + 2 \qquad \text{and} \qquad f^{-1}(x) = 3x - 6 \qquad (1)$$

**CAUTION**    In the context of functions, $f^{-1}(x)$ does not in general mean $\dfrac{1}{f(x)}$. For instance, regarding the pair of inverse functions in equations (1), it's certainly not true in general that $3x - 6 = \dfrac{1}{\frac{1}{3}x + 2}$. (For other examples, see Exercises 11 and 12 at the end of this section.) For reference now, in the box that follows, we rewrite the defining equations for inverse functions using the $f^{-1}$ notation. Figure 2 provides a graphic summary of these equations.

**Figure 2**
The action of inverse functions:
The set $A$ in the figure is both the domain of $f$ and the range of $f^{-1}$.
The set $B$ is both the domain of $f^{-1}$ and the range of $f$.

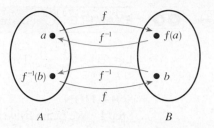

$$f[f^{-1}(x)] = x \qquad \text{for each } x \text{ in the domain of } f^{-1}$$

and

$$f^{-1}[f(x)] = x \qquad \text{for each } x \text{ in the domain of } f$$

---

**EXAMPLE 4   Using the definition of inverse functions**

Suppose $f(x) = 4x^3 + 7$. Find $f[f^{-1}(5)]$. (Assume that $f^{-1}$ exists and that 5 is in its domain.)

**SOLUTION**
As in Example 1, this is just an application of the definition of inverse functions. We have, by definition, $f[f^{-1}(x)] = x$ for every $x$ in the domain of $f^{-1}$. Replacing $x$ with 5 throughout this last equation, we immediately obtain

$$f[f^{-1}(5)] = 5$$

Note that we did not need to use the equation $f(x) = 4x^3 + 7$, nor did we need to find a formula for $f^{-1}(x)$.

---

**EXAMPLE 5   An equation to solve that involves inverse functions**

Solve the following equation for $x$, given that the domain of both $f$ and $f^{-1}$ is $(-\infty, \infty)$ and that $f(1) = -2$:

$$3 + f^{-1}(x - 1) = 4$$

**SOLUTION**

$$
\begin{aligned}
3 + f^{-1}(x - 1) &= 4 \\
f^{-1}(x - 1) &= 1 \\
f[f^{-1}(x - 1)] &= f(1) && \text{applying } f \text{ to both sides} \\
x - 1 &= f(1) && \text{definition of inverse function} \\
x = 1 + f(1) &= 1 + (-2) = -1
\end{aligned}
$$

---

We'll postpone a discussion until the end of this section as to which functions have inverses and which do not. For functions that do have inverses, however, there's a simple method that can often be used to determine those inverses. This method is illustrated in Example 6.

**EXAMPLE 6** Determining the inverse function

Let $f(x) = \dfrac{x-1}{3x+5}$. Find $f^{-1}(x)$.

**SOLUTION**

**Step 1** We begin by writing the given equation as

$$y = \frac{x-1}{3x+5} \tag{2}$$

We know that $f^{-1}$ interchanges the inputs and outputs of $f$, so to determine $y = f^{-1}(x)$, we first interchange the $x$'s and $y$'s in equation (2) and then solve for $y$. Interchanging gives us

$$x = \frac{y-1}{3y+5} \tag{3}$$

**Step 2** Now we solve equation (3) for $y$.

$$3xy + 5x = y - 1 \qquad \text{multiplying both sides of equation (3) by } 3y + 5$$

$$3xy - y = -5x - 1 \qquad \text{rearranging}$$

$$y(3x - 1) = -5x - 1$$

$$y = \frac{-5x - 1}{3x - 1}$$

Thus the inverse function is $y = (-5x - 1)/(3x - 1)$. Using function notation, we can write this result as

$$f^{-1}(x) = \frac{-5x - 1}{3x - 1}$$

**REMARK** Actually, we should call this result only a candidate for $f^{-1}$, because certain technical matters remain to be discussed. However, if you compute $f[f^{-1}(x)]$ and $f^{-1}[f(x)]$ and find they both do equal $x$, then the matter is settled, by definition. Exercise 21 at the end of this section asks you to carry out those calculations.

For reference, in the box that follows we summarize our procedure for calculating $f^{-1}(x)$.

---

**To Find $f^{-1}(x)$ for the Function $y = f(x)$**

**Step 1** Interchange $x$ and $y$ in the equation $y = f(x)$.

**Step 2** Solve the resulting equation for $y$.

---

CAUTION This method does not work for every function with an inverse. See the discussion of exponential and logarithmic functions in Chapter 5 and the discussions of trigonometric and inverse trigonometric functions in Chapters 6–8.

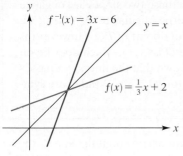

**Figure 3**

There is a certain type of symmetry that always occurs when we graph a function and its inverse. Consider, for example, the pair of inverse functions $f(x) = \frac{1}{3}x + 2$ and $f^{-1}(x) = 3x - 6$ that are graphed in Figure 3. (In Example 2 we verified that these were indeed inverse functions.) Note that the graphs of $f$ and $f^{-1}$ appear to be *symmetric about the line $y = x$*. That is, if the page were folded along the dashed line $y = x$ and held up to the light, then the graphs of $f$ and $f^{-1}$ would coincide. To say it differently, the graphs of $f$ and $f^{-1}$ are mirror images of one another about the line $y = x$. As background for the remainder of our work on inverse functions, we give a definition of symmetry about the line $y = x$ in the box that follows. (After you read the definition, note that the ideas involved are the same as those for symmetry about the $x$- or $y$-axis, as presented in Section 1.7.)

---

**DEFINITION** | **Symmetry about the Line y = x**

---

Refer to Figure 4. Two points $P$ and $Q$ are symmetric about the line $y = x$ provided that

1. $\overline{PQ}$ is perpendicular to the line $y = x$; and
2. the points $P$ and $Q$ are equidistant from the line $y = x$.

**Figure 4**

---

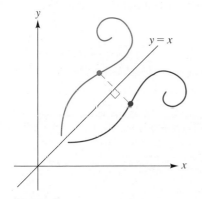

**Figure 5**
The two curves are symmetric about the line $y = x$.

This definition says that $P$ and $Q$ are symmetric about the line $y = x$ if $y = x$ is the perpendicular bisector of line segment $\overline{PQ}$. In Figure 4, we say that the two points $P$ and $Q$ are **reflections** of each other about the line $y = x$ and that $y = x$ is the **axis of symmetry**. In addition, we say that two curves are symmetric about $y = x$ if each point on one curve is the reflection of a corresponding point on the other curve, and vice versa; see Figure 5.

---

**EXAMPLE** **7** **Showing two given points are symmetric about y = x**

Verify that the points $P(4, 1)$ and $Q(1, 4)$ are symmetric about the line $y = x$; see Figure 6.

**SOLUTION**
We have to show that the line $y = x$ is the perpendicular bisector of the line segment $\overline{PQ}$. Now, the slope of $\overline{PQ}$ is

$$m = \frac{4 - 1}{1 - 4} = -1$$

**Figure 6**

We know that the slope of the line $y = x$ is 1. Since these two slopes are negative reciprocals, we conclude that the line $y = x$ is perpendicular to $\overline{PQ}$. Next, we must show that the line $y = x$ passes through the midpoint of $\overline{PQ}$. However (as you should check for yourself), the midpoint of $\overline{PQ}$ is $(\frac{5}{2}, \frac{5}{2})$, which does lie on the line $y = x$. (Why?) In summary, then, we've shown that the line $y = x$ passes through the midpoint of $\overline{PQ}$ and is perpendicular to $\overline{PQ}$. Thus $P$ and $Q$ are symmetric about the line $y = x$, as we wished to show.

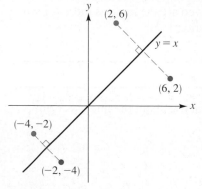

Figure 7
Two examples of the fact that $(a, b)$ and $(b, a)$ are symmetric about $y = x$

Just as we've shown that $(4, 1)$ and $(1, 4)$ are symmetric about the line $y = x$, we can also show that in general, $(a, b)$ and $(b, a)$ are always symmetric about the line $y = x$. Figure 7 displays two examples of this, and Exercise 51 at the end of this section asks you to supply a proof for the general situation.

Now let's see why the graphs of $f$ and $f^{-1}$ are always mirror images of each other about the line $y = x$. First, recall that the function $f^{-1}$ interchanges the inputs and outputs of $f$. Thus, $(a, b)$ is on the graph of $f$ if and only if $(b, a)$ is on the graph of $f^{-1}$. But as we have just stated, the points $(a, b)$ and $(b, a)$ are symmetric about the line $y = x$. It follows therefore that the graphs of $f$ and $f^{-1}$ are symmetric about the line $y = x$. For reference, we restate this useful fact in the box that follows.

**PROPERTY SUMMARY** **The Graphs of $f$ and $f^{-1}$**

The graphs of $y = f(x)$ and $y = f^{-1}(x)$ are symmetric about the line $y = x$.

  **EXAMPLE** 8 | **Using symmetry to sketch the graph of an inverse function**

The graph of a function $f$ consists of the line segment joining the points $(-2, -3)$ and $(-1, 4)$, as shown in Figure 8. Sketch a graph of $f^{-1}$.

**SOLUTION**
The graph of $f^{-1}$ is obtained by reflecting the graph of $f$ about the line $y = x$. The reflection of $(-2, -3)$ is $(-3, -2)$, and the reflection of $(-1, 4)$ is $(4, -1)$. To graph $f^{-1}$, then, we plot the reflected points $(-3, -2)$ and $(4, -1)$ and connect them with a line segment, as shown in Figure 9.

Figure 8          Figure 9

NOTE   When a linear function has an inverse the inverse function is also linear. See Exercise 52 at the end of this section. For reference, Figure 9 also shows the graphs of $f$ and $y = x$.

---

### EXAMPLE  9  Finding an inverse function and its graph

Let $g(x) = x^3$. Find $g^{-1}(x)$, and then, on the same set of axes, sketch the graphs of $g$, $g^{-1}$, and $y = x$.

**SOLUTION**
We begin by writing $y = x^3$, then switching $x$ and $y$ and solving for $y$. We first have

$$x = y^3$$

To solve this equation for $y$, we take the cube root of both sides to obtain

$$\sqrt[3]{x} = y$$

So the inverse function is $g^{-1}(x) = \sqrt[3]{x}$. We could graph the function $g^{-1}$ by plotting points, but the easier way is to reflect the graph of $g(x) = x^3$ about the line $y = x$; see Figure 10.

Figure 10

Earlier in this section, we mentioned that not every function has an inverse function. For instance, Tables 1(a) and 1(b) indicate what happens if we begin with the function defined by $F(x) = x^2$ and interchange the inputs and outputs. The resulting table, Table 1(b), does not define a function. For instance, the input 4 in Table 1(b) produces two distinct outputs, 2 and $-2$, but the definition of a function requires exactly one output for a given input.

Why didn't this difficulty arise when we looked for the inverse of $f(x) = 2x$ at the beginning of this section? The answer is that there is an essential difference between the functions defined by $f(x) = 2x$ and $F(x) = x^2$. With $f(x) = 2x$, different inputs never yield the same output. To put it another way, for the function $f(x) = 2x$, the only time it can happen that $f(a) = f(b)$ is when $a = b$. This condition guarantees

**TABLE 1(a)**
**F(x) = x²**

| x | y |
|---|---|
| 1 | 1 |
| 2 | 4 |
| 3 | 9 |
| −1 | 1 |
| −2 | 4 |
| −3 | 9 |

**TABLE 1(b)**
**Reversing the Inputs and Outputs**

| x | y |
|---|---|
| 1 | 1 |
| 4 | 2 |
| 9 | 3 |
| 1 | −1 |
| 4 | −2 |
| 9 | −3 |

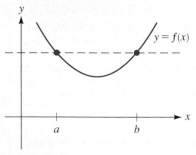

Figure 11

that interchanging the inputs and outputs of $f$ will yield a function. With $F(x) = x^2$, however, it *can* happen that $F(a) = F(b)$ and yet $a \neq b$. For instance,

$$F(2) = F(-2) \quad \text{because } 2^2 = 4 = (-2)^2$$

but, of course, $2 \neq -2$.

It's useful to have a name for functions such as $f(x) = 2x$, in which distinct inputs always yield distinct outputs. We call these types of functions *one-to-one* functions.

| DEFINITION | One-to-One |
|---|---|

A function $f$ is **one-to-one** provided that the following condition holds for all $a$ and $b$ in the domain of $f$:

If $f(a) = f(b)$ then $a = b$

**EXAMPLES**

$f(x) = 2x$ is one-to-one.
$F(x) = x^2$ is not one-to-one because $F(2) = F(-2)$, yet $2 \neq -2$.

Using graphs, there is an easy way to tell which functions are one-to-one:

### Horizontal Line Test

A function $f$ is one-to-one if and only if each horizontal line intersects the graph of $y = f(x)$ in at most one point.

Figure 11 will help you to see why the horizontal line test is valid. The figure shows a horizontal line intersecting the graph of a function $f$ at two distinct points with $x$-coordinates $a$ and $b$. From the graph, we see that $f(a) = f(b)$, even though $a \neq b$. Thus the function represented in Figure 11 is not one-to-one.

| EXAMPLE | 10 | Using the horizontal line test |
|---|---|---|

Use the horizontal line test to determine which functions in Figure 12 are one-to-one.

(a)

(b)

(c)

Figure 12

**SOLUTION**
The horizontal line test tells us that $F$ and $h$ are one-to-one, but $H$ is not.

The following theorem tells us that the functions with inverses are precisely the one-to-one functions. (The proof of the theorem isn't difficult, but we'll omit it here.)

**THEOREM**

A function $f$ has an inverse function $f^{-1}$ if and only if $f$ is one-to-one.

**EXAMPLE** | **11** | **Using one-to-one to determine whether a function has an inverse**

Which of the three functions in Figure 12 have inverse functions?

**SOLUTION**
According to our theorem, the functions with inverses are those that are one-to-one. In Example 10, we saw that $F$ and $h$ were one-to-one but $H$ was not. So $F$ and $h$ each have inverses, but $H$ does not.

# EXERCISE SET 3.6

**A**

1. If $h$ and $k$ are a pair of inverse functions, then (fill in the blanks).
   (a) $h[k(x)] = $ ____ for every $x$ in the domain of _____.
   (b) $k[h(x)] = $ _____ for every $x$ in the domain of _____.
2. Let $f(x) = x^2$ and $g(x) = 1/x$. Compute $f[g(x)]$ and $g[f(x)]$, and note that the results are identical. Then say why $f$ and $g$ do *not* qualify as a pair of inverse functions.
3. Verify that the given pairs of functions are inverse functions, as in Example 2.
   (a) $f(x) = 3x$; $g(x) = x/3$
   (b) $f(x) = 4x - 1$; $g(x) = \frac{1}{4}x + \frac{1}{4}$
   (c) $g(x) = \sqrt{x}$; $h(x) = x^2$ [Assume that the domain of both $g$ and $h$ is $[0, \infty)$.]
4. Which pairs of functions are inverses?
   (a) $f(x) = -3x + 2$; $g(x) = \frac{2}{3} - \frac{1}{3}x$
   (b) $F(x) = 2x + 1$; $G(x) = \frac{1}{2}x - 1$
   (c) $G(x) = x^3$; $H(x) = 1 - x^3$
   (d) $f(t) = t^3$; $g(t) = \sqrt[3]{t}$
5. (a) Use a graphing utility to graph the following three functions on the same set of axes.
   $$f(x) = \sqrt[3]{x^3 + 3} - 1$$
   $$g(x) = \sqrt[3]{x^3 + 1} - 3$$
   $$h(x) = \sqrt[3]{(x + 1)^3} - 3$$

If necessary, adjust the picture so that it shows true proportions.
   (b) Which two graphs appear to be symmetric about the line $y = x$? Use algebra (as in Example 2) to verify that the two functions are indeed inverses.

6. (a) Use a graphing utility to graph both $g(x) = \sqrt[3]{2 - x^3}$ and $y - x$ on the same set of axes.
   (b) What kind of symmetry do you observe? What does this tell you about the inverse for $g$? [If you are uncertain how to answer this last question, try coming back to it after working part (c).]
   (c) Starting with the equation $g(x) = \sqrt[3]{2 - x^3}$, follow the two-step procedure on page 198 to find $g^{-1}(x)$. What do you observe?

*In Exercises 7 and 8, suppose that $f$ and $g$ are a pair of inverse functions.*
7. If $f(7) = 12$, what is $g(12)$? (If you need a hint, reread Example 3.)
8. If $g(-2) = 0$, what is $f(0)$?

*In Exercises 9 and 10, let $f(x) = x^3 + 2x + 1$, and assume that $f^{-1}$ exists and has domain $(-\infty, \infty)$. Simplify each expression (as in Example 4).*
9. (a) $f[f^{-1}(4)]$                    (c) $(f \circ f^{-1})(\sqrt{2})$
   (b) $f^{-1}[f(-1)]$                   (d) $f[f^{-1}(t + 1)]$

10. (a) $f(0)$
   (b) $f^{-1}(1)$   *Hint:* Use the result in part (a).
   (c) $f(-1)$          (d) $f^{-1}(-2)$
11. Let $f(x) = 2x + 1$.
   (a) Find $f^{-1}(x)$.
   (b) Calculate $f^{-1}(5)$ and $1/f(5)$. Are your answers the same?
12. Let $g(t) = \dfrac{1}{t} + 1$.

   (a) Find $g^{-1}(t)$.
   (b) Calculate $g^{-1}(2)$ and $1/g(2)$, and note that the answers are not the same.
13. Let $f(x) = 3x - 1$.
   (a) Compute $f^{-1}(x)$.
   (b) Verify that $f[f^{-1}(x)] = x$ and that $f^{-1}[f(x)] = x$.
   (c) On the same set of axes, sketch the graphs of $f$, $f^{-1}$, and the line $y = x$. Note that the graphs of $f$ and $f^{-1}$ are symmetric about the line $y = x$.
14. Follow Exercise 13, but use $f(x) = \frac{1}{3}x - 2$.
15. Follow Exercise 13, but use $f(x) = \sqrt{x-1}$. [The domain of $f^{-1}$ will be $[0, \infty)$.]
16. Follow Exercise 13, but use $f(x) = 1/x$.
17. Let $f(x) = (x + 2)/(x - 3)$.
   (a) Find the domain and range of the function $f$.
   (b) Find $f^{-1}(x)$.
   (c) Find the domain and range of the function $f^{-1}$. What do you observe?
18. Let $f(x) = (2x - 3)/(x + 4)$. Find $f^{-1}(x)$. Find the domain and range for $f$ and $f^{-1}$. What do you observe?
19. Let $f(x) = 2x^3 + 1$. Find $f^{-1}(x)$.
20. In our discussion at the beginning of this section, we considered the functions $f(x) = 2x$ and $g(x) = x/2$. Verify that $f[g(x)] = x$ and that $g[f(x)] = x$. On the same set of axes, sketch the graphs of $f$, $g$, and $y = x$.
21. This exercise refers to the comments made at the end of Example 6. Compute $f[f^{-1}(x)]$ and $f^{-1}[f(x)]$ using the functions $f(x) = (x-1)/(3x+5)$ and $f^{-1}(x) = (-5x-1)/(3x-1)$. By actually carrying out the calculations, you'll find that the result in each case is $x$, which *proves* these are indeed inverse functions.
22. Let $f(x) = (x - 3)^3 - 1$.
   (a) Compute $f^{-1}(x)$.
   (b) On the same set of axes, sketch the graphs of $f$, $f^{-1}$, and the line $y = x$.   *Hint:* Sketch $f$ using the ideas of Section 3.4. Then reflect the graph of $y = f(x)$ in the line $y = x$ to obtain the graph of $y = f^{-1}(x)$.

*For Exercises 23 and 24, refer to the following figure, which shows the graph of a function $f$. (The axes are marked off in one-unit intervals.) In each case, graph the indicated function.*

23. (a) $y = f^{-1}(x)$          (c) $y = f^{-1}(x) - 2$
    (b) $y = f^{-1}(x - 2)$      (d) $y = f^{-1}(x - 2) - 2$
24. (a) $y = f^{-1}(-x)$          (c) $y = -f^{-1}(-x)$
    (b) $y = -f^{-1}(x)$          (d) $y = -f^{-1}(-x) - 1$

*In Exercises 25–28, assume that the domain of $f$ and $f^{-1}$ is $(-\infty, \infty)$. Solve the equation for $x$ or for $t$ (whichever is appropriate) using the given information.*
25. (a) $7 + f^{-1}(x - 1) = 9; f(2) = 6$
    (b) $4 + f(x + 3) = -3; f^{-1}(-7) = 0$
26. (a) $f^{-1}(2x + 3) = 5; f(5) = 13$
    (b) $f(1 - 2x) = -4; f^{-1}(-4) = -5$
27. $f^{-1}\left(\dfrac{t+1}{t-2}\right) = 12; f(12) = 13$

28. $f\left(\dfrac{1-2t}{1+2t}\right) = 7; f^{-1}(7) = -3$

*For Exercises 29–33, use the horizontal line test to determine whether the function is one-to-one (and therefore has an inverse). (You should be able to sketch the graph of each function on your own, without using a graphing utility.)*
29. $f(x) = -x^2 + 1$          30. $g(x) = x^3 - 1$
31. $g(x) = 5$ (for all $x$)
32. $f(x) = \begin{cases} x^2 & \text{if } -1 \le x \le 0 \\ x^2 + 1 & \text{if } x > 0 \end{cases}$

33. $g(x) = \begin{cases} x^2 & \text{if } -1 \le x < 0 \\ x^2 + 1 & \text{if } x \ge 0 \end{cases}$

34. Which of the six basic functions graphed in Figure 7 in Section 3.2 are one-to-one?

Ⓖ *In Exercises 35–40, use a graphing utility to graph each function and then apply the horizontal line test to see whether the function is one-to-one.*
35. $y = x^2 + 2x$          36. $y = x^3 + 2x$
37. $y = 2x^3 + x^2$   *Suggestion:* Begin with the standard viewing rectangle and then use a zoom-in view. (First looks can be deceiving.)
38. $y = 0.01x^4 - 1$          39. $y = 2x^5 + x - 1$
40. (a) $f(x) = x^3 + x^2 + x$
    (b) $g(x) = x^3 - x^2 + x$
    (c) $h(x) = x^3 - x^2 - x$

**B**

**G** **41. (a)** In the standard viewing rectangle, graph two functions

$$f(x) = x^3 + 1.73x^2 + x + 2$$

and

$$g(x) = x^3 + 1.74x^2 + x + 2$$

**(b)** Use the zoom feature of your graphing utility to find out whether either function is one-to-one.

**42.** Let $f(x) = \sqrt{x}$.

**(a)** Find $f^{-1}(x)$. What is the domain of $f^{-1}$? [The domain is not $(-\infty, \infty)$.]

**(b)** In each case, determine whether the given point lies on the graph of $f$ or $f^{-1}$.

    **(i)**    $(4, 2)$

    **(ii)**   $(2, 4)$

    **(iii)**  $(5, \sqrt{5})$

    **(iv)**  $(\sqrt{5}, 5)$

    **(v)**   $(a, f(a))$, where $a \geq 0$

    **(vi)**  $(f(a), a)$

    **(vii)** $(b, f^{-1}(b))$, where $b \geq 0$

    **(viii)** $(f^{-1}(b), b)$

**43.** In the following figure, determine the coordinates of the points $A$, $B$, $C$, and $D$. Express your answers in terms of the function $f$ and the number $a$. (Each dashed line through $A$ is parallel to an axis.)

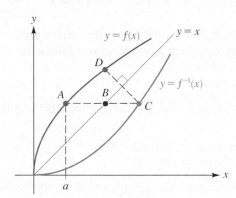

**44.** In the following figure, determine the coordinates of the points $A$, $B$, $C$, $D$, $E$, and $F$. Specify the answers in terms of the functions $f$ and $f^{-1}$ and the number $b$.

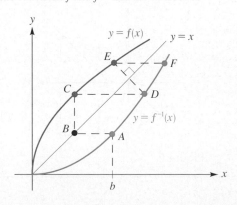

**45.** Let $f(x) = 3/(x - 1)$.

**(a)** Find the average rate of change of $f$ on the interval $[4, 9]$.

**(b)** Find $f^{-1}(x)$ and then compute the average rate of change of $f^{-1}$ on the interval $[f(4), f(9)]$. What do you observe?

**46.** The accompanying figure shows the graph of a function $f$ on the interval $[a, b]$. If the average rate of change of $f$ on the interval $[a, b]$ is $k$, show that the average rate of change of the function $f^{-1}$ on the interval $[f(a), f(b)]$ is $1/k$, where $k \neq 0$.

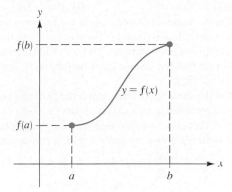

**47.** Suppose that $(a, b)$ is a point on the graph of $y = f(x)$. Match the functions defined in the left-hand column with the points in the right-hand column. For example, the appropriate match for (a) in the left-hand column is determined as follows. The graph of $y = f(x) + 1$ is obtained by translating the graph of $y = f(x)$ up one unit. Thus the point $(a, b)$ moves up to $(a, b + 1)$, and consequently, (E) is the appropriate match for (a).

**(a)** $y = f(x) + 1$               **(A)** $(-a, b)$

**(b)** $y = f(x + 1)$              **(B)** $(b, a)$

**(c)** $y = f(x - 1) + 1$        **(C)** $(a - 1, b)$

**(d)** $y = f(-x)$                **(D)** $(-b, a + 1)$

**(e)** $y = -f(x)$               **(E)** $(a, b + 1)$

**(f)** $y = -f(-x)$             **(F)** $(1 - a, b)$

**(g)** $y = f^{-1}(x)$              **(G)** $(-a, -b)$

**(h)** $y = f^{-1}(x) + 1$        **(H)** $(-b, 1 - a)$

**(i)** $y = f^{-1}(x - 1)$        **(I)** $(b, -a)$

**(j)** $y = f^{-1}(-x) + 1$     **(J)** $(a, -b)$

**(k)** $y = -f^{-1}(x)$         **(K)** $(b + 1, a)$

**(l)** $y = -f^{-1}(-x) + 1$    **(L)** $(a + 1, b + 1)$

**(m)** $y = 1 - f^{-1}(x)$      **(M)** $(b, a + 1)$

**(n)** $y = f(1 - x)$            **(N)** $(b, 1 - a)$

**48.** Let $f(x) = \dfrac{1}{1 - x}$. Show that the function $f \circ f$ is the inverse of $f$.

**49.** Let $f(x) = -\dfrac{2x + 2}{x}$.

**(a)** Find $f[f(x)]$.

**G** **(b)** Use a graphing utility to graph $y = f[f(x)]$. Display the graph using true proportions. What type of symmetry does the graph appear to have?

**(c)** The result in part (b) suggests that the inverse of the function $f \circ f$ is again $f \circ f$. Use algebra to show that this is indeed correct.

**50.** In this exercise you'll investigate the inverse of a composite function. In parts (b) and (c), which involve graphing, be sure to use the same size unit and scale on both axes so that symmetry about the line $y = x$ can be checked visually.

**(a)** Let $f(x) = 2x + 1$ and $g(x) = \frac{1}{4}x - 3$. Compute each of the following:

    **(i)** $f(g(x))$           **(iv)** $g^{-1}(x)$

    **(ii)** $g(f(x))$          **(v)** $f^{-1}(g^{-1}(x))$

    **(iii)** $f^{-1}(x)$        **(vi)** $g^{-1}(f^{-1}(x))$

Ⓖ **(b)** On the same set of axes, graph the two answers that you obtained in (i) and (v) of part (a). Note that the graphs are *not* symmetric about $y = x$. The conclusion here is that the inverse function for $f(g(x))$ is not $f^{-1}(g^{-1}(x))$.

Ⓖ **(c)** On the same set of axes, graph the two answers that you obtained in (i) and (vi) of part (a); also put the line $y = x$ into the picture. Note that the two graphs *are* symmetric about the line $y = x$. The conclusion here

is that the inverse function for $f(g(x))$ is $g^{-1}(f^{-1}(x))$. In fact, it can be shown that this result is true in general. For reference, then, we summarize this fact about the inverse of a composite function in the box that follows.

---

Inverse of a Composition

$$(f \circ g)^{-1} = g^{-1} \circ f^{-1}$$

---

**51.** Use the method of Example 7 to show that the points $(a, b)$ and $(b, a)$ are symmetric about the line $y = x$.

**52.** In this exercise you will show that if a linear function has an inverse, then the inverse function is also linear. Let $f(x) = mx + b$, where $m$ and $b$ are constants, with $m \neq 0$.

**(a)** Show $f^{-1}$ exists. *Hint*: Show $f$ is one-to-one.

**(b)** Find a formula for $f^{-1}(x)$.

**(c)** Explain why $f^{-1}$ is linear. In particular, what are the slope and $y$-intercept of the graph of $y = f^{-1}(x)$?

**(d)** What happens when $m = 0$?

---

## MINI PROJECT | A FREQUENTLY ASKED QUESTION ABOUT INVERSES

*Student*:  If $f[g(x)] = x$, isn't it automatically true then that $g[f(x)] = x$?

*Professor*:  No, that's only when you have a pair of inverse functions.

*Student*:  But in Example 2 and in similar homework problems, whenever I find that $f[g(x)] = x$, it *always* turns out that $g[f(x)] = x$.

This project provides an example of two functions $f$ and $g$ satisfying the following two conditions:

1.  The equation $g[f(x)] = x$ holds for every real number $x$.
2.  There are some real numbers $x$ for which $f[g(x)] \neq x$.

Figures A and B show these two functions $f$ and $g$; but you are not told which is which. Determine which function is $f$ and which is $g$. In investigating $f[g(x)]$ and $g[f(x)]$, be sure you cover all cases.

$$y = \begin{cases} x & \text{if } x \leq 0 \\ x+1 & \text{if } x > 0 \end{cases}$$

Figure A

$$y = \begin{cases} x & \text{if } x \leq 0 \\ 1 & \text{if } 0 < x \leq 1 \\ x-1 & \text{if } x > 1 \end{cases}$$

Figure B

## Chapter 3 | Summary of Principal Terms and Formulas

| Terms or notation | Page reference | Comments |
|---|---|---|
| **1.** Function | 132 | Given two nonempty sets $A$ and $B$, a function from $A$ to $B$ is a rule of correspondence that assigns to each element of $A$ exactly one element in $B$. |
| **2.** Domain | 133 | The domain of a function is the set of all inputs for that function. If $f$ is a function from $A$ to $B$, then the domain is the set $A$. |
| **3.** Range | 133 | The range of a function from $A$ to $B$ is the set of all elements in $B$ that are actually used as outputs. |
| **4.** $f(x)$ | 136 | Given a function $f$, the notation $f(x)$ denotes the output that results from the input $x$. |
| **5.** Graph of a function | 146 | The graph of a function $f$ consists of those points $(x, y)$ such that $x$ is in the domain of $f$ and $y = f(x)$. |
| **6.** Vertical line test | 147 | A graph in the $x$-$y$ plane represents a function $y = f(x)$ provided that any vertical line intersects the graph in at most one point. |
| **7.** Turning point | 159 | A turning point on a graph is a point where the graph changes from rising to falling, or vice versa. See, for example, Figure 1 on page 159. |
| **8.** Maximum value and minimum value | 159 | An output $f(a)$ is a maximum value of the function $f$ if $f(a) \geq f(x)$ for every $x$ in the domain of $f$. An output $f(b)$ is a minimum value if $f(b) \leq f(x)$ for every $x$ in the domain of $f$. |
| **9.** Increasing function | 159 | A function $f$ is increasing on an interval if the following condition holds: If $a$ and $b$ are in the interval and $a < b$, then $f(a) < f(b)$. Geometrically, this means that the graph is rising as we move in the positive $x$-direction. |
| **10.** Decreasing function | 159 | A function $f$ is decreasing on an interval if the following condition holds: If $a$ and $b$ are in the interval and $a < b$, then $f(a) > f(b)$. Geometrically, this means that the graph is falling as we move in the positive $x$-direction. |
| **11.** Average rate of change | 162 | The average rate of change, $\Delta f / \Delta x$, of a function $f$ on an interval $[a, b]$ is the slope of the line segment through the two points $(a, f(a))$ and $(b, f(b))$: $$\frac{\Delta f}{\Delta x} = \frac{f(b) - f(a)}{b - a}$$ |

| Terms or notation | Page reference | Comments |
|---|---|---|
| **12.** Techniques for graphing functions | 172 | The box on page 172 lists six techniques involving translation and reflection. For a comprehensive example, see Example 7 on pages 177–178. |
| **13.** $f \circ g$ | 183 | The composition of two functions $f$ and $g$: $(f \circ g)(x) = f[g(x)]$ |
| **14.** Iterates | 188 | Given a function $f$ and an input $x_0$, the iterates of $x_0$ are the numbers $f(x_0), f(f(x_0)), f(f(f(x_0))), \ldots$. The number $f(x_0)$ is called the first iterate, the number $f(f(x_0))$ is called the second iterate, and so on. The orbit of $x_0$ under the function $f$ is the list of numbers $$x_0, f(x_0), f(f(x_0)), \ldots$$ |
| **15.** Inverse functions | 195 | Two functions $f$ and $g$ are inverses of one another provided that the following two conditions are met. First, $f[g(x)] = x$ for each $x$ in the domain of $g$. Second, $g[f(x)] = x$ for each $x$ in the domain of $f$. |
| **16.** $f^{-1}$ | 196 | $f^{-1}$ denotes the inverse function for $f$. *Note*: In this context, $f^{-1}$ does not mean $1/f$. |
| **17.** One-to-one function | 202 | A function $f$ is said to be one-to-one provided that distinct inputs always yield distinct outputs. Geometrically, this means that every horizontal line intersects the graph of $y = f(x)$ in at most one point. Algebraically, this means that $f$ satisfies the following condition: If $a$ and $b$ are in the domain of $f$, and $f(a) = f(b)$, then $a = b$. The relationship between inverse functions and one-to-one functions is this: A function $f$ has an inverse if and only if $f$ is one-to-one. |

## Writing Mathematics

**1.** Section 3.6 on inverse functions begins with the following quotation from Professor R. P. Boas:

> If anybody ever told me why the graph of $y = x^{1/2}$ is the reflection of the graph of $y = x^2$ [$x \geq 0$] in a 45° line, it didn't sink in. To this day, there are textbooks that expect students to think that it is so obvious as to need no explanation.

Show your instructor that you are not in the dark about inverse functions. Write out an explanation of why the graphs of $y = x^{1/2}$ and $y = x^2$ ($x \geq 0$) are indeed reflections of one another in a 45° line. (As preparation for your writing, you'll probably need to look over Section 3.6 and make a few notes.)

2. Decide which of the following rules are functions. Write out your reasons in complete sentences. (In each case, assume that the domain is the set of students in your school.)
   **(a)** *F* is the rule that assigns to each person his or her brother.
   **(b)** *G* is the rule that assigns to each person his or her aunt.
   **(c)** *H* is the rule that assigns to each person his or her birth-mother.
   **(d)** *K* is the rule that assigns to each person his or her mother or father.

# Chapter 3 ▮ Review Exercises

1. **(a)** Find the domain of the function defined by
   $f(x) = \sqrt{15 - 5x}$.
   **(b)** Find the range of the function defined by
   $g(x) = (3 + x)/(2x - 5)$.
2. Let $f(x) = 3x^2 - 4x$ and $g(x) = 2x + 1$. Compute each of the following:
   **(a)** $(f - g)(x)$          **(c)** $f[g(-1)]$
   **(b)** $(f \circ g)(x)$
3. A **linear function** is a function defined by an equation of the form $F(x) = ax + b$, where *a* and *b* are real numbers. Suppose *f* and *g* are linear functions. Is the function $f \circ g$ a linear function?
4. A **quadratic function** is a function defined by an equation of the form $F(x) = ax^2 + bx + c$, where *a*, *b*, and *c* are real numbers and $a \neq 0$.
   **(a)** Give an example of quadratic functions *f* and *g* for which $f + g$ is also a quadratic function.
   **(b)** Give an example of quadratic functions *f* and *g* for which $f + g$ is not a quadratic function.
   **(c)** Suppose *f* and *g* are quadratic functions. Is the function $f \circ g$ a quadratic function?
5. **(a)** Compute $\dfrac{F(x) - F(a)}{x - a}$ given that $F(x) = 1/x$.
   **(b)** Compute $\dfrac{g(x + h) - g(x)}{h}$ for the function defined by $g(x) = x - 2x^2$.
6. The *y*-intercept for the graph of $y = f(x)$ is 4. What is the *y*-intercept for the graph of $y = -f(x) + 1$?
7. **(a)** Find $g^{-1}(x)$ given that $g(x) = \dfrac{1 - 5x}{3x}$.
   **(b)** The figure displays the graph of a function *f*. Sketch the graph of $f^{-1}$.

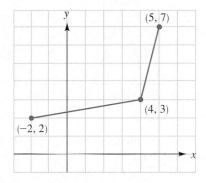

8. Refer to the function *f* in Exercise 7(b).
   **(a)** Compute $\Delta f / \Delta x$ on $[-2, 5]$.
   **(b)** Find the average rate of change of $f^{-1}$ on $[2, 7]$.
9. Graph each function and specify the intercepts.
   **(a)** $y = |x + 2| - 3$          **(b)** $y = \dfrac{1}{x + 2} - 1$
10. Refer to the following graph of $y = g(x)$. The domain of *g* is $[-5, 2]$.
    **(a)** What are the coordinates of the turning point(s)?
    **(b)** What is the maximum value of *g*?
    **(c)** Which input yields a minimum value for *g*?
    **(d)** On which interval(s) is *g* increasing?
    **(e)** Compute $\Delta g / \Delta x$ for each of the following intervals: $[-5, -3]$; $[-3, -2]$; $[-5, 2]$.

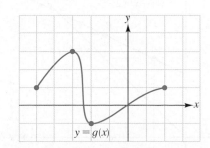

$y = g(x)$

**11.** Let $f(x) = 3x^2 - 2x$.
  **(a)** Find $f(-1)$.            **(b)** Find $f(1 - \sqrt{2})$.
**12.** Graph the function $G$ defined by

$$G(x) = \begin{cases} \sqrt{1 - x^2} & \text{if } -1 \leq x < 0 \\ \sqrt{x} & \text{if } x \geq 0 \end{cases}$$

**13.** Express the slope of a line passing through the points $(5, 25)$ and $(5 + h, (5 + h)^2)$ as a function of $h$.
**14.** Graph the function $y = |9 - x^2|$. Specify symmetry and intercepts.
**15.** The following figure shows the graph of a function $y = f(x)$. Sketch the graph of $y = f(-x)$.

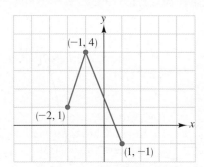

**16.** Given that the domains of $f$ and $f^{-1}$ are both $(-\infty, \infty)$ and that $f^{-1}(1) = -4$, solve the following equation for $t$: $2 + f(3t + 5) = 3$.
**17.** Let $f(x) = \frac{1}{2}x + 2$.
  **(a)** Compute the first three iterates of $x_0 = 1$.
  **(b)** Refer to the following figure. Explain why the $y$-coordinates of the points $A$, $B$, and $C$ are the iterates that you computed in part (a).
  **(c)** Determine the $y$-coordinate of the point where the lines $y = x$ and $y = \frac{1}{2}x + 2$ intersect.
  **(d)** If we continue the pattern of dashed lines in the figure, it appears that the iterates of $x_0 = 1$ will approach 4. Verify this empirically by using your calculator to compute the fourth through tenth iterates. (Round your final answers to three decimal places.)

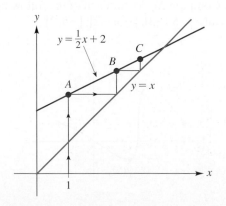

*In Exercises 18–34, sketch the graph and specify any x- or y-intercepts.*

**18.** $y = \dfrac{1}{x} + 1$           **19.** $f(x) = \dfrac{1}{x + 1}$

**20.** $y = \dfrac{1}{x + 1} + 1$        **21.** $y = |x + 3|$

**22.** $g(x) = -\sqrt{x - 4}$
**23.** $h(x) = \sqrt{1 - x^2}$
**24.** $y = 4 - \sqrt{-x}$
**25.** $y = (\sqrt{x})^2$
**26.** $f \circ g$, where $g(x) = x + 3$ and $f(x) = x^2$
**27.** $f \circ g$, where $g(x) = \sqrt{x - 1}$ and $f(x) = -x^2$

**28.** $f(x) = \begin{cases} \sqrt{1 - x^2} & \text{if } -1 \leq x \leq 0 \\ \sqrt{x} + 1 & \text{if } x > 0 \end{cases}$

**29.** $y = \begin{cases} 1/x & \text{if } 0 < x \leq 1 \\ 1/(x - 1) & \text{if } 1 < x \leq 2 \end{cases}$

**30.** $(y + |x| - 1)(y - |x| + 1) = 0$
**31.** $f^{-1}$, where $f(x) = \frac{1}{2}(x + 1)$
**32.** $g^{-1}$, where $g(x) = \sqrt[3]{x + 2}$
**33.** $f \circ f^{-1}$, where $f(x) = \sqrt{x - 2}$
**34.** $f^{-1} \circ f$, where $f(x) = \sqrt{x - 2}$

*In Exercises 35–40, find the domain of the function.*

**35.** $y = 1/(x^2 - 9)$         **36.** $y = x^3 - x^2$

**37.** $y = \sqrt{8 - 2x}$       **38.** $y = \dfrac{x}{6x^2 + 7x - 3}$

**39.** $y = \sqrt{x^2 - 2x - 3}$  **40.** $y = \sqrt{5 - x^2}$

*In Exercises 41–44, determine the range of the function.*

**41.** $y = \dfrac{x + 4}{3x - 1}$

**42.** $f \circ g$, where $f(x) = 1/x$ and $g(x) = 3x + 4$

**43.** $g \circ f$, where $f(x) = \dfrac{x + 2}{x - 1}$ and $g(x) = \dfrac{x + 1}{x + 4}$

**44.** $f^{-1}$, where $f(x) = \dfrac{x}{3x - 6}$

*In Exercises 45–52, express the function as a composition of two or more of the following functions:*

$$f(x) = \frac{1}{x} \quad g(x) = x - 1 \quad F(x) = |x| \quad G(x) = \sqrt{x}$$

**45.** $a(x) = \dfrac{1}{x - 1}$        **46.** $b(x) = \dfrac{1}{x} - 1$

**47.** $c(x) = \sqrt{x - 1}$            **48.** $d(x) = \sqrt{x} - 1$
**49.** $A(x) = (1/\sqrt{x}) - 1$         **50.** $B(x) = |x - 2|$
**51.** $C(x) = \sqrt[4]{x} - 1$          **52.** $D(x) = 1/\sqrt{x - 3}$

*For Exercises 53–80, compute the indicated quantity using the functions f, g, and F defined as follows:*

$$f(x) = x^2 - x \qquad g(x) = 1 - 2x \qquad F(x) = \frac{x-3}{x+4}$$

**53.** $f(-3)$
**54.** $f(1 + \sqrt{2})$
**55.** $F(3/4)$
**56.** $f(t)$
**57.** $f(-t)$
**58.** $g(2x)$
**59.** $f(x - 2)$
**60.** $g(x + h)$
**61.** $f(x^2)$
**62.** $f(x)/x \quad (x \neq 0)$
**63.** $[f(x)][g(x)]$
**64.** $f[f(x)]$
**65.** $f[g(x)]$
**66.** $g[f(3)]$
**67.** $(g \circ f)(x)$
**68.** $(g \circ f)(x) - (f \circ g)(x)$
**69.** $(F \circ g)(x)$
**70.** $\dfrac{g(x + h) - g(x)}{h}$
**71.** $\dfrac{f(x + h) - f(x)}{h}$
**72.** $\dfrac{F(x) - F(a)}{x - a}$
**73.** $F^{-1}(x)$
**74.** $F[F^{-1}(x)]$
**75.** $(g \circ g^{-1})(x)$
**76.** $g^{-1}(x)$
**77.** $g^{-1}(-x)$
**78.** $\dfrac{g^{-1}(x + h) \quad g^{-1}(x)}{h}$
**79.** $F^{-1}[F(22/7)]$
**80.** $T^{-1}(x)$, where $T(x) = f(x)/x \quad (x \neq 0)$

*In Exercises 81–94, refer to the graph of the function f in the figure. (The axes are marked off in one-unit intervals.)*

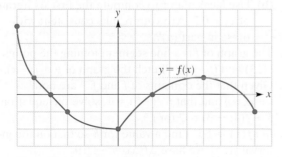

**81.** Is $f(0)$ positive or negative?
**82.** Specify the domain and range of $f$.
**83.** Find $f(-3)$.
**84.** Which is larger, $f(-5/2)$ or $f(-1/2)$?
**85.** Compute $f(0) - f(8)$.
**86.** Compute $|f(0) - f(8)|$.
**87.** Specify the coordinates of the turning points.
**88.** What are the minimum and the maximum values of $f$?
**89.** On which interval(s) is $f$ decreasing?
**90.** For which $x$-values is it true that $1 \leq f(x) \leq 4$?
**91.** What is the largest value of $f(x)$ when $|x| \leq 2$?

**92.** Is $f$ a one-to-one function?
**93.** Does $f$ possess an inverse function?
**94.** Compute $f[f(-4)]$.

*For Exercises 95–110, refer to the graphs of the functions f and g in the following figure. Assume that the domain of each function is [0, 10].*

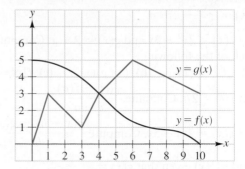

**95.** For which $x$-value is $f(x) = g(x)$?
**96.** For which $x$-values is it true that $g(x) \leq f(x)$?
**97.** (a) For which $x$-value is $f(x) = 0$?
     (b) For which $x$-value is $g(x) = 0$?
**98.** Compute $f(0) + g(0)$.
**99.** Compute each of the following.
     (a) $(f + g)(8)$      (c) $(fg)(8)$
     (b) $(f - g)(8)$      (d) $(f/g)(8)$
**100.** Compute each of the following.
     (a) $g[f(5)]$      (c) $(g \circ f)(5)$
     (b) $f[g(5)]$      (d) $(f \circ g)(5)$
**101.** Which is larger, $(f \circ f)(10)$ or $(g \circ g)(10)$?
**102.** Compute $g[f(10)] - f[g(10)]$.
**103.** For which $x$-values is it true that $f(x) \geq 3$?
**104.** For which $x$-values is it true that $|f(x) - 3| \leq 1$?
**105.** What is the largest number in the range of $g$?
**106.** Specify the coordinates of the highest point on the graph of each of the following equations.
     (a) $y = g(-x)$      (d) $y = f(-x)$
     (b) $y = -g(x)$      (e) $y = -f(x)$
     (c) $y = g(x - 1)$   (f) $y = -f(-x)$
**107.** On which intervals is the function $g$ decreasing?
**108.** What are the coordinates of the turning points of $g$?
**109.** For which values of $x$ in the interval $(4, 7)$ is the quantity $\dfrac{f(x) - f(5)}{x - 5}$ negative?
**110.** For which values of $x$ in the interval $(0, 5)$ is the quantity $\dfrac{f(x) - f(2)}{x - 2}$ positive?

# Chapter 3  Test

1. Find the domain of the function defined by
$f(x) = \sqrt{x^2 - 5x - 6}$.

2. Find the range of the function defined by
$$g(x) = \frac{2x - 8}{3x + 5}.$$

3. Let $f(x) = 2x^2 - 3x$ and $g(x) = 2 - x$. Compute each of the following:
   (a) $(f - g)(x)$     (b) $(f \circ g)(x)$     (c) $f[g(-4)]$

4. Let $f(t) = 2/t$. Compute $\dfrac{f(t) - f(a)}{t - a}$.

5. Let $g(x) = 2x^2 - 5x$. Compute $\dfrac{g(x + h) - g(x)}{h}$.

6. Find $g^{-1}(x)$ given that $g(x) = \dfrac{-4x}{6x + 1}$.

7. The graph of a function $f$ is a line segment joining the two points $(-3, 1)$ and $(5, 6)$. Determine the slope of the line segment that results from graphing the equation $y = -f^{-1}(x)$.

8. Graph each function and specify the intercepts:
   (a) $y = -|x - 3| + 1$     (b) $y = \dfrac{1}{x + 3} - 2$

9. The figure shows the graph of a function $g$ with domain $[-4, 2]$.

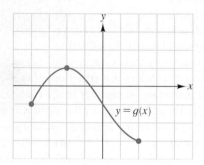

   (a) Specify the range of $g$.
   (b) What are the coordinates of the turning point?
   (c) What is the minimum value of $g$?
   (d) Which input yields a maximum value for $g$? What is that maximum value?
   (e) On which interval is $g$ decreasing?
   (f) Use the horizontal line test to say whether or not $g$ is one-to-one.

10. Let $f(x) = x^2 - 3x - 1$. Compute each of the following:
   (a) $f(-3/2)$     (b) $f(\sqrt{3} - 2)$

11. Graph the function $F$ defined by
$$F(x) = \begin{cases} |x + 1| & \text{if } x < -1 \\ -x^2 + 1 & \text{if } x > -1 \end{cases}$$

What is the domain of this function?

12. In the figure below, the graph of $f(x) = 1 - |2x - 1|$ is shown in red ($y = x$ is included also).

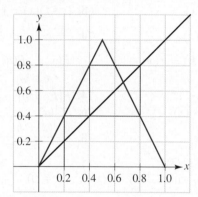

   (a) Use the figure to specify the first six iterates of $x_0 = 0.2$.
   (b) Use a calculator to compute the first six iterates of $x_0 = 0.2$. Are your results consistent with those in part (a)?

13. The graph of $f$ is a line segment joining the points $(1, 3)$ and $(5, -2)$. Sketch the graph of $y = f(-x)$.

14. Given that the domains of $f$ and $f^{-1}$ are both $(-\infty, \infty)$ and that $f^{-1}(-3) = 1$, solve the equation $5 + f(4t - 3) = 2$ for $t$.

15. Let $f(x) = 1/x$. Find a value for $b$ so that on the interval $[1, b]$, we have $\Delta f / \Delta x = -1/10$.

16. During the first five hours of a lab experiment, the temperature of a solution is given by
$$F(t) = 0.16t^2 - 1.6t + 35 \qquad (0 \le t \le 5)$$

where $t$ is measured in hours, $t = 0$ corresponds to the time that the experiment begins, and $F(t)$ is the temperature (in degrees Celsius) at time $t$.
   (a) Find (and simplify) a formula for $\Delta F / \Delta t$ over the interval $[a, 5]$.
   (b) Use the result in part (a) to compute the average rate of change of temperature during the period from $t = 4$ hr to $t = 5$ hr. (Be sure to include the units as part of the answer.)

# CHAPTER 4

# Polynomial and Rational Functions. Applications to Optimization

*POLYNOMIAL was used by François Viéta (1540–1603). The term RATIONAL FUNCTION was used by Joseph Louis Lagrange (1736–1813) in "Réflexions sur la résolution algébrique des équations," . . .—From Jeff Miller's website Earliest Known Uses of Some of the Words of Mathematics* (http://members.aol.com/jeff570/mathword.html)

In the previous chapter we studied some rather general rules for working with functions and graphs. With that as background we are ready to focus our attention on a few specific types of functions and their applications. Some contexts in which we'll use the functions and ideas introduced in this chapter are:

- Modeling data relating smoking and lung cancer
  (Example 5 in Section 4.1)
- Summarizing global trends in airline passenger miles using a quadratic model
  (Exercise 1 in Exercise Set 4.2)
- Modeling the spread of AIDS using linear and quadratic functions
  (Example 1 in Section 4.2)
- Finding the minimum value of a quadratic function to gain insight into how least-squares lines are defined and determined
  (Project at end of Section 4.5)
- Determining long-term behavior in a population model by computing the horizontal asymptote of a rational function
  (Example 7 in Section 4.7)

---

## 4.1  LINEAR FUNCTIONS

*I had a moment of mixed joy and anguish, when my mind took over. It raced well ahead of my body and drew my body compellingly forward. I felt that the moment of a lifetime had come.—* Dr. Roger Bannister, first person to run the mile in under four minutes, recalling the last lap of his record-breaking run at the Ilffley Road Track, Oxford, England, May 6, 1954. The quotation is from Roger Bannister, *The Four Minute Mile* (New York: Dodd, Mead & Co., 1955).

By a **linear function** we mean a function defined by an equation of the form

$$f(x) = Ax + B$$

where $A$ and $B$ are constants. In this chapter the constants $A$ and $B$ will always be real numbers. From our work in Chapter 1 we know that the graph of $y = Ax + B$ is a straight line.

*All decent functions are practically linear.—Professor Andrew Gleason*

**EXAMPLE** **1**    **Finding an equation defining a linear function**

Suppose that $f$ is a linear function. If $f(1) = 0$ and $f(2) = 3$, find an equation defining $f$.

**SOLUTION**
From the statement of the problem we know that the graph of $f$ is a straight line passing through the points $(1, 0)$ and $(2, 3)$. Thus the slope of the line is

$$m = \frac{y_2 - y_1}{x_2 - x_1} = \frac{3 - 0}{2 - 1} = 3$$

Now we can use the point–slope formula using the point $(1, 0)$ to find the required equation. We have

$$y - y_1 = m(x - x_1)$$
$$y - 0 = 3(x - 1)$$
$$y = 3x - 3$$

This is the equation defining $f$. If we wish, we can rewrite it using function notation: $f(x) = 3x - 3$.

One basic application of linear functions that occurs in business and economics is *linear* or *straight-line depreciation*. In this situation we assume that the value $V(t)$ of an asset (such as a machine or an apartment building) decreases linearly over time $t$:

$$V(t) = mt + b$$

where $t = 0$ corresponds to the time when the asset is new (or when its value is first assessed), and the slope $m$ is negative.

**EXAMPLE** **2**    **Using a linear model for depreciation**

A factory owner buys a new machine for \$8000. After ten years, the machine has a salvage value of \$500.
**(a)** Assuming linear depreciation (as indicated in Figure 1), find a formula for the value $V(t)$ of the machine after $t$ yr, where $0 \le t \le 10$.
**(b)** Use the depreciation function determined in part (a) to find the value of the machine after seven years.

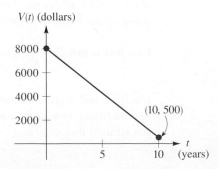

**Figure 1**

**SOLUTION**

**(a)** We need to determine $m$ and $b$ in the equation $V(t) = mt + b$. From Figure 1 we see that the $V$-intercept of the line segment is $b = 8000$. Furthermore, since the line segment passes through the two points $(10, 500)$ and $(0, 8000)$, the slope $m$ is

$$\frac{8000 - 500}{0 - 10} = -750$$

So we have $m = -750$ and $b = 8000$, and the required equation is

$$V(t) = -750t + 8000 \qquad (0 \le t \le 10)$$

**(b)** Substituting $t = 7$ in the equation $V(t) = -750t + 8000$ yields

$$V(7) = -750(7) + 8000 = -5250 + 8000 = 2750$$

Thus the value of the machine after seven years is $2750.

It is instructive to keep track of the units associated with the slope in Example 2. Repeating the slope calculation and keeping track of the units, we have

$$m = \frac{\$8000 - \$500}{0 \text{ yr} - 10 \text{ yr}} = -\$750/\text{yr} \qquad (1)$$

Thus slope is a *rate of change*. (We met this idea earlier, back in Section 1.6.) In this example the slope represents the rate of change of the value of the machine. Notice that the calculations in (1) are exactly those that we would have used in Chapter 3 to compute the *average* rate of change $\Delta V / \Delta t$. In the context of linear functions we often suppress the word "average" and refer simply to the *rate of change,* because no matter what two points we choose on the graph of a linear function, the slope will always be the same.

As a second example of slope as a rate of change, let us suppose that a small manufacturer of handmade running shoes knows that her total cost in dollars, $C(x)$, for producing $x$ pairs of shoes each business day is given by the linear function

$$C(x) = 10x + 50$$

Figure 2(a) displays a table and the graph for this function. Actually, since $x$ represents the daily number of pairs of shoes, $x$ can assume only whole-number values. So technically, the graph that should be given is the one in Figure 2(b). However,

| $x$ | 0 | 1 | 2 | 3 |
|---|---|---|---|---|
| $C(x)$ | 50 | 60 | 70 | 80 |

(a)

(b)

**Figure 2**

the graph in Figure 2(a) turns out to be useful in practice, and we shall follow this convention.

The slope of the line $C(x) = 10x + 50$ in Figure 2(a) is 10, the coefficient of $x$. To understand the units involved, let's calculate the slope using two of the points in Figure 2(a). Using the points $(0, 50)$ and $(1, 60)$ and keeping track of the units, we have

$$m = \frac{\$60 - \$50}{1 \text{ pair} - 0 \text{ pairs}} = \frac{\$10}{1 \text{ pair}} = \$10/\text{pair}$$

Again the slope is a rate. In this case the slope represents the rate of increase of cost; each additional pair of shoes produced costs the manufacturer $10.

In the study of economics a function that gives the cost $C(x)$ for producing $x$ units of a commodity is called a **cost function.** We define the **marginal cost** as the additional cost to produce one more unit. When the cost function is linear, the marginal cost is the slope of the corresponding line. In the preceding example the marginal cost is $10 per pair, and we see that the slope of the line in Figure 2(a) is 10 (dollars per pair).

---

**EXAMPLE 3    A cost function that is linear**

Suppose that the cost $C(x)$ in dollars of producing $x$ bicycles is given by the linear function

$$C(x) = 625 + 45x$$

**(a)** Find the cost of producing 10 bicycles.
**(b)** What is the marginal cost?
**(c)** Use the answers in parts (a) and (b) to find the cost of producing 11 bicycles. Then check the answer by evaluating $C(11)$.

**SOLUTION**
**(a)** Using $x = 10$ in the cost equation, we have

$$C(10) = 625 + 45(10) = 1075$$

Thus the cost of producing ten bicycles is $1075.
**(b)** Since $C$ is a linear function, the marginal cost is the slope, and we have

$$\text{marginal cost} = \$45 \text{ per bicycle}$$

**(c)** According to the result in part (b), each additional bicycle costs $45. Therefore we can compute the cost of 11 bicycles by adding $45 to the cost for 10 bicycles:

$$\text{cost of 11 bicycles} = \text{cost of 10 bicycles} + \text{marginal cost}$$
$$= \$1075 + \$45 = \$1120$$

So the cost of producing 11 bicycles is $1120. We can check this result by using the cost function $C(x) = 625 + 45x$ to compute $C(11)$ directly:

$$C(11) = 625 + 45(11)$$
$$= 625 + 495$$
$$= \$1120 \qquad \text{as obtained previously}$$

Interpreting slope as a rate of change is not restricted to applications in business or economics. Suppose, for example, that you are driving a car at a steady rate of 50 mph. Using the distance formula from elementary mathematics,

$$\text{distance} = \text{rate} \times \text{time}$$

or

$$d = rt$$

We have in this case $d = 50t$, where $d$ represents the distance traveled (in miles) in $t$ hours. In Figure 3 we show a graph of the linear function $d = 50t$. The slope of this line is 50, the coefficient of $t$. But 50 is also the given rate of speed, in miles per hour. So again, slope is a rate of change. In this case, slope is the **velocity,** or *rate of change of distance with respect to time.*

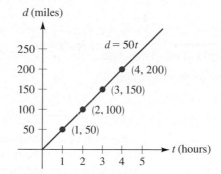

**Figure 3**
The slope of the line is the rate of change of distance with respect to time.

We conclude this section by indicating one way that linear functions are used in statistical applications. Tables 1 and 2 show the evolution of the world record for the one-mile run during the years 1911–1993. In case you're wondering why Table 1

| **TABLE 1**   Evolution of the Record for the Mile Run, 1911–1954 |||
|---|---|---|
| x (year) | y (time) | |
| 1911 | 4:15.4 | (John Paul Jones, United States) |
| 1913 | 4:14.6 | (John Paul Jones, United States) |
| 1915 | 4:12.6 | (Norman Taber, United States) |
| 1923 | 4:10.4 | (Paavo Nurmi, Finland) |
| 1931 | 4:09.2 | (Jules Ladoumegue, France) |
| 1933 | 4:07.6 | (Jack Lovelock, New Zealand) |
| 1934 | 4:06.8 | (Glen Cunningham, United States) |
| 1937 | 4:06.4 | (Sidney Wooderson, Great Britain) |
| 1942 | 4:06.2 | (Gunder Haegg, Sweden) |
| 1942 | 4:06.2 | (Arne Andersson, Sweden) |
| 1942 | 4:04.6 | (Gunder Haegg, Sweden) |
| 1943 | 4:02.6 | (Arne Andersson, Sweden) |
| 1944 | 4:01.6 | (Arne Andersson, Sweden) |
| 1945 | 4:01.4 | (Gunder Haegg, Sweden) |
| 1954 | 3:59.4 | (Roger Bannister, Great Britain) |
| 1954 | 3:58.0 | (John Landy, Australia) |

| **TABLE 2**   Evolution of the Record for the Mile Run, 1957–1993 |||
|---|---|---|
| x (year) | y (time) | |
| 1957 | 3:57.2 | (Derek Ibbotson, Great Britain) |
| 1958 | 3:54.5 | (Herb Elliott, Australia) |
| 1962 | 3:54.4 | (Peter Snell, New Zealand) |
| 1964 | 3:54.1 | (Peter Snell, New Zealand) |
| 1965 | 3:53.6 | (Michel Jazy, France) |
| 1966 | 3:51.3 | (Jim Ryun, United States) |
| 1967 | 3:51.1 | (Jim Ryun, United States) |
| 1975 | 3:51.0 | (Filbert Bayi, Tanzania) |
| 1975 | 3:49.4 | (John Walker, New Zealand) |
| 1979 | 3:49.0 | (Sebastian Coe, Great Britain) |
| 1980 | 3:48.8 | (Steve Ovett, Great Britain) |
| 1981 | 3:48.53 | (Sebastian Coe, Great Britain) |
| 1981 | 3:48.40 | (Steve Ovett, Great Britain) |
| 1981 | 3:47.33 | (Sebastian Coe, Great Britain) |
| 1985 | 3:46.32 | (Steve Cram, Great Britain) |
| 1993 | 3:44.39 | (Noureddine Morceli, Algeria) |

(a)   Scatter plot for the data in Table 1.

(b)   Scatter plot and regression line for the data in Table 1.

**Figure 4**

begins with 1911, John Paul Jones was the first twentieth-century runner to break the previous century's record of 4:15.6, set in 1895. Table 1 ends with the year 1954, the first year in which the "four-minute barrier" was broken. (See the quote by Roger Bannister at the beginning of this section.)

Let's begin by looking at the data in Table 1 graphically. In Figure 4(a) we've plotted the $(x, y)$ pairs given in the table. The resulting plot is called a **scatter diagram** or **scatter plot.**

A striking feature of the scatter diagram in Figure 4(a) is that the records do not appear to be leveling off; rather, they seem to be decreasing in an approximately linear fashion. Using the *least-squares technique* from the field of statistics, it can be shown that the linear function that best fits the data in Table 1 is

$$f(x) = -0.370x + 962.041 \qquad (2)$$

The graph of this line is shown in Figure 4(b). The line itself is referred to as the **regression line,** or the **least-squares line.**

General formulas for determining the regression line are given in Exercise 45. (The derivation, however, is not given, because that requires calculus.) Many graphing utilities and spreadsheet applications have features for computing regression lines when two columns or lists of numbers are entered. We'll cite but one example here using the popular spreadsheet program Microsoft *Excel*™. For more details or for other types of graphing utilities, see the user's manual that came with your graphing utility.

Suppose, for example, that we want to obtain a scatter plot and regression line for the four data points

$$(0, 1) \qquad (1, 2) \qquad (3, 6) \qquad (6, 7)$$

As indicated in Figure 5(a), we enter the $x$-$y$ pairs using adjacent columns of the *Excel* spreadsheet. (In the figure, the $x$-values are in column A and the $y$-values in column B.) Next, of the many chart types that *Excel* provides for displaying data vi-

| | A | B |
|---|---|---|
| 1 | 0 | 1 |
| 2 | 1 | 2 |
| 3 | 3 | 6 |
| 4 | 6 | 7 |

(a) Data

(b) Scatter plot

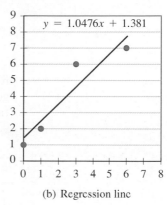

$y = 1.0476x + 1.381$

(b) Regression line

**Figure 5**
Using a spreadsheet application to obtain a regression line

sually, we choose the "Scatter" option and obtain the result shown in Figure 5(b). Finally, for the required regression line, we go to the "Add Trendline" menu and choose "Linear" along with "Display equation on chart." The final result is shown in Figure 5(c).

  **EXAMPLE  4   Using a regression line**

**(a)** The regression line given by equation (2) is based on records from 1911 through 1954. Use this regression line to estimate what the world record for the mile run might have been in 1999.

**(b)** Check the prediction against the actual 1999 record 3:43.13, set by Hicham El Guerrouj of Morocco. Compute the percentage error.

**SOLUTION**
**(a)** Substituting the value $x = 1999$ in equation (2) yields

$$f(1999) = -0.370(1999) + 962.041 \approx 222.41 \text{ sec}$$

$$= 3 \text{ min and } 42.41 \text{ sec}$$

**(b)** The prediction obtained in part (a) is 3:42.41, and the actual record is 3:43.13. Thus the actual record is slightly higher than the prediction, but the difference is less than one second. For computing the percentage error, let's first express the actual record of 3:43.13 in seconds. [From part (a) we already know the predicted record expressed in seconds.] We have

$$3 \text{ min and } 43.13 \text{ sec} = 3(60) \text{ sec} + 43.13 \text{ sec}$$
$$= 223.13 \text{ sec}$$

Now we're ready to compute the percentage error in the prediction:

$$\text{percentage error} = \frac{|(\text{actual value}) - (\text{predicted value})|}{\text{actual value}} \times 100$$
$$= \frac{|223.13 - 222.41|}{223.13} \times 100 \approx 0.32\%$$

The percentage error in the prediction is 0.32%.

**REMARK**   The prediction in this example has turned out to be extremely good. However, see part (c) in the next example for an important word of caution regarding predictions such as this.

---

| EXAMPLE | 5 | A regression line in a medical application |
|---|---|---|

The data in Table 3 are extracted from a 1954 paper on smoking and lung cancer that appeared in the journal *Danish Medical Bulletin*. In Table 3 the left-hand column of numbers shows annual cigarette consumption in 1930 for four countries. The right-hand column gives the mortality rates from lung cancer in those same countries 20 years later.

**TABLE 3    Cigarette Consumption and Lung Cancer**

| | Cigarette consumption for 1930 (per person) | Lung cancer deaths in 1950 (per 100,000 males) |
|---|---|---|
| Sweden | 320 | 11.1 |
| Netherlands | 444 | 28.3 |
| Finland | 1106 | 35.3 |
| England-Wales | 1200 | 53.0 |

Data extracted from "Bronchial Carcinoma—A Pandemic," by A. Nielsen and J. Clemmennsen, *Danish Medical Bulletin,* vol. 1 (1954), pp. 194–199. In some instances the indicated years 1930 and 1950 are only approximate. For instance, for Sweden, the mortality rate pertains to 1951, rather than 1950.

**(a)** Use a graphing utility to create a scatter plot and to find and graph the regression line. (Use the consumption data for the $x$-values and the mortality rates for the corresponding $y$-values.)

**(b)** The regression line gives a functional relationship between per capita cigarette consumption and lung cancer death rates. Use this relationship to obtain estimates for the mortality rates in 1950 for Denmark and Norway, given that the 1930 cigarette consumption figures for Denmark and Norway were 373 and 257, respectively.

**(c)** Compute the percentage error in each estimate, given that the actual death rates (per 100,000) in Denmark and Norway were 18.4 and 9.2, respectively.

Smokescreen? The figure is from a 1948 magazine ad for Camel cigarettes. A 1929 ad for Lucky Strike cigarettes announced "Many prominent athletes smoke Luckies all day long with no harmful effects to wind or physical condition." A 1953 ad by Liggett & Meyers said "It's so satisfying to know that a doctor reports no adverse effects to the nose, throat and sinuses from smoking Chesterfield."

Source: The University of Alabama Center for the Study of Tobacco and Society (Alan Blum, M.D.)

**Figure 6**

(a) Scatter plot

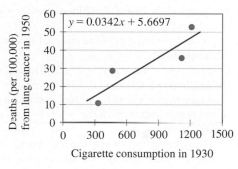

(b) Scatter plot with regression line

## SOLUTION

**(a)** See Figure 6 for the scatter plot and regression line.

**(b)** As indicated in Figure 6(b), the regression line is $y = 0.0342x + 5.697$.

For Denmark with $x = 373$:
$$y = 0.0342(373) + 5.6697$$
$$\approx 18.4$$

For Norway with $x = 257$:
$$y = 0.0342(257) + 5.6697$$
$$\approx 14.5$$

According to the calculations, the projected mortality rate for Denmark in 1950 is 18.4 deaths per 100,000; for Norway the projection is 14.5 per 100,000.

**(c)** For Denmark the projection is 18.4 and so is the actual death rate. So in this case we happen to have 0% error. For Norway we have

$$\text{percentage error} = \frac{|(\text{actual value}) - (\text{projected value})|}{\text{actual value}} \times 100$$

$$= \frac{|9.2 - 14.5|}{9.2} \times 100 \approx 58\%$$

In summary, for Denmark the projected death rate from lung cancer agrees with the actual rate. For Norway, however, there is a relatively large discrepancy between the projection and actual value; the percentage error there is 58%. This highlights one of the shortcomings in using a regression line. Without further analysis and the use of more advanced statistical concepts (and perhaps more data) it's difficult or impossible to know ahead of time how much one should rely on these projections.

# EXERCISE SET 4.1

## A

*In Exercises 1–8, find the linear functions satisfying the given conditions.*

1. $f(-1) = 0$ and $f(5) = 4$
2. $f(3) = 2$ and $f(-3) = -4$
3. $g(0) = 0$ and $g(1) = \sqrt{2}$
4. The graph passes through the points $(2, 4)$ and $(3, 9)$.
5. $f(\frac{1}{2}) = -3$ and the graph of $f$ is a line parallel to the line $x - y = 1$.
6. $g(2) = 1$ and the graph of $g$ is perpendicular to the line $6x - 3y = 2$.
7. The graph of the inverse function passes through the points $(-1, 2)$ and $(0, 4)$.
8. The $x$- and $y$-intercepts of the inverse function are 5 and $-1$, respectively.
9. Let $f(x) = 3x - 4$ and $g(x) = 1 - 2x$. Determine whether the function $f \circ g$ is linear.
10. Explain why there is no linear function with a graph that passes through all three of the points $(-3, 2)$, $(1, 1)$, and $(5, 2)$.
11. A factory owner buys a new machine for $20,000. After eight years, the machine has a salvage value of $1000. Find a formula for the value of the machine after $t$ years, where $0 \le t \le 8$.
12. A manufacturer buys a new machine costing $120,000. It is estimated that the machine has a useful lifetime of ten years and a salvage value of $4000 at that time.
    (a) Find a formula for the value of the machine after $t$ years, where $0 \le t \le 10$.
    (b) Find the value of the machine after eight years.
13. A factory owner installs a new machine costing $60,000. Its expected lifetime is five years, and at the end of that time the machine has no salvage value.
    (a) Find a formula for the value of the machine after $t$ years, where $0 \le t \le 5$.
    (b) Complete the following depreciation schedule.

| End of year | Yearly depreciation | Accumulated depreciation | Value $V$ |
|---|---|---|---|
| 0 | 0 | 0 | 60,000 |
| 1 | | | |
| 2 | | | |
| 3 | | | |
| 4 | | | |
| 5 | | 60,000 | 0 |

14. Let $x$ denote a temperature on the Celsius scale, and let $y$ denote the corresponding temperature on the Fahrenheit scale.
    (a) Find a linear function relating $x$ and $y$; use the facts that 32°F corresponds to 0°C and 212°F corresponds to 100°C. Write the function in the form $y = Ax + B$.

    (b) What Celsius temperature corresponds to 98.6°F?
    (c) Find a number $z$ for which $z$°F $= z$°C.
15. Suppose that the cost $C(x)$, in dollars, of producing $x$ electric fans is given by $C(x) = 450 + 8x$.
    (a) Find the cost to produce 10 fans.
    (b) Find the cost to produce 11 fans.
    (c) Use your answers in parts (a) and (b) to find the marginal cost. (Then check that your answer is the slope of the line.)
16. Suppose that the cost to a manufacturer of producing $x$ units of a certain motorcycle is given by $C(x) = 220x + 4000$, where $C(x)$ is in dollars.
    (a) Find the marginal cost.
    (b) Find the cost of producing 500 motorcycles.
    (c) Use your answers in parts (a) and (b) to find the cost of producing 501 motorcycles.
17. Suppose that the cost $C(x)$, in dollars, of producing $x$ compact discs is given by $C(x) = 0.5x + 500$.
    (a) Graph the given equation.
    (b) Compute $C(150)$.
    (c) If you add the marginal cost to the answer in part (b), you obtain a certain dollar amount. What does this amount represent?
18. The following graphs each relate distance and time for a moving object. Determine the velocity in each case.

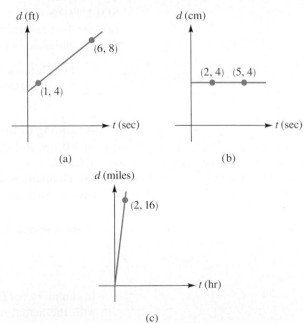

(a)

(b)

(c)

19. Two points $A$ and $B$ move along the $x$-axis. After $t$ sec, their positions are given by the equations

$$A: \quad x = 3t + 100$$
$$B: \quad x = 20t - 36$$

    (a) Which point is traveling faster, $A$ or $B$?

**(b)** Which point is farther to the right when $t = 0$?

**(c)** At what time $t$ do $A$ and $B$ have the same $x$-coordinate?

**20.** A point moves along the $x$-axis, and its $x$-coordinate after $t$ sec is $x = 4t + 10$. (Assume that $x$ is in centimeters.)

**(a)** What is the velocity?

**(b)** What is the $x$-coordinate when $t = 2$ sec?

**(c)** Use your answers in parts (a) and (b) to find the $x$-coordinate when $t = 3$ sec. *Hint*: What are the units of the velocity in part (a)? Check your answer by letting $t = 3$ in the given equation.

**21.** The following table gives the population of California in 1995 and in 1997.

| x (year) | y (population) |
|----------|----------------|
| 1995     | 31,493,525     |
| 1997     | 32,217,708     |

**(a)** Find the equation of the linear function whose graph passes through the two $(x, y)$ points given in the table.

**(b)** Use the linear function determined in part (a) to make a projection for the population of California in 2000. (Round your answer to the nearest 1000.)

**(c)** The actual California population for 2000 was 33,871,648. Does the linear function yield a projection that is too high or too low? Compute the percentage error.

**22.** The following table gives the population of Florida in 1985 and 1990.

| x (year) | y (population) |
|----------|----------------|
| 1985     | 11,351,118     |
| 1990     | 13,018,365     |

Follow the steps in Exercise 21 to make a projection for the population of Florida in 2000. For part (c) the actual population of Florida was 15,982,378.

**23.** The following table indicates total motion picture receipts (including video tape rentals) in the United States for the years 1994 and 1995.

**Motion Picture Receipts**

| x (year) | y (receipts) (in millions of dollars) |
|----------|----------------------------------------|
| 1994     | 53,504                                 |
| 1995     | 57,184                                 |

Source: U.S. Census Bureau, *Statistical Abstract of the United States: 1999*

**(a)** Find the equation of the linear function whose graph passes through the two $(x, y)$ points given in the table.

Ⓖ **(b)** Use a graphing utility to graph the line in part (a). Then use a TRACE or ZOOM feature to estimate what

motion picture receipts might have been for the year 1997.

**(c)** Compute the percentage error in the estimate in part (b), given that the actual figure for 1997 was $63,010 millions.

**24.** During the 1990s the percentage of TV households viewing cable and satellite TV programs increased while the percentage viewing network affiliate shows (ABC, CBS, NBC, and FOX) generally decreased. The following table shows the primetime ratings for the network affiliates in the years 1993 and 1995. (In the table the *rating percentage* is defined as the percentage of TV households viewing a TV program in an average minute.)

**Primetime Ratings for Network Affiliates**

| x (year) | y (rating percentage) |
|----------|------------------------|
| 1993     | 40.9                   |
| 1995     | 37.3                   |

Source: Nielsen Media Research, *1998 Report on Television*

**(a)** Find the equation of the linear function whose graph passes through the two $(x, y)$ points given in the table.

Ⓖ **(b)** Using a graphing utility to graph the line in part (a). Then use a TRACE or ZOOM feature to estimate what the rating percentage might have been for the year 1997.

**(c)** Compute the percentage error in the estimate in part (b), given that the actual figure for 1997, according to Nielsen Media Research, was 33.1.

*In general, the growth of plants or animals does not follow a linear pattern. For relatively short intervals of time, however, a linear function may provide a reasonable description of the growth. Exercises 25 and 26 provide examples of this.*

**25. (a)** In an experiment with sunflower plants, H. S. Reed and R. H. Holland measured the height of the plants every seven days for several months. [The experiment is reported in *Proceedings of the National Academy of Sciences*, vol. 5 (1919), p. 140.] The following data are from this experiment.

| x (number of days) | 21 | 49 |
|--------------------|-------|--------|
| y [average height (cm) of plants after x days] | 67.76 | 205.50 |

Find the linear function whose graph passes through the two points given in the table. (Round each number in the answer to two decimal places.)

**(b)** Use the linear function determined in part (a) to estimate the average height of the plants after 28 days. (Round your answer to two decimal places.)

*(continues)*

(c) In the experiment, Reed and Holland found that the average height after 28 days was 98.10 cm. Is your estimate in part (b) too high or too low? Compute the percentage error in your estimate.

(d) Follow parts (b) and (c) using $x = 14$ days. For the computation of percentage error, you need to know that Reed and Holland found that the average height after 14 days was 36.36 cm.

(e) As you've seen in parts (c) and (d), your estimates are quite close to the actual values obtained in the experiment. This indicates that for a relatively short interval, the growth function is nearly linear. Now repeat parts (b) and (c) using $x = 84$ days, which is a longer interval of time. You'll find that the linear function does a poor job in describing the growth of the sunflower plants. To compute the percentage error, you need to know that Reed and Holland determined the average height after 84 days to be 254.50 cm.

**26.** (a) The biologist R. Pearl measured the population of a colony of fruit flies (*Drosophila melanogaster*) over a period of 39 days. [The experiment is discussed in Pearl's book, *The Biology of Population Growth* (New York: Alfred Knopf, 1925).] Two of the measurements made by Pearl are given in the following table.

| $x$ (number of days) | 12 | 18 |
|---|---|---|
| $y$ (population) | 105 | 225 |

Find the linear function whose graph passes through the two points given in the table.

(b) Use the linear function determined in part (a) to estimate the population after 15 days. Then compute the percentage error in your estimate, given that the actual population after 15 days, as found by Pearl, was 152.

(c) Use the linear function determined in part (a) to estimate the population after 9 days. Then compute the percentage error in your estimate, given that after 9 days, Pearl found the actual population to be 39.

(d) As you've seen in parts (b) and (c), your estimates are quite close to the actual values obtained in the experiment. This indicates that for relatively short intervals of time, the growth is nearly linear. Now repeat part (b) using $x = 39$ days, which covers a longer interval of time. You'll find that the linear function does a poor job in describing the population growth. For the computation of percentage error, you need to know that Pearl determined the population after 39 days to be 938.

**27.** (a) On graph paper, plot the following points: $(1, 0)$, $(2, 3)$, $(3, 6)$, $(4, 7)$.

(b) In your scatter diagram from part (a), sketch a line that best seems to fit the data. Estimate the slope and the $y$-intercept of the line.

(c) The actual regression line in this case is $y = 2.4x - 2$. Add the graph of this line to your sketch from parts (a) and (b).

**28.** (a) On graph paper, plot the following points: $(1, 2)$, $(3, 2)$, $(5, 4)$, $(8, 5)$, $(9, 6)$.

(b) In your scatter diagram from part (a), sketch a line that best seems to fit the data.

(c) Using your sketch from part (b), estimate the $y$-intercept and the slope of the regression line.

(d) The actual regression line is $y = 0.518x + 1.107$. Check to see whether your estimates in part (c) are consistent with the actual $y$-intercept and slope. Graph this line along with the points given in part (a). (In sketching the line, use the approximation $y = 0.5x + 1.1$.)

**29.** The table in the following figure shows the population of Los Angeles over the years 1930–1990. The accompanying graph shows the corresponding scatter plot and regression line. The equation of the regression line is

$$f(x) = 37{,}546.068x - 71{,}238{,}863.429$$

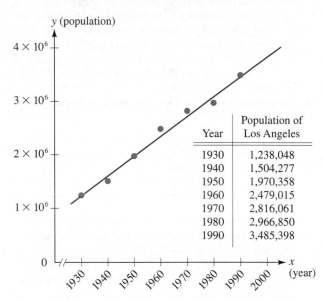

| Year | Population of Los Angeles |
|---|---|
| 1930 | 1,238,048 |
| 1940 | 1,504,277 |
| 1950 | 1,970,358 |
| 1960 | 2,479,015 |
| 1970 | 2,816,061 |
| 1980 | 2,966,850 |
| 1990 | 3,485,398 |

(a) Use the regression line to compute an estimate for what the population of Los Angeles might have been in 2000. (Round the answer to the nearest thousand.) Then compute the percentage error in the estimate, given that the actual figure for 2000 is 3.823 million.

(b) Find $f^{-1}(x)$.

(c) Use your answer in part (b) to estimate the year in which the population of Los Angeles might reach 4 million. *Hint:* For the function $f$, the inputs are years and the outputs are populations; for $f^{-1}$, the inputs are populations and the outputs are years.

**30.** Perhaps foreshadowing the end of the Cold War in the early 1990s, the number of nuclear warheads worldwide began to decrease after the year 1986 (when the number was at an all-time high). The following table indicates the global number of nuclear warheads over the years 1986–1992. The graph shows the corresponding scatter plot and regression line. The equation for the regression line is

$$f(x) = -2810.96x + 5,653,063.25$$

| Year | Number of nuclear warheads |
|------|---------------------------|
| 1986 | 69,075 |
| 1987 | 67,302 |
| 1988 | 65,932 |
| 1989 | 63,645 |
| 1990 | 60,642 |
| 1991 | 57,017 |
| 1992 | 53,136 |

Source of data: R. S. Norris and W. M. Arkin, *Bulletin of Atomic Scientists,* Nov./Dec. 1997

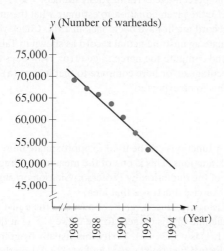

**(a)** Use the regression line to make a projection for the number of nuclear warheads in 1997. Then compute the percentage error, given that the actual number was 36,110.

**(b)** When might there be only (!) 10,000 nuclear warheads worldwide? Round the answer to the nearest integer. Also, if the trend were to continue, when would there be no warheads remaining?

**31.** The following table shows world grain production for selected years over the period 1950–1990.

| Year | World grain production (million tons) |
|------|---------------------------------------|
| 1950 | 631 |
| 1960 | 824 |
| 1970 | 1079 |
| 1980 | 1430 |
| 1990 | 1769 |

Source: Lester R. Brown et al. in *Vital Signs 1999* (New York: W. W. Norton & Co, 1999)

**G** **(a)** Use a graphing utility or spreadsheet to determine the equation of the regression line. For the *x*-*y* data pairs, use *x* for the year and *y* for the grain production. Create a graph showing both the scatter plot and regression line.

**(b)** Use the equation of the regression line to make a projection for the world grain production in 1993. Then compute the percentage error in your projection, given that the actual grain production in 1993 was 1714 million tons. *Remark:* Your projection will turn out to be higher than the actual figure. One (among many) reasons for this: In 1993 there was a drop in world grain production due largely to the effects of poor weather on the U.S. corn crop.

**(c)** Use the equation of the regression line to make a projection for the world grain production in 1998. Then compute the percentage error in your projection, given that the actual world grain production in 1998 was 1844 million tons. *Remark:* Again, your projection will turn out to be too optimistic. According to Lester Brown's *Vital Signs: 1999,* world grain production dropped in 1998 "due largely to severe drought and heat in Russia on top of an overall deterioration of that country's economy."

**32.** The following table shows global natural gas production for the years 1990–1996. The abbreviation "tcf" stands for *trillion cubic feet.*

| Year | Natural gas production (tcf) |
|------|------------------------------|
| 1990 | 71.905 |
| 1991 | 73.037 |
| 1992 | 73.219 |
| 1993 | 74.570 |
| 1994 | 75.190 |
| 1995 | 76.614 |
| 1996 | 80.045 |

Source: *BP Amoco Statistical Review of World Energy* (49th ed.) http://www.bp.com/worldenergy

**G** **(a)** Use a graphing utility or spreadsheet to determine the equation of the regression line. For the *x*-*y* data pairs, use *x* for the year and *y* for the natural gas production. Create a graph showing both the scatter plot and regression line.

**(b)** What are the units associated with the slope of the regression line in part (a)?

**G** **(c)** In your graph of the regression line, use a TRACE or ZOOM feature to make an estimate for natural gas production in the year 1999.

**(d)** The actual production figure for 1999 is 83.549 tcf. Is your estimate high or low? Compute the percentage error.

**(e)** The table above shows that global production of natural gas increased over the period 1990–1996, and in fact it still continues to increase each year. However, for purposes of making a very conservative estimate, let's assume for the moment that natural gas production levels off at its 1999 value of 83.549 tcf per year. According to the *BP Amoco Statistical Review of World Energy,* as of the end of 1999, proved world reserves of natural gas were 5171.8 tcf. Carry out the following calculation and interpret your answer. *Hint:* Keep track of the units.

$$\frac{5171.8 \text{ tcf}}{83.549 \text{ tcf/yr}} = \cdots$$

**33.** This exercise illustrates one of the pitfalls that can arise in using a regression line: large discrepancies can occur when the regression line is used to make long-term projections. The table in the following figure shows the population of California during the years 1860–1900. The graph displays the scatter plot of the data; the equation of the regression line is

$$f(x) = 28{,}632.69x - 52{,}928{,}780$$

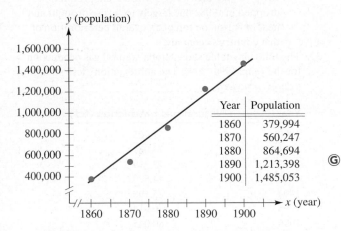

| Year | Population |
|------|-----------|
| 1860 | 379,994 |
| 1870 | 560,247 |
| 1880 | 864,694 |
| 1890 | 1,213,398 |
| 1900 | 1,485,053 |

As you can see from the scatter plot, the population growth over this period is very nearly linear.

**(a)** Use the regression line to estimate the population of California in 1990.

**(b)** According to the U.S. Bureau of the Census, the population of California in 1990 was 29,839,250. Is your estimate in part (a) close to this figure?

**34. (a)** The June 1976 issue of *Scientific American* magazine contained an article entitled "Future Performance in Footracing" by H. W. Ryder, H. J. Carr, and P. Herget. According to the authors of this article, "It appears likely that within 50 years the record [for the mile] will be down to 3:30." Use the regression line defined in equation (2) on page 218 to make a projection for the mile time in the year 2026 (which will be 50 years after the article appeared). Is your projection close to the one given in the *Scientific American* article?

**(b)** The regression line defined in equation (2) is based only on the data from Table 1. If we use all the data

from both Table 1 and Table 2, then the least-squares technique can be used to derive the following regression line:

$$f(x) = -0.400x + 1019.472$$

Use this equation to make a projection for the mile time in the year 2026. Which projection is closer to the value predicted in the *Scientific American* article, this one or the one calculated in part (a)?

**35.** The data in Table 2 on page 217 covers the years 1957–1993. The equation of the regression line for the data is

$$y = -0.318x + 858.955$$

**(a)** Use this equation to estimate what the mile record might have been for the year 1954. Then check Table 1 to see the actual record for 1954, which was set by John Landy. Is your estimate too high or too low? Compute the percentage error in your estimate.

**(b)** Use the given equation to estimate what the mile record might have been back in 1911. Check your estimate against the actual record as shown in Table 1, and compute the percentage error. How does the percentage error here compare to that in part (a)? Why is this to be expected?

**B**

**36.** Linear functions can be used to approximate more complicated functions. This is one of the meanings or implications of the quotation by Professor Gleason on page 213. This exercise illustrates that idea.

**(a)** Using calculus, it can be shown that the equation of the line that is tangent to the curve $y = x^2$ at the point $(1, 1)$ is $y = 2x - 1$. Verify this visually by graphing the two functions $y = x^2$ and $y = 2x - 1$ on the same set of axes. (*Suggestion:* Use a viewing rectangle that extends from $-2$ to 3 in the $x$-direction and from $-3$ to 4 in the $y$-direction.) Note that the tangent line is virtually indistinguishable from the curve in the immediate vicinity of the point $(1, 1)$.

**(b)** For numerical rather than visual evidence of how well the linear function $y = 2x - 1$ approximates the function $y = x^2$ in the immediate vicinity of $(1, 1)$, complete the following tables.

| $x$ | 0.9 | 0.99 | 0.999 |
|------|------|------|------|
| $x^2$ | | | |
| $2x - 1$ | | | |

| $x$ | 1.1 | 1.01 | 1.001 |
|------|------|------|------|
| $x^2$ | | | |
| $2x - 1$ | | | |

*In Exercises 37–40, let f and g be the linear functions defined by*

$$f(x) = Ax + B \quad (A \neq 0) \quad \text{and} \quad g(x) = Cx + D \quad (C \neq 0)$$

*In each case, compute the average rate of change of the given function on the interval [a, b].*

**37.** (a) $f$
(b) $f \circ f$
(c) $g \circ f$
(d) $f \circ g$

**38.** (a) $f^{-1}$
(b) $g^{-1}$

**39.** (a) $(f \circ g)^{-1}$
(b) $(g \circ f)^{-1}$

**40.** (a) $f^{-1} \circ g^{-1}$
(b) $g^{-1} \circ f^{-1}$

**41.** Show that the linear function $f(x) = mx$ satisfies the following identities:
(a) $f(a + b) = f(a) + f(b)$
(b) $f(ax) = af(x)$

**42.** Let $f$ be a linear function such that

$$f(a + b) = f(a) + f(b)$$

for all real numbers $a$ and $b$. Show that the graph of $f$ passes through the origin. *Hint*: Let $f(x) = Ax + B$ and show that $B = 0$.

**43.** Find a linear function $f(x) = mx + b$ such that $m$ is positive and $(f \circ f)(x) = 9x + 4$.

**44.** (a) Let $f$ be a linear function. Show that

$$f\left(\frac{x_1 + x_2}{2}\right) = \frac{f(x_1) + f(x_2)}{2}$$

(In words: The output of the average is the average of the outputs.)
(b) Show (by using an example) that the equation in part (a) does not hold for the function $f(x) = x^2$.

**45.** This exercise shows how to compute the slope and the $y$-intercept of the regression line. As an example, we'll work with the simple data set given in Exercise 27.

| x | 1 | 2 | 3 | 4 |
|---|---|---|---|---|
| y | 0 | 3 | 6 | 7 |

(a) Let $\Sigma x$ denote the sum of the $x$-coordinates in the data set, and let $\Sigma y$ denote the sum of the $y$-coordinates. Check that $\Sigma x = 10$ and $\Sigma y = 16$.
(b) Let $\Sigma x^2$ denote the sum of the squares of the $x$-coordinates, and let $\Sigma xy$ denote the sum of the products of the corresponding $x$- and $y$-coordinates. Check that $\Sigma x^2 = 30$ and $\Sigma xy = 52$.
(c) The slope $m$ and the $y$-intercept $b$ of the regression line satisfy the following pair of simultaneous equations [in the first equation, $n$ denotes the number of points $(x, y)$ in the data set]:

$$\begin{cases} nb + (\Sigma x)m = \Sigma y \\ (\Sigma x)b + (\Sigma x^2)m = \Sigma xy \end{cases}$$

In the present example these equations become

$$\begin{cases} 4b + 10m = 16 \\ 10b + 30m = 52 \end{cases}$$

Solve this pair of equations for $m$ and $b$, and check that your answers agree with the values in Exercise 27(c).

*In Exercises 46–49:*
(a) Use the method described in Exercise 45 to find the equation of the regression line for the given data set.
(b) For Exercises 48 and 49, if your graphing utility has a feature for computing regression lines, use it to check your answer in part (a).

**46.**
| x | 2 | 4 | 8 | 10 |
|---|---|---|---|---|
| y | −7 | −5 | −2 | −1 |

**47.**
| x | 1 | 2 | 3 | 4 | 5 |
|---|---|---|---|---|---|
| y | 2 | 3 | 9 | 9 | 11 |

**48.**
| x | 1 | 2 | 3 | 4 | 5 |
|---|---|---|---|---|---|
| y | 16 | 13.1 | 10.5 | 7.5 | 2 |

**49.**
| x | 520 | 740 | 560 | 610 | 650 |
|---|---|---|---|---|---|
| y | 81 | 98 | 83 | 88 | 95 |

## C

**50.** Suppose that $f$ is a linear function satisfying the condition $f(kx) = kf(x)$ for all real numbers $k$. Prove that the graph of $f$ passes through the origin.

**51.** (a) Find all linear functions $f$ satisfying the identity $f(f(x)) = 2x + 1$. (For your answer, rationalize any denominators containing radicals.)
(b) Find all linear functions $f$ satisfying the identity

$$f(f(f(x))) = 2x + 1$$

(Rationalize any denominators containing radicals.) *Hint*: Try the factoring formula, $x^3 - y^3 = (x - y)(x^2 + xy + y^2)$ from Appendix B.4.

**52.** Let $a$ and $b$ be real numbers, and suppose that the inequality $ax + b \leq 0$ has no solutions. What can you say about the linear function $f(x) = ax + b$? Answer in complete sentences and justify what you say.

**53.** Are there any linear functions $f$ satisfying the identity $f^{-1}(x) = f(f(x))$? If so, list them; if not, explain why not.

**54.** Let $f(x) = ax + b$, where $a$ and $b$ are positive numbers, and assume that the following equation holds for all values of $x$: $f(f(x)) = bx + a$. Show that $a + b = 1$.

# MINI PROJECT    WHO ARE BETTER RUNNERS, MEN OR WOMEN?

An oversimplified answer here would be to say that men are better because in any given event, the men's world record time is less than the women's. For instance, as of the year 2000, the men's and women's world records for the 100-m dash were 9.79 sec and 10.49 sec, respectively. This reasoning, however, ignores the fact that, historically, women have been training and competing on the world stage for far less time than men. Likewise, it's only relatively recently that women have been supported or sponsored to a degree approaching that for men. Indeed, currently, women's records are falling at a faster rate than men's. Complete the following research and calculations, then discuss this issue.

The following table gives the names of athletes who set world records in the 100-m dash over the years 1968–1999. (The table is restricted to times that were recorded electronically, rather than manually; 1968 was the year in which electric timing made its major debut (in the 1968 Olympics in Mexico City).

### Selected Record-Setting Performances in 100-m Dash, 1968–1999*

| Year | Men | Women |
|------|-----|-------|
| 1968 | James Hines, USA (10/14/68) | Wyomia Tyus, USA (10/15/68) |
| 1972 | | Renate Stecher, DDR (East Germany) (9/2/72) |
| 1976 | | Annegret Richter, FRG (West Germany) (7/25/76) |
| 1977 | | Marlies Oelsner (Göhr) DDR (7/1/77) |
| 1983 | Calvin Smith, USA (7/3/83) | Evelyn Ashford, USA (7/3/83) |
| 1984 | | Evelyn Ashford, USA (8/22/84) |
| 1988 | Carl Lewis, USA (9/24/88) | Florence Griffith-Joyner, USA (7/17/88) |
| 1991 | Carl Lewis, USA (8/25/91) | |
| 1994 | Leroy Burrell, USA (7/6/94) | |
| 1996 | Donovan Bailey, CAN (7/29/96) | |
| 1999 | Maurice Greene, USA (6/16/99) | |

*In cases in which the record was broken more than once in a given year, only the fastest performance is indicated.

**(a)** Using the library or the Internet, look up the 100-m times for each athlete in the table.

**(b)** For the men's records: Let $x$ represent the year, with $x = 0$ corresponding to 1960, and let $y$ represent the record time in that year. Find the regression line $y = f(x)$.

**(c)** For the women's records: Again, let $x$ represent the year, with $x = 0$ corresponding to 1960, and let $y$ represent the record time in that year. Find the regression line $y = g(x)$.

**(d)** Solve the equation $f(x) = g(x)$ to compute a projection for the year in which the men's and women's records might be equal. What would that common record be?

# 4.2 QUADRATIC FUNCTIONS

In the text and exercises for the previous section we saw examples in which data sets and their scatter plots were modeled using a linear function. Clearly, however, linear functions with their straight line graphs cannot be appropriate models for every data set. Consider, for instance, the scatter plot in Figure 1, which shows the daily trading volumes for Amazon.com stock in a particular month. It appears that no line could adequately summarize the situation. Next, in Figure 2, look at the data and scatter plot relating to the spread of AIDS. Here it appears that some sort of curve, rather than straight line, would be better for summarizing the trend in the data. As you'll see in a moment, one type of curve that does fit the data in Figure 2 quite well is obtained by graphing a *quadratic function*.

| $x$ years after 1980 | 4 | 5 | 6 | 7 | 8 | 9 | 10 |
|---|---|---|---|---|---|---|---|
| $y$ AIDS cases (millions) | 0.2 | 0.4 | 0.7 | 1.1 | 1.6 | 2.3 | 3.2 |

**Figure 1**
Daily number of shares of Amazon.com stock traded (i.e., sold) in March 2000. $x = 1$ corresponds to March 1.

**Figure 2**
Estimated cumulative number of AIDS cases worldwide, 1984–1990

Source: Joint United Nations Programme on HIV/AIDS

After the linear functions, the next simplest functions are the **quadratic functions,** which are defined by equations of the form

$$f(x) = ax^2 + bx + c \qquad (a \neq 0)$$

where $a$, $b$, and $c$ are constants and $a$ is not zero. (The word "quadratic" is derived from the Latin word for a square, *quadratus*.) We will see that the graph of any quadratic function is a curve called a **parabola** that is similar in shape to the basic $y = x^2$ graph. Figure 3 displays the graphs of two typical quadratic functions. Subsequent examples will demonstrate that the parabola opens upward when $a > 0$ and downward when $a < 0$. As Figure 3 indicates, the turning point on the parabola is called the **vertex.** The **axis of symmetry** of the parabola $y = ax^2 + bx + c$ is the vertical line passing through the vertex. (Mini Project 1 at the end of this section indicates how to *prove* that the graph does indeed have this symmetry.)

Figure 3      (a)          (b)

We mentioned in Section 4.1 that many graphing utilities have features for determining the regression line for a given set of data points. This is the line that best fits the data points. (We are using the phrase "best fits" in an intuitive sense here; the technical meaning is explained in a project at the end of Section 4.5.) In addition to fitting a linear function to a data set, many of these graphing utilities can fit other types of functions as well, including quadratics. In Example 1 we find and compare linear and quadratic models for the AIDS data in Figure 2. For details on using a graphing calculator to determine a quadratic function that best fits a data set, see the owner's manual that came with your graphing utility. [On a TI graphing calculator, go to the "STAT menu," choose "CALC," and then select "QuadReg" (which stands for *quadratic regression*). In Microsoft *Excel*™, go to the "Chart" menu, select "Add Trendline," then choose "Polynomial," and type in "2" for the order.]

| EXAMPLE | 1 | **Using linear and quadratic functions to model AIDS data** |
|---|---|---|

**(a)** Use a graphing utility to find and graph the linear and quadratic models for the AIDS data in Figure 2 on page 229.

**Figure 4**
Linear and quadratic models for
AIDS data from Figure 2

(a) Linear model
$y = 0.4893x - 2.0679$

(b) Quadratic model
$y = 0.0679x^2 - 0.4607x + 0.9857$

**(b)** Use each function to make projections for the years 1992 and 1997. Then use the following information to see which model is more accurate in each case. The cumulative numbers of AIDS cases in 1992 and 1997 were 5.5 million and 15.1 million, respectively.

**SOLUTION**
**(a)** See Figure 4.
**(b)** The results of the calculations (rounded to one decimal place) are shown in Table 1. As perspective in evaluating these models, keep in mind that they are obtained using the data in Figure 2, which covers the years 1984–1990. So we are using the models to project two years and seven years beyond the data, that is, beyond 1990. For 1992 both projections fall short of the actual figure, but the quadratic model is much closer. As you should compute for yourself, the percentage errors for the linear and quadratic projections for 1992 are approximately 31% and 5%, respectively. For 1997 both projections again fall short of the actual figure. The linear model is even farther off this time; it predicts less than half of the actual figure. The quadratic model is again closer to reality, but as you can check, the percentage error in this case is a relatively large 15%. In summary: The quadratic model works quite well in the short run (two years), but it misses the mark considerably for the longer term (seven years). The linear model misses badly in both cases. For a health professional or a United Nations administrator writing a budget proposal to deal with the AIDS epidemic in 1990, evidently even the quadratic model doesn't grow fast enough and so might mislead the

**TABLE 1   Comparison of Linear and Quadratic Models
for Cumulative Number of AIDS Cases Worldwide in 1992 and 1997**

| Year | Linear model $y = 0.4893x - 2.0679$ (millions) | Quadratic model $y = 0.0679x^2 - 0.4607x + 0.9857$ (millions) | Actual figures (millions) |
|---|---|---|---|
| 1992 ($x = 12$) | 3.8 | 5.2 | 5.5 |
| 1997 ($x = 17$) | 6.3 | 12.8 | 15.1 |

person into underfunding the project. (In later work we look at types of functions that grow faster than any quadratic. See, for example, Exercise 64 in Section 4.6, or see Section 5.1.)

In the next set of examples the main focus will be on graphing quadratic functions by hand, rather than with a graphing utility. The goal is to *understand* why the graphs look as they do and to see how they relate to the basic $y = x^2$. The techniques that we'll use in analyzing quadratic functions have already been developed in previous chapters. In particular, the following two topics are prerequisites for understanding the examples in this section:

- Completing the square—for a review see either Section 1.7 or 2.1
- Translations and reflections—for a review see Section 3.4

  **EXAMPLE** 2 **Graphing a quadratic function using completing the square and translation**

Graph the function $y = x^2 - 2x + 3$.

**SOLUTION**
The idea here is to use the technique of completing the square; this will enable us to obtain the required graph simply by shifting the basic $y = x^2$ graph. We begin by writing the given equation

$$y = x^2 - 2x \qquad + 3$$

To complete the square for the $x$-terms we want to add 1. (Check this.) Of course, to keep the equation in balance, we have to account for this by writing

$$y = (x^2 - 2x + 1) + 3 - 1 \qquad \text{adding zero to the right side}$$

or

$$y = (x - 1)^2 + 2$$

Now, as we know from Section 3.4, the graph of this last equation is obtained by moving the parabola $y = x^2$ one unit in the positive $x$-direction and two units in the positive $y$-direction. This shifts the vertex from the origin to the point $(1, 2)$. See Figure 5.

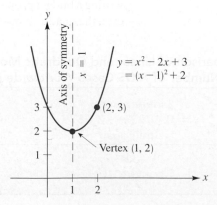

**Figure 5**

**NOTE**   As a guide to sketching the graph, you'll want to know the $y$-intercept. To find the $y$-intercept, substitute $x = 0$ in the given equation to obtain $y = 3$. Then, given the vertex $(1, 2)$ and the point $(0, 3)$, a reasonably accurate graph can be quickly sketched. [Actually, once you find that $(0, 3)$ is on the graph, you also know that the reflection of this point about the axis of symmetry is on the graph. This is why the point $(2, 3)$ is shown in Figure 5.]

Now we want to compare the graphs of $y = x^2$, $y = 2x^2$, and $y = \frac{1}{2}x^2$. The last two functions were not specifically discussed in the previous chapters, so for now you can graph them by first setting up tables. If you do this, rather than using a graphing utility, you'll gain some insight into why the graphs in Figure 6 look as they do. All three graphs are parabolas that open upward, but $y = 2x^2$ appears to be narrower than $y = x^2$, while $y = \frac{1}{2}x^2$ appears wider than $y = x^2$. Another way (besides setting up tables) to see why the graphs appear this way is to start from the inequalities $\frac{1}{2} < 1 < 2$. Then, assuming for the moment that $x \neq 0$, we can multiply through by the *positive* quantity $x^2$ to obtain

$$\frac{1}{2}x^2 < x^2 < 2x^2 \qquad \text{(provided that } x \neq 0)$$

This tells us that with the exception of the origin, the graph of $y = \frac{1}{2}x^2$ is *below* that of $y = x^2$, which in turn is *below* $y = 2x^2$. This is why, on any given interval (for example $-2 \leq x \leq 2$, as in Figure 6), the graph of $y = \frac{1}{2}x^2$ appears wider than $y = x^2$, which in turn appears wider than $y = 2x^2$.

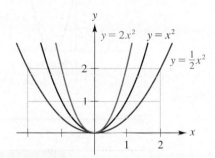

**Figure 6**

The observations that we've just made about the relative shapes of three parabolas also apply to $y = -x^2$, $y = -2x^2$, and $y = -\frac{1}{2}x^2$, except in these cases the parabolas open downward rather than upward. In the box that follows we summarize and generalize our observations up to this point.

**PROPERTY SUMMARY   The Graph of $y = ax^2$**

1. The graph of $y = ax^2$ is a parabola with vertex at the origin. It is similar in shape to $y = x^2$.
2. The parabola $y = ax^2$ opens upward if $a > 0$, downward if $a < 0$.
3. The parabola $y = ax^2$ is narrower than $y = x^2$ if $|a| > 1$, wider than $y = x^2$ if $|a| < 1$.

| EXAMPLE | 3 | Graphing parabolas that appear narrower than the basic $y = x^2$ |

Sketch the graphs of the following quadratic functions:
**(a)** $y = 3(x - 1)^2$;          **(b)** $y = -3(x - 1)^2$.

**SOLUTION**
**(a)** Because of the $x - 1$, we shift the basic parabola $y = x^2$ one unit to the right. The factor of 3 in the given equation tells us that we want to draw a parabola that is narrower than $y = x^2$ but that has the same vertex, $(1, 0)$. To see exactly how narrow to draw $y = 3(x - 1)^2$, we need to know another point on the graph other than the vertex, $(1, 0)$. An easy point to obtain is the $y$-intercept. Setting $x = 0$ in the equation yields $y = 3(0 - 1)^2 = 3$. Now that we know the vertex, $(1, 0)$, and the $y$-intercept, 3, we can sketch a reasonably accurate graph; see Figure 7(a).

**(b)** In part (a) we sketched the graph of $y = 3(x - 1)^2$. By reflecting that graph in the $x$-axis, we obtain the graph of $y = -3(x - 1)^2$, as shown in Figure 7(b).

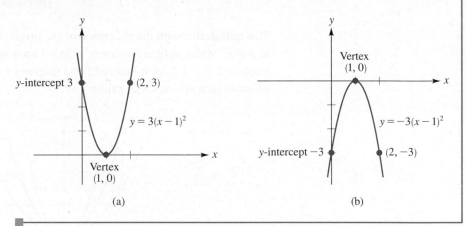

Figure 7          (a)                                                    (b)

| EXAMPLE | 4 | Analyzing a quadratic function |

Graph the function $f(x) = -2x^2 + 4x + 6$ and specify the vertex, axis of symmetry, maximum or minimum value of $f$, and $x$- and $y$-intercepts.

**SOLUTION**
The idea is to complete the square, as in Example 2. We have

$$
\begin{aligned}
y &= -2x^2 + 4x \qquad\quad + 6 \\
&= -2(x^2 - 2x \qquad) + 6 \\
&= -2(x^2 - 2x + 1) + 6 + 2 \qquad \text{adding } 0 = (-2)(1) + 2 \text{ to the} \\
&\qquad\qquad\qquad\qquad\qquad\qquad\quad \text{right-hand side} \\
&= -2(x - 1)^2 + 8 \tag{1}
\end{aligned}
$$

From equation (1) we see that the required graph is obtained simply by shifting the graph of $y = -2x^2$ "right 1, up 8," so that the vertex is $(1, 8)$. As a guide to sketching the graph, we want to compute the intercepts. The $y$-intercept is 6. (Why?) For the $x$-intercepts we replace $y$ with 0 in equation (1) to obtain

$$-2(x-1)^2 = -8$$
$$(x-1)^2 = 4$$
$$x - 1 = \pm 2$$
$$x = 1 \pm 2 = -1 \quad \text{or} \quad 3$$

Thus the $x$-intercepts are $x = -1$ and $x = 3$. Knowing these intercepts and the vertex, we can sketch the graph as in Figure 8. You should check for yourself that the information accompanying Figure 8 is correct.

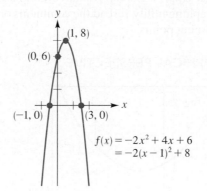

| $f(x) = -2x^2 + 4x + 6$ | |
|---|---|
| Vertex: | $(1, 8)$ |
| Axis of symmetry: | $x = 1$ |
| Maximum value of $f$: | 8 |
| $y$-intercept: | 6 |
| $x$-intercepts: | $-1$ and 3 |

$$f(x) = -2x^2 + 4x + 6$$
$$= -2(x-1)^2 + 8$$

Figure 8

The next three examples involve maximum and minimum values of functions. As background for this, we first summarize our basic technique for graphing parabolas.

## PROPERTY SUMMARY
### The Graph of the Parabola $y = ax^2 + bx + c$

By completing the square, the equation of the parabola $y = ax^2 + bx + c$ can always be rewritten in the form

$$y = a(x - h)^2 + k$$

In this form, the vertex of the parabola is $(h, k)$ and the axis of symmetry is the line $x = h$. The parabola opens upward if $a > 0$ and downward if $a < 0$.

**EXAMPLE 5**    Determining the input at which a quadratic function has a minimum value

The graph of the quadratic function $g(x) = x^2 - \frac{6}{7}x + 2$ is a parabola that opens upward because the coefficient of $x^2$ is positive. Thus it makes sense to talk about a minimum rather than maximum value for this function. Let $x_0$ denote the input for which $g(x_0)$ is minimum.

**(a)** Use a TRACE and/or ZOOM feature on a graphing utility to estimate $x_0$ to the nearest one-tenth. What is the corresponding estimate for $g(x_0)$?

**(b)** Use algebra to determine the exact value of $x_0$ and the minimum value of the function. Check that the results are consistent with the visual evidence in part (a).

**SOLUTION**

**(a)** From the preliminary view obtained in Figure 9(a), we can see that the input $x_0$ at which the function has a minimum is roughly 0.5, a bit less actually. The zoom-in view in Figure 9(b) reveals that $x_0$ is closer to 0.4 than to 0.5. So we have $x_0 \approx 0.4$, to the nearest tenth. Figure 9(b) shows that the output $g(x_0)$ is between 1.81 and 1.82, so certainly to the nearest tenth we can say that $g(x_0) \approx 1.8$. *Suggestion*: Before working this example with your own graphing utility, reread the comments on page 161 regarding zooming in on turning points.

**GRAPHICAL PERSPECTIVE**

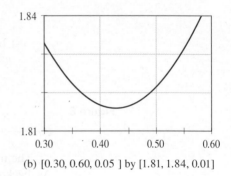

**Figure 9**
Zooming in on the turning point of $g(x) = x^2 - \frac{6}{7}x + 2$

(a) $[-1, 2, 0.5]$ by $[1, 4, 0.5]$          (b) $[0.30, 0.60, 0.05]$ by $[1.81, 1.84, 0.01]$

**(b)** By completing the square as in Example 4, we find that the given equation can be rewritten as

$$g(x) = \left( x - \frac{3}{7} \right)^2 + \frac{89}{49}$$

(You should verify this for yourself, using Example 4 as a model.) This last equation tells us that the vertex of the parabola is the point $(\frac{3}{7}, \frac{89}{49})$. Thus the minimum value of the function is $\frac{89}{49}$ and this minimum occurs at $x_0 = \frac{3}{7}$. Using a calculator now, you'll find that $\frac{3}{7} \approx 0.429$ and $\frac{89}{49} \approx 1.816$. Both of these values are consistent with the graphical estimates in part (a).

**Figure 10**
The minimum value occurs at $x_0$ for both of the functions $y = \sqrt[3]{f(x)}$ and $y = f(x)$.

For the previous two examples, keep in mind that we were able to find the maximum or minimum easily only because the functions were quadratics. In contrast, you cannot expect to find the minimum of $y = x^4 - 8x$ using the method of Examples 4 and 5 because it is not a quadratic function. In general, the techniques of calculus are required to find maxima and minima for functions other than quadratics. There are some cases, however, in which our present method can be adapted to functions that are closely related to quadratics. For instance, in the next example, we look for an input that minimizes a function of the form $y = \sqrt[3]{f(x)}$, where $f$ is a quadratic function. As indicated in Figure 10, we need only find the input that minimizes the quadratic function $y = f(x)$, because this same input also minimizes $y = \sqrt[3]{f(x)}$.

(The outputs of the two functions are, of course, different, but the point here is that the same *input* does the job for both functions.)

| EXAMPLE | 6 | Finding the minimum of a function that's related to a quadratic |
|---|---|---|

Let $f(x) = \sqrt[3]{x^2 - x + 1}$. Which $x$-value yields the minimum value for the function $f$? What is this minimum value?

**SOLUTION**

According to the remarks just prior to this example, the $x$-value that minimizes the function $f(x) = \sqrt[3]{x^2 - x + 1}$ will be the same $x$-value that minimizes the function $y = x^2 - x + 1$. To find this $x$-value, we complete the square, just as we've done previously in this section. We have

$$y = x^2 - x \qquad\quad + 1$$
$$= x^2 - x + \frac{1}{4} + 1 - \frac{1}{4}$$
$$= \left(x - \frac{1}{2}\right)^2 + \frac{3}{4}$$

This shows that the vertex of the parabola $y = x^2 - x + 1$ is $(1/2, 3/4)$. Since this parabola opens upward, we conclude that the input $x = 1/2$ will produce the minimum value for $y = x^2 - x + 1$ and also for $f(x) = \sqrt[3]{x^2 - x + 1}$. The minimum value of the function $f$ is

$$f(1/2) = \sqrt[3]{(1/2)^2 - (1/2) + 1}$$
$$= \sqrt[3]{3/4} \approx 0.91$$

In summary: The minimum value of the function $f$ occurs when $x = 1/2$. This minimum value is $\sqrt[3]{3/4}$, which is approximately 0.91. See Figure 11 for a graphical perspective.

**GRAPHICAL PERSPECTIVE**

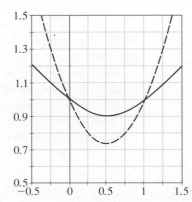

**Figure 11**
The dashed graph is $y = x^2 - x + 1$; the other is $f(x) = \sqrt[3]{x^2 - x + 1}$. The minimum value for both functions occurs when $x = 0.5$. The minimum value of $f$ is $\sqrt[3]{3/4}$, which is approximately 0.9.

**Figure 12**

| EXAMPLE | 7 | Finding inputs that maximize a function related to a quadratic |

As indicated in Figure 12, the maximum value of the function $y = -t^4 + 3t^2$ occurs when $t$ is between 1.0 and 1.5 and also when $t$ is between $-1.0$ and $-1.5$. Determine these $t$-values exactly, then obtain calculator approximations rounded to three decimal places.

**SOLUTION**
The substitution $t^2 = x$ will reduce this question to one about a quadratic function. If $t^2 = x$, then $t^4 = x^2$ and we have

$$
\begin{aligned}
y &= -t^4 + 3t^2 \\
&= -x^2 + 3x \\
&= -\left(x - \frac{3}{2}\right)^2 + \frac{9}{4} \qquad \text{completing the square, as we've done throughout this section (Check the algebra!)}
\end{aligned}
$$

The graph of this last equation is a parabola that opens downward, and the maximum occurs when $x$ is 3/2. So we have

$$
t^2 = x = \frac{3}{2}
$$

and therefore

$$
t = \pm\sqrt{\frac{3}{2}} = \pm\frac{\sqrt{3}}{\sqrt{2}} = \pm\frac{\sqrt{6}}{2} \approx \pm 1.225
$$

Note that these calculator values are consistent with Figure 12.

In many real-life applications in science and business, data are collected that can be arranged in an $x$-$y$ table of values. (We've seen examples in this and the previous section.) We conclude this section with a useful theorem that tells how to determine whether a given $x$-$y$ table can be generated by a linear function or a quadratic function (or neither). As background for the theorem, we explain what is meant by *first differences* and *second differences*. Suppose we have a list of numbers, say, 2, 7, 8, 4, 15. Then the list of **first differences** is a new list formed by subtracting adjacent members of the given list as follows:

$$
7 - 2(=5), \qquad 8 - 7(=1), \qquad 4 - 8(=-4), \qquad 15 - 4 = 11
$$

So, for this example, the list of first differences is 5, 1, $-4$, 11. The process can be summarized conveniently as shown in Figure 13.

Once we have the list of first differences, we can follow the same procedure to form the list of **second differences** as shown in Figure 14. For the second differences we are subtracting adjacent numbers in the list of first differences.

With the terminology we've now introduced, we are ready to state the theorem for determining whether or not a given table of $x$-$y$ values can be generated by a lin-

Original list ⟶ 2   7   8   4   15
First differences ⟶ 5   1   $-4$   11

**Figure 13**

Original list ⟶ 2   7   8   4   15
First differences ⟶ 5   1   $-4$   11
Second differences ⟶ $-4$   $-5$   15

**Figure 14**

ear or quadratic function. In the statement of the theorem, reference is made to $x$ values that are *equally spaced*. That means, for example, we could have $x = 1, 2, 3$, and so on, or $x = 5, 10, 15$, and so on, but not $x = 1, 2, 4, \ldots$.

---

**THEOREM   How to Determine Whether a Data Set Can Be Generated by a Linear or Quadratic Function**

Suppose we have a table of $x$-$y$ values and the $x$-values are equally spaced. Then:

(a) The data can be generated by a linear function if and only if the first differences of the $y$-values are constant.
(b) The data can be generated by a quadratic function if and only if the second differences of the $y$-values are constant.

---

The proof for part (a) of this theorem is outlined in Exercises 63 and 64. We omit the proof of part (b) because of the lengthy algebra that is involved.

---

**EXAMPLE   8   Using first and second differences**

The $x$-$y$ values in Figure 15 are generated by a linear function because the first differences of the $y$'s are constant. The $x$-$y$ values in Figure 16 are generated by neither a linear function nor a quadratic function because neither the first nor second differences are constant.

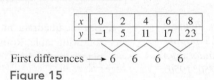

Figure 15

Figure 16

---

# EXERCISE SET 4.2

## A

*Exercises 1 and 2 require graphing utilities that can create scatter plots and compute linear and quadratic regression models.*

Ⓖ  **1.** The following table shows the number of air passenger miles flown worldwide for selected years from 1950 to 1985.

(a) Use a graphing utility to create a scatter plot for the data. Then determine the linear model and the quadratic model that fit the data as closely as possible. Add the graph of each model to your scatter plot.
(b) Use each model to make projections for the number of passenger miles for 1990 and for 1998.

*(continues)*

| Year $x$ ($x = 0$ is 1950) | 0 | 5 | 10 | 15 | 20 | 25 | 30 | 35 |
|---|---|---|---|---|---|---|---|---|
| Passenger miles $y$ (billions) | 16.94 | 36.90 | 65.94 | 119.78 | 278.57 | 421.83 | 658.88 | 827.19 |

Data computed from *Vital Signs 1999*, Lester R. Brown et al. (New York: W. W. Norton & Co., 1999)

(c) Use the following information to compute the percentage errors in the projections in part (b). For each case, which model produces the smaller percentage error? The number of passenger miles for 1990 and 1998 were 1145.94 billion and 1585.74 billion, respectively.

2. The following table shows the number of cellular phone subscribers worldwide over the years 1990–1995.

| Year x (x = 0 is 1990) | 0 | 1 | 2 | 3 | 4 | 5 |
|---|---|---|---|---|---|---|
| Cell phone subscribers (millions) | 11 | 16 | 23 | 34 | 55 | 91 |

Source: *Vital Signs, 2000,* Lester R. Brown et al. (New York: W. W. Norton & Co., 2000)

(a) Use a graphing utility to create a scatter plot for the data. Then determine the quadratic model that fit the data as closely as possible. Add the graph of the quadratic function to your scatter plot.

(b) Use the model to make projections for the number of cell phone subscribers for 1996 and for 1998. Which projection do you think might be more accurate? Now compute the percentage error in each projection using the following information. The number of cell phone subscribers in 1996 and 1998 were 142 million and 319 million, respectively.

*For Exercises 3 and 4, refer to the following figures. Figure A shows a scatter plot and quadratic model for the U.S. population over the period 1790–1950. Figure B shows similar information for the world population over the period 1750–1950. For both figures, x represents the number of years after 1750. (Thus x = 0 corresponds to the year 1750, and x = 200 corresponds to 1950.)*

$$y = 0.00572x^2 - 0.44741x + 12.70012$$

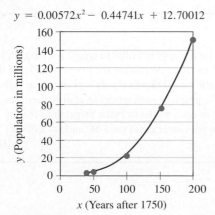

**Figure A**
Scatter plot and quadratic model for U.S. population, 1790–1950.

$$y = 0.000042x^2 - 0.000140x + 0.824000$$

**Figure B**
Scatter plot and quadratic model for world population, 1750–1950

3. Use the quadratic model in Figure A to complete the following table. Round each projection to two decimal places; round the percentage error to the nearest integer.

| | Projected U.S. population (millions) | Actual U.S. population (millions) | Projection too high or too low? | % error |
|---|---|---|---|---|
| 1970 | | 203.30 | | |
| 2000 | | 275.60 | | |

4. Use the quadratic model in Figure B to complete the following table. Round each projection to two decimal places; round the percentage error to the nearest integer.

| | Projected world population (billions) | Actual world population (billions) | Projection too high or too low? | % error |
|---|---|---|---|---|
| 1970 | | 3.708 | | |
| 2000 | | 6.080 | | |

*Afterword on Exercises 3 and 4*: For the time spans shown in Figures A and B, quadratic models describe both the U.S. and world populations quite well. That is, the graph of each quadratic function comes very close to the data points in the scatter plot. Exercise 3 shows that a quadratic model for the U.S. population does a reasonably good job of projecting the population figures 20 and even 50 years beyond the base data. Exercise 4, on the other hand, shows that the quadratic model is inappropriate for similar projections of the world population, because the quadratic model grows much too slowly. In Chapter 5 we study *exponential functions,* which can be much more appropriate for modeling very rapid growth.

*In Exercises 5–20, graph the quadratic function. Specify the vertex, axis of symmetry, maximum or minimum value, and intercepts.*

5. $y = (x + 2)^2$

6. $y = -(x + 2)^2$

7. $y = 2(x + 2)^2$

8. $y = 2(x + 2)^2 + 4$

9. $y = -2(x + 2)^2 + 4$

10. $y = x^2 + 6x - 1$

11. $f(x) = x^2 - 4x$

12. $F(x) = x^2 - 3x + 4$

13. $g(x) = 1 - x^2$

14. $y = 2x^2 + \sqrt{2}x$

15. $y = x^2 - 2x - 3$

16. $y = 2x^2 + 3x - 2$

17. $y = -x^2 + 6x + 2$

18. $y = -3x^2 + 12x$

19. $s = 2 + 3t - 9t^2$

20. $s = -\frac{1}{4}t^2 + t - 1$

*For Exercises 21–26, determine the input that produces the largest or smallest output (whichever is appropriate). State whether the output is largest or smallest.*

21. $y = 2x^2 - 4x + 11$

22. $f(x) = 8x^2 + x - 5$

23. $g(x) = -6x^2 + 18x$

24. $s = -16t^2 + 196t + 80$

25. $f(x) = x^2 - 10$

26. $h(x) = x^2 - 10x$

*In Exercises 27–30, find the maximum or minimum value for each function (whichever is appropriate). State whether the value is a maximum or minimum.*

27. $y = x^2 - 8x + 3$

28. $y = \frac{1}{2}x^2 + x + 1$

29. $y = -2x^2 - 3x + 2$

30. $y = -\frac{1}{3}x^2 - 2x$

*In Exercises 31–34, you are given a quadratic function.*

(a) *By looking at the coefficient of the square term, state whether the function has a maximum or a minimum value.*

Ⓖ (b) *Use a TRACE and/or ZOOM feature on a graphing utility to estimate the input $x_0$ for which the function obtains its maximum or minimum value. (Estimate to the nearest one-tenth, as in Example 5.) What is the corresponding estimate for the maximum or minimum value?*

(c) *Use algebra to determine the exact value of $x_0$ and the corresponding maximum or minimum value of the function. Check to see that the results are consistent with the graphical estimates obtained in part (b).*

31. $f(x) = 6x^2 - x - 4$

32. $g(t) = 40t - 7t^2$

33. $y = -9t^2 + 40t + 1$

34. $y = \sqrt{2}x^2 + 4x + 3$

35. How far from the origin is the vertex of the parabola $y = x^2 - 6x + 13$?

36. Find the distance between the vertices of the parabolas $y = -\frac{1}{2}x^2 + 4x$ and $y = 2x^2 - 8x - 1$.

*For Exercises 37–42, the functions f, g, and h are defined as follows:*

$$f(x) = 2x - 3 \qquad g(x) = x^2 + 4x + 1 \qquad h(x) = 1 - 2x^2$$

*In each exercise, classify the function as linear, quadratic, or neither.*

37. $f \circ g$

38. $g \circ f$

39. $g \circ h$

40. $h \circ g$

41. $f \circ f$

42. $h \circ h$

*In Exercises 43 and 44, determine the inputs that yield the minimum values for each function. Compute the minimum value in each case.*

43. (a) $f(x) = \sqrt{x^2 - 6x + 73}$

(b) $g(x) = \sqrt[3]{x^2 - 6x + 73}$

(c) $h(x) = x^4 - 6x^2 + 73$

44. (a) $F(x) = (4x^2 - 4x + 109)^{1/2}$

(b) $G(x) = (4x^2 - 4x + 109)^{1/3}$

(c) $H(x) = 4x^4 - 4x^2 + 109$

Ⓖ *For Exercises 45 and 46, first, use a graphing utility to estimate to the nearest one-tenth the maximum value of the function. Then use algebra to determine the exact value, and check that your answer is consistent with the graphical estimate.*

45. (a) $f(x) = \sqrt{-x^2 + 4x + 12}$

(b) $g(x) = \sqrt[3]{-x^2 + 4x + 12}$

(c) $h(x) = -x^4 + 4x^2 + 12$

46. (a) $F(x) = (27x - x^2)^{1/2}$

(b) $G(x) = (27x - x^2)^{1/3}$

(c) $H(x) = 27x^2 - x^4$

*In Exercises 47–50, determine whether the x-y values are generated by a linear function, a quadratic function, or neither.*

47.

| x | −4 | −2 | 0 | 2 | 4 |
|---|---|---|---|---|---|
| y | 25 | 3 | −4 | 7 | 33 |

48.

| x | 1 | 2 | 3 | 4 | 5 |
|---|---|---|---|---|---|
| y | −12 | −8.5 | −5 | −1.5 | 2 |

49.

| x | 0 | 1 | 2 | 3 | 4 |
|---|---|---|---|---|---|
| y | −21 | −3 | 7 | 9 | 3 |

50.

| x | 0.25 | 0.50 | 0.75 | 1.00 | 1.25 |
|---|---|---|---|---|---|
| y | −0.40 | −0.16 | 0.08 | 0.32 | 0.62 |

Ⓖ 51. On the same set of axes, graph the four parabolas $y = x^2$, $2x^2$, $3x^2$, and $8x^2$. Relative to your graphs, where do you think the graph of $y = 50x^2$ would fit in? After answering, check by adding the graph of $y = 50x^2$ to the picture.

Ⓖ 52. Graph the four parabolas $y = x^2$, $0.5x^2$, $0.25x^2$, and $0.125x^2$. Relative to your graphs, where do you think the graph of $y = 0.02x^2$ would fit in? After answering, check by adding the graph of $y = 0.02x^2$ to the picture.

**B**

53. Let $f(x) = x^2$. Find the average rate of change $\Delta f/\Delta x$ on the interval $[a, x]$.

**54.** If $f(x) = ax^2 + bx + c$, show that
$$\frac{f(x + h) - f(x)}{h} = 2ax + ah + b.$$

**55.** Find the $x$-coordinate of the vertex of the parabola $y = (x - a)(x - b)$. (Your answer will be in terms of the constants $a$ and $b$.)   *Hint*: It's easier here to rely on symmetry than on completing the square.

Ⓖ **56. (a)** Graph the two functions $y = x^2 + 4x$ and $y = x^2 - 4x$. How are the two graphs related (in terms of symmetry)?

**(b)** Follow part (a) using the two functions $y = -2x^2 + 3x + 4$ and $y = -2x^2 - 3x + 4$.

**(c)** Which one of the graphing techniques from Section 3.4 relates to what you have observed in parts (a) and (b)?

*In Exercises 57–60, find quadratic functions satisfying the given conditions.*

**57.** The graph passes through the origin, and the vertex is the point $(2, 2)$.   *Hint*: What do $h$ and $k$ stand for in the general equation $y = a(x - h)^2 + k$?

**58.** The graph is obtained by translating $y = x^2$ four units in the negative $x$-direction and three units in the positive $y$-direction.

**59.** The vertex is $(3, -1)$, and one $x$-intercept is 1.

**60.** The axis of symmetry is the line $x = 1$. The $y$-intercept is 1. There is only one $x$-intercept.

**61.** Let $g(x) = x^2 + bx$. Are there any values for $b$ for which the minimum value of this function is $-1$? If so, what are they? If not, explain why.

**62.** For which value of $c$ will the minimum value of the function $f(x) = x^2 + 2x + c$ be $\sqrt{2}$?

**63.** This exercise shows that if we have a table generated by a linear function and the $x$-values are equally spaced, then the first differences of the $y$-values are constant.

**(a)** In the following data table, the three $x$-entries are equally spaced. Compute the three entries in the $f(x)$ row assuming that $f$ is the linear function given by $f(x) = mx + b$. (Don't worry about the fact that your answers contain all four of the letters $m$, $b$, $a$, and $h$.)

| x | a | a + h | a + 2h |
|---|---|---|---|
| f(x) | | | |

**(b)** Compute the first differences for the three quantities that you listed in the $f(x)$ row in part (a). (The two first differences that you obtain should turn out to be equal, as required.)

**64.** Suppose we have a table of $x$-$y$ values with the $x$-values equally spaced. This exercise shows that if the first differences of the $y$-values are constant, then the table can be generated by a linear function.   *Note*: To show that the data points are generated by a linear function, it is enough to show that the points all lie on one nonvertical line.

Consider the following table with the $x$-values equally spaced by an amount $h \neq 0$. (We are assuming that $h$ is nonzero to guarantee that the three $x$-values are distinct.)

| x | a | a + h | a + 2h |
|---|---|---|---|
| y | $y_1$ | $y_2$ | $y_3$ |

Assuming that the first differences of the $y$-values are constant, we have $y_2 - y_1 = y_3 - y_2 = k$, where $k$ is a constant.

**(a)** Check that the slope of the line joining the two data points $(a, y_1)$ and $(a + h, y_2)$ is $k/h$.

**(b)** Likewise, check that the slope of the line joining the two data points $(a + h, y_2)$ and $(a + 2h, y_3)$ is $k/h$.

From parts (a) and (b), we conclude that the three data points lie on a nonvertical line, as required. (The slope $k/h$ is well defined because we assumed $h \neq 0$.)

**65.** The following table and scatter plot show global coal consumption for the years 1990–1995.

**Global Coal Consumption 1990–1995**

| Year x<br>x = 0 ↔ 1990 | Coal consumption y<br>(billion tons) |
|---|---|
| 0 | 3.368 |
| 1 | 3.285 |
| 2 | 3.258 |
| 3 | 3.243 |
| 4 | 3.261 |
| 5 | 3.311 |

Source: World Resources Institute

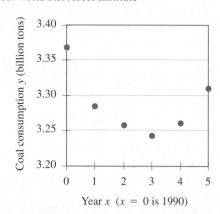

**(a)** Use a graphing utility to find a quadratic model for the data. Then use the model to make estimates for global coal consumption in 1989 and 1996.

**(b)** Use the following information to show that, in terms of percentage error, the 1996 estimate is better than the 1989 estimate, but in both cases the percentage error is less than 2%. The actual figures for coal consumption in 1989 and 1996 are 3.408 and 3.428 billion tons, respectively.

**(c)** Use the model to project worldwide coal consumption in 1998. Then show that the percentage error is more than 9%, given that the actual 1998 consumption was 3.329 billion tons.

**66.** *Driven by rising consumer demand and growing dissatisfaction with conventional farming practices, the organic agriculture industry is soaring.* — *Vital Signs 2000,* Lester R. Brown et al. (New York: W. W. Norton & Co., 2000)

The following table and scatter plot show the area devoted to organic farming in the European Union over the period 1988–1998. (One hectare equals 2.471 acres or 10,000 square meters.)

| Year x | Area y (million hectares) |
|--------|---------------------------|
| 1988 | 0.17 |
| 1990 | 0.34 |
| 1992 | 0.69 |
| 1994 | 1.15 |
| 1996 | 1.90 |
| 1998 | 3.17 |

Data from *Vital Signs 2000*

**(a)** In view of the scatter plot and the opening quotation, a quadratic model might be useful here, at least in

making short-term predictions. Indeed, if you look at the scatter plot without knowing that it was generated from real-life data, in the context of this section you might think that the points all lie exactly on the graph of a parabola. Show that this is not the case: Compute the second differences of the $y$-values in the given table, and note that they are not equal. (In fact, no two are equal.)

**(b)** In the following table, fill in the missing entries so that all six data points are generated by one quadratic function.  *Hint:* Work back from the second differences; you want them all to be equal.

| 1988 | 0.17 |
|------|------|
| 1990 | 0.34 |
| 1992 | 0.69 |
| 1994 | ? |
| 1996 | ? |
| 1998 | ? |

## C

**67.** By completing the square, show that the coordinates of the vertex of the parabola $y = ax^2 + bx + c$ are $(-b/2a, -D/4a)$, where $D = b^2 - 4ac$.

**68.** Compute the average of the two $x$-intercepts of the graph of $y = ax^2 + bx + c$. (Assume $b^2 - 4ac > 0$.) How does your answer relate to the result in Exercise 67?

**69.** Consider the quadratic function $y = px^2 + px + r$, where $p \neq 0$.
**(a)** Show that if the vertex lies on the $x$-axis, then $p = 4r$.
**(b)** Show that if $p = 4r$, then the vertex lies on the $x$-axis.

**70.** Let $f(x) = ax^2 + bx$, where $a \neq 0$ and $b \neq 0$. Find a value for $b$ such that the equation $f(f(x)) = 0$ has exactly three real roots.

---

**MINI PROJECT 1**

### HOW DO YOU KNOW THAT THE GRAPH OF A QUADRATIC FUNCTION IS ALWAYS SYMMETRIC ABOUT A VERTICAL LINE?

**(a)** A short answer that sweeps everything under the rug: The graph of the basic parabola $y = x^2$ is symmetric about a vertical axis, and the graph of $f(x) = ax^2 + bx + c$ inherits this type of symmetry. In a group, discuss the reasons supporting this short answer. (The discussion won't be complete without taking into account the following three concepts: completing the square, translations, and reflection in the $y$-axis.) After the discussion, write a paragraph or two answering, as carefully as you can, the question raised in the title of this mini project.

**(b)** Here's a completely different way to go about answering the question in the title of this mini project. An advantage to this alternative approach is that, as a by-product, it gives you the equation of the axis of symmetry without the need for completing the square. We start with the definition of what it means for the graph of $y = f(x)$ to be symmetric about a vertical line, say, $x = x_0$.

---

**DEFINITION** | **Symmetry about the Line $x = x_0$**

The graph of a function $f$ is symmetric about the line $x = x_0$ provided the following condition holds. Whenever $x_0 + h$ is in the domain of $f$, then so is $x_0 - h$ and

$$f(x_0 + h) = f(x_0 - h)$$

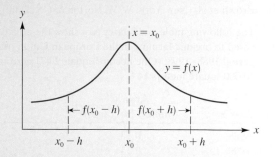

---

Now suppose we have a quadratic function

$$f(x) = ax^2 + bx + c \qquad (a \neq 0) \tag{1}$$

Because the domain is the set of all real numbers, we don't have to worry about the part of the definition in the box above regarding domain. Thus, to show that the graph of the quadratic function is symmetric about a line $x = x_0$ we need to find a value for $x_0$ so that the following equation holds for all values of $h$:

$$f(x_0 + h) = f(x_0 - h) \tag{2}$$

Now your job: Evaluate each side of equation (2) using the definition of $f$ in equation (1). Then solve the resulting equation for $x_0$. You should obtain $x_0 = -b/2a$. This shows that the graph of the quadratic function is indeed symmetric about a vertical line, namely, $x = -b/2a$.

---

# MINI PROJECT 2 | WHAT'S LEFT IN THE TANK?

**(a)** The following table shows global oil consumption for the years 1990–1995, 1998, and 1999. Using only the data for the years 1990–1995, use a graphing utility to find a linear model and a quadratic model for global oil consumption.

**(b)** Provide the detailed calculations to back up the following statements regarding the use of these models in projecting global oil consumption for the years 1998 and 1999.

For both 1998 and 1999 the linear model underestimates oil consumption, while the quadratic model overestimates. For both models, however, the percentage error is always less than 5%. For both years, the quadratic model gives the better projection (as measured by percentage error).

**Global Oil Consumption, 1990–1995, 1998, 1999**

| Year $x$ ($x = 0$ corresponds to 1990) | 0 | 1 | 2 | 3 | 4 | 5 | 8 | 9 |
|---|---|---|---|---|---|---|---|---|
| Global oil consumption $y$ (billion barrels) | 23.886 | 23.913 | 24.105 | 23.997 | 24.506 | 24.893 | 26.251 | 26.723 |

Source: U.S. Energy Information Administration

**(c)** Oil, as you know, is a nonrenewable energy resource; at some point in the future, it will be used up. When this will occur will depend on, among other things, consumption patterns and the amount of oil that exists on the planet. In this portion of the mini project you'll compute estimates for the *depletion date* for oil using three different consumption scenarios. On the basis of figures from the U.S. Geological Survey and the Energy Information Administration, we'll assume that in 1990 the total amount of oil remaining was 2886 billion barrels. [This estimate takes into account reserves and resources as of 1990, plus resources discovered in the 1990s, plus current estimates (at the end of the 1990s) for as yet undiscovered resources.]

*A consequence of the linear yearly consumption model:* Suppose that the consumption $y$ (in billions of barrels) in year $x$ is given by a linear function, $y = mx + b$. Then, using a result from Chapter 13 (Exercise 1 in Section 13.1), it can be shown that the total amount $A$ of oil consumed over the years $x = 0$ through $x = T$ is given by the quadratic model

$$A = \frac{m}{2}T^2 + \left(\frac{m}{2} + b\right)T + b$$

On the left side of this equation, replace $A$ with 2886; on the right side, replace $m$ and $b$ with the values that you obtained for the linear model in part (a). Now find the positive root of the resulting quadratic equation. (Use either the quadratic formula or a graphing utility.) The root represents the "life expectancy" of oil under this scenario. Round the answer to the nearest ten years and add to 1990 to get a depletion date for oil.

*A consequence of the quadratic yearly consumption model:* Suppose that the consumption $y$ (in billions of barrels) in year $x$ is given by a quadratic function, $y = ax^2 + bx + c$. Then, using a result from Chapter 13 (Exercise 5 in Section 13.1), it can be shown that the total amount $A$ of oil consumed over the years $x = 0$ through $x = T$ is given by the cubic model

$$A = \frac{a}{3}T^3 + \frac{a+b}{2}T^2 + \left(\frac{a+3b+6c}{6}\right)T + c$$

On the left side of this equation, replace $A$ with 2886; on the right side, replace $a$, $b$, and $c$ with the values that you obtained for the quadratic model in part (a). Now use a graphing utility to find the positive root of the resulting cubic equation. The root gives you the "life expectancy" of oil under this scenario. Round the answer to the nearest ten years and add to 1990 to get a depletion date for oil.

*Constant consumption model:* If you've done the preceding calculations correctly, you will have found that the depletion dates under both models occur within the present century. Now try the following "what if." Go back to the linear consumption model and redo the calculations using for $m$ the value 0 rather than the value from part (a). In terms of consumption, what's the interpretation of $m = 0$? What depletion date do you obtain?

**(d)** Write a paragraph or two summarizing the results from part (c). (Don't forget to include what the assumptions are in each case.)

# 4.3 USING ITERATION TO MODEL POPULATION GROWTH (Optional Section)

*Although I shall henceforth adopt the habit of referring to the variable X as "the population," there are countless situations outside population biology where . . . [iteration of functions] applies. . . . Examples in economics include models for the relationship between commodity quantity and price, for the theory of business cycles, and for the temporal sequences generated by various other economic quantities.*

*. . . I would therefore urge that people be introduced to, say, [the iteration process for $f(x) = kx(1 - x)$] early in their mathematical education. This equation can be studied phenomenologically by iterating it on a calculator, or even by hand. Its study does not involve as much conceptual sophistication as does elementary calculus. Such study would greatly enrich the student's intuition about nonlinear systems.* —Biologist Robert M. May, "Simple mathematical models with very complicated dynamics," *Nature*, vol. 261 (1976), pp. 459–467.

The size of a population or its genetic makeup may change from one generation to the next. In the study of *discrete dynamics* we use functions and the iteration process (from Section 3.5) to investigate and analyze changes such as these that occur over discrete intervals of time. We begin by introducing the notion of a *fixed point* of a function.

If we start with a function $f$ and an input $x$, it's usually not the case that $f(x)$ turns out to be the same as $x$ itself. That is, usually, the output is not the same as the input. But sometimes this does happen. Take, for example, the function $f(x) = 3x - 2$ and the input $x = 1$. Then we have

$$f(1) = 3(1) - 2 = 1$$

So for this particular function the input $x = 1$ is an instance where "input = output." The input $x = 1$ in this case is called a *fixed point* of the function $f(x) = 3x - 2$. In the box that follows, we give the general definition of a fixed point.

---

**DEFINITION** | **Fixed Point of a Function**

A fixed point of a function $f$ is an input $x$ in the domain of $f$ such that

$$f(x) = x$$

**EXAMPLE**

Both 0 and 1 are fixed points for $f(x) = x^2$ because $f(0) = 0^2 = 0$ and $f(1) = 1^2 = 1$.

---

**EXAMPLE** **1** **Finding fixed points**

Find the fixed points (if any) for each function:

**(a)** $f(x) = 1 - x$;  **(b)** $g(x) = 1 + x$;  **(c)** $h(x) = x^2 - x - 3$.

**SOLUTION**
**(a)** We're looking for a number $x$ such that $f(x) = x$. In view of the definition of $f$, this last equation becomes

$$1 - x = x$$

and therefore

$$x = \frac{1}{2}$$

This result shows that the function $f$ has one fixed point; it is $x = 1/2$.
**(b)** If $x$ is a fixed point of $g(x) = 1 + x$, we have

$$1 + x = x$$

But then subtracting $x$ from both sides of this last equation yields $1 = 0$, which is impossible. We conclude from this that there is no fixed point for the function $g(x) = 1 + x$.
**(c)** The fixed points (if any) are the solutions of the quadratic equation $x^2 - x - 3 = x$. Subtracting $x$ from both sides of this equation, we have

$$x^2 - 2x - 3 = 0$$
$$(x - 3)(x + 1) = 0$$

Looking at this last equation, we can see that there are two roots: 3 and $-1$. Each of these numbers is a fixed point for the given function $h(x) = x^2 - x - 3$. That is, $h(3) = 3$ and $h(-1) = -1$. [You should verify each of these last two statements for yourself by actually computing $h(3)$ and $h(-1)$.]

A fixed point of a function can be interpreted geometrically: It is the $x$-coordinate of a point where the graph of the given function intersects the line $y = x$. Figure 1 shows the fixed points for the functions in the example that we've just completed.

**Figure 1**
Fixed points for the functions in Example 1

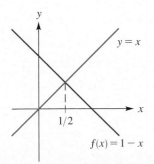

(a)  The fixed point of $f$ is 1/2.

(b)  The function $g$ has no fixed points.

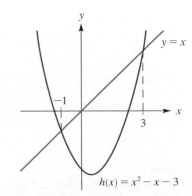

(c)  The fixed points of $h$ are $-1$ and 3.

Fixed points are related to the iteration process in several ways. Suppose that a number $a$ is a fixed point of the function $f$. Then by definition we have $f(a) = a$, which says that the first iterate of $a$ is equal to $a$ itself. Similarly, all of the subsequent iterates of the fixed point $a$ will be equal to $a$. For instance, for the second iterate we have

$$f(f(a)) = f(a) \qquad \text{substituting } a \text{ for } f(a) \text{ on the left-hand side}$$

$$= a \qquad \text{again because } f(a) = a$$

This shows that the second iterate is equal to $a$. The same type of calculation will show that any subsequent iterate of the fixed point $a$ is equal to $a$.

Another connection between fixed points and iteration is this: for some functions, a fixed point can be a "target value" for other iterates. We'll explain this using Figure 2.

Figure 2 shows the first four steps in the iteration process for $f(x) = \frac{1}{2}x + 2$ with $x_0 = 1$. (See Section 3.5 if you need to review graphical iteration.) As indicated in Figure 2, the input 4 is a fixed point for the function $f$, and the iteration process follows a staircase pattern that approaches the point $(4, 4)$. We say in this case that the iterates of $x_0 = 1$ **approach** the fixed point 4 and that this target value 4 is an **attracting fixed point** of the function $f$. Table 1 gives you a more numerical look at what is meant by saying that the iterates approach the target value 4.

In the table, notice, for example, that

$$x_5 \text{ differs from 4 by less than 0.1}$$

$$x_{10} \text{ differs from 4 by less than 0.01}$$

and $\qquad x_{15} \text{ differs from 4 by less than 0.0001}$

What's important here is that the differences between the iterates and 4 can be made as small as we please by carrying out the iteration process sufficiently far. The idea of a target value or *limit* is made more precise in calculus. But for our purposes, Figure 2 and Table 1 will certainly give you an intuitive understanding of the idea and what we mean by saying that the iterates approach 4.

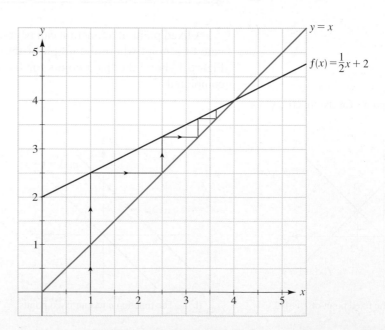

**Figure 2**
The first four steps in the iteration process for $f(x) = \frac{1}{2}x + 2$ with $x_0 = 1$

| **TABLE 1** | The Iterates Approach 4 | | |
|---|---|---|---|
| $x_1$ | 2.5 | | |
| $x_2$ | 3.25 | | |
| $x_3$ | 3.625 | | |
| $x_4$ | 3.8125 | $x_{11}$ | 3.9985 ... |
| $x_5$ | 3.906 ... | $x_{12}$ | 3.99926 ... |
| $x_6$ | 3.953 ... | $x_{13}$ | 3.99963 ... |
| $x_7$ | 3.976 ... | $x_{14}$ | 3.99981 ... |
| $x_8$ | 3.988 ... | $x_{15}$ | 3.999908 ... |
| $x_9$ | 3.9941 ... | $x_{20}$ | 3.9999971 ... |
| $x_{10}$ | 3.9970 ... | $x_{25}$ | 3.999999910 ... |

Figures 3 and 4 show two more ways in which the iteration process may relate to fixed points. In Figure 3 there is an attracting fixed point for the iterates of $x_0 = -0.1$, but this time the iteration process approaches the fixed point through a spiral pattern rather than a staircase pattern. To find the fixed point (and thereby determine the number that the iterates are approaching), we need to solve the quadratic equation $x^2 - 0.5 = x$. As you should check for yourself by means of the quadratic formula and then a calculator, the relevant root here is $(1 - \sqrt{3})/2 \approx -0.366$. Notice that this value is consistent with Figure 3. In Figure 4 the fixed point 1 is a **repelling fixed point** for the iterates of $x_0 = 1.25$. As Figure 4 indicates, the iterates of $x_0 = 1.25$ move farther and farther away from the value 1. Indeed, as you can check with a calculator, the first five iterates of 1.25 are as follows (we're rounding to two decimal places):

$$x_1 \approx 1.56 \qquad x_2 \approx 2.44 \qquad x_3 \approx 5.96 \qquad x_4 \approx 35.53 \qquad x_5 \approx 1262.18$$

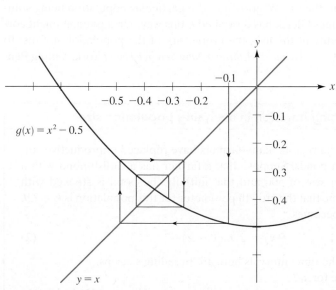

**Figure 3**
The iterates of $x_0 = -0.1$ under the function $g(x) = x^2 - 0.5$ approach the attracting fixed point $\frac{1}{2}(1 - \sqrt{3}) \approx -0.366$.

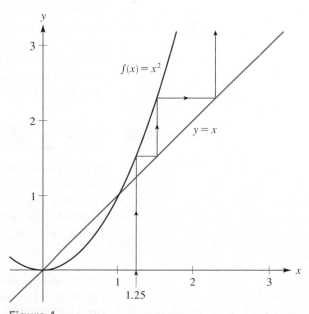

**Figure 4**
The iterates of $x_0 = 1.25$ under the function $f(x) = x^2$ move away from the repelling fixed point 1.

The iteration process for functions is often applied in the study of population growth. The word "population" here is used in a general sense. It needn't refer only to human populations. For instance, biological or ecological studies may involve animal, insect, or bacterial populations. (Also, see the quotation at the beginning of this section.) The following equation defines one type of quadratic function that has been studied extensively in this context:

$$f(x) = kx(1 - x) \tag{1}$$

In using this idealized model, we assume that the population size is measured by a number between 0 and 1, where 1 corresponds to the maximum possible population size in the given environment and 0 corresponds to the case in which the population has become extinct. We start with a given input $x_0$ ($0 \leq x_0 \leq 1$) that represents the fraction of the maximum population size that is initially present. For instance, if the maximum possible population of catfish in a pond is 100 and initially there were 70 catfish, then we would have $x_0 = 70/100 = 0.7$.

The next basic assumption in using equation (1) to model population size is that the iterates of $x_0$ represent the fraction of the maximum possible population present after each successive time interval. That is,

$f(x_0) = x_1$ is the fraction of the maximum population after the first time interval

$f(x_1) = x_2$ is the fraction of the maximum population after the second time interval

and, in general,

$f(x_{n-1}) = x_n$ is the fraction of the maximum population after the $n$th time interval

It is important to note that the function $f(x)$ does *not* represent the size of the population. The population size after $n$ time intervals is given by

$$x_n \cdot (\text{the maximum population}) = f(x_{n-1}) \cdot (\text{maximum population})$$

In a given study, the time intervals might be measured, for example, in years, in months, or in breeding seasons. The constant $k$ in equation (1) is the *growth parameter*; it is related to the rate of growth of the particular population being studied. Science writer James Gleick has described $k$ this way: "In a pond, it might correspond to the fecundity of the fish, the propensity of the population not just to boom but also to bust. . . ." [*Chaos: Making a New Science* (New York: Viking Penguin, Inc., 1988)]

**EXAMPLE 2    Using iteration in analyzing population size**

In the Mississippi Delta region, many farmers have replaced unproductive cotton fields with catfish ponds. Suppose that a farmer has a catfish pond with a maximum population size of 500 and that initially the pond is stocked with 50 catfish. Also, assume that the growth parameter for this population is $k = 2.9$, so that equation (1) becomes

$$f(x) = 2.9x(1 - x) \tag{2}$$

Finally, assume that the time intervals here are breeding seasons.

**(a)** What is the value for $x_0$?

**(b)** Use Figure 5 to estimate the iterates $x_1$ through $x_5$. Then use a calculator to compute these values. Round the final answers to three decimal places. Interpret the results.

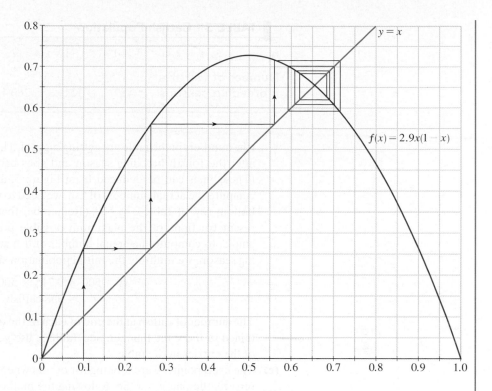

**Figure 5**
The first ten iterations of $x_0 = 0.1$
under $f(x) = 2.9x(1 - x)$

**(c)** As indicated in Figure 5, the iteration process is spiraling in on a fixed point of the function. (Figure 6 later in this section will demonstrate this in greater detail.) Find this fixed point and interpret the result.

**SOLUTION**

**(a)** $x_0 = \dfrac{\text{initial population}}{\text{maximum population}} = \dfrac{50}{500} = 0.1$

**(b)** In looking at Figure 5, it appears that $x_1$, the first iterate of $x_0$, is between 0.25 and 0.30, much closer to the former number than the latter. As an estimate, let's say that $x_1$ is about 0.26. This and the other estimates are given in Table 2. *Suggestion*: Make the estimates for yourself before looking at the estimates we give. Some slight discrepancies are okay. In the bottom row of Table 2 are the values of the iterates obtained using a calculator. You should verify these for yourself. (There should be no discrepancies here.)

The results in Table 2 tell us what is happening to the population through the first five breeding seasons. From an initial population of 50 catfish, the population size steadily increases through the first three breeding seasons

**TABLE 2**
**Iterates of $x_0 = 0.1$ under the Function $f(x) = 2.9x(1 - x)$**
**(calculator values rounded to three decimal places)**

|  | $x_1$ | $x_2$ | $x_3$ | $x_4$ | $x_5$ |
|---|---|---|---|---|---|
| From graph | 0.26 | 0.56 | 0.71 | 0.58 | 0.70 |
| From calculator | 0.261 | 0.559 | 0.715 | 0.591 | 0.701 |

**TABLE 3   Catfish Population**

| $n$ | 0 | 1 | 2 | 3 | 4 | 5 |
|---|---|---|---|---|---|---|
| Number of fish after $n$ breeding seasons | 50 | 131 | 280 | 358 | 296 | 351 |

(the numbers in the table are getting bigger). The population size then drops after the fourth breeding season and goes back up after the fifth season. (These facts can be deduced from Figure 5, as well as from Table 2.) To compute the actual numbers of fish, we need to multiply each number in the bottom row of Table 2 by 500. (Remember that the iterates in Table 2 represent fractions of the maximum possible population size 500.) For example, to compute the actual number of fish at the end of the third breeding season, we multiply the initial population size of 500 by $x_3$:

$$x_3 \times 500 \approx 0.715 \times 500$$
$$\approx 358 \text{ catfish}$$

The number of catfish at the end of each of the other breeding seasons is obtained in the same manner. See Table 3; use your calculator to check each of the entries in the table.

**(c)** The fixed point we are looking for occurs when the parabola in Figure 5 intersects the line $y = x$. So, following the method in Example 1, we need to solve the equation $2.9x(1 - x) = x$. We have

$$2.9x(1 - x) = x$$
$$-2.9x^2 + 1.9x = 0$$
$$x(-2.9x + 1.9) = 0$$

Therefore, $x = 0$ or $-2.9x + 1.9 = 0$, that is,

$$x = \frac{-1.9}{-2.9} = \frac{19}{29} \approx 0.655 \qquad \text{using a calculator and rounding to three decimal places}$$

This shows that there are two fixed points for the function $f$, namely, 0 and 19/29. Looking at Figure 5, we know that 19/29 is the fixed point that we are interested in here, not 0. So the iterates of $x_0 = 0.1$ are approaching the value 19/29, which is approximately 0.655.

We now summarize and interpret the results. There were initially 50 catfish in a pond that could hold at most 500. As we saw in part (b), the population size increases over the first three breeding seasons. After this, as Figure 5 shows, the population oscillates up and down but draws closer and closer to an equilibrium population corresponding to the fixed point $x = 19/29$. This equilibrium population is

$$\frac{19}{29} \times 500 \approx 328 \text{ catfish}$$

We conclude this section with some pictures indicating only three of the many possibilities that can arise in the iteration of quadratic functions of the form

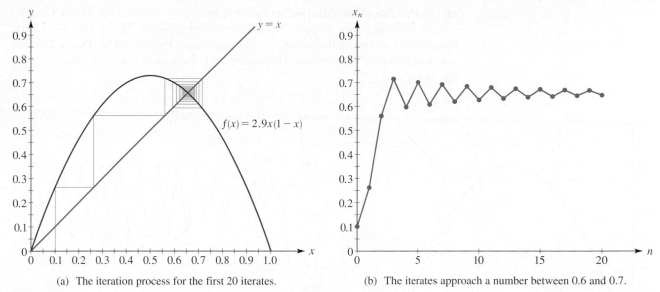

(a) The iteration process for the first 20 iterates.

(b) The iterates approach a number between 0.6 and 0.7.

**Figure 6**
The iteration of $f(x) = kx(1 - x)$ with growth parameter $k = 2.9$ and $x_0 = 0.1$

$f(x) = kx(1 - x)$. Figure 6 concerns the function with growth parameter $k = 2.9$ that we used in the catfish example: $f(x) = 2.9x(1 - x)$. In Figure 6(a) we've carried out the iteration of $x_0 = 0.1$ through the twentieth iterate. (In the catfish example, Figure 5 goes only as far as the tenth iterate.) Figure 6(a) indicates quite clearly that the iterates are indeed approaching a fixed point of the function. Figure 6(b) presents another way to visualize the long-term behavior of the iterates. Values of $n$ are marked on the horizontal axis, values of the iterates $x_n$ are marked on the vertical axis, and the points with coordinates $(n, x_n)$ are then plotted. For example, since $x_0 = 0.1$, we plot the point $(0, 0.1)$; and since $x_1 = 0.261$, we plot the point $(1, 0.261)$. The line segments in Figure 6(b) are drawn in only to help the eye see the pattern that is emerging. Three facts that can be inferred from Figure 6(b) are as follows: After the first few iterates, the iterates oscillate up and down; the magnitude of the oscillations is decreasing; and, in the long run, the iterates are approaching a number between 0.6 and 0.7. (In Example 2 we found this value to be approximately 0.655.)

Unlike the iteration pictured in Figure 6(a), Figure 7(a) shows a case in which the iteration process is spiraling away from, rather than toward, a fixed point. Again, we've used the initial input $x_0 = 0.1$, but this time the growth parameter is $k = 3.2$. As indicated in Figure 7(b), the long-term behavior of the iterates becomes quite predictable: they alternate between two values. Figure 7(b) shows that the smaller of these two values is between 0.5 and 0.6, while the larger is approximately 0.8. Exercise 36 gives you formulas for computing these two limiting values for the iterates. (They turn out to be, approximately, 0.513 and 0.799.)

In Figure 8, once again we take the initial input to be $x_0 = 0.1$, but this time the growth parameter is $k = 3.9$. Now the iterates seem to fluctuate widely with no apparent pattern, in sharp contrast to the previous two figures, in which there were clear patterns. Phenomena such as this are the subject of **chaos theory,** a new branch of twentieth-century mathematics with wide application. [For a readable and nontechnical introduction to this relatively new subject, see James Gleick's *Chaos: Making a New Science* (New York: Viking Penguin, Inc., 1988). For a little more detail on the mathematics, see the paperback by Donald M. Davis, *The Nature and Power of Mathematics* (Princeton, N.J.: Princeton University Press, 1993), pp. 314–363.]

(a) The iteration process for the first 25 iterates.

(b) The iterates alternately approach two numbers. These numbers are approximately 0.513 and 0.799.

**Figure 7**
The iteration of $f(x) = kx(1 - x)$ with growth parameter $k = 3.2$ and $x_0 = 0.1$

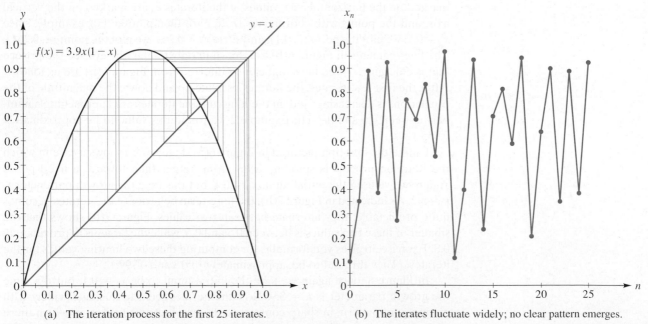

(a) The iteration process for the first 25 iterates.

(b) The iterates fluctuate widely; no clear pattern emerges.

**Figure 8**
The iteration of $kx(1 - x)$ with growth parameter $k = 3.9$ and $x_0 = 0.1$

# EXERCISE SET 4.3

## A

*In Exercises 1–16, find all real numbers (if any) that are fixed points for the given functions.*

1. $f(x) = -4x + 5$
2. $g(x) = 3x - 14$
3. $G(x) = \frac{1}{2} + x$
4. $F(x) = (7 - 2x)/8$
5. $h(x) = x^2 - 3x - 5$
6. $H(t) = 3t^2 + 18t - 6$
7. $f(t) = t^2 - t + 1$
8. $F(t) = t^2 - t - 1$
9. $k(t) = t^2 - 12$
10. $K(t) = t^2 + 12$
11. $T(x) = 1.8x(1 - x)$
12. $T(y) = 3.4y(1 - y)$
13. $g(u) = 2u^2 + 3u - 4$
14. $G(u) = 3u^2 - 4u - 2$
15. $f(x) = 7 + \sqrt{x - 1}$
16. $f(x) = \sqrt{10 + 3x} - 4$

Ⓖ *In Exercises 17–22:*

(a) *Graph each function along with the line $y = x$. Use the graph to determine how many (if any) fixed points there are for the given function.*

(b) *For those cases in which there are fixed points, use the zoom-in capability of the graphing utility to estimate the fixed point. (In each case, continue the zoom-in process until you are sure about the first three decimal places.)*

17. $f(x) = x^3 + 3x + 2$
18. $g(x) = x^3 - 3x + 2$
19. $h(x) = x^3 - 3x - 3.07$
20. $k(x) = x^3 - 3x - 3.08$
21. $s(t) = t^4 + 3t - 2$
22. $u(t) = t^4 + 3t + 2$

23. This exercise refers to the function $g(x) = x^2 - 0.5$ in Figure 3 in the text.

(a) Use the quadratic formula to verify that one of the fixed points of this function is $(1 - \sqrt{3})/2$, then use your calculator to check that this is approximately $-0.366$.

(b) According to the text, the iterates of $-0.1$ approach the value determined in part (a). Use your calculator: which is the first iterate to have the digit 3 in the first decimal place?

(c) Use your calculator: Which is the first iterate to have the digit 6 in the second decimal place?

24. This exercise refers to the function $f(x) = x^2$ in Figure 4 in the text. According to the text, the iterates of 1.25 move farther and farther away from the fixed point 1. In this exercise you'll see that iterates of other points even closer to the fixed point 1 nevertheless are still "repelled" by 1.

(a) Let $x_0 = 1.1$. Use your calculator: Which is the first iterate to exceed 10? Which is the first iterate to exceed one million?

(b) Let $x_0 = 1.001$. Use your calculator: Which is the first iterate to exceed 2? Which is the first iterate to exceed one million?

(c) Let $x_0 = 0.99$. Compute $x_1$ through $x_{10}$ to see that the iterates are indeed moving farther and farther away from the fixed point 1. What value are the iterates approaching? Is this value a fixed point of the function?

25. The accompanying figure shows the first eight steps in the iteration process for $f(x) = -0.7x + 2$, with $x_0 = 0.4$.

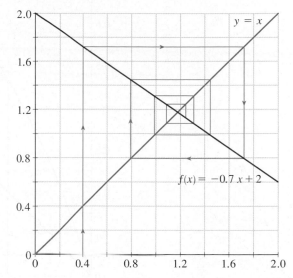

(a) Complete the following table. For the values obtained from the graph, estimate to the nearest one-tenth; for the calculator values, round the final answers to three decimal places.

| | $x_1$ | $x_2$ | $x_3$ | $x_4$ | $x_5$ | $x_6$ | $x_7$ | $x_8$ |
|---|---|---|---|---|---|---|---|---|
| From graph | | | | | | | | |
| From calculator | | | | | | | | |

(b) The figure shows that the iterates are approaching a fixed point of the function. Determine the exact value of this fixed point and then give a calculator approximation rounded to three decimal places.

(c) In the table for part (a), you used a calculator to compute the first eight iterates. Which of these iterates is the first to have the same digit in the first decimal place as the fixed point?

26. The figure on the next page shows the first six steps in the iteration process for $f(x) = 2.9x(1 - x)$, with $x_0 = 0.2$.

(a) Complete the following table. For the values obtained from the graph, estimate to the nearest 0.05, or closer if you can. For instance, to the nearest 0.05, the first iterate is 0.45. But, since the graph shows the iterate a bit above 0.45, the estimate 0.46 would be better. For the calculator work, round the final answers to three decimal places.

| | $x_1$ | $x_2$ | $x_3$ | $x_4$ | $x_5$ | $x_6$ |
|---|---|---|---|---|---|---|
| From graph | | | | | | |
| From calculator | | | | | | |

*(continues)*

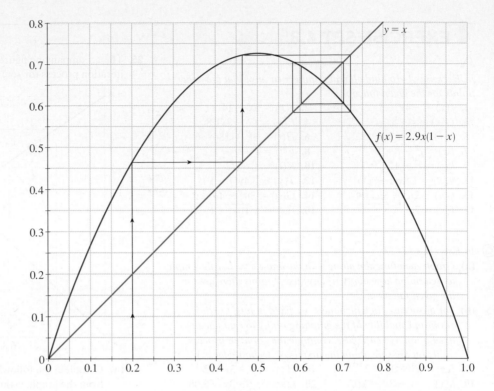

**Figure for Exercise 26**

(b) The figure shows that the iterates are approaching a fixed point of the function. Use the figure to estimate, to the nearest 0.05, a value for this fixed point. Then determine the exact value of this fixed point, and also give a calculator approximation rounded to three decimal places.

(c) In the table for part (a), you used a calculator to compute the first six iterates. Which of these iterates is the first to have the same digit in the first decimal place as the fixed point?   *Remark*: Agreement in the second decimal place doesn't occur until the 26th iterate.

*For Exercises 27 and 28, refer to the figure on page 257, which shows the first nine steps in the iteration process for $f(x) = 4x(1 - x)$, with $x_0 = 0.9$. (Qualitatively, note that this figure is quite different from those in the previous two exercises or in Figures 2 through 7 in the text. Here, no clear pattern in the iterates seems to emerge.)*

**27.** Complete the following table. For the values obtained from the graph, estimate to the nearest 0.05, or closer if you can. For instance, to the nearest 0.05, the first iterate is 0.35. But since the graph shows the iterate a bit above 0.35, the estimate 0.36 would be better. For the calculator work, round the final answers to three decimal places.

|  | $x_1$ | $x_2$ | $x_3$ | $x_4$ | $x_5$ | $x_6$ | $x_7$ | $x_8$ | $x_9$ |
|---|---|---|---|---|---|---|---|---|---|
| From graph |  |  |  |  |  |  |  |  |  |
| From calculator |  |  |  |  |  |  |  |  |  |

**28.** As in Exercise 27, we work with the function $f(x) = 4x(1 - x)$. Furthermore, in part (a) we use an input that is very close to the one in Exercise 27. As you will see, however, the results will be remarkably different. This phenomenon, whereby a very small change in the initial input results in a completely different pattern in the iterates, is called **sensitivity to initial conditions.** Sensitivity to initial conditions is one of the characteristic behaviors studied in chaos theory.

(a) For the initial input, use $x_0 = \frac{1}{8}(5 + \sqrt{5}) \approx 0.9045$. Note that this differs from the input in Exercise 27 by less than 0.01. (Exercise 36 shows how this seemingly off-the-wall input was obtained.) Use algebra (not a calculator!) to compute exact expressions for $x_1$ and $x_2$. What do you observe? What are $x_3$ and $x_4$? What's the general pattern here?   *Note*: If you were to use a calculator rather than algebra for all of this, due to rounding errors you could miss seeing the patterns.

(b) Take $x_0 = 0.905$. Use a calculator to compute $x_1$ through $x_{10}$. Round the final results to three decimal places. Is the behavior of the iterates more like that in Exercise 27 or in part (a) of this exercise?

*As background for Exercises 29–32, you need to have read Example 2 in this section. As in Example 2, assume that there is a catfish pond with a maximum population size of 500 catfish. Also assume, unless stated otherwise, that the initial population size is 50 catfish (so that $x_0 = 0.1$).*

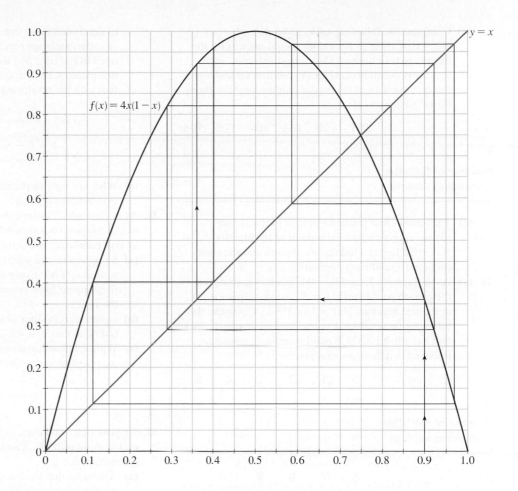

**Figure for
Exercises 27 and 28**

29. (a) In Example 2 we used a growth parameter of $k = 2.9$ and we computed the first five iterates of $x_0 = 0.1$. Now (under these same assumptions) compute $x_{21}$ through $x_{25}$, given that $x_{20} \approx 0.64594182$. Round your final answers to four decimal places.

   (b) Use the results in part (a) to complete the following table. [Compare your table to Table 3 in the text; note that the population size continues to oscillate up and down, but now the sizes of the oscillations are much smaller. This provides additional evidence that the population size is approaching an equilibrium value. (In Example 2 we determined this equilibrium size to be about 328 catfish.)]

| $n$ | 20 | 21 | 22 | 23 | 24 | 25 |
|---|---|---|---|---|---|---|
| Number of fish after $n$ breeding seasons | | | | | | |

   (c) In parts (a) and (b) and in Example 2 we worked with a growth parameter of 2.9, and we found that the iterates of $x_0 = 0.1$ were approaching a fixed point of the function. Now assume instead that the growth parameter is $k = 0.75$ (but, still, that $x_0 = 0.1$). Determine the iterates $x_1$ through $x_5$. (Round to five decimal places.) Are the iterates approaching a fixed point of the function $f(x) = 0.75x(1 - x)$? Interpret your results.

30. As in Example 2, take $x_0 = 0.1$, but now assume that the growth parameter is $k = 3$, so that equation (1) in the text becomes $f(x) = 3x(1 - x)$.

   (a) Complete the following tables. (Round the final answers for the iterates to three decimal places.) Notice that after the third breeding season, the population oscillates up and down, as in Example 2.

| $n$ | 0 | 1 | 2 | 3 | 4 | 5 |
|---|---|---|---|---|---|---|
| $x_n$ | 0.1 | | | | | |
| Number of fish after $n$ breeding seasons | 50 | | | | | |

| $n$ | 6 | 7 | 8 | 9 | 10 |
|---|---|---|---|---|---|
| $x_n$ | | | | | |
| Number of fish after $n$ breeding seasons | | | | | |

**(b)** Complete the following table, given that $x_{100} \approx 0.643772529$. Round your final answers for the iterates to four decimal places. In your results, note that the population continues to oscillate up and down, but that the sizes of the oscillations are less than those observed in part (a).

| $n$ | 101 | 102 | 103 | 104 | 105 | 106 |
|-----|-----|-----|-----|-----|-----|-----|
| $x_n$ | | | | | | |
| Number of fish after $n$ breeding seasons | | | | | | |

**(c)** The iterates that you computed in parts (a) and (b) are approaching a fixed point of the function $f(x) = 3x(1 - x)$. Find this fixed point and the corresponding equilibrium population size.

**31. (a)** As in Example 2, take $x_0 = 0.1$, but now assume that the growth parameter is $k = 3.1$, so that equation (1) in the text becomes $f(x) = 3.1x(1 - x)$. Complete the following three tables. For the third table, use the fact that $x_{20} \approx 0.56140323$. Round your final answers for the iterates to four decimal places.

| $n$ | 0 | 1 | 2 | 3 | 4 | 5 |
|-----|---|---|---|---|---|---|
| $x_n$ | 0.1 | | | | | |
| Number of fish after $n$ breeding seasons | 50 | | | | | |

| $n$ | 6 | 7 | 8 | 9 | 10 |
|-----|---|---|---|---|----|
| $x_n$ | | | | | |
| Number of fish after $n$ breeding seasons | | | | | |

| $n$ | 21 | 22 | 23 | 24 | 25 | 26 |
|-----|-----|-----|-----|-----|-----|-----|
| $x_n$ | | | | | | |
| Number of fish after $n$ breeding seasons | | | | | | |

**(b)** Your results in part (a) will show that the population size is oscillating up and down, but that the iterates don't seem to be approaching a fixed point. Indeed, determine the (nonzero) fixed point of the function $f(x) = 3.1x(1 - x)$. Then note that the successive iterates in part (a) actually move farther and farther away from this fixed point.

**(c)** It can be shown that the long-term behavior of the iterates in this case resembles the pattern in Figure 7(b) on page 254; that is, the iterates alternately approach two values. Use the following formulas, with $k = 3.1$,

to determine these two values $a$ and $b$ that the iterates are alternately approaching. (The formulas are developed in Exercise 36.) Round the answers to four decimal places. Check to see that your answers are consistent with the results in part (a).

$$a = \frac{1 + k + \sqrt{(k - 3)(k + 1)}}{2k}$$

$$b = \frac{1 + k - \sqrt{(k - 3)(k + 1)}}{2k}$$

**(d)** What are the two populations corresponding to these two numbers $a$ and $b$?

**32.** As in Example 2, assume that the maximum population size of the pond is 500 catfish, but now suppose that the growth parameter is $k = 0.6$.

**(a)** Suppose that the initial population is again 50 catfish, so that $x_0 = 0.1$. Compute the first ten iterates. Do they appear to be approaching a fixed point? Interpret the results.

**(b)** Follow part (a), but assume that the initial population is 450, so that $x_0 = 450/500 = 0.9$.

**(c)** What relationship do you see between the iterates in part (a) and in part (b)?

**B**

**33.** Suppose that $c$ and $d$ are inputs for a function $g$ and that $g(c) = d$ and $g(d) = c$. Then we say the set $\{c, d\}$ is a **2-cycle** for the function $g$.

**(a)** Assuming that $\{c, d\}$ is a 2-cycle for the function $g$, list the first six iterates of $c$ and the first six iterates of $d$. Describe in a complete sentence or two the pattern you see.

**(b)** The following figure shows the iteration process for the function $T(x) = 1 - |2x - 1|$, with initial input $x_0 = 0.4$. Use the figure to list the first six iterates of 0.4 under the function $T$.

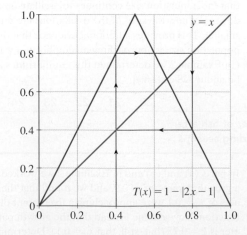

**(c)** In the following sentence, fill in the two blank spaces with numbers. The work in part (b) shows that {___, ___} is a 2-cycle for the function $T$.

**(d)** In part (b) you used a graph to list the first six iterates of $x_0 = 0.4$ under the function $T(x) = 1 - |2x - 1|$. Now, using a calculator (or just simple arithmetic), actually compute $x_1$ and $x_2$ and thereby check your results.

**34.** As background for this exercise, you need to have worked part (a) in the previous exercise so that you know the definition of a 2-cycle.

**(a)** The curve in the following figure is the graph of the function $Q(x) = x^2 - 7$. Use the figure to list the first six iterates of $-3$ under the function $Q$. Also, list the first six iterates of 2.

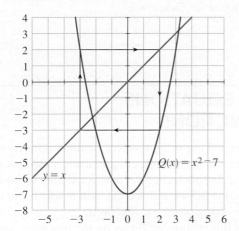

**(b)** In the following sentence, fill in the two blank spaces with numbers. The work in part (a) shows that {___, ___} is a 2-cycle for the function $Q$.

**(c)** In part (a) you used a graph to list the first six iterates of $-3$ under the function $Q$. Now, using the formula $Q(x) = x^2 - 7$, actually compute $x_1$ and $x_2$ and thereby check your results.

**(d)** Use your calculator to compute the first six iterates of $x_0 = -2.99$ under the function $Q(x) = x^2 - 7$. Note that the behavior of the iterates is vastly different than that observed in part (a), even though the initial inputs differ by only 0.01. (As pointed out in Exercise 28, this type of behavior is referred to as *sensitivity to initial conditions*.)

**35.** Let $f(x) = 4x(1 - x)$. In this exercise we find distinct inputs $a$ and $b$ such that $f(a) = b$ and $f(b) = a$. As indicated in Exercise 33, the set {$a, b$} is called a *2-cycle for the function f*.

**(a)** From the equation $f(a) = b$ and the definition of $f$, we have

$$4a(1 - a) = b \qquad (1)$$

Likewise, from the equation $f(b) = a$ and the definition of $f$, we have

$$4b(1 - b) = a \qquad (2)$$

Subtract equation (2) from equation (1) and show that the resulting equation can be written

$$4(b - a)(b + a - 1) = b - a \qquad (3)$$

**(b)** Divide both sides of equation (3) by the quantity $b - a$. (The quantity $b - a$ is nonzero because we are assuming that $a$ and $b$ are distinct.) Then solve the resulting equation for $b$ in terms of $a$. You should obtain

$$b = \frac{5}{4} - a \qquad (4)$$

**(c)** Use equation (4) to substitute for $b$ in equation (1). After simplifying, you should obtain

$$16a^2 - 20a + 5 = 0 \qquad (5)$$

**(d)** Use the quadratic formula to solve equation (5) for $a$. You should obtain

$$a = (5 \pm \sqrt{5})/8$$

**(e)** Using the positive root for the moment, suppose $a = (5 + \sqrt{5})/8$. Use this expression to substitute for $a$ in equation (4). Show that the result is $b = (5 - \sqrt{5})/8$. Now check that these values of $a$ and $b$ satisfy the conditions of the problem. That is, given that $f(x) = 4x(1 - x)$, show that

$$f\left[\frac{1}{8}(5 + \sqrt{5})\right] = \frac{1}{8}(5 - \sqrt{5})$$

and

$$f\left[\frac{1}{8}(5 - \sqrt{5})\right] - \frac{1}{8}(5 + \sqrt{5})$$

*Note*: If we'd begun part (e) by using the other root of the quadratic, namely, $a = (5 - \sqrt{5})/8$, then we would have found $b = (5 + \sqrt{5})/8$, so no new information would have been obtained. In summary, the 2-cycle for the function $f$ consists of the two numbers that are the roots of equation (5).

**36.** Let $f(x) = kx(1 - x)$ and assume that $k > 0$. Follow the method of Exercise 35 to show that the values of $a$ and $b$ for which $f(a) = b$ and $f(b) = a$ are given by the formulas

$$a = \frac{1 + k + \sqrt{(k - 3)(k + 1)}}{2k}$$

and

$$b = \frac{1 + k - \sqrt{(k - 3)(k + 1)}}{2k}$$

Note that for $k > 3$, both of these expressions represent real numbers (because the quantity beneath the radical sign is then positive). In summary: For all values of $k$ greater than 3, the function $f(x) = kx(1 - x)$ has a unique 2-cycle {$a, b$}, where $a$ and $b$ are given by the preceding formulas.

**37. (a)** Let $f(x) = 3.5x(1 - x)$. Use the formulas in Exercise 36 to find values for $a$ and $b$ such that $\{a, b\}$ is a 2-cycle for this function [that is, so that $f(a) = b$ and $f(b) = a$]. Exact answers are required, not calculator approximations.

**(b)** The figure on the right shows the iteration process for the 2-cycle determined in part (a). Use the answers in part (a) to specify the coordinates of the four points $P$, $Q$, $R$, and $S$.

**38.** Let $f(x) = 3.2x(1 - x)$. Use the formulas in Exercise 36 to determine the values of $a$ and $b$ such that $\{a, b\}$ is a 2-cycle for this function. Use a calculator to evaluate the answers and round to three decimal places. [You'll find that these are the two numbers referred to in the caption for Figure 7(b) in this section.]

**Figure for Exercise 37**

# 4.4   SETTING UP EQUATIONS THAT DEFINE FUNCTIONS

*I hope that I shall shock a few people in asserting that the most important single task of mathematical instruction in the secondary schools is to teach the setting up of equations to solve word problems.*
—George Polya (1887–1985)

*Each problem that I solved became a rule which afterwards served to solve other problems.* —René Descartes (1596–1650)

One of the first steps in problem solving often involves defining a function. The function then serves to describe or summarize a given situation in a way that is both concise and (one hopes) revealing. In this section we practice setting up equations that define such functions. In Section 4.5 we will use this skill in solving an important class of applied problems involving quadratic functions.

For many of the examples in this section we'll rely on the following four-step procedure to set up the required equation. You may eventually want to modify this procedure to fit your own style. The important point, however, is that it *is* possible to approach these problems in a systematic manner. A word of advice: You're accustomed to working mathematics problems in which the answers are numbers. In this section, the answers are functions (or, more precisely, equations defining functions); you may need to get used to this.

### Steps for Setting Up Equations

**Step 1**   After reading the problem carefully, draw a picture that conveys the given information.

**Step 2**   State in your own words, as specifically as you can, what the problem is asking for. (This usually requires rereading the problem.) Now, assuming that the problem asks you to find a particular quantity (or a formula for a particular quantity), assign a variable to denote that key quantity.

**Step 3**   Label any other quantities in your figure that appear relevant. Are there equations relating these quantities?

**Step 4**   Find an equation involving the key variable that you identified in Step 2. (Some people prefer to do this right after Step 2.) Now, as necessary, substitute in this equation using the auxiliary equations from Step 3 to obtain an equation involving only the required variables.

| EXAMPLE | 1 | The area of a rectangle as a function of its width |

The perimeter of a rectangle is 100 cm. Express the area of the rectangle in terms of the width.

**SOLUTION**
Let's follow our four-step procedure.

**Step 1** See Figure 1. The figure conveys the given information that the perimeter is 100 cm and that the width is $x$. (For the moment, ignore the label $L$ at the base of the rectangle; it enters the picture in Step 3, but it's not part of the given information.)

**Step 2** We want to express the area of the rectangle in terms of $x$, the width. Let $A$ stand for the area of the rectangle.

**Step 3** Call the length of the rectangle $L$, as indicated in Figure 1. Then, since the perimeter is given as 100 cm, we have

$$2x + 2L = 100$$
$$x + L = 50$$
$$L = 50 - x \qquad (1)$$

**Step 4** The area of a rectangle equals width times length:

$$\begin{aligned} A &= x \cdot L \\ &= x(50 - x) \qquad \text{substituting for } L \text{ using equation (1)} \\ &= 50x - x^2 \qquad (2) \end{aligned}$$

This is the required equation expressing the area of the rectangle in terms of the width $x$.

To emphasize this dependence of $A$ on $x$, we can use function notation to rewrite equation (2):

$$A(x) = 50x - x^2$$

The domain of this area function is the open interval $(0, 50)$. To see why this is so, first note that $x > 0$ because $x$ denotes a width. Furthermore, in view of equation (1), we must have $x < 50$; otherwise, $L$, the length, would be zero or negative.

Perimeter = 100 cm

$x$

$L$

**Figure 1**

| EXAMPLE | 2 | The perimeter of a rectangle as a function of its width |

A rectangle is inscribed in a circle of diameter 8 cm. Express the perimeter of the rectangle as a function of its width.

**SOLUTION**
We follow our four-step procedure.

**Step 1** See Figure 2. Notice that the diagonal of the rectangle is a diameter of the circle.

**Step 2** The problem asks us to come up with a formula or a function that gives us the perimeter of the rectangle in terms of $x$, the width. Let $P$ denote the perimeter.

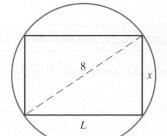

8

$x$

$L$

**Figure 2**

**Step 3**    Let $L$ denote the length of the rectangle, as shown in Figure 2. Then, by the Pythagorean theorem, we have

$$L^2 + x^2 = 8^2 = 64$$

This equation relates the length $L$ and the width $x$. Rather than leaving the equation in this form, however, we'll solve for $L$ in terms of $x$ (because the instructions for the problem ask for the perimeter in terms of the width $x$):

$$L^2 = 64 - x^2$$
$$L = \sqrt{64 - x^2} \tag{3}$$

**Step 4**    The perimeter of the rectangle is

$$P = 2x + 2L \tag{4}$$

This equation expresses $P$ in terms of $x$ and $L$. However, the problem asks for $P$ in terms of just $x$. Using equation (3) to substitute for $L$ in equation (4), we have

$$P = 2x + 2\sqrt{64 - x^2} \tag{5}$$

This is the required equation. It expresses the perimeter $P$ as a function of the width $x$, so if you know $x$, you can calculate $P$.

To emphasize this dependence of $P$ on $x$, we can employ function notation to rewrite equation (5):

$$P(x) = 2x + 2\sqrt{64 - x^2} \tag{6}$$

Before leaving this example, we need to specify the domain of the perimeter function in equation (6). An easy way to do this is to look again at Figure 2. Since $x$ represents a width, we certainly want $x > 0$. Furthermore, Figure 2 tells us that $x < 8$, because in any right triangle, a leg is always shorter than the hypotenuse. Putting these observations together, we conclude that the domain of the perimeter function in equation (6) is the open interval $(0, 8)$.

*Note*: Although it would make sense *algebraically* to use an input such as $x = -1$ in equation (6), it does not make sense in our *geometric* context, where $x$ denotes the width.

---

NOTE   In the following example we introduce the notation $P(x, y)$, which stands for the phrase "a point $P$ with coordinates $(x, y)$."

---

**EXAMPLE    3    Expressing a distance as a function of one variable**

Let $P(x, y)$ be a point on the curve $y = \sqrt{x}$. Express the distance from $P$ to the point $(1, 0)$ as a function of one variable.

**SOLUTION**
**Step 1**    See Figure 3.
**Step 2**    We want to express the length of the dashed line in Figure 3 in terms of $x$. Call this length $D$.

Figure 3

**Step 3**   There are no other quantities in Figure 3 that need labeling. But don't forget that we are given

$$y = \sqrt{x} \tag{7}$$

**Step 4**   By the distance formula we have

$$\begin{aligned} D &= \sqrt{(x - 1)^2 + (y - 0)^2} \\ &= \sqrt{x^2 - 2x + 1 + y^2} \end{aligned} \tag{8}$$

Now we can use equation (7) to eliminate $y$ in equation (8):

$$\begin{aligned} D(x) &= \sqrt{x^2 - 2x + 1 + (\sqrt{x})^2} \\ &= \sqrt{x^2 - 2x + 1 + x} \\ &= \sqrt{x^2 - x + 1} \end{aligned} \tag{9}$$

Equation (9) expresses the distance as a function of $x$, as required. What about the domain of this distance function? Since the $x$-coordinate of a point on the curve $y = \sqrt{x}$ can be any nonnegative number, the domain of the distance function is $[0, \infty)$.

**EXAMPLE 4**   **Expressing the area of a triangle as a function of one variable**

A point $P(x, y)$ lies in the first quadrant on the parabola $y = 16 - x^2$, as indicated in Figure 4. Express the area of the triangular region in Figure 4 as a function of one variable.

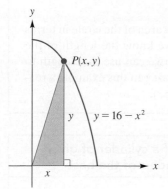

Figure 4

**SOLUTION**

**Step 1**   See Figure 4.

**Step 2**   We want to express the area of the shaded triangle in terms of $x$. Let $A$ denote the area of this triangle.

**Step 3**   Since the coordinates of $P$ are $(x, y)$, the base of our triangle is $x$ and the height is $y$. Also, $x$ and $y$ are related by the given equation

$$y = 16 - x^2 \tag{10}$$

**Step 4**   The area of a triangle equals $\frac{1}{2}$(base)(height):

$$A = \frac{1}{2}(x)(y)$$

so

$$\begin{aligned} A(x) &= \frac{1}{2}(x)(16 - x^2) \qquad \text{substituting for } y \text{ using equation (10)} \\ &= 8x - \frac{1}{2}x^3 \end{aligned}$$

This last equation expresses the area of the triangle as a function of $x$, as required. (Exercise 50 at the end of this section will ask you to specify the domain of this area function.)

| EXAMPLE | 5 | **Expressing the area of a circle as a function of the circumference** |
|---|---|---|

A piece of wire $x$ in. long is bent into the shape of a circle. Express the area of the circle in terms of $x$.

**SOLUTION**
**Step 1**   See Figure 5.
**Step 2**   We are supposed to express the area of the circle in terms of $x$, the circumference. Let $A$ denote the area.
**Step 3**   The general formula for circumference in terms of radius is $C = 2\pi r$. Since in our case the circumference is given as $x$, our equation becomes

$$x = 2\pi r \quad \text{or} \quad r = \frac{x}{2\pi} \tag{11}$$

**Step 4**   The general formula for the area of a circle in terms of the radius is

$$A = \pi r^2 \tag{12}$$

This expresses $A$ in terms of $r$, but we want $A$ in terms of $x$. So we replace $r$ in equation (12) by the quantity given in equation (11). This yields

$$A(x) = \pi \left( \frac{x}{2\pi} \right)^2 = \frac{\pi x^2}{4\pi^2} = \frac{x^2}{4\pi}$$

Thus we have

$$A(x) = \frac{x^2}{4\pi}$$

This is the required equation. It expresses the area of the circle in terms of the circumference $x$. In other words, if we know the length of the piece of wire that is to be bent into a circle, we can use that length to calculate what the area of the circle will be. *Note*: In this example a reasonable domain for the function $A(x)$ is $(0, \infty)$.

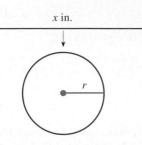

$x$ in.

$r$

Circumference is $x$ in.
**Figure 5**

| EXAMPLE | 6 | **Expressing the surface area of a cylinder of given volume as a function of the radius of the base** |
|---|---|---|

Figure 6 displays a right circular cylinder, along with the formulas for its volume $V$ and total surface area $S$. Given that the volume is 10 cm$^3$, express the surface area $S$ as a function of $r$, the radius of the base.

**SOLUTION**
**Step 1**   See Figure 6.
**Step 2**   We are given a formula that expresses the surface area $S$ in terms of both $r$ and $h$. We want to express $S$ in terms of just $r$.
**Step 3**   We are given that $V = 10$ and also that $V = \pi r^2 h$. Thus

$$\pi r^2 h = 10$$

and consequently, expressing $h$ in terms of $r$,

$$h = \frac{10}{\pi r^2} \tag{13}$$

Volume = 10 cm$^3$

$h$

$V = \pi r^2 h$
$S = 2\pi r^2 + 2\pi r h$
**Figure 6**

**Step 4**   We take the given formula for $S$, namely,

$$S = 2\pi r^2 + 2\pi rh$$

and replace $h$ with the quantity given in equation (13). We obtain

$$S(r) = 2\pi r^2 + 2\pi r\left(\frac{10}{\pi r^2}\right)$$

$$= 2\pi r^2 + \frac{20}{r}$$

This is the required equation. It expresses the total surface area in terms of the radius $r$. Since the only restriction on $r$ is that it be positive, the domain of the area function is $(0, \infty)$.

We have followed the same four-step procedure in Examples 1 through 6. Of course, no single method can cover all possible cases. As usual, common sense and experience are often necessary. Also, you should not feel compelled to follow this procedure at any cost. Keep this in mind as you study the last two examples in this section.

| EXAMPLE | 7 | Expressing a certain product as a function of a single variable |
|---|---|---|

Two numbers add up to 8. Express the product $P$ of these two numbers in terms of a single variable.

**SOLUTION**
If we call the two numbers $x$ and $8 - x$, then their product $P$ is given by

$$P(x) = x(8 - x) = 8x - x^2$$

That's it. This last equation expresses the product as a function of the variable $x$. Since there are no restrictions on $x$ (other than its being a real number), the domain of this function is $(-\infty, \infty)$.

| EXAMPLE | 8 | Expressing revenue as a function of one variable |
|---|---|---|

In economics, the revenue $R$ generated by selling $x$ units at a price of $p$ dollars per unit is given by

$$R = x \cdot p$$

price per unit
number of units

In Figure 7, we are given a hypothetical function relating the selling price of a certain item to the number of units sold. Such a function is called a **demand function.** Express the revenue as a function of $x$.

**Figure 7**

**SOLUTION**
More than anything else, this problem is an exercise in reading. After reading the problem several times, we find that it comes down to this:

given: $R = x \cdot p$ and $p = -\dfrac{1}{3}x + 40$ $(0 \le x \le 117)$

find: an equation expressing $R$ in terms of $x$

In view of this, we write

$$R = x \cdot p = x\left(-\dfrac{1}{3}x + 40\right)$$

Thus we have

$$R(x) = -\dfrac{1}{3}x^2 + 40x \qquad (0 \le x \le 117)$$

This is the required function. It allows us to calculate the revenue when we know the number of units sold. Note that this revenue function is a quadratic function.

QUESTION FOR REVIEW AND ALSO PREVIEW How would you find the maximum revenue in this case?

# EXERCISE SET 4.4

**A**

*In each exercise in Exercise Set 4.4 you are asked to express one variable as a function of another. Be sure to state a domain for the function that reflects the constraints of the problem.*

1. **(a)** The perimeter of a rectangle is 16 cm. Express the area of the rectangle in terms of the width $x$.
   *Suggestion*: First reread Example 1.
   **(b)** The area of a rectangle is 85 cm². Express the perimeter as a function of the width $x$.

2. A rectangle is inscribed in a circle of diameter 12 in.
   **(a)** Express the perimeter of the rectangle as a function of its width $x$. *Suggestion*: First reread Example 2.
   **(b)** Express the area of the rectangle as a function of its width $x$.

3. A point $P(x, y)$ is on the curve $y = x^2 + 1$.
   **(a)** Express the distance from $P$ to the origin as a function of $x$. *Suggestion*: First reread Example 3.

**(b)** In part (a), you expressed the length of a certain line segment as a function of $x$. Now express the slope of that line segment in terms of $x$.

4. A point $P(x, y)$ lies on the curve $y = \sqrt{x}$, as shown in the figure.

**(a)** Express the area of the shaded triangle as a function of $x$. *Suggestion*: First reread Example 4.

**(b)** Express the perimeter of the shaded triangle in terms of $x$.

**5.** A piece of wire $\pi y$ inches long is bent into a circle.
   **(a)** Express the area of the circle as a function of $y$. *Suggestion*: First reread Example 5.
   **(b)** If the original piece of wire were bent into a square instead of a circle, how would you express the area in terms of $y$?

**6.** The volume of a right circular cylinder is $12\pi$ in.$^3$.
   **(a)** Express the height as a function of the radius.
   **(b)** Express the total surface area as a function of the radius.

**7.** Two numbers add to 16.
   **(a)** Express the product of the two numbers in terms of a single variable. *Suggestion*: First reread Example 7.
   **(b)** Express the sum of the squares of the two numbers in terms of a single variable.
   **(c)** Express the difference of the cubes of the two numbers in terms of a single variable. (There are two answers.)
   **(d)** What happens when you try to express the average of the two numbers in terms of one variable?

**8.** The product of two numbers is 16. Express the sum of the squares of the two numbers as a function of a single variable.

**9.** Suppose we are given the following demand function relating the price $p$ in dollars to the number of units $x$ sold of a certain commodity:

$$p = 5 - \frac{x}{4} \qquad (p \text{ in dollars})$$

   **(a)** Graph this demand function.
   **(b)** How many units can be sold when the unit price is $3? Locate the point on the graph of the demand function that conveys this information.
   **(c)** To sell 12 items, how should the unit price be set? Locate the point on the graph of the demand function that conveys this information.
   **(d)** Find the revenue function corresponding to the given demand function. (Use the formula $R = x \cdot p$.) Graph the revenue function.
   **(e)** Find the revenue when $x = 2$, when $x = 8$, and when $x = 14$.
   **(f)** According to your graph in part (d), which $x$-value yields the greatest revenue? What is that revenue? What is the corresponding unit price?

**10.** In Example 1 we considered a rectangle with perimeter 100 cm. We found that the area of such a rectangle is given by $A(x) = 50x - x^2$, where $x$ is the width of the rectangle. Compute the numbers $A(1)$, $A(10)$, $A(20)$, $A(25)$, and $A(35)$. Which width $x$ seems to yield the largest area $A(x)$?

**11.** In Example 2 we considered a rectangle inscribed in a circle of diameter 8 cm. We found that the perimeter of such a rectangle is given by

$$P(x) = 2x + 2\sqrt{64 - x^2}$$

where $x$ is the width of the rectangle.
   **(a)** Use a calculator to complete the following table, rounding each answer to two decimal places.

| $x$ | 1 | 2 | 3 | 4 | 5 | 6 | 7 |
|---|---|---|---|---|---|---|---|
| $P(x)$ | | | | | | | |

   **(b)** In your table, what is the largest value for $P(x)$? What is the width $x$ in this case?
   **(c)** Using calculus, it can be shown that among all possible widths $x$, the width $x = 4\sqrt{2}$ cm yields the largest possible perimeter. Use a calculator to compute the perimeter in this case, and check to see that the value you obtain is indeed larger than all of the values obtained in part (a).

**12.** Let $2s$ denote the length of the side of an equilateral triangle.
   **(a)** Express the height of the triangle as a function of $s$.
   **(b)** Express the area of the triangle as a function of $s$.
   **(c)** Use the function you found in part (a) to determine the height of an equilateral triangle, each side of which is 8 cm long.
   **(d)** Use the function you found in part (b) to determine the area of an equilateral triangle, each side of which is 5 in. long.

**13.** If $x$ denotes the length of a side of an equilateral triangle, express the area of the triangle as a function of $x$.

**14.** The height of a right circular cylinder is twice the radius. Express the volume as a function of the radius.

**15.** Using the information given in Exercise 14, express the radius as a function of the volume.

**16.** The total surface area of a right circular cylinder is 14 in.$^2$. Express the volume as a function of the radius.

**17.** The volume $V$ and the surface area $S$ of a sphere of radius $r$ are given by the formulas $V = \frac{4}{3}\pi r^3$ and $S = 4\pi r^2$. Express $V$ as a function of $S$.

**18.** The base of a rectangle lies on the $x$-axis, while the upper two vertices lie on the parabola $y = 10 - x^2$. Suppose that the coordinates of the upper right vertex of the rectangle are $(x, y)$. Express the area of the rectangle as a function of $x$.

**19.** The hypotenuse of a right triangle is 20 cm. Express the area of the triangle as a function of the length $x$ of one of the legs.

**20.** **(a)** Express the area of the shaded triangle in the figure on the next page as a function of $x$.
   **(b)** Express the perimeter of the shaded triangle as a function of $x$.

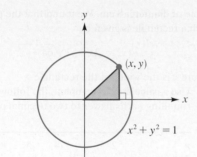

**Figure for
Exercise 20**

**21.** For the following figure, express the length $AB$ as a function of $x$.   *Hint*: Note the similar triangles.

**22.** Five hundred feet of fencing is available to enclose a rectangular pasture alongside a river, which serves as one side of the rectangle (so only three sides require fencing—see the figure). Express the area of the rectangular pasture as a function of $x$.

Ⓖ *For Exercises 23–30:*
   **(a)** *Is this a quadratic function? Use a graphing utility to draw the graph.*
   **(b)** *How many turning points are there within the given interval?*
   **(c)** *On the given interval, does the function have a maximum value? A minimum value?*

**23.** $A(x) = 50x - x^2,\quad 0 < x < 50$ (This is the function that we obtained in Example 1.)

**24.** $P(x) = 2x + 2\sqrt{64 - x^2},\quad 0 < x < 8$ (from Example 2)

**25.** $D(x) = \sqrt{x^2 - x + 1},\quad x \geq 0$ (from Example 3)

**26.** $A(x) = 8x - \frac{1}{2}x^3,\quad 0 < x < 4$ (from Example 4)

**27.** $S(r) = 2\pi r^2 + 20/r,\quad r > 0$ (from Example 6)

**28.** $R(x) = x(-\frac{1}{3}x + 40),\quad x \geq 0$ (from Example 8)

**29.** **(a)** $f(x) = x + \dfrac{1}{x},\quad x > 0$   **(b)** $g(x) = x - \dfrac{1}{x},\quad x > 0$

**30.** **(a)** $F(x) = \sqrt{x} - \dfrac{1}{x}$   **(b)** $G(x) = \sqrt{x} + \dfrac{1}{x}$

Ⓖ **31. (a)** Suppose that the product of two positive numbers is $\sqrt{11}$. Express the sum of the two numbers as a function of a single variable, and then use a graphing util-

ity to draw the graph. Based on the graph, does the sum have a minimum value or maximum value?
   **(b)** Suppose that the sum of two positive numbers is $\sqrt{11}$. Express the product of the two numbers as a function of a single variable. Without drawing a graph, explain why the product has a maximum value.

**B**

**32.** A piece of wire 4 m long is cut into two pieces, then each piece is bent into a square. Express the combined area of the two squares in terms of one variable.

**33.** A piece of wire 3 m long is cut into two pieces. Let $x$ denote the length of the first piece and $3 - x$ the length of the second. The first piece is bent into a square and the second into a rectangle in which the width is half the length. Express the combined area of the square and the rectangle as a function of $x$. Is the resulting function a quadratic function?

*In Exercises 34–37, refer to the following figure, which displays a right circular cone along with the formulas for the volume $V$ and the lateral surface area $S$.*

$$V = \frac{1}{3}\pi r^2 h$$

$$S = \pi r \sqrt{r^2 + h^2}$$

**34.** The volume of a right circular cone is $12\pi$ cm³.
   **(a)** Express the height as a function of the radius.
   **(b)** Express the radius as a function of the height.

**35.** Suppose that the height and radius of a right circular cone are related by the equation $h = \sqrt{3}r$.
   **(a)** Express the volume as a function of $r$.
   **(b)** Express the lateral surface area as a function of $r$.

**36.** The volume of a right circular cone is 2 ft.³ Show that the lateral surface area as a function of $r$ is given by

$$S = \frac{\sqrt{\pi^2 r^6 + 36}}{r}$$

**37.** In a certain right circular cone the volume is numerically equal to the lateral surface area.
   **(a)** Express the radius as a function of the height.
   **(b)** Express the height as a function of the radius.

**38.** A line is drawn from the origin $O$ to a point $P(x, y)$ in the first quadrant on the graph of $y = 1/x$. From point $P$, a line is drawn perpendicular to the $x$-axis, meeting the $x$-axis at $B$.
   **(a)** Draw a figure of the situation described.
   **(b)** Express the perimeter of $\triangle OPB$ as a function of $x$.

**(c)** Try to express the area of $\triangle OPB$ as a function of $x$. What happens?

**39.** A piece of wire 14 in. long is cut into two pieces. The first piece is bent into a circle, the second into a square. Express the combined total area of the circle and the square as a function of $x$, where $x$ denotes the length of the wire that is used for the circle.

**40.** A wire of length $L$ is cut into two pieces. The first piece is bent into a square, the second into an equilateral triangle. Express the combined total area of the square and the triangle as a function of $x$, where $x$ denotes the length of wire used for the triangle. (Here, $L$ is a constant, not another variable.)

**41.** An athletic field with a perimeter of $\frac{1}{4}$ mile consists of a rectangle with a semicircle at each end, as shown in the figure. Express the area of the field as a function of $r$, the radius of the semicircle.

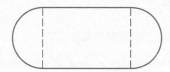

**42.** A square of side $x$ is inscribed in a circle. Express the area of the circle as a function of $x$.

**43.** An equilateral triangle of side $x$ is inscribed in a circle. Express the area of the circle as a function of $x$.

**44. (a)** Refer to the accompanying figure. An offshore oil rig is located at point $A$, which is 10 miles out to sea. An oil pipeline is to be constructed from $A$ to a point $C$ on the shore and then to an oil refinery at point $D$, farther up the coast. If it costs \$8000 per mile to lay the pipeline in the sea and \$2000 per mile on land, express the cost of laying the pipeline in terms of $x$, where $x$ is the distance from $B$ to $C$.

**(b)** Use a calculator and your result in part (a) to complete the following table, rounding the answers to the nearest 100 dollars.

| x (miles)     | 0 | 10 | 20 | 30 | 40 | 50 |
|---------------|---|----|----|----|----|----|
| Cost (dollars) |   |    |    |    |    |    |

**(c)** On the basis of the results in part (b), does it appear that the cost function is increasing, decreasing, or nei-

ther on the interval $0 \le x \le 50$? Which of the $x$-values in the table yields the lowest cost?

**(d)** Use a calculator and your result in part (a) to complete the following table, rounding the answers to the nearest 100 dollars.

| x (miles)      | 0 | 4 | 8 | 12 | 16 | 20 |
|----------------|---|---|---|----|----|----|
| Cost (dollars) |   |   |   |    |    |    |

**(e)** Again, answer the questions in part (c), but now take into account the results in part (d) also.

**45. (a)** An open-top box is constructed from a 6-by-8-inch rectangular sheet of tin by cutting out equal squares at each corner and then folding up the flaps, as shown in the figure. Express the volume of the box as a function of $x$, the length of the side of each cutout square.

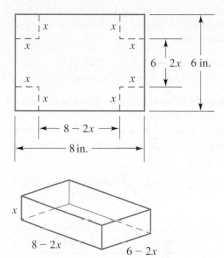

**(b)** Use a calculator and your result in part (a) to complete the following table. Round the answers to the nearest 0.5 in.$^3$.

| x (in.)        | 0 | 0.5 | 1.0 | 1.5 | 2.0 | 2.5 | 3.0 |
|----------------|---|-----|-----|-----|-----|-----|-----|
| Volume (in.$^3$) |   |     |     |     |     |     |     |

**(c)** On the basis of the results in part (b), which $x$-value in the interval $0 \le x \le 3$ appears to yield the largest volume for the box?

**(d)** Use a calculator and your result in part (a) to complete the following table. Round off the answers to the nearest 0.1 in.$^3$.

| x (in.)        | 0.8 | 0.9 | 1.0 | 1.1 | 1.2 | 1.3 | 1.4 |
|----------------|-----|-----|-----|-----|-----|-----|-----|
| Volume (in.$^3$) |     |     |     |     |     |     |     |

**(e)** Again, answer the questions in part (c), but now take into account the results in part (d), too.

**46.** Follow Exercise 45(a), but assume that the original piece of tin is a square, 12 in. on each side.

**47.** A Norman window is in the shape of a rectangle surmounted by a semicircle, as shown in the figure. Assume that the perimeter of the window is 32 ft.

**(a)** Express the area of the window as a function of $r$, the radius of the semicircle.

**(b)** The function you were asked to find in part (a) is a quadratic function, so its graph is a parabola. Does the parabola open upward or downward? Does it pass through the origin? Show that the vertex of the parabola is

$$\left(\frac{32}{\pi + 4}, \frac{512}{\pi + 4}\right)$$

**48.** Refer to the following figure. Express the lengths $CB$, $CD$, $BD$, and $AB$ in terms of $x$. *Hint:* Recall the theorem from geometry stating that in a 30°-60°-90° right triangle, the side opposite the 30° angle is half the hypotenuse.

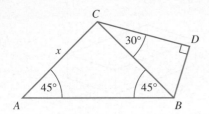

**49.** Refer to the following figure; let $s$ denote the ratio of $y$ to $z$.
**(a)** Express $y$ as a function of $s$.
**(b)** Express $s$ as a function of $y$.
**(c)** Express $z$ as a function of $s$.
**(d)** Express $s$ as a function of $z$.

**50.** Refer to Example 4.
**(a)** What is the $x$-intercept of the curve $y = 16 - x^2$ in Figure 4?
**(b)** What is the domain of the area function in Example 4, assuming that the point $P$ does not lie on the $x$- or $y$-axis?

**51.** The following figure shows the parabola $y = x^2$ and a line segment $\overline{AP}$ drawn from the point $A(0, -1)$ to the point $P(a, a^2)$ on the parabola.

**(a)** Express the slope of $\overline{AP}$ in terms of $a$.
**(b)** Show that the area of the shaded triangle in the figure is given by

$$\text{area} = \frac{a^5}{2(a^2 + 1)}$$

**52.** A rancher who wishes to fence off a rectangular area finds that the fencing in the east-west direction will require extra reinforcement due to strong prevailing winds. Fencing in the east-west direction will therefore cost $12 per (linear) yard, as opposed to a cost of $8 per yard for fencing in the north-south direction. Given that the rancher wants to spend $4800 on fencing, express the area of the rectangle as a function of its width $x$. (*Note:* In this problem by *width* we mean *the measure in yards of a side running in the east-west direction.*) The required function is in fact a quadratic, so its graph is a parabola. Does the parabola open upward or downward? By considering this graph, find which width $x$ yields the rectangle of largest area. What is this maximum area?

**C**

**53.** The following figure shows two concentric squares. Express the area of the shaded triangle as a function of $x$.

**54.** The following figure shows two concentric circles of radii $r$ and $R$. Let $A$ denote the area within the larger circle but outside the smaller one. Express $A$ as a function of $x$ (where $x$ is defined in the figure).

**55.** A straight line with slope $m$ ($m < 0$) passes through the point $(1, 2)$ and intersects the line $y = 4x$ at a point in the first quadrant. Let $A$ denote the area of the triangle bounded by $y = 4x$, the $x$-axis, and the given line of slope $m$. Express $A$ as a function of $m$.

**56.** A line with slope $m$ ($m < 0$) passes through the point $(a, b)$ in the first quadrant and intersects the line $y = Mx$ ($M > 0$) at another point in the first quadrant. Let $A$ denote the area of the triangle bounded by $y = Mx$, the

$x$-axis, and the given line with slope $m$. Show that $A$ can be written as

$$A = \frac{M(am - b)^2}{2m(m - M)}$$

**57.** A line with slope $m$ ($m < 0$) passes through the point $(a, b)$ in the first quadrant. Express the area of the triangle bounded by this line and the axes in terms of $m$.

**58.** One corner of a sheet of paper of width $a$ is folded over and just reaches the opposite side, as indicated in the figure. Express $L$, the length of the crease, in terms of $x$ and $a$.

# MINI PROJECT

## GROUP WORK ON FUNCTIONS OF TIME

In each of the examples and exercises of this section, the goal was to express a certain quantity as a function of a single variable. In the three problems that follow, that single variable will be time $t$. For each problem, after the group finds a solution, each individual should write up the solution on his or her own. (The problems are in order of increasing difficulty.)

1. **(a)** This problem is based on Example 1. So first, have someone in your group present the example.
   **(b)** Under the conditions of Example 1, assume the following additional information. The width $x$ is increasing at the rate of 3 cm/min, and at time $t = 0$ min, the width $x$ is 2 cm. Express the area of the rectangle as a function of time $t$.
   **(c)** During the time interval from $t = 0$ min to $t = 16$ min, when is the area of the rectangle increasing? When is it decreasing? Why are we using the value $t = 16$ min?

2. Starting at time $t = 0$ hr, two cars move away from the same intersection. Car $A$ goes north at 40 miles/hr, and car $B$ goes east at 30 miles/hr. Express the distance between the cars as a function of the time $t$. Is your result a linear function, a quadratic function, or neither?

3. Car $C$ passes through an intersection, heading north at 40 miles/hr. One quarter hour later, car $D$ goes through the intersection, heading east at 30 miles/hr. Express the distance between the two cars as a function of time. Is your result a linear function, a quadratic function, or neither?

## 4.5 MAXIMUM AND MINIMUM PROBLEMS

*. . . problems on maxima and minima, although new features in an English textbook, stand so little in need of apology with the scientific public that I offer none.*—G. Chrystal in his preface to *Textbook of Algebra* (1886)

*In daily life it is constantly necessary to choose the best possible (optimal) solution. A tremendous number of such problems arise in economics and in technology. In such cases it is frequently useful to resort to mathematics.*—V. K. Tikhomirov in *Stories about Maxima and Minima* (translated from the Russian by Abe Shenitzer) (Providence, R.I.: The American Mathematical Society, 1990)

### TABLE 1

| x | y | x + y | xy |
|---|---|---|---|
| −2 | 11 | 9 | −22 |
| −1 | 10 | 9 | −10 |
| 0 | 9 | 9 | 0 |
| 1 | 8 | 9 | 8 |
| 2 | 7 | 9 | 14 |
| 3 | 6 | 9 | 18 |
| 4 | 5 | 9 | (20) |

### TABLE 2

| x | y | x + y | xy |
|---|---|---|---|
| 1 | 8 | 9 | 8 |
| 1.5 | 7.5 | 9 | 11.25 |
| 2 | 7 | 9 | 14 |
| 2.5 | 6.5 | 9 | 16.25 |
| 3 | 6 | 9 | 18 |
| 3.5 | 5.5 | 9 | 19.25 |
| 4 | 5 | 9 | 20 |
| 4.5 | 4.5 | 9 | (20.25) |

You have already seen several examples of maximum and minimum problems in Section 4.2. Before reading further in the present section, you should first review Examples 5 through 7 on pages 235–238.

Actually, we begin this section's discussion of maximum and minimum problems at a more intuitive level. Consider, for example, the following question: If two numbers add to 9, what is the largest possible value of their product? To gain some insight here, we carry out a few preliminary calculations. See Table 1.

We have circled the 20 in the right-hand column of Table 1 because it *appears* to be the largest product. We say "appears" because our table is incomplete. For instance, what if we allowed *x*- and *y*-values that are not whole numbers? Might we get a product exceeding 20? Table 2 shows the results of some additional calculations along these lines.

As you can see from Table 2, there is a product exceeding 20, namely, 20.25. Now the question is, if we further expand our tables, can we find an even larger product, one exceeding 20.25? And here we have come about as far as we want to go using this approach involving arithmetic and tables. For no matter what candidate we come up with for the largest product, there will always be the question of whether we might do still better using a larger table.

Nevertheless, this approach was useful, for it showed us what is really at the heart of a typical maximum or minimum problem. Essentially, we are trying to sort through an infinite number of possible cases and pick out the required extreme case. In the example at hand, there are infinitely many pairs of numbers *x* and *y* adding to 9. We are asked to look at the products of all of these pairs and see which (if any!) is the largest. Example 1 shows how to apply our knowledge of quadratic functions to solve this problem in a definitive manner.

| EXAMPLE | 1 | Maximizing a product |
|---|---|---|

Two numbers add to 9. What is the largest possible value for their product?

**SOLUTION**
Call the two numbers *x* and 9 − *x*. Then their product *P* is given by

$$P = x(9 - x) = 9x - x^2$$

The graph of this quadratic function is the parabola in Figure 1. Note the accompanying calculations for the vertex. As Figure 1 and the accompanying

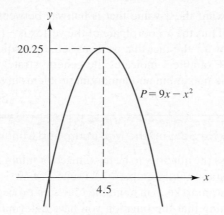

Vertex calculation (by completing the square):

$$P = -(x^2 - 9x)$$
$$= -\left(x^2 - 9x + \frac{81}{4}\right) + \frac{81}{4}$$
$$= -\left(x - \frac{9}{2}\right)^2 + \frac{81}{4}$$

The vertex is $\left(\frac{9}{2}, \frac{81}{4}\right)$

**Figure 1**

calculations show, the largest value of the product $P$ is 20.25. This is the required solution. (Note from the graph that there is no smallest value of $P$.)

In the example just completed, we used the technique of completing the square to determine the vertex of a parabola. Another way to determine the vertex, approximately at least, is to use a graphing utility, as in Example 5(a) in Section 4.2. There is a third method and we shall make use of it for the remaining examples in this section. This third method uses the *vertex formula* given in the box that follows. You should check with your instructor to see which of the three methods he or she wants you to use in a given context. We're going to use the vertex formula in the exposition here so that you can better focus on the problem-solving aspects of the examples.

---

**THEOREM   The Vertex Formula**

| | |
|---|---|
| The $x$-coordinate of the vertex of the parabola $y = ax^2 + bx + c$ $(a \neq 0)$ is given by | **EXAMPLE** For the parabola $y = 2x^2 - 12x + 5$ the $x$-coordinate of the vertex is |
| $$x = \frac{-b}{2a}$$ | $$x = \frac{-b}{2a} = \frac{-(-12)}{2(2)} = 3$$ |

---

The vertex formula can be derived by completing the square (see Exercise 67 on p. 243) or by using the method outlined in the first mini project at the end of Section 4.2. Here's another way, perhaps the simplest. The parabola $y = ax^2 + bx + c$ will have the same $x$-coordinate for its vertex as does $y = ax^2 + bx$ because the two graphs are just vertical translates of one another by a distance $|c|$. But due to symmetry, it's easy to find the $x$-coordinate of the vertex of $y = ax^2 + bx$. As Figure 2 indicates, the $x$-coordinate of the vertex is midway between the two $x$-intercepts. To find these $x$-intercepts, we have

$$ax^2 + bx = 0$$
$$x(ax + b) = 0$$
$$x = 0 \quad \bigg| \quad ax + b = 0$$
$$x = -\frac{b}{a}$$

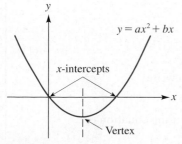

**Figure 2**

Now we want the $x$-value that is halfway between $x = 0$ and $x = -b/a$, namely, $\frac{1}{2}(-b/a)$. Thus the $x$-coordinate of the vertex is $-b/2a$, as we wished to show.

Except for the fact that we completed the square rather than using the vertex formula, Example 1 indicates the general strategy that we're going to follow for solving the maximum and minimum problems in this section.

### Strategy for Solving the Maximum and Minimum Problems in This Section

1. Express the quantity to be maximized or minimized in terms of a single variable. For instance, in Example 1 we found $P = 9x - x^2$. In setting up such functions, you'll want to keep in mind the four-step procedure used in Section 4.4.
2. Assuming that the function you have determined is a quadratic, note whether its graph, a parabola, opens upward or downward. Check whether this is consistent with the requirements of the problem. For instance, the parabola in Figure 1 opens downward; so it makes sense to look for a *largest*, not a smallest, value of $P$. Now use the vertex formula $x = -b/2a$ to locate the $x$-coordinate of the vertex. (If the function is not a quadratic but is closely related to a quadratic, these ideas may still apply. See, for instance, Examples 6 and 7 in Section 4.2.)
3. After you have determined the $x$-coordinate of the vertex, you must relate that information to the original question. In Example 1, for instance, we were asked for the product $P$, not for $x$.

---

| EXAMPLE | 2 | **Finding the dimensions of the rectangle with maximum area** |

Among all rectangles having a perimeter of 10 ft, find the dimensions (length and width) of the one with the greatest area.

### SOLUTION

First we want to set up a function that expresses the area of the rectangle in terms of a single variable. In doing this, we'll be guided by the four-step procedure that we used in Section 4.4. Figure 3(a) displays the given information. Our problem is to determine the dimensions of the rectangle that has the greatest area. As Figure 3(b) indicates, we can label the dimensions $x$ and $y$. Since the perimeter is given as 10 ft, we have

$$2x + 2y = 10$$
$$x + y = 5$$
$$y = 5 - x \qquad (1)$$

Letting $A$ denote the area of the rectangle, we can write

$$A = xy$$
$$A(x) = x(5 - x) \qquad \text{substituting for } y \text{ using equation (1)}$$
$$= 5x - x^2$$

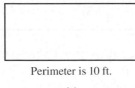

Perimeter is 10 ft.

(a)

$x$

$y$

Perimeter is 10 ft.

(b)

**Figure 3**

**GRAPHICAL PERSPECTIVE**

**Figure 4**
The graph of the area function,
$A(x) = 5x - x^2$, is a parabola that
opens downward. The maximum
area occurs when $x = 2.5$ ft.

This expresses the area of the rectangle in terms of the width $x$. Since the graph of this quadratic function is a parabola that opens downward, it does make sense to talk about the maximum. We calculate the $x$-coordinate of the vertex:

$$x = \frac{-b}{2a}$$

$$= \frac{-5}{2(-1)} = 2.5 \text{ ft}$$

This is the width of the rectangle with the greatest area. Now, the problem asks for the length and width of this rectangle, not its area. So we don't want to calculate $A(x)$; rather, we want $y$. Using equation (1), we have

$$y = 5 - x = 5 - 2.5 = 2.5 \text{ ft}$$

Thus among all rectangles having a perimeter of 10 ft, the one with the greatest area is actually the square with dimensions of 2.5 ft by 2.5 ft. See Figure 4 for a graphical view of this result.

| EXAMPLE | 3 | Finding the maximum height of a baseball |

Suppose that a baseball is tossed straight up and that its height as a function of time is given by the function

$$h(t) = -16t^2 + 64t + 6$$

where $h(t)$ is measured in feet, $t$ is in seconds, and $t = 0$ corresponds to the instant that the ball is released. What is the maximum height of the ball?

**SOLUTION**
The given function tells us how the height $h(t)$ of the ball depends upon the time $t$. We want to know the largest possible value for $h(t)$. Since the graph of the given height function is a parabola opening downward, we can determine the largest value of $h(t)$ just by finding the vertex of the parabola. We use the vertex formula $x = -b/2a$, letting $t$ play the role of $x$. This yields

$$t = \frac{-b}{2a} = \frac{-64}{2(-16)} = 2$$

Thus when $t = 2$ sec, the ball reaches its maximum height. To find that maximum height (and the problem does ask for height, not time), we substitute the value $t = 2$ in the equation $h(t) = -16t^2 + 64t + 6$ to obtain

$$h(2) = -16(2)^2 + 64(2) + 6$$
$$= 70 \text{ ft} \qquad \text{(Check the arithmetic.)}$$

The maximum height of the ball is 70 ft. See Figure 5 for a graphical perspective. *Caution*: The path of the baseball is not the parabola. Why?

**GRAPHICAL PERSPECTIVE**

**Figure 5**
The graph of the height function
$h(t) = -16t^2 + 64t + 6$ is a
parabola that opens downward.
The maximum height is 70 ft, and
this occurs when $t = 2$ sec.

In the next example we look for an input to minimize a function of the form $y = \sqrt{f(x)}$, where $f$ is a quadratic function with values that are always nonnegative.

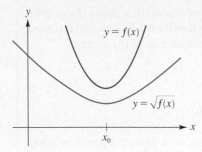

**Figure 6**
The same input $x_0$ minimizes both functions $y = f(x)$ and $y = \sqrt{f(x)}$ [provided $f(x)$ is nonnegative for all $x$].

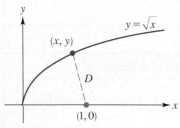

**Figure 7**

(There was an example similar to this in Section 4.2.) As indicated in Figure 6, we need only find the input that minimizes the quadratic function $y = f(x)$, because this same input also minimizes $y = \sqrt{f(x)}$. (The *outputs* of the two functions are different; but the same *input* serves to minimize both functions.)

| EXAMPLE | 4 | Working with a function that is closely related to a quadratic |
|---|---|---|

Which point on the curve $y = \sqrt{x}$ is closest to the point $(1, 0)$?

**SOLUTION**
In Figure 7 we let $D$ denote the distance from a point $(x, y)$ on the curve to the point $(1, 0)$. We are asked to find out exactly which point $(x, y)$ will make the distance $D$ as small as possible. Using the distance formula, we have

$$
\begin{aligned}
D &= \sqrt{(x - 1)^2 + (y - 0)^2} \\
&= \sqrt{x^2 - 2x + 1 + y^2}
\end{aligned}
\tag{2}
$$

This expresses $D$ in terms of both $x$ and $y$. To express $D$ in terms of $x$ alone, we use the given equation $y = \sqrt{x}$ to substitute for $y$ in equation (3). This yields

$$
\begin{aligned}
D(x) &= \sqrt{x^2 - 2x + 1 + (\sqrt{x})^2} \\
&= \sqrt{x^2 - x + 1}
\end{aligned}
$$

Now, according to the remarks just prior to this example, the $x$-value that minimizes the function $D(x) = \sqrt{x^2 - x + 1}$ is the same $x$-value that minimizes $y = x^2 - x + 1$. (Actually, to apply those remarks, we need to know that the expression $x^2 - x + 1$ is nonnegative for all inputs $x$. See Exercise 43 for this.) Since the graph of $y = x^2 - x + 1$ is a parabola that opens upward, the required $x$-value is the $x$-coordinate of the vertex, and we have

$$
x = \frac{-b}{2a} = \frac{-(-1)}{2(1)} = \frac{1}{2}
$$

Now that we have the $x$-coordinate of the vertex, we want to calculate the $y$-coordinate. [We don't want to calculate $D(x)$ because this particular problem asks us to specify a *point*, not a distance. Go back and reread the wording of the question if you are not clear on this.] Substituting $x = 1/2$ in the equation $y = \sqrt{x}$ yields

$$
y = \sqrt{\frac{1}{2}} = \sqrt{\frac{1}{2} \cdot \frac{2}{2}} = \frac{\sqrt{2}}{\sqrt{2^2}} = \frac{\sqrt{2}}{2}
$$

Thus, among all points on the curve $y = \sqrt{x}$, the point closest to $(1, 0)$ is $(1/2, \sqrt{2}/2)$. *Question*: Why would it not have made sense to ask instead for the point farthest from $(1, 0)$?

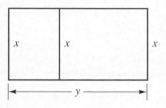

**Figure 8**

## EXAMPLE 5 Finding the dimensions that maximize an area

Suppose that you have 600 m of fencing with which to build two adjacent rectangular corrals. The two corrals are to share a common fence on one side, as shown in Figure 8. Find the dimensions $x$ and $y$ so that the total enclosed area is as large as possible.

**SOLUTION**

You have 600 m of fencing to be set up as shown in Figure 8. The question is how to choose $x$ and $y$ so that the total area is maximum. Since the total length of fencing is 600 m, we can relate $x$ and $y$ by writing

$$x + x + x + y + y = 600$$
$$3x + 2y = 600$$
$$2y = 600 - 3x$$
$$y = 300 - \frac{3}{2}x \qquad (4)$$

Letting $A$ denote the total area, we have

$$A = xy$$
$$A(x) = x\left(300 - \frac{3}{2}x\right) \qquad \text{using equation (4) to substitute for } y$$
$$= 300x - \frac{3}{2}x^2$$

This last equation expresses the area as a function of $x$. Note that the graph of this function is a parabola opening downward, so it does make sense to talk about a maximum. The $x$-coordinate of the vertex is

$$x = \frac{-b}{2a} = \frac{-300}{2(-3/2)} = \frac{300}{3} = 100$$

Now that we have the $x$-value that maximizes the area $A(x)$, the remaining dimension $y$ can be calculated by using equation (4):

$$y = 300 - \frac{3}{2}x = 300 - \frac{3}{2}(100) = 150$$

Thus by choosing $x$ to be 100 m and $y$ to be 150 m, the total area in Figure 8 will be as large as possible. Incidentally, note that the exact location of the fence dividing the two corrals does not influence our work or the final answer.

In the next example a demand function is given, and we want to maximize the revenue. As background, you should review Example 8 in Section 4.4.

## EXAMPLE 6 A maximization problem involving revenue

Suppose that the following demand function relates the selling price, $p$, of an item to the quantity sold, $x$:

$$p = -\frac{1}{3}x + 40 \qquad (p \text{ in dollars})$$

For which value of $x$ will the revenue be a maximum? Compute the corresponding unit price and maximum revenue.

**SOLUTION**
First, recall the formula for revenue given on page 265.

$$R = \text{numbers of units} \times \text{price per unit}$$

Using this, we have

$$R = x \cdot p$$
$$R(x) = x\left(-\frac{1}{3}x + 40\right) = -\frac{1}{3}x^2 + 40x \tag{5}$$

We want to know which value of $x$ yields the largest revenue $R(x)$. Since the graph of the revenue function in equation (5) is a parabola opening downward, the required $x$-value is the $x$-coordinate of the vertex of the parabola. We have

$$x = \frac{-b}{2a} = \frac{-40}{2(-1/3)} = \frac{20}{1/3} = 60$$

This tells us that to earn the maximum revenue, 60 items should be sold. We calculate the corresponding unit price by substituting $x = 60$ in the given equation $p = -\frac{1}{3}x + 40$. This yields

$$p = -\frac{1}{3}(60) + 40$$
$$= -20 + 40 = 20$$

Thus setting the price at $20 per item will maximize the revenue. That maximum revenue can be calculated by using $x = 60$ in equation (5). More simply, since we now have both values $x = 60$ and $p = 20$, we can compute

$$R = x \cdot p = 60 \times 20 = 1200$$

The maximum revenue is $1200.

**GRAPHICAL PERSPECTIVE**

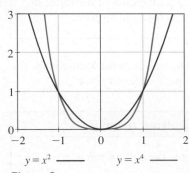

$y = x^2$ ——  $y = x^4$ ——

**Figure 9**

The next example, the last for this section, is similar to Example 3 in that we are looking for the minimum value of a function that, although not a quadratic function, is closely related to one. Also, in this example you'll see a translation of the function $y = x^4$. Since we have not yet studied this function, for background we show its graph along with that of the familiar $y = x^2$ in Figure 9. In the next section we do study functions of the form $y = x^n$, where $n$ is a positive integer.

**EXAMPLE 7  Minimizing the length of a connecting road**

Figure 10 shows portions of two train routes. One route follows the curve $y = x^4 + 10$, and the other follows $y = 4x^2$. Assume that distance along both axes is measured in miles. The railroad wants to construct a north-south maintenance road $\overline{PQ}$ between the two routes, as indicated in the figure. Where should

**Figure 10**
Portions of two train routes and a
north-south maintenance road $\overline{PQ}$

the road be located so that it is as short as possible? What is the minimum
length?

**SOLUTION**
We want to determine points $P$ and $Q$ on the curves $y = x^4 + 10$ and $y = 4x^2$,
respectively, so that the distance from $P$ to $Q$ is as small as possible. Since $P$ and
$Q$ lie on a north-south line, they have the *same* $x$-coordinate, and we can write
the coordinates of $P$ and $Q$ as

$$P(x, x^4 + 10) \quad \text{and} \quad Q(x, 4x^2)$$

The vertical distance $PQ$ between these two points is just the difference in the
$y$-coordinates:

$$PQ = (x^4 + 10) - 4x^2 = x^4 - 4x^2 + 10$$

So the function that we want to minimize is

$$y = x^4 - 4x^2 + 10 \tag{6}$$

The substitution $x^2 = t$ will transform this into a quadratic function. (You saw
this substitution technique before, in Example 7 of Section 4.2.) Note that if
$x^2 = t$, then $x^4 = t^2$, and equation (6) becomes

$$y = t^2 - 4t + 10 \tag{7}$$

Since the graph of equation (7) will be a parabola opening upward, the input $t$
that yields a minimum value for this function is

$$t = \frac{-b}{2a} = \frac{-(-4)}{2(1)} = 2$$

That gives us $t$, but what about $x$? Substituting the value $t = 2$ in the equation
$x^2 = t$ gives us $x^2 = 2$ and consequently $x = \sqrt{2}$. (We're using the positive square
root because $x$ is in the first quadrant.) With this value for $x$, we can calculate the
$y$-coordinates of $P$ and $Q$ as follows:

| $y$-coordinate of $P$: | $y$-coordinate of $Q$: |
|---|---|
| $(\sqrt{2})^4 + 10 = 4 + 10 = 14$ | $4(\sqrt{2})^2 = 8$ |

Putting things together now, the road should connect the points $P$ and $Q$ given by

$$P: (\sqrt{2}, 14) \approx (1.41, 14) \qquad \text{and} \qquad Q: (\sqrt{2}, 8) \approx (1.41, 8)$$

The length of the road is $14 - 8 = 6$ mi.

---

# EXERCISE SET 4.5

**A**

1. Two numbers add to 5. What is the largest possible value of their product?

2. Find two numbers adding to 20 such that the sum of their squares is as small as possible.

3. The difference of two numbers is 1. What is the smallest possible value for the sum of their squares?

4. For each quadratic function, state whether it would make sense to look for a highest or a lowest point on the graph. Then determine the coordinates of that point.
   - **(a)** $y = 2x^2 - 8x + 1$
   - **(b)** $y = -3x^2 - 4x - 9$
   - **(c)** $h = -16t^2 + 256t$
   - **(d)** $f(x) = 1 - (x + 1)^2$
   - **(e)** $g(t) = t^2 + 1$
   - **(f)** $f(x) = 1000x^2 - x + 100$

5. Among all rectangles having a perimeter of 25 m, find the dimensions of the one with the largest area.

6. What is the largest possible area for a rectangle with a perimeter of 80 cm?

7. What is the largest possible area for a right triangle in which the sum of the lengths of the two shorter sides is 100 in.?

8. The perimeter of a rectangle is 12 m. Find the dimensions for which the diagonal is as short as possible.

9. Two numbers add to 6.
   - **(a)** Let $T$ denote the sum of the squares of the two numbers. What is the smallest possible value for $T$?
   - **(b)** Let $S$ denote the sum of the first number and the square of the second. What is the smallest possible value for $S$?
   - **(c)** Let $U$ denote the sum of the first number and twice the square of the second number. What is the smallest possible value for $U$?
   - **(d)** Let $V$ denote the sum of the first number and the square of twice the second number. What is the smallest possible value for $V$?

10. Suppose that the height of an object shot straight up is given by $h = 512t - 16t^2$. (Here $h$ is in feet and $t$ is in seconds.) Find the maximum height and the time at which the object hits the ground.

11. A baseball is thrown straight up, and its height as a function of time is given by the formula $h = -16t^2 + 32t$ (where $h$ is in feet and $t$ is in seconds).
   - **(a)** Find the height of the ball when $t = 1$ sec and when $t = 3/2$ sec.
   - **(b)** Find the maximum height of the ball and the time at which that height is attained.
   - **(c)** At what times is the height 7 ft?

12. Find the point on the curve $y = \sqrt{x}$ that is nearest to the point $(3, 0)$.

13. Which point on the curve $y = \sqrt{x - 2} + 1$ is closest to the point $(4, 1)$? What is this minimum distance?

14. Find the coordinates of the point on the line $y = 3x + 1$ closest to $(4, 0)$.

15. **(a)** What number exceeds its square by the greatest amount?
    **(b)** What number exceeds twice its square by the greatest amount?

16. Suppose that you have 1800 m of fencing with which to build three adjacent rectangular corrals, as shown in the figure. Find the dimensions so that the total enclosed area is as large as possible.

17. Five hundred feet of fencing is available for a rectangular pasture alongside a river, the river serving as one side of the rectangle (so only three sides require fencing). Find the dimensions yielding the greatest area.

18. Let $A = 3x^2 + 4x - 5$ and $B = x^2 - 4x - 1$. Find the minimum value of $A - B$.

19. Let $R = 0.4x^2 + 10x + 5$ and $C = 0.5x^2 + 2x + 101$. For which value of $x$ is $R - C$ a maximum?

20. Suppose that the revenue generated by selling $x$ units of a certain commodity is given by $R = -\frac{1}{5}x^2 + 200x$. Assume that $R$ is in dollars. What is the maximum revenue possible in this situation?

**21.** Suppose that the function $p = -\frac{1}{4}x + 30$ relates the selling price $p$ of an item to the number of units $x$ that are sold. Assume that $p$ is in dollars. For which value of $x$ will the corresponding revenue be a maximum? What is this maximum revenue and what is the unit price?

**22.** The action of sunlight on automobile exhaust produces air pollutants known as *photochemical oxidants*. In a study of cross-country runners in Los Angeles, it was shown that running performances can be adversely affected when the oxidant level reaches 0.03 part per million. Suppose that on a given day, the oxidant level $L$ is approximated by the formula

$$L = 0.059t^2 - 0.354t + 0.557 \qquad (0 \le t \le 7)$$

where $t$ is measured in hours, with $t = 0$ corresponding to 12 noon, and $L$ is in parts per million. At what time is the oxidant level $L$ a minimum? At this time, is the oxidant level high enough to affect a runner's performance?

**23.** **(a)** Find the smallest possible value of the quantity $x^2 + y^2$ under the restriction that $2x + 3y = 6$.
   **(b)** Find the radius of the circle whose center is at the origin and that is tangent to the line $2x + 3y = 6$. How does this answer relate to your answer in part (a)?

**24.** **(a)** Find the coordinates of the vertex of the parabola $y = 2x^2 - 4x + 7$. Then, on the same set of axes, graph this parabola along with $y = x^2$.
   **(b)** Rework Example 7 using the two curves in part (a) rather than the two used in Example 7.

Ⓖ **25.** **(a)** Using a graphing utility, graph the two functions $y = x^4 + 2$ and $y = x^2$ in the viewing rectangle $[0, 4, 1] \times [0, 16, 2]$. If your graphing utility allows, include the $y$-axis gridlines in the picture; they'll be helpful in part (b).
Ⓖ **(b)** Suppose that we use the two functions in part (a) as the given functions in Example 7. On the basis of the graph in part (a), make a rough estimate for the minimum length of the road.
   **(c)** Use the technique of Example 7 to find the exact value for the minimum length.

**B**

**26.** Through a type of chemical reaction known as *autocatalysis*, the human body produces the enzyme trypsin from the enzyme trypsinogen. (Trypsin then breaks down proteins into amino acids, which the body needs for growth.) Let $r$ denote the rate of the chemical reaction in which trypsin is formed from trypsinogen. It has been shown experimentally that $r = kx(a - x)$, where $k$ is a positive constant, $a$ is the initial amount of trypsinogen, and $x$ is the amount of trypsin produced (so $x$ increases as the reaction proceeds). Show that the reaction rate $r$ is a maximum when $x = a/2$. In other words, the speed of the reaction is greatest when the amount of trypsin formed is half the original amount of trypsinogen.

**27.** **(a)** Let $x + y = 15$. Find the minimum value of the quantity $x^2 + y^2$.
   **(b)** Let $C$ be a constant and $x + y = C$. Show that the minimum value of $x^2 + y^2$ is $C^2/2$. Then use this result to check your answer in part (a).

**28.** Suppose that $A$, $B$, and $C$ are positive constants and that $x + y = C$. Show that the minimum value of $Ax^2 + By^2$ occurs when $x = BC/(A + B)$ and $y = AC/(A + B)$.

**29.** The following figure shows a square inscribed within a unit square. For which value of $x$ is the area of the inner square a minimum? What is the minimum area? *Hint:* Denote the lengths of the two segments that make up the base of the unit square by $t$ and $1 - t$. Now use the Pythagorean theorem and congruent triangles to express $x$ in terms of $t$.

**30.** **(a)** Show that the coordinates of the point on the line $y = mx + b$ that is closest to the origin are given by

$$\left(\frac{-mb}{1 + m^2}, \frac{b}{1 + m^2}\right)$$

   **(b)** Show that the perpendicular distance from the origin to the line $y = mx + b$ is $|b|/\sqrt{1 + m^2}$. *Suggestion:* Use the result in part (a).
   **(c)** Use part (b) to show that the perpendicular distance from the origin to the line $Ax + By + C = 0$ is $|C|/\sqrt{A^2 + B^2}$.

**31.** The point $P$ lies in the first quadrant on the graph of the line $y = 7 - 3x$. From the point $P$, perpendiculars are drawn to both the $x$-axis and the $y$-axis. What is the largest possible area for the rectangle thus formed?

**32.** Show that the largest possible area for the shaded rectangle shown in the figure is $-b^2/4m$. Then use this to check your answer to Exercise 31.

**33.** Show that the maximum possible area for a rectangle inscribed in a circle of radius $R$ is $2R^2$. *Hint:* Maximize the square of the area.

**34.** An athletic field with a perimeter of $\frac{1}{4}$ mile consists of a rectangle with a semicircle at each end, as shown in the figure. Find the dimensions $x$ and $r$ that yield the greatest possible area for the rectangular region.

**35.** A rancher who wishes to fence off a rectangular area finds that the fencing in the east-west direction will require extra reinforcement due to strong prevailing winds. Because of this, the cost of fencing in the east-west direction will be $12 per (linear) yard, as opposed to a cost of $8 per yard for fencing in the north-south direction. Find the dimensions of the largest possible rectangular area that can be fenced for $4800.

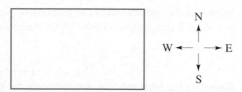

**36.** Let $f(x) = (x - a)^2 + (x - b)^2 + (x - c)^2$, where $a$, $b$, and $c$ are constants. Show that $f(x)$ will be a minimum when $x$ is the average of $a$, $b$, and $c$.

**37.** Let $y = a_1(x - x_1)^2 + a_2(x - x_2)^2$, where $a_1$, $a_2$, $x_1$, and $x_2$ are all constants. In addition, suppose that $a_1$ and $a_2$ are both positive. Show that the minimum of this function occurs when

$$x = \frac{a_1 x_1 + a_2 x_2}{a_1 + a_2}$$

**38.** Among all rectangles with a given perimeter $P$, find the dimensions of the one with the shortest diagonal.

**39.** By analyzing sales figures, the economist for a stereo manufacturer knows that 150 units of a compact disc player can be sold each month when the price is set at $p = \$200$ per unit. The figures also show that for each $10 hike in price, five fewer units are sold each month.
  **(a)** Let $x$ denote the number of units sold per month and let $p$ denote the price per unit. Find a linear function relating $p$ and $x$.    *Hint*: $\Delta p / \Delta x = 10/(-5) = -2$
  **(b)** The revenue $R$ is given by $R = xp$. What is the maximum revenue? At what level should the price be set to achieve this maximum revenue?

**40.** Let $f(x) = x^2 + px + q$, and suppose that the minimum value of this function is 0. Show that $q = p^2/4$.

**41.** Among all possible inputs for the function $f(t) = -t^4 + 6t^2 - 6$, which ones yield the largest output?

**42.** Let $f(x) = x - 3$ and $g(x) = x^2 - 4x + 1$.
  **(a)** Find the minimum value of $g \circ f$.
  **(b)** Find the minimum value of $f \circ g$.
  **(c)** Are the results in parts (a) and (b) the same?

**43.** This exercise completes a detail mentioned in Example 4. In that example we used the result that the input minimizing the function $D(x) = \sqrt{x^2 - x + 1}$ is the same input that minimizes the function $y = x^2 - x + 1$. For this result to be applicable, we need to know that the quantity $x^2 - x + 1$ is nonnegative for all $x$. Parts (a) and (b) each suggest a way to verify that this is indeed the case. [Actually, parts (a) and (b) both show that the quantity $x^2 - x + 1$ is positive for all $x$.]
  **(a)** Use the fact that $x^2 - x + 1$ can be written as $(x - \frac{1}{2})^2 + \frac{3}{4}$ to explain (in complete sentences) why the quantity $x^2 - x + 1$ is positive for all inputs $x$.
  **(b)** Compute the discriminant of the quadratic $x^2 - x + 1$ and explain why the graph of $y = x^2 - x + 1$ has no $x$-intercepts. Then use this fact to explain why the quantity $x^2 - x + 1$ is always positive.    *Hint*: Is the graph of the parabola $y = x^2 - x + 1$ U-shaped up or U-shaped down?

**44.** Let $f(x) = (x - 1)^2 - 4$.
  **(a)** Sketch the graph of the function $f$ and note that the minimum value occurs when $x$ is 1.
  **(b)** Although the minimum value of the function $f$ occurs when $x = 1$, the minimum value of the function $y = \sqrt{f(x)}$ does not occur when $x = 1$. Explain why this does not contradict the statement in the caption to Figure 6 on page 276.
  **(c)** Find the value(s) of $x$ that minimize the function $y = \sqrt{f(x)}$.    *Hint*: What is the domain of $y = \sqrt{f(x)}$?

**45.** A piece of wire 16 in. long is to be cut into two pieces. Let $x$ denote the length of the first piece and $16 - x$ the length of the second. The first piece is to be bent into a circle and the second piece into a square.
  **(a)** Express the total combined area $A$ of the circle and the square as a function of $x$.
  **(b)** For which value of $x$ is the area $A$ a minimum?
  **(c)** Using the $x$-value that you found in part (b), find the ratio of the lengths of the shorter to the longer piece of wire.    *Answer*: $\pi/4$

**46.** A 30-in. piece of string is to be cut into two pieces. The first piece will be formed into the shape of an equilateral triangle and the second piece into a square. Find the length of the first piece if the combined area of the triangle and the square is to be as small as possible.

*Exercises 47–52 are maximum-minimum problems in which the function that you set up will not turn out to be a quadratic, nor will it be closely related to one. Thus the vertex formula will not be applicable.*

**(a)** *Set up the appropriate function to be maximized or minimized just as you have practiced in this section and Section 4.4.*

ⓖ **(b)** *Use a graphing utility to draw the graph of the function and determine, as least approximately, the number or numbers that the problem asks for. (General techniques for determining the exact values are developed in calculus.)*

*Exercises 47–52 are quoted from the following calculus textbooks with the permission of the publishers.*

EXERCISE  TEXT
**47.** *Calculus: A New Horizon,* 6th ed., Howard Anton (New York: John Wiley & Sons, 1998)

**48.** *Calculus,,* 6th ed., Roland E. Larson et al. (Boston: Houghton Mifflin, 1997)

**49.** *Calculus and Analytic Geometry,* 5th ed., Sherman K. Stein and Anthony Barcellos (New York: McGraw-Hill, 1992)

**50.** *Calculus with Analytic Geometry,* 5th ed., C. H. Edwards, Jr. and David E. Penney (Upper Saddle River, N.J.: Prentice-Hall, 1997)

**51.** *Calculus: One and Several Variables,* 8th ed., Saturnino L. Salas and Garret J. Etgen (New York: John Wiley & Sons, 1998)

**52.** *Calculus,* 5th ed., James Stewart (Pacific Grove, Calif.: Brooks/Cole, 2003)

**47.** A cylindrical can, open at the top, is to hold $500 \text{ cm}^3$ of liquid. Find the height and radius that minimize the amount of material needed to manufacture the can.

**48.** A power station is on one side of a river that is $1/2$ mi. wide, and a factory is 6 mi. downstream on the other side. It costs $6 per foot to run power lines overland and $8 per foot to run them underwater. Find the most economical path for the transmission line from the power station to the factory.

**49.** What point on the parabola $y = x^2$ is closest to the point $(3, 0)$?

**50.** A rectangle of fixed perimeter 36 is rotated about one of its sides, thus sweeping out a figure in the shape of a right circular cylinder. [Refer to the accompanying figure.] What is the maximum possible volume of that cylinder?

**51.** Let $ABC$ be a triangle with vertices $A(-3, 0)$, $B(0, 6)$, $C(3, 0)$. Let $P$ be a point on the line segment that joins $B$ to the origin. Find the position of $P$ that minimizes the sum of the distances between $P$ and the vertices.

**52.** A fence 8 ft tall runs parallel to a tall building at a distance of 4 ft from the building. What is the length of the shortest ladder that will reach from the ground over the fence to the wall of the building?

## C

ⓖ **53. (a)** Use a graphing utility to graph the parabolas $y = x^2 - 2x$, $y = x^2 + 2x$, $y = x^2 - 3x$, and $y = x^2 + 3x$. Check visually that, in each case, the vertex of the parabola appears to lie on the curve $y = -x^2$.

  **(b)** Prove that for all real numbers $k$, the vertex of the parabola $y = x^2 + kx$ lies on the curve $y = -x^2$.

ⓖ **54. (a)** Graph the four parabolas $y = x^2 + 2kx + 1$ corresponding to $k = 2, 3, 0.75, 1.5$. Among the four parabolas, which one appears to have the vertex closest to the origin?

  **(b)** Let $f(x) = x^2 + 2kx + 1$. Find a positive value for $k$ so that the distance from the origin to the vertex of the parabola is as small as possible. Check that your answer is consistent with your observations in part (a).

**55.** The figure shows a rectangle inscribed in a given triangle of base $b$ and height $h$. Find the ratio of the area of the triangle to the area of the rectangle when the area of the rectangle is maximum.

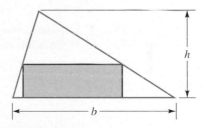

**56.** A Norman window is in the shape of a rectangle surmounted by a semicircle, as shown in the figure. Assume that the perimeter of the window is $P$, a constant. Show that the area of the window is a maximum when both $x$ and $r$ are equal to $P/(\pi + 4)$. Show that this maximum area is $\frac{1}{2}P^2/(\pi + 4)$.

**57.** A triangle is inscribed in a semicircle of diameter $2R$, as shown in the figure. Show that the smallest possible value for the area of the shaded region is $(\pi - 2)R^2/2$.

*Hint*: The area of the shaded region is a minimum when the area of the triangle is a maximum. Find the value of $x$ that maximizes the *square* of the area of the triangle. This will be the same $x$ that maximizes the area of the triangle.

**58. (a)** Complete the following table. Which $x$-$y$ pair in the table yields the smallest sum $x + y$?

| $x$ | 0.5 | 1 | 1.5 | 2 | 2.5 | 3 | 3.5 |
|---|---|---|---|---|---|---|---|
| $y$ | | | | | | | |
| $xy$ | 12 | 12 | 12 | 12 | 12 | 12 | 12 |
| $x + y$ | | | | | | | |

**(b)** Find two positive numbers with a product of 12 and as small a sum as possible. *Hint*: The quantity that you need to minimize is $x + (12/x)$, where $x > 0$. But

$$x + \frac{12}{x} = \left( \sqrt{x} - \sqrt{\frac{12}{x}} \right)^2 + 2\sqrt{12}$$

This last expression is minimized when the quantity within parentheses is zero. Why?

**(c)** Use a calculator to verify that the two numbers obtained in part (b) produce a sum that is smaller than any of the sums obtained in part (a).

**59.** What is the smallest possible value for the sum of a positive number and its reciprocal? *Hint*: After setting up the appropriate function, adapt the hint given in Exercise 58(b).

**60.** Suppose that $a$ and $b$ are positive numbers whose sum is 1.
**(a)** Find the maximum possible value of the product $ab$.
**(b)** Prove that $\left( 1 + \frac{1}{a} \right)\left( 1 + \frac{1}{b} \right) \geq 9$.

# PROJECT | THE LEAST-SQUARES LINE

*The great advances in mathematical astronomy made during the early years of the nineteenth century were due in no small part to the development of the method of least squares. The same method is the foundation for the calculus of errors of observation now occupying a place of great importance in the scientific study of social, economic, biological, and psychological problems.* — A Source Book in Mathematics, by David Eugene Smith (New York: Dover Publications, 1959)

*Of all the principles which can be proposed . . .* [for finding the line or curve that best fits a data set], *I think there is none more general, more exact, and more easy of application than . . . rendering the sum of the squares of the errors a minimum.* —Adrien Marie Legendre (1752–1833) [Legendre and Carl Friedrich Gauss (1777–1855) developed the least-squares method independently.]

When we worked with the least-squares (or regression) line in Section 4.1, we said that this is the line that "best fits" the given set of data points. In this project we explain the meaning of "best fits," and we use quadratic functions to gain some insight into how the least-squares line is calculated. *Suggestion*: Two or three people could volunteer to study the text here and then present the material to another group or to the class at large. The presentation will be deemed successful if the audience can then work on their own the two exercises at the end of this project.

Suppose that we have a data point $(x_i, y_i)$ and a line $y = f(x) = mx + b$ (not necessarily the least-squares line). As indicated in Figure A, we define the *deviation $e_i$* of this line from the data point as

$$e_i = y_i - f(x_i)$$

**Figure A**

In Figure A, where the data point is above the line, the deviation $e_i$ represents the vertical distance between the data point and the line. If the data point were below the line, then the deviation $y_i - f(x_1)$ would be the negative of that distance. Think of $e_i$ as the *error* made if $f(x_i)$ were used as a prediction for the value of $y_i$.

Figure B and the accompanying calculations show two examples using this definition. For the data point $(x_1, y_1) = (4, 3)$, the result $e_1 = 2$ does represent the vertical distance between the data point and the line. For the data point $(8, 2)$, the deviation is $e_2 = -1$, and the absolute value of this gives the vertical distance between the data point and the line.

For the data point $(x_1, y_1) = (4, 3)$:
$$e_1 = y_1 - f(x_1)$$
$$= 3 - \left(\tfrac{1}{2}(4) - 1\right) = 2$$

For the data point $(x_2, y_2) = (8, 2)$:
$$e_2 = y_2 - f(x_2)$$
$$= 2 - \left(\tfrac{1}{2}(8) - 1\right) = -1$$

**Figure B**

Now suppose we have a given data set and a line. One way to measure how closely this line fits the data would be to simply add up all the deviations. The problem with this, however, is that positive and negative deviations would tend to cancel one another out. For this reason, we use the sum of the squares of the deviations as the measure of how closely a line fits a data set. (The sum of the absolute values of the deviations would be another alternative, but in calculus, squares are easier to work with than absolute values.)

As an example, suppose we have the following data set:

| $x$ | 1 | 2 | 3 |
|---|---|---|---|
| $y$ | 2 | 4 | 5 |

or equivalently

$$(x_1, y_1) = (1, 2)$$
$$(x_2, y_2) = (2, 4)$$
$$(x_3, y_3) = (3, 5)$$

---

**DEFINITION** | **Line of Best Fit**

---

Suppose we have a set of $n$ data points $(x_1, y_1)$, $(x_2, y_2)$, $(x_3, y_3)$, ..., $(x_n, y_n)$. For any line, let $E$ denote the sum of the squares of the deviations:

$$E = e_1^2 + e_2^2 + e_3^2 + \cdots + e_n^2$$

Then the **line of best fit** is that line for which $E$ is as small as possible. (It can be shown that there is only one such line.) The line of best fit is also known as the **least-squares line** or the **regression line.**

---

Then, for any line $y = mx + b$ we have

$$e_1 = 2 - [m(1) + b] \qquad e_2 = 4 - [m(2) + b] \qquad e_3 = 5 - [m(3) + b]$$
$$= 2 - m - b \qquad\qquad = 4 - 2m - b \qquad\qquad = 5 - 3m - b$$

Now, by definition, for the least-squares line we want to find the values for $m$ and $b$ so that the quantity $E = e_1^2 + e_2^2 + e_3^2$ is as small as possible. Using the expressions we've just calculated for $e_1$, $e_2$, and $e_3$, we have

$$\begin{aligned} E &= e_1^2 + e_2^2 + e_3^2 \\ &= (2 - m - b)^2 + (4 - 2m - b)^2 + (5 - 3m - b)^2 \end{aligned} \qquad (1)$$

Equation (1) expresses $E$ as a function of *two* variables, $m$ and $b$. In all the work we've done previously on maximum-minimum problems, we were always able to express one variable in terms of the other, and then apply our knowledge of quadratics. In this case, though, $m$ and $b$ are not related, so that strategy doesn't work here. In fact, in general, the methods of calculus are required to handle a two-variable maximum-minimum problem. Therefore to make this problem accessible within our context, we'll assume the result (from calculus) that in this problem $b$ turns out to be $2/3$. Go ahead now and make the substitution $b = 2/3$ in equation (1). After simplifying, you'll have a quadratic function, and you know how to find the value of $m$ that minimizes the function. Then, with both $m$ and $b$ known, you have determined the least-squares line $y = mx + b$. As a visual check, graph the data set along with the least-squares line. See whether things look reasonable. Finally, use a graphing utility to compute the least-squares line and check your answer.

## EXERCISES

*In each case you are given a data set and the value for b in the least-squares line $y = mx + b$. Find the equation of the least-squares line using the method indicated above. Check your answer using an appropriate graphing utility. Then graph the data set along with the least-squares line. In Exercise 2, in reporting the final answer, round both b and m to two decimal places.*

**1.** (*Easy numbers*)

| $x$ | 1 | 2 | 3 |
|-----|---|---|----|
| $y$ | 2 | 5 | 11 |

$b = -3$

**2.** (*"Actual" numbers*) The data in the following table are from a study relating air pollution and incidence of respiratory disease. The data were collected in five cities over the years 1955, 1957, and 1958. The subjects were women working in RCA factories. In the table, $x$ denotes the average concentration of particulate sulfates ("sulfur dust") in the air of the given city, measured in micrograms per cubic meter ($\mu g/m^3$). The variable $y$ denotes the number of absences due to respiratory disease per 1000 employees per year. (Only absences lasting more than seven days were counted.)

$b = -20.8117$

| City | $x$ Concentration of suspended particulate sulfates ($\mu g/m^3$) | $y$ Number of respiratory disease related absences per 1000 employees per year |
|---|---|---|
| Cincinnati, Oh. | 7.4 | 18.5 |
| Indianapolis, Ind. | 13.2 | 44.2 |
| Woodbridge, N.J. | 13.6 | 50.3 |
| Camden, N.J. | 17.1 | 58.3 |
| Harrison, N.J. | 19.8 | 85.7 |

Source: F. Curtis Dohan, "Air Pollutants and Incidence of Respiratory Disease," *Archives of Environmental Health*, 3(1961), pp. 387–395

# 4.6 POLYNOMIAL FUNCTIONS

*After a few hitches or twitches, the polynomial functions settle down to behavior in which things simply get bigger or smaller. An example is $f(x) = x^2$. Just once, as the values of x approach 0, the graph of this function dips downward to alter its shape; thereafter it ascends solemnly like a helium-filled balloon.* —David Berlinski, *A Tour of the Calculus* (New York: Vintage Books, 1995)

We can rephrase the definitions of linear and quadratic functions using the terminology for polynomials that was reviewed in Section 1.3. A function $f$ is *linear* if $f(x)$ is a polynomial of degree 1:

$$f(x) = a_1x + a_0 \qquad \text{where } a_0 \text{ and } a_1 \text{ are constants} \tag{1}$$

A function $f$ is *quadratic* if $f(x)$ is a polynomial of degree 2:

$$f(x) = a_2x^2 + a_1x + a_0 \qquad \text{where } a_0, a_1 \text{ and } a_2 \text{ are constants, with } a_2 \text{ not zero} \tag{2}$$

In the box that follows, we give the general definition for a polynomial function of degree $n$.

---

| **DEFINITION** | **Polynomial Function** |

A **polynomial function** is a function defined by an equation of the form

$$f(x) = a_n x^n + a_{n-1} x^{n-1} + \cdots + a_1 x + a_0$$

where $n$ is a nonnegative integer and the $a_i$'s are constants. If $a_n \neq 0$, the **degree** of the polynomial function is $n$, the largest exponent on the input variable.

**EXAMPLES**

$$f(x) = 2x^3 - 3x^2 + x - 4$$
(degree 3)

$$g(u) = 3u^7 - \sqrt{3}u^2 - \pi$$
(degree 7)

$$L(x) = 5x + 1 \quad \text{(degree 1)}$$

---

A nonzero constant function, for example, $y = 7$ for all $x$, is a polynomial function of *degree zero*. (Think of the defining equation $y = 7$ as $y = 7x^0$.) The one polynomial function for which degree is not defined is the *zero function*: $f(x) = 0$ for all $x$. (What does the graph of that function look like?)

A function of the form $y = x^n$, where $n$ is any real-number constant, is called a **power function.** If we only consider exponents $n$ that are nonnegative integers, then these power functions are the simplest polynomial functions. In a sense, they are the building blocks for all other polynomial functions. Figure 1 shows examples of power functions with which we are already familiar. Our focus here is on the power functions in Figures 1(a) through 1(d), where $n$ is a nonnegative integer.

When $n$ is an integer greater than 3, the graph of $y = x^n$ resembles the graph of $y = x^2$ or $y = x^3$, depending on whether $n$ is even or odd. Consider, for instance, the graph of $y = x^4$, shown in Figure 2 along with the graph of $y = x^2$. Just as with

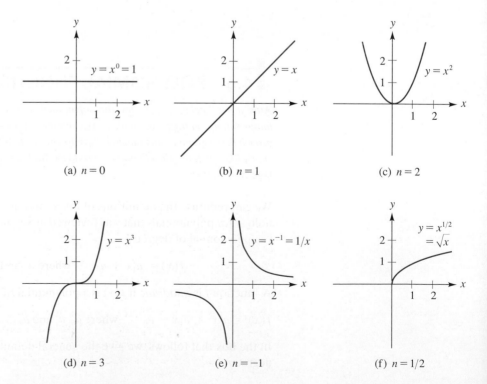

**Figure 1**
Some familiar power functions
$y = x^n$, where $n$ is a real number

(a) $n = 0$

(b) $n = 1$

(c) $n = 2$

(d) $n = 3$

(e) $n = -1$

(f) $n = 1/2$

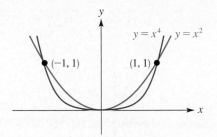

**Figure 2**

$y = x^2$, the graph of $y = x^4$ is a symmetric, U-shaped curve passing through the three points $(-1, 1)$, $(1, 1)$, and $(0, 0)$. However, in the interval $-1 < x < 1$, the graph of $y = x^4$ is flatter than that of $y = x^2$. Similarly, the graph of $y = x^6$ in this interval would be flatter still. (*Note*: Exercise 65 at the end of this section asks you to show why this is true.) The data in Table 1 illustrate this behavior. Figure 3 displays the graphs of $y = x^2$, $y = x^4$, and $y = x^6$ for the interval $0 \le x \le 1$.

**TABLE 1**

| x | 0.2 | 0.4 | 0.6 | 0.8 | 1.0 |
|------|----------|----------|----------|----------|-----|
| $x^2$ | 0.04 | 0.16 | 0.36 | 0.64 | 1.0 |
| $x^4$ | 0.0016 | 0.0256 | 0.1296 | 0.4096 | 1.0 |
| $x^6$ | 0.000064 | 0.004096 | 0.046656 | 0.262144 | 1.0 |

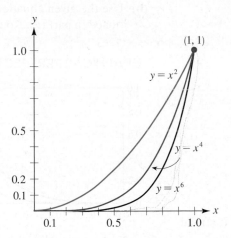

**Figure 3**

Incidentally, Figure 3 indicates one of the practical difficulties you may encounter in trying to draw an accurate graph of $y = x^n$. Suppose, for instance, that you want to graph $y = x^6$ and the lines you draw are 0.01 cm thick. Also suppose that you use the same scale on both axes, taking the common unit to be 1 cm. Then, in the first quadrant, your graph of $y = x^6$ will be indistinguishable from the $x$-axis when $x^6 < 0.01$, or $x < \sqrt[6]{0.01} \approx 0.46$ cm (using a calculator). This explains why sections of the graphs in Figure 3 appear horizontal.

For $|x| > 1$, the graph of $y = x^4$ rises more rapidly than that of $y = x^2$. Similarly, the graph of $y = x^6$ rises still more rapidly. This is shown in Figures 4(a) and (b). (Note the different scales used on the $y$-axes in the two figures.)

**Figure 4**

(a)

(b)

| EXAMPLE | 1 | Comparing average rates of change of two power functions |
|---|---|---|

Let $f(x) = x^4$ and $g(x) = x^8$.
**(a)** Use Figure 5 to estimate and compare the averages rates of change of $f$ and $g$ on the interval $[0, 0.8]$ and on the interval $[0, 1.25]$.
**(b)** Use the given equations for $f$ and $g$ to compute the rates of change mentioned in part (a). Round the answers to three decimal places.

**GRAPHICAL PERSPECTIVE**

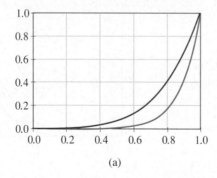

**Figure 5**
Two views of $f(x) = x^4$ (red) and
$g(x) = x^8$ (blue)

(a)

(b)

**SOLUTION**
**(a)** Refer to Figure 5(a). On the interval $[0, 0.8]$ we have $g(0) = 0$, and from the graph, $g(0.8)$ is roughly 0.2. So on this interval we have

$$\frac{\Delta g}{\Delta x} = \frac{g(0.8) - g(0)}{0.8 - 0} \approx \frac{0.2 - 0}{0.8} = 0.25$$

Also on the interval $[0, 0.8]$, $f(0) = 0$ and $f(0.8) \approx 0.4$. Thus we have

$$\frac{\Delta f}{\Delta x} = \frac{f(0.8) - f(0)}{0.8 - 0} \approx \frac{0.4 - 0}{0.8} = 0.5$$

In summary, on the interval $[0, 0.8]$, the average rate of change of $g$ is approximately 0.25, which is half of the value estimated for the average rate of change of $f$.

Exercise 45 asks you to follow this same procedure for the interval $[0, 1.25]$ shown in Figure 5(b). The exercise asks you to show that the estimates for this interval are $\Delta g/\Delta x \approx 4$ and $\Delta f/\Delta x \approx 2$. So, on this interval, it's $g$ rather than $f$ that has the larger average rate of change. The estimate for the average rate of change of $g$ is twice the value estimated for the average rate of change of $f$.

**(b)** For the interval $[0, 0.8]$,

$$\frac{\Delta g}{\Delta x} = \frac{g(0.8) - g(0)}{0.8 - 0} = \frac{(0.8)^8 - 0^8}{0.8} \qquad \frac{\Delta f}{\Delta x} = \frac{f(0.8) - f(0)}{0.8 - 0} = \frac{(0.8)^4 - 0^4}{0.8}$$

$$= (0.8)^7 \approx 0.210 \quad \text{rounding to} \qquad\qquad = (0.8)^3 = 0.512 \quad \text{(exactly)}$$

three decimal places

Exercise 46(a) asks you to carry out similar calculations for the interval $[0, 1.25]$ to obtain the results $\Delta g/\Delta x \approx 4.768$ and $\Delta f/\Delta x \approx 1.953$.

As was mentioned earlier, when $n$ is odd, the graph of $y = x^n$ resembles that of $y = x^3$. In Figure 6 we compare the graphs of $y = x^3$ and $y = x^5$. Notice that both curves pass through $(0, 0)$, $(1, 1)$, and $(-1, -1)$. For reasons similar to those explained for even $n$, the graph of $y = x^5$ is flatter than that of $y = x^3$ in the interval $-1 < x < 1$, and the graph of $y = x^7$ is flatter still. For $|x| > 1$, the graph of $y = x^5$ is steeper than that of $y = x^3$, and that of $y = x^7$ is steeper still. (See Exercise 65 at the end of this section.)

**Figure 6**

---

## EXAMPLE 2 Translating the graph of a power function

Sketch the graph of $y = (x + 2)^5$ and specify the $y$-intercept.

**SOLUTION**
The graph of $y = (x + 2)^5$ is obtained by moving the graph of $y = x^5$ two units to the left. As a guide to drawing the curve, we recall that $y = x^5$ passes through the points $(0, 0)$, $(1, 1)$, and $(-1, -1)$. Thus $y = (x + 2)^5$ must pass through $(-2, 0)$, $(-1, 1)$, and $(-3, -1)$, as shown in Figure 7.

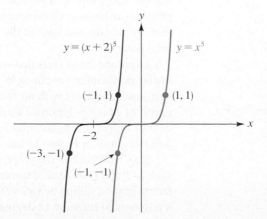

**Figure 7**

Although the curve rises and falls very sharply, it is important to realize that it is never really vertical. For instance, the curve eventually crosses the $y$-axis. To find the $y$-intercept, we set $x = 0$ to obtain $y = 2^5 = 32$. Thus the $y$-intercept is 32.

In Section 4.2 we observed the effect of the constant $a$ on the graph of $y = ax^2$. Those same comments apply to the graph of $y = ax^n$. For instance, the graph of $y = \frac{1}{2}x^4$ is wider than that of $y = x^4$, whereas the graph of $y = -\frac{1}{2}x^4$ is obtained by reflecting the graph of $y = \frac{1}{2}x^4$ in the $x$-axis.

### EXAMPLE 3    Translating a reflection of a power function

Graph the function $y = -2(x - 3)^4$.

**SOLUTION**
We begin with the graph of $y = -2x^4$, in Figure 8(a). The points $(1, -2)$ and $(-1, -2)$ are obtained by substituting $x = 1$ and $x = -1$, respectively, in the equation $y = -2x^4$. Now if we replace $x$ with $x - 3$ in the equation $y = -2x^4$, we have $y = -2(x - 3)^4$, which we can graph by translating the graph in Figure 8(a) to the right 3 units; see Figure 8(b).

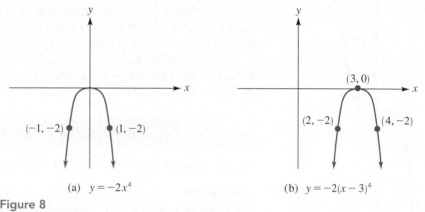

(a)  $y = -2x^4$          (b)  $y = -2(x - 3)^4$

**Figure 8**

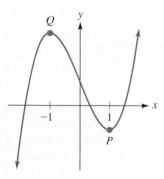

(a)  $y = x^3 - 3x + 1$

(b)  $y = -(x + 1)^3 + 1$

**Figure 9**

In principle, we can obtain the graph of any polynomial function by setting up a table and plotting a sufficient number of points. Indeed, this is just the way a graphing calculator or computer operates. However, to *understand* why the graphs look as they do, we want to discuss some additional methods for graphing polynomial functions.

There are three facts that we shall need. By way of example, look at the graphs of the polynomial functions in Figure 9. First, notice that both graphs are unbroken, smooth curves with no "corners." As in shown in calculus, this is true for the graph of every polynomial function. In contrast, the graphs in Figures 10 and 11 cannot represent polynomial functions. The graph in Figure 10 has a break in it, and the graph in Figure 11 has what's called a **cusp.**

Now look back at the graph in Figure 9(a). Recall (from Section 3.2) that points such as $P$ and $Q$ are called **turning points.** These are points where the graph changes from rising to falling or vice versa. It is a fact (proved in calculus) that the graph of a polynomial function of degree $n$ has *at most* $n - 1$ turning points. For instance, in

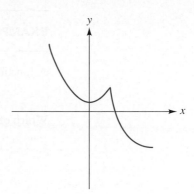

**Figure 10**
Since the graph has a break, it cannot represent a polynomial function.

**Figure 11**
Since the graph has a cusp, it cannot represent a polynomial function.

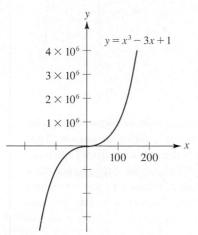

**Figure 12**
When $|x|$ is very large, the graph of $y = x^3 - 3x + 1$ appears indistinguishable from that of $y = x^3$.

Figure 9(a) there are two turning points, and the degree of the polynomial is 3. However, as Figure 9(b) indicates, we needn't have any turning points at all.

A third property of polynomial functions concerns their behavior when $|x|$ is very large. We'll illustrate this property using the function $y = x^3 - 3x + 1$, graphed in Figure 9(a). Now, in Figure 9(a), the $x$-values are relatively small; for instance, the $x$-coordinates of $P$ and $Q$ are 1 and $-1$, respectively. In Figure 12, however, we show the graph of this same function using units of 100 on the $x$-axis. On this scale, the graph appears indistinguishable from that of $y = x^3$. In particular, note that as $|x|$ gets very large, $|y|$ grows very large.

It's easy to see why the function $y = x^3 - 3x + 1$ resembles $y = x^3$ when $|x|$ is very large. First, let's rewrite the equation $y = x^3 - 3x + 1$ as

$$y = x^3\left(1 - \frac{3}{x^2} + \frac{1}{x^3}\right)$$

Now, when $|x|$ is very large, both $3/x^2$ and $1/x^3$ are close to zero. So we have

$$y \approx x^3(1 - 0 + 0)$$
$$\approx x^3 \qquad \text{when } |x| \text{ is very large}$$

The same technique that we've just used in analyzing $y = x^3 - 3x + 1$ can be applied to any (nonconstant) polynomial function. The result is summarized in item 3 in the following box.

## PROPERTY SUMMARY   Graphs of Polynomial Functions

1. The graph of a polynomial function of degree 2 or greater is an unbroken smooth curve. (For degrees 1 and 0, the graph is a line.)
2. The graph of a polynomial function of degree $n$ has at most $n - 1$ turning points.
3. For the graph of any polynomial function (other than a constant function), as $|x|$ gets very large, $|y|$ grows very large. If

$$f(x) = a_n x^n + a_{n-1} x^{n-1} + \cdots + a_1 x + a_0 \qquad (a_n \neq 0)$$

then

$$f(x) \approx a_n x^n \qquad \text{when } |x| \text{ is very large}$$

EXAMPLE 4    **Choosing a plausible graph for a given polynomial function**

A function $f$ is defined by

$$f(x) = -x^3 + x^2 + 9x + 9$$

Which of the graphs in Figure 13 might represent this function?

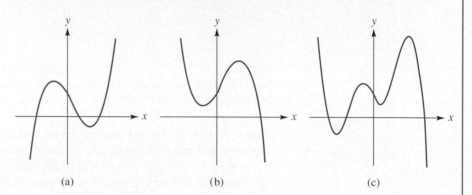

Figure 13          (a)                    (b)                    (c)

**SOLUTION**
When $|x|$ is very large, $f(x) \approx -x^3$. This rules out the graph in Figure 13(a). The graph in Figure 13(c) can also be ruled out, but for a different reason. That graph has four turning points, whereas the graph of the cubic function $f$ can have at most two turning points. The graph in Figure 13(b), on the other hand, does have two turning points; furthermore, that graph does behave like $y = -x^3$ when $|x|$ is very large. The graph in Figure 13(b) might be (in fact, it is) the graph of the given function $f$.

■

EXAMPLE 5    **Comparing polynomials of the same degree**

**GRAPHICAL PERSPECTIVE**

Figure 14
$f(x) = x^4$ (blue) and
$g(x) = x^4 - 3x^3 + 5x + 4$ (red) in
the viewing rectangle $[-3, 3, 1]$
by $[-3, 12, 3]$

Consider the two polynomial functions $f$ and $g$ defined by

$$f(x) = x^4 \qquad g(x) = x^4 - 3x^3 + 5x + 4$$

(a) With a graphing utility, find a viewing rectangle that highlights the differences between these two functions.

(b) Find a sequence of viewing rectangles demonstrating that as $x$ gets larger and larger, the graph of $g$ looks more and more like the graph of $f$.

**SOLUTION**
(a) The view in Figure 14 indicates that the graph of $g$ has three turning points, while the graph of $f$ has but one. The graph of $f$ is symmetric about the $y$-axis; the graph of $g$ is not.

(b) See the three views in Figure 15. For the scale and size used in Figure 15(c), the two graphs are virtually indistinguishable from one another.

## GRAPHICAL PERSPECTIVE

(a) [−5, 5, 5] by [0, 200, 50]    (b) [−10, 10, 5] by [0, 5000, 1000]    (c) [−100, 100, 50] by [0, 5 × 10⁷, 10⁷]

**Figure 15**
In views (a) and (b), the blue graph is $f(x) = x^4$ and the red is $g(x) = x^4 - 3x^2 + 5x + 4$. In view (c), both graphs are black; they are indistinguishable from one another at this scale and size.

We can use our work on solving inequalities (in Section 2.6) to graph polynomial functions that are in factored form. Consider, for example, the function

$$f(x) = x(x + 1)(x - 3)$$

First of all, by inspection we see that $f(x) = 0$ when $x = 0$, $x = -1$, or $x = 3$. These are the $x$-intercepts for the graph. Also, note that the $y$-intercept is 0. (Why?) Next, we want to know what the graph looks like in the intervals between the $x$-intercepts. To do this, we solve the two inequalities $f(x) > 0$ and $f(x) < 0$ using the technique in Section 2.6. Table 2 shows the results. (You should check these results for yourself; if you need a review, the details of this example are worked out on pages 114–115.)

Now we interpret the results in Table 2 graphically. When $x$ is in either of the intervals $(-\infty, -1)$ or $(0, 3)$, the graph lies below the $x$-axis (because $f(x) < 0$); and when $x$ is in either of the intervals $(-1, 0)$ or $(3, \infty)$, the graph lies above the $x$-axis (because $f(x) > 0$). This information is summarized in Figure 16(a). The three dots in the figure indicate the $x$-intercepts of the graph. The shaded regions are the **excluded regions** through which the graph cannot pass. The graph must pass only through the unshaded regions (and through the three $x$-intercepts). In Figure 16(b) we have drawn a rough sketch of a curve satisfying these conditions.

### TABLE 2

| Interval | $x(x + 1)(x - 3)$ |
|---|---|
| $(-\infty, -1)$ | negative |
| $(-1, 0)$ | positive |
| $(0, 3)$ | negative |
| $(3, \infty)$ | positive |

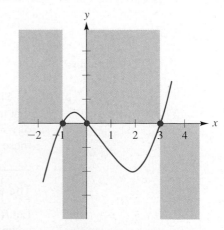

(a)  The $x$-intercepts and the excluded regions for the graph of $f(x) = x(x + 1)(x - 3)$

(b)  A rough graph of $f(x) = x(x + 1)(x - 3)$

**Figure 16**

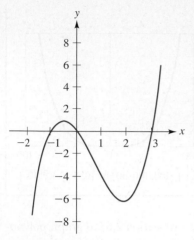

**Figure 17**
$f(x) = x(x + 1)(x - 3)$

Notice that to draw a smooth curve satisfying the conditions of Figure 16(a), we need at least two turning points: one between $x = -1$ and $x = 0$ and another between $x = 0$ and $x = 3$. On the other hand, since the degree of $f(x)$ is 3, there can be no more than two turning points. Thus Figure 16(b) has exactly two turning points. As another check on our rough sketch, we note that for large values of $|x|$, the graph indeed resembles that of $y = x^3$. (We are using the third property in the summary box on page 293.)

Although the precise location of the turning points is a matter for calculus, we can nevertheless improve upon the sketch in Figure 16(b) by computing $f(x)$ for some specific values of $x$. Some reasonable choices in this case are the inputs $-2, -\frac{1}{2}, 1, 2$, and 4. As you can check, the resulting points on the graph are $(-2, -10)$, $(-\frac{1}{2}, \frac{7}{8})$, $(1, -4)$, $(2, -6)$, and $(4, 20)$. We can now sketch the graph, as shown in Figure 17.

In the example just concluded, the polynomial $f(x) = x(x + 1)(x - 3)$ has no *repeated factors*. That is, none of the factors is squared, cubed, or raised to a higher power. Now let us look at two examples in which there are repeated factors. The observations we make will help us in determining the general shape of a graph without the need for plotting a large number of individual points. In Figure 18(a), we show the graph of $g(x) = x(x + 1)(x - 3)^2$. Notice that in the immediate vicinity of the intercept at $x = 3$, the graph has the same general shape as that of $y = A(x - 3)^2$.

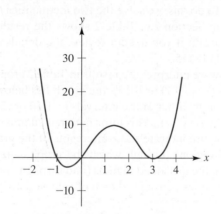

(a) $g(x) = x(x + 1)(x - 3)^2$
Near the $x$-intercept at 3, the graph has the same general shape as that of $y = A(x - 3)^2$.

(b) $h(x) = x(x + 1)(x - 3)^3$
Near the $x$-intercept at 3, the graph has the same general shape as that of $y = A(x - 3)^3$.

**Figure 18**

Similarly, in Figure 18(b) we show the graph of $h(x) = x(x + 1)(x - 3)^3$; notice that in the immediate vicinity of $x = 3$, the graph has the same general shape as that of $y = A(x - 3)^3$. In the box that follows, we state the general principle underlying these observations. (The principle can be justified using calculus.)

---

### The Behavior of a Polynomial Function Near an x-Intercept

Let $f(x)$ be a polynomial and suppose that $(x - a)^n$ is a factor of $f(x)$. [Furthermore, assume that none of the other factors of $f(x)$ contains $(x - a)$.] Then, in the immediate vicinity of the $x$-intercept at $a$, the graph of $y = f(x)$ closely resembles that of $y = A(x - a)^n$.

---

The principle that we have just stated is easy to apply because we already know how to graph functions of the form $y = A(x - a)^n$. The next example shows how this works.

| EXAMPLE | 6 | **Determining the shape of the graph of a polynomial function near an x-intercept** |

Describe the behavior of each function in the immediate vicinity of the indicated $x$-intercept.

**(a)** $f(x) = \frac{1}{2}(x - 3)(x - 1)^3$; intercept: $x = 1$

**(b)** $g(x) = (x + 1)(x + 4)(x + 3)^2$; intercept: $x = -3$

**SOLUTION**

**(a)** We make the following observation:

$$f(x) = \frac{1}{2}\underbrace{(x - 3)}(x - 1)^3$$

$\uparrow$

When $x$ is close to 1,
this factor is close
to $1 - 3$, or $-2$.

So if $x$ is very close to 1, we have the approximation

$$f(x) \approx \frac{1}{2}(1 - 3)(x - 1)^3 = \frac{1}{2}(-2)(x - 1)^3 = -(x - 1)^3$$

Thus in the immediate vicinity of $x = 1$ the graph of $f$ closely resembles $y = -(x - 1)^3$. Notice the technique we used to obtain this result. We retained the factor corresponding to the intercept $x = 1$, and we approximated the remaining factor using the value $x = 1$. See Figure 19.

**(b)** We use the approximation technique shown in part (a).

$$g(x) = \underbrace{(x + 1)}\underbrace{(x + 4)}(x + 3)^2$$

When $x$ is close to $-3$, $\uparrow$    $\uparrow$ When $x$ is close to $-3$,
this factor is close                this factor is close
to $-3 + 1$, or $-2$.                to $-3 + 4$, or 1.

Thus when $x$ is close to $-3$, we have the approximation

$$g(x) \approx (-3 + 1)(-3 + 4)(x + 3)^2 = -2(x + 3)^2$$

This tells us that in the immediate vicinity of $x = -3$, the graph of $g$ resembles $y = -2(x + 3)^2$. See Figure 20.

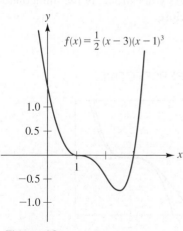

**Figure 19**

When $x$ is close to 1, the graph of $f(x) = \frac{1}{2}(x - 3)(x - 1)^3$ closely resembles $y = -(x - 1)^3$.

**Figure 20**
When $x$ is close to $-3$, the graph of
$g(x) = (x + 1)(x + 4)(x + 3)^2$
closely resembles $y = -2(x + 3)^2$.

The technique introduced in Example 6, whereby we approximate the behavior of the factored polynomial near each $x$-intercept, allows us to draw by hand a reasonably accurate graph. (Of course, some judicious point plotting is necessary too, as mentioned previously.) It's interesting though, to use a graphing utility to confirm visually just how well that simple approximation technique does work. As an example, consider the polynomial function $f$ defined by

$$f(x) = 2(x + 1)(x - 2)^3$$

Near the $x$-intercept $x = 2$, our approximation technique yields

$$f(x) \approx 2(2 + 1)(x - 2)^3$$
$$f(x) \approx 6(x - 2)^3 \qquad \text{near } x = 2$$

In Figure 21 we've used a graphing utility to plot both the graph of $f$ and the graph of the approximating polynomial $y = 6(x - 2)^2$. As you can see, in the immediate vicinity of $x = 2$, the two graphs are remarkably close.

**GRAPHICAL PERSPECTIVE**

**Figure 21**
$f(x) = 2(x + 1)(x - 2)^3$
and $y = 6(x - 2)^3$

— $f(x) = 2(x + 1)(x - 2)^3$
— $y = 6(x - 2)^3$

# EXERCISE SET 4.6

**A**

1. Which of the functions in Figure 1 on page 288 are polynomial functions?
2. (a) Give an example of a power function that is not a polynomial function.
   (b) Give an example of a polynomial function that is not a power function.
3. Let $f(x) = x^2$ and $g(x) = x^3$.
   (a) Either by hand or with a graphing utility, on the same set of axes draw the graphs of $f$ and $g$ on the interval $[0, 1]$.
   (b) Compute and compare the average rates of change of $f$ and $g$ on the interval $[0, 1]$ and on the interval $[0, 1/2]$.
4. Let $f(t) = t^4$ and $g(t) = t^5$.
   (a) Using a graphing utility, draw the graphs of $f$ and $g$ on the same set of axes.
   (b) Which of the three types of symmetry discussed on page 58 does the graph of each function possess?
   (c) Compute the average rate of change of each function on the interval $[-2, 2]$.
   (d) Explain why each answer in part (c) is predictable from the symmetry of the graph.

*In Exercises 5–16, sketch the graph of each function and specify all x- and y-intercepts.*

5. $y = (x - 2)^2 + 1$
6. $y = -3x^4$
7. $y = -(x - 1)^4$
8. $y = -(x + 2)^3$
9. $y = (x - 4)^3 - 2$
10. $y = -(x - 4)^3 - 2$
11. $y = -2(x + 5)^4$
12. $y = -2x^4 + 5$
13. $y = (x + 1)^5/2$
14. $y = \frac{1}{2}x^5 + 1$
15. $y = -(x - 1)^3 - 1$
16. $y = x^8$

*In Exercises 17–20, give a reason (as in Example 4) why each graph cannot represent a polynomial function of degree 3.*

17.

18.

19.

20.

*In Exercises 21–24, give a reason why each graph cannot represent a polynomial function that has the highest-degree term $2x^5$.*

21.

22.

23.

24.

**G** *For Exercises 25 and 26:*
   (a) *With a graphing utility, find a viewing rectangle that highlights the differences between the two functions, as in Example 5.*
   (b) *Find a sequence of viewing rectangles demonstrating that as x gets larger and larger, the graph of g looks more and more like the graph of f.*
25. $f(x) = 2x^2, g(x) = 2x^2 - 12x - 5$
26. $f(x) = 4x^3, g(x) = 4x^3 + 72x^2 + 420x + 805$

*In Exercises 27–34:*
   (a) *Determine the x- and y-intercepts and the excluded regions for the graph of the given function. Specify your results using a sketch similar to Figure 16(a). In Exercises 31–34, you will first need to factor the polynomial.*
   (b) *Graph each function.*
27. $y = (x - 2)(x - 1)(x + 1)$
28. $y = (x - 3)(x + 2)(x + 1)$
29. $y = 2x(x - 2)(x - 1)$
30. $y = (x - 3)(x - 2)(x + 2)$
31. $y = x^3 - 4x^2 - 5x$
32. $y = x^3 - 9x$
33. $y = x^3 + 3x^2 - 4x - 12$
34. $y = x^3 - 5x^2 - x + 5$

*In Exercises 35–44:*
   (a) *Determine the x- and y-intercepts and the excluded regions for the graph of the given function. Specify your results using a sketch similar to Figure 16(a).*
   (b) *Describe the behavior of the function at each x-intercept that corresponds to a repeated factor. Specify your results using a sketch similar to the left-hand portion of Figure 20.*
   (c) *Graph each function.*
35. $y = x^3(x + 2)$
36. $y = (x - 1)(x - 4)^2$
37. $y = 2(x - 1)(x - 4)^3$
38. $y = (x - 1)^2(x - 4)^2$
39. $y = (x + 1)^2(x - 1)(x - 3)$
40. $y = x^2(x - 4)(x + 2)$

**41.** $y = -x^3(x - 4)(x + 2)$   **42.** $y = 4(x - 2)^2(x + 2)^3$
**43.** $y = -4x(x - 2)^2(x + 2)^3$   **44.** $y = -3x^3(x + 1)^4$
**45.** This exercise refers to Example 1(a) in the text. Use Figure 5(b) to obtain the following estimates: on the interval $[0, 1.25]$, $\Delta g/\Delta x \approx 4$, and $\Delta f/\Delta x \approx 2$.

## B

**46. (a)** This exercise refers to Example 1(b), in which $f(x) = x^4$ and $g(x) = x^8$. Show that on the interval $[0, 1.25]$, we have $\Delta g/\Delta x \approx 4.768$ and $\Delta f/\Delta x \approx 1.953$.
   **(b)** Let $f(x) = x^4$ and $g(x) = x^8$, as in part (a). Find a positive constant $b$ so that on the interval $[0, b]$, the average rate of change of $g$ is 100 times the average rate of change of $f$. Give two forms for the answer: an exact expression and a decimal approximation rounded to three decimal places.

*In Exercises 47–50, first use the graph to estimate the x-intercepts. Then use algebra to determine each x-intercept. If an intercept involves a radical, give that answer as well as a calculator approximation rounded to three decimal places. Be sure to check that your results are consistent with the initial graphical estimates.*

**47.**

$y = x^3 - 3x^2 - 5x$

**48.**

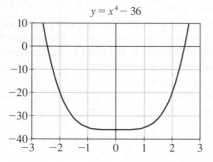

$y = x^4 - 36$

**49.**

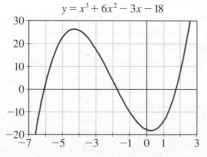

$y = x^3 + 6x^2 - 3x - 18$

*Hint*: Factor $x^3 + 6x^2 - 3x - 18$ by grouping.

**50.**

$y = x^4 - 2x^2 - 5$

*For Exercises 51 and 52:*

Ⓖ **(a)** *Use a graphing utility to draw a graph of each function.*
Ⓖ **(b)** *For each x-intercept, zoom in until you can estimate it accurately to the nearest one-tenth.*
   **(c)** *Use algebra to determine each x-intercept. If an intercept involves a radical, give that answer as well as a calculator approximation rounded to three decimal places. Check to see that your results are consistent with the graphical estimates obtained in part (b).*

**51.** $N(t) = t^7 + 8t^4 + 16t$   **52.** $W(u) = 2u^4 - 17u^2 + 35$

*In Exercises 53–58, six functions are defined as follows:*

$$f(x) = x \qquad g(x) = x^2 \qquad h(x) = x^3$$
$$F(x) = x^4 \qquad G(x) = x^5 \qquad H(x) = x^6$$

*Refer also to the following figure.*

**53.** The six graphs in the figure are the graphs of the six given functions for the interval $[0, 1]$, but the graphs are not labeled. Which is which?
**54.** For which x-values in $[0, 1]$ will the graph of $g$ lie strictly below the horizontal line $y = 0.1$? Use a calculator to evaluate your answer. Round off the result to two significant figures.

**55.** Follow Exercise 54, using the function $H$ instead of $g$.

**56.** Find a number $t$ in $[0, 1]$ such that the vertical distance between $f(t)$ and $g(t)$ is $1/4$.

**57.** Is there a number $t$ in $[0, 1]$ such that the vertical distance between $g(t)$ and $F(t)$ is $0.26$?

**58.** Find all numbers $t$ in $[0, 1]$ such that $F(t) = G(t) + H(t)$.

**59.** The figure shows the graphs of $y = 4x$ and $y = x^2/100$ in a standard viewing rectangle.

(a) Do the graphs intersect anywhere other than at the origin?

Ⓖ (b) Use a graphing utility to support your answer in part (a).

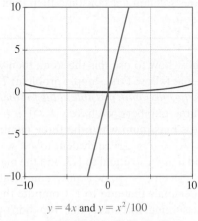

$y = 4x$ and $y = x^2/100$

$[-10, 10, 5]$ by $[-10, 10, 5]$

**60. (a)** Factor the expression $4x^2 - x^4$. Then use the techniques explained in this section to graph the function defined by $y = 4x^2 - x^4$.

(b) Find the coordinates of the turning points. *Hint*: As in previous sections, use the substitution $x^2 = t$.

**61. (a)** Graph the function $D(x) = x^2 - x^4$.

(b) Find the turning points of the graph. (See the hint in Exercise 60.)

(c) On the same set of axes, sketch the graphs of $y = x^2$ and $y = x^4$ for $0 \le x \le 1$. What is the maximum vertical distance between the graphs?

**62. (a)** An open-top box is to be constructed from a 6-by-8-in. rectangular sheet of tin by cutting out equal squares at each corner and then folding up the resulting flaps. Let $x$ denote the length of the side of each cutout square. Show that the volume $V(x)$ is

$$V(x) = x(6 - 2x)(8 - 2x)$$

(b) What is the domain of the volume function in part (a)? [The answer is *not* $(-\infty, \infty)$.]

Ⓖ (c) Use a graphing utility to graph the volume function, taking into account your answer in part (b).

Ⓖ (d) By zooming in on the turning point, estimate to the nearest one-hundredth the maximum volume.

**63.** The point $P$ is in the first quadrant on the graph of $y = 1 - x^4$. From $P$, perpendiculars are drawn to the $x$- and $y$-axes, thus forming a rectangle.

(a) Express the area of the rectangle as a function of a single variable.

Ⓖ (b) Use a graphing utility to graph the area function. Then, using the ZOOM feature, estimate to the nearest hundredth the maximum possible area for the rectangle.

**64.** In Example 1 in Section 4.2 we used a graphing utility to determine linear and quadratic functions to model the AIDS data in Figure 2 on page 229. We then used these models to make projections for the years 1992 and 1997. For both models and both years we found that the projections were too low. We also saw that the quadratic projections were more accurate than the linear ones, as measured by percentage error.

Ⓖ (a) Use a graphing utility to find a polynomial of degree 3 (a *cubic model*) that best fits the data in Figure 2 on page 229.

(b) Use the cubic model to make projections for the cumulative number of AIDS cases in 1992 and 1997.

(c) Are the projections higher or lower than the actual figures given in Example 1 in Section 4.2? Compute the percentage error for each projection. In each case, which is the better predictor, the quadratic or the cubic model?

**C**

**65. (a)** Show that for $m$ and $n$ positive integers with $m < n$ the following inequalities hold:

$$\text{if } 0 \le x \le 1 \quad \text{then } 0 \le x^n \le x^m$$

and

$$\text{if } x > 1 \quad \text{then } x^m < x^n$$

(b) Using part (a), explain why for $m$ and $n$ positive *even* integers, with $m < n$, the graph of $y = x^n$ lies below the graph of $y = x^m$ for $-1 < x < 1$ while the graph of $y = x^n$ lies above the graph of $y = x^m$ for $|x| > 1$.

(c) Using part (a), explain why for $m$ and $n$ positive *odd* integers, with $m < n$, the graph of $y = x^n$ lies above the graph of $y = x^m$ for $x > 1$ and $-1 < x < 0$ and lies below the graph of $y = x^m$ for $x < -1$ and $0 < x < 1$.

# PROJECT

**FINDING SOME MAXIMUM VALUES WITHOUT USING CALCULUS**

In Section 4.2 it was stated that, *in general*, the techniques of calculus are required to find maximum or minimum values for functions that are not quadratics. Nevertheless, there are a number of cases involving polynomials or quotients of polynomials where algebra, rather than calculus, will suffice. The following theorem can be used to find maximum values in certain types of problems. (One way to establish this theorem is indicated at the end of this project.)

---

### THEOREM

If the sum of three positive quantities $s$, $t$, and $u$ is constant, then their product $stu$ is maximum if and only if $s = t = u$.

---

We'll give three examples that show how to use this theorem; then you can try your hand at the three problems that follow. First sample problem: *The sum of three positive numbers is 1. What is the maximum possible value for their product?* Letting $s$, $t$, and $u$ denote the three numbers, we have $s + t + u = 1$. According to the theorem, the product is maximum when the three numbers are equal. So in that case, the equation $s + t + u = 1$ is equivalent to $s + s + s = 1$, which implies $s = 1/3$. Therefore $t$ and $u$ are also equal to 1/3, and the maximum possible value for the product is $stu = (\frac{1}{3})(\frac{1}{3})(\frac{1}{3}) = \frac{1}{27}$. As a quick empirical check, pick any three positive fractions or decimals that add to 1. Compute the product, and check that it's less than $\frac{1}{27}$ (assuming, of course, that you didn't pick all three numbers to be 1/3).

Second sample problem: *Let $f(x) = 2x(4 - x)^2$. By using the standard graphing techniques discussed in Section 4.6, we find that the general shape for the graph of $f$ is as shown in Figure A. One turning point, $(4, 0)$, is on the x-axis; the second turning point is in the first quadrant, with an x-coordinate between 0 and 4. Find the exact coordinates of this second turning point.* First, note that the three factors comprising $f(x)$, namely, $2x$, $(4 - x)$, and $(4 - x)$ again, do have a constant sum: $2x + (4 - x) + (4 - x) = 8$. Furthermore, on the open interval $0 < x < 4$, each of these factors is positive. Thus our theorem in the box is applicable. The maximum value of the product $f(x) = 2x(4 - x)^2$ on the open interval $0 < x < 4$ occurs when the three factors are equal. Setting $2x = 4 - x$, we obtain $3x = 4$, and consequently, $x = 4/3$. This is the required x-coordinate of the turning point. For the y-coordinate we have $f(\frac{4}{3}) = 2(\frac{4}{3})(4 - \frac{4}{3})^2$. As you can verify, that works out to $\frac{512}{27}$. In summary, the coordinates of the turning point are $(\frac{4}{3}, \frac{512}{27})$.

Third sample problem: *According to Figure B, the graph of the polynomial function defined by $g(x) = x^2(1 - x)$ has a turning point in the first quadrant. Find the x-coordinate of that turning point.* First, note that on the open interval $0 < x < 1$, each of the three factors $x$, $x$ again, and $1 - x$ is positive. However, as you can check, the sum of the three factors is not constant. We can work around this by writing

$$(x)(x)(1 - x) = 4\left[\left(\frac{x}{2}\right)\left(\frac{x}{2}\right)(1 - x)\right]$$

**Figure A**
$f(x) = 2x(4 - x)^2$

### GRAPHICAL PERSPECTIVE

**Figure B**
$g(x) = x^2(1 - x)$

Now notice that the three factors in brackets do have a constant sum. For a maximum then, we require that $\frac{x}{2} = 1 - x$. Solving this last equation yields $x = 2/3$, the required $x$-coordinate.

## EXERCISES

1. **(a)** First, sketch a graph of the function $f(x) = x^2(6 - 2x)$ using the standard techniques from Section 4.6. Then, use the ideas presented above to find the exact coordinates of the turning point in the first quadrant.
   **(b)** Follow part (a), but use $g(x) = x^2(6 - 3x)$.
2. An open-top box is to be constructed from a 16-inch square sheet of cardboard by cutting out congruent squares at each corner and then folding up the flaps. See the following figure. Express the volume of the box as a function of a single variable. Then find the maximum possible volume for the box.

3. When a person coughs, the radius $r$ of the trachea (windpipe) decreases. In a paper, "The Human Cough" (Lexington, Mass.: COMAP, Inc., 1979), Philip Tuchinsky developed the following model for the average velocity of air through the trachea during a cough:

$$v(r) = c(r_0 - r)r^2 \qquad (\tfrac{1}{2}r_0 \le r \le r_0)$$

In this formula the variable $r$ represents the radius of the trachea; the constant $r_0$ is the normal radius when the person is not coughing; $c$ is a positive constant (which, among other things, depends upon the length of the person's trachea); and $v(r)$ is the average velocity of the air in the trachea. Show that $v(r)$ is a maximum when $r = \frac{2}{3}r_0$. In other words, according to this model, in coughing to clear the air passages, the most effective cough occurs when the radius contracts to two-thirds its normal size.

## ESTABLISHING THE THEOREM

Exercise 44 in Section 2.3 outlines a proof of the following result, known as the *arithmetic-geometric mean inequality* for three numbers:

> If $a$, $b$, and $c$ are nonnegative real numbers, then $\sqrt[3]{abc} \le (a + b + c)/3$, with equality holding if and only if $a = b = c$.

On your own or through a group discussion, determine why our theorem in the box at the beginning of this project is a consequence of the arithmetic-geometric mean inequality. Then, on your own, write a paragraph carefully explaining this. (You are not being asked here to prove the arithmetic-geometric mean inequality.)

## 4.7 RATIONAL FUNCTIONS

*We shall not attempt to explain the numerous situations in life sciences where the study of such graphs is important nor the chemical reactions which give rise to the rational functions $r(x)$. . . . Let it suffice to mention that, to the experimental biochemist, theoretical results concerning the shapes of rational functions are of considerable interest.*
—W. G. Bardsley and R. M. W. Wood in "Critical Points and Sigmoidicity of Positive Rational Functions," *The American Mathematical Monthly*, vol. 92 (1985), pp. 37–42.

After the polynomial functions, the next simplest functions are the **rational functions.** These are functions defined by equations of the form

$$y = \frac{f(x)}{g(x)}$$

where $f(x)$ and $g(x)$ are polynomials. In general, throughout this section, when we write a function such as $y = f(x)/g(x)$, we assume that $f(x)$ and $g(x)$ contain no common factors (other than constants). (Exercises 44 and 45 ask you to consider several cases in which $f(x)$ and $g(x)$ do contain common factors.) Also, for each of the examples that we discuss, the degree of the numerator $f(x)$ is less than or equal to the degree of the denominator $g(x)$. (A case in which the degree of $f(x)$ exceeds the degree of $g(x)$ is developed in the exercises.)

We'll use the graphs in Figure 1 to introduce some of the ideas and terminology involved in analyzing rational functions. Figure 1(a) shows the familiar rational function $y = 1/x$ that we graphed in Section 3.2. The graph of $y = 1/x$ differs from the graph of every polynomial function in two important aspects. First, the graph has a break in it; it is composed of two distinct pieces or **branches.** (Recall from Sec-

### GRAPHICAL PERSPECTIVE

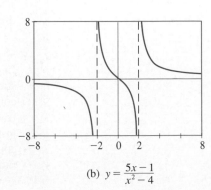

**Figure 1**
Graphs of two rational functions

(a) $y = \frac{1}{x}$

(b) $y = \frac{5x - 1}{x^2 - 4}$

tion 4.6 that the graph of a polynomial function never has a break or gap in it.) In general, the graph of a rational function has one more branch than the number of distinct real values for which the denominator is zero. In Figure 1(b), for example, there are two distinct numbers for which the denominator is zero (what are they?), and the graph has three branches.

The second way that the graph of $y = 1/x$ differs from that of a polynomial function is related to the *asymptotes*. A line is an **asymptote** for a curve if the distance between the line and the curve approaches zero as we move out farther and farther along the line. In Figure 1(a) the $x$-axis is a horizontal asymptote for the curve; the $y$-axis is a vertical asymptote. In Figure 1(b) the $x$-axis is a horizontal asymptote, and each of the lines $x = 2$ and $x = -2$ is a vertical asymptote. Note that 2 and $-2$ are also the $x$-values for which the denominator $x^2 - 4$ is zero. In general, this type of correspondence will always occur for a rational function $y = f(x)/g(x)$ as long as the two polynomials have no common factors (other than constants). Thus to find the vertical asymptotes for the graph of $y = f(x)/g(x)$, just find the $x$-values for which the denominator is zero. What if there are no real-number values for $x$ that make the denominator zero? Then the graph of the rational function has no vertical asymptotes. Figure 2 shows such an example.

**GRAPHICAL PERSPECTIVE**

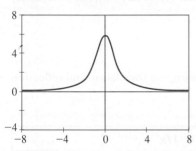

**Figure 2**
$y = 6/(1 + x^2)$
There are no real numbers $x$ for which the denominator is zero. The graph has no vertical asymptotes, and there is no break in the graph.

We can use the functions in Figures 1(b) and 2 as examples in determining domain and intercepts. For the domain of the function $y = (5x - 1)/(x^2 - 4)$ in Figure 1(b), rewrite the equation with the denominator in factored form:

$$y = \frac{5x - 1}{(x - 2)(x + 2)}$$

In this form, we can see than any $x$-value other than $-2$ or 2 will yield an unambiguous output value for $y$. Thus the domain consists of all real numbers except for $-2$ and 2. [Note that the graph in Figure 1(b) supports this conclusion.] Using interval notation, the domain is

$$(-\infty, -2) \cup (-2, 2) \cup (2, \infty)$$

For the function in Figure 2, $y = 6/(x^2 + 1)$, the denominator is never zero. (Why?) Thus any real number $x$ is an appropriate input, and the domain is the set of all real numbers.

Now look back at Figure 1(b). Here we can see that the $x$- and $y$-intercepts are each close to zero, if not zero. To calculate the $y$-intercept, set $x = 0$ in the given equation. That yields

$$y = \frac{5(0) - 1}{0^2 - 4} = \frac{1}{4}$$

Thus, the $y$-intercept is $1/4$. For the $x$-intercept in Figure 1(b), set $y = 0$ in the given equation:

$$0 = \frac{5x - 1}{x^2 - 4}$$

The fraction in this last equation, like any fraction, can only be zero if the numerator is zero (and the denominator isn't zero). Setting $5x - 1$ equal to zero gives us $x = 1/5$, which is the required $x$-intercept. By the way, this simple idea that a fraction can only be zero when the numerator is zero can tell you right away, even before seeing a graph, that some rational functions have no $x$-intercepts. For instance, the numerator of $y = 6/(x^2 + 1)$ is certainly never zero, and therefore the graph of $y = 6/(x^2 + 1)$ has no $x$-intercepts. (See Figure 2.)

If $k$ is a positive constant, the graph of $y = k/x$ resembles that of $y = 1/x$. Figure 3 shows the graphs of $y = 1/x$ and $y = 4/x$.

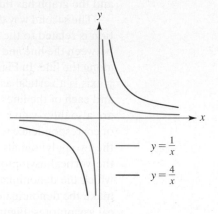

$$ y = \frac{1}{x} $$

$$ y = \frac{4}{x} $$

**Figure 3**

Once we know about the graph of $y = k/x$, we can graph any rational function of the form

$$ y = \frac{ax + b}{cx + d} $$

The next three examples show how this is done using the translation and reflection techniques explained in Section 3.4.

$$ y = \frac{1}{x-1} $$

Asymptote: $x = 1$

**Figure 4**
The graph of $y = 1/(x - 1)$

---

**EXAMPLE**    **1**    **Graphing a translate of $y = 1/x$**

Graph: $y = 1/(x - 1)$.

**SOLUTION**
By translating the graph of $y = 1/x$ one unit to the right, we obtain the graph of $y = 1/(x - 1)$, shown in Figure 4. Notice that the horizontal asymptote is unchanged by the translation. However, the vertical asymptote moves one unit to the right. (The $y$-intercept is $-1$; why?)

---

**EXAMPLE**    **2**    **Two graphs obtained from that of $y = 2/x$**

Graph: $y = 2/(x - 1)$ and $y = -2/(x - 1)$.

**SOLUTION**
The graph of $y = 2/(x - 1)$ has the same basic shape and location as the graph of $y = 1/(x - 1)$ shown in Figure 4. As a further guide to sketching $y = 2/(x - 1)$, we can pick several convenient $x$-values on either side of the asymptote $x = 1$ and then compute the corresponding $y$-values. After doing this, we obtain the graph shown in Figure 5(a). By reflecting this graph about the $x$-axis, we obtain the graph of $y = -2/(x - 1)$, which is shown in Figure 5(b).

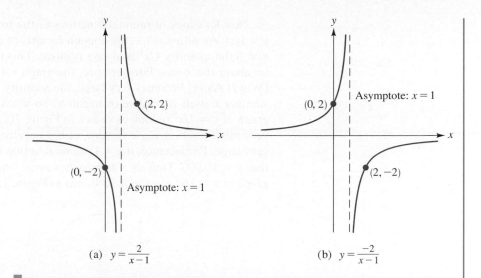

Figure 5

(a) $y = \dfrac{2}{x-1}$

(b) $y = \dfrac{-2}{x-1}$

 **EXAMPLE** 3 **Long division as an aid in graphing**

Graph: $y = \dfrac{4x-2}{x-1}$.

**SOLUTION**
First, as you can readily check, the $x$- and $y$-intercepts are $1/2$ and $2$, respectively. Next, using long division, we find that

$$\frac{4x-2}{x-1} = 4 + \frac{2}{x-1}$$

[If you need a review of (or reintroduction to) the long division process from basic or intermediate algebra, see Section 12.2.] We conclude that the required graph can be obtained by moving the graph of $y = 2/(x-1)$ up four units in the $y$-direction; see Figure 6. Notice that the vertical asymptote is still $x = 1$, but the horizontal asymptote is now $y = 4$ instead of the $x$-axis.

Figure 6

The graph of $y = \dfrac{4x-2}{x-1}$

Now let's look at rational functions of the form $y = 1/x^n$. First we'll consider $y = 1/x^2$. As with $y = 1/x$, the domain consists of all real numbers except $x = 0$. For $x \neq 0$ the quantity $1/x^2$ is always positive. This means that the graph will always lie above the $x$-axis. Furthermore, the graph will be symmetric about the $y$-axis. (Why?) As $|x|$ becomes very large, the quantity $1/x^2$ approaches zero; this is true whether $x$ itself is positive or negative. So when $|x|$ is very large, we expect the graph of $y = 1/x^2$ to look as shown in Figure 7(a). On the other hand, when $x$ is a very small fraction, close to zero, either negative or positive, the quantity $1/x^2$ is very large. For instance, if $x = 1/10$, we find that $y = 100$, and if $x = 1/100$, we find that $y = 10,000$. Thus as $x$ approaches zero, from the right or from the left, the graph of $y = 1/x^2$ must look as shown in Figure 7(b).

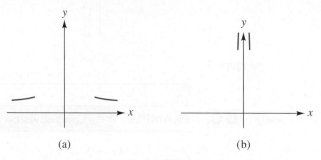

Figure 7

(a)          (b)

Now, by plotting several points and taking Figures 7(a) and 7(b) into account, we obtain the graph of $y = 1/x^2$, shown in Figure 8. Also, by following a similar line of reasoning, we find that the graph of $y = 1/x^3$ looks as shown in Figure 9. Note that the graph of $y = 1/x^3$ is symmetric about the origin, and the graph of $y = 1/x^2$ is symmetric about the $y$-axis.

In general, when $n$ is an even integer greater than 2, the graph of $y = 1/x^n$ resembles that of $y = 1/x^2$. When $n$ is an odd integer greater than 3, the graph of $y = 1/x^n$ resembles that of $y = 1/x^3$.

Figure 8
The graph of $y = 1/x^2$

Figure 9
The graph of $y = 1/x^3$

---

**EXAMPLE**   **4**    **A graph based on that of $y = 1/x^2$**

Graph: $y = -1/(x + 3)^2$.

**SOLUTION**
Refer to Figure 10. Begin with the graph of $y = 1/x^2$. By moving the graph three units to the left, we obtain the graph of $y = 1/(x + 3)^2$. Then by re-

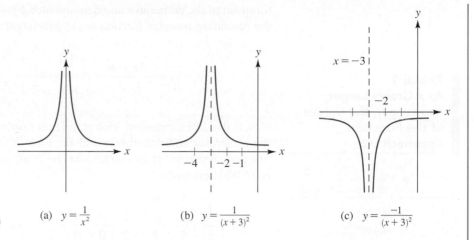

Figure 10

(a) $y = \dfrac{1}{x^2}$

(b) $y = \dfrac{1}{(x+3)^2}$

(c) $y = \dfrac{-1}{(x+3)^2}$

flecting the graph of $y = 1/(x + 3)^2$ about the $x$-axis, we get the graph of $y = -1/(x + 3)^2$.

*Question*: What are the $y$-intercepts in Figures 10(b) and 10(c)?

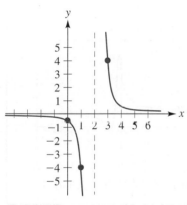

Figure 11
The graph of $y = 4/(x - 2)^3$

### EXAMPLE 5   A graph based on that of $y = 1/x^3$

Graph: $y = 4/(x - 2)^3$.

**SOLUTION**
Moving the graph of $y = 1/x^3$ two units to the right gives us the graph of the function $y = 1/(x - 2)^3$. The graph of $y = 4/(x - 2)^3$ will have the same basic shape and location. As a further guide to sketching the required graph, we can pick several convenient $x$-values near the asymptote $x = 2$ and compute the corresponding $y$-values. Using $x = 0, x = 1$, and $x = 3$, we find that the points $(0, -\frac{1}{2})$, $(1, -4)$, and $(3, 4)$ are on the graph. With this information, the graph can be sketched as in Figure 11.

As we have seen in Examples 1 through 5, the vertical asymptotes of $y = f(x)/g(x)$ are found by solving the equation $g(x) = 0$, provided that $f$ and $g$ are polynomials with no common factors other than constants. In Example 6 we determine the horizontal asymptote by comparing the highest powers of $x$ in the numerator and denominator.

### EXAMPLE 6   Finding a horizontal asymptote

Determine the horizontal asymptote for the graph of $y = \dfrac{x^2 - 5x + 6}{2x^2 - 4x + 3}$.

**SOLUTION**
The strategy is to factor out the highest power of $x$ that occurs in the numerator and do the same for the denominator. Then reduce the ratio of powers of $x$ fac-

tored out of the numerator and denominator. Finally, determine the behavior of the remaining complex fraction as $|x|$ gets larger and larger. We have

$$y = \frac{x^2 - 5x + 6}{2x^2 - 4x + 3} = \frac{x^2\left(1 - \dfrac{5}{x} + \dfrac{6}{x^2}\right)}{x^2\left(2 - \dfrac{4}{x} + \dfrac{3}{x^2}\right)} = \frac{1 - \dfrac{5}{x} + \dfrac{6}{x^2}}{2 - \dfrac{4}{x} + \dfrac{3}{x^2}}$$

Now, in that last expression, look at the four resulting fractions appearing within the numerator and denominator of the main fraction: $5/x$, $6/x^2$, $4/x$, and $3/x^2$. The point is that as $|x|$ gets larger and larger, all four of those fractions approach zero. We therefore have

$$y = \frac{1 - \dfrac{5}{x} + \dfrac{6}{x^2}}{2 - \dfrac{4}{x} + \dfrac{3}{x^2}} \approx \frac{1 - 0 + 0}{2 - 0 + 0} = \frac{1}{2} \qquad \text{as } |x| \text{ gets larger and larger}$$

This tells us that the line $y = 1/2$ is a horizontal asymptote for the graph of the given function. See Table 1 and Figure 12 for numerical and graphical perspectives.

### TABLE 1
### As x Grows Larger and Larger, the Values of the Function Approach 0.5

| $x$ | $y = \dfrac{x^2 - 5x + 6}{2x^2 - 4x + 3}$ |
|---|---|
| 10 | 0.343558 … |
| $10^2$ | 0.484925 … |
| $10^3$ | 0.498499 … |
| $10^4$ | 0.499849 … |
| $10^5$ | 0.499984 … |
| $10^6$ | 0.499998 … |

**GRAPHICAL PERSPECTIVE**

(a) $[-8, 8, 8]$ by $[-1, 3, 1]$

(b) $[-25, 25, 25]$ by $[-1, 3, 1]$

**Figure 12**
Two views of the rational function
$y = \dfrac{x^2 - 5x + 6}{2x^2 - 4x + 3}$ (red) with horizontal asymptote $y = 1/2$ (blue)

---

### EXAMPLE 7 Using rational functions to model bacterial growth

A group of agricultural scientists has been studying how the growth of a particular type of bacteria is affected by the acidity level of the soil. One colony of the bacteria is placed in a soil that is slightly acidic. A second colony of the same size is placed in a neutral soil. Suppose that after analyzing the data, the scientists determine that the size of each population over time can be modeled by the following functions.

colony in neutral soil:  $y = (2t + 1)/(t + 1)$   $t \geq 0$
colony in acidic soil:  $y = (4t + 3)/(t^2 + 3)$   $t \geq 0$

In both cases, $y$ represents the population, in thousands, after $t$ hours. Figure 13 shows the graphs of these two population functions over the first hour of the

**Figure 13**
Population models for two colonies of bacteria

experiment. (Note from both the graphs and the equations that each colony begins with 1000 bacteria.) Find the horizontal asymptotes for each graph and thereby determine the long-term behavior of each colony.

**SOLUTION**

*Colony in neutral soil:*

$$y = \frac{2t + 1}{t + 1}$$

$$= \frac{t(2 + 1/t)}{t(1 + 1/t)} \qquad \begin{array}{l} \text{factoring out } t \\ \text{from the top} \\ \text{and bottom} \end{array}$$

$$= \frac{2 + 1/t}{1 + 1/t}$$

$$\approx \frac{2 + 0}{1 + 0} = 2 \qquad \begin{array}{l} \text{as } t \text{ gets larger} \\ \text{and larger} \end{array}$$

*Colony in acidic soil:*

$$y = \frac{4t + 3}{t^2 + 3}$$

$$= \frac{t^2(4/t + 3/t^2)}{t^2(1 + 3/t^2)} \qquad \begin{array}{l} \text{factoring out } t^2 \\ \text{from the top} \\ \text{and bottom} \end{array}$$

$$= \frac{4/t + 3/t^2}{1 + 3/t^2}$$

$$\approx \frac{0 + 0}{1 + 0} = 0 \qquad \begin{array}{l} \text{as } t \text{ gets larger} \\ \text{and larger} \end{array}$$

For the colony in neutral soil, the horizontal asymptote for the growth function is $y = 2$. So in the long run, this colony approaches a population of 2000. For the colony in acidic soil, the horizontal asymptote is $y = 0$ and the population approaches extinction (or becomes extinct, depending on the interpretation). See Figure 14.

**GRAPHICAL PERSPECTIVE**

**Figure 14**
Snapshots of the population functions after $t = 8$ hr and $t = 24$ hr. The vertical axis is the population $y$, in thousands.

$$\text{———} \quad y = (2t + 1)/(t + 1) \quad \text{(colony in neutral soil)}$$
$$\text{———} \quad y = (4t + 3)/(t^2 + 3) \quad \text{(colony in slightly acidic soil)}$$

**EXAMPLE  8   Graphing a rational function**

Graph the function $y = \dfrac{x^2 - x - 6}{x^2 - x - 2} = \dfrac{(x - 3)(x + 2)}{(x + 1)(x - 2)}$.

**SOLUTION**

By looking at the factored form of the fraction, we see that the $x$-intercepts are 3 and $-2$. Also, the vertical asymptotes are the lines $x = -1$ and $x = 2$. For the $y$-intercept it's a bit simpler to set $x = 0$ in the unfactored, rather than factored, expression. As you can check, the result in either case is that the $y$-intercept is 3. The horizontal asymptote works out to be the line $y = 1$; you should verify this for yourself using the method demonstrated in the previous two examples.

Now we want to see how the graph looks in the immediate vicinity of the $x$-intercepts and the vertical asymptotes. To do this, we use the approximation technique explained in the previous section for polynomial functions. Let's start with the $x$-intercept at $x = 3$. As in Section 4.6, we'll retain the factor $x - 3$ and approximate the remaining factors using $x = 3$. So for $x$ near 3 we have

$$y = \frac{(x - 3)(x + 2)}{(x + 1)(x - 2)} \approx \frac{(x - 3)(3 + 2)}{(3 + 1)(3 - 2)} = \frac{5}{4}(x - 3)$$

Thus in the immediate vicinity of the $x$-intercept $x = 3$, the required graph will closely resemble the line $y = \frac{5}{4}(x - 3)$. The remaining calculations for approximating the graph near the other $x$-intercept and near the two vertical asymptotes are carried out in exactly the same manner. As Exercise 43 will ask you to verify, the results are

$$x \text{ near } 3: \quad y \approx \frac{5}{4}(x - 3) \qquad x \text{ near } -1: \quad y \approx \frac{4/3}{x + 1}$$

$$x \text{ near } -2: \quad y \approx -\frac{5}{4}(x + 2) \qquad x \text{ near } 2: \quad y \approx \frac{-4/3}{x - 2}$$

We summarize these results as follows. As the graph passes through the points $(3, 0)$ and $(-2, 0)$, it resembles the lines $y = \frac{5}{4}(x - 3)$ and $y = -\frac{5}{4}(x + 2)$, respectively. Near the vertical asymptote $x = -1$, the graph has the same basic shape as $y = 1/(x + 1)$, and near the vertical asymptote $x = 2$, the graph resembles $y = -1/(x - 2)$; see Figure 15.

**Figure 15**

The graph of $y = \dfrac{(x - 3)(x + 2)}{(x + 1)(x - 2)}$
near its $x$-intercepts and vertical asymptotes

**Figure 16**

The graph of $y = \dfrac{(x-3)(x+2)}{(x+1)(x-2)}$ near $x$-intercepts and its horizontal and vertical asymptotes

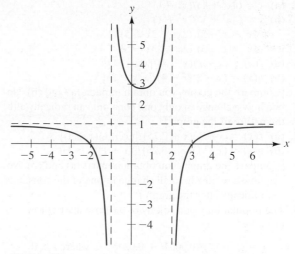

**Figure 17**

The graph of $y = \dfrac{(x-3)(x+2)}{(x+1)(x-2)}$

| TABLE 2 When $\|x\|$ Is Large, $y$ Is Less Than 1 | |
| --- | --- |
| $x$ | $y$ |
| 10 | 0.95 |
| 100 | 0.99 |
| −10 | 0.96 |
| −100 | 0.9996 |

Finally, we want to find out how the graph approaches the horizontal asymptote $y = 1$. Perhaps the simplest way is to do some calculations. In Table 2 we have computed the outputs for some relatively large values of $|x|$. From the table we see that when $|x|$ is large, $y$ is less than 1. Graphically, this means that the curve approaches the asymptote $y = 1$ from below. In Figure 16 we summarize what we have discovered up to this point. Then, using Figure 16 as a guide, we can sketch the required graph, as shown in Figure 17.

NOTE   In this example the coordinates of the lowest point on the graph in the interval $-1 < x < 2$ can be found by applying algebraic techniques. See Exercise 46 for the details.

# EXERCISE SET 4.7

**A**

*In Exercises 1–8:*

**(a)** *Find the domain, x- and y-intercepts, vertical asymptotes, and horizontal asymptotes for each rational function.*

Ⓖ **(b)** *Use a graphing utility to graph the function. Check to see that the graph is consistent with your results in part (a).*

**1.** $y = (3x + 15)/(4x - 12)$
**2.** $y = (x + 6)(x + 4)/(x - 1)^2$
**3.** $y = (6x^2 - 5x + 1)/(2x^2)$
**4.** $y = x/(x^2 + x + 1)$
**5.** $y = (x^2 - 9)/(4x^2 - 1)$
**6.** $y = (x^2 - 9)/(4x^2 + 1)$
**7.** $y = (3x^2 - 2x - 8)/(2x^3 + x^2 - 3x)$
**8.** $y = (x^3 - 27)/(x^4 - 2x^3 + 9x^2 - 18x)$

*In Exercises 9–34, sketch the graph of each rational function. Specify the intercepts and the asymptotes.*

**9.** $y = 1/(x + 4)$
**10.** $y = -1/(x + 4)$
**11.** $y = 3/(x + 2)$
**12.** $y = -3/(x + 2)$
**13.** $y = -2/(x - 3)$
**14.** $y = (x - 1)/(x + 1)$
**15.** $y = (x - 3)/(x - 1)$
**16.** $y = 2x/(x + 3)$
**17.** $y = (4x - 2)/(2x + 1)$
**18.** $y = (3x + 2)/(x - 3)$
**19.** $y = 1/(x - 2)^2$
**20.** $y = -1/(x - 2)^2$
**21.** $y = 3/(x + 1)^2$
**22.** $y = -3/(x + 1)^2$
**23.** $y = 1/(x + 2)^3$
**24.** $y = -1/(x + 2)^3$
**25.** $y = -4/(x + 5)^3$
**26.** $y = x/[(x + 1)(x - 3)]$
**27.** $y = -x/[(x + 2)(x - 2)]$
**28.** $y = 2x/(x + 1)^2$
**29.** **(a)** $y = 3x/[(x - 1)(x + 3)]$
   **(b)** $y = 3x^2/[(x - 1)(x + 3)]$

**30. (a)** $y = (4x^2 + 1)/(x^2 - 1)$
   **(b)** $y = (4x^2 + 1)/(x^2 + 1)$
**31.** $y = (4x^2 + x - 5)/(2x^2 - 3x - 5)$
**32.** $y = (4x^2 - x - 3)/(2x^2 - 3x - 5)$
**Ⓖ 33. (a)** $f(x) = (x - 2)(x - 4)/[x(x - 1)]$
   **(b)** $g(x) = (x - 2)(x - 4)/[x(x - 3)]$
   [Compare the graphs you obtain in parts (a) and (b). Notice how a change in only one constant can radically alter the nature of the graph.]
**Ⓖ 34. (a)** $f(x) = (x - 1)(x + 2.75)/[(x + 1)(x + 3)]$
   **(b)** $g(x) = (x - 1)(x + 3.25)/[(x + 1)(x + 3)]$
   [Compare the graphs you obtain in parts (a) and (b). Notice how a relatively small change in one of the constants can radically alter the graph.]
**35.** The population $y$ of a colony of bacteria after $t$ hr is given by

$$y = (t + 12)/(0.0004t + 0.024) \qquad \text{where } t \geq 0$$

   **(a)** Find the initial population (that is, the population when $t = 0$ hr).
   **(b)** Determine the long-term behavior of the population (as in Example 7).
**36.** The population $y$ (in thousands) of a colony of bacteria after $t$ hr is given by

$$y = (6t + 12)/(2t + 1) \qquad \text{where } t \geq 0$$

   **(a)** Find the initial population and the long-term population. Which is larger?
 **(b)** Use a graphing utility to graph the population function. Is the function increasing or decreasing? Check that your response here is consistent with your answers in part (a).

## B

**37.** A desktop publisher designing a small rectangular poster decides to make the area 500 in.$^2$ The margins on the top and bottom of the poster are to be 3 in. and 4 in., respectively. The left and right margins are each to be 1.5 in.

|◄——— $x$ ———►|

   **(a)** Express the area of the printed portion of the poster as a function of $x$, the width of the entire poster. (The gray region in the figure represents the printed area.)

Ⓖ **(b)** Use a graphing utility to graph the area function that you found in part (a).

Ⓖ **(c)** Use a ZOOM feature to estimate (to the nearest one-tenth) the width $x$ for which the printed area is a maximum. What is the corresponding length of the poster in this case?

**38.** The accompanying figure gives formulas for the volume $V$ and total surface area $S$ of a circular cylinder with radius $r$ and height $h$. For a cylinder of given volume we are interested in finding the dimensions that minimize the surface area.

$$V = \pi r^2 h$$
$$S = 2\pi r^2 + 2\pi rh$$

   **(a)** Assume that the volume of the cylinder is 1000 cm$^3$. Express the surface area as a function of the radius. After combining terms in your answer, show that the resulting function can be written

$$S(r) = \frac{2\pi r^3 + 2000}{r} \qquad (r > 0)$$

Ⓖ **(b)** Use a graphing utility to graph the surface area function obtained in part (a).

Ⓖ **(c)** Estimate, to the nearest one-hundredth, the radius $r$ that minimizes the surface area. What is the corresponding value for $h$?

*In Exercises 39–42, graph the functions. Note: In each case, the graph crosses its horizontal asymptote once. To find the point where the rational function $y = f(x)$ crosses its horizontal asymptote $y = k$, you'll need to solve the equation $f(x) = k$.*

**39.** $y = \dfrac{(x - 4)(x + 2)}{(x - 1)(x - 3)}$

**40.** $y = \dfrac{(x - 1)(x - 3)}{(x + 1)^2}$

**41.** $y = \dfrac{(x + 1)^2}{(x - 1)(x - 3)}$

**42.** $y = \dfrac{2x^2 - 3x - 2}{x^2 - 3x - 4}$

**43.** (This exercise refers to Example 8.) Let

$$y = \frac{(x - 3)(x + 2)}{(x + 1)(x - 2)}$$

Verify each of the following approximations.
   **(a)** When $x$ is close to $-2$, then $y \approx -\frac{5}{4}(x + 2)$.
   **(b)** When $x$ is close to $-1$, then $y \approx \dfrac{4/3}{x + 1}$.
   **(c)** When $x$ is close to 2, then $y \approx \dfrac{-4/3}{x - 2}$.

*In Exercises 44 and 45, graph the functions. Notice in each case that the numerator and denominator contain at least one common factor. Thus you can simplify each quotient; but don't lose track of the domain of the function as it was initially defined.*

**44.** (a) $y = \dfrac{x+2}{x+2}$   (c) $y = \dfrac{x-1}{(x-1)(x-2)}$

   (b) $y = \dfrac{x^2-4}{x-2}$

**45.** (a) $y = \dfrac{x^2-9}{x+3}$

   (b) $y = \dfrac{x^2-5x+6}{x^2-2x-3}$

   (c) $y = \dfrac{(x-1)(x-2)(x-3)}{(x-1)(x-2)(x-3)(x-4)}$

**46.** This exercise shows you how to determine the coordinates of the lowest point on the middle branch of the curve in Figure 17. The basic idea is as follows. Suppose that the required coordinates are $(h, k)$. Then the horizontal line $y = k$ is the unique horizontal line intersecting the curve in one and only one point. (Any other horizontal line intersects the curve either in two points or not at all.) In steps (a) through (c) that follow, we use these observations to determine the point $(h, k)$.

   **(a)** Given any horizontal line $y = k$, its intersection with the curve in Figure 17 is determined by solving the following pair of simultaneous equations:

   $$\begin{cases} y = k \\ y = \dfrac{x^2-x-6}{x^2-x-2} \end{cases}$$

   In the second equation of the system, replace $y$ with $k$ and show that the resulting equation can be written

   $$(k-1)x^2 - (k-1)x + (6-2k) = 0 \qquad (1)$$

   **(b)** If $k$ is indeed the required $y$-coordinate, then equation (1) must have exactly one real solution. Set the discriminant of the quadratic equation equal to zero to obtain

   $$(k-1)^2 - 4(k-1)(6-2k) = 0$$

   and deduce from this that $k = 1$ or $k = 25/9$. The solution $k = 1$ can be discarded. (To see why, look at Figure 17.)

   **(c)** Using the value $y = 25/9$, show that the corresponding $x$-coordinate is $1/2$. Thus, the required point is $(\frac{1}{2}, \frac{25}{9})$.

**47.** Graph the function $y = x/(x-3)^2$. Use the technique explained in Exercise 46 to find the coordinates of any turning points on the graph.

**48.** Graph the function $y = 2/(x-x^2)$. Use the technique explained in Exercise 46 to find the coordinates of any turning points on the graph.

*An asymptote that is neither horizontal nor vertical is called a **slant** or **oblique asymptote**. For example, as indicated in the*

*following figure, the line $y = x$ is a slant asymptote for the graph of $y = (x^2 + 1)/x$. To understand why the line $y = x$ is an asymptote, we carry out the indicated division and write the function in the form*

$$y = x + \frac{1}{x} \qquad (2)$$

*From equation (2) we see that if $|x|$ is very large then $y \approx x + 0$; that is, $y \approx x$, as we wished to show. Equation (2) actually tells us more than this. When $|x|$ is very close to zero, equation (2) yields $y \approx 0 + (1/x)$. In other words, as we approach the y-axis, the curve looks more and more like the graph of $y = 1/x$. In general, if we have a rational function $f(x)/g(x)$ in which the degree of $f(x)$ is 1 greater than the degree of $g(x)$, then the graph has a slant asymptote that is obtained as follows. Divide $f(x)$ by $g(x)$ to obtain an equation of the form*

$$\frac{f(x)}{g(x)} = (mx + b) + \frac{h(x)}{g(x)}$$

*where the degree of $h(x)$ is less than the degree of $g(x)$. Then the equation of the slant asymptote is $y = mx + b$. (For instance, using the previous example, we have $y = mx + b - x$ and $h(x)/g(x) = 1/x$.) In Exercises 49–51, you are asked to graph functions that have slant asymptotes.*

**49.** Let $y = F(x) = \dfrac{x^2 + x - 6}{x - 3}$.

   **(a)** Use long division to show that

   $$\frac{x^2 + x - 6}{x - 3} = (x + 4) + \frac{6}{x - 3}$$

   **(b)** The result in part (a) shows that the line $y = x + 4$ is a slant asymptote for the graph of the function $F$. Verify this fact empirically by completing the following two tables.

| $x$ | $x + 4$ | $\dfrac{x^2 + x - 6}{x - 3}$ |
|---|---|---|
| 10 | | |
| 100 | | |
| 1000 | | |

*(continues)*

| $x$ | $x + 4$ | $\dfrac{x^2 + x - 6}{x - 3}$ |
|-----|---------|------------------------------|
| $-10$ | | |
| $-100$ | | |
| $-1000$ | | |

**(c)** Determine the vertical asymptote and the $x$- and $y$-intercepts of the graph of $F$.

**(d)** Graph the function $F$. (Use the techniques in this section along with the fact that $y = x + 4$ is a slant asymptote.)

**(e)** Use the technique explained in Exercise 46 to find the coordinates of the two turning points on the graph of $F$.

**50. (a)** Show that the line $y = x - 2$ is a slant asymptote for the graph of $F(x) = x^2/(x + 2)$.

**(b)** Sketch the graph of $F$.

**51.** Show that the line $y = -x$ is a slant asymptote for the graph of $y = (1 - x^2)/x$. Then sketch the graph of this function.

**52.** Let $f(x) = (x^3 + 2x^2 + 1)/(x^2 + 2x)$.

Ⓖ **(a)** Graph the function $f$ using a viewing rectangle extending from $-5$ to $5$ in both the $x$- and $y$-directions.

Ⓖ **(b)** Add the graph of the line $y = x$ to your picture in part (a). Note that to the right of the origin, as $x$ increases, the graph of $f$ begins to look more and more like the line $y = x$. This also occurs to the left of the origin as $x$ decreases.

**(c)** The results in part (b) suggest that the line $y = x$ may be an asymptote for the graph of $f$. Verify this visually by changing the viewing rectangle so that it extends from $-20$ to $20$ in both the $x$- and the $y$-directions. What do you observe?

**(d)** Using algebra, verify the identity

$$\frac{x^3 + 2x^2 + 1}{x^2 + 2x} = \frac{1}{x^2 + 2x} + x$$

Then explain why, for large values of $|x|$, the graph of $f$ looks more and more like the line $y = x$.  *Hint:* Substitute some large numbers (such as 100 or 1000) into the expression $1/(x^2 + 2x)$. What happens?

**53.** Let $f(x) = (x^5 + 1)/x^2$.

Ⓖ **(a)** Graph the function $f$ using a viewing rectangle that extends from $-4$ to $4$ in the $x$-direction and from $-8$ to $8$ in the $y$-direction.

Ⓖ **(b)** Add the graph of the curve $y = x^3$ to your picture in part (a). Note that as $|x|$ increases (that is, as $x$ moves away from the origin), the graph of $f$ looks more and more like the curve $y = x^3$. For additional perspective, first change the viewing rectangle so that $y$ extends from $-20$ to $20$. (Retain the $x$-settings for the moment.) Describe what you see. Next, adjust the viewing rectangle so that $x$ extends from $-10$ to $10$ and $y$ extends from $-100$ to $100$. Summarize your observations.

**(c)** In the text we said that a line is an asymptote for a curve if the distance between the line and the curve approaches zero as we move further and further out along the curve. The work in part (b) illustrates that a *curve* can behave like an asymptote for another curve. In particular, part (b) illustrates that the distance between the curve $y = x^3$ and the graph of the given function $f$ approaches zero as we move further and further out along the graph of $f$. That is, the curve $y = x^3$ is an "asymptote" for the graph of the given function $f$. Complete the following two tables for a numerical perspective on this. In the tables, $d$ denotes the vertical distance between the curve $y = x^3$ and the graph of $f$:

$$d = \left| \frac{x^5 + 1}{x^2} - x^3 \right|$$

| $x$ | 5 | 10 | 50 | 100 | 500 |
|-----|---|-----|-----|------|------|
| $d$ | | | | | |

| $x$ | $-5$ | $-10$ | $-50$ | $-100$ | $-500$ |
|-----|------|-------|-------|--------|--------|
| $d$ | | | | | |

**(d)** Parts (b) and (c) have provided both a graphical and a numerical perspective. For an algebraic perspective that ties together the previous results, verify the following identity, and then use it to explain why the results in parts (b) and (c) were inevitable:

$$\frac{x^5 + 1}{x^2} = x^3 + \frac{1}{x^2}$$

## PROJECT

### FINDING SOME MINIMUM VALUES WITHOUT USING CALCULUS

In this project you'll solve some minimum problems that involve rational functions. The theorem that we'll rely on is given in the box that follows. Methods for establishing this theorem are indicated in Question 3 at the end of this project. (This theorem can be stated in a more general form for $n$ positive quantities, rather than two or three, but we won't need that for the applications in this project.)

---

### THEOREM   On Minimum Sums

(a) If the product of two positive quantities $s$ and $t$ is constant, then their sum $s + t$ is a minimum if and only if $s = t$.

(b) If the product of three positive quantities $s$, $t$, and $u$ is constant, then their sum $s + t + u$ is a minimum if and only if $s = t = u$.

---

First, just to get a feeling for what part (a) of the theorem is saying, complete the following two tables, and in each case note which pair of numbers $a$ and $b$ yields the smallest sum.

| $a$ | $b$ | $ab$ | $a + b$ |
|-----|-----|------|---------|
| 1 | 36 | | |
| 2 | 18 | | |
| 3 | 12 | | |
| 4 | 9 | | |
| 6 | 6 | | |

| $a$ | $b$ | $ab$ | $a + b$ |
|-----|-----|------|---------|
| 1 | 12 | | |
| 2 | 6 | | |
| 3 | 4 | | |
| $3\frac{1}{2}$ | $3\frac{3}{7}$ | | |
| $2\sqrt{3}$ | $2\sqrt{3}$ | | |

**1.** Use part (a) of the theorem to solve the following problems.

   **(a)** Find the smallest possible value for the sum of a positive number and its reciprocal.

   **(b)** The accompanying figure shows a line with slope $m$ ($m < 0$) passing through the point $(2, 1)$. Find the smallest possible area for the triangle that is formed. *Hint*: First use the point–slope formula to write the equation of a line with slope $m$ that passes through the point $(2, 1)$. Next, find the $x$- and $y$-intercepts of the line in terms of $m$. Then express the area of the triangle in terms of $m$ and find a way to apply part (a) of the theorem.

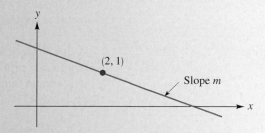

2. Use part (b) of the theorem to solve the following problems.

   (a) After using a graphing utility to estimate the minimum value of the function $f(x) = x^2 + \dfrac{1}{x}$ for $x > 0$, find the exact value for this minimum.

   *Hint*: Write $x^2 + \dfrac{1}{x}$ as $x^2 + \dfrac{1}{2x} + \dfrac{1}{2x}$.

   (b) Use a graphing utility to estimate the minimum value of the function $g(x) = (2x^3 + 3)/x$ for $x > 0$. Then find the exact minimum. (Adapt the hint in the previous exercise.)

   (c) A box with a square base and no top is to be constructed. The volume is to be 27 ft$^3$. Find the dimensions of the box so that the surface area is a minimum.

   (d) In Exercise 38 on page 314, a graphing utility is used to estimate the minimum possible surface area for a circular cylinder with a volume 1000 cm$^3$. Find the exact value for this minimum. Also confirm the following fact: For the values of $r$ and $h$ that yield the minimum surface area, we have $2r = h$.

3. (a) *Proof for part (a) of the theorem:*   Verify that the following simple identity holds for all real numbers $a$ and $b$.

   $$(a + b)^2 = 4ab + (a - b)^2$$

   Then use this identity to explain why part(a) of the theorem is valid. *Suggestion*: First discuss the reasoning within a group; then, on your own, write a paragraph carefully explaining the reasoning in your own words.

   (b) *Proof for part (b) of the theorem:*   Use the result in Exercise 44 of Section 2.3 to explain why part (b) of the theorem is valid.

# Chapter 4

# Summary of Principal Terms

| Terms | Page reference | Comments |
|---|---|---|
| **1.** Linear function | 213 | A linear function is a function of the form $f(x) = Ax + B$, where $A$ and $B$ are constants. The graph of a linear function is a straight line. An important idea that arose in several of the examples is that the slope of a line can be interpreted as a rate of change. Two instances of this are marginal cost and velocity. |
| **2.** Quadratic function | 230 | A quadratic function is a function of the form $f(x) = ax^2 + bx + c$, where $a$, $b$, and $c$ are constants and $a$ is not zero. The graph of a quadratic function is a parabola. See the Property Summaries on pages 233 and 235. |
| **3.** Fixed point | 246 | A fixed point of a function $f$ is an input $x$ in the domain of $f$ such that $f(x) = x$. For example, $x = 1$ is a fixed point for $f(x) = \sqrt{x}$ because $f(1) = \sqrt{1} = 1$. |

| Terms | Page reference | Comments |
|---|---|---|
| **4.** Vertex formula | 273 | The $x$-coordinate of the vertex of the parabola $y = ax^2 + bx + c$ is given by $x = -b/2a$. |
| **5.** Polynomial function | 288 | A polynomial function is a function of the form $$f(x) = a_n x^n + a_{n-1} x^{n-1} + \cdots + a_1 x + a_0$$ where $n$ is a nonnegative integer and $a_0, a_1, \ldots,$ and $a_n$ are constants. Three basic properties of polynomial functions are summarized in the box on page 293. If $a_n \neq 0$, the degree of the polynomial is $n$, the largest exponent on the input variable. |
| **6.** Rational function | 304 | A rational function is a function of the form $y = f(x)/g(x)$, where $f(x)$ and $g(x)$ are polynomials. |
| **7.** Asymptote | 305 | A line is said to be an asymptote for a curve if the distance between the line and the curve approaches zero as we move out farther and farther along the line. |

## Writing Mathematics

1. At the start of Section 4.6 is a quotation by David Berlinski describing polynomial functions. Reread the quotation, and then write a paragraph or two explaining its contents using the ideas and terminology from Section 4.6. With the aid of a graphing utility, use examples as appropriate to illustrate your points.
2. Consider the following two problems.

### PROBLEM 1
The perimeter of a rectangle is 2 m.
(i) Express the area as a function of the width $w$.
(ii) Find the maximum possible area.

### PROBLEM 2
The area of a rectangle is 2 m$^2$.
(i) Express the perimeter as a function of the width $w$.
(ii) Find the minimum possible perimeter.

   **(a)** After working out Problem 1 for yourself, write out the solution in complete sentences, as if you were explaining it to a classmate or to your instructor. Be sure to let the reader know where you are headed and why each of the main steps is necessary.
   **(b)** After working out part (i) of Problem 2 for yourself, write out the solution to part (i) in complete sentences.
   **(c)** Explain why the methods of Section 4.5 are not applicable for solving part (ii) of Problem 2.

**(d)** The following result is known as the *arithmetic-geometric mean inequality:*

> *For all nonnegative real numbers a and b we have $a + b \geq 2\sqrt{ab}$, with equality holding if and only if $a = b$.*

By working with classmates or your instructor, find a way to apply this result in part (ii) of Problem 2. Then write out your solution in complete sentences. How does your final answer here compare with that in Problem 1?

---

## Chapter 4          Review Exercises

1. Find $G(0)$ if $G$ is a linear function such that $G(1) = -2$ and $G(-2) = -11$.

2. **(a)** Let $f(x) = 3x^2 + 6x - 10$. For which input $x$ is the value of the function a minimum? What is that minimum value?

   **(b)** Let $g(t) = 6t^2 - t^4$. For which input $t$ is the value of the function a maximum?

3. Suppose the function $p = -\frac{1}{8}x + 100$ $(0 \leq x \leq 12)$ relates the selling price $p$ of an item to the quantity $x$ that is sold. Assume that $p$ is in dollars. What is the maximum revenue possible in this situation?

4. Graph the function $y = -1(x + 1)^3$.

5. Graph the function $y = (x - 4)(x - 1)(x + 1)$.

6. Graph the function $f(x) = x^2 + 4x - 5$. Specify the vertex, the $x$- and $y$-intercepts, and the axis of symmetry.

7. A factory owner buys a new machine for $1000. After five years, the machine has a salvage value of $100. Assuming linear depreciation, find a formula for the value $V$ of the machine after $t$ yr, where $0 \leq t \leq 5$.

8. Graph the function $y = 2(x - 3)^4$. Does the graph cross the $y$-axis? If so, where?

9. Graph the function $y = (3x + 5)/(x + 2)$. Specify all intercepts and asymptotes.

10. What is the largest area possible for a right triangle in which the sum of the lengths of the two shorter sides is 12 cm?

11. Graph the function $y = x/[(x + 2)(x - 4)]$.

12. Let $P(x, y)$ be a point [other than $(-1, -1)$] on the graph of $f(x) = x^3$. Express the slope of the line passing through the points $P$ and $(-1, -1)$ as a function of $x$. Simplify your answer as much as possible.

13. A rectangle is inscribed in a circle. The circumference of the circle is 12 cm. Express the perimeter of the rectangle as a function of its width $w$.

14. Give a reason why each of the following two graphs cannot represent a polynomial function with highest-degree term $-\frac{1}{3}x^3$.

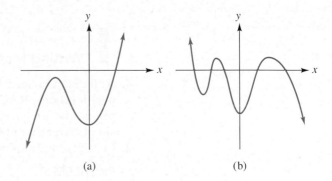

(a)                          (b)

*In Exercises 15–18, find equations for the linear functions satisfying the given conditions. Write each answer in the form $f(x) = mx + b$.*

15. $f(4) = -1$ and the graph of $f$ is parallel to the line $3x - 8y = 16$.

16. The graph passes through $(6, 1)$ and the $x$-intercept is twice the $y$-intercept.

17. $f(-3) = 5$, and the graph of the inverse function passes through $(2, 1)$.

18. The graph of $f$ passes through the vertices of the two parabolas $y = x^2 + 4x + 1$ and $y = \frac{1}{2}x^2 + 9x + \frac{81}{2}$.

*In Exercises 19–22, graph the quadratic functions. In each case, specify the vertex and the x- and y-intercepts.*

**19.** $y = x^2 + 2x - 3$    **20.** $f(x) = x^2 - 2x - 15$

**21.** $f(x) = 2x^2 - 2x + 1$    **22.** $y = -3x^2 + 12x$

**23.** Find the distance between the vertices of the two parabolas $y = x^2 - 4x + 6$ and $y = -x^2 - 4x - 5$.

**24.** Find the value of $a$, given that the maximum value of the function $f(x) = ax^2 + 3x - 4$ is 5.

**25.** Suppose that an object is thrown vertically upward (from ground level) with an initial velocity of $v_0$ ft/sec. It can be shown that the height $h$ (in feet) after $t$ sec is given by the formula $h = v_0 t - 16t^2$.

    **(a)** At what time does the object reach its maximum height? What is that maximum height?

    **(b)** At what time does the object strike the ground?

**26.** Let $f(x) = 4x^2 - x + 1$ and $g(x) = (x - 3)/2$.

    **(a)** For which input will the value of the function $f \circ g$ be a minimum?

    **(b)** For which input will the value of $g \circ f$ be a minimum?

**27.** Find all values of $b$ such that the minimum distance from the point $(2, 0)$ to the line $y = \frac{4}{3}x + b$ is 5.
*Hint:* Use the formula from Exercise 94 on page 77.

**28.** What number exceeds one-half its square by the greatest amount?

**29.** Suppose that $x + y = \sqrt{2}$. Find the minimum value of the quantity $x^2 + y^2$.

**30.** For which numbers $t$ will the value of $9t^2 - t^4$ be as large as possible?

**31.** Find the maximum area possible for a right triangle with a hypotenuse of 15 cm. *Hint:* Let $x$ denote the length of one leg. Show that the area is $A = x\sqrt{225 - x^2}/2$. Now work with $A^2$.

**32.** For which point $(x, y)$ on the curve $y = 1 - x^2$ is the sum $x + y$ a maximum?

**33.** Let $f(x) = x^2 - (a^2 + 2a)x + 2a^3$, where $0 < a < 2$. For which value of $a$ will the distance between the $x$-intercepts of the graph of $y = f(x)$ be a maximum?

**34.** Suppose that the function $p = 160 - \frac{1}{5}x$ relates the selling price $p$ of an item to the quantity $x$ that is sold. Assume that $p$ is in dollars. For which value of $x$ will the revenue $R$ be a maximum? What is the selling price $p$ in this case?

**35.** A piece of wire 16 cm long is cut into two pieces. Let $x$ denote the length of the first piece and $16 - x$ the length of the second. The first piece is formed into a rectangle in which the length is twice the width. The second piece of wire is also formed into a rectangle, but with the length three times the width. For which

value of $x$ is the total area of the two rectangles a minimum?

**36.** Find all real numbers that are fixed points of the given functions.

    **(a)** $f(x) = x^2 - 8$    **(c)** $y = 4x - x^3$

    **(b)** $g(x) = x^2 + 8$    **(d)** $y = 8x^2 - x - 15$

**37.** In the following figure, $PQRS$ is a square with sides parallel to the coordinate axes. The coordinates of points $A$ and $B$ are $A(a, 0)$ and $B(b, 0)$. Show that $f(a) = b$ and $f(b) = a$.

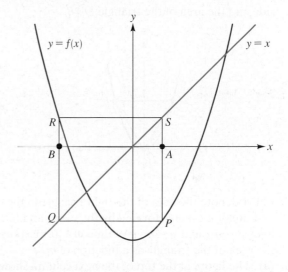

**38.** Let $f(x) = x^2 - 2$. Find two numbers $a$ and $b$ $(a \neq b)$ such that $f(a) = b$ and $f(b) = a$. *Hint:* To simplify the algebra, see part (a) of Exercise 35 on page 259.

*In Exercises 39–50, graph each function and specify the x- and y-intercepts and asymptotes, if any.*

**39.** $y = (x + 4)(x - 2)$    **40.** $y = (x + 4)(x - 2)^2$

**41.** $y = -x^2(x + 1)$    **42.** $y = -x^3(x + 1)$

**43.** $y = x(x - 2)(x + 2)$    **44.** $y = \dfrac{1 - 2x}{x}$

**45.** $y = \dfrac{-1}{(x - 1)^2}$    **46.** $y = \dfrac{x + 1}{x + 2}$

**47.** $y = \dfrac{x - 2}{x - 3}$    **48.** $y = \dfrac{x}{(x - 2)(x + 4)}$

**49.** $y = \dfrac{x^2 - 2x + 1}{x^2 - 4x + 4}$    **50.** $y = \dfrac{x(x - 2)}{(x - 4)(x + 4)}$

**51.** The range of the function $y = x^2 - 2x + k$ is the interval $[5, \infty)$. Find the value of $k$.

**52.** Find a value for $b$ such that the range of the function $f(x) = x^2 + bx + b$ is the interval $[-15, \infty)$.

**53.** Find the range of the function $y = \dfrac{(x-1)(x-3)}{x-4}$.

*Hint*: Solve the equation for $x$ in terms of $y$ using the quadratic formula. If you're careful with the algebra, you will find that the expression under the resulting radical sign is $y^2 - 8y + 4$. The range of the given function can then be found by solving the inequality $y^2 - 8y + 4 \geq 0$.

**54.** In the following figure, triangle $OAB$ is equilateral and $\overline{AB}$ is parallel to the $x$-axis. Find the length of a side and the area of the triangle $OAB$.

**55.** Let $A$ denote the area of the right triangle in the first quadrant that is formed by the $y$-axis and the lines $y = mx$ and $y = m$. (Assume $m > 0$.) Express the area of the triangle as a function of $m$.

**56. (a)** The figure at the top of the next column shows the parabola $y = x^2 - 6x$ and a circle that passes through the vertex and $x$-intercepts of the parabola. Find the center and radius of the circle.

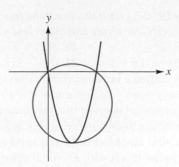

**(b)** Suppose that a circle passes through the vertex and $x$-intercepts of a parabola $y = x^2 - 2bx$, where $b > 0$. Show that the circumference of the circle as a function of $b$ is $c = \pi b^2 + \pi$.

**57.** In the accompanying figure, the radius of the circle is $OC = 1$. Express the area of $\triangle ABC$ as a function of $x$.

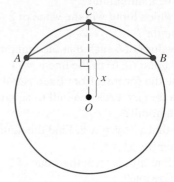

**58. (a)** Factor the expression $x^3 - 3x^2 + 4$.
*Hint*: Subtract and add 1, then factor by grouping.

**(b)** Use the factorization from part (a) to graph the function $y = x^3 - 3x^2 + 4$. Check your result using a graphing utility.

# Chapter 4    Test

**1.** A linear function $L$ satisfies the conditions $L(-2) = -4$ and $L(5) = 1$. Find $L(0)$.

**2. (a)** Let $F(x) = 4x - 2x^2$. What is the maximum value for this function? On which interval is this function increasing?

**(b)** Let $G(t) = 9t^4 + 6t^2 + 2$. For which value of $t$ is this function a minimum?

**3.** Let $f(x) = (x - 3)(x + 4)^2$.

**(a)** Determine the intercepts and the excluded regions for the graph of $f$.

**(b)** Determine the behavior of $f$ when $x$ is very close to $-4$.

**(c)** Sketch the graph of $f$.

4. Graph each function:
   (a) $y = -1/(x - 3)^3$
   (b) $y = -1/(x - 3)^2$

5. Graph the function $y = -x^2 + 7x + 6$. Specify the intercepts, the axis of symmetry, and the coordinates of the turning point.

6. Suppose that the function $p = -\frac{1}{6}x + 80$
   $(0 \le x \le 400)$ relates the selling price of an item to the quantity $x$ that is sold. Assume that $p$ is in dollars. What is the maximum revenue possible in this situation? Which price $p$ generates this maximum revenue?

7. The price of a new machine is $14,000. After ten years, the machine has a salvage value of $750. Assuming linear depreciation, find a formula for the value of the machine after $t$ yr, where $0 \le t \le 10$.

8. Graph the function $y = -\frac{1}{2}(3 - x)^3$. Specify the intercepts. *Hint*: First graph $y = -\frac{1}{2}(x - 3)^3$.

9. Graph the function $y = (2x - 3)/(x + 1)$. Specify the intercepts and asymptotes.

10. (a) Suppose that $P(x, y)$ is a point on the line $y = 3x - 1$ and $Q$ is the point $(-1, 3)$. Express the length $PQ$ as a function of $x$.
    (b) For which value of $x$ is the length $PQ$ a minimum?

11. Let $f(x) = x(x - 2)/(x^2 - 9)$.
    (a) Find the vertical and the horizontal asymptotes.
    (b) Use a sketch to show the behavior of $f$ near the $x$-intercepts.
    (c) Use a sketch to show the behavior of $f$ near the asymptotes.
    (d) Sketch the graph of $f$.

12. A rectangle is inscribed in a semicircle of diameter 8 cm. (See the accompanying figure.) Express the area of the rectangle as a function of the width $w$ of the rectangle.

8 cm

13. Explain why each of the following graphs cannot represent a polynomial function with highest-degree term $-x^3$.

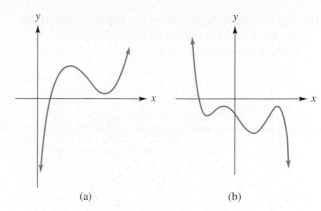

(a)                    (b)

14. The following table shows U.S. expenditures for national defense for the years 1992–1995.

**Federal Budget Outlays for National Defense, 1992–1995**

| Year $t$ ($t = 0$ is 1990) | 2 | 3 | 4 | 5 |
|---|---|---|---|---|
| Expenditures $y$ (billions of dollars) | 298.4 | 291.1 | 281.6 | 272.1 |

Source: U.S. Office of Management and Budget

(a) Draw (by hand) a scatter plot of the data. (Show the portion of the $y$-axis from 270 to 300, in increments of 5.) You'll see that the data points appear to fall roughly on a straight line. Sketch in a line that seems to fit the data. Estimate the slope of the line. (Include the units for the slope.)

(b) Use a graphing utility to determine the equation of the line that best fits the data. Is your slope estimate in part (a) close to the slope obtained here?

(c) Use the least-squares equation obtained in part (b) to make estimates for what the expenditures might have been for 1996 and for 1999. Then compare the percentage errors in these two estimates, given that the actual expenditures (in billions of dollars) for 1996 and 1999 were 265.8 and 276.7, respectively.

*Problems 15 and 16, which follow, are based on the work in Optional Section 4.3.*

15. Find the real numbers (if any) that are fixed points of the given functions.
    (a) $f(x) = 2x(1 - x)$
    (b) $g(x) = (4x - 1)/(3x + 6)$

**16.** The following figure shows the first six steps in the iteration process for the function $f(x) = 0.6 - x^2$ with initial input $x_0 = 0.2$.

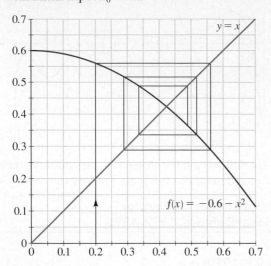

**(a)** Use the figure and your calculator to complete the following table. For your answers from the graph, try to estimate to the nearest 0.02 (or 0.01). For the calculator answers, round to three decimal places.

|  | $x_1$ | $x_2$ | $x_3$ | $x_4$ | $x_5$ | $x_6$ |
|---|---|---|---|---|---|---|
| From graph |  |  |  |  |  |  |
| From calculator |  |  |  |  |  |  |

**(b)** Compute the two fixed points of the function $f(x) = 0.6 - x^2$. Give two forms for each answer: an exact expression involving a radical and a calculator approximation rounded to four decimal places. Which fixed point do the iterates in part (a) approach?

**(c)** Use your calculator to compute the first six iterates of $x_0 = 1$. Do the iterates seem to approach either of the fixed points determined in part (b)?

# Exponential and Logarithmic Functions

*... in 1958 ... C. D. Keeling of The Scripps Institution of Oceanography ... began a series of painstaking measurements of $CO_2$ concentration on a remote site at what is now the Mauna Loa Observatory in Hawaii. His observations, continued to the present, show an exponential growth of atmospheric carbon dioxide. ... Keeling's observations have been duplicated at other stations in various parts of the world over shorter periods of time. In all sets of observations, the exponential increase is clear. ...* — Gordon MacDonald in "Scientific Basis for the Greenhouse Effect," from *The Challenge of Global Warming*, Dean Edwin Abrahamson, ed. (Washington, D.C.: Island Press, 1989)

In this chapter we study two major types of functions with widespread applications: the *exponential functions* and their inverses, the *logarithmic functions*. Exponential functions are functions of the form $y = ab^{cx}$ where $a$, $b$, and $c$ are constants (with $b$ positive and not equal to 1). As an introductory example, suppose that when you were born your parents opened a savings account in your name. Assume that the initial deposit was $100, with an annual interest rate of 8%, compounded twice a year. (If you are unfamiliar with compound interest, the details are in Section 5.6; but you won't need that to understand the point of the present discussion.) Under these conditions the dollar amount $y$ in the account after $x$ years is given by the exponential function $y = 100 \times 1.04^{2x}$. In Table 1 we show the amount in the account at five-year intervals for the first 30 years. Figure 1(a) shows a graph of the function $y = 100 \times 1.04^{2x}$ and the data points from Table 1. For comparison, Figure 1(b) shows the same scatter plot along with a quadratic function fitted to the data (using the quadratic regression option on a graphing utility). Over this relatively short interval of time, it appears that there is not much of a difference between the two models. For longer time intervals, however, the situation changes drastically.

Table 2 shows additional values for the exponential function $y = 100 \times 1.04^{2x}$ at ten-year intervals. In Figure 2 we've plotted these data points along with the original data set, and we show the exponential and quadratic models. As you can see, over the longer time interval, the quadratic function is no longer a good model for the amount of money in your account; the quadratic grows too slowly to keep pace with the exponential. Indeed, this is one of the key features of exponential growth: Eventually, it will outpace not only a quadratic, but any polynomial, no matter how high the degree.

Some of the applications you will see in this chapter for logarithmic or exponential functions involve:

- Modeling the temperature of a cup of coffee (Project in Section 5.2)
- Using the Richter scale to quantify the size of an earthquake (Example 8 in Section 5.3)

| TABLE 1 | $100 Invested at 8% per Year, Compounded Semiannually | | | | | | |
|---|---|---|---|---|---|---|---|
| x (years) | 0 | 5 | 10 | 15 | 20 | 25 | 30 |
| y (dollars) | 100 | 148.02 | 219.11 | 324.34 | 480.10 | 710.67 | 1051.96 |

(a) Exponential function

$$y = 100 \times 1.04^{2x}$$

(b) Quadratic function fitted to the data in Table 1.

$$y = 0.894x^2 + 1.395x + 108.09$$

**Figure 1**
Initially, the exponential and quadratic models appear quite similar (but see Figure 2).

| TABLE 2 | Amount in the Account After 40, 50, and 60 Years | | |
|---|---|---|---|
| x (years) | 40 | 50 | 60 |
| y (dollars) | 2304.98 | 5050.50 | 11066.26 |

**Figure 2**
The exponential function eventually grows much faster than the quadratic.

- Computing the annual yield (= effective rate) for money earning compound interest (Example 4 in Section 5.6)
- Analyzing world population growth (Examples 2–4 in Section 5.7)
- Describing the increasing levels of carbon dioxide in the atmosphere (Example 5 and Exercises 15 and 16 in Section 5.7)

## 5.1 EXPONENTIAL FUNCTIONS

**TABLE 1**

| x (day number) | y (amount earned that day) |
|---|---|
| 1 | 2¢ (= $2^1$) |
| 2 | 4¢ (= $2^2$) |
| 3 | 8¢ (= $2^3$) |
| 4 | 16¢ (= $2^4$) |
| 5 | 32¢ (= $2^5$) |
| . | . |
| . | . |
| . | . |
| x | $2^x$ |

We begin with an example. Suppose that your mathematics instructor, in an effort to improve classroom attendance, offers to pay you each day for attending class! Suppose you are to receive 2¢ on the first day you attend class, 4¢ the second day, 8¢ the third day, and so on, as shown in Table 1. How much money will you receive for attending class on the 30th day?

As you can see by looking at Table 1, the amount y earned on day x is given by the rule, or *exponential function,*

$$y = 2^x$$

Thus on the 30th day (when $x = 30$) you will receive

$$y = 2^{30} \text{ cents}$$

If you use a calculator, you will find this amount to be well over 10 million dollars! The point here is simply this: Although we begin with a small amount, $y = 2¢$, repeated doubling quickly leads to a very large amount. In other words, the exponential function grows very rapidly.

Before leaving this example, we mention a simple method for quickly estimating numbers such as $2^{30}$ (or any power of two) in terms of the more familiar powers of ten. Begin by observing that

$$2^{10} \approx 10^3 \quad \text{(a useful coincidence, worth remembering)}$$

Now just cube both sides to obtain

$$(2^{10})^3 \approx (10^3)^3 \quad \text{or} \quad 2^{30} \approx 10^9$$

Thus $2^{30}$ is about one billion. To convert this number of cents to dollars, we divide by 100 or $10^2$ to obtain

$$\frac{10^9}{10^2} = 10^7 \text{dollars}$$

which is 10 million dollars, as mentioned before.

**EXAMPLE** 1 **Estimating a power of 2**

Estimate $2^{40}$ in terms of a power of 10.

**SOLUTION**
Take the basic approximation $2^{10} \approx 10^3$ and raise both sides to the fourth power. This yields

$$(2^{10})^4 \approx (10^3)^4$$

or

$$2^{40} \approx 10^{12} \quad \text{as required}$$

**EXAMPLE 2** Estimating an exponent

Estimate the power to which 10 must be raised to yield 2.

**SOLUTION**

We begin with our approximation

$$10^3 \approx 2^{10}$$

Raising both sides to the power 1/10 yields

$$(10^3)^{1/10} \approx (2^{10})^{1/10}$$

and, consequently,
$$10^{3/10} \approx 2$$

Thus the power to which 10 must be raised to yield 2 is approximately 3/10.

In Appendix B.3 we define the expression $b^x$, where $x$ is a rational number. We also state that if $x$ is irrational, then $b^x$ can be defined so that the usual properties of exponents continue to hold. Although a rigorous definition of irrational exponents requires concepts from calculus, we can nevertheless convey the basic idea by means of an example. (We need to do this before we give the general definition for exponential functions.)

How shall we assign a meaning to $2^{\sqrt{2}}$, for example? The basic idea is to evaluate the expression $2^x$ successively by using rational numbers $x$ that are closer and closer to $\sqrt{2}$. Table 2 displays the results of some calculations along these lines.

**TABLE 2** Values of $2^x$ for Rational Numbers $x$ Approaching $\sqrt{2}$ (= 1.41421356 . . .)

| $x$ | 1.4 | 1.41 | 1.414 | 1.4142 | 1.41421 | 1.414213 |
|---|---|---|---|---|---|---|
| $2^x$ | 2.6 . . . | 2.65 . . . | 2.664 . . . | 2.6651 . . . | 2.66514 . . . | 2.665143 . . . |

The data in the table suggest that as $x$ approaches $\sqrt{2}$, the corresponding values of $2^x$ approach a unique real number, call it $t$, with a decimal expansion that begins as 2.665. Furthermore, by continuing this process we can obtain (in theory, at least) as many places in the decimal expansion of $t$ as we wish. The value of the expression $2^{\sqrt{2}}$ is then defined to be this number $t$. The following results (stated here without proof) summarize this discussion and also pave the way for the definition we will give for exponential functions.

**PROPERTY SUMMARY** Real Number Exponents

Let $b$ denote an arbitrary positive real number. Then:

1. For each real number $x$, the quantity $b^x$ is a unique real number.
2. When $x$ is irrational, we can approximate $b^x$ as closely as we wish by evaluating $b^r$, where $r$ is a rational number sufficiently close to the number $x$.
3. The properties of rational exponents continue to hold for irrational exponents.
4. If $b^x = b^y$ and $b \neq 1$, then $x = y$.

| EXAMPLE | 3 | Simplifying expressions containing irrational exponents |
|---|---|---|

Use the properties of exponents to simplify each expression:

**(a)** $\left(3^{\sqrt{2}}\right)^{\sqrt{2}}$;  **(b)** $\left(3^{\sqrt{2}}\right)^2$.

**SOLUTION**

**(a)** $\left(3^{\sqrt{2}}\right)^{\sqrt{2}} = 3^{\sqrt{2} \times \sqrt{2}} = 3^2 = 9$

**(b)** $\left(3^{\sqrt{2}}\right)^2 = \left(3^2\right)^{\sqrt{2}}$   (Why?)

$\qquad = 9^{\sqrt{2}}$

| EXAMPLE | 4 | An equation with the unknown in the exponent |
|---|---|---|

Solve the equation $4^x = 8$.

**SOLUTION**

First let's estimate $x$, just to get a feeling for what kind of answer to expect. Since $4^1 = 4$, which is less than 8, and $4^2 = 16$, which is more than 8, we know that our final answer should be a number between 1 and 2. To obtain this answer, we take advantage of the fact that both 4 and 8 are powers of 2. Using this fact, we can write the given equation as

$$\left(2^2\right)^x = 2^3$$
$$2^{2x} = 2^3$$
$$2x = 3 \qquad \text{using Property 4 on page 328}$$
$$x = \frac{3}{2}$$

Note that the answer $x = 3/2$ is indeed between 1 and 2, as we estimated.

For the remainder of this section, $b$ denotes an arbitrary positive constant other than 1. In the box that follows, we define the exponential function with base $b$.

| DEFINITION | The Exponential Function with Base $b$   ($b > 0$, $b \neq 1$) |
|---|---|

Let $b$ denote an arbitrary positive constant other than 1. The **exponential function with base $b$** is defined by the equation

$$y = b^x$$

**Note:** In many applications, functions of the form $y = ab^{kx}$, where $a$, $b$, and $k$ are constants, with $b \neq 1$, are also called exponential functions.

EXAMPLES
1. The equations $y = 2^x$ and $y = 3^x$ define the exponential functions with bases 2 and 3, respectively.
2. The equation $y = (1/2)^x$ defines the exponential functions with base $1/2$.
3. The equations $y = x^2$ and $y = x^3$ do not define exponential functions.

To help with our analysis of exponential functions, let's set up a table and use it to graph the exponential function $y = 2^x$. This is done in Figure 1. In drawing a

**Figure 1**

smooth and unbroken curve, we are actually relying on the results in the Property Summary box on the previous page. The key features of the exponential function $y = 2^x$ and its graph are:

1. The domain of $y = 2^x$ is the set of all real numbers. The range is the set of all *positive* real numbers.
2. The $y$-intercept of the graph is 1. The graph has no $x$-intercept.
3. For $x > 0$, the function increases or grows very rapidly. For $x < 0$, the graph rapidly approaches the $x$-axis; the $x$-axis is a horizontal asymptote for the graph. (Recall from Section 4.7 that a line is an **asymptote** for a curve if the separation distance between the curve and the line approaches zero as we move farther and farther out along the line.)

You should memorize the basic shape and features of the graph of $y = 2^x$ so that you can sketch it as needed without first setting up a table. The next example shows why this is useful.

**EXAMPLE 5   Sketching graphs related to that of $y = 2^x$**

Graph each of the following functions. In each case specify the domain, the range, the intercept(s), and the asymptote:
**(a)** $y = -2^x$;  **(b)** $y = 2^{-x}$;  **(c)** $y = (1/2)^x$;  **(d)** $y = 2^{-x} - 2$.

**SOLUTION**

**(a)** Recall that $-2^x$ means $-(2^x)$, not $(-2)^x$. The graph of $y = -2^x$ is obtained by reflecting the graph of $y = 2^x$ in the $x$-axis. See Figure 2(a).
**(b)** Similarly, the graph of $y = 2^{-x}$ is obtained from the graph of $y = 2^x$ by reflection in the $y$-axis. See Figure 2(b).
**(c)** Next, regarding $y = (1/2)^x$, observe that

$$\left(\frac{1}{2}\right)^x = \frac{1^x}{2^x} = \frac{1}{2^x} = 2^{-x}$$

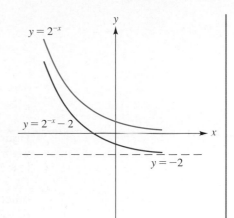

| $y = -2^x$ | | $y = 2^{-x} \left(\text{also } y = \left(\frac{1}{2}\right)^x\right)$ | | $y = 2^{-x} - 2$ |
|---|---|---|---|---|
| Domain: $(-\infty, \infty)$ | | Domain: $(-\infty, \infty)$ | | Domain: $(-\infty, \infty)$ |
| Range: $(-\infty, 0)$ | | Range: $(0, \infty)$ | | Range: $(-2, \infty)$ |
| $y$-intercept: $-1$ | | $y$-intercept: $1$ | | $y$-intercept: $-1$ |
| $x$-intercept: none | | $x$-intercept: none | | $x$-intercept: $-1$ |
| Asymptote: $x$-axis | | Asymptote: $x$-axis | | Asymptote: $y = -2$ |
| (a) | | (b) | | (c) |

**Figure 2**

In other words, $y = \left(\frac{1}{2}\right)^x$ is really the same function as $y = 2^{-x}$, which we already graphed in Figure 2(b).

**(d)** Finally, to graph $y = 2^{-x} - 2$, take the graph of $y = 2^{-x}$ in Figure 2(b) and move it two units in the negative $y$-direction, as shown in Figure 2(c). Note that the asymptote and $y$-intercept will also move down two units. To find the $x$-intercept, we set $y = 0$ in the given equation to obtain

$$2^{-x} - 2 = 0$$
$$2^{-x} = 2^1$$
$$-x = 1 \qquad \text{using Property 4 on page 328}$$
$$x = -1$$

Thus the $x$-intercept is $-1$.

In the next example we apply our knowledge about the graph of $y = 2^x$ to solve an equation. In particular, we use the fact that the graph of $y = 2^x$ always lies above the $x$-axis; for no value of $x$ is $2^x$ ever zero.

**EXAMPLE** | 6 | **Using the fact that $2^x$ is always positive to solve an equation**

Consider the equation

$$x^3 2^x - 3(2^x) = 0 \tag{1}$$

The graph in Figure 3 indicates that equation (1) has a positive root between 0 and 2. However, the viewing rectangle does not tell us whether equation (1) has

**GRAPHICAL PERSPECTIVE**

**Figure 3**
$y = x^3 2^x - 3(2^x)$
$[-8, 2, 2]$ by $[-5, 10, 5]$

other roots. (For instance, perhaps there is a negative root somewhere to the left of $-8$). By solving the equation, find out whether there are any roots other than the one between 0 and 2. For each root, give both an exact expression and a calculator approximation rouded to two decimal places.

**SOLUTION**

**(a)** On the left-hand side of equation (1) the common term $2^x$ can be factored out. This yields

$$2^x(x^3 - 3) = 0 \qquad (2)$$

Now applying the zero-product property in equation (2), we have

$$2^x = 0 \qquad \text{or} \qquad x^3 - 3 = 0$$

The equation $2^x = 0$ has no solutions because $2^x$ is positive for all values of $x$. From the equation $x^3 - 3 = 0$ we conclude that $x^3 = 3$, and therefore $x = \sqrt[3]{3}$. With a calculator we find that $\sqrt[3]{3} \approx 1.44$. This is the root between 0 and 2 in Figure 3. The algebra that we've carried out indicates that this is the only root of the given equation.

---

**GRAPHICAL PERSPECTIVE**

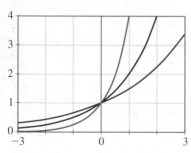

**Figure 4**
$y = 1.5^x \qquad y = 2^x \qquad y = 4^x$
$[-3, 3, 1]$ by $[0, 4, 1]$

Now what about exponential functions with bases other than 2? As Figure 4 indicates, the graphs are similar to $y = 2^x$. The graph of $y = 4^x$ rises more rapidly than $y = 2^x$ when $x$ is positive. For negative $x$-values, the graph of $y = 4^x$ is below that of $y = 2^x$. You can see why this happens by taking $x = -1$, for example, and comparing the values of $4^x$ and $2^x$. If $x = -1$, then

$$2^x = 2^{-1} = \frac{1}{2} \qquad \text{but} \qquad 4^x = 4^{-1} = \frac{1}{4}$$

Therefore $4^x < 2^x$ when $x = -1$. In general $0 < 2^x < 4^x$ for $x > 0$, so $0 < 1/4^x < 1/2^x$ or $0 < 4^{-x} < 2^{-x}$ for $x > 0$. Reflecting in the $y$-axis by replacing $x$ by its opposite we obtain $0 < 4^x < 2^x$ when $x < 0$. Notice also in Figure 4 all three graphs have the same $y$-intercept of 1. This follows from the fact that $b^0 = 1$ for any positive number $b$.

The exponential functions in Figure 4 all have bases larger than 1. To see examples in which the bases are in the interval $0 < b < 1$, we need only reflect the graphs in Figure 4 in the $y$-axis. For instance, the reflection of $y = 4^x$ in the $y$-axis gives us the graph of $y = 4^{-x} = 1/4^x$. (We discussed the idea behind this in Example 5; see Figure 2(b), for instance.)

In the box that follows, we summarize what we've learned up to this point regarding the exponential function $y = b^x$.

## ▋PROPERTY SUMMARY   The Exponential Function $y = b^x$

Domain:   $(-\infty, \infty)$
Range:   $(0, \infty)$
$y$-intercept:   1
$x$-intercept:   none
Asymptote:   $x$-axis

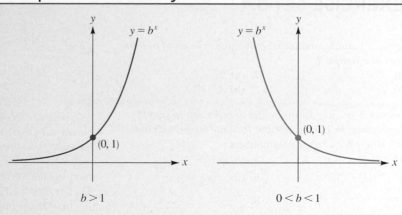

$b > 1$          $0 < b < 1$

*Note*: The function defined by the equation $y = b^x$ for positive constant $b \neq 1$ is called the *exponential function with base b*.

    **EXAMPLE**   **7**   **Reflecting and translating the graph of an exponential function**

Graph the function $y = -3^{-x} + 1$.

**SOLUTION**
The required graph is obtained by reflecting and translating the graph of $y = 3^x$, as shown in Figure 5.

Begin with $y = 3^x$.

Reflect $y = 3^x$ in the $y$-axis to obtain $y = 3^{-x}$.

Reflect $y = 3^{-x}$ in the $x$-axis to obtain $y = -3^{-x}$.

Translate $y = -3^{-x}$ up one unit to obtain $y = -3^{-x} + 1$. Note that the $y$-intercept is 0 and the asymptote is the line $y = 1$.

**Figure 5**

# EXERCISE SET 5.1

## A

*In Exercises 1 and 2, estimate each quantity in terms of powers of ten, as in Example 1.*

**1. (a)** $2^{30}$
   **(b)** $2^{50}$

**2. (a)** $2^{90}$
   **(b)** $4^{50}$

*In Exercises 3–10, use the properties of exponents to simplify each expression. In Exercises 9 and 10, write the answers in the form $b^n$, where b and n are real numbers.*

**3.** $(5^{\sqrt{3}})^{\sqrt{3}}$

**4.** $(\sqrt{2}^{\sqrt{2}})^{\sqrt{2}}$

**5.** $(4^{1+\sqrt{2}})(4^{1-\sqrt{2}})$

**6.** $(3^{2+\sqrt{5}})(3^{2-\sqrt{5}})$

**7.** $\dfrac{2^{4+\pi}}{2^{1+\pi}}$

**8.** $\dfrac{10^{\pi+2}}{10^{\pi-2}}$

**9.** $(\sqrt{5}^{\sqrt{2}})^2$

**10.** $[(\sqrt{3})^{\pi}]^4$

*In Exercises 11 and 12, solve each equation, as in Example 4.*

**11. (a)** $3^x = 27$
   **(b)** $9^t = 27$
   **(c)** $3^{1-2y} = \sqrt{3}$
   **(d)** $3^z = 9\sqrt{3}$

**12. (a)** $2^x = 32$
   **(b)** $2^t = 1/4$
   **(c)** $2^{3y+1} = \sqrt{2}$
   **(d)** $8^{z+1} = 32\sqrt{2}$

*In Exercises 13–16, specify the domain of the function.*

**13.** $y = 2^x$

**14.** $y = 1/2^x$

**15.** $y = 1/(2^{x-1})$

**16.** $y = 1/(2^x - 1)$

*In Exercises 17–24, graph the pair of functions on the same set of axes.*

**17.** $y = 2^x; y = 2^{-x}$

**18.** $y = 3^x; y = 3^{-x}$

**19.** $y = 3^x; y = -3^x$

**20.** $y = 4^x; y = -4^x$

**21.** $y = 2^x; y = 3^x$

**22.** $y = (1/3)^x; y = 3^x$

**23.** $y = (1/2)^x; y = (1/3)^x$

**24.** $y = (1/2)^{-x}; y = (1/3)^{-x}$

*For Exercises 25–32, graph the function and specify the domain, range, intercept(s), and asymptote.*

**25.** $y = -2^x + 1$

**26.** $y = -3^x + 3$

**27.** $y = 3^{-x} + 1$

**28.** $y = 3^{-x} - 3$

**29.** $y = 2^{x-1}$

**30.** $y = 2^{x-1} - 1$

**31.** $y = 3^{x+1} + 1$

**32.** $y = 1 - 3^{x-1}$

*For Exercises 33–38:*

**(a)** *Use paper and pencil to determine the intercepts and asymptotes for the graph of each function.*

Ⓖ **(b)** *Use a graphing utility to graph each function. Your results in part (a) will be helpful in choosing an appropriate viewing rectangle that shows the essential features of the graph.*

**33.** $y = -3^{x-2}$

**34.** $y = -3^{x-2} + 1$

**35.** $y = 4^{-x} - 4$

**36.** $y = 4 + (1/4)^x$

**37.** $y = 10^{x-1}$

**38.** $y = -10^{x-1} + 0.5$

*For Exercises 39–42, solve the equation, as in Example 6.*

**39.** $3x(10^x) + 10^x = 0$

**40.** $4x^2(2^x) - 9(2^x) = 0$

**41.** $3(3^x) - 5x(3^x) + 2x^2(3^x) = 0$

**42.** $\dfrac{(x+4)10^x}{x-3} = 2x(10^x)$

## B

*Exercises 43 and 44 provide some simple examples of an important idea that was presented in the chapter introduction: Exponential growth eventually outpaces polynomial growth (no matter how high the degree of the polynomial). In each case, carry out the calculations needed to verify the given statement.*

**43.** Let $f(x) = 1.125x^2 - 0.75x + 1$ and $g(x) = 2^x$.

**(a)** On the interval [0, 2], both functions have the same average rate of change. This is also true for the interval [2, 4].

**(b)** On the interval [4, 6], however, $\Delta g/\Delta x$ is more than twice $\Delta f/\Delta x$. And on the interval [6, 8], $\Delta g/\Delta x$ is more than six times $\Delta f/\Delta x$.

**(c)** On the interval [10, 12], the average rate of change of the exponential function is 64 times that of the quadratic function.

**44.** Let $g(x) = x^4$ and $h(x) = 3^x$.

**(a)** On the interval [0, 5], the average rate of change of g is more than two and one-half times the average rate of change of h. On the interval [5, 10], however, the average rate of change of h is more than six times that for g.

**(b)** On the interval [10, 15] the average rate of change of the exponential function is more than 350 times that of the polynomial function.

**45.** Let $f(x) = 2^x$. Show that

$$\frac{f(x+h) - f(x)}{h} = 2^x\left(\frac{2^h - 1}{h}\right)$$

**46.** Let $\phi(t) = 1 + a^t$. Show that $\dfrac{1}{\phi(t)} + \dfrac{1}{\phi(-t)} = 1$.

**47.** Let $f(x) = 2^x$ and let g denote the function that is the inverse of f.

**(a)** On the same set of axes, sketch the graphs of f, g, and the line $y = x$.

**(b)** Using the graph you obtained in part (a), specify the domain, range, intercept, and asymptote for the function g.

**48.** Let $S(x) = (2^x - 2^{-x})/2$ and $C(x) = (2^x + 2^{-x})/2$. Compute $[C(x)]^2 - [S(x)]^2$.

*For Exercises 49–56, refer to the following figure, which shows portions of the graphs of $y = 2^x$, $y = 3^x$, and $y = 5^x$. In each case:* **(a)** *use the figure to estimate the indicated quantity; and* **(b)** *use a calculator to compute the indicated quantity, rounding the result to two decimal places.*

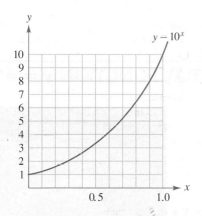

$y = 5^x$   $y = 3^x$   $y = 2^x$

$y = 2.0 \rightarrow$

$y = 1.5 \rightarrow$

$y = 1.0 \rightarrow$

$x = 0$      $x = 0.5$      $x = 1.0$

the viewing rectangle so that $x$ extends from $-100$ to 100 and $y$ extends from 0 to 100,000.

Ⓖ **62.** Follow the general procedure in Exercise 61, but use the two functions $y = 2^x - 2^{-x}$ and $y = x^3$.

Ⓖ **63.** As background for this exercise, reread Example 2 in the text. (The example shows how to estimate the value of $x$ for which $10^x = 2$.)

   **(a)** In the same picture, graph the two functions $y = 10^x$ and $y = 2$. Use a viewing rectangle in which $x$ runs from 0 to 1 and $y$ runs from 0 to 10.

   **(b)** Explain how your picture in part (a) supports the answer 3/10 that was obtained in Example 2.

**49.** $\sqrt{2}$   *Hint:* $\sqrt{2} = 2^{1/2}$     **50.** $\sqrt[5]{2}$

**51.** $2^{3/5}$                               **52.** $\sqrt[5]{8}$   *Hint:* $8^{1/5} = 2^?$

**53.** $\sqrt{3}$      **54.** $\sqrt[3]{3}$      **55.** $5^{3/10}$        **56.** $\sqrt[4]{5}$

## C

**64.** This exercise serves as a preview for the work on logarithms in Section 5.3. Follow Steps (a)–(f) to complete the table. (Notice that one entry in the table is already filled in. Reread Example 2 in the text to see how that entry was obtained.)

   **(a)** Fill in the entries in the right-hand column corresponding to $x = 1$ and $x = 10$.

   **(b)** Note that 4 and 8 are powers of 2. Use this information along with the approximation $10^{0.3} \approx 2$ to find the entries in the table corresponding to $x = 4$ and $x = 8$.

   **(c)** Find the entry corresponding to $x = 5$.
   *Hint:* $5 = 10/2 \approx 10/10^{0.3}$

   **(d)** Find the entry corresponding to $x = 7$.
   *Hint:* $7^2 \approx 50 = 5 \times 10$; now make use of your answer in part (c).

   **(e)** Find the entry corresponding to $x = 3$.
   *Hint:* $3^4 \approx 80 = 8 \times 10$

   **(f)** Find the entries corresponding to $x = 6$ and $x = 9$.
   *Hint:* $6 = 3 \times 2$ and $9 = 3^2$

*In Exercises 57–60, refer to the following graph of the exponential function $y = 10^x$. Use the graph to estimate (to the nearest tenth) the solution of each equation. (After we've studied logarithmic functions later in the chapter, we will be able to obtain precise solutions.)*

$y$

$y = 10^x$

10
9
8
7
6
5
4
3
2
1

0.5        1.0        $x$

*Remark:* This table is called a *table of logarithms to the base 10*. We say, for example, that the logarithm of 2 to the base 10 is (about) 0.3. We write this symbolically as $\log_{10} 2 \approx 0.3$.

**57.** $10^x = 2$   **58.** $10^x = 4$   **59.** $10^x = 5$   **60.** $10^x = 8$

Ⓖ **61.** If you add two quadratic functions, the result is again a quadratic function (assuming that the $x^2$-terms don't add to zero). For example, if $f(x) = x^2 + 2x$ and $g(x) = 2x^2 - 1$, then the sum is $(f + g)(x) = 3x^2 + 2x - 1$, another quadratic. But this is not the case for exponential functions. To explore a visual example, consider the function $y = 2^x + 2^{-x}$. This is the sum of the two exponentials $y = 2^x$ and $y = (1/2)^x$.

   **(a)** Graph the function $y = 2^x + 2^{-x}$ in the standard viewing rectangle. As you can see, the resulting graph is U-shaped.

   **(b)** For comparison, add the graph of $y = x^2$ to your picture. Note that (at this scale) the graphs are very similar for $|x| > 2$.

   **(c)** Actually, the graph of $y = 2^x + 2^{-x}$ rises much more steeply than does $y = x^2$. To demonstrate this, change

| $x$ | Exponent to which 10 must be raised to yield $x$ |
|-----|--------------------------------------------------|
| 1   |                                                  |
| 2   | $\approx 0.3$                                     |
| 3   |                                                  |
| 4   |                                                  |
| 5   |                                                  |
| 6   |                                                  |
| 7   |                                                  |
| 8   |                                                  |
| 9   |                                                  |
| 10  |                                                  |

## MINI PROJECT

### USING DIFFERENCES TO COMPARE EXPONENTIAL AND POLYNOMIAL GROWTH

In the chapter introduction (on pages 325–326), you saw an example comparing and contrasting exponential and quadratic growth models. Another way to compare exponential growth and quadratic growth (or, more generally, polynomial growth) uses the idea of *differences,* as discussed at the end of Section 4.2.

**(a)** Appoint a member of the group in which you are working to summarize for the group the definitions and results on differences on page 239.

**(b)** Just as second differences are obtained by subtracting adjacent first differences, *third differences* are obtained by subtracting adjacent second differences. For the cubic polynomial function $y = x^3$, set up a table of x-y values using $x = 0, 1, 2, \ldots, 6$. Then compute the first, second, and third differences. What do you observe?

**(c)** For the exponential function $y = 2^x$, set up a table of x-y values using $x = 0, 1, 2, \ldots, 6$. Then compute the first, second, and third differences. What do you observe? Write a paragraph summarizing your observations and contrasting the results with what occurs in the case of linear and quadratic functions and the cubic function in part (b).

## 5.2 THE EXPONENTIAL FUNCTION $y = e^x$

*Why did he* [the Swiss mathematician Leonhard Euler (1707–1783)] *choose the letter* e? *There is no general consensus. According to one view, Euler chose it because it is the first letter of the word* exponential. *More likely, the choice came to him naturally as the first "unused" letter of the alphabet, since the letters* a, b, c, *and* d *frequently appear elsewhere in mathematics. It seems unlikely that Euler chose the letter because it is the initial of his own name, as occasionally has been suggested: he was an extremely modest man . . .*
—Eli Maor, e: The Story of a Number (Princeton, N.J.: Princeton University Press, 1994)

The shape of the Gateway Arch in St. Louis is based on the *catenary curve,* which is defined in terms of the exponential function $y = e^x$. For details see Exercises 55 and 56. (Photo from Scenics of America/Photo Link)

From the standpoint of calculus and scientific applications, one particular base for exponential functions is by far the most useful. This base is a certain irrational

## TABLE 1

| $x$ | $f(x) = (1 + \frac{1}{x})^x$ |
|-----|------------------------------|
| $10^1$ | 2.59374246 |
| $10^2$ | 2.70481382 |
| $10^3$ | 2.71692393 |
| $10^4$ | 2.71814592 |
| $10^5$ | 2.71826823 |
| $10^6$ | 2.71828046 |
| $10^7$ | 2.71828169 |

As $x$ grows larger and larger, the values of $[1 + (1/x)]^x$ approach the number $e$. [Compare the digits in the right column with those in the expression for $e$ given in equation (1).]

## GRAPHICAL PERSPECTIVE

$f(x) = [1 + (1/x)]^x$ for $x > 0$ ——

$y = e$ ——

**Figure 1**
The line $y = e$ is an asymptote for the graph of $f(x) = [1 + (1/x)]^x$. As $x$ gets larger and larger, the values of $[1 + (1/x)]^x$ approach the number $e$.

number that lies between 2 and 3 and is denoted by the letter $e$. To ten decimal places, without rounding off, the value of $e$ is

$$e = 2.7182818284 \ldots \tag{1}$$

For most purposes of approximation and simple estimation, all you need to remember is that

$$e \approx 2.7$$

At the precalculus level, it's hard to escape the feeling that $y = 2^x$ or $y = 10^x$ is by far more simple and more natural than $y = e^x$. At the end of this section we'll explain why the function $y = e^x$ makes life simpler, not more complex.

There are several different (but equivalent) ways that the number $e$ can be defined. One way involves investigating the values of the function $f(x) = [1 + (1/x)]^x$ as $x$ becomes larger and larger. As indicated in Table 1, the values of this function get closer and closer to $e$ as $x$ gets larger and larger. Indeed, in some calculus books, the number $e$ is *defined* as the target value or *limit* of the function $f(x) = [1 + (1/x)]^x$ as $x$ grows ever larger. Now admittedly, we have not defined here the meaning of the terms *target value* or *limit*; that's a topic for calculus. Nevertheless, Table 1 will give you a reasonable, if intuitive, appreciation of the idea. In Figure 1 we give a graphical interpretation.

One more comment about Table 1 and the number $e$: In Section 5.6 you'll see that the data in Table 1 can be interpreted in terms of banking and compound interest. For this reason the constant $e$ is sometimes called "the banker's constant."

In calculus the number $e$ is sometimes introduced in a way that involves slopes of lines. You know that the graph of each exponential function $y = b^x$ passes through the point $(0, 1)$. Figure 2(a) shows the exponential function $y = 2^x$ along with a line that is tangent to the curve at the point $(0, 1)$. By carefully measuring rise and run, it can be shown that the slope of this tangent line is about 0.7. Figure 2(b) shows a similar situation with the curve $y = 3^x$. Here the slope of the tangent line through $(0, 1)$ is approximately 1.1. Now, since the slope of the tangent to $y = 2^x$ is a bit less than 1 while that for $y = 3^x$ is a bit more than 1, it seems reasonable to suppose that there is a number between 2 and 3, call it $e$, with the property that the

**Figure 2**

(a)    (b)

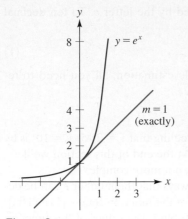

**Figure 3**
The slope of the tangent to the curve
$y = e^x$ at the point $(0, 1)$ is $m = 1$.

slope of the tangent through $(0, 1)$ is exactly 1. See Figure 3 at left and the Property Summary box that follows (see Figure 4).

---

**PROPERTY SUMMARY   The Exponential Function $y = e^x$**

Domain:   $(-\infty, \infty)$
Range:   $(0, \infty)$
$y$-intercept:   1
Asymptote:   $x$-axis

**Figure 4**

---

**REMARK**   It's certainly not obvious that defining $e$ to be the unique number with the property that the slope of the tangent line to the graph of $y = e^x$ at the point $(0, 1)$ is exactly 1 is equivalent to the definition of $e$ as the limit of the function $f(x) = (1 + 1/x)^x$ as $x$ grows ever larger. The methods of calculus are required to demonstrate that the definitions are indeed equivalent. (For an informal justification, however, see Exercise 62.)

**EXAMPLE   1   Sketching graphs related to that of $y = e^x$**

Graph each of the following functions, specifying the domain, range, intercept, and asymptote:
**(a)** $y = e^{x-1}$;       **(b)** $y = -e^{x-1}$;       **(c)** $y = -e^{x-1} + 1$.

**SOLUTION**
**(a)** We begin with the graph of $y = e^x$ (as in Figure 4). Moving the graph to the right one unit yields the graph of $y = e^{x-1}$, shown in Figure 5(a). The $x$-axis is still an asymptote for this translated graph, but the $y$-intercept will no longer be 1. To find the $y$-intercept, we replace $x$ with 0 in the given equation to obtain

$$y = e^{-1} = \frac{1}{e} \approx 0.37 \qquad \text{using a calculator}$$

**(b)** Reflecting the graph from part (a) in the $x$-axis yields the graph of $y = -e^{x-1}$; see Figure 5(b). Note that under this reflection, the $y$-intercept moves from $1/e$ to $-1/e$.
**(c)** Translating the graph in Figure 5(b) up one unit produces the graph of $y = -e^{x-1} + 1$, shown in Figure 5(c). Under this translation, the asymptote moves from $y = 0$ (the $x$-axis) to $y = 1$. Also, the $y$-intercept moves from

(a)

Domain: $(-\infty, \infty)$
Range: $(0, \infty)$
y-intercept: $1/e$
Asymptote: x-axis

(b)

Domain: $(-\infty, \infty)$
Range: $(-\infty, 0)$
y-intercept: $-1/e$
Asymptote: x-axis

(c)

Domain: $(-\infty, \infty)$
Range: $(-\infty, 1)$
x-intercept: $1$
y-intercept: $(-1/e) + 1$
Asymptote: $y = 1$

**Figure 5**

$-1/e$ to $(-1/e) + 1 \approx 0.63$. The x-intercept in Figure 5(c) is obtained by setting $y = 0$ in the equation $y = -e^{x-1} + 1$. This yields

$$0 = -e^{x-1} + 1$$
$$e^{x-1} = 1$$
$$e^{x-1} = e^0$$
$$x - 1 = 0 \quad \text{(Why?)}$$
$$x = 1$$

Near the beginning of this section we said that using $e$ as the base for an exponential function makes things simpler. To explain the context in which this is true, we introduce the concept of the *instantaneous rate of change* of a function. We are going to rely on examples and numerical calculations. A more rigorous development properly belongs to calculus. Our first two examples will involve simple polynomial functions; then we'll move on to the exponential function $f(x) = e^x$. In Table 2(a) we've calculated the average rates of change of the function $f(x) = x^2$ on a sequence of increasingly short intervals, each interval having 1 as the left endpoint. Table 2(b) shows similar calculations with intervals that have 1 as the right endpoint.

**TABLE 2    The Average Rates of Change Approach 2**

| Interval | $\Delta f/\Delta x$ for $f(x) = x^2$ | Interval | $\Delta f/\Delta x$ for $f(x) = x^2$ |
|---|---|---|---|
| [1, 1.1] | 2.1 | [0.9, 1] | 1.9 |
| [1, 1.01] | 2.01 | [0.99, 1] | 1.99 |
| [1, 1.001] | 2.001 | [0.999, 1] | 1.999 |
| [1, 1.0001] | 2.0001 | [0.9999, 1] | 1.9999 |
| [1, 1.00001] | 2.00001 | [0.99999, 1] | 1.99999 |
| (a) | | (b) | |

From the tables we make the following observation: As the lengths of the intervals get smaller and smaller, the average rates of change get closer and closer to 2. We say in this case that the **instantaneous rate of change** of the function $f(x) = x^2$ at $x = 1$ is 2.

In Tables 3(a) and (b), we are looking for the instantaneous rate of change of the function $g(x) = x^3$ at $x = 2$. From the tables, it appears that as the lengths of the intervals get smaller and smaller, the average rates of change get closer and closer to 12. We say that the instantaneous rate of change of $g(x) = x^3$ at $x = 2$ is 12.

| ■ TABLE 3    The Average Rates of Change Approach 12 | | | |
|---|---|---|---|
| Interval | $\Delta g/\Delta x$ for $g(x) = x^3$ | Interval | $\Delta g/\Delta x$ for $g(x) = x^3$ |
| [2, 2.1] | 12.61 | [1.9, 2] | 11.41 |
| [2, 2.01] | 12.0601 | [1.99, 2] | 11.9401 |
| [2, 2.001] | 12.006001 | [1.999, 2] | 11.994001 |
| [2, 2.0001] | 12.00060001 | [1.9999, 2] | 11.99940001 |
| [2, 2.00001] | 12.0000600001 | [1.99999, 2] | 11.9999400001 |
| (a) | | (b) | |

For a more intuitive example of instantaneous rate of change, something closer to your experience, suppose you are driving a car, and at a particular instant the speedometer reads 45 mi/hr. At that instant the instantaneous rate of change of distance with respect to time is 45 mi/hr. We say that the *instantaneous velocity* at that instant is 45 mi/hr. (For a specific example relating average velocity and instantaneous velocity, go back to Section 3.3 and see Example 6 and the related Exercise 36.)

Now we are prepared to say what is so special about the exponential function $f(x) = e^x$. For reference, we state this result in the box that follows. (Remember, we are leaving the precise definitions and the proofs to calculus; we content ourselves here with examples.)

---

**THEOREM    The Instantaneous Rate of Change of the Function $f(x) = e^x$**

Let $a$ be any real number. Then the instantaneous rate of change of the function $f(x) = e^x$ at $x = a$ is $e^a$. In other words, at each point on the graph of $f(x) = e^x$, the instantaneous rate of change is just the $y$-coordinate of the point. Furthermore, the *only* functions with this property are the exponential function $f(x) = e^x$ and constant multiples of this function (that is, functions of the form $y = ce^x$, where $c$ is a constant).

**EXAMPLES**

1. At $x = 1$ the instantaneous rate of change of
   $$f(x) = e^x \quad \text{is} \quad e^1 = e$$

2. At $x = 2$ the instantaneous rate of change of
   $$f(x) = e^x \quad \text{is} \quad e^2$$

---

Table 4 provides a numerical check on Example 2 in the box above. (Exercise 29 asks you to complete a similar table for intervals in which 2 is the right, rather than left, endpoint.)

| TABLE 4 | |
|---|---|
| **The Average Rates of Change Approach $e^2 = 7.3890560\ldots$** | |
| Interval | $\Delta f / \Delta x$ for $f(x) = e^x$ (7 decimal places, no rounding) |
| [2, 2.1] | 7.7711381 |
| [2, 2.01] | 7.4261248 |
| [2, 2.001] | 7.3927518 |
| [2, 2.0001] | 7.3894255 |
| [2, 2.00001] | 7.3890930 |
| [2, 2.000001] | 7.3890597 |

**EXAMPLE 2**   **Average and instantaneous rates of change of a population**

In a biology experiment, let $N(t)$ be the number of bacteria in a colony after $t$ hours, where $t = 0$ corresponds to the time the experiment begins. Suppose that during the period from $t = 4$ hours to $t = 8$ hours the number of bacteria is modeled by the exponential function $N(t) = e^t$. (See Figure 6.)

**GRAPHICAL PERSPECTIVE**

**Figure 6**
$N(t) = e^t, 4 \leq t \leq 8$

**(a)** Find the average rate of change of the population over the time period $5 \leq t \leq 7$.

**(b)** What is the instantaneous rate of change of the population at the instant $t = 7$ hours?

**SOLUTION**

**(a)** On the interval from $t = 5$ to $t = 7$ hours, we have

$$\frac{\Delta N}{\Delta t} = \frac{e^7 - e^5}{7 - 5} \quad \text{bacteria/hour}$$

$$\approx 474 \quad \text{bacteria/hour} \quad \text{using a calculator and rounding}$$

Thus on average over this 2-hour time period, the population is increasing at a rate of 474 bacteria/hour.

**(b)** Applying the theorem in the box on page 340, the instantaneous rate of change of the function $N(t) = e^t$ at $t = 7$ is $e^7$. Thus at the instant when $t = 7$ hours, the population is changing at a rate of

$$e^7 \quad \text{bacteria/hour}$$

$$\approx 1097 \quad \text{bacteria/hour} \quad \text{using a calculator and rounding}$$

# EXERCISE SET 5.2

## A

Ⓖ *In Exercises 1–8, answer* True *or* False. *You do not need a calculator for these exercises. Rather, use the fact that e is approximately 2.7.*

**1.** $e < 1/2$  **2.** $e < 5/2$  **3.** $\sqrt{e} < 1$  **4.** $e^2 < 4$
**5.** $e^2 < 9$  **6.** $e^3 < 27$  **7.** $e^{-1} < 0$  **8.** $e^0 = 1$

*For Exercises 9 and 10, you are given some simple rational approximations for the irrational numbers $\pi$ and e. In each case, use a calculator to find out how many decimal places of the approximation agree with the irrational number.* *Remark: Each of the approximations in Exercise 10 is the best rational approximation using numerators and denominators less than 1000.*

**9. (a)** $\pi \approx 22/7$ **10. (a)** $\pi \approx 355/113$
   **(b)** $e \approx 19/7$    **(b)** $e \approx 878/323$

*In Exercises 11–20, graph the function and specify the domain, range, intercept(s), and asymptote.*

**11.** $y = e^x$ **12.** $y = e^{-x}$
**13.** $y = -e^x$ **14.** $y = -e^{-x}$
**15.** $y = e^x + 1$ **16.** $y = e^{x+1}$
**17.** $y = e^{x+1} + 1$ **18.** $y = e^{x-1} - 1$
**19.** $y = e - e^x$ **20.** $y = e^{-x} - e$

Ⓖ *In Exercises 21 and 22, first tell what translations or reflections are required to obtain the graph of the given function from that of $y = e^x$. Then graph the given function along with $y = e^x$ and check that the picture is consistent with what you've said.*

**21. (a)** $y = e^{x+2}$ **22. (a)** $y = 1 - e^{-x}$
   **(b)** $y = e^{-x+2}$    **(b)** $y = 1 - e^{-x+1}$

*In Exercises 23 and 24, let $f(x) = x^2$, $g(x) = 2^x$, and $h(x) = e^x$. In each case, carry out the calculations needed to verify the given statement.*

**23.** On the interval $[0, 1]$: The average rate of change of $h$ is about 1.7 times that of $g$. The functions $f$ and $g$ have the same average rate of change on the interval $[0, 1]$.

**24.** On the interval $[9, 10]$: The average rate of change of $g$ is more than 25 times greater than that of $f$. The average rate of change of $h$ is approximately 733 times that of $f$.

Ⓖ **25.** In this exercise we compare three functions:

$$y = 2^x \qquad y = e^x \qquad y = 3^x$$

**(a)** Begin by graphing all three functions in the standard viewing rectangle. The picture confirms three facts that you know from the text: on the positive $x$-axis, the functions increase very rapidly; on the negative $x$-axis, the graphs approach the asymptote (which is the $x$-axis) as you move to the left; the $y$-intercept in each case is 1.

**(b)** To compare the functions for positive values of $x$, use a viewing rectangle in which $x$ extends from 0 to 3 and $y$ extends from 0 to 10. Note that the graph of $e^x$ is

bounded between the graphs of $2^x$ and $3^x$, just as the number $e$ is between 2 and 3. In particular, the picture that you obtain demonstrates the following fact: For positive values of $x$,

$$2^x < e^x < 3^x$$

**(c)** To see the graphs more clearly when $x$ is negative, change the viewing rectangle so that $x$ extends from $-3$ to 0 and $y$ extends from 0 to 1. Again, note that the graph of $e^x$ is bounded between the graphs of $2^x$ and $3^x$, but now the graph of $3^x$ is the bottom (rather than the top) curve in the picture. This demonstrates the following fact: For negative values of $x$,

$$3^x < e^x < 2^x$$

**(d)** Explain how the result in part (c) follows from the result in part (b).

**26.** This exercise introduces the approximation

$$e^x \approx x + 1 \qquad \text{provided that } x \text{ is close to zero}$$

This approximation has an important consequence when we study population growth in Section 5.7. (The details are in Exercise 61 in Section 5.7.)

**(a)** Use the information in Figure 3 to explain why the equation of the line tangent to the curve $y = e^x$ at the point $(0, 1)$ is $y = x + 1$.

Ⓖ **(b)** Verify visually that the line $y = x + 1$ is tangent to the curve $y = e^x$ at the point $(0, 1)$ by using a graphing utility to display the graphs of both functions in the same standard viewing rectangle. Note that the curve and the line are virtually indistinguishable in the immediate vicinity of the point $(0, 1)$.

Ⓖ **(c)** Zoom in on the point $(0, 1)$; use a viewing rectangle in which $x$ extends from $-0.05$ to 0.05 and $y$ extends from 0.95 to 1.05. Again, note that the line and the curve are virtually indistinguishable in the immediate vicinity of the point $(0, 1)$. For a numerical look at this, complete the following table. In the columns for $e^x$ and $e^x - (x + 1)$, round each entry to four decimal places. When you are finished, observe that the closer $x$ is to 0, the closer the agreement between the two quantities $x + 1$ and $e^x$.

| $x$ | $x + 1$ | $e^x$ | $e^x - (x + 1)$ |
|---|---|---|---|
| $-0.04$ | | | |
| $-0.03$ | | | |
| $-0.02$ | | | |
| $-0.01$ | | | |
| $0.00$ | | | |
| $0.01$ | | | |
| $0.02$ | | | |
| $0.03$ | | | |
| $0.04$ | | | |

**27.** Complete the following two tables. On the basis of the results you obtain, what would you say is the instantaneous rate of change of the function $f(x) = x^2$ at $x = 3$?

| Interval | $\Delta f/\Delta x$ for $f(x) = x^2$ | Interval | $\Delta f/\Delta x$ for $f(x) = x^2$ |
|---|---|---|---|
| [3, 3.1] | | [2.9, 3] | |
| [3, 3.01] | | [2.99, 3] | |
| [3, 3.001] | | [2.999, 3] | |
| [3, 3.0001] | | [2.9999, 3] | |
| [3, 3.00001] | | [2.99999, 3] | |

**28.** Tables 2(a) and 2(b) on page 339 were used to determine the instantaneous rate of change of $f(x) = x^2$ at $x = 1$. Set up and complete similar tables to find the instantaneous rate of change of $g(x) = x^3$ at $x = 1$.

**29.** Let $f(x) = e^x$. Complete the following table. In the right column, give the average rates of change to six decimal places without rounding. Note that the average rates of change seem to approach $e^2 = 7.3890560. \ldots$ This result along with Table 4 in the text supports a statement in the box on page 340: The instantaneous rate of change of $f(x) = e^x$ at $x = 2$ is $e^2$.

| Interval | $\Delta f/\Delta x$ for $f(x) = e^x$ |
|---|---|
| [1.9, 2] | |
| [1.99, 2] | |
| [1.999, 2] | |
| [1.9999, 2] | |
| [1.99999, 2] | |
| [1.999999, 2] | |
| [1.9999999, 2] | |

Ⓖ

**30.** Complete a table similar to the one shown in Exercise 29, but use the function $h(x) = 3^x$, rather than $f(x) = e^x$. Note that the average rates of change do *not* approach $3^2 = 9$. What does this have to do with the statements in the box on page 340? (Explain using complete sentences.)

*Exercises 31 and 32 refer to Example 2 in the text. Round all answers to the nearest integer. (Don't forget to include units with your answers.)*

**31. (a)** Find the average rate of change of the population over the time period $5 \le t \le 6$.

**(b)** What is the instantaneous rate of change of the population at $t = 5$ hr? At $t = 5.5$ hr?

**32. (a)** Find the average rate of change of the population over the time period $4 \le t \le 6$.

**(b)** What is the instantaneous rate of change of the population at $t = 6$ hr?

**33.** As is indicated in the accompanying figure, the three points $P$, $Q$, and $R$ lie on the graph of $y = e^x$, and the

$x$-coordinates of these points are $-1$, $0$, and $0.5$, respectively. Use the theorem in the box on page 340 to specify the instantaneous rate of change of the function $y = e^x$ at each of these points. For one of the points, a numerical answer can be obtained without a calculator. For the other points, give two forms of each answer: an exact expression involving $e$ and a calculator approximation rounded to two decimal places.

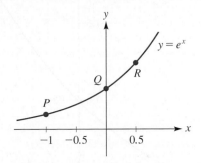

**34.** Suppose that during the first hour and 15 minutes of a physics experiment, the surface temperature of a small iron block is modeled by the exponential function $f(t) = 15e^t$, where $f(t)$ is the Celsius temperature $t$ hours after the experiment begins.

Ⓖ **(a)** Use a graphing utility to graph the function $f(t) = 15e^t$ over the interval $0 \le t \le 1.25$.

**(b)** Compute the average rate of change of temperature over the second half hour of the experiment (i.e., over the interval $0.5 \le t \le 1$). Round the answer to one decimal place.

**(c)** Use one of the facts in the box on page 340 to determine the instantaneous rate of change of temperature: 30 minutes after the start of the experiment; 1 hour after the start of the experiment. Round each answer to one decimal place.

# B

*In Exercises 35–42, decide which of the following properties apply to each function. (More than one property may apply to a function.)*

**A.** The function is increasing for $-\infty < x < \infty$.
**B.** The function is decreasing for $-\infty < x < \infty$.
**C.** The function has a turning point.
**D.** The function is one-to-one.
**E.** The graph has an asymptote.
**F.** The function is a polynomial function.
**G.** The domain of the function is $(-\infty, \infty)$.
**H.** The range of the function is $(-\infty, \infty)$.

**35.** $y = e^x$       **36.** $y = e^{-x}$
**37.** $y = -e^x$      **38.** $y = e^{|x|}$
**39.** $y = x + e$     **40.** $y = x^2 + e$
**41.** $y = x/e$       **42.** $y = e/x$

In Exercises 43–50, refer to the following graph of $y = e^x$. In each case, use the graph to estimate the indicated quantity to the nearest tenth (or closer, if it seems appropriate). Also, use a calculator to obtain a second estimate. Round the calculator values to three decimal places.

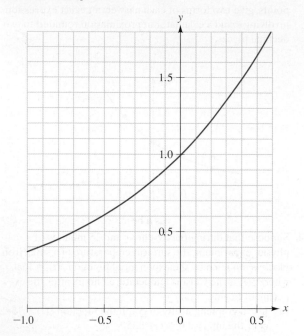

**43.** $e^{0.1}$    **44.** $e^{-0.1}$    **45.** $e^{-0.3}$

**46.** $e^{0.4}$    **47.** $e^{-1}$    **48.** $\sqrt{e}$

**49.** $1/\sqrt{e}$   Hint: Rewrite this expression using a rational exponent, that is, $1/\sqrt{e} = e^?$.

**50.** $\sqrt[5]{e}$

**51. (a)** Use the graph preceding Exercise 43 to estimate the value of $x$ for which $e^x = 1.5$.
  **(b)** One of the keys on your calculator will allow you to solve the equation in part (a) for $x$; it is the "ln" key. Use your calculator to compute $\ln(1.5)$. Round your answer to three decimal places and check to see that it is consistent with the value obtained graphically in part (a).   Remark: The "ln" function, which is called the *natural logarithm* function, is discussed in detail in the next section.

**52.** Follow Exercise 51 using the equation $e^x = 0.6$ (rather than $e^x = 1.5$).

**53.** Follow Exercise 51 using the equation $e^x = 1.8$.

**54.** Follow Exercise 51 using the equation $e^x = 0.4$.

**55.** The **hyperbolic cosine function,** denoted by **cosh,** is defined by the equation

$$\cosh(x) = \frac{1}{2}(e^x + e^{-x})$$

  **(a)** Without a calculator, find $\cosh(0)$. Using a calculator, find $\cosh(1)$ and $\cosh(-1)$, rounding the answers to two decimal places.

  **(b)** What is the domain of the function cosh?   Hint: Visualize the graphs of $y = e^x$ and $y = e^{-x}$.
  **(c)** Show that $\cosh(-x) = \cosh(x)$. What does this say about the graph of $y = \cosh(x)$?
  **(d)** Use a graphing utility to graph $y = \cosh(x)$. Check that the picture is consistent with your answer in part (c).

**56.** (Continuation of Exercise 55.) Suppose that a flexible cable of uniform density is suspended between two supports, as indicated in Figure A. (Example: a telephone line between two phone poles.) Using calculus and physics, it can be shown that the curve formed is a portion of the graph of $y = a \cosh(x/a)$, where $a$ is a constant. See Figure B. (The actual value for $a$ depends on the tension in the cable and the density of the cable.) The graph of an equation of the form $y = a \cosh(x/a)$ is called a **catenary** (from the Latin *catena,* meaning *chain*).

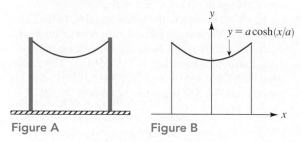

Figure A          Figure B

  **(a)** Use a graphing utility to graph the four catenaries $y = a \cosh(x/a)$ corresponding to $a = 0.2, 1, 3,$ and $5$. Describe (in complete sentences) how the shape and location of the curve changes as the value of $a$ increases.
  **(b)** The Gateway Arch in St. Louis (shown on page 336) is built in the form of an inverted catenary. The equation for the curve is given in Figure C. In this equation both $x$ and $y$ are measured in feet. Find the height of the Gateway Arch, then determine the width by using a graphing utility to graph the equation given in Figure C.   Remark: The Gateway Arch is the tallest monument in the U.S. National Park System. Designed by architect Eero Saarinen and completed in 1965, the Gateway Arch commemorates the Louisiana Purchase, and more generally, the westward expansion of the United States over the period 1803–1890.

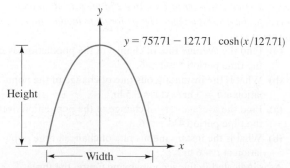

Figure C
Gateway Arch design. Distance on axes is measured in feet.

**57.** The **hyperbolic sine function,** denoted by **sinh,** is defined by the equation

$$\sinh(x) = \frac{1}{2}(e^x - e^{-x})$$

*Note:* For speaking and reading purposes, *sinh* is pronounced as "cinch."

**(a)** Without a calculator, find sinh(0). Using a calculator, find sinh(1) and sinh(−1), rounding the answers to two decimal places.

**(b)** What is the domain of the function sinh?

**(c)** Show that sinh(−x) = −sinh(x). What does this say about the graph of $y = \sinh(x)$?

Ⓖ **(d)** Use a graphing utility to graph $y = \sinh(x)$. Check that the picture is consistent with your answer in part (c).

Ⓖ **(e)** How many points are there where the two curves $y = \sinh(x)$ and $y = x^3$ intersect?

**58.** For this exercise you need to know the definitions of the functions cosh and sinh, which were given in Exercises 55 and 57, respectively.

Ⓖ **(a)** Use a graphing utility to graph the equation $y = \cosh(x) + \sinh(x)$. What do you observe?

**(b)** Use algebra to show why the graph in part (a) looks as it does. [That is, use the definitions of cosh(x) and sinh(x) to simplify the quantity cosh(x) + sinh(x).]

**59.** The following figure shows portions of the graphs of the exponential functions $y = e^x$ and $y = \pi^x$.

**(a)** Use the figure (not your calculator) to determine which number is larger, $e^\pi$ or $\pi^e$.

**(b)** Use your calculator to check your answer in part (a). *Remark:* The number $e^\pi$ is known to be irrational. This was proven by the Russian mathematician A. O. Gelfond in 1929. It is still not known, however, whether $\pi^e$ is irrational.

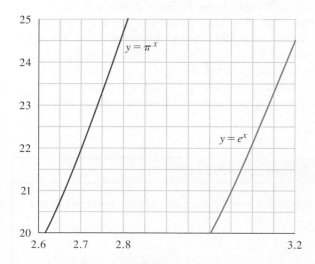

**60. (a)** Use your calculator to approximate the numbers $e\pi$ and $e + \pi$. *Remark:* It is not known whether these numbers are rational or irrational.

**(b)** Use your calculator to approximate $(e^{\pi\sqrt{163}})^{1/3}$. *Remark:* Contrary to the evidence on your calculator, it is known that this number is irrational.

**61.** Let $f(x) = e^x$. Let $L$ denote the function that is the inverse of $f$.

**(a)** On the same set of axes, sketch the graphs of $f$ and $L$. *Hint:* You do not need the equation for $L(x)$.

**(b)** Specify the domain, range, intercept, and asymptote for the function $L$ and its graph.

**(c)** Graph each of the following functions. Specify the intercept and asymptote in each case.
   **(i)** $y = -L(x)$   **(ii)** $y = L(-x)$   **(iii)** $y = L(x-1)$

**62.** The text mentioned two ways to define the number $e$. One involved the expression $(1 + 1/x)^x$ and the other involved a tangent line. In this exercise you'll see that these two approaches are, in fact, related. For convenience, we'll write the expression $(1 + 1/x)^x$ using the letter $n$ rather than $x$ (so that we can use $x$ for something else in a moment.) Thus, we have

$$(1 + 1/n)^n \approx e \qquad \text{as } n \text{ becomes larger and} \qquad (1)$$
$$\text{larger without bound}$$

Working from this approximation, we'll obtain evidence that the slope of the tangent to the curve $y = e^x$ at $x = 0$ is 1. (A rigorous proof requires calculus.)

**(a)** Define $x$ by the equation $x = 1/n$. As $n$ becomes larger and larger without bound, what happens to the corresponding values of $x$? Complete the following table.

| $n$ | $10^2$ | $10^3$ | $10^6$ | $10^9$ |
|---|---|---|---|---|
| $x$ | | | | |

**(b)** Substitute $x = 1/n$ in approximation (1) to obtain

$$(1 + x)^{1/x} \approx e \qquad \text{as } x \text{ approaches 0}$$

Next, raise both sides to the power $x$ to obtain

$$(1 + x) \approx e^x \qquad \text{as } x \text{ approaches 0} \qquad (2)$$

Approximation (2) says that the curve $y = e^x$ looks more and more like the line $y = 1 + x$ as $x$ approaches 0. For numerical perspective on this, complete the following tables. These results suggest (but do not *prove*) that the line $y = 1 + x$ is tangent to the curve $y = e^x$ at $x = 0$. Thus, the results suggest that the slope of the tangent to $y = e^x$ at $x = 0$ is 1.

| $x$ | 0.3 | 0.2 | $10^{-1}$ | $10^{-2}$ | $10^{-3}$ | $10^{-4}$ |
|---|---|---|---|---|---|---|
| $x + 1$ | | | | | | |
| $e^x$ | | | | | | |

| $x$ | $-0.3$ | $-0.2$ | $-10^{-1}$ | $-10^{-2}$ | $-10^{-3}$ | $-10^{-4}$ |
|---|---|---|---|---|---|---|
| $x + 1$ | | | | | | |
| $e^x$ | | | | | | |

## C

*For Exercises 63 and 64, you need to know the definitions of the functions cosh and sinh given in Exercises 55 and 57, respectively.*

**63.** Consider the following two equations:

$$[\cosh(x)]^2 - 2[\sinh(x)]^2 = 1 \qquad [\cosh(x)]^2 - [\sinh(x)]^2 = 1$$

Ⓖ

(a) One of the given equations is an identity, and the other is not. Use a graphing utility to determine which equation is *not* an identity. For that equation, make a conjecture about the root(s). Then use the definitions of $\cosh(x)$ and $\sinh(x)$ to verify algebraically that your conjecture is valid.

(b) For the other equation, use the definitions of $\cosh(x)$ and $\sinh(x)$ to prove that the equation is indeed an identity.

**64.** Consider the following three equations:

$$[\cosh(x)]^2 = \frac{1}{2}[\cosh(2x) + 1] \qquad [\sinh(x)]^2 = \frac{1}{2}[\cosh(2x) - 1]$$

$$[\sinh(x)]^2 = \frac{1}{2}[\sinh(2x) + 1]$$

Ⓖ

(a) Only one of the three equations is not an identity. Use a graphing utility to find out which. For that equation, are there any values of $x$ for which the equation becomes a true statement? If so, use the graphing utility to estimate to the nearest hundredth each such value.

(b) For each of the other two equations, use the definitions of $\cosh(x)$ and $\sinh(x)$ to prove that the equation is indeed an identity.

---

## PROJECT    | COFFEE TEMPERATURE

Suppose that a cup of hot coffee at a temperature of $T_0$ is set down to cool in a room where the temperature is kept at $T_1$. Then the temperature of the coffee as it cools can be modeled by the function

$$f(t) = (T_0 - T_1)e^{kt} + T_1 \qquad\qquad (1)$$

Here, $f(t)$ is the temperature of the coffee after $t$ minutes; $t = 0$ corresponds to the initial instant when the temperature of the hot coffee is $T_0$; and $k$ is a (negative) constant that depends, among other factors, on the dimensions of the cup and the material from which it is constructed. [This model is derived in calculus. It is based on *Newton's law of cooling*: The rate of change of temperature of a cooling object is *proportional* to the difference between the temperature of the object and the surrounding temperature. (*Note: y is proportional to x* means $y = kx$ for some constant $k$.)]

After studying the following example, solve Problem A below by applying equation (1) and using the technique shown in the example. Then try your hand at Problem B. You won't be able to complete Problem B using the techniques developed in this text up to now. In complete sentences, explain exactly at which point you get stuck. What would you have to know how to do to complete the solution? (In the next section we discuss *logarithms,* which will allow us to complete Problem B.) For now, use a graphing utility to obtain an approximate answer for Problem B.

---

**EXAMPLE**    |   **Coffee Temperature Project**

Given that the graph of the function $y = ae^{kx}$ passes through the points $(0, 2)$ and $(3, 5)$, find $y$ when $x = 7$.

**SOLUTION**

Substituting $x = 0$ and $y = 2$ in the given equation yields $2 = ae^0$, and therefore $a = 2$. Next, substituting $x = 3$ and $y = 5$ in the equation $y = 2e^{kx}$ yields $5 = 2e^{k(3)}$, or $e^{3k} = 2.5$. This last equation can be rewritten $(e^k)^3 = 2.5$. Taking the cube root of both sides gives us

$$e^k = 2.5^{1/3} \qquad (2)$$

The original function can now be written as follows

$$\begin{aligned} y &= 2e^{kx} = 2(e^k)^x \\ &= 2(2.5^{1/3})^x \qquad \text{using equation (2)} \end{aligned}$$

That is, $y = 2(2.5^{x/3})$. In this form, we can calculate $y$ when $x$ is given. In particular then, when $x = 7$, we obtain

$$\begin{aligned} y &= 2(2.5^{7/3}) \\ &\approx 16.97 \qquad \text{using a calculator} \end{aligned}$$

---

## PROBLEM A

Suppose that a cup of hot coffee at a temperature of 185°F is set down to cool in a room where the temperature is kept at 70°F. What is the temperature of the coffee ten minutes later?

## PROBLEM B

Suppose that a cup of hot coffee at a temperature of 185°F is set down to cool in a room where the temperature is kept at 70°F. How long will it take for the coffee to cool to 140°F?

---

# 5.3 LOGARITHMIC FUNCTIONS

*But if logarithms have lost their role as the centerpiece of computational mathematics, the logarithmic function remains central to almost every branch of mathematics, pure or applied. It shows up in a host of applications, ranging from physics and chemistry to biology, psychology, art, and music.* —Eli Maor in *e: The Story of a Number* (Princeton, N.J.: Princeton University Press, 1994)

*[John Napier] hath set my head and hands a work with his new and admirable logarithms. I hope to see him this summer, if it please God, for I never saw book that pleased me better, or made me more wonder.* —Henry Briggs, March 10, 1615

*It has been thought that the earliest reference to the logarithmic curve was made by the Italian Evangelista Torricelli in a letter on the year 1644, but Paul Tannery made it practically certain that Descartes knew the curve in 1639.* —Florian Cajori in *A History of Mathematics*, 4th ed. (New York: Chelsea Publishing Co., 1985)

*For the number whose logarithm is unity, let* e *be written, . . .* —Leonhard Euler in a letter written in 1727 or 1728

In the previous two sections we studied exponential functions. Now we consider functions that are inverses of exponential functions. These inverse functions are called *logarithmic functions*.

**Figure 1**
The exponential function $y = b^x$ is one-to-one.

Having said this, let's back up for a moment to review briefly some of the basic ideas behind inverse functions (as discussed in Section 3.6). We start with a given function $F$, for example, $F(x) = 3x$, that is one-to-one. (That is, for each output there is only one input.) Then, by interchanging the inputs and outputs, we obtain a new function, the so-called inverse function. In the case of $F(x) = 3x$, it's easy to find an equation defining the inverse function. We just interchange $x$ and $y$ in the equation $y = 3x$ to obtain $x = 3y$. Solving for $y$ in this last equation then gives us $y = \frac{1}{3}x$, which defines the inverse function. Using function notation, we can summarize the situation by writing $F(x) = 3x$ and $F^{-1}(x) = \frac{1}{3}x$.

In the preceding paragraph we saw that a particular linear function had an inverse, and we found a formula for that inverse. Now let's repeat that same reasoning, beginning with an exponential function. First, we must make sure the exponential function $f$ defined by $f(x) = b^x$ is one-to-one. We can see this by applying the horizontal line test, as indicated in Figure 1. Next, since $f(x) = b^x$ is one-to-one, it has an inverse function. Let's study this inverse.

We begin by writing the exponential function $f(x) = b^x$ in the form

$$y = b^x \qquad (1)$$

Then, to obtain an equation for $f^{-1}$, we interchange $x$ and $y$ in equation (1). This gives us

$$x = b^y \qquad (2)$$

The crucial step now is to express equation (2) in words:

$$y \text{ is the exponent to which } b \text{ must be raised to yield } x. \qquad (3)$$

Statement (3) defines the function that is the inverse of $y = b^x$. Now we introduce a notation that will allow us to write this statement in a more compact form.

---

**DEFINITION** | $\log_b x$

We define the expression $\log_b x$ to mean "the exponent to which $b$ must be raised to yield $x$." ($\log_b x$ is read *log base b of x* or *the logarithm of x to the base b*.)

**EXAMPLES**
(a) $\log_2 8 = 3$, since 3 is the exponent to which 2 must be raised to yield 8.
(b) $\log_{10}(1/10) = -1$, since $-1$ is the exponent to which 10 must be raised to yield $1/10$.
(c) $\log_5 1 = 0$, since 0 is the exponent to which 5 must be raised to yield 1.

---

**TABLE 1**

| Exponential form of equation | Logarithmic form of equation |
|---|---|
| $8 = 2^3$ | $\log_2 8 = 3$ |
| $\frac{1}{9} = 3^{-2}$ | $\log_3 \frac{1}{9} = -2$ |
| $1 = e^0$ | $\log_e 1 = 0$ |
| $a = b^c$ | $\log_b a = c$ |

Using this notation, statement (3) becomes

$$y = \log_b x$$

Since (2) and (3) are equivalent, we have the following important relationship.

$$\boxed{y = \log_b x \qquad \text{is equivalent to} \qquad x = b^y}$$

We say that the equation $y = \log_b x$ is in **logarithmic form** and that the equivalent equation $x = b^y$ is in **exponential form.** Table 1 displays some examples.

Let us now summarize our discussion up to this point.

1. According to the horizontal line test, the function $f(x) = b^x$ is one-to-one and therefore possesses an inverse. This inverse function is written

$$f^{-1}(x) = \log_b x$$

2. $\log_b a = c$ means that $a = b^c$.

To graph the function $y = \log_b x$, we recall from Section 3.5 that the graph of a function and its inverse are reflections of one another about the line $y = x$. Thus to graph $y = \log_b x$, we need only reflect the curve $y = b^x$ about the line $y = x$. This is shown in Figure 2 for the case $b > 1$.

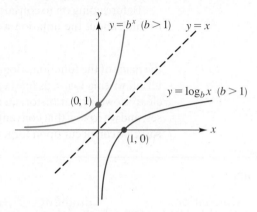

**Figure 2**

NOTE   For the rest of this chapter we assume that the base $b$ is greater than 1 when we use the expression $\log_b x$.

With the aid of Figure 2 we can make the following observations about the function $y = \log_b x$.

**PROPERTY SUMMARY**
**The Logarithmic Function $y = \log_b x$   ($b > 1$)**

Domain:   $(0, \infty)$
Range:   $(-\infty, \infty)$
$y$-intercept:   none
$x$-intercept:   1
Asymptote:   $y$-axis

**Figure 3**

One aspect of the function $y = \log_b x$ may not be immediately apparent to you from Figures 2 and 3: The function grows or increases *very* slowly. Consider $y = \log_2 x$, for example. Let's ask how large $x$ must be before the curve reaches the height $y = 10$ (see Figure 4).

**Figure 4**

To answer this question, we substitute $y = 10$ in the equation $y = \log_2 x$:

$$10 = \log_2 x$$

Writing this equation in exponential form yields

$$x = 2^{10} = 1024$$

In other words, we must go out beyond 1000 on the $x$-axis before the curve $y = \log_2 x$ reaches a height of 10 units. Exercise 63 at the end of this section asks you to show that the graph of $y = \log_2 x$ doesn't reach a height of 100 until $x$ is greater than $10^{30}$. (Numbers as large as $10^{30}$ rarely occur in any of the sciences. For instance, the distance in inches to the Andromeda galaxy is less than $10^{24}$.) The point we are emphasizing is this: The graph of $y = \log_2 x$ (or $\log_b x$) is always rising, but very slowly.

Before going on to consider some numerical examples, let's pause for a moment to think about the notation we've been using. In the expression

$$\log_b x$$

the name of the function is $\log_b$ and the input is $x$. To emphasize this, we might be better off writing $\log_b x$ as $\log_b(x)$, so that the similarity to the familiar $f(x)$ notation is clear. However, for historical reasons* the convention is to suppress the parentheses, and we follow that convention here. In the box that follows, we indicate some errors that can occur upon forgetting that $\log_b$ is the name of a function, not a number.

## ERRORS TO AVOID

| Error | Correction | Comment |
|---|---|---|
| $\dfrac{\log_2 8}{\log_2 4} = \dfrac{8}{4}$ | $\dfrac{\log_2 8}{\log_2 4} = \dfrac{3}{2}$ | $\log_2$ is the name of a function. It is not a factor that can be "cancelled" from the numerator and denominator. |
| $\dfrac{\log_2 16}{16} = \log_2$ | $\dfrac{\log_2 16}{16} = \dfrac{4}{16} = \dfrac{1}{4}$ | This "equation" is nonsense. On the left-hand side there is a quotient of two real numbers, which is a real number. On the right-hand side is the name of a function. |

We conclude this section with a set of examples involving logarithms and logarithmic functions. In one way or another, every example makes use of the key fact that the equation $\log_b a = c$ is equivalent to $b^c = a$.

### EXAMPLE 1   Comparing two logarithms by using the definition

Which quantity is larger: $\log_3 10$ or $\log_7 40$?

**SOLUTION**
First we estimate $\log_3 10$. This quantity represents the exponent to which 3 must be raised to yield 10. Since $3^2 = 9$ (less than 10), but $3^3 = 27$ (more than 10), we conclude that the quantity $\log_3 10$ lies between 2 and 3. In a similar way we can

---

*The notation *log* was introduced in 1624 by the astronomer Johannes Kepler (1571–1630). In Leonhard Euler's text *Introduction to Analysis of the Infinite,* first published in 1748, appears the statement, "It has been customary to designate the logarithm of $y$ by the symbol $\log y$."

estimate $\log_7 40$; this quantity represents the exponent to which 7 must be raised to yield 40. Since $7^1 = 7$ (less than 40) while $7^2 = 49$ (more than 40), we conclude that the quantity $\log_7 40$ lies between 1 and 2. It now follows from these two estimates that $\log_3 10$ is larger than $\log_7 40$.

**EXAMPLE 2**  **Evaluating a logarithmic expression**

Evaluate $\log_4 32$.

**SOLUTION**

Let $y = \log_4 32$. The exponential form of this equation is $4^y = 32$. Now, since both 4 and 32 are powers of 2, we can rewrite the equation $4^y = 32$ using the same base on both sides:

$$(2^2)^y = 2^5$$
$$2^{2y} = 2^5$$
$$2y = 5 \qquad \text{using Property 4 on page 328}$$
$$y = \frac{5}{2} \qquad \text{as required}$$

**EXAMPLE 3**  **Sketching the graph of a logarithmic function and its reflection**

Graph the following equations:
**(a)** $y = \log_{10} x$;      **(b)** $y = -\log_{10} x$.

**SOLUTION**

**(a)** The function $y = \log_{10} x$ is the inverse function for the exponential function $y = 10^x$. Thus we obtain the graph of $y = \log_{10} x$ by reflecting the graph of $y = 10^x$ in the line $y = x$; see Figure 5(a).

**(b)** To graph $y = -\log_{10} x$, we reflect the graph of $y = \log_{10} x$ in the $x$-axis; see Figure 5(b).

(a)

(b)

**Figure 5**

**EXAMPLE** 4 | **Finding the domain of a function defined by a logarithm**

Find the domain of the function $f(x) = \log_2(12 - 4x)$.

**SOLUTION**
As you can see by looking back at Figure 3 on page 349, the inputs for the logarithmic function must be positive. So, in the case at hand, we require that the quantity $12 - 4x$ be positive. Consequently, we have

$$12 - 4x > 0$$
$$-4x > -12$$
$$x < 3$$

Therefore the domain of the function $f(x) = \log_2(12 - 4x)$ is the interval $(-\infty, 3)$.

The next example concerns the exponential function $y = e^x$ and its inverse function, $y = \log_e x$. Many books, as well as calculators, abbreviate the expression $\log_e x$ by $\ln x$, read *natural log of x*.\* For reference and emphasis we repeat this fact in the following box. (Incidentally, on most calculators, "log" is an abbreviation for $\log_{10}$.)

**DEFINITION** | The "ln" Notation for Base e Logarithms

$\ln x$ means $\log_e x$

**EXAMPLES**
1. $\ln e = 1$ because $\ln e$ stands for $\log_e e$, which equals 1.
2. $\ln(e^2) = 2$ because $\ln(e^2)$ stands for $\log_e(e^2)$, which equals 2.
3. $\ln 1 = 0$ because $\ln 1$ stands for $\log_e 1$, which equals 0. (The exponential form of the equation $\ln 1 = 0$ is $e^0 = 1$.)

**EXAMPLE** 5 | **Sketching the graph of ln x and a translation**

Graph the following functions:
**(a)** $y = \ln x$; **(b)** $y = \ln(x - 1)$.

**SOLUTION**
**(a)** The function $y = \ln x$ $(=\log_e x)$ is the inverse of $y = e^x$. Thus its graph is obtained by reflecting the graph of $y = e^x$ in the line $y = x$, as in Figure 6(a).
**(b)** To graph $y = \ln(x - 1)$, we take the graph of $y = \ln x$ and move it one unit in the positive $x$-direction; see Figure 6(b).

---

\*According to the historian Florian Cajori, the notation $\ln x$ was used by (and perhaps first introduced by) Irving Stringham in his text *Uniplanar Algebra* (San Francisco: University Press, 1893).

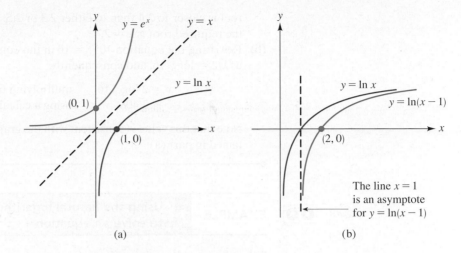

Figure 6

(a)

(b)

---

**EXAMPLE** 6 **Solving an equation involving an exponential function**

Consider the equation $10^{x/2} = 16$.

**(a)** Use a graphing utility to show that the equation has exactly one root. Then estimate the root to the nearest one-tenth (by finding an appropriate viewing rectangle).

**(b)** Solve the given equation algebraically by rewriting it in logarithmic form. Give two forms for the answer: an exact expression and a calculator approximation rounded to three decimal places. Check to see that the result is consistent with the graphical estimate obtained in part (a).

**SOLUTION**

**(a)** Figure 7(a) shows a viewing rectangle in which the graphs of $y = 10^{x/2}$ and $y = 16$ intersect. The $x$-coordinate of this intersection point is a root of the given equation. As you can check by zooming out from this view, there are no other intersection points, and thus no other roots of the given equation.

   From Figure 7(a) we know that the required root is between 2 and 3, a bit closer to 2 than to 3. This suggests that we try a viewing rectangle with $x$ running from 2 to 2.5, as indicated in Figure 7(b). This view shows that the

**GRAPHICAL PERSPECTIVE**

$y = 10^{x/2}$    $y = 16$

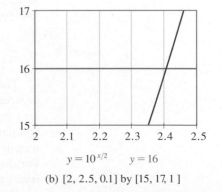

$y = 10^{x/2}$    $y = 16$

Figure 7       (a) [−1, 3, 1] by [0, 20, 10]       (b) [2, 2.5, 0.1] by [15, 17, 1]

root is closer to 2.4 than to either 2.3 or 2.5. Thus to the nearest one-tenth the required root is $x \approx 2.4$.

**(b)** Rewriting the equation $10^{x/2} = 16$ in the equivalent logarithmic form gives us $x/2 = \log_{10} 16$, and consequently,

$$x = 2 \log_{10} 16 \qquad \text{multiplying both sides by 2}$$
$$\approx 2.408 \qquad \text{using a calculator}$$

Note that this value is consistent with the graphical estimate 2.4 that was obtained in part (a).

| EXAMPLE | 7 | **Using the natural logarithm function to solve an equation** |

Solve the equation $e^{2t-5} = 5000$. Give two forms for the answer: an exact expression and a calculator approximation rounded to three decimal places.

**SOLUTION**
Rewriting the equation in logarithmic form yields $2t - 5 = \ln 5000$. Consequently, we have

$$2t = 5 + \ln 5000$$
$$t = (5 + \ln 5000)/2 \qquad \text{dividing by 2}$$
$$\approx 6.759 \qquad \text{using a calculator}$$

*Remark*: This result says that, for the function $y = e^{2t-5}$, a relatively small input of about 6.8 produces a very large output of 5000. This is a reminder of the fact that exponential functions grow very rapidly (when the exponents are positive and the base is greater than 1).

The next example indicates one of the many ways that logarithmic functions occur in applications. Geologists record the vibrations from an earthquake on a device known as a *seismograph*. Figure 8 shows a (simplified) output from a seismograph during an earthquake.

**Figure 8**

The maximum amplitude of the shock wave provides a measure of the intensity or strength of the particular earthquake. One of the problems faced by the American geologist Charles F. Richter (1900–1985) in devising a meaningful scale for comparing the sizes of earthquakes had to do with the fact that the maximum amplitudes for different earthquakes can vary greatly, by factors of thousands or more. For instance, an earthquake so small that most people would not feel it might register a maximum amplitude of 0.2 mm, whereas a destructive (yet not major) quake might register a maximum amplitude of 1000 mm. But a comparison scale for rating earthquakes that ranged from 0.2 to 1000, say, would not be especially useful; the wide range of numbers would make it nonintuitive. For instance, you might ask a friend to rate on a scale of 1 to 10 a movie he or she had seen, but you wouldn't want to use a scale of 1 to 1000. It would be nonintuitive and not especially informative in most cases. On the other hand, if we introduce a logarithm function in this example, we have $\log_{10} 0.2 \approx -0.7$ and $\log_{10} 1000 = 3$. So while the original amplitudes range numerically from (approximately) 0 to 1000, the logs range from (approximately) $-1$ to 3, a much smaller, more manageable scale in this case. This is the observation that Dr. Richter used in defining his scale for comparing earthquakes. In his words:

> . . . *the range between the largest and smallest magnitudes seemed unmanageably large. Dr. Beno Gutenberg [1889–1960] then made the natural suggestion to plot the amplitudes logarithmically.*

Charles F. Richter in an interview by Henry Spall of the U.S. Geological Survey, http://wwwneic.cr.usgs.gov/neis/seismology/people/int_richter.html

In its simplest form, the Richter magnitude $M$ of an earthquake is defined by the equation

$$M = \log_{10}\left(\frac{A}{A_0}\right)$$

where $A$ is the maximum amplitude recorded on a standard seismograph located 100 km from the epicenter of the earthquake, and the constant $A_0$ is the maximum amplitude of a certain standard intensity earthquake. In Example 8 we use this definition to compare the intensities of two earthquakes. *Remark*: Richter introduced this formula for the magnitude of an earthquake in 1935. Beginning in 1936, he worked with Gutenberg to modify the formula to account for different types of seismographs located at arbitrary distances from the epicenter of the quake. For more information about earthquakes and hands-on experience in computing the Richter magnitude of an earthquake, see the following *VirtualEarthquake* web pages by Professor Gary Novak:

http://vcourseware.calstatela.edu/VirtualEarthquake/VQuakeIntro.html

---

**EXAMPLE 8    Using the Richter magnitude scale**

---

The Richter magnitudes for two large earthquakes are given in Table 2. Use the formula $M = \log_{10}(A/A_0)$ to determine how many times stronger was the earthquake in India than the earthquake in California. Assume that $A$ (the maximum amplitude on the seismograph) is a measure of the strength of an earthquake.

**TABLE 2    Data for Two Earthquakes**

| Location of earthquake | Date | Richter magnitude $M$ |
|---|---|---|
| Northridge, California | January 17, 1994 | 6.8 |
| Gujarat Province, India | January 26, 2001 | 7.9 |

**SOLUTION**

We begin by solving the Richter magnitude equation $M = \log_{10}(A/A_0)$ for $A$. We want to do this so that we can compare the values of $A$ for the two quakes. Rewriting the equation in its equivalent exponential form yields $A/A_0 = 10^M$, and therefore

$$A = A_0 10^M$$

Now, using this last equation and the values of $M$ given in Table 2, we have

For Northridge quake: | For Gujarat quake:
$$A = A_0 10^{6.8} \qquad\qquad A = A_0 10^{7.9}$$

Computing the ratio of these two $A$-values gives us

$$\frac{A\text{-value for Gujarat}}{A\text{-value for Northridge}} = \frac{A_0 10^{7.9}}{A_0 10^{6.8}} = 10^{7.9-6.8} = 10^{1.1}$$

$$\approx 12.6 \qquad \text{using a calculator}$$

In summary, the quake in India was more than 12 times stronger than the one in California, even though the Richter magnitudes differ by only 1.1. *Remark*: The Richter scale is an example of what we call a *logarithmic scale*. Exercise 45 asks you to show that if the Richter magnitudes of two quakes differ by an amount $d$, then the larger quake is $10^d$ (not just $d$) times stronger than the smaller quake. Other applications of logarithmic scales are given in Exercises 46–52.

---

# EXERCISE SET 5.3

**A**

*In Exercises 1–4, fill in the blanks.*

1. If $f$ and $g$ are inverse functions, then:
   (a) $f[g(x)] = $ _____ for each $x$ in the domain of $g$.
   (b) $g[f(x)] = $ _____ for each $x$ in the domain of _____.
2. Suppose that $f$ and $g$ are inverse functions, 5 is in the domain of $f$, and 3 is in the domain of $g$. Then $f[g(3)] = $ _____, and $g[f(5)] = $ _____.
3. (a) The functions $f(x) = 2^x$ and $g(x) = $ _____ are inverse functions.
   (b) In view of part (a) we have $2^{\log_2 x} = $ _____ for each positive number $x$, and $\log_2(2^x) = $ _____ for all real numbers $x$.
   (c) So, for example, without calculating, I know that $2^{\log_2 99} = $ _____ and also that $\log_2(2^{-\pi}) = $ _____.
4. (a) The functions $f(x) = e^x$ and $g(x) = $ _____ are inverse functions.
   (b) In view of part (a) we have $e^{\ln x} = $ _____ for each positive number $x$, and $\ln(e^x) = $ _____ for all real numbers $x$.
   (c) So, for example, without calculating, I know that $e^{\ln 99} = $ _____ and also that $\ln(e^{-\pi}) = $ _____.

*Exercises 5–8 provide additional review on the inverse function concept. The exercises do not explicitly involve logarithmic functions (but may be helpful to you because we've defined logarithmic functions in terms of inverse functions).*

5. Which of the following functions are one-to-one and therefore possess an inverse?
   (a) $y = x + 1$
   (b) $y = (x + 1)^2$
   (c) $y = (x + 1)^3$
6. Let $f(x) = 4x - 5$.
   (a) Find $f^{-1}(x)$.
   (b) Find $f[f^{-1}(x)]$.
   (c) Find $[f(x)][f^{-1}(x)]$.
   (d) Note that your answers for parts (b) and (c) are not the same (or at least they shouldn't be). Of the two expressions given in parts (b) and (c), which one is involved in the definition of an inverse function?
7. Let $f(x) = x^3 + 5x + 1$. Given that $f^{-1}$ exists and 6 is in the domain of $f^{-1}$, evaluate $f[f^{-1}(6)]$.
8. The graph of $y = f(x)$ is a line segment joining the two points $(3, -2)$ and $(-1, 5)$. Specify the corresponding endpoints for the graph of:
   (a) $y = f^{-1}(x)$
   (b) $y = f^{-1}(x - 1)$

*In Exercises 9 and 10, write each equation in logarithmic form.*

**9.** (a) $9 = 3^2$
    (b) $1000 = 10^3$
    (c) $7^3 = 343$
    (d) $\sqrt{2} = 2^{1/2}$

**10.** (a) $1/125 = 5^{-3}$
    (b) $e^0 = 1$
    (c) $5^x = 6$
    (d) $e^{3t} = 8$

*In Exercises 11 and 12, write each equation in exponential form.*

**11.** (a) $\log_2 32 = 5$
    (b) $\log_{10} 1 = 0$
    (c) $\log_e \sqrt{e} = 1/2$
    (d) $\ln(1/e) = -1$

**12.** (a) $\ln u = s$
    (b) $\log_a b = c$

*In Exercises 13 and 14, complete the tables.*

**13.**

| x | 1 | 10 | $10^2$ | $10^3$ | $10^{-1}$ | $10^{-2}$ | $10^{-3}$ |
|---|---|----|--------|--------|-----------|-----------|-----------|
| $\log_{10} x$ | | | | | | | |

**14.**

| x | 1 | e | $e^2$ | $e^3$ | $e^{-1}$ | $e^{-2}$ | $e^{-3}$ |
|---|---|---|-------|-------|----------|----------|----------|
| $\ln x$ | | | | | | | |

*In Exercises 15 and 16, rely on the definition of $\log_b x$ (in the box on page 348) to decide which of the two quantities is larger.*

**15.** (a) $\log_5 30$ or $\log_8 60$
    (b) $\ln 17$ or $\log_{10} 17$

**16.** (a) $\log_9 80$ or $\ln(e^2)$
    (b) $\log_2 3$ or $\log_3 2$

*In Exercises 17 and 18, evaluate each expression.*

**17.** (a) $\log_9 27$
    (b) $\log_4(1/32)$
    (c) $\log_5 5\sqrt{5}$

**18.** (a) $\log_{25}(1/625)$
    (b) $\log_{16}(1/64)$
    (c) $\log_{10} 10$
    (d) $\log_2 8\sqrt{2}$

*In Exercises 19 and 20, solve each equation for x by converting to exponential form. In Exercises 19(b) and 20, give two forms for each answer: one involving e and the other a calculator approximation rounded to two decimal places.*

**19.** (a) $\log_4 x = -2$
    (b) $\ln x = -2$

**20.** (a) $\log_5 x = e$
    (b) $\ln x = -e$

*In Exercises 21 and 22, find the domain of each function.*

**21.** (a) $y = \log_4 5x$
    (b) $y = \log_{10}(3 - 4x)$
    (c) $y = \ln(x^2)$
    (d) $y = (\ln x)^2$
    (e) $y = \ln(x^2 - 25)$

**22.** (a) $y = \ln(2 - x - x^2)$
    (b) $y = \log_{10} \dfrac{2x + 3}{x - 5}$

**23.** In the accompanying figure, what are the coordinates of the four points $A$, $B$, $C$, and $D$?

**24.** In the accompanying figure, what are the coordinates of the points $A$, $B$, $C$, and $D$?

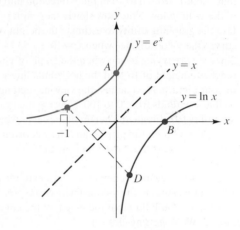

*In Exercises 25–30, graph each function and specify the domain, range, intercept(s), and asymptote.*

**25.** (a) $y = \log_2 x$
    (b) $y = -\log_2 x$
    (c) $y = \log_2(-x)$
    (d) $y = -\log_2(-x)$

**26.** (a) $y = \ln x$
    (b) $y = -\ln x$
    (c) $y = \ln(-x)$
    (d) $y = -\ln(-x)$

**27.** $y = -\log_3(x - 2) + 1$

**28.** $y = -\log_{10}(x + 1)$

**29.** $y = \ln(x + e)$

**30.** $y = \ln(-x) + e$

*In Exercises 31 and 32, simplify each expression.*

**31.** (a) $\ln e^4$
    (b) $\ln(1/e)$
    (c) $\ln \sqrt{e}$

**32.** (a) $\ln e$
    (b) $\ln e^{-2}$
    (c) $(\ln e)^{-2}$

*For Exercises 33–40:*

Ⓖ (a) *Use a graphing utility to estimate the root(s) of the equation to the nearest one-tenth (as in Example 6).*

    (b) *Solve the given equation algebraically by first rewriting it in logarithmic form. Give two forms for each answer: an exact expression and a calculator approximation rounded to three decimal places. Check to see that each result is consistent with the graphical estimate obtained in part (a).*

**33.** $10^x = 25$

**34.** $10^{2x-1} = 145$

**35.** $10^{x^2} = 40$

**36.** $(10^x)^2 = 40$

**37.** $e^{2t+3} = 10$

**38.** $e^{t-1} = 16$

**39.** $e^{1-4t} = 12.405$

**40.** $e^{3x^2} = 112$

Ⓖ **41.** Use graphs to help answer the following questions.

    **(a)** For which $x$-values is $\ln x < \log_{10} x$?

    **(b)** For which $x$-values is $\ln x > \log_{10} x$?

    **(c)** For which $x$-values is $e^x < 10^x$?

    **(d)** For which $x$-values is $e^x > 10^x$?

Ⓖ **42.** This exercise demonstrates the very slow growth of the natural logarithm function $y = \ln x$. We consider the following question: How large must $x$ be before the graph of $y = \ln x$ reaches a height of 10?

    **(a)** Graph the function $y = \ln x$ using a viewing rectangle that extends from 0 to 10 in the $x$-direction and 0 to 12 in the $y$-direction. Note how slowly the graph rises. Use the graphing utility to estimate the height of the curve (the $y$-coordinate) when $x = 10$.

    **(b)** Since we are trying to see when the graph of $y = \ln x$ reaches a height of 10, add the horizontal line $y = 10$ to your picture. Next, adjust the viewing rectangle so that $x$ extends from 0 to 100. Now use the graphing utility to estimate the height of the curve when $x = 100$. [As both the picture and the $y$-coordinate indicate, we're still not even halfway to 10. Go on to part (c).]

    **(c)** Change the viewing rectangle so that $x$ extends to 1000, then estimate the $y$-coordinate corresponding to $x = 1000$. (You'll find that the height of the curve is almost 7. We're getting closer.)

    **(d)** Repeat part (c) with $x$ extending to 10,000. (You'll find that the height of the curve is over 9. We're almost there.)

    **(e)** The last step: Change the viewing rectangle so that $x$ extends to 100,000, then use the graphing utility to estimate the $x$-value for which $\ln x = 10$. As a check on your estimate, rewrite the equation $\ln x = 10$ in exponential form, and evaluate the expression that you obtain for $x$.

*In Exercises 43 and 44, Richter magnitudes of earthquakes are given. Follow the method of Example 8 to determine how many times stronger one quake was than the other.*

**43.**

| Location of earthquake | Date | Richter magnitude $M$ |
|---|---|---|
| Bombay, India | September 29, 1993 | 6.4 |
| (15 mi. east of) San Salvador, El Salvador | February 13, 2001 | 6.6 |

**44.**

| Location of earthquake | Date | Richter magnitude $M$ |
|---|---|---|
| Napa, California | September 3, 2000 | 5.2 |
| Sumatra, Indonesia | June 4, 2000 | 8.0 |

## B

*As background for Exercises 45 and 46, you need to have read Example 8.*

**45.** Suppose that an earthquake has a Richter magnitude of $M_0$, and a second earthquake has a magnitude of $M_0 + d$ (where $d > 0$). Show that the second earthquake is $10^d$ times stronger than the first earthquake.

**46.** In 1956 the geologists Gutenberg and Richter developed the following formula for estimating the amount of energy $E$ released in an earthquake: $\log_{10} E = 4.4 + (1.5)M$, where $E$ is the energy in joules and $M$ is the Richter magnitude. Now refer to the following table, and let $E_1$ denote the energy of the quake in the Philippines and $E_2$ the energy of the quake in Washington. Compute the ratio $E_1/E_2$ to compare the energies of the two quakes.

| Location of earthquake | Date | Richter magnitude $M$ |
|---|---|---|
| Mindanao, Philippines | January 1, 2001 | 7.5 |
| (northeast of) Olympia, Washington | February 28, 2001 | 6.8 |

**47.** The intensity of the sounds that the human ear can detect varies over a very wide range of values. For instance, a whisper from 1 meter away has an intensity of approximately $10^{-10}$ watts per square meter (W/m$^2$), whereas, from a distance of 50 meters, the intensity of a launch of the Space Shuttle is approximately $10^8$ W/m$^2$. For a sound with intensity $I$, the sound level $\beta$ is defined by

$$\beta = 10 \log_{10}(I/I_0)$$

where the constant $I_0$ is the sound intensity of a barely audible sound at the threshold of hearing. The units for the sound level $\beta$ are *decibels,* abbreviated dB.

    **(a)** Solve the equation $\beta = 10 \log_{10}(I/I_0)$ for $I$ by first dividing by 10 and then converting to exponential form.

    **(b)** The sound level for a power lawnmower is $\beta = 100$ db, and that for a cat purring is $\beta = 10$ db. Use your result in part (a) to determine how many times more intense is the power mower sound than the cat's purring.

**48.** A sound level of $\beta = 120$ db is at the threshold of pain. (Some loud rock concerts reach this level.) The sound intensity that corresponds to $\beta = 120$ db is 1 W/m$^2$. Use this information and the equation $\beta = 10 \log_{10}(I/I_0)$ to determine $I_0$, the intensity of a barely audible sound at the threshold of hearing. What is the decibel level, $\beta$, of a barely audible sound?

*In Exercises 49–52, use the following information on pH. Chemists define pH by the formula $pH = -\log_{10}[H^+]$, where $[H^+]$ is the hydrogen ion concentration measured in moles per liter. For example, if $[H^+] = 10^{-5}$, then $pH = 5$. Solutions with a pH of 7 are said to be neutral; a pH below 7 indicates an acid; and a pH above 7 indicates a base. (A calculator is helpful for Exercises 49 and 50.)*

**49.** **(a)** For some fruit juices, $[H^+] = 3 \times 10^{-4}$. Determine the pH and classify these juices as acid or base.
  **(b)** For sulfuric acid, $[H^+] = 1$. Find the pH.
**50.** An unknown substance has a hydrogen ion concentration of $3.5 \times 10^{-9}$. Classify the substance as acid or base.
**51.** What is the hydrogen ion concentration for black coffee if the pH is 5.9?
**52.** A chemist adds some acid to a solution changing the pH from 6 to 4. By what factor does the hydrogen ion concentration change?   *Note:* Lower pH corresponds to higher hydrogen ion concentration.

*In Exercises 53–60, decide which of the following properties apply to each function. (More than one property may apply to a function.)*
**A.** The function is increasing for $-\infty < x < \infty$.
**B.** The function is decreasing for $-\infty < x < \infty$.
**C.** The function has a turning point.
**D.** The function is one-to-one.
**E.** The graph has an asymptote.
**F.** The function is a polynomial function.
**G.** The domain of the function is $(-\infty, \infty)$.
**H.** The range of the function is $(-\infty, \infty)$.
**53.** $y = \ln x$          **54.** $y = \ln(-x)$
**55.** $y = -\ln x$         **56.** $y = \ln|x|$
**57.** $y = \ln x + e$      **58.** $y = x + \ln e$
**59.** $y = -\ln(-x)$       **60.** $y = (\ln x)^2$
**61.** Let $f(x) = e^{x+1}$. Find $f^{-1}(x)$ and sketch its graph. Specify any intercept or asymptote.
**62.** Let $g(t) = \ln(t - 1)$. Find $g^{-1}(t)$ and draw its graph. Specify any intercept or asymptote.
**63.** Estimate a value for $x$ such that $\log_2 x = 100$. Use the approximation $10^3 \approx 2^{10}$ to express your answer as a power of 10.          *Answer:* $10^{30}$
**64.** **(a)** How large must $x$ be before the graph of $y = \ln x$ reaches a height of $y = 100$?
  **(b)** How large must $x$ be before the graph of $y = e^x$ reaches a height of **(i)** $y = 100$? **(ii)** $y = 10^6$?
Ⓖ **65.** This exercise uses the natural logarithm and a regression line (i.e., a linear function) to find a simple formula relating the following two quantities:

$x$: the average distance of a planet from the sun
$y$: the period of a planet (i.e., the time required for a planet to make one complete revolution around the sun)

**(a)** Complete the following table. (In the table the abbreviation AU stands for *astronomical unit*, a unit of distance. By definition, one AU is the average distance from the earth to the sun.

| Planet | $x$ Average distance from the sun (AU) | $y$ Period (years) | ln $x$ | ln $y$ |
|---|---|---|---|---|
| Mercury | 0.387 | 0.241 | | |
| Venus | 0.723 | 0.615 | | |
| Earth | 1.000 | 1.000 | | |
| Mars | 1.523 | 1.881 | | |
| Jupiter | 5.202 | 11.820 | | |

**(b)** Use a graphing utility to obtain a scatter plot and a regression equation $Y = AX + B$ for the pairs of numbers $(\ln x, \ln y)$. After some rounding, you should obtain $A = 1.5$ and $B = 0$. Thus the quantities $\ln x$ and $\ln y$ are related as follows:

$$\ln y = 1.5 \ln x$$

**(c)** Show that the equation obtained in part (b) can be simplified to

$$y = x^{1.5} \qquad (1)$$

**(d)** Equation (1) was obtained using data for the first five planets from the sun. Complete the following table to see how well equation (1) fits the data for the remaining planets.

| Planet | $x$ (AU) | $y$ (years) [calculated from eqn. (1)] | $y$ (years) (from astronomical observations) |
|---|---|---|---|
| Saturn | 9.555 | | 29.46 |
| Uranus | 19.22 | | 84.01 |
| Neptune | 30.11 | | 164.79 |
| Pluto | 39.44 | | 248.50 |

*Remark*: Equation (1) is approximately *Kepler's third law of planetary motion*. According to George F. Simmons in *Calculus Gems* (New York: McGraw-Hill, Inc., 1992), "Kepler had struggled for more than twenty years to find this connection between a planet's *distance* from the sun and the *time* required to complete its orbit. He published his discovery in 1619 in a work entitled *Harmonices Mundi* (The Harmonies of the World)."

Ⓖ **66.** This exercise uses the natural logarithm and a regression line to find a simple formula relating the following two quantities.

$x$: the average distance of a planet from the sun

$y$: the average orbital velocity of the planet

**(a)** Complete the following table.

| Planet | $x$<br>Average distance from the sun (millions of miles) | $y$<br>Average orbital velocity (miles/sec) | ln $x$ | ln $y$ |
|--------|------|------|------|------|
| Mercury | 35.98 | 29.75 | | |
| Venus | 67.08 | 21.76 | | |
| Earth | 92.96 | 18.51 | | |
| Mars | 141.64 | 14.99 | | |

**(b)** Use a graphing utility to obtain a scatter plot and a regression equation $Y = AX + B$ for the pairs of numbers (ln $x$, ln $y$). You will find that $A = -0.500$ and $B = 5.184$. Thus the quantities ln $x$ and ln $y$ are related as follows:

$$\ln y = -0.500 \ln x + 5.184$$

**(c)** Show that the equation obtained in part (b) can be rewritten in the form

$$y = \frac{e^{5.184}}{\sqrt{x}} \qquad (2)$$

*Hint:* Convert from logarithmic to exponential form.

**(d)** Equation (2) was obtained using data for the first four planets from the sun. Complete the following table to see how well equation (2) fits the data for the remaining planets. (Round the answers to two decimal places.)

| Planet | $x$<br>Average distance from the sun (millions of miles) | $y$<br>Average orbital velocity (miles/sec) [calculated from eqn. (2)] | $y$<br>Average orbital velocity (miles/sec) (from astronomical observations) |
|--------|------|------|------|
| Jupiter | 483.63 | | 8.12 |
| Saturn | 888.22 | | 5.99 |
| Uranus | 1786.55 | | 4.23 |
| Neptune | 2799.06 | | 3.38 |
| Pluto | 3700.75 | | 2.95 |

Ⓖ **67.** *Logarithmic regression:* In Sections 4.1 and 4.2 we looked at applications in which linear functions or quadratic functions were used to model data sets. In each case we used a graphing utility to obtain the equation of the linear function or quadratic function that "best fitted" the data. In this exercise we use a function of the form $y = a + b \ln x$ to model a given data set, and we compare a projection made with this model to one based on a linear model.

**(a)** The following table gives the population of Los Angeles County at ten-year intervals over the period 1950–

1990. Use a graphing utility to obtain a scatter plot for the data, and then use the *logarithmic regression* option on the graphing utility to find a function of the form $y = a + b \ln x$ that best fits the data. (Let $x = 50$ correspond to 1950. The reason we don't use the seemingly simpler choice $x = 0$ for 1950 is that $x = 0$ is not in the domain of the function $y = a + b \ln x$.) Display the graph of the function and the scatter plot on the same screen.

**Population of Los Angeles County**

| Year | 1950 | 1960 | 1970 | 1980 | 1990 |
|------|------|------|------|------|------|
| Population (millions) | 4.152 | 6.040 | 7.032 | 7.478 | 8.863 |

Source: U.S. Bureau of the Census

**(b)** Follow part (a), but use a linear model. Display the scatter plot and the graphs of the linear and logarithmic models on the same screen.

**(c)** Use each model to make a projection for what the population might have been in the year 2000.

**(d)** According to the U.S. Bureau of the Census, the population of Los Angeles County in 2000 was 9.519 million. Which answer in part (c) is closer to this? Compute the percentage error for each projection.

**68.** This exercise indicates one of the ways the natural logarithm function is used in the study of prime numbers. Recall that a prime number is a natural number greater than 1 with no factors other than itself and 1. For example, the first ten prime numbers are 2, 3, 5, 7, 11, 13, 17, 19, 23, and 29.

**(a)** Let $P(x)$ denote the number of prime numbers that do not exceed $x$. For instance, $P(6) = 3$, since there are three prime numbers (2, 3, and 5) that do not exceed 6. Compute $P(10)$, $P(18)$, and $P(19)$.

**(b)** According to the **prime number theorem,** $P(x)$ can be approximated by $x/(\ln x)$ when $x$ is large and, in fact, the ratio $\dfrac{P(x)}{x/(\ln x)}$ approaches 1 as $x$ grows larger and larger. Verify this empirically by completing the following table. Round your results to three decimal places. (These facts were discovered by Carl Friedrich Gauss in 1792, when he was 15 years old. It was not until 1896, more than 100 years later, that the prime number theorem was formally proved by the French mathematician J. Hadamard and also by the Belgian mathematician C. J. de la Vallée-Poussin.)

| $x$ | $P(x)$ | $\dfrac{x}{\ln x}$ | $\dfrac{P(x)}{x/\ln x}$ |
|-----|--------|------|------|
| $10^2$ | 25 | | |
| $10^4$ | 1229 | | |
| $10^6$ | 78498 | | |
| $10^8$ | 5761455 | | |
| $10^9$ | 50847534 | | |
| $10^{10}$ | 455052512 | | |

**(c)** In 1808 A. M. Legendre found that he could improve upon Gauss's approximation for $P(x)$ by using the expression $x/(\ln x - 1.08366)$ rather than $x/(\ln x)$. Complete the following table to see how well Legendre's expression approximates $P(x)$. Round your results to four decimal places.

| $x$ | $P(x)$ | $\dfrac{x}{\ln x - 1.08366}$ | $\dfrac{P(x)}{x/(\ln x - 1.08366)}$ |
|---|---|---|---|
| $10^2$ | 25 | | |
| $10^4$ | 1229 | | |
| $10^6$ | 78498 | | |
| $10^8$ | 5761455 | | |
| $10^9$ | 50847534 | | |
| $10^{10}$ | 455052512 | | |

**C**

**69. (a)** Find the domain of the function $f$ defined by
$$f(x) = \ln(\ln x).$$
**(b)** Find $f^{-1}(x)$ for the function $f$ in part (a).
**70.** Find the domain of the function $g$ defined by
$$g(x) = \ln(\ln(\ln x)).$$
**71.** Let $g(x) = \ln(\ln(\ln x))$.
**(a)** Using a graphing utility, display the graph of $g$, first in the standard viewing rectangle, then in the viewing rectangle $[0, 100, 10]$ by $[-5, 5, 1]$.
**(b)** Find the range of the function $g$. (See Example 4 in Section 3.1 if you need a hint on how to begin.)
**(c)** Could you have guessed the answer in part (b) from the graphs in part (a)?

---

## MINI PROJECT | MORE COFFEE

As a prerequisite for this mini project, someone in your group or in the class at large needs to have completed the Section 5.2 project that dealt with the temperature of a cooling cup of coffee. This is a continuation (a completion, actually) of Problem B in that project. As a start here, have that person present a detailed summary of the questions, methods, and results from the Section 5.2 project. Then, for this mini project: Use the techniques from both Sections 5.2 and 5.3 to work out a complete solution to Problem B. Round the answer to the nearest one second. Check that your result is consistent with the approximation from the graphing utility obtained in the Section 5.2 project.

---

# 5.4   PROPERTIES OF LOGARITHMS

*. . . he [John Napier] invented the word "logarithms," using two Greek words, . . . arithmos, "number" and logos, "ratio." It is impossible to say exactly what he had in mind when making up this word.*—Alfred Hooper in *Makers of Mathematics* (New York: Random House, Inc., 1948)

A few basic properties of logarithms are used repeatedly. In this section we will state these properties, discuss their proofs, and then look at examples.

### Properties of Logarithms

1. (a) $\log_b b = 1$      (b) $\log_b 1 = 0$
2. $\log_b PQ = \log_b P + \log_b Q$
   *The log of a product is the sum of the logs of the factors.*
3. $\log_b(P/Q) = \log_b P - \log_b Q$
   *The log of a quotient is the log of the numerator minus the log of the denominator.*
   As a useful particular case, we have $\log_b(1/Q) = -\log_b Q$.
4. $\log_b P^n = n \log_b P$
5. $b^{\log_b P} = P$
6. $\log_b b^x = x$, for all real numbers $x$.

*Note:* $P$ and $Q$ are assumed to be positive in Properties 2–6.

In essence, each of these properties follows from the equivalence of the two equations $y = \log_b x$ and $b^y = x$. For instance, the equivalent exponential forms for Properties 1(a) and 1(b) are $b^1 = b$ and $b^0 = 1$, respectively, both of which are certainly valid.

To prove Property 2, we begin by letting $x = \log_b P$. The equivalent exponential form of this equation is

$$P = b^x \tag{1}$$

Similarly, we let $y = \log_b Q$. The exponential form of this equation is

$$Q = b^y \tag{2}$$

If we multiply equation (1) by equation (2), we get

$$PQ = b^x b^y$$

and therefore

$$PQ = b^{x+y} \tag{3}$$

Next we write equation (3) in its equivalent logarithmic form. This yields

$$\log_b PQ = x + y$$

But using the definitions of $x$ and $y$, this last equation is equivalent to

$$\log_b PQ = \log_b P + \log_b Q$$

That completes the proof of Property 2.

The proof of Property 3 is quite similar to the proof given for Property 2. Exercise 72(a) asks you to carry out the proof of Property 3.

We turn now to the proof of Property 4. We begin by letting $x = \log_b P$. In exponential form, this last equation becomes

$$b^x = P \tag{4}$$

Now we raise both sides of equation (4) to the power $n$. This yields

$$(b^x)^n = b^{nx} = P^n$$

The logarithmic form of this last equation is

$$\log_b P^n = nx$$

or (from the definition of $x$)

$$\log_b P^n = n \log_b P$$

The proof of Property 4 is now complete.

Property 5 is again just a restatement of the meaning of $\log_b P$. To derive this property, let $x = \log_b P$. Therefore

$$b^x = P$$

Now, in this last equation, we simply replace $x$ with $\log_b P$. The result is

$$b^{\log_b P} = P \qquad \text{as required}$$

Finally, Property 6 follows from the meaning of the logarithm $\log_b b^x = x$ since $x$ is the power to which $b$ must be raised to get $b^x$.

Now let's see how these properties are used. To begin with, we display some simple numerical examples in the box that follows.

## ▌PROPERTY SUMMARY   Properties of Logarithms

| Property | Example |
|---|---|
| $\log_b P + \log_b Q = \log_b PQ$ | Simplify:   $\log_{10} 50 + \log_{10} 2$ |
| | Solution:   $\log_{10} 50 + \log_{10} 2 = \log_{10}(50 \cdot 2)$ |
| | $\qquad\qquad\qquad\qquad\qquad = \log_{10} 100$ |
| | $\qquad\qquad\qquad\qquad\qquad = 2$ |
| $\log_b P - \log_b Q = \log_b \dfrac{P}{Q}$ | Simplify:   $\log_8 56 - \log_8 7$ |
| | Solution:   $\log_8 56 - \log_8 7 = \log_8 \dfrac{56}{7}$ |
| | $\qquad\qquad\qquad\qquad\qquad = \log_8 8 = 1$ |
| $\log_b P^n = n \log_b P$ | Simplify:   $\log_2 \sqrt[5]{16}$ |
| | Solution:   $\log_2 \sqrt[5]{16} = \log_2(16^{1/5})$ |
| | $\qquad\qquad\qquad\quad = \dfrac{1}{5} \log_2 16 = \dfrac{4}{5}$ |
| $b^{\log_b P} = P$ | Simplify:   $3^{\log_3 7}$ |
| | Solution:   $3^{\log_3 7} = 7$ |

The examples in the box showed how we can simplify or shorten certain expressions involving logarithms. The next example is also of this type.

| **EXAMPLE** | **1** | **Using log properties to shorten expressions** |
|---|---|---|

Express as a single logarithm with a coefficient of 1:

$$\frac{1}{2}\log_b x - \log_b(1 + x^2)$$

**SOLUTION**

$\dfrac{1}{2}\log_b x - \log_b(1 + x^2) = \log_b x^{1/2} - \log_b(1 + x^2)$   using Property 4 on page 361

$$= \log_b \frac{x^{1/2}}{1 + x^2} \qquad\qquad \text{using Property 3}$$

This last expression is the required answer.

Property 2 says that the logarithm of a product of two factors is equal to the sum of the logarithms of the two factors. This can be generalized to any number of factors. For instance, with three factors we have

$\log_b(ABC) = \log_b[A(BC)]$

$\qquad\qquad\quad = \log_b A + \log_b BC \qquad\qquad$ using Property 2

$\qquad\qquad\quad = \log_b A + \log_b B + \log_b C \qquad$ using Property 2 again

The next example makes use of this idea.

**EXAMPLE** 2 **Using log properties to shorten expressions**

Express as a single logarithm with a coefficient of 1:

$$\ln(x^2 - 9) + 2 \ln \frac{1}{x + 3} + 4 \ln x \qquad (x > 3)$$

**SOLUTION**

$$\ln(x^2 - 9) + 2 \ln \frac{1}{x + 3} + 4 \ln x = \ln(x^2 - 9) + \ln\left[\left(\frac{1}{x + 3}\right)^2\right] + \ln x^4$$

$$= \ln(x^2 - 9) + \ln \frac{1}{(x + 3)^2} + \ln x^4$$

$$= \ln\left[(x^2 - 9) \cdot \frac{1}{(x + 3)^2} \cdot x^4\right]$$

$$= \ln \frac{(x^2 - 9)x^4}{(x + 3)^2}$$

This last expression can be simplified still further by factoring the quantity $x^2 - 9$ as $(x - 3)(x + 3)$. Then a factor of $x + 3$ can be divided out of the numerator and denominator of the fraction. The result is

$$\ln(x^2 - 9) + 2 \ln \frac{1}{x + 3} + 4 \ln x = \ln \frac{(x - 3)x^4}{x + 3}$$

$$= \ln \frac{x^5 - 3x^4}{x + 3}$$

In the examples we have considered so far, we've used the properties of logarithms to shorten given expressions. We can also use these properties to expand an expression. (This is useful in calculus.)

**EXAMPLE** 3 **Using log properties to expand expressions**

Write each of the following quantities as sums and differences of simpler logarithmic expressions. Express each answer in such a way that no logarithm of products, quotients, or powers appears.

**(a)** $\log_{10} \sqrt{3x}$      **(b)** $\log_{10} \sqrt[3]{\dfrac{2x}{3x^2 + 1}}$      **(c)** $\ln \dfrac{x^2\sqrt{2x - 1}}{(2x + 1)^{3/2}}$

**SOLUTION**

**(a)** $\log_{10} \sqrt{3x} = \log_{10}(3x)^{1/2} = \frac{1}{2}\log_{10}(3x)$

$$= \frac{1}{2}(\log_{10} 3 + \log_{10} x)$$

**(b)** $\log_{10} \sqrt[3]{\dfrac{2x}{3x^2 + 1}} = \log_{10}\left[\left(\dfrac{2x}{3x^2 + 1}\right)^{1/3}\right]$

$$= \frac{1}{3}\log_{10} \frac{2x}{3x^2 + 1}$$

$$= \frac{1}{3}[\log_{10} 2x - \log_{10}(3x^2 + 1)]$$

$$= \frac{1}{3}[\log_{10} 2 + \log_{10} x - \log_{10}(3x^2 + 1)]$$

**(c)** $\ln \dfrac{x^2\sqrt{2x-1}}{(2x+1)^{3/2}} = \ln \dfrac{x^2(2x-1)^{1/2}}{(2x+1)^{3/2}}$

$$= \ln x^2 + \ln(2x-1)^{1/2} - \ln(2x+1)^{3/2}$$

$$= 2\ln x + \tfrac{1}{2}\ln(2x-1) - \tfrac{3}{2}\ln(2x+1)$$

---

**EXAMPLE 4  Practice applying the log properties**

Given that $\log_b 2 = A$ and $\log_b 6 = B$, express each of the following in terms of $A$ and/or $B$.

**(a)** $\log_b 8$  **(c)** $\log_b 12$  **(e)** $\log_{\sqrt{b}} 2$

**(b)** $\log_b \sqrt{6}$  **(d)** $\log_b 3$  **(f)** $\log_b(b/36)$

**SOLUTION**

**(a)** $\log_b 8 = \log_b 2^3 = 3\log_b 2 = 3A$

**(b)** $\log_b \sqrt{6} = \log_b 6^{1/2} = \tfrac{1}{2}\log_b 6 = \tfrac{1}{2}B$

**(c)** $\log_b 12 = \log_b(2 \times 6) = \log_b 2 + \log_b 6 = A + B$

**(d)** $\log_b 3 = \log_b(6/2) = \log_b 6 - \log_b 2 = B - A$

**(e)** Let $\log_{\sqrt{b}} 2 = x$. (So we want to express $x$ in terms of $A$ and/or $B$.) Writing this equation in exponential form, we have $(\sqrt{b})^x = 2$, and therefore

$$(b^{1/2})^x = 2$$
$$b^{x/2} = 2$$

Now we rewrite this last equation in logarithmic form to obtain $\log_b 2 = x/2$, and therefore

$$x = 2\log_b 2 = 2A$$

**(f)** $\log_b(b/36) = \log_b b - \log_b 36$

$$= 1 - \log_b 6^2 = 1 - 2\log_b 6 = 1 - 2B$$

---

**EXAMPLE 5  Using the property $\log_b P^n = n\log_b P$ to find an x-intercept**

Figure 1 shows the graph of $y = 2^x - 3$. (The axes are marked off in one-unit intervals.) As indicated in the figure, the x-intercept of the curve is between 1 and 2. Determine both an exact expression for this x-intercept and a calculator approximation rounded to two decimal places.

**SOLUTION**

Setting $y$ equal to zero in the given equation yields $2^x - 3 = 0$, or $2^x = 3$. Notice that the unknown, $x$, appears in the exponent. To solve for $x$, we take the logarithm of both sides of the equation. (Base $e$ logarithms are used in the following computations; Exercise 71 asks you to check that the use of base 10 logarithms produces an equivalent answer.) We have

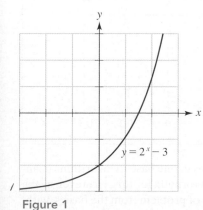

**Figure 1**

$$\ln 2^x = \ln 3$$
$$x \ln 2 = \ln 3 \qquad \text{using Property 4 on page 361}$$
$$x = \frac{\ln 3}{\ln 2} \approx 1.58 \qquad \text{CAUTION: } \frac{\ln 3}{\ln 2} \neq \ln 3 - \ln 2$$

Alternatively, we could express $2^x = 3$ in logarithmic form to obtain the solution $x = \log_2 3$ and then use the change of base formula on page 367 to obtain a decimal approximation.

**EXAMPLE 6** **Using the property $\log_b P^n = n \log_b P$ to solve an equation**

Solve for $x$: $4^{5x+2} = 70$. Use a calculator to evaluate the final answer; round to three decimal places.

**SOLUTION**
The fact that the unknown appears in the exponent suggests that Property 4 (the property that "brings down" the exponent) may be useful. To put Property 4 into play, we'll take the logarithm of both sides of the given equation. Either base 10 or base $e$ logarithms can be used here (because they're both on the calculator). Since we used base $e$ logarithms in the previous example, let's use base 10 here just for the sake of variety. (You can check for yourself at the end that base $e$ logarithms will yield the same numerical answer.)

Taking the base 10 logarithm of both sides of the given equation, we have

$$\log_{10} 4^{5x+2} = \log_{10} 70$$
$$(5x + 2)\log_{10} 4 = \log_{10} 70 \qquad \text{using Property 4}$$
$$5x + 2 = (\log_{10} 70)/(\log_{10} 4)$$
$$x = \frac{[(\log_{10} 70)/(\log_{10} 4)] - 2}{5}$$
$$x \approx 0.213$$

The required solution is approximately 0.213. Figure 2 shows a graphical interpretation of this result.

**GRAPHICAL PERSPECTIVE**

**Figure 2**
The curve $y = 4^{5x+2}$ intersects the line $y = 70$ at a point whose $x$-coordinate is slightly greater than 0.2. Example 6 shows that this $x$-coordinate is 0.213 (rounded to three decimal places).

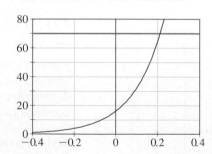

It is sometimes necessary to convert logarithms in one base to logarithms in another base. After the next example, we will state a formula for this. However, as the next example indicates, it is easy to work this type of problem from the basics, without relying on a formula.

| EXAMPLE | 7 | Changing bases |

Express $\log_2 5$ in terms of base 10 logarithms.

**SOLUTION**
Let $z = \log_2 5$. The exponential form of this equation is

$$2^z = 5$$

We now take the base 10 logarithm of each side of this equation to obtain

$$\log_{10} 2^z = \log_{10} 5$$
$$z \log_{10} 2 = \log_{10} 5 \qquad \text{using Property 4 on page 361}$$
$$z = \frac{\log_{10} 5}{\log_{10} 2}$$

Given our definition of $z$, this last equation can be written

$$\log_2 5 = \frac{\log_{10} 5}{\log_{10} 2}$$

This is the required answer.

The method shown in Example 7 can be used to convert between any two bases. Exercise 72(b) at the end of this section asks you to follow this method, using letters rather than numbers, to arrive at the following general formula.

**PROPERTY SUMMARY   Change of Base for Logarithms**

| Formula | Examples |
|---|---|
| $\log_a x = \dfrac{\log_b x}{\log_b a}$ | $\log_2 3 = \dfrac{\log_{10} 3}{\log_{10} 2} = \dfrac{\ln 3}{\ln 2} \qquad \log_{10} e = \dfrac{\ln e}{\ln 10} = \dfrac{1}{\ln 10}$ |

| EXAMPLE | 8 | Changing bases to simplify an expression |

Simplify the product $(\log_2 10)(\log_{10} 2)$.

**SOLUTION**
We'll use the change-of-base formula so that both factors in the given product involve logarithms with the same base. Expressing the first factor, $\log_2 10$, in terms of base 10 logarithms, we have

$$\log_2 10 = \frac{\log_{10} 10}{\log_{10} 2} = \frac{1}{\log_{10} 2}$$

and therefore $\qquad (\log_2 10)(\log_{10} 2) = \dfrac{1}{\log_{10} 2}(\log_{10} 2) = 1$

So the given product is equal to 1. [Using the same method, one can show that, in general, $(\log_a b)(\log_b a) = 1$.]

Examples 1–8 have dealt with applications of the properties of logarithms. However, you also need to understand what the properties *don't* say. For instance, Property 3 does not apply to an expression such as $\dfrac{\log_{10} 5}{\log_{10} 2}$. [Property 3 *would* apply if the expression were $\log_{10}(5/2)$.] In the box that follows, we list some errors to avoid in working with logarithms.

---

### ERRORS TO AVOID

| Error | Correction | Comment |
|---|---|---|
| $\log_b(x + y) = \log_b x + \log_b y$ | $\log_b(xy) = \log_b x + \log_b y$ | In general, there is no simple identity involving $\log_b(x + y)$. This is similar to the situation for $\sqrt{x + y}$ (which is not equal to $\sqrt{x} + \sqrt{y}$). |
| $\dfrac{\log_b x}{\log_b y} = \log_b x - \log_b y$ | $\log_b\left(\dfrac{x}{y}\right) = \log_b x - \log_b y$ | In general, there is no simple identity involving the quotient $(\log_b x)/(\log_b y)$. |
| $(\ln x)^3 = 3 \ln x$ | $(\ln x)^3 = (\ln x)(\ln x)(\ln x)$ | $(\ln x)^3$ is not the same as $\ln(x^3)$. Regarding the latter, we do have $\ln(x^3) = 3 \ln x$, where $x > 0$. |
| $\ln \dfrac{x}{2} = \dfrac{\ln x}{2}$ | $\ln \dfrac{x}{2} = \ln x - \ln 2 \quad$ for $x > 0$ <br><br> and <br><br> $\dfrac{\ln x}{2} = \dfrac{1}{2} \ln x = \ln \sqrt{x} \quad$ for $x > 0$ | The confusion between $\ln \dfrac{x}{2}$ and $\dfrac{\ln x}{2}$ is sometimes due simply to careless handwriting. |

---

## EXERCISE SET 5.4

### A

*In Exercises 1–10, simplify the expression by using the definition and properties of logarithms.*

**1.** $\log_{10} 70 - \log_{10} 7$    **2.** $\log_{10} 40 + \log_{10}(5/2)$

**3.** $\log_7 \sqrt{7}$    **4.** $\log_9 25 - \log_9 75$

**5.** $\log_3 108 + \log_3(3/4)$    **6.** $\ln e^3 - \ln e$

**7.** $-\frac{1}{2} + \ln \sqrt{e}$    **8.** $e^{\ln 3} + e^{\ln 2} - e^{\ln e}$

**9.** $2^{\log_2 5} - 3 \log_5 \sqrt[3]{5}$    **10.** $\log_b b^b$

*In Exercises 11–19, write the expression as a single logarithm with a coefficient of 1.*

**11.** $\log_{10} 30 + \log_{10} 2$    **12.** $2 \log_{10} x - 3 \log_{10} y$

**13.** $\log_5 6 + \log_5(1/3) + \log_5 10$

**14.** $p \log_b A - q \log_b B + r \log_b C$

**15. (a)** $\ln 3 - 2 \ln 4 + \ln 32$

**(b)** $\ln 3 - 2(\ln 4 + \ln 32)$

**16. (a)** $\log_{10}(x^2 - 16) - 3 \log_{10}(x + 4) + 2 \log_{10} x$

**(b)** $\log_{10}(x^2 - 16) - 3[\log_{10}(x + 4) + 2 \log_{10} x]$

**17.** $\log_b 4 + 3[\log_b(1 + x) - \frac{1}{2} \log_b(1 - x)]$

**18.** $\ln(x^3 - 1) - \ln(x^2 + x + 1)$

**19.** $4 \log_{10} 3 - 6 \log_{10}(x^2 + 1) + \frac{1}{2}[\log_{10}(x + 1) - 2 \log_{10} 3]$

*In Exercises 20–26, write the quantity using sums and differences of simpler logarithmic expressions. Express the answer so that logarithms of products, quotients, and powers do not appear.*

**20. (a)** $\log_{10} \sqrt{(x + 1)(x + 2)}$

**(b)** $\ln \sqrt{\dfrac{(x + 1)(x + 2)}{(x - 1)(x - 2)}}$

**21. (a)** $\log_{10} \dfrac{x^2}{1 + x^2}$

**(b)** $\ln \dfrac{x^2}{\sqrt{1 + x^2}}$

**22. (a)** $\log_b \dfrac{\sqrt{1 - x^2}}{x}$

**(b)** $\ln \dfrac{x\sqrt[3]{4x + 1}}{\sqrt{2x - 1}}$

**23. (a)** $\log_{10} \sqrt{9 - x^2}$

**(b)** $\ln \dfrac{\sqrt{4 - x^2}}{(x - 1)(x + 1)^{3/2}}$

**24. (a)** $\log_b \sqrt[3]{\dfrac{x + 3}{x}}$

**(b)** $\ln \dfrac{1}{\sqrt{x^2 + x + 1}}$

**25. (a)** $\log_b \sqrt{x/b}$

**(b)** $2\ln \sqrt{(1 + x^2)(1 + x^4)(1 + x^6)}$

**26. (a)** $\log_b \sqrt[3]{\dfrac{(x-1)^2(x-2)}{(x+2)^2(x+1)}}$   **(b)** $\ln\left(\dfrac{e-1}{e+1}\right)^{3/2}$

In Exercises 27–36, suppose b is a positive constant greater than 1, and let A, B, and C be defined as follows:

$$\log_b 2 = A \qquad \log_b 3 = B \qquad \log_b 5 = C$$

In each case, use the properties of logarithms to evaluate the given expression in terms of A, B, and/or C. (In Exercises 31–36, use the change-of-base formula.)

**27. (a)** $\log_b 6$

**(b)** $\log_b(1/6)$

**(c)** $\log_b 27$

**(d)** $\log_b(1/27)$

**29. (a)** $\log_b(5/3)$

**(b)** $\log_b 0.6$

**(c)** $\log_b(5/9)$

**(d)** $\log_b(5/16)$

**31. (a)** $\log_3 b$

**(b)** $\log_3(10b)$

**33. (a)** $\log_{3b} 2$

**(b)** $\log_{3b} 15$

**35. (a)** $(\log_b 5)(\log_5 b)$

**(b)** $(\log_b 6)(\log_6 b)$

**28. (a)** $\log_b 10$

**(b)** $\log_b 100$

**(c)** $\log_b 0.01$

**(d)** $\log_b 0.3$

**30. (a)** $\log_b \sqrt{5}$

**(b)** $\log_b \sqrt{15}$

**(c)** $\log_b \sqrt[3]{0.4}$

**(d)** $\log_b \sqrt[4]{60}$

**32. (a)** $\log_{b^2} 5$

**(b)** $\log_{\sqrt{b}} 2$

**34. (a)** $\log_{5b} 1.2$

**(b)** $\log_{5b} 2.5$

**36. (a)** $\log_{2b} 6 + \log_{2b}(1/6)$

**(b)** $\log_{18}(1/b)$

In Exercises 37 and 38, suppose that $\log_{10} A = a$, $\log_{10} B = b$, and $\log_{10} C = c$. Express the following logarithms in terms of a, b, and c.

**37. (a)** $\log_{10} AB^2C^3$

**(b)** $\log_{10} 10\sqrt{A}$

**(c)** $\log_{10} \sqrt{10}ABC$

**(d)** $\log_{10}(10A/\sqrt{BC})$

**38. (a)** $\log_{10} A + 2\log_{10}(1/A)$

**(b)** $\log_{10}(A/10)$

**(c)** $\log_{10} \dfrac{100\,A^2}{B^4\sqrt[3]{C}}$

**(d)** $\log_{10} \dfrac{(AB)^5}{C}$

In Exercises 39 and 40, suppose that $\ln x = t$ and $\ln y = u$. Write each expression in terms of t and u.

**39. (a)** $\ln(ex)$

**(b)** $\ln xy - \ln(x^2)$

**(c)** $\ln\sqrt{xy} + \ln(x/e)$

**(d)** $\ln(e^2 x\sqrt{y})$

**40. (a)** $\ln(e^{\ln x})$

**(b)** $e^{\ln(\ln xy)}$

**(c)** $\ln\left(\dfrac{ex}{y}\right) - \ln\left(\dfrac{y}{ex}\right)$

**(d)** $\dfrac{(\ln x)^3 - \ln(x^4)}{\left(\ln \dfrac{x}{e^2}\right)\ln(xe^2)}$

In Exercises 41 and 42, graph the equations and determine the x-intercepts (as in Example 5).

**41. (a)** $y = 2^x - 5$

**(b)** $y = 2^{x/2} - 5$

**42. (a)** $y = 3^{x-1} - 2$

**(b)** $y = 3^{1-x} - 4$

In Exercises 43–48, solve the equations. Express the answers in terms of natural logarithms.

**43.** $5 = 2e^{2x-1}$   Suggestion: First divide by 2.

**44.** $3e^{1+t} = 2$        **45.** $2^x = 13$           **46.** $5^{3x-1} = 27$

**47.** $10^x = e$            **48.** $10^{2x+3} = 280$

In Exercises 49 and 50, solve the equations. Give two forms for each answer: one involving base 10 logarithms and the other a calculator approximation rounded to three decimal places.

**49.** $3^{x^2-1} = 12$                   **50.** $2^{9-x^2} = 430.5389$

In Exercises 51–56, express the quantity in terms of base 10 logarithms.

**51.** $\log_2 5$                **52.** $\log_5 10$                **53.** $\ln 3$

**54.** $\ln 10$               **55.** $\log_b 2$                **56.** $\log_2 b$

In Exercises 57–61, express the quantity in terms of natural logarithms.

**57.** $\log_{10} 6$       **58.** $\log_2 10$       **59.** $\log_{10} e$

**60.** $\log_b 2$, where $b = e^2$        **61.** $\log_{10}(\log_{10} x)$

**62.** Give specific examples showing that each statement is false.

**(a)** $\log(x + y) = \log x + \log y$

**(b)** $(\log x)/(\log y) = \log x - \log y$

**(c)** $(\log x)(\log y) = \log x + \log y$

**(d)** $(\log x)^k = k \log x$

**63.** True or false?

**(a)** $\log_{10} A + \log_{10} B - \frac{1}{2}\log_{10} C = \log_{10}(AB/\sqrt{C})$

**(b)** $\log_e \sqrt{e} = 1/2$

**(c)** $\ln \sqrt{e} = 1/2$

**(d)** $\ln x^3 = \ln 3x$

**(e)** $\ln x^3 = 3 \ln x$

**(f)** $\ln 2x^3 = 3 \ln 2x$

**(g)** $\log_a c = b$ means $a^b = c$.

**(h)** $\log_5 24$ is between $5^1$ and $5^2$.

**(i)** $\log_5 24$ is between 1 and 2.

**(j)** $\log_5 24$ is closer to 1 than to 2.

**(k)** The domain of $g(x) = \ln x$ is the set of all real numbers.

**(l)** The range of $g(x) = \ln x$ is the set of all real numbers.

**(m)** The function $g(x) = \ln x$ is one-to-one.

Use a calculator for Exercises 64–66.

**64. (a)** Check Property 2 using the values $b = 10$, $P = \pi$, and $Q = \sqrt{2}$.

**(b)** Let $P = 3$ and $Q = 4$. Show that $\ln(P + Q) \neq \ln P + \ln Q$.

**(c)** Check Property 3 using the values $b = 10$, $P = 2$, and $Q = 3$.

**(d)** If $P = 10$ and $Q = 20$, show that $\ln(PQ) \neq (\ln P)(\ln Q)$.

**(e)** Check Property 3 using natural logarithms and the values $P = 17$ and $Q = 76$.

**(f)** Show that $(\log_{10} 17)/(\log_{10} 76) \neq \log_{10} 17 - \log_{10} 76$.

**65. (a)** Check Property 4 using the values $b = 10$, $P = \pi$, and $n = 7$.

**(b)** Using the values given for $b$, $P$, and $n$ in part (a), show that $\log_b P^n \neq (\log_b P)^n$.

*(continues)*

(c) Verify Property 5 using the values $b = 10$ and $P = 1776$.

(d) Verify that $\ln 2 + \ln 3 + \ln 4 = \ln 24$.

(e) Verify that

$$\log_{10} A + \log_{10} B + \log_{10} C = \log_{10}(ABC)$$

using the values $A = 11$, $B = 12$, and $C = 13$.

(f) Let $f(x) = e^x$ and $g(x) = \ln x$. Compute $f[g(2345.6)]$.

(g) Let $f(x) = 10^x$ and $g(x) = \log_{10} x$. Compute $g[f(0.123456)]$.

**66.** Evaluate $[\frac{1}{\pi} \ln(640320^3 + 744)]^2$. *Remark*: Contrary to the empirical evidence from your calculator, it is known that this number is irrational.

**67.** *The approximation* $\ln(1 + x) \approx x$: As indicated in the accompanying graph, the values of $\ln(1 + x)$ and $x$ are very close to one another for small positive values of $x$.

Using your calculator, complete the table to obtain numerical evidence of this. For your answers, report the first six decimal places of the calculator display (don't round off).

| $x$ | 0.1 | 0.05 | 0.005 | 0.0005 |
|---|---|---|---|---|
| $\ln(1 + x)$ | | | | |

**68.** As indicated in the figure, the graph of $y = ae^{bx}$ passes through the two points $(2, 10)$ and $(8, 80)$. Follow steps (a) through (c) to determine the values of the constants $a$ and $b$.

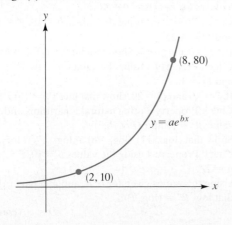

(a) Since the point $(8, 80)$ lies on the graph, the pair of values $x = 8$ and $y = 80$ satisfies the equation $y = ae^{bx}$; that is,

$$80 = ae^{8b} \qquad (1)$$

Similarly, since the point $(2, 10)$ lies on the graph, we have

$$10 = ae^{2b} \qquad (2)$$

Now use equations (1) and (2) to show that $b = (\ln 8)/6$.

(b) In equation (2), substitute for $b$ using the expression obtained in part (a). Show that the resulting equation can be written $10 = a(e^{\ln 8})^{1/3}$.

(c) Use one of the properties of logarithms to simplify the right-hand side of the equation in part (b), then solve for $a$. (You should obtain $a = 5$.)

*In Exercises 69 and 70, you are given the coordinates of two points on the graph of the curve $y = ae^{bx}$. In each case, determine the values of $a$ and $b$. Hint: Use the method explained in Exercise 68.*

**69.** $(-2, 324)$ and $(1/2, 4/3)$     **70.** $(1, 2)$ and $(4, 8)$

**71.** (a) Use base 10 logarithms to solve the equation $2^x - 3 = 0$.

(b) Use your calculator to evaluate the answer in part (a). Also use the calculator to evaluate $(\ln 3)/(\ln 2)$.

(c) Prove that $(\log_{10} 3)/(\log_{10} 2) = (\ln 3)/(\ln 2)$.

**72.** (a) Prove that $\log_b(P/Q) = \log_b P - \log_b Q$.

*Hint*: Study the proof of Property 2 in the text.

(b) Prove the **change-of-base formula:**

$$\log_a x = \frac{\log_b x}{\log_b a}$$

*Hint*: Use the method of Example 7 in the text.

**73.** Show that $\log_b \dfrac{\sqrt{3} + \sqrt{2}}{\sqrt{3} - \sqrt{2}} = 2 \log_b(\sqrt{3} + \sqrt{2})$.

**74.** (a) Show that $\log_b(P/Q) + \log_b(Q/P) = 0$.

(b) Simplify: $\log_a x + \log_{1/a} x$.

**75.** Simplify: $b^{3\log_b x}$.

**76.** Is there a constant $k$ such that the equation $e^x = 2^{kx}$ holds for all values of $x$?

**77.** Prove that $\log_b a = 1/(\log_a b)$.

**78.** Simplify: $(\log_2 3)(\log_3 4)(\log_4 5)$.

**79.** (a) Without using your calculator, show that

$$\frac{1}{\log_2 \pi} + \frac{1}{\log_5 \pi} > 2.$$ *Hint*: Convert to base $\pi$ logarithms.

(b) Without using your calculator, show that

$$\log_\pi 2 + \frac{1}{\log_\pi 2} > 2$$

*Hint*: First explain, in complete sentences, how you know that the quantity $\log_\pi 2$ is positive. Then apply the inequality given in Exercise 40(b) in Section 2.3.

(c) Use your calculator (and the change-of-base formula) to find out which of the two quantities is larger:

$$\frac{1}{\log_2 \pi} + \frac{1}{\log_5 \pi} \qquad \text{or} \qquad \log_\pi 2 + \frac{1}{\log_\pi 2}$$

**80.** A function $f$ with domain $(1, \infty)$ is defined by the equation $f(x) = \log_x 2$.
  **(a)** Find a value for $x$ such that $f(x) = 2$.
  **(b)** Is the number that you found in part (a) a fixed point of the function $f$?

## C

**81.** Prove that $(\log_a x)/(\log_{ab} x) = 1 + \log_a b$.
**82.** Simplify $a^x$ when $x = \log_b(\log_b a)/\log_b a$.
**83.** If $a^2 + b^2 = 7ab$, where $a$ and $b$ are positive, show that

$$\log\left[\frac{1}{3}(a + b)\right] = \frac{1}{2}(\log a + \log b)$$

no matter which base is used for the logarithms (but it is understood that the same base is used throughout).

**84.** Let $f(x) = \ln\left(1 - \frac{1}{x^2}\right)$.
  **(a)** Use the properties of logarithms (and some algebra) to show that

$$f(2) + f(3) + f(4) = \ln\frac{5}{8}$$

  **(b)** Use a calculator to check the result in part (a).

---

# 5.5 EQUATIONS AND INEQUALITIES WITH LOGS AND EXPONENTS

*Initially, [John] Napier [1550–1617] called logarithms "artificial numbers" but later coined the term logarithm, meaning "number of the ratio."*—Ronald Calinger, ed., *Classics of Mathematics* (Englewood Cliffs, N.J.: Prentice Hall, 1995)

*. . . we would like to give a value for z, such that $a^z = y$. This value of z, insofar as it is viewed as a function of y, it is called the LOGARITHM of y.*—Leonhard Euler (1707–1783), *Introductio in analysin infinitorum* (Lausanne: 1748) [This classic text has been translated by John D. Blanton (Berlin: Springer-Verlag, 1988).]

In Examples 2 through 9 in this section we illustrate some of the more common approaches for solving equations and inequalities involving exponential and logarithmic expressions. Although there is no single technique that can be used to solve every equation or inequality of this type, the methods in this section do have much in common: they all rely on the definition and the basic properties of logarithms.

Actually, in the previous two sections we've already solved some equations involving exponential expressions. So as background for the work to follow, you might want to review the following four examples. *Study suggestion*: Try solving for yourself the following four equations before you turn back to the text's solution.

| EXAMPLE | EQUATION |
|---|---|
| Example 6 in Section 5.3 | $10^{x/2} - 16$ |
| Example 7 in Section 5.3 | $e^{2t-5} = 5000$ |
| Example 5 in Section 5.4 | $2^x - 3 = 0$ |
| Example 6 in Section 5.4 | $4^{5x+2} = 70$ |

---

**EXAMPLE** **1** **Reviewing some possibilities for roots**

Consider the following two equations:

$$(\ln x)^2 = 2 \ln x \tag{1}$$
$$\ln(x^2) = 2 \ln x \tag{2}$$

**(a)** Is either one of the values $x = 1$ or $x = 2$ a root of equation (1)?
**(b)** Is either one of the values $x = 1$ or $x = 2$ a root of equation (2)?

**SOLUTION**
**(a)** To see whether the value $x = 1$ satisfies equation (1), we have

$$(\ln 1)^2 = 2 \ln 1$$
$$0^2 = 2(0) \qquad \text{True}$$

Thus $x = 1$ is a root of equation (1). To see whether $x = 2$ is a root, we write

$$(\ln 2)^2 = 2 \ln 2$$
$$\ln 2 = 2 \qquad \text{dividing through by } \ln 2 \ (\neq 0)$$

This last equation is not valid. You can see this by using a calculator or, more directly, by rewriting the equation in exponential form to obtain $e^2 = 2$, which is clearly false. (Why?) Consequently, the value $x = 2$ is not a solution of equation (1).

**(b)** You've seen equation (2) before, or at least one very much like it. It's an example of one of the basic properties of logarithms that we studied in the previous section. That is, we know from the previous section that the equation $\ln(x^2) = 2 \ln x$ holds for every value of $x$ in the domain of the function $y = \ln x$. In particular, then, since both $x = 1$ and $x = 2$ are in the domain of the function $y = \ln x$, we can conclude immediately, without any work required, that both of the values 1 and 2 satisfy equation (2).

The example that we have just completed serves to remind us of the difference between a *conditional equation* and an *identity*. An identity is true for all values of the variable in its domain. For example, the equation $\ln(x^2) = 2 \ln x$ is an identity; it is true for every positive real number $x$. In contrast to this, a conditional equation is true only for some (or perhaps even none) of the values of the variable. Equation (1) in Example 1 is a conditional equation; we saw that it is true when $x = 1$ and false when $x = 2$. The equation $2^x = -1$ is an example of a conditional equation that has no real-number root. (Why?) Most of the equations that we solve in this section are conditional equations, but watch for a few identities to pop up in the examples and exercises. It can make your work much easier.

  **EXAMPLE** **2** **An equation where unknown appears in exponent**

Find all real-number roots of the equation $4^x = 3^{2x+1}$.

**SOLUTION**
Taking the natural logarithm of both sides of the given equation, we have

$$\ln(4^x) = \ln(3^{2x+1})$$

and therefore

$$x \ln 4 = (2x + 1)\ln 3$$
$$x \ln 4 = 2x \ln 3 + \ln 3$$
$$x(\ln 4 - 2 \ln 3) = \ln 3$$
$$x = \frac{\ln 3}{\ln 4 - 2 \ln 3}$$

Using a calculator now, we find that $x$ is approximately $-1.355$. In Figure 1 we show a graphical check of this solution. Exercise 88 asks you to check the solution algebraically.

## GRAPHICAL PERSPECTIVE

**Figure 1**
The curves $y = 4^x$ and $y = 3^{2x+1}$ intersect at a point whose $x$-coordinate is between $-1.4$ and $-1.3$. In Example 2 we found this $x$-value to be $-1.355$ (rounded to three decimal places). (Question: Which of the two graphs in the figure represents $y = 4^x$?)

---

**EXAMPLE** **3** **Some equations involving the natural logarithm**

Find all real-number roots of the following equations:
**(a)** $\ln(\ln x) = 2$;     **(b)** $e^{\ln x} = -2$;     **(c)** $e^{\ln x} = 2$.

**SOLUTION**
**(a)** For convenience we let $t$ stand for $\ln x$. Then the given equation becomes

$$\ln t = 2$$

Rewriting this equation in exponential form, we have

$$t = e^2$$

or, in view of the definition of $t$,

$$\ln x = e^2$$

Now we rewrite this last equation in exponential form to obtain

$$x = e^{e^2}$$
$$\approx 1618.2 \qquad \text{using a calculator}$$

As Exercise 85 asks you to verify, the value $x = e^{e^2}$ indeed checks in the original equation.

**(b)** Think for a moment about the graph of the basic exponential function $y = e^x$. The graph is always above the $x$-axis. This tells us that $e$ raised to any exponent is never negative. Consequently, the equation $e^{\ln x} = -2$ has no real-number solution.

**(c)** From Section 5.2 (as well as Section 5.3) we know that $e^{\ln x} = x$ for all positive numbers $x$, so the given equation $e^{\ln x} = 2$ becomes simply $x = 2$, and we are done.

---

In the next example we solve equations involving logarithms by converting them to exponential form. For part (b) of the example you need to recall the quadratic formula.

  **EXAMPLE** **4** **Equations involving base 10 logarithms**

Find all real-number roots of the following equations:
**(a)** $\log_{10}(x^2 - 2) = 3$;     **(b)** $\log_{10}(x^2 - 2x) = 3$.

**SOLUTION**

**(a)** Converting to exponential form, we have

$$x^2 - 2 = 10^3$$

and therefore

$$x^2 = 1002$$

or

$$x = \pm\sqrt{1002} \approx \pm 31.65$$

As Exercise 86(a) asks you to check, both of the values $\pm\sqrt{1002}$ satisfy the given equation.

**(b)** Again we begin by converting to exponential form. This yields

$$x^2 - 2x = 1000$$

and therefore

$$x^2 - 2x - 1000 = 0$$

Now we apply the quadratic formula:

$$x = \frac{-b \pm \sqrt{b^2 - 4ac}}{2a} = \frac{2 \pm \sqrt{(-2)^2 - 4(1)(-1000)}}{2}$$

$$= \frac{2 \pm \sqrt{4004}}{2} = \frac{2 \pm \sqrt{4(1001)}}{2}$$

$$= \frac{2 \pm 2\sqrt{1001}}{2} = 1 \pm \sqrt{1001}$$

As Exercise 86(b) asks you to verify, both of the numbers $1 + \sqrt{1001}$ and $1 - \sqrt{1001}$ satisfy the given equation. Using a calculator, we find that these two values are approximately 32.6 and −30.6, respectively. In Figure 2 we show a graphical check of the solutions that we've determined in this example.

**GRAPHICAL PERSPECTIVE**

(a)   $y = \log_{10}(x^2 - 2)$

(b)   $y = \log_{10}(x^2 - 2x)$

**Figure 2**
In (a) the figure shows that the curve $y = \log_{10}(x^2 - 2)$ intersects the horizontal line $y = 3$ at two points whose x-coordinates are approximately 30 and −30. In part (a) of Example 4 we found these two numbers to be 31.65 and −31.65, respectively (rounded to two decimal places). Similarly, in (b) the figure shows that the curve $y = \log_{10}(x^2 - 2x)$ intersects the horizontal line $y = 3$ at two points, one with an x-coordinate slightly greater than 30, the other with an x-coordinate very close to −30. In part (b) of the example we found these two x-coordinates to be 32.6 and −30.6, respectively (rounded to one decimal place).

If you look over both parts of the example just completed, you'll see that we used the same general procedure in both cases: Convert from logarithmic to exponential form, then solve the resulting quadratic equation. The next example works in the other direction: First we solve a quadratic equation, then we isolate the variable by converting from exponential to logarithmic form.

| EXAMPLE 5 | An equation in quadratic form that involves exponentials |
|---|---|

As indicated in Figure 3, the graph of the function $y = 2(3^{2x}) - 3^x - 3$ has an $x$-intercept between 0.25 and 0.50. Find the exact value of this intercept and also a calculator approximation rounded to three decimal places.

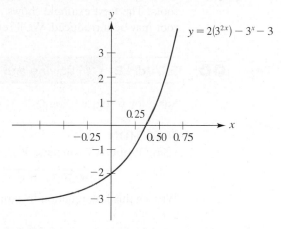

$y = 2(3^{2x}) - 3^x - 3$

**Figure 3**

**SOLUTION**

We need to solve the equation $2(3^{2x}) - 3^x - 3 = 0$. The observation that helps here is that $3^{2x}$ can be written as $(3^x)^2$. This lets us rewrite the equation as

$$2(3^x)^2 - 3^x - 3 = 0$$

Now, for convenience, we let $t = 3^x$ so that the equation becomes

$$2t^2 - t - 3 = 0$$

or

$$(2t - 3)(t + 1) = 0 \qquad \text{Check the factoring.}$$

$$2t - 3 = 0 \qquad \bigg| \qquad t + 1 = 0$$

$$t = \frac{3}{2} \qquad \bigg| \qquad t = -1$$

Using the value $t = 3/2$ in the equation $t = 3^x$ gives us

$$3^x = \frac{3}{2}$$

We can solve this last equation by taking the logarithm of both sides. Using base $e$ logarithms, we have

$$\ln(3^x) = \ln 1.5$$

and therefore

$$x \ln 3 = \ln 1.5$$

Dividing both sides of this last equation by the quantity ln 3, we obtain $x = (\ln 1.5)/(\ln 3)$. As Exercise 87 asks you to verify, this value for $x$ indeed checks in the original equation.

Now, what about the other value for $t$ that we found? With $t = -1$ we have $3^x = -1$, but that is impossible. (Why?) Consequently, there is only one root of the given equation, namely, $x = (\ln 1.5)/(\ln 3)$. This is the required $x$-intercept for the graph shown in Figure 3. Using a calculator, we find that $\ln (1.5)/(\ln 3) \approx 0.369$. Note that this value is consistent with Figure 3, in which the $x$-intercept appears to be roughly halfway between 0.25 and 0.50.

When we solved equations in earlier chapters of this text, we learned that some techniques, such as squaring both sides of an equation, may introduce extraneous roots. The next example shows another type of situation in which an extraneous root may be introduced. We'll return to this point after the example.

**EXAMPLE 6    Solving and then checking for extraneous roots**

Solve for $x$: $\log_3 x + \log_3(x + 2) = 1$.

**SOLUTION**
Using Property 2 (on page 361), we can write the given equation as

$$\log_3[x(x + 2)] = 1 \qquad \text{or} \qquad \log_3(x^2 + 2x) = 1$$

Writing this last equation in exponential form yields

$$x^2 + 2x = 3^1$$
$$x^2 + 2x - 3 = 0$$
$$(x + 3)(x - 1) = 0$$

Thus we have

$$x + 3 = 0 \qquad \text{or} \qquad x - 1 = 0$$

and, consequently,

$$x = -3 \qquad \text{or} \qquad x = 1$$

Now let's check these values in the original equation to see whether they are indeed solutions.

If $x = -3$, the equation becomes

$$\underbrace{\log_3(-3)} + \underbrace{\log_3(-1)} \stackrel{?}{=} 1$$

Neither expression is defined, since the domain of the logarithm function does not contain negative numbers.

If $x = 1$, the equation becomes

$$\log_3 1 + \log_3 3 \stackrel{?}{=} 1$$
$$0 + 1 \stackrel{?}{=} 1 \qquad \text{True}$$

Thus the value $x = 1$ is a solution of the original equation, but $x = -3$ is not.

In the example we just concluded, an extraneous solution ($x = -3$) was generated along with the correct solution, $x = 1$. How did this happen? It happened because in the second line of the solution, we used the property $\log_b PQ = \log_b P + \log_b Q$, which is valid only when both $P$ and $Q$ are positive. In the box that follows, we generalize this remark about extraneous solutions.

> ## PROPERTY SUMMARY
> ### Extraneous Solutions for Logarithmic Equations
>
> Using the properties of logarithms (on page 361) to solve logarithmic equations may introduce extraneous solutions that do not check in the original equation. (This occurs because the logarithm function requires positive inputs, but in solving an equation, we may not know ahead of time the sign of an input involving a variable.) Therefore it is always necessary to check any candidates for solutions that are obtained in this manner.

Earlier in this book, in Sections 2.3 and 2.4, we learned how to solve inequalities involving polynomials. Those same techniques, along with the properties of logarithms, are often useful in solving inequalities involving logarithmic and exponential expressions. In the box that follows, we list some additional facts that are helpful in solving these types of inequalities.

## PROPERTY SUMMARY   Inequalities Involving Exponential and Logarithmic Functions

For each of the following, assume that $b$ is a positive constant greater than 1.

1. (Refer to Figure 4.)
   (a) If $p < q$ then $b^p < b^q$.
   (b) Conversely, if $b^p < b^q$ then $p < q$.

2. (Refer to Figure 5.) Assume that $p$ and $q$ are positive.
   (a) If $p < q$ then $\log_b p < \log_b q$.
   (b) Conversely, if $\log_b p < \log_b q$ then $p < q$.

Figure 4

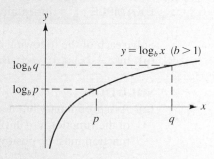

Figure 5

---

### EXAMPLE   7   An inequality involving an exponential function

Solve the inequality $2(1 + 0.4^x) < 5$.

**SOLUTION**
Dividing both sides by 2, we have

$$1 + 0.4^x < 5/2$$
$$0.4^x < 3/2$$
$$\ln(0.4^x) < \ln(3/2) \qquad \text{using Property 2(a) above}$$
$$x \ln(0.4) < \ln(3/2)$$

Now, to isolate $x$, we want to divide both sides of this last inequality by the quantity $\ln(0.4)$, which is negative. (Without relying on a calculator, how do you know that this quantity is negative?) Since dividing both sides by a negative quantity reverses the inequality, we obtain

$$x > \frac{\ln(3/2)}{\ln(0.4)}$$

So the solution set consists of all real numbers greater than $\dfrac{\ln(3/2)}{\ln(0.4)}$.

Using a calculator to evaluate this last expression, we find that it is approximately $-0.443$. With this approximation, we can use interval notation to write the solution set as $(-0.443, \infty)$. See Figure 6 for a graphical view of this solution.

### GRAPHICAL PERSPECTIVE

**Figure 6**
The graph of the equation $y = 2(1 + 0.4^x)$ indicates that the solution set of the inequality $2(1 + 0.4^x) < 5$ is an interval of the form $(a, \infty)$, where $a$ is approximately $-0.5$. In Example 7 we found that this value of $a$ is $(\ln 1.5)/(\ln 0.4) \approx -0.443$ (rounded to three decimal places).

---

### EXAMPLE 8  Inequalities with logarithmic and exponential functions

Solve each of the following inequalities:
**(a)** $\ln(2 - 3x) \le 1$;     **(b)** $e^{2-3x} \le 1$.

**SOLUTION**
**(a)** As a preliminary but necessary first step, we need to determine the domain of the function $y = \ln(2 - 3x)$. Since the inputs for the natural logarithm function must be positive, we require $2 - 3x > 0$, and therefore

$$-3x > -2 \qquad \text{or} \qquad x < \frac{2}{3}$$

Now we turn to the given inequality $\ln(2 - 3x) \le 1$. Applying Property 1(a) on the previous page to this inequality, we can write

$$e^{\ln(2-3x)} \le e^1$$

and, consequently,

$$2 - 3x \le e$$
$$-3x \le e - 2$$
$$x \ge \frac{e-2}{-3} = \frac{2-e}{3}$$

Putting things together now, we want $x$ to be greater than or equal to $(2 - e)/3$ but less than $2/3$. Thus the solution set is the interval $\left[\dfrac{2-e}{3}, \dfrac{2}{3}\right)$.

**NOTE**   For this interval notation to make sense, the fraction $(2 - e)/3$ must be smaller than $2/3$. Although you can verify this using a calculator, you can also explain it without relying on a calculator. Exercise 89 asks you to do this.

**(b)** Since the domain of the exponential function is the set of all real numbers, there is no preliminary restriction on $x$, as there was in part (a). Taking the natural logarithm of both sides of the given inequality [as in Property 2(a) on page 377], we obtain

$$\ln(e^{2-3x}) \le \ln(1)$$

and therefore

$$2 - 3x \le 0$$
$$-3x \le -2$$
$$x \ge \frac{2}{3}$$

The solution set of the given inequality is the interval $[2/3, \infty)$.

**EXAMPLE 9**   Taking domain into account in determining the solution set

**(a)** Determine the domain of the function $f(x) = \log_{10} x + \log_{10}(x - 2)$.
**(b)** Solve the inequality $\log_{10} x + \log_{10}(x - 2) \le \log_{10} 24$.

**SOLUTION**
**(a)** As you know, the logarithm function requires positive inputs. So for the expression $\log_{10} x$ we require $x > 0$, whereas for the expression $\log_{10}(x - 2)$ we require

$$x - 2 > 0 \quad \text{and therefore} \quad x > 2$$

In summary, then, we want $x$ to be greater than zero, and at the same time, we need to have $x$ greater than 2. Notice now that if $x$ is greater than 2, it's automatically true that $x$ is greater than zero. Thus the domain of the given function $f$ consists of all real numbers greater than 2.
**(b)** On the left-hand side of the given inequality, we can use one of the basic properties of logarithms to write

$$\log_{10} x + \log_{10}(x - 2) = \log_{10}[x(x - 2)] = \log_{10}(x^2 - 2x)$$

With this result the given inequality becomes

$$\log_{10}(x^2 - 2x) \le \log_{10} 24$$

and therefore

$$x^2 - 2x \le 24 \quad \text{using Property 2(b) on page 377}$$

or

$$x^2 - 2x - 24 \le 0 \tag{1}$$

Inequality (1) is one of the types of inequalities that you learned to solve earlier in this text (in Section 2.4). As Exercise 90 at the end of this section asks you to show, the solution set for inequality (1) is the closed interval

$[-4, 6]$. This closed interval, however, is not the solution set for the original inequality; we need to take into account the result in part (a). Putting things together, then, we want only those numbers in the interval $[-4, 6]$ that are greater than 2. Consequently, the solution set for the given inequality is the interval $(2, 6]$. Figure 7 shows a graphical view of this result.

**Figure 7**

The curve $y = \log_{10} x + \log_{10}(x - 2)$ is below the horizontal line $y = \log_{10} 24$ when $2 < x < 6$. At $x = 6$ the curve and the line intersect. Thus the solution set of the inequality $\log_{10} x + \log_{10}(x - 2) \le \log_{10} 24$ is the interval $(2, 6]$.

## EXERCISE SET 5.5

**A**

*To help you get started, Exercises 1–10 correlate directly with Examples 2–6 as shown in the chart. (Thus, if you need help in any of Exercises 1–10, first consult the indicated example.)*

| Exercise | 1, 2 | 3, 4 | 5, 6 | 7, 8 | 9, 10 |
|---|---|---|---|---|---|
| Based on Example No. | 2 | 3(a) | 4(a) | 4(b) | 5 |

*In Exercises 1–41, find all the real-number roots of each equation. In each case, give an exact expression for the root and also (where appropriate) a calculator approximation rounded to three decimal places.*

**1.** $5^x = 3^{2x-1}$

**2.** $7^{-4x} = 2^{1+3x}$

**3.** $\ln(\ln x) = 1.5$

**4.** $\log_3[\log_3(2x)] = -2$

**5.** $\log_{10}(x^2 + 36) = 2$

**6.** $\log_2(2x^2 - 4) = 5$

**7.** $\log_{10}(2x^2 - 3x) = 2$

**8.** $\log_9(x^2 + x) = 0.5$

**9.** $10^{2x} + 3(10^x) - 10 = 0$

**10.** $3(2^{2x}) - 11(2^x) - 4 = 0$

**11.** (a) $\ln(x^3) = 3 \ln x$
    (b) $(\ln x)^3 = 3 \ln x$

**12.** (a) $(\log_{10} x)^2 = 2 \log_{10} x$
    (b) $\log_{10}(x^2) = 2 \log_{10} x$

**13.** (a) $\log_3 6x = \log_3 6 + \log_3 x$
    (b) $\log_3 6x = 6 \log_3 x$

**14.** (a) $\ln x = (\log_{10} x)/(\log_{10} e)$
    (b) $\ln x = (\log_{10} e)/(\log_{10} x)$

**15.** $7^{\log_7 2x} = 2x$

**16.** $7^{\log_7 2x} = 7$

**17.** $\log_2(\log_3 x) = -1$

**18.** $\ln[\ln(\ln x)] = 1$

**19.** $\ln 4 - \ln x = (\ln 4)/(\ln x)$

**20.** $\log_5 x - \log_5 10 = \log_5(x/10)$

**21.** $\ln(3x^2) = 2 \ln(3x)$

**22.** $\ln(3x^2) = 2 \ln(\sqrt{3}x)$

**23.** $\log_{16} \dfrac{x + 3}{x - 1} = \dfrac{1}{2}$

**24.** $\log_{\sqrt{2}} \dfrac{1 - 4x}{1 + 4x} = 4$

**25.** (a) $e^{2x} + 2e^x + 1 = 0$
    (b) $e^{2x} - 2e^x + 1 = 0$
    (c) $e^{2x} - 2e^x - 3 = 0$
    (d) $e^{2x} - 2e^x - 4 = 0$

**26.** (a) $4e^{6x} - 12e^{3x} + 9 = 0$
    (b) $4e^{6x} + 12e^{3x} + 9 = 0$
    (c) $4e^{6x} - 16e^{3x} - 9 = 0$
    (d) $e^{6x} - 12e^{3x} - 9 = 0$

**27.** $e^x - e^{-x} = 1$   *Hint*: Multiply both side by $e^x$.

**28.** $e^x + e^{-x} = 2$

**29.** $2^{5x} = 3^x(5^{x+3})$

**30.** $e^{3x} = 10^{2x}(2^{1-x})$

**31.** $\log_6 x + \log_6(x + 1) = 1$

**32.** $\log_6 x + \log_6(x + 1) = 0$

**33.** $\log_9(x + 1) = \frac{1}{2} + \log_9 x$

**34.** $\log_2(x + 4) = 2 - \log_2(x + 1)$

**35.** $\log_{10}(2x + 4) + \log_{10}(x - 2) = 1$

**36.** $\ln x + \ln(x + 1) = \ln 12$

**37.** $\log_{10}(x + 3) - \log_{10}(x - 2) = 2$

**38.** $\ln(x + 1) = 2 + \ln(x - 1)$

**39.** $\log_{10}(x + 1) = 2 \log_{10}(x - 1)$

**40.** $\log_2(2x^2 + 4) = 5$

**41.** $\log_{10}(x - 6) + \log_{10}(x + 3) = 1$

**42.** Solve for $x$ in terms of $a$:
    $\log_2(x + a) - \log_2(x - a) = 1$.

**43.** Solve for $x$ in terms of $y$:
    (a) $\log_{10} x - y = \log_{10}(3x - 1)$;
    (b) $\log_{10}(x - y) = \log_{10}(3x - 1)$.

**44.** Solve for $x$ in terms of $b$: $\log_b(1 - 3x) = 3 + \log_b x$.

In Exercises 45–50, you are given an equation of the form $\ln x = f(x)$. In each case the equation cannot be solved using the algebraic techniques of this section.

(a) Without using a graphing utility, determine how many roots the equation has by sketching the graphs of $y = \ln x$ and $y = f(x)$ in the same coordinate system.

G (b) Use a graphing utility to draw the graphs on the same screen. Then, by zooming in on each point where the graphs intersect, estimate to the nearest hundredth each root of the equation $\ln x = f(x)$.

45. $\ln x = -x$      46. $\ln x = (x - 2)^2$
47. $\ln x = 1/(x + 1)$      48. $\ln x = e^{-x}$
49. $\ln x = |x - 2|$      50. $\ln x = -|x - 2|$

In Exercises 51–66, solve the inequalities. Where appropriate, give an exact answer as well as a decimal approximation.

51. $3(2 - 0.6^x) \le 1$      52. $6(5 - 1.6^x) \ge 13$
53. $4(10 - e^x) \le -3$      54. $\frac{2}{3}(1 - e^{-x}) \le -3$
55. $\ln(2 - 5x) > 2$      56. $3 \log_{10}(4x + 3) < 1$
57. $e^{2+x} \ge 100$      58. $4^{5-x} > 15$
59. $2^x > 0$      60. $\log_2 x \ge 0$
61. $\log_2 \dfrac{2x - 1}{x} < 0$      62. $\ln \dfrac{3x - 2}{4x + 1} > \ln 4$
63. $e^{x^2 - 4x} \ge e^5$      64. $10^{-x^2} \le 10^{-12}$
65. $e^{(1/x) - 1} > 1$      66. $e^{1/(x-1)} > 1$

67. (a) Specify the domain of the function $y = \ln x + \ln(x - 4)$.
    (b) Solve the inequality $\ln x + \ln(x - 4) \le \ln 21$.
68. (a) Specify the domain of the function $y = \ln x + \ln(x + 2)$.
    (b) Solve the inequality $\ln x + \ln(x + 2) \le \ln 35$.
69. Solve the inequality
    $\log_2 x + \log_2(x + 1) - \log_2(2x + 6) < 0$.
70. Solve the inequality $\log_{10}(x^2 - 6x - 6) > 0$.

## B

71. Find all roots of the equation $\log_2 x = \log_x 2$, or explain why there are none.
72. Solve the equation $\log_2 x = \log_x 3$. For each root, give an exact expression and a calculator approximation rounded to two decimal places.
G 73. Use a graphing utility to graph the two functions $y = \ln(x^2)$ and $y = 2 \ln x$, first separately, then in the same viewing rectangle. What do you observe? What does this have to do with the statements made in the text in the solution of Example 1(b)?
G 74. (a) Graph the two functions $f(x) = (\ln x)/(\ln 3)$ and $g(x) = \ln x - \ln 3$. (Use a viewing rectangle in which $x$ extends from 0 to 10 and $y$ extends from $-5$ to 5.) Why aren't the two graphs identical? That is, doesn't one of the basic log identities say that $(\ln a)/(\ln b) = \ln a - \ln b$?
    (b) Your picture in part (a) indicates that
$$\frac{\ln x}{\ln 3} > \ln x - \ln 3 \quad (0 < x \le 10)$$
Find a viewing rectangle in which
$(\ln x)/(\ln 3) \le \ln x - \ln 3$.

(c) Use the picture that you obtain in part (b) to estimate the value of $x$ for which $(\ln x)/(\ln 3) = \ln x - \ln 3$.
(d) Solve the equation $(\ln x)/(\ln 3) = \ln x - \ln 3$ algebraically and use the result to check your estimate in part (c).

In Exercises 75–84, solve each equation. In Exercises 79–84, solve for $x$ in terms of the other letters.

75. $3(\ln x)^2 - \ln(x^2) - 8 = 0$      76. $x^{1 + \log_x 16} = 4x^2$
77. $\log_6 x = \dfrac{1}{\dfrac{1}{\log_2 x} + \dfrac{1}{\log_3 x}}$      78. $\dfrac{\ln(\sqrt{x + 4} + 2)}{\ln \sqrt{x}} = 2$
79. $\alpha \ln x + \ln \beta = 0$      80. $3 \ln x = \alpha + 3 \ln \beta$
81. $y = Ae^{kx}$      82. $\beta = 10 \log_{10}(x/x_0)$
83. $y = a/(1 + be^{-kx})$      84. $T = T_1 + (T_0 - T_1)e^{-kx}$

In Exercises 85–88, you are given an equation and a root that was obtained in an example in the text. In each case: (a) verify (algebraically) that the root indeed satisfies the equation; and (b) use a calculator to check that the root satisfies the equation.

85. [From Example 3(a)]   $\ln(\ln x) = 2; x = e^{e^2}$
86. (a) [From Example 4(a)]   $\log_{10}(x^2 - 2) = 3; x = \pm\sqrt{1002}$
    (b) [From Example 4(b)]   $\log_{10}(x^2 - 2x) = 3;$
    $x = 1 + \sqrt{1001}$
87. (From Example 5)   $2(3^{2x}) - 3^x - 3 = 0; x = (\ln 1.5)/\ln 3$
    Hint: Use the change of base formula on page 367 to express $(\ln 1.5)/\ln 3$ as a logarithm base 3.
88. (From Example 2)   $4^x = 3^{2x+1}; x = (\ln 3)/(\ln 4 - 2 \ln 3)$
    Hint: First show that $4^{\ln 3} = 3^{\ln 4}$ and then use it to write the left-hand side as a power of 3.
89. [From Example 8(a)]   Explain, in one or two complete sentences, how you know (without using a calculator) that the fraction $(2 - e)/3$ is less than $2/3$.
90. [From Example 9(b)]   Solve the inequality $x^2 - 2x - 24 \le 0$. You should find that the solution set is the closed interval $[-4, 6]$.

## C

In Exercises 91 and 92, solve the inequalities.

91. $\log_\pi[\log_4(x^2 - 5)] < 0$   Hint: In the expression $\log_b y$, $y$ must be positive.
92. $\dfrac{1}{\log_2 x} + \dfrac{1}{\log_3 x} + \dfrac{1}{\log_4 x} > 2$   (for $x > 1$)

In Exercises 93 and 94, solve the equations.

93. $x^{(x^x)} = (x^x)^x$   Hint: There are two solutions.
94. $(\pi x)^{\log_{10} \pi} = (ex)^{\log_{10} e}$
95. Solve for $x$ (assuming that $a > b > 0$):
$$(a^4 - 2a^2b^2 + b^4)^{x-1} = (a - b)^{2x}(a + b)^{-2}$$
    Answer:   $x = \dfrac{\ln(a - b)}{\ln(a + b)}$
96. Let $f(x) = \ln(x + \sqrt{x^2 + 1})$. Find $f^{-1}(x)$.
97. Suppose that $\log_{10} 2 = a$ and $\log_{10} 3 = b$. Solve for $x$ in terms of $a$ and $b$:
$$6^x = \frac{10}{3} - 6^{-x}$$

*S = Pe$^{rt}$. This result is remarkable both because of its simplicity and the occurrence of e. (Who would expect that number to pop up in finance theory?)* —Philip Gillett in *Calculus and Analytic Geometry,* 3rd ed. (Lexington, Mass.: D.C. Heath, 1988)

## 5.6 COMPOUND INTEREST

We begin this section by considering how money accumulates in a savings account. Eventually, this will lead us back to the number $e$ and to functions of the form $y = ae^{bx}$.

The following idea from arithmetic is a prerequisite for our discussion. To increase a given quantity by, say, 15%, we multiply the quantity by 1.15. For instance, suppose that we want to increase $100 by 15%. The calculations can be written as

$$100 + 0.15(100) = 100(1 + 0.15) = 100(1.15)$$

Similarly, to increase a quantity by 30%, we would multiply by 1.30, and so on. The next example displays some calculations involving percentage increase. The results might surprise you unless you're already familiar with this topic.

---

**EXAMPLE** 1 **Computing percentage increase**

An amount of $100 is increased by 15%, and then the new amount is increased by 15%. Is this the same as an overall increase of 30%?

**SOLUTION**
To increase $100 by 15%, we multiply by 1.15 to obtain $100(1.15). Now to increase this new amount by 15%, we multiply it by 1.15 to obtain

$$[(\$100)(1.15)](1.15) = \$100(1.15)^2 = \$132.25$$

Alternatively, if we increase the original $100 by 30%, we obtain

$$\$100(1.30) = \$130$$

Comparing, we see that the result of two successive 15% increases is greater than the result of a single 30% increase.

---

Now let's look at another example and use it to introduce some terminology. Suppose that you place $1000 in a savings account at 10% interest *compounded annually.* This means that at the end of each year, the bank contributes to your account 10% of the amount that is in the account at that time. Interest compounded in this manner is called **compound interest.** The original deposit of $1000 is called the **principal,** denoted $P$. The interest rate, expressed as a decimal, is denoted by $r$. Thus, $r = 0.10$ in this example. The variable $A$ is used to denote the **amount** in the account at any given time. The calculations displayed in Table 1 show how the account grows.

We can learn several things from Table 1. First, consider how much interest is paid each year.

| | |
|---|---|
| Interest paid for first year: | $1100 − $1000 = $100 |
| Interest paid for second year: | $1210 − $1100 = $110 |
| Interest paid for third year: | $1331 − $1210 = $121 |

Thus the interest earned each year is not a constant; it increases each year.

## TABLE 1

| Time period | Algebra | Arithmetic |
|---|---|---|
| After 1 year | $A = P(1 + r)$ | $A = 1000(1.10)$ <br> $= \$1100$ |
| After 2 years | $A = [P(1 + r)](1 + r)$ <br> $= P(1 + r)^2$ | $A = 1100(1.10)$ <br> $= \$1210$ |
| After 3 years | $A = [P(1 + r)^2](1 + r)$ <br> $= P(1 + r)^3$ | $A = 1210(1.10)$ <br> $= \$1331$ |

If you look at the algebra in Table 1, you can see what the general formula should be for the amount after $t$ years.

### Compound Interest Formula (interest compounded annually)

Suppose that a principal of $P$ dollars is invested at an annual rate $r$ that is compounded annually. Then the amount $A$ after $t$ years is given by

$$A = P(1 + r)^t$$

  **EXAMPLE  2   Interest compounded annually**

Suppose that \$2000 is invested at $7\frac{1}{2}\%$ interest compounded annually. How many years will it take for the money to double?

**SOLUTION**
In the formula $A = P(1 + r)^t$, we use the given values $P = \$2000$ and $r = 0.075$. We want to find how long it will take for the money to double; that is, we want to find $t$ when $A = \$4000$. Making these substitutions in the formula, we obtain

$$4000 = 2000(1 + 0.075)^t$$

and therefore

$$2 = 1.075^t \qquad \text{dividing by 2000}$$

We can solve this exponential equation by taking the logarithm of both sides. We use base $e$ logarithms. (Base 10 would also be convenient here.) This yields

$$\ln 2 = \ln 1.075^t$$

and, consequently,

$$\ln 2 = t \ln 1.075 \quad \text{(Why?)}$$

To isolate $t$, we divide both sides of this last equation by $\ln 1.075$. This yields

$$t = \frac{\ln 2}{\ln 1.075} \approx 9.6 \, \text{years}$$

Now, assuming that the bank computes the compound interest only at the end of the year, we must round the preliminary answer of 9.6 years and say that when

**TABLE 2**
$A = 2000(1.075)^t$

| $t$ (years) | $A$ (dollars) |
|---|---|
| 9 | 3834.48 |
| 10 | 4122.06 |

$t = 10$ years, the initial $2000 will have *more than* doubled. Table 2 adds some perspective to this. The table shows that after 9 years, something less than $4000 is in the account; whereas after 10 years, the amount exceeds $4000.

In Example 2 the interest was compounded annually. In practice, though, the interest is usually computed more often. For instance, a bank may advertise a rate of 8% per year *compounded semiannually*. This means that after half a year, the interest is compounded at 4%, and then after another half year, the interest is again compounded at 4%. (If you review Example 1, you'll see that two compoundings, each at a rate of $r/2$, is not the same as one compounding at the rate $r$. The former scheme yields more money overall than the latter.) In the case of a rate of 8% per year compounded semiannually, we say that the *periodic interest rate* is 4%. Similarly, if the interest rate of 8% per year were compounded four times per year, then the periodic interest rate would be 2 ($= 8/4$) percent. In Table 3 we show examples of this terminology, assuming an annual rate of $r\%$. Note that, in general, the **periodic interest rate** is equal to $r/n$, where $r$ is the annual interest rate and $n$ is the number of times per year that the interest is compounded.

**TABLE 3    Periodic Interest Rates, Assuming an Annual Rate of $r\%$***

| | $n$ (number of times per year that interest is compounded) | Periodic interest rate (%) |
|---|---|---|
| Annually | 1 | $r$ |
| Semiannually | 2 | $r/2$ |
| Quarterly | 4 | $r/4$ |
| Monthly | 12 | $r/12$ |
| Daily (assuming 360-day year) | 360 | $r/360$ |
| Daily (assuming 365-day year) | 365 | $r/365$ |

*Regarding the last two rows of the table: Some banks base their calculations on a 360-day rather than 365-day year.

The compound interest formula

$$A = P(1 + r)^t \tag{1}$$

that we worked with in Example 2 can be generalized to cover the cases that we've just been discussing, in which the interest is compounded more than once per year. The general formula is given in the box that follows.

---

**Compound Interest Formula (interest compounded $n$ times per year)**

Suppose that a principal of $P$ dollars is invested at an annual rate $r$ that is compounded $n$ times per year. Then the amount $A$ after $t$ years is given by

$$A = P\left(1 + \frac{r}{n}\right)^{nt} \tag{2}$$

Note that the quantity $r/n$ in parentheses is the periodic interest rate, and the exponent $nt$ represents the total number of compoundings.

---

Although we won't derive equation (2) from scratch, note that it is obtained from equation (1) as follows: In equation (1), replace the annual interest rate $r$ by the periodic interest rate $r/n$; in equation (1), replace $t$ (which not only represents time, but also the number of compoundings) with the quantity $nt$, which also represents the total number of compoundings.

---

**EXAMPLE** 3  **Comparing annual to quarterly compounding**

Suppose that $1000 is placed in a savings account at 10% per annum. How much is in the account at the end of 1 year if the interest is: **(a)** compounded once each year ($n = 1$); and **(b)** compounded quarterly ($n = 4$)?

**SOLUTION**
We use the formula $A = P[1 + (r/n)]^{nt}$.
**(a)**  For $n = 1$ we obtain

$$A = 1000\left(1 + \frac{0.10}{1}\right)^{(1)(1)}$$
$$= 1000(1.1)$$
$$= \$1100$$

**(b)**  For $n = 4$ we obtain

$$A = 1000\left(1 + \frac{0.10}{4}\right)^{4(1)}$$
$$= 1000(1.025)^4$$
$$= \$1103.81 \qquad \text{using a calculator}$$

Notice that compounding the interest quarterly rather than annually yields the greater amount. This is in agreement with our observations in Example 1.

---

The results in Example 3 will serve to illustrate some additional terminology used by financial institutions. In that example, the interest for the year under quarterly compounding was

$$\$1103.81 - \$1000 = \$103.81$$

Now, $103.81 is 10.381% of $1000. We say in this case that the **effective rate** of interest is 10.381%. The given rate of 10% per annum compounded once a year is called the **nominal rate.** (The nominal rate and the effective rate are also referred to as the *annual rate* and the *annual yield,* respectively.) The next example further illustrates these ideas.

---

  **EXAMPLE** 4  **Computing the effective rate**

A bank offers a nominal interest rate of 6% per annum for certain accounts. Compute the effective rate if interest is compounded monthly.

**SOLUTION**
Let $P$ denote the principal, which earns 6% ($r = 0.06$) compounded monthly ($n = 12$). Then with $t = 1$, our formula yields

$$A = P\left(1 + \frac{0.06}{12}\right)^{12(1)} \approx P(1.0617) \qquad \text{using a calculator}$$

This shows that the effective interest rate is about 6.17%.

There are two rather natural questions to ask on first encountering compound interest calculations:

**Question 1**    For a fixed period of time (say, one year), does more and more frequent compounding of interest continue to yield greater and greater amounts?

**Question 2**    Is there a limit on how much money can accumulate in a year when interest is compounded more and more frequently?

The answer to both of these questions is yes. If you look back over Example 1, you'll see evidence for the affirmative answer to Question 1. For additional evidence, and for the answer to Question 2, let's do some calculations. To keep things as simple as possible, suppose a principal of $1 is invested for 1 year at the nominal rate of 100% per annum. (More realistic figures could be used here, but the algebra becomes more cluttered.) With these data our formula becomes

$$A = 1\left(1 + \frac{1}{n}\right)^{n(1)} \quad \text{or} \quad A = \left(1 + \frac{1}{n}\right)^{n}$$

Now, as we know from Section 5.2, the expression $\left(1 + \frac{1}{n}\right)^{n}$ approaches the value $e$ as $n$ grows larger and larger; see Table 4.

**TABLE 4    Results of Compounding Interest More and More Frequently**

| Number of compoundings, $n$ | Amount, $\left(1 + \frac{1}{n}\right)^{n}$ |
|---|---|
| $n = 1$ (annually) | $[1 + (1/1)]^{1} = 2$ |
| $n = 2$ (semiannually) | $[1 + (1/2)]^{2} = 2.25$ |
| $n = 4$ (quarterly) | $[1 + (1/4)]^{4} \approx 2.44$ |
| $n = 12$ (monthly) | $[1 + (1/12)]^{12} \approx 2.61$ |
| $n = 365$ (daily) | $[1 + (1/365)]^{365} \approx 2.7146$ |
| $n = 8760$ (hourly) | $[1 + (1/8760)]^{8760} \approx 2.7181$ |
| $n = 525{,}600$ (each minute) | $[1 + (1/525{,}600)]^{525{,}600} \approx 2.71827$ |
| $n = 31{,}536{,}000$ (each second) | $[1 + (1/31{,}536{,}000)]^{31{,}536{,}000} \approx 2.71828$ |

Table 4 shows that the amount does increase with the number of compoundings. But assuming that the bank rounds to the nearest penny, Table 4 also shows that there is no difference between compounding hourly, compounding each minute, and compounding each second. In each case, the rounded amount is $2.72.

Some banks advertise interest compounded not monthly, daily, or even hourly, but *continuously,* that is, at each instant. The formula (derived in calculus) for the amount earned under continuous compounding of interest is as follows.

### Compound Interest Formula (interest compounded continuously)

Suppose that a principal of $P$ dollars is invested at an annual rate $r$ that is compounded continuously. Then the amount $A$ after $t$ years is given by

$$A = Pe^{rt}$$

**EXAMPLE 5 Continuous compounding of interest**

A principal of $1600 is placed in a savings account at 5% per annum compounded continuously. Assuming no subsequent withdrawals or deposits, when will the balance reach $2400?

**SOLUTION**

Substitute the values $A = 2400$, $P = 1600$, and $r = 0.05$ in the formula $A = Pe^{rt}$ to obtain $2400 = 1600e^{0.05t}$. To isolate the time $t$ in this last equation, first divide both sides by 1600. This yields

$$1.5 = e^{0.05t}$$

and therefore

$$0.05t = \ln 1.5 \qquad \text{converting from exponential to logarithmic form}$$
$$t = \frac{\ln 1.5}{0.05}$$

Using a calculator now to evaluate this last expression, we find $t \approx 8.1$ years. In summary, it will take slightly longer that 8 years 1 month for the balance to reach $2400. *Suggestion:* You can use a graphing utility to check this result. Graph the function $A = 1600e^{0.05t}$ along with the horizontal line $A = 2400$ in an appropriate viewing rectangle. Is it then the first or second coordinate of the intersection point that you want to estimate?

In the next example we compare the results of continuous compounding and annual compounding of interest.

**EXAMPLE 6 Comparing continuous to annual compounding**

A principal of $100 is deposited in Account #1 at 6% per annum, compounded continuously. At the same time, another principal of $100 is deposited in Account #2 at 6% per annum, compounded only once a year. Use a graphing utility to determine how long it will take until the amount in Account #1 exceeds that in Account #2 by (at least) ten dollars.

**GRAPHICAL PERSPECTIVE**

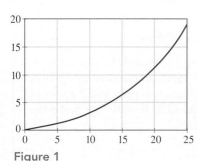

**Figure 1**
$f(t) = 100e^{0.06t} - 100(1.06^t)$
[0, 25, 5] by [0, 20, 5]

**SOLUTION**

The amount in Account #1 after $t$ years is given by $A = 100e^{0.06t}$; for Account #2 the amount is $A = 100(1 + 0.06)^t = 100(1.06)^t$. Define $f(t)$ to be the *difference* between the amounts in each account at time $t$:

$$f(t) = 100e^{0.06t} - 100(1.06)^t$$

We want to know when the difference $f(t)$ exceeds ten dollars. Using a graphing utility as in Figure 1, we find that when $t = 15$, the difference is less than 10, whereas when $t = 20$, the difference is more than 10.

At this point, we can either zoom in on the portion of the graph corresponding to $15 \leq t \leq 20$, or we can use the TABLE feature of the graphing utility. For this example we'll use the TABLE feature to evaluate the amount in each account

**TABLE 5**

| $t$ | Account #1<br>$A = 100e^{0.06t}$ | Account #2<br>$A = 100(1.06)^t$ | Difference<br>$100e^{0.06t} - 100(1.06^t)$ |
|-----|------|------|------|
| 15 | 245.96 | 239.66 | 6.30 |
| 16 | 261.17 | 254.04 | 7.13 |
| 17 | 277.32 | 269.28 | 8.04 |
| 18 | 294.47 | 285.43 | 9.03 |
| 19 | 312.68 | 302.56 | 10.12 |
| 20 | 332.01 | 320.71 | 11.30 |

and the difference $f(t)$ corresponding to the years $t = 15$ to $t = 20$. The results are shown in Table 5. You should verify these results for yourself. (For help on the TABLE feature, consult the owner's manual for your graphing utility.)

As Table 5 indicates, after 18 years, the accounts differ by less than ten dollars, but after 19 years the difference is more than ten dollars. In summary, it takes 19 years (to the nearest year) before the accounts differ by at least ten dollars. *Remark*: An algebraic solution for this example would involve solving the inequality $100e^{0.06t} - 100(1.06^t) \geq 10$. This can't be done, however, using any of the algebraic techniques of this chapter. (Try it!)

In the next example we compare the nominal rate with the effective rate under continuous compounding of interest.

**EXAMPLE 7   Nominal and effective rates under continuous compounding**

(a) Given a nominal rate of 8% per annum compounded continuously, compute the effective interest rate.
(b) Given an effective rate of 8% per annum, compute the nominal rate compounded continuously.

**SOLUTION**
(a) With the values $r = 0.08$ and $t = 1$, the formula $A = Pe^{rt}$ yields

$$A = Pe^{0.08(1)}$$
$$A \approx P(1.08329) \qquad \text{using a calculator}$$

This shows that the effective interest rate is approximately 8.33% per year.
(b) We now wish to compute the nominal rate $r$, given an effective rate of 8% per year. An effective rate of 8% means that the initial principal $P$ grows to $P(1.08)$ by the end of the year. Thus in the formula $A = Pe^{rt}$ we make the substitutions $A = P(1.08)$ and $t = 1$. This yields

$$P(1.08) = Pe^{r(1)}$$

Dividing both sides of this last equation by $P$, we have

$$1.08 = e^r$$

**TABLE 6**
**Comparison of Nominal and Effective Rates in Example 7**

| Nominal rate (% per annum) | Effective rate (% per per annum) |
|---|---|
| 8 | 8.33 |
| 7.70 | 8 |

To solve this equation for $r$, we rewrite it in its equivalent logarithmic form:

$$r = \ln(1.08)$$
$$r \approx 0.07696 \qquad \text{using a calculator}$$

Thus, a nominal rate of about 7.70% per annum compounded continuously yields an effective rate of 8%. Table 6 summarizes these results.

Now we come to one of the remarkable and characteristic features of compound interest and of growth governed by the formula $A = Pe^{rt}$. By the **doubling time** we mean, as the name implies, the amount of time required for a given principal to double. The surprising fact here is that the doubling time does not depend on the principal $P$. To see why this is so in the continuous compounding case, we begin with the formula

$$A = Pe^{rt}$$

We are interested in the time $t$ at which $A = 2P$. Replacing $A$ by $2P$ in the formula yields

$$2P = Pe^{rt}$$
$$2 = e^{rt}$$
$$rt = \ln 2$$
$$t = \frac{\ln 2}{r}$$

Denoting the doubling time by $T_2$, we have the following formula.

---

**Doubling Time under Continuous Compounding**

$$\text{Doubling time} = T_2 = \frac{\ln 2}{r}$$

---

As you can see, the formula for the doubling time $T_2$ does not involve $P$, but only $r$. Thus at a given rate under continuous compounding, $2 and $2000 would both take the same amount of time to double. (This idea takes some getting used to.) *Note*: For compound interest other than continuous compounding, the doubling time is also independent of the principal, but the formula is a little more complicated.

---

**EXAMPLE 8 Computing the doubling time**

Compute the doubling time $T_2$ when a sum is invested at an interest rate of 4% per annum compounded continuously.

**SOLUTION**

$$T_2 = \frac{\ln 2}{r} = \frac{\ln 2}{0.04} \approx 17.3 \text{ years} \qquad \text{using a calculator}$$

---

There is a convenient approximation that allows us to estimate doubling times easily. As you can check with a calculator, we have $\ln 2 \approx 0.7$. Using this approximation in the doubling time formula, we have

$$T_2 \approx \frac{0.7}{r}$$

where $r$ (as usual) is the annual interest rate expressed as a decimal. Now let $R$ be the annual interest rate expressed as a percentage, so that $R = 100r$. Then we can write

$$T_2 \approx \frac{0.7}{r} = \frac{0.7}{r} \times \frac{100}{100} = \frac{70}{100r} = \frac{70}{R}$$

That is,

$$T_2 \approx \frac{70}{R} \qquad \text{where } R \text{ is the annual rate expressed as a percentage}$$

This is the so-called *rule of 70* for estimating doubling times. For instance, for an annual percentage rate of 10%, we estimate the doubling time as $T_2 \approx 70/10 = 7$ years. As another example, let's use this rule of 70 to rework Example 8, in which the annual interest rate is 4%. We have

$$T_2 \approx \frac{70}{4} = \frac{35}{2} = 17.5 \text{ years}$$

This is quite close to the actual doubling time of 17.3 years computed in Example 8. *Remark*: A slightly less accurate approximation that's often used in business is the *rule of 72, $T_2 \approx 72/R$*. The number 72 is used instead of 70 simply because there are more numbers that divide into 72 evenly than into 70.

The rule of 70 for estimating doubling times is useful when you want to sketch a graph of the function $A = Pe^{rt}$ without relying on a graphing utility. As an example, suppose that a principal of $1000 is invested at 10% per annum compounded continuously. Then the function that we wish to graph is

$$A = 1000e^{0.1t}$$

Approximating the doubling time using the rule of 70 gives us

$$T_2 \approx \frac{70}{R} = \frac{70}{10} = 7 \text{ years}$$

Now we just set up a table showing the results of doubling $1000 every 7 years, plot the points, and then join them with a smooth curve. See Figure 2.

| $t$ | $A$ |
|-----|-----|
| 0 | 1000 |
| 7 | 2000 |
| 14 | 4000 |
| 21 | 8000 |
| 28 | 16,000 |

**Figure 2**
Applying the rule of 70 to sketch a graph

# EXERCISE SET 5.6

**A**

1. You invest $800 at 6% interest compounded annually. How much is in the account after 4 years, assuming that you make no subsequent withdrawal or deposit?

2. A sum of $1000 is invested at an interest rate of $5\frac{1}{2}$% compounded annually. How many years will it take until the sum exceeds $2500? (First find out when the amount equals $2500; then round off as in Example 2.)

3. At what interest rate (compounded annually) will a sum of $4000 grow to $6000 in 5 years?

4. A bank pays 7% interest compounded annually. What principal will grow to $10,000 in 10 years?

5. You place $500 in a savings account at 5% compounded annually. After 4 years you withdraw all your money and take it to a different bank, which advertises a rate of 6% compounded annually. What is the balance in this new account after 4 more years? (As usual, assume that no subsequent withdrawal or deposit is made.)

6. A sum of $3000 is placed in a savings account at 6% per annum. How much is in the account after 1 year if the interest is compounded **(a)** annually? **(b)** semiannually? **(c)** daily?

7. A sum of $1000 is placed in a savings account at 7% per annum. How much is in the account after 20 years if the interest is compounded **(a)** annually? **(b)** quarterly?

8. Your friend invests $2000 at $5\frac{1}{4}$% per annum compounded semiannually. You invest an equal amount at the same yearly rate, but compounded daily. How much larger is your account than your friend's after 8 years?

9. You invest $100 at 6% per annum compounded quarterly. How long will it take for your balance to exceed $120? (Round your answer up to the next quarter.)

10. A bank offers an interest rate of 7% per annum compounded daily. What is the effective rate?

11. What principal should you deposit at $5\frac{1}{2}$% per annum compounded semiannually so as to have $6000 after 10 years?

12. You place a sum of $800 in a savings account at 6% per annum compounded continuously. Assuming that you make no subsequent withdrawal or deposit, how much is in the account after 1 year? When will the balance reach $1000?

13. A principal of $600 dollars is placed in a savings account at 6.5% per annum compounded continuously.

   **(a)** Use a graphing utility to estimate how long it will take for the balance to reach $800. (Adapt the suggestion at the end of Example 5.)

   **(b)** Use algebra (as in Example 5) to determine how long it will take for the balance to reach $800.

14. A principal of $4000 dollars is invested at 8% per annum compounded continuously.

   **(a)** Use a graphing utility to estimate how long it will take for the balance to increase by 25%. (That is, you want a balance of $4000 + $1000 = $5000.) (Adapt the suggestion at the end of Example 5.)

   **(b)** Use algebra, rather than a graphing utility, to solve the problem in part (a).

15. A principal of $3500 is deposited in Account #1 at 7% per annum, compounded continuously. At the same time, another principal of $3500 is deposited in Account #2 at 7% per annum, compounded semiannually. Use a graphing utility to determine how long it will take until the amount in Account #1 exceeds that in Account #2 by (at least) $200. (Follow the method of Example 6).

16. A principal of $1000 is deposited in Account #1 at 8% per annum, compounded continuously. At the same time, a principal of $1200 is deposited in Account #2 at 6% per annum, compounded once per year. Use a graphing utility to determine how long it will take until the amount in Account #1 exceeds that in Account #2. Give your answer to the nearest whole number of years, rounded upward.

17. A bank offers an interest rate of $6\frac{1}{2}$% per annum compounded continuously. What principal will grow to $5000 in 10 years under these conditions?

18. Given a nominal rate of 6% per annum, compute the effective rate under continuous compounding of interest.

19. Suppose that under continuous compounding of interest, the effective rate is 6% per annum. Compute the nominal rate.

20. You have two savings accounts, each with an initial principal of $1000. The nominal rate on both accounts is $5\frac{1}{4}$% per annum. In the first account, interest is compounded semiannually. In the second account, interest is compounded continuously. How much more is in the second account after 12 years?

21. You want to invest $10,000 for 5 years, and you have a choice between two accounts. The first pays 6% per annum compounded annually. The second pays 5% per annum compounded continuously. Which is the better investment?

22. Suppose that a certain principal is invested at 6% per annum compounded continuously.

   **(a)** Use the rule of 70, $T_2 \approx 70/R$, to estimate the doubling time.

   **(b)** Compute the doubling time using the formula $T_2 = (\ln 2)/r$.

   **(c)** Do your answers in (a) and (b) differ by more than 2 months?

23. A sum of $1500 is invested at 5% per annum compounded continuously.

   **(a)** Estimate the doubling time.

   **(b)** Compute the actual doubling time.

   **(c)** Let $d_1$ and $d_2$ denote the actual and estimated doubling times, respectively. Define $d$ by $d = |d_1 - d_2|$. What percentage is $d$ of the actual doubling time?

24. A sum of $5000 is invested at 10% per annum compounded continuously.

   **(a)** Estimate the doubling time.

*(continues)*

**(b)** Estimate the time required for the $5000 to grow to $40,000.

**25.** After carrying out the calculations in this problem, you'll see one of the reasons why some governments impose inheritance taxes and why laws are passed to prohibit savings accounts from being passed from generation to generation without restriction. Suppose that a family invests $1000 at 8% per annum compounded continuously. If this account were to remain intact, being passed from generation to generation, for 300 years, how much would be in the account at the end of those 300 years?

**26.** A principal of $500 is invested at 7% per annum compounded continuously.
   **(a)** Estimate the doubling time.
   **(b)** Sketch a graph similar to the one in Figure 2, showing how the amount increases with time.

**27.** A principal of $7000 is invested at 5% per annum compounded continuously.

   **(a)** Estimate the doubling time.
   **(b)** Sketch a graph showing how the amount increases with time.

**28.** In one savings account, a principal of $1000 is deposited at 5% per annum. In a second account, a principal of $500 is deposited at 10% per annum. Both accounts compound interest continuously.
   **(a)** Estimate the doubling time for each account.
   **(b)** On the same set of axes, sketch graphs showing the amount of money in each account over time. Give the (approximate) coordinates of the point where the two curves meet. In financial terms, what is the significance of this point? (In working this problem, assume that the initial deposits in each account were made at the same time.)
   **(c)** During what period of time does the first account have the larger balance?

---

# PROJECT

## LOAN PAYMENTS

*Amortize: Gradual paying off of a debt by making regular equal payments to cover interest and principal.* —http://www.moneywords.com

*Amortize: (obsolete) To deaden, render as if dead, destroy.* —Oxford English Dictionary

*The goode werkes that men don whil thay ben in good lif ben al amortised by synne folwyng.* —Chaucer (ca. 1386), as quoted in the Oxford English Dictionary

**(a)** In this first part of the project, we'll imagine a loan scenario and explain how the calculations work from month to month. Suppose that when you graduate college, you are shopping for a new car. You decide that you'll need a loan of $15,000 toward the purchase of the particular model that you are interested in. The car dealer tells you that he can arrange this loan for you. It's a four-year loan at 6% per annum, compounded monthly. The dealer says that the monthly payments will each be $283.40.

In the following table we will explain how the entries in the row for monthly payment #1 are obtained. Then, as a check on your understanding of the process, you should fill in the next two rows yourself. (Tables of this form are called *amortization schedules*.)

| Monthly payment # | Monthly payment | Portion of payment toward interest | Portion of payment toward principal | Loan balance |
|---|---|---|---|---|
| 0 | | | | $15,000.00 |
| 1 | $283.40 | $75.00 | $208.40 | $14,791.60 |
| 2 | $283.40 | | | |
| 3 | $283.40 | | | |

*Portion of monthly payment #1 toward interest:* Each month, a portion of your $283.40 payment is used to pay off the previous month's interest on the unpaid loan balance. Then, whatever is left from the $283.40 is used as a payment on the actual loan balance. We are assuming a rate of 6% per annum compounded monthly. So the interest on an unpaid balance of $P$ dollars for one month is

$$\text{interest} = P(1 + r/n)^{nt} - P$$
$$= P[(1 + 0.06/12)^{12(1/12)} - 1] = P[(1 + 0.06/12) - 1]$$
$$= 0.005P$$

For payment #1 then, we have

$$\text{interest} = 0.005P = 0.005(\$15{,}000) = \$75.00$$

*Portion of monthly payment #1 toward principal:*
$283.40 − $75.00 = $208.40

*Loan balance:* $15,000 − $208.40 = $14,791.60

The calculations corresponding to monthly payments #2 and #3 are now carried out in the same manner. In starting your work for monthly payment #2, remember that your unpaid balance now is $P = \$14{,}791.60$, rather than $P = \$15{,}000$. As a check on your work, after monthly payment #2 the loan balance should turn out to be $14,582.16.

**(b)** There are formulas (that we won't derive) from the mathematics of finance relating the loan amount, the monthly payments, and the interest rate. One such formula, which applies to our example (with monthly compounding and monthly payments) is

$$L = M\frac{1 - (1 + p)^{-n}}{p} \tag{1}$$

where $L$ is the loan amount, $p$ is the periodic interest rate, and $n$ is the total number of compoundings in the life of the loan (or, equivalently in our case, the length of the loan, in months). Use equation (1) to calculate what the monthly payments $M$ should be for the example in part (a). Did the car dealer give you the correct figure?

**(c)** Solve equation (1) for $n$ in terms of the other variables. Then use the result to compute an answer for the following problem: You are thinking of taking out a bank loan of $315,848 toward the purchase of a beachfront condominium. In your notes, you've written down that the interest rate is $7\frac{1}{2}\%$ per annum, compounded monthly, and that the monthly payments would be $953.90. You forgot, however, to write down the amount of time required to pay off the loan. Compute the required time.

**(d)** You graduate, and the government reminds you that the time has come to begin repaying your student loan of $L = \$5800$. You have 4 years to repay this loan; the interest is compounded monthly; and the monthly payments are $M = \$113.88$. Find the periodic interest rate $p$ and then the annual rate $r = 12p$. *Hint:* Substitute the given numerical values for $L$ and $M$ into equation (1) and then convince yourself that you cannot solve for $p$ using the algebraic techniques you learned in this chapter. Now use a graphing utility and the ZOOM feature to find $p$. It may take some work to find an appropriate viewing rectangle.

Drawing by Professor Ann Jones, University of Colorado, Boulder. From the cover of *The Physics Teacher*, vol. 14, no. 7 (October 1976).

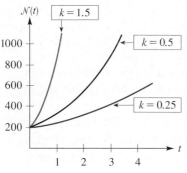

**Figure 1**
The graph of $\mathcal{N}(t) = 200e^{kt}$ for $k = 0.25$, $k = 0.5$, and $k = 1.5$

# 5.7   EXPONENTIAL GROWTH AND DECAY

In newspapers and in everyday speech, the term "exponential growth" is used rather loosely to describe any situation involving rapid growth. In the sciences, however, **exponential growth** refers specifically to growth governed by functions of the form $y = ae^{bx}$, where $a$ and $b$ are positive constants. For example, since the function $A = Pe^{rt}$ (discussed in the previous section) has this general form, we say that money grows exponentially under continuous compounding of interest. Similarly, in the sciences, **exponential decay** refers specifically to decrease or decay governed by functions of the form $y = ae^{bx}$, where $a$ is positive and $b$ is negative. As examples in this section, we shall consider population growth, global warming, and radioactive decay.

Under ideal conditions involving unlimited food and space, the size of a population of bacteria is modeled by a function of the form

$$\mathcal{N}(t) = \mathcal{N}_0 e^{kt}$$

In this *growth law*, $\mathcal{N}(t)$ is the population at time $t$, and $k$ is a positive constant related to (but not equal to) the growth rate of the population. The constant $k$ is referred to as the **growth constant.** The number $\mathcal{N}_0$ is also a constant; it represents the size of the population at time $t = 0$. You can see that this is the case by substituting $t = 0$ in the equation $\mathcal{N}(t) = \mathcal{N}_0 e^{kt}$. This yields

$$\mathcal{N}(0) = \mathcal{N}_0 e^0 = \mathcal{N}_0 \cdot 1 = \mathcal{N}_0$$

That is, $\mathcal{N}(0) = \mathcal{N}_0$, which says that the population at time $t = 0$ is indeed $\mathcal{N}_0$. Figure 1 shows three examples. In each case the initial population size is $\mathcal{N}_0 = 200$, and we've graphed the growth laws using three different values for the growth constant $k$.

*A remark about notation*: In science texts the growth law is often written as

$$\mathcal{N} = \mathcal{N}_0 e^{kt} \qquad \text{rather than} \qquad \mathcal{N}(t) = \mathcal{N}_0 e^{kt}$$

In both cases the quantity on the left-hand side of the equation represents the population at time $t$. For ease in writing, we follow this convention too, in Examples 5 and 7. (For the record: The difference between the use of $\mathcal{N}$ in the two equations is this. On the left-hand side of the equation $\mathcal{N}(t) = \mathcal{N}_0 e^{kt}$, $\mathcal{N}$ is the name of the function. On the left-hand side of the equation $\mathcal{N} = \mathcal{N}_0 e^{kt}$, $\mathcal{N}$ serves as a dependent variable, just like the "$y$" in $y = x^2$.)

| EXAMPLE | 1 | Modeling bacterial growth |

Suppose that at the start of an experiment in a biology lab, 1200 bacteria are present in a colony. Two hours later, the size of the population is found to be 1440. Assume that the population size grows exponentially.

**(a)** Determine the growth constant $k$ and the growth law for this population.

**(b)** How many bacteria were there 1.5 hours after the experiment began? Round the answer to the nearest 5 (that is, nearest multiple of 5).

**(c)** When will the population size reach 4800?

**SOLUTION**

**(a)** The initial population size $\mathcal{N}_0$ is 1200, so the equation $\mathcal{N}(t) = \mathcal{N}_0 e^{kt}$ becomes

$$\mathcal{N}(t) = 1200 e^{kt}$$

We are also told that after 2 hours, the size of the population is 1440. Using this information in equation (1) gives us

$$\mathcal{N}(2) = 1200 e^{k(2)}$$
$$1440 = 1200 e^{2k}$$

and therefore

$$e^{2k} = \frac{1400}{1200} = \frac{6}{5}$$

To isolate $k$, we rewrite this last equation in logarithmic form (or take the natural logarithm of both sides) to obtain $2k = \ln(1440/1200)$, and consequently,

$$k = \frac{\ln(6/5)}{2} \tag{2}$$
$$\approx 0.09116 \qquad \text{using a calculator and rounding to five decimal places}$$

The growth law for the population is therefore

$$\mathcal{N}(t) = 1200 e^{kt} \qquad \text{where } k \text{ is given by equation (2)} \tag{3}$$

Notice that in our statement of the growth law we referenced the exact expression for $k$ rather than the calculator approximation. In parts (b) and (c) of this problem we don't round during the intermediate steps. This is standard procedure in scientific calculations because rounding errors can, in general, build up and adversely effect the accuracy of the final result.

**(b)** Substituting $t = 1.5$ in the growth law [that's equation (3)] yields

$$\mathcal{N}(1.5) = 1200 e^{k(1.5)} \qquad \text{where } k = \frac{\ln(6/5)}{2}$$

With a calculator now, you should verify that $\mathcal{N}(1.5) \approx 1375.8$. In our context, $\mathcal{N}(1.5)$ must be a whole number because it represents the number of bacteria. Furthermore, the problem asks us to round to the nearest 5. In summary then, after 1.5 hours the population is 1375.

**(c)** We want to find out when the population reaches 4800. Replacing $\mathcal{N}(t)$ with 4800 in equation (3), we have $4800 = 1200 e^{kt}$, and therefore $4 = e^{kt}$. Rewriting this last equation in logarithmic form gives us

$$kt = \ln 4$$
$$t = \frac{\ln 4}{k} \approx 15.207 \qquad \begin{array}{l}\text{using the expression for } k \\ \text{in equation (2) and a calculator}\end{array}$$

Thus it takes approximately 15.2 hours for the size of the population to reach 4800. As you can check with arithmetic, this is 15 hours 12 minutes. See Figure 2 for a graphical solution to this part of the example.

**GRAPHICAL PERSPECTIVE**

(a) [0, 20, 4] by [0, 6000, 2000]

(b) [15.0, 15.5, 0.1] by [4600, 5000, 100]

**Figure 2**
In both viewing rectangles the red graph is the population growth function determined in part (a) of Example 1. The blue graph is the horizontal line $\mathcal{N}(t) = 4800$. The viewing rectangle in Figure 2(a) shows that the population reaches 4800 at a time that is roughly halfway between $t = 14$ and $t = 16$ hours. The zoom-in view in Figure 2(b) shows the time to be 15.2 hours, to the nearest tenth of an hour.

In Example 2 and in exercises we are going to use the function $\mathcal{N}(t) = \mathcal{N}_0 e^{kt}$ as a model for the size of human populations. But in order to do that in a reasonably honest way (short of bringing in calculus), first we need to introduce the concept of a *relative growth rate.* Suppose that in a biology lab you obtain the following population figures in successive hours for a colony of bacteria:

3 P.M.:   12,000 bacteria      4 P.M.:   15,000 bacteria

Let us compute the percentage increase in the population over this 1-hour interval. We have

$$\text{percentage increase} = \frac{\text{change in population}}{\text{initial population}} \times 100$$

$$= \frac{15{,}000 - 12{,}000}{12{,}000} \times 100 = \frac{1}{4} \times 100 = 25\%$$

We say in this case that the **average relative growth rate** of the population is 25%/hour. In this section and in the exercises we will shorten the phrase *average relative growth rate* to simply **relative growth rate.** Just as the interest rate in banking is sometimes expressed as a percentage and sometimes as a decimal, so too with the relative growth rate. In the example we are using, then, the decimal form of the relative growth rate is 0.25/hour. Whether expressed as a percentage or a decimal, the relative growth rate over a unit of time is a measure of how the population increases (or decreases) compared to its starting value.

There is a relationship between the growth constant $k$ in the equation $\mathcal{N}(t) = \mathcal{N}_0 e^{kt}$ and the relative growth rate. To demonstrate this, we'll use the growth function obtained in Example 1. In Table 1, we've computed the relative growth rates (in decimal form) for this function over successive 1-hour time intervals.

We make two observations about the results in Table 1.

- The relative growth rates all are equal.
- The relative growth rate (0.095) is approximately equal to the growth constant $k$ (0.091).

**TABLE 1** Relative Growth Rates for the Function in Example 1 over Successive 1-Hour Intervals*

| $t$ | Relative growth rate on interval $[t, t + 1]$ | Calculator value (rounded to 3 places) |
|---|---|---|
| 0 | $\dfrac{\mathcal{N}(1) - \mathcal{N}(0)}{\mathcal{N}(0)}$ | 0.095 |
| 1 | $\dfrac{\mathcal{N}(2) - \mathcal{N}(1)}{\mathcal{N}(1)}$ | 0.095 |
| 2 | $\dfrac{\mathcal{N}(3) - \mathcal{N}(2)}{\mathcal{N}(2)}$ | 0.095 |
| 3 | $\dfrac{\mathcal{N}(4) - \mathcal{N}(3)}{\mathcal{N}(3)}$ | 0.095 |

*The function is given by $\mathcal{N}(t) = 1200e^{kt}$, where $k = \dfrac{\ln(1440/1200)}{2} = 0.09116\ldots$

The observation that the relative growth rates all turn out to be the same seems surprising at first. This is, however, one of the characteristic features of exponential growth and not only a coincidence. To see why, we compute $[\mathcal{N}(t + 1) - \mathcal{N}(t)]/\mathcal{N}(t)$ for the function $\mathcal{N}(t) = \mathcal{N}_0 e^{kt}$. We have

$$\frac{\mathcal{N}(t + 1) - \mathcal{N}(t)}{\mathcal{N}(t)} = \frac{\mathcal{N}_0 e^{k(t+1)} - \mathcal{N}_0 e^{kt}}{\mathcal{N}_0 e^{kt}}$$

$$= \frac{\mathcal{N}_0 e^{kt}(e^k - 1)}{\mathcal{N}_0 e^{kt}} \qquad \text{since } e^{k(t+1)} = e^{kt+k} = e^{kt}e^k \qquad (4)$$

$$= e^k - 1$$

This shows that the relative growth rate over every interval $[t, t + 1]$ is the constant $e^k - 1$; the value does not depend upon $t$.

The second of the two observations we made was that the relative growth rate was nearly the same as the growth constant $k$. It turns out that this is true for every exponential growth function provided $k$ is close to zero. (Exercise 61 will help you to see why this is so.) For this reason, in using the exponential growth law $\mathcal{N}(t) = \mathcal{N}_0 e^{kt}$ to model human populations, we'll simply use the relative growth rate for the value of $k$. This is convenient to do, since most of the available data report growth in terms of a relative growth rate. Furthermore, since the census figures themselves are, in general, not precise, it wouldn't be particularly meaningful to quibble over a fraction of a percent in this context. See Table 2.

| **EXAMPLE** | **2** | **Using an exponential growth model for world population growth** |
|---|---|---|

The Population Reference Bureau, www.prb.org, estimates that in the year 1900 the size of the world's population was 1.628 billion, with a relative growth rate of about 0.7%/year.

**TABLE 2** Comparison of Relative Growth Rate $e^k - 1$ [from Equation (4)] to Growth Constant $k$ (computed assuming exponential growth)*

| Country | Relative growth rate for year 2000 | | $k$ |
| | as percentage | as decimal | |
|---|---|---|---|
| Liberia | 3.2 | 0.032 | 0.03149... |
| United States | 0.6 | 0.006 | 0.00598... |
| Sweden | -0.1 | -0.001 | -0.00099... |

*When the numbers are close to zero, the relative growth rate (in decimal form) is a good approximation for $k$.

Source for relative growth rates: Population Reference Bureau, www.prb.org

**TABLE 3**

| Year | World population |
|---|---|
| 1925 | 1.963 |
| 2000 | 6.067 |

Source: Population Reference Bureau

**(a)** Use the exponential growth model to make population projections for the years 1925 and 2000.

**(b)** Use the data in Table 3 to compute the percentage errors in the projections, and summarize the results.

**SOLUTION**

**(a)** Let $t = 0$ correspond to 1900. The initial population is $N_0 = 1.628$, in units of one billion. For the value of $k$, we convert the given relative growth rate 0.7%/year into its decimal form, which is 0.007/year. With these values, the growth law becomes $N(t) = 1.628e^{0.007t}$. Now we're ready to compute.

| For 1925, $t = 25$ | For 2000, $t = 100$ |
|---|---|
| $N(25) = 1.628e^{0.007(25)}$ | $N(100) = 1.628e^{0.007(100)}$ |
| $\approx 1.939$ using a calculator | $\approx 3.278$ using a calculator |

The exponential model projects a world population of 1.939 billion in 1925 and 3.278 billion in 2000.

**(b)** For 1925 the projection is 1.939 billion, whereas the figure from Table 3 is 1.963 billion. The percentage error in the projection is then

$$\text{percentage error} = \frac{|\text{actual value} - \text{estimate}|}{\text{actual value}} \times 100$$

$$= \frac{|1.963 \text{ billion} - 1.939 \text{ billion}|}{1.963 \text{ billion}} \times 100$$

$$\approx 1.2\% \quad \text{using a calculator}$$

As you should check now for yourself using the year 2000 figures, the percentage error in the projection for 2000 is 46.0%. *Remark*: In both cases the exponential projection is too low. However, the projection for 1925 *is* quite close, with a percentage error of only about 1%. In the case of the year 2000 projection, the model is way off; the percentage error is 46%.

**EXAMPLE** **3** **More on world population growth**

In the previous example we found that from 1900 to 2000, the world population grew faster than what was predicted by an exponential growth model with a relative growth rate of 0.7%/year. Actually, as you might well expect, the relative growth rate was not constant over the course of the entire century. But, assuming that it had been, find the value of the growth constant $k$ that would yield an accurate projection for the year 2000. (The year 2000 population is given in Table 3.)

**SOLUTION**

Again we let $t = 0$ correspond to 1900, and we have $\mathcal{N}_0 = 1.628$, in units of one billion. Our exponential growth law is $\mathcal{N}(t) = 1.628e^{kt}$. We want to find $k$ so that the population in the year 2000 is 6.067 billion (according to Table 3). The year 2000 corresponds to $t = 100$, so we have

$$\mathcal{N}(100) = 1.628e^{k(100)}$$
$$6.067 = 1.628e^{100k}$$
$$\frac{6.067}{1.628} = e^{100k}$$

Writing this last equation in logarithmic form gives us

$$100\,k = \ln\frac{6.067}{1.628}$$

and therefore

$$k = \frac{\ln\dfrac{6.067}{1.628}}{100} \approx 0.0131\ldots \qquad \text{using a calculator}$$

Thus rounding to three decimal places, the required value of $k$ is approximately 0.013. The corresponding relative growth rate in percent form is then 1.3%/year. *Note*: If you try checking this result using the approximation $k = 0.013$, you'll find that the population projection falls short of the required 6.067 billion. Don't round until the end. A good way to do this with your calculator is to first evaluate $k = (\ln\frac{6.067}{1.628})/100$, then *store* the result, and use the stored value in computing $1.628e^{k(100)}$. (If necessary, see your calculator owner's manual on how to store and then recall a constant.)

In the next example we compute the *doubling time* for a population that is growing exponentially. As the name indicates, the **doubling time** for a population is the amount of time required for the size of the population to double. Now, in the previous section we developed a formula for the doubling time $T_2$ of an amount of money under continuous compounding of interest. That formula is $T_2 = (\ln 2)/r$, where $r$ is annual interest rate. The same formula is applicable now, because in both cases the underlying assumption is that of exponential growth. In the current context, the growth constant $k$ plays the role of the annual interest rate $r$. Thus for a population that grows exponentially, the doubling time is $T_2 = (\ln 2)/k$. Note that the doubling time depends only upon the growth constant $k$ and not upon the initial population size $\mathcal{N}_0$. For reference we state the formula for doubling time in the box that follows.

---

**Doubling Time Formula**

Suppose that a population grows exponentially. Then the doubling time $T_2$ is given by

$$T_2 = \frac{\ln 2}{k}$$

where $k$ is the growth constant.

---

**EXAMPLE**   **4**   **Computing a doubling time**

According to the *Global Data Files* of the U.S. Bureau of the Census, the size of the world population in 1950 was approximately 2.555 billion, with an annual growth rate of 1.47%/year. Estimate the doubling time, assuming exponential growth at 1.47%/year.

**SOLUTION**
Converting 1.47% to a decimal, we have $k = 0.0147$. The doubling time is therefore

$$T_2 = \frac{\ln 2}{k} = \frac{\ln 2}{0.0147}$$
$$\approx 47 \text{ years} \qquad \text{using a calculator and rounding to the nearest year}$$

The exponential model predicts a doubling time of approximately 47 years. That would be the year 1950 + 47 = 1997. Note the fact that the 1950 population size was not needed in this computation. *Remark*: It's interesting to check this model against the actual data. The model predicts that the size of the population in 1997 is 2 × 2.555 billion = 5.110 billion. The actual figure from the U.S. census is 5.847 billion. So the model projects too low a population for 1997. To put it another way, it actually took less than 47 years for the 1950 population to double in size. Indeed, a further check of the census data shows that the size of the population reached (our projected) 5.110 billion back in 1988.

In the next example we use the exponential growth model to describe the concentration of the so-called greenhouse gas carbon dioxide in the earth's atmosphere. As background, we quote from an article on the front page of the *New York Times,* June 7, 2001. The headline under which the article appears is "Panel Tells Bush Global Warming Getting Worse."

A panel of top American scientists declared today that global warming was a real problem, and was getting worse . . . . In a much anticipated report from the National Academy of Sciences, 11 leading atmospheric scientists, including previous skeptics about global warming, reaffirmed the mainstream scientific view that the earth's atmosphere was getting warmer and that human activity was largely responsible. "Greenhouse gases are accumulating in the earth's atmosphere as a result of human activities, causing surface air temperatures and subsurface ocean temperature to rise," the report said.

*New York Times* article by Katharine Q. Seelye with Andrew C. Revkin, June 7, 2001

| EXAMPLE | 5 | Using an exponential model for carbon dioxide levels in the atmosphere |

The following statements about the increasing levels of carbon dioxide in the atmosphere appear in the book *The Challenge of Global Warming,* edited by Dean Edwin Abrahamson (Washington, D.C.: Island Press, 1989).

> Carbon dioxide, the single most important greenhouse gas, accounts for about half of the warming that has been experienced as a result of past emissions* and also for half of the projected future warming. The present [1988] concentration is now about 350 parts per million (ppm) and is increasing about 0.4% . . . per year. . . .

Assuming that the concentration of carbon dioxide in the atmosphere continues to increase exponentially at 0.4% per year, estimate when the concentration might reach 600 ppm. (This would be roughly twice the level estimated to exist prior to the Industrial Revolution.)

**SOLUTION**

Let $t = 0$ correspond to the year 1988. In the formula $\mathcal{N} = \mathcal{N}_0 e^{kt}$, we want to determine the time $t$ when $\mathcal{N} = 600$. Using the values $\mathcal{N}_0 = 350$, $\mathcal{N} = 600$, and $k = 0.004$, we have

$$600 = 350\, e^{0.004t} \quad \text{or} \quad \frac{600}{350} = \frac{12}{7} = e^{0.004t}$$

and, consequently,

$$\ln(12/7) = 0.004t$$
$$t = \frac{\ln(12/7)}{0.004} \approx 135 \qquad \text{using a calculator and rounding to the nearest whole number}$$

Now, 135 years beyond the base year of 1988 is 2123. Rounding once more, we summarize our result this way: If the carbon dioxide levels continue to increase exponentially at 0.4% per year, then the concentration will reach 600 ppm by approximately 2125. (*Note:* We round our result to the nearest five years because of the uncertainty in both the initial concentration of 350 ppm and the 0.4% rate of increase.)

In Examples 1 through 4 we used the function $\mathcal{N}(t) = \mathcal{N}_0 e^{kt}$ to describe population growth. In Example 5 we used the function to model the increasing levels of carbon dioxide in the atmosphere. And in the previous section a function of this form was used to describe how a sum of money grows under continuous compounding of interest. It is a remarkable fact that the same basic function, but now with $k < 0$, describes radioactive decay. How do scientists know that this is the appropriate model for radioactive decay? We mention two reasons: one empirical, one theoretical. As early as 1900–1903, the physicist Ernest Rutherford (Nobel prize, 1908) and the chemist Frederick Soddy (Nobel prize, 1921) carried out experiments measuring radioactive decay. They found that an equation of the form

---

*The two principal sources of these emissions are the burning of fossil fuels and the burning of vegetation in the tropics.

$\mathcal{N} = \mathcal{N}_0 e^{kt}$, with $k < 0$, indeed aptly described their data. Alternatively, on theoretical grounds, it can be argued that the decay rate at time $t$ must be proportional to the amount $\mathcal{N}(t)$ of the radioactive substance present. Under this condition, calculus can be used to show that a law of exponential decay applies. (Exercise 63 demonstrates the converse: Assuming that the law of exponential decay applies, then the rate of decay must be proportional to the amount of the substance present.)

In discussing radioactive decay, it is convenient to introduce the term *half-life*. As you'll see, this is analogous to the concept of *doubling time* for exponential growth.

---

| **DEFINITION** | **Half-life** |
|---|---|

The **half-life** of a radioactive substance is the time required for half of a given sample to disintegrate. The half-life is an intrinsic property of the substance; it does not depend on the given sample size.

**EXAMPLE**
Iodine-131 is a radioactive substance with a half-life of 8 days. Suppose that 2 g are present initially. Then:

at $t = 0$, 2 g are present;

at $t = 8$ days, 1 g is left;

at $t = 16$ days, $\frac{1}{2}$ g is left;

at $t = 24$ days, $\frac{1}{4}$ g is left;

at $t = 32$ days, $\frac{1}{8}$ g is left;

---

**TABLE 4**

| $t$ (days) | $\mathcal{N}(t)$ (amount) |
|---|---|
| 0 | $\mathcal{N}_0$ |
| 8 | $\mathcal{N}_0/2$ |
| 16 | $\mathcal{N}_0/4$ |
| 24 | $\mathcal{N}_0/8$ |
| 32 | $\mathcal{N}_0/16$ |

Just as we used the idea of doubling time to graph an exponential growth function in the previous section, we can use the half-life to graph an exponential decay function. Consider, for example, the radioactive substance iodine-131, which has a half-life of 8 days. Table 4 shows what fraction of an initial amount remains at 8-day intervals. Using the data in this table, we can draw the graph of the decay function $\mathcal{N}(t) = \mathcal{N}_0 e^{kt}$ for iodine-131 (see Figure 3). Notice that we are able to construct this graph without specifically evaluating the decay constant $k$. (The next example shows how to determine $k$.)

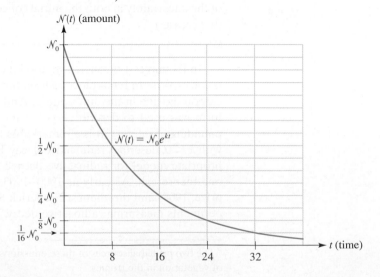

**Figure 3**
The exponential decay function for iodine-131

---

**EXAMPLE 6 Using the exponential decay formula**

Hospitals utilize the radioactive substance iodine-131 in the diagnosis of the thyroid gland. The half-life of iodine-131 is 8 days.

**(a)** Determine the *decay constant k* for iodine-131.

**(b)** If a hospital acquires 2 g of iodine-131, how much of this sample will remain after 20 days?

**(c)** How long will it be until only 0.01 g remains?

**SOLUTION**

**(a)** We use the half-life information to find the value of the decay constant $k$. Substituting $t = 8$ in the decay law $\mathcal{N}(t) = \mathcal{N}_0 e^{kt}$ yields

$$\mathcal{N}(8) = \mathcal{N}_0 e^{k(8)}$$

$$\frac{1}{2}\mathcal{N}_0 = \mathcal{N}_0 e^{8k} \qquad \text{A half-life of 8 days means that } \mathcal{N}(8) = \tfrac{1}{2}\mathcal{N}_0.$$

$$\frac{1}{2} = e^{8k} \qquad \text{dividing both sides by } \mathcal{N}_0$$

In logarithmic form, this last equation becomes

$$8k = \ln\frac{1}{2} \qquad \text{and therefore} \qquad k = \frac{\ln\frac{1}{2}}{8} = \frac{-\ln 2}{8}$$

$$\approx -0.08664 \qquad \text{rounding to five places}$$

**(b)** We are given $\mathcal{N}_0 = 2$ g and we want to find $\mathcal{N}(20)$, the amount remaining after 20 days. First, before using algebra and a calculator, let's estimate the answer to get a feeling for the situation. The half-life is 8 days. This means that after 8 days, 1 g remains; after 16 days, 0.5 g remains; and after 24 days, 0.25 g remains. Since 20 is between 16 and 24, it follows that after 20 days, the amount remaining will be between 0.5 g and 0.25 g. Now for the actual calculations: Substitute the values $\mathcal{N}_0 = 2$ and $t = 20$ in the decay law $\mathcal{N}(t) = \mathcal{N}_0 e^{kt}$ to obtain

$$\mathcal{N}(20) = 2e^{k(20)} \qquad \text{where } k = \frac{-\ln 2}{8}$$

$$\approx 0.354 \text{ g} \qquad \text{using a calculator}$$

Thus after 20 days, approximately 0.35 g of the iodine-131 remains. Note that this amount is indeed between 0.5 g and 0.25 g as we first estimated.

**(c)** We want to find the time $t$ for which $\mathcal{N}(t) = 0.01$ g. Substituting 0.01 for $\mathcal{N}(t)$ in the decay law gives us

$$0.01 = 2e^{kt} \qquad \text{and therefore} \qquad 0.005 = e^{kt}$$

The logarithmic form of this last equation is $kt = \ln(0.005)$, from which we conclude that

$$t = \frac{\ln(0.005)}{k} \qquad \text{where } k = \frac{-\ln 2}{8}$$

$$\approx 61.2 \text{ days} \qquad \text{using a calculator}$$

In Example 6(a) we found that the decay constant for iodine-131 is given by $k = -(\ln 2)/8$. Notice that the denominator in this expression is the half-life of iodine-131. By following the same reasoning used in Example 6(a), we find that the decay constant for any radioactive substance is always $-\ln 2$ divided by the half-life. For reference, this useful fact is restated in the box that follows.

---

**| PROPERTY SUMMARY   A Formula for the Decay Constant $k$**

| Formula | Example |
|---|---|
| $k = \dfrac{-\ln 2}{\text{half-life}}$ | The half-life of strontium-90 is 28 years, and therefore $k = -(\ln 2)/28$. |

---

**EXAMPLE    7    Calculations and estimates for radioactivity**

An article on nuclear energy appeared in the January 1976 issue of *Scientific American*. The author of the article was Hans Bethe (1906–2005), a Nobel prize winner in physics. At one point in the article, Professor Bethe discussed the disposal (through burial) of radioactive waste material from a nuclear reactor. The particular waste product under discussion was plutonium-239.

> . . . Plutonium-239 has a half-life of nearly 25,000 years, and 10 half-lives are required to cut the radioactivity by a factor of 1000. Thus, the buried wastes must be kept out of the biosphere for 250,000 years.

**(a)** Supply the detailed calculations to support the statement that 10 half-lives are required before the radioactivity is reduced by a factor of 1000.
**(b)** Show how the figure of 10 half-lives can be obtained by estimation, as opposed to detailed calculation.

**SOLUTION**

**(a)** Let $\mathcal{N}_0$ denote the initial amount of plutonium-239 at time $t = 0$. Then the amount $\mathcal{N}$ present at time $t$ is given by $\mathcal{N} = \mathcal{N}_0 e^{kt}$. We wish to determine $t$ when $\mathcal{N} = \frac{1}{1000}\mathcal{N}_0$. First, since the half-life is 25,000 years, we have $k = -(\ln 2)/25{,}000$. Now, substituting $\frac{1}{1000}\mathcal{N}_0$ for $\mathcal{N}$ in the decay law gives us

$$\frac{1}{1000}\mathcal{N}_0 = \mathcal{N}_0 e^{kt} \qquad \text{where } k \text{ is } -(\ln 2)/25{,}000$$

$$\frac{1}{1000} = e^{kt}$$

$$kt = \ln \frac{1}{1000} \qquad \text{converting from exponential to logarithmic form}$$

$$t = \frac{-\ln 1000}{k} = \frac{-\ln 1000}{\dfrac{-\ln 2}{25{,}000}} = \frac{25{,}000 \ln 1000}{\ln 2}$$

Using a calculator, we obtain the value 249,114.6 years; however, given the time scale involved, it would be ludicrous to announce the answer in this form. Instead, we round off the answer to the nearest thousand years and say that after 249,000 years, the radioactivity will have decreased by a factor of 1000. Notice that this result is consistent with Professor Bethe's ballpark estimate of 10 half-lives, or 250,000 years

**(b)** After 1 half-life:   $\mathcal{N} = \dfrac{\mathcal{N}_0}{2}$

After 2 half-lives:   $\mathcal{N} = \dfrac{1}{2}\left(\dfrac{\mathcal{N}_0}{2}\right) = \dfrac{\mathcal{N}_0}{2^2}$

After 3 half-lives:   $\mathcal{N} = \dfrac{1}{2}\left(\dfrac{\mathcal{N}_0}{2^2}\right) = \dfrac{\mathcal{N}_0}{2^3}$

Following this pattern, we see that after 10 half-lives we should have

$$\mathcal{N} = \dfrac{\mathcal{N}_0}{2^{10}}$$

However, as we noted in the first section of this chapter, $2^{10}$ is approximately 1000. Therefore we have

$$\mathcal{N} \approx \dfrac{\mathcal{N}_0}{1000} \qquad \text{after 10 half-lives}$$

This is in agreement with Professor Bethe's statement.

# EXERCISE SET 5.7

## A

*In Exercises 1 and 2, assume that the populations grow exponentially, that is, according to the law $\mathcal{N}(t) = \mathcal{N}_0 e^{kt}$.*

**1.** At the start of an experiment, 2000 bacteria are present in a colony. Two hours later, the population is 3800.
 **(a)** Determine the growth constant $k$.
 **(b)** Determine the population five hours after the start of the experiment.
 **(c)** When will the population reach 10,000?

**2.** At the start of an experiment, $2 \times 10^4$ bacteria are present in a colony. Eight hours later, the population is $3 \times 10^4$.
 **(a)** Determine the growth constant $k$.
 **(b)** What was the population two hours after the start of the experiment?
 **(c)** How long will it take for the population to triple?

**3.** The figure in the next column shows the graph of an exponential growth function $\mathcal{N}(t) = \mathcal{N}_0 e^{kt}$. Determine the values of $\mathcal{N}_0$ and $k$.

**4.** Suppose that you are helping a friend with his homework on the growth law, $\mathcal{N}(t) = \mathcal{N}_0 e^{kt}$, and on his paper you see the equation $e^k = -0.75$. How do you know at this point that your friend must have made an error?

**TABLE A**

| Region | 1995 Population (billions) | Percentage of population in 1995 | Relative growth rate (%/year) | Year 2000 population (billions) | Percentage of world population in 2000 |
|---|---|---|---|---|---|
| World | 5.702 | 100 | 1.5 | ? | ? |
| More developed regions | 1.169 | ? | 0.2 | ? | ? |
| Less developed regions | 4.533 | ? | 1.9 | ? | ? |

**TABLE B**

| Country | 1995 Population (millions) | Relative growth rate (%/year) | Year 2000 population (millions) | Percentage increase in population |
|---|---|---|---|---|
| United States | 263.2 | 0.7 | ? | ? |
| People's Republic of China | 1218.8 | 1.1 | ? | ? |
| Mexico | 93.7 | 2.2 | ? | ? |

*In Exercises 5 and 6:* **(a)** *Complete the table; and* **(b)** *use the information that is given to compute the percentage errors in the population projections in part (a). Round each answer to one decimal place. [The populations projections are in the second column from the right in Tables A and B.] The data in Exercises 5 and 6 are from The Population Reference Bureau,* www.prb.org.

5. **(a)** See Table A.
   **(b)** Year 2000 population in billions: world, 6.067; more developed, 1.184; less developed 4.883
6. **(a)** See Table B.
   **(b)** Year 2000 population in millions: United States, 275.6; People's Republic of China, 1264.5; Mexico, 99.6
7. As of the year 2000, the African nation of Chad had one of the highest population growth rates in the world, 3.3%/year. At the other extreme in 2000, the United Kingdom had one of the lowest (positive) growth rates, 0.1%/year. (There are countries with zero or with negative growth rates.)
   **(a)** In 2000 the sizes of the populations of Chad and the United Kingdom were 8.0 million and 59.8 million, respectively. Write the exponential growth law for each country, letting $t = 0$ correspond to 2000.
   **(b)** Assuming exponential growth, when would the two countries have populations of the same size? Round the answer to the nearest five years. *Hint*: Equate the two expressions for $N(t)$ obtained in part (a).
8. In 2000 the nations of Mali and Cuba had similar size populations: Mali 11.2 million, Cuba 11.1 million. However, the relative growth rate for Mali was 3.1%/year, whereas that for Cuba was 0.7%/year.
   **(a)** Assuming exponential growth at the given rates, make projections for each population in the year 2015.
   **(b)** When might the population of Mali reach 20 million? What would the population of Cuba be at that time?

9. In 2000 the nations of Niger and Portugal had similar size populations: Niger 10.1 million, Portugal 10.0 million. However, the relative growth rate for Niger was 3.0%/year, whereas that for Portugal was only 0.1%/year.
   **(a)** Assuming exponential growth at the given rates, make projections for each population in the year 2015.
   **(b)** When might the population of Niger reach 15 million? What would the population of Portugal be at that time?
10. The population of Guatemala in 2000 was 12.7 million.
    **(a)** Assuming exponential growth, what value for $k$ would lead to a population of 20 million one quarter of a century later (that is, in 2025)? *Remark*: The answer you obtain is, in fact, less than the actual year 2000 growth rate, which was about 2.9%/year.
    **(b)** Again, assuming a population of 12.7 million in 2000, what value for $k$ would lead to a population of 20 million, one century later (that is, in 2100)?

*As background for Exercises 11 and 12, here's a reminder of what we found in Example 2. Starting with data for the year 1900, we saw two cases where the world population had grown faster than what was predicted by an exponential model. In Exercises 11 and 12, you'll work with more recent data for the base year and find that now the population is, in fact, growing slower than the exponential model predicts.*

11. According to the U.S. Bureau of the Census, the world population in 1975 was 4.088 billion, with a relative growth rate of 1.75%/year.
    **(a)** Use an exponential growth model to predict the year 2000 population.
    **(b)** According to Table 3 in the text, the world population in 2000 was 6.067 billion. Is your projection in part (a) higher or lower than this? Compute the percentage

error in the projection and round the answer to the nearest one percent.

**12.** Follow Exercise 11, but start from the following data. In 1990, the world population was 5.284 billion, with a relative growth rate of 1.56%/year.

**13.** In each case, you are given the relative growth rate of a country or region in the year 2000. Compute the doubling time for the population (assuming an exponential growth model). Round the answer to the nearest whole number of years.
(a) United States: 0.6%/year
(b) Tajikistan: 1.6%/year
(c) Cambodia: 2.6%/year
(d) Palestinian Territory: 3.7%/year

**14.** Refer to the following table, which gives global populations and relative growth rates for the year 2000. Assume an exponential growth model.

| | 2000 Population (billions) | Relative growth rate (%/year) |
|---|---|---|
| World | 6.067 | 1.4 |
| More developed regions | 1.184 | 0.1 |
| Less developed regions | 4.883 | 1.7 |

Source: Population Reference Bureau

(a) Compute the doubling time for the world population, and give the year in which that population would be reached. (Round each answer to the nearest year.)
(b) Follow part (a) for the more developed regions.
(c) Follow part (a) for the less developed regions.

**15.** In Example 5 in the text we modeled the concentration of carbon dioxide in the atmosphere using an exponential growth model with $k = 0.4$%/year and $N_0 = 350$ ppm, where $t = 0$ corresponds to 1988.
(a) A more precise value for $N_0$ is 351.31 ppm. Using this value in the exponential growth model, complete the following table of projected values for the atmospheric carbon dioxide concentrations. Round the answers to one decimal place.

| Year | 1998 ($t = 10$) | 2000 ($t = 12$) |
|---|---|---|
| Atmospheric concentration of carbon dioxide (ppm) | | |

Source for data: C. D. Keeling and T. P. Whorf, Scripps Institution of Oceanography

(b) The actual values for 1998 and 2000 were 366.7 ppm and 368.4 ppm, respectively. For each of these two years, say whether the exponential model projects too high or two low a value, and compute the percentage error.

**16.** For this exercise refer to the following table, which gives the atmospheric concentrations of carbon dioxide ($CO_2$) for selected years over the latter half of the 20th century.

| Year | 1960 | 1985 | 1990 | 1995 | 1999 |
|---|---|---|---|---|---|
| Atmospheric concentration of carbon dioxide (ppm) | 316.75 | 345.73 | 354.04 | 360.91 | 368.37 |

Source: C. D. Keeling and T. P. Whorf, Scripps Institution of Oceanography

(a) Let $t = 0$ correspond to 1960, and assume an exponential growth model $N = 316.75e^{kt}$. Use the information for 1999 in the table to find the growth constant $k$.
(b) Use the growth law determined in part (a) to make a projection for the $CO_2$ concentration in 1985. Then, referring to the table, say whether the exponential model predicts too high or low a figure, and compute the percentage error.
(c) Follow part (b) for the year 1990 and 1995.
(d) Why do you think that the year 1999 was not included in part (c)?

**17.** According to figures from the U.S. Bureau of the Census, in 2000, the size of the population of the state of New York was more than three times larger than that of Arizona. However, New York had one of the lower growth rates in the nation, and Arizona had the second highest.
(a) Use the data in the following table to specify an exponential growth model for each state. (Let $t = 0$ correspond to the year 2000.)

| State | Population in 2000 (millions) | Relative growth rate (%/year) |
|---|---|---|
| New York | 18.976 | 0.6 |
| Arizona | 5.131 | 4.0 |

(b) Assuming continued exponential growth, when would the two states have populations of the same size? Round the answer to the nearest five years. *Hint:* Equate the two expressions for $N(t)$ obtained in part (a).

**18.** The following table gives the population size and relative growth rates in 2000 for three states. Use exponential models to project the population of each state in the year 2010, listing the results from largest to smallest. Does the order remain the same as it was in 2000?

| State | Population in 2000 (millions) | Relative growth rate (%/year) |
|---|---|---|
| Iowa | 2.926 | 0.54 |
| Arkansas | 2.673 | 1.37 |
| Nevada | 1.998 | 6.63 |

**19.** Lester R. Brown, in his book *State of the World 1985* (New York: W. W. Norton and Co., 1985), makes the following statement:

> The projected [population] growth for North America, all of Europe, and the Soviet Union is less than the additions expected in either Bangladesh or Nigeria.

In this exercise, you are asked to carry out the type of calculations that could be used to support Lester Brown's projection for the period 1990–2025. The source of the data in the following table is the Population Division of the United Nations.

| Region | 1990 Population (millions) | Projected relative growth rate (%/year) | 2025 Projected population (millions) |
|---|---|---|---|
| North America | 275.2 | 0.7 | ? |
| (Former) Soviet Union | 291.3 | 0.7 | ? |
|  | 291.3 | 0.7 | ? |
| Europe | 499.5 | 0.2 | ? |
| Nigeria | 113.3 | 3.1 | ? |

(a) Complete the table, assuming that the populations grow exponentially and that the indicated growth rates are valid over the period 1990–2025.

(b) According to the projections in part (a), what will be the net increase in Nigeria's population over the period 1990–2025?

(c) According to the projections in part (a), what will be the net increase in the combined populations of North America, the (former) Soviet Union, and Europe over the period 1990–2025?

(d) Compare your answers in parts (b) and (c). Do your results support or contradict Lester Brown's projection?

**20.** The *2000 World Population Data Sheet* (published by the Population Reference Bureau, Washington, D.C.) lists ten nations with populations exceeding 100 million. (See Exercise 21 regarding a possible eleventh nation.) The populations, in order of decreasing size, along with relative growth rates, are listed in the accompanying table. Over a decade ago, in 1987, the U.S. Bureau of the Census made the following statement in its analysis of world population data: "The latest projections suggest that India's population may surpass China's in less than 60 years, or before today's youngsters in both countries reach old age." Using the data in the table, and assuming exponential growth, make projections for the populations of India and China in the year 2050 (which would be roughly 60 years after that statement by the Bureau of the Census). Do your results for China and India support the projection by the Bureau of the Census?

| Country | 2000 Population (millions) | Relative growth rate (%/year) |
|---|---|---|
| 1. China | 1264.5 | 0.9 |
| 2. India | 1002.1 | 1.8 |
| 3. United States | 275.6 | 0.6 |
| 4. Indonesia | 212.2 | 1.6 |
| 5. Brazil | 170.1 | 1.5 |
| 6. Pakistan | 150.6 | 2.8 |
| 7. Russia | 145.2 | −0.6 |
| 8. Bangladesh | 128.1 | 1.8 |
| 9. Japan | 126.9 | 0.2 |
| 10. Nigeria | 123.3 | 2.8 |

Source: Population Reference Bureau, www.prb.org

**21.** The population figures in Exercise 20 are actually for mid-2000. As of that time, the population of Mexico was 99.6 million, with a relative growth rate of 2.0%/year. Let $t = 0$ correspond to June 2000 and use the exponential growth model $N(t) = 99.6e^{0.02t}$ to verify that $N(0.5) > 100$. Interpret the result.

**22.** In 2000 the Philippines and Germany had similar size populations, but very different growth rates. The population of the Philippines was 80.3 million, with a relative growth rate of 2.0%/year. The population of Germany was 82.1 million, with a relative "growth" rate of −0.1%/year. Using exponential models, make a projection for the population of Germany in the year when the Philippine population has doubled.

*In Exercises 23 and 24, use the half-life information to complete each table. (The formula $N = N_0 e^{kt}$ is not required.)*

**23. (a)** Uranium-228: half-life = 550 seconds

| t (seconds) | 0 | 550 | 1100 | 1650 | 2200 |
|---|---|---|---|---|---|
| N (grams) | 8 | | | | |

**(b)** Uranium-238: half-life = $4.9 \times 10^9$ years

| t (years) | 0 | | | | |
|---|---|---|---|---|---|
| N (grams) | 10 | 5 | 2.5 | 1.25 | 0.625 |

**24. (a)** Polonium-210: half-life = 138.4 days

| t (years) | 0 | 138.4 | 276.8 | 415.2 | |
|---|---|---|---|---|---|
| N (grams) | 0.4 | | | | 0.025 |

**(b)** Polonium-214: half-life = $1.63 \times 10^{-4}$ second

| t (seconds) | 0 | | | | $6.52 \times 10^{-4}$ |
|---|---|---|---|---|---|
| N (grams) | 0.1 | 0.05 | 0.025 | 0.0125 | |

25. The half-life of iodine-131 is 8 days. How much of a one-gram sample will remain after 7 days?

26. The half-life of strontium-90 is 28 years. How much of a 10-g sample will remain after **(a)** 1 year? **(b)** 10 years?

27. The radioactive isotope sodium-24 is used as a tracer to measure the rate of flow in an artery or vein. The half-life of sodium-24 is 14.9 hours. Suppose that a hospital buys a 40-g sample of sodium-24.
    **(a)** How much of the sample will remain after 48 hours?
    **(b)** How long will it be until only 1 gram remains?

28. The radioactive isotope carbon-14 is used as a tracer in medical and biological research. Compute the half-life of carbon-14 given that the decay constant $k$ is $-1.2097 \times 10^{-4}$. (The units for $k$ here are such that your half-life answer will be in years.)

29. **(a)** The half-life of radium-226 is 1620 years. Sketch a graph of the decay function for radium-226, similar to that shown in Figure 3.
    **(b)** The half-life of radium-A is 3 min. Sketch a graph of the decay function for radium-A.

30. **(a)** The half-life of thorium-232 is $1.4 \times 10^{10}$ years. Sketch a graph of the decay function.
    **(b)** The half-life of thorium-A is 0.16 sec. Sketch a graph of the decay function.

31. The half-life of plutonium-241 is 13 years.
    **(a)** How much of an initial 2-g sample remains after 5 years?
    **(b)** Find the time required for 90% of the 2-g sample to decay. *Hint*: If 90% has decayed, then 10% remains.

32. The half-life of radium-226 is 1620 years.
    **(a)** How much of a 2-g sample remains after 100 years?
    **(b)** Find the time required for 80% of the 2-g sample to decay.

33. The half-life of thorium-229 is 7340 years.
    **(a)** Compute the time required for a given sample to be reduced by a factor of 1000. Show detailed calculations, as in Example 7(a).
    **(b)** Express your answer in part (a) in terms of half-lives.
    **(c)** As in Example 7(b), estimate the time required for a given sample for thorium-229 to be reduced by a factor of 1000. Compare your answer with that obtained in part (b).

34. The Chernobyl nuclear explosion (in the former Soviet Union, on April 26, 1986) released large amounts of radioactive substances into the atmosphere. These substances included cesium-137, iodine-131, and strontium-90. Although the radioactive material covered many countries, the actual amount and intensity of the fallout varied greatly from country to country, due to vagaries of the weather and the winds. One area that was particularly hard hit was Lapland, where heavy rainfall occurred just when the Chernobyl cloud was overhead.
    **(a)** Many of the pastures in Lapland were contaminated with cesium-137, a radioactive substance with a half-

life of 33 years. If the amount of cesium-137 was found to be ten times the normal level, how long would it take until the level returned to normal? *Hint*: Let $\mathcal{N}_0$ be the amount that is ten times the normal level. Then you want to find the time when $\mathcal{N}(t) = \mathcal{N}_0/10$.
    **(b)** Follow part (a), but assume that the amount of cesium-137 was 100 times the normal level.
    *Remark*: Several days after the explosion, it was reported that the level of cesium-137 in the air over Sweden was 10,000 times the normal level. Fortunately there was little or no rainfall.

35. Strontium-90, with a half-life of 28 years, is a radioactive waste product from nuclear fission reactors. One of the reasons great care is taken in the storage and disposal of this substance stems from the fact that strontium-90 is, in some chemical respects, similar to ordinary calcium. Thus strontium-90 in the biosphere, entering the food chain via plants or animals, would eventually be absorbed into our bones.
    **(a)** Compute the decay constant $k$ for strontium-90.
    **(b)** Compute the time required if a given quantity of strontium-90 is to be stored until the radioactivity is reduced by a factor of 1000.
    **(c)** Using half-lives, estimate the time required for a given sample to be reduced by a factor of 1000. Compare your answer with that obtained in (b).

36. **(a)** Suppose that a certain country violates the ban against above-ground nuclear testing and, as a result, an island is contaminated with debris containing the radioactive substance iodine-131. A team of scientists from the United Nations wants to visit the island to look for clues in determining which country was involved. However, the level of radioactivity from the iodine-131 is estimated to be 30,000 times the safe level. Approximately how long must the team wait before it is safe to visit the island? The half-life of iodine-131 is 8 days.
    **(b)** Rework part (a), assuming instead that the radioactive substance is strontium-90 rather than iodine-131. The half-life of strontium-90 is 28 years. Assume, as before, that the initial level of radioactivity is 30,000 times the safe level. (This exercise underscores the difference between a half-life of 8 days and one of 28 years.)

37. An article that appeared in the August 13, 1994, *New York Times* reported

    German authorities have discovered . . . a tiny sample of weapons-grade nuclear material believed to have been smuggled out of Russia to interest foreign governments or terrorist groups that might want to build atomic bombs. . . . [the police] said they had seized the material, .028 ounces of highly enriched uranium-235, in June in . . . Bavaria . . . and have since arrested . . . [six] suspects. . . .

Suppose that the suspects, in an attempt to avoid arrest, had thrown the 0.028 ounces of uranium-235 into the Danube River, where it would sink to the bottom. How many ounces of the uranium-235 would still be in the river after 1000 years? The half-life of uranium-235 is $7.1 \times 10^8$ years.

**38.** In 1969 the United States National Academy of Sciences issued a report entitled *Resources and Man.* One conclusion in the report is that a world population of 10 billion "is close to (if not above) the maximum that an intensively managed world might hope to support with some degree of comfort and individual choice." (The figure "10 billion" is sometimes referred to as the *carrying capacity* of the Earth.)

   **(a)** When the report was issued in 1969, the world population was about 3.6 billion, with a relative growth rate of 2% per year. Assuming continued exponential growth at this rate, estimate the year in which the Earth's carrying capacity of 10 billion might be reached.

   **(b)** Repeat the calculations in part (a) using the following more recent data: In 2000 the world population was about 6.0 billion, with a relative growth rate of 1.4% per year. How does your answer compare with that in part (a)?

**39.** The following extract is from an article by Kim Murphy that appeared in the *Los Angeles Times* on September 14, 1994.

> CAIRO—Over a chorus of reservations from Latin America and Islamic countries still troubled about abortion and family issues, nearly 180 nations adopted a wide-ranging plan Tuesday on global population, the first in history to obtain partial endorsement from the Vatican.
>
> The plan, approved on the final day of the U.N. population conference here, for the first time tries to limit the growth of the world's population by preventing it from exceeding 7.2 billion people over the next two decades.

   **(a)** In 1995 the world population was 5.7 billion, with a relative growth rate of 1.6%/year. Assuming continued exponential growth at this rate, make a projection for the world population in the year 2020. Round off the answer to one decimal place. How does your answer compare to the target value of 7.2 billion mentioned in the article?

   **(b)** As in part (a), assume that in 1995 the world population was 5.7 billion. Determine a value for the growth constant $k$ so that exponential growth throughout the years 1995–2020 leads to a world population of 7.2 billion in the year 2020.

**G  40.** Economists define the **gross domestic product (GDP)** as the total market value of a nation's goods and services produced (within the borders of the nation) over a specified

period of time. The GDP is one of the key measures of a nation's economic health. Table A gives the annual GDP for the United States for the period 1950–1990, at 10-year intervals. In Figures A and B we show scatter plots for the data along with regression functions that model the data. Figure A uses a linear model, Figure B an exponential model. In each case, the years are on the horizontal axis, with $t = 0$ corresponding to 1900. In this exercise you'll use a graphing utility to obtain the specific equations for these models and for two other models as well. You'll also compare projections using the various models.

**TABLE A    Gross Domestic Product (GDP) in Constant 1996 Dollars**

| Year $t$ ($t = 0 \leftrightarrow 1900$) | 50 | 60 | 70 | 80 | 90 |
|---|---|---|---|---|---|
| GDP (billions of dollars) | 1686.6 | 2376.7 | 3578.0 | 4900.9 | 6707.9 |

Source: U.S. Bureau of Economic Analysis, http://www.bea.gov

**Figure A**
Linear model    $y = at + b$

**Figure B**
Exponential model    $y = ab^t$
or $y = Ae^{Bt}$

   **(a)** Use a graphing utility to create your own scatter plot of the data in Table A. Then, use the regression or trend line options of the graphing utility to obtain the specific equations for the linear model in Figure A and the exponential model in Figure B. (For the exponential model, you can report your answer in either one of the two forms indicated in the caption for Figure B, depending on what your graphing utility provides.) For comparison, graph both models in the same viewing rectangle.

**(b)** Use the regression or trend line options of the graphing utility to obtain the equation for a quadratic model $y = at^2 + bt + c$. Show the graph of the quadratic model with the scatter plot. Now repeat this process for a power model $y = at^b$.

**(c)** Use the functions that you determined in parts (a) and (b) to complete Table B, showing what each model projects for the gross domestic product in the indicated year. (Round each projection to one decimal place.) Then, in each row, circle the projection that is closest to the actual value given at the end of that row. Finally, compute the percentage error for each projection that you circled.

**TABLE B  Gross Domestic Product (GDP) Projections Using Various Models**

| Year | GDP (billion $) linear model | GDP (billion $) exponential model | GDP (billion $) quadratic model | GDP (billion $) power model | GDP (billion $) actual |
|---|---|---|---|---|---|
| 1995 | | | | | 7543.8 |
| 1999 | | | | | 8875.8 |
| 2001 | | | | | 9333.8 |

## B

**41.** *Depletion of Nonrenewable Resources*: Suppose that the world population grows exponentially. Then, as a first approximation, it is reasonable to assume that the use of nonrenewable resources, such as petroleum and coal, also grows exponentially. Under these conditions, the following formula can be derived (using calculus):

$$A = \frac{A_0}{k}(e^{kT} - 1)$$

where $A$ is the amount of the resource consumed from time $t = 0$ to $t = T$, the quantity $A_0$ is the amount of the resource consumed during the year $t = 0$, and $k$ is the relative growth rate of annual consumption.

**(a)** Show that solving the formula for $T$ yields

$$T = \frac{\ln[(Ak/A_0) + 1]}{k}$$

This formula gives the "life expectancy" $T$ for a given resource. In the formula, $A_0$ and $k$ are as previously defined, and $A$ represents the total amount of the resource available.

**(b)** Over the years 1965–1972, world oil consumption grew exponentially. In this part of the exercise, you'll compute the life expectancy of oil, assuming continued exponential growth. Let $t = 0$ correspond to 1972. In that year, worldwide consumption of oil was approximately 18.7 billion barrels, with a relative growth rate of 7%/year. The global reserves of oil at that time were estimated to be 700 billion barrels. Compute the life expectancy $T$ of oil under this exponential growth scenario and specify the *depletion year* ($= 1972 + T$). If the relative growth had been only 1%/year, what would the depletion year be?

**(c)** Beginning with the first Arab oil embargo of 1973–1974, worldwide oil consumption ceased to grow exponentially. In fact, oil consumption actually decreased over the years 1973–1975, and it decreased again for 1979–1983, following the second Arab oil embargo. More recently, as indicated by the following data, scatter plot, and regression line, worldwide oil consumption has been increasing in a linear fashion. Use a graphing utility and the data in the table to determine the equation $y = mt + b$ for the regression line.

| Year $t$ ($t = 0 \leftrightarrow 1993$) | 0 | 1 | 2 | 3 |
|---|---|---|---|---|
| Global oil consumption $y$ (billion barrels) | 23.997 | 24.506 | 24.893 | 25.450 |

| Year $t$ ($t = 0 \leftrightarrow 1993$) | 4 | 5 | 6 |
|---|---|---|---|
| Global oil consumption $y$ (billion barrels) | 26.123 | 26.251 | 26.723 |

**(d)** If yearly consumption of a nonrenewable resource is given by a linear function $y = mt + b$, then it can be shown that the life expectancy $T$ of the resource is given by the following formula,

$$T = \frac{-b + \sqrt{b^2 + 2mA}}{m}$$

where $A$ represents the total amount of the resource available (that is, the world reserves) in the year corresponding to $t = 0$. (The derivation does not require calculus, but we shall omit giving it here.) In 1993, world reserves of oil were estimated to be 1007 billion barrels. Using this value for $A$ and the values of $m$ and $b$ determined in part (c), estimate the life expectancy for oil and the depletion date ($=1993 + T$). (Aside: The figure we've given here for the estimated world reserves in 1993 is greater than the one we gave for 1972. This reflects improved technology in locating oil fields and in extracting the oil.)

*For Exercises 42 and 43, refer to the following table. (Data compiled from United States Geological Survey, World Resources Institute, and the* World Almanac, 2000.)

| Resource | 1999 world consumption (million metric tons) | 1999 world reserves (million metric tons) | Relative growth rate (%/year) |
|---|---|---|---|
| Aluminum (in bauxite) | 23.1 | 34,000 | 3.0 |
| Copper | 12.6 | 650 | 2.4 |

**42. (a)** Suppose that the consumption of aluminum were growing exponentially. Use the formula for $T$ in Exercise 41 to compute the life expectancy of aluminum and the depletion year.

**(b)** What if the world reserves for aluminum were actually twice that listed in the table, and the relative growth rate were half that in the table? Compute the depletion year under this scenario.

**(c)** Suppose that from 1999 onward, consumption of aluminum stopped increasing exponentially and stabilized at the 1999 level of 23.1 million metric tons per year. How many years would it take to deplete the world reserves of 34,000 million metric tons?

**43.** Follow Exercise 42, using copper instead of aluminum.

Ⓖ **44.** The following table and scatter plots display data for the number of fixed-line phone connections worldwide and the number of cell phone subscribers over the years 1985–1998. As indicated by the scatter plots, the number of cell phone subscribers is far less than the number of phone lines, but it is increasing at a faster rate.

**(a)** Use the regression option on a graphing utility or spreadsheet to find a quadratic model $y = at^2 + bt + c$ describing the number of phone lines over the period 1985–1998 ($t = 0$ to $t = 13$). Similarly, find an exponential model of the form $y = ab^t$ or $y = Ae^{Bt}$ describing the number of cell phone subscribers. Then use the graphing utility to display the scatter plots and the two models in the same viewing rectangle.

**(b)** By finding an appropriate viewing rectangle, make a projection for the year in which there would be as many cell phone subscribers as phone lines.

| Year $t$ $t$ ($t = 0 \leftrightarrow 1985$) | Phone lines (millions) | Cell phone subscribers (millions) |
|---|---|---|
| 0 | 407 | 1 |
| 1 | 426 | 1 |
| 2 | 446 | 2 |
| 3 | 469 | 4 |
| 4 | 493 | 7 |
| 5 | 520 | 11 |
| 6 | 546 | 16 |
| 7 | 574 | 23 |
| 8 | 606 | 34 |
| 9 | 645 | 55 |
| 10 | 691 | 91 |
| 11 | 738 | 142 |
| 12 | 788 | 215 |
| 13 | 844 | 319 |

Source: International Telecommunications Union data as reported in *Vital Signs 2000,* Lester Brown et al. (New York: W. W. Norton & Co., 2000)

**45.** The age of some rocks can be estimated by measuring the ratio of the amounts of certain chemical elements within the rock. The method known as the *rubidium–strontium method* will be discussed here. This method has been used in dating the moon rocks brought back on the Apollo missions.

Rubidium-87 is a radioactive substance with a half-life of $4.7 \times 10^{10}$ years. Rubidium-87 decays into the substance strontium-87, which is stable (nonradioactive). We are going to derive the following formula for the age of a rock:

$$T = \frac{\ln[(\mathcal{N}_s/\mathcal{N}_r) + 1]}{-k}$$

where $T$ is the age of the rock, $k$ is the decay constant for rubidium-87, $\mathcal{N}_s$ is the number of atoms of strontium-87 now present in the rock, and $\mathcal{N}_r$ is the number of atoms of rubidium-87 now present in the rock.

**(a)** Assume that initially, when the rock was formed, there were $\mathcal{N}_0$ atoms of rubidium-87 and none of strontium-87. Then, as time goes by, some of the rubidium atoms decay into strontium atoms, but the total number of atoms must still be $\mathcal{N}_0$. Thus, after $T$ years, we have $\mathcal{N}_0 = \mathcal{N}_r + \mathcal{N}_s$ or, equivalently,

$$\mathcal{N}_s = \mathcal{N}_0 - \mathcal{N}_r \qquad (1)$$

However, according to the law of exponential decay for the rubidium-87, we must have $\mathcal{N}_r = \mathcal{N}_0 e^{kT}$. Solve this equation for $\mathcal{N}_0$ and then use the result to eliminate $\mathcal{N}_0$ from equation (1). Show that the result can be written

$$\mathcal{N}_s = \mathcal{N}_r e^{-kT} - \mathcal{N}_r \qquad (2)$$

**(b)** Solve equation (2) for $T$ to obtain the formula given at the beginning of this exercise.

**46.** (Continuation of Exercise 45)
**(a)** The half-life of rubidium-87 is $4.7 \times 10^{10}$ years. Compute the decay constant $k$.
**(b)** Analysis of lunar rock samples taken on the Apollo 11 mission showed the strontium–rubidium ratio to be

$$\frac{\mathcal{N}_s}{\mathcal{N}_r} = 0.0588$$

Estimate the age of these lunar rocks.

**47.** (Continuation of Exercise 45) Analysis of the so-called genesis rock sample taken on the Apollo 15 mission revealed a strontium–rubidium ratio of 0.0636. Estimate the age of this rock.

**48.** *Radiocarbon Dating*: Because rubidium-87 decays so slowly, the technique of rubidium–strontium dating is generally considered effective only for objects older than 10 million years. In contrast, archeologists and geologists rely on the *radiocarbon dating* method in assigning ages ranging from 500 to 50,000 years.

Two types of carbon occur naturally in our environment. carbon-12, which is nonradioactive, and carbon-14, which has a half-life of 5730 years. All living plant and animal tissue contains both types of carbon, always in the same ratio. (The ratio is one part carbon-14 to $10^{12}$ parts carbon-12.) As long as the plant or animal is living, this ratio is maintained. When the organism dies, however, no new carbon-14 is absorbed, and the amount of carbon-14 begins to decrease exponentially. Since the amount of carbon-14 decreases exponentially, it follows that the level of radioactivity also must decrease exponentially. The formula describing this situation is

$$\mathcal{N} = \mathcal{N}_0 e^{kT}$$

where $T$ is the age of the sample, $\mathcal{N}$ is the present level of radioactivity (in units of disintegrations per hour per gram of carbon), and $\mathcal{N}_0$ is the level of radioactivity $T$ years ago, when the organism was alive. Given that the half-life of carbon-14 is 5730 years and that $\mathcal{N}_0 = 920$ disintegrations per hour per gram, show that the age $T$ of a sample is given by

$$T = \frac{5730 \ln(\mathcal{N}/920)}{\ln(1/2)}$$

*In Exercises 49–54, use the formula derived in Exercise 48 to estimate the age of each sample.   Note: Some technical complications arise in interpreting such results. Studies have shown that the ratio of carbon-12 to carbon-14 in the air (and therefore in living matter) has not in fact been constant over time. For instance, air pollution from factory smokestacks tends to increase the level of carbon-12. In the other direction, nuclear bomb testing increases the level of carbon-14.*

**49.** Prehistoric cave paintings were discovered in the Lascaux cave in France. Charcoal from the site was analyzed and the level of radioactivity was found to be $\mathcal{N} = 141$ disintegrations per hour per gram. Estimate the age of the paintings.

**50.** Before radiocarbon dating was used, historians estimated that the tomb of Vizier Hemaka, in Egypt, was constructed about 4900 years ago. After radiocarbon dating became available, wood samples from the tomb were analyzed, and it was determined that the radioactivity level was 510 disintegrations per hour per gram. Estimate the age of the tomb on the basis of this reading and compare your answer to the figure already mentioned.

**51.** Before radiocarbon dating, scholars believed that agriculture (farming, as opposed to the hunter-gatherer existence) in the Middle East began about 6500 years ago. However, when radiocarbon dating was used to study an ancient farming settlement at Jericho, the radioactivity level was found to be in the range $\mathcal{N} = 348$ disintegrations per hour per gram of carbon. On the basis of this evidence, estimate the age of the site, and compare your answer to the figure mentioned at the beginning of this exercise. Round your answer to the nearest 100 years. (Similar analyses in Iraq, Turkey, and other countries have since shown that agriculture was firmly established at least 9000 years ago.)

**52. (a)** Analyses of some ancient campsites in the Western Hemisphere reveal a carbon-14 radioactivity level of $\mathcal{N} = 226$ disintegrations per hour per gram of carbon. Show that this implies an age of 11,500 years, to the nearest 500 years.   *Remark*: An age of 11,500 years corresponds to the last Ice Age, when the sea level was significantly lower than it is today. According to the *Clovis hypothesis,* this was the time humans first entered the Western Hemisphere, across what would have been a land bridge extending over what is now the Bering Strait. (The name "Clovis" refers to Clovis, New Mexico. In 1933 a spearpoint and bones were discovered there that were subsequently found to be about 11,500 years old.)

**(b)** In the article "Coming to America" (*Time Magazine,* May 3, 1993), Michael D. Lemonick describes some of the evidence indicating that the Clovis hypothesis is not valid:

A team led by University of Kentucky archeologist Tom Dillehay discovered indisputable traces . . . [in Monte Verde, in southern Chile] of a human settlement that was inhabited between 12,800 and

12,300 years ago. Usually all scientists can find from that far back are stones and bones. In this case, thanks to a peat layer that formed during the late Pleistocene era, organic matter [to which radiocarbon dating can be applied] was mummified and preserved as well.

What range for the carbon-14 radioactivity level $\mathcal{N}$ corresponds to the ages mentioned in this article? (That is, compute the values of $\mathcal{N}$ corresponding to $T = 12{,}800$ and $T = 12{,}300$.)

53. The Dead Sea Scrolls are a collection of ancient manuscripts discovered in caves along the west bank of the Dead Sea. (The discovery occurred by accident when an Arab herdsman of the Taamireh tribe was searching for a stray goat.) When the linen wrappings on the scrolls were analyzed, the carbon-14 radioactivity level was found to be 723 disintegrations per hour per gram. Estimate the age of the scrolls using this information. Historical evidence suggests that some of the scrolls date back somewhere between 150 B.C. and A.D. 40. How do these dates compare with the estimate derived using radiocarbon dating?

54. **(a)** According to Exercise 48, the formula for the age $T$ of a sample in terms of the radioactivity level $\mathcal{N}$ is
$$T = \frac{5730 \ln(\mathcal{N}/920)}{\ln(1/2)}.$$
Solve this equation for $\mathcal{N}$ and show that the result can be written $\mathcal{N} = 920(2^{-T/5730})$.

**(b)** The famous prehistoric stone monument Stonehenge is located 8 miles north of Salisbury, England. Excavations and radiocarbon dating have led anthropologists and archeologists to distinguish three periods in the building of Stonehenge: period I, 2800 years ago; period II, 2100 years ago; and period III, 2000 years ago. Use the formula in part (a) to compute the carbon-14 radioactivity levels that would have led the scientists to assign these ages.

*Exercises 55–60 introduce a model for population growth that takes into account limitations on food and the environment. This is the* **logistic growth model,** *named and studied by the nineteenth century Belgian mathematician and sociologist Pierre Verhulst. (The word "logistic" has Latin and Greek origins meaning "calculation" and "skilled in calculation," respectively. However, that is not why Verhulst named the curve as he did. See Exercise 56 for more about this.)*

*In the logistic model that we'll study, the initial population growth resembles exponential growth. But then, at some point, owing perhaps to food or space limitations, the growth slows down and eventually levels off, and the population approaches an equilibrium level. The basic equation that we'll use for logistic growth is*
$$\mathcal{N} = \frac{P}{1 + ae^{-bt}}$$

*where $\mathcal{N}$ is the population at time t, P is the equilibrium population (or the upper limit for population), and a and b are positive constants.*

55. The following figure shows the graph of the logistic function $\mathcal{N}(t) = 4/(1 + 8e^{-t})$. Note that in this equation the equilibrium population $P$ is 4 and that this corresponds to the asymptote $\mathcal{N} = 4$ in the graph.

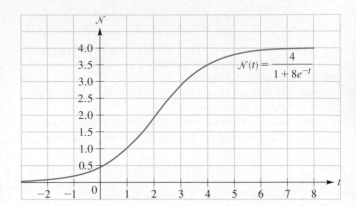

**(a)** Use the graph and your calculator to complete the following table. For the values that you read from the graph, estimate to the nearest 0.25. For the calculator values, round to three decimal places.

| | $\mathcal{N}(-1)$ | $\mathcal{N}(0)$ | $\mathcal{N}(1)$ | $\mathcal{N}(4)$ | $\mathcal{N}(5)$ |
|---|---|---|---|---|---|
| From graph | | | | | |
| From calculator | | | | | |

**(b)** As indicated in the graph, the line $\mathcal{N} = 4$ appears to be an asymptote for the curve. Confirm this empirically by computing $\mathcal{N}(10)$, $\mathcal{N}(15)$, and $\mathcal{N}(20)$. Round each answer to eight decimal places.

**(c)** Use the graph to estimate, to the nearest integer, the value of $t$ for which $\mathcal{N}(t) = 3$.

**(d)** Find the exact value of $t$ for which $\mathcal{N}(t) = 3$. Evaluate the answer using a calculator, and check that it is consistent with the result in part (c).

G 56. (Continuation of Exercise 55) The author's ideas for this exercise are based on Professor Bonnie Shulman's article "Math-Alive! Using Original Sources to Teach Mathematics in Social Context," *Primus*, vol. VIII (March 1998).

**(a)** The function $\mathcal{N}$ in Exercise 55 expresses population as a function of time. But as pointed out by Professor Shulman, in Verhulst's original work it was the other way around; he expressed time as a function of population. In terms of our notation, we would say that he was studying the function $\mathcal{N}^{-1}$. Given $\mathcal{N}(t) = 4/(1 + 8e^{-t})$, find $\mathcal{N}^{-1}(t)$.

**(b)** Use a graphing utility to draw the graphs of $\mathcal{N}$, $\mathcal{N}^{-1}$, and the line $y = x$ in the viewing rectangle $[-3, 8, 2]$ by $[-3, 8, 2]$. Use true portions. (Why?)

**(c)** In the viewing rectangle $[0, 5, 1]$ by $[-3, 2, 1]$, draw the graphs of $y = \mathcal{N}^{-1}(t)$ and $y = \ln t$. Note that the two graphs have the same general shape and characteristics. In other words, Verhulst's logistic function (our $\mathcal{N}^{-1}$) appears log-like, or *logistique*, as Verhulst actually named it in French. (For details, both historical and mathematical, see the paper by Professor Shulman cited above.)

**57.** The following figure shows the graph of a logistic function $\mathcal{N}(t) = P/(1 + ae^{-bt})$. As indicated in the figure, the graph passes through the two points $(0, 1)$ and $(1, 2)$, and the asymptote is $\mathcal{N} = 5$. In this exercise we determine the values of the constants $P$, $a$, and $b$.

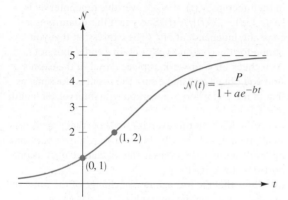

**(a)** As indicated in the figure, the logistic curve approaches an equilibrium population of 5. By definition, this is the value of the constant $P$, so the equation becomes

$$\mathcal{N}(t) = 5/(1 + ae^{-bt})$$

Now use the fact that the graph passes through the point $(0, 1)$ to obtain an equation that you can solve for $a$. Solve the equation; you should obtain $a = 4$.

**(b)** With $P = 5$ and $a = 4$, the logistic equation becomes $\mathcal{N}(t) = 5/(1 + 4e^{-bt})$. Use the fact that the graph of this equation passes through the point $(1, 2)$ to show that $b = \ln(8/3) \approx 0.9808$.

**58.** Biologist H. G. Thornton carried out an experiment in the 1920s to measure the growth of a colony of bacteria in a closed environment. As is common in the biology lab, Thornton measured the area of the colony, rather than count the number of individuals. (The reasoning is that the actual population size is directly proportional to the area, and the area is much easier to measure.) The following table and scatter plot summarize Thornton's measurements. Notice that the data points in the scatter plot suggest a logistic growth curve.

| Days | 0 | 1 | 2 | 3 | 4 | 5 |
|---|---|---|---|---|---|---|
| Area of colony (cm²) | 0.24 | 2.78 | 13.53 | 36.30 | 47.50 | 49.40 |

Source: H. G. Thornton, *Annals of Applied Biology*, 1922, p. 265

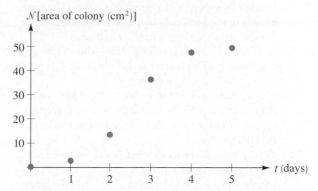

**(a)** Use the technique shown in Exercise 57 to determine a logistic function $\mathcal{N}(t) = P/(1 + ae^{-bt})$ with a graph that passes through Thornton's two points $(0, 0.24)$ and $(2, 13.53)$. Assume that the equilibrium population is $P = 50$. Round the final values of $a$ and $b$ to two decimal places.

**(b)** Use the logistic function that you determined in part (a) to estimate the area of the colony after 1, 3, 4, and 5 days. Round your estimates to one decimal place. If you compare your estimates to the results that Thornton obtained in the laboratory, you'll see there is good agreement.

**(c)** Use the logistic function that you determined in part (a) to estimate the time at which the area of the colony was 10 cm². Express your answer in terms of days and hours, and round to the nearest half-hour.

**59.** The following data on the growth of *Lupinus albus*, a plant in the pea family, are taken from an experiment that was summarized in the classic text by Sir D'Arcy Wentworth Thompson, *On Growth and Form* (New York: Dover Publications, Inc., 1992).

| Day | 4 | 6 | 8 | 10 | 12 |
|---|---|---|---|---|---|
| length (mm) | 10.5 | 23.3 | 42.2 | 77.9 | 107.4 |

| Day | 14 | 16 | 18 | 20 | 21 |
|---|---|---|---|---|---|
| length (mm) | 132.3 | 149.7 | 158.1 | 161.4 | 161.6 |

**(a)** Follow Exercise 57 to determine an equation for a logistic function that models these data. Assume $P = 162$, $\mathcal{N}(0) = 1$, and $\mathcal{N}(10) = 77.9$.

**(b)** Using the model that you determined in part (a), compute $\mathcal{N}(4)$, $\mathcal{N}(8)$, $\mathcal{N}(12)$, and $\mathcal{N}(16)$. Round the answers to one decimal place. In each case, say whether your answer is higher or lower than the actual value.

(c) For the logistic model in general, it can be shown (using calculus) that the population is growing fastest at the instant when it reaches half the equilibrium level $P$. Use this fact to determine when the population in this experiment is growing fastest. Give your answer in the form $d$ days, $h$ hours, with the number of hours rounded to the nearest half-hour.

G **60.** This exercise requires a graphing utility with a logistic regression feature. (This feature is included on the Texas Instruments *TI-83 Plus,* for example.)

(a) Use a graphing utility to create a scatter plot for the data in Exercise 59. Next, use the logistic regression option to find the equation of the logistic model that best fits the data.

(b) On the basis of the model that you determined in part (a), what is the equilibrium population $P$? (Remember that $P$ has to be an integer.) Add the graph of the horizontal line $\mathcal{N} = P$ to the picture obtained in part (a).

(c) In the initial stages of logistic growth (when the population is small compared to the equilibrium level $P$), the growth resembles exponential growth. Demonstrate this as follows. Use a graphing utility to find an exponential growth model fitting only the first three data pairs in the table in Exercise 59. Add the graph of this exponential model to the picture that you obtained in part (b). Also include the graph of the horizontal line $\mathcal{N} = P/2$. Now (in complete sentences), summarize what you see.

**61. (a)** Let $\mathcal{N}(t) = \mathcal{N}_0 e^{kt}$. Show that $[\mathcal{N}(t + 1) - \mathcal{N}(t)]/\mathcal{N}(t) = e^k - 1$. (This is actually done in detail in the text. So, ideally, you should look back only if you get stuck or want to check your answer.)

**(b)** Assume as given the following approximation, which was introduced in Exercise 26 of Section 5.2.

$$e^x \approx x + 1 \qquad \text{provided } x \text{ is close to zero}$$

Use this approximation to explain why $e^k - 1 \approx k$, provided that $k$ is close to zero. *Remark*: Combining this result with that in part (a), we conclude that the relative growth rate for the function $\mathcal{N}(t) = \mathcal{N}_0 e^{kt}$ is approximately equal to the growth constant $k$. As explained in the text, this is one of the reasons why in applications we've not distinguished between the relative growth rate and the decay constant $k$.

**62.** In the text we showed that the relative growth rate for the function $\mathcal{N}(t) = \mathcal{N}_0 e^{kt}$ is constant for all time intervals of unit length, $[t, t + 1]$. Recall that we did this by computing the relative change $[\mathcal{N}(t + 1) - \mathcal{N}(t)]/\mathcal{N}(t)$ and noting that the result was a constant, independent of $t$. (If you've completed the previous exercise, you've done this calculation for yourself.) Now consider a time interval of arbitrary length, $[t, t + d]$. The relative change in the function $\mathcal{N}(t) = \mathcal{N}_0 e^{kt}$ over this time interval is $[\mathcal{N}(t + d) - \mathcal{N}(t)]/\mathcal{N}(t)$. Show that this quantity is a constant, independent of $t$. (The expression that you obtain for the constant will contain $e$ and $d$, but not $t$. As a check on your work, replace $d$ by 1 in the expression you obtain and make sure the result is the same as that in the text where we worked with intervals of length $d = 1$.)

**63.** Let $\mathcal{N} = \mathcal{N}_0 e^{kt}$. In this exercise we show that if $\Delta t$ is very small, then $\Delta \mathcal{N}/\Delta t \approx k\mathcal{N}$. In other words, over very small intervals of time, the average rate of change of $\mathcal{N}$ is proportional to $\mathcal{N}$ itself.

**(a)** Show that the average rate of change of the function $\mathcal{N} = \mathcal{N}_0 e^{kt}$ on the interval $[t, t + \Delta t]$ is given by

$$\frac{\Delta \mathcal{N}}{\Delta t} = \frac{\mathcal{N}_0 e^{kt}(e^{k\Delta t} - 1)}{\Delta t} = \frac{\mathcal{N}(e^{k\Delta t} - 1)}{\Delta t}$$

**(b)** In Exercise 26 of Section 5.2 we saw that $e^x \approx x + 1$ when $x$ is close to zero. Thus, if $\Delta t$ is sufficiently small, we have $e^{k\Delta t} \approx k\,\Delta t + 1$. Use this approximation and the result in part (a) to show that $\Delta \mathcal{N}/\Delta t \approx kN$ when $\Delta t$ is sufficiently close to zero.

# PROJECT

## A VARIABLE GROWTH CONSTANT?

Ⓖ As background for this project you need to have worked Exercise 39 in this section regarding the United Nation's proposed population limits. Or, if you are working in a group, have a group member present a summary of the problem and the results.

Over the past few decades, world population growth rates have, in general, been decreasing. (Over the period 1970–2000, for example, the rate fell from 2.0%/year to 1.4%/year.) In this project we consider a modification of the exponential model that takes this declining growth rate into account. In particular, we consider a growth equation of the form

$$N(t) = N_0 e^{[f(t)]t} \tag{1}$$

where the function $f$ in the exponent describes the changing relative growth rate.

**(a)** The following table lists some relative growth rates for the world's population over the period 1985–2000. Set up a scatter plot for the information in the table, subject to the following specifications. For the horizontal time-axis, let $t = 0$ correspond to 1980. For the relative growth rates, use the decimal form, rather than the given percentage. Then use a graphing utility to determine the equation of the regression line $f(t) = mt + b$.

| Year | 1980 | 1985 | 1990 | 1995 | 2000 |
|------|------|------|------|------|------|
| Relative growth rate (%/year) | 1.8 | 1.8 | 1.7 | 1.6 | 1.4 |

Source: Population Reference Bureau

**(b)** In 1980 the world population was 4.448 billion. Use this value for $N_0$ in equation (1). Also, in equation (1), replace $f(t)$ by the quantity $mt + b$ determined in part (a). Now, use a graphing utility to graph the resulting population growth model for the period 1980 to 2020 (that is, $t = 0$ to $t = 40$). Use the graph to decide whether or not (according to this model) the projected population in 2020 exceeds United Nation's proposed limit of 7.2 billion.

**(c)** For purposes of comparison, add the graph of an exponential growth model to the viewing rectangle. For the model, use the value of $N_0$ given in part (b) and choose a year from the table to obtain $k$. (The value of $k$ obtained will differ slightly depending on the year you choose.) Does this model project a population excess of 7.2 billion in 2020?

**(d)** Switch to the viewing rectangle [0, 50, 200] by [0, 8, 4]. Give a description, in complete sentences, of the general behavior of the population after 2020 as projected by the model $N(t) = N_0 e^{[f(t)]t}$ in part (b). What do you think about this scenario?

# Chapter 5

## Summary of Principal Terms and Formulas

| Term, notation, or formula | Page reference | Comments |
|---|---|---|
| **1.** Exponential function with base $b$ | 329 | The exponential function with base $b$ is defined by the equation $y = b^x$. It is understood here that the base $b$ is a positive number other than 1. More generally, functions of the form $y = ab^{cx}$ are also referred to as exponential functions. |
| **2.** The number $e$ | 337 | The irrational number $e$ is one of the basic constants in mathematics, as is the irrational number $\pi$. To five decimal places, the value of $e$ is 2.71828. In calculus $e$ is the base most commonly used for exponential functions. The graph of the exponential function $y = e^x$ is shown in the box on page 338. |
| **3.** Instantaneous rate of change of the function $y = e^x$ | 340 | The concept of the instantaneous rate of change of a function is introduced on pages 339–340. One of the distinguishing characteristics of the function $y = e^x$ is that the instantaneous rate of change at any point on the graph is just the $y$-coordinate of that point. See the examples in the box on page 340. |
| **4.** $\log_b x$ | 348 | The expression $\log_b x$ denotes the exponent to which $b$ must be raised to yield $x$. The equation $\log_b x = y$ is equivalent to $b^y = x$. |
| **5.** $\ln x$ | 352 | The expression $\ln x$ means $\log_e x$. Logarithms to the base $e$ are known as *natural logarithms*. For the graph of $y = \ln x$, see Figure 6(a) in Section 5.3. |
| **6.** $\log_a x = \dfrac{\log_b x}{\log_b a}$ | 367 | This is the change-of-base formula for converting logarithms from one base to another. |
| **7.** $A = P\left(1 + \dfrac{r}{n}\right)^{nt}$ | 384 | This formula gives the amount $A$ that accumulates after $t$ years when a principal of $P$ dollars is invested at an annual rate $r$ that is compounded $n$ times per year. |
| **8.** $A = Pe^{rt}$ | 386 | This formula gives the amount $A$ that accumulates after $t$ years when a principal of $P$ dollars is invested at an annual rate $r$ that is compounded continuously. |
| **9.** Doubling time; rule of 70 | 389 | For money earning compound interest, the doubling time $T_2$ is the length of time required for an amount to double. As can be seen from the formula $T_2 = (\ln 2)/r$, the doubling time does not depend on the initial amount, but only on the interest rate $r$. (In the formula, the interest rate is expressed as a decimal.) The *rule of 70* gives an approximate value for the doubling time: $T_2 \approx 70/R$, where $R$ is the interest rate expressed as a percentage. |

| Term, notation, or formula | Page reference | Comments |
|---|---|---|
| **10.** $N = N_0 e^{kt}$    $(k > 0)$ | 394 | This is the exponential growth model, where $N_0$ is the size of the population at time $t = 0$, and $k$ is a constant called the *growth constant*. In the applications we studied, we used the value of the relative growth rate for $k$. (As is explained in the text, the two quantities are approximately equal when their values are near zero.) |
| **11.** $N = N_0 e^{kt}$    $(k < 0)$ | 401 | In this exponential decay model for radioactive substances, $N_0$ is the amount of the substance present at $t = 0$, and $k$ is the decay constant. |
| **12.** Half-life | 402 | The half-life of a radioactive substance is the time required until only half of the initial amount remains. For a given radioactive substance the half-life is independent of the amount initially present, as evidenced by the formula *half-life* $= -(\ln 2)/k$. |

## Writing Mathematics

1. In Section 5.3 we defined logarithmic functions in terms of inverse functions.
   **(a)** Explain in general what is meant by a pair of inverse functions.
   **(b)** Assuming a knowledge of the function $f(x) = 2^x$, explain how to define and then graph the function $g(x) = \log_2 x$.

2. A student who was trying to simplify the expression $\dfrac{\ln(e^3)}{\ln(e^2)}$ wrote

$$\frac{\ln(e^3)}{\ln(e^2)} = \ln(e^3) - \ln(e^2) = 3 - 2 = 1$$

   **(a)** What is the error here? What do you think is the most probable reason for making this error?
   **(b)** Give the correct solution.

3. A student who wanted to simplify the expression $\dfrac{100}{\log_{10} 100}$ wrote

$$\frac{100}{\log_{10} 100} = \frac{\overset{1}{\cancel{100}}}{\log_{10} \underset{1}{\cancel{100}}} = \frac{1}{\log_{10}}$$

   Explain why this is nonsense, and then indicate the correct solution.

4. Look over the following method for solving the equation $\ln x^2 = 6$:

$$2 \ln x = 6$$
$$\ln x = 3$$
$$x = e^3$$

   As you can check, $e^3$ is a root of the given equation. The value $-e^3$, however, is also a root. Why is it that the demonstrated method fails to produce this root? Find a method that does produce both roots.

# Chapter 5 | Review Exercises

1. Which is larger, $\log_5 126$ or $\log_{10} 999$?
2. Graph the function $y = 3^{-x} - 3$. Specify the domain, range, intercept(s), and asymptote.
3. Suppose that the population of a colony of bacteria increases exponentially. If the population at the start of an experiment is 8000, and 4 hours later it is 10,000, how long (from the start of the experiment) will it take for the population to reach 12,000? (Express the answer in terms of base $e$ logarithms.)
4. Express $\log_{10} 2$ in terms of base $e$ logarithms.
5. Let $f$ be the function defined by

$$f(x) = \begin{cases} 2^{-x} & \text{if } x < 0 \\ x^2 & \text{if } x \geq 0 \end{cases}$$

   Sketch the graph of $f$ and then use the horizontal line test to determine whether $f$ is one-to-one.
6. Estimate $2^{60}$ in terms of an integral power of 10.
7. Solve for $x$:   $\ln(x + 1) - 1 = \ln(x - 1)$.
8. Suppose that $5000 is invested at 8% interest compounded annually. How many years will it take for the money to double? Make use of the approximations $\ln 2 \approx 0.7$ and $\ln 1.08 \approx 0.08$ to obtain a numerical answer.
9. On the same set of axes, sketch the graphs of $y = e^x$ and $y = \ln x$. Specify the domain and range for each function.
10. Solve for $x$: $xe^x - 2e^x = 0$.
11. Simplify: $\log_9(1/27)$.
12. Given that $\ln A = a$, $\ln B = b$, and $\ln C = c$, express $\ln[(A^2\sqrt{B})/C^3]$ in terms of $a$, $b$, and $c$.
13. The half-life of plutonium-241 is 13 years. What is the decay constant? Use the approximation $\ln(1/2) \approx -0.7$ to obtain a numerical answer.
14. Express as a single logarithm with a coefficient of 1: $3 \log_{10} x - \log_{10}(1 - x)$.
15. Solve for $x$, leaving your answer in terms of base $e$ logarithms:   $5e^{2-x} = 12$.
16. Let $f(x) = e^{x+1}$. Find a formula for $f^{-1}(x)$ and specify the domain of $f^{-1}$.
17. Suppose that in 1995 the population of a certain country was 2 million and increasing with a relative growth rate of 2%/year. Estimate the year in which the population will reach 3 million.
18. Simplify: $\ln e + \ln \sqrt{e} + \ln 1 + \ln e^{\ln 10}$.

19. A principal of $1000 is deposited at 10% per annum, compounded continuously. Estimate the doubling time and then sketch a graph that shows how the amount increases with time.
20. Simplify: $\ln(\log_8 56 - \log_8 7)$.

*In Exercises 21–32, graph the function and specify the asymptote(s) and intercepts(s).*

21. $y = e^x$
22. $y = -e^{-x}$
23. $y = \ln x$
24. $y = \ln(x + 2)$
25. $y = 2^{x+1} + 1$
26. $y = \log_{10}(-x)$
27. $y = (1/e)^x$
28. $y = (1/2)^{-x}$
29. $y = e^{x+1} + 1$
30. $y = -\log_2(x + 1)$
31. $y = \ln(e^x)$
32. $y = e^{\ln x}$

*In Exercises 33–49, solve the equation for $x$. (When logarithms appear in your answer, leave the answer in that form, rather than using a calculator.)*

33. $\log_4 x + \log_4(x - 3) = 1$
34. $\log_3 x + \log_3(2x + 5) = 1$
35. $\ln x + \ln(x + 2) = \ln 15$
36. $\log_6 \dfrac{x + 4}{x - 1} = 1$
37. $\log_2 x + \log_2(3x + 10) - 3 = 0$
38. $2 \ln x - 1 = 0$
39. $3 \log_9 x = 1/2$
40. $e^{2x} = 6$
41. $e^{1-5x} = 3\sqrt{e}$
42. $2^x = 100$
43. $\log_{10} x - 2 = \log_{10}(x - 2)$
44. $\log_{10}(x^2 - x - 10) = 1$
45. $\ln(x + 2) = \ln x + \ln 2$
46. $\ln(2x) = \ln 2 + \ln x$
47. $\ln x^4 = 4 \ln x$
48. $(\ln x)^4 = 4 \ln x$
49. $\log_{10} x = \ln x$
50. Solve for $x$: $(\ln x)/(\ln 3) = \ln x - \ln 3$. Use a calculator to evaluate your result and round to the nearest integer.       *Answer:*   206,765

*In Exercises 51–66, simplify the expression without using a calculator.*

51. $\log_{10}\sqrt{10}$
52. $\log_7 1$
53. $\ln \sqrt[5]{e}$
54. $\log_3 54 - \log_3 2$
55. $\log_{10} \pi - \log_{10} 10\pi$
56. $\log_2 2$
57. $10^t$, where $t = \log_{10} 16$
58. $e^{\ln 5}$
59. $\ln(e^4)$
60. $\log_{10}(10^{\sqrt{2}})$
61. $\log_{12} 2 + \log_{12} 18 + \log_{12} 4$

**62.** $(\log_{10} 8)/(\log_{10} 2)$

**63.** $(\ln 100)/(\ln 10)$

**64.** $\log_5 2 + \log_{1/5} 2$

**65.** $\log_2 \sqrt{16 \sqrt[3]{2\sqrt{2}}}$

**66.** $\log_{1/8}(1/16) + \log_5 0.02$

*In Exercises 67–70, express the quantity in terms of a, b, and c, where $a = \log_{10} A$, $b = \log_{10} B$, and $c = \log_{10} C$.*

**67.** $\log_{10} A^2 B^3 \sqrt{C}$

**68.** $\log_{10} \sqrt[3]{AC/B}$

**69.** $16 \log_{10} \sqrt{A} \sqrt[4]{B}$

**70.** $6 \log_{10}[B^{1/3}/(A\sqrt{C})]$

*In Exercises 71–76, find consecutive integers n and n + 1 such that the given expression lies between n and n + 1. Do not use a calculator.*

**71.** $\log_{10} 209$     **72.** $\ln 2$     **73.** $\log_6 100$

**74.** $\log_{10}(1/12)$     **75.** $\log_{10} 0.003$     **76.** $\log_3 244$

**77. (a)** On the same set of axes, graph the curves $y = \ln(x + 2)$ and $y = \ln(-x) - 1$. According to your graph, in which quadrant do the two curves intersect?

    **(b)** Find the x-coordinate of the intersection point.

**78.** The curve $y = ae^{bt}$ passes through the point (3, 4) and has a y-intercept of 2. Find a and b.

**79.** A certain radioactive substance has a half-life of T years. Find the decay constant (in terms of T).

**80.** Find the half-life of a certain radioactive substance if it takes T years for one-third of a given sample to disintegrate. (Your answer will be in terms of T.)

**81.** A radioactive substance has a half-life of M minutes. What percentage of a given sample will remain after 4M minutes?

**82.** At the start of an experiment, a colony of bacteria has initial population a. After b hours, there are c bacteria present. Determine the population d hours after the start of the experiment.

**83.** The half-life of a radioactive substance is d days. If you begin with a sample weighing b grams, how long will it be until c grams remain?

**84.** Find the half-life of a radioactive substance if it takes D days for P percent of a given sample to disintegrate.

*In Exercises 85–90, write the expression as a single logarithm with a coefficient of 1.*

**85.** $\log_{10} 8 + \log_{10} 3 - \log_{10} 12$

**86.** $4 \log_{10} x - 2 \log_{10} y$

**87.** $\ln 5 - 3 \ln 2 + \ln 16$

**88.** $\ln(x^4 - 1) - \ln(x^2 - 1)$

**89.** $a \ln x + b \ln y$

**90.** $\ln(x^3 + 8) - \ln(x + 2) - 2 \ln(x^2 - 2x + 4)$

*In Exercises 91–98, write the quantity using sums and differences of simpler logarithmic expressions. Express the answer so that logarithms of products, quotients, and powers do not appear.*

**91.** $\ln \sqrt{(x - 3)(x + 4)}$

**92.** $\log_{10} \dfrac{x^2 - 4}{x + 3}$

**93.** $\log_{10} \dfrac{x^3}{\sqrt{1 + x}}$

**94.** $\ln \dfrac{x^2 \sqrt{2x + 1}}{2x - 1}$

**95.** $\ln \left( \dfrac{1 + 2e}{1 - 2e} \right)^3$

**96.** $\log_{10} \sqrt[3]{x \sqrt{1 + y^2}}$

**97.** Suppose that A dollars are invested at R% compounded annually. How many years will it take for the money to double?

**98.** A sum of $2800 is placed in a savings account at 9% per annum. How much is in the account after 2 years if the interest is compounded quarterly?

**99.** A bank offers an interest rate of 9.5% per annum, compounded monthly. Compute the effective interest rate.

**100.** A sum of D dollars is placed in an account at R% per annum, compounded continuously. When will the balance reach E dollars?

**101.** Compute the doubling time for a sum of D dollars invested at R% per annum, compounded continuously.

**102.** Your friend invests D dollars at R% per annum, compounded semiannually. You invest an equal amount at the same yearly rate, but compounded daily. How much larger is your account than your friend's after T years?

**103. (a)** You invest $660 at 5.5% per annum, compounded quarterly. How long will it take for your balance to reach $1000? Round off your answer to the next quarter of a year.

    **(b)** You invest D dollars at R% per annum, compounded quarterly. How long will it take for your balance to reach nD dollars? (Assume that n > 1.)

*In Exercises 104–107, find the domain of each function.*

**104. (a)** $y = \ln x$     **105. (a)** $y = \log_{10} \sqrt{x}$

    **(b)** $y = e^x$              **(b)** $y = \sqrt{\log_{10} x}$

**106. (a)** $f \circ g$, where $f(x) = \ln x$ and $g(x) = e^x$

    **(b)** $g \circ f$, where f and g are as in part (a)

**107.** $y = \dfrac{2 + \ln x}{2 - \ln x}$

**108.** Find the range of the function defined by $y = \dfrac{e^x + 1}{e^x - 1}$.

# Chapter 5    Test

1. Graph the function $y = 2^{-x} - 3$. Specify the domain, range, intercepts, and asymptote.
2. Suppose that the population of a colony of bacteria increases exponentially. At the start of an experiment there are 6000 bacteria, and 1 hour later the population is 6200. How long (from the start of the experiment) will it take for the population to reach 10,000? Give two forms for the answer: one in terms of base $e$ logarithms and the other a calculator approximation rounded to the nearest hour.
3. Which is larger, $\log_2 17$ or $\log_3 80$? Explain the reasons for your answer.
4. Express $\log_2 15$ in terms of base $e$ logarithms.
5. Estimate $2^{40}$ in terms of an integral power of 10.
6. Suppose that $9500 is invested at 6% interest, compounded annually. How long will it take for the amount in the account to reach $12,000?
7. **(a)** For which values of $x$ is the identity $e^{\ln x} = x$ valid?
   **(b)** On the same set of axes, graph $y = e^x$ and $y = \ln x$.
8. Given that $\log_{10} A = a$ and $\log_{10} B = b$, express $\log_{10}(A^3/\sqrt{B})$ in terms of $a$ and $b$.
9. Simplify each expression:
   **(a)** $\log_5(1/\sqrt{5})$
   **(b)** $\ln e^2 + \ln 1 - e^{\ln 3}$
10. Solve for $x$: $x^3 e^x - 4xe^x = 0$.
11. The half-life of a radioactive substance is 4 days.
    **(a)** Find the decay constant.
    **(b)** How much of an initial 2-g sample will remain after 10 days?

12. Express as a single logarithm with a coefficient of 1: $2 \ln x - \ln \sqrt[3]{x^2 + 1}$.
13. Solve for $x$, leaving your answer in terms of base $e$ logarithms: $-2e^{3x-1} = 9$.
14. Let $g(x) = \log_{10}(x - 1)$. Find a formula for $g^{-1}(x)$ and specify the range of $g^{-1}$.
15. A principal of $12,000 is deposited at 6% per annum, compounded continuously.
    **(a)** Use the rule of 70 to estimate the doubling time.
    **(b)** Sketch a graph showing how the amount increases with time.
16. **(a)** For which values of $x$ is it true that $\ln(x^2) = 2 \ln x$?
    **(b)** For which values of $x$ is it true that $(\ln x)^2 = 2 \ln x$?
17. Let $f(x) = e^x$.
    **(a)** Compute the average rate of change of the function $f$ over the interval $[\ln 3, \ln 4]$. Give two forms for the answer: an expression simplified as much as possible and a calculator approximation rounded to two decimal places.
    **(b)** Specify the instantaneous rate of change of the function $f$ at the point on the graph where $x = \ln 4$.
18. Solve for $x$: $\frac{1}{2} - \log_{16}(x - 3) = \log_{16} x$.
19. Solve for $x$: $6e^{2x} - 5e^x = 6$.
20. Solve each inequality:
    **(a)** $5(4 - 0.3^x) > 12$
    **(b)** $\ln x + \ln(x - 3) \le \ln 4$

# 6 CHAPTER

# Trigonometric Functions of Angles

*The origins of trigonometry are obscure. There are some problems in the Rhind papyrus [ca. 1650 B.C.] that involve the cotangent of the dihedral angles at the base of a pyramid, and . . . the Babylonian cuneiform tablet Plimpton 322 essentially contains a remarkable table of secants. It may be that modern investigations into the mathematics of ancient Mesopotamia will reveal an appreciable development of practical trigonometry.* —Howard Eves in *An Introduction to the History of Mathematics,* 6th ed. (Philadelphia: Saunders College Publishing, 1990)

In general, there are two approaches to trigonometry at the precalculus level. One approach centers on the study of triangles. Indeed, the word "trigonometry" is derived from two Greek words, *trigonon,* meaning "triangle," and *metria,* meaning "measurement." It is with this triangle approach that we begin the chapter. The second approach, which is in a sense a generalization of the first, we will take up in Chapters 7 and 8. Before getting down to specifics, we offer the following bird's-eye view of Chapters 6, 7, and 8 in terms of functions. As you'll see in subsequent chapters, a real familiarity with both approaches to trigonometry is necessary.

| | Inputs for the Functions | Outputs | Emphasis |
|---|---|---|---|
| *Chapter 6* | angles | real numbers | The trigonometric functions are used to study triangles. |
| *Chapters 7 and 8* | real numbers | real numbers | The objects of study are the trigonometric functions themselves. |

*It is certain that the division of the ecliptic into 360 degrees . . . [was] adopted by the Greeks from Babylon. . . . [But] It was Hipparchus [ca. 180–ca. 125 B.C.] who first divided the circle in general into 360 parts or degrees, and the introduction of this division coincides with his invention of trigonometry.* —Sir Thomas Heath in *A History of Greek Mathematics,* vol. II (London: Oxford University Press, 1921)

## 6.1 TRIGONOMETRIC FUNCTIONS OF ACUTE ANGLES

In elementary geometry an **angle** is a figure formed by two rays with a common endpoint. As is indicated in Figure 1, the common endpoint is called the **vertex** of the angle. There are several conventions used in naming angles; Figure 2 indicates some of these. In Figure 2 the symbol $\theta$ is the lowercase Greek letter *theta.* Greek letters are often used to name angles. For reference, the Greek alphabet is given in the endpapers at the back of this book. The $\angle$ symbol that you see in Figure 2 stands for the word "angle." When three letters are used in naming an angle, as with $\angle ABC$ in Figure 2, the middle letter always indicates the vertex of the angle.

Vertex
**Figure 1**

Notations for the angle at $B$:
$\theta$, $\angle\theta$, $\angle B$, $\angle ABC$, $\angle CBA$

**Figure 2**

... [the English clergyman and mathematician] *William Oughtred* [1574–1660] *introduced a vast array of characters into mathematics. ... In the* Trigonometria *(1657), he employed $\angle$ for angle. ...* —Florian Cajori in *A History of Mathematical Notations*, vol. I (La Salle, Ill.: The Open Court Publishing Co., 1928)

There are several ways to indicate the size of (that is, the amount of rotation in) an angle. In this chapter we use the familiar units of *degrees.* Recall that 360 degrees is the measure of an angle obtained by rotating a ray through one complete circle. The symbol for degrees is °. For comparison, Figure 3 displays angles of various degrees. In this section we will not make any distinction whether the rotation generating an angle is clockwise or counterclockwise; in a subsequent section this distinction will be important. The angles in Figures 3(a) and 3(b) are **acute angles;** these are angles with degree measure $\theta$ satisfying $0° < \theta < 90°$. The angle in Figure 3(d) is an **obtuse angle,** that is, an angle with degree measure $\theta$ satisfying $90° < \theta < 180°$.

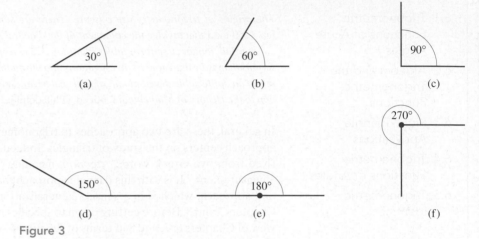

**Figure 3**

The degree is subdivided into two smaller units: the **minute,** which is 1/60 of a degree; and the **second,** which is 1/60 of a minute. The abbreviations for minutes and seconds are ′ and ″, respectively. Thus we have

$$1° = 60' \qquad \text{There are 60 minutes in one degree.}$$

and

$$1' = 60'' \qquad \text{There are 60 seconds in one minute.}$$

Until modern handheld calculators became commonplace (in the 1970s and 1980s), these subdivisions of the degree were widely used. Nowadays, however, the convention in most scientific applications is to use ordinary decimal notation for the fractional parts of a degree, and this is the convention we follow in this text. (We mention in passing that minutes and seconds are still widely used in some portions of astronomy and in navigation.)

One more convention: Suppose, for example, that the measure of angle $\theta$ is 70°. We can write this as

$$\text{measure } \angle\theta = 70° \qquad \text{or just} \qquad m\angle\theta = 70°$$

For ease of notation and speech, however, we will usually write

$$\angle\theta = 70° \qquad \text{or simply} \qquad \theta = 70°$$

as shorthand for "$\theta$ is an angle whose measure is 70°."

We are going to define the six *trigonometric functions.* As indicated by the title of this section, the inputs for these functions will be acute angles. The outputs will be real numbers. In a later section we'll make a transition so that angles of any size can serve as inputs, and in Chapter 7 we'll make another transition, this time to real-number inputs.

For reasons that are more historical* than mathematical, the trigonometric functions have names that are words rather than single letters such as *f*. Using words rather than single letters for naming functions is by no means peculiar to trigonometry. For example, $\log_b x$ denotes the logarithmic function with base *b*. The names of the six trigonometric functions, along with their abbreviations, are as follows.

| NAME OF FUNCTION | ABBREVIATION |
| --- | --- |
| cosine | cos |
| sine | sin |
| tangent | tan |
| secant | sec |
| cosecant | csc |
| cotangent | cot |

Now an acute angle can always be placed in a right triangle as shown in Figure 4. The six trigonometric functions are defined in the box that follows.

---

**DEFINITIONS** | **Trigonometric Functions of an Acute Angle**

Let $\theta$ be an acute angle placed in a right triangle (as shown in Figure 4); then

$$\cos \theta = \frac{\text{length of side adjacent to angle } \theta}{\text{length of hypotenuse}}$$

$$\sin \theta = \frac{\text{length of side opposite to angle } \theta}{\text{length of hypotenuse}}$$

$$\tan \theta = \frac{\text{length of side opposite to angle } \theta}{\text{length of side adjacent to angle } \theta}$$

$$\sec \theta = \frac{\text{length of hypotenuse}}{\text{length of side adjacent to angle } \theta}$$

$$\csc \theta = \frac{\text{length of hypotenuse}}{\text{length of side opposite to angle } \theta}$$

$$\cot \theta = \frac{\text{length of side adjacent to angle } \theta}{\text{length of side opposite to angle } \theta}$$

---

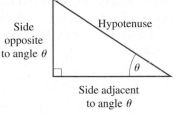

Figure 4

The definitions that we have just given are often called the right triangle definitions of the trigonometric functions. Our work for the next several sections will be devoted to exploring these definitions and their consequences. Here are four preliminary observations that will help you to understand and memorize the definitions.

1. An expression such as $\cos \theta$ really means $\cos(\theta)$, where cos or cosine is the name of the function and $\theta$ is an input. It is for historical rather than mathematical reasons that the parentheses are suppressed.

---

*For a discussion of the names of the trigonometric functions, see Howard Eves, *An Introduction to the History of Mathematics,* 6th ed., pp. 236–237 (Philadelphia: Saunders College Publishing, 1990).

2. For convenience and ease of memorization the phrases in the definition that describe the sides of the triangle are often shortened to one word. For example, the expression for the cosine would be written

$$\cos \theta = \frac{\text{adjacent}}{\text{hypotenuse}}$$

3. There are three pairs of reciprocals in the definitions: cos and sec, sin and csc, and tan and cot. To be more explicit, we have

$$\sec \theta = \frac{\text{hypotenuse}}{\text{adjacent}} = \frac{1}{\dfrac{\text{adjacent}}{\text{hypotenuse}}} = \frac{1}{\cos \theta}$$

Similarly,

$$\csc \theta = \frac{1}{\sin \theta} \quad \text{and} \quad \cot \theta = \frac{1}{\tan \theta}$$

4. For acute angles the values of the trigonometric functions are always positive since they are ratios of lengths.

The definitions that we have just given for the trigonometric functions involve ratios of sides in a right triangle. The fact that *ratios* are involved is important. We'll use two examples to explain and emphasize this. Figure 5 shows two right triangles; both contain the same angle $\theta$. From Figure 5(a) we have

$$\tan \theta = \frac{\text{opposite}}{\text{adjacent}} = \frac{BC}{AC}$$

Now the question is: Will Figure 5(b) give us the same value for $\tan \theta$? [It had better, otherwise tan will not qualify as a function. (Why?)] Indeed, Figure 5(b) does give us the same value for $\tan \theta$. Elementary geometry* tells us that $\triangle ABC$ is similar to $\triangle A'B'C'$. Then, because corresponding sides of similar triangles are proportional, we have

$$\frac{BC}{AC} = \frac{B'C'}{A'C'} \tag{1}$$

Now look at the ratio on the right-hand side of equation (1); it represents $\tan \theta$ as we would calculate it in Figure 5(b). The left-hand side of the equation, as we've already seen from Figure 5(a), represents $\tan \theta$. In summary, similar triangles and equation (1) tell us that we obtain the same value for $\tan \theta$ whether we use Figure 5(a) or Figure 5(b).

The point of the example we've just concluded is this: For a given acute angle $\theta$, the values of the trigonometric functions depend on the ratios of the lengths of the sides but not on the size of the particular right triangle in which $\theta$ resides. For emphasis the next example makes this same point.

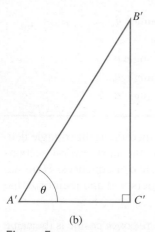

(a)

(b)

**Figure 5**

---

*If two angles of one triangle are congruent to two corresponding angles of another triangle, then the triangles are similar.

| EXAMPLE | 1 | Comparing trigonometric ratios for similar triangles |

Figure 6 shows two right triangles. The first right triangle has sides 5, 12, and 13. The second right triangle is similar to the first (the angles are the same), but each side is 10 times longer than the corresponding side in the first triangle. Calculate and compare the values of $\sin \theta$, $\cos \theta$, and $\tan \theta$ for both triangles.

**Figure 6**

**SOLUTION**

SMALL TRIANGLE

$$\sin \theta = \frac{\text{opposite}}{\text{hypotenuse}} = \frac{5}{13}$$

$$\cos \theta = \frac{\text{adjacent}}{\text{hypotenuse}} = \frac{12}{13}$$

$$\tan \theta = \frac{\text{opposite}}{\text{adjacent}} = \frac{5}{12}$$

LARGE TRIANGLE

$$\sin \theta = \frac{50}{130} = \frac{5}{13}$$

$$\cos \theta = \frac{120}{130} = \frac{12}{13}$$

$$\tan \theta = \frac{50}{120} = \frac{5}{12}$$

OBSERVATION    The corresponding values for $\sin \theta$, $\cos \theta$, and $\tan \theta$ are the same for both triangles.

| EXAMPLE | 2 | Calculating trigonometric functions of an acute angle |

Let $\theta$ be the acute angle indicated in Figure 7. Determine the six quantities $\cos \theta$, $\sin \theta$, $\tan \theta$, $\sec \theta$, $\csc \theta$, and $\cot \theta$.

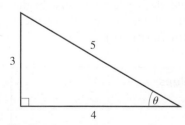

**Figure 7**

**SOLUTION**
We use the definitions:

$$\cos \theta = \frac{\text{adjacent}}{\text{hypotenuse}} = \frac{4}{5} \qquad \sec \theta = \frac{\text{hypotenuse}}{\text{adjacent}} = \frac{5}{4}$$

$$\sin \theta = \frac{\text{opposite}}{\text{hypotenuse}} = \frac{3}{5} \qquad \csc \theta = \frac{\text{hypotenuse}}{\text{opposite}} = \frac{5}{3}$$

$$\tan \theta = \frac{\text{opposite}}{\text{adjacent}} = \frac{3}{4} \qquad \cot \theta = \frac{\text{adjacent}}{\text{opposite}} = \frac{4}{3}$$

Note the pairs of answers that are reciprocals. (As was mentioned before, this helps in memorizing the definitions.)

---

**EXAMPLE** **3** **Calculating sine and cosine**

Let $\beta$ be the acute angle indicated in Figure 8. Find $\sin \beta$ and $\cos \beta$.

**SOLUTION**
In view of the definitions we need to know the length of the hypotenuse in Figure 8. If we call this length $h$, then by the Pythagorean theorem we have

$$h^2 = 3^2 + 1^2 = 10$$
$$h = \sqrt{10}$$

Therefore

$$\sin \beta = \frac{\text{opposite}}{\text{hypotenuse}} = \frac{3}{\sqrt{10}} = \frac{3\sqrt{10}}{10}$$

and

$$\cos \beta = \frac{\text{adjacent}}{\text{hypotenuse}} = \frac{1}{\sqrt{10}} = \frac{\sqrt{10}}{10}$$

Figure 8

In the next example we use a calculator to evaluate the trigonometric functions for a particular acute-angle input. All scientific calculators allow for two common units of angle measurement: the degree and the *radian*. Radian measure is discussed in Chapter 7; for the present chapter, though, we are using degree measure exclusively. So before working through the next example on your own, you need to check that your calculator is set in the "degree mode" rather than the "radian mode." If necessary, consult the user's manual for your calculator on this point.

One more calculator-related detail: For most calculators, when you want to evaluate a function, first you enter the name of the function then you enter the input. On these calculators, the keystrokes for evaluating $\sin 40°$ are as follows:

$\boxed{\sin}$ 40 $\boxed{\text{ENTER}}$     name of function before input

If your calculator is set in degree mode it should display a value that begins 0.6427. . . . (If it does not display such a value, you will need to consult the user's manual to find out how to evaluate the trigonometric functions.)

---

**EXAMPLE** **4** **Calculating approximate values of trigonometric functions**

Use a calculator to evaluate $\cos 40°$, $\sin 40°$, and $\tan 40°$. Round the results to three decimal places.

**SOLUTION**
With the calculator set in the degree mode, the sequence of keystrokes and the results (rounded to three decimal places) are as follows. You should verify each of these results for yourself.

| EXPRESSION | KEYSTROKES | OUTPUT |
|---|---|---|
| cos 40° | cos 40 ENTER | 0.766 |
| sin 40° | sin 40 ENTER | 0.643 |
| tan 40° | tan 40 ENTER | 0.839 |

In the next example we use a calculator to evaluate the three functions secant, cosecant, and cotangent for a particular input. These three functions are referred to as the **reciprocal functions.** This is because, from observation 3 on page 426, it follows that

$$\sec \theta = \frac{1}{\cos \theta} \qquad \csc \theta = \frac{1}{\sin \theta} \qquad \cot \theta = \frac{1}{\tan \theta}$$

So, for example, although most calculators do not have a key labeled "sec," we can nevertheless evaluate the secant function by using the cosine key cos and then the reciprocal key 1/x or $x^{-1}$.

---

**EXAMPLE 5   Calculating approximate values of the reciprocal functions**

Use a calculator to evaluate sec 10°, csc 10°, and cot 10°. Round the results to three decimal places.

**SOLUTION**
As in the previous example, we first check that the calculator is in the degree mode. Then the sequence of keystrokes and the results are as follows (again, you should verify each of these results for yourself):

| EXPRESSION | KEYSTROKES | OUTPUT |
|---|---|---|
| sec 10° | ( cos 10 ) $x^{-1}$ ENTER | 1.015 |
| csc 10° | ( sin 10 ) $x^{-1}$ ENTER | 5.759 |
| cot 10° | ( tan 10 ) $x^{-1}$ ENTER | 5.671 |

---

There are certain angles for which we can evaluate the trigonometric functions without using a calculator. Three such angles are 30°, 45°, and 60°. We focus on these particular angles for now, not because they are somehow more fundamental than others, but because a ready knowledge of their trigonometric values will provide a useful source of examples in our subsequent work.

To obtain the trigonometric values for angles of 30° and 60°, we rely on the following theorem from geometry. (For a proof of this theorem, see Exercise 43.)

---

**THEOREM   The 30°-60° Right Triangle**

In a 30°-60° right triangle the length of the side opposite the 30° angle is half the length of the hypotenuse. (See Figure 9.)

---

Figure 9

If we let $y$ denote the length of the unmarked side in Figure 9, then (according to the Pythagorean theorem) we have $y^2 + x^2 = (2x)^2$ and, consequently,

$$y^2 = 4x^2 - x^2 = 3x^2$$
$$y = \sqrt{3}x$$

Our 30°-60° right triangle can now be labeled as in Figure 10. From this figure the required trigonometric values can be written down by inspection. We will list only the values of the cosine, sine, and tangent, since the remaining three values are just the reciprocals of these.

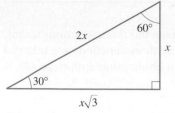

**Figure 10**

$$\cos 30° = \frac{x\sqrt{3}}{2x} = \frac{\sqrt{3}}{2} \qquad\qquad \cos 60° = \frac{x}{2x} = \frac{1}{2}$$

$$\sin 30° = \frac{x}{2x} = \frac{1}{2} \qquad\qquad \sin 60° = \frac{x\sqrt{3}}{2x} = \frac{\sqrt{3}}{2}$$

$$\tan 30° = \frac{x}{x\sqrt{3}} = \frac{1}{\sqrt{3}} = \frac{\sqrt{3}}{3} \qquad \tan 60° = \frac{x\sqrt{3}}{x} = \sqrt{3}$$

There are two observations to be made here. First, the final answers do not involve $x$. Once again this shows that for a given angle, it is the *ratios* of the sides that determine the trigonometric values, not the size of the triangle. Second, notice that

$$\sin 30° = \cos 60° \qquad \text{and} \qquad \sin 60° = \cos 30°$$

It is easy to see that this is no coincidence. The terms "opposite" and "adjacent" are relative ones. As a glance at Figure 10 shows, the side opposite to one acute angle in a right triangle is automatically adjacent to the other acute angle. We'll return to this point again in the next section.

Another angle for which we can compute the trigonometric values without the aid of a calculator is 45°. Figure 11 shows a 45°-45° right triangle. Since the base angles of this triangle are equal, it follows from a theorem of geometry that the sides opposite those angles are equal so the triangle is isosceles. The two equal sides are indicated by the use of the letter $x$ twice in Figure 11. If we now use $y$ to denote the length of the unmarked side in Figure 11, we have

$$y^2 = x^2 + x^2 = 2x^2 \qquad \text{and, consequently,} \qquad y = \sqrt{2}x$$

Our 45°-45° right triangle can now be labeled as in Figure 12, and the trigonometric values can then be obtained by inspection. As before, we list only the values for cosine, sine, and tangent, since the remaining three are just the reciprocals of these.

**Figure 11**

**Figure 12**

$$\cos 45° = \frac{x}{x\sqrt{2}} = \frac{1}{\sqrt{2}} = \frac{\sqrt{2}}{2}$$

$$\sin 45° = \frac{x}{x\sqrt{2}} = \frac{1}{\sqrt{2}} = \frac{\sqrt{2}}{2}$$

$$\tan 45° = \frac{x}{x} = 1$$

Table 1 summarizes the results we've now obtained for angles of 30, 45, and 60 degrees. These results should be memorized.

**TABLE 1**

| $\theta$ | $\sin \theta$ | $\cos \theta$ | $\tan \theta$ |
|---|---|---|---|
| 30° | $\dfrac{1}{2}$ | $\dfrac{\sqrt{3}}{2}$ | $\dfrac{\sqrt{3}}{3}$ |
| 45° | $\dfrac{\sqrt{2}}{2}$ | $\dfrac{\sqrt{2}}{2}$ | 1 |
| 60° | $\dfrac{\sqrt{3}}{2}$ | $\dfrac{1}{2}$ | $\sqrt{3}$ |

# EXERCISE SET 6.1

## A

*In Exercises 1–4, use the definitions (as in Example 2) to evaluate the six trigonometric functions of **(a)** θ and **(b)** β. In cases in which a radical occurs in a denominator, rationalize the denominator.*

**1.**  **2.**

**3.**  **4.**

*In Exercises 5–12, suppose that △ABC is a right triangle with ∠C = 90°.*

**5.** If $AC = 3$ and $BC = 2$, find the following quantities.
  **(a)** cos $A$, sin $A$, tan $A$
  **(b)** sec $B$, csc $B$, cot $B$

**6.** If $AC = 6$ and $BC = 2$, find the following quantities.
  **(a)** cos $A$, sin $A$, tan $A$
  **(b)** sec $B$, csc $B$, cot $B$

**7.** If $AB = 13$ and $BC = 5$, compute the values of the six trigonometric functions of angle $B$.

**8.** If $AB = 3$ and $AC = 1$, compute the values of the six trigonometric functions of angle $A$.

**9.** If $AC = 1$ and $BC = 3/4$, compute each quantity.
  **(a)** sin $B$, cos $A$
  **(b)** sin $A$, cos $B$
  **(c)** (tan $A$)(tan $B$)

**10.** If $AC = BC = 4$, compute the following.
  **(a)** sec $A$, csc $A$, cot $A$
  **(b)** sec $B$, csc $B$, cot $B$
  **(c)** (cot $A$)(cot $B$)

**11.** If $AB = 25$ and $AC = 24$, compute each of the required quantities.
  **(a)** cos $A$, sin $A$, tan $A$
  **(b)** cos $B$, sin $B$, tan $B$
  **(c)** (tan $A$)(tan $B$)

**12.** If $AB = 1$ and $BC = \sqrt{3}/2$, compute the following.
  **(a)** cos $A$, sin $B$
  **(b)** tan $A$, cot $B$
  **(c)** sec $A$, csc $B$

*In Exercises 13–18, use a calculator to compute cos θ, sin θ, and tan θ for the given value of θ. Round each result to three decimal places.*

**13.** $θ = 65°$  **14.** $θ = 21°$
**15.** $θ = 38.5°$  **16.** $θ = 12.4°$
**17.** $θ = 80.06°$  **18.** $θ = 0.99°$

*In Exercises 19–24, use a calculator to compute sec θ, csc θ, and cot θ (as in Example 5) for the given value of θ. Round each result to three decimal places.*

**19.** $θ = 20°$  **20.** $θ = 40°$
**21.** $θ = 17.5°$  **22.** $θ = 18.5°$
**23.** $θ = 1°$  **24.** $θ = 89.9°$

*In Exercises 25–36, verify that each equation is correct by evaluating each side. Do not use a calculator. The purpose of Exercises 25–36 is twofold. First, doing the problems will help you to review the values in Table 1 of this section. Second, the exercises serve as an algebra review.* Note: *In the exercises, notation such as* $\sin^2 θ$ *stands for* $(\sin θ)^2$. *This common notational convention will be discussed in the next section.*

**25.** $\cos 60° = \cos^2 30° - \sin^2 30°$

**26.** $\cos 60° = 1 - 2\sin^2 30°$

**27.** $\sin^2 30° + \sin^2 45° + \sin^2 60° = 3/2$

**28.** $\sin 30° \cos 60° + \cos 30° \sin 60° = 1$

**29.** $2\sin 30° \cos 30° = \sin 60°$

**30.** $2\sin 45° \cos 45° = 1$

**31.** $\sin 30° = \sqrt{(1 - \cos 60°)/2}$

**32.** $\cos 30° = \sqrt{(1 + \cos 60°)/2}$

**33.** $\tan 30° = \dfrac{\sin 60°}{1 + \cos 60°}$

**34.** $\tan 30° = \dfrac{1 - \cos 60°}{\sin 60°}$

**35.** $1 + \tan^2 45° = \sec^2 45°$

**36.** $1 + \cot^2 60° = \csc^2 60°$

**37. (a)** Use a calculator to evaluate cos 30° and cos 45°. Give your answers to as many decimal places as your calculator allows.

  **(b)** In Table 1 there are expressions for cos 30° and cos 45°. Use your calculator to evaluate these expressions, and check to see that the results agree with those in part (a).

**38. (a)** Use a calculator to evaluate tan 30° and tan 60°. Give your answers to as many decimal places as your calculator allows.

  **(b)** In Table 1 there are expressions for tan 30° and tan 60°. Use your calculator to evaluate these expressions, and check to see that the results agree with those in part (a).

## B

*In Exercises 39 and 40, refer to the following figure. In the figure, the arc is a portion of a circle with center O and radius r.*

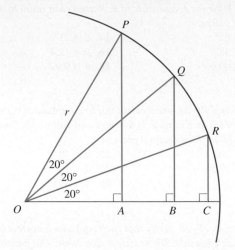

39. (a) Use the figure and the right-triangle definition of sine to explain (in complete sentences) why $\sin 20° < \sin 40° < \sin 60°$.
    (b) Use a calculator to verify that $\sin 20° < \sin 40° < \sin 60°$.
40. (a) Use the figure and the right-triangle definition of cosine to explain (in complete sentences) why $\cos 20° > \cos 40° > \cos 60°$.
    (b) Use a calculator to verify that $\cos 20° > \cos 40° > \cos 60°$.

*For Exercises 41 and 42, refer to the following figure. In each case, say which of the two given quantities is larger. If the quantities are equal, say so. In either case, be able to support your conclusion.*

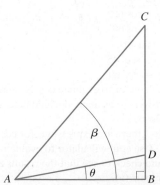

41. (a) $\cos \theta, \cos \beta$
    (b) $\sec \theta, \sec \beta$
42. (a) $\tan \theta, \tan \beta$
    (b) $\cot \theta, \cot \beta$
43. The following figure shows a 30°–60° right triangle, △*ABC*. Prove that $AC = 2AB$. *Suggestion:* Construct △*DBC* as shown, congruent to △*ABC*. Then note that △*ADC* is equilateral. *Note:* This exercise provides a proof of the theorem on page 429.

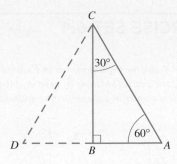

44. This exercise shows how to obtain radical expressions for sin 15° and cos 15°. In the figure, assume that $AB = BD = 2$.

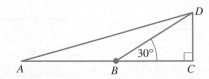

(a) In the right triangle *BCD*, note that $DC = 1$ because $\overline{DC}$ is opposite the 30° angle and $BD = 2$. Use the Pythagorean theorem to show that $BC = \sqrt{3}$.
(b) Use the Pythagorean theorem to show that $AD = 2\sqrt{2 + \sqrt{3}}$.
(c) Show that the expression for *AD* in part (b) is equal to $\sqrt{6} + \sqrt{2}$. *Hint:* Two nonnegative quantities are equal if and only if their squares are equal.
(d) Explain why $\angle BAD = \angle BDA$.
(e) According to a theorem from geometry, an exterior angle of a triangle is equal to the sum of the two nonadjacent interior angles. Apply this to △*ABD* with exterior angle $DBC = 30°$, and show that $\angle BAD = 15°$.
(f) Using the figure and the values that you have obtained for the lengths, conclude that

$$\sin 15° = \frac{1}{\sqrt{6} + \sqrt{2}} \qquad \cos 15° = \frac{2 + \sqrt{3}}{\sqrt{6} + \sqrt{2}}$$

(g) Rationalize the denominators in part (f) to obtain

$$\sin 15° = \frac{\sqrt{6} - \sqrt{2}}{4} \qquad \cos 15° = \frac{\sqrt{6} + \sqrt{2}}{4}$$

(h) Use your calculator to check the results in part (g).
45. If an angle $\theta$ is an integral multiple of 3°, then the real number $\sin \theta$ is either rational or expressible in terms of radicals. You've already seen examples of this with the angles 30°, 45°, and 60°. The accompanying table gives the values of $\sin \theta$ for some multiples of 3°. Use your calculator to check the entries in the table. *Remark:* If $\theta$ is an integral number of degrees but not a multiple of 3°, then the real number $\sin \theta$ cannot be expressed in terms of radicals within the real-number system.

| $\theta$ | $\sin \theta$ |
|----------|---------------|
| 3° | $\frac{1}{16}\left[(\sqrt{6}+\sqrt{2})(\sqrt{5}-1)-2(\sqrt{3}-1)\sqrt{5+\sqrt{5}}\right]$ |
| 6° | $\frac{1}{8}(\sqrt{30-6\sqrt{5}}-\sqrt{5}-1)$ |
| 9° | $\frac{1}{8}(\sqrt{10}+\sqrt{2}-2\sqrt{5-\sqrt{5}})$ |
| 12° | $\frac{1}{8}(\sqrt{10+2\sqrt{5}}-\sqrt{15}+\sqrt{3})$ |
| 15° | $\frac{1}{4}(\sqrt{6}-\sqrt{2})$ |
| 18° | $\frac{1}{4}(\sqrt{5}-1)$ |

**46. (a)** Use the expression for sin 18° given in Exercise 45 to show that the number sin 18° is a root of the quadratic equation $4x^2 + 2x - 1 = 0$.

**(b)** Use the expression for sin 15° given in Exercise 45 to show that the number sin 15° is a root of the equation $16x^4 - 16x^2 + 1 = 0$.

# PROJECT

## TRANSITS OF VENUS AND THE SCALE OF THE SOLAR SYSTEM

*Almost every High School child knows that the Sun is 93 million miles (or 150 million Kilometres) away from the Earth. Despite the incredible immensity of this figure in comparison with everyday scales—or perhaps even because it is so hard to grasp—astronomical data of this kind is accepted on trust by most educated people. Very few pause to consider how it could be possible to measure such a distance . . . and few are aware of the heroic efforts which attended early attempts at measuring it.* —David Sellers, *The Transit of Venus & the Quest for the Solar Parallax* (Maga Velda Press, 2001)

A transit of Venus occurs when the planet Venus crosses a line of sight from Earth to the Sun. For over four hundred years, transits of Venus have caused excitement among astronomers, explorers, and the interested public. From the seventeenth through the twenty-first century transits occurred in 1631, 1639, 1761, 1769, 1874, 1882, and 2004. The next transit, in 2012, will be the last of the current century and will be visible from the western United States. Inspired by a paper presented by Edmond Halley (1656–1742) to the Royal Society in 1716, expeditions set out to distant locations all over the Earth to observe the transits of 1761 and 1769. Among famous explorers and mapmakers of the eighteenth century, Charles Mason and Jeremiah Dixon observed the 1761 transit from South Africa, and Captain James Cook observed the 1769 transit from Tahiti. When the data from the observations was processed, the value of the solar parallax was determined to be between 8.5 and 8.9 seconds of arc. The modern value is 8.794148 arc seconds.

Halley's method used complicated tools from spherical trigonometry. In this project, we will see how observations of a transit of Venus and some basic plane trigonometry can be used to estimate the solar parallax and the distance from Earth to the Sun. This project can be done as an individual or group activity but may be more fun with a group.

Figure A shows the geometric relationship between the **solar parallax,** angle $\alpha$, the distance $r_e$, from Earth to the Sun, and the radius $R$ of the Earth. The notation $r_e$ comes from thinking of the distance from Earth to the Sun as the radius of the Earth's orbit. Figure A is not drawn to scale. It greatly exaggerates angle $\alpha$, and $r_e$ is really about 25,000 times larger than $R$.

**EXERCISE 1**   Use the right triangle definition of the sine function to derive the formula

$$r_e = \frac{R}{\sin \alpha} \tag{i}$$

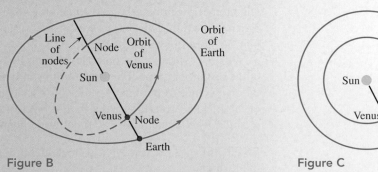

Figure A

for the distance from Earth to the Sun in terms of the solar parallax and the radius of Earth.

More than 2000 years ago Eratosthenes calculated that the circumference of Earth was about 250,000 stades. While the precise length of a stade is not known, an estimate of about 160 meters gives a circumference of 40,000 kilometers. (For a short, very readable account of Eratosthenes' life and work, see pp. 13–21 of Kitty Ferguson's book quoted in the margin.)

**EXERCISE 2** Assuming a circumference of 40,000 kilometers, show that the radius $R$ of the Earth is about 6400 kilometers. (The modern value is 6371 kilometers.)

**EXERCISE 3** After the data from the expeditions of 1761 and 1769 were analyzed, the best estimate for the solar parallax was about 8.7 arc seconds. Assuming $\alpha$ is 8.7 arc seconds, use formula (i) to find the distance from Earth to the Sun. (Don't forget to convert 8.7 arc seconds to degrees.) How does it compare with a modern value of 149,600,000 km?

A transit of Venus occurs when Earth, Venus, and the Sun lie along a straight line. This happens because the orbits of both planets lie in planes containing the Sun, but it happens only rarely because the orbital plane of Venus is tilted about 3.4 degrees to the plane of Earth's orbit. See Figure B. A transit occurs when the three bodies line up along the **line of nodes** as illustrated in Figure B and Figure C. Transits occur in pairs, about eight years apart, about once per century. Although the orbits of Earth and Venus are not quite circular, in our discussion we'll assume that they are circles centered at the center of the Sun; a top view would resemble Figure C.

Figure B

Figure C

Figure D, like Figure A, is greatly exaggerated. It shows the geometric situation during a transit of Venus as seen by two symmetrically placed observers on

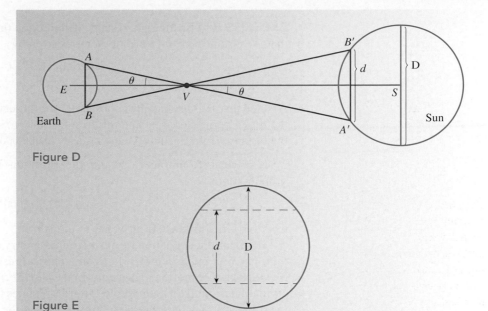

**Figure D**

**Figure E**

Earth. The observer at point $A$ sees Venus as a dark spot on the Sun at point $A'$, and the observer at $B$ sees Venus at the point $B'$.

Observer $B$ would see Venus transit the Sun, that is, move across the face of the Sun, along the path indicated by the upper dashed line in Figure E. Similarly, observer $A$ would see Venus transit the Sun along the lower dashed line. In principle, the ratio $d/D$ can be measured from a careful drawing. The eighteenth-century observers recorded the time of the first contact of Venus with the solar disk, the time that Venus separated from the solar disk, and their geographical position (latitude and longitude). This data was used to calculate $d/D$.

**EXERCISE 4**   The value of the ratio $d/D$ calculated as a result of the eighteenth-century measurements was about 0.0260. To an observer on Earth the full diameter of the Sun subtends an angle of about 31.5 minutes of arc. Use this information to show that angle $\theta$ is about 24.6 arc seconds (0.00683 degrees). *Hint*: Use a proportion.

Since the radii of both the Earth and the Sun are very small compared to the distance between their centers we can capture the geometric information needed to estimate the radius of Earth's orbit in the simplified triangle diagram in Figure F, where the points have the same meaning as in Figure D. The simplification involves positioning the centers of the Earth and Sun at the midpoints of their corresponding chords rather than at the centers of the bodies. The errors introduced are negligible.

**Figure F**

**EXERCISE 5** Use the right triangle definition of the tangent function to show that the distance $a$ from Earth to Venus is given by

$$a = \frac{\text{length of } AE}{\tan \theta}$$

Assume that the distance from observer $A$ to observer $B$ is 10,000 km and use the result from Exercise 4 and this formula for $a$ to show that, during a transit, the distance from Earth to Venus is about 42,000,000 km.

It is clear from Figure F and the result of Exercise 5 that with our simplifications

$$r_e - r_v = a = 42,000,000 \tag{ii}$$

where $r_v$ = the distance from Venus to the Sun.

To get another equation we move from geometry to physics. We use Kepler's third law, first published in 1616 as an empirical result, and later derived from Newton's laws of motion and gravity. In the case of circular orbits, for two planets in orbit around the Sun, Kepler's third law states that the cube of the ratio of the orbital radii equals the square of the ratio of the orbital periods. For Earth and Venus this implies

$$\left(\frac{r_e}{r_v}\right)^3 = \left(\frac{T_e}{T_v}\right)^2 \tag{iii}$$

where $T_e$ and $T_v$ are the orbital periods of Earth and Venus, respectively.

**EXERCISE 6** Use $T_e = 365$ (Earth) days for the orbital period of Earth and $T_v = 225$ (Earth) days for the orbital period of Venus in equation (iii) to show

$$r_e = 1.381 r_v \tag{iv}$$

**EXERCISE 7** Solve the system of equations (ii) and (iv) and compare your result for the radius of Earth's orbit with your result from Exercise 3.

This completes our work on using the observations of a transit of Venus to determine the radii of the orbits of Earth and Venus. You might want to review your work on this project shortly before the next transit of Venus on June 6, 2012.

We conclude with a historical note. From centuries of observations the orbital periods of the six innermost planets were known by Kepler's time. It follows from the derivation of equation (ii) and Kepler's third law that if we can find a value for the distance between any two planets in the solar system, then we can find values for *all* of the orbital radii. The first measurement of an interplanetary distance, from Earth to Mars (not to Venus), was made almost 100 years before the transits of Venus discussed in this project. Based on a 1672 measurement of the "parallax of Mars" (the angle with vertex at the center of Mars and rays to two widely separated observers on Earth) by Cassini in Paris and Rocher in what is now French Guiana, Cassini determined a value of 140,000,000 km for the distance from Earth to the Sun. One hundred years later the expeditions for the transits of Venus significantly improved this value.

# 6.2   ALGEBRA AND THE TRIGONOMETRIC FUNCTIONS

In this section we are going to practice the algebra involved in working with the trigonometric functions. This will help to pave the way both for the applications in the next section and for some of the more analytical parts of trigonometry in the next chapter. We begin by listing some common notational conventions.

## Notational Conventions

*Albert Girard (1595–1632), who seems to have lived chiefly in Holland, . . . interested himself in spherical trigonometry and trigonometry. In 1626, he published a treatise on trigonometry that contains the earliest use of our abbreviations* sin, tan, *and* sec *for* sine, tangent, *and* secant. —Howard Eves in *An Introduction to the History of Mathematics,* 6th ed. (Philadelphia: Saunders College Publishing, 1990)

1. An expression such as $\sin \theta$ really means $\sin(\theta)$, where sin or sine is the name of the function and $\theta$ is an input. It is for historical rather than mathematical reasons that the parentheses are suppressed. An exception to this, however, occurs in expressions such as $\sin(A + B)$, where the parentheses are necessary.
2. Parentheses are often omitted in multiplication. For example, the product $(\sin \theta)(\cos \theta)$ is usually written $\sin \theta \cos \theta$. Similarly, $2(\sin \theta)$ is written $2 \sin \theta$.
3. The quantity $(\sin \theta)^n$ is usually written $\sin^n \theta$. For example, $(\sin \theta)^2$ is written $\sin^2 \theta$. The same convention also applies to the other five trigonometric functions.*

---

**EXAMPLE** | **1** | **Algebraic simplification of trigonometric expressions**

**(a)** Combine like terms: $3 \sin^2 \theta \cos \theta - 5 \sin^2 \theta \cos \theta$.
**(b)** Carry out the multiplication: $(2 \sin \theta - 3 \cos \theta)^2$.

**SOLUTION**
**(a)** We do this in the same way we would simplify the algebraic expression $3S^2C - 5S^2C$. Since

$$3S^2C - 5S^2C = -2S^2C$$

we have

$$3 \sin^2 \theta \cos \theta - 5 \sin^2 \theta \cos \theta = -2 \sin^2 \theta \cos \theta$$

**(b)** We do this in the same way that we would expand $(2S - 3C)^2$. Since

$$(2S - 3C)^2 = 4S^2 - 12SC + 9C^2$$

we have

$$(2 \sin \theta - 3 \cos \theta)^2 = 4 \sin^2 \theta - 12 \sin \theta \cos \theta + 9 \cos^2 \theta$$

---

**EXAMPLE** | **2** | **Factoring trigonometric expressions**

Factor: $\tan^2 A + 5 \tan A + 6$.

---

*A single exception to this convention occurs when $n = -1$. The meaning of the expression $\sin^{-1} x$ will be explained in Section 4 in Chapter 8.

**SOLUTION**

PRELIMINARY SOLUTION    To help us focus on the algebra that is actually involved, let's replace each occurrence of the quantity $\tan A$ by the letter $T$. Then

$$T^2 + 5T + 6 = (T + 3)(T + 2)$$

ACTUAL SOLUTION

$$\tan^2 A + 5 \tan A + 6 = (\tan A + 3)(\tan A + 2)$$

*Note*: After you are accustomed to working with trigonometric expressions, you should be able to eliminate the preliminary step.

---

**EXAMPLE   3    Simplifying trigonometric expressions**

Add: $\sin \theta + \dfrac{1}{\cos \theta}$.

**SOLUTION**

PRELIMINARY SOLUTION

$$S + \frac{1}{C} = \frac{S}{1} + \frac{1}{C} = \frac{S}{1} \cdot \frac{C}{C} + \frac{1}{C}$$

$$= \frac{SC}{C} + \frac{1}{C} = \frac{SC + 1}{C}$$

ACTUAL SOLUTION

$$\sin \theta + \frac{1}{\cos \theta} = \frac{\sin \theta}{1} + \frac{1}{\cos \theta} = \frac{\sin \theta}{1} \cdot \frac{\cos \theta}{\cos \theta} + \frac{1}{\cos \theta}$$

$$= \frac{\sin \theta \cos \theta}{\cos \theta} + \frac{1}{\cos \theta} = \frac{\sin \theta \cos \theta + 1}{\cos \theta}$$

---

There are numerous identities involving the trigonometric functions. Recall that an **identity** is an equation that is satisfied by all relevant values of the variables concerned. Two examples of identities are $(x - y)(x + y) = x^2 - y^2$ and $x^3 = x^4/x$. The first of these is true no matter what real numbers are used for $x$ and $y$; the second is true for all real numbers except $x = 0$. For now, in the context of right-triangle trigonometry, we'll consider only a few of the most basic identities.

---

**▌PROPERTY SUMMARY    Basic Right-Triangle Identities**

| Identity | Examples |
|---|---|
| 1. $\sin^2 \theta + \cos^2 \theta = 1$ | 1. $\sin^2 30° + \cos^2 30° = 1$ <br> $\sin^2 19° + \cos^2 19° = 1$ |
| 2. $\dfrac{\sin \theta}{\cos \theta} = \tan \theta$ | 2. $\dfrac{\sin 60°}{\cos 60°} = \tan 60°$ |
| 3. $\sin(90° - \theta) = \cos \theta; \quad \cos(90° - \theta) = \sin \theta$ | 3. $\sin 70° = \cos 20°; \quad \sin 20° = \cos 70°$ |
| 4. $\sec \theta = \dfrac{1}{\cos \theta}; \quad \csc \theta = \dfrac{1}{\sin \theta}; \quad \cot \theta = \dfrac{1}{\tan \theta}$ | 4. $\cot 40° = \dfrac{1}{\tan 40°}$ |

**Figure 1**

The fourth set of identities in the box follows directly from observation 3 on page 426. For the proofs of the other identities we refer to Figure 1.

**Proof That $\sin^2 \theta + \cos^2 \theta = 1$.**  Looking at Figure 1, we have $\sin \theta = a/c$ and $\cos \theta = b/c$. Thus

$$\sin^2 \theta + \cos^2 \theta = \left(\frac{a}{c}\right)^2 + \left(\frac{b}{c}\right)^2 = \frac{a^2}{c^2} + \frac{b^2}{c^2} = \frac{a^2 + b^2}{c^2}$$

$$= \frac{c^2}{c^2} \qquad \text{using } a^2 + b^2 = c^2, \text{ the Pythagorean theorem}$$

$$= 1 \qquad \text{as required.}$$

**Proof That $(\sin \theta)/(\cos \theta) = \tan \theta$.**  Again with reference to Figure 1, we have, by definition, $\sin \theta = a/c$, $\cos \theta = b/c$ and $\tan \theta = a/b$. Therefore

$$\frac{\sin \theta}{\cos \theta} = \frac{a/c}{b/c} = \frac{a}{c} \cdot \frac{c}{b}$$

$$= \frac{a}{b} = \tan \theta \qquad \text{as required.}$$

**Proof That $\sin(90° - \theta) = \cos \theta$.**  First of all, since the sum of the angles in any triangle is 180°, we have

$$\theta + \beta + 90° = 180°$$

$$\beta = 90° - \theta$$

Then $\sin(90° - \theta) = \sin \beta = b/c$. But also (by definition) $\cos \theta = b/c$. Thus

$$\sin(90° - \theta) = \cos \theta$$

since both expressions equal $b/c$. This is what we wanted to prove.

The proof that $\cos(90° - \theta) = \sin \theta$ is entirely similar, so we omit it. We can conveniently summarize these last two results by recalling the notion of complementary angles. Two acute angles are said to be **complementary** provided that their sum is 90°. Thus the two angles $\theta$ and $90° - \theta$ are complementary. In view of this, we can restate the last two results as follows:

---

If two angles are complementary, then the sine of (either) one equals the cosine of the other.

---

Incidentally, this result gives us an insight into the origin of the term "cosine": it is a shortened form of the phrase "complement's sine."

| EXAMPLE | 4 | Finding the value of a trigonometric function |

Suppose that $B$ is an acute angle and $\cos B = \frac{2}{5}$. Find $\sin B$ and $\tan B$.

**SOLUTION**
We'll show two methods. The first uses the identities $\sin^2 B + \cos^2 B = 1$ and $(\sin B)/(\cos B) = \tan B$. The second makes direct use of the Pythagorean theorem.

**First Method.** Replace $\cos B$ with $\frac{2}{5}$ in the identity $\sin^2 B + \cos^2 B = 1$. This yields

$$\sin^2 B + \left(\frac{2}{5}\right)^2 = 1$$

$$\sin^2 B = 1 - \frac{4}{25} = \frac{21}{25}$$

$$\sin B = \sqrt{\frac{21}{25}} = \frac{\sqrt{21}}{5} \qquad \text{or} \qquad \sin B = -\frac{\sqrt{21}}{5}$$

Since the sine of an acute angle is positive (see observation 4 on page 426), we choose the positive solution. It follows that

$$\sin B = \frac{\sqrt{21}}{5}$$

CAUTION  In a later section we'll extend the definitions of the trigonometric functions to include angles that are not acute. In those cases some of the trigonometric values will not be positive; we will then need to pay more attention to the matter of signs.

For $\tan B$ we have

$$\tan B = \frac{\sin B}{\cos B} = \frac{\sqrt{21}/5}{2/5} = \frac{\sqrt{21}}{2}$$

**Alternative Method.**  Since $\cos B = \dfrac{2}{5} = \dfrac{\text{adjacent}}{\text{hypotenuse}}$, we can work with a right triangle labeled as in Figure 2. Using the Pythagorean theorem, we have $2^2 + x^2 = 5^2$, from which it follows that $x = \sqrt{21}$. Consequently,

$$\sin B = \frac{\text{opposite}}{\text{hypotenuse}} = \frac{x}{5} = \frac{\sqrt{21}}{5}$$

and

$$\tan B = \frac{\text{opposite}}{\text{adjacent}} = \frac{x}{2} = \frac{\sqrt{21}}{2} \qquad \text{as obtained previously}$$

**Figure 2**

One of the many uses for the identities in this section is in simplifying trigonometric expressions. In the example that follows, we use the identity $\sin^2 A + \cos^2 A = 1$.

---

**EXAMPLE  5  Using identities to simplify trigonometric expressions**

Combine and simplify: $\dfrac{\sin A}{\cos A} + \dfrac{\cos A}{\sin A}$.

**SOLUTION**

The common denominator is $\cos A \sin A$. Therefore we have

$$\frac{\sin A}{\cos A} + \frac{\cos A}{\sin A} = \frac{\sin A}{\cos A} \cdot \frac{\sin A}{\sin A} + \frac{\cos A}{\sin A} \cdot \frac{\cos A}{\cos A}$$

$$= \frac{\sin^2 A}{\cos A \sin A} + \frac{\cos^2 A}{\sin A \cos A}$$

$$= \frac{\sin^2 A + \cos^2 A}{\cos A \sin A}$$

$$= \frac{1}{\cos A \sin A}$$

This is the required result. If we wish, we can write this answer in an alternative form that doesn't involve fractions:

$$\frac{1}{\cos A \sin A} = \frac{1}{\cos A} \cdot \frac{1}{\sin A} = \sec A \csc A$$

One of the most useful techniques for simplifying a trigonometric expression is first to rewrite the expression in terms of sines and cosines and then to carry out appropriate algebraic simplifications. This is demonstrated in Examples 6 through 8.

---

**EXAMPLE 6 Simplifying trigonometric expressions**

Express in terms of sines and cosines and simplify the expression

$$\csc A \tan A \cos^2 A$$

**SOLUTION**

$$\csc A \tan A \cos^2 A = \frac{1}{\overset{\,}{\underset{1}{\sin A}}} \cdot \frac{\overset{1}{\sin A}}{\cos A} \cdot \cos^2 A$$

$$= \frac{\cos^2 A}{\cos A} = \cos A$$

---

**EXAMPLE 7 Simplifying trigonometric expressions**

Simplify the expression $\dfrac{1 - \tan^2 B}{1 + \tan^2 B}$.

**SOLUTION**

$$\frac{1 - \tan^2 B}{1 + \tan^2 B} = \frac{1 - \dfrac{\sin^2 B}{\cos^2 B}}{1 + \dfrac{\sin^2 B}{\cos^2 B}} \qquad \text{Since } \tan B = (\sin B)/(\cos B), \text{ it follows that } \tan^2 B = (\sin^2 B)/(\cos^2 B).$$

$$= \frac{(\cos^2 B)\left(1 - \dfrac{\sin^2 B}{\cos^2 B}\right)}{(\cos^2 B)\left(1 + \dfrac{\sin^2 B}{\cos^2 B}\right)} \qquad \text{multiplying both the numerator and the denominator by } \cos^2 B$$

$$= \frac{\cos^2 B - \sin^2 B}{\cos^2 B + \sin^2 B}$$

$$= \frac{\cos^2 B - \sin^2 B}{1} = \cos^2 B - \sin^2 B$$

  **EXAMPLE** 8 **Simplifying trigonometric expressions**

Express in terms of sines and cosines and simplify the expression $\dfrac{\tan(90° - A)}{\cos A \sin A}$.

**SOLUTION**

$$\frac{\tan(90° - A)}{\cos A \sin A} = \frac{\dfrac{\sin(90° - A)}{\cos(90° - A)}}{\cos A \sin A} \qquad \text{applying the identity } \tan \theta = (\sin \theta)/(\cos \theta)$$

$$= \frac{\dfrac{\cos A}{\sin A}}{\cos A \sin A} \qquad \text{(Why?)}$$

$$= \frac{\cos A}{\sin A} \cdot \frac{1}{\cos A \sin A} = \frac{1}{\sin^2 A}$$

The given expression is therefore equal to $1/\sin^2 A$. We can also write this as $\csc^2 A$.

# EXERCISE SET 6.2

**A**

*In Exercises 1–12, carry out the indicated operations.*

**1. (a)** $-SC + 12SC$
   **(b)** $-\sin \theta \cos \theta + 12 \sin \theta \cos \theta$

**2. (a)** $10SC + 4SC - 16SC$
   **(b)** $10 \sin \theta \cos \theta + 4 \sin \theta \cos \theta - 16 \sin \theta \cos \theta$

**3. (a)** $4C^3 S - 12C^3 S$
   **(b)** $4 \cos^3 \theta \sin \theta - 12 \cos^3 \theta \sin \theta$

**4. (a)** $-C^2 S^2 + (2SC)^2$
   **(b)** $-\cos^2 \theta \sin^2 \theta + (2 \sin \theta \cos \theta)^2$

**5. (a)** $(1 + T)^2$
   **(b)** $(1 + \tan \theta)^2$

**6. (a)** $(3 - 2T)^2$
   **(b)** $(3 - 2 \tan \theta)^2$

**7. (a)** $(T + 3)(T - 2)$
   **(b)** $(\tan \theta + 3)(\tan \theta - 2)$

**8. (a)** $(S^2 - 3)(S^2 + 3)$
   **(b)** $(\sec^2 \theta - 3)(\sec^2 \theta + 3)$

**9. (a)** $\dfrac{S - C}{C - S}$
   **(b)** $\dfrac{\sin \theta - \cos \theta}{\cos \theta - \sin \theta}$

**10. (a)** $\dfrac{5 - 2T}{2T - 5}$
   **(b)** $\dfrac{5 - 2 \tan \theta}{2 \tan \theta - 5}$

**11. (a)** $C + \dfrac{2}{S}$

**(b)** $\cos A + \dfrac{2}{\sin A}$

**12. (a)** $\dfrac{1}{S} - \dfrac{3}{C}$

**(b)** $\dfrac{1}{\sin A} - \dfrac{3}{\cos A}$

*In Exercises 13–18, factor each expression.*

**13. (a)** $T^2 + 8T - 9$

**(b)** $\tan^2 \beta + 8 \tan \beta - 9$

**15. (a)** $4C^2 - 1$

**(b)** $4 \cos^2 B - 1$

**17. (a)** $9S^2 T^3 + 6ST^2$

**(b)** $9 \sec^2 B \tan^3 B + 6 \sec B \tan^2 B$

**18. (a)** $5C^2 c^2 - 15Cc.$

**(b)** $5 \csc^2 B \cot^2 B - 15 \csc B \cot B$

**14. (a)** $3S^2 + 2S - 8$

**(b)** $3 \sec^2 \beta + 2 \sec \beta - 8$

**16. (a)** $16S^3 - 9S^2$

**(b)** $16 \sin^3 B - 9 \sin^2 B$

*In Exercises 19–30, use the given information to determine the values of the remaining five trigonometric functions. (Assume that all of the angles are acute.) When radicals appear in a denominator, rationalize the denominator. In Exercises 19–24, use either of the methods shown in Example 4. In Exercises 25–30, use the second method shown in Example 4.*

**19.** $\sin \theta - 3/4$

**20.** $\sin \theta = 2/5$

**21.** $\cos \beta = \sqrt{3}/5$

**22.** $\cos \beta = \sqrt{7}/3$

**23.** $\sin A = 5/13$

**24.** $\cos A = 8/17$

**25.** $\tan B = 4/3$

**26.** $\tan B = 5$

**27.** $\sec C = 3/2$

**28.** $\csc C = \sqrt{5}/2$

**29.** $\cot \alpha = \sqrt{3}/3$

**30.** $\cot \alpha - \sqrt{3}/2$

*In Exercises 31–34, use the first method shown in Example 4 and a calculator to determine the values of the remaining five trigonometric functions. (In each case, $\theta$ denotes an acute angle.) Round the final answers to three decimal places.*

**31.** $\cos \theta = 0.4626$

**32.** $\sin \theta = 0.5917$

**33.** $\tan \theta - 1.1998$

**34.** $\sec \theta - 2.3283$

*In Exercises 35–56, write in terms of sine and cosine and simplify each expression.*

**35.** $\dfrac{\sin^2 A - \cos^2 A}{\sin A - \cos A}$    *Hint*: Factor the numerator.

**36.** $\dfrac{\sin^4 A - \cos^4 A}{\cos A - \sin A}$

**37.** $\sin^2 \theta \cos \theta \csc^3 \theta \sec \theta$

**38.** $\sin \theta \csc \theta \tan \theta$

**39.** $\cot B \sin^2 B \cot B$

**40.** $\dfrac{3 \sin \theta + 6}{\sin^2 \theta - 4}$

**41.** $\dfrac{\cos^2 A + \cos A - 12}{\cos A - 3}$

**42.** $\dfrac{\cos A - 2 \sin A \cos A}{\cos^2 A - \sin^2 A + \sin A - 1}$

**43.** $\dfrac{\tan \theta}{\sec \theta - 1} + \dfrac{\tan \theta}{\sec \theta + 1}$

**44.** $\cot \theta + \dfrac{1 - 2 \cos^2 \theta}{\sin \theta \cos \theta}$

**45.** $\sec A \csc A - \tan A - \cot A$

**46.** $(\sec A + \tan A)(\sec A - \tan A)$

**47.** $\dfrac{\cot^2 \theta}{\csc^2 \theta} + \dfrac{\tan^2 \theta}{\sec^2 \theta}$

**48.** $\dfrac{\tan \theta + \tan \theta \sin \theta - \cos \theta \sin \theta}{\sin \theta \tan \theta}$

**49.** $\dfrac{\cos(90° - \theta)}{\cos \theta}$

**50.** $\sin^2(90° - \beta) + \cos^2(90° - \beta)$

**51.** $\dfrac{\cos^2(90° - A)}{\sin^2(90° - A)} - \dfrac{1}{\cos^2 A}$

**52.** $\dfrac{\cos(90° - A)}{\csc A} + \dfrac{\sin(90° - A)}{\sec A}$

**53.** $1 - \sin(90° - \theta)\cos \theta$

**54.** $\dfrac{\cos A \tan A}{\tan(90° - A)} - \dfrac{1}{\sin(90° - A)}$

**55.** $\dfrac{\dfrac{\cos \theta + 1}{\cos \theta} + 1}{\dfrac{\cos \theta - 1}{\cos \theta} - 1}$

**56.** $\dfrac{\dfrac{\cot \beta + 1}{\cot \beta} + 1}{\dfrac{\cot \beta - 1}{\cot \beta} - 1}$

**B**

**57.** Suppose that

$$A \sin \theta + \cos \theta = 1 \quad \text{and} \quad B \sin \theta - \cos \theta = 1$$

Show that $AB = 1$.    *Hint*: Solve the first equation for $A$, the second for $B$, and then compute $AB$.

**58.** If $\sin \alpha + \cos \alpha = a$ and $\sin \alpha - \cos \alpha = b$, show that

$$\tan \alpha = \frac{a + b}{a - b}$$

**59.** If $a \sin^2 \theta + b \cos^2 \theta = 1$, show that

$$\sin^2 \theta = \frac{1 - b}{a - b} \quad \text{and} \quad \tan^2 \theta = \frac{b - 1}{1 - a}$$

**60.** This exercise shows how to obtain radical expressions for $\sin 18°$ and $\cos 18°$, using the following figure.

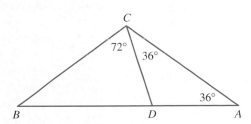

**(a)** Find $\angle B$, $\angle BDC$, and $\angle ADC$.

**(b)** Why does $AC = BC = BD$?

*For the rest of this problem, assume that $AD = 1$.*

**(c)** Why does $CD = 1$?

**(d)** Let $x$ denote the common lengths $AC$, $BC$, and $BD$. Use similar triangles to deduce that $x/(1 + x) = 1/x$. Then show that $x = (1 + \sqrt{5})/2$.

**(e)** In $\triangle BDC$, draw an altitude from $B$ to $\overline{DC}$, meeting $\overline{DC}$ at $F$. Use right triangle $BFC$ to conclude that $\sin 18° = 1/(1 + \sqrt{5})$.

**(f)** Rationalize the denominator in part (e) to obtain $\sin 18° = \tfrac{1}{4}(\sqrt{5} - 1)$.

*(continues)*

**(g)** Use the identity $\sin^2 \theta + \cos^2 \theta = 1$, along with part (f), to show that

$$\cos 18° = \frac{1}{4}\sqrt{10 + 2\sqrt{5}}$$

**(h)** Use your calculator to check the results in parts (f) and (g).

*Note*: In the project at the end of this section the result in part (f) is used as the basis for a compass and straightedge construction of a regular pentagon.

**61.** Suppose that $\beta$ is an acute angle and

$$\sin \beta = \frac{m^2 - n^2}{m^2 + n^2} \qquad (m > n > 0)$$

Show that

$$\cos \beta = \frac{2mn}{m^2 + n^2} \qquad \text{and} \qquad \tan \beta = \frac{m^2 - n^2}{2mn}$$

## PROJECT

## CONSTRUCTING A REGULAR PENTAGON

This is intended as a group project to create a poster explaining a compass and straightedge construction of a regular pentagon. (Recall that *regular* means that all of the sides are equal and all of the angles are equal.) In the first part you are going to construct a regular pentagon by first constructing a regular decagon and then connecting every other vertex. The second part asks you to write a short paper explaining why the construction is valid. Although the construction given here is somewhat awkward, its justification is fairly straightforward. In the Writing Mathematics section at the end of Chapter 8 a shorter and more elegant construction is described. The third part provides some history of the construction of regular *n*-gons.

**(a)** As background you should review the ruler and compass construction for the perpendicular bisector of a line segment. The construction proceeds as follows.

Draw a line segment, and label the endpoints $A$ and $D$. Construct the perpendicular bisector, and denote the midpoint of $AD$ by $C$. Set your compass to the length of $AC$, which is 1 unit for this construction, and mark a point two units from $C$ along the perpendicular bisector. Label this point $B$, and draw the line segment $AB$. With your compass still set to the length of $AC$, draw a unit circle somewhere away from triangle $ABC$. Set the needle tip of your compass at $B$, and let $E$ denote the point on $AB$ that is 1 unit from $B$. Bisect the line segment $AE$, and label the midpoint $F$. The length of $AF$ will be one side of a regular decagon inscribed in the unit circle. Mark ten consecutive points around the unit circle spaced this distance apart. These are the vertices of a regular decagon. Connecting every other vertex completes this construction of a regular pentagon.

**(b)** As background for this part you should review parts (a) though (f) of Exercise 60 in Exercise Set 6.2. To complete this part of the project, write a careful justification for the construction described in part (a). You should use a mixture of English sentences, equations, and figures similar to the exposition in this textbook. A brief sketch of the beginning of a justification follows:

It is straightforward to show that the line segment $AF$ described in part (a) has length $(\sqrt{5} - 1)/2$. From Exercise 60(f) in Section 6.2, $\sin 18° = (\sqrt{5} - 1)/4$. This implies, in a few steps, that an isosceles triangle with two sides of length 1 and the third side of length $(\sqrt{5} - 1)/2$ has a vertex angle of 36°.

**(c)** Carl Friedrich Gauss (1777–1855) was one of the greatest mathematicians in history. In the last section of his great work on number theory, *Disquisitiones Arithmeticae,* published in 1801, he discusses the problem of constructing regular $n$-gons. He first deals with regular polygons with a prime number, $p$, of sides and proves that if $p$ is of the form $p = 2^{2^k} + 1$, where $k$ is a nonnegative integer, then a regular $p$-gon is constructible, that is, can be constructed using a compass and straightedge. Then he gives an explicit construction for a regular 17-gon. In the quotation to the left Gauss warns the reader that a regular $p$-gon is *not* constructible if $p$ is not a prime of the form $p = 2^{2^k} + 1$ but that the limits of the book do not allow him to present the proof. The first published proof was by Pierre L. Wantzel in 1837. The numbers $F_k = 2^{2^k} + 1$ are called Fermat numbers after Pierre de Fermat (1601–1665). $F_0$ through $F_4$ are prime, but it remains an open problem as to whether or not there are any other *prime* Fermat numbers. Gauss also notes that constructions for regular polygons with 3, 4, 5, and 15 sides and those that are easily constructed from these, with $2^m \cdot 3$, $2^m \cdot 4$, $2^m \cdot 5$, or $2^m \cdot 15$ sides, for $m$ a positive integer, were known since Euclid's time but that no new constructible polygons had been found for 2000 years (until his discoveries of 1796).

*WE CAN SHOW WITH ALL RIGOR THAT THESE HIGHER-DEGREE EQUATIONS CANNOT BE AVOIDED IN ANY WAY NOR CAN THEY BE REDUCED TO LOWER-DEGREE EQUATIONS. The limits of the present work exclude this demonstration here, but we issue this warning lest anyone attempt to achieve geometric constructions for sections other than the one suggested by our theory (e.g. sections into 7, 11, 13, 19, etc. parts) and so spend his time uselessly.*
—Carl Friedrich Gauss in *Disquisitions Arithmeticae,* 1801. [Translation by Arthur A. Clarke, S. J. (New Haven and London: Yale University Press, 1966)]

Assuming a regular $n$-gon is constructible, explain why a regular polygon of $2^m \cdot n$ sides, where $m$ is a positive integer, is constructible.

Gauss's *Disquisitiones Arithmeticae* consists of 366 numbered articles separated into seven sections. In the last article he makes a statement equivalent to the assertion that a regular polygon of $n$ sides is constructible if and only if

$$n = 2^k p_1 p_2 \cdots p_l$$

where $p_1, p_2, \ldots, p_l$ are distinct (no two are equal) prime Fermat numbers and $k$ is a nonnegative integer. He finishes the article with a list of the 37 constructible regular polygons with 300 or fewer sides.

List the 12 constructible regular polygons with 25 or fewer sides. When you finish, you might try to find the 25 remaining constructible regular polygons with 300 or fewer sides, thus completing Gauss's list.

## 6.3 RIGHT-TRIANGLE APPLICATIONS

We began this chapter in Section 6.1 by defining the six trigonometric functions of an acute angle $\theta$. Then in Section 6.2 we looked at some of the algebra that is involved in working with the trigonometric functions. Now we are ready to apply these ideas in solving some basic problems involving right triangles.

**Figure 1**

| EXAMPLE | 1 | **Using trigonometric functions to find a side in a right triangle** |

Use one of the trigonometric functions to find $x$ in Figure 1.

**SOLUTION**
Relative to the given 30° angle, $x$ is the adjacent side. The length of the hypotenuse is 100 cm. Since the adjacent side and the hypotenuse are involved, we use the cosine function here:

$$\cos 30° = \frac{\text{adjacent}}{\text{hypotenuse}} = \frac{x}{100}$$

Consequently,

$$x = 100 \cos 30° = (100) \cdot (\sqrt{3}/2) = 50\sqrt{3} \text{ cm}$$

This is the result we are looking for.

We used the cosine function in Example 1 because the adjacent side and the hypotenuse were involved. We could instead use the secant. In that case, again with reference to Figure 1, the calculations look like this:

$$\sec 30° = \frac{\text{hypotenuse}}{\text{adjacent}} = \frac{100}{x}$$

$$\frac{2}{\sqrt{3}} = \frac{100}{x}$$

$$2x = 100\sqrt{3}$$

$$x = \frac{100\sqrt{3}}{2} = 50\sqrt{3} \text{ cm} \qquad \text{as was obtained previously}$$

| EXAMPLE | 2 | **Using trigonometric functions to find a side in a right triangle** |

Find $y$ in Figure 1.

**SOLUTION**
As you can see from Figure 1, the side of length $y$ is opposite the 30° angle. Furthermore, we are given the length of the hypotenuse. Since the opposite side and the hypotenuse are involved, we use the sine function. This yields

$$\sin 30° = \frac{\text{opposite}}{\text{hypotenuse}} = \frac{y}{100}$$

and therefore

$$y = 100 \sin 30° = (100) \cdot (1/2) = 50 \text{ cm}$$

This is the required answer. Actually, we could have obtained this particular result much faster by recalling that in the 30°–60° right triangle, the side opposite the 30° angle, namely, $y$, is half of the hypotenuse. That is $y = 100/2 = 50$ cm, as was obtained previously.

**EXAMPLE** **3** **A right-triangle application**

A ladder that is leaning against the side of a building forms an angle of 50° with the ground. If the foot of the ladder is 12 ft from the base of the building, how far up the side of the building does the ladder reach? See Figure 2.

**SOLUTION**
In Figure 2 we have used $y$ to denote the required distance. Notice that $y$ is opposite the 50° angle, while the given side is adjacent to that angle. Since the opposite and adjacent sides are involved, we'll use the tangent function. (The cotangent function could also be used.) We have

$$\tan 50° = \frac{y}{12} \quad \text{and therefore} \quad y = 12 \tan 50°$$

Without the use of a calculator or tables, this is our final answer. On the other hand, using a calculator, we find that $y = 14$ ft, to the nearest foot.

**Figure 2**

In the next example we derive a useful formula for the area of a triangle. The formula can be used when we are given two sides and the included angle but not the height.

**EXAMPLE** **4** **A trigonometric formula for the area of a triangle**

Show that the area of the triangle in Figure 3 is given by

$$A = \frac{1}{2}ab \sin \theta$$

**SOLUTION**
In Figure 3, if $h$ denotes the length of the altitude, then we have

$$\sin \theta = \frac{h}{a} \quad \text{and therefore} \quad h = a \sin \theta$$

This value for $h$ can now be used in the usual formula for the area of a triangle:

$$A = \frac{1}{2}bh = \frac{1}{2}b(a \sin \theta) = \frac{1}{2}ab \sin \theta$$

**Figure 3**

The formula that we just derived in Example 4 is worth remembering. In words, the formula states that *the area of a triangle is equal to half the product of the lengths of two of the sides times the sine of the included acute angle.* In Section 6.4 we will see that the formula remains valid even when the included angle is not an acute angle.

Figure 4

Figure 5

**EXAMPLE 5** Using the trigonometric formula to find the area of a triangle

Find the area of the triangle in Figure 4.

**SOLUTION**
From Example 4 the area is given by the formula $A = \frac{1}{2}ab \sin \theta$. Here we let $a = 3$ cm, $b = 12$ cm, and $\theta = 60°$. Then

$$A = \frac{1}{2}(3)(12) \sin 60° = (18)\frac{\sqrt{3}}{2}$$
$$= 9\sqrt{3} \text{ cm}^2$$

This is the required area.

**EXAMPLE 6** The area of a regular pentagon

Figure 5 shows a regular pentagon inscribed in a circle of radius 2 in. (*Regular* means that all of the sides are equal and all of the angles are equal.) Find the area of the pentagon.

**SOLUTION**
The idea here is first to find the area of triangle *BOA* by using the area formula from Example 4. Then, since the pentagon is composed of five such identical triangles, the area of the pentagon will be five times the area of triangle *BOA*. We will make use of the result from geometry that, in a regular *n*-sided polygon, the central angle is $360°/n$. In our case we therefore have

$$\angle BOA = \frac{360°}{5} = 72°$$

We can now find the area of triangle *BOA*:

$$\text{area} = \frac{1}{2}ab \sin \theta$$
$$= \frac{1}{2}(2)(2)\sin 72° = 2 \sin 72° \text{ in.}^2$$

The area of the pentagon is five times this, or $10 \sin 72°$ in.$^2$. (Using a calculator, this is about 9.51 in.$^2$. )

Now we introduce some terminology that will be used in the next two examples. Suppose that a surveyor sights an object at a point above the horizontal, as indicated in Figure 6(a). Then the angle between the line of sight and the horizontal is called the **angle of elevation**. The **angle of depression** is similarly defined for an object below the horizontal, as shown in Figure 6(b).

Figure 6                    (a)                    (b)

---

**EXAMPLE** **7** **Using the angle of depression to find a distance**

A helicopter hovers 800 ft directly above a small island that is off the California coast. From the helicopter the pilot takes a sighting to a point $P$ directly ashore on the mainland, at the water's edge. If the angle of depression is 35°, how far off the coast is the island? See Figure 7.

Figure 7

**SOLUTION**

Let $x$ denote the distance from the island to the mainland. Then, as you can see from Figure 7, we have $\theta + 35° = 90°$, from which it follows that $\theta = 55°$. Now we can write

$$\tan 55° = \frac{x}{800}$$

or

$$x = 800 \tan 55° \approx 1150 \text{ ft} \qquad \text{using a calculator and rounding to the nearest 50 feet}$$

**EXAMPLE** 8 **Finding the altitude of a satellite**

Two satellite-tracking stations, located at points $A$ and $B$ in California's Mojave Desert, are 200 miles apart. At a prearranged time, both stations measure the angle of elevation of a satellite as it crosses the vertical plane containing $A$ and $B$. This means that $A$, $B$, and $S$ lie in a plane perpendicular to the ground. (See Figure 8.) If the angles of elevation from $A$ and from $B$ are $\alpha$ and $\beta$, respectively, express the altitude $h$ of the satellite in terms of $\alpha$ and $\beta$.

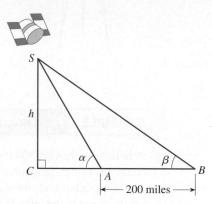

Figure 8

**SOLUTION**
We want to express the length $h = SC$ in Figure 8 in terms of the angles $\alpha$ and $\beta$. Note that $\overline{SC}$ is a side of both of the right triangles $SCA$ and $SCB$. Working first in the right triangle $SCB$, we have

$$\cot \beta = \frac{CA + 200}{h}$$

or

$$h \cot \beta = CA + 200 \qquad (1)$$

We can eliminate $CA$ from equation (1) as follows. Looking at right triangle $SCA$, we have

$$\cot \alpha = \frac{CA}{h} \qquad \text{and thus} \qquad CA = h \cot \alpha$$

Using this last equation to substitute for $CA$ in equation (1), we obtain

$$h \cot \beta = h \cot \alpha + 200$$
$$h \cot \beta - h \cot \alpha = 200$$
$$h(\cot \beta - \cot \alpha) = 200$$
$$h = \frac{200}{\cot \beta - \cot \alpha} \text{ miles} \qquad \text{as required}$$

| EXAMPLE | 9 | Expressing lengths and area using trigonometric functions |

The arc shown in Figure 9 is a portion of the unit circle, $x^2 + y^2 = 1$. Express the following quantities in terms of $\theta$:

**(a)** $OA$;     **(b)** $AB$;     **(c)** $OC$;     **(d)** The area of $\triangle OAC$.

**SOLUTION**
**(a)** In right triangle $OAB$,

$$\cos\theta = \frac{OA}{OB} = \frac{OA}{1}$$
$$OA = \cos\theta$$

**(b)** In right triangle $OAB$,

$$\sin\theta = \frac{AB}{OB} = \frac{AB}{1}$$
$$AB = \sin\theta$$

**(c)** In right triangle $OAC$, we have $\cos\theta = OC/OA$, and therefore

$$OC = OA\cos\theta = (\cos\theta)(\cos\theta) = \cos^2\theta$$

**(d)** area $\triangle OAC = \frac{1}{2}(OA)(OC)(\sin\theta)$     using the formula area $= \frac{1}{2}ab\sin\theta$

$= \frac{1}{2}(\cos\theta)(\cos^2\theta)(\sin\theta)$     using the results from parts (a) and (c)

$= \frac{1}{2}\cos^3\theta\sin\theta$

**Figure 9**

# EXERCISE SET 6.3

**A**

*For Exercises 1–6, refer to the following figure. (However, each problem is independent of the others.)*

**1.** If $\angle A = 30°$ and $AB = 60$ cm, find $AC$ and $BC$.
**2.** If $\angle A = 60°$ and $AB = 12$ cm, find $AC$ and $BC$.
**3.** If $\angle B = 60°$ and $AC = 16$ cm, find $BC$ and $AB$.
**4.** If $\angle B = 45°$ and $AC = 9$ cm, find $BC$ and $AB$.

**5.** If $\angle B = 50°$ and $AB = 15$ cm, find $BC$ and $AC$. (Round your answers to one decimal place.)
**6.** If $\angle A = 25°$ and $AC = 100$ cm, find $BC$ and $AB$. (Round your answers to one decimal place.)
**7.** A ladder 18 ft long leans against a building. The ladder forms an angle of 60° with the ground.
   **(a)** How high up the side of the building does the ladder reach? [Here and in part (b), give two forms for your answers: one with radicals and one (using a calculator) with decimals, rounded to two places.]
   **(b)** Find the horizontal distance from the foot of the ladder to the base of the building.
**8.** From a point level with and 1000 ft away from the base of the Washington Monument, the angle of elevation to the top of the monument is 29.05°. Determine the height of the monument to the nearest half foot.

**9.** Refer to the following figure. At certain times, the planets Earth and Mercury line up in such a way that $\angle EMS$ is a right angle. At such times, $\angle SEM$ is found to be 21.16°. Use this information to estimate the distance $MS$ of Mercury from the Sun. Assume that the distance from the Earth to the Sun is 93 million miles. (Round your answer to the nearest million miles. Because Mercury's orbit is not really circular, the actual distance of Mercury from the Sun varies from about 28 million miles to 43 million miles.)

**10.** Determine the distance $AB$ across the lake shown in the figure, using the following data: $AC = 400$ m, $\angle C = 90°$, and $\angle CAB = 40°$. Round the answer to the nearest meter.

**11.** A building contractor wants to put a fence around the perimeter of a flat lot that has the shape of a right triangle. One angle of the triangle is 41.4°, and the length of the hypotenuse is 58.5 m. Find the length of fencing required. Round the answer to one decimal place.

**12.** Suppose that the contractor in Exercise 11 reviews his notes and finds that it is not the hypotenuse that is 58.5 m but rather the side opposite the 41.4° angle. Find the length of fencing required in this case. Again, round the answer to one decimal place.

*For Exercises 13 and 14, refer to the following diagram for the roof of a house. In the figure, x is the length of a rafter measured from the top of a wall to the top of the roof; θ is the acute angle between a rafter and the horizontal; and h is the vertical distance from the top of the wall to the top of the roof.*

**13.** Suppose that $\theta = 39.4°$ and $x = 43.0$ ft.
   **(a)** Determine $h$. Round the answer to one decimal place.
   **(b)** The *gable* is the triangular region bounded by the rafters and the attic floor. Find the area of the gable. Round the final answer to one decimal place.

**14.** Suppose that $\theta = 34°$ and $h = 36.5$ ft.
   **(a)** Determine $x$. Round the answer to one decimal place.
   **(b)** Find the area of the gable. Round the final answer to one decimal place. [See Exercise 13(b) for the definition of gable.]

*In Exercises 15 and 16, find the area of the triangle. In Exercise 16, use a calculator and round the final answer to two decimal places.*

**15.**    **16.**

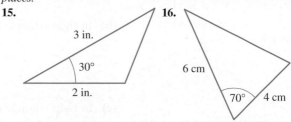

*In Exercises 17–22, determine the area of the shaded region, given that the radius of the circle is 1 unit and the inscribed polygon is a regular polygon. Give two forms for each answer: an expression involving radicals or the trigonometric functions; a calculator approximation rounded to three decimal places.*

**17.**    **18.**

**19.**    **20.**

**21.**    **22.**

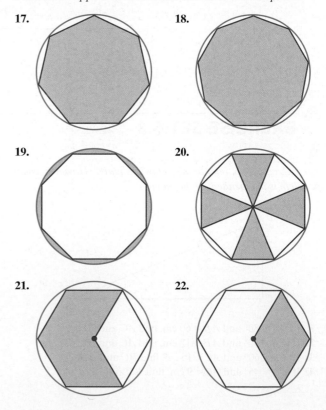

23. Show that the perimeter of the pentagon in Example 6 is 20 sin 36°. *Hint:* In Figure 5, draw a perpendicular from $O$ to $\overline{AB}$.

24. In triangle $OAB$, lengths $OA = OB = 6$ in. and $\angle AOB = 72°$. Find $AB$. *Hint:* Draw a perpendicular from $O$ to $AB$. Round the answer to one decimal place.

25. The accompanying figure shows two ships at points $P$ and $Q$, which are in the same vertical plane as an airplane at point $R$. When the height of the airplane is 3500 ft, the angle of depression to $P$ is 48°, and that to $Q$ is 25°. Find the distance between the two ships. Round the answer to the nearest 10 feet.

26. An observer in a lighthouse is 66 ft above the surface of the water. The observer sees a ship and finds the angle of depression to be 0.7°. Estimate the distance of the ship from the base of the lighthouse. Round the answer to the nearest 5 feet.

27. From a point on ground level, you measure the angle of elevation to the top of a mountain to be 38°. Then you walk 200 m farther away from the mountain and find that the angle of elevation is now 20°. Find the height of the mountain. Round the answer to the nearest meter.

28. A surveyor stands 30 yd from the base of a building. On top of the building is a vertical radio antenna. Let $\alpha$ denote the angle of elevation when the surveyor sights to the top of the building. Let $\beta$ denote the angle of elevation when the surveyor sights to the top of the antenna. Express the length of the antenna in terms of the angles $\alpha$ and $\beta$.

29. In $\triangle ACD$, you are given $\angle C = 90°$, $\angle A = 60°$, and $AC = 18$ cm. If $B$ is a point on $\overline{CD}$ and $\angle BAC = 45°$, find $BD$. Express the answer in terms of a radical (rather than using a calculator).

30. The radius of the circle in the following figure is 1 unit. Express the lengths $OA$, $AB$, and $DC$ in terms of $\alpha$.

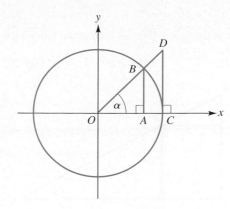

31. The arc in the next figure is a portion of the unit circle, $x^2 + y^2 = 1$.
    (a) Express the following angles in terms of $\theta$: $\angle BOA$, $\angle OAB$, $\angle BAP$, $\angle BPA$. (Assume that $\theta$ is in degrees.)
    (b) Express the following lengths in terms of $\sin \theta$ and $\cos \theta$: $AO$, $AP$, $OB$, $BP$.

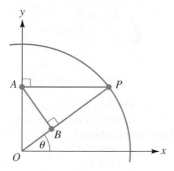

32. In the following figure, suppose that $AD = 1$. Find the length of each of the other line segments in the figure. When radicals appear in an answer, leave the answer in that form rather than using a calculator.

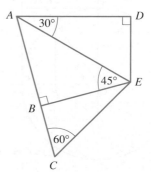

## B

**33.** Refer to the figure. Express each of the following lengths as a function of $\theta$.

   **(a)** $BC$          **(b)** $AB$          **(c)** $AC$

**34.** In the following figure, $AB = 8$ in. Express $x$ as a function of $\theta$.   *Hint:* First work Exercise 33.

**35.** In the figure, line segment $\overline{BA}$ is tangent to the unit circle at $A$. Also, $\overline{CF}$ is tangent to the circle at $F$. Express the following lengths in terms of $\theta$.

   **(a)** $DE$          **(c)** $CF$          **(e)** $AB$

   **(b)** $OE$          **(d)** $OC$          **(f)** $OB$

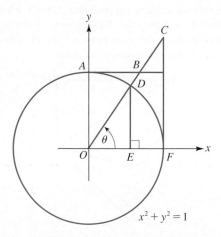

$$x^2 + y^2 = 1$$

**36.** At point $P$ on Earth's surface, the moon is observed to be directly overhead, while at the same time at point $T$, the moon is just visible. See the following figure.

   **(a)** Show that $MP = \dfrac{OT}{\cos \theta} - OP$.

   **(b)** Use a calculator and the following data to estimate the distance $MP$ from the earth to the moon: $\theta = 89.05°$

and $OT = OP = 4000$ miles. Round your answer to the nearest thousand miles. (Because the moon's orbit is not really circular, the actual distance varies from about 216,400 miles to 247,000 miles.)

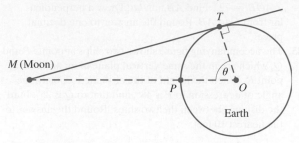

**37.** Refer to the figure below. Let $r$ denote the radius of the moon.

   **(a)** Show that $r = \left( \dfrac{\sin \theta}{1 - \sin \theta} \right) PS.$

   **(b)** Use a calculator and the following data to estimate the radius $r$ of the moon: $PS = 238{,}857$ miles and $\theta = 0.257°$. Round your answer to the nearest 10 miles.

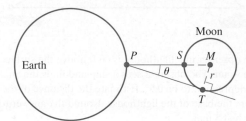

**38.** Figure A shows a regular hexagon inscribed in a circle of radius 1. Figure B shows a regular heptagon (seven-sided polygon) inscribed in a circle of radius 1. In Figure A, a line segment drawn from the center of the circle perpendicular to one of the sides is called an **apothem** of the polygon.

   **Figure A**             **Figure B**

   **(a)** Show that the length of the apothem in Figure A is $\sqrt{3}/2$.

   **(b)** Show that the length of one side of the heptagon in Figure B is $2 \sin(180°/7)$.

   **(c)** Use a calculator to evaluate the expressions in parts (a) and (b). Round each answer to four decimal places, and note how close the two values are. Approximately two thousand years ago, Heron of Alexandria made use of this coincidence when he used the length of the apothem of the hexagon to approximate the length of the side of the heptagon. (The apothem of the hexagon can be constructed with ruler and compass; the side of the regular heptagon cannot.)

**39. (a)** Using right triangles, show that the area of a regular $n$-gon inscribed in a circle of radius 1 unit is given by

$$A_n = n \sin \frac{180°}{n} \cos \frac{180°}{n}$$

**(b)** Using the area formula from Example 4, again show that the area of a regular $n$-gon inscribed in a circle of radius 1 unit is given by

$$A_n = \frac{n}{2} \sin \frac{360°}{n}$$

*Comment*: The results in (a) and (b) imply an interesting "double-angle formula" that we will discuss in Section 8.4.

**(c)** Use the formula in part (b) and a calculator to complete the following table.

| $n$ | 5 | 10 | 50 | 100 | 1000 | 5000 | 10,000 |
|-----|---|----|----|-----|------|------|--------|
| $A_n$ | | | | | | | |

**(d)** Explain why the successive values of $A_n$ in your table get closer and closer to $\pi$.

**40.** The figure shows a regular pentagon and a regular hexagon, with a common side of length 2 cm. Compute the area within the hexagon but outside of the pentagon. Round the answer to two decimal places.

2 cm

**C**

**41.** In the accompanying figure, the smaller circle is tangent to the larger circle. Ray $PQ$ is a common tangent and ray $PR$ passes through the centers of both circles. If the radius of the smaller circle is $a$ and the radius of the larger circle is $b$, show that $\sin \theta = (b - a)/(a + b)$. Then, using the identity $\sin^2 \theta + \cos^2 \theta = 1$, show that $\cos \theta = 2\sqrt{ab}/(a + b)$.

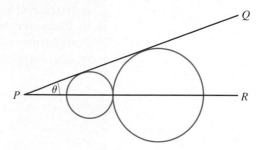

**42.** A vertical tower of height $h$ stands on level ground. From a point $P$ at ground level and due south of the tower, the angle of elevation to the top of the tower is $\theta$. From a point $Q$ at ground level and due west of the tower, the angle of elevation to the top of the tower is $\beta$. If $d$ is the distance between $P$ and $Q$, show that

$$h = \frac{d}{\sqrt{\cot^2 \theta + \cot^2 \beta}}$$

**43.** The following problem is taken from *An Elementary Treatise on Plane Trigonometry*, 8th ed., by R. D. Beasley (London: Macmillan and Co.; first published in 1884):

The [angle of] elevation of a tower standing on a horizontal plane is observed; $a$ feet nearer it is found to be 45°; $b$ feet nearer still it is the complement of what it was at the first station; shew that the height of the tower is $ab/(a - b)$ feet.

# PROJECT | SNELL'S LAW AND AN ANCIENT EXPERIMENT

*"The 'lifting' effect produced by refraction is the basis for one of the earliest recorded experiments in optics, one which was known to the ancient Greeks. A coin is placed in the bottom of an empty vessel and the eye of an observer is placed in such a position that the coin is hidden below the edge of the vessel. If water is poured into the vessel the coin appears to rise and come into view."*—Francis Weston Sears in *Optics* (Reading, Mass.: Addison-Wesley Publishing Company, Inc., 1958)

In this group project you will learn some of the basic ideas of geometrical optics, a subject first studied by the ancient Greeks, advanced by artists and mathematicians of the Renaissance, and further developed by mathematicians and physicists from the seventeenth through the twentieth and into the twenty-first century. Major contributors include Archimedes, Descartes, Fermat, Huygens, Newton, Gauss, Hamilton, Fresnel, Einstein, and Born.

We now discuss some of the basic principles. The first one is the notion of a light ray. When traveling through a uniform transparent medium (such as a vacuum, water, plastic, or glass) light travels along straight line paths called **light rays.**

The second principle is that light rays bend when passing from one medium to another, for example, when passing from water to air. The amount of bending is determined by the Law of Refraction, usually referred to as Snell's Law after its discoverer, Willebrod Snell (1580–1626). When a light ray traveling in a transparent medium intersects the boundary with another transparent medium, its direction changes as indicated in Figure A.

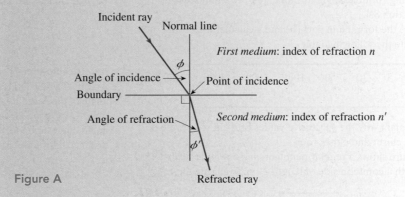

Figure A

Using the terminology introduced in Figure A we can state **Snell's Law** in two parts:

**I.** The incident ray, the refracted ray and the line normal (or perpendicular) to the boundary at the point of incidence all lie in the same plane.

**II.** The angle of incidence and the angle of refraction are related by the equation

$$n \sin \phi = n' \sin \phi'$$

The **index of refraction** of a vacuum is defined to be 1. For other materials it may be determined empirically by precise measurement of angles. Air has an index of refraction very close to 1, for water it's about 4/3, and for many glasses and plastics it's about 3/2.

*Note:* Although it is often left out of statements of Snell's Law, part I is essential because light rays travel in three-dimensional space where three lines can intersect at a point, but not lie in the same plane. (You should think of an example.)

The third principle concerns vision. The eye can see a light source if and only if light rays pass from the source into the pupil of the eye. In Figure B, the eye labeled $E$ can see the light source $S$ because rays pass from the source to the eye through the gap in the blackened surrounding sphere. However, the eye labeled

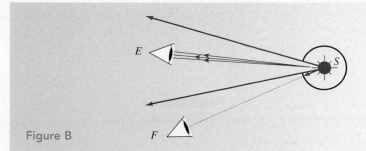

Figure B

*F* can't see *S* because light traveling along the line of sight *SF* is blocked before reaching the eye.

Our fourth principle is that an object appears to be located in the direction determined by the rays entering the eye from the object. This is illustrated in Figure C(i), where one ray from the fish's mouth at *A* appears to come from the direction of *A'*.

While the single ray in Figure C(i) suffices to give the apparent direction to the fish's mouth, it is not sufficient to determine the distance to *A'*. To determine this distance we must consider several rays coming from point *A*. Figure C(ii) shows several such rays which, after bending at the water's surface, all appear to come from point *A'*. The fact that all of the rays entering the eye from point *A* appear to come from a single point after refraction is quite surprising. We will examine this in more detail below.

(i)                                      (ii)

Figure C

Although the principles we've stated do not completely define geometric optics, they are sufficient to allow us to analyze the experiment discussed in the opening quotation. Figure D shows a greatly exaggerated eye looking vertically downward to the point at the center of a coin lying at the bottom of a cup of water. The solid red rays emerge from this point and enter the eye after bending at the water's surface. The ray emerging from the center of the coin to the center of the eye is called the **chief ray.** On the right side of the figure, one ray emerging from the center of the coin is shown refracted at the surface of the water and entering the pupil of the eye. The dashed line extends the part of this ray in air *back* through the water intersecting the chief ray. We could perform this same construction for any other non-chief ray in Figure D. Our goal is to show that all

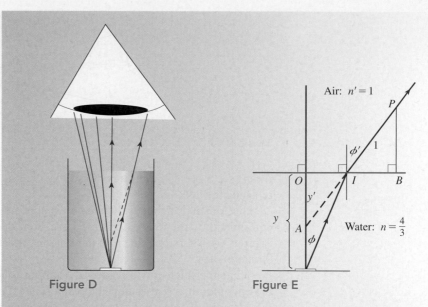

Figure D          Figure E

the dashed extensions would intersect the chief ray at approximately the same point.

In Figure E we lay out the geometry for a typical ray in great detail.

## EXERCISE 1

**(a)** Show that a ray emerging from the coin making an angle $\phi$ with the vertical intersects the air-water boundary with angle of incidence $\phi$. Then show that angle $BPI$ is equal to the angle of refraction $\phi'$.

**(b)** Show that the length of line segment $IB$ is $\sin \phi'$, which by Snell's law is $n \sin \phi$, then show that the length of $PB$ is $\sqrt{1 - n^2 \sin^2 \phi}$. *Caution*: Pay attention to the direction of the rays in Figure E.

**(c)** Show that the length of line segment $OI$ is $y \tan \phi$.

**(d)** Show that triangles $IOA$ and $IBP$ are similar.

**(e)** Use parts (a) through (d) to show that $y' = \dfrac{y \tan \phi \sqrt{1 - n^2 \sin^2 \phi}}{n \sin \phi}$ and

simplify to show

$$y' = \frac{\sqrt{1 - n^2 \sin^2 \phi}}{\cos \phi} \frac{1}{n} y$$

The last formula allows us to compute the point at which the center of the coin would appear to be located if we just consider the chief ray and a particular ray emerging from the center point at an angle $\phi$ to the vertical. To complete your investigation, you need to see if other rays entering the eye from the center of the coin appear to be coming from the same (or nearly the same) point.

**EXERCISE 2** Letting $n$ equal 4/3 compute, to four decimal places, the value of $\dfrac{\sqrt{1 - n^2 \sin^2 \phi}}{\cos \phi} \dfrac{1}{n}$ for $\phi = 0.25, 0.5, 1$, and 2 degrees. Based on these values, is it reasonable to conclude that the center of a coin in a cup filled with water to a depth of $y$ centimeters would appear to be at a depth of $y' = (3/4)y$ centimeters? If the water is 10 centimeters deep how far above the table will the coin appear to rise? What do you think would happen if instead of water we use an oil with an index of refraction of $3/2$?

The situation of the ancient Greek experiment is illustrated in Figure F. An observer looking into the empty cup cannot see the coin, but looking into the full cup will see the coin. Although the observer is not looking straight down, it turns out that the refraction at the water's surface will still cause the coin to appear to rise from the bottom of the cup to a position about three-fourths of the actual depth below the surface.

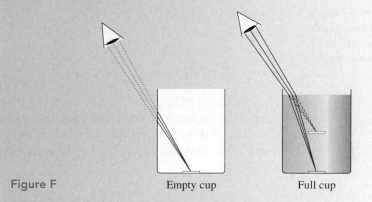

Figure F          Empty cup          Full cup

**EXERCISE 3** Do the experiment. Get an empty cup. Place a coin in the bottom of the cup (a little gum or honey to keep it from moving might be helpful). Have an observer stand where he or she can see the coin and then move back until the coin is just barely hidden by the rim of the cup. Have another member of your group pour water into the cup, stopping frequently to allow the observer to describe what he or she sees. Have yet another member write down these observations.

## 6.4 TRIGONOMETRIC FUNCTIONS OF ANGLES

*Be clear about the signs of the functions. Your calculator will show them to you correctly, but you still need to be able to figure them out for yourself, quadrant by quadrant.* —David Halliday and Robert Resnick in *Fundamentals of Physics,* 3rd ed. (New York: John Wiley and Sons, 1988)

Recall that the definitions of the trigonometric functions given in Section 6.1 apply only to acute angles. That is, as defined on page 425, the domains of trigonometric functions consist of all angles $\theta$ such that $0° < \theta < 90°$. In this section we want to expand our definitions of the trigonometric functions to include angles of any size. To do this, we will need to be more explicit than we have been about angles and their size or measure.

For analytical purposes we think of the two rays that form an angle as having been originally coincident; then while one ray is held fixed, the other is rotated to

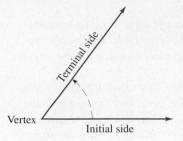

**Figure 1**

**Figure 2**
Angles generated by a counter-clockwise rotation have positive measure. Angles generated by a clockwise rotation have negative measure.

create the given angle. As Figure 1 indicates, the fixed ray is called the **initial side** of the angle, and the rotated ray is called the **terminal side.** By convention we take the measure of an angle to be **positive** if the rotation is counterclockwise (as in Figure 1) and **negative** if the rotation is clockwise. For example, the measure of the angle in Figure 2(a) is *positive* 30 degrees because the rotation is counterclockwise, whereas the measure of the angle in Figure 2(b) is *negative* 30 degrees because the rotation is clockwise. Figure 2(c) shows an angle of 390°.

(a)                    (b)                    (c)

In our development of trigonometry it will be convenient to have a *standard position* for angles. In a rectangular coordinate system an angle is in **standard position** if the vertex is located at (0, 0) and the initial side of the angle lies along the positive horizontal axis. Figure 3 shows examples of angles in standard position.

**Figure 3**
Examples of angles in standard position

Now we are ready to extend our definitions of the trigonometric functions to accommodate angles of any size. We begin by placing the angle $\theta$ in standard position and drawing in the **unit circle** $x^2 + y^2 = 1$, as shown in Figure 4. (Recall from Chapter 1 that the equation $x^2 + y^2 = 1$ represents the circle of radius 1, with center at the origin.) Notice the notation $P(x, y)$ in Figure 4; this stands for the point $P$, with coordinates $(x, y)$, where the terminal side of angle $\theta$ intersects the unit circle. With this notation, we define the six trigonometric functions of $\theta$ as follows.

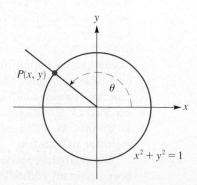

**Figure 4**
$P(x, y)$ denotes the point where the terminal side of angle $\theta$ intersects the unit circle.

| DEFINITION | Trigonometric Functions of Angles |
|---|---|

$$\cos \theta = x \qquad\qquad \sec \theta = \frac{1}{x} \quad (x \neq 0)$$

$$\sin \theta = y \qquad\qquad \csc \theta = \frac{1}{y} \quad (y \neq 0)$$

$$\tan \theta = \frac{y}{x} \quad (x \neq 0) \qquad \cot \theta = \frac{x}{y} \quad (y \neq 0)$$

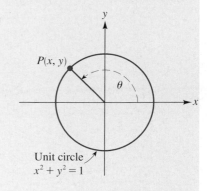

Unit circle
$x^2 + y^2 = 1$

Even before turning to some examples, we make three initial observations concerning our new definitions. The first two observations will help you to memorize the definitions. The third observation will help you to see why these new definitions are consistent with our previous work on right-triangle trigonometry.

1. $\cos \theta$ is the first coordinate of the point where the terminal side of angle $\theta$ intersects the unit circle; $\sin \theta$ is the second coordinate. (You can remember this by noting that, alphabetically, cosine comes before sine.)
2. Just as with the right-triangle definitions, we have the same three pairs of reciprocals: $\cos \theta$ and $\sec \theta$, $\sin \theta$ and $\csc \theta$, and $\tan \theta$ and $\cot \theta$.
3. For the cases in which the angle $\theta$ is acute, these definitions are really equivalent to the original right-triangle definitions. Consider, for instance, the acute angle $\theta$ in Figure 5. According to our "new" definition of sine, we have

$$\sin \theta = y$$

On the other hand, applying the original right-triangle definition to Figure 5 yields

$$\sin \theta = \frac{\text{opposite}}{\text{hypotenuse}} = \frac{y}{1} = y$$

Thus in both cases we obtain the same result. Using Figure 5, you should check for yourself that the same agreement also occurs for the other trigonometric functions.

**Figure 5**

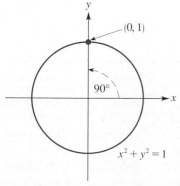

**Figure 6**

| EXAMPLE | 1 | Using the unit circle to calculate trigonometric functions of 90° |
|---|---|---|

Compute $\cos 90°$, $\sin 90°$, $\tan 90°$, $\sec 90°$, $\csc 90°$, and $\cot 90°$.

**SOLUTION**
We place the angle $\theta = 90°$ in standard position. Then, as Figure 6 indicates, the terminal side of the angle meets the unit circle at the point $(0, 1)$. Now we apply the definitions:

$$(0, 1)$$
By definition, $\cos 90°$    By definition, $\sin 90°$
is this number.      is this number.

Thus

$$\cos 90° = 0 \quad \text{and} \quad \sin 90° = 1$$

For the remaining trigonometric functions of 90° we have

$$\tan 90° = \frac{y}{x} = \frac{1}{0} \quad \text{undefined}$$

$$\sec 90° = \frac{1}{x} = \frac{1}{0} \quad \text{undefined}$$

$$\csc 90° = \frac{1}{y} = \frac{1}{1} = 1$$

$$\cot 90° = \frac{x}{y} = \frac{0}{1} = 0$$

These are the required results.

---

| EXAMPLE | 2 | **Using the unit circle to calculate trigonometric functions of −180°** |

Evaluate the trigonometric functions of −180°.

**SOLUTION**

The results can be read off from Figure 7.

$$\cos(-180°) = x = -1 \qquad \sec(-180°) = \frac{1}{x} = \frac{1}{-1} = -1$$

$$\sin(-180°) = y = 0 \qquad \csc(-180°) = \frac{1}{y} = \frac{1}{0} \quad \text{undefined}$$

$$\tan(-180°) = \frac{y}{x} = \frac{0}{-1} = 0 \qquad \cot(-180°) = \frac{x}{y} = \frac{-1}{0} \quad \text{undefined}$$

**Figure 7**

In the two examples we have just concluded, we evaluated the trigonometric functions for $\theta = 90°$ and $\theta = -180°$. In the same manner the trigonometric functions can be evaluated just as easily for any angle that is an integral multiple of 90°. Table 1 shows the results of such calculations. Exercise 14 at the end of this section asks you to make these calculations for yourself.

**TABLE 1**

| $\theta$ | $\cos \theta$ | $\sin \theta$ | $\tan \theta$ | $\sec \theta$ | $\csc \theta$ | $\cot \theta$ |
|---|---|---|---|---|---|---|
| **0°** | 1 | 0 | 0 | 1 | undefined | undefined |
| **90°** | 0 | 1 | undefined | undefined | 1 | 0 |
| **180°** | −1 | 0 | 0 | −1 | undefined | undefined |
| **270°** | 0 | −1 | undefined | undefined | −1 | 0 |
| **360°** | 1 | 0 | 0 | 1 | undefined | undefined |

## EXAMPLE 3    Using the unit circle to approximate cosine and sine

Use Figure 8 to approximate the following trigonometric values to within successive tenths. Then use a calculator to check your answers. Round the calculator values to two decimal places.

**(a)** cos 160° and sin 160°        **(b)** cos(−40°) and sin(−40°)

### SOLUTION

**(a)** Figure 8 shows that (the terminal side of) an angle of 160° in standard position meets the unit circle at a point in Quadrant II. Letting $(x, y)$ denote the coordinates of that point, we have (from Figure 8)

$$-1.0 < x < -0.9 \quad \text{and} \quad 0.3 < y < 0.4$$

But by definition, cos 160° = $x$ and sin 160° = $y$, and, consequently,

$$-1.0 < \cos 160° < -0.9 \quad \text{and} \quad 0.3 < \sin 160° < 0.4$$

     The corresponding calculator results are cos 160° ≈ −0.94 and sin 160° ≈ 0.34. Note that the estimations we obtained from Figure 8 are consistent with these calculator values. (When you check these calculator values for yourself, be sure that your calculator is set in the degree mode.)

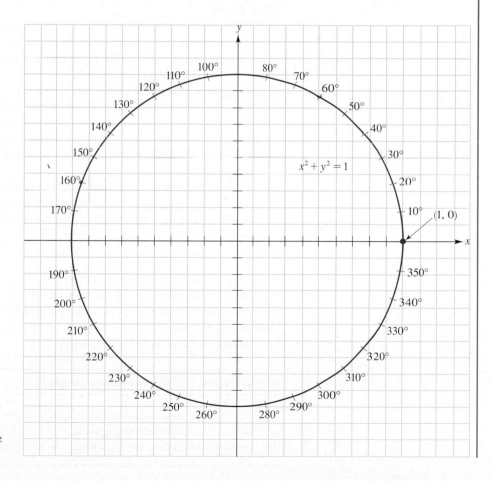

**Figure 8**
Degree measure on the unit circle
for angles in standard position

**(b)** As you can verify using Figure 8, the terminal side of an angle of $-40°$ intersects the unit circle at the same point as does the terminal side of an angle of $320°$. Letting $(x, y)$ denote the coordinates of that point, we have (from Figure 8)

$$0.7 < x < 0.8 \quad \text{and} \quad -0.7 < y < -0.6$$

and, consequently,

$$0.7 < \cos(-40°) < 0.8 \quad \text{and} \quad -0.7 < \sin(-40°) < -0.6$$

The corresponding calculator values here are $\cos(-40°) \approx 0.77$ and $\sin(-40°) \approx -0.64$. Again, note that the estimations we obtain from Figure 8 are consistent with these calculator values.

| EXAMPLE | 4 | Using the unit circle to visually estimate cosine and sine |
|---|---|---|

In each case, use Figure 8 to determine which quantity is larger. Then use a calculator to check the answer.

**(a)** $\sin 80°$ or $\cos 80°$ **(b)** $\sin 110°$ or $\sin 290°$ **(c)** $\cos 20°$ or $\cos 40°$

**SOLUTION**
**(a)** In Figure 8, look at the point on the unit circle corresponding to $80°$. The $y$-coordinate (which is $\sin 80°$) is nearly 1, but the $x$-coordinate ($\cos 80°$) is less than 0.2. So $\sin 80° > \cos 80°$. Indeed, a calculator shows that $\sin 80° \approx 0.98$ and $\cos 80° \approx 0.17$.
**(b)** In Figure 8, look at the points on the unit circle corresponding to $110°$ and $290°$. The $y$-coordinate for $110°$ is positive, while the $y$-coordinate for $290°$ is negative. In other words, $\sin 110°$ is positive, and $\sin 290°$ is negative. So (without even worrying about the decimal places) we have $\sin 110° > \sin 290°$. A calculator check shows that $\sin 110° \approx +0.94$ and $\sin 290° \approx -0.94$.
**(c)** Look at the points on the unit circle corresponding to $20°$ and $40°$. The $x$-coordinate for $20°$ is larger than the $x$-coordinate for $40°$. Therefore $\cos 20° > \cos 40°$. A calculator check confirms this: $\cos 20° \approx 0.94$ and $\cos 40° \approx 0.77$.

In evaluating the trigonometric functions, we'd like to take advantage, as much as possible, of the symmetry in Figure 8. To do this, we introduce the concept of a *reference angle*. (Even when we are using a calculator with the trigonometric functions, there are times, nevertheless, when we will need the reference angle concept. For instance, see Example 2(c) in Section 7.4.)

**DEFINITION** | The Reference Angle

Let $\theta$ be an angle in standard position, and suppose that $\theta$ is not an integer multiple of $90°$. The **reference angle** associated with $\theta$ is the acute angle (with positive measure) formed by the $x$-axis and the terminal side of the angle $\theta$.

The reference angle for 135° is 45° [180° − 135° = 45°].

The reference angle for 300° is 60° [360° − 300° = 60°].

The reference angle for 210° is 30° [210° − 180° = 30°].

The reference angle for −45° is 45°.

**Figure 9**

In Figure 9 angles are indicated by dashed arcs, and their respective reference angles are indicated by solid arcs. The first part of Figure 9 shows how to find the reference angle for $\theta = 135°$ in standard position. Then we find the acute angle between the $x$-axis and the terminal side of $\theta$. As you can see, in this case this acute angle is 45°. So the reference angle associated with $\theta = 135°$ is 45°. In the same way you should work through the remaining three parts of Figure 9.

Now let's look at an example to see how reference angles are used in evaluating the trigonometric functions. Suppose that we want to evaluate cos 150°. In Figure 10(a) we've placed the angle $\theta = 150°$ in standard position. As you can see, the reference angle for 150° is 30°.

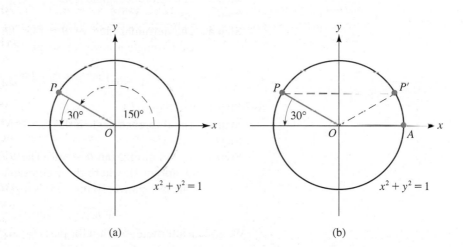

**Figure 10**　(a)　(b)

By definition the value of cos 150° is the $x$-coordinate of the point $P$ in Figure 10(a). To find this $x$-coordinate, we reflect the line segment $\overline{OP}$ in the $y$-axis; the reflected line segment is the segment $\overline{OP'}$ in Figure 10(b). Since $\angle P'OA = 30°$, the $x$-coordinate of the point $P'$ is by definition cos 30°, or $\sqrt{3}/2$. The $x$-coordinate of $P$ is then the negative of this, that is, the $x$-coordinate of $P$ is $-\sqrt{3}/2$. It follows now, again by definition, that the value of cos 150° is $-\sqrt{3}/2$.

The same method that we have just used to evaluate cos 150° can be used to evaluate any of the trigonometric functions when the angles are not multiples of 90°. The following four steps summarize this method.

**Step 1** Draw (or refer to) a sketch of the angle and reference angle.
**Step 2** Determine the reference angle associated with the given angle.
**Step 3** Evaluate the given trigonometric function of the reference angle.
**Step 4** Affix the appropriate sign determined by the quadrant of the terminal side of the angle in standard position.

The next two examples illustrate this procedure.

**EXAMPLE 5   Using the four-step procedure**

Evaluate the following quantities:
**(a)** $\sin 135°$;       **(b)** $\cos 135°$;       **(c)** $\tan 135°$.

**SOLUTION**
As Figure 11 indicates, the reference angle associated with 135° is 45°.

**(a) Step 1** See Figure 11.
   **Step 2** The reference angle is 45°.
   **Step 3** $\sin 45° = \sqrt{2}/2$
   **Step 4** The terminal side of $\theta = 135°$ lies in Quadrant II, where the $y$-coordinate is positive, so $\sin 135°$ is positive. We therefore have

$$\sin 135° = \sin 45° = \frac{\sqrt{2}}{2}$$

**(b) Step 1** See Figure 11.
   **Step 2** The reference angle is 45°.
   **Step 3** $\cos 45° = \sqrt{2}/2$
   **Step 4** The terminal side of $\theta = 135°$ lies in Quadrant II, where the $x$-coordinate is negative, so $\cos 135°$ is negative. We therefore have

$$\cos 135° = -\cos 45° = -\frac{\sqrt{2}}{2}$$

**(c) Step 1** See Figure 11.
   **Step 2** The reference angle is 45°.
   **Step 3** $\tan 45° = 1$
   **Step 4** By definition, $\tan \theta = y/x$. The terminal side of $\theta = 135°$ lies in Quadrant II, where the $y$-coordinate is positive and the $x$-coordinate is negative, so $\tan 135°$ is negative. We therefore have

$$\tan 135° = -\tan 45° = -1$$

We give an alternate solution for parts (a) and (c) of Example 5 using a right triangle picture rather than a unit circle picture. We again use the four-step procedure.

**(a) Step 1** See Figure 12.
   **Step 2** The reference angle is 45°.
   **Step 3** $\sin 45° = \dfrac{\text{opposite}}{\text{hypotenuse}} = \dfrac{1/\sqrt{2}}{1} = \dfrac{\sqrt{2}}{2}$
   **Step 4** The terminal side of $\theta = 135°$ lies in Quadrant II, where the $y$-coordinate is positive, so $\sin 135°$ is positive. We therefore have

$$\sin 135° = \sin 45° = \frac{\sqrt{2}}{2}$$

**Figure 11**

**Figure 12**

**(c)  Step 1**  See Figure 12.

   **Step 2**  The reference angle is 45°.

   **Step 3**  $\tan 45° = \dfrac{\text{opposite}}{\text{adjacent}} = \dfrac{1/\sqrt{2}}{1/\sqrt{2}} = 1$

   **Step 4**  The terminal side of $\theta = 135°$ lies in Quadrant II, where the $x$-coordinates are negative and $y$-coordinates are positive, so tan 135° is negative. We therefore have

$$\tan 135° = -\tan 45° = -1$$

*Note*: Remember in a right triangle each side has *positive* length and each non-right angle is *acute*. In Figure 12, $\theta = 135°$ is *not* an acute angle of the right triangle, but the reference angle, 45°, is an acute angle of the triangle. Also we labeled the length of the horizontal side with a positive number.

| EXAMPLE | 6 | Finding the values of trigonometric functions of an angle with negative measure |

Evaluate the following quantities:

**(a)**  $\cos(-120°)$;        **(b)**  $\cot(-120°)$;        **(c)**  $\sec(-120°)$.

**SOLUTION**

As Figure 13 shows, the reference angle for −120° is 60°.

**(a)  Step 1**  See Figure 13.

   **Step 2**  The reference angle for −120° is 60°.

   **Step 3**  $\cos 60° = 1/2$

   **Step 4**  The terminal side of $\theta = -120°$ lies in Quadrant III, where the $x$-coordinate is negative, so cos(−120°) is negative. We therefore have

$$\cos(-120°) = -\cos(60°) = -\frac{1}{2}$$

**(b)  Step 1**  See Figure 13.

   **Step 2**  The reference angle for −120° is 60°.

   **Step 3**  $\cot 60° = \sqrt{3}/3$

   **Step 4**  By definition, $\cot \theta = x/y$. Now, the terminal side of $\theta = -120°$ lies in Quadrant III, where the $x$-coordinate is negative and the $y$-coordinate is negative. Thus cot(−120°) is positive. We therefore have

$$\cot(-120°) = \cot(60°) = \frac{\sqrt{3}}{3}$$

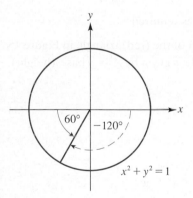

Figure 13

**(c)**  We could follow our four-step procedure here, but in this case there is a faster method. In part (a) of this example we found that $\cos(-120°) = -1/2$. Therefore, since $\sec \theta$ is the reciprocal of $\cos \theta$, we have

$$\sec(-120°) = \frac{1}{\cos(-120°)} = \frac{1}{(-1/2)} = -2$$

In this section we have used the unit circle to generalize our definitions of the trigonometric functions to accommodate angles of any size. We conclude this section with an application that relies on both the unit circle definitions (page 461) and the acute angle or right triangle definitions (page 425). Recall that in the previous section we found that the area of a triangle is given by the formula $A = \frac{1}{2}ab\sin\theta$, where $a$ and $b$ are the lengths of two sides and $\theta$ is the angle included between those two sides. When we derived this result in the previous section, we were assuming that $\theta$ was an acute angle. In fact, however, the formula is still valid when $\theta$ is an obtuse angle (an angle between 90° and 180°). To establish this result, we'll need to rely on the following identity:

$$\sin(180° - \theta) = \sin\theta$$

We will use Figure 14 to establish this identity for the case in which $\theta$ is an obtuse angle. (Exercise 61 shows you how to prove this identity when $\theta$ is an acute angle, and Section 8.1 discusses identities such as this from a more general point of view.) Figure 14 shows an obtuse angle $\theta$ in standard position. Let us apply our four-step procedure to determine $\sin\theta$. (As you'll see, the end result will be the required identity.)

**Step 1**  Refer to Figure 15.
**Step 2**  The reference angle for $\theta$ is $180° - \theta$.
**Step 3**  The sine of the reference angle is $\sin(180° - \theta)$.
**Step 4**  $\sin\theta$ is positive because the terminal side of $\theta$ lies in Quadrant II. Therefore we have

$$\sin\theta = \sin(180° - \theta) \qquad \text{as required}$$

Figure 14

We are now prepared to show that the area $A$ of the (red) triangle in Figure 15 is given by $A = \frac{1}{2}ab\sin\theta$. The area of any triangle is given by $A = \frac{1}{2}(\text{base})(\text{height})$. Thus, referring to Figure 15, we have

$$A = \frac{1}{2}bh \qquad (1)$$

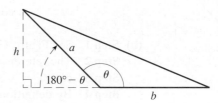

Figure 15

Also from Figure 15 we have

$$\sin(180° - \theta) = \frac{\text{opposite}}{\text{hypotenuse}} = \frac{h}{a}$$
$$h = a\sin(180° - \theta)$$
$$h = a\sin\theta \qquad \text{using the identity } \sin(180° - \theta) = \sin\theta \qquad (2)$$

Now we can use equation (2) to substitute for $h$ in equation (1). This yields

$$A = \frac{1}{2}b(a\sin\theta) = \frac{1}{2}ab\sin\theta$$

The formula that we've just derived is a useful one. We will use it in later work to prove the *law of sines*. For reference, we summarize the result in the box that follows.

---

### Formula for the Area of a Triangle

If $a$ and $b$ are lengths of two sides of a triangle and $\theta$ is the angle included between those two sides, then the area of the triangle is given by

$$\text{area} = \frac{1}{2}ab \sin \theta$$

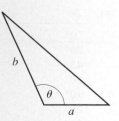

**In Words**   The area of a triangle equals one-half the product of the lengths of two sides times the sine of the included angle.

---

# EXERCISE SET 6.4

## A

*In Exercises 1–8, sketch each angle in standard position and specify the reference angle.*

1. (a) $110°$
   (b) $-110°$
2. (a) $160°$
   (b) $-160°$
3. (a) $200°$
   (b) $200°$
4. (a) $225°$
   (b) $-225°$
5. (a) $300°$
   (b) $-300°$
6. (a) $325°$
   (b) $-325°$
7. (a) $60°$
   (b) $-60°$
8. (a) $460°$
   (b) $-460°$

*In Exercises 9–13, use the definitions (not a calculator) to evaluate the six trigonometric functions of the angle. If a value is undefined, state this.*

9. $270°$
10. $450°$
11. $-270°$
12. $-720°$
13. $540°$
14. Use the definitions of the trigonometric functions to complete the table. (When you are finished, check your results against the values shown in Table 1 on page 462.)

| $\theta$ | $\cos \theta$ | $\sin \theta$ | $\tan \theta$ | $\sec \theta$ | $\csc \theta$ | $\cot \theta$ |
|---|---|---|---|---|---|---|
| 0° | | | | | | |
| 90° | | | | | | |
| 180° | | | | | | |
| 270° | | | | | | |
| 360° | | | | | | |

*In Exercises 15–28, use Figure 8 to approximate within successive tenths the given trigonometric values. Then use a calculator to approximate the values to the nearest hundredth.*

15. $\sin 10°$ and $\sin(-10°)$
16. $\cos 10°$ and $\cos(-10°)$
17. $\cos 80°$ and $\cos(-80°)$
18. $\sin 80°$ and $\sin(-80°)$
19. $\sin 120°$ and $\sin(-120°)$
20. $\cos 120°$ and $\cos(-120°)$
21. $\sin 150°$ and $\sin(-150°)$
22. $\cos 150°$ and $\cos(-150°)$
23. $\cos 220°$ and $\cos(-220°)$
24. $\sin 220°$ and $\sin(-220°)$
25. $\cos 310°$ and $\cos(-310°)$
26. $\sin 310°$ and $\sin(-310°)$
27. $\sin(40° + 360°)$
28. $\cos(40° + 360°)$

*In Exercises 29–40, use Figure 8 (on page 463) to determine which quantity is larger. Then use a calculator to check the answer. For the calculator values, round to two decimal places.*

29. $\sin 70°$ or $\cos 70°$
30. $\sin 60°$ or $\sin 70°$
31. $\cos 170°$ or $\cos 160°$
32. $\sin 190°$ or $\cos 190°$
33. $\cos 280°$ or $\cos 290°$
34. $\sin 160°$ or $\sin 170°$
35. $\sin 10°$ or $\sin(-10°)$
36. $\sin 190°$ or $\sin(-190°)$
37. $\sin 80°$ or $\sin 110°$
38. $\sin 230°$ or $\sin 320°$
39. $\sin(-80°)$ or $\cos(-110°)$
40. $\sin(-230°)$ or $\cos(-230°)$

*In Exercises 41–50, evaluate each expression using the method shown in Examples 5 and 6.*

41. (a) $\cos 315°$
    (b) $\cos(-315°)$
    (c) $\sin 315°$
    (d) $\sin(-315°)$
42. (a) $\cos 240°$
    (b) $\cos(-240°)$
    (c) $\sin 240°$
    (d) $\sin(-240°)$
43. (a) $\cos 300°$
    (b) $\cos(-300°)$
    (c) $\sin 300°$
    (d) $\sin(-300°)$
44. (a) $\cos 150°$
    (b) $\cos(-150°)$
    (c) $\sin 150°$
    (d) $\sin(-150°)$
45. (a) $\cos 210°$
    (b) $\cos(-210°)$
    (c) $\sin 210°$
    (d) $\sin(-210°)$
46. (a) $\cos 585°$
    (b) $\cos(-585°)$
    (c) $\sin 585°$
    (d) $\sin(-585°)$
47. (a) $\cos 390°$
    (b) $\cos(-390°)$
    (c) $\sin 390°$
    (d) $\sin(-390°)$
48. (a) $\cos 405°$
    (b) $\cos(-405°)$
    (c) $\sin 405°$
    (d) $\sin(-405°)$

**49. (a)** sec 600°  **(c)** tan 600°
  **(b)** csc(−600°)  **(d)** cot(−600°)
**50. (a)** sec 330°  **(c)** tan 330°
  **(b)** csc(−330°)  **(d)** cot(−330°)

*In Exercises 51 and 52, complete the tables.*

**51.**

| $\theta$ | sin $\theta$ | cos $\theta$ | tan $\theta$ |
|---|---|---|---|
| 0° | | | |
| 30° | | | |
| 45° | | | |
| 60° | | | |
| 90° | | | |
| 120° | | | |
| 135° | | | |
| 150° | | | |
| 180° | | | |

**52.**

| $\theta$ | sin $\theta$ | cos $\theta$ | tan $\theta$ |
|---|---|---|---|
| 180° | | | |
| 210° | | | |
| 225° | | | |
| 240° | | | |
| 270° | | | |
| 300° | | | |
| 315° | | | |
| 330° | | | |
| 360° | | | |

*Exercises 53–56, use the given information to determine the area of each triangle.*

**53.** Two of the sides are 5 cm and 7 cm, and the angle between those sides is 120°.

**54.** Two of the sides are 3 m and 6 m, and the included angle is 150°.

**55.** Two of the sides are 21.4 cm and 28.6 cm, and the included angle is 98.5°. (Round the final answer to one decimal place.)

**56.** Two of the sides are 5.98 cm and 8.05 cm, and the included angle is 107.1°. (Round the answer to one decimal place.)

**57.** The following figure shows an equilateral triangle inscribed in a circle of radius 12 cm. Use the method of Example 6 in Section 6.3 to compute the area of the triangle. Give two forms for your answer: one with a square root and the other a calculator approximation rounded to two decimal places.

**58.** An equilateral triangle is inscribed in a circle of radius 8 cm. Compute the area of the shaded region in each of the following figures. Round your final answers to three decimal places.

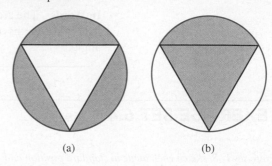

(a)                    (b)

# B

**59. (a)** Complete the following table, using the words "positive" or "negative" as appropriate.

| | Terminal side of angle $\theta$ lies in | | | |
|---|---|---|---|---|
| | Quadrant I | Quadrant II | Quadrant III | Quadrant IV |
| cos $\theta$ and sec $\theta$ | positive | negative | | |
| sin $\theta$ and csc $\theta$ | | | | |
| tan $\theta$ and cot $\theta$ | | | | |

**(b)** The mnemonic (memory device) ASTC (*a*ll *s*tudents *t*ake *c*alculus) is sometimes used to recall the signs of the trigonometric values in each quadrant:

**A**  All are positive in Quadrant I.
**S**  Sine is positive in Quadrant II.
**T**  Tangent is positive in Quadrant III.
**C**  Cosine is positive in Quadrant IV.

Check the validity of this mnemonic against your chart in part (a).

**60.** The value of tan $\theta$ is undefined when $\theta = 90°$. Use a calculator to complete the following tables to investigate the behavior of tan $\theta$ as $\theta$ approaches 90°. Round each value to the nearest integer.

**(a)**

| $\theta$ | 89° | 89.9° | 89.99° | 89.999° |
|---|---|---|---|---|
| $\tan \theta$ | | | | |

**(b)**

| $\theta$ | 91° | 90.1° | 90.01° | 90.001° |
|---|---|---|---|---|
| $\tan \theta$ | | | | |

**61.** In the text we derived the identity $\sin(180° - \theta) = \sin \theta$ in the case when $\theta$ is an obtuse angle, and used it to show that the same formula for the area of a triangle that was derived in Section 6.3 for acute angles also works for obtuse angles.

*Note*: If $\theta$ is an acute angle, then $180° - \theta$ is an obtuse angle.

**(a)** Sketch a figure showing the obtuse angle $180° - \theta$ in standard position. Note that the terminal side of the angle $180° - \theta$ lies in the second quadrant.

**(b)** What is the reference angle for the angle $180° - \theta$?

**(c)** Use Steps (a) and (b) to conclude that $\sin(180° - \theta) = \sin \theta$.

**62.** Check that the identity $\sin(180° - \theta) \sin \theta$ is valid in the three cases $\theta = 0°$, $\theta = 90°$, and $\theta = 180°$.

*Note*: This exercise completes the verification of the identity $\sin(180° - \theta) = \sin \theta$ for all $\theta$ from 0° to 180°.

*For Exercises 63 and 64, refer to the following figure.*

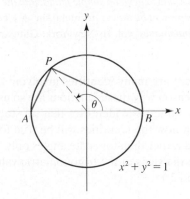

**63.** Express the area of $\triangle ABP$ as a function of $\theta$.

**64. (a)** Express the slope of $\overline{PB}$ as a function of $\theta$.

**(b)** Express the slope of $\overline{PA}$ as a function of $\theta$.

**(c)** Using the expressions obtained in parts (a) and (b), compute the product of the two slopes.

**(d)** What can you conclude from your answer in part (c)?

*As background for Exercises 65–70, you need to have studied logarithms in Sections 5.3 and 5.4.*

**65. (a)** Choose (at random) an angle $\theta$ such that $0° < \theta < 90°$. Then with this value of $\theta$, use your calculator to verify that $\log_{10}(\sin^2 \theta) = 2 \log_{10}(\sin \theta)$.

**(b)** For which values of $\theta$ in the interval $0° \le \theta \le 180°$ is the equation in part (a) valid?

**66. (a)** Choose (at random) an angle $\theta$ such that $0° < \theta < 90°$. Then with this value of $\theta$, use your calculator to verify that $\log_{10}(\cos^2 \theta) = 2 \log_{10}(\cos \theta)$.

**(b)** For which values of $\theta$ in the interval $0° \le \theta \le 180°$ is the equation in part (a) valid?

*For Exercises 67 and 68, let*

$$\left.\begin{array}{l} S(\theta) = \sin \theta \\ C(\theta) = \cos \theta \end{array}\right\} \quad 0° \le \theta \le 360°$$
$$L(x) = \ln x$$

**67.** What is the domain of the function $(L \circ S)(\theta)$?

**68.** What is the domain of the function $(L \circ C)(\theta)$?

**69. (a)** Choose (at random) an angle $\theta$ such that $0° < \theta < 90°$. Then with this value of $\theta$, use your calculator to verify that

$$\ln\sqrt{1 - \cos \theta} + \ln\sqrt{1 + \cos \theta} = \ln(\sin \theta)$$

**(b)** Use the properties of logarithms to prove that if $0° < \theta < 90°$, then

$$\ln\sqrt{1 - \cos \theta} + \ln\sqrt{1 + \cos \theta} = \ln(\sin \theta)$$

**(c)** For which values of $\theta$ in the interval $0° \le \theta \le 360°$ is the equation in part (b) valid?

**70. (a)** Choose (at random) an angle $\theta$ such that $0° < \theta < 90°$. Then with this value of $\theta$, use your calculator to verify that

$$\ln\sqrt{1 - \sin \theta} + \ln\sqrt{1 + \sin \theta} = \ln(\cos \theta)$$

**(b)** Use the properties of logarithms to prove that the equation in part (a) holds for all acute angles $(0° < \theta < 90°)$.

**(c)** Does the equation in part (a) hold if $\theta = 90°$? If $\theta = 0°$?

**(d)** For which values of $\theta$ in the interval $0° \le \theta \le 360°$ is the equation in part (a) valid?

**71.** *Formula for* $\sin(\alpha + \beta)$ In the following figure, $\overline{AD} \perp \overline{BC}$ and $AD = 1$.

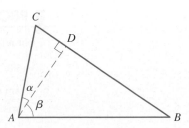

**(a)** Show that $AC = \sec \alpha$ and $AB = \sec \beta$.

*(continues)*

**(b)** Show that

$$\text{area } \triangle ADC = \frac{1}{2} \sec \alpha \sin \alpha$$

$$\text{area } \triangle ADB = \frac{1}{2} \sec \beta \sin \beta$$

$$\text{area } \triangle ABC = \frac{1}{2} \sec \alpha \sec \beta \sin(\alpha + \beta)$$

**(c)** The sum of the areas of the two smaller triangles in part (b) equals the area of $\triangle ABC$. Use this fact and the expressions given in part (b) to show that

$$\sin(\alpha + \beta) = \sin \alpha \cos \beta + \cos \alpha \sin \beta$$

**(d)** Use the formula in part (c) to compute $\sin 75°$.
*Hint*: $75° = 30° + 45°$

**(e)** Show that $\sin 75° \neq \sin 30° + \sin 45°$.

**(f)** Compute $\sin 105°$ and then check that $\sin 105° \neq \sin 45° + \sin 60°$.

**C**

**72.** Use the figure to prove the following theorem: The area of a quadrilateral is equal to one-half of the product of the diagonals times the sine of the included angle. *Hint*: Find the areas of each of the four triangles that make up the quadrilateral. Show that the sum of those areas is $\frac{1}{2}(\sin \theta)[qs + rq + rp + ps]$. Then factor the quantity within the brackets.

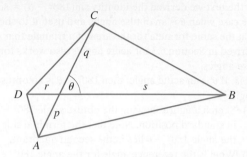

# 6.5 TRIGONOMETRIC IDENTITIES

*A special name for the function which we call the sine is first found in the works of Āryabhata (ca. 510). . . .*

*It is further probable, from the efforts made to develop simple tables, that the Hindus were acquainted with the principles which we represent by the . . . [formula] $\sin^2 \phi + \cos^2 \phi = 1$. . . .*
—David Eugene Smith in *History of Mathematics,* vol. II (New York: Ginn and Company, 1925)

As we mentioned in Section 6.2, there are many identities involving the trigonometric functions. In fact, that's one reason why these functions are so useful. In the box that follows, we list some of the same basic identities that we studied in Section 6.2. Keep in mind, however, that now the identities will be true for all angles for which the expressions are defined rather than for acute angles only. This means that we will need to pay attention to the signs of the trigonometric values. (You'll see how this works in Examples 1 and 2.)

**▮ PROPERTY SUMMARY   Basic Trigonometric Identities**

For all appropriate values of $\theta$:

1. $\sin^2 \theta + \cos^2 \theta = 1$

2. $\dfrac{\sin \theta}{\cos \theta} = \tan \theta$

3. $\sec \theta = \dfrac{1}{\cos \theta}; \quad \csc \theta = \dfrac{1}{\sin \theta}; \quad \cot \theta = \dfrac{1}{\tan \theta}$

The second and the third identities in the box are immediate consequences of the unit-circle definitions of the trigonometric functions. To see why the first identity in the box is valid, consider Figure 1. Since the point $P(x, y)$ lies on the unit circle, we have

$$x^2 + y^2 = 1$$

But by definition, $x = \cos \theta$ and $y = \sin \theta$. Therefore we have

$$\cos^2 \theta + \sin^2 \theta = 1$$

which is essentially what we wished to show. Incidentally, you should also become familiar with the equivalent forms of this identity:

$$\cos^2 \theta = 1 - \sin^2 \theta \qquad \text{and} \qquad \sin^2 \theta = 1 - \cos^2 \theta$$

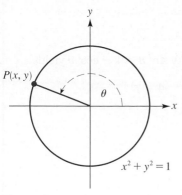

**Figure 1**

| EXAMPLE | 1 | Using identities to calculate trigonometric functions |

Given $\sin \theta = 2/3$ and $90° < \theta < 180°$, find $\cos \theta$ and $\tan \theta$.

**SOLUTION**
Substituting $\sin \theta = 2/3$ into the identity $\sin^2 \theta + \cos^2 \theta = 1$ yields

$$\left(\frac{2}{3}\right)^2 + \cos^2 \theta = 1$$

$$\cos^2 \theta = 1 - \left(\frac{2}{3}\right)^2 = \frac{5}{9}$$

$$\cos \theta = \pm\sqrt{\frac{5}{9}} = \frac{\pm\sqrt{5}}{3}$$

(Note that we could have started with $\cos^2 \theta = 1 - \sin^2 \theta$.)

To decide whether to choose the positive or the negative value, note that the given inequality $90° < \theta < 180°$ tells us that the terminal side of $\theta$ lies in the second quadrant. Since $x$-coordinates are negative in Quadrant II, we choose the negative value here. Thus

$$\cos \theta = \frac{-\sqrt{5}}{3}$$

For $\tan \theta$ we have

$$\tan \theta = \frac{y}{x} = \frac{\sin \theta}{\cos \theta} = \frac{2/3}{-\sqrt{5}/3}$$

$$= -\frac{2}{\sqrt{5}} = -\frac{2\sqrt{5}}{5}$$

 | EXAMPLE | 2 | Using identities to calculate trigonometric functions |

Suppose that

$$\cos \theta = \frac{t}{2}$$

where $270° < \theta < 360°$. Express the other five trigonometric values as functions of $t$. Note that for $270° < \theta < 360°$, $t$ must be positive. Why? In fact, $0 < t < 2$. Why?

**SOLUTION**
Replacing $\cos \theta$ with the quantity $t/2$ in the identity $\sin^2 \theta = 1 - \cos^2 \theta$ yields

$$\sin^2 \theta = 1 - \left(\frac{t}{2}\right)^2 = 1 - \frac{t^2}{4} = \frac{4 - t^2}{4}$$

and, consequently,

$$\sin \theta = \pm \frac{\sqrt{4 - t^2}}{2}$$

To decide whether to choose the positive or the negative value here, note that the given inequality $270° < \theta < 360°$ tells us that the terminal side of $\theta$ lies in the fourth quadrant. Since $y$-coordinates are negative in Quadrant IV, we choose the negative value here. Thus

$$\sin \theta = -\frac{\sqrt{4 - t^2}}{2}$$

To obtain $\tan \theta$, we use the identity $\tan \theta = (\sin \theta)/(\cos \theta)$. This yields

$$\tan \theta = \frac{-\sqrt{4 - t^2}/2}{t/2} = -\frac{\sqrt{4 - t^2}}{t}$$

We can now find the remaining three values simply by taking reciprocals:

$$\sec \theta = \frac{1}{\cos \theta} = \frac{2}{t}$$

$$\csc \theta = \frac{1}{\sin \theta} = -\frac{2}{\sqrt{4 - t^2}} = -\frac{2\sqrt{4 - t^2}}{4 - t^2} \qquad \text{rationalizing the denominator}$$

$$\cot \theta = \frac{1}{\tan \theta} = -\frac{t}{\sqrt{4 - t^2}} = -\frac{t\sqrt{4 - t^2}}{4 - t^2} \qquad \text{rationalizing the denominator}$$

We give an alternative solution for Example 2 based on a right-triangle picture rather than identities. We draw an angle $\theta$ between $270°$ and $360°$ in standard position and complete a right triangle as shown in Figure 2. Let $\tilde{\theta}$ denote the reference angle. For convenience, since the trigonometric functions are ratios, we can use a length of 2 units for the hypotenuse. Since $\theta$ is in Quadrant IV, $\cos \theta = t/2$ is positive, so $t$ is positive; also $\cos \theta = \cos \tilde{\theta}$. So we label the length of the adjacent side $t$, and we have

$$\cos \theta = \cos \tilde{\theta} = \frac{t}{2}$$

From the right triangle,

$$\text{opposite} = \sqrt{2^2 - t^2} = \sqrt{4 - t^2}$$

**Figure 2**

So

$$\sin \theta = -\sin \tilde{\theta} = -\frac{\text{opposite}}{\text{hypotenuse}} = -\frac{\sqrt{4 - t^2}}{2}$$

$$\tan \theta = -\tan \tilde{\theta} = -\frac{\text{opposite}}{\text{adjacent}} = -\frac{\sqrt{4 - t^2}}{t}$$

The rest follows as in the previous solution.

In the next five examples we are asked to show that certain trigonometric equations are, in fact, identities. The procedures here will be very much like those in our work on simplifying trigonometric expressions in Section 6.2, but now we have an advantage. In each case we are given an answer toward which to work. The identities in the next five examples should not be memorized; they are too specialized. Instead, concentrate on the proofs themselves, noting where the fundamental identities (such as $\sin^2 \theta + \cos^2 \theta = 1$) come into play. Remember that the identities are true only for values of the variable for which all expressions are defined.

**EXAMPLE** **3** **Proving an identity by expressing all trigonometric functions in terms of sine and cosine**

Prove that the equation $\csc A \tan A \cos A = 1$ is an identity.

**SOLUTION**
We begin with the left-hand side and express each factor in terms of sines or cosines:

$$\csc A \tan A \cos A = \frac{1}{\sin A} \cdot \frac{\overset{1}{\cancel{\sin A}}}{\cancel{\cos A}} \cdot \overset{1}{\cancel{\cos A}}$$

$$= 1 \qquad \text{as required}$$

**EXAMPLE** **4** **Proving an identity by expressing all trigonometric functions in terms of sine and cosine**

Prove that $1 - \dfrac{\cot^2 \theta}{\csc^2 \theta} = \sin^2 \theta$.

**SOLUTION**
We'll work with the left-hand side, expressing everything in terms of sines and cosines and then simplifying (as in Section 6.2).

$$1 - \frac{\cot^2 \theta}{\csc^2 \theta} = 1 - \frac{(\cos^2 \theta)/(\sin^2 \theta)}{1/\sin^2 \theta}$$

Since $\tan \theta = (\sin \theta)/(\cos \theta)$, it follows that $\tan^2 \theta = (\sin^2 \theta)/(\cos^2 \theta)$ and, consequently, $\cot^2 \theta = (\cos^2 \theta)/(\sin^2 \theta)$.

$$= 1 - \frac{\cos^2 \theta}{1}$$

multiplying both numerator and denominator of the fraction by $\sin^2 \theta$

$$= 1 - \cos^2 \theta = \sin^2 \theta$$

| EXAMPLE | 5 | **Proving an identity by expressing all trigonometric functions in terms of sine and cosine** |
|---|---|---|

Prove that $\cos^2 B - \sin^2 B = \dfrac{1 - \tan^2 B}{1 + \tan^2 B}$.

**SOLUTION**

We begin with the right-hand side this time; it is the more complicated expression, and it is easier to express $\tan^2 B$ in terms of $\sin B$ and $\cos B$ than it is to express $\sin^2 B$ and $\cos^2 B$ in terms of $\tan B$. As in previous examples we write everything in terms of sines and cosines.

$$\frac{1 - \tan^2 B}{1 + \tan^2 B} = \frac{1 - \dfrac{\sin^2 B}{\cos^2 B}}{1 + \dfrac{\sin^2 B}{\cos^2 B}} = \frac{\cos^2 B\left(1 - \dfrac{\sin^2 B}{\cos^2 B}\right)}{\cos^2 B\left(1 + \dfrac{\sin^2 B}{\cos^2 B}\right)}$$

$$= \frac{\cos^2 B - \sin^2 B}{\cos^2 B + \sin^2 B} = \frac{\cos^2 B - \sin^2 B}{1} = \cos^2 B - \sin^2 B$$

| EXAMPLE | 6 | **An algebraic technique for creating a difference of squares** |
|---|---|---|

Prove that $\dfrac{\cos \theta}{1 - \sin \theta} = \dfrac{1 + \sin \theta}{\cos \theta}$.

**SOLUTION**

The suggestions given in the previous examples are not applicable here. Everything is already in terms of sines and cosines. Furthermore, neither side appears more complicated than the other. A technique that does work here is to begin with the left-hand side and "rationalize" the denominator to obtain a perfect square. We do this by multiplying numerator and denominator by the same quantity, namely, $1 + \sin \theta$. Doing so gives us

$$\frac{\cos \theta}{1 - \sin \theta} = \frac{\cos \theta}{1 - \sin \theta} \cdot \frac{1 + \sin \theta}{1 + \sin \theta}$$

$$= \frac{(\cos \theta)(1 + \sin \theta)}{1 - \sin^2 \theta}$$

$$= \frac{(\cos \theta)(1 + \sin \theta)}{\cos^2 \theta} = \frac{1 + \sin \theta}{\cos \theta}$$

This identity could also be proven by starting on the right-hand side and rationalizing the numerator.

The general strategy for each of the proofs in Examples 3 through 6 was the same. In each case we worked with one side of the given equation, and we transformed it into equivalent expressions until it was identical to the other side of the equation. This is not the only strategy that can be used.

Before we describe an alternative strategy, a warning is in order. Establishing an identity is *not* like solving an equation. When solving an equation, we begin with an assumption that there is a value for the variable that makes the left-hand and right-hand sides equal. Then, using operations such as adding the same quantity to both sides or multiplying both sides by the same nonzero quantity, we derive a series of equivalent equations until the original equation is solved.

On the other hand, an identity is an assertion that two functions are equal, that is, their function values are equal for *all* values of the variable in their common domain. To prove an identity, we *cannot assume* that the left-hand and right-hand sides are equal, since that is precisely what we are trying to prove; so we cannot use the same techniques that we use to solve an equation.

In proving an identity, it is important to separately transform the left-hand side into the right-hand side or the right-hand side into the left-hand side, as in Examples 3 through 6. Another strategy that can be used in establishing identities is to separately transform each side to a common expression. We use this strategy in the next example.

---

**EXAMPLE 7** Proving an identity by showing that both sides equal the same expression

Prove that $\dfrac{1}{1 - \cos \beta} + \dfrac{1}{1 + \cos \beta} = 2 + 2 \cot^2 \beta.$

**SOLUTION**

$$\text{Left-hand side} = \frac{1(1 + \cos \beta) + 1(1 - \cos \beta)}{(1 - \cos \beta)(1 + \cos \beta)}$$

$$= \frac{2}{1 - \cos^2 \beta}$$

$$\text{Right-hand side} = 2 + \frac{2 \cos^2 \beta}{\sin^2 \beta}$$

$$= \frac{2 \sin^2 \beta + 2 \cos^2 \beta}{\sin^2 \beta}$$

$$= \frac{2(\sin^2 \beta + \cos^2 \beta)}{1 - \cos^2 \beta}$$

$$= \frac{2}{1 - \cos^2 \beta}$$

We've now established the required identity by showing that both sides are equal to the same expression.

---

# EXERCISE SET 6.5

## A

*In Exercises 1–8, use the given information to determine the remaining five trigonometric values. Rationalize any denominators that contain radicals.*

**1.** (a) $\sin \theta = 1/5, 90° < \theta < 180°$
  (b) $\sin \theta = -1/5, 180° < \theta < 270°$

**2.** (a) $\cos \theta = -3/4, 90° < \theta < 180°$
  (b) $\cos \theta = 3/4, 270° < \theta < 360°$

**3.** (a) $\cos \theta = 5/13, 0° < \theta < 90°$
  (b) $\cos \theta = -5/13, 180° < \theta < 270°$

**4.** (a) $\sin \theta = \sqrt{3}/6, 0° < \theta < 90°$
  (b) $\sin \theta = -\sqrt{3}/6, 270° < \theta < 360°$

5. $\csc A = -3, 270° < A < 360°$   *Hint*: First find $\sin A$.
6. $\csc A = 6/5, 90° < A < 180°$
7. $\sec B = -3/2, 180° < B < 270°$
8. $\sec B = 25/24, 270° < B < 360°$

*In Exercises 9–14, use the given information to express the remaining five trigonometric values as functions of t or u. Assume that t and u are positive. Rationalize any denominators that contain radicals.*

9. $\cos \theta = t/3, 270° < \theta < 360°$
10. $\cos \theta = -2t/5, 90° < \theta < 180°$
11. $\sin \theta = -3u, 180° < \theta < 270°$
12. $\sin \theta = -u^3, 270° < \theta < 360°$
13. $\cos \theta = u/\sqrt{3}, 0° < \theta < 90°$
14. $\sin \theta = 2u/\sqrt{7}, 0° < \theta < 90°$

*In Exercises 15–36, prove that the equations are identities.*

15. $\sin \theta \cos \theta \sec \theta \csc \theta = 1$
16. $\tan^2 A + 1 = \sec^2 A$
17. $(\sin \theta \sec \theta)/(\tan \theta) = 1$
18. $\tan \beta \sin \beta = \sec \beta - \cos \beta$
19. $(1 - 5 \sin x)/\cos x = \sec x - 5 \tan x$
20. $\dfrac{1}{\sin \theta} - \sin \theta = \cot \theta \cos \theta$
21. $(\cos A)(\sec A - \cos A) = \sin^2 A$
22. $\dfrac{\sin \theta}{\csc \theta} + \dfrac{\cos \theta}{\sec \theta} = 1$
23. $(1 - \sin \theta)(\sec \theta + \tan \theta) = \cos \theta$
24. $(\cos \theta - \sin \theta)^2 + 2 \sin \theta \cos \theta = 1$
25. $(\sec \alpha - \tan \alpha)^2 = \dfrac{1 - \sin \alpha}{1 + \sin \alpha}$
26. $\dfrac{\sin B}{1 + \cos B} + \dfrac{1 + \cos B}{\sin B} = 2 \csc B$
27. $\sin A + \cos A = \dfrac{\sin A}{1 - \cot A} - \dfrac{\cos A}{\tan A - 1}$
28. $(1 - \cos C)(1 + \sec C) = \tan C \sin C$
29. $\csc^2 \theta + \sec^2 \theta = \csc^2 \theta \sec^2 \theta$
30. $\cos^2 \theta - \sin^2 \theta = 1 - 2 \sin^2 \theta$
31. $\sin A \tan A = \dfrac{1 - \cos^2 A}{\cos A}$
32. $\dfrac{\cot A - 1}{\cot A + 1} = \dfrac{1 - \tan A}{1 + \tan A}$
33. $\cot^2 A + \csc^2 A = -\cot^4 A + \csc^4 A$
34. $\dfrac{\cot^2 A - \tan^2 A}{(\cot A + \tan A)^2} = 2 \cos^2 A - 1$
35. $\dfrac{\sin A - \cos A}{\sin A} + \dfrac{\cos A - \sin A}{\cos A} = 2 - \sec A \csc A$
36. $\tan A \tan B = \dfrac{\tan A + \tan B}{\cot A + \cot B}$

**B**

37. Only one of the following two equations is an identity. Decide which equation this is, and give a proof to show that it is, indeed, an identity. For the other equation, give an

example showing that it is not an identity. (For example, to show that the equation $\sin \theta + \cos \theta = 1$ is not an identity, let $\theta = 30°$. Then the equation becomes $1/2 + \sqrt{3}/2 = 1$, which is false.)

   (a) $\dfrac{\csc^2 \alpha - 1}{\csc^2 \alpha} = \cos \alpha$

   (b) $(\sec^2 \alpha - 1)(\csc^2 \alpha - 1) = 1$

38. Follow the directions given in Exercise 37.

   (a) $(\csc \beta - \cot \beta)^2 = \dfrac{1 + \cos \beta}{1 - \cos \beta}$

   (b) $\cot \beta + \dfrac{\sin \beta}{1 + \cos \beta} = \csc \beta$

39. Prove the identity $\dfrac{\sin \theta}{1 - \cos \theta} = \dfrac{1 + \cos \theta}{\sin \theta}$ in two ways.

   (a) Adapt the method of Example 6.
   (b) Begin with the left-hand side, and multiply numerator and denominator by $\sin \theta$.

*In Exercises 40–44, prove that the equations are identities.*

40. $\dfrac{2 \sin^3 \beta}{1 - \cos \beta} = 2 \sin \beta + 2 \sin \beta \cos \beta$

   *Hint*: Write $\sin^3 \beta$ as $(\sin \beta)(\sin^2 \beta)$.

41. $\dfrac{\sec \theta - \csc \theta}{\sec \theta + \csc \theta} = \dfrac{\tan \theta - 1}{\tan \theta + 1}$

42. $1 - \dfrac{\sin^2 \theta}{1 + \cot \theta} - \dfrac{\cos^2 \theta}{1 + \tan \theta} = \sin \theta \cos \theta$

43. $(\sin^2 \theta)(1 + n \cot^2 \theta) = (\cos^2 \theta)(n + \tan^2 \theta)$

44. $(r \sin \theta \cos \phi)^2 + (r \sin \theta \sin \phi)^2 + (r \cos \theta)^2 = r^2$

45. (a) Factor the expression $\cos^3 \theta - \sin^3 \theta$.
   (b) Prove the identity

   $$\dfrac{\cos \phi \cot \phi - \sin \phi \tan \phi}{\csc \phi - \sec \phi} = 1 + \sin \phi \cos \phi$$

46. Prove the following identities. (These two identities, along with $\sin^2 \theta + \cos^2 \theta = 1$, are known as the *Pythagorean identities*. They will be discussed in the next chapter.)

   (a) $\tan^2 \theta = \sec^2 \theta - 1$   (b) $\cot^2 \theta = \csc^2 \theta - 1$

47. If $\tan \alpha \tan \beta = 1$ and $\alpha$ and $\beta$ are acute angles, show that $\sec \alpha = \csc \beta$.   *Hint*: Make use of the identities in Exercise 46.

48. Refer to the figure. Express the slope $m$ of the line as a function of $\theta$.   *Hint*: What are the coordinates of the point $P$?

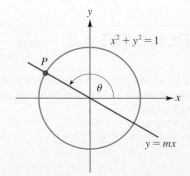

**49.** Suppose that $\sin \theta = (p - q)/(p + q)$, where $p$ and $q$ are positive and $90° < \theta < 180°$. (Note that $p > q$. Why?) Show that

$$\tan \theta = \frac{q - p}{2\sqrt{qp}}$$

**50.** In this exercise you will use the unit-circle definitions of sine and cosine, along with the identity $\sin^2 \theta + \cos^2 \theta = 1$ to prove a surprising geometric result. In the figure, we show an equilateral triangle inscribed in the unit circle $x^2 + y^2 = 1$. The vertices of the equilateral triangle are $A\left(-\frac{1}{2}, -\frac{\sqrt{3}}{2}\right)$, $B(1, 0)$, and $C\left(-\frac{1}{2}, \frac{\sqrt{3}}{2}\right)$. Prove that for any point $P$ on the unit circle, the sum of the squares of the distances from $P$ to the three vertices is 6. *Hint*: Let the coordinates of $P$ be $(\cos \theta, \sin \theta)$.

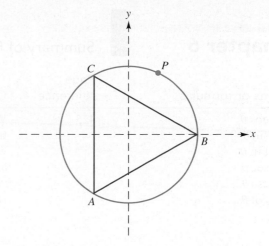

# MINI PROJECT | IDENTITIES AND GRAPHS

An identity is an assertion that two functions are equal for every value in their common domain. In this mini project you will use your graphing utility to visualize identities.

Ⓖ **EXERCISE**

Graph each pair of equations. If a pair of graphs suggests an identity, then state the identity clearly with a carefully stated domain. If a pair does not suggest an identity then exhibit a counterexample, that is, a value of the domain variable at which the function values are not the same. For trigonometric functions the variables represent angles in *degrees*. So, in parts (e) through (j), make sure you are working in degree mode and try starting with a window of $[-360, 360, 30]$ by $[-1, 1, 0.25]$ and then vary the size.

**(a)** $y = x^2 + 2x + 1$   and   $y = (x + 1)^2$

**(b)** $y = \dfrac{t^2 - 9}{t + 3}$   and   $y = t - 3$

**(c)** $y = \sqrt{x^2 + 9}$   and   $y = x + 3$

**(d)** $y = \dfrac{|p - 1|}{p - 1}$   and   $y = \begin{cases} -1, & \text{if } p < 1 \\ 1, & \text{if } p > 1 \end{cases}$

**(e)** $y = \cos^2 \theta + \sin^2 \theta$   and   $y = 1$

**(f)** $y = \sec^2 \alpha - 1$   and   $y = \tan^2 \alpha$

**(g)** $y = \sin 2\theta$   and   $y = 2 \sin \theta$

**(h)** $y = \cos 2\beta$   and   $y = \cos^2 \beta - \sin^2 \beta$

**(i)** $y = \cos(\alpha - 60°)$   and   $y = \cos \alpha - \cos 60°$

**(j)** $y = \cos 3\theta + \sqrt{3} \sin 3\theta$   and   $y = 2 \cos(3\theta - 60°)$

# Chapter 6

## Summary of Principal Terms and Formulas

| Terms or formulas | Page reference | Comments |
|---|---|---|
| **1.** $\cos\theta$<br>$\sin\theta$<br>$\tan\theta$<br>$\sec\theta$<br>$\csc\theta$<br>$\cot\theta$ | 425 | When $\theta$ is an acute angle in a right triangle, the six trigonometric functions of $\theta$ are defined as follows. (In these definitions, the word "adjacent" means "the length of the side adjacent to angle $\theta$." The same conventions apply to the words "opposite" and "hypotenuse.")<br><br>$$\cos\theta = \frac{\text{adjacent}}{\text{hypotenuse}} \qquad \sec\theta = \frac{\text{hypotenuse}}{\text{adjacent}}$$<br>$$\sin\theta = \frac{\text{opposite}}{\text{hypotenuse}} \qquad \csc\theta = \frac{\text{hypotenuse}}{\text{opposite}}$$<br>$$\tan\theta = \frac{\text{opposite}}{\text{adjacent}} \qquad \cot\theta = \frac{\text{adjacent}}{\text{opposite}}$$ |
| **2.** $\sin^n\theta$ | 437 | $\sin^n\theta$ means $(\sin\theta)^n$. The same convention also applies to the other five trigonometric functions. |
| **3.** $\sin^2\theta + \cos^2\theta = 1$<br>$(\sin\theta)/(\cos\theta) = \tan\theta$<br>$\sin(90° - \theta) = \cos\theta$<br>$\cos(90° - \theta) = \sin\theta$<br>$\sec\theta = 1/\cos\theta$<br>$\csc\theta = 1/\sin\theta$<br>$\cot\theta = 1/\tan\theta$ | 438, 472 | These are some of the most fundamental trigonometric identities. (We'll see many more in the following chapter.) With the exception of the third and fourth identities in this list, we discussed these identities in the context of both right-triangle and unit-circle trigonometry. Although the third and fourth identities were discussed only in the context of right triangles, you'll see in Chapter 8 that these two identities indeed hold for all angles. |
| **4.** $A = \frac{1}{2}ab\sin\theta$ | 447, 468 | The area of a triangle equals one-half of the product of the lengths of two sides times the sine of the included angle. |
| **5.** Initial side of an angle<br>Terminal side of an angle | 460 | We think of the two rays that form an angle as having been originally coincident; then, while one ray is held fixed, the other is rotated to create the given angle. The fixed ray is the initial side of the angle, and the rotated ray is the terminal side. (See Figure 1 on page 460.) The measure of an angle is *positive* if the rotation is counterclockwise and *negative* if the rotation is clockwise. (See Figure 2 on page 460.) |
| **6.** Standard position | 460 | In a rectangular coordinate system an angle is in standard position if the vertex is located at $(0, 0)$ and the initial side of the angle lies along the positive horizontal axis. For examples, see Figure 3 on page 460. |

| Terms or formulas | Page reference | Comments |
|---|---|---|
| **7.** $\cos\theta$ $\sin\theta$ $\tan\theta$ $\sec\theta$ $\csc\theta$ $\cot\theta$ | 460–461 | If $\theta$ is an angle in standard position and $P(x, y)$ is the point where the terminal side of the angle meets the unit circle, then the six trigonometric functions of $\theta$ are defined as follows. $$\cos\theta = x \qquad\qquad \sec\theta = \frac{1}{x}\ (x \neq 0)$$ $$\sin\theta = y \qquad\qquad \csc\theta = \frac{1}{y}\ (y \neq 0)$$ $$\tan\theta = \frac{y}{x}\ (x \neq 0) \qquad \cot\theta = \frac{x}{y}\ (y \neq 0)$$ |
| **8.** Reference angle | 464 | Let $\theta$ be an angle in standard position in an $x$-$y$ coordinate system, and suppose that $\theta$ is not an integer multiple of 90°. The reference angle associated with $\theta$ is the acute angle (with positive measure) formed by the $x$–axis and the terminal side of the angle $\theta$. |
| **9.** The four-step procedure for evaluating the trigonometric functions | 466 | The following four-step procedure can be used to evaluate the trigonometric functions of angles that are not multiples of 90°.<br><br>**Step 1** Draw and label an appropriate picture.<br>**Step 2** Determine the reference angle associated with the given angle.<br>**Step 3** Evaluate the given trigonometric function using the reference angle for the input.<br>**Step 4** Affix the appropriate sign to the number found in Step 2. (See Examples 5 and 6 on pages 466–467.)<br><br>For the right-triangle version of the four step procedure, remember that each side has *positive* length and each *non*-right angle is *acute*. |

## Writing Mathematics

**1.** A student who wanted to simplify the expression $\dfrac{30°}{\sin 30°}$ wrote

$$\frac{30°}{\sin 30°} = \frac{\cancel{30°}}{\sin\cancel{30°}} = \frac{1}{\sin}$$

Explain why this is nonsense, and then indicate the correct solution.

**2.** Determine whether each of the following statements is TRUE or FALSE. In each case, write out your reason or reasons in complete sentences. If you draw a diagram to accompany your writing, be sure that you clearly label any parts of the diagram to which you refer in the writing.

**(a)** If $\theta$ is an angle in standard position and $180° < \theta < 270°$, then $\tan\theta < \sin\theta$.

**(b)** If $\theta$ is an acute angle in a right triangle, then $\sin\theta < 1$.

**(c)** If $\theta$ is an acute angle in a right triangle, then $\tan\theta < 1$.

**(d)** For all angles $\theta$, we have $\sin \theta = \sqrt{1 - \cos^2 \theta}$.

**(e)** For all acute angles $\theta$, we have $\sin \theta = \sqrt{1 - \cos^2 \theta}$.

**(f)** The formula for the area of a triangle, $A = \frac{1}{2}ab \sin \theta$, is not valid when $\theta$ is a right angle.

**(g)** Every angle $\theta$ satisfying $0° < \theta < 180°$ is an allowable input for the sine function.

**(h)** Every angle $\theta$ satisfying $0° < \theta < 180°$ is an allowable input for the tangent function.

**3.** A student who was asked to simplify the expression $\sin^2 33° + \sin^2 57°$ wrote $\sin^2 33° + \sin^2 57° = \sin^2(33° + 57°) = \sin^2 90° = 1^2 = 1$.

    **(a)** Where is the error?

    **(b)** What is the correct answer?

**4.** **(a)** Use a calculator to evaluate the quantity $4 \sin 18° \cos 36°$.

    **(b)** The following *very* short article, with the accompanying figure, appeared in *The Mathematical Gazette,* Vol. XXIII (1939), p. 211. On your own or with a classmate, study the article and fill in the missing details. Then, strictly on your own, rewrite the article in a paragraph (or two at the most). Write as if you were explaining to a friend or classmate why $4 \sin 18° \cos 36° = 1$.

> *To prove that* $4 \sin 18° \cos 36° = 1$.
> In the figure, $\sin 18° = \frac{1}{2}a/b$, $\cos 36° = \frac{1}{2}b/a$. Multiply.

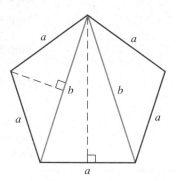

---

# Chapter 6 | Review Exercises

*For Exercises 1–16, evaluate each expression. (Don't use a calculator.)*

**1.** $\sin 135°$    **2.** $\cos(-60°)$    **3.** $\tan(-240°)$

**4.** $\sin 450°$    **5.** $\csc 210°$    **6.** $\sec 225°$

**7.** $\sin 270°$    **8.** $\cot(-330°)$    **9.** $\cos(-315°)$

**10.** $\cos 180°$    **11.** $\cos 1800°$    **12.** $\sec 120°$

**13.** $\csc 240°$    **14.** $\csc(-45°)$    **15.** $\sec 780°$

**16.** $\sin^2 33° + \sin^2 57°$

**17.** Simplify: $\ln(\sin^2 17° + \cos^2 17°) - \cos(\ln e^\pi)$.

**18.** If $\theta = 45°$, find each of the following.

    **(a)** $\cos \theta$    **(d)** $\cos 3\theta$    **(g)** $\cos(-\theta)$

    **(b)** $\cos^3 \theta$    **(e)** $\cos(2\theta/3)$    **(h)** $\cos^3 5\theta$

    **(c)** $\cos 2\theta$    **(f)** $(\cos 3\theta)/3$

*In Exercises 19–31, the lengths of the three sides of a triangle are denoted a, b, and c; the angles opposite these sides are A, B, and C, respectively. In each exercise, use the given information to find the required quantities.*

| GIVEN | FIND |
|---|---|
| **19.** $B = 90°$, $A = 30°$, $b = 1$ | $a$ and $c$ |
| **20.** $B = 90°$, $A = 60°$, $a = 1$ | $c$ and $b$ |
| **21.** $B = 90°$, $\sin A = 2/5$, $a = 7$ | $b$ |
| **22.** $B = 90°$, $\sec C = 4$, $c = \sqrt{2}$ | $b$ |

| GIVEN | FIND |
|---|---|
| **23.** $B = 90°$, $\cos A = 3/8$ | $\sin A$ and $\cot A$ |
| **24.** $B = 90°$, $b = 1$, | $a$ |
| $\tan C = \sqrt{5}$ | |
| **25.** $b = 4$, $c = 5$, | area of $\triangle ABC$ |
| $A = 150°$ | |
| **26.** $A = 120°$, $b = 8$ | $c$ |
| area $\triangle ABC = 12\sqrt{3}$ | |
| **27.** $c = 4$, $a = 2$, $B = 90°$ | $\sin^2 A + \cos^2 B$ |
| **28.** $B = 90°$, $2a = b$ | $A$ |
| **29.** $A = 30°$, $B = 120°$, | $a$ |
| $b = 16$ | |
| **30.** $a = 7$, $b = 8$, | area of $\triangle ABC$ |
| $\sin C = 1/4$ | |
| **31.** $a = b = 5$, | $c$ and area of $\triangle ABC$ |
| $\sin(\frac{1}{2}C) = 9/10$ | |

**32.** For the following figure, show that
$$y = x[\tan(\alpha + \beta) - \tan \beta]$$

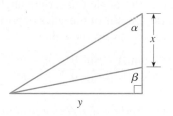

**33.** For the following figure, show that
$$y = \frac{x}{\cot \alpha - \cot \beta}$$

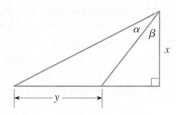

**34.** For the following figure, show that
$$\cot \theta = \frac{a}{b} + \cot \alpha$$

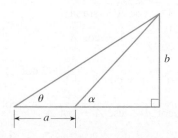

**35.** Suppose that $\theta$ is an acute angle in a right triangle and $\sin \theta = \dfrac{2p^2q^2}{p^4 + q^4}$. Find $\cos \theta$ and $\tan \theta$.

**36.** This problem is adapted from the text *An Elementary Treatise on Plane Trigonometry*, by R. D. Beasley, first published in 1884.
  **(a)** Prove the following identity, which will be used in part (b): $1 + \tan^2 \alpha = \sec^2 \alpha$.
  **(b)** Suppose that $\alpha$ and $\theta$ are acute angles and $\tan \theta = \dfrac{1 + \tan \alpha}{1 - \tan \alpha}$. Express $\sin \theta$ and $\cos \theta$ in terms of $\alpha$.   *Hint*: Draw a right triangle, label one of the angles $\theta$, and let the lengths of the sides opposite and adjacent to $\theta$ be $1 + \tan \alpha$ and $1 - \tan \alpha$, respectively.
      *Answer*:   $\sin \theta = (\cos \alpha + \sin \alpha)/\sqrt{2}$
               $\cos \theta = (\cos \alpha - \sin \alpha)/\sqrt{2}$

*In Exercises 37– 46, convert each expression into one involving only sines and cosines and then simplify. (Leave your answers in terms of sines and/or cosines.)*

**37.** $\dfrac{\sin A + \cos A}{\sec A + \csc A}$      **38.** $\dfrac{\csc A \sec A}{\sec^2 A + \csc^2 A}$

**39.** $\dfrac{\sin A \sec A}{\tan A + \cot A}$      **40.** $\cos A + \tan A \sin A$

**41.** $\dfrac{\cos A}{1 - \tan A} + \dfrac{\sin A}{1 - \cot A}$

**42.** $\dfrac{1}{\sec A - 1} \div \dfrac{1}{\sec A + 1}$

**43.** $(\sec A + \csc A)^{-1}[(\sec A)^{-1} + (\csc A)^{-1}]$

**44.** $\dfrac{\dfrac{\tan^2 A - 1}{\tan^3 A + \tan A}}{\dfrac{\tan A + 1}{\tan^2 A + 1}}$

**45.** $\dfrac{\dfrac{\sin A + \cos A}{\sin A - \cos A} - \dfrac{\sin A - \cos A}{\sin A + \cos A}}{\dfrac{\sin A + \cos A}{\sin A - \cos A} + \dfrac{\sin A - \cos A}{\sin A + \cos A}}$

**46.** $\dfrac{\sin A \tan A - \cos A \cot A}{\sec A - \csc A}$

*In Exercises 47–50, refer to the figure at the top of the next page. This figure shows a highly magnified view of the point P, where the terminal side of an angle of 10° (in standard position) meets the unit circle.*

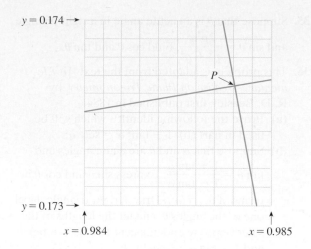

$y = 0.174 \rightarrow$

$P$

$y = 0.173 \rightarrow$

$x = 0.984$          $x = 0.985$

**47.** Using the figure, estimate the value of cos 10° to four decimal places. (Then use a calculator to check your estimate.)

**48.** Use your estimate in Exercise 47 to evaluate each of the following.
(a) cos 170°      (b) cos 190°      (c) cos 350°

**49.** Using the figure, estimate the value of sin 10° to four decimal places. (Then use a calculator to check your estimate.)

**50.** Use your estimate in Exercise 49 to evaluate each of the following.
(a) sin(−10°)
(b) sin(−190°)
(c) sin(−370°)

*In Exercises 51–60, use the given information to find the required quantities.*

| GIVEN | FIND |
|---|---|
| **51.** $\cos \theta = 3/5$, | $\sin \theta$ and $\tan \theta$ |
| $0° < \theta < 90°$ | |
| **52.** $\sin \theta = -12/13$, | $\cos \theta$ |
| $180° < \theta < 270°$ | |
| **53.** $\sec \theta = 25/7$, | $\tan \theta$ |
| $270° < \theta < 360°$ | |
| **54.** $\cot \theta = 4/3$, | $\sin \theta$ |
| $0° < \theta < 90°$ | |
| **55.** $\csc \theta = 13/12$, | $\cot \theta$ |
| $0° < \theta < 90°$ | |
| **56.** $\sin \theta = 1/5$, | $\cos(90° - \theta)$ |
| $0° < \theta < 90°$ | |
| **57.** $\cos \theta = 5t$, | $\tan(90° - \theta)$ |
| $0° < \theta < 90°$ | |
| **58.** $\sin \theta = -\sqrt{5}u$, | $\sec \theta$ |
| $90° < \theta < 270°$ | |

| GIVEN | FIND |
|---|---|
| **59.** $\tan \theta = \dfrac{\sqrt{2} - 1}{\sqrt{2} + 1}$, | $\sin \theta$ |
| $0° < \theta < 90°$ | |
| **60.** $\cos \theta = \dfrac{2u}{u^2 + 1}$, | $\tan \theta$ |
| $0° < \theta < 90°$ | |

**61.** Suppose $\theta$ is an acute angle and $\tan \theta + \cot \theta = 2$. Show that $\sin \theta + \cos \theta = \sqrt{2}$.

**62.** A 100-ft vertical antenna is on the roof of a building. From a point on the ground, the angles of elevation to the top and the bottom of the antenna are 51° and 37°, respectively. Find the height of the building.

**63.** In an isosceles triangle, the two base angles are each 35°, and the length of the base is 120 cm. Find the area of the triangle.

**64.** Find the perimeter and the area of a regular pentagon inscribed in a circle of radius 9 cm.

**65.** In triangle $ABC$, let $a$ be the length of the side opposite angle $A$, and let $h$ denote the length of the altitude from $A$ to $\overline{BC}$. Show that $h = a/(\cot B + \cot C)$.

**66.** The length of each side of an equilateral triangle is $2a$. Show that the radius of the inscribed circle is $a/\sqrt{3}$ and the radius of the circumscribed circle is $2a/\sqrt{3}$.

**67.** From a helicopter $h$ ft above the sea, the angle of depression to the pilot's horizon is $\theta$. Show that $\cot \theta = R/\sqrt{2Rh + h^2}$, where $R$ is the radius of the Earth.

**68.** In triangle $ABC$, angle $C$ is a right angle. If $a$, $b$, and $c$ denote the lengths of the sides opposite angles $A$, $B$, and $C$, respectively, show that

$$\frac{\sin A - \sin B}{\sin A + \sin B} = \frac{a - b}{a + b}$$

*In Exercises 69–78, show that each equation is an identity.*

**69.** $\sin^2(90° - \theta) \csc \theta - \tan^2(90° - \theta) \sin \theta = 0$

**70.** $\cos A \cot A = \csc A - \sin A$

**71.** $\sec A - 1 = (\sec A)(1 - \cos A)$

**72.** $\dfrac{\cot A - 1}{\cot A + 1} = \dfrac{\cos A - \sin A}{\cos A + \sin A}$

**73.** $\dfrac{\sin A}{\csc A - \cot A} = 1 + \cos A$

**74.** $\dfrac{1}{1 - \cos A} + \dfrac{1}{1 + \cos A} = 2 + 2\cot^2 A$

**75.** $\dfrac{1}{\csc A - \cot A} - \dfrac{1}{\csc A + \cot A} = 2\cot A$

**76.**
$$\frac{1}{1+\sin^2 A}+\frac{1}{1+\cos^2 A}+\frac{1}{1+\sec^2 A}+\frac{1}{1+\csc^2 A}=2$$

**77.** $\dfrac{\sec A - \tan A}{\sec A + \tan A} = \left(\dfrac{\cos A}{1+\sin A}\right)^2$

**78.** $\dfrac{1-\sin\theta\cos\theta}{\cos\theta(\sec\theta-\csc\theta)}\cdot\dfrac{\sin^2\theta-\cos^2\theta}{\sin^3\theta+\cos^3\theta}=\sin\theta$

**79.** The radius of the circle in the following figure is one unit. The line segment $\overline{PT}$ is tangent to the circle at $P$, and $\overline{PN}$ is perpendicular to $\overline{OT}$. Express each of the following lengths in terms of $\theta$.

(a) $PN$     (c) $PT$     (e) $NA$
(b) $ON$     (d) $OT$     (f) $NT$

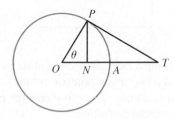

**80.** Refer to the figure accompanying Exercise 79.
(a) Show that the ratio of the area of triangle $ONP$ to the area of triangle $NPT$ is $\cot^2\theta$.
(b) Show that the ratio of the area of triangle $NPT$ to the area of triangle $OPT$ is $\sin^2\theta$.

**81.** Refer to the following figure. From a point $R$, two tangent lines are drawn to a circle of radius 1. These tangents meet the circle at the points $P$ and $Q$. At the midpoint of the circular arc $\overset{\frown}{PQ}$, a third tangent line is drawn, meeting the other two tangents at $T$ and $U$, as shown. Express the area of triangle $RTU$ as a function of $\theta$ (where $\theta$ is defined in the figure).

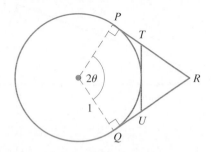

**82.** Suppose that in $\triangle ABC$, angle $C$ is a right angle. Let $a$, $b$, and $c$ denote the lengths of the sides opposite angles $A$, $B$, and $C$, respectively. Use the right-triangle definitions of sine and cosine to prove that
$$\frac{a^2\cos^2 B - b^2\cos^2 A}{a^2 - b^2} = 1$$

**83.** The following figure shows a semicircle with radius $AO = 1$.

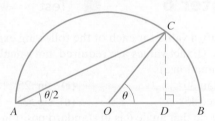

(a) Use the figure to derive the formula
$$\tan\frac{\theta}{2}=\frac{\sin\theta}{1+\cos\theta}$$
*Hint*: Show that $CD = \sin\theta$ and $OD = \cos\theta$. Then look at right triangle $ADC$ to find $\tan(\theta/2)$.

(b) Use the formula developed in part (a) to show that
(i) $\tan 15° = \dfrac{1}{2+\sqrt{3}} = 2 - \sqrt{3};$
(ii) $\tan 22.5° = \sqrt{2} - 1$.

**84.** This exercise outlines geometric derivations of formulas
$$\sin 2\theta = 2\sin\theta\cos\theta \qquad \cos 2\theta = 2\cos^2\theta - 1$$

Refer to the figure, which shows a semicircle with diameter $\overline{SV}$ and radius $UV = 1$. In each case, supply the reasons for the given statement.
(a) $TU = \cos 2\theta$
(b) $TV = 1 + \cos 2\theta$
(c) $WT = \sin 2\theta$
(d) $WV = 2\cos\theta$    *Hint*: Use right triangle $SWV$.
(e) $SW = 2\sin\theta$
(f) $\sin\theta = \dfrac{\sin 2\theta}{2\cos\theta}$

*Hint*: Use $\triangle WTV$ and the results in parts (c) and (d).
(g) $\sin 2\theta = 2\sin\theta\cos\theta$
(h) $\cos\theta = \dfrac{1+\cos 2\theta}{2\cos\theta}$    *Hint*: Use $\triangle WTV$.
(i) $\cos 2\theta = 2\cos^2\theta - 1$

# Chapter 6  Test

1. Specify a value for each of the following expressions. (Exact values are required, not calculator approximations.)
   (a) $\tan 30°$        (c) $\sin^2 25° + \cos^2 25°$
   (b) $\sec 45°$        (d) $\sin 53° - \cos 37°$

2. Suppose that angle $\theta$ is in standard position and the terminal side of the angle is in the third quadrant. Which of the following are positive?
   (a) $\sec \theta$        (b) $\csc \theta$        (c) $\cot \theta$

3. Evaluate each of the following:
   (a) $\cdot \sin(-270°)$        (c) $\tan 720°$
   (b) $\cos 180°$

4. Factor: $2 \cot^2 \theta + 11 \cot \theta + 12$.

5. Find the area of a triangle in which the lengths of two sides are 8 cm and 9 cm and the angle included between those two sides is $150°$.

6. Evaluate each of the following (exact values required, not calculator approximations):
   (a) $\sin(-225°)$        (c) $\sec 120°$
   (b) $\tan 330°$

7. If $\sin \theta = -\sqrt{5}/5$ and $180° < \theta < 270°$, find $\cos \theta$ and $\tan \theta$.

8. If $\sin \theta = -u/3$ and $270° < \theta < 360°$, express $\cos \theta$ and $\cot \theta$ as functions of $u$.

9. Simplify: $\dfrac{\dfrac{\cos \theta + 1}{\cos \theta} + 1}{\dfrac{\cos \theta - 1}{\cos \theta} - 1}$.

10. A regular nine-sided polygon is inscribed in a circle of radius 3 m. Find the area of the polygon. Give two forms of the answer: one in terms of a trigonometric function and the other a calculator approximation rounded to three decimal places.

11. Express each term using sines and cosines and simplify as much as possible:
$$\frac{\cot^2 \theta}{\csc^2 \theta} + \frac{\tan^2 \theta}{\sec^2 \theta}$$

12. In the figure, $\angle DAB = 25°$, $\angle CAB = 55°$, and $AB = 50$ cm. Find $CD$. Leave your answer in terms of the trigonometric functions (rather than using a calculator).

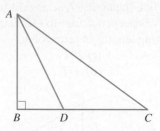

13. Without using a calculator, determine in each case which of the two trigonometric values is the larger. State your reasons.   *Hint*: Sketch each pair of angles in standard position.
   (a) $\sin 5°$ or $\sin 85°$
   (b) $\sin 5°$ or $\cos 5°$
   (c) $\tan 175°$ or $\tan 185°$

14. In $\triangle ABC$ (shown in the figure), $\angle A = 20°$, $AB = 3.25$ cm, and $AC = 2.75$ cm. Complete steps (a) and (b) to determine the length $CB$.
   (a) Find $AD$, $DB$, and $CD$. Leave your answers in terms of the trigonometric functions.
   (b) Find $CB$ by applying the Pythagorean theorem in $\triangle CDB$. For your final answer, use a calculator and round to two decimal places.

# Trigonometric Functions of Real Numbers

*Trigonometric functions were originally introduced and tabulated in calculations in astronomy and navigation and were used extensively in surveying. What is more important* [now], *they describe a periodic process, like the vibration of a string, the tides, planetary motion, alternating currents, or the emission of light by atoms.* —From *The Mathematical Sciences,* edited by the Committee on Support of Research in the Mathematical Sciences with the collaboration of George Boehm (Cambridge, Mass.: The M.I.T. Press, 1969)

As the opening quotation indicates, the trigonometric functions play an important role in many of the modern applications of mathematics. In these applications the inputs for the functions are real numbers rather than angles. To make the transition from angle inputs to real-number inputs, we introduce *radian measure* for angles in Sections 7.1 and 7.2. Then in Section 7.3 we use radian measure to restate the definitions of the trigonometric functions in such a way that the domains are indeed sets of real numbers. Among other advantages, this allows us to analyze the trigonometric functions using the graphing techniques from Chapter 3. Graphs relating to the sine and cosine functions are discussed in Sections 7.4 and 7.5. The next Section, 7.6, shows how these graphs are used in the study of *simple harmonic motion.* The last section of the chapter, 7.7, focuses on the graphs of the tangent, the cotangent, the secant, and the cosecant functions.

## 7.1 RADIAN MEASURE

*Degree measure, traditionally used to measure the angles of a geometric figure, has one serious drawback. It is artificial. There is no intrinsic connection between a degree and the geometry of a circle. Why 360 degrees for one revolution? Why not 400? or 100?* —*Calculus, One and Several Variables,* 7th ed., by S. L. Salas and Einar Hille, revised by Garret J. Etgen (New York: John Wiley and Sons, Inc., 1995)

In elementary geometry, angles are measured using the familiar units of degrees. However, for the more analytical portions of trigonometry and for calculus, *radian measure* is most often used. The radian measure of an angle is defined as follows.

---

**DEFINITION** | **The Radian Measure of an Angle**

---

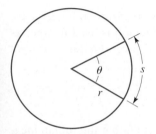

**Figure 1**
The radian measure $\theta$ is defined by the equation $\theta = s/r$.

Place the vertex of the angle at the center of a circle of radius $r$. Let $s$ denote the length of the arc intercepted by the angle, as indicated in Figure 1. The **radian measure** $\theta$ of the angle is the ratio of the arc length $s$ to the radius $r$.

**487**

In symbols,

$$\theta = \frac{s}{r} \tag{1}$$

In this definition it is assumed that $s$ and $r$ have the same linear units.

**EXAMPLE** **1** **Calculating the radian measure of an angle**

Determine the radian measure for each angle in Figure 2.

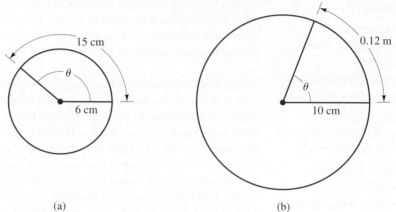

**Figure 2**          (a)                              (b)

**SOLUTION**

In Figure 2(a) we have $r = 6$ cm, $s = 15$ cm, and therefore

$$\theta = \frac{s}{r} = \frac{15 \text{ cm}}{6 \text{ cm}} = \frac{5}{2}$$

So for the angle in Figure 2(a) we obtain $\theta = 5/2$ radians. In the calculations just completed, notice that although both $s$ and $r$ have the dimensions of length, the resulting radian measure $s/r$ is simply a real number with no dimensions. (The dimensions "cancel out." *Note:* When we write $\theta = 5/2$ radians, we do not think of radians as a dimension, but we are indicating that we are interpreting the *ratio* 5/2 as the measure of an angle.)

Before carrying out the calculations for the radian measure in Figure 2(b), we have to arrange matters so that the same unit of length is used for the radius and the arc length. Converting the arc length $s$ to centimeters, we have $s = 12$ cm, and, consequently,

$$\theta = \frac{s}{r} = \frac{12 \text{ cm}}{10 \text{ cm}} = \frac{6}{5}$$

Thus in Figure 2(b) we have $\theta = 6/5$ radians. Again, note that the radian measure $s/r$ is dimensionless. (Check for yourself that the same answer is obtained if we use meters rather than centimeters for the common unit of measurement.)

At first it might appear to you that the radian measure depends on the radius of the particular circle that we use. But as you will see, this is not the case. To gain some experience in working with the definition of radian measure, let's calculate the radian measure of the right angle in Figure 3. We begin with the formula $\theta = s/r$. Now, since $\theta$ is a right angle, the arc length $s$ is one-quarter of the entire circumference. Thus

**Figure 3**

$$s = \frac{1}{4}(2\pi r) = \frac{\pi r}{2} \tag{2}$$

Using equation (2) to substitute for $s$ in equation (1), we get

$$\theta = \frac{\pi r/2}{r} = \frac{\pi r}{2} \times \frac{1}{r} = \frac{\pi}{2}$$

We commonly write

$$90° = \frac{\pi}{2} \text{ radians} \tag{3}$$

So the right angle $\theta$ in Figure 3 has degree measure 90° and radian measure $\pi/2$ radians. (Notice that the radius $r$ does not appear in our answer.)

For practical reasons we would like to be able to convert rapidly between degree and radian measure. Multiplying both sides of equation (3) by 2 yields

$$180° = \pi \text{ radians} \tag{4}$$

Equation (4) is useful and should be memorized. For instance, dividing both sides of equation (4) by 6 yields

$$\frac{180°}{6} = \frac{\pi}{6} \text{ radians}$$

or

$$30° = \frac{\pi}{6} \text{ radians}$$

Similarly, dividing both sides of equation (4) by 4 and 3, respectively, yields

$$45° = \frac{\pi}{4} \text{ radians} \qquad \text{and} \qquad 60° = \frac{\pi}{3} \text{ radians}$$

And multiplying both sides of equation (4) by 2 gives us

$$360° = 2\pi \text{ radians}$$

Figure 4 summarizes some of these results.

**Figure 4**

| EXAMPLE | 2 | An important observation |
|---|---|---|

**(a)** Express 1° in radian measure.
**(b)** Express 1 radian in terms of degrees.

**SOLUTION**
**(a)** We can solve equation (4) for 1 degree by dividing both sides by 180 to yield

$$1° = \frac{\pi}{180} \text{ radian} \qquad (\approx 0.017 \text{ radian})$$

**(b)** Similarly, we can solve equation (4) for 1 radian by dividing both sides by $\pi$ to yield

$$1 \text{ radian} = \frac{180°}{\pi}$$

In other words, 1 radian is approximately 180°/3.14, or 57.3°.

From the results in Example 2 we have the following rules for converting between radians and degrees.

To convert from degrees to radians, multiply by $\pi/180°$. To convert from radians to degrees, multiply by $180°/\pi$.

| EXAMPLE | 3 | Converting from degrees to radians |
|---|---|---|

Convert 150° to radians.

**SOLUTION**

$$150° \left( \frac{\pi}{180°} \right) = \frac{5\pi}{6} \qquad \text{reducing the fraction}$$

Thus

$$150° = \frac{5\pi}{6} \text{ radians}$$

| EXAMPLE | 4 | Converting from radians to degrees |
|---|---|---|

Convert $11\pi/6$ radians to degrees.

**SOLUTION**

$$\frac{11\pi}{6} \left( \frac{180°}{\pi} \right) = \frac{(11)(180°)}{6} = 11(30°) = 330°$$

So $11\pi/6$ radians = 330°.

We saw in Example 2(b) that 1 radian is approximately 57°. It is also important to be able to visualize an angle of 1 radian without thinking in terms of degree measure. This is done as follows. In the equation $\theta = s/r$, we let $\theta = 1$. This yields $1 = s/r$, and, consequently, $r = s$. In other words, in any circle, 1 radian is the measure of the central angle that intercepts an arc equal in length to the radius of the circle. In the box that follows we summarize this result. Figure 5 displays angles of 1, 2, and 3 radians.

## PROPERTY SUMMARY    Radian Measure

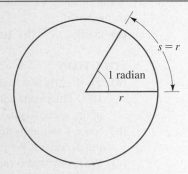

In a circle, 1 radian is the measure of the central angle that intercepts an arc equal in length to the radius of the circle.

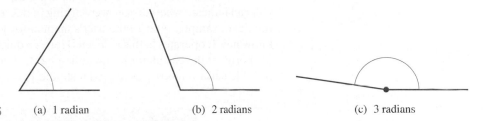

Figure 5       (a)  1 radian                           (b)  2 radians                           (c)  3 radians

From now on, when we specify the measure of an angle, we will assume that the units are radians unless the degree symbol is explicitly used. (This convention is also used in calculus.) For instance, the equation $\theta = 2$ means that $\theta$ is 2 radians. Similarly, the expression $\sin(\pi/6)$ refers to the sine of $\pi/6$ radians.

  **EXAMPLE**  5    **Finding values of trigonometric functions of angles in radians**

Evaluate the following quantities:

**(a)**  $\sin \dfrac{\pi}{6}$;        **(b)**  $\cos 2\pi$.

**SOLUTION**

**(a)**  $\dfrac{\pi}{6}$ radians $= 30°$; therefore

$$\sin \frac{\pi}{6} = \sin 30° = \frac{1}{2} \qquad \text{because } \sin 30° = \tfrac{1}{2}$$

**(b)** $2\pi$ radians $= 360°$; therefore

$$\cos 2\pi = \cos 360° = 1 \qquad \text{because } \cos 360° = 1$$

---

| EXAMPLE | 6 | Finding signs of trigonometric functions of angles in radians |
|---|---|---|

Without using a calculator, determine whether the following values are positive or negative:

**(a)** $\cos 3$;      **(b)** $\sin 1$;      **(c)** $\tan 6$.

**SOLUTION**

**(a)** 3 is slightly less than $\pi$, and $\pi$ radians is $180°$, so 3 radians is slightly less that $180°$. Thus in standard position the terminal side of an angle of 3 radians lies in the second quadrant. Therefore $\cos 3$ is negative.

**(b)** Since 1 radian is approximately $60°$ [as we saw in Example 2(b) and in Figure 5], $\sin 1$ is positive.

**(c)** We know that 6 radians is slightly less than $2\pi$ radians, which is one revolution, or $360°$. Thus, in standard position, the terminal side of an angle of 6 radians lies in the fourth quadrant. Consequently, $\tan 6$ is negative.

---

As we mentioned in Chapter 6, all scientific calculators have keys with which you can indicate whether you are working in degrees or radians. In preparation for the next example, refer to the user's manual for your calculator to make sure you know how it operates in this respect. [Here's a quick way to find out whether you've properly set the calculator in the radian mode. Compute $\sin(\pi/6)$ and see whether the calculator reads 0.5, as indeed it should.]

---

| EXAMPLE | 7 | Using the unit circle to visually estimate cosine and sine |
|---|---|---|

Use Figure 6 to approximate to within successive tenths the following trigonometric values. Then use a calculator to check your answers. Round off the calculator values to two decimal places:

**(a)** $\cos 3$ and $\sin 3$;      **(b)** $\cos(-3)$ and $\sin(-3)$.

**SOLUTION**

**(a)** Figure 6 shows that (the terminal side of ) an angle of 3 radians in standard position meets the unit circle at a point in the second quadrant. Letting $(x, y)$ denote the coordinates of that point, we have (using the grid in Figure 6)

$$-1.0 < x < -0.9 \qquad \text{and} \qquad 0.1 < y < 0.2$$

But by definition, $\cos 3 = x$ and $\sin 3 = y$, so, consequently,

$$-1.0 < \cos 3 < -0.9 \qquad \text{and} \qquad 0.1 < \sin 3 < 0.2$$

The corresponding calculator values here are

$$\cos 3 \approx -0.99 \qquad \text{and} \qquad \sin 3 \approx 0.14$$

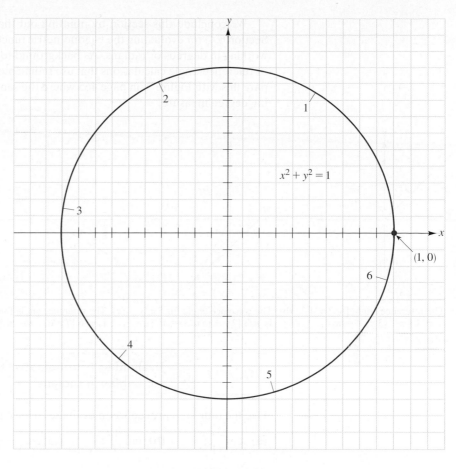

**Figure 6**
Radian measure on the unit circle
for angles in standard position

Note that the estimates we obtained from Figure 6 are consistent with these calculator values. (When you verify these calculator values for yourself, be sure that the calculator is set in the radian mode.)

**(b)** In Figure 6 we want to know where the terminal side of an angle of $-3$ radians intersects the unit circle. There is no marker for this point in Figure 6. We can, nevertheless, locate the point by using symmetry. Let $(x, y)$ denote the point corresponding to 3 radians, determined in part (a). By reflecting the point in the $x$-axis, we obtain the point corresponding to $-3$ radians. This means that the required point will have the same $x$-coordinate as the point in part (a), while the $y$-coordinate will be just the negative of that in part (a). So, given that

$$-1.0 < \cos 3 < -0.9 \qquad \text{and} \qquad 0.1 < \sin 3 < 0.2$$

we conclude that

$$-1.0 < \cos(-3) < -0.9 \qquad \text{and} \qquad -0.2 < \sin(-3) < -0.1$$

For the corresponding calculator values here, we obtain

$$\cos(-3) \approx -0.99 \qquad \text{and} \qquad \sin(-3) \approx -0.14$$

Again, note that the estimates from Figure 6 are consistent with these calculator values. When you verify these calculator values for yourself, remember that the calculator should be in the radian mode.

We conclude this section by pointing out that our four-step procedure (from Section 6.4) for evaluating the trigonometric functions is applicable whether we are working in degrees or radians. As background for this, Figure 7 displays examples of reference-angle calculations that use radian measure. You should carefully compare this with Figure 9 on page 465 where the same calculations are carried out using degree measure.

(a) The reference angle for $3\pi/4$ is $\pi/4$ $[\pi - (3\pi/4) = \pi/4]$.

(b) The reference angle for $5\pi/3$ is $\pi/3$ $[2\pi - (5\pi/3) = \pi/3]$.

(c) The reference angle for $7\pi/6$ is $\pi/6$ $[7\pi/6 - \pi = \pi/6]$.

(d) The reference angle for $-\pi/4$ is $\pi/4$.

**Figure 7**

| EXAMPLE | 8 | Evaluating trigonometric functions for angles in radians |

Use the four-step procedure to evaluate each of the following expressions:

(a) $\cos\dfrac{3\pi}{4}$;    (b) $\tan\dfrac{7\pi}{6}$;    (c) $\csc\left(-\dfrac{\pi}{4}\right)$.

**SOLUTION**

(a) **Step 1**  See Figure 7(a).

   **Step 2**  The reference angle for $3\pi/4$ is $\pi/4$.

   **Step 3**  $\cos(\pi/4) = \sqrt{2}/2$

   **Step 4**  $\cos\theta$ is the $x$-coordinate of a point on the unit circle. The terminal side of $\theta = 3\pi/4$ lies in Quadrant II, where $x$-coordinates are negative. Consequently, we have $\cos(3\pi/4) = -\cos(\pi/4) = -\sqrt{2}/2$.

(b) **Step 1**  See Figure 7(c).

   **Step 2**  The reference angle for $7\pi/6$ is $\pi/6$.

   **Step 3**  $\tan(\pi/6) = \sqrt{3}/3$ (How do we know this?)

   **Step 4**  By definition, $\tan\theta = y/x$. Now, the terminal side of $\theta = 7\pi/6$ lies in Quadrant III, in which both $x$ and $y$ are negative. Thus the quotient $y/x$ is positive, and we conclude that $\tan(7\pi/6) = \tan(\pi/6) = \sqrt{3}/3$.

(c) **Step 1**  See Figure 7(d).

   **Step 2**  The reference angle for $-\pi/4$ is $\pi/4$.

   **Step 3**  $\csc(\pi/4) = \dfrac{1}{\sin(\pi/4)} = \dfrac{1}{1/\sqrt{2}} = \sqrt{2}$

   **Step 4**  By definition, $\csc\theta = 1/y$. Now, the terminal side of $\theta = -\pi/4$ lies in Quadrant IV, in which $y$ is negative. Consequently $1/y$ is negative, and we have $\csc(-\pi/4) = -\csc(-\pi/4) = -\sqrt{2}$.

# EXERCISE SET 7.1

## A

In Exercises 1–4, use the definition $\theta = s/r$ to determine the radian measure of each angle.

**1.**

5 cm

$\theta$

2 cm

**2.**

2 cm

$\theta$

3 cm

**3.**

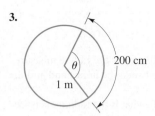

200 cm

$\theta$

1 m

**4.**

$r = 1.0013$ cm

$r$

$\theta$

0.0367 m

In Exercises 5–8, convert to radian measure. Express your answers both in terms of $\pi$ and as decimal approximations rounded to two decimal places.

**5. (a)** 45°     **(b)** 90°     **(c)** 135°
**6. (a)** 30°     **(b)** 150°    **(c)** 300°
**7. (a)** 0°      **(b)** 360°    **(c)** 450°
**8. (a)** 36°     **(b)** 35°     **(c)** 720°

In Exercises 9–12, convert the radian measures to degrees.

**9. (a)** $\pi/12$     **(b)** $\pi/6$     **(c)** $\pi/4$
**10. (a)** $3\pi$      **(b)** $3\pi/2$    **(c)** $2\pi$
**11. (a)** $\pi/3$     **(b)** $5\pi/3$    **(c)** $4\pi$
**12. (a)** $5\pi/6$    **(b)** $11\pi/6$   **(c)** 0

In Exercises 13 and 14, convert the radian measures to degrees. Round the answers to two decimal places.

**13. (a)** 2     **(b)** 3     **(c)** $\pi^2$
**14. (a)** 1.32  **(b)** 0.96  **(c)** $1/\pi$

**15.** Suppose that the radian measure of an angle is $3/2$. Without using a calculator or tables, determine if this angle is larger or smaller than a right angle.   *Hint:* What is the radian measure of a right angle?

**16.** Two angles in a triangle have radian measure $\pi/5$ and $\pi/6$. What is the radian measure of the third angle?

For Exercises 17 and 18, refer to the following figure, which shows all of the angles from 0° to 360° that are multiples of 30° or 45°.

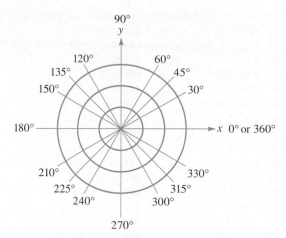

**17.** In the figure, relabel the angles in Quadrants I and II using radian measure.
**18.** In the figure, relabel the angles in Quadrants III and IV using radian measure.

In Exercises 19 and 20, complete the tables.

**19.**

| $\theta$ | $\sin \theta$ | $\cos \theta$ | $\tan \theta$ |
|---|---|---|---|
| 0 | | | |
| $\pi/2$ | | | |
| $\pi$ | | | |
| $3\pi/2$ | | | |
| $2\pi$ | | | |

**20.**

| $\theta$ | $\csc \theta$ | $\sec \theta$ | $\cot \theta$ |
|---|---|---|---|
| 0 | | | |
| $\pi/2$ | | | |
| $\pi$ | | | |
| $3\pi/2$ | | | |
| $2\pi$ | | | |

In Exercises 21–30, use Figure 6 to approximate the given trigonometric values to within successive tenths. Then use a calculator to compute the values to the nearest hundredth.

**21.** cos 1 and sin 1
**22.** cos 2 and sin 2
**23.** $\cos(-1)$ and $\sin(-1)$
**24.** $\cos(-2)$ and $\sin(-2)$
**25.** cos 4 and sin 4

26. cos 5 and sin 5
27. cos(−4) and sin(−4)
28. cos(−5) and sin(−5)
29. sin(1 + 2π)
30. sin(2 + 2π)

*In Exercises 31–40, evaluate each expression (as in Example 8).*

31. (a) cos(π/3)     (c) sin(π/3)
    (b) cos(−π/3)    (d) sin(−π/3)
32. (a) cos(5π/3)    (c) sin(5π/3)
    (b) cos(−5π/3)   (d) sin(−5π/3)
33. (a) cos(4π/3)    (c) sin(4π/3)
    (b) cos(−4π/3)   (d) sin(−4π/3)
34. (a) cos(2π/3)    (c) sin(2π/3)
    (b) cos(−2π/3)   (d) sin(−2π/3)
35. (a) cos(5π/4)    (c) sin(5π/4)
    (b) cos(−5π/4)   (d) sin(−5π/4)
36. (a) cos(17π/6)   (c) sin(17π/6)
    (b) cos(17π/6)   (d) sin(−17π/6)
37. (a) sec(4π/3)    (c) tan(4π/3)
    (b) csc(−4π/3)   (d) cot(−4π/3)
38. (a) sec(7π/4)    (c) tan(7π/4)
    (b) csc(−7π/4)   (d) cot(−7π/4)
39. (a) sec(17π/6)   (c) tan(17π/6)
    (b) csc(−17π/6)  (d) cot(−17π/6)
40. (a) sec(3π/4)    (c) tan(3π/4)
    (b) csc(−3π/4)   (d) cot(−3π/4)

# B

41. Suppose that you have two sticks and a piece of wire, each of length 1 ft, fastened at the ends to form an equilateral triangle; see Figure A. If side $\overline{BC}$ is bent out to form an

arc of a circle with center $A$, then the angle at $A$ will decrease from 60° to something less. See Figure B. What is the measure of this new angle at $A$ in both radians and degrees?

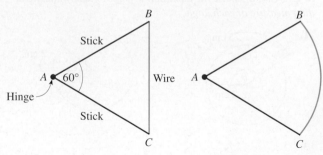

Figure A          Figure B

42. (a) When a clock reads 4:00, what is the radian measure of the (smaller) angle between the hour hand and the minute hand?
    (b) When a clock reads 5:30, what is the radian measure of the (smaller) angle between the hour hand and the minute hand?
43. Are there any real numbers $x$ with the property that $x$ degrees equals $x$ radians? If so, find them; if not, explain why not.
44. Are there any real numbers $x$ with the property that $x$ degrees equals $2x$ radians? If so, find them; if not, explain why not.

## 7.2 RADIAN MEASURE AND GEOMETRY

*. . . I wrote to him* [to Alexander J. Ellis, in 1874], *and he declared at once for the form "radian," on the ground that it could be viewed as a contraction for "radial angle. . . ."*—Thomas Muir, in a letter appearing in the April 7, 1910, issue of *Nature*

*I shall be very pleased to send Dr. Muir a copy of my father's examination questions of June, 1873, containing the word* radian. *. . . It thus appears that* radian *was thought of independently by Dr. Muir and my father, and, what is really more important than the exact form of the name, they both independently thought of the necessity of giving a name to the unit-angle.*—James Thomson, in a letter appearing in the June 16, 1910, issue of *Nature*

One of the advantages in using radian measure in precalculus and calculus is that many formulas then take on especially simple forms. The two basic formulas in the box that follows are examples of this.

## PROPERTY SUMMARY  Formulas for Arc Length and Sector Area

1. *Arc Length Formula*
   (Refer to Figure 1.) In a circle of radius $r$, the arc length $s$ determined by a central angle of radian measure $\theta$ is given by

   $$s = r\theta$$

   In this formula it is assumed that $s$ and $r$ have the same linear units.

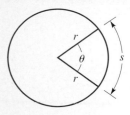

Figure 1

2. *Sector Area Formula*
   (Refer to Figure 2, in which the shaded region is a *sector.*) In a circle of radius $r$, the area $A$ of a sector with central angle of radian measure $\theta$ is given by

   $$A = \frac{1}{2}r^2\theta$$

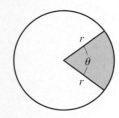

Figure 2

The arc length formula is a direct consequence of the definition of radian measure. Recall from the previous section that the defining equation for radian measure is $\theta = s/r$. Multiplying both sides of this equation by $r$ yields $\theta r = s$; that is, $s = r\theta$, which is the arc length formula.

To derive the sector area formula, we'll rely on the following two facts from elementary geometry. First, the area of a circle of radius $r$ is $\pi r^2$. Second, the area $A$ of a sector is directly proportional to the measure $\theta$ of its central angle. (For example, if you double the angle, the area of the sector is doubled.) The statement that the area $A$ is directly proportional to the angle $\theta$ is expressed algebraically as

$$A = k\theta \tag{1}$$

To determine the value of the constant $k$, we use the fact that when $\theta = 2\pi$, the sector is actually a full circle with area $\pi r^2$. Substituting the values $\theta = 2\pi$ and $A = \pi r^2$ in equation (1) yields

$$\pi r^2 = k(2\pi)$$

and therefore

$$k = \frac{1}{2}r^2$$

Using this last value for $k$ in equation (1), we obtain $A = \frac{1}{2}r^2\theta$, as required. The next three examples indicate how the arc length formula and the sector area formula are used in calculations.

### EXAMPLE  1  Calculating arc length

Compute the indicated arc lengths in Figures 3(a) and 3(b). Express the answers both in terms of $\pi$ and as decimal approximations rounded to two decimal places.

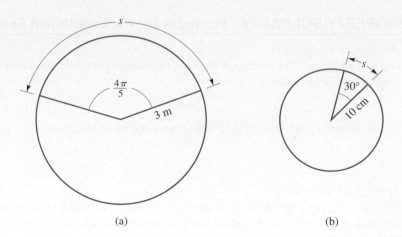

**Figure 3**

(a)                                                              (b)

**SOLUTION**

**(a)** We use the formula $s = r\theta$ with $r = 3$ m and $\theta = 4\pi/5$. This yields

$$s = (3 \text{ m})\left(\frac{4\pi}{5}\right) = \frac{12\pi}{5} \text{ m}$$

Using a calculator, we find that this is approximately 7.54 m.

**(b)** To apply the formula $s = r\theta$, the angle measure $\theta$ must first be expressed in radians (because the formula is just a restatement of the definition of radian measure). We've seen previously that $30° = \pi/6$ radians. So we have

$$s = r\theta = (10 \text{ cm})\left(\frac{\pi}{6}\right) = \frac{5\pi}{3} \text{ cm}$$

Before picking up the calculator, note that we can obtain a quick approximation here: Since $\pi \approx 3$, we have $s \approx 5(3/3) = 5$ cm. With a calculator now, we obtain $s = \frac{5\pi}{3}$ cm $\approx 5.24$ cm.

---

**EXAMPLE  2    Calculating the area of a sector**

Compute the area of the sector in Figure 4.

**Figure 4**

**SOLUTION**

We first convert 120° to radians:

$$120°\left(\frac{\pi}{180°}\right) = \frac{2\pi}{3} \text{ radians}$$

We then have

$$A = \frac{1}{2}r^2\theta$$

$$= \frac{1}{2}(5 \text{ cm})^2\left(\frac{2\pi}{3}\right) = \frac{25\pi}{3} \text{ cm}^2 \qquad (\approx 26.18 \text{ cm}^2)$$

**EXAMPLE 3 Calculating the area of a segment of a circle**

A **segment** of a circle is a region bounded by an arc of the circle and its chord. Compute the area of the segment (the shaded region) in Figure 5. Give two forms for the answer: an exact expression involving $\pi$ and a calculator approximation rounded to two decimal places.

**SOLUTION**

Although we have not developed an explicit formula for the area of a segment, notice in Figure 5 that $\triangle OPQ$ and the shaded segment, taken together, form a sector of the circle. So we have

$$\text{area of segment} = (\text{area of sector } OPQ) - (\text{area of } \triangle OPQ)$$

For the area of the sector we compute

$$\text{area of sector } OPQ = \frac{1}{2}r^2\theta = \frac{1}{2}(2^2)\left(\frac{3\pi}{5}\right)$$
$$= \frac{6\pi}{5} \text{ cm}^2$$

For the area of the triangle we use the formula $A = \frac{1}{2}ab \sin \theta$ (from Section 6.4):

$$\text{area of } \triangle OPQ = \frac{1}{2}(2)(2)\sin\frac{3\pi}{5} = 2\sin\frac{3\pi}{5} \text{ cm}^2$$

Putting things together now, we obtain

$$\text{area of segment} = \left(\frac{6\pi}{5} - 2\sin\frac{3\pi}{5}\right) \text{ cm}^2$$
$$\approx 1.87 \text{ cm}^2$$

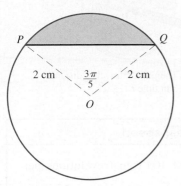

**Figure 5**

The next example indicates how radian measure is used in the study of rotating objects. As a prerequisite for this example, we first define the terms *angular speed* and *linear speed*.

---

**DEFINITION** | **Angular Speed and Linear Speed**

---

Suppose that a wheel rotates about its axis at a constant rate.

1. Refer to Figure 6(a) on the next page. If a radial line turns through an angle $\theta$ in time $t$, then the **angular speed** of the wheel [denoted by the Greek letter $\omega$ (*omega*)] is defined to be

$$\text{angular speed} = \omega = \frac{\theta}{t}$$

2. Refer to Figure 6(b). If a point $P$ on the rotating wheel travels a distance $d$ in time $t$, then the **linear speed** of $P$, denoted by $v$, is defined to be

$$\text{linear speed} = v = \frac{d}{t}$$

**Figure 6**

(a) A radial line turns through an angle $\theta$ in time $t$.

(b) The point $P$ travels a distance $d$ in time $t$.

**EXAMPLE** **4** **Calculating angular and linear speed**

A circular gear in a motor rotates at the rate of 100 rpm (revolutions per minute).
**(a)** What is the angular speed of the gear in radians per minute?
**(b)** Find the linear speed of a point on the gear 4 cm from the center.

**SOLUTION**
**(a)** Each revolution of the gear is $2\pi$ radians. So in 100 revolutions there are

$$\theta = 100(2\pi) = 200\pi \text{ radians}$$

Consequently, we have

$$\omega = \frac{\theta}{t} = \frac{200\pi \text{ radians}}{1 \text{ min}} = 200\pi \text{ radians/min}$$

**(b)** We can use the formula $s = r\theta$ to find the distance traveled by the point in 1 minute. Using $r = 4$ cm and $\theta = 200\pi$, we obtain

$$s = r\theta = 4(200\pi) = 800\pi \text{ cm}$$

The linear speed is therefore

$$v = \frac{d}{t} = \frac{800\pi \text{ cm}}{1 \text{ min}}$$
$$= 800\pi \text{ cm/min} \qquad (\approx 2513 \text{ cm/min})$$

There is a simple equation relating linear speed and angular speed. [Actually, as you'll see, the explanation we are about to give is just a repetition of the reasoning used in Example 4(b).] We refer back to Figure 6, in which the radial line turns through an angle $\theta$ in time $t$. Now we make two additional assumptions. First, we assume that the angle $\theta$ is measured in radians (so that we can apply the formula $s = r\theta$). Second, we assume that the point $P$ is a distance $r$ from the center of the circle. That is, the radius of the circular path is $r$. Then, according to our arc length formula, the distance $d$ in Figure 6(b) is given by $d = r\theta$. So we have

$$v = \frac{d}{t} = \frac{r\theta}{t} = r \times \frac{\theta}{t}$$
$$= r\omega \qquad \text{using the definition of } \omega$$

We have now shown that $v = r\omega$. For reference we record this result in the box that follows.

### Linear Speed and Angular Speed

Suppose that an object travels at a constant rate along a circular path of radius $r$. Then the linear speed $v$ and the angular speed $\omega$ are related by the equation

$$v = r\omega$$

In this equation the angular speed $\omega$ must be expressed in radians per unit time.

We can use the formula $v = r\omega$ to rework Example 4(b) in a more concise fashion. Recall that we wanted to find the linear speed $v$ of a point 4 cm from the center. To do this, we need only substitute the values $r = 4$ cm and $\omega = 200\pi$ radians/min [from part (a) of the example] in the formula $v = r\omega$. This yields

$$v = r\omega$$
$$= (4 \text{ cm})(200\pi \text{ radians/min}) \tag{2}$$
$$= 800\pi \text{ cm/min} \quad \text{(as obtained previously)} \tag{3}$$

Notice how the units work in equations (2) and (3). Although radians appear in equation (2), they do not appear in the final answer in equation (3); the units for the linear speed are simply cm/min. We drop the radians from the final result because, as was pointed out in Section 7.1, radian measure is unitless.*

## EXERCISE SET 7.2

**A**

*In Exercises 1– 4, find the arc length s in each case.*

**1.**

**2.**

**3.**

**4.**

*In Exercises 5 and 6, find the area of the sector determined by the given radius r and central angle $\theta$. Express the answer both in terms of $\pi$ and as a decimal approximation rounded to two decimal places.*

**5. (a)** $r = 6$ cm; $\theta = 2\pi/3$    **(c)** $r = 24$ m; $\theta = \pi/20$
     **(b)** $r = 5$ m; $\theta = 80°$         **(d)** $r = 1.8$ cm; $\theta = 144°$

**6. (a)** $r = 4$ cm; $\theta = \pi/10$    **(c)** $r = 21$ ft; $\theta = 11\pi/6$
     **(b)** $r = 16$ m; $\theta = 5°$          **(d)** $r = 4.2$ in.; $\theta = 170°$

**7.** In a circle of radius 1 cm, the area of a certain sector is $\pi/5$ cm$^2$. Find the radian measure of the central angle. Express the answer in terms of $\pi$ rather than as a decimal approximation.

**8.** In a circle of radius 3 m, the area of a certain sector is 20 m$^2$. Find the degree measure of the central angle. Round the answer to two decimal places.

*In Exercises 9 and 10, find **(a)** the perimeter of the sector; and **(b)** the area of the sector. In each case, use a calculator to evaluate the answer and round to two decimal places.*

---

*Many physics texts gloss over this point in the calculations. One text that does provide sufficient emphasis here is *Physics,* 7th ed., by John D. Cutnell and Kenneth W. Johnson (New York: John Wiley & Sons, Inc., 1995). In that text, the authors state, "In calculations, therefore, the radian is treated as a unitless number and has no effect on other units that it multiplies or divides."

**9.**

30°

5 in.

**10.**

3 m

135°

*In Exercises 11 and 12, compute the area of the shaded segment of the circle. Give two forms for each answer: an exact expression and a calculator approximation rounded to two decimal places. In the figure for Exercise 11, recall the following convention (mentioned in Section 7.1): If degree measure is not explicitly indicated, assume that radian measure is used.*

**11.**                                    **12.**

1.4   6 cm

120°

3 m

*In Exercises 13–18, you are given the rate of rotation of a wheel as well as its radius. In each case, determine the following:* **(a)** *the angular speed, in units of radians/sec;* **(b)** *the linear speed, in units of cm/sec, of a point on the circumference of the wheel; and* **(c)** *the linear speed, in cm/sec, of a point halfway between the center of the wheel and the circumference.*

**13.** 6 revolutions/sec; $r = 12$ cm

**14.** 15 revolutions/sec; $r = 20$ cm

**15.** 1080°/sec; $r = 25$ cm

**16.** 2160°/sec; $r = 60$ cm

**17.** 500 rpm; $r = 45$ cm

**18.** 1250 rpm; $r = 10$ cm

**19.** For this problem, assume that the earth is a sphere with a radius of 3960 miles and a rotation rate of 1 revolution per 24 hours.

    **(a)** Find the angular speed. Express your answer in units of radians/sec, and round to two significant digits.

    **(b)** Find the linear speed of a point on the equator. Express the answer in units of miles per hour, and round to the nearest 10 mph.

**20.** A wheel 3 ft in diameter makes $x$ revolutions. Find $x$, given that the distance traveled by a point on the circumference of the wheel is 22619 ft. (Round your answer to the nearest whole number.)

**B**

*In Exercises 21 and 22, suppose that a belt drives two wheels of radii r and R, as indicated in the figure.*

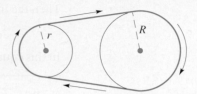

r    R

**21.** If $r = 6$ cm, $R = 10$ cm, and the angular speed of the larger wheel is 100 rpm, determine each of the following:

    **(a)** the angular speed of the larger wheel in radians per minute;

    **(b)** the linear speed of a point on the circumference of the larger wheel;

    **(c)** the angular speed of the smaller wheel in radians per minute.    *Hint:* Because of the belt, the linear speed of a point on the circumference of the larger wheel is equal to the linear speed of a point on the circumference of the smaller wheel.

    **(d)** The angular speed of the smaller wheel in rpm.

**22.** Follow Exercise 21, assuming that $r = 5$ cm, $R = 15$ cm, and the angular speed of the larger wheel is 1800 rpm.

*The latitude of a point P on the surface of the Earth is specified by means of the angle θ in the figure. For instance, the latitude of Paris, France, is 48°52′ N. The letter N is used here to indicate that the location is north of, rather than south of, the equator. (Recall that the notation 52′ indicates 52/60 of one degree.) In Exercises 23–28, use the arc length formula (and your calculator) to determine the distance $\overset{\frown}{PE}$ from the given location P to the equator. Assume that the Earth is a sphere with radius $OP = OE = 3960$ miles. Round each answer to the nearest 10 miles.*

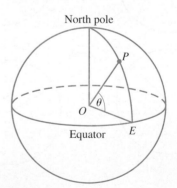

North pole

P

θ

O

Equator    E

**23.** Point Barrow, Alaska:    71°23′ N

**24.** Singapore:    1°17′ N

**25.** Honolulu:    21°19′ N

**26.** Lagos:    6°27′ N

**27.** Washington, D.C.:    38°54′ N

**28.** Fairbanks, Alaska:    64°51′ N

**29.** Many of the window designs used in gothic architecture involve circles, sectors, and segments of circles. The **equilateral arch** in Figure A is an example of this. Figure B shows how the arch is designed. Starting with the equilateral triangle $ABC$, circular arc $\overset{\frown}{AC}$ is drawn with center $B$ and radius $AB$. Similarly, circular arc $\overset{\frown}{BC}$ is drawn with center $A$ and radius $AB$.

Figure A

Figure B

**(a)** Let $s$ denote the length of a side of the equilateral triangle in Figure B. Express the perimeter of the equilateral arch in terms of $s$.

**(b)** Express the area of the equilateral arch in terms of $s$.

**30.** Closely related to the equilateral arch in Exercise 29 is the **equilateral curved triangle** shown in Figure C. Just as with the equilateral arch in Exercise 29, the design begins with the equilateral triangle $ABC$. Circular arcs are then constructed on each side of the triangle, following the method explained in Exercise 29.

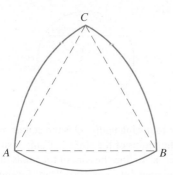

Figure C

**(a)** In Figure C, let $s$ denote the length of a side of the equilateral triangle $ABC$. Express the perimeter and the area of the equilateral curved triangle in terms of $s$.

**(b)** Show that the area of the equilateral triangle $ABC$ is approximately 61% of the area of the equilateral curved triangle $ABC$.

**31.** Figure D shows one of the gothic window designs used in Wells Cathedral in England. (The cathedral was constructed in the mid-thirteenth century.) Figure E indicates how the design is formed. We start with the equilateral $\triangle ABC$ and construct the equilateral arch $ABC$. Next, the midpoints of the three sides of $\triangle ABC$ are joined to create four smaller equilateral triangles. The two equilateral triangles $ADF$ and $FEC$ are then used to construct the two smaller equilateral arches shown in Figure E. And finally, the equilateral triangle $DBE$ is used to construct the equilateral curved triangle within the top half of the figure.

**(a)** Let $s$ denote the length of a side of the equilateral triangle $ABC$. Express the area of each of the equilateral arches $ABC$ and $ADF$ in terms of $s$. Also, find the ratio of the area of arch $ADF$ to arch $ABC$.

**(b)** Express the area of the equilateral curved triangle $DBE$ in terms of $s$.

**(c)** Express the area of the curved figure $DEF$ in terms of $s$. (By "the curved figure $DEF$" we mean the region bounded by the circular arcs $\overset{\frown}{DE}$, $\overset{\frown}{EF}$, and $\overset{\frown}{FD}$.)

**(d)** Express the area of the curved figure $BEC$ in terms of $s$.

Figure D

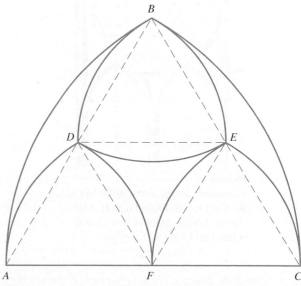

Figure E

**32.** Figure F shows a gothic window design from the cathedral at Reims, France. (The cathedral was constructed during the years 1211–1311.) Figure G indicates how the design is formed. Triangle *ABC* is equilateral and arch *ABC* is the corresponding equilateral arch. Equilateral triangle *GID*, congruent to triangle *ABC*, is constructed such that *D* is the midpoint of $\overline{AB}$, and $\overline{GI}$ is parallel to $\overline{AB}$. The points *E* and *F* are the midpoints of segments $\overline{DG}$ and $\overline{DI}$, respectively. The two small arches at the bottom of the figure are equilateral arches corresponding to the equilateral triangles *GHE* and *HIF*. For the circle in the figure, the center is *D* and the radius is $AD(= ED = FD)$.

**(a)** Let *s* denote the length of a side in each of the two equilateral triangles *ABC* and *GID*. Find the area and the perimeter (in terms of *s*) of the curved figure *AJBCA*. *Hint:* For the area, subtract the area of the semicircle *AJB* from the area of the equilateral arch *ABC*.

**(b)** Express (in terms of *s*) the area and the perimeter of equilateral arch *GHE*.

**(c)** Show that the area of the curved figure *EHF* is $s^2(2\sqrt{3} - \pi)/8$.

**(d)** Express (in terms of *s*) the perimeter and the area of the curved figure *FBI*.

**Figure G**

**Figure F**
A window design in the cathedral at Reims, France. From Hans H. Hofstätter, *Living Architecture: Gothic* (Office du Livre, S. A., 1970)

**33. (a)** The following figure shows a segment with central angle $\alpha$ in a circle of radius *r*. (Assume that $\alpha$ is in radians.) Show that the area *A* of the segment is given by

$$A = \frac{1}{2}r^2(\alpha - \sin \alpha)$$

**(b)** In the following figure, *O* is the center of the circle, and the radius of the circle is 1 unit. Use the formula in part (a) to find the sum of the areas of the two shaded segments. Give two forms for the answer: an exact expression involving $\pi$ and a calculator approximation rounded to two decimal places.

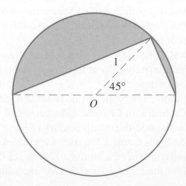

**34.** In the following figure, arc $ABC$ is a portion of a circle with center $D(0, -1)$ and radius $\overline{DC}$. The shaded crescent-shaped region is called a **lune.** Verify the following result, which was discovered (and proved) by the Greek mathematician Hippocrates of Chios approximately 2500 years ago. The area of the lune is equal to the area of the square $OCED$. *Hint:* In computing the area of the lune, make use of the formula given in Exercise 33(a) for the area of a segment.

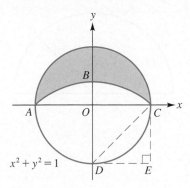

**35.** In the following figure, $\overline{AB}$ is a chord in a circle of radius 1. The length of $\overline{AB}$ is $d$, and $\overline{AB}$ subtends an angle $\theta$ at the center of the circle, as shown.

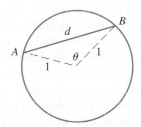

In this exercise we derive the following formula for the length $d$ of the chord in terms of the angle $\theta$:

$$d = \sqrt{2 - 2\cos\theta}$$

(The derivation of this formula does not require any knowledge of radian measure. The formula is developed here for use in Exercise 36.)

**(a)** We place the figure in an $x$-$y$ coordinate system and orient it so that the angle $\theta$ is in standard position and the point $B$ is located at $(1, 0)$. (See the following figure.) What are the coordinates of the point $A$ (in terms of $\theta$)?

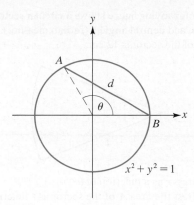

**(b)** Use the formula for the distance between two points to show that $d = \sqrt{2 - 2\cos\theta}$.

**36.** In the following figure, arc $ABC$ is a semicircle with diameter $\overline{AC}$, and arc $CDE$ is a semicircle with diameter $\overline{CE}$.

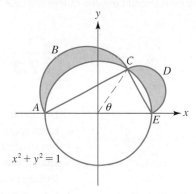

**(a)** Find the area of the lune $CDE$ assuming that $\theta = 60°$. Give two forms for the answer: an exact expression involving $\pi$ and a calculator approximation rounded to three decimal places. *Hint:* Use the formulas in Exercises 33(a) and 35.

**(b)** Follow part (a) for lune $ABC$, again assuming that $\theta = 60°$.

**(c)** Find the area of $\triangle ACE$ (still assuming that $\theta = 60°$). Then use the results in parts (a) and (b) to verify that the area of $\triangle ACE$ is equal to the sum of the areas of the lunes $CDE$ and $ABC$.

*Remark:* In this exercise we used the value $\theta = 60°$. Actually, the result in part (c) holds in general: For any angle $\theta$ between $0°$ and $180°$, the sum of the areas of the two lunes is equal to the area of the triangle. As with the result in Exercise 34, this fact was discovered and proved by the ancient Greek mathematician Hippocrates of Chios. According to Professor George F. Simmons in his text *Calculus Gems* (New York: McGraw-Hill Book Co., 1992), these results appear "to be the earliest precise determination of the area of a region bounded by curves."

**37.** The accompanying figure shows a circular sector with radius $r$ cm and central angle $\theta$ (radian measure). The perimeter of the sector is 12 cm.

(a) Express $r$ as a function of $\theta$.
(b) Express the area $A$ of the sector as a function of $\theta$. Is this a quadratic function?
(c) Express $\theta$ as a function of $r$.
(d) Express the area $A$ of the sector as a function of $r$. Is this a quadratic function?
(e) For which value of $r$ is the area $A$ a maximum? What is the corresponding value of $\theta$ in this case?

**38.** The following figure shows a semicircle of radius 1 unit and two adjacent sectors, $AOC$ and $COB$.
(a) Show that the product $P$ of the areas of the two sectors is given by

$$P = \frac{\pi\theta}{4} - \frac{\theta^2}{4}$$

Is this a quadratic function?
(b) For what value of $\theta$ is $P$ a maximum?

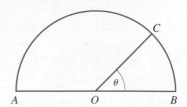

---

## 7.3 TRIGONOMETRIC FUNCTIONS OF REAL NUMBERS

In calculus and in the sciences many of the applications of the trigonometric functions require that the inputs be real numbers, rather than angles. By making a small but crucial change in our viewpoint, we can define the trigonometric functions in such a way that the inputs are real numbers. As background for our discussion, recall that radian measure is defined by the equation $\theta = s/r$. In this definition, $s$ and $r$ are assumed to have the same linear units (for example, centimeters) and therefore the ratio $s/r$ is a real number with no units. For example, in Figure 1 the radius is 3 cm, the arc length is 6 cm, and so the radian measure $\theta$ is given by

$$\theta = \frac{6 \text{ cm}}{3 \text{ cm}} = 2 \qquad \text{(a real number)}$$

In the previous chapter (Section 6.4) the definitions of the trigonometric functions were based on the unit circle, so let's look at radian measure in that context. In the equation $\theta = s/r$, we set $r = 1$. This yields

$$\theta = \frac{s}{1} = s \qquad \text{(just as before, a real number)}$$

**Figure 1**

Thus, in the unit circle, the radian measure of the angle is equal to the measure of the intercepted arc. For reference we summarize this important observation in Figure 2. (We've used the letter $t$, rather than our usual $\theta$, to emphasize the fact that both the radian measure of the angle and the measure of the intercepted arc are given by the same *real number*.)

**Figure 2**
In the unit circle, the radian measure of an angle equals the measure of the intercepted arc.

The conventions regarding the measurement of arc length on the unit circle are the same as those introduced in the previous chapter for angles. As Figure 3 (on the next page) indicates, we measure from the point $(1, 0)$, and we assume that the positive direction is counterclockwise.

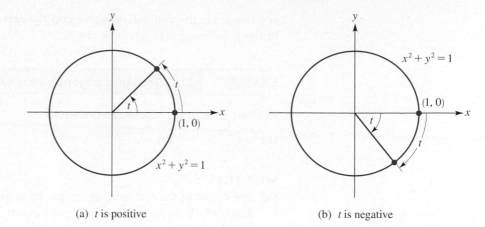

**Figure 3**
The positive direction is counter-clockwise.

(a)  *t* is positive

(b)  *t* is negative

In the definitions that follow, you may think of *t* as either the measure of an arc or the radian measure of an angle. But in both cases, and this is the point, *t* denotes a real number.

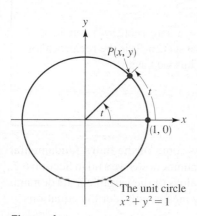

**Figure 4**

---

**DEFINITION** | **Trigonometric Functions of Real Numbers**

(Refer to Figure 4.) Let $P(x, y)$ denote the point on the unit circle that has arc length measure *t* from $(1, 0)$. (Note that in Figure 4, $0 < t < \pi/2$.) Let $P(x, y)$ denote the point where the terminal side of the angle with radian measure *t* intersects the unit circle. Then the six trigonometric functions of the real number *t* are defined as follows.

$$\cos t = x \qquad\qquad \sec t = \frac{1}{x} \quad (x \neq 0)$$

$$\sin t = y \qquad\qquad \csc t = \frac{1}{y} \quad (y \neq 0)$$

$$\tan t = \frac{y}{x} \quad (x \neq 0) \qquad \cot t = \frac{x}{y} \quad (y \neq 0)$$

---

Note that there is nothing essentially new here as far as evaluating the trigonometric functions. For instance, $\sin(\pi/2)$ is still equal to 1. What is different now is that the inputs are real numbers:

$$\sin \frac{\pi}{2} = 1$$

name of function ⟶ ⬆ ⬆
input (a real number) ⟶ �752; �718; ⟵ output (a real number)

As was explained in Section 7.1, the four-step procedure for evaluating the trigonometric functions is valid whether we are working in degrees or radians. When radian measure is used, the reference angle is sometimes referred to as the **reference number** to emphasize the fact that a radian angle measure (such as $\pi/4$ or 3) is indeed a real number. In the next example we evaluate trigonometric functions with real number inputs. As you'll see, however, there are no new techniques for you to learn in this context. As we've said, the new definition amounts to a change in viewpoint more than anything else.

| EXAMPLE | 1 | Calculating trigonometric functions of real numbers |

Evaluate each of the following expressions:

**(a)** $\cos \dfrac{2\pi}{3}$;       **(b)** $\sec \dfrac{2\pi}{3}$.

**SOLUTION**
**(a)** The cosine of the real number $2\pi/3$ is, by definition, the cosine of $2\pi/3$ radians, which we can evaluate by means of our four-step procedure.
   **Step 1**   See Figure 5.
   **Step 2**   The reference angle for $2\pi/3$ is $\pi/3$.
   **Step 3**   $\cos(\pi/3) = 1/2$
   **Step 4**   $\cos t$ is the $x$-coordinate, and in Quadrant II, $x$-coordinates are negative. Thus since the terminal side of $t = 2\pi/3$ is in Quadrant II, $\cos(2\pi/3)$ is negative. Consequently, we have

$$\cos \frac{2\pi}{3} = -\cos \frac{\pi}{3} = -\frac{1}{2}$$

**(b)** We could use the four-step procedure to evaluate $\sec(2\pi/3)$ but in this case it is much more direct simply to note that $\sec(2\pi/3)$ is the reciprocal of $\cos(2\pi/3)$, which we evaluated in part (a). Thus we have

$$\sec \frac{2\pi}{3} = -2$$

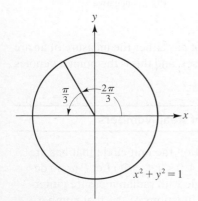

Figure 5

For the remainder of this section we discuss some of the more fundamental identities for the trigonometric functions of real numbers. As we said in Section 6.2, an **identity** is an equation that is satisfied by all values of the variable in its domain. As a demonstration of what this definition really means, consider the equation

$$\sin^2 t + \cos^2 t = 1$$

As we'll prove in a moment (and as you should already expect from the previous chapter), this equation is an identity. The domain of the variable $t$ in this case is the set of all real numbers. So if we pick a real number at random, say, $t = 17$, then it follows that the equation

$$\sin^2 17 + \cos^2 17 = 1$$

is true. You should take a minute now to confirm this empirically with your calculator. That is, actually compute the left-hand side of the preceding equation and check that the result is indeed 1. The point is, no matter what real number we choose for $t$, the resulting equation will be true.

As an example of an equation that is not an identity, consider the *conditional equation*

$$2 \sin t = 1 \tag{1}$$

As you can check (without a calculator), this equation is true when $t = \pi/6$ but false when $t = \pi/3$. Thus equation (1) is *not* satisfied by *all* values of the variable in its domain. In other words, equation (1) is not an identity. In a later section, we'll work with conditional equations such as equation (1). When we do that, we will be trying to solve these equations; that is, we'll want to find just which values of the variable (if any) do satisfy the equation.

QUESTION FOR REVIEW AND PREVIEW   Can you find some real numbers other than $\pi/6$ that also satisfy equation (1)?

There are five identities that are immediate consequences of the unit-circle definitions of the trigonometric functions. For example, using the unit-circle definitions, we have

$$\tan t = \frac{y}{x} \qquad \text{definition of } \tan t$$

$$= \frac{\sin t}{\cos t} \qquad \text{definitions of } \sin t \text{ and } \cos t$$

Thus we have $\tan t = (\sin t)/(\cos t)$. This identity and four others are listed in the box that follows.

---

## Consequences of the Definitions

$$\sec t = \frac{1}{\cos t} \qquad \csc t = \frac{1}{\sin t} \qquad \cot t = \frac{1}{\tan t}$$

$$\tan t = \frac{\sin t}{\cos t} \qquad \cot t = \frac{\cos t}{\sin t}$$

---

The next identities that we consider are the three *Pythagorean identities*. The term "Pythagorean" is used here because, as you'll see, the proofs of the identities rely on the unit-circle definitions of the trigonometric functions; and the equation of the unit circle essentially is derived from the Pythagorean theorem.

---

## The Pythagorean Identities

$$\sin^2 t + \cos^2 t = 1$$

$$\tan^2 t + 1 = \sec^2 t$$

$$\cot^2 t + 1 = \csc^2 t$$

---

To establish the identity $\sin^2 t + \cos^2 t = 1$, we think of the real number $t$, for the moment, as the radian measure of an angle in standard position, as indicated in Figure 6. Now we proceed exactly as in the previous chapter, when we proved this identity in the context of angles. Since the point $(x, y)$ in Figure 6 lies on the unit circle, we have

$$x^2 + y^2 = 1$$

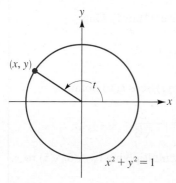

**Figure 6**
A real number $t$ interpreted as the radian measure of an angle in standard position

Now, replacing $x$ by $\cos t$ and $y$ by $\sin t$ gives us

$$\cos^2 t + \sin^2 t = 1$$

which is what we wished to show. You should also be familiar with two other ways of writing this identity:

$$\cos^2 t = 1 - \sin^2 t \quad \text{and} \quad \sin^2 t = 1 - \cos^2 t$$

To prove the second of the Pythagorean identities, we begin with the identity $\sin^2 t + \cos^2 t = 1$ and divide both sides by the quantity $\cos^2 t$ to obtain

$$\frac{\sin^2 t}{\cos^2 t} + \frac{\cos^2 t}{\cos^2 t} = \frac{1}{\cos^2 t} \quad \text{assuming that } \cos t \neq 0$$

and, consequently,

$$\tan^2 t + 1 = \sec^2 t \quad \text{as required}$$

Since the proof of the third Pythagorean identity is similar, we omit it here.

---

**EXAMPLE 2 Finding values of trigonometric functions**

If $\sin t = 2/3$ and $\pi/2 < t < \pi$, compute $\cos t$ and $\tan t$.

**SOLUTION**

$$\cos^2 t = 1 - \sin^2 t \qquad \text{using the first Pythagorean identity}$$
$$= 1 - \left(\frac{2}{3}\right)^2 \qquad \text{substituting}$$
$$= 1 - \frac{4}{9} = \frac{5}{9}$$

Consequently,

$$\cos t = \frac{\sqrt{5}}{3} \quad \text{or} \quad \cos t = -\frac{\sqrt{5}}{3}$$

Now, since $\pi/2 < t < \pi$, it follows that $\cos t$ is negative. (Why?) Thus

$$\cos t = -\frac{\sqrt{5}}{3} \quad \text{as required}$$

To compute $\tan t$, we use the identity $\tan t = (\sin t)/(\cos t)$ to obtain

$$\tan t = \frac{2/3}{-\sqrt{5}/3} = \frac{2}{3} \times \frac{3}{-\sqrt{5}} = -\frac{2}{\sqrt{5}}$$

If required, we can rationalize the denominator (by multiplying by $\sqrt{5}/\sqrt{5}$) to obtain

$$\tan t = -\frac{2\sqrt{5}}{\sqrt{5}}$$

**EXAMPLE** 3   **Finding values of trigonometric functions**

If $\sec t = -5/3$ and $\pi < t < 3\pi/2$, compute $\cos t$ and $\tan t$.

**SOLUTION**
Since $\cos t$ is the reciprocal of $\sec t$, we have $\cos t = -3/5$. We can compute $\tan t$ using the second Pythagorean identity as follows:

$$\tan^2 t = \sec^2 t - 1$$
$$= \left(-\frac{5}{3}\right)^2 - 1 = \frac{16}{9}$$

Therefore

$$\tan t = \frac{4}{3} \quad \text{or} \quad \tan t = -\frac{4}{3}$$

Since $t$ is between $\pi$ and $3\pi/2$, $\tan t$ is positive. (Why?) Thus

$$\tan t = \frac{4}{3}$$

Example 4 shows how certain radical expressions can be simplified with an appropriate trigonometric substitution. (This technique is often useful in calculus.)

**EXAMPLE** 4   **Using a trigonometric substitution to rationalize a square root**

In the expression $u/\sqrt{u^2 - 1}$, make the substitution $u = \sec \theta$ and show that the resulting expression is equal to $\csc \theta$. (Assume that $0 < \theta < \pi/2$.)

**SOLUTION**
Replacing $u$ by $\sec \theta$ in the given expression yields

$$\frac{u}{\sqrt{u^2 - 1}} = \frac{\sec \theta}{\sqrt{\sec^2 \theta - 1}}$$
$$= \frac{\sec \theta}{\sqrt{\tan^2 \theta}} \quad \text{using the second Pythagorean identity}$$
$$= \frac{\sec \theta}{\tan \theta} = \frac{1/\cos \theta}{\sin \theta/\cos \theta}$$
$$= \frac{1}{\sin \theta} = \csc \theta$$

*Question*: Where did we use the condition $0 < \theta < \pi/2$?

As we saw in Chapter 6, one technique for simplifying trigonometric expressions involves first writing everything in terms of sines and cosines. However, this is not necessarily the most efficient method. As the next example indicates, the second and third Pythagorean identities can be quite useful in this context.

**EXAMPLE** | 5 | **Using trigonometric identities to simplify trigonometric expressions**

Simplify the expression $\dfrac{\csc t + \csc t \cot^2 t}{\sec^2 t - \tan^2 t}$

**SOLUTION**

$$\frac{\csc t + \csc t \cot^2 t}{\sec^2 t - \tan^2 t} = \frac{(\csc t)(1 + \cot^2 t)}{1}$$

> factoring out the common factor in the numerator and applying the second Pythagorean identity in the denominator

$$= (\csc t)(\csc^2 t)$$

> applying the third Pythagorean identity

$$= \csc^3 t$$

$f(t) = t^2$

**Figure 7**
The graph of an even function is symmetric about the $y$-axis.

As background for the next set of identities, we define the terms "even function" and "odd function." A function $f$ is said to be an **even function** provided

$$f(-t) = f(t) \qquad \text{for every value of } t \text{ in the domain of } f$$

The function defined by $f(t) = t^2$ serves as a simple example of an even function. Whether we use $t$ or $-t$ for the input, the output is the same. For instance,

$$f(5) = 5^2 = 25 \qquad \text{and also} \qquad f(-5) = (-5)^2 = 25$$

The graph of an even function is always symmetric about the $y$-axis. (This follows directly from the symmetry tests in Chapter 1 on page 59.) For example, in Figure 7 we show the graph of the even function $f(t) = t^2$.

A function $f$ is said to be an **odd function** provided

$$f(-t) = -f(t) \qquad \text{for every value of } t \text{ in the domain of } f$$

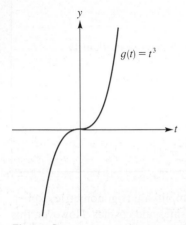

$g(t) = t^3$

The function defined by $g(t) = t^3$ is an odd function. For instance, if you compute $g(5)$ and $g(-5)$, you'll find that the outputs are the negatives of one another. (Check this.) The graph of an odd function is always symmetric about the origin. (Again, this follows from the symmetry tests in Chapter 1.) In Figure 8 we display the graph of the odd function $g(t) = t^3$.

*Note*: The domains of both even and odd functions must have the property that if $t$ is in the domain, then $-t$ is also in the domain.

Now let's return to our development of trigonometric identities. The three identities in the box that follows can be interpreted using the terminology we've just been discussing.

**Figure 8**
The graph of an odd function is symmetric about the origin.

---

**The Opposite-Angle Identities**

$$\cos(-t) = \cos t$$

$$\sin(-t) = -\sin t$$

$$\tan(-t) = -\tan t$$

---

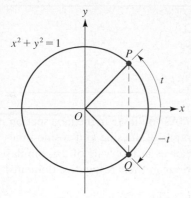

$x^2 + y^2 = 1$

**Figure 9**

To see why the first two of these identities are true, consider Figure 9. We'll assume that $0 < t < \pi/2$, so Figure 9 shows an arc of length $t$ terminating in Quadrant I. By definition the coordinates of the points $P$ and $Q$ in Figure 9 are as follows:

$$P: \quad (\cos t, \sin t)$$
$$Q: \quad (\cos(-t), \sin(-t))$$

However, as you can see by looking at Figure 9, the $x$-coordinates of $P$ and $Q$ are the same, while the $y$-coordinates are negatives of each other. Thus,

$$\cos(-t) = \cos t$$

and

$$\sin(-t) = -\sin t \qquad \text{as we wished to show}$$

Now we can establish the third identity, involving $\tan(-t)$, as follows:

$$\tan(-t) = \frac{\sin(-t)}{\cos(-t)}$$
$$= \frac{-\sin t}{\cos t} = -\frac{\sin t}{\cos t} = -\tan t$$

Although we assumed that the arc terminated in Quadrant I the argument we used will work no matter where the arc terminates. To check this, you should try the last argument with a $t$ such that $P$ is not in Quadrant I.

The opposite-angle identities tell us that the cosine function is an even function and that the sine and tangent functions are odd functions.

**EXAMPLE   6   Using the opposite-angle identities**

(a) If $\sin t = -0.76$, find $\sin(-t)$.
(b) If $\cos s = -0.29$, find $\cos(-s)$.
(c) If $\sin u = 0.54$, find $\sin^2(-u) + \cos^2(-u)$.

**SOLUTION**
(a) $\sin(-t) = -\sin t$
$\qquad\qquad = -(-0.76) = 0.76$
(b) $\cos(-s) = \cos s = -0.29$
(c) The opposite-angle identities are unnecessary here, and so too is the given value of $\sin u$, for, according to the first Pythagorean identity, we have

$$\sin^2(-u) + \cos^2(-u) = 1$$

The final identities that we are going to discuss in this section are simply consequences of the fact that the circumference $C$ of the unit circle is $2\pi$. (Substituting $r = 1$ in the formula $C = 2\pi r$ gives us $C = 2\pi$.) Thus if we begin at any point $P$ on the unit circle and travel a distance of $2\pi$ units along the perimeter, we return to the same point $P$. In other words, arc lengths of $t$ and $t + 2\pi$ [measured from $(1, 0)$, as usual] yield the same terminal point on the unit circle. Since the trigonometric functions are defined in terms of the coordinates of that point $P$, we obtain the following identities.

## Periodicity of Sine and Cosine

$$\sin(t + 2\pi) = \sin t$$

$$\cos(t + 2\pi) = \cos t$$

These two identities are true for all real numbers $t$. As you'll see in the next section, they provide important information about the graphs of the sine and cosine functions; the graphs of both functions repeat themselves at intervals of $2\pi$. Similar identities hold for the other trigonometric functions in their respective domains:

$$\tan(t + 2\pi) = \tan t \qquad \csc(t + 2\pi) = \csc t$$

$$\cot(t + 2\pi) = \cot t \qquad \sec(t + 2\pi) = \sec t$$

---

**EXAMPLE 7 Using periodicity to find a value of sine**

Evaluate: $\sin \dfrac{5\pi}{2}$.

**SOLUTION**
First, simply as a matter of arithmetic, we observe that $5\pi/2 = \pi/2 + 2\pi$. Thus in view of our earlier remarks we have

$$\sin \frac{5\pi}{2} = \sin \frac{\pi}{2} = 1$$

■

---

The preceding set of identities can be generalized as follows. If we start at a point $P$ on the unit circle and make two complete counterclockwise revolutions, the arc length we travel is $2\pi + 2\pi = 4\pi$. Similarly, for three complete revolutions the arc length traversed is $3(2\pi) = 6\pi$. And, in general, if $k$ is any integer, the arc length for $k$ complete revolutions is $2k\pi$. (When $k$ is positive, the revolutions are counterclockwise; when $k$ is negative, the revolutions are clockwise.) Consequently, we have the following identities.

---

For any real number $t$ and any integer $k$, the following identities hold:

$$\sin(t + 2k\pi) = \sin t \qquad \text{and} \qquad \cos(t + 2k\pi) = \cos t$$

---

**EXAMPLE 8 Using periodicity to find a value of cosine**

Evaluate: $\cos(-17\pi)$.

**SOLUTION**
$$\cos(-17\pi) = \cos(\pi - 18\pi) = \cos \pi = -1$$

■

# EXERCISE SET 7.3

## A

*In Exercises 1–8, evaluate each expression (as in Example 1).*

1. (a) $\cos(11\pi/6)$      (c) $\sin(11\pi/6)$
   (b) $\cos(-11\pi/6)$    (d) $\sin(-11\pi/6)$
2. (a) $\cos(2\pi/3)$      (c) $\sin(2\pi/3)$
   (b) $\cos(-2\pi/3)$    (d) $\sin(-2\pi/3)$
3. (a) $\cos(\pi/6)$      (c) $\sin(\pi/6)$
   (b) $\cos(-\pi/6)$    (d) $\sin(-\pi/6)$
4. (a) $\cos(13\pi/4)$      (c) $\sin(13\pi/4)$
   (b) $\cos(-13\pi/4)$    (d) $\sin(-13\pi/4)$
5. (a) $\cos(5\pi/4)$      (c) $\sin(5\pi/4)$
   (b) $\cos(-5\pi/4)$    (d) $\sin(-5\pi/4)$
6. (a) $\cos(9\pi/4)$      (c) $\sin(9\pi/4)$
   (b) $\cos(-9\pi/4)$    (d) $\sin(-9\pi/4)$
7. (a) $\sec(5\pi/3)$      (c) $\tan(5\pi/3)$
   (b) $\csc(-5\pi/3)$    (d) $\cot(-5\pi/3)$
8. (a) $\sec(7\pi/4)$      (c) $\tan(7\pi/4)$
   (b) $\csc(-7\pi/4)$    (d) $\cot(-7\pi/4)$
9. (a) List four positive real-number values of $t$ for which $\cos t = 0$.
   (b) List four negative real-number values of $t$ for which $\cos t = 0$.
10. (a) List four positive real numbers $t$ such that $\sin t = 1/2$.
    (b) List four positive real numbers $t$ such that $\sin t = -1/2$.
    (c) List four negative real number $t$ such that $\sin t = 1/2$.
    (d) List four negative real numbers $t$ such that $\sin t = -1/2$.

*In Exercises 11–14, use a calculator to evaluate the six trigonometric functions using the given real-number input. (Round the results to two decimal places.)*

11. (a) 2.06        (b) $-2.06$
12. (a) 0.55        (b) $-0.55$
13. (a) $\pi/6$        (b) $\pi/6 + 2\pi$
14. (a) 1000        (b) $1000 - 2\pi$

*In Exercises 15–22, check that both sides of the identity are indeed equal for the given values of the variable t. For part (c) of each problem, use your calculator.*

15. $\sin^2 t + \cos^2 t = 1$      16. $\tan^2 t + 1 = \sec^2 t$
    (a) $t = \pi/3$                  (a) $t = 3\pi/4$
    (b) $t = 5\pi/4$                  (b) $t = -2\pi/3$
    (c) $t = -53$                    (c) $t = \sqrt{5}$
17. $\cot^2 t + 1 = \csc^2 t$      18. $\cos(-t) = \cos t$
    (a) $t = -\pi/6$                  (a) $t = \pi/6$
    (b) $t = 7\pi/4$                  (b) $t = -5\pi/3$
    (c) $t = 0.12$                    (c) $t = -4$
19. $\sin(-t) = -\sin t$      20. $\tan(-t) = -\tan t$
    (a) $t = 3\pi/2$                  (a) $t = -4\pi/3$
    (b) $t = -5\pi/6$                  (b) $t = \pi/4$
    (c) $t = 13.24$                  (c) $t = 1000$

21. $\sin(t + 2\pi) = \sin t$      22. $\cos(t + 2\pi) = \cos t$
    (a) $t = 5\pi/3$                  (a) $t = -5\pi/3$
    (b) $t = -3\pi/2$                  (b) $t = \pi$
    (c) $t = \sqrt{19}$                (c) $t = -\sqrt{3}$

*In Exercises 23 and 24, show that the equation is not an identity by evaluating both sides using the given value of t and noting that the results are unequal.*

23. $\cos 2t = 2 \cos t; t = \pi/6$
24. $\sin 2t = 2 \sin t; t = \pi/2$
25. If $\sin t = -3/5$ and $\pi < t < 3\pi/2$, compute $\cos t$ and $\tan t$.
26. If $\cos t = 5/13$ and $3\pi/2 < t < 2\pi$, compute $\sin t$ and $\cot t$.
27. If $\sin t = \sqrt{3}/4$ and $\pi/2 < t < \pi$, compute $\tan t$.
28. If $\sec s = -\sqrt{13}/2$ and $\sin s > 0$, compute $\tan s$.
29. If $\tan \alpha = 12/5$ and $\cos \alpha > 0$, compute $\sec \alpha$, $\cos \alpha$, and $\sin \alpha$.
30. If $\cot \theta = -1/\sqrt{3}$ and $\cos \theta < 0$, compute $\csc \theta$ and $\sin \theta$.
31. In the expression $\sqrt{9 - x^2}$, make the substitution $x = 3 \sin \theta$ $(0 < \theta < \frac{\pi}{2})$, and show that the result is $3 \cos \theta$.
32. Make the substitution $u = 2 \cos \theta$ in the expression $1/\sqrt{4 - u^2}$, and simplify the result. (Assume that $0 < \theta < \pi$.)
33. In the expression $1/(u^2 - 25)^{3/2}$, make the substitution $u = 5 \sec \theta$ $(0 < \theta < \frac{\pi}{2})$, and show that the result is $(\cot^3 \theta)/125$.
34. In the expression $1/(x^2 + 5)^2$, replace $x$ by $\sqrt{5} \tan \theta$ and show that the result is $(\cos^4 \theta)/25$.
35. In the expression $1/\sqrt{u^2 + 7}$, let $u = \sqrt{7} \tan \theta$, where $0 < \theta < \pi/2$, and simplify the result.
36. In the expression $\sqrt{x^2 - a^2}/x$ $(a > 0)$, let $x = a \sec \theta$ $(0 < \theta < \frac{\pi}{2})$, and simplify the result.
37. (a) If $\sin t = 2/3$, find $\sin(-t)$.
    (b) If $\sin \phi = -1/4$, find $\sin(-\phi)$.
    (c) If $\cos \alpha = 1/5$, find $\cos(-\alpha)$.
    (d) If $\cos s = -1/5$, find $\cos(-s)$.
38. (a) If $\sin t = 0.35$, find $\sin(-t)$.
    (b) If $\sin \phi = -0.47$, find $\sin(-\phi)$.
    (c) If $\cos \alpha = 0.21$, find $\cos(-\alpha)$.
    (d) If $\cos s = -0.56$, find $\cos(-s)$.
39. If $\cos t = -1/3$ $(\frac{\pi}{2} < t < \pi)$, compute the following:
    (a) $\sin(-t) + \cos(-t)$      (b) $\sin^2(-t) + \cos^2(-t)$
40. If $\sin(-s) = 3/5$ $(\pi < s < \frac{3\pi}{2})$, compute:
    (a) $\sin s$              (c) $\cos s$
    (b) $\cos(-s)$          (d) $\tan s + \tan(-s)$

*In Exercises 41 and 42, use one of the identities $\cos(t + 2\pi k) = \cos t$ or $\sin(t + 2\pi k) = \sin t$ to evaluate each expression.*

41. (a) $\cos(\frac{\pi}{4} + 2\pi)$      (c) $\sin(\frac{\pi}{2} - 6\pi)$
    (b) $\sin(\frac{\pi}{3} + 2\pi)$

**42.** (a) $\sin(17\pi/4)$     (e) $\tan(-7\pi/4)$
    (b) $\sin(-17\pi/4)$     (f) $\cos(7\pi/4)$
    (c) $\cos 11\pi$        (g) $\sec(\frac{11\pi}{6} + 2\pi)$
    (d) $\cos(53\pi/4)$     (h) $\csc(2\pi - \frac{\pi}{3})$

*In Exercises 43–46, use the Pythagorean identities to simplify the given expressions.*

**43.** $\dfrac{\sin^2 t + \cos^2 t}{\tan^2 t + 1}$      **44.** $\dfrac{\sec^2 t - 1}{\tan^2 t}$

**45.** $\dfrac{\sec^2 \theta - \tan^2 \theta}{1 + \cot^2 \theta}$      **46.** $\dfrac{\csc^4 \theta - \cot^4 \theta}{\csc^2 \theta + \cot^2 \theta}$

*In Exercises 47–54, prove that the equations are identities.*

**47.** $\csc t = \sin t + \cot t \cos t$

**48.** $\sin^2 t - \cos^2 t = \dfrac{1 - \cot^2 t}{1 + \cot^2 t}$

**49.** $\dfrac{1}{1 + \sec s} + \dfrac{1}{1 - \sec s} = -2\cot^2 s$

**50.** $\dfrac{1 + \tan s}{1 - \tan s} = \dfrac{\sec^2 s + 2\tan s}{2 - \sec^2 s}$

**51.** $\dfrac{\sec s + \cot s \csc s}{\cos s} = \csc^2 s \sec^2 s$

**52.** $(\tan \theta)(1 - \cot^2 \theta) + (\cot \theta)(1 - \tan^2 \theta) = 0$

**53.** $(\cos \alpha \cos \beta - \sin \alpha \sin \beta)(\cos \alpha \cos \beta + \sin \alpha \sin \beta)$
$$= \cos^2 \alpha - \sin^2 \beta$$

**54.** $\cot \theta + \tan \theta + 1 = \dfrac{\cot \theta}{1 - \tan \theta} + \dfrac{\tan \theta}{1 - \cot \theta}$

**55.** If $\sec t = 13/5$ and $3\pi/2 < t < 2\pi$, evaluate
$$\frac{2\sin t - 3\cos t}{4\sin t - 9\cos t}$$

**56.** If $\sec t = (b^2 + 1)/2b$ and $\pi < t < 3\pi/2$, find $\tan t$ and $\sin t$. (*Note*: $b$ is negative. Why?) You should assume that $b < -1$.

## B

**57.** Use the accompanying figure to explain why the following four identities are valid. (The identities can be used to provide an algebraic foundation for the reference-angle technique that we've used to evaluate the trigonometric functions.)

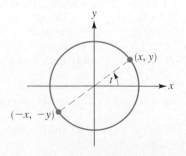

   (i) $\sin(t + \pi) = -\sin t$     (iii) $\cos(t + \pi) = -\cos t$
   (ii) $\sin(t - \pi) = -\sin t$     (iv) $\cos(t - \pi) = -\cos t$

**58.** Use two of the results in Exercise 57 to verify the identity $\tan(t + \pi) = \tan t$. (You'll see the graphical aspect of this identity in Section 7.7.)

**59.** In the equation $x^4 + 6x^2y^2 + y^4 = 32$, make the substitutions
$$x = X\cos\frac{\pi}{4} - Y\sin\frac{\pi}{4} \quad \text{and} \quad y = X\sin\frac{\pi}{4} + Y\cos\frac{\pi}{4}$$
and show that the result simplifies to $X^4 + Y^4 = 16$. (*Hint*: Evaluate the trigonometric functions, simplify the expressions for $x$ and $y$, take out the common factor, and then substitute.)

**60.** Suppose that $\tan \theta = 2$ and $0 < \theta < \pi/2$.
   (a) Compute $\sin \theta$ and $\cos \theta$.
   (b) Using the values obtained in part (a), make the substitutions
$$x = X\cos\theta - Y\sin\theta \quad \text{and} \quad y = X\sin\theta + Y\cos\theta$$
in the expression $7x^2 - 8xy + y^2$, and simplify the result.

**61.** In this exercise, we are going to find the minimum value of the function
$$f(t) = \tan^2 t + 9\cot^2 t \qquad 0 < t < \frac{\pi}{2}$$
   (a) Set your calculator in the radian mode and complete the table. Round the values you obtain to two decimal places.

| t | 0.2 | 0.4 | 0.6 | 0.8 | 1.0 | 1.2 | 1.4 |
|---|---|---|---|---|---|---|---|
| f(t) | | | | | | | |

   (b) Of the seven outputs you calculated in part (a), which is the smallest? What is the corresponding input?
   (c) Prove that $\tan^2 t + 9\cot^2 t = (\tan t - 3\cot t)^2 + 6$.
   (d) Use the identity in part (c) to explain why $\tan^2 t + 9\cot^2 t \geq 6$.
   (e) The inequality in part (d) tells us that $f(t)$ is never less than 6. Furthermore, in view of part (c), $f(t)$ will equal 6 when $\tan t - 3\cot t = 0$. From this last equation, show that $\tan^2 t = 3$, and conclude that $t = \pi/3$. In summary, the minimum value of $f$ is 6, and this occurs when $t = \pi/3$. How do these values compare with your answers in part (b)?

**62.** Let $f(\theta) = \sin\theta\cos\theta$ $(0 \leq \theta \leq \frac{\pi}{2})$.
   (a) Set your calculator in the radian mode and complete the table. Round the results to two decimal places.

| $\theta$ | 0 | $\frac{\pi}{10}$ | $\frac{\pi}{5}$ | $\frac{\pi}{4}$ | $\frac{3\pi}{10}$ | $\frac{2\pi}{5}$ | $\frac{\pi}{2}$ |
|---|---|---|---|---|---|---|---|
| $f(\theta)$ | | | | | | | |

**(b)** What is the largest value of $f(\theta)$ in your table in part (a)?

**(c)** Show that $\sin \theta \cos \theta \le 1/2$ for all real numbers $\theta$ in the interval $0 \le \theta \le \pi/2$.    *Hint:* Use the inequality $\sqrt{ab} \le (a + b)/2$ [given in Exercise 40(b) on page 111], with $a = \sin \theta$ and $b = \cos \theta$.

**(d)** Does the inequality $\sin \theta \cos \theta \le \frac{1}{2}$ hold for all real numbers $\theta$?

**63.** Consider the equation

$$2 \sin^2 t - \sin t = 2 \sin t \cos t - \cos t$$

**(a)** Evaluate each side of the equation when $t = \pi/6$.

**(b)** Evaluate each side of the equation when $t = \pi/4$.

**(c)** Is the given equation an identity?

**64.** Suppose that

$$f(t) = (\sin t \cos t)(2 \sin t - 1)(2 \cos t - 1)(\tan t - 1)$$

**(a)** Compute each of the following: $f(0), f(\pi/6), f(\pi/4), f(\pi/3),$ and $f(\pi/2)$.

**(b)** Is the equation $f(t) = 0$ an identity?

*In Section 7.2 we pointed out that one of the advantages in using radian measure is that many formulas then take on particularly simple forms. Another reason for using radian measure is that the trigonometric functions can be closely approximated by very simple polynomial functions. To see examples of this, complete the tables in Exercises 65–68. Round (or, for exact values, simply report) the answers to six decimal places. In Exercises 67 and 68, note that the higher-degree polynomial provides the better approximation.    Note: The approximating polynomials in Exercises 65–68 are known as **Taylor polynomials,** after the English mathematician Brook Taylor (1685–1731). The theory of Taylor polynomials is developed in calculus.*

**65. (a)**

| $t$ | $1 - \frac{1}{2}t^2$ | $\cos t$ |
|-----|----------------------|----------|
| 0.02 | | |
| 0.05 | | |
| 0.1 | | |
| 0.2 | | |
| 0.3 | | |

Ⓖ **(b)** On the same set of axes, graph the functions $1 - \frac{1}{2}t^2$ and $\cos t$. Use a window extending from $-\pi$ to $\pi$ in the $x$-direction and $-1$ to 1 in the $y$-direction. What do you observe?

**66. (a)**

| $t$ | $t - \frac{1}{6}t^3$ | $\sin t$ |
|-----|----------------------|----------|
| 0.02 | | |
| 0.05 | | |
| 0.1 | | |
| 0.2 | | |
| 0.3 | | |

Ⓖ **(b)** On the same set of axes, graph the functions $t - \frac{1}{6}t^3$ and $\sin t$. Use a window extending from $-\pi$ to $\pi$ in the $x$-direction and $-1$ to 1 in the $y$-direction. What do you observe?

**67. (a)**

| $x$ | $\frac{1}{3}x^3 + x$ | $\frac{2}{15}x^5 + \frac{1}{3}x^3 + x$ | $\tan x$ |
|-----|----------------------|----------------------------------------|----------|
| 0.1 | | | |
| 0.2 | | | |
| 0.3 | | | |
| 0.4 | | | |
| 0.5 | | | |

Ⓖ **(b)** On the same set of axes, graph the functions $\frac{1}{3}x^3 + x$, $\frac{5}{12}x^5 + \frac{1}{3}x^3 + x$, and $\tan x$. Use a window extending from $-\pi$ to $\pi$ in the $x$-direction and $-10$ to 10 in the $y$-direction. What do you observe?

**68. (a)**

| $x$ | $x^2 + x$ | $\frac{1}{3}x^3 + x^2 + x$ | $e^x \sin x$ |
|-----|-----------|----------------------------|--------------|
| 0.1 | | | |
| 0.2 | | | |
| 0.3 | | | |
| 0.4 | | | |
| 0.5 | | | |

Ⓖ **(b)** On the same set of axes, graph the functions $x^2 + x$, $\frac{1}{3}x^3 + x^2 + x$, and $e^x \sin x$. Use a window extending from $-\pi$ to $\pi$ in the $x$-direction and $-10$ to 10 in the $y$-direction. What do you observe?

**69.** The figure on the following page shows two $x$-$y$ coordinate systems. (The same unit of length is used on all four axes.) In the coordinate system on the left, the curve is a portion of the unit circle

$$x^2 + y^2 = 1$$

and $A$ is the point $(1, 0)$. The points $B, C, D, E,$ and $F$ are located on the circle according to the information in the following table.

| arc | $\overset{\frown}{AB}$ | $\overset{\frown}{AC}$ | $\overset{\frown}{AD}$ | $\overset{\frown}{AE}$ | $\overset{\frown}{AF}$ |
|-----|------|------|------|------|------|
| length | $\frac{\pi}{12}$ | $\frac{\pi}{6}$ | $\frac{\pi}{4}$ | $\frac{\pi}{3}$ | $\frac{5\pi}{12}$ |

Determine the $y$-coordinates of the points $P, Q, R, S,$ and $T$. Give an exact expression for each answer and, where appropriate, a calculator approximation rounded to three decimal places.

Figure for Exercise 69

# PROJECT

## A LINEAR APPROXIMATION FOR THE SINE FUNCTION

In this project we derive the following very important property of the sine function:

> For real numbers $\theta$, the ratio $\dfrac{\sin \theta}{\theta}$ approaches 1 as $\theta$ approaches zero.

In the phrase "as $\theta$ approaches zero" (in the domain of $\sin \theta$) it is important to understand that $\theta$ cannot be zero because we can't substitute zero for $\theta$ in our trigonometric ratio.

To begin we need a preliminary result:

> For real numbers $\theta$, $\cos \theta$ approaches 1 as $\theta$ approaches zero.

**EXERCISE 1**   Convince yourself that this preliminary result is true in each of the following ways.

Ⓖ **(a)** By looking at the graph of $y = \cos \theta$, for $-\pi/4 < \theta < \pi/4$, in a $\theta$-$y$ coordinate system.

**(b)** By looking at a point $(\cos \theta, \sin \theta)$ on the unit circle.

In both parts (a) and (b), be sure to consider $\theta$ approaching zero through both positive and negative values.

Now consider real numbers $\theta$ approaching zero through positive values. Eventually $\theta < \pi/2$ so we may assume $0 < \theta < \pi/2$. In Figure A we have the unit circle with various labeled points:

$O$   is the origin.

$A$   is the point $(1, 0)$.

$P$   is the point on the unit circle corresponding to the number $\theta$, or, equivalently, the angle with radian measure $\theta$.

$B$   is the point at the foot of the perpendicular from $P$ to the $x$-axis.

$Q$   is the vertex of $\triangle OAQ$ lying on the terminal side of angle $\theta$ outside the unit circle; the line through $Q$ and $A$ is tangent to the circle.

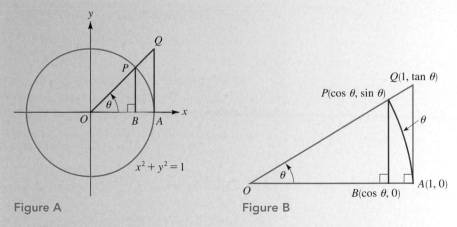

**Figure A**          **Figure B**

**EXERCISE 2**  In Figure A explain why $\angle OAQ$ is a right angle. Then explain why

$$P = (\cos\theta, \sin\theta), \quad B = (\cos\theta, 0), \quad \text{and} \quad Q = (1, \tan\theta)$$

The information from Exercise 2 is shown in Figure B.

**EXERCISE 3**  In Figure B (where $0 < \theta < \pi/2$) explain why $\sin\theta \le \theta$. (*Hint*: Draw the line segment from $P$ to $A$ and argue that its length is less than $\theta$, the length of the circular arc from $P$ to $A$. Use $\triangle PBA$ to complete your explanation.) Then show that

$$\frac{\sin\theta}{\theta} \le 1 \tag{i}$$

Inequality (i) provides a nice upper bound for $(\sin\theta)/\theta$. Considering the arc length interpretation of radian measure our derivation of (i) seems quite natural. However, we do not know of a similar elementary method for obtaining a lower bound. The standard approach uses an area inequality.

**EXERCISE 4**  In Figure B explain why

$$\text{area of circular sector } OAP \le \text{area of triangle } OAQ \tag{ii}$$

**EXERCISE 5**  Show the following:
**(a)**  area of circular sector $OAP = \frac{1}{2}\theta$
**(b)**  area of triangle $OAQ = \frac{1}{2}\tan\theta$

Substituting the values from Exercise 5 into inequality (ii) we have

$$\frac{1}{2}\theta \le \frac{1}{2}\tan\theta \tag{iii}$$

**EXERCISE 6**  Use inequality (iii) to show

$$\cos\theta \le \frac{\sin\theta}{\theta} \tag{iv}$$

Be careful to explain why the sense of inequality (iii) is preserved.

Combining inequalities (i) and (iv) we have

$$\cos \theta \le \frac{\sin \theta}{\theta} \le 1 \qquad \text{(v)}$$

As $\theta$ approaches zero through positive values, the quantity $(\sin \theta)/\theta$ is "sandwiched" between the two quantities $\cos \theta$ and 1, which both approach 1. This leads us to conclude that

$$\frac{\sin \theta}{\theta} \text{ approaches 1 as } \theta \text{ approaches zero through positive values} \qquad \text{(vi)}$$

**EXERCISE 7**    As $\theta$ approaches zero through negative values, eventually $-\pi/2 < \theta < 0$. Let $\theta = -\alpha$.
**(a)**  Explain why $0 < \alpha < \pi/2$.
**(b)**  Show that $(\sin \theta)/\theta = (\sin \alpha)/\alpha$.

Continuing with the notation of Exercise 7, as $\theta$ approaches zero through negative values, $\alpha$ approaches zero through positive values. Then $(\sin \theta)/\theta$ approaches the same quantity that $(\sin \alpha)/\alpha$ approaches. We know by the argument preceding Exercise 7 that $(\sin \alpha)/\alpha$ approaches 1 as $\alpha$ approaches zero through positive values. Thus

$$\frac{\sin \theta}{\theta} \text{ approaches 1 as } \theta \text{ approaches zero through negative valucs} \qquad \text{(vii)}$$

Combining (vi) and (vii), we conclude that

$$\text{For real numbers } \theta, \frac{\sin \theta}{\theta} \text{ approaches 1 as } \theta \text{ approaches zero.} \qquad \text{(viii)}$$

An important interpretation of (viii) is that for a nonzero real number $\theta$ close to zero, $(\sin \theta)/\theta$ is close to 1, or equivalently, $\sin \theta$ is close to $\theta$. We say

$$\sin \theta \approx \theta \qquad \text{for } |\theta| \approx 0 \qquad \text{(ix)}$$

We interpret (ix) by saying $\sin \theta$ can be approximated by the linear function $\theta$ for $\theta$ near zero.

**EXERCISE 8**
**(a)**  For what real numbers $\theta$ "near" zero is the percentage error introduced by using $\theta$ as an approximation for $\sin \theta$ at most 1%? At most 5%? What are the corresponding angles in degrees?
**(b)**  In Figure B, if the degree measure of the angle $\theta$ is 30°, what are the lengths of the circular arc from $P$ to $A$ and the line segment from $P$ to $B$? What is the percentage error introduced by using the length of the arc as an approximation for the length of the vertical line segment?

Ⓖ  **EXERCISE 9**    For $-\pi/4 < \theta < \pi/4$, graph $y = \sin \theta$ and $y = \theta$ in a $\theta$-$y$ coordinate system. Note that the graph of $y = \sin \theta$ is very close to the graph of $y = \theta$ for $\theta$ near 0. This is the graphical interpretation of the approximation in (ix).

**EXERCISE 10**

**(a)** Show that

$$\frac{\tan \theta}{\theta} = \frac{\sin \theta}{\theta} \cdot \frac{1}{\cos \theta} \qquad \text{for } \theta \neq 0$$

**(b)** Use the identity in part (a) to show that $(\tan \theta)/\theta$ approaches 1 as $\theta$ approaches zero.

**(c)** Explain why

$$\tan \theta \approx \theta \qquad \text{for} \qquad |\theta| \approx 0 \qquad \qquad (x)$$

What is the functional interpretation of (x)?

Ⓖ **(d)** For $-\pi/4 < \theta < \pi/4$, graph $y = \tan \theta$ and $y = \theta$. Use these graphs to explain the graphical interpretation of the approximation in (x).

---

# 7.4   GRAPHS OF THE SINE AND COSINE FUNCTIONS

Our focus in this section is on the sine and cosine functions. As preparation for the discussion, we want to understand what is meant by the term "periodic function." By way of example both of the functions in Figure 1 are **periodic.** That is, their graphs display patterns that repeat themselves at regular intervals.

In Figure 1(a) the graph of the function $f$ repeats itself every six units. We say that *the period of $f$ is* 6. Similarly, the period of $g$ in Figure 1(b) is $2\pi$. In both cases, notice that the period represents the minimum number of units that we must travel along the horizontal axis before the graph begins to repeat itself. Because of this, we can state the definition of a periodic function as follows.

(a) The graph of $f$

(b) The graph of $g$

**Figure 1**

---

**DEFINITION** | **A Periodic Function and Its Period**

---

A non-constant function $f$ is said to be **periodic** if there is a number $p > 0$ such that

$$f(x + p) = f(x)$$

for all $x$ in the domain of $f$. The smallest such number $p$ is called the **period** of $f$.

---

We also want to define the term "amplitude" as it applies to periodic functions. For a function such as $g$ in Figure 1(b), in which the graph is centered about the horizontal axis, the amplitude is simply the maximum height of the graph above the horizontal axis. Thus the amplitude of $g$ is 4. More generally, we define the amplitude of any periodic function as follows.

---

| **DEFINITION** | **Amplitude** |
|---|---|

Let $f$ be a periodic function and let $m$ and $M$ denote, respectively, the minimum and maximum values of the function. Then the **amplitude** of $f$ is the number

$$\frac{M - m}{2}$$

---

For the function $g$ in Figure 1(b) this definition tells us that the amplitude is $\dfrac{4 - (-4)}{2} = 4$, which agrees with our previous value. Check for yourself now that the amplitude of the function in Figure 1(a) is 1.

Periodic functions are used throughout the sciences to analyze or describe a variety of phenomena ranging from the vibrations of an electron to the variations in the size of an animal population as it interacts with its environment. Figures 2 through 4 display some examples of periodic functions.

**Figure 2**
The surface temperature of the star Delta Cephei is a periodic function of time. The period is 5.367 days. The amplitude is $(6800 - 5400)/2 = 700$ degrees Kelvin.

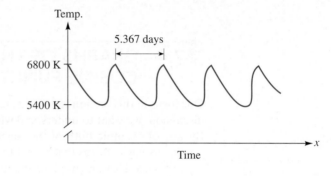

**Figure 3**
Electrical activity of the heart and blood pressure as periodic functions of time. The figure shows (a) a typical ECG (electrocardiogram) and (b) the corresponding graph of arterial blood pressure. [Adapted from *Physics for the Health Sciences* by C. R. Nave and B. C. Nave (Philadelphia: W. B. Saunders Co., 1975)]

(a)

(b)

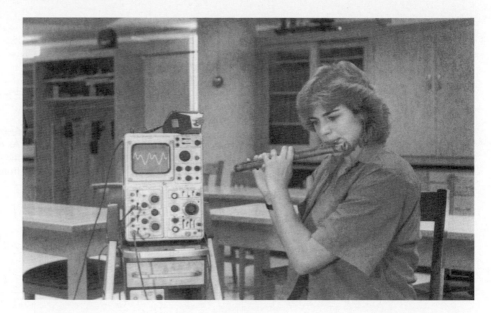

The sound wave generated by a note played on the bamboo flute is a periodic function. The sound wave is recorded on an oscilloscope. (Photograph by Professor Vern Ostdiek)

(a)  The sound wave generated by a tuning fork vibrating at 440 vibrations per second (On the piano, this note corresponds to the first A above middle C.)

(b)  The sound wave generated by a tuning fork vibrating at 880 vibrations per second [This note is an A one octave above that in part (a).]

**Figure 4**
Sound waves

(c)  The sound wave generated by simultaneously striking the tuning forks in parts (a) and (b)

Let us now graph the sine function $f(\theta) = \sin \theta$. We are assuming that $\theta$ is a real number, so the domain of the sine function is the set of all real numbers. Even before making any calculations, we can gain strong intuitive insight into how the graph must look by carrying out the following experiment. After drawing the unit circle, $x^2 + y^2 = 1$, place your fingertip at the point $(1, 0)$ and then move your finger

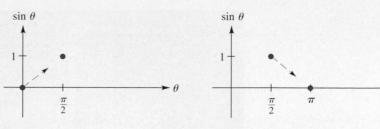

(a) As $\theta$ increases from 0 to $\pi/2$, the $y$-coordinate ($\sin \theta$) increases from 0 to 1.

(b) As $\theta$ increases from $\pi/2$ to $\pi$, the $y$-coordinate decreases from 1 back down to 0.

(c) As $\theta$ increases from $\pi$ to $3\pi/2$, the $y$-coordinate decreases from 0 to $-1$.

(d) As $\theta$ increases from $3\pi/2$ to $2\pi$, the $y$-coordinate increases from $-1$ back up to 0.

**Figure 5**

counterclockwise around the circle. As you do this, keep track of what happens to the $y$-coordinate of your fingertip. (The $y$-coordinate is $\sin \theta$.) If we think of $\theta$ as the radian measure of an angle, the $y$-coordinate of your fingertip is $\sin \theta$.

Figure 5 tells us a great deal about the sine function: where the function is increasing and decreasing, where the graph crosses the $x$-axis, and where the high and low points of the graph occur. Furthermore, since at $\theta = 2\pi$ we've returned to our starting point (1, 0), additional counterclockwise trips around the unit circle will just result in repetitions of the pattern established in Figure 5. This insight can be used to prove that the period of the function $y = \sin \theta$ is indeed $2\pi$.

As informative as Figure 5 is, however, there is not enough information there to tell us the precise shape of the required graph. For instance, all three of the curves in Figure 6 fit the specifications described in Figure 5.

Now let's set up a table so that we can accurately sketch the graph of $y = \sin \theta$. Since the sine function is periodic (as we've just observed) with period $2\pi$, our

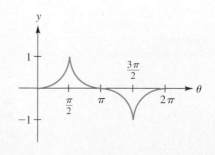

**Figure 6**

**TABLE 1**

| $\theta$ | 0 | $\dfrac{\pi}{6}$ | $\dfrac{\pi}{3}$ | $\dfrac{\pi}{2}$ | $\dfrac{2\pi}{3}$ | $\dfrac{5\pi}{6}$ | $\pi$ | $\dfrac{7\pi}{6}$ | $\dfrac{4\pi}{3}$ | $\dfrac{3\pi}{2}$ | $\dfrac{5\pi}{3}$ | $\dfrac{11\pi}{6}$ | $2\pi$ |
|---|---|---|---|---|---|---|---|---|---|---|---|---|---|
| $\sin\theta$ | 0 | $\dfrac{1}{2}$ | $\dfrac{\sqrt{3}}{2}$ | 1 | $\dfrac{\sqrt{3}}{2}$ | $\dfrac{1}{2}$ | 0 | $-\dfrac{1}{2}$ | $-\dfrac{\sqrt{3}}{2}$ | $-1$ | $-\dfrac{\sqrt{3}}{2}$ | $-\dfrac{1}{2}$ | 0 |

table need contain only values of $\theta$ between 0 and $2\pi$, as shown in Table 1. This will establish the basic pattern for the graph.

In plotting the points obtained from Table 1, we use the approximation $\sqrt{3}/2 \approx 0.87$. Rather than approximating $\pi$, however, we mark off units on the horizontal axis in terms of $\pi$. The resulting graph is shown in Figure 7. By continuing this same pattern to the left and right, we obtain the complete graph of $f(\theta) = \sin\theta$, as indicated in Figure 8.

**Figure 7**

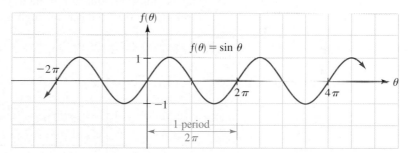

**Figure 8**

Before going on to analyze the sine function or to study the graphs of the other trigonometric functions, we're going to make a slight change in the notation we've been using. To conform with common usage, we will use $x$ instead of $\theta$ on the horizontal axis, and we will use $y$ for the vertical axis. The sine function is then written simply as $y = \sin x$, where the real number $x$ denotes the radian measure of an angle or, equivalently, the length of the corresponding arc on the unit circle. For reference we redraw Figures 7 and 8 using this familiar $x$-$y$ notation, as shown in Figure 9.

You should memorize the graph of the sine curve in Figure 9(b) so that you can sketch it without first setting up a table. Of course, once you know the shape and the location of the basic cycle shown in Figure 9(a), you automatically know the graph of the full sine curve in Figure 9(b). *Note:* The graph of $y = \sin x$ on an interval of length $2\pi$, the period of the sine function, is called a *cycle* of the graph of $y = \sin x$.

(a) The basic cycle of $y = \sin x$          (b) The period of $y = \sin x$ is $2\pi$

**Figure 9**

We can use the graphs in Figure 9 to help us list some of the key properties of the sine function.

---

**PROPERTY SUMMARY   The Sine Function: $y = \sin x$**

1. The domain of the sine function is the set of all real numbers. The range of the sine function is the closed interval $[-1, 1]$, and we have

$$-1 \leq \sin x \leq 1 \qquad \text{for all } x$$

2. The sine function is an odd periodic function with period $2\pi$. The amplitude is 1.

3. The graph of $y = \sin x$ consists of repetitions, over the entire domain, of the **basic sine wave** shown in Figure 10. The basic sine wave crosses the $x$-axis at the beginning, middle, and end of the cycle. The curve reaches its highest point one-quarter of the way through the cycle and its lowest point three-quarters of the way through the cycle.

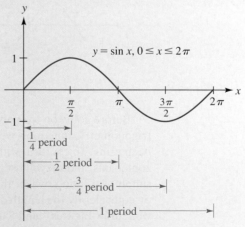

**Figure 10**
The basic sine wave

---

*Note:* The graph of $y = \sin x$ is symmetric about the origin.

| EXAMPLE | 1 | **Finding coordinates of turning points and intercepts of the graph of y = sin x** |

Figure 11 shows a portion of the graph of $y = \sin x$.

**(a)** What are the coordinates of the three turning points $A$, $B$, and $C$? Here, and in part (b), report the answers both in terms of $\pi$ and as calculator approximations rounded to three decimal places.

**(b)** What are the $x$-intercepts at $D$ and $E$?

**Figure 11**

**SOLUTION**

**(a)** From Figure 10 (which you should also memorize) we know that the coordinates of the point $A$ are $(\pi/2, 1)$. Therefore since the period of the sine function is $2\pi$, the coordinates of $B$ and $C$ are as follows:

$$\text{Coordinates of } B: \quad \left(\frac{\pi}{2} + 2\pi, 1\right) \quad \text{or} \quad \left(\frac{5\pi}{2}, 1\right)$$

$$\text{Coordinates of } C: \quad \left(\frac{\pi}{2} - 2\pi, 1\right) \quad \text{or} \quad \left(-\frac{3\pi}{2}, 1\right)$$

As you should now check for yourself, the calculator approximations here are

$$A(1.571, 1) \qquad B(7.854, 1) \qquad C(-4.712, 1)$$

**(b)** From Figure 10 we also know the $x$-coordinate at $D$, it is $\pi$. Since the point $E$ is $2\pi$ units to the right of $D$, the $x$-coordinate of $E$ is $\pi + 2\pi = 3\pi$. Using a calculator, we have

$$x\text{-intercept at } D: \quad 3.142$$
$$x\text{-intercept at } E: \quad 9.425$$

We could obtain the graph of the cosine function by setting up a table, just as we did with the sine function. A more interesting and informative way to proceed, however, is to use the identity

$$\cos x = \sin\left(x + \frac{\pi}{2}\right) \tag{1}$$

(Exercise 63 at the end of this section outlines a geometric proof of this identity. Also, after studying Section 8.1, you'll see a simple way to prove this identity algebraically.) From our work on graphing functions in Chapter 3, we can interpret equation (1) geometrically. Equation (1) tells us that the graph of $y = \cos x$ is obtained by translating the sine curve $\pi/2$ units to the left. The result is shown in Figure 12(a). Figure 12(b) displays one complete cycle of the cosine curve, from $x = 0$ to $x = 2\pi$.

As with the sine function, you should memorize the graph and the basic features of the cosine function, which are summarized in the box that follows.

(a)

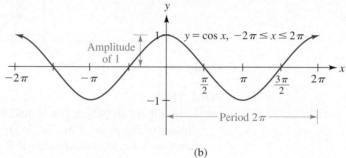

**Figure 12**

(b)

---

## PROPERTY SUMMARY The Cosine Function: $y = \cos x$

1. The domain of the cosine function is the set of all real numbers. The range of the cosine function is the closed interval $[-1, 1]$, and we have

$$-1 \le \cos x \le 1 \qquad \text{for all } x$$

2. The cosine function is an even periodic function with period $2\pi$. The amplitude is 1.

3. The graph of $y = \cos x$ consists of repetitions, over the entire domain, of the **basic cosine wave** shown in Figure 13. The basic cosine wave crosses the $x$-axis one-quarter of the way and again three-quarters of the way through the basic cycle. The curve reaches its highest point at the beginning and end of the basic cycle and reaches its lowest point half-way through the basic cycle.

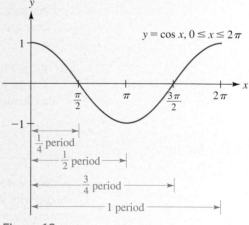

**Figure 13**
The basic cosine wave

---

*Note*: The graph of $y = \cos x$ is symmetric about the $y$-axis.

In the next example we use a graph to estimate roots of equations involving the cosine function. We also use a calculator to obtain more accurate results. As you'll see, the calculator portion of the work involves more than just button pushing. You'll need to use the reference-angle concept, and you'll need to apply the following property of inverse functions (from Section 3.6).

$$f^{-1}(f(x)) = x \qquad \text{for every } x \text{ in the domain of } f$$

| EXAMPLE | 2 | **Finding approximate solutions of cos x = ±0.8 visually and with a calculator** |

**(a)** Use the graph in Figure 14 to estimate a root of the equation

$$\cos x = 0.8$$

in the interval $0 \leq x \leq \pi/2$.

**(b)** Use a calculator to obtain a more accurate value for the root in part (a). Round the answer to three decimal places.

**(c)** Use the reference-angle concept to find all solutions to the equation $\cos x = 0.8$ in the interval $0 \leq x \leq 2\pi$. Round the answer to three decimal places.

**(d)** Use the reference-angle concept and a calculator to find all solutions of the equation $\cos x = -0.8$ within the interval $0 \leq x \leq 2\pi$. Again, round the answer to three decimal places.

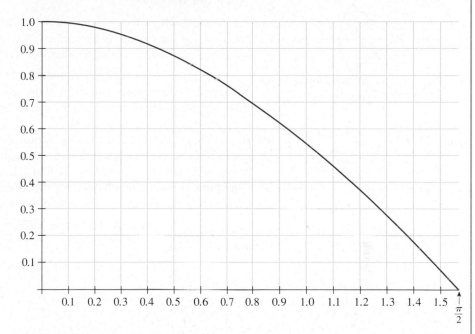

**Figure 14**
$y = \cos x, \ 0 \leq x \leq \pi/2$

**SOLUTION**

**(a)** In Figure 14, look at the point where the horizontal line $y = 0.8$ intersects the curve $y = \cos x$. The $x$-coordinate of this point, call it $x_1$, is the root we are looking for. (Why?) Using Figure 14, we estimate that $x_1$ is approximately halfway between $x = 0.6$ and $x = 0.7$. So our estimate for the root is $x_1 \approx 0.65$.

**(b)** We can determine the root $x_1$ by using the *inverse cosine function*. We will discuss the inverse cosine function in detail in Chapter 8. Just as the notation $f^{-1}$ denotes the inverse of a function $f$, so the notation $\cos^{-1}$ is often used to denote the inverse cosine function. Starting with the equation $\cos x_1 = 0.8$, we apply the inverse cosine to both sides to obtain

$$\cos^{-1}(\cos x_1) = \cos^{-1}(0.8)$$

and therefore

$$x_1 = \cos^{-1}(0.8)$$

We use a calculator, set in the radian mode, to evaluate the expression $\cos^{-1}(0.8)$. The keystrokes are as follows. (If these keystrokes don't work on your calculator, be sure to check the user's manual.)

| EXPRESSION | KEYSTROKES | OUTPUT |
|---|---|---|
| $\cos^{-1}(0.8)$ | [2nd] [cos] 0.8 [ENTER] | 0.644 |

Note that the value 0.644 is consistent with the estimate $x_1 \approx 0.65$ that was obtained graphically in part (a).

**(c)** To find another root of the equation, we use the fact that the cosine is positive in Quadrant IV as well as in Quadrant 1. The root $x_1 \approx 0.644$ is the radian measure of a first-quadrant angle (because $0.644 < \pi/2$). As is indicated in Figure 15, we let $x_2$ denote the radian measure of the fourth-quadrant angle that has $x_1$ for its reference angle. Then we have $\cos x_2 = \cos x_1 = 0.8$. That is, $x_2$ is also a solution of the equation $\cos x = 0.8$. The calculations for $x_2$ now run as follows:

$$\begin{aligned} x_2 &= 2\pi - x_1 \\ &= 2\pi - \cos^{-1}(0.8) \\ &\approx 5.640 \qquad \text{using a calculator (radian mode) and} \\ & \qquad\qquad\quad \text{rounding to three decimal places} \end{aligned}$$

We have now determined two roots of the equation $\cos x = 0.8$ in the interval $0 \le x \le 2\pi$. There are no other roots in this interval because the cosine is negative in Quadrants II and III.

**(d)** In part (b) we determined a first-quadrant angle $x_1$ satisfying the equation $\cos x = 0.8$. Now we want solutions for the equation $\cos x = -0.8$. Since the cosine is negative in Quadrants II and III, we therefore want angles in Quadrants II and III that have $x_1$ for the reference angle. As is indicated in Figure 16, these angles are $\pi - x_1$ and $\pi + x_1$. Computing, we have

$$\pi - x_1 = \pi - \cos^{-1}(0.8) \approx 2.498$$

and

$$\pi + x_1 = \pi + \cos^{-1}(0.8) \approx 3.785$$

**Figure 15**

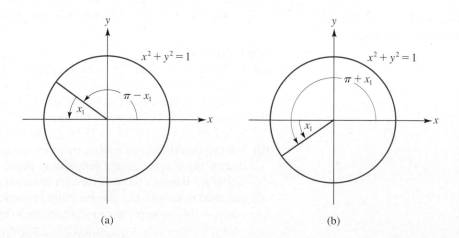

(a)                    (b)

**Figure 16**
The reference angle for both
$\pi - x_1$ and $\pi + x_1$ is $x_1$.

In summary, the equation $\cos x = -0.8$ has two roots in the closed interval $[0, 2\pi]$. These roots are approximately 2.498 and 3.785. In Figure 17,

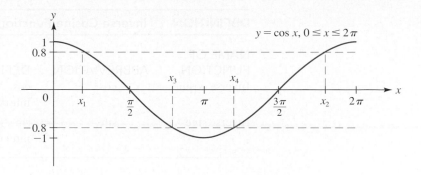

**Figure 17**
Summary of Example 2.
The roots of the equation
$\cos x = 0.8$ in the interval $[0, 2\pi]$
are $x_1 \approx 0.644$ and $x_2 \approx 5.640$. The
roots of the equation $\cos x \approx -0.8$
in the interval $[0, 2\pi]$ are $x_3 \approx 2.498$
and $x_4 \approx 3.785$.

which summarizes this example, these two roots are denoted by $x_3$ and $x_4$, respectively.

In part (b) of the example just concluded, we used a calculator to find a number $x$ such that $\cos x = 0.8$. As was indicated in the example, the function that outputs such a number is called the inverse cosine function. There are two standard abbreviations for the name of this function, and a third abbreviation that is used on some types of calculators. The two standard abbreviations are $\cos^{-1}$ and arccos (read *arc cos*). In the next chapter we will analyze the inverse cosine function in some detail. But for our present purposes you need only know the following definition:

---

$\cos^{-1}(x)$ denotes the unique number in the interval $[0, \pi]$ whose cosine is $x$.

---

As examples of this notation, we have

$$\cos^{-1}\left(\frac{1}{2}\right) = \frac{\pi}{3} \qquad \text{because } \cos\frac{\pi}{3} = \tfrac{1}{2} \text{ and } 0 < \tfrac{\pi}{3} < \pi$$

$$\cos^{-1}\left(\frac{1}{2}\right) \neq \frac{5\pi}{3} \qquad \text{because although } \cos\frac{5\pi}{3} = \tfrac{1}{2}, \text{ the number } \tfrac{5\pi}{3}$$
$$\text{is not in the required interval } [0, \pi]$$

$$\cos^{-1}\left(-\frac{1}{2}\right) = \frac{2\pi}{3} \qquad \text{because } \cos\frac{2\pi}{3} = -\tfrac{1}{2} \text{ and } 0 < \tfrac{2\pi}{3} < \pi,$$

$$\cos^{-1}(0.8) \approx 0.644 \qquad \text{as we saw in Example 2}$$

In Example 2, Figure 17 tells us that the number $x_1$ is in the interval $[0, \pi]$ but $x_2$ is not. That is why the keystrokes on page 530 gave us the value for $x_1$ rather than $x_2$. (We then used the reference-angle or reference-number concept to obtain $x_2$.)

For some of the exercises in this section you will need to use the *inverse sine function*, rather than the inverse cosine function that we have just been discussing. For reference, we define both functions in the box that follows. (These functions are discussed at greater length in the next chapter.)

| DEFINITION | Inverse Cosine Function and Inverse Sine Function | |
|---|---|---|
| **NAME OF FUNCTION** | **ABBREVIATION** | **DEFINITION** |
| Inverse cosine | $\cos^{-1}$ | $\cos^{-1}(x)$ is the (unique) number in the interval $[0, \pi]$ whose cosine is $x$. |
| Inverse sine | $\sin^{-1}$ | $\sin^{-1}(x)$ is the (unique) number in the interval $[-\frac{\pi}{2}, \frac{\pi}{2}]$ whose sine is $x$. |

# EXERCISE SET 7.4

**A**

*In Exercises 1–8, specify the period and amplitude for each function.*

**1.**

**2.**

**3.**

**4.**

**5.**

**6.**

**7.**

**8.**

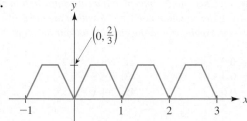

*In Exercises 9–18, refer to the graph of y = sin x in the following figure. Specify the coordinates of the indicated points. Give the x-coordinates both in terms of π and as calculator approximations rounded to three decimal places.*

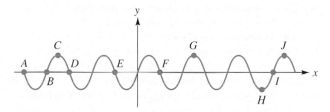

| | |
|---|---|
| **9.** *C* | **10.** *F* |
| **11.** *G* | **12.** *A* |
| **13.** *B* | **14.** *J* |
| **15.** *D* | **16.** *H* |
| **17.** *E* | **18.** *I* |

*In Exercises 19–22, state whether the function y = sin x is increasing or decreasing on the given interval. (The terms increasing and decreasing are explained on page 159.)*

**19.** $3\pi/2 < x < 2\pi$

**20.** $-\pi/2 < x < \pi/2$

**21.** $5\pi/2 < x < 7\pi/2$

**22.** $-5\pi/2 < x < -2\pi$

*In Exercises 23–32, refer to the graph of y = cos x in the following figure. Specify the coordinates of the indicated points. Give the x-coordinates both in terms of π and as calculator approximations rounded to three decimal places.*

| | |
|---|---|
| **23.** *J* | **24.** *H* |
| **25.** *A* | **26.** *G* |
| **27.** *E* | **28.** *D* |
| **29.** *I* | **30.** *F* |
| **31.** *B* | **32.** *C* |

*In Exercises 33–36, state whether the function y = cos x is increasing or decreasing on the given interval.*

**33.** $0 < x < \pi$          **34.** $6\pi < x < 7\pi$

**35.** $-\pi/2 < x < 0$     **36.** $-5\pi/2 < x < -2\pi$

*In Exercises 37–39, use a graphing utility to obtain several different views of y = sin x and y = cos x. If you are using a graphics calculator, make sure it is set for the radian mode (rather than the degree mode).*

Ⓖ **37. (a)** Graph $y = \sin x$ using a viewing rectangle that extends from −7 to 7 in the x-direction and from −3 to 3 in the y-direction. Note that there is an x-intercept between 3 and 4. Using your knowledge of the sine function (and not the graphing utility), what is the exact value for this x-intercept?

     **(b)** Refer to the graph that you obtained in part (a). How many turning points do you see? Note that one of the turning points occurs when x is between 1 and 2. What is the exact x-coordinate for this turning point?

     **(c)** Add the graph of $y = \cos x$ to your picture. How many turning points do you see for $y = \cos x$? Note that one of the turning points occurs between $x = 6$ and $x = 7$. What is the exact x-coordinate for this turning point?

     **(d)** Your picture in part (c) indicates that the graphs of $y = \sin x$ and $y = \cos x$ are just translates of one another. By what distance would we have to shift the graph of $y = \sin x$ to the left for it to coincide with the graph of $y = \cos x$?

     **(e)** Most graphing utilities have an option that will let you mark off the units on the x-axis in terms of π. Check your instruction manual if necessary, and then, for the picture that you obtained in part (c), change the x-axis units to multiples of $\pi/2$. Use the resulting picture to confirm your answers to the questions in parts (a) through (c) regarding x-intercepts and turning points.

Ⓖ **38.** This exercise presents an interesting fact about the graph of $y = \sin x$ that is useful in numerical work.

*(continues)*

(a) In the standard viewing rectangle, graph the function $y = \sin x$ along with the line $y = x$. Notice that the two graphs appear to be virtually identical in the vicinity of the origin. Actually, the only point that the two graphs have in common is $(0, 0)$, but very near the origin, the distance between the two graphs is less than the thickness of the lines or dots that your graphing utility draws. To underscore this fact, zoom in on the origin several times. What do you observe?

(b) The work in part (a) can be summarized as follows. (Recall that the symbol $\approx$ means "is approximately equal to.")

---

$$\sin x \approx x \qquad \text{when } |x| \text{ is close to } 0$$

---

To see numerical evidence that supports this result, complete the following tables.

| x | 0.253 | 0.0253 | 0.00253 | 0.000253 |
|---|---|---|---|---|
| sin x | | | | |
| x − sin x | | | | |

| x | −0.253 | −0.0253 | −0.00253 | −0.000253 |
|---|---|---|---|---|
| sin x | | | | |
| x − sin x | | | | |

(c) The numerical evidence in part (b) suggests that for $x$ positive and close to 0, $\sin x < x$. State the corresponding result for $x$ negative and close to 0. Now on the same set of axes draw, without a calculator, the graphs of $y = x$ and $y = \sin x$.

Ⓖ **39. (a)** Graph the function $y = \cos x$ in the standard viewing rectangle, and look at the arch-shaped portion of the curve between $-\pi/2$ and $\pi/2$. This portion of the cosine curve has the general shape of a parabola. Could it actually be a portion of a parabola? Go on to part (b).

(b) Calculus shows that the answer to the question raised in part (a) is "no." But calculus also shows that there is a parabola, $y = 1 - 0.5x^2$, that closely resembles the cosine curve in the vicinity of $x = 0$. To see this, graph the parabola $y = 1 - 0.5x^2$ and the curve $y = \cos x$ in the standard viewing rectangle. Describe, in a complete sentence or two, what you observe.

(c) Complete the following table to see numerical evidence that strongly supports your observations in part (b).

| x | 1 | 0.5 | 0.1 | 0.01 | 0.001 |
|---|---|---|---|---|---|
| cos x | | | | | |
| 1 − 0.5x² | | | | | |

*In Exercises 40–45 you are given an equation of the form*

$$\cos x = k \qquad \text{where } k \geq 0$$

(a) *Use the graph in Figure 14 (on page 529) to estimate (to the nearest 0.05) a root of the equation within the interval $0 \leq x \leq \pi/2$.*

(b) *Use a calculator to obtain a more accurate value for the root in part (a). Round the answer to four decimal places.*

(c) *Use the reference-angle concept and a calculator to find another root of the equation (within the interval $0 \leq x \leq 2\pi$).*

(d) *Use the reference-angle concept and a calculator to find all solutions of the equation $\cos x = -k$ within the interval $0 \leq x \leq 2\pi$. Again, round the answers to four decimal places.*

**40.** $\cos x = 0.7$      **41.** $\cos x = 0.9$
**42.** $\cos x = 0.4$      **43.** $\cos x = 0.3$
**44.** $\cos x = 0.6$      **45.** $\cos x = 0.55$

*In Exercises 46–51 you are given an equation of the form*

$$\sin x = k \qquad \text{where } k > 0$$

(a) *Use the graph in Figure A on the next page to estimate (to the nearest 0.05) a root of the equation within the interval $0 \leq x \leq \pi/2$.*

(b) *Use a calculator (with the inverse sine function) to obtain a more accurate value for the root in part (a). Round the answer to four decimal places.*

(c) *Use the reference-angle concept and a calculator to find another root of the equation (within the interval $0 \leq x \leq 2\pi$). Round the answer to four decimal places.*

(d) *Use the reference-angle concept and a calculator to find all solutions of the equation $\sin x = -k$ within the interval $0 \leq x \leq 2\pi$. Round the answer to four decimal places.*

**46.** $\sin x = 0.1$      **47.** $\sin x = 0.6$
**48.** $\sin x = 0.4$      **49.** $\sin x = 0.2$
**50.** $\sin x = 0.85$      **51.** $\sin x = 0.7$

Ⓖ **52.** In Example 2 in Section 7.4 we determined two roots $x_1$ and $x_2$ of the equation $\cos x = 0.8$ in the interval $0 \leq x \leq 2\pi$. The values were $x_1 \approx 0.644$ and $x_2 \approx 5.640$. Check these results graphically as follows. Using a viewing rectangle extending from $x = 0$ to $x = 2\pi$, graph the curve $y = \cos x$ along with the horizontal line $y = 0.8$. Then use the graphing utility (with repeated zooms) to estimate the $x$-coordinates of the two points where the curve $y = \cos x$ intersects the line $y = 0.8$. What do you observe?

Ⓖ **53.** In Example 2(d) we determined two roots $x_3$ and $x_4$ of the equation $\cos x = -0.8$ in the interval $0 \leq x \leq 2\pi$. The values were $x_3 \approx 2.498$ and $x_4 \approx 3.785$. Use the procedure indicated in Exercise 52 to check these results graphically.

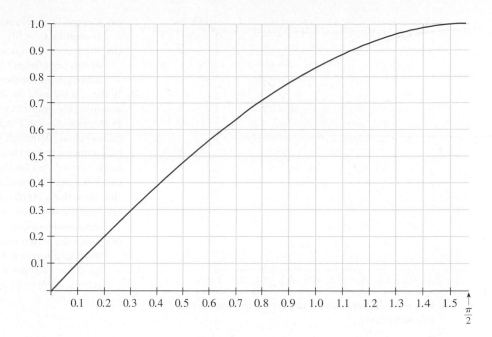

**Figure A**
$y = \sin x, 0 \le x \le \pi/2$

*In Exercises 54 and 55, use graphs (as in Example 2) to esti-mate the roots of each equation for $0 \le x \le 2\pi$. Zoom in close enough on the intersection points until you are sure about the first two decimal places in each root. Then use a calculator, as in Example 2, to determine more accurate values for the roots. Round the calculator values to four decimal places.*

G **54.** (a) $\cos x = 0.351$
    (b) $\cos x = -0.351$

G **55.** (a) $\sin x = 0.687$
    (b) $\sin x = -0.687$

## B

*In Exercises 56–60 refer to the following figure, which shows the graphs of $y = \sin x$ and $y = \cos x$ on the closed interval $[0, 2\pi]$.*

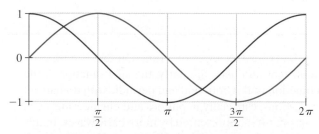

**56. (a)** When the value of $\sin x$ is a maximum, what is the corresponding value of $\cos x$?
   **(b)** When the value of $\cos x$ is a maximum, what is the corresponding value of $\sin x$?

**57.** Follow Exercise 56, but replace the word "maximum" with "minimum."

**58. (a)** For which $x$-values in the interval $0 \le x \le 2\pi$ is $\sin x = \cos x$?   *Hint*: Refer to Table 1 on page 430.

**(b)** For which $x$-values in the interval $0 \le x \le 2\pi$ is $\sin x < \cos x$?

**59.** Specify an open interval in which both the sine and cosine functions are decreasing.

**60.** Specify an open interval in which the sine function is decreasing but the cosine function is increasing.

*As a prerequisite for Exercises 61 and 62, you need to have studied Section 4.3 on iteration and population growth. In particular, you should be familiar with Example 2 on pages 250–252.*

**61.** As in Example 2 in Section 4.3, suppose a farmer has a fishpond with a maximum population size of 500, and suppose that initially the pond is stocked with 50 fish. Unlike Example 2, however, assume that the growth equation is

$$f(x) = \cos x \qquad (0 \le x \le 1)$$

Finally, as in Example 2, assume that the time intervals are breeding seasons.

**(a)** Use the iteration diagram on the next page and your calculator to complete the following table. For the values obtained from the graph, estimate to the nearest 0.05 (or closer, if it seems appropriate). For the calculator values, round the final answers to five decimal places. As usual, check to see that the calculator results are consistent with the estimates obtained from the graph.

| | $x_1$ | $x_2$ | $x_3$ | $x_4$ | $x_5$ | $x_6$ | $x_7$ |
|---|---|---|---|---|---|---|---|
| From graph | | | | | | | |
| From calculator | | | | | | | |

*(continues)*

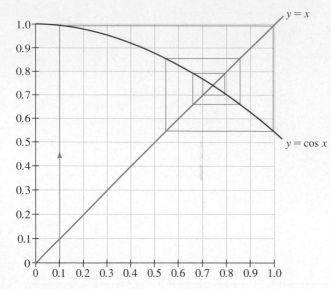

**(b)** Use the calculator results in part (a) to complete the following table.

| $n$ | 0 | 1 | 2 | 3 | 4 | 5 | 6 | 7 |
|---|---|---|---|---|---|---|---|---|
| Number of fish after $n$ breeding seasons | 50 | | | | | | | |

**(c)** As indicated in the figure accompanying part (a), the iteration process is spiraling in on a fixed point between 0.7 and 0.8. Using calculus (or simply a calculator), it can be shown that this fixed point is 0.7391 (rounded to four decimal places). What is the corresponding equilibrium population?

**62.** Suppose that in Exercise 61, instead of $f(x) = \cos x$, we use $g(x) = \sin x$ ($0 \le x \le 1$) for the growth function.

**(a)** Complete a table similar to the one in Exercise 61(b) (assuming $x_0 = 50$).

**(b)** What do you think would be the long-term behavior of this population? *Hint:* Think graphically. Is there a fixed point for the function $g(x) = \sin x$?

**63.** In the text we used the identity $\cos\theta = \sin(\theta + \pi/2)$ in obtaining the graph of $y = \cos x$ from that of $y = \sin x$. In this exercise you'll derive this identity. Refer to the figure below. (Although the figure shows the angle of radian measure $\theta$ in the first quadrant, the proof can be easily carried over for the other quadrants as well.)

**(a)** What are the coordinates of $C$?

**(b)** Show that $\triangle AOB$ and $\triangle COD$ are congruent.

**(c)** Use the results in parts (a) and (b) to show that the coordinates of $A$ are $(-\sin\theta, \cos\theta)$.

**(d)** Since the radian measure of $\angle DOA$ is $\theta + \pi/2$, the coordinates of $A$ (by definition) are $(\cos(\theta + \frac{\pi}{2}), \sin(\theta + \frac{\pi}{2}))$. Now explain why $\cos\theta = \sin(\theta + \frac{\pi}{2})$ and $-\sin\theta = \cos(\theta + \frac{\pi}{2})$.

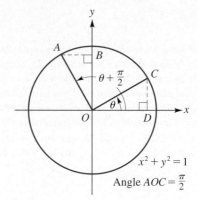

Angle $AOC = \frac{\pi}{2}$

---

## PROJECT   ▌ MAKING WAVES

The cosine function is the prototypical example of a function that is both even and periodic with domain all real numbers. Similarly, the sine function is the prototypical example of a function that is both odd and periodic with domain all real numbers. In many applications, especially in physics and engineering, even and odd periodic phenomena are often represented by more basic waves. In this project we examine square waves, sawtooth waves, and triangular waves.

We begin with a square wave. Consider the function $f$ defined by $f(x) = 1$, for $0 < x < 1$, graphed in Figure A. We want to extend this function to be an odd and periodic function with domain all real numbers. First we extend this function to be an odd function. We get

$$f(x) = \begin{cases} 1, & 0 < x < 1 \\ -1, & -1 < x < 0 \end{cases}$$

**Figure A**
A graph of $f(x) = 1$ for $0 < x < 1$

This extended version of $f$ is an odd function, since its domain, $(-1, 0) \cup (0, 1)$, is symmetric about zero and for each $x$ in its domain $f(-x) = -f(x)$. For example, if $x = \frac{1}{2}$, then $f(\frac{1}{2}) = 1$ and $f(-\frac{1}{2}) = -1 = -f(\frac{1}{2})$. Notice the graph of this extended version of $f$, shown in Figure B, is symmetric about the origin as is true for any odd function.

Next, we extend again to obtain a periodic version of this odd function. We have

$$f(x) = \begin{cases} 1, & 0 < x < 1 \\ -1, & -1 < x < 0 \end{cases} \quad \text{and} \quad f(x + 2) = f(x)$$

for all noninteger real numbers $x$. Note that $f$ is still an odd function and is also a periodic function with period 2. Its graph is shown in Figure C.

**Figure B**
A graph of
$$f(x) = \begin{cases} 1, & 0 < x < 1 \\ -1, & -1 < x < 0 \end{cases}$$

**Figure C**
A graph of
$$f(x) = \begin{cases} 1, & 0 < x < 1 \\ -1, & -1 < x < 0 \end{cases} \quad \text{and} \quad f(x + 2) = f(x) \text{ for noninteger real numbers } x$$

To complete our task, we define $f(x) = 0$ for all integers $x$. So we obtain
$$f(x) = \begin{cases} 1, & 0 < x < 1 \\ -1, & -1 < x < 0 \end{cases}, f(x + 2) = f(x), \text{ for noninteger real number } x, \text{ and}$$
$f(x) = 0$ for integer $x$.

This final version of $f$ is an odd periodic function of period 2 with domain all real numbers. Its graph, shown in Figure D, is called a **square wave.**

**Figure D**
A graph of
$$f(x) = \begin{cases} 1, & 0 < x < 1 \\ -1, & -1 < x < 0 \end{cases}, \quad f(x) = 0 \quad \text{for integer } x, \text{ and } f(x + 2) = f(x)$$

The next two problems guide you through the construction of a sawtooth wave and a triangular wave.

1. *Sawtooth wave:* Consider the function $g$ defined by $g(x) = x$ for $0 \le x < 1$.
   (a) Graph $y = g(x)$.
   (b) Extend $g$ to be an odd function for $-1 < x < 1$. Graph this odd version of $g$.
   (c) Extend the odd version of $g$ to be a periodic function with period 2. Graph this odd and periodic version of $g$.
   (d) Finally extend the odd and periodic version of $g$ to have domain all real numbers. Graph this odd and periodic version of $g$ with domain all real numbers. This graph is called a **sawtooth wave.**
2. *Triangular wave:* Consider the function $h$ defined by $h(x) = x$ for $0 \le x \le 1$.
   (a) Graph $y = h(x)$.
   (b) Extend $h$ to be an even function for $-1 \le x \le 1$. Graph this even version of $h$.
   (c) Extend the even version of $h$ to be a periodic function with period 2. Notice the domain is all real numbers. Graph this even and periodic version of $h$ with domain all real numbers. This graph is called a **triangular wave.**

## 7.5 GRAPHS OF $y = A \sin(Bx - C)$ AND $y = A \cos(Bx - C)$

The graphs of $y = \sin x$ and $y = \cos x$ are the building blocks we need for graphing functions of the form

$$y = A \sin(Bx - C) \quad \text{and} \quad y = A \cos(Bx - C)$$

As a first example, consider $y = 2 \sin x$. To obtain the graph of $y = 2 \sin x$ from that of $y = \sin x$, we multiply each $y$-coordinate on the graph of $y = \sin x$ by 2. As is indicated in Figure 1, this changes the amplitude from 1 to 2, but it does not affect the period, which remains $2\pi$. As a second example, Figure 2 shows the graphs of $y = \cos x$ and $y = \frac{1}{2} \cos x$. Note that the amplitude of $y = \frac{1}{2} \cos x$ is $\frac{1}{2}$ and the period is, again, $2\pi$. More generally, graphs of functions of the form $y = A \sin x$ and $y = A \cos x$ always have an amplitude of $|A|$ and a period of $2\pi$.

*Note:* The complete graph of $y = 2 \sin x$ is obtained by repeating, over the entire domain, the basic cycle shown in Figure 1. The complete graph for $y = \frac{1}{2} \cos x$ is obtained similarly.

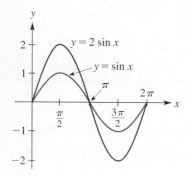

**Figure 1**
The amplitude of $y = 2 \sin x$ is 2. Both $y = \sin x$ and $y = 2 \sin x$ have a period of $2\pi$.

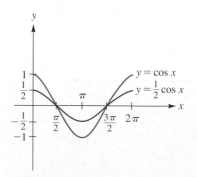

**Figure 2**
The amplitude of $y = \frac{1}{2} \cos x$ is $\frac{1}{2}$. Both $y = \cos x$ and $y = \frac{1}{2} \cos x$ have a period of $2\pi$.

---

**EXAMPLE** **1** **Graphing a function of the form $y = A \sin x$**

Graph the function $y = -2 \sin x$ over one period. On which interval(s) is the function decreasing?

**SOLUTION**
In Section 3.4 we saw that the graph of $y = -f(x)$ is obtained from that of $y = f(x)$ by reflection about the $x$-axis. Thus we need only take the graph of $y = 2 \sin x$ from Figure 1 and reflect it about the $x$-axis; see Figure 3. Note that

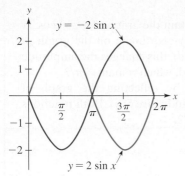

**Figure 3**

both functions have an amplitude of 2 and a period of $2\pi$. From the graph in Figure 3, we can see that the function $y = -2 \sin x$ is decreasing on the intervals $(0, \frac{\pi}{2})$ and $(\frac{3\pi}{2}, 2\pi)$.

We have just seen that functions of the form $y = A \sin x$ and $y = A \cos x$ have an amplitude of $|A|$ and a period of $2\pi$. The next two examples show how to analyze functions of the form $y = A \sin Bx$ and $y = A \cos Bx$ $(B > 0)$. As you'll see, these functions have an amplitude of $|A|$ and a period of $2\pi/B$.

**EXAMPLE** **2** **Graphing a function of the form $y = \cos Bx$**

Graph the function $y = \cos 3x$ over one period.

**SOLUTION**
We know that the cosine curve $y = \cos x$ begins its basic pattern when $x = 0$ and completes that pattern when $x = 2\pi$. Thus $y = \cos 3x$ will begin its basic pattern when $3x = 0$, and it will complete that pattern when $3x = 2\pi$. From the equation $3x - 0$ we conclude that $x = 0$, and from the equation $3x = 2\pi$ we conclude that $x = 2\pi/3$. Thus the graph of $y = \cos 3x$ begins its basic pattern at $x = 0$ and completes the pattern at $x = 2\pi/3$. This tells us that the period is $2\pi/3$. Next, in preparation for drawing the graph, we divide the period into quarters, as shown in Figure 4(a). In Figure 4(b) we've plotted the points with $x$-coordinates shown in Figure 4(a). (We've also plotted the point on the curve corresponding to $x = 0$, where the basic pattern is to begin.) From Figure 4(b) we can see that the amplitude is going to be 1. Now, with the points in Figure 4(b) as a guide, we can sketch one cycle of $y = \cos 3x$, as shown in Figure 4(c).

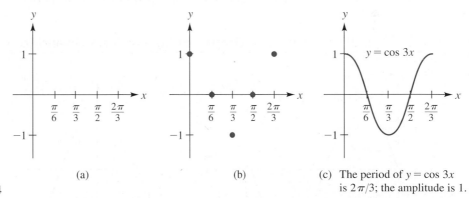

(a)  (b)  (c) The period of $y = \cos 3x$ is $2\pi/3$; the amplitude is 1.

**Figure 4**

**EXAMPLE** **3** **Graphing functions of the form $y = A \cos Bx$**

Graph each function over one period:

**(a)** $y = \dfrac{1}{2} \cos 3x$;  **(b)** $y = -\dfrac{1}{2} \cos 3x$.

**SOLUTION**

(a) In Example 2 we graphed $y = \cos 3x$. To obtain the graph of $y = \frac{1}{2}\cos 3x$ from that of $y = \cos 3x$, we multiply each $y$-coordinate on the graph of $y = \cos 3x$ by 1/2. As is indicated in Figure 5(a), this changes the amplitude from 1 to 1/2, but it does not affect the period, which remains $2\pi/3$.

(b) The graph of $y = -\frac{1}{2}\cos 3x$ is obtained by reflecting the graph of $y = \frac{1}{2}\cos 3x$ about the $x$-axis, as is indicated in Figure 5(b). Both functions have a period of $2\pi/3$ and an amplitude of 1/2.

(a)

(b) The period of $y = -\frac{1}{2}\cos 3x$ is $2\pi/3$; the amplitude is 1/2.

**Figure 5**

Before looking at more examples, let's take a moment to summarize where we are. Our work in Examples 2 and 3(a) shows how to graph $y = \frac{1}{2}\cos 3x$. The same technique that we used in those examples can be applied to any function of the form $y = A \cos Bx$ or $y = A \sin Bx$. As indicated in the box that follows, for both functions the amplitude is $|A|$, and the period is $2\pi/B$. (Exercise 56 asks you to use the method of Example 2 to show that the period is indeed $2\pi/B$.)

**PROPERTY SUMMARY** The Graphs of (a) $y = A \sin Bx$ and (b) $y = A \cos Bx$ $(B > 0)$

(a)

(b)

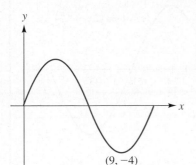

**Figure 6**

**EXAMPLE** 4    **Using a graph of $y = A \sin Bx$ to determine $A$ and $B$**

In Figure 6 a function of the form $y = A \sin Bx$ $(B > 0)$ is graphed for one period. Determine the values of $A$ and $B$.

**SOLUTION**
From the figure we see that the amplitude is 4. Also from the figure we know that three-fourths of the period is 9, so

$$\frac{3}{4}\left(\frac{2\pi}{B}\right) = 9$$

$$\frac{\pi}{2B} = 3$$

$$B = \frac{\pi}{6} \qquad \text{(Check the algebra in the last two lines.)}$$

In summary, we have $A = 4$ and $B = \pi/6$; the equation of the curve is $y = 4 \sin(\pi x/6)$.

**EXAMPLE** 5    **Graphing a function of the form $y = A \sin(Bx - C)$**

Graph the function $y = 4 \sin\left(2x - \dfrac{2\pi}{3}\right)$ over one period.

**SOLUTION**
The technique here is to factor the quantity within parentheses so that the coefficient of $x$ is 1. We'll then be able to graph the function using a simple translation, as in Chapter 3. We have

$$y = 4 \sin\left(2x - \frac{2\pi}{3}\right)$$

$$= 4 \sin\left[2\left(x - \frac{\pi}{3}\right)\right] \tag{1}$$

Now note that equation (1) is obtained from $y = 4 \sin 2x$ by replacing $x$ with $x - \pi/3$. Thus the graph of equation (1) is obtained by translating the graph of $y = 4 \sin 2x$ a distance of $\pi/3$ units to the right. Figure 7(a) on the next page shows the graph of $y = 4 \sin 2x$ over one period. By translating this graph $\pi/3$ units to the right, we obtain the required graph, as shown in Figure 7(b). Note that the translated graph has the same amplitude and period as the original graph. Also, as a matter of arithmetic, you should check for yourself that each of the $x$-coordinates shown in Figure 7(b) is obtained simply by adding $\pi/3$ to a corresponding $x$-coordinate in Figure 7(a). For example, in Figure 7(a) the cycle ends at $x = \pi$; in Figure 7(b) the cycle ends at $\pi + \pi/3 = 4\pi/3$.

*Note*: In Figure 7(b) the labeled $x$-coordinates can be found by using a common denominator of 12 and then reducing.

(b) $y = 4 \sin 2x$
Period: $2\pi/B = \pi$
Amplitude: $|A| = 4$

(b) $y = 4 \sin\left(2x - \frac{2\pi}{3}\right) = 4 \sin\left[2\left(x - \frac{\pi}{3}\right)\right]$
The graph is obtained by translating the graph of $y = 4 \sin 2x$ a distance of $\pi/3$ units to the right. The period and amplitude are still $\pi$ and 4, respectively.

**Figure 7**

In Example 5 we used translation to graph the function $y = 4 \sin\left(2x - \frac{2\pi}{3}\right)$. In particular, we translated the graph of $y = 4 \sin 2x$ so that the starting point of the basic cycle was shifted from $x = 0$ to $x = \pi/3$. The number $\pi/3$ in this case is called the *phase shift* of the function. In the box that follows, we define phase shift, and we generalize the results of the graphing technique used in Example 5.

---

**PROPERTY SUMMARY** $y = A \sin(Bx - C)$ and $y = A \cos(Bx - C)$ $(B > 0, C \ne 0)$

The graphs of (a) $y = A \sin(Bx - C)$ and (b) $y = A \cos(Bx - C)$ are obtained by horizontally translating the graphs of $y = A \sin Bx$ and $y = A \cos Bx$, respectively, so that the starting point of the basic cycle is shifted from $x = 0$ to $x = C/B$. The number $C/B$ is called the **phase shift** for each of the functions $y = A \sin(Bx - C)$ and $y = A \cos(Bx - C)$. The amplitude and the period for these functions are $|A|$ and $2\pi/B$, respectively.

(a)

(b)

**EXAMPLE 6     Finding amplitude, period, and phase shift**

Specify the amplitude, period, and phase shift for each function:

**(a)** $f(x) = 3 \cos(4x - 5)$;     **(b)** $g(x) = -2 \cos\left(\pi x + \dfrac{2\pi}{3}\right)$.

**SOLUTION**

**(a)** By comparing the given equation with $y = A \cos(Bx - C)$, we see that $A = 3$, $B = 4$, and $C = 5$. Consequently, we have

$$\text{amplitude} = |A| = 3$$

$$\text{period} = \frac{2\pi}{B} = \frac{2\pi}{4} = \frac{\pi}{2}$$

$$\text{phase shift} = \frac{C}{B} = \frac{5}{4}$$

For purposes of review, let's also calculate the phase shift without explicitly relying on the expression $C/B$. In the equation $f(x) = 3 \cos(4x - 5)$, we can factor a 4 out of the parentheses to obtain

$$f(x) = 3 \cos\left[4\left(x - \frac{5}{4}\right)\right].$$

This last equation tells us that we can obtain the graph of $f$ by translating the graph of $y = 3 \cos 4x$. In particular, the translation shifts the starting point of the basic cycle from $x = 0$ to $x = 5/4$. The number $5/4$ is the phase shift, as obtained previously.

**(b)** We have $A = -2$, $B = \pi$, and $C = -2\pi/3$, and therefore

$$\text{amplitude} = |A| = 2$$

$$\text{period} = \frac{2\pi}{B} = \frac{2\pi}{\pi} = 2$$

$$\text{phase shift} = \frac{C}{B} = \frac{-2\pi/3}{\pi} = -\frac{2}{3}$$

**EXAMPLE 7     Graphing a function of the form $y = A \cos(Bx - C)$**

Graph the following function over one period:

$$g(x) = -2 \cos\left(\pi x + \frac{2\pi}{3}\right).$$

**SOLUTION**

Our strategy is first to obtain the graph of $y = 2 \cos\left(\pi x + \frac{2\pi}{3}\right)$. The graph of $g$ can then be obtained by a reflection about the $x$-axis. We have

$$y = 2 \cos\left(\pi x + \frac{2\pi}{3}\right) = 2 \cos\left[\pi\left(x + \frac{2}{3}\right)\right]$$

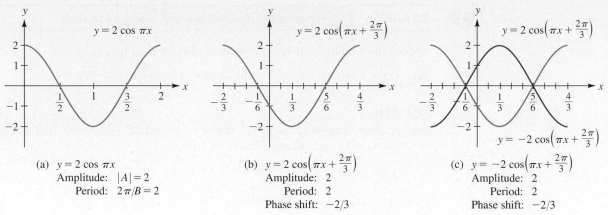

(a) $y = 2 \cos \pi x$
Amplitude: $|A| = 2$
Period: $2\pi/B = 2$

(b) $y = 2 \cos\left(\pi x + \frac{2\pi}{3}\right)$
Amplitude: 2
Period: 2
Phase shift: $-2/3$

(c) $y = -2 \cos\left(\pi x + \frac{2\pi}{3}\right)$
Amplitude: 2
Period: 2
Phase shift: $-2/3$

Figure 8

Now the graph of this last equation is obtained by translating the graph of $y = 2 \cos \pi x$ a distance of 2/3 unit to the left. Figures 8(a) and 8(b) show the graphs of $y = 2 \cos \pi x$ and $y = 2 \cos\left[\pi\left(x + \frac{2}{3}\right)\right]$. By reflecting the graph of this last equation about the $x$-axis, we obtain the graph of $g$. See Figure 8(c).

In previous chapters we've used several types of functions to model real-life data sets: Linear and quadratic functions were used in Chapter 4; exponential and log functions were used in Chapter 5. The functions that we've graphed in this section are often used in modeling data where a variable repeats itself at regular or near-regular intervals. In the next example, we use a trigonometric function of the form $y = A \sin(Bt - C) + D$ to approximate average monthly temperatures.

### EXAMPLE 8 Modeling data using a trigonometric function

Table 1 shows the average monthly temperatures for Minneapolis–St. Paul, and Figure 9 shows a scatter plot based on this data. The numbers on the horizontal

**TABLE 1 Average Monthly Temperatures for Minneapolis–St. Paul (The monthly averages were computed using daily maximum temperatures.)**

| Month | Jan. | Feb. | Mar. | Apr. | May | June | July | Aug. | Sept. | Oct. | Nov. | Dec. |
|---|---|---|---|---|---|---|---|---|---|---|---|---|
| Temperature (°F) | 20.7 | 26.6 | 39.2 | 56.5 | 69.4 | 78.8 | 84.0 | 80.7 | 70.7 | 58.8 | 41.0 | 25.5 |

Source: Robert B. Thomas, *The Old Farmers' Almanac, 1996* (Dublin, New Hampshire: Yankee Publishing, Inc., 1995)

Figure 9

$t$-axis indicate months: January is $t = 1$, February is $t = 2$, and so on; the next January is $t = 13$. Find a periodic function of the form $y = A \sin(Bt - C) + D$ whose values approximate the monthly temperatures in Table 1.

**SOLUTION**
We need to compute the four constants $A$, $B$, $C$, and $D$ in the equation $y = A \sin(Bt - C) + D$. We'll do this in four steps, one step for each required constant.

**Step 1** *Computing A*  For the amplitude $A$, we'll use the equation $A = (M - m)/2$ (from Section 7.2). According to Table 1, the maximum average temperature is $M = 84.0°$ and the minimum is $m = 20.7°$. Therefore

$$A = \frac{M - m}{2} = \frac{84.0 - 20.7}{2} = 31.65$$

**Step 2** *Computing B*  We know from our work in this section that the period is given by $2\pi/B$. So, assuming that the period of the average temperature function is 12 months, we have $2\pi/B = 12$, and therefore

$$12B = 2\pi \quad \text{or} \quad B = \frac{\pi}{6}$$

**Step 3** *Computing C*  Now that we know $B$, we can compute $C$ by considering the phase shift $C/B$. If there were no phase shift, a maximum for the sine wave would occur one-quarter of the way through the period at $t = \frac{1}{4}(12)$, which is 3. As you can see in Figure 9, however, a maximum occurs when $t = 7$, four units to the right of $t = 3$. Thus, the phase shift here is 4 and we have

$$\frac{C}{B} = 4 \quad \text{or} \quad C = 4B$$

Substituting $B = \pi/6$ in this last equation then yields

$$C = 4\left(\frac{\pi}{6}\right) = \frac{2\pi}{3}$$

**Step 4** *Computing D*  Substituting the values we've found for $A$, $B$, and $C$ in the equation $y = A \sin(Bt - C) + D$ yields

$$y = 31.65 \sin\left(\frac{\pi}{6}t - \frac{2\pi}{3}\right) + D \tag{2}$$

One way to determine a value for $D$ is to use the data pair $t = 1, y = 20.7$ from Table 1 and substitute in equation (2). This yields

$$20.7 = 31.65 \sin\left(\frac{\pi}{6} - \frac{2\pi}{3}\right) + D$$

$$= 31.65 \sin\left(-\frac{\pi}{2}\right) + D$$

$$= -31.65 + D \quad \text{using } \sin(-\pi/2) = -1$$

and consequently, $D = 20.7 + 31.65 = 52.35$.

In summary now, our function that approximates the average monthly temperatures is

$$y = 31.65 \sin\left(\frac{\pi}{6}t - \frac{2\pi}{3}\right) + 52.35$$

Figure 10(a) shows the graph of this equation along with the scatter plot from Figure 9. As you can see, the curve does a fairly good job in approximating the values from the scatter plot. *Remark*: More advanced techniques from the field of statistics yield a slightly different sine wave that does an even better job in modeling the temperature data. See Figure 10(b).

**Figure 10(a)**
The scatter plot for average monthly temperatures along with the graph of the function obtained in Example 8,
$y = 31.65 \sin(\frac{\pi}{6}t - \frac{2\pi}{3}) + 52.35$

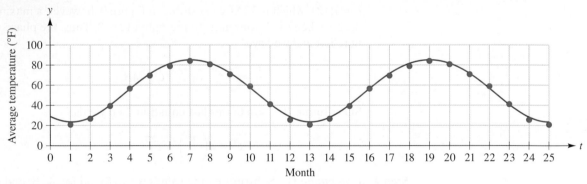

**Figure 10(b)**
The scatter plot for average monthly temperatures along with the graph of the function
$y = 31.139 \sin(0.521t - 2.086) + 54.157$. This function was obtained using the SinReg
(sine regression) algorithm on the Texas Instruments TI-83 Graphing Calculator.

# EXERCISE SET 7.5

**A**

*In Exercises 1–8, graph the functions for one period. In each case, specify the amplitude, period, x-intercepts, and interval(s) on which the function is increasing.*

**1.** (a) $y = 2 \sin x$
   (b) $y = -\sin 2x$

**2.** (a) $y = 3 \sin x$
   (b) $y = \sin 3x$

**3.** (a) $y = \cos 2x$
   (b) $y = 2 \cos 2x$

**4.** (a) $y = \cos (x/2)$
   (b) $y = -\frac{1}{2} \cos(x/2)$

**5.** (a) $y = 3 \sin(\pi x/2)$
   (b) $y = -3 \sin(\pi x/2)$

**6.** (a) $y = 2 \sin \pi x$
   (b) $y = -2 \sin \pi x$

**7.** (a) $y = \cos 2\pi x$
   (b) $y = -4 \cos 2\pi x$

**8.** (a) $y = -2 \cos(x/4)$
   (b) $y = -2 \cos(\pi x/4)$

Ⓖ  **9.** Set the viewing rectangle so that it extends from 0 to $2\pi$ in the *x*-direction and from $-4$ to 4 in the *y*-direction. On the same set of axes, graph the four functions $y = \sin x$, $y = 2 \sin x$, $y = 3 \sin x$, and $y = 4 \sin x$. What is the amplitude in each case? What is the period?

Ⓖ  **10. (a)** Without using a graphing utility, specify the amplitude and the period for each of the following four functions: $y = \cos x$, $y = 2 \cos x$, $y = 3 \cos x$, and $y = 4 \cos x$.

　　 **(b)** Check your answers in part (a) by graphing the four functions. (Use the viewing rectangle specified in Exercise 1.)

Ⓖ  **11. (a)** Without using a graphing utility, specify the amplitude and the period for $y = 2 \sin \pi x$ and for $y = \sin 2\pi x$.

　　 **(b)** Check your answers in part (a) by graphing the two functions. (Use a viewing rectangle that extends from 0 to 2 in the *x*-direction and from $-2$ to 2 in the *y*-direction.)

*In Exercises 12–15, graph the function for one period. Specify the amplitude, period, x-intercepts, and interval(s) on which the function is increasing.*

**12.** $y = 1 + \sin 2x$ 　　　**13.** $y = \sin(x/2) - 2$
**14.** $y = 1 - \cos(\pi x/3)$ 　　**15.** $y = -2 - 2\cos 3\pi x$

*In Exercises 16–31, determine the amplitude, period, and phase shift for the given function. Graph the function over one period. Indicate the x-intercepts and the coordinates of the highest and lowest points on the graph.*

**16.** $f(x) = \sin\left(x - \frac{\pi}{6}\right)$ 　　**17.** $g(x) = \cos\left(x + \frac{\pi}{3}\right)$
**18.** $F(x) = -\cos\left(x + \frac{\pi}{4}\right)$ 　**19.** $G(x) = -\sin(x + 2)$
**20.** $y = \sin\left(2x - \frac{\pi}{2}\right)$ 　　**21.** $y = \sin\left(3x + \frac{\pi}{2}\right)$
**22.** $y = \cos(2x - \pi)$ 　　　**23.** $y = \cos\left(x - \frac{\pi}{2}\right)$
**24.** $y = 3 \sin\left(\frac{1}{2}x + \frac{\pi}{6}\right)$ 　　**25.** $y = -2\sin(\pi x + \pi)$
**26.** $y = 4 \cos\left(3x - \frac{\pi}{4}\right)$ 　　**27.** $y = \cos(x + 1)$
**28.** $y = \frac{1}{2}\sin\left(\frac{\pi x}{2} - \pi^2\right)$ 　**29.** $y = \cos\left(2x - \frac{\pi}{3}\right) + 1$
**30.** $y = 1 - \cos\left(2x - \frac{\pi}{3}\right)$ 　**31.** $y = 3 \cos\left(\frac{2x}{3} + \frac{\pi}{6}\right)$

*For Exercises 32–39:*

**(a)** *Using pencil and paper, not a graphing utility, determine the amplitude, period, and (where appropriate) phase shift for each function.*

**(b)** *Use a graphing utility to graph each function for two complete cycles. [In choosing an appropriate viewing rectangle, you will need to use the information obtained in part (a).]*

**(c)** *Use the graphing utility to estimate the coordinates of the highest and the lowest points on the graph.*

**(d)** *Use the information obtained in part (a) to specify the exact values for the coordinates that you estimated in part (c).*

Ⓖ  **32.** $y = -2.5 \cos(3x + 4)$ 　Ⓖ **33.** $y = -2.5 \cos(3\pi x + 4)$
Ⓖ  **34.** $y = -2.5 \cos\left(\frac{1}{3}x + 4\right)$ 　Ⓖ **35.** $y = -2.5 \cos\left(\frac{1}{3}\pi x + 4\right)$
Ⓖ  **36.** $y = \sin(0.5x - 0.75)$ 　Ⓖ **37.** $y = \sin(0.5x + 0.75)$
Ⓖ  **38.** $y = 0.02 \cos(100\pi x - 4\pi)$
Ⓖ  **39.** $y = 0.02 \cos(0.01\pi x - 4\pi)$

*In Exercises 40–45, determine whether the equation for the graph has the form $y = A \sin Bx$ or $y = A \cos Bx$ (with $B > 0$) and then find the values of A and B.*

**40.**

$(3\pi, -2)$

**41.**

$\left(\frac{\pi}{3}, 1.5\right)$

**42.**

$(1, 0)$

**43.**

$(5, 1)$

**44.**

$(5\pi, 4)$

**45.**

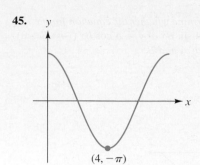

$(4, -\pi)$

*In each of Exercises 46–50, you are given a table of average monthly temperatures and a scatter plot based on the data. Use the methods of Example 8 to find a periodic function of the form $y = A \sin(Bt - C) + D$ whose values approximate the monthly temperatures. The data in these exercises, as well as in Exercise 51, are from the Global Historical Climatology Network, and can be accessed on the internet through the following website created by Robert Hoare:* http://www.worldclimate.com/.

**46.**

**Average Monthly Temperatures for Phoenix, Arizona (based on daily maximums)**

| Month | Temperature (°F) |
| --- | --- |
| Jan. | 65.5 |
| Feb. | 70.2 |
| Mar. | 75.2 |
| Apr. | 84.6 |
| May | 93.2 |
| June | 102.7 |
| July | 105.1 |
| Aug. | 103.1 |
| Sept. | 98.6 |
| Oct. | 88.2 |
| Nov. | 74.7 |
| Dec. | 66.4 |

**47.**

**Average Monthly Temperatures for Bangor, Maine**

| Month | Temperature (°F) |
| --- | --- |
| Jan. | 18.0 |
| Feb. | 20.8 |
| Mar. | 30.7 |
| Apr. | 42.6 |
| May | 54.1 |
| June | 62.8 |
| July | 68.5 |
| Aug. | 67.3 |
| Sept. | 58.1 |
| Oct. | 47.1 |
| Nov. | 36.9 |
| Dec. | 23.7 |

**48.**

**Average Monthly Temperatures for Cape Town, South Africa**

| Month | Temperature (°F) |
| --- | --- |
| Jan. | 69.8 |
| Feb. | 70.0 |
| Mar. | 67.8 |
| Apr. | 63.1 |
| May | 58.8 |
| June | 55.6 |
| July | 54.3 |
| Aug. | 55.4 |
| Sept. | 57.7 |
| Oct. | 61.2 |
| Nov. | 64.8 |
| Dec. | 67.8 |

**49.**

**Average Monthly Temperatures
for Beira, Mozambique**

| Month | Temperature (°F) |
|---|---|
| Jan. | 81.3 |
| Feb. | 81.3 |
| Mar. | 80.1 |
| Apr. | 77.5 |
| May | 73.0 |
| June | 69.4 |
| July | 68.7 |
| Aug. | 70.2 |
| Sept. | 73.4 |
| Oct. | 76.6 |
| Nov. | 79.0 |
| Dec. | 80.4 |

*Hint*: In Step 3 of the solution, since both Jan. ($t = 1$) and Feb. ($t = 2$) yield the same maximum temperature, use $t = 1.5$ for the corresponding input.

**50.** The following two scatter plots and table display average temperature data for two locations with very different climates. Dar es Salaam is south of the Equator, in Tanzania, on the Indian Ocean; Tiksi is in Russia, far north of the Arctic Circle, on the Arctic Ocean.

**Average Monthly Temperatures for Dar es Salaam, Tanzania, and Tiksi, Russia**

| Month | Temperature (°F) Dar es Salaam | Temperature (°F) Tiksi |
|---|---|---|
| Jan. | 81.3 | −24.2 |
| Feb. | 81.7 | −18.7 |
| Mar. | 80.8 | −13.4 |
| Apr. | 79.0 | −1.4 |
| May | 77.2 | 19.9 |
| June | 75.0 | 37.8 |
| July | 73.9 | 43.9 |
| Aug. | 74.3 | 43.9 |
| Sept. | 75.2 | 34.2 |
| Oct. | 77.0 | 11.8 |
| Nov. | 79.2 | −10.4 |
| Dec. | 81.1 | −18.5 |

(a) Use the methods of Example 8 to find a periodic function of the form $y = A \sin(Bt - C) + D$ whose values approximate the monthly temperatures for Dar es Salaam.

(b) Follow part (a) for Tiksi.

(c) By looking at the scatter plot for temperatures in Dar es Salaam, say if the average rate of change of temperature over the interval from January through July is positive or negative.

(d) Use the table of values to compute the average rate of change of temperature in Dar es Salaam over the interval from January through July. Be sure to include units as part of your answer, and check that the sign is consistent with your response in part (c).

(e) By looking at the scatter plot for temperatures in Tiksi, say if the average rate of change of temperature over the interval from January through July is positive or negative.

(f) Use the table of values to compute the average rate of change of temperature in Tiksi over the interval from January through July. As before, be sure to include units as part of your answer, and check that the sign is consistent with your response in part (e).

**51.** The scatter plot on the next page displays average monthly temperatures for Death Valley, California. (The averages were obtained using daily maximums.) Use the methods of Example 8 to find a periodic function of the form $y = A \sin(Bt - C) + D$ whose values approximate the monthly temperatures. (No table is given; you will need to rely on the scatter plot and make estimates.)

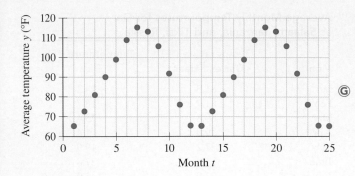

**B**

52. In Section 8.2 you'll see the identity $\sin^2 x = \frac{1}{2} - \frac{1}{2}\cos 2x$. Use this identity to graph the function $y = \sin^2 x$ for one period.

53. In Section 8.2 you'll see the identity $\cos^2 x = \frac{1}{2} + \frac{1}{2}\cos 2x$. Use this identity to graph the function $y = \cos^2 x$ for one period.

54. In Section 8.2 we derive the identity $\sin 2x = 2\sin x \cos x$. Use this to graph $y = \sin x \cos x$ for one period.

55. In Section 8.2 we derive the identity $\cos 2x = \cos^2 x - \sin^2 x$. Use this to graph $y = \cos^2 x - \sin^2 x$ for one period.

56. In Example 2 we showed that the period of $y = \cos 3x$ is $2\pi/3$. Use the same method to show that the period of $y = A \cos Bx$ is $2\pi/B$.

G 57. Let $F(x) = \sin x$, $G(x) = x^2$, and $H(x) = x^3$. Which, if any, of the following four composite functions have graphs that do not go below the $x$-axis? First, try to answer without using a graphing utility, then use the graphing utility to check yourself. (You will learn more this way than if you were to draw the graphs immediately.)

$$y = G(F(x)) \qquad y = F(G(x))$$
$$y = F(H(x)) \qquad y = H(F(x))$$

G 58. (a) Graph the two functions $y = \sin x$ and $y = \sin(\sin x)$ in the standard viewing rectangle. Then for a closer look, switch to a viewing rectangle extending from 0 to $2\pi$ in the $x$-direction and from $-1$ to 1 in the $y$-direction. Compare the two graphs; write out your observations in complete sentences.

   (b) Use the graphing utility to estimate the amplitude of the function $y = \sin(\sin x)$.

   (c) Using your knowledge of the sine function, explain why the amplitude of the function $y = \sin(\sin x)$ is the number $\sin 1$. Then evaluate $\sin 1$ and use the result to check your approximation in part (b).

G 59. Let $f(x) = e^{x/20}(\sin x)$.

   (a) Graph the function $f$ using a viewing rectangle that extends from $-5$ to 5 in both the $x$- and the $y$-directions. Note that the resulting graph resembles a sine curve.

   (b) Change the viewing rectangle so that $x$ extends from 0 to 50 and $y$ extends from $-10$ to 10. Describe what you see. Is the function periodic?

   (c) Add the graphs of the two functions $y = e^{x/20}$ and $y = -e^{x/20}$ to your picture in part (b). Describe what you see.

G 60. For this exercise, use the standard viewing rectangle.

   (a) Graph the function $y = \ln(\sin^2 x)$.

   (b) Graph the function $y = \ln(1 - \cos x) + \ln(1 + \cos x)$.

   (c) Explain why the two graphs are identical.

---

## PROJECT | FOURIER SERIES

In the project at the end of Section 7.4 we discussed square waves, sawtooth waves, and triangular waves. In this project we use the idea of superposition of waves to find a "trigonometric" way to describe a square wave.

We start with the square wave given by $y = f(x)$ where

$$f(x) = \begin{cases} 1, & 0 < x < 1 \\ -1, & -1 < x < 0 \end{cases}$$

$f(x) = 0$   for all integers $x$      and      $f(x + 2) = f(x)$      (i)

This square wave is shown in Figure A.

Now, $f$ is an odd function, periodic with period 2, and has domain all real numbers. That $f$ is periodic suggests it might be related to more familiar periodic waves, for example, sine waves and cosine waves. Since $f$ is an odd function we might be able to describe $f$ by using only sine waves. And since the domain of $f$ is all real numbers, our description of $f$ using sine waves should coincide with $f$ for most, if not all, real numbers.

**Figure A**

A graph of $f(x) = \begin{cases} 1, & 0 < x < 1 \\ -1, & -1 < x < 0 \end{cases}$,   $f(x) = 0$   for integer $x$, and $f(x + 2) = f(x)$

It turns out that $f$ can be expressed by adding together *infinitely* many sine waves. In fact, using methods from calculus, it can be shown that

$$f(x) = \frac{4}{\pi} \sin \pi x + \frac{4}{3\pi} \sin 3\pi x + \frac{4}{5\pi} \sin 5\pi x + \frac{4}{7\pi} \sin 7\pi x + \cdots \quad (ii)$$

for all real numbers $x$. The symbol "$\cdots$" means there are infinitely many more terms that in this case follow the given pattern. So we are expressing $f(x)$ as an *infinite series*, a sum of infinitely many terms. (While we will study some infinite series of numbers in Chapter 13, it should be noted that the right-hand side of equation (ii) is an infinite series of functions.) The particular infinite series on the right-hand side of equation (ii) is called the **Fourier series** for the function $f$. Notice that the Fourier series for $f$ consists of sine waves of different periods, but that 2, the period of the given square wave, is an integer multiple of each period. When we superimpose or add up the waves, we obtain the function $f$ of period 2.

Figure B shows the graphs of the first three partial sums of the Fourier series for $f$ on the closed interval $[-3, 3]$ along with the graph of the square wave.

Notice that as we add more and more terms of the Fourier series, we appear to obtain better approximations to $f$.

It turns out that equation (ii) is valid for all real numbers $x$, that is, for each real number $x$, the Fourier series for $f$ yields the function value $f(x)$. This fact leads us to a famous formula for $\pi$ discovered by Gottfried Wilhelm Leibniz (ca. 1700), who along with Isaac Newton is credited with the invention of calculus. Using equation (ii), let $x = 1/2$. Then for the square wave $f(1/2) = 1$. And

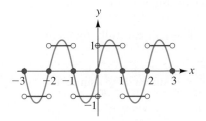

Graph of $y = \frac{4}{\pi} \sin \pi x$

Graph of $y = \frac{4}{\pi} \sin \pi x + \frac{4}{3\pi} \sin 3\pi x$

Graph of $y = \frac{4}{\pi} \sin \pi x + \frac{4}{3\pi} \sin 3\pi x + \frac{4}{5\pi} \sin 5\pi x$

**Figure B**

the Fourier series with $x = 1/2$ becomes

$$\frac{4}{\pi}\sin\frac{\pi}{2} + \frac{4}{3\pi}\sin\frac{3\pi}{2} + \frac{4}{5\pi}\sin\frac{5\pi}{2} + \frac{4}{7\pi}\sin\frac{7\pi}{2} + \cdots$$

$$= \frac{4}{\pi} - \frac{4}{3\pi} + \frac{4}{5\pi} - \frac{4}{7\pi} + \cdots = \frac{4}{\pi}\left(1 - \frac{1}{3} + \frac{1}{5} - \frac{1}{7} + \cdots\right)$$

So

$$f\left(\frac{1}{2}\right) = \frac{4}{\pi}\left(1 - \frac{1}{3} + \frac{1}{5} - \frac{1}{7} + \cdots\right) \quad \text{or} \quad 1 = \frac{4}{\pi}\left(1 - \frac{1}{3} + \frac{1}{5} - \frac{1}{7} + \cdots\right)$$

Multiplying each side of this last equation by $\pi/4$, we obtain Leibniz's formula for $\pi$,

$$\frac{\pi}{4} = 1 - \frac{1}{3} + \frac{1}{5} - \frac{1}{7} + \cdots$$

(It should be noted that Leibniz's formula is an inefficient way to calculate $\pi$. See also Exercises 86 and 87 on page 632. Also Leibniz derived his formula by a much different method than the one just presented.)

For many years Fourier series were commonly used by mathematicians, chiefly Daniel Bernoulli and Leonhard Euler, to analyze wave phenomena, among other things. But, it was not until the publication of Joseph Fourier's classic treatise, *Théorie Analytique de la Chlaleur* ("The Analytic Theory of Heat") in 1822 that the series that now bear his name were used in a systematic way to solve problems in the theory and application of heat conduction. Much of the development of mathematics in the nineteenth and well into the twentieth century was driven by the desire to place Fourier's methods on a rigorous foundation.

Fourier's idea that almost all important functions that arise in mathematical models of real-world phenomena can be represented as a superposition of sine and cosine functions has been of central importance in many physical theories and engineering applications. Modern optics, information theory, communication technology, celestial mechanics (and yes, rocket science), geophysics, meteorology, analysis of structures, and sound systems all rely on Fourier's idea. Terms such as "frequency response" and "bandwidth" from the mathematical theory of Fourier analysis have entered into common usage. The "bass" and "treble" controls on your sound system directly adjust the amplitudes of terms in a Fourier series.

## EXERCISES

**1. (a)** Look at equation (ii) on page 551. What are the next three terms of the Fourier series for $f$?

   **(b)** On the same set of axes, for $0 \leq x \leq 1$, graph carefully *by hand* the equations

$$y = \frac{4}{\pi}\sin\pi x, \qquad y = \frac{4}{3\pi}\sin 3\pi x, \qquad y = \frac{4}{\pi}\sin\pi x + \frac{4}{3\pi}\sin 3\pi x$$

   and compare with Figure B.

   **(c)** Using a graphing utility, graph each of the first seven partial sums. (Figure B shows graphs of the first three.) For each graph, use the zoom facility to estimate the slope near the origin and the deviation of the bump at $x = 1/2$ from the square wave value, one. As the number of terms of the partial sums increase, what happens to the slopes near the origin and to the deviation of the bump?

Ⓖ (d) Compare your graph of the seventh partial sum with the graphs in Figure B. What do you notice?

**2.** Consider the triangular wave defined by

$$g(x) = \begin{cases} x, & 0 \le x \le 1 \\ -x, & -1 \le x < 0 \end{cases} \quad \text{and} \quad g(x + 2) = g(x) \quad \text{for all real numbers } x$$

(a) Graph $y = g(x)$.

(b) Is $g$ an even function, an odd function, or neither even nor odd? Is $g$ a periodic function? If yes what is the period of $g$? What is the domain of $g$?

(c) The Fourier series of $g$ should consist only of cosine waves. Why? What is true about the periods of all of the cosine waves?

Ⓖ (d) It can be shown that

$$g(x) = \frac{1}{2} - \frac{4}{\pi^2} \cos \pi x - \frac{4}{3^2 \pi^2} \cos 3\pi x$$

$$- \frac{4}{5^2 \pi^2} \cos 5\pi x - \frac{4}{7^2 \pi^2} \cos 7\pi x - \cdots$$

for all real numbers $x$. Graph the fourth partial sum of the Fourier series for $g$, and compare your graph with the triangular wave. The fit of the fourth partial sum of this series to the triangular wave should be comparable to the fit of the third partial sum in Figure B to the square wave. Which do you think gives a better fit? Why?

(e) In the series in part (d), let $x = 1$ and obtain a well-known formula due to Daniel Bernoulli (among others).

$$\frac{\pi^2}{8} = 1 + \frac{1}{9} + \frac{1}{25} + \frac{1}{49} + \frac{1}{81} + \frac{1}{121} + \cdots$$

**3.** In this exercise we sketch a (nonrigorous) derivation of one of the most celebrated formulas of eighteenth-century mathematics, discovered by Euler in 1736.

(a) Start with the series

$$S = 1 + \frac{1}{2^2} + \frac{1}{3^2} + \frac{1}{4^2} + \frac{1}{5^2} + \frac{1}{6^2} + \cdots$$

and regroup it into a sum of two series, one, $S_1$, with odd denominators and the other, $S_2$, with even denominators. So $S = S_1 + S_2$.

(b) Note that $S_1 = \pi^2/8$ by Exercise 2(e). Also note that $S_2 = (1/4)S$. So $S = (\pi^2/8) + (1/4)S$.

(c) Solve the last equation for $S$ to obtain $S = \pi^2/6$, that is,

$$\frac{\pi^2}{6} = 1 + \frac{1}{2^2} + \frac{1}{3^2} + \frac{1}{4^2} + \frac{1}{5^2} + \frac{1}{6^2} + \cdots$$

which is Euler's formula for the sum of the squares of the reciprocals of the positive integers.

# 7.6 SIMPLE HARMONIC MOTION

*s*-axis

**Figure 1**

*Amongst the most important classes of motions which we have to consider in Natural Philosophy, there is one, namely,* Harmonic Motion, *which is of such immense use, not only in ordinary kinetics, but in the theories of sound, light, heat, etc., that we make no apology for entering here into considerable detail regarding it.* —Sir William Thomson (Lord Kelvin) and Peter Tait in *Treatise on Natural Philosophy* (Cambridge University Press, 1879)

Figure 1 shows a mass attached to a spring hung from the ceiling. If we pull the mass down a bit and then release it, the resulting up-and-down oscillations are referred to as **simple harmonic motion.** (We are neglecting the effects of friction and air resistance here.) Other examples of simple harmonic motion (or combinations of simple harmonic motions) include the vibration of a string or of a column of air in a musical instrument and the vibration of an atom in a solid. Furthermore, the mathematics used in describing or analyzing these mechanical oscillations is the same as that used in studying electromagnetic oscillations (such as radio waves, microwaves, or the alternating electrical current in your house).

To analyze the motion of a mass attached to a spring, we set up a coordinate system as shown in Figure 1, in which the equilibrium position of the mass (the position before we pull it down) corresponds to $s = 0$. Now suppose that we pull the mass down to $s = -2$ and release it. If we take a sequence of "snapshots" at one-second time intervals, we will obtain the type of result shown in Figure 2.

**Figure 2**
Snapshots of a mass–spring system taken at one-second intervals

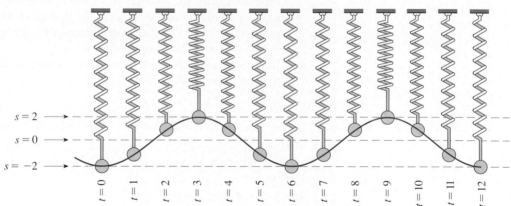

The curve in Figure 2 shows how the coordinate $s$ of the mass changes over time. As you can see, the curve resembles the graphs of $y = A \sin(Bx - C)$ and $y = A \cos(Bx - C)$ that we considered in the previous section. Indeed, using calculus, it can be shown that simple harmonic motion is characterized by either one of these types of equations. For example, for the simple harmonic motion depicted in Figure 2, it can be shown that an appropriate equation relating the position $s$ and the time $t$ is

$$s = -2 \cos \frac{\pi t}{3} \qquad (1)$$

Using equation (1) and Figure 2, we can give a physical interpretation to the term *period.* From Figure 2 we see that it takes 6 seconds for the mass to return to its starting position at $s = -2$. Then in the next 6 seconds, the same motion is repeated, and so on. We say that the **period** of the motion is 6 seconds. That is, it takes 6 seconds for the motion to go through one complete cycle. Notice that this agrees numerically with the period we calculate using equation (1) and the expression $2\pi/B$ from Section 7.5:

$$\text{period} = \frac{2\pi}{B} = \frac{2\pi}{\pi/3} = 6$$

In simple harmonic motion the **frequency** $f$ is the number of complete cycles per unit time, and it is given by

$$\text{frequency} = f = \frac{1}{\text{period}}$$

For instance, for the motion in Figure 2 we have

$$f = \frac{1}{\text{period}} = \frac{1}{6} \text{ cycles per second}$$

We mention in passing that 1 cycle per second (cps) is known as a *hertz,* abbreviated Hz. This unit is named after the German physicist Heinrich Hertz (1857–1894), who was the first person to produce and study radio waves.* Although you might not have realized it, you have probably heard this unit mentioned (implicitly, at least) many times on the radio. For example, when a radio station advertises itself as "98.1 on the FM dial," this refers to radio waves with a frequency of 98.1 million hertz.

From Figure 2 we can see that the mass moves back and forth between $s = -2$ and $s = 2$. In other words, the maximum displacement of the mass from its equilibrium position (at $s = 0$) is two units. We say that the **amplitude** of the motion is two units. Notice that this agrees with the amplitude we would calculate using equation (1).

| EXAMPLE | 1 | A spring–mass system |
|---|---|---|

A mass on a smooth tabletop is attached to a spring, as shown in Figure 3. The coordinate system has been chosen so that the equilibrium position of the mass corresponds to $s = 0$. Assume that the mass moves in simple harmonic motion described by

$$s = 5 \cos \frac{\pi t}{4}$$

where $s$ is in centimeters and $t$ is in seconds.

Figure 3

---

*For background and details, see the interesting article "Heinrich Hertz" by Philip and Emily Morrison in the December 1957 issue of *Scientific American.*

**(a)** Graph the function $s = 5 \cos(\pi t/4)$ over the interval $0 \leq t \leq 16$. Specify the amplitude, the period, and the frequency of the motion.

**(b)** Use the graph to determine the times in this interval at which the mass is farthest from the origin.

**(c)** When during this interval of time is the mass passing through the equilibrium position?

**SOLUTION**

**(a)** Using the techniques developed in Section 7.5, we obtain the graph shown in Figure 4. From the graph (or from the given equation) we have

$$\text{amplitude} = 5 \text{ cm}$$
$$\text{period} = 8 \text{ sec}$$
$$\text{frequency} = \frac{1}{8} \text{ cycles/sec}$$

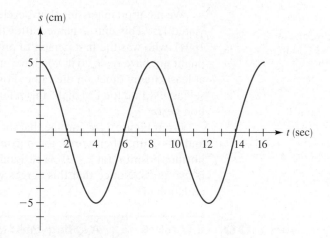

**Figure 4**

**(b)** The distance of the mass from the origin is given by $|s|$. According to Figure 4, the maximum value of $|s|$ is 5, and this occurs when $t = 0$ sec, 4 sec, 8 sec, 12 sec, and 16 sec.

**(c)** We are given that the equilibrium position of the mass is $s = 0$. From Figure 4 we see that $s$ is zero when $t = 2$ sec, 6 sec, 10 sec, and 14 sec.

---

# EXERCISE SET 7.6

**A**

*For Exercises 1 and 2, suppose that we have a spring–mass system as shown in Figure 3 on page 555.*

**1.** Assume that the simple harmonic motion is described by the equation $s = 4 \cos(\pi t/2)$, where $s$ is in centimeters and $t$ is in seconds.

**(a)** Specify the $s$-coordinate of the mass at each of the following times: $t = 0$ sec, 0.5 sec, 1 sec, and 2 sec. (One of these coordinates will involve a radical sign; for this case, use a calculator and round the final answer to two decimal places.)

**(b)** Find the amplitude, the period, and the frequency of this motion. Sketch the graph of $s = 4 \cos(\pi t/2)$ over the interval $0 \leq t \leq 8$.

**(c)** Use your graph to determine the times in this interval at which the mass is farthest from the origin.

**(d)** When during the interval of time $0 \leq t \leq 8$ is the mass passing through the origin?

**(e)** When during the interval of time $0 \leq t \leq 8$ is the mass moving to the right? *Hint*: The mass is moving to the right when the $s$-coordinate is increasing. Use the graph to see when $s$ is increasing.

**2.** Assume that the simple harmonic motion is described by the equation $s = -6\cos(\pi t/6)$, where $s$ is in centimeters and $t$ is in seconds.

(a) Complete the table. (For coordinates that involve radical signs, use a calculator and round the result to two decimal places.)

| t (sec) | 1 | 2 | 3 | 4 | 5 | 6 | 7 | 8 | 9 | 10 | 11 | 12 |
|---------|---|---|---|---|---|---|---|---|---|----|----|----|
| s (cm)  |   |   |   |   |   |   |   |   |   |    |    |    |

(b) Find the amplitude, period, and frequency of this motion. Sketch the graph of $s = -6\cos(\pi t/6)$ over the interval $0 \le t \le 24$.

(c) Use your graph to determine the times in this interval at which the mass is farthest from the equilibrium position.

(d) When during the interval of time $0 \le t \le 24$ is the mass passing through the origin?

(e) When during the interval of time $0 \le t \le 24$ is the mass moving to the left?   *Hint*: The mass is moving to the left when the $s$-coordinate is decreasing. Use the graph to see when $s$ is decreasing.

*In Exercises 3 and 4, suppose that we have a spring–mass system, as shown in Figure 1 on page 554.*

**3.** Assume that the simple harmonic motion is described by the equation $s = -3\cos(\pi t/3)$, where $s$ is in feet, $t$ is in seconds, and the equilibrium position of the mass is $s = 0$.

(a) Specify the amplitude, period, and frequency for this simple harmonic motion, and sketch the graph of the function $s = -3\cos(\pi t/3)$ over the interval $0 \le t \le 12$.

(b) When during the interval of time $0 \le t \le 12$ is the mass moving upward?   *Hint*: The mass is moving upward when the $s$-coordinate is increasing. Use the graph to see when $s$ is increasing.

(c) When during the interval of time $0 \le t \le 12$ is the mass moving downward?   *Hint*: The mass is moving downward when the $s$-coordinate is decreasing. Use the graph to see when $s$ is decreasing.

(d) For this harmonic motion it can be shown (using calculus) that the velocity $v$ of the mass is given by

$$v = \pi \sin \frac{\pi t}{3}$$

where $t$ is in seconds and $v$ is in feet per second. Graph this velocity function over the interval $0 \le t \le 12$.

(e) Use your graph of the velocity function from part (d) to find the times during this interval when the velocity is zero. At these times, where is the mass? (That is, what are the $s$-coordinates?)

(f) Use your graph of the velocity function to find the times when the velocity is maximum. Where is the mass at these times?

(g) Use your graph of the velocity function to find the times when the velocity is minimum. Where is the mass at these times?

(h) On the same set of axes, graph the velocity function $v = \pi \sin(\pi t/3)$ and the position function $s = -3\cos(\pi t/3)$ for $0 \le t \le 12$.

**4.** Assume that the simple harmonic motion is described by the equation $s = 4\cos(2t/3)$, where $s$ is in feet, $t$ is in seconds, and the equilibrium position of the mass is $s = 0$.

(a) Specify the amplitude, period, and frequency for this simple harmonic motion, and sketch the graph of the function $s = 4\cos(2t/3)$ over the interval $0 \le t \le 6\pi$.

(b) When during the interval of time $0 \le t \le 6\pi$ is the mass moving upward?   *Hint*: The mass is moving upward when the $s$-coordinate is increasing. Use the graph to see when $s$ is increasing.

(c) When during the interval of time $0 \le t \le 6\pi$ is the mass moving downward?   *Hint*: The mass is moving downward when the $s$-coordinate is decreasing. Use the graph to see when $s$ is decreasing.

(d) For this harmonic motion, it can be shown (using calculus) that the velocity $v$ of the mass is given by $v = \frac{8}{3}\sin(2t/3)$, where $t$ is in seconds and $v$ is in ft/sec. Graph this velocity function over the interval $0 \le t \le 6\pi$.

(e) Use your graph of the velocity function from part (d) to find the times during this interval when the velocity is zero. At these times, where is the mass? (That is, what are the $s$-coordinates?)

(f) Use your graph of the velocity function to find the times when the velocity is maximum. Where is the mass at these times?

(g) Use your graph of the velocity function to find the times when the velocity is minimum. Where is the mass at these times?

**5.** The voltage in a household electrical outlet is given by

$$V = 170\cos(120\pi t)$$

where $V$ is measured in volts and $t$ in seconds.

(a) Specify the amplitude and the frequency for this oscillation.

(b) Graph the function $V = 170\cos(120\pi t)$ for two complete cycles beginning at $t = 0$.

(c) For which values of $t$ in part (b) is the voltage maximum?

**B**

**6.** The following figure (on the next page) shows a simple pendulum consisting of a string with a weight attached at one end and the other end suspended from a fixed point. As indicated in the figure, the angle between the vertical and the pendulum is denoted by $\theta$ (where $\theta$ is in radians). Suppose that we pull the pendulum out from the equilibrium position (where $\theta = 0$) to a position $\theta = \theta_0$. Now we release the pendulum so that it swings back and forth. Then (neglecting friction and assuming that $\theta_0$ is a small angle), it can be shown that the angle $\theta$ at time $t$ is very closely approximated by

$$\theta = \theta_0 \cos(t\sqrt{g/L})$$

where $L$ is the length of the pendulum, $g$ is a constant (the acceleration due to gravity), and $t$ is the time in seconds.

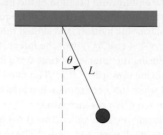

(a) What are the amplitude, the period, and the frequency for the motion defined by the equation $\theta = \theta_0 \cos(t\sqrt{g/L})$? Assume that $t$ is in seconds, $L$ is in meters, and $g$ is in m/sec$^2$.

(b) Use your results in part (a) to answer these two questions. Does the period of the pendulum depend upon the amplitude? Does the period depend upon the length $L$?

(c) Graph the function $\theta = \theta_0 \cos(t\sqrt{g/L})$ for two complete cycles beginning at $t = 0$ and using the following values for the constants:

$$\theta_0 = 0.1 \text{ radian} \qquad L = 1 \text{ m} \qquad g = 9.8 \text{ m/sec}^2$$

(d) For which values of $t$ during these two cycles is the weight moving to the right? *Hint:* The weight is moving to the right when $\theta$ is increasing; use your graph in part (c) to see when this occurs.

(e) The velocity $V$ of the weight as it oscillates back and forth is given by

$$V = -\theta_0 \sqrt{g/L} \sin(t\sqrt{g/L})$$

where $V$ is in m/sec. Graph this function for two complete cycles using the values of the constants given in part (c).

(f) At which times during these two cycles is the velocity maximum? What is the corresponding value of $\theta$ in each case?

(g) At which times during these two cycles is the velocity minimum? What is the corresponding value of $\theta$ in each case?

(h) At which times during these two cycles is the velocity zero? What is the corresponding value of $\theta$ in each case?

7. Refer to Figure A. Suppose that the point $P$ travels counterclockwise around the unit circle at a constant angular speed of $\pi/3$ radians/sec. Assume that at time $t = 0$ sec, the location of $P$ is $(1, 0)$.

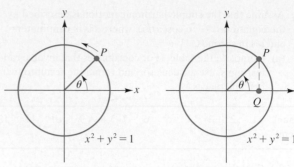

**Figure A**          **Figure B**

(a) Complete the table.

| $t$ (sec) | 0 | 1 | 2 | 3 | 4 | 5 | 6 | 7 |
|-----------|---|---|---|---|---|---|---|---|
| $\theta$ (radians) | | | | | | | | |

(b) Now (for each position of the point $P$) suppose that we draw a perpendicular from $P$ to the $x$-axis, meeting the $x$-axis at $Q$, as indicated in Figure B. The point $Q$ is called the *projection* of the point $P$ on the $x$-axis. As the point $P$ moves around the circle, the point $Q$ will move back and forth along the diameter of the circle. What is the $x$-coordinate of the point $Q$ at each of the times listed in the table for part (a)?

(c) Draw a sketch showing the location of the points $P$ and $Q$ when $t = 1$ sec.

(d) Draw sketches as in part (c) for $t = 2, 3$, and 4 sec.

(e) The $x$-coordinate of $Q$ is always equal to $\cos\theta$. Why?

(f) If you look back at your table in part (a), you'll see that the relation between $\theta$ and $t$ is $\theta = \pi t/3$. Thus the $x$-coordinate of $Q$ at time $t$ is given by

$$x = \cos\frac{\pi t}{3}$$

This tells us that as the point $P$ moves around the circle at a constant angular speed, the point $Q$ oscillates in simple harmonic motion along the $x$-axis. Graph this function for two complete cycles, beginning at $t = 0$. Specify the amplitude, the period, and the frequency for the motion.

(g) Using calculus, it can be shown that the velocity of the point $Q$ at time $t$ is given by

$$V = -\frac{\pi}{3} \sin\frac{\pi t}{3}$$

Graph this function for two complete cycles, beginning at $t = 0$.

(h) Use the graph in part (g) to determine the times (during the first two cycles) when the velocity of the point $Q$ is zero. What are the corresponding $x$-coordinates of $Q$ in each case?

**(i)** Use the graph in part (g) to determine the times (during the first two cycles) when the velocity of the point $Q$ is maximum. Where is $Q$ located at these times?

**(j)** Use the graph in part (g) to determine the times (during the first two cycles) when the velocity of the point $Q$ is minimum. Where is $Q$ located at these times?

## PROJECT

### THE MOTION OF A PISTON

*To see the way a machine works, you can take the the covers off and look inside. But to understand what goes on, you need to get to know the principles that govern its actions.* — David Macaulay, *The Way Things Work* (Boston Mass.: Houghton Mifflin Company, 1988)

In this project we examine a simple linkage that exhibits an oscillatory motion that is somewhat more complicated than simple harmonic motion. The tools that we've developed in the last two chapters will enable us to derive a function describing this motion. This function provides a very good mathematical model for the motion of a piston in a conventional internal combustion car engine. Although you won't need to be familiar with car engines to follow the mathematics, your appreciation of its applicability would be greatly enhanced if someone in your group could explain how a crankshaft piston and cylinder move in a car engine. The internet or a reference such as the one quoted above might be useful.

Figure A shows a line segment $OC$ of length R rotating counterclockwise about the fixed origin $O$ and another line segment $CP$ of length L, with L greater than R. The line segments are thought of as being linked together at point C as if they were flat rods with a pin through them so that they can rotate freely about $C$, their common endpoint. The point $P$ is constrained to move along the $x$-axis. As the line segment $OC$ rotates about the origin, the point $P$ moves back and forth along the $x$-axis. The two figures illustrate the configuration at two different rotation positions. In the language of car engines the origin would be the center of a cross-section of the crankshaft, the segment $OC$ would be a crank arm, the segment $CP$ would be a piston rod, and point $P$ would be the center of a cross-section of a wrist pin.

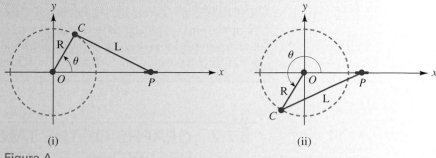

(i)                                    (ii)

Figure A

**EXERCISE 1**   Let $f(\theta)$ equal the $x$-coordinate of the point $P$ when the line segment $OC$ is at an angle $\theta$ (measured in radians) from the positive $x$-axis. What are the maximum and minimum values of $f$ and at what values of $\theta$ do they occur?

**EXERCISE 2**   Figure B can be used to derive a formula for $f(\theta)$. Express the lengths of $OA$ and $CA$ in terms of R and $\theta$. Now use the Pythagorean theorem

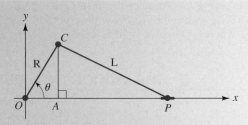

**Figure B**

to express the length of $AP$ in terms of R, L, and $\theta$. Since, in Figure B, $f(\theta)$ equals the length of line segment $OP$ we have

$$f(\theta) = R \cos\theta + \sqrt{L^2 - R^2 \sin^2\theta}$$

How do the maximum and minimum value for $f$ compare with your answers from Exercise 1? Explain why this derivation would work when point $C$ is in the second quadrant.

Ⓖ **EXERCISE 3** For given values of L and R, graph the indicated functions, for $0 \le \theta \le 4\pi$, on the same set of axes and zoom in near the maximum, minimum, and any other interesting points. Write short notes of your observations. $f(\theta)$ is the function derived in the previous exercise.
**(a)** Let L = 20 cm and R = 4 cm. Graph $y = L$, $y = L + R \cos\theta$, and $y = f(\theta)$.
**(b)** Let L = 20 cm and R = 10 cm. Graph $y = L$, $y = L + R \cos\theta$, and $y = f(\theta)$.
**(c)** Let L = 20 cm and R = 10 cm. Graph $y = 1.868\,R + R \cos\theta$, and $y = f(\theta)$.
**(d)** Let L = 20 cm and R = 10 cm. Graph $y = 1.868\,R + R \cos\theta + 0.1339\,R \cos 2\theta$, and $y = f(\theta)$.

In parts (c) and (d) the functions graphed with $f$ are the second and third partial sums of the Fourier series for $f$. If you did the project on Fourier series at the end of Section 7.5, note how much better the third partial sum of the Fourier series is as an approximation to $f$ here than in Figure B of that project.

Finally, let's apply the result of Exercise 2 to a typical automotive situation.

**EXERCISE 4** Given that segment $OC$ is rotating at 3000 revolutions per minute (rpm) let $g(t)$ be the $x$-coordinate of the point $P$ at time $t$ seconds and find a formula for $g(t)$. (*Hint*: Find $\theta$ in terms of $t$ and substitute into the formula for $f(\theta)$.) What would the formula be for $k$ revolutions per minute?

# 7.7 GRAPHS OF THE TANGENT AND THE RECIPROCAL FUNCTIONS

*A third . . . function, the tangent of $\theta$, or tan $\theta$, is of secondary importance, in that it is not associated with wave phenomena. Nevertheless, it enters into the body of analysis so prominently that we cannot ignore it.* —Samuel E. Urner and William B. Orange in *Elements of Mathematical Analysis* (Boston: Ginn and Co., 1950)

We have seen in the previous sections that the sine and cosine functions are periodic. The remaining four trigonometric functions are also periodic, but their

## TABLE 1

| x | 0 | $\dfrac{\pi}{6}$ | $\dfrac{\pi}{4}$ | $\dfrac{\pi}{3}$ | $\dfrac{5\pi}{12}$ (= 75°) | $\dfrac{17\pi}{36}$ (= 85°) | $\dfrac{89\pi}{180}$ (= 89°) | $\dfrac{\pi}{2}$ |
|---|---|---|---|---|---|---|---|---|
| tan x | 0 | $\dfrac{\sqrt{3}}{3} \approx 0.58$ | 1 | $\sqrt{3} \approx 1.73$ | 3.73 | 11.43 | 57.29 | undefined |

graphs differ significantly from those of sine and cosine. In particular, the graphs of $y = \tan x$, cot $x$, csc $x$, and sec $x$ all possess vertical asymptotes.

We'll obtain the graph of the tangent function by a combination of both point-plotting and symmetry considerations. Table 1 displays a list of values for $y = \tan x$ using $x$-values in the interval $[0, \pi/2)$.

*Note*: As $x$ increases from 0 to $\pi/2$, the values of tan $x$ increase slowly at first then more and more rapidly.

As is indicated in Table 1, tan $x$ is undefined when $x = \pi/2$. This follows from the identity

$$\tan x = \frac{\sin x}{\cos x} \tag{1}$$

When $x = \pi/2$, the denominator in this identity is zero. Indeed, when $x$ is equal to any odd integral multiple of $\pi/2$ (for example, $\pm 3\pi/2$, $\pm 5\pi/2$), the denominator in equation (1) will be zero, and, consequently, tan $x$ will be undefined.

Because tan $x$ is undefined when $x = \pi/2$, we want to see how the graph behaves as $x$ gets closer and closer to $\pi/2$. This is why the $x$-values $5\pi/12$, $17\pi/36$, and $89\pi/180$ are used in Table 1. In Figure 1 we've used the data in Table 1 to draw the graph of $y = \tan x$ for $0 \le x < \pi/2$. As the figure indicates, the vertical line $x = \pi/2$ is an asymptote for the graph.

The graph of $y = \tan x$ can now be completed without further need for tables or a calculator. First, the identity $\tan(-x) = -\tan x$ (from Section 7.3) tells us that the tangent is an odd function so the graph of $y = \tan x$ is symmetric about the origin. After reflecting the graph in Figure 1 about the origin, we can draw the graph of $y = \tan x$ on the interval $\left(-\frac{\pi}{2}, \frac{\pi}{2}\right)$, as shown in Figure 2.

Now, to complete the graph of $y = \tan x$, we use the identity

$$\tan(s + \pi) = \tan s \tag{2}$$

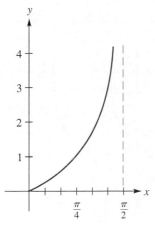

**Figure 1**
$y = \tan x$, $0 \le x < \pi/2$

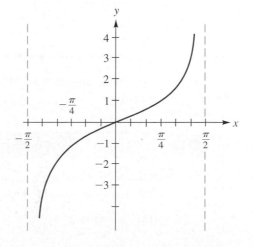

**Figure 2**
$y = \tan x$, $-\pi/2 < x < \pi/2$
The graph is symmetric about the origin. The lines $x = \pm \pi/2$ are asymptotes.

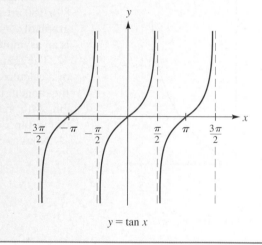

Looking at Figure 3, we can see why this identity is valid. By definition, the coordinates of $P$ and $Q$ are

$$P(\cos s, \sin s) \qquad \text{and} \qquad Q(\cos(s + \pi), \sin(s + \pi))$$

On the other hand, the points $P$ and $Q$ are symmetric about the origin, so the coordinates of $Q$ are just the negatives of the coordinates of $P$. That is,

$$\cos(s + \pi) = -\cos s \qquad \text{and} \qquad \sin(s + \pi) = -\sin s$$

Consequently, we have

$$\tan(s + \pi) = \frac{\sin(s + \pi)}{\cos(s + \pi)} = \frac{-\sin s}{-\cos s}$$

$$= \frac{\sin s}{\cos s} = \tan s \qquad \text{as required}$$

**Figure 3**

[Although Figure 3 shows the angle with radian measure $s$ terminating in Quadrant I, our proof is valid for the other quadrants as well. (Draw a figure for yourself and verify this.)]

Identity (2) tells us that the graph of $y = \tan x$ must repeat itself at intervals of length $\pi$. Taking this fact into account, along with Figure 2, we conclude that the period of $y = \tan x$ is exactly $\pi$. Our final graph of $y = \tan x$ is shown in the Property Summary Box that follows.

## PROPERTY SUMMARY   The Tangent Function: $y = \tan x$

Domain:   The set of all real numbers other than

$$\pm\frac{\pi}{2}, \pm\frac{3\pi}{2}, \pm\frac{5\pi}{2}, \ldots$$

Range:   $(-\infty, \infty)$

Period:   $\pi$

Asymptotes:   $x = \pm\dfrac{\pi}{2}, x = \pm\dfrac{3\pi}{2}, x = \pm\dfrac{5\pi}{2}, \ldots$

$x$-intercepts:   $0, \pm\pi, \pm2\pi, \pm3\pi, \ldots$

*Note*: The $x$-intercepts occur midway between consecutive vertical asymptotes

$y = \tan x$

*Note*: The tangent is an odd function so the graph of $y = \tan x$ is symmetric about the origin.

    **EXAMPLE**   **1**   **Finding periods, asymptotes, and intercepts**

Graph the following functions for one period. In each case, specify the period, the asymptotes, and the intercepts:

**(a)**  $y = \tan\left(x - \dfrac{\pi}{4}\right)$;        **(b)**  $y = -\tan\left(x - \dfrac{\pi}{4}\right)$.

(a)  $y = \tan x$
Period:  $\pi$
Asymptotes:  $x = \pm\pi/2$
x-intercept:  0
y-intercept:  0

(b)  $y = \tan\left(x - \frac{\pi}{4}\right)$
Period:  $\pi$
Asymptotes:  $x = -\pi/4$
                    $x = 3\pi/4$
x-intercept:  $\pi/4$
y-intercept:  $-1$

(c)  $y = -\tan\left(x - \frac{\pi}{4}\right)$
Period:  $\pi$
Asymptotes:  $x = -\pi/4$
                    $x = 3\pi/4$
x-intercept:  $\pi/4$
y-intercept:  1

**Figure 4**

**SOLUTION**
We begin with the graph of one period of $y = \tan x$, as shown in Figure 4(a). By translating this graph $\pi/4$ units to the right, we obtain the graph of $y = \tan(x - \frac{\pi}{4})$, in Figure 4(b). With this translation, note that the left asymptote shifts from $x = -\pi/2$ to $x = -\pi/2 + \pi/4 = -\pi/4$; the right asymptote shifts from $x = \pi/2$ to $x = \pi/2 + \pi/4 = 3\pi/4$; and the x-intercept shifts from 0 to $\pi/4$.

For the y-intercept of $y = \tan(x - \frac{\pi}{4})$ we replace x with 0 in the equation. This yields

$$y = \tan\left(0 - \frac{\pi}{4}\right) = \tan\left(-\frac{\pi}{4}\right) = -\tan\frac{\pi}{4} = -1$$

Finally, for the graph of $y = -\tan(x - \frac{\pi}{4})$ we need only reflect the graph in Figure 4(b) about the x-axis; see Figure 4(c).

---

**EXAMPLE**  **2**   **Graphing a function of the form $y = \tan Bx$**

Graph the function $y = \tan(x/2)$ for one period.

**SOLUTION**
First we refer back to Figure 2, which shows the basic pattern for one period of $y = \tan x$. In this basic pattern the asymptotes occur when the radian measure of the angle equals $-\pi/2$ or $\pi/2$. Consequently, for $y = \tan(x/2)$, the asymptotes occur when $x/2 = -\pi/2$ and when $x/2 = \pi/2$. From the equation $x/2 = -\pi/2$ we conclude that $x = -\pi$, and from the equation $x/2 = \pi/2$ we conclude that $x = \pi$. Thus the asymptotes for $y = \tan(x/2)$ are $x = -\pi$ and $x = \pi$. The distance between these asymptotes, namely, $2\pi$, is the period of $y = \tan(x/2)$. This is twice the period of $y = \tan x$, so basically, we want to draw a curve with the same general shape as $y = \tan x$ but twice as wide; see Figure 5. Note that the graph in Figure 5 passes through the origin, since when $x = 0$, we have

$$y = \tan\frac{0}{2} = \tan 0 = 0$$

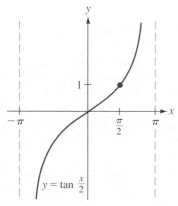

$y = \tan\frac{x}{2}$

**Figure 5**

The graph of the cotangent function can be obtained from that of the tangent function by means of the identity

$$\cot x = -\tan\left(x - \frac{\pi}{2}\right) \tag{3}$$

(Exercise 57 shows how to derive this identity.) According to identity (3), the graph of $y = \cot x$ can be obtained by first translating the graph of $y = \tan x$ to the right $\pi/2$ units and then reflecting the translated graph about the $x$-axis. When this is done, we obtain the graph shown in the box that follows.

---

**PROPERTY SUMMARY   The Cotangent Function: $y = \cot x$**

Domain:   The set of all real numbers other than $0, \pm\pi, \pm2\pi, \ldots$

Range:   $(-\infty, \infty)$

Period:   $\pi$

Asymptotes:   $x = 0, x = \pm\pi, x = \pm2\pi, \ldots$

$x$-intercepts:   $\pm\dfrac{\pi}{2}, \pm\dfrac{3\pi}{2}, \pm\dfrac{5\pi}{2}, \ldots$

*Note*: The $x$-intercepts occur midway between consecutive vertical asymptotes.

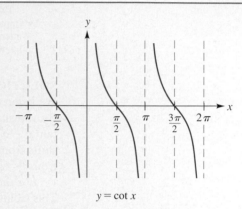

$y = \cot x$

---

*Note*: The cotangent is an odd function so the graph of $y = \cot x$ is symmetric about the origin.

  **EXAMPLE 3   Graphing functions of the form $y = A \cot Bx$**

Graph each of the following functions for one period:

**(a)** $y = \cot \pi x;$      **(b)** $y = \dfrac{1}{2} \cot \pi x;$      **(c)** $y = -\dfrac{1}{2} \cot \pi x.$

**SOLUTION**

**(a)** Looking at the graph of $y = \cot x$ in the Property Summary above, we see that one complete pattern or cycle of the graph occurs between the asymptotes $x = 0$ and $x = \pi$. Now, for the function we are given, $x$ has been replaced by $\pi x$. Thus the corresponding asymptotes occur when $\pi x = 0$ and when $\pi x = \pi$, in other words, when $x = 0$ and when $x = 1$; see Figure 6(a).

**(b)** The graph of $y = \frac{1}{2} \cot \pi x$ will have the same general shape as that of $y = \cot \pi x$, but each $y$-coordinate on $y = \frac{1}{2} \cot \pi x$ will be one-half of the corresponding coordinate on $y = \cot \pi x$; see Figure 6(b).

**(c)** The graph of $y = -\frac{1}{2} \cot \pi x$ is obtained by reflecting the graph of $y = \frac{1}{2} \cot \pi x$ about the $x$-axis; see Figure 6(c).

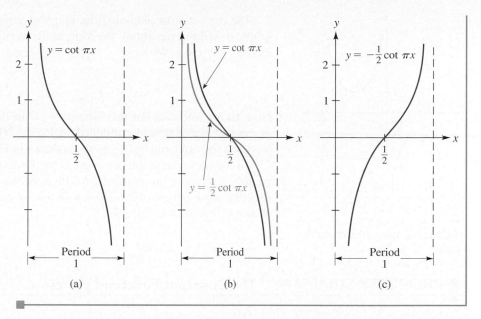

**Figure 6**

(a)          (b)          (c)

We conclude this section with a discussion of the graphs of $y = \csc x$ and $y = \sec x$. We will obtain these graphs in a series of easy steps, relying on the ideas of symmetry and translation. First consider the function $y = \csc x$. In Figure 7(a) we've set up a table and used it to sketch the graph of $y = \csc x$ on the interval $[\frac{\pi}{2}, \pi)$. Note that $\csc x$ is undefined when $x = \pi$. (Why?)

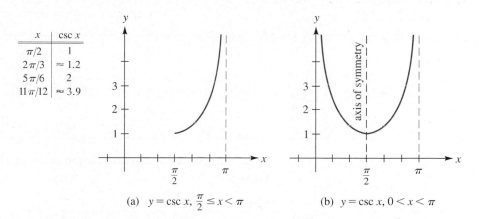

**Figure 7**

(a)  $y = \csc x,\ \frac{\pi}{2} \le x < \pi$        (b)  $y = \csc x,\ 0 < x < \pi$

As Figure 7(a) indicates, the vertical line $x = \pi$ is an asymptote for the graph. The graph in Figure 7(a) can be extended to the interval $(0, \pi)$ by means of the identity

$$\csc\left(\frac{\pi}{2} + s\right) = \csc\left(\frac{\pi}{2} - s\right)$$

(Exercise 59 shows you how to verify this identity.) This identity tells us that, starting at $x = \pi/2$, whether we travel a distance $s$ to the right or a distance $s$ to the left, the value of $y = \csc x$ is the same. In other words, the graph of $y = \csc x$ is symmetric about the line $x = \pi/2$. In view of this symmetry we can sketch the graph of $y = \csc x$ on the interval $(0, \pi)$, as shown in Figure 7(b).

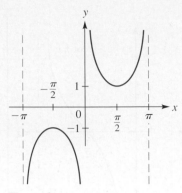

**Figure 8**

$y = \csc x, \; -\pi < x < \pi$

The graph is symmetric about the origin.

The next step in obtaining the graph of $y = \csc x$ is to use the fact that the graph is symmetric about the origin. To verify this, we need to check that $\csc(-x) = -\csc x$. We have

$$\csc(-x) = \frac{1}{\sin(-x)} = \frac{1}{-\sin x} = -\csc x \qquad \text{as required}$$

Now, taking into account this symmetry about the origin and the portion of the graph that we've already obtained in Figure 7(b), we can sketch the graph of $y = \csc x$ over the interval $(-\pi, \pi)$, as shown in Figure 8.

To complete the graph of $y = \csc x$, we observe that the values of $\csc x$ must repeat themselves at intervals of $2\pi$. This is because $\csc x = 1/(\sin x)$, and the sine function has a period of $2\pi$. In view of this we can draw the graph of $y = \csc x$ as shown in the box that follows.

---

**PROPERTY SUMMARY   The Cosecant Function: $y = \csc x$**

Domain:   All real numbers other than
         $0, \pm\pi, \pm 2\pi, \ldots$
Range:    $(-\infty, -1] \cup [1, \infty)$
Period:   $2\pi$
Asymptotes:   $x = 0, x = \pm\pi, x = \pm 2\pi, \ldots$
Intercepts:   None

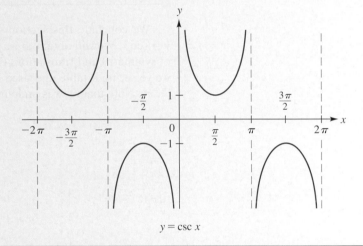

$y = \csc x$

---

*Note*: The cosecant is an odd function so the graph of $y = \csc x$ is symmetric about the origin.

---

  **EXAMPLE   4   Graphing a function of the form $y = \csc Bx$**

Graph the function $y = \csc(x/3)$ for one period.

**SOLUTION**
Since $\csc(x/3) = 1/\sin(x/3)$, it will be helpful first to graph one period of $y = \sin(x/3)$. This is done in Figure 9(a) using the techniques of Section 7.5. Note that the period of $y = \sin(x/3)$ is $6\pi$. This is also the period of $y = \csc(x/3)$, because $\csc(x/3)$ and $\sin(x/3)$ are just reciprocals. The asymptotes for $y = \csc(x/3)$ occur when $\sin(x/3) = 0$. From Figure 9(a) we see that $\sin(x/3) = 0$ when $x = 0$, when $x = 3\pi$, and when $x = 6\pi$. These asymptotes are sketched in Figure 9(b). The colored points in Figure 9(b) indicate where the value of $\sin(x/3)$ is 1 or $-1$;

(a) $y = \sin \dfrac{x}{3}$

(b) The asymptotes for $y = \csc(x/3)$ occur when $\sin(x/3) = 0$.

(c) $y = \csc \dfrac{x}{3}$

Figure 9

the graph of $y = \csc(x/3)$ must pass through these points. (Why?) Finally, using the points and the asymptotes in Figure 9(b), we can sketch the graph of $y = \csc(x/3)$, as shown in Figure 9(c).

In Section 7.4 we used the identity

$$\cos x = \sin\left( x + \frac{\pi}{2} \right) \tag{4}$$

to graph the cosine function. This identity tells us that the graph of $y = \cos x$ can be obtained by translating the graph of $y = \sin x$ to the left by $\pi/2$ units. Now, from identity (4) it follows that

$$\sec x = \csc\left( x + \frac{\pi}{2} \right)$$

This last identity tells us that the graph of $y = \sec x$ can also be obtained by a translation. In this case, by translating the graph of $y = \csc x$ a distance of $\pi/2$ units to the left, we obtain the graph of $y = \sec x$, as shown in the box that follows.

## PROPERTY SUMMARY   The Secant Function: $y = \sec x$

Domain:  All real numbers other than
$$\pm\frac{\pi}{2}, \pm\frac{3\pi}{2}, \pm\frac{5\pi}{2}, \dots$$

Range:  $(-\infty, -1] \cup [1, \infty)$

Period:  $2\pi$

Asymptotes:  $x = \pm\dfrac{\pi}{2}, x = \pm\dfrac{3\pi}{2},$
$$x = \pm\frac{5\pi}{2}, \dots$$

$y$-intercept:  1

$x$-intercept:  None

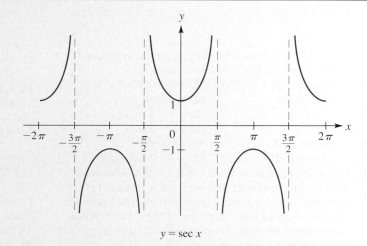

$y = \sec x$

*Note:* The secant is an even function so the graph of $y = \sec x$ is symmetric about the $y$-axis.

# EXERCISE SET 7.7

## A

*In Exercises 1–12, graph each function for one period, and show (or specify) the intercepts and asymptotes.*

**1. (a)** $y = \tan(x + \frac{\pi}{4})$        **2. (a)** $y = \tan(x - \frac{\pi}{3})$
   **(b)** $y = -\tan(x + \frac{\pi}{4})$           **(b)** $y = -\tan(x - \frac{\pi}{3})$
**3. (a)** $y = \tan(x/3)$               **4. (a)** $y = 2 \tan \pi x$
   **(b)** $y = -\tan(x/3)$                  **(b)** $y = -2 \tan \pi x$
**5.** $y = \frac{1}{2} \tan(\pi x/2)$          **6.** $y = -\frac{1}{2} \tan 2\pi x$
**7.** $y = \cot(\pi x/2)$              **8.** $y = \cot 2\pi x$
**9.** $y = -\cot(x - \frac{\pi}{4})$        **10.** $y = \cot(x + \frac{\pi}{6})$
**11.** $y = \frac{1}{2} \cot 2x$             **12.** $y = -\frac{1}{2} \cot(x/2)$

G **13.** Graph the function $y = \tan x$. Use a viewing rectangle that extends from $-5$ to $5$ in both the $x$- and the $y$-directions. What are the exact values for the $x$-intercepts shown in your graph?

G **14.** In graphing the tangent function in the text, we used the identity $\tan(x + \pi) = \tan x$. Check this identity by graphing the two equations $y = \tan x$ and $y = \tan(x + \pi)$ and noting that the graphs indeed appear to be identical.

*In Exercises 15–20, graph each function. Adjust the viewing rectangle as necessary so that the graph is shown for at least two periods.*

G **15. (a)** $y = \tan(x/4)$      G **16. (a)** $y = \cot(2x)$
   **(b)** $y = \tan(4x)$              **(b)** $y = \cot(x/2)$
G **17. (a)** $y = 0.5 \tan \pi x$   G **18. (a)** $y = 0.25 \cot x$
   **(b)** $y = 0.5 \tan(\pi x + \frac{\pi}{3})$    **(b)** $y = 0.25 \cot(x + \frac{\pi}{4})$
   **(c)** $y = 0.5 \tan(\pi x + 1)$     **(c)** $y = -0.25 \cot(x + \frac{\pi}{4})$
G **19. (a)** $y = 0.4 \tan(x/2)$    G **20. (a)** $y = 0.2 \cot(3x)$
   **(b)** $y = 0.4 \tan(x/3)$           **(b)** $y = -0.2 \cot(4x)$
   **(c)** $y = 0.4 \tan(x/5)$           **(c)** $y = -0.2 \cot(12x)$

*In Exercises 21–32, graph each function for one period, and show (or specify) the intercepts and asymptotes.*

**21.** $y = \csc(x - \frac{\pi}{4})$          **22.** $y = \csc(x - \frac{\pi}{6})$
**23.** $y = -\csc(x/2)$              **24.** $y = 2 \csc x$
**25.** $y = \frac{1}{3} \csc \pi x$            **26.** $y = -\frac{1}{2} \csc 2\pi x$
**27.** $y = -\sec x$                 **28.** $y = -2 \sec x$
**29.** $y = \sec(x - \pi)$            **30.** $y = \sec(x + 1)$
**31.** $y = 3 \sec(\pi x/2)$           **32.** $y = -2 \sec(\pi x/3)$

G **33.** Graph the functions $y = \sin x$ and $y = \csc x$ in the standard viewing rectangle. [For $\csc x$, use $1 \div (\sin x)$.] Observe that $|\sin x| \leq 1$, while $|\csc x| \geq 1$. At which points in the picture do we have $\sin x = \csc x$? Why? (*Hint:* Which two numbers are their own reciprocals?) There are no points where $\sin x = -\csc x$. Why?

G **34.** Graph the functions $y = \cos x$ and $y = \sec x$ in the standard viewing rectangle. [For $\sec x$, use $1 \div (\cos x)$.] Observe that $|\cos x| \leq 1$, while $|\sec x| \geq 1$. At which points in the picture do we have $\cos x = \sec x$? Why? (*Hint:* Which two numbers are their own reciprocals?) There are no points where $\cos x = -\sec x$. Why?

*In Exercises 35–38, graph each function for two periods. Specify the intercepts and the asymptotes.*

**35. (a)** $y = 2 \sin(3\pi x - \frac{\pi}{6})$
   **(b)** $y = 2 \csc(3\pi x - \frac{\pi}{6})$
**36. (a)** $y = -\frac{1}{2} \sin(\pi x + \frac{\pi}{3})$
   **(b)** $y = -\frac{1}{2} \csc(\pi x + \frac{\pi}{3})$
**37. (a)** $y = -3 \cos(2\pi x - \frac{\pi}{4})$
   **(b)** $y = -3 \sec(2\pi x - \frac{\pi}{4})$
**38. (a)** $y = \cos(3x + \frac{\pi}{3})$
   **(b)** $y = \sec(3x + \frac{\pi}{3})$

*In Exercises 39–42, graph each pair of functions on the same set of axes. Adjust the viewing rectangle as necessary so that the graphs are shown for at least two periods.*

G **39.** $Y_1 = 0.6 \sin(x/2)$      G **40.** $Y_1 = -1.2 \sin(\pi x/3)$
   $Y_2 = 0.6 \csc(x/2)$           $Y_2 = -1.2 \csc(\pi x/3)$
G **41.** $Y_1 = 3 \cos(2x - \frac{\pi}{6})$   G **42.** $Y_1 = -1.5 \cos(\pi x - \frac{\pi}{6})$
   $Y_2 = 3 \sec(2x - \frac{\pi}{6})$         $Y_2 = -1.5 \sec(\pi x - \frac{\pi}{6})$

## B

*For Exercises 43–46, six functions are defined as follows:*

$$f(x) = \sin x \qquad g(x) = \csc x \qquad h(x) = \pi x - \frac{\pi}{6}$$

$$F(x) = \cos x \qquad G(x) = \sec x \qquad H(x) = \pi x + \frac{\pi}{4}$$

*In each case, graph the indicated function for one period.*

**43. (a)** $f \circ h$           **44. (a)** $F \circ H$
   **(b)** $g \circ h$              **(b)** $G \circ H$
**45. (a)** $f \circ H$           **46. (a)** $F \circ h$
   **(b)** $g \circ H$              **(b)** $G \circ h$

*For Exercises 47–50, four functions are defined as follows:*

$$f(x) = \csc x \qquad T(x) = \tan x$$

$$g(x) = \sec x \qquad A(x) = |x|$$

*In each case, graph the indicated function over the interval $[-2\pi, 2\pi]$.*

**47.** $A \circ T$              **48.** $A \circ g$
**49.** $A \circ f$              **50.** $f \circ A$

Ⓖ **51.** In this exercise we compare the graphs of $f(x) = \tan x$ and $g(x) = x^3$ on the open interval $-\pi/2 < x < \pi/2$. On the same set of axes, graph these two functions for $-\pi/2 < x < \pi/2$. Then answer the following questions.
(a) Which of the two graphs appears to be horizontal as it passes through the origin?
(b) When $x$ is in the open interval $(0, \frac{\pi}{2})$, which quantity is larger, $\tan x$ or $x^3$? Why is your choice reasonable? (*Hint*: $x^3$ is finite at $x = \pi/2$.)
(c) When $x$ is in the open interval $(-\frac{\pi}{2}, 0)$, which quantity is larger, $\tan x$ or $x^3$? Why is your choice reasonable?

Ⓖ **52.** Graph the two functions $y = \tan^2 x$ and $y = \sec^2 x - 1$. What do you observe? What does this demonstrate?

Ⓖ **53.** Graph the two functions $y = \cot^2 x$ and $y = \csc^2 x - 1$. What do you observe? What does this demonstrate?

Ⓖ **54. (a)** Graph the two functions $y = \tan x$ and $y = x$ in the standard viewing rectangle. Observe that $\tan x$ and $x$ are very close to one another when $x$ is close to zero. In fact, the approximation $\tan x \approx x$ is often used in applications when it is known that $x$ is close to zero.
(b) To obtain a better view of $y = \tan x$ and $y = x$ near the origin, adjust the viewing rectangle so that $x$ extends from $-\pi/2$ to $\pi/2$ and $y$ extends from $-2$ to $2$. Again, note that when $x$ is close to zero, the values of $\tan x$ are indeed close to $x$. To see numerical evidence of this, complete the following table.

| $x$ | 0.000123 | 0.01 | 0.05 | 0.1 | 0.2 | 0.3 | 0.4 | 0.5 |
|---|---|---|---|---|---|---|---|---|
| $\tan x$ | | | | | | | | |

| $x$ | $-0.000123$ | $-0.01$ | $-0.05$ | $-0.1$ | $-0.2$ | $-0.3$ | $-0.4$ | $-0.5$ |
|---|---|---|---|---|---|---|---|---|
| $\tan x$ | | | | | | | | |

(c) The numerical evidence in part (b) suggests that for $x$ positive and close to 0, $\tan x > x$. State the corresponding result for $x$ negative and close to 0. Then on the same set of axes, draw, without a calculator, the graphs of $y = x$ and $y = \tan x$.
(d) If you study *Taylor polynomials* in calculus, you'll see that an even better approximation to $\tan x$ is

$$\tan x \approx x + \frac{1}{3}x^3 \qquad \text{when } x \text{ is close to } 0$$

Add the graph of $y = x + \frac{1}{3}x^3$ to the picture that you obtained in part (b). Describe what you see.
(e) To see numerical evidence of how well $\tan x$ is approximated by $x + \frac{1}{3}x^3$, add a third row to the table you worked out in part (b); in this third row, show the values for $x + \frac{1}{3}x^3$. When you've completed the table, note that the new values are much closer to $\tan x$ than were the values of $x$.

Ⓖ **55. (a)** Graph the equations $y = \tan x$ and $y = 2$ in the standard viewing rectangle.
(b) Use the graph to give a rough estimate for the smallest positive root of the equation $\tan x = 2$.
*Answer:* $x \approx 1$
(c) Use the graphing utility to determine the root more accurately, say, through the first four decimal places.
(d) Let $r$ denote the root that you determined in part (c). Is the number $r + \pi$ also a root of the equation $\tan x = 2$?

Ⓖ **56. (a)** Graph the equations $y = \tan x$ and $y = x$ in the standard viewing rectangle. Use the graph to give a rough estimate for the smallest positive root of the equation $\tan x = x$.
*Answer:* Something between 4 and 5, call it 4.5
(b) Use the graphing utility to determine the root more accurately, say, through the first four decimal places.
(c) Let $r$ denote the root that you determined in part (b). Is the number $r + \pi$ also a root of the equation $\tan x = x$?

**57.** In the text we used the identity

$$\cot s = -\tan\left(s - \frac{\pi}{2}\right)$$

to obtain the graph of $y = \cot x$ from that of $y = \tan x$. The following steps show one way to derive this identity. (Although the accompanying figure shows the angle with radian measure $s$ terminating in the first quadrant, the proof is valid no matter where the angle terminates.) In the figure, $\overline{PO} \perp \overline{QO}$.

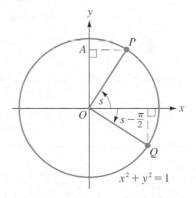

(a) Why are the coordinates of $P$ and $Q$ as follows?

$$P(\cos s, \sin s) \qquad \text{and} \qquad Q\left(\cos\left(s - \frac{\pi}{2}\right), \sin\left(s - \frac{\pi}{2}\right)\right)$$

(b) Using congruent triangles [and without reference to part (a)], explain why the $y$-coordinate of $Q$ is the negative of the $x$-coordinate of $P$, and the $x$-coordinate of $Q$ equals the $y$-coordinate of $P$.

(*continues*)

**(c)** Use the results in parts (a) and (b) to conclude that

$$\sin\left(s - \frac{\pi}{2}\right) = -\cos s \quad \text{and} \quad \cos\left(s - \frac{\pi}{2}\right) = \sin s$$

**(d)** Use the result in part (c) to show that

$$\cot s = -\tan\left(s - \frac{\pi}{2}\right)$$

**58.** In the text we obtained the graph of the cotangent function from that of the tangent by means of the identity $\cot x = -\tan(x - \frac{\pi}{2})$. Verify this identity graphically by graphing the two functions $y = \cot x$ and $y = -\tan(x - \frac{\pi}{2})$ and noting that the graphs indeed appear to be identical.

**59.** In this exercise we verify the identity $\csc(\frac{\pi}{2} + s) = \csc(\frac{\pi}{2} - s)$. Refer to the figure at the right, in which $\angle AOB = \angle BOC = s$ radians. [Although the figure shows $s$ in the interval $0 < s < \pi/2$, a similar proof will work for other intervals as well. (A proof that does not depend upon a picture can be given using the formula for $\sin(s + t)$, which is developed in Section 8.1.)]

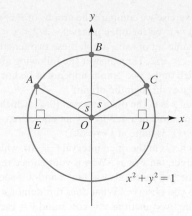

**(a)** Show that the triangles $AOE$ and $COD$ are congruent and, consequently, that $AE = CD$.

**(b)** Explain why the $y$-coordinates of the points $C$ and $A$ are $\sin(\frac{\pi}{2} - s)$ and $\sin(\frac{\pi}{2} + s)$, respectively.

**(c)** Use parts (a) and (b) to conclude that $\sin(\frac{\pi}{2} + s) = \sin(\frac{\pi}{2} - s)$. It follows from this that $\csc(\frac{\pi}{2} + s) = \csc(\frac{\pi}{2} - s)$, as required.

# Chapter 7 █ Summary of Principal Formulas and Terms

| Terms or formulas | Page reference | Comments |
|---|---|---|
| **1.** $\theta = \dfrac{s}{r}$ | 487–488 | This equation defines the *radian measure* $\theta$ of an angle. We assume here that the vertex of the angle is placed at the center of a circle of radius $r$ and that $s$ is the length of the intercepted arc. See Figure 1 in Section 7.1. |
| **2.** $s = r\theta$ | 497 | This formula expresses the arc length $s$ on a circle in terms of the radius $r$ and the radian measure $\theta$ of the central angle subtended by the arc. |
| **3.** $A = \dfrac{1}{2}r^2\theta$ | 497 | This formula expresses the area of a sector of a circle in terms of the radius $r$ and the radian measure $\theta$ of the central angle. |
| **4.** $\omega = \dfrac{\theta}{t}$ <br> $v = \dfrac{d}{t}$ <br> $v = r\omega$ | 499–501 | Suppose that a wheel rotates about its axis at a constant rate. If a radial line on the wheel turns through an angle of measure $\theta$ in time $t$, then the *angular speed* $\omega$ of the wheel is defined by $\omega = \theta/t$. If a point on the rotating wheel travels a distance $d$ in time $t$, then the linear speed $v$ of the point is defined by $v = d/t$. If the angular speed $\omega$ is expressed in radians per unit time, then the linear and angular speeds are related by $v = r\omega$. |

| Terms or formulas | Page reference | Comments |
|---|---|---|
| **5.** $\cos t$ <br> $\sin t$ <br> $\tan t$ <br> $\sec t$ <br> $\csc t$ <br> $\cot t$ | 507 | Let $P(x, y)$ denote the point on the unit circle such that the arc length from $(1, 0)$ is $t$. Or equivalently, let $P(x, y)$ denote the point where the terminal side of the angle with radian measure $t$ intersects the unit circle. Then the six trigonometric functions of the real number $t$ are defined as follows: $$\cos t = x \qquad\qquad \sec t = \frac{1}{x} \quad (x \neq 0)$$ $$\sin t = y \qquad\qquad \csc t = \frac{1}{y} \quad (y \neq 0)$$ $$\tan t = \frac{y}{x} \quad (x \neq 0) \qquad \cot t = \frac{x}{y} \quad (y \neq 0)$$ |
| **6.** $\sec t = \dfrac{1}{\cos t} \qquad \csc t = \dfrac{1}{\sin t}$ <br><br> $\cot t = \dfrac{1}{\tan t} \qquad \tan t = \dfrac{\sin t}{\cos t}$ <br><br> $\cot t = \dfrac{\cos t}{\sin t}$ | 509 | These five identities are direct consequences of the definitions of the trigonometric functions. |
| **7.** $\sin^2 t + \cos^2 t = 1$ <br> $\tan^2 t + 1 = \sec^2 t$ <br> $\cot^2 t + 1 = \csc^2 t$ | 509 | These are the three *Pythagorean identities*. |
| **8.** Even function, <br> odd function | 512 | A function is an *even function* if $f(-t) = f(t)$ for every value of $t$ in the domain of $f$. <br><br> A function is an *odd function* if $f(-t) = -f(t)$ for every value of $t$ in the domain of $f$. |
| **9.** $\cos(-t) = \cos t$ <br> $\sin(-t) = -\sin t$ <br> $\tan(-t) = -\tan t$ | 512 | These three identities are sometimes referred to as the *opposite-angle identities*. In each case, a trigonometric function of $-t$ is expressed in terms of that same function of $t$. Cosine is an *even* function; sine and tangent are *odd* functions. |
| **10.** Periodic function | 521 | A non-constant function $f$ is periodic if there is a positive number $p$ such that the equation $f(x + p) = f(x)$ holds for all $x$ in the domain of $f$. The smallest such number $p$ is called the *period* of $f$. Important examples: The period of $y = \sin x$ is $2\pi$; the period of $y = \cos x$ is $2\pi$; the period of $y = \tan x$ is $\pi$. |
| **11.** Amplitude | 522 | Let $m$ and $M$ denote the smallest and the largest values, respectively, of the periodic function $f$. Then the *amplitude* of $f$ is defined to be the number $\frac{1}{2}(M - m)$. Important examples: The amplitude for both $y = \sin x$ and $y = \cos x$ is 1; amplitude is not defined for the function $y = \tan x$. |

| Terms or formulas | Page reference | Comments |
|---|---|---|
| **12.** Period $= \dfrac{2\pi}{B}$ | 542 | This formula gives the period for the functions $y = A \sin(Bx - C)$ and $y = A \cos(Bx - C)$. |
| **13.** Phase shift $= \dfrac{C}{B}$ | 542 | The phase shift serves as a guide in graphing functions of the form $y = A \sin(Bx - C)$ or $y = A \cos(Bx - C)$. For instance, to graph one complete cycle of $y = A \sin(Bx - C)$, first sketch one complete cycle of $y = A \sin Bx$, beginning at $x = 0$. Then draw a curve with exactly the same shape, but beginning at $x = C/B$ rather than $x = 0$. This will represent one cycle of $y = A \sin(Bx - C)$. |
| **14.** Simple harmonic motion | 554 | Oscillation described by an equation of the form $y = A \sin(Bx - C)$ or $y = A \cos(Bx - C)$ is referred to as *simple harmonic motion*. The standard example for simple harmonic motion is the motion of a mass on the end of a spring (neglecting friction), as depicted in Figures 1 and 3 in Section 7.6. |
| **15.** Period, frequency, and amplitude for simple harmonic motion | 555 | The amplitude for simple harmonic motion is the maximum displacement from the equilibrium position. The period is the time required for one complete cycle of the motion. The frequency $f$, measured in cycles per second, is computed from the equation $f = 1/\text{period}$. |

## Writing Mathematics

1. Say whether the statement is TRUE or FALSE. Write out your reason or reasons in complete sentences. If you draw a diagram to accompany your writing, be sure that you clearly label any parts of the diagram to which you refer.
   **(a)** If $t$ is a real number less than $\pi$, then $\cos t$ is positive.
   **(b)** The equation $1 + \tan^2 t = \sec^2 t$ is true for every real number $t$.
   **(c)** If $t$ is a positive real number, then $\cos^2 t$ is a positive real number.
   **(d)** Between any two consecutive turning points, the graph of $y = \sin x$ is decreasing.
   **(e)** If $a$ and $b$ are real numbers and $\ln(\sin a) = \ln(\sin b)$, then $\sin a = \sin b$.
   **(f)** If $a$ and $b$ are real numbers and $\ln(\sin a) = \ln(\sin b)$, then $a = b$.
   **(g)** If $a$ and $b$ are real numbers and $\sin(\ln a) = \sin(\ln b)$, then $\ln a = \ln b$.
2. Let $f(x) = x + \sin x$. This function has an interesting property: The iterates can be used to obtain better and better approximations to the number $\pi$. The following table, for instance, shows the first five iterates of $x_0 = 0.8$. As you can see, the fifth iterate is indeed an excellent approximation to $\pi$. In fact, the fifth iterate, $x_5$, agrees with $\pi$ through the first 15 decimal places. [As you'll see in part (a), this behavior is not peculiar to $x_0 = 0.8$. Any value for $x_0$ between 0 and $\pi$ will produce similar results.]

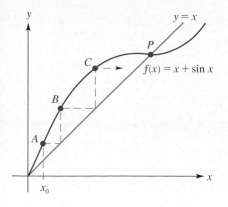

| $x_1$ | 1.5173560908 ... |
|---|---|
| $x_2$ | 2.5159285012 ... |
| $x_3$ | 3.1015642481 ... |
| $x_4$ | 3.1415819650 ... |
| $x_5$ | 3.1415926535 ... |

Iterates of $x_0 = 0.8$ for the function $f(x) = x + \sin x$

**(a)** Use your calculator to set up three tables of iterates, similar to the given table, using $x_0 = 0.9$, $x_0 = 1.5$, and $x_0 = 2$. Describe the results.

**(b)** Use the figure in the margin to explain why the successive iterates approach the number $\pi$.

# Chapter 7 | Review Exercises

1. Evaluate the following.
   **(a)** $\sin(5\pi/3)$      **(b)** $\cot(11\pi/6)$
2. Graph the function $y = 3 \cos 3\pi x$ over the interval $-\frac{1}{3} \le x \le \frac{1}{3}$. Specify the $x$-intercepts and the coordinates of the highest point on the graph.
3. Simplify the following expression:

$$\cos t - \cos(-t) + \sin t - \sin(-t)$$

4. In the expression $1/\sqrt{4 - t^2}$, make the substitution $t = 2 \cos x$ and simplify the result. Assume that $0 < x < \pi$.
5. Graph the equation $y = \sec(2\pi x - 3)$ for one complete cycle.
6. If $\sec t = -5/3$ and $\pi < t < 3\pi/2$, compute $\cot t$.
7. Graph the function $y = -\sin(2x - \pi)$ for one complete period. Specify the amplitude, period, and phase shift.
8. Graph $y = -\frac{1}{2} \tan(\pi x/3)$ over one period.

*In Exercises 9–20, evaluate each expression without using a calculator or tables.*

9. $\cos \pi$
10. $\sin(-3\pi/2)$
11. $\csc(2\pi/3)$
12. $\tan(\pi/3)$
13. $\tan(11\pi/6)$
14. $\cos 0$
15. $\sin(\pi/6)$
16. $\sec(3\pi/4)$
17. $\cot(5\pi/4)$
18. $\tan(-7\pi/4)$
19. $\csc(-5\pi/6)$
20. $\sin^2(\pi/7) + \cos^2(\pi/7)$

*Exercises 21–30 are calculator exercises. (Set your calculator to the radian mode.) In Exercises 21–26, where*

*numerical answers are required, round your results to three decimal places.*

21. Evaluate $\sin 1$.
22. Evaluate $\cos 2$.
23. Evaluate $\sin(3\pi/2)$.
24. Evaluate $\sin(0.78)$.
25. Evaluate $\sin(\sin 0.0123)$.
26. Evaluate $\sin[\sin(\sin 0.0123)]$.
27. Verify that $\sin^2 1776 + \cos^2 1776 = 1$.
28. Verify that $\sin 14 = 2 \sin 7 \cos 7$.
29. Verify that $\cos(0.5) = \cos^2(0.25) - \sin^2(0.25)$.
30. Verify that $\cos(0.3) = [\frac{1}{2}(1 + \cos 0.6)]^{1/2}$.
31. In the expression $\sqrt{25 - x^2}$, make the substitution $x = 5 \sin \theta$ $(0 < \theta < \frac{\pi}{2})$ and simplify the result.
32. In the expression $(49 + x^2)^{1/2}$, make the substitution $x = 7 \tan \theta$ $(0 < \theta < \frac{\pi}{2})$ and simplify the result.
33. In the expression $(x^2 - 100)^{1/2}$, make the substitution $x = 10 \sec \theta$ $(0 < \theta < \frac{\pi}{2})$ and simplify the result.
34. In the expression $(x^2 - 4)^{-3/2}$, make the substitution $x = 2 \sec \theta$ $(0 < \theta < \frac{\pi}{2})$ and simplify the result.
35. In the expression $(x^2 + 5)^{-1/2}$, make the substitution $x = \sqrt{5} \tan \theta$ $(0 < \theta < \frac{\pi}{2})$ and simplify the result.
36. If $\sin \theta = -5/13$ and $\pi < \theta < 3\pi/2$, compute $\cos \theta$.
37. If $\cos \theta = 8/17$ and $\sin \theta$ is negative, compute $\tan \theta$.
38. If $\sec \theta = -25/7$ and $\pi < \theta < 3\pi/2$, compute $\cot \theta$.
39. In the figure on the next page, $P$ is the center of the circle, which has radius $\sqrt{2}$ units. If the radian measure of angle $BPA$ is $\theta$, express the area of the

shaded region in terms of $\theta$. Simplify your answer as much as possible.

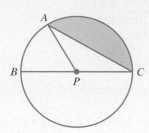

**40.** Express the area of the shaded region in the following figure in terms of $r$ and $\theta$. (Assume that $\theta$ is in radians.)

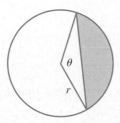

**41.** In the following figure, $ABCD$ is a square, each side of which is 1 cm. The two arcs are portions of circles with radii of 1 cm and with centers $A$ and $C$. Find the area of the shaded region.   *Hint*: Draw $\overline{BD}$ and use your result from Exercise 40.

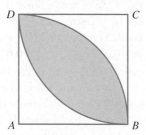

*In Exercises 42–46, a function of the form $y = A \sin Bx$ or $y = A \cos Bx$ is graphed for one period. Determine the equation in each case. (Assume that $B > 0$.)*

**42.**

$(6, -3)$

**43.**

$4$

$(\pi, 0)$

**44.**

$(3\pi, -6)$

**45.**

$\left(\dfrac{\pi}{2}, -2\right)$

**46.**

$(2\pi, -3)$

*In Exercises 47–52, sketch the graph of each function for one complete cycle. In each case, specify the x-intercepts and the coordinates of the highest and lowest points on the graph.*

**47.** $y = -3 \cos 4x$       **48.** $y = 2 \sin(3\pi x/4)$

**49.** $y = 2 \sin\left(\frac{\pi x}{2} - \frac{\pi}{4}\right)$     **50.** $y = -\sin(x - 1)$

**51.** $y = 3 \cos\left(\frac{\pi x}{3} - \frac{\pi}{3}\right)$     **52.** $y = -2 \cos(x + \pi)$

*In Exercises 53–56, sketch the graph of each function for one period.*

**53. (a)** $y = \tan(\pi x/4)$     **54. (a)** $y = 2 \cot 2x$
   **(b)** $y = \cot(\pi x/4)$        **(b)** $y = 2 \tan 2x$

**55. (a)** $y = 3 \sec(x/4)$     **56. (a)** $y = \sec \pi x$
   **(b)** $y = 3 \csc(x/4)$        **(b)** $y = \csc \pi x$

**57.** A mass on a tabletop is attached to a spring, as shown in the figure. The coordinate system has been chosen so that the equilibrium position of the mass corresponds to $s = 0$. Assume that the mass moves in simple harmonic motion described by the equation $s = -2.5 \cos(\pi t/8)$, where $s$ is in centimeters and $t$ is in seconds.

**(a)** Graph two complete cycles of the function $s = -2.5 \cos(\pi t/8)$ beginning at $t = 0$. Specify the amplitude, period, and frequency of the motion.

**(b)** Use the graph to determine the times in this interval at which the mass is farthest from the equilibrium position.

**(c)** When during this interval of time is the mass passing through the equilibrium position?

**58.** In the following figure, the arc is a portion of a circle with center $O$ and radius 1. Use the figure to prove the following result: If $\alpha$ and $\beta$ are acute angles (radian measure) with $\beta > \alpha$, then $\sin \beta - \sin \alpha < \beta - \alpha$.

*Hint:* The area of the segment of the circle determined by chord $\overline{AB}$ is less than the area of the segment determined by chord $\overline{AC}$.

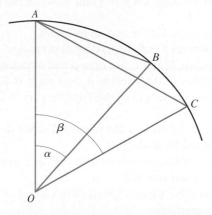

**59.** In the following figure, the arc is a portion of a circle with center $O$ and radius 1, and $\angle OAE = \pi/2$. Use the figure to prove the following result: If $\alpha$ and $\beta$ are acute angles (radian measure) with $\beta > \alpha$, then $\tan \beta - \tan \alpha > \beta - \alpha$.   *Hint:* The area of region $ABDA$ is less than the area of region $ABCEDA$.

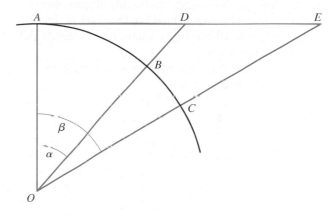

# Chapter 7        Test

**1.** Evaluate each expression without using a calculator or tables.
   **(a)** $\cos(4\pi/3)$
   **(b)** $\csc(-5\pi/6)$
   **(c)** $\sin^2(3\pi/4) + \cos^2(3\pi/4)$

**2.** In the expression $1/\sqrt{16 - t^2}$, make the substitution $t = 4 \sin u$ and simplify the result. Assume that $0 < u < \pi/2$.

**3.** Graph the function $y = 0.5 \sec(4\pi x - 1)$ for one complete cycle.

4. Graph the function $y = -\sin(3x - \frac{\pi}{4})$ for one complete cycle. Specify the amplitude, period, and phase shift.

5. Graph the function $y = 3\tan(\pi x/4)$ on the interval $0 \le x \le 4$.

6. (a) Convert $175°$ to radian measure.
   (b) Convert 5 radians to degree measure.

7. Two points $B$ and $C$ are on a circle of radius 5 cm. The center of the circle is $A$, and angle $BAC$ is $75°$.
   (a) Find the length of the (shorter) arc of the circle from $B$ to $C$.
   (b) Find the area of the (smaller) sector determined by angle $BAC$.

8. A wheel rotates about its axis with an angular speed of 25 revolutions/sec.
   (a) Find the angular speed of the wheel in radians/sec.
   (b) Find the linear speed of a point on the wheel that is 5 cm from the center.

9. Prove that the following equation is an identity:

$$\frac{\cot\theta}{1 + \tan(-\theta)} + \frac{\tan\theta}{1 + \cot(-\theta)} = \cot\theta + \tan\theta + 1$$

10. A point moves in simple harmonic motion along the $x$-axis. The $x$-coordinate of the point at time $t$ is given by $x = 10\cos(\pi t/3)$, where $t$ is in seconds and $x$ is in centimeters.
    (a) Graph this function for two complete cycles, beginning at $t = 0$.

    (b) At what times during these two cycles is the point passing through the origin? At what times is the point farthest from the origin?

11. Evaluate each expression. (Show your work or supply reasons; *don't* use a calculator.)
    (a) $\sin^2 13 + \cos^2 13$
    (b) $\sin 5 + \sin(-5)$
    (c) $\tan 1 + \tan(-1 - 2\pi)$

12. The following figure shows the graph of $y = \sin x$ for $0 \le x \le 1.6$.

    (a) Use the graph to estimate, to the nearest tenth, a root of the equation $\sin x = 0.9$.
    (b) Use a calculator to obtain a more accurate value for the root in part (a). Round the answer to four decimal places.
    (c) Use the reference-angle concept and a calculator to find another root of the equation $\sin x = 0.9$ in the interval $0 \le x \le 2\pi$. Round the answer to four decimal places.

*... through the improvements in algebraic symbolism ... trigonometry became, in the 17th century, largely an analytic science, and as such it entered the field of higher mathematics.* —David Eugene Smith in *History of Mathematics* (New York: Ginn and Company, 1925)

This chapter is devoted to some of the more algebraic (as opposed to geometric) portions of trigonometry. In Section 8.1 we develop six basic identities known as the *addition formulas*. Then, in the next two sections, we consider a number of identities that follow rather directly from these addition formulas. In Section 8.4 we return to a topic that was introduced briefly in the previous chapter: solving trigonometric equations. In solving many of these equations, we'll use the identities developed in the previous sections. We also make use of the inverse trigonometric functions that were introduced in the previous chapter (in Section 7.4). In the last section of this chapter, Section 8.5, we take a more careful look at the inverse trigonometric functions and their properties.

## 8.1 THE ADDITION FORMULAS

For any real numbers $r$, $s$, and $t$ it is always true that $r(s + t) = rs + rt$. This is the so-called **distributive law** for real numbers. If $f$ is a function, however, it is not true in general that $f(s + t) = f(s) + f(t)$. For example, consider the cosine function. It is not true in general that $\cos(s + t) = \cos s + \cos t$. For instance, with $s = \pi/6$ and $t = \pi/3$ we have

$$\cos\left(\frac{\pi}{6} + \frac{\pi}{3}\right) \overset{?}{=} \cos\frac{\pi}{6} + \cos\frac{\pi}{3}$$

$$\cos\frac{\pi}{2} \overset{?}{=} \cos\frac{\pi}{6} + \cos\frac{\pi}{3}$$

$$0 \overset{?}{=} \frac{\sqrt{3}}{2} + \frac{1}{2} \quad \text{(No!)}$$

In this section we will see just what $\cos(s + t)$ does equal. The correct formula for $\cos(s + t)$ is one of a group of important trigonometric identities called the **addition formulas.** We begin with the four addition formulas for sine and cosine.

*It has long been recognized that the addition formulas are the heart of trigonometry. Indeed, Professor Rademacher and others have shown that the entire body of trigonometry can be derived from the assumption that there exist functions S and C such that*

1. $S(x - y)$
$= S(x)C(y) - C(x)S(y)$
2. $C(x - y)$
$= C(x)C(y) + S(x)S(y)$
3. $\lim\limits_{x \to 0^+} \dfrac{S(x)}{x} = 1$

—Professor Frederick H. Young in his article, "The Addition Formulas" from *The Mathematics Teacher*, vol. L (1957), pp. 45–48.

---

### The Addition Formulas for Sine and Cosine

$$\sin(s + t) = \sin s \cos t + \cos s \sin t$$
$$\sin(s - t) = \sin s \cos t - \cos s \sin t$$
$$\cos(s + t) = \cos s \cos t - \sin s \sin t$$
$$\cos(s - t) = \cos s \cos t + \sin s \sin t$$

---

Our strategy for deriving these formulas will be as follows. First we'll prove the fourth formula, which takes some effort. The other three formulas are then relatively easy to derive from the fourth one. As background for our discussion, you will need to recall that the distance $d$ between two points $(x_1, y_1)$ and $(x_2, y_2)$ is given by $d = \sqrt{(x_2 - x_1)^2 + (y_2 - y_1)^2}$.

To prove the fourth formula in the box, we use Figure 1. The idea behind the proof is as follows.* We begin in Figure 1(a) with the unit circle and the angles $s$, $t$, and $s - t$. Then we rotate $\triangle OPQ$ about the origin until the point $P$ coincides with the point $(1, 0)$, as indicated in Figure 1(b). Although this rotation changes the coordinates for the points $P$ and $Q$, it certainly has no effect upon the length of the line segment $\overline{PQ}$. Thus whether we calculate $PQ$ using the coordinates in Figure 1(a) or those in Figure 1(b), the results must be the same. As you'll see, by equating the two expressions for $PQ$, we will obtain the required formula.

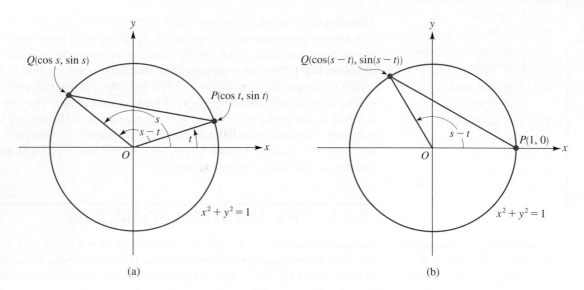

**Figure 1**
(a)                                    (b)

Applying the distance formula in Figure 1(a), we have

$$PQ = \sqrt{(\cos s - \cos t)^2 + (\sin s - \sin t)^2}$$
$$= \sqrt{\cos^2 s - 2 \cos s \cos t + \cos^2 t + \sin^2 s - 2 \sin s \sin t + \sin^2 t}$$
$$= \sqrt{2 - 2 \cos s \cos t - 2 \sin s \sin t} \quad \text{(Why?)} \tag{1}$$

Next, applying the distance formula in Figure 1(b), we have

$$PQ = \sqrt{[\cos(s - t) - 1]^2 + [\sin(s - t) - 0]^2}$$
$$= \sqrt{\cos^2(s - t) - 2 \cos(s - t) + 1 + \sin^2(s - t)}$$

The right-hand side of this last equation can be simplified by using the fact that $\cos^2(s - t) + \sin^2(s - t) = 1$. We then have

$$PQ = \sqrt{2 - 2 \cos(s - t)} \tag{2}$$

*This idea for the proof can be traced back to the great French mathematician Augustin-Louis Cauchy (1789–1857).

From equations (1) and (2) we conclude that

$$2 - 2\cos(s - t) = 2 - 2\cos s \cos t - 2 \sin s \sin t$$
$$-2\cos(s - t) = -2\cos s \cos t - 2 \sin s \sin t$$
$$\cos(s - t) = \cos s \cos t + \sin s \sin t$$

This completes the proof of the fourth addition formula. Before deriving the other three addition formulas, let's look at some applications of this result.

---

**EXAMPLE 1** Using an addition formula: the cosine of a difference

Simplify the expression $\cos 2\theta \cos \theta + \sin 2\theta \sin \theta$.

**SOLUTION**
According to the identity that we just proved, we have

$$\cos 2\theta \cos \theta + \sin 2\theta \sin \theta = \cos(2\theta - \theta) = \cos \theta$$

Thus the given expression is equal to $\cos \theta$.

---

**EXAMPLE 2** The cosine of a difference

Simplify $\cos(\theta - \pi)$.

**SOLUTION**
We use the formula for $\cos(s - t)$ with $s$ and $t$ replaced by $\theta$ and $\pi$, respectively. This yields

$$\cos(s - t) = \cos s \cos t + \sin s \sin t$$
$$\updownarrow \quad \updownarrow$$
$$\cos(\theta - \pi) = \cos \theta \cos \pi + \sin \theta \sin \pi$$
$$= (\cos \theta)(-1) + (\sin \theta)(0) = -\cos \theta$$

Thus the required simplification is $\cos(\theta - \pi) = -\cos \theta$.

---

In Example 2 we found that $\cos(\theta - \pi) = -\cos \theta$. This type of identity is often referred to as a **reduction formula.** The next example develops two basic reduction formulas that we will need to use later in this section.

---

**EXAMPLE 3** Cofunction identities

Prove the following identities:

**(a)** $\cos\left(\dfrac{\pi}{2} - \alpha\right) = \sin \alpha$;　　**(b)** $\sin\left(\dfrac{\pi}{2} - \beta\right) = \cos \beta$.

**SOLUTION**

**(a)** $\cos\left(\dfrac{\pi}{2} - \alpha\right) = \cos\dfrac{\pi}{2}\cos \alpha + \sin\dfrac{\pi}{2}\sin \alpha$

$$= (0)\cos \alpha + (1)\sin \alpha = \sin \alpha$$

This proves the identity. Incidentally, if we use degree measure instead of radian measure, this identity states that $\cos(90° - \alpha) = \sin \alpha$ as we saw in Section 6.2.

**(b)** Since the identity $\cos(\frac{\pi}{2} - \alpha) = \sin \alpha$ holds for all values of $\alpha$, we can simply replace $\alpha$ by the quantity $\frac{\pi}{2} - \beta$ to obtain

$$\cos\left[\frac{\pi}{2} - \left(\frac{\pi}{2} - \beta\right)\right] = \sin\left(\frac{\pi}{2} - \beta\right)$$

$$\cos\left(\frac{\pi}{2} - \frac{\pi}{2} + \beta\right) = \sin\left(\frac{\pi}{2} - \beta\right)$$

$$\cos \beta = \sin\left(\frac{\pi}{2} - \beta\right)$$

This proves the identity.

The two identities in Example 3 are worth memorizing. For simplicity we replace both $\alpha$ and $\beta$ by the single $\theta$ to get the following formulas.

$$\cos\left(\frac{\pi}{2} - \theta\right) = \sin \theta \qquad \text{and} \qquad \sin\left(\frac{\pi}{2} - \theta\right) = \cos \theta$$

In the formulas in the preceding box, the arguments on the left-hand side and right-hand side, $\pi/2 - \theta$, and $\theta$, respectively, add up to $\pi/2$, so the angles or numbers are complementary. Then the boxed formulas express the idea that cosine and sine are *cofunctions:* The function value of one function at a number is equal to the cofunction's value at the complementary number. Similar formulas hold for tangent and cotangent as well as for secant and cosecant.

In Examples 2 and 3, radian measure was used. However, if you look back at Figure 1 and the derivation of the formula for $\cos(s - t)$, you will see that the derivation makes no reference, implicit or explicit, to a specific system of angle measurement. (For instance, the derivation does not involve the formula $s = r\theta$, which does require radian measure.) Thus the formula for $\cos(s - t)$ is also valid when angles are measured in degrees. In the next example we apply the formula in just such a case.

  **EXAMPLE** | 4 | **Using the cosine of a difference**

Use the formula for $\cos(s - t)$ to determine the exact value of $\cos 15°$.

**SOLUTION**
First observe that $15° = 45° - 30°$. Then we have

$\cos 15° = \cos(45° - 30°)$

$\qquad = \cos 45° \cos 30° + \sin 45° \sin 30° \qquad$ using the formula for $\cos(s - t)$
$\qquad\qquad\qquad\qquad\qquad\qquad\qquad\qquad\qquad$ with $s = 45°$ and $t = 30°$

$\qquad = \left(\dfrac{\sqrt{2}}{2}\right)\left(\dfrac{\sqrt{3}}{2}\right) + \left(\dfrac{\sqrt{2}}{2}\right)\left(\dfrac{1}{2}\right)$

$\qquad = \dfrac{\sqrt{6}}{4} + \dfrac{\sqrt{2}}{4} = \dfrac{\sqrt{6} + \sqrt{2}}{4}$

Thus the exact value of $\cos 15°$ is $(\sqrt{6} + \sqrt{2})/4$.

Now let's return to our derivations of the addition formulas. Using the fourth addition formula, we can easily derive the third formula as follows. In the formula

$$\cos(s - t) = \cos s \cos t + \sin s \sin t$$

we replace $t$ by the quantity $-t$. This is permissible because the formula holds for all real numbers. We obtain

$$\cos[s - (-t)] = \cos s \cos(-t) + \sin s \sin(-t)$$

On the right-hand side of this equation we can use the identities developed for $\cos(-t)$ and $\sin(-t)$ in Section 7.3. Doing this yields

$$\cos(s + t) = (\cos s)(\cos t) + (\sin s)(-\sin t)$$

which is equivalent to

$$\cos(s + t) = \cos s \cos t - \sin s \sin t$$

This is the third addition formula, as we wished to prove.

Next we derive the formula for $\sin(s + t)$. We have

$$\sin(s + t) = \cos\left[\frac{\pi}{2} - (s + t)\right] \qquad \text{replacing } \theta \text{ by } s + t \text{ in the identity } \sin\theta = \cos(\frac{\pi}{2} - \theta)$$

$$= \cos\left[\left(\frac{\pi}{2} - s\right) - t\right]$$

$$= \cos\left(\frac{\pi}{2} - s\right)\cos t + \sin\left(\frac{\pi}{2} - s\right)\sin t \quad \text{(Why?)}$$

$$= \sin s \cos t + \cos s \sin t \quad \text{(Why?)}$$

This proves the first addition formula.

Finally, we can use the first addition formula to prove the second one as follows:

$$\sin(s - t) = \sin[s + (-t)]$$

$$= \sin s \cos(-t) + \cos s \sin(-t)$$

$$= (\sin s)(\cos t) + (\cos s)(-\sin t)$$

$$= \sin s \cos t - \cos s \sin t$$

This completes the proofs of the four addition formulas for sine and cosine.

---

| **EXAMPLE 5** | **Using an addition formula to calculate a value of a trigonometric function** |

If $\sin s = 3/5$ $(0 < s < \frac{\pi}{2})$ and $\sin t = -\sqrt{3}/4$ $(\pi < t < \frac{3\pi}{2})$, compute $\sin(s - t)$.

**SOLUTION**

$$\sin(s - t) = \underbrace{\sin s}_{\uparrow} \cos t - \cos s \underbrace{\sin t}_{\uparrow} \tag{3}$$

$$\text{given as } 3/5 \qquad \text{given as } -\sqrt{3}/4$$

In view of equation (3) we need to find only $\cos t$ and $\cos s$. These can be determined by using the Pythagorean identity $\cos^2\theta = 1 - \sin^2\theta$. We have

$$\cos^2 t = 1 - \sin^2 t$$

$$= 1 - \left(\frac{-\sqrt{3}}{4}\right)^2 = 1 - \frac{3}{16} = \frac{13}{16}$$

Therefore

$$\cos t = \frac{\sqrt{13}}{4} \quad \text{or} \quad \cos t = -\frac{\sqrt{13}}{4}$$

We choose the negative value here for cosine, since it is given that $\pi < t < 3\pi/2$. Thus

$$\cos t = -\frac{\sqrt{13}}{4}$$

Similarly, to find $\cos s$, we have

$$\cos^2 s = 1 - \sin^2 s = 1 - \left(\frac{3}{5}\right)^2 = \frac{16}{25}$$

Therefore

$$\cos s = \frac{4}{5} \quad \cos s \text{ is positive, since } 0 < s < \pi/2$$

Finally, we substitute the values we've obtained for $\cos t$ and $\cos s$, along with the given data, back into equation (3). This yields

$$\sin(s - t) = \left(\frac{3}{5}\right)\left(\frac{-\sqrt{13}}{4}\right) - \left(\frac{4}{5}\right)\left(\frac{-\sqrt{3}}{4}\right)$$

$$= \frac{-3\sqrt{13}}{20} + \frac{4\sqrt{3}}{20} = \frac{-3\sqrt{13} + 4\sqrt{3}}{20}$$

In the box that follows, we list the two addition formulas for the tangent function. As you'll see, these two formulas follow directly from the addition formulas for sine and cosine.

## Addition Formulas for Tangent

$$\tan(s + t) = \frac{\tan s + \tan t}{1 - \tan s \tan t}$$

$$\tan(s - t) = \frac{\tan s - \tan t}{1 + \tan s \tan t}$$

*Note*: These formulas are valid only for values of $s$ and $t$ that are in the domain of the tangent function and for which the denominators are nonzero.

To prove the formula for $\tan(s + t)$, we begin with

$$\tan(s + t) = \frac{\sin(s + t)}{\cos(s + t)}$$

$$= \frac{\sin s \cos t + \cos s \sin t}{\cos s \cos t - \sin s \sin t} \tag{4}$$

Now we divide both numerator and denominator on the right-hand side of equation (4) by the quantity $\cos s \cos t$. This yields

$$\tan(s + t) = \dfrac{\dfrac{\sin s \cancel{\cos t}}{\cos s \cancel{\cos t}} + \dfrac{\cancel{\cos s} \sin t}{\cancel{\cos s} \cos t}}{\dfrac{\cancel{\cos s \cos t}}{\cancel{\cos s \cos t}} - \dfrac{\sin s \sin t}{\cos s \cos t}} = \dfrac{\tan s + \tan t}{1 - \tan s \tan t}$$

This proves the formula for $\tan(s + t)$. The formula for $\tan(s - t)$ can be deduced from this with the aid of the identity $\tan(-t) = -\tan t$, which was derived in Section 7.3. We have

$$\tan(s - t) = \tan[s + (-t)]$$

$$= \dfrac{\tan s + \tan(-t)}{1 - \tan s \tan(-t)} = \dfrac{\tan s + (-\tan t)}{1 - (\tan s)(-\tan t)}$$

$$= \dfrac{\tan s - \tan t}{1 + \tan s \tan t} \qquad \text{as required}$$

---

**EXAMPLE 6 Using an addition formula for tangent**

Simplify the expression $\dfrac{\tan \frac{\pi}{9} + \tan \frac{2\pi}{9}}{1 - \tan \frac{\pi}{9} \tan \frac{2\pi}{9}}$.

**SOLUTION**

$$\dfrac{\tan \frac{\pi}{9} + \tan \frac{2\pi}{9}}{1 - \tan \frac{\pi}{9} \tan \frac{2\pi}{9}} = \tan\left(\dfrac{\pi}{9} + \dfrac{2\pi}{9}\right) \qquad \text{using the formula for } \tan(s + t)$$

$$= \tan \dfrac{3\pi}{9} = \tan \dfrac{\pi}{3} = \sqrt{3}$$

---

**EXAMPLE 7 Using an addition formula for tangent**

Compute $\tan \frac{\pi}{12}$, using the fact that $\frac{\pi}{12} = \frac{\pi}{3} - \frac{\pi}{4}$.

**SOLUTION**

$$\tan \dfrac{\pi}{12} = \tan\left(\dfrac{\pi}{3} - \dfrac{\pi}{4}\right)$$

$$= \dfrac{\tan \frac{\pi}{3} - \tan \frac{\pi}{4}}{1 + \tan \frac{\pi}{3} \tan \frac{\pi}{4}} \qquad \begin{array}{l} \text{using the formula for } \tan(s - t) \\ \text{with } s = \pi/3 \text{ and } t = \pi/4 \end{array}$$

$$= \dfrac{\sqrt{3} - 1}{1 + \sqrt{3}(1)}$$

So $\tan \dfrac{\pi}{12} = \dfrac{\sqrt{3} - 1}{\sqrt{3} + 1}$. We can write this answer in a more compact form by rationalizing the denominator. As you can check, the result is $\tan \dfrac{\pi}{12} = 2 - \sqrt{3}$.

# EXERCISE SET 8.1

## A

*In Exercises 1–10, use the addition formulas for sine and cosine to simplify the expression.*

1. $\sin \theta \cos 2\theta + \cos \theta \sin 2\theta$
2. $\sin \frac{\pi}{6} \cos \frac{\pi}{3} + \cos \frac{\pi}{6} \sin \frac{\pi}{3}$
3. $\sin 3\theta \cos \theta - \cos 3\theta \sin \theta$
4. $\sin 110° \cos 20° - \cos 110° \sin 20°$
5. $\cos 2u \cos 3u - \sin 2u \sin 3u$
6. $\cos 2u \cos 3u + \sin 2u \sin 3u$
7. $\cos \frac{2\pi}{9} \cos \frac{\pi}{18} + \sin \frac{2\pi}{9} \sin \frac{\pi}{18}$
8. $\cos \frac{3\pi}{10} \cos \frac{\pi}{5} - \sin \frac{3\pi}{10} \sin \frac{\pi}{5}$
9. $\sin(A + B) \cos A - \cos(A + B) \sin A$
10. $\cos(s - t) \cos t - \sin(s - t) \sin t$

*In Exercises 11–14, simplify each expression (as in Example 2).*

11. $\sin(\theta - \frac{3\pi}{2})$
12. $\cos(\frac{3\pi}{2} + \theta)$
13. $\cos(\theta + \pi)$
14. $\sin(\theta - \pi)$
15. Expand $\sin(t + 2\pi)$ using the appropriate addition formula, and check to see that your answer agrees with the formula in the first box on page 514.
16. Follow the directions in Exercise 15, but use $\cos(t + 2\pi)$.
17. Use the formula for $\cos(s + t)$ to compute the exact value of $\cos 75°$.
18. Use the formula for $\sin(s - t)$ to compute the exact value of $\sin \frac{\pi}{12}$.
19. Use the formula for $\sin(s + t)$ to find $\sin \frac{7\pi}{12}$.
20. Determine the exact value of **(a)** $\sin 105°$ and **(b)** $\cos 105°$.

*In Exercises 21–24, use the addition formulas for sine and cosine to simplify each expression.*

21. $\sin(\frac{\pi}{4} + s) - \sin(\frac{\pi}{4} - s)$
22. $\sin(t + \frac{\pi}{6}) - \sin(t - \frac{\pi}{6})$
23. $\cos(\frac{\pi}{3} - \theta) - \cos(\frac{\pi}{3} + \theta)$
24. $\cos(\theta - \frac{\pi}{4}) + \cos(\theta + \frac{\pi}{4})$

*In Exercises 25–28, compute the indicated quantity using the following data.*

$$\sin \alpha = \frac{12}{13} \quad \text{where } \frac{\pi}{2} < \alpha < \pi$$

$$\cos \beta = -\frac{3}{5} \quad \text{where } \pi < \beta < \frac{3\pi}{2}$$

$$\cos \theta = \frac{7}{25} \quad \text{where } -2\pi < \theta < -\frac{3\pi}{2}$$

25. **(a)** $\sin(\alpha + \beta)$
    **(b)** $\cos(\alpha + \beta)$
26. **(a)** $\sin(\alpha - \beta)$
    **(b)** $\cos(\alpha - \beta)$
27. **(a)** $\sin(\theta - \beta)$
    **(b)** $\sin(\theta + \beta)$
28. **(a)** $\cos(\alpha + \theta)$
    **(b)** $\cos(\alpha - \theta)$
29. Suppose that $\sin \theta = 1/5$ and $0 < \theta < \pi/2$.
    **(a)** Compute $\cos \theta$.
    **(b)** Compute $\sin 2\theta$. *Hint*: $\sin 2\theta = \sin(\theta + \theta)$
30. Suppose that $\cos \theta = 12/13$ and $3\pi/2 < \theta < 2\pi$.
    **(a)** Compute $\sin \theta$.
    **(b)** Compute $\cos 2\theta$. *Hint*: $\cos 2\theta = \cos(\theta + \theta)$

31. Given $\tan \theta = -2/3$, where $\pi/2 < \theta < \pi$, and $\csc \beta = 2$, where $0 < \beta < \pi/2$, find $\sin(\theta + \beta)$ and $\cos(\beta - \theta)$.
32. Given $\sec s = 5/4$, where $\sin s < 0$, and $\cot t = -1$, where $\pi/2 < t < \pi$, find $\sin(s - t)$ and $\cos(s + t)$.

*In Exercises 33–36, prove that each equation is an identity.*

33. $\sin(t + \frac{\pi}{4}) = (\sin t + \cos t)/\sqrt{2}$
34. $\cos(t + \frac{\pi}{4}) = (\cos t - \sin t)/\sqrt{2}$
35. $\sin(t + \frac{\pi}{4}) + \cos(t + \frac{\pi}{4}) = \sqrt{2} \cos t$
36. $\sec(\alpha + \beta) = \dfrac{\sec \alpha \sec \beta}{1 - \tan \alpha \tan \beta}$

*In Exercises 37–40, use the given information to compute* $\tan(s + t)$ *and* $\tan(s - t)$.

37. $\tan s = 2$ and $\tan t = 3$
38. $\tan s = 1/2$ and $\tan t = 1/3$
39. $s = 3\pi/4$ and $\tan t = -4$
40. $s = 7\pi/4$ and $\tan t = -2$

*In Exercises 41–46, use the addition formulas for tangent to simplify each expression.*

41. $\dfrac{\tan t + \tan 2t}{1 - \tan t \tan 2t}$
42. $\dfrac{\tan \frac{\pi}{5} - \tan \frac{\pi}{30}}{1 + \tan \frac{\pi}{5} \tan \frac{\pi}{30}}$
43. $\dfrac{\tan 70° - \tan 10°}{1 + \tan 70° \tan 10°}$
44. $\dfrac{2 \tan \frac{\pi}{12}}{1 - \tan^2 \frac{\pi}{12}}$
45. $\dfrac{\tan(x - y) + \tan y}{1 - \tan(x - y) \tan y}$
46. $[\tan(\theta + \pi)][\tan(\theta - \pi)] + 1$
47. Compute $\tan \frac{7\pi}{12}$ and rationalize the answer.
    *Hint*: $\frac{7\pi}{12} = \frac{\pi}{3} + \frac{\pi}{4}$
48. Compute $\tan 15°$ using the fact that $15° = 45° - 30°$. Then check that your answer is consistent with the result in Example 7.

## B

*In Exercises 49–58, prove that each equation is an identity.*

49. $\dfrac{\sin(s + t)}{\cos s \cos t} = \tan s + \tan t$
50. $\dfrac{\cos(s - t)}{\cos s \sin t} = \cot t + \tan s$
51. $\cos(A - B) - \cos(A + B) = 2 \sin A \sin B$
52. $\sin(A - B) + \sin(A + B) = 2 \sin A \cos B$
53. $\cos(A + B) \cos(A - B) = \cos^2 A - \sin^2 B$
54. $\sin(A + B) \sin(A - B) = \cos^2 B - \cos^2 A$
55. $\cos(\alpha + \beta) \cos \beta + \sin(\alpha + \beta) \sin \beta = \cos \alpha$
56. $\cos(\theta + \frac{\pi}{4}) + \sin(\theta - \frac{\pi}{4}) = 0$
57. $\tan 2\theta = \dfrac{2 \tan \theta}{1 - \tan^2 \theta}$
58. $\tan(\frac{\pi}{4} + \theta) - \tan(\frac{\pi}{4} - \theta) = 2 \tan 2\theta$
    *Hint*: Use the addition formulas for tangent and the result in Exercise 57.

*In Exercises 59–61, you are asked to derive expressions for the average rates of change of the functions* $\sin x$, $\cos x$, *and* $\tan x$. *In each case, assume that the interval is* $[x, x + h]$. *(The results are used in calculus in the study of derivatives.)*

**59.** Let $f(x) = \sin x$. Show that

$$\frac{\Delta f}{\Delta x} = (\sin x)\left(\frac{\cos h - 1}{h}\right) + (\cos x)\left(\frac{\sin h}{h}\right)$$

**60.** Let $g(x) = \cos x$. Show that

$$\frac{\Delta g}{\Delta x} = (\cos x)\left(\frac{\cos h - 1}{h}\right) - (\sin x)\left(\frac{\sin h}{h}\right)$$

**61.** Let $T(x) = \tan x$. Show that

$$\frac{\Delta T}{\Delta x} = \frac{\tan h}{h} \cdot \frac{\sec^2 x}{1 - \tan h \tan x}$$

**62.** Let $\theta$ be the acute angle defined by the following figure.

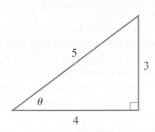

Use an addition formula and the figure to show that $5 \sin(x + \theta) = 4 \sin x + 3 \cos x$.

**63.** Let $a$ and $b$ be positive constants, and let $\theta$ be the acute angle (in radian measure) defined by the following figure.

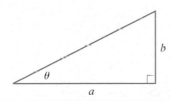

(a) Use an addition formula and the figure to show that $\sqrt{a^2 + b^2} \sin(x + \theta) = a \sin x + b \cos x$.

(b) Use the result in part (a) to specify the maximum value of the function $f(x) = a \sin x + b \cos x$.

**64.** (a) Use an addition formula to show that $2 \sin(x + \frac{\pi}{6}) = \cos x + \sqrt{3} \sin x$.

(b) Use the result in part (a) to graph the function $f(x) = \cos x + \sqrt{3} \sin x$ for one period.

**65.** (a) Use an addition formula to show that $\sqrt{2} \cos(x - \frac{\pi}{4}) = \cos x + \sin x$.

(b) Use the result in part (a) to graph the function $f(x) = \cos x + \sin x$ for one period.

**66.** Let $A$, $B$, and $C$ be the angles of a triangle, so that $A + B + C = \pi$.

(a) Show that $\sin(A + B) = \sin C$.

(b) Show that $\cos(A + B) = -\cos C$.

(c) Show that $\tan(A + B) = -\tan C$.

**67.** Suppose that $A$, $B$, and $C$ are the angles of a triangle, so that $A + B + C = \pi$. Show that

$$\cos^2 A + \cos^2 B + \cos^2 C + 2 \cos A \cos B \cos C = 1$$

**68.** Prove that

$$\frac{\sin(\alpha - \beta)}{\cos \alpha \cos \beta} + \frac{\sin(\beta - \gamma)}{\cos \beta \cos \gamma} + \frac{\sin(\gamma - \alpha)}{\cos \gamma \cos \alpha} = 0$$

**69.** Suppose that $a^2 + b^2 = 1$ and $c^2 + d^2 = 1$. Prove that $|ac + bd| \le 1$.   *Hint:* Let $a = \cos \theta$, $b = \sin \theta$, $c = \cos \phi$, and $d = \sin \phi$.

*In Exercises 70–72, simplify the expression.*

**70.** $\cos(\frac{\pi}{6} + t) \cos(\frac{\pi}{6} - t) - \sin(\frac{\pi}{6} + t) \sin(\frac{\pi}{6} - t)$
   *Hint:* If your solution relies on four separate addition formulas, then you are doing this the hard way.

**71.** $\sin(\frac{\pi}{3} - t) \cos(\frac{\pi}{3} + t) + \cos(\frac{\pi}{3} - t) \sin(\frac{\pi}{3} + t)$

**72.** $\dfrac{\tan(A + 2B) - \tan(A - 2B)}{1 + \tan(A + 2B) \tan(A - 2B)}$

**73.** If $\alpha + \beta = \pi/4$, show that $(1 + \tan \alpha)(1 + \tan \beta) = 2$.

*Exercises 74 and 75 outline simple geometric derivations of the formulas for* $\sin(\alpha + \beta)$ *and* $\cos(\alpha + \beta)$ *in the case in which* $\alpha$ *and* $\beta$ *are acute angles, with* $\alpha + \beta < 90°$. *The exercises rely on the accompanying figures, which are constructed as follows. Begin, in Figure A, with* $\alpha = \angle GAD$, $\beta = \angle HAG$, *and* $AH = 1$. *Then, from H, draw perpendiculars to* $\overline{AD}$ *and to* $\overline{AG}$, *as shown in Figure B. Finally, draw* $\overline{FE} \perp \overline{BH}$ *and* $\overline{FC} \perp \overline{AD}$.

**Figure A**

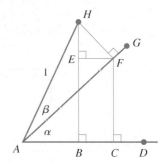

**Figure B**

**74.** *Formula for* $\sin(\alpha + \beta)$.   Supply the reasons or steps behind each statement.

(a) $BH = \sin(\alpha + \beta)$

(b) $FH = \sin \beta$   (c) $\angle BHF = \alpha$

(d) $EH = \cos \alpha \sin \beta$   *Hint:* Use $\triangle EFH$ and the result in part (b).

(e) $AF = \cos \beta$   (f) $CF = \sin \alpha \cos \beta$

(g) $\sin(\alpha + \beta) = \sin \alpha \cos \beta + \cos \alpha \sin \beta$
   *Hint:* $\sin(\alpha + \beta) = BH = EH + CF$

**75.** *Formula for* $\cos(\alpha + \beta)$.   Supply the reasons or steps behind each statement.

(a) $\cos(\alpha + \beta) = AB$

(b) $AC = \cos \alpha \cos \beta$
   *Hint:* Use $\triangle ACF$ and the result in Exercise 74(e).

(*continues*)

(c) $EF = \sin \alpha \sin \beta$

(d) $\cos(\alpha + \beta) = \cos \alpha \cos \beta - \sin \alpha \sin \beta$

*Hint*: $AB = AC - BC$

**76.** Let $S$ and $C$ be two functions. Assume that the domain for both $S$ and $C$ is the set of all real numbers and that $S$ and $C$ satisfy the following two identities.

$$S(x - y) = S(x)C(y) - C(x)S(y) \qquad (1)$$
$$C(x - y) = C(x)C(y) + S(x)S(y) \qquad (2)$$

Also, suppose that the function $S$ is not identically zero. That is,

$$S(x) \neq 0 \qquad \text{for at least one real number } x \qquad (3)$$

(a) Show that $S(0) = 0$. *Hint*: In identity (1), let $x = y$.

(b) Show that $C(0) = 1$. *Hint*: In identity (1), let $y = 0$.

(c) Explain (in complete sentences) why it was necessary to use condition (3) in the work for part (b).

(d) Prove the identity $[C(x)]^2 + [S(x)]^2 = 1$.
*Hint*: In identity (2), let $y = x$.

(e) Show that $C$ is an even function and $S$ is an odd function. That is, prove the identities $C(-x) = C(x)$ and $S(-x) = -S(x)$.
*Hint*: Write $-x$ as $0 - x$.

*In Exercises 77–80, prove the identities.*

**77.** $\dfrac{\sin(A + B)}{\sin(A - B)} = \dfrac{\tan A + \tan B}{\tan A - \tan B}$

**78.** $\dfrac{\cos(A + B)}{\cos(A - B)} = \dfrac{1 - \tan A \tan B}{1 + \tan A \tan B}$

**79.** $\cot(A + B) = \dfrac{\cot A \cot B - 1}{\cot A + \cot B}$

**80.** $\cot(A - B) = \dfrac{\cot A \cot B + 1}{\cot B - \cot A}$

**81.** Let $f(t) = \cos^2 t + \cos^2(t + \frac{2\pi}{3}) + \cos^2(t - \frac{2\pi}{3})$.

(a) Complete the table. (Use a calculator.)

| $t$ | 1 | 2 | 3 | 4 |
|---|---|---|---|---|
| $f(t)$ | | | | |

(b) On the basis of your results in part (a), make a conjecture about the function $f$. Prove that your conjecture is correct.

## C

**82.** (a) Use your calculator to check that
$\tan 50° - \tan 40° = 2 \tan 10°$.

(b) Part (a) is a specific example of a more general identity. State the identity and prove it.

**83.** If $\tan B = \dfrac{n \sin A \cos A}{1 - n \sin^2 A}$, show that
$\tan(A - B) = (1 - n)\tan A$.

**84.** If triangle $ABC$ is not a right triangle, and $\cos A = \cos B \cos C$, show that $\tan B \tan C = 2$.

**85.** (a) The angles of a triangle are $A = 20°$, $B = 50°$, and $C = 110°$. Use your calculator to compute the sum $\tan A + \tan B + \tan C$ and then the product $\tan A \tan B \tan C$. What do you observe?

(b) The angles of a triangle are $\alpha = \pi/10$, $\beta = 3\pi/10$, and $\gamma = 3\pi/5$. Use your calculator to compute $\tan \alpha + \tan \beta + \tan \gamma$ and $\tan \alpha \tan \beta \tan \gamma$.

(c) If triangle $ABC$ is not a right triangle, prove that $\tan A + \tan B + \tan C = \tan A \tan B \tan C$.

## PROJECT | THE DESIGN OF A FRESNEL LENS

Before the invention of the Fresnel lens lighthouse beacons were visible from a distance of only four or five miles out at sea. To form a beam of light visible from significantly further than five miles required construction of a lens system, based on the then conventional design, that would be unfeasibly large and heavy—not to mention expensive—and was beyond the manufacturing capabilities of the time. In 1822 Augustin Fresnel revolutionized the design and construction of lighthouse beacons by inventing a lens that was both thin and lightweight, which could form a beam of light that could be seen from twenty or more miles away. Today Fresnel lenses are used in traffic lights, overhead projectors, and on the rear windows of buses and motor homes.

In this group project we use trigonometric identities and Snell's law to design a Fresnel lens. As background, you will need to read the discussion of geometric optics and Snell's law in the project at the end of Section 6.3.

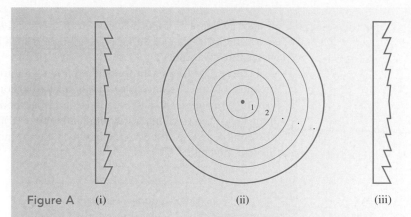

**Figure A**   (i)                              (ii)                              (iii)

Figure A shows cross-sectional views of a *positive* or *converging* Fresnel lens on the left and a *negative* or *diverging* lens on the right. The cross-sections are taken along a diameter of the lens. The front view (ii) would be the same for both. A **groove** is the annular region between two consecutive concentric circles seen when looking at the front of a Fresnel lens. In Figure A(ii) groove number 1 lies between the center dot and the smallest circle, groove number 2 lies between the smallest circle and the next one out, and so on.

The lenses commonly seen on the the rear windows of vehicles are diverging lenses, but most uses of Fresnel lenses, as in traffic lights and overhead projectors, require a converging lens. The optical situation is a little simpler for converging lenses, so that's what we'll study in this project. However, the groove angle formula we derive applies to both converging and diverging Fresnel lenses.

**Figure B**          (i)                                                                (ii)

Figure B shows the basic design problem. We are given two points lying along an axis through the center of the lens and perpendicular to the flat surface of the lens. Point $A$ is at a distance $s_1$ to the left of the lens and point $B$ is at a distance $s_2$ to the right of the lens. The lens is made of a material of index of refraction $n$. The design goal is to ensure that light rays emerging from point $A$ go through point $B$ after refraction by the lens. Figure B(i) shows a ray from $A$ striking the flat surface of the lens at a distance $r$ from the center of the lens and, after refraction at that surface, striking the slanted groove surface where it is again refracted. The **groove angle** $\beta$ is measured from the vertical as is shown in an enlarged view in Figure B(ii). Given $s_1$, $s_2$, and $n$, we need to show how, for each value of $r$, we can find a groove angle $\beta$ such that after refraction the ray passes through point $B$.

Figure C(i) shows a simplified version of Figure B, in which we ignore the thickness of the lens since it is usually negligible compared to $s_1$ and $s_2$. We also introduce the angles $\theta_1$ and $\theta_2$, and (using what theorem from geometry?) show them, measured from the horizontal, in Figure C(ii). As in Figure B, Figure C(ii) is an enlarged view of the region in which the ray indicated in Figure C(i) passes through the lens.

**Figure C**  (i)  (ii)

We are now ready to derive a formula for $\beta$. Figure D shows the path of the ray through the lens with all the relevant angles labeled. Angles $\varphi_1$ and $\varphi_1'$ denote the angles of incidence and refraction at the first surface, and angles $\varphi_2'$ and $\varphi_2$ denote the angles of incidence and refraction at the second surface.

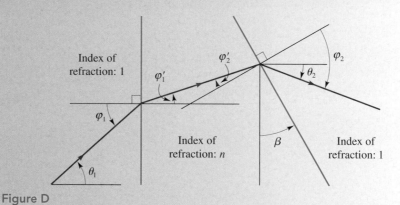

**Figure D**

## EXERCISE 1

**(a)** Given $r$, $s_1$, and $s_2$, explain how to use a calculator to find $\theta_1$ and $\theta_2$.

**(b)** Explain why $\varphi_1 = \theta_1$, $\varphi_2 = \beta + \theta_2$, and $\varphi_1' + \varphi_2' = \beta$.

**(c)** Using Snell's law and part (b) show that

$$\sin \theta_1 = n \sin \varphi_1' \qquad \text{(i)}$$
$$n \sin \varphi_2' = \sin(\beta + \theta_2) \qquad \text{(ii)}$$
$$n \sin \varphi_2' = n \sin(\beta - \varphi_1') \qquad \text{(iii)}$$

and conclude that

$$n \sin(\beta - \varphi_1') = \sin(\beta + \theta_2) \qquad \text{(iv)}$$

**(d)** Use an addition formula for sine and a Pythagorean identity to show that

$$n \sin(\beta - \varphi_1') = (\sin \beta)(n\sqrt{1 - \sin^2 \varphi_1'}) - (\cos \beta)(n \sin \varphi_1') \qquad \text{(v)}$$

Use equation (i) to obtain

$$n \sin(\beta - \varphi_1') = (\sin \beta) \sqrt{n^2 - \sin^2 \theta_1} - \cos \beta \sin \theta_1 \qquad \text{(vi)}$$

Then use equations (iv) and (vi) and an addition formula for sine to obtain

$$(\sin \beta) \sqrt{n^2 - \sin^2 \theta_1} - \cos \beta \sin \theta_1 = \sin \beta \cos \theta_2 + \cos \beta \sin \theta_2 \qquad \text{(vii)}$$

**(e)** It is surprising that equation (vii) can be be solved for $\beta$ in a few steps. Divide both sides by $\cos \beta$ and solve for $\tan \beta$ to derive the Fresnel lens groove angle formula

$$\tan \beta = \frac{\sin \theta_1 + \sin \theta_2}{\sqrt{n^2 - \sin^2 \theta_1} - \cos \theta_2} \qquad \text{(viii)}$$

**EXERCISE 2**   An optical designer must design a Fresnel lens 80 millimeters in diameter to gather light from a lamp 100 mm from the lens and cause it to pass through a small opening 400 mm from the lens on the side opposite the lamp. The index of refraction of the lens material is 1.50. She lets $s_1 = 100$ mm and $s_2 = 400$ mm, decides to make the width of each groove 0.4 mm, and calculates that there will be 100 grooves. (How?)

She writes a computer program to generate a file containing the 100 groove angles, in degrees, which will be the input to another computer program that will generate commands for a computer-controlled machine (a lathe in this case) that will produce the lens. Before trying to make the lens she decides to calculate the groove angle for grooves numbered 1, 25, 50, and 100, and use the calculated values to check the output of her program. She makes a table with column headings $r$ in mm and $\theta_1$, $\theta_2$, and $\beta$ in degrees. Her first $r$-value is 0.200 mm and her second is 9.800 mm and she calculates $\theta_1$, $\theta_2$, and $\beta$ to four decimal places. Your job as her assistant is to produce your own version of the table as another check of her work. Use the results of Exercise 1 parts (a) and (e) to produce the table.

## 8.2   THE DOUBLE-ANGLE FORMULAS

*Ptolemy (ca. 150) knew substantially the sine of half an angle . . . and it is probable that Hipparchus (ca. 140 B.C.) and certain that Varahamihira (ca. 505) knew the relation that we express as* $\sin \frac{\phi}{2} = \sqrt{(1 - \cos \phi)/2}$.—David Eugene Smith in *History of Mathematics* (New York: Ginn and Company, 1925)

There are a number of basic identities that follow from the addition formulas. In the following two boxes we summarize some of the most useful of these.

### The Double-Angle Formulas

1.  $\sin 2\theta = 2 \sin \theta \cos \theta$
2.  $\cos 2\theta = \cos^2 \theta - \sin^2 \theta$
3.  $\tan 2\theta = \dfrac{2 \tan \theta}{1 - \tan^2 \theta}$

### The Half-Angle Formulas

1. $\sin \dfrac{s}{2} = \pm\sqrt{\dfrac{1 - \cos s}{2}}$

2. $\cos \dfrac{s}{2} = \pm\sqrt{\dfrac{1 + \cos s}{2}}$

3. $\tan \dfrac{s}{2} = \dfrac{\sin s}{1 + \cos s}$

*Note:* In the half-angle formulas the $\pm$ symbol is intended to mean either positive or negative but not both, and the sign before the radical is determined by the quadrant in which the angle (or arc) $s/2$ terminates.

The identities for $\sin 2\theta$, $\cos 2\theta$, and $\tan 2\theta$ are all derived in the same way: We replace $2\theta$ by $(\theta + \theta)$ and use the appropriate addition formula. For instance, for $\sin 2\theta$ we have

$$\sin 2\theta = \sin(\theta + \theta) = \sin \theta \cos \theta + \cos \theta \sin \theta$$
$$= 2 \sin \theta \cos \theta$$

This establishes the formula for $\sin 2\theta$. (Exercise 33 asks you to carry out the corresponding derivations for $\cos 2\theta$ and $\tan 2\theta$.)

---

**EXAMPLE 1    Using double-angle formulas**

If $\sin \theta = 4/5$ and $\pi/2 < \theta < \pi$, find the quantities $\cos \theta$, $\sin 2\theta$, and $\cos 2\theta$.

**SOLUTION**
We have

$$\cos^2 \theta = 1 - \sin^2 \theta = 1 - \left(\frac{4}{5}\right)^2 = \frac{9}{25}$$

Consequently, $\cos \theta = 3/5$ or $\cos \theta = -3/5$. We want the negative value for the cosine here, since $\pi/2 < \theta < \pi$. Thus

$$\cos \theta = -\frac{3}{5}$$

Now that we know the values of $\cos \theta$ and $\sin \theta$, the double-angle formulas can be used to determine $\sin 2\theta$ and $\cos 2\theta$. We have

$$\sin 2\theta = 2 \sin \theta \cos \theta = 2\left(\frac{4}{5}\right)\left(-\frac{3}{5}\right) = -\frac{24}{25}$$

and

$$\cos 2\theta = \cos^2 \theta - \sin^2 \theta$$
$$= \left(-\frac{3}{5}\right)^2 - \left(\frac{4}{5}\right)^2 = \frac{9}{25} - \frac{16}{25} = -\frac{7}{25}$$

The required quantities are therefore $\cos \theta = -3/5$, $\sin 2\theta = -24/25$, and $\cos 2\theta = -7/25$.

### EXAMPLE 2 Using a double-angle formula

If $x = 4 \sin \theta$, $0 < \theta < \pi/2$, express $\sin 2\theta$ in terms of $x$.

**SOLUTION**
The given equation is equivalent to $\sin \theta = x/4$, so we have

$$\sin 2\theta = 2 \sin \theta \cos \theta = 2\left(\frac{x}{4}\right)\cos \theta$$

$$= \frac{x}{2}\sqrt{1 - \sin^2 \theta} \qquad \text{(Why is the positive root appropriate?)}$$

$$= \frac{x}{2}\sqrt{1 - \frac{x^2}{16}} = \frac{x}{2}\sqrt{\frac{16 - x^2}{16}} = \frac{x\sqrt{16 - x^2}}{8}$$

At the start of this section we listed formulas for $\cos 2\theta$ and for $\sin 2\theta$. There are also formulas for $\cos 3\theta$ and for $\sin 3\theta$:

$$\cos 3\theta = 4 \cos^3 \theta - 3 \cos \theta \qquad \sin 3\theta = 3 \sin \theta - 4 \sin^3 \theta$$

In the next example we derive the formula for $\cos 3\theta$, and Exercise 40 asks you to derive the formula for $\sin 3\theta$. Although these formulas needn't be memorized, they are useful. For instance, Exercise 89 in Section 8.4 shows how the formula for $\cos 3\theta$ can be used to solve certain types of cubic equations. *Historical note*: The identities for $\cos 3\theta$ and $\sin 3\theta$ are usually attributed to the French mathematician François Viète (1540–1603). Recent research, however, has shown that a geometric version of the formula for $\sin 3\theta$ was developed much earlier by the Persian mathematican and astronomer Jashmid al-Kāshi (d. 1429). (For background and details, see the article by Professor Farhad Riahi, "An Early Iterative Method for the Determination of $\sin 1°$," in *The College Mathematics Journal,* vol. 26, January 1995, pp. 16–21.)

### EXAMPLE 3 Using double-angle formulas to prove an identity

Prove the following identity:

$$\cos 3\theta = 4 \cos^3 \theta - 3 \cos \theta$$

**SOLUTION**
$$\cos 3\theta = \cos(2\theta + \theta)$$
$$= \underbrace{\cos 2\theta} \cos \theta - \underbrace{\sin 2\theta} \sin \theta$$
$$(\cos^2 \theta - \sin^2 \theta) \qquad (2 \sin \theta \cos \theta)$$
$$= (\cos^2 \theta - \sin^2 \theta)\cos \theta - (2 \sin \theta \cos \theta)\sin \theta$$
$$= \cos^3 \theta - \sin^2 \theta \cos \theta - 2 \sin^2 \theta \cos \theta$$

Collecting like terms now gives us

$$\cos 3\theta = \cos^3 \theta - 3 \sin^2 \theta \cos \theta$$

Finally, we replace $\sin^2 \theta$ by the quantity $1 - \cos^2 \theta$. This yields

$$\begin{aligned}
\cos 3\theta &= \cos^3 \theta - 3(1 - \cos^2 \theta)\cos \theta \\
&= \cos^3 \theta - 3 \cos \theta + 3 \cos^3 \theta \\
&= 4 \cos^3 \theta - 3 \cos \theta \qquad \text{as required}
\end{aligned}$$

In the box that follows, we list several alternate ways of writing the formula for $\cos 2\theta$. Formulas (3) and (4) are quite useful in calculus.

---

**Equivalent Forms of the Formula $\cos 2\theta = \cos^2 \theta - \sin^2 \theta$**

1. $\cos 2\theta = 2 \cos^2 \theta - 1$        3. $\cos^2 \theta = \dfrac{1 + \cos 2\theta}{2}$

2. $\cos 2\theta = 1 - 2 \sin^2 \theta$        4. $\sin^2 \theta = \dfrac{1 - \cos 2\theta}{2}$

---

One way to prove identity (1) is as follows:

$$\begin{aligned}
\cos 2\theta &= \cos^2 \theta - \sin^2 \theta \\
&= \cos^2 \theta - (1 - \cos^2 \theta) \\
&= \cos^2 \theta - 1 + \cos^2 \theta \\
&= 2 \cos^2 \theta - 1 \qquad \text{as required}
\end{aligned}$$

In this last equation, if we add 1 to both sides and then divide by 2, the result is identity (3). (Verify this.) The proofs for (2) and (4) are similar; see Exercise 34.

  **EXAMPLE 4**    **Expressing a power of cosine in terms of cosines of multiple angles**

Express $\cos^4 t$ in a form that does not involve powers of the trigonometric functions.

**SOLUTION**

$$\begin{aligned}
\cos^4 t = (\cos^2 t)^2 &= \left( \frac{1 + \cos 2t}{2} \right)^2 \qquad \text{using the formula for } \cos^2 \theta \\
&= \frac{1 + 2 \cos 2t + \cos^2 2t}{4} \\
&= \frac{1 + 2 \cos 2t + \frac{1}{2}(1 + \cos 4t)}{4} \qquad \text{using the formula for } \cos^2 \theta \text{ with } \theta = 2t
\end{aligned}$$

An easy way to simplify this last expression is to multiply both the numerator and the denominator by 2. As you should check for yourself, the final result is

$$\cos^4 t = \frac{3 + 4 \cos 2t + \cos 4t}{8}$$

The last three formulas we are going to prove in this section are the **half-angle formulas** which follow.

$$\cos \frac{s}{2} = \pm \sqrt{\frac{1 + \cos s}{2}}$$

$$\sin \frac{s}{2} = \pm \sqrt{\frac{1 - \cos s}{2}}$$

$$\tan \frac{s}{2} = \frac{\sin s}{1 + \cos s}$$

To derive the formula for $\cos(s/2)$, we begin with one of the alternative forms of the cosine double-angle formula:

$$\cos^2 \theta = \frac{1 + \cos 2\theta}{2} \qquad \text{or} \qquad \cos \theta = \pm \sqrt{\frac{1 + \cos 2\theta}{2}}$$

Since this identity holds for all values of $\theta$, we may replace $\theta$ by $s/2$ to obtain

$$\cos \frac{s}{2} = \pm \sqrt{\frac{1 + \cos 2(s/2)}{2}} = \pm \sqrt{\frac{1 + \cos s}{2}}$$

This is the required formula for $\cos(s/2)$. To derive the formula for $\sin(s/2)$, we follow exactly the same procedure, except that we begin with the identity $\sin^2 \theta = \frac{1}{2}(1 - \cos 2\theta)$. [Exercise 34(c) asks you to complete the proof.] In both formulas the sign before the radical is determined by the quadrant in which the angle or arc $s/2$ terminates.

---

**EXAMPLE   5   Using a half-angle formula**

Evaluate $\cos 105°$ using a half-angle formula.

**SOLUTION**

$$\cos 105° = \cos \frac{210°}{2} = \pm \sqrt{\frac{1 + \cos 210°}{2}} \qquad \begin{array}{l} \text{using the formula for} \\ \cos(s/2) \text{ with } s = 210° \end{array}$$

$$= \pm \sqrt{\frac{1 + (-\sqrt{3}/2)}{2}}$$

$$= \pm \sqrt{\frac{1 - (\sqrt{3}/2)}{2} \cdot \frac{2}{2}} = \pm \sqrt{\frac{2 - \sqrt{3}}{4}}$$

$$= \frac{\pm \sqrt{2 - \sqrt{3}}}{2}$$

So

$$\cos \theta = \frac{\sqrt{2 - \sqrt{3}}}{2} \qquad \text{or} \qquad \frac{-\sqrt{2 - \sqrt{3}}}{2} \qquad \text{(Which one?)}$$

We choose the negative value here, since the terminal side of $105°$ lies in Quadrant II. Thus we finally obtain

$$\cos 105° = \frac{-\sqrt{2 - \sqrt{3}}}{2}$$

Our last task is to establish the formula for $\tan(s/2)$. To do this, we first prove the equivalent identity, $\tan\theta = \dfrac{\sin 2\theta}{1 + \cos 2\theta}$.

**Proof That** $\tan\theta = \dfrac{\sin 2\theta}{1 + \cos 2\theta}$.

$$\frac{\sin 2\theta}{1 + \cos 2\theta} = \frac{2\sin\theta\cos\theta}{2\cos^2\theta} \qquad \text{using the identity } \cos 2\theta = 2\cos^2\theta - 1 \text{ in the denominator}$$

$$= \frac{\sin\theta}{\cos\theta} = \tan\theta$$

If we now replace $\theta$ by $s/2$ in the identity $\tan\theta = \dfrac{\sin 2\theta}{1 + \cos 2\theta}$, the result is

$$\tan\frac{s}{2} = \frac{\sin s}{1 + \cos s}$$

This is the half-angle formula for the tangent.

We conclude this section with a summary of the principal trigonometric identities developed in this section and in Chapter 7. For completeness the list also includes two sets of trigonometric identities that we did not discuss in this section. These are the so-called **product-to-sum formulas** and **sum-to-product formulas.** Proofs and applications of these formulas are discussed in the next section.

---

## ▌PROPERTY SUMMARY   Principal Trigonometric Identities

1. Consequences of the definitions

   (a) $\csc\theta = \dfrac{1}{\sin\theta}$      (b) $\sec\theta = \dfrac{1}{\cos\theta}$      (c) $\cot\theta = \dfrac{1}{\tan\theta}$

   (d) $\tan\theta = \dfrac{\sin\theta}{\cos\theta}$      (e) $\cot\theta = \dfrac{\cos\theta}{\sin\theta}$

2. The Pythagorean identities

   (a) $\sin^2\theta + \cos^2\theta = 1$      (b) $\tan^2\theta + 1 = \sec^2\theta$      (c) $\cot^2\theta + 1 = \csc^2\theta$

3. The opposite-angle formulas

   (a) $\sin(-\theta) = -\sin\theta$      (b) $\cos(-\theta) = \cos\theta$      (c) $\tan(-\theta) = -\tan\theta$

4. The reduction formulas

   (a) $\sin(\theta + 2\pi k) = \sin\theta$      (b) $\cos(\theta + 2\pi k) = \cos\theta$      (c) $\sin(\frac{\pi}{2} - \theta) = \cos\theta$

   (d) $\cos(\frac{\pi}{2} - \theta) = \sin\theta$

5. The addition formulas

   (a) $\sin(s + t) = \sin s\cos t + \cos s\sin t$      (b) $\sin(s - t) = \sin s\cos t - \cos s\sin t$

   (c) $\cos(s + t) = \cos s\cos t - \sin s\sin t$      (d) $\cos(s - t) = \cos s\cos t + \sin s\sin t$

   (e) $\tan(s + t) = \dfrac{\tan s + \tan t}{1 - \tan s\tan t}$      (f) $\tan(s - t) = \dfrac{\tan s - \tan t}{1 + \tan s\tan t}$

6. The double-angle formulas

   (a) $\sin 2\theta = 2\sin\theta\cos\theta$      (b) $\cos 2\theta = \cos^2\theta - \sin^2\theta$      (c) $\tan 2\theta = \dfrac{2\tan\theta}{1 - \tan^2\theta}$

7. The half-angle formulas

(a) $\sin\dfrac{\theta}{2} = \pm\sqrt{\dfrac{1 - \cos\theta}{2}}$   (b) $\cos\dfrac{\theta}{2} = \pm\sqrt{\dfrac{1 + \cos\theta}{2}}$   (c) $\tan\dfrac{\theta}{2} = \dfrac{\sin\theta}{1 + \cos\theta}$

8. The product-to-sum formulas

(a) $\sin A \sin B = \frac{1}{2}[\cos(A - B) - \cos(A + B)]$   (b) $\sin A \cos B = \frac{1}{2}[\sin(A + B) + \sin(A - B)]$

(c) $\cos A \cos B = \frac{1}{2}[\cos(A + B) + \cos(A - B)]$

9. The sum-to-product formulas

(a) $\sin\alpha + \sin\beta = 2\sin\dfrac{\alpha + \beta}{2}\cos\dfrac{\alpha - \beta}{2}$   (b) $\sin\alpha - \sin\beta = 2\cos\dfrac{\alpha + \beta}{2}\sin\dfrac{\alpha - \beta}{2}$

(c) $\cos\alpha + \cos\beta = 2\cos\dfrac{\alpha + \beta}{2}\cos\dfrac{\alpha - \beta}{2}$   (d) $\cos\alpha - \cos\beta = -2\sin\dfrac{\alpha + \beta}{2}\sin\dfrac{\alpha - \beta}{2}$

# EXERCISE SET 8.2

## A

*In Exercises 1–8, use the given information to evaluate each expression.*

**1.** $\cos\varphi = 7/25$   $(0° < \varphi < 90°)$
  (a) $\sin 2\varphi$   (b) $\cos 2\varphi$   (c) $\tan 2\varphi$
**2.** $\cos\varphi = 3/5$   $(0° < \varphi < 90°)$
  (a) $\sin 2\varphi$   (b) $\cos 2\varphi$   (c) $\tan 2\varphi$
**3.** $\tan u = -4$   $\left(\frac{3\pi}{2} < u < 2\pi\right)$
  (a) $\sin 2u$   (b) $\cos 2u$   (c) $\tan 2u$
**4.** $\cot s = 2$   $\left(\pi < s < \frac{3\pi}{2}\right)$
  (a) $\sin 2s$   (b) $\cos 2s$   (c) $\tan 2s$
**5.** $\sin\alpha = \sqrt{3}/2$   $(0° < \alpha < 90°)$
  (a) $\sin(\alpha/2)$   (b) $\cos(\alpha/2)$   (c) $\tan(\alpha/2)$
**6.** $\cos\beta = -1/8$   $(180° < \beta < 270°)$
  (a) $\sin(\beta/2)$   (b) $\cos(\beta/2)$   (c) $\tan(\beta/2)$
**7.** $\cos\theta = -7/9$   $\left(\frac{\pi}{2} < \theta < \pi\right)$
  (a) $\sin(\theta/2)$   (b) $\cos(\theta/2)$   (c) $\tan(\theta/2)$
**8.** $\cos\theta = 12/13$   $\left(\frac{3\pi}{2} < \theta < 2\pi\right)$
  (a) $\sin(\theta/2)$   (b) $\cos(\theta/2)$   (c) $\tan(\theta/2)$

*In Exercises 9–12, use the given information to compute each of the following:*

(a) $\sin 2\theta$   (c) $\sin(\theta/2)$
(b) $\cos 2\theta$   (d) $\cos(\theta/2)$

**9.** $\sin\theta = 3/4$   and   $\pi/2 < \theta < \pi$
**10.** $\cos\theta = 2/5$   and   $3\pi/2 < \theta < 2\pi$
**11.** $\cos\theta = -1/3$   and   $180° < \theta < 270°$
**12.** $\sin\theta = -1/10$   and   $270° < \theta < 360°$

*In Exercises 13–16, use an appropriate half-angle formula to evaluate each quantity.*

**13.** (a) $\sin(\pi/12)$   **14.** (a) $\sin(\pi/8)$
   (b) $\cos(\pi/12)$      (b) $\cos(\pi/8)$
   (c) $\tan(\pi/12)$      (c) $\tan(\pi/8)$

**15.** (a) $\sin 105°$   **16.** (a) $\sin 165°$
   (b) $\cos 105°$      (b) $\cos 165°$
   (c) $\tan 105°$      (c) $\tan 165°$

*In Exercises 17–24, refer to the two triangles and compute the quantities indicated.*

**17.** (a) $\sin 2\theta$   (b) $\cos 2\theta$   (c) $\tan 2\theta$
**18.** (a) $\sin 2t$   (b) $\cos 2t$   (c) $\tan 2t$
**19.** (a) $\sin 2\beta$   (b) $\cos 2\beta$   (c) $\tan 2\beta$
**20.** (a) $\sin 2s$   (b) $\cos 2s$   (c) $\tan 2s$
**21.** (a) $\sin(\theta/2)$   (b) $\cos(\theta/2)$   (c) $\tan(\theta/2)$
**22.** (a) $\sin(s/2)$   (b) $\cos(s/2)$   (c) $\tan(s/2)$
**23.** (a) $\sin(\beta/2)$   (b) $\cos(\beta/2)$   (c) $\tan(\beta/2)$
**24.** (a) $\sin(t/2)$   (b) $\cos(t/2)$   (c) $\tan(t/2)$

*In Exercises 25–28, use the given information to express $\sin 2\theta$ and $\cos 2\theta$ in terms of $x$.*

**25.** $x = 5\sin\theta$   $\left(0 < \theta < \frac{\pi}{2}\right)$
**26.** $x = \sqrt{2}\cos\theta$   $\left(0 < \theta < \frac{\pi}{2}\right)$
**27.** $x - 1 = 2\sin\theta$   $\left(0 < \theta < \frac{\pi}{2}\right)$
**28.** $x + 1 = 3\sin\theta$   $\left(\frac{\pi}{2} < \theta < \pi\right)$

*In Exercises 29–32, express each quantity in a form that does not involve powers of the trigonometric functions (as in Example 4).*

**29.** $\sin^4\theta$   **30.** $\cos^6\theta$
**31.** $\sin^4(\theta/2)$   **32.** $\sin^6(\theta/4)$

33. Prove each of the following double-angle formulas. *Hint*: As in the text, replace $2\theta$ with $\theta + \theta$, and use an appropriate addition formula.
    (a) $\cos 2\theta = \cos^2 \theta - \sin^2 \theta$
    (b) $\tan 2\theta = \dfrac{2 \tan \theta}{1 - \tan^2 \theta}$

34. (a) Beginning with the identity $\cos 2\theta = \cos^2 \theta - \sin^2 \theta$, prove that $\cos 2\theta = 1 - 2 \sin^2 \theta$.
    (b) Using the result in part (a), prove that $\sin^2 \theta = (1 - \cos 2\theta)/2$.
    (c) Derive the formula for $\sin(s/2)$ as follows: using the identity in part (b), replace $\theta$ with $s/2$, and then take square roots.

# B

*In Exercises 35–50, prove that the given equations are identities.*

35. $\cos 2s = \dfrac{1 - \tan^2 s}{1 + \tan^2 s}$

36. $1 + \cos 2t = \cot t \sin 2t$

37. $\cos \theta = 2 \cos^2(\theta/2) - 1$

38. $\dfrac{\sin 2\theta}{\sin \theta} - \dfrac{\cos 2\theta}{\cos \theta} = \sec \theta$

39. $\sin^4 \theta = \dfrac{3 - 4 \cos 2\theta + \cos 4\theta}{8}$

40. $\sin 3\theta = 3 \sin \theta - 4 \sin^3 \theta$

41. $\sin 2\theta = \dfrac{2 \tan \theta}{1 + \tan^2 \theta}$

42. $2 \csc 2\theta = \dfrac{\csc^2 \theta}{\cot \theta}$

43. $\sin 2\theta = 2 \sin^3 \theta \cos \theta + 2 \sin \theta \cos^3 \theta$

44. $\cot \theta = \dfrac{1 + \cos 2\theta}{\sin 2\theta}$

45. $\dfrac{1 + \tan(\theta/2)}{1 - \tan(\theta/2)} = \tan \theta + \sec \theta$

46. $\tan \theta + \cot \theta = 2 \csc 2\theta$

47. $2 \sin^2(45° - \theta) = 1 - \sin 2\theta$

48. $(\sin \theta - \cos \theta)^2 = 1 - \sin 2\theta$

49. $1 + \tan \theta \tan 2\theta = \tan 2\theta \cot \theta - 1$

50. $\tan(\frac{\pi}{4} + \theta) - \tan(\frac{\pi}{4} - \theta) = 2 \tan 2\theta$

51. If $\tan \alpha = 1/11$ and $\tan \beta = 5/6$, find $\alpha + \beta$, given that $0 < \alpha < \pi/2$ and $0 < \beta < \pi/2$. *Hint*: Compute $\tan(\alpha + \beta)$.

52. Let $z = \tan \theta$ for $-\pi/2 < \theta < \pi/2$. Show that
    (a) $\cos 2\theta = \dfrac{1 - z^2}{1 + z^2}$ and $\sin 2\theta = \dfrac{2z}{1 + z^2}$
    (b) Explain why these formulas give the correct signs for $\cos 2\theta$ and $\sin 2\theta$.

53. (a) Use a calculator to verify that the value $x = \cos 20°$ is a root of the cubic equation $8x^3 - 6x - 1 = 0$.
    (b) Use the identity $\cos 3\theta = 4 \cos^3 \theta - 3 \cos \theta$ (from Example 3 on page 591) to prove that $\cos 20°$ is a root of the cubic equation $8x^3 - 6x - 1 = 0$. *Hint*: In the given identity, substitute $\theta = 20°$.

54. (a) Use a calculator to verify that the value $x = \sin \frac{5\pi}{18}$ is a root of the cubic equation $8x^3 - 6x + 1 = 0$.

(b) Use the identity $\sin 3\theta = 3 \sin \theta - 4 \sin^3 \theta$ (from Exercise 40) to prove that $\sin \frac{5\pi}{18}$ is a root of the equation $8x^3 - 6x + 1 = 0$. *Hint*: In the identity, substitute $\theta = 5\pi/18$.

55. The following figure shows a semicircle with radius $AO = 1$.

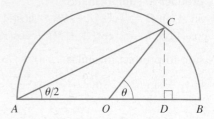

(a) Use the figure to derive the formula
$$\tan \frac{\theta}{2} = \frac{\sin \theta}{1 + \cos \theta} \qquad \left(0 < \theta < \frac{\pi}{2}\right)$$
*Hint*: Show that $CD = \sin \theta$ and $OD = \cos \theta$. Then look at right triangle $ADC$ to find $\tan(\theta/2)$.

(b) Use the formula developed in part (a) to show that
    (i) $\tan 15° = \dfrac{1}{2 + \sqrt{3}} = 2 - \sqrt{3}$
    (ii) $\tan(\pi/8) = \sqrt{2} - 1$

56. In this exercise we'll use the accompanying figure to prove the following identities:
$$\cos 2\theta = 2 \cos^2 \theta - 1$$
$$\sin 2\theta = 2 \sin \theta \cos \theta$$
$$\cos 3\theta = 4 \cos^3 \theta - 3 \cos \theta$$
$$\sin 3\theta = 3 \sin \theta - 4 \sin^3 \theta$$

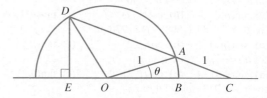

[The figure and the technique in this exercise are adapted from the article by Wayne Dancer, "Geometric Proofs of Multiple Angle Formulas," in *American Mathematical Monthly*, vol. 44 (1937), pp. 366–367.] The figure is constructed as follows. We start with $\angle AOB = \theta$ in standard position in the unit circle, as shown. The point $C$ is chosen on the extended diameter such that $CA = 1$. Then $\overline{CA}$ is extended to meet the circle at $D$, and radius $\overline{DO}$ is drawn. Finally, from $D$ a perpendicular is drawn to the diameter, as shown.

Supply the reason or reasons that justify each of the following statements.
(a) $\angle ACO = \theta$
(b) $\angle DAO = 2\theta$ *Hint*: $\angle DAO$ is an exterior angle to $\triangle AOC$.

**(c)** $\angle ODA = 2\theta$  **(d)** $\angle DOE = 3\theta$

**(e)** From $O$, draw a perpendicular to $\overline{CD}$, meeting $\overline{CD}$ at $F$. From $A$, draw a perpendicular to $\overline{OC}$, meeting $\overline{OC}$ at $G$. Then $GC = OG = \cos\theta$ and $FA = DF = \cos 2\theta$.

**(f)** $\cos\theta = \dfrac{1 + \cos 2\theta}{2\cos\theta}$  *Hint:* Use $\triangle CFO$.

**(g)** $\cos 2\theta = 2\cos^2\theta - 1$  *Hint:* In the equation in part (f), solve for $\cos 2\theta$.

**(h)** $OF = \sin 2\theta$

**(i)** $\sin 2\theta = 2\sin\theta\cos\theta$  *Hint:* Find $\sin\theta$ in $\triangle CFO$, and then solve the resulting equation for $\sin 2\theta$.

**(j)** $DC = 1 + 2\cos 2\theta$ and $EO = \cos 3\theta$

**(k)** $\cos\theta = \dfrac{2\cos\theta + \cos 3\theta}{1 + 2\cos 2\theta}$  *Hint:* Compute $\cos\theta$ in $\triangle CDE$, and then use part (j).

**(l)** $\cos 3\theta = 4\cos^3\theta - 3\cos\theta$  *Hint:* Use the results in parts (k) and (g).

**(m)** $DE = \sin 3\theta$

**(n)** $\sin 3\theta = 3\sin\theta - 4\sin^3\theta$  *Hint:* Compute $\sin\theta$ in $\triangle CDE$.

**57.** Prove the following identities involving products of cosines. *Suggestion.* In each case, begin with the right-hand side and use the double-angle formula for the sine.

**(a)** $\cos\theta\cos 2\theta = \dfrac{\sin 4\theta}{4\sin\theta}$

**(b)** $\cos\theta\cos 2\theta\cos 4\theta = \dfrac{\sin 8\theta}{8\sin\theta}$

**(c)** $\cos\theta\cos 2\theta\cos 4\theta\cos 8\theta = \dfrac{\sin 16\theta}{16\sin\theta}$

**58. (a)** Use your calculator to evaluate the expression $\cos 72°\cos 144°$. Then follow steps (b) through (d) to *prove* that $\cos 72°\cos 144° = -1/4$.

**(b)** Multiply the expression $\cos 72°\cos 144°$ by the quantity $(\sin 72°)/(\sin 72°)$, which equals 1. Show that the result can be written

$$\frac{\frac{1}{2}\sin 144°\cos 144°}{\sin 72°}$$

**(c)** Explain why the expression obtained in part (b) is equal to

$$\frac{\frac{1}{4}\sin 288°}{\sin 72°}$$

**(d)** Use the reference-angle concept to explain why the expression in part (c) is equal to $-1/4$, as required.

**59. (a)** Use your calculator to evaluate the expression $\cos 72° + \cos 144°$. Then follow steps (b) through (d) to *prove* that $\cos 72° + \cos 144° = -1/2$.

**(b)** Use the observation

$$\cos 72° + \cos 144° = \cos(108° - 36°) + \cos(108° + 36°)$$

and the addition formulas for cosine to show that

$$\cos 72° + \cos 144° = 2\cos 108°\cos 36°$$

**(c)** Use the reference-angle concept to explain why $\cos 108°\cos 36° = \cos 72°\cos 144°$.

**(d)** Use parts (b) and (c) and the identity in Exercise 58(a) to conclude that $\cos 72° + \cos 144° = -1/2$, as required.

**60.** In the figure below, the points $A_1$, $A_2$, $A_3$, $A_4$, and $A_5$ are the vertices of a regular pentagon. Follow steps (a) through (c) to show that

$$(A_1A_2)(A_1A_3)(A_1A_4)(A_1A_5) = 5$$

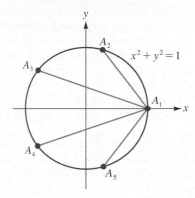

[This is a particular case of a general result due to Roger Cotes (1682–1716): Suppose that a regular $n$-gon is inscribed in the unit circle. Let the vertices of the $n$-gon be $A_1, A_2, A_3, \ldots, A_n$. Then the product $(A_1A_2)(A_1A_3)\cdots(A_1A_n)$ is equal to $n$, the number of sides of the polygon.]

**(a)** What are the coordinates of the points $A_2$, $A_3$, $A_4$, and $A_5$? (Give your answers in terms of sines and cosines.)

**(b)** Show that

$$(A_1A_2)(A_1A_3)(A_1A_4)(A_1A_5)$$
$$= (2 - 2\cos 72°)(2 - 2\cos 144°)$$

**(c)** Show that the expression on the right-hand side of the equation in part (b) is equal to 5.  *Hint:* Use the equations given in Exercises 58(a) and 59(a).

*For Exercises 61 and 62, refer to the following figures. Figure A shows an equilateral triangle inscribed in the unit circle. Figure B shows a regular pentagon inscribed in the unit circle. In both figures, the coordinates of the point $P$ are $(x, 0)$.*

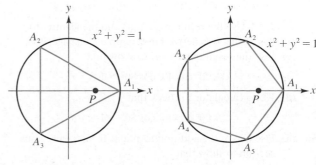

Figure A          Figure B

**61.** For Figure A, show that $(PA_1)(PA_2)(PA_3) = 1 - x^3$.

**62.** For Figure B, show that

$$(PA_1)(PA_2)(PA_3)(PA_4)(PA_5) = 1 - x^5$$

*Hints*: First find the coordinates of $A_2$ and $A_3$ in terms of sines and cosines. Next, show that

$(PA_1)(PA_2)(PA_3)(PA_4)(PA_5)$
$= (1 - x)[(1 - 2x \cos 72° + x^2)(1 - 2x \cos 144° + x^2)]$

Then expand the expression within the brackets and simplify using the equations in Exercises 58(a) and 59(a).
*Remark*: The results in Exercises 61 and 62 are particular cases of the following theorem of Roger Cotes: Suppose that a regular $n$-gon $A_1A_2A_3 \cdots A_n$ is inscribed in the unit circle. Suppose that $A_1$ is the point $(1, 0)$ and that $P$ is a point with coordinates $(x, 0)$, where $0 \le x \le 1$. Then the product $(PA_1)(PA_2)(PA_3) \cdots (PA_n)$ is equal to $1 - x^n$.

*In Exercises 63 and 64, the results and the techniques are taken from the article by Zalman Usiskin, "Products of Sines," which appeared in* The Two-Year College Mathematics Journal, *vol. 10 (1979), pp. 334–340.*

**63. (a)** Use your calculator to check that

$$\sin 18° \sin 54° = 1/4$$

**(b)** Supply reasons for each of the following steps to prove that the equation in part (a) is indeed correct.
**(i)** $\sin 72° = 2 \sin 36° \cos 36° = 2 \sin 36° \sin 54°$
**(ii)** $\sin 72° = 4 \sin 18° \cos 18° \sin 54°$
$= 4 \sin 18° \sin 72° \sin 54°$
**(iii)** $1/4 = \sin 18° \sin 54°$

**64. (a)** Use your calculator to check that

$$\sin 10° \sin 50° \sin 70° = 1/8$$

**(b)** Prove that the equation in part (a) is indeed correct.
*Hint*: Use the technique in Exercise 63; begin with the equation $\sin 80° = 2 \sin 40° \cos 40°$.

**65. (a)** Use two of the addition formulas from the previous section to show that

$$\cos(60° - \theta) \cos(60° + \theta) = (4 \cos^2 \theta - 3)/4$$

**(b)** Show that

$$\cos \theta \cos(60° - \theta) \cos(60° + \theta) = (\cos 3\theta)/4$$

*Hint*: Use the result in part (a) and the identity for $\cos 3\theta$ that was derived in Example 3 on page 591.

**(c)** Use the result in part (b) to show that

$$\cos 20° \cos 40° \cos 80° = 1/8$$

**(d)** Use a calculator to check that

$$\cos 20° \cos 40° \cos 80° = 1/8$$

**66. (a)** Use two of the addition formulas from the previous section to show that

$$\sin(60° - \theta) \sin(60° + \theta) = \frac{3 - 4 \sin^2 \theta}{4}$$

**(b)** Show that

$$\sin \theta \sin(60° - \theta) \sin(60° + \theta) = \frac{\sin 3\theta}{4}$$

*Hint*: Use the result in part (a) and the identity for $\sin 3\theta$ in Exercise 40.

**(c)** Use the result in part (b) to show that
$\sin 20° \sin 40° \sin 80° = \sqrt{3}/8$.

**(d)** Use a calculator to check that
$\sin 20° \sin 40° \sin 80° = \sqrt{3}/8$.

## C

**67.** In this exercise we show that the irrational number $\cos \frac{2\pi}{7}$ is a root of the cubic equation

$$8x^3 + 4x^2 - 4x - 1 = 0$$

**(a)** Prove the following two identities:

$$\cos 3\theta = 4 \cos^3 \theta - 3 \cos \theta$$
$$\cos 4\theta = 8 \cos^4 \theta - 8 \cos^2 \theta + 1$$

**(b)** Let $\theta = 2\pi/7$. Use the reference-angle concept [not the formulas in part (a)] to explain why $\cos 3\theta = \cos 4\theta$.

**(c)** Now use the formulas in part (a) to show that if $\theta = 2\pi/7$, then

$$8 \cos^4 \theta - 4 \cos^3 \theta - 8 \cos^2 \theta + 3 \cos \theta + 1 = 0$$

**(d)** Show that the equation in part (c) can be written

$$(\cos \theta - 1)(8 \cos^3 \theta + 4 \cos^2 \theta - 4 \cos \theta - 1) = 0$$

Conclude that the value $x = \cos \frac{2\pi}{7}$ satisfies the equation $8x^3 + 4x^2 - 4x - 1 = 0$.

**(e)** Use your calculator (in the radian mode) to check that $x = \cos \frac{2\pi}{7}$ satisfies the cubic equation $8x^3 + 4x^2 - 4x - 1 = 0$. *Remark*: An interesting fact about the real number $\cos \frac{2\pi}{7}$ is that it cannot be expressed in terms of radicals within the real-number system.

**68.** *Calculation of* $\sin 18°$, $\cos 18°$, *and* $\sin 3°$.
**(a)** Prove that $\cos 3\theta = 4 \cos^3 \theta - 3 \cos \theta$.
**(b)** Supply a reason for each statement.
**(i)** $\sin 36° = \cos 54°$
**(ii)** $2 \sin 18° \cos 18° = 4 \cos^3 18° - 3 \cos 18°$
**(iii)** $2 \sin 18° = 4 \cos^2 18° - 3$
**(c)** In equation (iii), replace $\cos^2 18°$ by $1 - \sin^2 18°$ and then solve the resulting equation for $\sin 18°$. Thus show that $\sin 18° = \frac{1}{4}(\sqrt{5} - 1)$.
**(d)** Show that $\cos 18° = \frac{1}{4}\sqrt{10 + 2\sqrt{5}}$.
**(e)** Show that $\sin 3°$ is equal to

$$\frac{1}{16}[(\sqrt{5} - 1)(\sqrt{6} + \sqrt{2}) - 2(\sqrt{3} - 1)\sqrt{5 + \sqrt{5}}]$$

*Hint*: $3° = 18° - 15°$
**(f)** Use your calculator to check the results in parts (c), (d), and (e).

# 8.3   THE PRODUCT-TO-SUM AND SUM-TO-PRODUCT FORMULAS

*In the summer of 1580, . . . [the Polish mathematician Paul Wittich] went for a short time to Uraniborg to work with Tycho Brache. He soon showed himself to be a skillful mathematician, for with Tycho he discovered—or, more precisely, rediscovered—the method of prosthaphaeresis, by which the products and quotients of trigonometric functions . . . can be replaced by simpler sums and differences.*

*The method of prosthaphaeresis originated with Johann Werner [a German astronomer, mathematician, and geographer (1468–1522)], who developed it in conjunction with the law of cosines for sides of a spherical triangle.* —Charles C. Gillispie (ed.), *Dictionary of Scientific Biography,* vol. XIV (New York: Charles Scribner's Sons, 1976)

The addition formulas for sine and cosine (from Section 8.1) can be used to establish identities concerning sums and products of sines and cosines. These identities are useful at times for simplifying expressions in trigonometry and in calculus. We begin with the three *product-to-sum formulas.*

---

The Product-to-Sum Formulas

$$\sin A \sin B = \frac{1}{2}[\cos(A - B) - \cos(A + B)]$$

$$\sin A \cos B = \frac{1}{2}[\sin(A - B) + \sin(A + B)]$$

$$\cos A \cos B = \frac{1}{2}[\cos(A - B) + \cos(A + B)]$$

---

To derive the first identity in the box, we write down the addition formulas for $\cos(A - B)$ and for $\cos(A + B)$:

$$\cos A \cos B + \sin A \sin B = \cos(A - B) \qquad (1)$$

$$\cos A \cos B - \sin A \sin B = \cos(A + B) \qquad (2)$$

If we subtract equation (2) from equation (1), we have

$$2 \sin A \sin B = \cos(A - B) - \cos(A + B)$$

Now, dividing both sides of this last equation by 2, we obtain the required identity:

$$\sin A \sin B = \frac{1}{2}[\cos(A - B) - \cos(A + B)]$$

The derivations of the remaining two product-to-sum formulas are entirely similar. (See Exercise 42.)

---

**EXAMPLE** **1**   **Changing a product of sines to a difference of cosines**

Use the formula for $\sin A \sin B$ to simplify the expression $\sin 15° \sin 75°$.

**SOLUTION**
In the identity for $\sin A \sin B$ we substitute the values $A = 15°$ and $B = 75°$. This yields

$$\sin 15° \sin 75° = \frac{1}{2}[\cos(15° - 75°) - \cos(15° + 75°)]$$

$$= \frac{1}{2}[\cos(-60°) - \cos(90°)]$$

$$= \frac{1}{2}\left(\frac{1}{2} - 0\right) = \frac{1}{4}$$

| EXAMPLE | 2 | Changing a product of a sine and a cosine to a sum of sines |

Convert the product $\sin 4x \cos 3x$ to a sum.

**SOLUTION**
Using the formula for $\sin A \cos B$ with $A = 4x$ and $B = 3x$, we have

$$\sin 4x \cos 3x = \frac{1}{2}[\sin(4x - 3x) + \sin(4x + 3x)]$$

$$= \frac{1}{2}[\sin x + \sin 7x]$$

$$= \frac{1}{2}\sin x + \frac{1}{2}\sin 7x$$

*Note*: This result is *not* equal to $\sin(x/2) + \sin(7x/2)$.

| EXAMPLE | 3 | Changing a product of cosines to a sum of cosines |

Simplify the following expression.

$$\cos\left(s + \frac{\pi}{4}\right)\cos\left(s - \frac{\pi}{4}\right)$$

**SOLUTION**
In the formula

$$\cos A \cos B = \frac{1}{2}[\cos(A - B) + \cos(A + B)]$$

we will let $A = s + \pi/4$ and $B = s - \pi/4$. Notice that with these values for $A$ and $B$, we have

$$A - B = \frac{\pi}{2} \qquad \text{and} \qquad A + B = 2s$$

Consequently,

$$\cos\left(s + \frac{\pi}{4}\right)\cos\left(s - \frac{\pi}{4}\right) = \frac{1}{2}\left(\cos\frac{\pi}{2} + \cos 2s\right)$$

$$= \frac{1}{2}(0 + \cos 2s) = \frac{1}{2}\cos 2s$$

As we saw in Examples 1 and 3, converting a product into a sum can produce in some instances a much simpler form of a given expression. Of course, there are times when it may be more useful to proceed in the other direction. That is, there are times when we want to convert a sum (or a difference) into a product. The following *sum-to-product formulas* are useful here.

---

**The Sum-to-Product Formulas**

$$\sin \alpha + \sin \beta = 2 \sin \frac{\alpha + \beta}{2} \cos \frac{\alpha - \beta}{2}$$

$$\sin \alpha - \sin \beta = 2 \cos \frac{\alpha + \beta}{2} \sin \frac{\alpha - \beta}{2}$$

$$\cos \alpha + \cos \beta = 2 \cos \frac{\alpha + \beta}{2} \cos \frac{\alpha - \beta}{2}$$

$$\cos \alpha - \cos \beta = -2 \sin \frac{\alpha + \beta}{2} \sin \frac{\alpha - \beta}{2}$$

---

Each of these formulas can be derived from one of the product-to-sum formulas that are listed on page 599. For instance, to derive the formula for $\cos \alpha - \cos \beta$, we begin with

$$\sin A \sin B = \frac{1}{2}[\cos(A - B) - \cos(A + B)] \tag{3}$$

If we let

$$A + B = \alpha \tag{4}$$

and

$$A - B = \beta \tag{5}$$

then we have

$$A = \frac{\alpha + \beta}{2} \qquad \text{adding equations (4) and (5) and then dividing by 2}$$

and

$$B = \frac{\alpha - \beta}{2} \qquad \text{subtracting equation (5) from equation (4) and then dividing by 2}$$

Now we use these last two equations and also equations (4) and (5) to substitute in equation (3). The result is

$$\sin \frac{\alpha + \beta}{2} \sin \frac{\alpha - \beta}{2} = \frac{1}{2}(\cos \beta - \cos \alpha)$$

or, after multiplying by 2,

$$2 \sin \frac{\alpha + \beta}{2} \sin \frac{\alpha - \beta}{2} = \cos \beta - \cos \alpha$$

This last equation is equivalent to

$$\cos \alpha - \cos \beta = -2 \sin \frac{\alpha + \beta}{2} \sin \frac{\alpha - \beta}{2}$$

This is the fourth sum-to-product formula, as required. (For the derivation of the remaining three sum-to-product formulas, see Exercises 43–45.)

---

EXAMPLE | 4 | **Using the sum-to-product formulas**

Convert each expression to a product and simplify where possible:
**(a)** $\sin 50° + \sin 70°$; **(b)** $\cos \theta - \cos 5\theta$.

**SOLUTION**
**(a)** In the formula

$$\sin \alpha + \sin \beta = 2 \sin \frac{\alpha + \beta}{2} \cos \frac{\alpha - \beta}{2}$$

we set $\alpha = 50°$ and $\beta = 70°$. Then we have

$$\sin 50° + \sin 70° = 2 \sin \frac{50° + 70°}{2} \cos \frac{50° - 70°}{2}$$
$$= 2 \sin 60° \cos(-10°)$$
$$= \sqrt{3} \cos 10° \quad \text{using the identity } \cos(-\theta) = \cos \theta$$

**(b)** Using the formula

$$\cos \alpha - \cos \beta = -2 \sin \frac{\alpha + \beta}{2} \sin \frac{\alpha - \beta}{2}$$

we have

$$\cos \theta - \cos 5\theta = -2 \sin \frac{\theta + 5\theta}{2} \sin \frac{\theta - 5\theta}{2}$$
$$= -2 \sin 3\theta \sin(-2\theta)$$
$$= 2 \sin 3\theta \sin 2\theta \quad \text{using the identity } \sin(-t) = -\sin t$$

---

EXAMPLE | 5 | **Expressing a sum of a sine and a cosine as a scaled and shifted cosine function**

**(a)** Use a sum-to-product formula to show that

$$\sin x + \cos x = \sqrt{2} \cos \left( x - \frac{\pi}{4} \right)$$

**(b)** Use the identity in part (a) to graph the function $y = \sin x + \cos x$.

**SOLUTION**
**(a)** Using the identity $\cos x = \sin(\frac{\pi}{2} - x)$, we have

$$\sin x + \cos x = \sin x + \sin \left( \frac{\pi}{2} - x \right)$$
$$= 2 \sin \frac{x + (\frac{\pi}{2} - x)}{2} \cos \frac{x - (\frac{\pi}{2} - x)}{2}$$
$$= 2 \sin \frac{\pi}{4} \cos \left( x - \frac{\pi}{4} \right) \quad \text{Check the algebra.}$$
$$= \sqrt{2} \cos \left( x - \frac{\pi}{4} \right)$$

Actually, there is an easier way to obtain this identity. Expand $\cos(x - \pi/4)$ using an addition formula, then multiply the result by $\sqrt{2}$; the result will be $\cos x + \sin x$. We use the sum-to-product formula in this example because we want to begin with $\cos x + \sin x$ and work toward a form that can be graphed using the techniques of the previous chapter.

**(b)** In view of the identity established in part (a), we need to graph only the function $y = \sqrt{2} \cos(x - \frac{\pi}{4})$. This is a function of the form $y = A \cos(Bx - C)$, which we studied in Section 7.5. In Figure 1 we show the graph of $y = \sqrt{2} \cos(x - \frac{\pi}{4})$. You should verify for yourself (using the techniques of Section 7.5) that the amplitude, period, and phase shift indicated in Figure 1 are indeed correct.

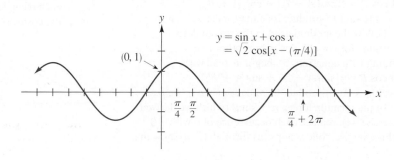

**Figure 1**
The graph of $y = \sin x + \cos x$ or
$y = \sqrt{2} \cos(x - \pi/4)$
Amplitude:  $\sqrt{2}$
Period:  $2\pi$
Phase shift:  $\pi/4$

---

# EXERCISE SET 8.3

**A**

*In Exercises 1–22, use a product-to-sum formula to convert each expression to a sum or difference. Simplify where possible.*

**1.** $\cos 70° \cos 20°$
**2.** $\cos 50° \cos 40°$
**3.** $\sin 5° \sin 85°$
**4.** $\sin 130° \sin 10°$
**5.** $\sin 20° \cos 10°$
**6.** $\cos 18° \sin 72°$
**7.** $\cos \frac{\pi}{5} \cos \frac{4\pi}{5}$
**8.** $\cos \frac{5\pi}{12} \cos \frac{\pi}{12}$
**9.** $\sin \frac{2\pi}{7} \sin \frac{5\pi}{7}$
**10.** $\sin \frac{3\pi}{8} \sin \frac{\pi}{8}$
**11.** $\sin \frac{7\pi}{12} \cos \frac{\pi}{12}$
**12.** $\cos \frac{7\pi}{8} \sin \frac{\pi}{8}$
**13.** $\sin 3x \sin 4x$
**14.** $\cos 5x \cos 2x$
**15.** $\sin 6\theta \cos 5\theta$
**16.** $\sin \frac{2\theta}{3} \sin \frac{5\theta}{3}$
**17.** $\cos \frac{\theta}{2} \sin \frac{3\theta}{2}$
**18.** $\cos \frac{t}{4} \cos \frac{3t}{4}$
**19.** $\sin(2x + y) \sin(2x - y)$
**20.** $\cos(\theta + \frac{\pi}{6}) \cos(\theta - \frac{\pi}{6})$
**21.** $\sin 2t \cos(s - t)$
**22.** $\cos(\alpha + 2\beta) \sin(2\alpha - \beta)$

*In Exercises 23–34, convert each expression into a product and simplify where possible.*

**23.** $\cos 35° + \cos 55°$
**24.** $\cos 50° - \cos 10°$
**25.** $\sin \frac{\pi}{5} - \sin \frac{3\pi}{10}$
**26.** $\sin \frac{\pi}{12} + \sin \frac{11\pi}{12}$
**27.** $\cos 5\theta - \cos 3\theta$
**28.** $\sin \frac{5\theta}{2} - \sin \frac{\theta}{2}$
**29.** $\sin 35° + \cos 65°$   *Hint*: Use the identity $\cos \theta = \sin(90° - \theta)$.
**30.** $\cos \frac{3\pi}{8} - \sin \frac{\pi}{8}$   *Hint*: Use the identity $\cos \theta = \sin(\frac{\pi}{2} - \theta)$.
**31.** $\sin(\frac{\pi}{3} + 2\theta) - \sin(\frac{\pi}{3} - 2\theta)$
**32.** $\cos(\frac{5\pi}{12} + \theta) + \cos(\frac{\pi}{12} - \theta)$

**33.** $\dfrac{\cos \frac{5\pi}{12} + \sin \frac{5\pi}{12}}{\cos \frac{\pi}{12} - \sin \frac{\pi}{12}}$
**34.** $\dfrac{\sin 47° + \cos 17°}{\cos 47° + \sin 17°}$

*In Exercises 35–38, prove that the equations are identities.*

**35.** $\dfrac{\sin s + \sin t}{\cos s + \cos t} = \tan\left(\dfrac{s + t}{2}\right)$
**36.** $\dfrac{\cos[(n - 2)\theta] - \cos n\theta}{\sin[(n - 2)\theta] + \sin n\theta} = \tan \theta$
**37.** $\dfrac{\sin 2x + \sin 2y}{\cos 2x + \cos 2y} = \tan(x + y)$
**38.** $\sin(\theta + \phi) \sin(\theta - \phi) = \sin^2 \theta - \sin^2 \phi$

*In Exercises 39 and 40, convert each sum to a product.*

**39.** $\cos 7\theta + \cos 5\theta + \cos 3\theta + \cos \theta$
*Hint*: The given expression can be written $(\cos 7\theta + \cos 5\theta) + (\cos 3\theta + \cos \theta)$. After converting the quantities in parentheses to products, look for a common term to factor out.
**40.** $\sin 2\theta + \sin 4\theta + \sin 6\theta + \sin 8\theta$
**41. (a)** Express the quantity $\sqrt{2} \, [\sin(x/2) + \cos(x/2)]$ in the form $A \cos(Bx - C)$.
   **(b)** Use your result in part (a) to graph the function $f(x) = \sqrt{2}[\sin(x/2) + \cos(x/2)]$ for two complete cycles. Specify the amplitude, period, and phase shift.

**B**

42. **(a)** Derive the product-to-sum formula for $\cos A \cos B$.
    *Hint*: Add equations (1) and (2) in the text on page 599.

    **(b)** Derive the product-to-sum formula for $\sin A \cos B$.
    *Hint*: Start by writing down the two addition formulas for $\sin(A + B)$ and $\sin(A - B)$, then add the two equations.

43. Derive the sum-to-product formula for $\cos \alpha + \cos \beta$.
    *Hint*: Follow the method used in the text to derive the formula for $\cos \alpha - \cos \beta$, but rather than beginning with equation (3), begin instead with $\cos A \cos B = \frac{1}{2}[\cos(A - B) + \cos(A + B)]$.

44. Derive the sum-to-product formula for $\sin \alpha + \sin \beta$.
    *Hint*: Follow the method used in the text to derive the formula for $\cos \alpha - \cos \beta$, but rather than beginning with equation (3), begin instead with $\sin A \cos B = \frac{1}{2}[\sin(A - B) + \sin(A + B)]$.

45. Derive the sum-to-product formula for $\sin \alpha - \sin \beta$.
    *Hint*: In the formula for $\sin \alpha + \sin \beta$ (which we derived in Exercise 44), replace each occurrence of $\beta$ with $-\beta$.

46. For this exercise, follow steps (a) through (c) to show that

$$\cos \frac{\pi}{7} \cos \frac{2\pi}{7} \cos \frac{3\pi}{7} = \frac{1}{8}$$

   **(a)** Start with the expression on the left side of the given equation and multiply both the numerator and the denominator by the quantity $\sin \frac{\pi}{7}$. Show that the resulting expression can be written as

$$\frac{\frac{1}{2} \sin \frac{2\pi}{7} \cos \frac{2\pi}{7} \cos \frac{3\pi}{7}}{\sin \frac{\pi}{7}}$$

   **(b)** Explain why the expression obtained in part (a) is equal to

$$\frac{\frac{1}{4} \sin \frac{4\pi}{7} \cos \frac{3\pi}{7}}{\sin \frac{\pi}{7}}$$

   **(c)** Now use a product-to-sum formula to simplify the numerator of the expression in part (b). Then conclude that the original expression is indeed equal to 1/8, as we wished to show.

47. The following problem appears in *Problems in Elementary Mathematics* by V. Lidsky et al. (Moscow: MIR Publishers, 1973).

Simplify the following expression:

$$\frac{1}{2 \sin 10°} - 2 \sin 70°$$

**C**

*In Exercises 48–50, assume that $A + B + C = 180°$. Prove that each equation is an identity.*

48. $\sin 2A + \sin 2B + \sin 2C = 4 \sin A \sin B \sin C$
49. $\cos A + \cos B + \cos C = 1 + 4 \sin(A/2) \sin(B/2) \sin(C/2)$
50. $\sin A + \sin B + \sin C = 4 \cos(A/2) \cos(B/2) \cos(C/2)$
51. **(a)** The accompanying figure shows three triangles. For each triangle, use a calculator to verify that the sum of the cosines of the angles of the triangle is less than 3/2.

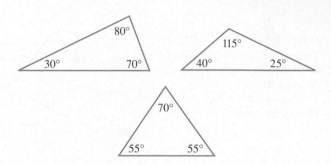

   **(b)** What is the sum of the cosines of the three angles in an equilateral triangle?

   **(c)** Let $A$, $B$, and $C$ denote the three angles of a triangle, so that $A + B + C = 180°$. The following sequence of steps proves the inequality $\cos A + \cos B + \cos C \leq 3/2$. Supply the reasons or calculations that support each step. [The proof, by W. O. J. Moser, appeared in *The American Mathematical Monthly*, vol. 67 (1960), p. 695.]

   **(i)** $\cos A + \cos B + \cos C$
   $= 2 \cos[(A + B)/2] \cos[(A - B)/2] + \cos C$
   **(ii)** $\leq 2 \cos[(A + B)/2] + \cos C$
   **(iii)** $= 2 \cos[(180° - C)/2] + \cos C$
   **(iv)** $= 2 \cos[90° - (C/2)] + \cos C$
   **(v)** $= 2 \sin(C/2) + [1 - 2 \sin^2(C/2)]$
   **(vi)** $= (3/2) - 2[\sin(C/2) - (1/2)]^2$
   **(vii)** $\leq 3/2$

# PROJECT

## SUPERPOSITION

In Example 5 of Section 8.3 we saw how to use a sum-to-product formula to combine a cosine wave and a sine wave with the same amplitude, the same period, and no phase shift into a single cosine wave with the same period but a bigger amplitude and a phase shift. By using exactly the same argument, you can show that

$$a \cos Bx + a \sin Bx = \sqrt{2}a \cos\left(Bx - \frac{\pi}{4}\right)$$

What happens if the original waves have different amplitudes? The previous approach does not apply because to use a sum-to-product formula requires that the original waves have the same amplitude. It is not hard to imagine that we should obtain a single wave with a bigger amplitude and the same period. It turns out that the new cosine wave will exhibit a phase shift.

Let's assume that there is a way to combine the waves as desired and see what that requires. So suppose that

$$a \cos Bx + b \sin Bx = A \cos(Bx + C) \qquad \text{(i)}$$

Here we assume that $a$, $b$, and $B$ are constants with $B$ positive and $a$ and $b$ nonzero. We want to express $A$ and $C$ in terms of $a$ and $b$. Using the cosine addition formula to expand $\cos(Bx + C)$, we have

$$\cos(Bx + C) = \cos Bx \cos C - \sin Bx \sin C$$

Substituting this into the right-hand side of equation (i) and rearranging, we obtain

$$a \cos Bx + b \sin Bx = (A \cos C) \cos Bx + (-A \sin C) \sin Bx \qquad \text{(ii)}$$

We want to choose $A$ and $C$ so that equation (ii) is true for all real numbers, that is, equation (ii) is an identity. Comparing the numerical coefficients of $\cos Bx$ and $\sin Bx$ on both sides of equation (ii), we choose $A$ and $C$ such that

$$A \cos C = a \qquad \text{and} \qquad -A \sin C = b \qquad \text{(iii)}$$

For equation (ii) to be an identity, it can be shown that these are in fact the *only* possible choices for $A$ and $C$. (We will use a similar argument in our discussion of partial fractions in Chapter 12.) Equations (iii) imply that

$$\begin{aligned} a^2 + b^2 &= (A \cos C)^2 + (-A \sin C)^2 \\ &= A^2 \cos^2 C + A^2 \sin^2 C \\ &= A^2 (\cos^2 C + \sin^2 C) \\ &= A^2 \end{aligned}$$

Let's take $A = \sqrt{a^2 + b^2}$. Equations (iii) also imply that

$$\frac{b}{a} = \frac{-A \sin C}{A \cos C} = -\tan C$$

Let's take $C$ in the open interval between $-\pi/2$ and $\pi/2$ so that $\tan C = -b/a$. These conditions allow us to find a unique number for $C$. (See Section 8.5 on inverse trigonometric functions for a discussion of the inverse tangent function.) The notation $C = \tan^{-1}(-b/a)$ means "$C$ is the unique number in the interval $(-\frac{\pi}{2}, \frac{\pi}{2})$ such that $\tan C = -b/a$." $C$ can be numerically approximated using the inverse tangent function on your calculator. We summarize

$$a \cos Bx + b \sin Bx = A \cos(Bx + C)$$

where

$$A = \sqrt{a^2 + b^2} \quad \text{and} \quad C = \tan^{-1}\left(-\frac{b}{a}\right) \qquad \text{(iv)}$$

The process of adding wave functions is called **superposition** and (iv) is an example of a **superposition formula.** Superposition is an essential feature of many physical phenomena involving waves, including acoustics (sound waves), optics (electromagnetic waves), radio (also electromagnetic waves), and surface waves (water waves). The exercises below use and extend the concepts developed on superposition.

## EXERCISES

1. Use the method of Example 5 in Section 8.3 to show

$$a \cos Bx + a \sin Bx = \sqrt{2}a \cos\left(Bx - \frac{\pi}{4}\right)$$

2. Use formula (iv) to redo problem 1.
3. **(a)** Use formula (iv) to show that $3 \cos 4x + \sqrt{3} \sin 4x = 2\sqrt{3} \cos(4x - \frac{\pi}{6})$.
   **(b)** Use a graphing utility to graph the left-hand side of the identity in part (a), and estimate the amplitude and phase shift. How do your estimates compare with the exact values?
4. **(a)** Use formula (iv) to show $2 \cos 3x + 5 \sin 3x = \sqrt{29} \cos(3x + C)$, where $C$ is in the interval $(-\frac{\pi}{2}, \frac{\pi}{2})$ and $\tan C = -5/2$.
   **(b)** Use a calculator to find $C$ correct to two decimal places.
   **(c)** Use a graphing utility to graph the left-hand side of the identity in part (a) and estimate the amplitude and phase shift. How do your estimates compare with the values from (a) and (b)?
5. What happens if the waves have different phase shifts? Use the method of derivation of formula (iv) to show that

$$a \cos(Bx + D) + b \sin(Bx + E) = A \cos(Bx + C)$$

where

$$A = \sqrt{a^2 + b^2 + 2ab \sin(E - D)}$$

and

$$\tan C = -\frac{b \cos E - a \sin D}{a \cos D + b \sin E} \quad \text{with } C \text{ in } (-\frac{\pi}{2}, \frac{\pi}{2})$$

## 8.4 TRIGONOMETRIC EQUATIONS

In this section we consider some techniques for solving equations involving the trigonometric functions. As usual, by a **solution** or **root** of an equation we mean a value of the variable for which the equation becomes a true statement.

| EXAMPLE 1 | Determining whether a given number is a solution of a trigonometric equation |
|---|---|

Consider the trigonometric equation $\sin x + \cos x = 1$. Is $x = \pi/4$ a solution? Is $x = \pi/2$ a solution?

**SOLUTION**
To see whether the value $x = \pi/4$ satisfies the given equation, we write

$$\sin \frac{\pi}{4} + \cos \frac{\pi}{4} \stackrel{?}{=} 1$$
$$\frac{\sqrt{2}}{2} + \frac{\sqrt{2}}{2} \stackrel{?}{=} 1$$
$$\sqrt{2} \stackrel{?}{=} 1 \quad (\text{No})$$

Thus $x = \pi/4$ is not a solution. In a similar fashion we can check to see whether $x = \pi/2$ is a solution:

$$\sin \frac{\pi}{2} + \cos \frac{\pi}{2} \stackrel{?}{=} 1$$
$$1 + 0 \stackrel{?}{=} 1 \quad (\text{Yes})$$

Thus $x = \pi/2$ is a solution.

The example that we've just concluded serves to remind us of the difference between a *conditional equation* and an *identity*. An identity is true for all values of the variable in its domain. For example, the equation $\sin^2 t + \cos^2 t = 1$ is an identity: It is true for every real number $t$. In contrast to this, a conditional equation is true only for some (or perhaps even none) of the values of the variable. The equation in Example 1 is a conditional equation; we saw that it is false when $x = \pi/4$ and true when $x = \pi/2$. The equation $\sin t = 2$ is an example of a conditional equation that has no solution. (Why?) The equations that we are going to solve in this section are conditional equations that involve the trigonometric functions. In general, there is no single technique that can be used to solve every trigonometric equation. In the examples that follow, we illustrate some of the more common approaches to solving trigonometric equations. As background for Example 2, you should review Example 2 in Section 7.4. (In that example we obtained solutions for the trigonometric equation $\cos x = 0.8$.)

| EXAMPLE 2 | Solving a trigonometric equation |
|---|---|

Consider the equation

$$\sin x = \frac{1}{2} \tag{1}$$

(a) Use your knowledge of the sine function (and not a calculator) to find all solutions of equation (1) in the open interval $(0, 2\pi)$.

(b) Use a calculator to find all solutions of equation (1) in the open interval $(0, 2\pi)$. Check that the answers are consistent with those in part (a).

(c) Find all real-number solutions of equation (1).

**SOLUTION**

(a) First of all, we know from earlier work that $\sin(\pi/6) = 1/2$. So one solution of equation (1) is certainly $x_1 = \pi/6$. To find another solution, we note that in Quadrant II, as well as in Quadrant I, $\sin x$ is positive. In Quadrant II the angle with a reference angle of $\pi/6$ is $5\pi/6$; see Figure 1. Thus $\sin(5\pi/6) = 1/2$, and we conclude that $x_2 = 5\pi/6$ is also a solution of equation (1). Since $\sin x$ is negative in Quadrants III and IV, we needn't look there for solutions. In summary, then, the solutions of the equation $\sin x = 1/2$ in the open interval $(0, 2\pi)$ are $x_1 = \pi/6$ and $x_2 = 5\pi/6$.

(b) We can determine a root of equation (1) by using a calculator and the *inverse sine function*, denoted by $\sin^{-1}$. Applying the inverse sine function to both sides of equation (1) yields

$$\sin^{-1}(\sin x) = \sin^{-1}\left(\frac{1}{2}\right)$$

and therefore

$$x = \sin^{-1}\left(\frac{1}{2}\right)$$

Now we use a calculator, set in the radian mode, to evaluate the expression $\sin^{-1}(1/2)$. (If these keystrokes don't work on your calculator, be sure to check the instruction manual.)

| EXPRESSION | KEYSTROKES | OUTPUT |
|---|---|---|
| $\sin^{-1}(0.5)$ | [2nd] [sin] 0.5 [ENTER] | 0.52359 . . . |

This gives us a root 0.52359 . . . for equation (1). Indeed, this is the decimal approximation for the root $x_1 = \pi/6$ that we determined in part (a). Take a moment to confirm this fact; that is, use your calculator to verify that $\pi/6 = 0.52359. . . .$

As explained in part (a), there is another root, one in Quadrant II. Taking the calculator value 0.52359 . . . for our reference angle, the second-quadrant root then is

$$\pi - 0.52359 . . . = 2.61799 . . .$$

This is the decimal approximation for the root $x_2 = 5\pi/6$ that we determined in part (a). (Use your calculator to verify that $5\pi/6 = 2.61799. . . .$)

(c) We can use the results in part (a), along with the fact that the sine function is periodic, to specify all real number solutions for the given equation. Since the period of the sine function is $2\pi$, we have

$$\sin(x + 2k\pi) = \sin x \qquad \text{for every integer } k$$

Consequently, since $\sin \frac{\pi}{6} = \frac{1}{2}$, we know that $\sin(\frac{\pi}{6} + 2k\pi)$ is also equal to $1/2$. In other words, for every integer $k$ the quantity $\pi/6 + 2k\pi$ is a solu-

**Figure 1**

$$\sin \frac{\pi}{6} = \sin \frac{5\pi}{6} = \frac{1}{2}$$

tion of the given equation. Following the same reasoning, the quantity $5\pi/6 + 2k\pi$ is also a solution of the given equation for every integer $k$. In summary, there are infinitely many real-number solutions of the equation $\sin x = 1/2$. These solutions are given by the expressions

$$\frac{\pi}{6} + 2k\pi \quad \text{and} \quad \frac{5\pi}{6} + 2k\pi \quad \text{where } k \text{ is an integer}$$

Figure 2 shows some of these solutions; they are the $x$-coordinates of the points where the sine curve intersects the line $y = 1/2$.

**GRAPHICAL PERSPECTIVE**

**Figure 2**
A view of the curve $y - \sin x$ for $-1.5\pi \le x \le 3.5\pi$

The $x$-coordinates of the points where the curve $y = \sin x$ intersects the line $y = 1/2$ are solutions of the equation $\sin x = 1/2$. This view shows five of the solutions: $-7\pi/6, \pi/6, 5\pi/6, 13\pi/6,$ and $17\pi/6$.

In part (b) of the example just concluded, we indicated how the inverse sine function can be used to solve a simple trigonometric equation. In the next section the inverse sine function is analyzed in detail. But for our present work with this function, you need to know only the following definition:

$\sin^{-1}(x)$ denotes the unique number in the interval $\left[-\frac{\pi}{2}, \frac{\pi}{2}\right]$ whose sine is $x$.

As examples of this definition, we have

$$\sin^{-1}\!\left(\frac{\sqrt{3}}{2}\right) = \frac{\pi}{3} \qquad \text{since } \pi/3 \text{ is the unique number in the interval } \left[-\frac{\pi}{2}, \frac{\pi}{2}\right] \text{ whose sine is } \sqrt{3}/2$$

$$\sin^{-1}\!\left(\frac{\sqrt{3}}{2}\right) \ne \frac{2\pi}{3} \qquad \text{Although } \sin(2\pi/3) = \sqrt{3}/2, \text{ the number } 2\pi/3 \text{ is not in the required interval } \left[-\frac{\pi}{2}, \frac{\pi}{2}\right].$$

For some of the exercises in this section you'll need to use the inverse cosine function (which we worked with in Section 7.4) or the *inverse tangent function,* rather than the inverse sine function that we've just been discussing. For reference we define the three functions in the box that follows. (All three functions are discussed at greater length in the next section.)

| DEFINITION | Inverse Trigonometric Functions | |
|---|---|---|
| **NAME OF FUNCTION** | **ABBREVIATION** | **DEFINITION** |
| Inverse cosine | $\cos^{-1}$ | $\cos^{-1}(x)$ is the unique number in the interval $[0, \pi]$ whose cosine is $x$. |
| Inverse sine | $\sin^{-1}$ | $\sin^{-1}(x)$ is the unique number in the interval $\left[-\frac{\pi}{2}, \frac{\pi}{2}\right]$ whose sine is $x$. |
| Inverse tangent | $\tan^{-1}$ | $\tan^{-1}(x)$ is the unique number in the interval $\left(-\frac{\pi}{2}, \frac{\pi}{2}\right)$ whose tangent is $x$. |

The next two examples show how factoring can be used to solve a trigonometric equation.

### EXAMPLE 3 Solving a trigonometric equation by factoring

Find all real-number solutions of the equation

$$\cos^2 x + \cos x - 2 = 0$$

**SOLUTION**
By factoring the expression on the left-hand side, we obtain

$$(\cos x + 2)(\cos x - 1) = 0$$

Therefore

$$\cos x = -2 \quad \text{or} \quad \cos x = 1$$

We discard the result $\cos x = -2$ because the value of $\cos x$ is never less than $-1$. From the equation $\cos x = 1$ we conclude that $x = 0$ is the only solution in the interval $[0, 2\pi)$. Since the cosine function has period $2\pi$, all solutions are given by $x = 0 + 2\pi k = 2\pi k$, where $k$ is an integer.

### EXAMPLE 4 Solving a trigonometric equation by factoring

Find all solutions of the equation $\tan^2 \theta + \tan \theta - 6 = 0$ in the interval $[0, 2\pi]$. Round the final answers to three decimal places.

**SOLUTION**
By factoring, we have

$$(\tan \theta - 2)(\tan \theta + 3) = 0$$

and therefore

$$\tan \theta = 2 \quad \text{or} \quad \tan \theta = -3$$

Applying the inverse tangent function to both sides of the equation $\tan \theta = 2$ gives us

$$\tan^{-1}(\tan \theta) = \tan^{-1}(2)$$

and, consequently,

$$\theta = \tan^{-1}(2)$$
$$\approx 1.107 \qquad \text{using a calculator set in the radian mode}$$

Now, since the period of the tangent function is $\pi$, we can find another root of the equation $\tan \theta = 2$ just by adding $\pi$ to the root $\tan^{-1}(2)$. This gives us

$$\tan^{-1}(2) + \pi \approx 4.249 \qquad \text{using a calculator set in the radian mode}$$

Note that this root is also in the required interval $[0, 2\pi]$. However, adding $\pi$ again to this value will take us out of the interval $[0, 2\pi]$. So let's turn to the other equation that we obtained through factoring: $\tan \theta = -3$. Applying the inverse tangent function to both sides of the equation $\tan \theta = -3$ gives us

$$\tan^{-1}(\tan \theta) = \tan^{-1}(-3)$$

and therefore

$$\begin{aligned} \theta &= \tan^{-1}(-3) \\ &= -1.2490457\ldots \qquad \text{using a calculator} \end{aligned}$$

Although this last value is a root of the equation $\tan \theta = -3$, it is not in the required interval $[0, 2\pi]$. To generate a root that does belong to this interval, we add $\pi$ (the period of the tangent function) to the quantity $\tan^{-1}(-3)$ to obtain

$$\tan^{-1}(-3) + \pi \approx 1.893 \qquad \text{using a calculator}$$

Still another root can be obtained by again adding $\pi$.

$$\tan^{-1}(-3) + 2\pi \approx 5.034$$

Adding $\pi$ again would take us out of the interval $[0, 2\pi]$, so we stop here. Let's summarize our results. In the interval $[0, 2\pi]$ there are four roots of the equation $\tan^2 \theta + \tan \theta - 6 = 0$. They are

$$\begin{aligned} \tan^{-1}(2) &\approx 1.107 \\ \tan^{-1}(2) + \pi &\approx 4.249 \\ \tan^{-1}(-3) + \pi &\approx 1.893 \\ \tan^{-1}(-3) + 2\pi &\approx 5.034 \end{aligned}$$

For a graphical check of these results, see Figure 3, which shows the graph of the equation $y = \tan^2 \theta + \tan \theta - 6$. The $\theta$-intercepts of the graph are the roots of the equation $\tan^2 \theta + \tan \theta - 6 = 0$. In the figure, note that each intercept is consistent with one of the roots that we have determined. For instance, the largest intercept in Figure 3 is approximately 5.0. This corresponds to the root $\tan^{-1}(-3) + 2\pi \approx 5.034$.

## GRAPHICAL PERSPECTIVE

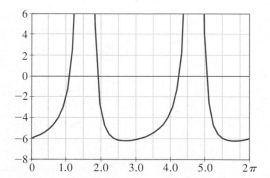

**Figure 3**
A view of $y = \tan^2 \theta + \tan \theta - 6$
for $0 \le \theta \le 2\pi$

In some equations more than one trigonometric function is present. A common approach here is to express the various functions in terms of a single function. The next example demonstrates this technique.

**EXAMPLE 5** **Using a trigonometric identity to solve an equation**

Find all real-number solutions of the equation

$$3 \tan^2 x - \sec^2 x - 5 = 0$$

**SOLUTION**

We use the Pythagorean identity $\tan^2 x + 1 = \sec^2 x$ to substitute for $\sec^2 x$ in the given equation. This gives us

$$3 \tan^2 x - (\tan^2 x + 1) - 5 = 0$$
$$2 \tan^2 x - 6 = 0$$
$$2 \tan^2 x = 6$$
$$\tan^2 x = 3$$
$$\tan x = \pm \sqrt{3}$$

Since the period of the tangent function is $\pi$, we need to find only those values of $x$ between 0 and $\pi$ that satisfy $\tan x = \pm \sqrt{3}$. The other solutions will then be obtained by adding multiples of $\pi$ to these solutions. Now, in Quadrant I the tangent is positive, and we know that $\tan x = \sqrt{3}$ when $x = \pi/3$. In Quadrant II $\tan x$ is negative, and we know that $\tan 2\pi/3 = -\sqrt{3}$, since the reference angle for $2\pi/3$ is $\pi/3$. Thus the solutions between 0 and $\pi$ are $x = \pi/3$ and $x = 2\pi/3$. It follows that all of the solutions to the equation $3 \tan^2 x - \sec^2 x - 5 = 0$ are given by

$$x = \frac{\pi}{3} + \pi k \qquad \text{and} \qquad x = \frac{2\pi}{3} + \pi k \qquad \text{where } k \text{ is an integer}$$

The technique used in Example 5, that is, expressing the various functions in terms of a single function, is most useful when it does not involve introducing a radical expression. For instance, consider the equation $\sin s + \cos s = 1$. Although we could begin by replacing $\cos s$ by the expression $\pm \sqrt{1 - \sin^2 s}$, it turns out to be easier in this situation to begin by squaring both sides of the given equation. This is done in the next example.

**EXAMPLE 6** **Squaring both sides to solve a trigonometric equation**

Find all solutions of the equation $\sin s + \cos s = 1$ satisfying $0° \leq s < 360°$.

**SOLUTION**

Squaring both sides of the equation yields

$$(\sin s + \cos s)^2 = 1^2$$
$$\sin^2 s + 2 \sin s \cos s + \cos^2 s = 1$$

⌐⎯ These add to 1. ⎯⌐

Consequently, we have

$$2 \sin s \cos s = 0$$

From this last equation we conclude that $\sin s = 0$ or $\cos s = 0$. When $\sin s = 0$, we know that $s = 0°$ or $s = 180°$. And when $\cos s = 0$, we know that $s = 90°$ or $s = 270°$. Now we must go back and check which (if any) of these values is a solution to the *original* equation. This must be done because squaring both sides in the process of solving an equation may introduce extraneous roots.

| | | |
|---|---|---|
| $s = 0°$ | $\sin 0° + \cos 0° \overset{?}{=} 1$ | |
| | $0 + 1 \overset{?}{=} 1$ | True |
| $s = 90°$ | $\sin 90° + \cos 90° \overset{?}{=} 1$ | |
| | $1 + 0 \overset{?}{=} 1$ | True |
| $s = 180°$ | $\sin 180° + \cos 180° \overset{?}{=} 1$ | |
| | $0 + (-1) \overset{?}{=} 1$ | False |
| $s = 270°$ | $\sin 270° + \cos 270° \overset{?}{=} 1$ | |
| | $-1 + 0 \overset{?}{=} 1$ | False |

We conclude that the only solutions of the equation $\sin s + \cos s = 1$ on the interval $0° \le s < 360°$ are $s = 0°$ and $s = 90°$.

*Note*: The equation $2 \sin s \cos s = 0$ is equivalent to $\sin 2s = 0$. (Why?) Then $2s = 0°$ or $180°$. So $s = 0°$ or $90°$. As before, both are solutions of the equation.

In the example that follows, we consider an equation that involves a multiple of the unknown angle.

| EXAMPLE | 7 | Solving a trigonometric equation that involves a multiple of an angle |
|---|---|---|

Solve the equation $\sin 3x = 1$ on the interval $0 \le x \le 2\pi$.

**SOLUTION**
We know that $\sin(\pi/2) = 1$. Thus one solution can be found by writing $3x = \pi/2$, from which we conclude that $x = \pi/6$. We can look for other solutions in the required interval by writing, more generally,

$$3x = \frac{\pi}{2} + 2\pi k$$
$$= \frac{\pi + 4\pi k}{2}$$

and therefore

$$x = \frac{\pi + 4\pi k}{6}$$

Thus when $k = 1$, we obtain

$$x = \frac{\pi + 4\pi(1)}{6} = \frac{5\pi}{6}$$

With $k = 2$ we have

$$x = \frac{\pi + 4\pi(2)}{6} = \frac{9\pi}{6} = \frac{3\pi}{2}$$

And with $k = 3$ we have

$$x = \frac{\pi + 4\pi(3)}{6} = \frac{13\pi}{6} \qquad \text{which is greater than } 2\pi$$

We conclude that the solutions of $\sin 3x = 1$ on the interval $0 \le x \le 2\pi$ are $\pi/6, 5\pi/6$, and $3\pi/2$.

In Example 7, notice that we did not need to make use of a formula for $\sin 3x$, even though the expression $\sin 3x$ did appear in the given equation. In the next example, however, we do make use of the identity $\sin 2x = 2 \sin x \cos x$.

| EXAMPLE | 8 | Transforming an equation in order to use a trigonometric identity |

Solve the equation $\sin x \cos x = 1$.

**SOLUTION**
We could begin by squaring both sides. (See Exercise 83.) However, with the double-angle formula for sine in mind, we can proceed as follows. We multiply both sides of the given equation by 2. This yields

$$2 \sin x \cos x = 2$$

and, consequently,

$$\sin 2x = 2 \qquad \text{using the double-angle formula}$$

This last equation has no solution, since the value of the sine function never exceeds 1. Thus the equation $\sin x \cos x = 1$ has no solution.

For the last example in this section we look at another case in which a calculator is required.

| EXAMPLE | 9 | Transforming an equation in both sine and cosine to an equation in only the tangent function |

Find all angles $\theta$ in the interval $0° \le \theta \le 360°$ that satisfy the following equation: $2 \sin \theta = \cos \theta$.

**SOLUTION**
We first want to rewrite the given equation using a single function, rather than both sine and cosine. The easiest way to do this is to divide both sides by $\cos \theta$. Nothing is lost here in assuming $\cos \theta \ne 0$. (If $\cos \theta$ were zero, then $\theta$ would be 90° or 270°; but neither of those angles is a solution of the given equation.) Dividing both sides of the given equation by $\cos \theta$, we have

$$\frac{2 \sin \theta}{\cos \theta} = \frac{\cos \theta}{\cos \theta}$$
$$2 \tan \theta = 1$$
$$\tan \theta = 0.5$$

From experience we know that none of the angles with which we are familiar (the multiples of 30° and 45°) has a value of 0.5 for the tangent. Therefore, as in Example 4, we use the inverse tangent function and a calculator. First, applying the inverse tangent function to both sides of the equation $\tan \theta = 0.5$, we have

$$\tan^{-1}(\tan \theta) = \tan^{-1}(0.5)$$

and therefore

$$\theta = \tan^{-1}(0.5)$$

Now, according to the statement of the problem, our answers are to be in degrees, not radians. So before using the calculator to evaluate the expression $\tan^{-1}(0.5)$, we first set the calculator in the degree mode. Then, as you should check for yourself, we obtain

$$\theta = \tan^{-1}(0.5) \approx 26.6° \qquad \text{using a calculator set in the degree mode}$$

To find another angle $\theta$ satisfying the equation $\tan \theta = 0.5$, we use the fact that the period of the tangent is $\pi$ radians, which is 180°. Thus a second solution (rounded to one decimal place) is

$$26.6° + 180° = 206.6°$$

Adding another 180° to this last value will take us out of the specified interval $0° \le \theta \le 360°$, so we stop here. In summary, there are two angles between 0° and 360° satisfying the given equation $2 \sin \theta = \cos \theta$. They are approximately, to one decimal place, 26.6° and 206.6°. For a graphical check of these results, see Figure 4, which shows the graphs of the equations $y = 2 \sin \theta$ and $y = \cos \theta$ for $0° \le \theta \le 360°$. (In Figure 4 we are viewing the horizontal axis as the $\theta$-axis, where $\theta$ is measured in degrees.) The graphs intersect at two points. The $\theta$-coordinates of these points are solutions of the equation $2 \sin \theta = \cos \theta$. The figure shows that at one of the intersection points, $\theta$ is slightly less than 30°, while at the other intersection point, $\theta$ is slightly less than 210°. These observations are consistent with the numerical values that we have obtained for the roots.

GRAPHICAL PERSPECTIVE

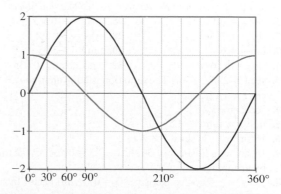

**Figure 4**
Graphs of $y = 2 \sin \theta$ and
$y = \cos \theta$ for $0° \le \theta \le 360°$

# EXERCISE SET 8.4  ⬤www

## A

1. Is $\theta = \pi/2$ a solution of $2\cos^2\theta - 3\cos\theta = 0$?
2. Is $x = 15°$ a solution of $(\sqrt{3}/3)\cos 2x + \sin 2x = 1$?
3. Is $x = 3\pi/4$ a solution of $\tan^2 x - 3\tan x + 2 = 0$?
4. Is $t = 2\pi/3$ a solution of $2\sin t + 2\cos t = \sqrt{3} - 1$?

*In Exercises 5–22, determine all solutions of the given equations. Express your answers using radian measure.*

5. $\sin\theta = \sqrt{3}/2$
6. $\sin\theta = \sqrt{2}/2$
7. $\sin\theta = -1/2$
8. $\sin\theta + (\sqrt{2}/2) = 0$
9. $\cos\theta = -1$
10. $\cos\theta = 1/2$
11. $\tan\theta = \sqrt{3}$
12. $\tan\theta + (\sqrt{3}/3) = 0$
13. $\tan x = 0$
14. $2\sin^2 x - 3\sin x + 1 = 0$
15. $2\cos^2\theta + \cos\theta = 0$
16. $\sin^2 x - \sin x - 6 = 0$
17. $\cos^2 t \sin t - \sin t = 0$
18. $\cos\theta + 2\sec\theta = -3$
19. $2\cos^2 x - \sin x - 1 = 0$
20. $2\cot^2 x + \csc^2 x - 2 = 0$
21. $\sqrt{3}\sin t - \sqrt{1 + \sin^2 t} = 0$
22. $\sec\alpha + \tan\alpha = \sqrt{3}$

Ⓖ 23. **(a)** Graph the equation $y = \cos^2 x + \cos x - 2$. Use a viewing rectangle extending from 0 to 10 in the $x$-direction and from $-3$ to 3 in the $y$-direction.
    **(b)** The picture obtained in part (a) indicates that the graph has an $x$-intercept between 6 and 7. By zooming in on this $x$-intercept, or by using a solve key, obtain the first two decimal places of this intercept.
    **(c)** According to Example 3, what is the exact value of the $x$-intercept that you approximated in part (b)?

Ⓖ 24. **(a)** Graph the equation $y = \tan^2 x + \tan x - 6$ for $0 \le x \le 2\pi$.
    **(b)** By zooming in on each $x$-intercept of the graph in part (a), estimate the roots of the equation $\tan^2 x + \tan x - 6 = 0$. Then check that your estimates are consistent with the values obtained in Example 4.

*In Exercises 25–38, use a calculator to find all solutions in the interval $(0, 2\pi)$. Round the answers to two decimal places.*

25. $\cos x = 0.184$
26. $\cos t = -0.567$
27. $\sin x = 1/\sqrt{5}$
28. $\sin t = -0.301$
29. $\tan x = 6$
30. $\tan t = -5.25$
31. $\sin t = 5\cos t$
32. $\sin x \cos x = 0.035$
33. $\sec t = 2.24$   *Hint*: The equation is equivalent to $\cos t = 1/(2.24)$.
34. $\cot x = -3.27$
35. $\tan^2 x + \tan x - 12 = 0$
36. $15\sin^2 x - 26\sin x + 8 = 0$
37. $16\sin^3 x - 12\sin^2 x + 36\sin x - 27 = 0$   *Hint*: Factor by grouping.
38. $3\cos^3 x - 9\cos^2 x + \cos x - 3 = 0$   *Hint*: Factor by grouping.

*In Exercises 39–44, find all solutions in the interval $0° \le \theta \le 360°$. Where necessary, use a calculator and round to one decimal place.*

39. $\sin\theta = 1/4$
40. $\cos\theta = -4/5$
41. $9\tan^2\theta - 16 = 0$
42. $5\sin^2\theta + 13\sin\theta - 6 = 0$
43. $\cos^2\theta - \cos\theta - 1 = 0$   *Hint*: You'll need to use the quadratic formula.
44. $\tan^2\theta - \tan\theta - 1 = 0$

*In Exercises 45–52, determine all of the solutions in the interval $0° \le \theta < 360°$.*

45. $\cos 3\theta = 1$
46. $\tan 2\theta = -1$
47. $\sin 3\theta = -\sqrt{2}/2$
48. $\sin(\theta/2) = 1/2$
49. $\sin 2\theta = -2\cos\theta$
50. $2\sin^2\theta - \cos 2\theta = 0$
51. $\sin 2\theta = \sqrt{3}\cos 2\theta$   *Hint*: Divide by $\cos 2\theta$.
52. $\sin\theta = \cos(\theta/2)$.   *Hint*: $\sin\theta = 2\sin(\theta/2)\cos(\theta/2)$

Ⓖ *In Exercises 53–74, solve the equations on the interval $[0, 2\pi]$ as follows. Graph the expression on each side of the equation and then zoom in on the intersection points until you are certain of the first three decimal places in each answer. For instance, for Exercise 53, when you graph the two equations $y = \cos x$ and $y = 0.623$ on the interval $[0, 2\pi]$, you'll see that there are two intersection points. The $x$-coordinates of these points are roots of the equation $\cos x = 0.623$.*

53. $\cos x = 0.623$
54. $\sin x = -0.438$
55. $\cos x = \tan x$
56. $\cos x = \tan 2x$
57. $\cos^2 x = 2\sin x$
58. $\cos^3 x = 2\sin x$
59. $\cos 2x + 1 = \cos(2x + 1)$
60. $\cos 2x + 0.9 = \cos(2x + 1)$
61. $\cos(x/2) = \cos(x^2/2)$
62. $\cos(x/2) = \cos(x^2/12)$
63. $2\sin x - 3\cos x = \tan(x/4)$
64. $2\sin x + 3\cos x = \tan(x/4)$
65. $\sqrt{x} = \tan x$
66. $x^2 = \tan x$
67. $\sin(\cos x) = \sin x$
68. $\cos(\sin x) = \sin x$
69. $\tan x = x$
70. $\cos x = x$
71. $\sin^3 x + \cos^3 x = 0.5$
72. $\sin^3 x - \cos^3 x = 0.5$
73. $1 - \tan^2 x = 2\sin(x/5)$
74. $1 - \tan^2 x = 2\sin(x/6)$

## B

75. Find all solutions of the equation $\tan 3x - \tan x = 0$ in the interval $0 \le x < 2\pi$.   *Hint*: Write $\tan 3x = \tan(2x + x)$ and use the addition formula for tangent.
76. Find all solutions of the equation $2\sin x = 1 - \cos x$ in the interval $0° \le x < 360°$. Use a calculator and round the answer(s) to one decimal place.
77. Find all solutions of the equation $\cos(x/2) = 1 + \cos x$ in the interval $0 \le x < 2\pi$.
78. Find all solutions of the equation

$$\sin 3x \cos x + \cos 3x \sin x = \frac{\sqrt{3}}{2}$$

in the interval $0 < x < 2\pi$.

**79.** Find all real numbers $\theta$ for which

$$\sec 4\theta + 2 \sin 4\theta = 0$$

**80.** Consider the equation $\sin^2 x - \cos^2 x = 7/25$.
   **(a)** Solve the equation for $\cos x$.
   **(b)** Find all of the solutions of the equation satisfying $0 < x < \pi$.
   **(c)** Solve the original equation by means of a double-angle formula and use the result to check your answers in part (b).

**81.** Find a solution of the equation $4 \sin \theta - 3 \cos \theta = 2$ in the interval $0° < \theta < 90°$. *Hint:* Add $3 \cos \theta$ to both sides, then square.

**82.** Find all solutions of the equation

$$\sin^3 \theta \cos \theta - \sin \theta \cos^3 \theta = -\frac{1}{4}$$

in the interval $0 < \theta < \pi$. *Hint:* Factor the left-hand side, then use the double-angle formulas.

**83.** Consider the equation $\sin x \cos x = 1$.
   **(a)** Square both sides and then replace $\cos^2 x$ by $1 - \sin^2 x$. Show that the resulting equation can be written $\sin^4 x - \sin^2 x + 1 = 0$.
   **(b)** Show that the equation $\sin^4 x - \sin^2 x + 1 = 0$ has no solutions. Conclude from this that the original equation has no real-number solutions.

**84.** The accompanying figure shows a portion of the graph of the periodic function

$$f(x) = \sin(1 + \sin x)$$

Find the $x$-coordinates of the turning points $P$, $Q$, and $R$. Round the answers to three decimal places. *Hint:* You may use the fact that the $x$-coordinate of $Q$ is halfway between the $x$-coordinates of $P$ and $R$.

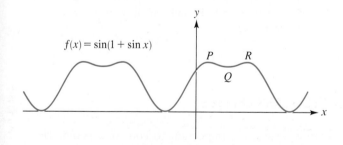

**85.** **(a)** Find the smallest solution of $\cos x = 0.412$ in the interval $(1000, \infty)$. (Round the answer to three decimal places.) *Hint:* Use a calculator to approximate a solution of $\cos x = 0.412$. Use this solution to approximate the other solution in the interval $[0, 2\pi]$. Use these solutions to finish the problem. (Don't round off your intermediate results.)
   **(b)** Find the smallest solution of $\cos x = -0.412$ in the interval $(1000, \infty)$.

**⒢ 86. (a)** Graph the function $y = \sin(\pi x/180)$ in the standard viewing rectangle. Describe what you see.
   **(b)** Change the viewing rectangle so that $x$ extends from 0 to 360. The graph that you obtain is the graph of $y = \sin x$, where $x$ is now measured in degrees.
   **(c)** According to Example 6, there are two solutions of the equation $\sin s + \cos s = 1$ in the interval $0° \le s < 360°$. Confirm this by graphing the two equations

$$y = \sin \frac{\pi x}{180} + \cos \frac{\pi x}{180}$$

   and

$$y = 1 \qquad \text{for } 0 \le x \le 360$$

   and noting that there are two intersection points. (In Example 6 the intersection point at $x = 360$ is excluded.)
   **(d)** In Example 6 we saw that $90°$ is a solution of the equation $\sin s + \cos s = 1$ in the interval $0° \le s < 360°$. Confirm this by zooming in on the appropriate intersection point in part (c) and checking the $x$-coordinate.

**87.** The accompanying figure shows a graph of the function $f(x) = x + 0.4 \sin(2\pi x)$ on the interval $0 \le x \le 1.5$. (Functions of this form occur in mathematical biology in the study of rhythmic behaviors, such as heartbeat.) Using calculus, it can be shown that the $x$-coordinates of the turning points of this function are found by solving the equation

$$1 + 0.8\pi \cos(2\pi x) = 0$$

Use this fact to find the $x$-coordinates of the turning points $P$, $Q$, and $R$ in the figure. Round the answers to three decimal places.

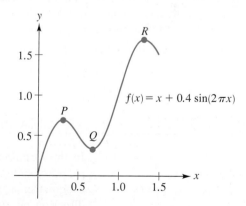

**88.** (As background for this exercise, you need to know the definitions of *fixed point* and *iterate* from Section 4.3.) The figure on the next page shows a view of the function $f(x) = x + 0.4 \sin(2\pi x)$ along with the line $y = x$.

(a) From the figure it appears that the value $x = 0.5$ is a fixed point for the function $f$. Confirm this algebraically by solving the equation $f(x) = x$ on the interval $0 \le x \le 1$.

(b) Compute the first ten iterates of $x_0 = 0.25$ under the function $f$. Round the answers to four decimal places. Describe any patterns that you detect. Are the iterates approaching the fixed point $x = 0.5$?

(c) Follow part (b) using $x_0 = 0.45$.

## C

89. In this exercise you will see how certain cubic equations can be solved by using the following identity (which we proved in Example 3 in Section 8.2):

$$4 \cos^3 \theta - 3 \cos \theta = \cos 3\theta \qquad (1)$$

For example, suppose that we wish to solve the equation

$$8x^3 - 6x - 1 = 0 \qquad (2)$$

To transform this equation into a form in which the stated identity is useful, we make the substitution $x = a \cos \theta$, where $a$ is a constant to be determined. With this substitution, equation (2) can be written

$$8a^3 \cos^3 \theta - 6a \cos \theta = 1 \qquad (3)$$

In equation (3) the coefficient of $\cos^3 \theta$ is $8a^3$. Since we want this coefficient to be 4 [as it is in equation (1)], we divide both sides of equation (3) by $2a^3$ to obtain

$$4 \cos^3 \theta - \frac{3}{a^2} \cos \theta = \frac{1}{2a^3} \qquad (4)$$

Next, a comparison of equations (4) and (1) leads us to require that $3/a^2 = 3$. Thus $a = \pm 1$. For convenience we choose $a = 1$; equation (4) then becomes

$$4 \cos^3 \theta - 3 \cos \theta = \frac{1}{2} \qquad (5)$$

Comparing equation (5) with the identity in (1) leads us to the equation

$$\cos 3\theta = \frac{1}{2}$$

As you can check, the solutions here are of the form

$$\theta = 20° + 120k° \qquad \text{and} \qquad \theta = 100° + 120k°$$

Thus

$$x = \cos(20° + 120k°) \qquad \text{and} \qquad x = \cos(100° + 120k°)$$

Now, however, as you can again check, only three of the angles yield distinct values for $\cos \theta$, namely, $\theta = 20°$, $\theta = 140°$, and $\theta = 260°$. Thus the solutions of the equation $8x^3 - 6x - 1 = 0$ are given by $x = \cos 20°$, $x = \cos 140°$, and $x = \cos 260°$.    *Note:* If you choose $a = -1$, your solutions will be equivalent to those we found with $a = 1$.

Use the method just described to solve the following equations.

(a) $x^3 - 3x + 1 = 0$

    *Answers:*  $2 \cos 40°$, $-2 \cos 20°$, $2 \cos 80°$

(b) $x^3 - 36x - 72 = 0$

(c) $x^3 - 6x + 4 = 0$    *Answers:*  $2, -1 \pm \sqrt{3}$

(d) $x^3 - 7x - 7 = 0$ (Round your answers to three decimal places.)

## MINI PROJECT    |    ASTIGMATISM AND EYEGLASS LENSES

In the manufacture of eyeglass lenses it is important to control a geometric property called *surface astigmatism*. We will not need to know what surface astigmatism is in order to do this project, but we do need to know that there is a direction on the lens associated with surface astigmatism called the *axis of astigmatism*. The angle that this line makes with a horizontal reference line is the **angle of the astigmatism axis** and is shown as angle $\theta$ in Figure A. A measurement of $\theta$ is called an axis measurement; it is given in degrees and always lies in the closed interval from 0 to 180 degrees.

Figure A

A certain manufacturer uses an accurate measuring instrument to measure surface astigmatism, but instead of measuring the axis angle $\theta$, the device produces data containing two numbers $a$ and $b$ that are equal to $\sin 2\theta$ and $\cos 2\theta$, respectively. An engineer has decided that a computer program is needed to take the output data from the measuring instrument as its input and produce the axis angle $\theta$ as its output. Your group has been asked to come up with a step-by-step procedure for finding the angle $\theta$ given the data $a$ and $b$.

One approach is to find all of the solutions in an appropriate interval to the pair of equations $\sin 2\theta = a$ and $\cos 2\theta = b$. Then, among the values of $\theta$ that satisfy both equations choose one that is between 0 and 180 degrees. Another approach uses an identity that arose in the proof of the half-angle formula for the tangent in Section 8.2. Choose one of these approaches and write a step-by-step procedure to find, to the nearest degree, the correct value of $\theta$ between 0 and 180 degrees. Use your procedure on the following four test cases: $a = 0.5000$ and $b = 0.8660$, $a = 0.5000$ and $b = -0.8660$, $a = -0.5000$ and $b = 0.8660$, and $a = -0.5000$ and $b = -0.8660$. Show for each case what values result at each step of your step-by-step procedure.

## 8.5   THE INVERSE TRIGONOMETRIC FUNCTIONS

*The notation* $\cos^{-1}\theta$ *must not be understood to signify* $1/\cos\theta$. —John Herschel in *Philosophical Transactions of London,* 1813

In previous sections we introduced the three inverse trigonometric functions $y = \sin^{-1} x$, $y = \cos^{-1} x$, and $y = \tan^{-1} x$. Because we were using these functions as tools to solve equations, our emphasis there was more computational than theoretical. Now we want to take a second look at these functions, this time from a more conceptual point of view. As background for this work, you should be familiar with the material on inverse functions in Section 3.6.

As is indicated in Figure 1(a), the sine function in not one-to-one. Therefore there is no inverse function. However, let us now consider the **restricted sine function:**

$$y = \sin x \qquad \left( -\frac{\pi}{2} \le x \le \frac{\pi}{2} \right)$$

The restricted sine function has domain $[-\frac{\pi}{2}, \frac{\pi}{2}]$ and range $[-1, 1]$. And, as is indicated in Figure 1(b), the restricted sine function *is* one-to-one, and therefore the

(a) The horizontal line test shows that the sine function is not one-to-one.

(b) By restricting the domain of the sine function to the closed interval $\left[-\frac{\pi}{2}, \frac{\pi}{2}\right]$, we obtain the restricted sine function. The horizontal line test shows that the restricted sine function is one-to-one.

**Figure 1**

inverse function does exist in this case. We refer to the inverse of the restricted sine function as the **inverse sine function.**

Two notations are commonly used to denote the inverse sine function:

$$y = \sin^{-1} x \qquad \text{and} \qquad y = \arcsin x$$

Initially, at least, we will use the notation $y = \sin^{-1} x$. Basic facts about inverse functions tell us that:

the domain of $\sin^{-1} x$ = the range of the restricted sine function = $[-1, 1]$, and

the range of $\sin^{-1} x$ = the domain of the restricted sine function = $\left[-\frac{\pi}{2}, \frac{\pi}{2}\right]$

The graph of $y = \sin^{-1} x$ is easily obtained by using the fact that the graph of a function and its inverse are reflections of one another about the line $y = x$. Figure 2(a) shows the graph of the restricted sine function and its inverse, $y = \sin^{-1} x$. Figure 2(b) shows the graph of $y = \sin^{-1} x$ alone. From Figure 2(b) we see that the domain of $y = \sin^{-1} x$ is the interval $[-1, 1]$, while the range is $\left[-\frac{\pi}{2}, \frac{\pi}{2}\right]$.

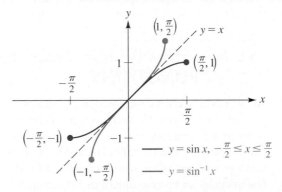

(a) The graphs of a function and its inverse are mirror images of one another about the line $y = x$.

(b) The inverse sine function.

**Figure 2**

What exactly is $\sin^{-1} x$? To see, we begin with the restricted sine function:

$$y = \sin x \qquad \left(-\frac{\pi}{2} \le x \le \frac{\pi}{2}\right)$$

As was explained in Section 3.6, the inverse function is obtained by interchanging $x$ and $y$ (the inputs and the outputs). So for the inverse function $y = \sin^{-1} x$ we have

$$x = \sin y \qquad \left( -\frac{\pi}{2} \le y \le \frac{\pi}{2} \right) \qquad (1)$$

Equation (1) tells us that $y = \sin^{-1} x$, is the number in the interval $[-\frac{\pi}{2}, \frac{\pi}{2}]$ whose sine is $x$. So values of $\sin^{-1} x$ are computed according to the following rule.

---

$\sin^{-1} x$ is that number in the interval $[-\frac{\pi}{2}, \frac{\pi}{2}]$ whose sine is $x$.

---

### EXAMPLE 1 Finding some exact values of the inverse sine

Evaluate:

**(a)** $\sin^{-1}\left(\dfrac{1}{2}\right)$;      **(b)** $\sin^{-1}\left(-\dfrac{1}{2}\right)$.

**SOLUTION**
**(a)** $\sin^{-1}(1/2)$ is that number in the interval $[-\frac{\pi}{2}, \frac{\pi}{2}]$ whose sine is $1/2$. Since $\pi/6$ is in $[-\frac{\pi}{2}, \frac{\pi}{2}]$ and $\sin(\pi/6) = 1/2$, we conclude that $\sin^{-1}(1/2) = \pi/6$.
**(b)** Since $\sin(-\pi/6) = -1/2$ and $-\pi/6$ is in the interval $[-\frac{\pi}{2}, \frac{\pi}{2}]$, we conclude that $\sin^{-1}(-1/2) = -\pi/6$.

*Note*: $\sin(5\pi/6) = 1/2$, but $5\pi/6$ is not in the interval $[-\frac{\pi}{2}, \frac{\pi}{2}]$, so $\sin^{-1}(1/2) \ne 5\pi/6$. Similarly, $\sin(7\pi/6) = -1/2$, but $\sin^{-1}(-1/2) \ne 7\pi/6$. (Why?)

We can use the result in Example 1(a) to see why the notation *arcsin* is used for the inverse sine function. With the arcsin notation the result in Example 1(a) can be written

$$\operatorname{arcsin} \frac{1}{2} = \frac{\pi}{6}$$

Now, as Figure 3 indicates, the length of the arc whose sine is $1/2$ is $\pi/6$. This is the idea behind the arcsin notation.

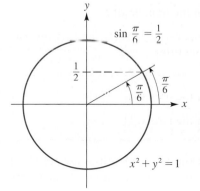

Figure 3

### EXAMPLE 2 Finding approximate values of the inverse sine

Evaluate arcsin(3/4). Round the answer to three decimal places.

**SOLUTION**
The quantity arcsin(3/4) is that number (or arc length, or angle in radians) in the interval $[-\frac{\pi}{2}, \frac{\pi}{2}]$ whose sine is $3/4$. Since we're not familiar with an angle with a sine of $3/4$, we use a calculator. As in previous sections, we show keystrokes for the most common type of calculator. (If these keystrokes don't work on your calculator, be sure to check the instruction manual.)

| EXPRESSION | KEYSTROKES | OUTPUT |
|---|---|---|
| arcsin(0.75) | [2nd] [sin] 0.75 [ENTER] | 0.84806 . . . |

Now, rounding to three decimal places, our result is

$$\arcsin \frac{3}{4} \approx 0.848$$

---

**EXAMPLE** **3**   **Explaining a common notational confusion**

Show that the following expressions are not equal:

$$\sin^{-1} 0 \qquad \text{and} \qquad \frac{1}{\sin 0}$$

**SOLUTION**

The quantity $\sin^{-1} 0$ is that number in the interval $[-\frac{\pi}{2}, \frac{\pi}{2}]$ whose sine is 0. Since 0 is in the interval $[-\frac{\pi}{2}, \frac{\pi}{2}]$ and $\sin 0 = 0$, we conclude that

$$\sin^{-1} 0 = 0$$

On the other hand, since $\sin 0 = 0$, the expression $1/(\sin 0)$ is not even defined. Thus the two given expressions certainly are not equal.

---

If $f$ and $f^{-1}$ are any pair of inverse functions, then by definition,

$$f[f^{-1}(x)] = x \qquad \text{for every } x \text{ in the domain of } f^{-1}$$

and

$$f^{-1}[f(x)] = x \qquad \text{for every } x \text{ in the domain of } f$$

Applying these facts to the restricted sine function, $y = \sin x$, and its inverse, $y = \sin^{-1} x$, we obtain the following two basic identities.

---

$$\sin(\sin^{-1} x) = x \qquad \text{for every } x \text{ in the interval } [-1, 1]$$

$$\sin^{-1}(\sin x) = x \qquad \text{for every } x \text{ in the interval } [-\frac{\pi}{2}, \frac{\pi}{2}]$$

---

You should convince yourself in words that these two identities are true. For example, $\sin(\sin^{-1} x) =$ the sine of (the number between $-\pi/2$ and $\pi/2$, inclusive, whose sine is $x$) $= x$, provided that $x$ is in the domain of $\sin^{-1} x =$ the range of $\sin x =$ the interval $[-1, 1]$. Now try to verify in words the second identity.

The following example indicates that the domain restrictions accompanying these two identities cannot be ignored.

---

    **EXAMPLE** **4**   **Calculations involving the inverse sine**

Compute each quantity that is defined.

**(a)** $\sin^{-1}\left(\sin \frac{\pi}{4}\right)$   **(b)** $\sin^{-1}(\sin 2)$

**(c)** $\sin(\sin^{-1} 2)$   **(d)** $\sin[\sin^{-1}(-1/\sqrt{5})]$

**SOLUTION**

**(a)** Since $\pi/4$ lies in the domain of the restricted sine function, the identity $\sin^{-1}(\sin x) = x$ is applicable here. Thus

$$\sin^{-1}\left(\sin\frac{\pi}{4}\right) = \frac{\pi}{4}$$

CHECK   $\sin\frac{\pi}{4} = \sqrt{2}/2$.

Therefore

$$\sin^{-1}\left(\sin\frac{\pi}{4}\right) = \sin^{-1}\left(\frac{\sqrt{2}}{2}\right) = \frac{\pi}{4}$$

**(b)** The number 2 is not in the domain of the restricted sine function, so the identity $\sin^{-1}(\sin x) = x$ does not apply in this case. However, $\pi - 2$ is in the first quadrant (see Figure 4), so it is in the domain of the restricted sine function and $\sin 2 = \sin(\pi - 2)$, so

$$\sin^{-1}(\sin 2) = \sin^{-1}[\sin(\pi - 2)] = \pi - 2$$

Thus $\sin^{-1}(\sin 2)$ is equal to $\pi - 2$, not 2.

**(c)** The number 2 is not in the domain of the inverse sine function. Thus the expression $\sin(\sin^{-1} 2)$ is undefined.

**(d)** The identity $\sin(\sin^{-1} x) = x$ is applicable here. (Why?) Thus

$$\sin\left[\sin^{-1}\left(-\frac{1}{\sqrt{5}}\right)\right] = -\frac{1}{\sqrt{5}}$$

**Figure 4**

**EXAMPLE  5    From a trigonometric to an algebraic expression**

If $\sin\theta = x/3$ and $0 < \theta < \pi/2$, express the quantity $\theta - \sin 2\theta$ as a function of $x$.

**SOLUTION**

The given conditions tell us that $\theta = \sin^{-1}(x/3)$. That expresses $\theta$ in terms of $x$. To express $\sin 2\theta$ in terms of $x$, we have

$$\sin 2\theta = 2\sin\theta\cos\theta = 2(\sin\theta)\sqrt{1 - \sin^2\theta} \qquad \text{since } \cos\theta = +\sqrt{1 - \sin^2\theta}$$
$$\text{(Why?)}$$

$$= 2\left(\frac{x}{3}\right)\sqrt{1 - \frac{x^2}{9}} = \frac{2x}{3}\sqrt{\frac{9 - x^2}{9}}$$

$$= \frac{2x\sqrt{9 - x^2}}{9}$$

Now, combining the results, we have

$$\theta - \sin 2\theta = \sin^{-1}\left(\frac{x}{3}\right) - \frac{2x\sqrt{9 - x^2}}{9}$$

We turn now to the inverse cosine function. We'll define it by following the same general procedure that we used to define the inverse sine. We begin by defining the **restricted cosine function:**

$$y = \cos x \quad (0 \le x \le \pi) \quad \text{with domain } [0, \pi] \text{ and range } [-1, 1]$$

As is indicated by the horizontal line test in Figure 5, the restricted cosine function is one-to-one, and therefore the inverse function exists. We denote the **inverse cosine function** by

$$y = \cos^{-1} x \quad \text{or} \quad y = \arccos x$$

Then the domain of $\cos^{-1} x$ = the range of the restricted cosine function = $[-1, 1]$, and the range of $\cos^{-1} x$ = the domain of the restricted cosine function = $[0, \pi]$.

The graph of $y = \cos^{-1} x$ is obtained by reflecting the graph of the restricted cosine function about the line $y = x$. Figure 6(a) displays the graph of the restricted cosine function along with $y = \cos^{-1} x$. Figure 6(b) shows the graph of $y = \cos^{-1} x$ alone. From Figure 6(b) we see that the domain of $y = \cos^{-1} x$ is the interval $[-1, 1]$, while the range is $[0, \pi]$.

**Figure 5**
The restricted cosine function is one-to-one.

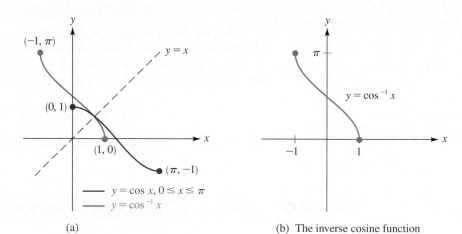

**Figure 6**

(a)

(b) The inverse cosine function

As was stated in the previous section, the values of $\cos^{-1} x$ are computed according to the following rule.

---

$\cos^{-1} x$ is that number in the interval $[0, \pi]$ whose cosine is $x$.

---

To see why this is so, we begin with the restricted cosine function:

$$y = \cos x \quad (0 \le x \le \pi)$$

Then for the inverse function, $y = \cos^{-1} x$, we interchange $x$ and $y$ (the inputs and the outputs) to obtain

$$x = \cos y \quad (0 \le y \le \pi)$$

This last equation tells us that $y = \cos^{-1} x$ is that number in the interval whose cosine is $x$. This is what we wished to show.

As we mentioned previously, the defining equations for inverse functions are

$$f[f^{-1}(x)] = x \quad \text{for every } x \text{ in the domain of } f^{-1}$$

and

$$f^{-1}[f(x)] = x \qquad \text{for every } x \text{ in the domain of } f$$

In the particular case of the restricted cosine function and the inverse cosine function, these two identities read as follows.

$$\cos(\cos^{-1} x) = x \qquad \text{for every } x \text{ in the interval } [-1, 1]$$
$$\cos^{-1}(\cos x) = x \qquad \text{for every } x \text{ in the interval } [0, \pi]$$

Again you should convince yourself in words that these two identities are true.

### EXAMPLE 6   Calculations involving the inverse cosine

Compute each of the following:

**(a)** $\cos^{-1}(0)$;   **(b)** $\cos\left(\arccos \dfrac{2}{3}\right)$;   **(c)** $\arccos(\cos 4)$.

**SOLUTION**

**(a)** $\cos^{-1}(0)$ is that number in the interval $[0, \pi]$ whose cosine is 0. Since $\pi/2$ is in $[0, \pi]$ and $\cos(\pi/2) = 0$, we have

$$\cos^{-1}(0) = \frac{\pi}{2}$$

**(b)** Since the number $2/3$ is in the domain of the inverse cosine function, the identity $\cos(\arccos x) = x$ is applicable. Thus,

$$\cos\left(\arccos \frac{2}{3}\right) = \frac{2}{3}$$

**(c)** The number 4 is not in the domain of the restricted cosine function, so the identity $\cos^{-1}(\cos x) = x$ does not apply in this case. However, since $2\pi - 4$ is in the second quadrant (see Figure 7), it is in the domain of the restricted cosine function and $\cos 4 = \cos(2\pi - 4)$, so

$$\cos^{-1}(\cos 4) = \cos^{-1}[\cos(2\pi - 4)] = 2\pi - 4$$

Thus $\cos^{-1}(\cos 4)$ is equal to $2\pi - 4$, not 4.

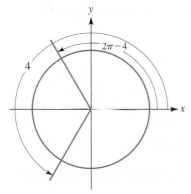

Figure 7

### EXAMPLE 7   An identity involving the inverse cosine

Show that $\sin(\cos^{-1} x) = \sqrt{1 - x^2}$ for $-1 \le x \le 1$.

**SOLUTION**
We use the identity $\sin y = \sqrt{1 - \cos^2 y}$, which is valid for $0 \le y \le \pi$. Substituting $\cos^{-1} x$ for $y$ in this identity, we obtain

$$\sin(\cos^{-1}x) = \sqrt{1 - [\cos(\cos^{-1} x)]^2}$$
$$= \sqrt{1 - x^2} \qquad \text{as required}$$

Before leaving this example, we point out an alternate method of solution that is useful when the restriction on $x$ is $0 < x < 1$. In this case we let $\theta = \cos^{-1} x$. Then $\theta$ is the radian measure of the acute angle whose cosine is $x$, and we can sketch $\theta$ as shown in Figure 8. The sides of the triangle in Figure 8 have been labeled in such a way that

$$\cos \theta = \frac{\text{adjacent}}{\text{hypotenuse}} = \frac{x}{1} = x$$

**Figure 8**

Then, by the Pythagorean theorem we find that the third side of the triangle is $\sqrt{1 - x^2}$. We therefore have

$$\sin \theta = \frac{\text{opposite}}{\text{hypotenuse}} = \frac{\sqrt{1 - x^2}}{1} = \sqrt{1 - x^2}$$

Just as there is a basic identity connecting $\sin x$ and $\cos x$, $\sin^2 x + \cos^2 x = 1$, there is also an identity connecting $\sin^{-1} x$ and $\cos^{-1} x$.

$$\sin^{-1} x + \cos^{-1} x = \frac{\pi}{2} \qquad \text{for every } x \text{ in the closed interval } [-1, 1]$$

We can use Figure 9 to see why this identity is valid when $0 < x < 1$. (Exercise 61 shows you how to establish this identity for all values of $x$ from $-1$ to 1.) In Figure 9, assume that $\theta$ and $\beta$ are the radian measures of the indicated acute angles. Then we have

**Figure 9**

$$\sin \theta = \frac{x}{1} = x \qquad \text{and} \qquad \cos \beta = \frac{x}{1} = x$$

and therefore

$$\theta = \sin^{-1} x \qquad \text{and} \qquad \beta = \cos^{-1} x$$

But from Figure 9 we know that $\theta + \beta = \pi/2$. So, we have $\sin^{-1} x + \cos^{-1} x = \pi/2$, as required.

Now let us turn to the definition of the inverse tangent function. We begin by defining the **restricted tangent function:**

$$y = \tan x \qquad \left( -\frac{\pi}{2} < x < \frac{\pi}{2} \right) \qquad \text{with domain } \left( -\frac{\pi}{2}, \frac{\pi}{2} \right) \text{ and range } R$$

Figure 10 shows the graph of the restricted tangent function. As you can check by applying the horizontal line test, the restricted tangent function is one-to-one. This tells us that the inverse function exists. The two common notations for this **inverse tangent function** are

$$y = \tan^{-1} x \qquad \text{or} \qquad y = \arctan x$$

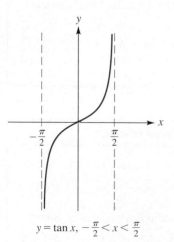

$y = \tan x, \ -\frac{\pi}{2} < x < \frac{\pi}{2}$

**Figure 10**

The restricted tangent function

The domain of $\tan^{-1} x = R$, and the range of $\tan^{-1} x =$ the interval $\left( -\frac{\pi}{2}, \frac{\pi}{2} \right)$. Why? Furthermore, if we follow the same line of reasoning used previously for the inverse sine and the inverse cosine, we obtain the following properties of the inverse tangent function.

$\tan^{-1} x$ is that number in the interval $\left(-\frac{\pi}{2}, \frac{\pi}{2}\right)$ whose tangent is $x$.

$$\tan(\tan^{-1} x) = x \qquad \text{for every real number } x$$

$$\tan^{-1}(\tan x) = x \qquad \text{for every } x \text{ in the open interval } \left(-\frac{\pi}{2}, \frac{\pi}{2}\right)$$

The graph of $y = \tan^{-1} x$ is obtained in the same way that we obtained the graphs of the inverse sine and the inverse cosine. That is, we use the fact that the graphs of a function and its inverse are mirror images of one another about the line $y = x$. In Figure 11(a) we've reflected the graph of the restricted tangent function about the line $y = x$ to obtain the graph of $y = \tan^{-1} x$. In Figure 11(b) we show the graph of $y = \tan^{-1} x$ alone.

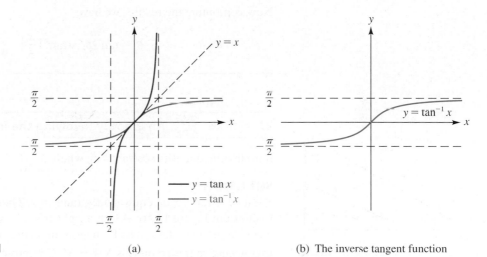

**Figure 11**                 (a)                         (b)  The inverse tangent function

From the graph in Figure 11(b) we can see that the domain of the inverse tangent function is the set of all real numbers, and the range is the open interval $\left(-\frac{\pi}{2}, \frac{\pi}{2}\right)$.

**EXAMPLE   8   Calculations involving the inverse tangent**

Evaluate:
**(a)** $\tan^{-1}(-1)$;        **(b)** $\tan(\tan^{-1}\sqrt{5})$.

**SOLUTION**
**(a)** The quantity $\tan^{-1}(-1)$ is that number in the interval $\left(-\frac{\pi}{2}, \frac{\pi}{2}\right)$ whose tangent is $-1$. Since $-\pi/4$ is in $\left(-\frac{\pi}{2}, \frac{\pi}{2}\right)$ and $\tan(-\pi/4) = -1$, we have $\tan^{-1}(-1) = -\pi/4$.

**(b)** The identity $\tan(\tan^{-1} x) = x$ holds for all real numbers $x$. We therefore have $\tan(\tan^{-1} \sqrt{5}) = \sqrt{5}$.

| EXAMPLE | 9 | Transforming a trigonometric expression to an algebraic expression |
|---|---|---|

If $\tan\theta = x/3$ and $0 < \theta < \pi/2$, express the quantity $\theta - \tan 2\theta$ as a function of $x$.

**SOLUTION**
The given equation tells us that $\theta = \tan^{-1}(x/3)$. That expresses $\theta$ in terms of $x$. To express $\tan 2\theta$ in terms of $x$, we have

$$\tan 2\theta = \frac{2\tan\theta}{1 - \tan^2\theta} = \frac{2(x/3)}{1 - (x/3)^2}$$

$$= \frac{2x/3}{1 - (x^2/9)} = \frac{6x}{9 - x^2} \qquad \text{multiplying numerator and denominator by 9}$$

Now, combining the results, we have

$$\theta - \tan 2\theta = \tan^{-1}\frac{x}{3} - \frac{6x}{9 - x^2}$$

| EXAMPLE | 10 | An identity involving the inverse tangent |
|---|---|---|

Simplify the quantity $\sec(\tan^{-1} x)$, where $x > 0$.

**SOLUTION**
We let $\theta = \tan^{-1} x$ or, equivalently, $\tan\theta = x$. Then $0 < \theta < \pi/2$. Why? Now, as is shown in Figure 12, we sketch a right triangle with an acute angle $\theta$ (in radians) whose tangent is $x$. The Pythagorean theorem tells us that the length of the hypotenuse in this triangle is $\sqrt{1 + x^2}$. Consequently, we have

$$\sec(\tan^{-1} x) = \sec\theta = \frac{\text{hypotenuse}}{\text{adjacent}} = \frac{\sqrt{1 + x^2}}{1} = \sqrt{1 + x^2}$$

**Figure 12**
$\theta = \tan^{-1} x \ (x > 0)$ or $\tan\theta = x$

*Note*: In both Examples 7 and 10 we found that a trigonometric function with an inverse trigonometric function for its input could be expressed in terms of quadratic and square root functions. This is explored further in Exercises 38 through 41 at the end of this section.

When suitable restrictions are placed on the domains of the secant, cosecant, and cotangent, corresponding inverse functions can be defined. However, with the exception of the inverse secant, these are rarely, if ever, encountered in calculus. Therefore we omit a discussion of these functions here. (For the inverse secant function, see the project at the end of this section.)

Let's take a moment now to review our work in this section. The sine, cosine, and tangent functions are not one-to-one functions. However, with suitable restrictions on the domains, we do obtain one-to-one functions. The graphs of these restricted versions of the sine, cosine, and tangent functions are shown in Figures 1(b), 5, and 10, respectively. It is the inverses of these restricted functions that are the focus in this section. In the three boxes that follow, we summarize the key properties of the inverse sine, the inverse cosine, and the inverse tangent.

## ▌PROPERTY SUMMARY   Inverse Sine Function: $y = \sin^{-1} x$   or   $y = \arcsin x$

1. *Domain, range, and graph:*   The domain of the inverse sine function is the closed interval $[-1, 1]$. The range is the closed interval $[-\frac{\pi}{2}, \frac{\pi}{2}]$.

2. *Defining equations:*   The function $y = \sin^{-1} x$ is the inverse of the restricted sine function. (The restricted sine function is defined by the equation $y = \sin x$ along with the restriction $-\pi/2 \le x \le \pi/2$.) Since the restricted sine function and the function $y = \sin^{-1} x$ are inverses of each other, we have

$$\sin(\sin^{-1}x) = x \qquad \text{for every } x \text{ in the interval } [-1, 1]$$

and

$$\sin^{-1}(\sin x) = x \qquad \text{for every } x \text{ in the interval } [-\tfrac{\pi}{2}, \tfrac{\pi}{2}]$$

3. *Computing* $\sin^{-1} x$:   $\sin^{-1} x$ is that number in the interval $[-\frac{\pi}{2}, \frac{\pi}{2}]$ whose sine is $x$.

## ▌PROPERTY SUMMARY   Inverse Cosine Function $y = \cos^{-1} x$   or   $y = \arccos x$

1. *Domain, range, and graph:*   The domain of the inverse cosine function is the closed interval $[-1, 1]$. The range is the closed interval $[0, \pi]$.

2. *Defining equations:*   The function $y = \cos^{-1} x$ is the inverse of the restricted cosine function. (The restricted cosine function is defined by the equation $y = \cos x$ along with the restriction $0 \le x \le \pi$.) Since the restricted cosine function and the function $y = \cos^{-1} x$ are inverses of each other, we have

$$\cos(\cos^{-1} x) = x \qquad \text{for every } x \text{ in the interval } [-1, 1] \qquad \qquad \textit{(continues)}$$

and

$$\cos^{-1}(\cos x) = x \qquad \text{for every } x \text{ in the interval } [0, \pi]$$

3. *Computing* $\cos^{-1} x$:   $\cos^{-1} x$ is that number in the interval $[0, \pi]$ whose cosine is $x$.

---

## PROPERTY SUMMARY   Inverse Tangent Function: $y = \tan^{-1} x$   or   $y = \arctan x$

1. *Domain, range, and graph:*   The domain of the inverse tangent function is the set of all real numbers, $(-\infty, \infty)$. The range is the open interval $\left(-\frac{\pi}{2}, \frac{\pi}{2}\right)$.

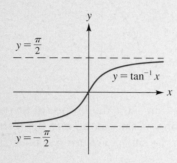

2. *Defining equations:*   The function $y = \tan^{-1} x$ is the inverse of the restricted tangent function. (The restricted tangent function is defined by the equation $y = \tan x$ along with the restriction $-\pi/2 < x < \pi/2$.) Since the restricted tangent function and the function $y = \tan^{-1} x$ are inverses of each other, we have

$$\tan(\tan^{-1} x) = x \qquad \text{for every real number } x$$

and

$$\tan^{-1}(\tan x) = x \qquad \text{for every } x \text{ in the interval } \left(-\frac{\pi}{2}, \frac{\pi}{2}\right)$$

3. *Computing* $\tan^{-1} x$:   $\tan^{-1} x$ is that number in the interval $\left(-\frac{\pi}{2}, \frac{\pi}{2}\right)$ whose tangent is $x$.

---

## EXERCISE SET 8.5

**A**

*In Exercises 1–20, evaluate each of the quantities that is defined, but do not use a calculator or tables. If a quantity is undefined, say so.*

**1.** $\sin^{-1}(\sqrt{3}/2)$

**2.** $\cos^{-1}(-1)$

**3.** $\tan^{-1} \sqrt{3}$

**4.** $\arccos(-\sqrt{2}/2)$

**5.** $\arctan(-1/\sqrt{3})$

**6.** $\arcsin(-1)$

**7.** $\tan^{-1} 1$

**8.** $\sin^{-1} 0$

**9.** $\cos^{-1} 2\pi$

**10.** $\arctan 0$

**11.** $\sin[\sin^{-1}(\frac{1}{4})]$

**12.** $\cos[\cos^{-1}(\frac{4}{3})]$

**13.** $\cos[\cos^{-1}(\frac{3}{4})]$

**14.** $\tan(\arctan 3\pi)$

**15.** $\arctan[\tan(-\frac{\pi}{7})]$

**16.** $\sin(\arcsin 2)$

**17.** $\arcsin(\sin \frac{\pi}{2})$

**18.** $\arccos(\cos \frac{\pi}{8})$

**19.** $\arccos(\cos 2\pi)$

**20.** $\sin^{-1}(\sin \frac{3\pi}{2})$

Ⓖ **21. (a)** Graph the function $y = \arcsin x$ using a viewing rectangle that extends from $-2$ to $2$ in both the $x$- and the $y$-directions. Then use the graphing utility to estimate the maximum and the minimum values of the function.

**(b)** What are the exact maximum and minimum values of the function $y = \arcsin x$? (If you need help answering this, refer to the graph in the first box on page 629.) Check that your estimates in part (a) are consistent with these results.

Ⓖ **22.** Using the viewing rectangle specified in Exercise 21, graph the function $f(x) = \sin(\arcsin x)$. What do you observe? What identity does this demonstrate?

Ⓖ **23. (a)** In the standard viewing rectangle, graph the function $y = \arctan x$.

(b) According to the text, the graph in part (a) has two horizontal asymptotes. What are the equations for these two asymptotes? Add the graphs of the two asymptotes to the picture obtained in part (a). Finally, to emphasize the fact that the two lines are indeed asymptotes, change the viewing rectangle so that $x$ extends from $-50$ to $50$. What do you observe?

*In Exercises 24–33, evaluate the given quantities without using a calculator or tables.*

**24.** $\tan[\sin^{-1}(\frac{4}{5})]$

**25.** $\cos(\arcsin\frac{2}{7})$

**26.** $\sin(\tan^{-1} 1)$

**27.** $\sin[\tan^{-1}(-1)]$

**28.** $\tan(\arccos\frac{5}{13})$

**29.** $\cos[\sin^{-1}(\frac{2}{3})]$

**30.** $\cos(\arctan\sqrt{3})$

**31.** $\sin[\cos^{-1}(\frac{1}{3})]$

**32.** $\sin[\arccos(-\frac{1}{3})]$

**33.** $\tan(\arcsin\frac{20}{29})$

**34.** Use a calculator to evaluate each of the following quantities. Express your answers to two decimal places without rounding them.

(a) $\sin^{-1}(\frac{3}{4})$

(b) $\cos^{-1}(\frac{2}{3})$

(c) $\tan^{-1}\pi$

(d) $\tan^{-1}(\tan^{-1}\pi)$

*In Exercises 35–37, evaluate the given expressions without using a calculator or tables.*

**35.** $\csc[\sin^{-1}(\frac{1}{2}) - \cos^{-1}(\frac{1}{2})]$

**36.** $\sec[\cos^{-1}(\sqrt{2}/2) + \sin^{-1}( 1)]$

**37.** $\cot[\cos^{-1}(-1/2) + \cos^{-1}(0) + \tan^{-1}(1/\sqrt{3})]$

Ⓖ **38.** In Example 7 we proved the identity $\sin(\cos^{-1} x) = \sqrt{1 - x^2}$ for $-1 \le x \le 1$. Demonstrate this identity visually by graphing the two functions $y = \sin(\cos^{-1} x)$ and $y = \sqrt{1 - x^2}$ and noting that the graphs appear to be identical.

Ⓖ **39.** In Example 10 we found that $\sec(\tan^{-1} x) = \sqrt{1 + x^2}$ for $x > 0$. Actually, this identity is valid for all real numbers. Demonstrate this visually by graphing the two functions $y = \sec(\tan^{-1} x)$ and $y = \sqrt{1 + x^2}$.

**40.** Show that $\cos(\sin^{-1} x) = \sqrt{1 - x^2}$ for $-1 \le x \le 1$. *Suggestion:* Use the method of Example 7 in the text.

Ⓖ **41.** Demonstrate the identity $\cos(\sin^{-1} x) = \sqrt{1 - x^2}$ for $-1 \le x \le 1$ by graphing the two functions $y = \cos(\sin^{-1} x)$ and $y = \sqrt{1 - x^2}$ and noting that the graphs appear to be identical.

**42.** If $\sin\theta = 2x$ and $0 < \theta < \pi/2$, express $\theta + \cos 2\theta$ as a function of $x$.

**43.** If $\sin\theta = 3x/2$ and $0 < \theta < \pi/2$, express $\frac{1}{4}\theta - \sin 2\theta$ as a function of $x$.

**44.** If $\cos\theta = x - 1$ and $0 < \theta < \pi/2$, express $2\theta - \cos 2\theta$ as a function of $x$.

**45.** If $\tan\theta = \frac{1}{2}(x - 1)$ and $0 < \theta < \pi/2$, express $\theta - \cos\theta$ as a function of $x$.

**46.** If $\tan\theta = \frac{1}{3}(x + 1)$ and $0 < \theta < \pi/2$, express $2\theta + \tan 2\theta$ as a function of $x$.

## B

*In Exercises 47–56, use the graphing techniques from Section 3.4 to sketch the graph of each function.*

**47.** (a) $y = -\sin^{-1} x$

(b) $y = \sin^{-1}(-x)$

(c) $y = -\sin^{-1}(-x)$

**48.** (a) $y = -\cos^{-1} x$

(b) $y = \cos^{-1}(-x)$

(c) $y = -\cos^{-1}(-x)$

**49.** (a) $f(x) = \arccos(x + 1)$

(b) $g(x) = \arccos x + \frac{\pi}{2}$

**50.** (a) $F(x) = \arcsin(x - 1)$

(b) $G(x) = \arcsin x - \frac{\pi}{4}$

**51.** (a) $y = \arcsin(2 - x) + \frac{\pi}{2}$

(b) $y = -\arcsin(2 - x) + \frac{\pi}{2}$

**52.** (a) $y = \cos^{-1}(1 - x)$

(b) $y = -\cos^{-1}(1 - x) - \pi$

**53.** (a) $y = -\tan^{-1} x$

(b) $y = \tan^{-1}(-x)$

(c) $y = -\tan^{-1}(-x)$

**54.** (a) $y = \arctan(x + 3)$

(b) $y = \arctan x + \pi/2$

(c) $y = -\arctan(-x) + \pi/2$

**55.** $f(x) = -\arctan(1 - x) - \pi/2$

**56.** $y = \tan^{-1}(2 - x) + \pi/4$

**57.** Evaluate $\sin(2 \tan^{-1} 4)$.  *Hint:* $\sin 2\theta = 2 \sin\theta \cos\theta$

**58.** Evaluate $\cos[2 \sin^{-1}(\frac{5}{13})]$.

**59.** Evaluate $\sin(\arccos\frac{3}{5} - \arctan\frac{7}{13})$.  *Suggestion:* Use the formula for $\sin(x - y)$.

**60.** Show that $\sin[\sin^{-1}(\frac{1}{3}) + \sin^{-1}(\frac{1}{4})] = (\sqrt{15} + 2\sqrt{2})/12$.

**61.** In the text we showed that $\sin^{-1} x + \cos^{-1} x = \pi/2$ for $x$ in the open interval $(0, 1)$. Follow steps (a) and (b) to show that this identity actually holds for every $x$ in the closed interval $[-1, 1]$.

(a) Let $\alpha = \sin^{-1} x$ and $\beta = \cos^{-1} x$. Explain why $-\pi/2 \le \alpha + \beta \le 3\pi/2$.  *Hint:* What are the ranges of the inverse sine and the inverse cosine functions?

(b) Use the addition formula for sine to show that $\sin(\alpha + \beta) = 1$. Conclude [with the help of part (a)] that $\alpha + \beta = \pi/2$, as required.

Ⓖ **62.** Using the viewing rectangle specified in Exercise 21, graph the function $g(x) = \sin^{-1} x + \cos^{-1} x$. What do you observe? What is the exact value for the $y$-intercept of the graph? What identity does this demonstrate?

*In Exercises 63 and 64, solve the given equations.*

**63.** $\cos^{-1} t = \sin^{-1} t$  *Hint:* Compute the cosine of both sides.

**64.** $\sin^{-1}(3t - 2) = \sin^{-1} t - \cos^{-1} t$

**65.** Show that $\arctan x + \arctan y = \arctan\dfrac{x + y}{1 - xy}$ when $x$ and $y$ are positive and $xy < 1$.

**66.** Use the identity in Exercise 65 to show that the following equations are correct.

(a) $\arctan\frac{1}{2} + \arctan\frac{1}{3} = \frac{\pi}{4}$

(b) $\arctan\frac{1}{4} + \arctan\frac{3}{5} = \frac{\pi}{4}$

(c) $2 \arctan\frac{1}{3} + \arctan\frac{1}{7} = \frac{\pi}{4}$

  *Hint:* $2 \arctan\frac{1}{3} = \arctan\frac{1}{3} + \arctan\frac{1}{3}$

(d) $\arctan\frac{1}{2} + \arctan\frac{1}{5} + \arctan\frac{1}{8} = \frac{\pi}{4}$

*In Exercises 67 and 68, solve the given equations.*

**67.** $2 \tan^{-1} x = \tan^{-1} \dfrac{1}{4x}$    *Hint:* Compute the tangent of both sides.

**68.** $2 \tan^{-1} \sqrt{t - t^2} = \tan^{-1} t + \tan^{-1}(1 - t)$

**69.** Consider the equation $\cos^{-1} x = \tan^{-1} x$.

  **(a)** Explain why $x$ cannot be negative or zero.

  **(b)** As you can see in the accompanying figure, the graphs of $y = \cos^{-1} x$ and $y = \tan^{-1} x$ intersect at a point in Quadrant I. By solving the equation $\cos^{-1} x = \tan^{-1} x$, show that the $x$-coordinate of this intersection point is given by

$$x = \sqrt{\dfrac{\sqrt{5} - 1}{2}}$$

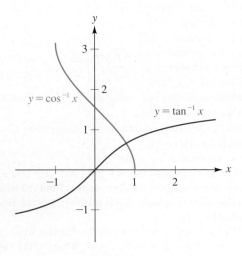

  **(c)** Use the result in part (b) along with your calculator to specify the coordinates of the intersection point.

Ⓖ *In Exercises 70–85, use graphs to determine whether there are solutions for each equation in the interval $[0, 1]$. If there are solutions, use the graphing utility to find them accurately to two decimal places.*

**70.** $\cos^{-1} x = \tan^{-1} x$       **71.** $x = \arccos x$

**72.** $\cos^{-1} x = x^2$

**73.** **(a)** $1.3(x - \frac{1}{2})^2 = \cos^{-1} x$

    **(b)** $1.4(x - \frac{1}{2})^2 = \cos^{-1} x$

**74.** $\tan^{-1} x = \sin 3x$

**75.** **(a)** $\arccos x = 2 \sin 3x$       **76.** **(a)** $\sin(2.3x) = \arctan x$

    **(b)** $\arccos x = 2 \sin 4x$          **(b)** $\sin(2.2x) = \arctan x$

**77.** **(a)** $1/(\tan^{-1} x + \sin^{-1} x) = \sin 2x$

    **(b)** $1/(\tan^{-1} x + \sin^{-1} x) = \sin 3x$

**78.** **(a)** $1/(\sin^{-1} x + \cos^{-1} x) = 4x^3$

    **(b)** $1/(\sin^{-1} x + \cos^{-1} x) = 5x^3$

**79.** $\sin^{-1} x = \cos^{-1} x$

**80.** $\sin^{-1} x = \sin^{-1}(\sin^{-1} x)$

**81.** $\cos^{-1} x = \cos^{-1}(\cos^{-1} x)$

**82.** $\cos^{-1}(\sin^{-1} x) = \sin^{-1}(\cos^{-1} x)$

**83.** $1/(\sin x) = \sin^{-1} x$

**84.** $1/(\cos x) = \cos^{-1} x$

**85.** $1/(\tan x) = \tan^{-1} x$

*In Exercises 86 and 87 we make use of some simple geometric figures to evaluate sums involving the inverse tangent function. The idea here is taken from the note by Professor Edward M. Harris entitled* Behold! Sums of Arctan *(The College Mathematics Journal, vol. 18 no. 2, p. 141).*

**86.** In this exercise we use the following figure to show that $\tan^{-1}(\frac{2}{3}) + \tan^{-1}(\frac{1}{5}) = \frac{\pi}{4}$.

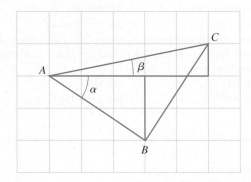

  **(a)** Show that $\angle ABC = \pi/2$.    *Hint:* Compute the slopes of $\overline{AB}$ and $\overline{BC}$. (Assume that the grid lines are marked off at one-unit intervals.)

  **(b)** Show that $AB = BC$ and conclude that $\angle BAC = \pi/4$.

  **(c)** Now explain why $\alpha = \tan^{-1}(\frac{2}{3})$, $\beta = \tan^{-1}(\frac{1}{5})$, and $\tan^{-1}(\frac{2}{3}) + \tan^{-1}(\frac{1}{5}) = \frac{\pi}{4}$.

**87.** In this exercise we use the accompanying figure to show that $\tan^{-1} 1 + \tan^{-1} 2 + \tan^{-1} 3 = \pi$.

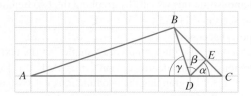

  **(a)** By computing slopes, show that $\overline{DE} \perp \overline{BC}$ and $\overline{AB} \perp \overline{BD}$. (Assume that the grid lines are at one-unit intervals.)

  **(b)** Determine the following lengths: $DE$, $CE$, $BE$, $AB$, and $BD$.

  **(c)** Show that $\tan \alpha = 1$, $\tan \beta = 2$, and $\tan \gamma = 3$. Then explain why $\tan^{-1} 1 + \tan^{-1} 2 + \tan^{-1} 3 = \pi$.

*Note:* It's possible to do part (c) without first doing part (b). Try it.

## PROJECT

### INVERSE SECANT FUNCTIONS

It is interesting to note that the property of periodicity, fundamental to the importance and usefulness of the sine, cosine, and tangent functions, is precisely what prevents these functions from being one-to-one and therefore having inverse functions. So in Section 8.5 we restricted the domains of these functions to obtain one-to-one versions and proceeded to construct the inverse sine, inverse cosine, and inverse tangent functions, systematically following our development of inverse functions from Chapter 3. The domains we chose are the ones that are traditionally used for this purpose.

In the case of the secant function there are two common choices of domain. These result in two one-to-one versions of the secant function, each with its own distinct inverse secant function. Before we start, keep in mind that our choice of domain is made to satisfy two conditions: We need a version of the function that is both one-to-one and has the same range as the unrestricted secant function.

The secant function is not one-to-one. Why? Looking at the graph of $y = \sec x$ where the secant's range is obtained, we can restrict the domain to the union of intervals $[0, \frac{\pi}{2}) \cup [\pi, \frac{3\pi}{2})$ to obtain a version of secant with the correct range. We have our first restricted secant function:

$$y = \sec x$$

with

$$\text{domain} = [0, \tfrac{\pi}{2}) \cup [\pi, \tfrac{3\pi}{2}) \quad \text{and} \quad \text{range} = (-\infty, -1] \cup [1, \infty)$$

which is one-to-one. Its graph is shown in Figure A(i).

(i)  The graph of $y = \sec x$ for $x$ in $[0, \frac{\pi}{2}) \cup [\pi, \frac{3\pi}{2})$

(ii)  The graph of $y = \sec^{-1} x$

Figure A

This secant function has an inverse, denoted $\sec^{-1} x$ or arcsec, with

$$\text{domain of } \sec^{-1} = \text{range of the restricted secant} = (-\infty, -1] \cup [1, \infty)$$

and

$$\text{range of sec}^{-1} = \text{domain of the restricted secant} = [0, \tfrac{\pi}{2}) \cup [\pi, \tfrac{3\pi}{2})$$

The graph of $y = \sec^{-1} x$ is shown in Figure A(ii) and can be obtained by reflecting the graph in Figure A(i) about the line with equation $y = x$. (Try it.)

What is $\sec^{-1} x$? Start with the equation $y = \sec x$. Interchange $x$ and $y$ to get $x = \sec y$. What does the $y$ in this last equation represent? The last equation tells us that $y = \sec^{-1} x$ is the unique number in the domain of the restricted secant, $[0, \tfrac{\pi}{2}) \cup [\pi, 3\tfrac{\pi}{2})$, whose secant is $x$.

---

**EXAMPLE  I    Values of some expressions involving the inverse secant**

**(a)** $\sec^{-1} 2 = $ the unique number in $[0, \tfrac{\pi}{2}) \cup [\pi, \tfrac{3\pi}{2})$ whose secant is $2 = \tfrac{\pi}{3}$

**(b)** $\text{arcsec}(-\sqrt{2}) = $ the unique number in $[0, \tfrac{\pi}{2}) \cup [\pi, \tfrac{3\pi}{2})$ whose secant is $-\sqrt{2} = \tfrac{5\pi}{4}$

**(c)** $\sec[\sec^{-1}(5)] = $ the secant of (the unique number in $[0, \tfrac{\pi}{2}) \cup [\pi, \tfrac{3\pi}{2})$ whose secant is 5) $= 5$

**(d)** $\sec^{-1}(\sec \tfrac{2}{3}) = $ the unique number in $[0, \tfrac{\pi}{2}) \cup [\pi, \tfrac{3\pi}{2})$ whose secant is $\sec \tfrac{2}{3} = \tfrac{2}{3}$

---

**EXAMPLE  II    Evaluating expressions involving the inverse secant**

**(a)** $\sin[\sec^{-1}(\tfrac{5}{2})]$

Let $\theta = \sec^{-1}(\tfrac{5}{2})$, then $\theta$ is in $[0, \tfrac{\pi}{2})$ and $\sec \theta = \tfrac{5}{2}$. Using the right triangle labeled in Figure B, we have

$$\sin\left[\sec^{-1}\left(\frac{5}{2}\right)\right] = \sin \theta = \frac{\text{opposite}}{\text{hypotenuse}} = \frac{\sqrt{21}}{5}$$

Alternatively, using identities,

$$\cos \theta = \frac{1}{\sec \theta} = \frac{1}{5/2} = \frac{2}{5}$$

So

$$\sin \theta = \sqrt{1 - \cos^2 \theta} = \sqrt{1 - (2/5)^2} = \frac{\sqrt{21}}{5} \qquad \text{Why the positive square root?}$$

**(b)** $\tan[\sec^{-1}(-\tfrac{8}{3})]$

Let $\theta = \sec^{-1}(-\tfrac{8}{3})$ and let $\tilde{\theta}$ be its reference angle. Then $\theta$ is in Quadrant III and $\sec \theta = -\tfrac{8}{3}$. Using the right triangle labeled in Figure C, we have

$$\tan\left[\sec^{-1}\left(-\frac{8}{3}\right)\right] = \tan \theta = \tan \tilde{\theta} = \frac{\text{opposite}}{\text{adjacent}} = \frac{\sqrt{55}}{3}$$

Figure B

Figure C

Alternatively, using identities,

$$\sec \theta = -\frac{8}{3}$$

So

$$\tan \theta = \sqrt{\sec^2 \theta - 1} = \sqrt{(-8/3)^2 - 1} = \frac{\sqrt{55}}{3} \qquad \text{Why the positive}$$
square root?

Now we construct a second version of the inverse secant by restricting the secant's domain in a different way. We'll use a capital S to distinguish this version from our previous version of a restricted secant. Let

$$y = \text{Sec } x$$

with

$$\text{domain} = [0, \tfrac{\pi}{2}) \cup (\tfrac{\pi}{2}, \pi] \qquad \text{and} \qquad \text{range} = (-\infty, -1] \cup [1, \infty)$$

Then Sec $x$ is one-to-one as can be seen from its graph in Figure D(i). So this Secant function has an inverse denoted $\text{Sec}^{-1}$ or Arcsec, with

$$\text{domain of Sec}^{-1} = \text{range of the restricted Secant} = (-\infty, -1] \cup [1, \infty)$$

and

$$\text{range of Sec}^{-1} = \text{domain of the restricted Secant} = [0, \tfrac{\pi}{2}) \cup (\tfrac{\pi}{2}, \pi]$$

The graph of $y = \text{Sec}^{-1} x$ is shown in Figure D(ii) and can be obtained by reflecting the graph in Figure D(i) about the line with equation $y = x$. (Try it.)

(i) The graph of $y = \text{Sec } x$ for $x$ in
$\left[0, \tfrac{\pi}{2}\right) \cup \left(\tfrac{\pi}{2}, \pi\right]$

(ii) The graph of $y = \text{Sec}^{-1} x$

**Figure D**

What is $\text{Sec}^{-1} x$? This time, $y = \text{Sec}^{-1} x =$ the unique number in the restricted domain of Secant, $[0, \tfrac{\pi}{2}) \cup (\tfrac{\pi}{2}, \pi]$, whose *Secant* is $x$.

### EXAMPLE III  Values of some expressions involving the second version of the inverse secant

You can show that $\text{Sec}^{-1} 2 = \frac{\pi}{3}$, $\text{Sec}[\text{Sec}^{-1}(5)] = 5$, and $\text{Sec}^{-1}(\text{Sec}\,\frac{2}{3}) = \frac{2}{3}$ as in Example I. However, $\text{Arcsec}(-\sqrt{2}) = $ the unique number in $[0, \frac{\pi}{2}) \cup (\frac{\pi}{2}, \pi]$ whose secant is $-\sqrt{2} = \frac{3\pi}{4}$, *not* $\frac{5\pi}{4}$ as in Example I.

**NOTE**   $\text{Sec}^{-1} x = \sec^{-1} x$ for $x \geq 1$, but $\text{Sec}^{-1} x = 2\pi - \sec^{-1} x$ for $x \leq -1$.

### EXAMPLE IV  Evaluating expressions involving the second version of the inverse secant

$\sin[\text{Sec}^{-1}(\frac{5}{2})] = \sqrt{21}/5$ as in Example II(a). Or, by the previous note,

$$\sin\left[\text{Sec}^{-1}\left(\frac{5}{2}\right)\right] = \sin\left[\sec^{-1}\left(\frac{5}{2}\right)\right] = \frac{\sqrt{21}}{5}$$

But, $\text{Sec}^{-1}(-\frac{8}{3})$ is in $(\frac{\pi}{2}, \pi]$, $\sec^{-1}(-\frac{8}{3})$ is in $[\pi, \frac{3\pi}{2})$, and neither equals $\pi$. (Why?) So $\text{Sec}^{-1}(-\frac{8}{3}) \neq \sec^{-1}(-\frac{8}{3})$, and in fact $\tan[\text{Sec}^{-1}(-\frac{8}{3})] \neq \tan[\sec^{-1}(-\frac{8}{3})]$. To evaluate $\tan[\text{Sec}^{-1}(-\frac{8}{3})]$, let $\theta = \text{Sec}^{-1}(-\frac{8}{3})$ and let $\tilde{\theta}$ be its reference angle. Then $\theta$ is in $(\frac{\pi}{2}, \pi]$ and $\text{Sec}\,\theta = -\frac{8}{3}$. Using the right triangle labeled in Figure E, we have

$$\tan[\text{Sec}^{-1}(-\tfrac{8}{3})] = \tan\theta = -\tan\tilde{\theta} = -\frac{\text{opposite}}{\text{adjacent}} = -\frac{\sqrt{55}}{3} \qquad \text{Why is } \tan\theta = -\tan\tilde{\theta}?$$

Alternatively, using identities, $\sec\theta = -\frac{8}{3}$, so

$$\tan\theta = -\sqrt{\sec^2\theta - 1} = -\sqrt{(-8/3)^2 - 1} = -\frac{\sqrt{55}}{3} \qquad \text{Why the negative square root?}$$

**Figure E**

## EXERCISES

In each of these exercises the secant and the Secant are the restricted versions defined in this project, so the inverse secant and the inverse Secant are the corresponding inverse functions.

1. Evaluate the following quantities:
   (a) $\sec^{-1}(0)$        (c) $\text{arcsec}(-1)$        (e) $\text{arcsec}\,\sqrt{2}$
   (b) $\sec^{-1}(-2/\sqrt{3})$    (d) $\sec[\sec^{-1}(10)]$    (f) $\sec^{-1}(\sec 4)$

2. Evaluate the following quantities:
   (a) $\cos[\sec^{-1}(\frac{6}{5})]$      (b) $\sin[\text{arcsec}(-5)]$      (c) $\tan[\sec^{-1}(-\frac{7}{3})]$

3. Evaluate the following quantities:
   (a) $\text{Sec}^{-1}(1)$        (c) $\text{Arcsec}(-2)$        (e) $\text{Sec}[\text{Sec}^{-1}(15)]$
   (b) $\text{Sec}^{-1}(\text{Sec}\,2)$    (d) $\sin[\text{Sec}^{-1}(\frac{13}{5})]$    (f) $\tan[\text{Sec}^{-1}(-\frac{15}{7})]$

4. Prove

$$\text{Sec}^{-1} x = \sec^{-1} x \qquad \text{for } x \geq 1$$

   and

$$\text{Sec}^{-1} x = 2\pi - \sec^{-1} x \qquad \text{for } x \leq -1$$

**5.** Use the result in Exercise 4 to show that

$$\tan[\text{Sec}^{-1}(-\tfrac{8}{3})] = \tan[\sec^{-1}(-\tfrac{8}{3})] = -\sqrt{55}/3$$

**6.** Explain why each of the following statements is true:

(a) $\sec[\text{Sec}^{-1}(3)] = 3$

(b) $\sec[\text{Sec}^{-1}(-3)]$ is undefined

(c) $\text{Sec}[\sec^{-1}(8)] = 8$

(d) $\text{Sec}[\sec^{-1}(-8)]$ is undefined

(e) $\text{Sec}^{-1}[\sec(\tfrac{4}{3})] = \tfrac{4}{3}$

(f) $\sec^{-1}[\text{Sec}\,\tfrac{3\pi}{4}] = \tfrac{5\pi}{4}$

(g) $\sec^{-1}(\text{Sec}\,2) = 2\pi - 2$

# Chapter 8

## Summary of Principal Terms and Formulas

| Terms or formulas | Page reference | Comments |
|---|---|---|
| **1.** $\sin(s + t)$ $= \sin s \cos t + \cos s \sin t$ <br><br> $\sin(s - t)$ $= \sin s \cos t - \cos s \sin t$ <br><br> $\cos(s + t)$ $= \cos s \cos t - \sin s \sin t$ <br><br> $\cos(s - t)$ $= \cos s \cos t + \sin s \sin t$ | 577 | These identities are referred to as the *addition formulas* for sine and cosine. |
| **2.** $\cos(\tfrac{\pi}{2} - \theta) = \sin\theta$ <br><br> $\sin(\tfrac{\pi}{2} - \theta) = \cos\theta$ | 579 | These two identities, called *reduction formulas,* hold for all real numbers $\theta$. In terms of angles, the identities state that the sine of an angle is equal to the cosine of its complement. |
| **3.** $\tan(s + t) = \dfrac{\tan s + \tan t}{1 - \tan s \tan t}$ <br><br> $\tan(s - t) = \dfrac{\tan s - \tan t}{1 + \tan s \tan t}$ | 582 | These are the *addition formulas* for tangent. |
| **4.** $\sin 2\theta = 2 \sin\theta \cos\theta$ <br><br> $\cos 2\theta = \cos^2\theta - \sin^2\theta$ <br><br> $\tan 2\theta = \dfrac{2 \tan\theta}{1 - \tan^2\theta}$ | 589 | These are the *double-angle formulas.* There are four other forms of the double-angle formula for cosine. They appear in the box on page 592. |
| **5.** $\sin\dfrac{s}{2} = \pm\sqrt{\dfrac{1 - \cos s}{2}}$ <br><br> $\cos\dfrac{s}{2} = \pm\sqrt{\dfrac{1 + \cos s}{2}}$ <br><br> $\tan\dfrac{s}{2} = \dfrac{\sin s}{1 + \cos s}$ | 590 | These three identities are referred to as the *half-angle formulas.* In the case of the half-angle formulas for sine and cosine the sign before the radical is determined by the quadrant in which the angle or arc $s/2$ terminates. |

| Terms or formulas | Page reference | Comments |
|---|---|---|
| **6.** $\sin A \sin B$ <br> $= \frac{1}{2}[\cos(A - B) - \cos(A + B)]$ <br><br> $\sin A \cos B$ <br> $= \frac{1}{2}[\sin(A - B) + \sin(A + B)]$ <br><br> $\cos A \cos B$ <br> $= \frac{1}{2}[\cos(A - B) + \cos(A + B)]$ | 599 | These *product-to-sum* identities are derived from the addition formulas for sine and cosine. |
| **7.** $\sin \alpha + \sin \beta$ <br> $= 2 \sin \dfrac{\alpha + \beta}{2} \cos \dfrac{\alpha - \beta}{2}$ <br><br> $\sin \alpha - \sin \beta$ <br> $= 2 \cos \dfrac{\alpha + \beta}{2} \sin \dfrac{\alpha - \beta}{2}$ <br><br> $\cos \alpha + \cos \beta$ <br> $= 2 \cos \dfrac{\alpha + \beta}{2} \cos \dfrac{\alpha - \beta}{2}$ <br><br> $\cos \alpha - \cos \beta$ <br> $= -2 \sin \dfrac{\alpha + \beta}{2} \sin \dfrac{\alpha - \beta}{2}$ | 601 | These are the *sum-to-product* identities. |
| **8.** The restricted sine function | 619 | The domain of the function $y = \sin x$ is the set of all real numbers. By allowing inputs only from the closed interval $\left[-\frac{\pi}{2}, \frac{\pi}{2}\right]$. we obtain the restricted sine function. (See Figure 1 on page 620.) The motivation for restricting the domain is that the restricted sine function is one-to-one, and therefore the inverse function exists. |
| **9.** $\sin^{-1} x$ or arcsin $x$ | 620 | $\sin^{-1} x$ is that number in the interval $\left[-\frac{\pi}{2}, \frac{\pi}{2}\right]$ whose sine is $x$. The basic properties of the inverse sine function are summarized in the first box on page 629. |
| **10.** The restricted cosine function | 624 | The domain of the function $y = \cos x$ is the set of all real numbers. By allowing inputs only from the closed interval $[0, \pi]$, we obtain the restricted cosine function. (See Figure 5 on page 624.) The motivation for restricting the domain is that the restricted cosine function is one-to-one, and therefore the inverse function exists. |
| **11.** $\cos^{-1} x$ or arccos $x$ | 624 | $\cos^{-1} x$ is that number in the interval $[0, \pi]$ whose cosine is $x$. The basic properties of the inverse cosine function are summarized in a box on pages 629–630. |
| **12.** The restricted tangent function | 626 | The tangent function, $y = \tan x$, is not one-to-one. However, by allowing inputs only from the open interval $\left(-\frac{\pi}{2}, \frac{\pi}{2}\right)$ we obtain the restricted tangent function, which is one-to-one. (See Figure 10 on page 626.) Since the restricted tangent function is one-to-one, the inverse function exists. |

| Terms or formulas | Page reference | Comments |
|---|---|---|
| **13.** $\tan^{-1} x$ or arctan $x$ | 626 | $\tan^{-1} x$ is that number in the interval $\left(-\frac{\pi}{2}, \frac{\pi}{2}\right)$ whose tangent is $x$. The basic properties of the inverse tangent function are summarized in a box on page 630. |

## Writing Mathematics

1. Say whether the statement is TRUE or FALSE. Write out your reason or reasons in complete sentences. If you draw a diagram to accompany your writing, be sure that you clearly label any parts of the diagram to which you refer.
   (a) The equation $\tan^2 t + 1 = \sec^2 t$ is true for every real number $t$.
   (b) There is no real number $x$ satisfying the equation $\cos(\frac{\pi}{4} + x) = 2$.
   (c) There is no real number $x$ satisfying the equation $\cos(\frac{\pi}{4} + x) = \cos x$.
   (d) For every number $x$ in the closed interval $[-1, 1]$, we have $\sin^{-1} x = 1/\sin x$.
   (e) There is no real number $x$ for which $\sin^{-1} x - 1/\sin x$.   *Hint*: Draw a careful sketch of the graphs of the inverse sine function and the cosecant function on the interval $0 < x \le 1$.
   (f) The equation $\sin(x + y) = \sin x \cos y + \cos x \sin y$ holds for all real numbers $x$ and $y$.
   (g) The equation $\tan(x + y) = \dfrac{\tan x + \tan y}{1 - \tan x \tan y}$ holds for all real numbers $x$ and $y$.

2. There is a formula for calculating the angle between two given lines in the $x$–$y$ plane. The derivation of this formula relies on the identity for $\tan(s - t)$. Find a book on analytic geometry in the library. Look up this formula; find out how it is derived and how to use it. You can work with a classmate or your instructor. Then on your own, write a summary of what you have learned. Include an example (like the ones in this precalculus text) explaining how the formula is applied in a specific case.

3. This exercise consists of two parts. In the first part you are going to follow some simple instructions to construct a regular pentagon. In the second part, you'll write a paper explaining why the construction is valid.
   (a) Use the following instructions to make a poster showing a regular pentagon inscribed in the unit circle. The poster should also show the steps used in the construction.

   Draw a unit circle. Label the origin $O$; let $B$ and $C'$ denote the points $(1, 0)$ and $(0, 1)$, respectively; let $C$ be the midpoint of $OC'$; and let $A$ denote the point where the bisector of $\angle OCB$ meets the $x$-axis. From $A$, draw a line segment straight up to the unit circle, meeting the unit circle at a point $P$. Then the line segment joining $B$ and $P$ will be one side of a regular pentagon inscribed in the unit circle.

   *Remark*: This is perhaps the simplest geometric construction known for the regular pentagon. The ancient Greek mathematicians had a more complicated method. The construction given here was discovered (only) a century ago by H. W. Richmond; it appeared in the *Quarterly Journal of Mathematics,* vol. 26 (1893), pp. 296–297.

**(b)** With a group of classmates or your instructor, work out the details in the following terse justification for the construction in part (a). Then, on your own, carefully write out the justification in full detail. This will involve a mixture of English sentences and equations, much like the exposition in this textbook. At each of the main steps, be sure to tell the reader where you are going and what that step will accomplish.

We want to show that $\angle POB = 72°$. Let $\angle OCB = \theta$. From right triangle $OCB$ we get $\sin\theta = 2\sqrt{5}/5$ and $\cos\theta = \sqrt{5}/5$. Using these values in the half-angle formula for tangent then yields (after simplifying) $\tan(\theta/2) = (\sqrt{5}-1)/2$. Next, from right triangle $OCA$ we have $OA = \frac{1}{2}\tan(\theta/2)$. From these last two equations we conclude that $OA = (\sqrt{5}-1)/4$. However, according to Exercise 68(c) in Section 8.2, $\sin 18° = (\sqrt{5}-1)/4$. It now follows that $OA = \cos 72°$, and therefore $\angle POB = 72°$.

(In working out the details, you can assume the result from Exercise 68(c) in Section 8.2.)

# Chapter 8     Review Exercises

*In Exercises 1–32, prove that the equations are identities.*

**1.** $\cot(x+y) = \dfrac{\cot x \cot y - 1}{\cot x + \cot y}$

**2.** $\cos 2x = \dfrac{1 - \tan^2 x}{1 + \tan^2 x}$

**3.** $\sin 2x = \dfrac{2\tan x}{1 + \tan^2 x}$

**4.** $\sin^2 x - \sin^2 y = \sin(x+y)\sin(x-y)$

**5.** $\tan^2 x - \tan^2 y = \dfrac{\sin(x+y)\sin(x-y)}{\cos^2 x \cos^2 y}$

**6.** $2\csc 2x = \sec x \csc x$

**7.** $(\sin x)[\tan(x/2) + \cot(x/2)] = 2$

**8.** $\tan(x + \frac{\pi}{4}) = (1 + \tan x)/(1 - \tan x)$

**9.** $\tan(\frac{\pi}{4} + x) - \tan(\frac{\pi}{4} - x) = 2\tan 2x$

**10.** $\dfrac{\cot x - 1}{\cot x + 1} = \dfrac{1 - \sin 2x}{\cos 2x}$

**11.** $2\sin\left(\dfrac{\pi}{4} - \dfrac{x}{2}\right)\cos\left(\dfrac{\pi}{4} - \dfrac{x}{2}\right) = \cos x$

**12.** $\dfrac{\tan(x+y) - \tan y}{1 + \tan(x+y)\tan y} = \tan x$

**13.** $\dfrac{1 - \tan(\frac{1}{4}\pi - t)}{1 + \tan(\frac{1}{4}\pi - t)} = \tan t$

**14.** $\tan(\frac{1}{4}\pi + \frac{1}{2}t) = \tan t + \sec t$

**15.** $\dfrac{\tan(\alpha - \beta) + \tan\beta}{1 - \tan(\alpha - \beta)\tan\beta} = \tan\alpha$

**16.** $(1 + \tan\theta)[1 + \tan(\frac{1}{4}\pi - \theta)] = 2$

**17.** $\tan 3\theta = \dfrac{3t - t^3}{1 - 3t^2}$, where $t = \tan\theta$

**18.** $\sin 2t = \sin(t + \frac{2}{3}\pi)\cos(t - \frac{2}{3}\pi)$
$\qquad\qquad\qquad + \cos(t + \frac{2}{3}\pi)\sin(t - \frac{2}{3}\pi)$

**19.** $\tan 2x + \sec 2x = \dfrac{\cos x + \sin x}{\cos x - \sin x}$

**20.** $\cos^4 x - \sin^4 x = \cos 2x$

**21.** $2\sin x + \sin 2x = \dfrac{2\sin^3 x}{1 - \cos x}$

**22.** $1 + \tan x \tan(x/2) = \sec x$

**23.** $\tan\dfrac{x}{2} = \dfrac{1 - \cos x + \sin x}{1 + \cos x + \sin x}$

**24.** $\dfrac{\sin 3x}{\sin x} - \dfrac{\cos 3x}{\cos x} = 2$

**25.** $\sin(x+y)\cos y - \cos(x+y)\sin y = \sin x$

**26.** $\dfrac{\sin x + \sin 2x}{\cos x - \cos 2x} = \cot\dfrac{x}{2}$

**27.** $\dfrac{1 - \tan^2(x/2)}{1 + \tan^2(x/2)} = \cos x$

**28.** $4\sin(x/4)\cos(x/4)\cos(x/2) = \sin x$

**29.** $\sin 4x = 4 \sin x \cos x - 8 \sin^3 x \cos x$

**30.** $\cos 4x = 8 \cos^4 x - 8 \cos^2 x + 1$

**31.** $\sin 5x = 16 \sin^5 x - 20 \sin^3 x + 5 \sin x$

**32.** $\cos 5x = 16 \cos^5 x - 20 \cos^3 x + 5 \cos x$

*In Exercises 33–41, establish the identities by applying the sum-to-product formulas.*

**33.** $\sin 80° - \sin 20° = \cos 50°$

**34.** $\sin 65° + \sin 25° = \sqrt{2} \cos 20°$

**35.** $\dfrac{\cos x - \cos 3x}{\sin x + \sin 3x} = \tan x$

**36.** $\dfrac{\sin 3° + \sin 33°}{\cos 3° + \cos 33°} = \tan 18°$

**37.** $\sin(5\pi/12) + \sin(\pi/12) = \sqrt{6}/2$

**38.** $\cos 10° - \sin 10° = \sqrt{2} \sin 35°$

**39.** $\dfrac{\cos 3y + \cos(2x - 3y)}{\sin 3y + \sin(2x - 3y)} = \cot x$

**40.** $\dfrac{\sin 10° - \sin 50°}{\cos 50° - \cos 10°} = \sqrt{3}$

**41.** $\dfrac{\sin 40° - \sin 20°}{\cos 20° - \cos 40°} = \dfrac{\sin 10° - \sin 50°}{\cos 50° - \cos 10°}$

**42.** Suppose that $a$ and $b$ are in the open interval $(0, \pi/2)$ and $a \neq b$. If $\sin a + \sin b = \cos a + \cos b$, show that $a + b = \pi/2$.   *Hint:* Begin with the sum-to-product formulas.

**43.** Refer to the figure. Using calculus, it can be shown that the area of the first-quadrant region under the curve $y = 1/(1 + x^2)$ from $x = 0$ to $x = a$ is given by the expression $\tan^{-1} a$. Use this fact to carry out the following calculations.

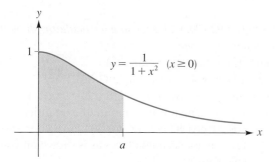

$y = \dfrac{1}{1 + x^2}$   $(x \geq 0)$

**(a)** Find the area of the first-quadrant region under the curve $y = 1/(1 + x^2)$ from $x = 0$ to $x = 1$.

**(b)** Find a value of $a$ so that the area of the first-quadrant region under the curve from $x = 0$ to $x = a$ is: (i) 1.5; (ii) 1.56; (iii) 1.57. In each case, round your answer to the nearest integer.

**44.** The figure at the top of the next column shows the graph of the curve $y = 1/\sqrt{1 - x^2}$ for $0 \leq x < 1$.

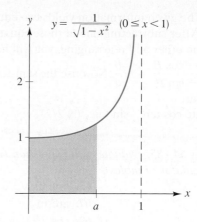

$y = \dfrac{1}{\sqrt{1 - x^2}}$   $(0 \leq x < 1)$

Using calculus it can be shown that the area of the first-quadrant region bounded by this curve, the coordinate axes, and the line $x = a$ is given by $\sin^{-1} a$. Use this fact to carry out the following calculations.

**(a)** Find the area of the first-quadrant region under this curve from $x = 0$ to $x = \sqrt{2}/2$. Give both the exact form of the answer and a calculator approximation rounded to three decimal places.

**(b)** Find a value of $a$ so that the area of the first-quadrant region under the curve from $x = 0$ to $x = a$ is 1.5. Round your answer to three decimal places.

*In Exercises 45–61, find all solutions of each equation in the interval $[0, 2\pi)$. In cases in which a calculator is necessary, round the answers to two decimal places.*

**45.** $\tan x = 4.26$      **46.** $\tan x = -4.26$

**47.** $\csc x = 2.24$      **48.** $\sin(\sin x) = \pi/6$

**49.** $\tan^2 x - 3 = 0$      **50.** $\cot^2 x - \cot x = 0$

**51.** $1 + \sin x = \cos x$      **52.** $2 \sin 3x - \sqrt{3} = 0$

**53.** $\sin x - \cos 2x + 1 = 0$      **54.** $\sin x + \sin 2x = 0$

**55.** $3 \csc x - 4 \sin x = 0$

**56.** $2 \sin^2 x + \sin x - 1 = 0$

**57.** $2 \sin^4 x - 3 \sin^2 x + 1 = 0$

**58.** $\sec^2 x - \sec x - 2 = 0$      **59.** $\sin^4 x + \cos^4 x = 5/8$

**60.** $4 \sin^2 2x + \cos 2x - 2 \cos^2 x - 2 = 0$

**61.** $\cot x + \csc x + \sec x = \tan x$   *Suggestion:* If you use sines and cosines, the given equation becomes $\cos^2 x - \sin^2 x + \cos x + \sin x = 0$, which can be factored.

**62.** If $A$ and $B$ both are solutions of the equation $a \cos x + b \sin x = c$, show that

$$\tan\left[\frac{1}{2}(A + B)\right] = \frac{b}{a}$$

*(continues)*

*Hint*: The given information yields two equations. After subtracting one of those equations from the other and rearranging, you will have $\dfrac{\cos A - \cos B}{\sin A - \sin B} = -\dfrac{b}{a}$. Now use the sum-to-product formulas.

**63.** Evaluate $\cos \tan^{-1} \sin \tan^{-1}(\sqrt{2}/2)$.

*In Exercises 64–85, evaluate each expression (without using a calculator or tables).*

**64.** $\cos^{-1}(-\sqrt{2}/2)$  
**65.** $\arctan(\sqrt{3}/3)$  
**66.** $\sin^{-1} 0$  
**67.** $\arcsin \frac{1}{2}$  
**68.** $\arctan \sqrt{3}$  
**69.** $\cos^{-1}(\frac{1}{2})$  
**70.** $\tan^{-1}(-1)$  
**71.** $\cos^{-1}(-\frac{1}{2})$  
**72.** $\sin(\sin^{-1} 1)$  
**73.** $\cos[\cos^{-1}(\frac{2}{7})]$  
**74.** $\sin^{-1}(\sin \frac{\pi}{7})$  
**75.** $\cos^{-1}(\cos 5)$  
**76.** $\sin^{-1}(\sin 2)$  
**77.** $\sin[\tan^{-1}(-1)]$  
**78.** $\sin[\arccos(-\frac{1}{2})]$  
**79.** $\sec[\cos^{-1}(\sqrt{2}/3)]$  
**80.** $\cot[\cos^{-1}(\frac{1}{2})]$  
**81.** $\tan[\frac{\pi}{4} + \sin^{-1}(\frac{5}{13})]$  
**82.** $\sin(\frac{3\pi}{2} + \arccos \frac{3}{5})$  
**83.** $\tan(2 \tan^{-1} 2)$  
**84.** $\sin[2 \sin^{-1}(\frac{4}{5})]$  
**85.** $\cos[\frac{1}{2} \cos^{-1}(\frac{4}{5})]$  

**86.** In this exercise we investigate the relationship between the variables $x$ and $\theta$ in the accompanying figure. (Assume that $\theta$ is in radians.)

**(a)** Refer to the figure. Show that

$$\theta = \tan^{-1}\left(\frac{10}{x}\right) - \tan^{-1}\left(\frac{4}{x}\right)$$

**(b)** Use your calculator to complete the following table. (Round the results to two decimal places.) Which $x$-value in the table yields the largest value for $\theta$?

| $x$ | 0.1 | 1 | 2 | 3 | 10 | 100 |
|-----|-----|---|---|---|----|-----|
| $\theta$ | | | | | | |

**(c)** As indicated in the following graph, the value of $x$ that makes $\theta$ as large as possible is a number between 5 and 10, closer to 5 than to 10.

Using calculus, it can be shown that this value of $x$ is, in fact, $2\sqrt{10}$. Use your calculator to evaluate $2\sqrt{10}$; check that the result is consistent with the given graph. What is the corresponding value of $\theta$ in this case? Also, give the coordinates of the highest point on the accompanying graph. Round both coordinates to two decimal places.

**(d)** What is the degree measure for the angle $\theta$ obtained in part (c)? Round the answer to one decimal place.

*In Exercises 87–91, show that each equation is an identity.*

**87.** $\tan(\tan^{-1} x + \tan^{-1} y) = (x + y)/(1 - xy)$  
**88.** $\tan^{-1}(x/\sqrt{1 - x^2}) = \sin^{-1} x$  
**89.** $\sin(2 \arctan x) = 2x/(1 + x^2)$  
**90.** $\cos(2 \cos^{-1} x) = 2x^2 - 1$  
**91.** $\sin[\frac{1}{2} \sin^{-1}(x^2)] = \sqrt{\frac{1}{2} - \frac{1}{2}\sqrt{1 - x^4}}$  

*In Exercises 92–94, without using a calculator, show that each statement is true.*

**92.** $\tan^{-1}(\frac{1}{3}) + \tan^{-1}(\frac{1}{5}) = \tan^{-1}(\frac{4}{7})$  
**93.** $\arcsin(4\sqrt{41}/41) + \arcsin(\sqrt{82}/82) = \pi/4$  
**94.** $\tan[\sin^{-1}(\frac{1}{3}) + \cos^{-1}(\frac{1}{2})] = \frac{1}{5}(8\sqrt{2} + 9\sqrt{3})$  

**95. (a)** Use a calculator to compute the quantity $\cos 20° \cos 40° \cos 60° \cos 80°$. Give your answer to as many decimal places as is shown on your calculator.

**(b)** Now use a product-to-sum formula to *prove* that the display on your calculator is the exact value of the given expression, not an approximation.

**96.** In this exercise we will use the accompanying figure to derive the half-angle formula for sine:

$$\sin \frac{\theta}{2} = \pm\sqrt{\frac{1}{2}(1 - \cos \theta)}$$

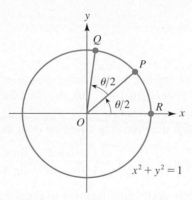

Our derivation will make use of the formula for the distance between two points and the identity $\sin^2 t + \cos^2 t = 1$. However, we will not rely on an addition formula for sine, as we did in Section 8.2.

**(a)** Explain why the coordinates of $P$ and $Q$ are $P(\cos \frac{\theta}{2}, \sin \frac{\theta}{2})$ and $Q(\cos \theta, \sin \theta)$.

**(b)** Use the distance formula to show that

$$(PQ)^2 = 2 - 2 \cos \frac{\theta}{2} \cos \theta - 2 \sin \frac{\theta}{2} \sin \theta$$

and

$$(PR)^2 = 2 - 2 \cos \frac{\theta}{2}$$

**(c)** Explain why $\triangle POR$ is congruent to $\triangle QOP$.

**(d)** From part (c), it follows that $(PQ)^2 = (PR)^2$. By equating the expressions for $(PQ)^2$ and $(PR)^2$ [obtained in part (b)], show that

$$\sin \frac{\theta}{2} \sin \theta = \left( \cos \frac{\theta}{2} \right)(1 - \cos \theta)$$

**(e)** Square both sides of the equation obtained in part (d); then replace $\cos^2(\theta/2)$ by $1 - \sin^2(\theta/2)$ and show that the resulting equation can be written

$$[\sin^2(\theta/2)](2 - 2 \cos \theta) = (1 - \cos \theta)^2$$

**(f)** Solve the equation in part (e) for the quantity $\sin \frac{\theta}{2}$. You should obtain

$$\sin \frac{\theta}{2} = \pm \sqrt{\tfrac{1}{2}(1 - \cos \theta)} \qquad \text{as required}$$

*In Exercises 97–99, prove that the equations are identities. (These identities appear in* Trigonometry and Double Algebra, *by August DeMorgan, published in 1849.)*

**97.** $\sin 2\theta = 2/(\cot \theta + \tan \theta)$

**98.** $\sin 2\theta = \dfrac{\tan(45° + \theta) - \tan(45° - \theta)}{\tan(45° + \theta) + \tan(45° - \theta)}$

**99.** $\cos 2\theta = 1/(1 + \tan 2\theta \tan \theta)$

**100.** Prove the following two identities. These identities were given by the Swiss mathematician Leonhard Euler in 1748.

  **(a)** $\tan 2\theta = \dfrac{2 \tan \theta}{1 - \tan^2 \theta}$

  **(b)** $\cot 2\theta = \dfrac{\cot \theta - \tan \theta}{2}$

**101.** Prove the following two identities. These identities were given by the Swiss mathematician Johann Heinrich Lambert in 1765.

  **(a)** $\sin 2\theta = \dfrac{2 \tan \theta}{1 + \tan^2 \theta}$

  **(b)** $\cos 2\theta = \dfrac{1 - \tan^2 \theta}{1 + \tan^2 \theta}$

**102.** Prove the following identity, which was essentially given by the German mathematician Johann Müller (known as "Regiomontanus") around 1464.

$$\frac{\sin A + \sin B}{\sin A - \sin B} = \frac{\tan[\frac{1}{2}(A + B)]}{\tan[\frac{1}{2}(A - B)]}$$

**103.** Prove the following identity, given by the Austrian mathematician George Joachim Rhaeticus in 1569.

$$\cos n\theta = \cos[(n - 2)\theta] - 2 \sin \theta \sin[(n - 1)\theta]$$

**104.** Suppose that $x + \dfrac{1}{x} = 2 \cos \theta$.

  **(a)** Show that $x^2 + \dfrac{1}{x^2} = 2 \cos 2\theta$.

  **(b)** Show that $x^3 + \dfrac{1}{x^3} = 2 \cos 3\theta$.

# Chapter 8  Test

1. Use an appropriate addition formula to simplify the expression $\sin(\theta + \frac{3\pi}{2})$.

2. Compute $\cos 2t$ given that $\sin t = -2\sqrt{5}/5$ and $3\pi/2 < t < 2\pi$.

3. Compute $\tan(\theta/2)$ given that $\cos\theta = -5/13$ and $\pi < \theta < 3\pi/2$.

4. Use a calculator to find all solutions of the equation $\sin x = 3\cos x$ in the interval $(0, 2\pi)$.

5. Find all solutions of the equation

$$2\sin^2 x + 7\sin x + 3 = 0$$

on the interval $0 \le x \le 2\pi$.

6. If $\cos\alpha = 2/\sqrt{5}$ ($\frac{3\pi}{2} < \alpha < 2\pi$) and $\sin\beta = 4/5$ ($\frac{\pi}{2} < \beta < \pi$), compute $\sin(\beta - \alpha)$.

7. Find all solutions of the equation $\sin(x + 30°) = \sqrt{3}\sin x$ on the interval $0° < x < 90°$.

8. If $\csc\theta = -3$ and $\pi < \theta < 3\pi/2$, compute $\sin(\theta/2)$.

9. On the same set of axes, sketch the graphs of the restricted sine function and the function $y = \sin^{-1} x$. Specify the domain and the range for each function.

10. Compute each of the following quantities:
    (a) $\sin^{-1}[\sin(\pi/10)]$ (b) $\sin^{-1}(\sin 2\pi)$

11. Compute $\cos(\arcsin\frac{3}{4})$.

12. Prove that the following equation is an identity:

$$\tan\left(\frac{\pi}{4} + \frac{\theta}{2}\right) = \frac{1 + \cos\theta + \sin\theta}{1 + \cos\theta - \sin\theta}$$

13. Use a product-to-sum formula to simplify the expression $\sin(7\pi/24)\cos(\pi/24)$.

14. Use the sum-to-product formulas to simplify the expression

$$\frac{\sin 3\theta + \sin 5\theta}{\cos 3\theta + \cos 5\theta}$$

15. Simplify the following expression:
    $\sec(\arctan\sqrt{x^2 - 1})$. (Assume that $x > 1$.)

16. Sketch a graph of the function $y = \tan^{-1} x$, and specify the domain and the range.

# Additional Topics In Trigonometry

*The subject of trigonometry is an excellent example of a branch of mathematics . . . which was motivated by both practical and intellectual interests—surveying, map-making, and navigation on the one hand, and curiosity about the size of the universe on the other. With it the Alexandrian mathematicians triangulated the universe and rendered precise their knowledge about the Earth and the heavens.*—Morris Klein in *Mathematics in Western Culture* (New York: Oxford University Press, 1953)

In this chapter we develop six topics that require a background in basic trigonometry. The first two of these topics, discussed in Section 9.1, are the law of sines and the law of cosines. These laws relate the angles and the lengths of the sides in any triangle. The next two sections, 9.2 and 9.3, introduce the important topic of vectors, first from a geometric standpoint, then from an algebraic standpoint. In Sections 9.4 through 9.6 we expand on some of the ideas in Chapters 2 and 3 on graphs and equations. The topics presented here are parametric equations and polar coordinates.

## 9.1 THE LAW OF SINES AND THE LAW OF COSINES

*The ratio of the sides of a triangle to each other is the same as the ratio of the sines of the opposite angles.*—Bartholomaus Pitiscus (1561–1613) in his text, *Trigonometriae sive de dimensione triangulorum libri quinque.* This text was first published in Frankfort, Germany, in 1595, and according to several historians of mathematics, it was the first satisfactory textbook on trigonometry.

In this section we discuss two formulas relating the sides and the angles in any triangle: the *law of sines* and the *law of cosines*. These formulas can be used to determine an unknown side or angle using given information about the triangle. As you will see, which formula to apply in a particular case depends on what data are initially given.

We will usually follow the convention of denoting the angles of a triangle by *A*, *B*, and *C* and the lengths of the corresponding opposite sides by *a*, *b*, and *c*; see Figure 1 on the next page. With this notation we are ready to state the law of sines.

### The Law of Sines

In any triangle the ratio of the sine of an angle to the length of its opposite side is constant:

$$\frac{\sin A}{a} = \frac{\sin B}{b} = \frac{\sin C}{c}$$

Figure 1

Equivalently,

$$\frac{a}{\sin A} = \frac{b}{\sin B} = \frac{c}{\sin C}$$

*Note*: The numerical value of the constant ratio $a/\sin A$ is not used directly in typical applications of the law of sines. However, the geometric meaning of this constant is derived in Exercise 47 at the end of this section.

The proof of the law of sines is easy. We use the following result from Section 6.4: The area of any triangle is equal to half the product of two sides times the sine of the included angle. Thus with reference to Figure 1 we have

$$\frac{1}{2}bc \sin A = \frac{1}{2}ac \sin B = \frac{1}{2}ab \sin C$$

since each of these three expressions equals the area of triangle $ABC$. Now we just multiply through by the quantity $2/abc$ to obtain

$$\frac{\sin A}{a} = \frac{\sin B}{b} = \frac{\sin C}{c}$$

which completes the proof.

*Note*: To use the law of sines effectively, we must know one angle and the length of its opposite side plus one additional angle or side. Why?

---

**EXAMPLE** **1** **Using the law of sines to find a length**

Find the length $x$ in Figure 2.

**SOLUTION**
We have an angle, 30°; the length of its opposite side, 20 cm; and one more angle, 135°. So the law of sines applies. We have

$$\frac{\sin 30°}{20} = \frac{\sin 135°}{x}$$

length of side opposite } ↑        ↑ { length of side opposite
the 30° angle                          the 135° angle

$$x \sin 30° = 20 \sin 135°$$

$$x = \frac{20 \sin 135°}{\sin 30°} = \frac{20(\sqrt{2}/2)}{1/2} = 20\sqrt{2} \text{ cm}$$

Figure 2

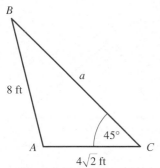

Figure 3

| EXAMPLE | 2 | **Using the law of sines to find a length** |

Find the length $y$ in Figure 3.

**SOLUTION**
We have an angle, 75°; the length of its opposite side, 10.2 in.; and one more angle, 62°. So the law of sines applies. To find $y$, we need to determine the angle $\theta$ in Figure 3. Since the sum of the angles in any triangle is 180°, we have

$$\theta = 180° - (75° + 62°) = 43°$$

Now, using the law of sines, we obtain

$$\frac{y}{\sin 43°} = \frac{10.2}{\sin 75°}$$

$$y = \frac{10.2 \sin 43°}{\sin 75°}$$

This is the exact answer. For an approximation a calculator yields

$$y \approx 7.2 \text{ in.}$$

Using given measurements in a triangle to find the remaining measurements is called solving the triangle. This is what we are asked to do in the next example.

| EXAMPLE | 3 | **Using the law of sines to solve a triangle** |

In $\triangle ABC$ we are given $\angle C = 45°$, $b = 4\sqrt{2}$ ft, and $c = 8$ ft. Solve the triangle; that is, determine the remaining side and angles.

**SOLUTION**
First let's draw a preliminary sketch conveying the given data; see Figure 4. (The sketch must be considered tentative. At the outset we don't know whether the other angles are acute or even whether the given data are compatible.) We have an angle, 45°, and the length of its opposite side, 8 ft. Since we have $b = 4\sqrt{2}$ ft, we can use the law of sines to find $B$. Thus

$$\frac{\sin B}{4\sqrt{2}} = \frac{\sin 45°}{8}$$

Then

$$\sin B = \frac{4\sqrt{2} \sin 45°}{8} = \frac{4\sqrt{2}(\sqrt{2}/2)}{8} = \frac{1}{2}$$

So

$$\sin B = \frac{1}{2}$$

From our previous work we know that one possibility for $B$ is 30°, since $\sin 30° = 1/2$. However, there is another possibility. Since the reference angle for

Figure 4

150° is 30°, we know that sin 150° is also equal to 1/2. Which angle do we want? For the problem at hand this is easy to answer. Since angle $C$ is given as 45°, angle $B$ cannot equal 150°, for the sum of 45° and 150° exceeds 180°. We conclude that

$$\angle B = 30°$$

Next, since $\angle B = 30°$ and $\angle C = 45°$, we have

$$\angle A = 180° - (30° + 45°) = 105°$$

Finally, we use the law of sines to find $a$. From the equation $a/\sin A = c/\sin C$ we have

$$a = \frac{c \sin A}{\sin C} = \frac{8 \sin 105°}{\sin 45°} = \frac{8 \sin 105°}{1/\sqrt{2}}$$
$$= 8\sqrt{2} \sin 105° \text{ ft} \approx 10.9 \text{ ft}$$

In the preceding example, two possibilities arose for the angle $B$: both 30° and 150°. However, it turned out that the value 150° was incompatible with the given information in the problem. In Exercise 13 at the end of this section you will see a case in which both of two possibilities are compatible with the given data. This results in two distinct solutions to the problem. In contrast to this, Exercise 11(a) shows a case in which there is no triangle fulfilling the given conditions. For these reasons the case in which we are given two sides and an angle opposite one of them is sometimes referred to as the **ambiguous case.**

Now we turn to the law of cosines.

## The Law of Cosines

In any triangle the square of the length of any side equals the sum of the squares of the lengths of the other two sides minus twice the product of the lengths of those other two sides times the cosine of their included angle.

$$a^2 = b^2 + c^2 - 2bc \cos A$$

$$b^2 = c^2 + a^2 - 2ca \cos B$$

$$c^2 = a^2 + b^2 - 2ab \cos C$$

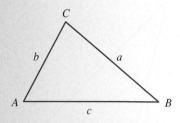

Before looking at a proof of this law, we make two preliminary comments. First, it is important to understand that the three equations in the box all follow the same pattern. For example, look at the first equation:

$$\underbrace{a^2 = b^2 + c^2 - 2bc \cos A}$$

side and opposite angle

sides that include this angle

Now check for yourself that the other two equations also follow this pattern. It is the pattern that is important here; after all, not every triangle is labeled $ABC$.

The second observation is that the law of cosines is a generalization of the Pythagorean theorem. In fact, look what happens to the equation

$$a^2 = b^2 + c^2 - 2bc \cos A$$

when angle $A$ is a right angle:

$$a^2 = b^2 + c^2 - 2bc \underbrace{\cos 90°}_{0}$$

$$a^2 = b^2 + c^2 \qquad \text{which is the Pythagorean theorem}$$

Now let us prove the law of cosines:

$$a^2 = b^2 + c^2 - 2bc \cos A$$

(The other two equations can be proved in the same way. Indeed, just relabeling the figure would suffice.) The proof that we give uses coordinate geometry in a very nice way to complement the trigonometry. We begin by placing angle $A$ in standard position, as indicated in Figure 5. (So in the figure, angle $A$ is then identified with angle $CAB$.) Then if $u$ and $v$ denote the lengths indicated in Figure 5, the coordinates of $C$ are $(u, v)$, and we have

$$\cos A = \frac{\text{adjacent}}{\text{hypotenuse}} = \frac{u}{b} \qquad \text{and therefore} \qquad u = b \cos A$$

Similarly, we have

$$\sin A = \frac{\text{opposite}}{\text{hypotenuse}} = \frac{v}{b} \qquad \text{and therefore} \qquad v = b \sin A$$

Thus the coordinates of $C$ are

$$(b \cos A, b \sin A)$$

(Exercise 44 at the end of this section asks you to check that these represent the coordinates of $C$ even when angle $A$ is not acute.)

Now we use the distance formula,

$$d = \sqrt{(x_2 - x_1)^2 + (y_2 - y_1)^2}$$

or, equivalently,

$$d^2 = (x_2 - x_1)^2 + (y_2 - y_1)^2$$

to compute the square of the distance $a$ between the points $C\,(b \cos A, b \sin A)$ and $B\,(c, 0)$. We have

$$a^2 = (b \cos A - c)^2 + (b \sin A - 0)^2$$
$$= b^2 \cos^2 A - 2bc \cos A + c^2 + b^2 \sin^2 A$$
$$= b^2 \underbrace{(\cos^2 A + \sin^2 A)}_{1} - 2bc \cos A + c^2$$
$$= b^2 + c^2 - 2bc \cos A$$

completing our proof of the law of cosines.

Figure 5

7 cm

120°

8 cm

**Figure 6**

**EXAMPLE** | **4** | **Using the law of cosines to find a length**

Compute the length $x$ in Figure 6.

**SOLUTION**
Note the law of sines does not apply. Why? The law of cosines is directly applicable. We have

$$x^2 = 7^2 + 8^2 - 2(7)(8)\cos 120°$$
$$= 49 + 64 - 112\left(-\frac{1}{2}\right) = 169$$
$$x = \sqrt{169} = 13 \text{ cm}$$

The law of cosines can be used effectively if we know the lengths of the sides of a triangle. For example, if the equation $a^2 = b^2 + c^2 - 2bc \cos A$ is solved for $\cos A$, the result is

$$\cos A = \frac{b^2 + c^2 - a^2}{2bc}$$

This expresses the cosine of an angle in a triangle in terms of the lengths of the sides. In a similar fashion we obtain the corresponding formulas

$$\cos B = \frac{c^2 + a^2 - b^2}{2ca} \quad \text{and} \quad \cos C = \frac{a^2 + b^2 - c^2}{2ab}$$

These alternative forms for the law of cosines are used in the next example.

**EXAMPLE** | **5** | **Using the law of cosines to find angles**

In triangle $ABC$ the sides are $a = 3$ units, $b = 5$ units, and $c = 7$ units. Find the angles. (Use degree measure.)

**SOLUTION**
Figure 7 summarizes the given data. We have

$$\cos A = \frac{b^2 + c^2 - a^2}{2bc} = \frac{5^2 + 7^2 - 3^2}{2(5)(7)} = \frac{65}{70} = \frac{13}{14}$$

$B$

$c = 7$

$a = 3$

$C$

$b = 5$

$A$

**Figure 7**

Now that we know $\cos A = 13/14$, we can find $\angle A$ by using a calculator to compute $\cos^{-1}(13/14)$. Since we are required to give the answer in degree measure, we first set the calculator to the degree mode. Then we obtain

$$\cos^{-1}(13/14) \approx 21.7867893 \quad \text{using a calculator set in the degree mode}$$

and therefore

$$\angle A \approx 21.8° \quad \text{rounding to one decimal place}$$

Why is there no second possible angle $\angle A$? In a similar manner we have

$$\cos B = \frac{c^2 + a^2 - b^2}{2ca} = \frac{7^2 + 3^2 - 5^2}{2(7)(3)} = \frac{33}{42} = \frac{11}{14}$$

So cos $B = 11/14$, and a calculator then yields $\angle B \approx 38.2132107° \approx 38.2°$.

At this point we can find $\angle C$ in either of two ways. Each has its advantage. The first way is to begin by computing cos $C$ in the same way that we found cos $A$ and cos $B$. As you can check, the result is cos $C = -1/2$. A calculator is not needed in this case. We know from previous work that $\angle C$ must be 120°. The second method that can be used relies on the fact that the sum of the angles in a triangle is 180°. Thus we have

$$\angle C = 180° - \angle A - \angle B$$
$$\approx 180° - 21.7867893° - 38.2132107°$$
$$\approx 120.0°$$

This way is quicker than the first method. The disadvantage, however, is that we know that $\angle C$ is only approximately 120°. The first method (using the cosine law) is longer, but it tells us that $\angle C$ is exactly 120°. In summary, then, the three required angles are

$$\angle A \approx 21.8° \qquad \angle B \approx 38.2° \qquad \angle C = 120°$$

Alternatively, after finding angle $\angle A$, we could have used the law of sines to find a second angle, say, $\angle B$. In this example, given the lengths of all three sides, there will be no ambiguity in $\angle B$. Why? Finally, we could find $\angle C$ using the law of sines, the law of cosines, or the fact that the sum of the angles in a triangle is 180°.

We conclude this section with an example indicating how the law of sines and the law of cosines are used in navigation. In this example you'll see the term *bearing* used in specifying the location of one point relative to another. To explain this term, we refer to Figure 8.

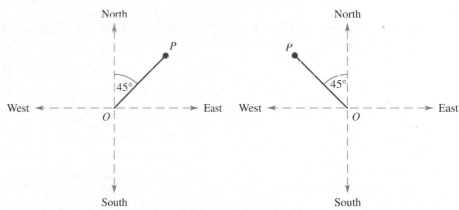

**Figure 8**    (a)  The bearing of $P$ from $O$ is N45°E.        (b)  The bearing of $P$ from $O$ is N45°W.

In Figure 8(a) the bearing of $P$ from $O$ is N45°E (read "north, 45° east"). This bearing tells us the *acute* angle between line segment $\overline{OP}$ and the north–south line through $O$. In Figure 8(b) the bearing of $P$ from $O$ is N45°W (read "north, 45° west"). Again, note that the bearing gives us the acute angle between line segment $\overline{OP}$ and the north–south line through $O$. Figure 9 provides additional examples of this terminology.

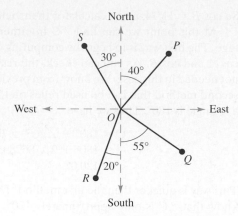

The bearing of $P$ from $O$ is N40°E.

The bearing of $Q$ from $O$ is S55°E.

The bearing of $R$ from $O$ is S20°W.

The bearing of $S$ from $O$ is N30°W.

**Figure 9**
The bearing is specified by means of the acute angle measured from the north–south line.

  **EXAMPLE 6** Using the law of sines and the law of cosines in navigation

A small fire is sighted from ranger stations $A$ and $B$. The bearing of the fire from station $A$ is N35°E, and the bearing of the fire from station $B$ is N49°W. Station $A$ is 1.3 miles due west of station $B$.

**(a)** How far is the fire from each ranger station?

**(b)** At fire station $C$, which is 1.5 miles from $A$, there is a helicopter that can be used to drop water on the fire. If the bearing of $C$ from $A$ is S42°E, find the distance from $C$ to the fire, and find the bearing of the fire from $C$.

**SOLUTION**

**(a)** In Figure 10 we have sketched the situation involving ranger stations $A$ and $B$ and the fire (denoted by $F$).

We compute the angles of $\triangle ABF$ as follows.

$$\angle FAB = 90° - 35° = 55° \qquad \angle FBA = 90° - 49° = 41°$$
$$\angle F = 180° - (55° + 41°) = 84°$$

We can now use the law of sines in $\triangle ABF$ to compute $AF$ and $BF$.

**Figure 10**

$$\frac{AF}{\sin \angle FBA} = \frac{AB}{\sin \angle F} \qquad\qquad \frac{BF}{\sin \angle FAB} = \frac{AB}{\sin \angle F}$$

and therefore

$$AF = \frac{AB \sin \angle FBA}{\sin \angle F} \qquad\qquad BF = \frac{AB \sin \angle FAB}{\sin \angle F}$$

or

$$AF = \frac{(1.3)\sin 41°}{\sin 84°} \qquad\qquad BF = \frac{(1.3)\sin 55°}{\sin 84°}$$

We use a calculator to evaluate these expressions for $AF$ and $BF$. As you should check for yourself, the results (rounded to the nearest tenth of a mile) are

$$AF \approx 0.9 \text{ miles} \qquad \text{and} \qquad BF \approx 1.1 \text{ miles}$$

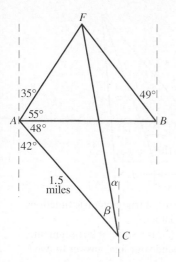

Figure 11

**(b)** We draw a sketch of the situation, as shown in Figure 11. In Figure 11 we can compute $CF$, the distance from the helicopter to the fire, using the law of cosines in $\triangle CAF$. First, note that $\angle CAF = 48° + 55° = 103°$. So we have

$$CF = \sqrt{AC^2 + AF^2 - 2 \cdot AC \cdot AF \cdot \cos 103°}$$

$$= \sqrt{1.5^2 + \left(\frac{1.3 \sin 41°}{\sin 84°}\right)^2 - 2(1.5)\left(\frac{1.3 \sin 41°}{\sin 84°}\right)\cos 103°}$$

$$\approx 1.9 \text{ miles} \qquad \text{using a calculator and rounding to one decimal place}$$

To find the bearing of the fire at $F$ from the fire station at $C$, we need to determine the angle $\alpha$ in Figure 11. First we find the angle $\beta$. Using the law of sines in $\triangle CAF$, we have

$$\frac{\sin \beta}{AF} = \frac{\sin 103°}{CF}$$

and therefore

$$\sin \beta = \frac{AF \cdot \sin 103°}{CF}$$

Before using the inverse sine function and a calculator to compute $\beta$, we note from Figure 11 that $\beta$ is an acute angle (because $\beta$ is an angle in $\triangle CAF$, and in that triangle, $\angle CAF$ is greater than 90°). So in this particular application of the law of sines there is no ambiguity. We have then

$$\beta = \sin^{-1}\left(\frac{AF \cdot \sin 103°}{CF}\right)$$

Now, on the right-hand side of this last equation we substitute the expressions we obtained previously for $AF$ and $CF$; then, using a calculator set in the degree mode, we obtain

$$\beta \approx 26° \qquad \text{rounding to the nearest degree}$$

(You should verify this calculator value for yourself.) Now that we know $\beta$, we can determine the bearing of the fire from station $C$. From Figure 11 we have

$$\alpha + \beta = 42° \quad \text{(Why?)}$$

and therefore

$$\alpha = 42° - \beta = 42° - 26° = 16° \qquad \text{to the nearest degree}$$

In summary now, fire station $C$ is approximately 1.9 miles from the fire, and the bearing of the fire from station $C$ is N16°W.

# EXERCISE SET 9.1

**A**

In Exercises 1–8, assume that the vertices and the lengths of the sides of a triangle are labeled as in Figure 1 on page 646. For Exercises 1–4, leave your answers in terms of radicals or the trigonometric functions; that is, don't use a calculator. In Exer- cises 5–8, use a calculator and round your final answers to one decimal place.

1. If $\angle A = 60°$, $\angle B = 45°$, and $BC = 12$ cm, find $AC$.
2. If $\angle A = 30°$, $\angle B = 135°$, and $BC = 4$ cm, find $AC$.
3. If $\angle B = 100°$, $\angle C = 30°$, and $AB = 10$ cm, find $BC$.

4. If $\angle A = \angle B = 35°$, and $AB = 16$ cm, find $AC$ and $BC$.
5. If $\angle A = 36°$, $\angle B = 50°$, and $b = 12.61$ cm, find $a$ and $c$.
6. If $\angle B = 81°$, $\angle C = 55°$, and $b = 6.24$ cm, find $c$ and $a$.
7. If $a = 29.45$ cm, $b = 30.12$ cm, and $\angle B = 66°$, find the remaining side and angles of the triangle.
8. If $a = 52.15$ cm, $c = 42.90$ cm, and $\angle A = 125°$, find the remaining side and angles of the triangle.

*In Exercises 9 and 10, use degree measure for your answers. In parts (c) and (d), use a calculator and round the results to one decimal place.*

9. (a) In $\triangle ABC$, $\sin B = \sqrt{2}/2$. What are the possible values for $\angle B$?
   (b) In $\triangle DEF$, $\cos E = \sqrt{2}/2$. What are the possible values for $\angle E$?
   (c) In $\triangle GHI$, $\sin H = 1/4$. What are the possible values for $\angle H$?
   (d) In $\triangle JKL$, $\cos K = -2/3$. What are the possible values for $\angle K$?

10. (a) In $\triangle ABC$, $\sin B = \sqrt{3}/2$. What are the possible values for $\angle B$?
    (b) In $\triangle DEF$, $\cos E = -\sqrt{3}/2$. What are the possible values for $\angle E$?
    (c) In $\triangle GHI$, $\sin H = 2/9$. What are the possible values for $\angle H$?
    (d) In $\triangle JKL$, $\cos K = 2/3$. What are the possible values for $\angle K$?

11. (a) Show that there is no triangle satisfying the conditions $a = 2.0$ ft, $b = 6.0$ ft, and $\angle A = 23.1°$
    *Hint*: Try computing $\sin B$ using the law of sines.
    (b) If $a = 2.0$ ft, $b = 3.0$ ft, $\angle A = 23.1°$, and $\angle B$ is obtuse, show that $c = 1.1$ ft.

12. (a) Show that there is no triangle with $a = 2$, $b = 3$, and $\angle A = 42°$.
    (b) Is there any triangle in which $a = 2$, $b = 3$, and $\angle A = 41°$?

13. Let $b = 1$, $a = \sqrt{2}$, and $\angle B = 30°$.
    (a) Use the law of sines to show that $\sin A = \sqrt{2}/2$. Conclude that $\angle A = 45°$ or $\angle A = 135°$.
    (b) Assuming that $\angle A = 45°$, determine the remaining parts of $\triangle ABC$.
    (c) Assuming that $\angle A = 135°$, determine the remaining parts of $\triangle ABC$.
    (d) Find the areas of the two triangles.

14. Let $a = 30$, $b = 36$, and $\angle A = 20°$.
    (a) Show that $\angle B = 24.23°$ or $\angle B = 155.77°$ (rounding to two decimal places).
    (b) Determine the remaining parts for each of the two possible triangles. Round your final results to two decimal places. [However, in your calculations, do *not* work with rounded values. (Why?)]
    (c) Find the areas of the two triangles.

15. Find the lengths $a$, $b$, $c$, and $d$ in the following figure.

Leave your answers in terms of trigonometric functions (rather than using a calculator).

16. In the following figure, $\overline{PQR}$ is a straight line segment. Find the distance $PR$. Round your final answer to two decimal places.

17. Two points $P$ and $Q$ are on opposite sides of a river (see the sketch). From $P$ to another point $R$ on the same side is 300 ft. Angles $PRQ$ and $RPQ$ are found to be 20° and 120°, respectively. Compute the distance from $P$ to $Q$, across the river. (Round your answer to the nearest foot.)

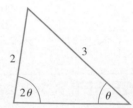

18. Determine the angle $\theta$ in the accompanying figure. Round your answer to two decimal places.

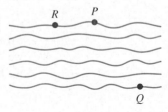

*In Exercises 19–22, use the law of cosines to determine the length x in each figure. For Exercises 19 and 20, leave your answers in terms of radicals. In Exercises 21 and 22, use a calculator and round the answers to one decimal place.*

**19. (a)**

5 cm
$x$
60°
8 cm

**(b)**

5 cm
$x$
120°
8 cm

**20. (a)**

4 cm
$x$
30°
10 cm

**(b)**

4 cm
$x$
150°
10 cm

**21. (a)**

7.3 cm
40°
$x$
11.5 cm

**(b)**

7.3 cm
140°
11.5 cm
$x$

**22. (a)**

1.2 m
$x$
72°
1.2 m

**(b)**

1.2 m
$x$
108°
1.2 m

*In Exercises 23 and 24, refer to the following figure.*

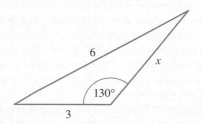

6
$x$
130°
3

**23.** In applying the law of cosines to the figure, a student incorrectly writes $x^2 = 3^2 + 6^2 - 2(3)(6)\cos 130°$. Why is this incorrect? What is the correct equation?

**24.** In applying the law of cosines to the figure, a student writes $6^2 = 3^2 + x^2 + 6x \cos 50°$. Why is this correct?

*In Exercises 25 and 26, use the given information to find the cosine of each angle in $\triangle ABC$.*

**25.** $a = 6$ cm, $b = 7$ cm, $c = 10$ cm

**26.** $a = 17$ cm, $b = 8$ cm, $c = 15$ cm (For this particular triangle, you can check your answers, because there is an alternative method of solution that does not require the law of cosines.)

*In Exercises 27–30, compute each angle of the given triangle. Where necessary, use a calculator and round to one decimal place.*

**27.** $a = 7, b = 8, c = 13$      **28.** $a = 33, b = 7, c = 37$

**29.** $a = b = 2/\sqrt{3}, c = 2$      **30.** $a = 36, b = 77, c = 85$

*In Exercises 31–34, round each answer to one decimal place.*

**31.** A regular pentagon is inscribed in a circle of radius 1 unit. Find the perimeter of the pentagon. *Hint:* First find the length of a side using the law of cosines.

**32.** Find the perimeter of a regular nine-sided polygon inscribed in a circle of radius 4 cm. (See the hint for Exercise 31.)

**33.** In $\triangle ABC$, $\angle A = 40°$, $b = 6.1$ cm, and $c = 3.2$ cm.
   **(a)** Find $a$ using the law of cosines.
   **(b)** Find $\angle C$ using the law of sines.
   **(c)** Find $\angle B$.

**34.** In parallelogram $ABCD$ you are given $AB = 6$ in., $AD = 4$ in., and $\angle A = 40°$. Find the length of each diagonal.

35. Town $B$ is 26 miles from town $A$ at a bearing of S15°W. Town $C$ is 54 miles from town $A$ at a bearing of S7°E. Compute the distance from town $B$ to town $C$. Round your final answer to the nearest mile.

36. Town $C$ is 5 miles due east of town $D$. Town $E$ is 12 miles from town $C$ at a bearing (from $C$) of N52°E.
    (a) How far apart are towns $D$ and $E$? (Round to the nearest one-half mile.)
    (b) Find the bearing of town $E$ from town $D$. (Round the angle to the nearest degree.)

37. An airplane crashes in a lake and is spotted by observers at lighthouses $A$ and $B$ along the coast. Lighthouse $B$ is 1.50 miles due east of lighthouse $A$. The bearing of the airplane from lighthouse $A$ is S20°E; the bearing of the plane from lighthouse $B$ is S42°W. Find the distance from each lighthouse to the crash site. (Round your final answers to two decimal places.)

38. (Continuation of Exercise 37) A rescue boat is in the lake, three-fourths of a mile from lighthouse $B$ and at a bearing of S35°E from lighthouse $B$.
    (a) Find the distance from the rescue boat to the airplane. Express your answer using miles and feet, with the portion in feet rounded to the nearest 10 feet.
    (b) Find the bearing of the plane from the rescue boat. (Your answer should have the form of S$\theta$°W. Round $\theta$ to two decimal places.)

39. (Refer to the following figure.) When the Sun is viewed from Earth, it subtends an angle of $\theta = 32'$ ($= 32/60$ degree). Assuming that the distance $d$ from Earth to the Sun is 92,690,000 miles, use the law of cosines to compute the diameter $D$ of the Sun. Round the answer to the nearest ten thousand miles.

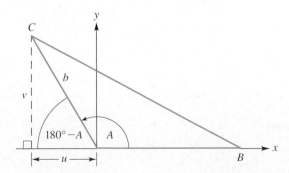

40. Compute the lengths $CD$ and $CE$ in the accompanying figure. Round the final answers to two decimal places.

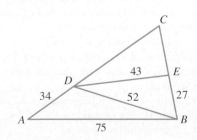

**B**

41. (a) Let $m$ and $n$ be positive numbers, with $m > n$. Furthermore, suppose that in triangle $ABC$ the lengths $a$, $b$, and $c$ are given by

$$a = 2mn + n^2 \qquad b = m^2 - n^2$$
$$c = m^2 + n^2 + mn$$

Show that $\cos C = -1/2$, and conclude that $\angle C = 120°$.

(b) Give an example of a triangle in which the lengths of the sides are whole numbers and one of the angles is 120°. (Specify the three sides; you needn't find the other angles.)

42. If the lengths of two adjacent sides of a parallelogram are $a$ and $b$, and if the acute angle formed by these two sides is $\theta$, show that the product of the lengths of the two diagonals is given by the expression

$$\sqrt{(a^2 + b^2)^2 - 4a^2b^2 \cos^2 \theta}$$

43. Two trains leave the railroad station at noon. The first train travels along a straight track at 90 mph. The second train travels at 75 mph along another straight track that makes an angle of 130° with the first track. At what time are the trains 400 miles apart? Round your answer to the nearest minute.

44. In this exercise you will complete a detail mentioned in the text in the proof of the law of cosines. Let the positive numbers $u$ and $v$ denote the lengths indicated in the figure at the top of the next column, so that the coordinates of $C$ are $(-u, v)$. Show that $u = -b \cos A$ and $v = b \sin A$. Conclude from this that the coordinates of $C$ are

$$(b \cos A, b \sin A)$$

*Hint:* Use the right-triangle definitions for cosine and sine along with the addition formulas for $\cos(180° - \theta)$ and $\sin(180° - \theta)$.

45. In the following figure, $ABCD$ is a square, $AB = 1$, and $\angle EAB = \angle EBA = 15°$. Show that $\triangle CDE$ is equilateral. *Hint:* First use the law of sines to find $AE$. Then use the law of cosines to find $DE$.

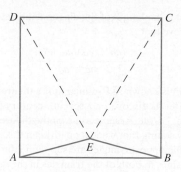

**46.** Use steps (a) through (c) to show that the area of any triangle *ABC* is given by the following expression:

$$\frac{a^2 - b^2}{2} \cdot \frac{\sin A \sin B}{\sin(A - B)}$$

**(a)** Use the law of sines to show that
$(a^2 - b^2)\sin A \sin B = ab(\sin^2 A - \sin^2 B)$.

**(b)** Prove the trigonometric identity
$\sin(A - B)\sin(A + B) = \sin^2 A - \sin^2 B$.

**(c)** Use the results in parts (a) and (b) to show that
$\frac{a^2 - b^2}{2} \cdot \frac{\sin A \sin B}{\sin(A - B)} = \frac{1}{2} ab \sin C$, which is the area of $\triangle ABC$, as required.

*As background for Exercises 47 and 48, refer to the figure below. The smaller circle in the figure is the **inscribed circle** for $\triangle ABC$. Each side of $\triangle ABC$ is tangent to the inscribed circle. The larger circle is the **circumscribed circle** for $\triangle ABC$. The circumscribed circle is the circle passing through the three vertices of the triangle.*

*In Exercises 47 and 48 you will derive expressions for the radii of the circumscribed circle and the inscribed circle for $\triangle ABC$. In these exercises, assume as given the following two results from geometry:*

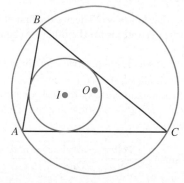

**i.** *The three angle bisectors of the angles of a triangle meet in a point. This point (labeled I in the figure) is the center of the inscribed circle.*

**ii.** *The perpendicular bisectors of the sides of a triangle meet in a point. This point (labeled O in the figure) is the center of the circumscribed circle.*

**47.** The following figure shows the circumscribed circle for $\triangle ABC$. The point $O$ is the center of the circle, and $\mathcal{R}$ is the radius.

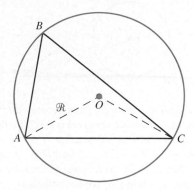

In this exercise you will derive the formulas for the radius $\mathcal{R}$ of the circumscribed circle for $\triangle ABC$:

$$\mathcal{R} = \frac{a}{2 \sin A} = \frac{b}{2 \sin B} = \frac{c}{2 \sin C}$$

**(a)** According to a theorem from geometry, the measure of $\angle AOC$ is twice the measure of $\angle B$. What theorem is this? (State the theorem using complete sentences.)

**(b)** Draw a perpendicular from $O$ to $\overline{AC}$, meeting $\overline{AC}$ at $T$. Explain why $AT = TC = b/2$. (As usual, $b$ denotes the length of the side opposite angle $B$.)
*Hint:* Result (i) or (ii) above may be useful.

**(c)** Explain why $\triangle ATO$ is congruent to $\triangle CTO$.

**(d)** Use the results in parts (a) and (c) to show that $\angle COT = \angle B$.

**(e)** Use the result in part (d) to show that $\mathcal{R} = b/(2 \sin B)$. From this we can conclude (by the law of sines) that

$$\mathcal{R} = \frac{a}{2 \sin A} = \frac{b}{2 \sin B} = \frac{c}{2 \sin C} \quad \text{as required}$$

**(f)** In the figure that we used for parts (a) through (e), the center of the circle falls within $\triangle ABC$. Draw a figure in which the center lies outside of $\triangle ABC$ and prove that the equation $\mathcal{R} = b/(2 \sin B)$ is true in this case, too.

**(g)** Two triangles have the same numerical value for the ratio that appears in the law of sines (the length of a side to the sine of its opposite angle). What geometric property do the two triangles have in common?

**48.** In this exercise you will show that the radius $r$ of the inscribed circle for $\triangle ABC$ is given by

$$r = 4\mathcal{R} \sin \frac{A}{2} \sin \frac{B}{2} \sin \frac{C}{2}$$

In the figure on the following page, the inscribed circle (with center $I$) is tangent to side $\overline{AC}$ at the point $D$.

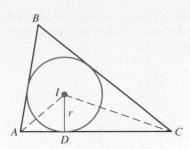

**(a)** According to a theorem from geometry, $\overline{ID}$ is perpendicular to $\overline{AC}$. What theorem is this? (State the theorem using complete sentences.)

**(b)** Show that $AD = r \cot(A/2)$ and $DC = r \cot(C/2)$. *Hint:* Result (i) or (ii) on page 657 may be useful.

**(c)** Use the results in part (b) to show that

$$r = \frac{b}{\cot(A/2) + \cot(C/2)}$$

*Hint:* From the figure we have $b = AD + DC$. (As usual, the letter $b$ denotes the length $AC$ in $\triangle ABC$.)

**(d)** Show that

$$r = \frac{b \sin(A/2) \sin(C/2)}{\sin[(A + C)/2]}$$

*Hint:* Begin with the expression for $r$ in part (c), and convert to sines and cosines. Then simplify and use an addition formula.

**(e)** Show that

$$r = \frac{b \sin(A/2) \sin(C/2)}{\cos(B/2)}$$

*Hint:* Begin with the expression for $r$ in part (d), and use the fact that $A + B + C = 180°$.

**(f)** From Exercise 47 we have $b = 2\mathcal{R} \sin B$. Use this to substitute for $b$ in part (e). Show that the resulting equation can be written

$$r = 4\mathcal{R} \sin \frac{A}{2} \sin \frac{B}{2} \sin \frac{C}{2} \qquad \text{as required}$$

**49.** The following figure shows a quadrilateral with sides $a$, $b$, $c$, and $d$ inscribed in a circle.

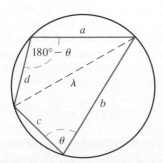

If $\lambda$ denotes the length of the diagonal indicated in the figure, prove that

$$\lambda^2 = \frac{(ab + cd)(ac + bd)}{bc + ad}$$

This result is known as **Brahmagupta's theorem.** It is named after its discoverer, a seventh-century Hindu mathematician. *Hint:* Assume as given the theorem from geometry stating that when a quadrilateral is inscribed in a circle, the opposite angles are supplementary. Apply the law of cosines in both of the triangles in the figure to obtain expressions for $\lambda^2$. Then eliminate $\cos \theta$ from one equation.

**50.** Prove the following identity for $\triangle ABC$:

$$\frac{\cos A}{a} + \frac{\cos B}{b} + \frac{\cos C}{c} = \frac{a^2 + b^2 + c^2}{2abc}$$

*Suggestion:* Use the law of cosines to substitute for $a^2$, for $b^2$, and for $c^2$ in the numerator of the expression on the right-hand side.

**51.** In $\triangle ABC$, suppose that $a^4 + b^4 + c^4 = 2(a^2 + b^2)c^2$. Find $\angle C$. (There are two answers.) *Hint:* Solve the given equation for $c^2$.

**52.** In this section we have seen that the cosines of the angles in a triangle can be expressed in terms of the lengths of the sides. For instance, for $\cos A$ in $\triangle ABC$, we obtained $\cos A = (b^2 + c^2 - a^2)/2bc$. This exercise shows how to derive corresponding expressions for the sines of the angles. For ease of notation in this exercise, let us agree to use the letter $T$ to denote the following quantity:

$$T = 2(a^2b^2 + b^2c^2 + c^2a^2) - (a^4 + b^4 + c^4)$$

Then the sines of the angles in $\triangle ABC$ are given by

$$\sin A = \frac{\sqrt{T}}{2bc} \qquad \sin B = \frac{\sqrt{T}}{2ac} \qquad \sin C = \frac{\sqrt{T}}{2ab}$$

In the steps that follow, we'll derive the first of these three formulas, the derivations for the other two being entirely similar.

**(a)** In $\triangle ABC$, why is the positive root always appropriate in the formula $\sin A = \sqrt{1 - \cos^2 A}$?

**(b)** In the formula in part (a), replace $\cos A$ by $(b^2 + c^2 - a^2)/2bc$ and show that the result can be written

$$\sin A = \frac{\sqrt{4b^2c^2 - (b^2 + c^2 - a^2)^2}}{2bc}$$

**(c)** On the right-hand side of the equation in part (b), carry out the indicated multiplication. After combining like terms, you should obtain $\sin A = \sqrt{T}/2bc$, as required.

**53.** In the two easy steps that follow, we derive the law of sines by using the formulas obtained in Exercise 52. (Since the formulas in Exercise 52 were obtained using the law of cosines, we are, in essence, showing how to derive the law of sines from the law of cosines.)

(a) Use the formulas in Exercise 52 to check that each of the three fractions $(\sin A)/a$, $(\sin B)/b$, and $(\sin C)/c$ is equal to $\sqrt{T}/2abc$.

(b) Conclude from part (a) that

$$(\sin A)/a = (\sin B)/b = (\sin C)/c$$

**54.** In this exercise you are going to use the law of cosines and the law of sines to determine the area of the shaded equilateral triangle in Figure A. Begin by labeling points, as shown in Figure B.

Figure A        Figure B

(a) Apply the law of cosines in $\triangle ABE$ to show that $AE = \sqrt{7}$.

(b) Apply the law of sines in $\triangle ABE$ to show that $\sin(\angle AEB) = (3\sqrt{3})/(2\sqrt{7})$.

(c) Apply the law of sines in $\triangle CFB$ to show that $\sin(\angle FBC) = (\sqrt{3})/(2\sqrt{7})$. *Hint:* $\triangle AEB$ is congruent to $\triangle BFC$, so $BF = AE$.

(d) Apply the law of sines in $\triangle QEB$ to show that $QE = 1/\sqrt{7}$.

(e) Apply the law of sines in $\triangle QEB$ to show that $QB = 3/\sqrt{7}$.

(f) Show that $PQ = 3\sqrt{7}/7$.
*Hint:* $PQ = AE - (QE + AP)$, and by symmetry, $AP = QB$.

(g) Use the result in part (f) to find the area of equilateral triangle $PQR$.

**55.** This exercise is adapted from a problem proposed by Professor Norman Schaumberger in the May 1990 issue of *The College Mathematics Journal*. In the accompanying figure, radius $OA = 1$ and $\angle AFC = 60°$. Follow steps (a) through (f) to prove that

$$AD \cdot AB - AE \cdot AC = BC$$

(a) Let $\angle BAF = \alpha$; show that $AD = 2 \cos \alpha$.
*Hint:* In isosceles triangle $AOD$, drop a perpendicular from $O$ to side $\overline{AD}$.

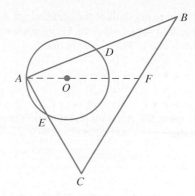

(b) Let $\angle CAF = \beta$; show that $AE = 2 \cos \beta$.

(c) Explain why $\angle B = 60° - \alpha$ and $\angle C = 120° - \beta$.

(d) Using the law of sines, show that

$$AB = \frac{BC \sin(120° - \beta)}{\sin(\alpha + \beta)}$$

and

$$AC = \frac{BC \sin(60° - \alpha)}{\sin(\alpha + \beta)}$$

(e) Using the results in parts (a), (b), and (d), verify that

$$AD \cdot AB - AE \cdot AC$$
$$= BC \cdot \left[\frac{2 \cos \alpha \sin(120° - \beta) - 2 \cos \beta \sin(60° - \alpha)}{\sin(\alpha + \beta)}\right]$$

(f) To complete the proof, you need to show that the quantity in brackets in part (e) is equal to 1. In other words, you want to show that

$$2 \cos \alpha \sin(120° - \beta) - 2 \cos \beta \sin(60° - \alpha)$$
$$= \sin(\alpha + \beta)$$

Use the addition formulas for sine to prove that this last equation is indeed an identity.

## C

**56.** *Heron's formula:* Approximately 2000 years ago, Heron of Alexandria derived a formula for the area of a triangle in terms of the lengths of the sides. A more modern derivation of Heron's formula is indicated in the steps that follow.

(a) Use the expression for $\sin A$ in Exercise 52(b) to show that

$$\sin^2 A = \frac{(a - b + c)(a + b - c)(b + c - a)(b + c + a)}{4b^2c^2}$$

*Hint:* Use difference-of-squares factoring repeatedly.
*(continues)*

**(b)** Let $s$ denote one-half of the perimeter of $\triangle ABC$. That is, let $s = \frac{1}{2}(a + b + c)$. Using this notation (which is due to Euler), verify that

**(i)** $a + b + c = 2s$

**(ii)** $-a + b + c = 2(s - a)$

**(iii)** $a - b + c = 2(s - b)$

**(iv)** $a + b - c = 2(s - c)$

Then, using this notation and the result in part (a), show that

$$\sin A = \frac{2\sqrt{s(s - a)(s - b)(s - c)}}{bc}$$

*Note*: Since $\sin A$ is positive (Why?), the positive root is appropriate here.

**(c)** Use the result in part (b) and the formula area $\triangle ABC = \frac{1}{2}bc \sin A$ to conclude that

$$\text{area } \triangle ABC = \sqrt{s(s - a)(s - b)(s - c)}$$

This is Heron's formula. For historical background and a purely geometric proof, see *An Introduction to the History of Mathematics,* 6th ed., by Howard Eves (Philadelphia: Saunders College Publishing, 1990), pp. 178 and 194.

**57.** In this exercise you will derive a formula for the length of an angle bisector in a triangle. (The formula will be needed in Exercise 58.) Let $f$ denote the length of the bisector of angle $C$ in $\triangle ABC$, as shown in the following figure.

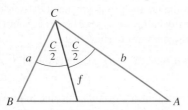

**(a)** Explain why

$$\frac{1}{2}af \sin \frac{C}{2} + \frac{1}{2}bf \sin \frac{C}{2} = \frac{1}{2}ab \sin C$$

*Hint*: Use areas.

**(b)** Show that

$$f = \frac{2ab \cos(C/2)}{a + b}$$

**(c)** By the law of cosines, $\cos C = (a^2 + b^2 - c^2)/2ab$. Use this to show that

$$\cos \frac{C}{2} = \frac{1}{2}\sqrt{\frac{(a + b - c)(a + b + c)}{ab}}$$

**(d)** Show that the length of the angle bisector in terms of the sides is given by

$$f = \frac{\sqrt{ab}}{a + b}\sqrt{(a + b - c)(a + b + c)}$$

**58.** In triangle $XYZ$ (in the accompanying figure), $\overline{SX}$ bisects angle $ZXY$ and $\overline{TY}$ bisects angle $ZYX$. In this exercise you are going to prove the following theorem, known as the **Steiner–Lehmus theorem:** If the lengths of the angle bisectors $\overline{SX}$ and $\overline{TY}$ are equal, then $\triangle XYZ$ is isosceles (with $XZ = YZ$).

**(a)** Let $x$, $y$, and $z$ denote the lengths of the sides $\overline{YZ}$, $\overline{XZ}$, and $\overline{XY}$, respectively. Use the formula in Exercise 57(d) to show that the equation $TY = SX$ is equivalent to

$$\frac{\sqrt{xz}}{x + z}\sqrt{(x + z - y)(x + z + y)}$$
$$= \frac{\sqrt{yz}}{y + z}\sqrt{(y + z - x)(y + z + x)} \quad (1)$$

**(b)** What common factors do you see on both sides of equation (1)? Divide both sides of equation (1) by those common factors. You should obtain

$$\frac{\sqrt{x}}{x + z}\sqrt{x + z - y} = \frac{\sqrt{y}}{y + z}\sqrt{y + z - x} \quad (2)$$

**(c)** Clear equation (2) of fractions, and then square both sides. After combining like terms and then grouping, the equation can be written

$$(3x^2yz - 3xy^2z) + (x^3y - xy^3)$$
$$+ (x^2z^2 - y^2z^2) + (xz^3 - yz^3) = 0 \quad (3)$$

**(d)** Show that equation (3) can be written

$$(x - y)[3xyz + xy(x + y) + x^2(x + y) + z^3] = 0$$

Now notice that the quantity in brackets in this last equation must be positive. (Why?) Consequently, $x - y = 0$, and so $x = y$, as required.

*Remark*: This theorem has a fascinating history, beginning in 1840 when C. L. Lehmus first proposed the theorem to the great Swiss geometer Jacob Steiner (1796–1863). For background (and much shorter proofs!), see either of the following references: *Scientific American,* vol. 204 (1961), pp. 166–168; *American Mathematical Monthly,* vol. 70 (1963), pp. 79–80.

**59.** Show that

$$\text{area } \triangle ABC = \frac{a^2 \sin 2B + b^2 \sin 2A}{4}$$

**60.** For any triangle $ABC$, show that

$$\frac{\sin(A - B)}{\sin(A + B)} = \frac{a^2 - b^2}{c^2}$$

# 9.2 VECTORS IN THE PLANE: A GEOMETRIC APPROACH

*The idea of a parallelogram of velocities may be found in various ancient Greek authors, and the concept of a parallelogram of forces was not uncommon in the sixteenth and seventeenth centuries.* —Michael J. Crowe in *A History of Vector Analysis* (Notre Dame, Ind.: University of Notre Dame Press, 1967)

*Vector notation is compact. If we can express a law of physics in vector form we usually find it easier to understand and to manipulate mathematically.* —David Halliday and Robert Resnick in *Fundamentals of Physics,* 3rd ed. (New York: John Wiley and Sons, Inc., 1988)

Certain quantities, such as temperature, length, and mass, can be specified by means of a single number (assuming that a system of units has been agreed on). We call these quantities **scalars.** On the other hand, quantities such as force and velocity are characterized by both a *magnitude* (a positive number) and a *direction.* We call these quantities **vectors.**

Geometrically, a vector is a directed line segment or arrow. The vector in Figure 1, for instance, represents a wind velocity of 5 mph from the west. The length of this vector represents the magnitude of the wind velocity, while the direction of the vector indicates the direction of the wind velocity. As another example, the vector in Figure 2 represents a force acting on an object: The magnitude of the force is 3 pounds, and the force acts at an angle of 135° with the horizontal.

**Figure 1**
A vector representing a wind velocity of 5 mph from the west

**Figure 2**
A vector representing a force of 3 lb acting at an angle of 135° with the horizontal

**Figure 3**

In a moment we are going to discuss the important concept of vector addition, but first let us agree on some matters of notation. Suppose that we have a vector drawn from a point $P$ to a point $Q$, as shown in Figure 3. The point $P$ in Figure 3 is called the **initial point** of the vector, and $Q$ is the **terminal point.** We can denote this vector by the notation

$$\overrightarrow{PQ}$$

We sometimes think of the vector $\overrightarrow{PQ}$ as the *directed* line segment from $P$ to $Q$.

The length or **magnitude** of the vector $\overrightarrow{PQ}$ is denoted by $|\overrightarrow{PQ}|$. On the printed page, vectors are often indicated by boldface letters, such as **a**, **A**, and **v**.

A word about notation. As has perhaps already occurred to you, the same vertical bars that we are using to denote the length of a vector are also used to denote the absolute value of a real number. It will be clear from the context which meaning is intended. Some books avoid this situation by using double bars to indicate the length of a vector: $\|\mathbf{v}\|$. In this text we use the notation $|\mathbf{v}|$ simply because that is the one found in most calculus books.

If two vectors **a** and **b** have the same length and the same direction, we say that they are *equal*, and we write $\mathbf{a} = \mathbf{b}$; see Figure 4. Notice that our definition for vector equality involves magnitude and direction but not location. Thus when it is convenient to do so, we are free to move a given vector to another location, provided that we do not alter the magnitude or the direction.

(a) $\mathbf{a} = \mathbf{b}$

(b) $\mathbf{c} \neq \mathbf{d}$
The magnitudes are the same but the directions are not.

(c) $\mathbf{u} \neq \mathbf{v}$
The directions are the same but the magnitudes are not.

(d) $\mathbf{p} \neq \mathbf{q}$
Neither the magnitudes nor the directions are the same.

**Figure 4**

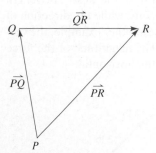

**Figure 5**

As motivation for the definition of vector addition, let's suppose that an object moves from a point $P$ to a point $Q$. Then we can represent this *displacement* by the vector $\vec{PQ}$. (Indeed, the word "vector" is derived from the Latin *vectus,* meaning "carried.") Now suppose that after moving from $P$ to $Q$, the object moves from $Q$ to $R$. We represent this displacement by the vector $\vec{QR}$. Then, as you can see in Figure 5, the net effect is a displacement from $P$ to $R$. We say in this case that the vector $\vec{PR}$ is the **sum** or **resultant** of the vectors $\vec{PQ}$ and $\vec{QR}$, and we write

$$\vec{PQ} + \vec{QR} = \vec{PR}$$

These ideas are formalized in the definition that follows.

---

**DEFINITION** | **Vector Addition**

---

Let **u** and **v** be two vectors. Position **v** (without changing its magnitude or direction) so that its initial point coincides with the terminal point of **u**, as in Figure 6(a). Then, as is indicated in Figure 6(b), the vector $\mathbf{u} + \mathbf{v}$ is the directed line segment from the initial point of **u** to the terminal point of **v**. The vector $\mathbf{u} + \mathbf{v}$ is called the **sum** or **resultant** of **u** and **v**.

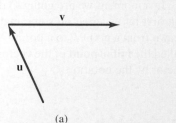

**Figure 6**      (a)                    (b)

---

**EXAMPLE** | **1** | **Adding two vectors geometrically**

---

Refer to Figure 7.
**(a)** Determine the initial and terminal points of $\mathbf{u} + \mathbf{v}$.  **(b)** Compute $|\mathbf{u} + \mathbf{v}|$.

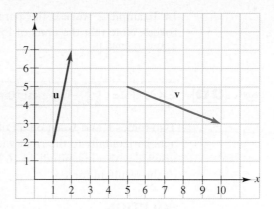

**Figure 7**

### SOLUTION

(a) According to the definition, we first need to move **v** (without changing its length or direction) so that its initial point coincides with the terminal point of **u**. From Figure 7 we see that this can be accomplished by moving each point of **v** three units in the negative $x$-direction and two units in the positive $y$-direction. Figure 8(a) shows the new location of **v**, and Figure 8(b) indicates the sum **u** + **v**. From Figure 8(b) we see that the initial and terminal points of **u** + **v** are (1, 2) and (7, 5), respectively.

(b) We can use the distance formula to determine $|\mathbf{u} + \mathbf{v}|$. Using the points (1, 2) and (7, 5) that were obtained in part (a), we have

$$|\mathbf{u} + \mathbf{v}| = \sqrt{(7 - 1)^2 + (5 - 2)^2} = \sqrt{45} = \sqrt{9 \cdot 5} = 3\sqrt{5}$$

(a)

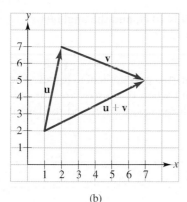

(b)

**Figure 8**

One important consequence of our definition for vector addition is that this operation is *commutative*. That is, for any two vectors **u** and **v** we have

$$\mathbf{u} + \mathbf{v} = \mathbf{v} + \mathbf{u}$$

Figure 9 indicates why this is so. Vector addition can also be carried out by using the **parallelogram law.** In Figure 9, to determine **u** + **v**, position **u** and **v** so that their initial points coincide. Then, as is indicated in Figure 10, the vector **u** + **v** is the directed diagonal of the parallelogram determined by **u** and **v**.

It is a fact, verified experimentally, that if two forces **F** and **G** act on an object, the net effect is the same as if just the resultant **F** + **G** acted on the object.

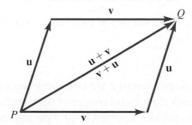

**Figure 9**
The upper triangle shows the sum **u** + **v**, while the lower triangle shows the sum **v** + **u**. Since in both cases the resultant is $\overrightarrow{PQ}$, it follows that **u** + **v** = **v** + **u**.

**Figure 10**
The parallelogram law for vector addition

In Example 2 we use the parallelogram law to compute the resultant of two forces. Note that the units of force used in this example are **newtons** (N), where $1 \text{ N} \approx 0.2248 \text{ lb}$.

**EXAMPLE** 2 **The resultant of two perpendicular forces**

Two forces **F** and **G** act on an object. As is indicated in Figure 11, the force **G** acts horizontally to the right with a magnitude of 12 N, while **F** acts vertically upward with a magnitude of 16 N. Determine the magnitude and the direction of the resultant force.

**SOLUTION**
We complete the parallelogram, as shown in Figure 12. Now we need to calculate the length of **F** + **G** and the angle $\theta$. Applying the Pythagorean theorem in Figure 12, we have

$$|\mathbf{F} + \mathbf{G}| = \sqrt{12^2 + 16^{16}} = \sqrt{144 + 256} = \sqrt{400} = 20$$

Also from Figure 12 we have

$$\tan \theta = \frac{16}{12} = \frac{4}{3}$$

Consequently,

$$\theta = \tan^{-1}\frac{4}{3} \approx 53.1° \qquad \text{using a calculator set in degree mode}$$

Summarizing our results, the magnitude of **F** + **G** is 20 N, and the angle $\theta$ between **F** + **G** and the horizontal is (approximately) 53.1°.

**Figure 11**

**Figure 12**

In Example 2 we determined the resultant for two perpendicular forces. The next example shows how to compute the resultant when the forces are not perpendicular. Our calculations will make use of both the law of sines and the law of cosines.

**EXAMPLE** 3 **The resultant of two forces**

Determine the resultant of the two forces in Figure 13. (Round the answers to one decimal place.)

**SOLUTION**
As in the previous example, we complete the parallelogram. In Figure 14 the angle in the lower right-hand corner of the parallelogram is 140°. This is because the sum of two adjacent angles in any parallelogram is always 180°. Letting $d$

**Figure 13**

**Figure 14**

denote the length of the diagonal in Figure 14, we can use the law of cosines to write

$$d^2 = 15^2 + 5^2 - 2(15)(5) \cos 140°$$
$$d = \sqrt{250 - 150 \cos 140°} = \sqrt{250 + 150 \cos 40°} \quad \text{(Why?)}$$
$$= \sqrt{25(10 + 6 \cos 40°)} = 5\sqrt{10 + 6 \cos 40°}$$
$$\approx 19.1 \quad \text{using a calculator}$$

So the magnitude of the resultant is 19.1 N (to one decimal place). To specify the direction of the resultant, we need to determine the angle $\theta$ in Figure 14. Using the law of sines, we have

$$\frac{\sin \theta}{5} = \frac{\sin 140°}{d}$$

and, consequently,

$$\sin \theta = \frac{5 \sin 40°}{d} \quad \text{(Why?)}$$
$$= \frac{5 \sin 40°}{5\sqrt{10 + 6 \cos 40°}} = \frac{\sin 40°}{\sqrt{10 + 6 \cos 40°}}$$

Using a calculator now, we obtain

$$\theta = \sin^{-1}\left(\frac{\sin 40°}{\sqrt{10 + 6 \cos 40°}}\right) \approx 9.7°$$

In summary, the magnitude of the resultant force is about 19.1 N, and the angle $\theta$ between the resultant and the 15 N force is approximately 9.7°.

As background for the next example we introduce the notion of *components* of a vector. (You will see this concept again in the next section in a more algebraic context.) Suppose that the initial point of a vector $\mathbf{v}$ is located at the origin of a rectangular coordinate system, as shown in Figure 15. Now suppose we draw perpendiculars from the terminal point of $\mathbf{v}$ to the axes, as indicated by the blue dashed lines in Figure 15. Then the coordinates $v_x$ and $v_y$ are called the **components** of the vector $\mathbf{v}$ in the $x$- and $y$-directions, respectively. For an example involving components, refer to Figure 12. The horizontal component of the vector $\mathbf{F} + \mathbf{G}$ is 12 N, and the vertical component is 16 N.

Figure 15

## EXAMPLE 4  Finding vertical and horizontal components

Determine the horizontal and vertical components of the velocity vector $\mathbf{v}$ in Figure 16.

**SOLUTION**
From Figure 16 we can write

$$\cos 30° = \frac{\text{adjacent}}{\text{hypotenuse}} = \frac{v_x}{70}$$

Figure 16

and, consequently,

$$v_x = (\cos 30°)(70) = \frac{\sqrt{3}}{2}(70)$$

$$= 35\sqrt{3} \approx 61 \text{ cm/sec} \qquad \text{to two significant digits}$$

Similarly, we have

$$\sin 30° = \frac{v_y}{70}$$

and therefore

$$v_y = (\sin 30°)(70) = 35 \text{ cm/sec}$$

So the $x$-component of the velocity is about 61 cm/sec, and the $y$-component is 35 cm/sec.

Figure 17

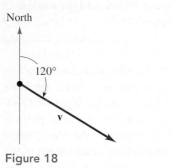

Figure 18

Our last example in this section will indicate how vectors are used in navigation. First, however, let's introduce some terminology. Suppose that an airplane has a **heading** of *due east*. This means that the airplane is pointed directly east, and if there were no wind effects, the plane would indeed travel due east with respect to the ground. The **air speed** is the speed of the airplane relative to the air, whereas the **ground speed** is the plane's speed relative to the ground. Again, if there were no wind effects, then the air speed and the ground speed would be equal. Now suppose that the heading and air speed of an airplane are represented by the velocity vector **V** in Figure 17. (The direction of **V** is the heading; the magnitude of **V** is the air speed.) Also suppose that the wind velocity is represented by the vector **W** in Figure 17. Then the vector sum **V** + **W** represents the actual velocity of the plane with respect to the ground. The direction of **V** + **W** is called the **course;** it is the direction in which the airplane is moving with respect to the ground. The magnitude of **V** + **W** is the ground speed (which was defined previously). The angle $\theta$ in Figure 17, from the heading to the course, is called the **drift angle.**

In navigation, directions are given in terms of the angle measured clockwise from true north. For example, the direction of the velocity vector **v** in Figure 18 is 120°.

---

## EXAMPLE 5 Using vectors in navigation

[Refer to Figure 19(a).] The heading and air speed of an airplane are 60° and 250 mph, respectively. If the wind is 40 mph from 150°, find the ground speed, the drift angle, and the course.

**SOLUTION**
In Figure 19(a) the vector $\overrightarrow{OA}$ represents the air speed of 250 mph and the heading of 60°. The vector $\overrightarrow{OW}$ represents a wind of 40 mph from 150°. Also, angle $WOA = 90°$. (Why?) In Figure 19(b) we have completed the parallelogram to obtain the vector sum $\overrightarrow{OA} + \overrightarrow{OW} = \overrightarrow{OB}$. The length of $\overrightarrow{OB}$ represents the

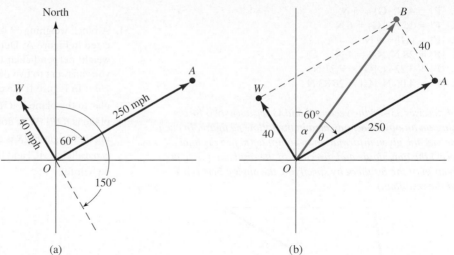

**Figure 19**        (a)                                (b)

ground speed, and $\theta$ is the drift angle. Because triangle $BOA$ is a right triangle, we have

$$\tan \theta = \frac{40}{250} = \frac{4}{25} \qquad \bigg| \qquad |\overrightarrow{OB}| = \sqrt{250^2 + 40^2}$$
$$\theta = 9.1° \qquad \qquad \approx 253.2$$

From these calculations we conclude that the ground speed is approximately 253.2 mph and the drift angle is about 9.1°. We still need to compute the course (that is, the direction of vector $\overrightarrow{OB}$). From Figure 19(b) we have

$$\alpha = 60° - \theta \approx 60° - 9.1° = 50.9°$$

Thus the course is 50.9°, to one decimal place. (We are using the convention, mentioned previously, that directions are given in terms of the angle measured clockwise from true north.)

# EXERCISE SET 9.2

## A

*In Exercises 1–26, assume that the coordinates of the points P, Q, R, S, and O are as follows:*

$$P(-1, 3) \qquad Q(4, 6) \qquad R(4, 3) \qquad S(5, 9) \qquad O(0, 0)$$

*For each exercise, draw the indicated vector (using graph paper) and compute its magnitude. In Exercises 7–20, compute the sums using the definition given on page 662. In Exercises 21–26, use the parallelogram law to compute the sums.*

1. $\overrightarrow{PQ}$
2. $\overrightarrow{QP}$
3. $\overrightarrow{SQ}$
4. $\overrightarrow{QS}$
5. $\overrightarrow{OP}$
6. $\overrightarrow{PO}$
7. $\overrightarrow{PQ} + \overrightarrow{QS}$
8. $\overrightarrow{SQ} + \overrightarrow{QP}$
9. $\overrightarrow{OP} + \overrightarrow{PQ}$
10. $\overrightarrow{OS} + \overrightarrow{SQ}$
11. $(\overrightarrow{OS} + \overrightarrow{SQ}) + \overrightarrow{QP}$
12. $(\overrightarrow{OS} + \overrightarrow{SP}) + \overrightarrow{PR}$
13. $\overrightarrow{OP} + \overrightarrow{QS}$
14. $\overrightarrow{QS} + \overrightarrow{PO}$
15. $\overrightarrow{SR} + \overrightarrow{PO}$
16. $\overrightarrow{OS} + \overrightarrow{QO}$
17. $\overrightarrow{OP} + \overrightarrow{RQ}$
18. $\overrightarrow{OP} + \overrightarrow{QR}$
19. $\overrightarrow{SQ} + \overrightarrow{RO}$
20. $\overrightarrow{SQ} + \overrightarrow{OR}$
21. $\overrightarrow{OP} + \overrightarrow{OR}$
22. $\overrightarrow{OP} + \overrightarrow{OQ}$
23. $\overrightarrow{RP} + \overrightarrow{RS}$
24. $\overrightarrow{QP} + \overrightarrow{QR}$
25. $\overrightarrow{SO} + \overrightarrow{SQ}$
26. $\overrightarrow{SQ} + \overrightarrow{SR}$

*In Exercises 27–32 the vectors $\mathbf{F}$ and $\mathbf{G}$ denote two forces that act on an object: $\mathbf{G}$ acts horizontally to the right, and $\mathbf{F}$ acts vertically upward. In each case, use the information that is given to compute $|\mathbf{F} + \mathbf{G}|$ and $\theta$, where $\theta$ is the angle between $\mathbf{G}$ and the resultant.*

27. $|\mathbf{F}| = 4$ N, $|\mathbf{G}| = 5$ N
28. $|\mathbf{F}| = 15$ N, $|\mathbf{G}| = 6$ N
29. $|\mathbf{F}| = |\mathbf{G}| = 9$ N
30. $|\mathbf{F}| = 28$ N, $|\mathbf{G}| = 1$ N
31. $|\mathbf{F}| = 3.22$ N, $|\mathbf{G}| = 7.21$ N
32. $|\mathbf{F}| = 4.06$ N, $|\mathbf{G}| = 26.83$ N

*In Exercises 33–38 the vectors **F** and **G** represent two forces acting on an object, as indicated in the following figure. In each case, use the given information to compute (to two decimal places) the magnitude and direction of the resultant. (Give the direction of the resultant by specifying the angle θ between **F** and the resultant.)*

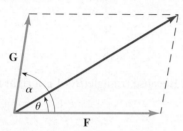

33. $|\mathbf{F}| = 5$ N, $|\mathbf{G}| = 4$ N, $\alpha = 80°$
34. $|\mathbf{F}| = 8$ N, $|\mathbf{G}| = 10$ N, $\alpha = 60°$
35. $|\mathbf{F}| = 16$ N, $|\mathbf{G}| = 25$ N, $\alpha = 35°$
36. $|\mathbf{F}| = 4.24$ N, $|\mathbf{G}| = 9.01$ N, $\alpha = 45°$
37. $|\mathbf{F}| = 50$ N, $|\mathbf{G}| = 25$ N, $\alpha = 130°$
38. $|\mathbf{F}| = 1.26$ N, $|\mathbf{G}| = 2.31$ N, $\alpha = 160°$

*In Exercises 39–46 the initial point for each vector is the origin, and θ denotes the angle (measured counterclockwise) from the x-axis to the vector. In each case, compute the horizontal and vertical components of the given vector. (Round your answers to two decimal places.)*

39. The magnitude of **V** is 16 cm/sec, and $\theta = 30°$.
40. The magnitude of **V** is 40 cm/sec, and $\theta = 60°$.
41. The magnitude of **F** is 14 N, and $\theta = 75°$.
42. The magnitude of **F** is 23.12 N, and $\theta = 52°$.
43. The magnitude of **V** is 1 cm/sec, and $\theta = 135°$.
44. The magnitude of **V** is 12 cm/sec, and $\theta = 120°$.
45. The magnitude of **F** is 1.25 N, and $\theta = 145°$.
46. The magnitude of **F** is 6.34 N, and $\theta = 175°$.

*In Exercises 47–50, use the given flight data to compute the ground speed, the drift angle, and the course. (Round your answers to two decimal places.)*

47. The heading and air speed are 30° and 300 mph, respectively; the wind is 25 mph from 120°.
48. The heading and air speed are 45° and 275 mph, respectively; the wind is 50 mph from 135°.
49. The heading and air speed are 100° and 290 mph, respectively; the wind is 45 mph from 190°.
50. The heading and air speed are 90° and 220 mph, respectively; the wind is 80 mph from **(a)** 180°; **(b)** 90°.

**B**

51. A block weighing 12 lb rests on an inclined plane, as indicated in Figure A. Determine the components of the weight perpendicular to and parallel to the plane. Round your answers to two decimal places.

    *Hint:* In Figure B the component of the weight perpendicular to the plane is $|\overrightarrow{OR}|$; the component parallel to the plane is $|\overrightarrow{OP}|$. Why does angle $QOR$ equal 35°? (Observing that angle $POR$ is a right angle, that line segment $PO$ is parallel to $AC$, and that $OQ$ is perpendicular to $AB$ may be helpful.)

**Figure A**

**Figure B**

*In Exercises 52 and 53 you are given the weight of a block on an inclined plane, along with the angle θ that the inclined plane makes with the horizontal. In each case, determine the components of the weight perpendicular to and parallel to the plane. (Round your answers to two decimal places where necessary.)*

52. 15 lb; $\theta = 30°$
53. 12 lb; $\theta = 10°$
54. A block rests on an inclined plane that makes an angle of 20° with the horizontal. The component of the weight parallel to the plane is 34.2 lb.
    **(a)** Determine the weight of the block. (Round your answer to one decimal place.)
    **(b)** Determine the component of the weight perpendicular to the plane. (Round your answer to one decimal place.)
55. In Section 9.3 we will see that vector addition is associative. That is, for any three vectors **A**, **B**, and **C**, we have $(\mathbf{A} + \mathbf{B}) + \mathbf{C} = \mathbf{A} + (\mathbf{B} + \mathbf{C})$. In this exercise you are going to check that this property holds in a particular case.

Let **A**, **B**, and **C** be the vectors with initial and terminal points as follows:

| Vector | Initial point | Terminal point |
|---|---|---|
| **A** | $(-1, 2)$ | $(2, 4)$ |
| **B** | $(1, 2)$ | $(3, 0)$ |
| **C** | $(6, 2)$ | $(4, -3)$ |

**(a)** Use the definition of vector addition on page 662 to determine the initial and terminal points of $(\mathbf{A} + \mathbf{B}) + \mathbf{C}$.  *Suggestion*: Use graph paper.

**(b)** Use the definition of vector addition to determine the initial and terminal points of $\mathbf{A} + (\mathbf{B} + \mathbf{C})$. [Your answers should agree with those in part (a).]

---

# PROJECT | VECTOR ALGEBRA USING VECTOR GEOMETRY

In the previous section we defined vectors and vector addition geometrically and showed that vector addition is commutative, that is, if **u** and **v** are vectors then $\mathbf{u} + \mathbf{v} = \mathbf{v} + \mathbf{u}$. What happens if we want to add three vectors? Let **u**, **v**, and **w** be vectors. How should we define the sum $\mathbf{u} + \mathbf{v} + \mathbf{w}$? Addition was defined for two vectors at a time. That leads to two possible "groupings" of the three terms. We might add **u** and **v** first, then add **w** to their sum. In symbols we write $(\mathbf{u} + \mathbf{v}) + \mathbf{w}$, where the parentheses are grouping symbols, as in algebra, indicating what operation is done first. Alternatively we might add **v** and **w** first, then add their sum to **u**. In symbols we write $\mathbf{u} + (\mathbf{v} + \mathbf{w})$. Of course, we would like $(\mathbf{u} + \mathbf{v}) + \mathbf{w}$ to equal $\mathbf{u} + (\mathbf{v} + \mathbf{w})$. If this is true, then we can write the sum $\mathbf{u} + \mathbf{v} + \mathbf{w}$ without ambiguity.

**EXERCISE 1**  Draw three distinct (unequal) vectors **u**, **v**, and **w**. Use the definition of vector addition to compute $(\mathbf{u} + \mathbf{v}) + \mathbf{w}$ and $\mathbf{u} + (\mathbf{v} + \mathbf{w})$. Convince yourself that the resulting sums are equal. So we have

$$(\mathbf{u} + \mathbf{v}) + \mathbf{w} = \mathbf{u} + (\mathbf{v} + \mathbf{w}) \qquad \text{(i)}$$

the *associative property* of vector addition.

Now we want to define a vector with the property that when we add it to any vector **v**, it leaves **v** unchanged. This new vector is called the **zero vector**, denoted **O**. So

$$\mathbf{v} + \mathbf{O} = \mathbf{v} \qquad \text{(ii)}$$

According to equation (ii), the zero vector is a vector with no direction and whose magnitude is zero. It can be shown that the zero vector is unique, that is, **O** is the *only* vector with the property that $\mathbf{v} + \mathbf{O} = \mathbf{v}$ for *all* vectors **v**.

**EXERCISE 2**  Explain why the zero vector must have no direction and have magnitude zero.

The next exercise provides a motivation for a definition of the multiplication of a vector by a positive real number.

**EXERCISE 3**  Draw a nonzero vector **v**. Then draw the vector $\mathbf{v} + \mathbf{v}$. What are the direction and magnitude of $\mathbf{v} + \mathbf{v}$?

On the basis of Exercise 3 it is natural to call the vector $\mathbf{v} + \mathbf{v}$, $2\mathbf{v}$, that is, $\mathbf{v} + \mathbf{v} = 2\mathbf{v}$. Similarly, for any *positive* real number $k$ the vector $k\mathbf{v}$ is *defined* to be the vector with the same direction as $\mathbf{v}$ and whose magnitude is $k$ times the magnitude of $\mathbf{v}$. In symbols, $|k\mathbf{v}| = k|\mathbf{v}|$.

Now start with a nonzero vector $\mathbf{v}$. Consider a new vector with the "opposite" direction of $\mathbf{v}$ and the same magnitude as $\mathbf{v}$. By opposite direction we mean that this new vector is represented by an arrow whose initial point is the terminal point of $\mathbf{v}$ and whose terminal point is the initial point of $\mathbf{v}$. This vector is called the **opposite** of $\mathbf{v}$, denoted $-\mathbf{v}$. Clearly, given $\mathbf{v}$, the vector $-\mathbf{v}$ is unique.

**EXERCISE 4**  Draw a nonzero vector $\mathbf{v}$ and its opposite, $-\mathbf{v}$. Then draw the vector $\mathbf{v} + (-\mathbf{v})$ to show

$$\mathbf{v} + (-\mathbf{v}) = \mathbf{O} \tag{iii}$$

Now we want to define $k\mathbf{v}$, where $k$ is a *negative* real number.

**EXERCISE 5**  Draw a nonzero vector $\mathbf{v}$. Then draw a vector with the opposite direction of $\mathbf{v}$ and with magnitude twice that of $\mathbf{v}$. On the basis of our definition of $-\mathbf{v}$, show that we can construct the desired vector by adding two copies of $-\mathbf{v}$, that is, $(-\mathbf{v}) + (-\mathbf{v})$.

Exercises 5 and 3 suggest it is natural to denote this new vector by the symbol $-2\mathbf{v}$, that is, $(-\mathbf{v}) + (-\mathbf{v}) = -2\mathbf{v}$. The $-2$ indicates the vector $-2\mathbf{v}$ has direction opposite that of $\mathbf{v}$ and magnitude $|-2| = 2$ times that of $\mathbf{v}$. This leads us to define, for a negative real number $k$, the vector $k\mathbf{v}$ as the vector with direction opposite that of $\mathbf{v}$ and magnitude $|k|$ times that of $\mathbf{v}$. In symbols, $|k\mathbf{v}| = |k||\mathbf{v}|$. Note that $|k|$ is the absolute value of the number $k$ and $|\mathbf{v}|$ is the magnitude of the vector $\mathbf{v}$. Note also that for $k$ positive we have $|k\mathbf{v}| = k|\mathbf{v}| = |k||\mathbf{v}|$, too.

This leads us to a definition.

---

**DEFINITION** | Scalar Multiplication

---

Given a nonzero vector $\mathbf{v}$ and a nonzero real number $k$, the vector $k\mathbf{v}$ is the vector of magnitude $|k\mathbf{v}| = |k||\mathbf{v}|$ whose direction is the same as that of $\mathbf{v}$ if $k$ is positive and opposite that of $\mathbf{v}$ if $k$ is negative. If either $\mathbf{v} = \mathbf{O}$ or $k = 0$, then we define $k\mathbf{v}$ to be the zero vector, that is, we define $k\mathbf{O} = \mathbf{O}$ and $0\mathbf{v} = \mathbf{O}$. "Multiplying" a vector by a real number is called **scalar multiplication.**

---

**EXERCISE 6**  For any vector $\mathbf{v}$, explain why $1\mathbf{v} = \mathbf{v}$ and $-1\mathbf{v} = -\mathbf{v}$.

Now we want to define *subtraction* of vectors. In arithmetic we define the difference of two numbers to be the number you add to the number subtracted to get the number you started with. For example, $8 - 5 = 3$, since $5 + 3 = 8$, that is, $3$ [or $(8 - 5)$] is what you add to $5$ to get $8$. Now let $\mathbf{u}$ and $\mathbf{v}$ be vectors and consider a new vector called the **difference** of $\mathbf{u}$ and $\mathbf{v}$, denoted by $\mathbf{u} - \mathbf{v}$. By analogy to subtraction of numbers, we define the difference $\mathbf{u} - \mathbf{v}$ to be the vector that you add to $\mathbf{v}$ to get $\mathbf{u}$. See Figure A.

**Figure A**
**u** − **v** is the vector that
you add to **v** to get **u**.

**EXERCISE 7**   Draw two vectors **u** and **v** with different directions and with **v** not equal to the opposite of **u**. Show

$$\mathbf{u} - \mathbf{v} = \mathbf{u} + (-\mathbf{v}) \tag{iv}$$

So we can think of subtracting as adding the opposite.

**EXERCISE 8**   We outline an algebraic derivation of the formula **u** − **v** = **u** + (−**v**.) According to the definition of **u** − **v**, we need to verify that adding **u** + (−**v**) to **v** results in **u**. Give reasons for each step.

$$\begin{aligned} \mathbf{v} + [\mathbf{u} + (-\mathbf{v})] &= \mathbf{v} + [(-\mathbf{v}) + \mathbf{u}] \\ &= [\mathbf{v} + (-\mathbf{v})] + \mathbf{u} \\ &= \mathbf{O} + \mathbf{u} \\ &= \mathbf{u} \end{aligned}$$

**EXERCISE 9**   Here are *examples* of more vector algebra properties. Draw two nonzero vectors **u** and **v** with different directions and **v** not equal to the opposite of **u**.
**(a)** Show 2(**u** + **v**) = 2**u** + 2**v**.
**(b)** Show (2 + 3)**u** = 2**u** + 3**u**.
**(c)** Show 2(3**u**) = (2 · 3)**u**.

Parts (a), (b), and (c) are specific examples of the following vector algebra properties. For any two vectors **u** and **v** and any two scalars $k$ and $l$,

$$k(\mathbf{u} + \mathbf{v}) = k\mathbf{u} + k\mathbf{v} \tag{v}$$
$$(k + l)\mathbf{u} = k\mathbf{u} + l\mathbf{u} \tag{vi}$$
$$k(l\mathbf{u}) = (kl)\mathbf{u} \tag{vii}$$

**EXERCISE 10**   For any vector **v**, show that −3**v** = (−3)**v**. *Hint:* −3**v** is the opposite of 3**v**, that is, −3**v** is the unique vector to add to 3**v** to get the zero vector. Use the result from Exercise 9(b) to show that 3**v** + [(−3)**v**] = **O**. Then (−3)**v** must be −3**v**.

# 9.3   VECTORS IN THE PLANE: AN ALGEBRAIC APPROACH

*A great many of the mathematical ideas that apply to physics and engineering are collected in the concept of vector spaces. This branch of mathematics has applications in such practical problems as calculating the vibrations of bridges and airplane wings. Logical extensions to spaces of infinitely many dimensions are widely used in modern theoretical physics as well as*

**Figure 1**

**Figure 2**

**Figure 3**
The vector $\overrightarrow{OP}$ is denoted by $\langle a, b \rangle$. The coordinates $a$ and $b$ are the components of the vector.

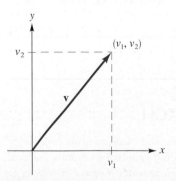

**Figure 4**

*in many branches of mathematics itself.*—From *The Mathematical Sciences,* edited by the Committee on Support of Research in the Mathematical Sciences with the collaboration of George Boehm (Cambridge, Mass.: The M.I.T. Press, 1969)

The geometric concept of a vector in the plane can be recast in an algebraic setting. This is useful both for computational purposes and (as our opening quotation implies) for more advanced work.

Consider an *x-y* coordinate system and a vector $\overrightarrow{OP}$ with initial point the origin, as shown in Figure 1. We call $\overrightarrow{OP}$ the **position vector** (or **radius vector**) of the point *P*. Most of our work in this section will involve such position vectors. There is no loss of generality in focusing on these types of vectors, for, as is indicated in Figure 2, each vector **v** in the plane is equal to a unique position vector $\overrightarrow{OP}$.

If the coordinates of the point *P* are (*a*, *b*), we call *a* and *b* the **components** of the vector $\overrightarrow{OP}$, and we use the notation

$$\langle a, b \rangle$$

to denote this vector (see Figure 3). The number *a* is the **horizontal component** or ***x*-component** of the vector; *b* is the **vertical component** or ***y*-component.**

In the previous section we said that two vectors are equal provided that they have the same length and the same direction. For vectors $\langle a, b \rangle$ and $\langle c, d \rangle$ this implies that

$$\langle a, b \rangle = \langle c, d \rangle \quad \text{if any only if} \quad a = c \quad \text{and} \quad b = d$$

(If you've studied complex numbers in a previous course, notice the similarity here. Two complex numbers are equal provided that their corresponding real and imaginary parts are equal; two vectors are equal provided that their corresponding components are equal.)

It's easy to calculate the length of a vector **v** when its components are given. Suppose that $\mathbf{v} = \langle v_1, v_2 \rangle$. Applying the Pythagorean theorem in Figure 4, we have

$$|\mathbf{v}|^2 = v_1^2 + v_2^2$$

and consequently,

$$|\mathbf{v}| = \sqrt{v_1^2 + v_2^2}$$

Although Figure 4 shows the point $(v_1, v_2)$ in Quadrant I, you can check for yourself that the same formula results when $(v_1, v_2)$ is located in any of the other three quadrants. We therefore have the following general formula.

---

**The Length of a Vector**

If $\mathbf{v} = \langle v_1, v_2 \rangle$, then

$$|\mathbf{v}| = \sqrt{v_1^2 + v_2^2}$$

---

| EXAMPLE | 1 | Finding the length of a vector |

Compute the length of the vector $\mathbf{v} = \langle 2, -4 \rangle$.

(a)

(b)

**Figure 5**

**SOLUTION**

$$|\mathbf{v}| = \sqrt{v_1^2 + v_2^2} = \sqrt{2^2 + (-4)^2} = \sqrt{20} = 2\sqrt{5}$$

If the coordinates of the points $P$ and $Q$ are $P(x_1, y_1)$ and $Q(x_2, y_2)$, then

$$\overrightarrow{PQ} = \langle x_2 - x_1, y_2 - y_1 \rangle$$

To derive this formula, we first construct the right triangle shown in Figure 5(a). Now we let $R$ denote the point $(x_2 - x_1, y_2 - y_1)$ and draw the position vector $\overrightarrow{OR}$ shown in Figure 5(b). Since the right triangles in Figures 5(a) and 5(b) are congruent (Why?) and have corresponding legs that are parallel, we have

$$\overrightarrow{PQ} = \overrightarrow{OR} = \langle x_2 - x_1, y_2 - y_1 \rangle$$

as required. We can summarize this result as follows. For any vector $\mathbf{v}$ we have

$x$-component of $\mathbf{v}$:
($x$-coordinate of terminal point) − ($x$-coordinate of initial point)
$y$-component of $\mathbf{v}$:
($y$-coordinate of terminal point) − ($y$-coordinate of initial point)

**EXAMPLE** **2** **Finding the components of a vector**

Let $P$ and $Q$ be the points $P(3, 1)$ and $Q(7, 4)$. Sketch $\overrightarrow{PQ}$, find the components of $\overrightarrow{PQ}$, and sketch the position vector for $\overrightarrow{PQ}$.

**SOLUTION**

Plot the points $P$ and $Q$ and draw the vector $\overrightarrow{PQ}$ as shown in Figure 6.

$x$-component of $\overrightarrow{PQ} = x$-coordinate of $Q$ − $x$-coordinate of $P$
$= 7 - 3 = 4$
$y$-component of $\overrightarrow{PQ} = y$-coordinate of $Q$ − $y$-coordinate of $P$
$= 4 - 1 = 3$

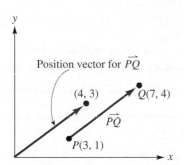

**Figure 6**

Consequently, $\overrightarrow{PQ} = \langle 4, 3 \rangle$. The position vector for $\overrightarrow{PQ}$ is shown in Figure 6.

Vector addition is particularly simple to carry out when the vectors are in component form. Indeed, we can use the parallelogram law to verify the following result.

**THEOREM** **Vector Addition**

If $\mathbf{u} = \langle u_1, u_2 \rangle$ and $\mathbf{v} = \langle v_1, v_2 \rangle$, then $\mathbf{u} + \mathbf{v} = \langle u_1 + v_1, u_2 + v_2 \rangle$.

This theorem tells us that vector addition can be carried out *componentwise;* in other words, to add two vectors, just add the corresponding components. For example,

$$\langle 1, 2 \rangle + \langle 3, 7 \rangle = \langle 4, 9 \rangle$$

**Figure 7**

To see why this theorem is valid, consider Figure 7, where we have completed the parallelogram. (*Caution:* In reading the derivation that follows, don't confuse notation such as $OA$ with $\vec{OA}$; recall that $OA$ denotes the length of the line segment $\overline{OA}$. Since the $x$-component of $\mathbf{u}$ is $u_1$, we have

$$OB = u_1$$

Also,

$$BC = OA = v_1$$

Therefore,

$$OC = OB + BC = u_1 + v_1$$

But $OC$ is the $x$-component of the vector $\vec{OP}$, and by the parallelogram law, $\vec{OP} = \mathbf{u} + \mathbf{v}$. In other words, the $x$-component of $\mathbf{u} + \mathbf{v}$ is $u_1 + v_1$, as we wished to show. The fact that the $y$-component of $\mathbf{u} + \mathbf{v}$ is $u_2 + v_2$ is proved in a similar fashion.

The vector $\langle 0, 0 \rangle$ is called the **zero vector,** and it is denoted by $\mathbf{0}$. Notice that for any vector $\mathbf{v} = \langle v_1, v_2 \rangle$ we have

$$\mathbf{v} + \mathbf{0} = \mathbf{v} \qquad \text{because} \qquad \langle v_1, v_2 \rangle + \langle 0, 0 \rangle = \langle v_1, v_2 \rangle$$

and

$$\mathbf{0} + \mathbf{v} = \mathbf{v} \qquad \text{because} \qquad \langle 0, 0 \rangle + \langle v_1, v_2 \rangle = \langle v_1, v_2 \rangle$$

Thus the sum of a given vector and the zero vector is the given vector. In other words, adding the zero vector to a given vector leaves the given vector unchanged. So for the operation of vector addition the zero vector plays the same role as does the real number zero in addition of real numbers. There are, in fact, several other ways in which vector addition resembles ordinary addition of real numbers. We'll return to this point again near the end of this section.

In the box that follows, we define an operation called **scalar multiplication,** in which a vector is "multiplied" by a real number (a **scalar**) to obtain another vector.

(a) The vectors $\mathbf{v}$ and $3\mathbf{v}$ have the same direction. The length of $3\mathbf{v}$ is three times that of $\mathbf{v}$.

---

**DEFINITION** | Scalar Multiplication

For each real number $k$ and each vector $\mathbf{v} = \langle x, y \rangle$, we define a vector $k\mathbf{v}$ by the equation

$$k\mathbf{v} = k\langle x, y \rangle = \langle kx, ky \rangle$$

**EXAMPLES**

If $\mathbf{v} = \langle 2, 1 \rangle$, then

$$2\mathbf{v} = \langle 4, 2 \rangle \qquad 3\mathbf{v} = \langle 6, 3 \rangle$$

$$0\mathbf{v} = \langle 0, 0 \rangle = \mathbf{0}$$

$$-1\mathbf{v} = \langle -2, -1 \rangle$$

---

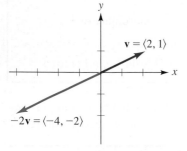

(b) The vectors $\mathbf{v}$ and $-2\mathbf{v}$ have opposite directions. The length of $-2\mathbf{v}$ is twice that of $\mathbf{v}$.

**Figure 8**

In geometric terms, the length of $k\mathbf{v}$ is $|k|$ times the length of $\mathbf{v}$. (See Exercise 60 at the end of this section.) The vectors $\mathbf{v}$ and $k\mathbf{v}$ have the same direction if $k > 0$ and opposite directions if $k < 0$. For example, let $\mathbf{v} = \langle 2, 1 \rangle$. In Figure 8(a) we show the vectors $\mathbf{v}$ and $3\mathbf{v}$, while in Figure 8(b) we show $\mathbf{v}$ and $-2\mathbf{v}$.

---

**EXAMPLE** **3** **Vector algebra**

Let $\mathbf{v} = \langle 3, 4 \rangle$ and $\mathbf{w} = \langle -1, 2 \rangle$. Compute each of the following:
**(a)** $\mathbf{v} + \mathbf{w}$; **(b)** $-2\mathbf{v} + 3\mathbf{w}$; **(c)** $|-2\mathbf{v} + 3\mathbf{w}|$.

**SOLUTION**

**(a)** $\mathbf{v} + \mathbf{w} = \langle 3, 4 \rangle + \langle -1, 2 \rangle = \langle 3 - 1, 4 + 2 \rangle = \langle 2, 6 \rangle$

**(b)** $-2\mathbf{v} + 3\mathbf{w} = -2\langle 3, 4 \rangle + 3\langle -1, 2 \rangle = \langle -6, -8 \rangle + \langle -3, 6 \rangle$
$$= \langle -9, -2 \rangle$$

**(c)** $|-2\mathbf{v} + 3\mathbf{w}| = |\langle -9, -2 \rangle| = \sqrt{(-9)^2 + (-2)^2} = \sqrt{85}$

Figure 9

For each vector $\mathbf{v}$ we define a vector $-\mathbf{v}$, called the **negative** or **opposite** of $\mathbf{v}$, by the equation

$$-\mathbf{v} = -1\mathbf{v}$$

Thus if $\mathbf{v} = \langle a, b \rangle$, then $-\mathbf{v} = \langle -a, -b \rangle$. As is indicated in Figure 9, the vectors $\mathbf{v}$ and $-\mathbf{v}$ have the same length but opposite directions.

We can use the ideas in the preceding paragraph to define **vector subtraction.** Given two vectors $\mathbf{u}$ and $\mathbf{v}$, we define a vector $\mathbf{u} - \mathbf{v}$ by the equation

$$\mathbf{u} - \mathbf{v} = \mathbf{u} + (-\mathbf{v}) \tag{1}$$

First let's see what equation (1) is saying in terms of components; then we will indicate a simple geometric interpretation of vector subtraction.

If $\mathbf{u} = \langle u_1, u_2 \rangle$ and $\mathbf{v} = \langle v_1, v_2 \rangle$, then equation (1) tells us that

$$\mathbf{u} - \mathbf{v} = \langle u_1, u_2 \rangle + \langle -v_1, -v_2 \rangle$$
$$= \langle u_1 + (-v_1), u_2 + (-v_2) \rangle$$

That is,

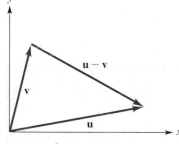

Figure 10

$$\mathbf{u} - \mathbf{v} = \langle u_1 - v_1, u_2 - v_2 \rangle \tag{2}$$

In other words, to subtract one vector from another, just subtract the corresponding components.

Vector subtraction can be interpreted geometrically. According to the formula in the first box on page 673, the right-hand side of equation (2) represents a vector drawn from the terminal point of $\mathbf{v}$ to the terminal point of $\mathbf{u}$. Figure 10 summarizes this fact, and Figure 11 provides a geometric comparison of vector addition and vector subtraction.

Figure 10 also indicates the algebraic significance of the difference $\mathbf{u} - \mathbf{v}$ as the vector we need to *add* to what is subtracted, $\mathbf{v}$, to get back what we started with, $\mathbf{u}$.

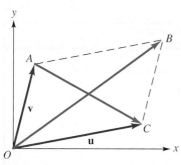

Figure 11
$\mathbf{u} + \mathbf{v}$ and $\mathbf{u} - \mathbf{v}$ are the directed diagonals of parallelogram $OABC$:
$\mathbf{u} + \mathbf{v} = \overrightarrow{OB}$ and $\mathbf{u} - \mathbf{v} = \overrightarrow{AC}$.

**EXAMPLE 4 Vector subtraction**

Let $\mathbf{u} = \langle 5, 3 \rangle$ and $\mathbf{v} = \langle -1, 2 \rangle$. Compute $3\mathbf{u} - \mathbf{v}$.

**SOLUTION**
$$3\mathbf{u} - \mathbf{v} = 3\langle 5, 3 \rangle - \langle -1, 2 \rangle$$
$$= \langle 15, 9 \rangle - \langle -1, 2 \rangle = \langle 15 - (-1), 9 - 2 \rangle = \langle 16, 7 \rangle$$

The next three examples deal with unit vectors. By definition any vector of length 1 is called a **unit vector.** Two particularly useful unit vectors are as follows.

**Figure 12**

$$\mathbf{i} = \langle 1, 0 \rangle \qquad \text{and} \qquad \mathbf{j} = \langle 0, 1 \rangle$$

These are shown in Figure 12.

Any vector $\mathbf{v} = \langle x, y \rangle$ can be uniquely expressed in terms of the unit vectors $\mathbf{i}$ and $\mathbf{j}$ as follows:

$$\langle x, y \rangle = x\mathbf{i} + y\mathbf{j} \qquad\qquad (3)$$

To verify equation (3), we have

$$x\mathbf{i} + y\mathbf{j} = x\langle 1, 0 \rangle + y\langle 0, 1 \rangle$$
$$= \langle x, 0 \rangle + \langle 0, y \rangle = \langle x, y \rangle$$

---

### EXAMPLE 5 Unit vectors and components

**(a)** Express the vector $\langle 3, -7 \rangle$ in terms of the unit vectors $\mathbf{i}$ and $\mathbf{j}$.
**(b)** Express the vector $\mathbf{v} = -4\mathbf{i} + 5\mathbf{j}$ in component form.

**SOLUTION**
**(a)** Using equation (3), we can write

$$\langle 3, -7 \rangle = 3\mathbf{i} + (-7)\mathbf{j} = 3\mathbf{i} - 7\mathbf{j}$$

*Note*: In the last step we used the fact that $(-7)\mathbf{j} = -7\mathbf{j}$ and the definition of vector subtraction.

**(b)** $\mathbf{v} = -4\mathbf{i} + 5\mathbf{j} = -4\langle 1, 0 \rangle + 5\langle 0, 1 \rangle$
$\qquad = \langle -4, 0 \rangle + \langle 0, 5 \rangle = \langle -4, 5 \rangle$

Thus the component form of $\mathbf{v}$ is $\langle -4, 5 \rangle$.

---

### EXAMPLE 6 Finding a unit vector

Find a unit vector $\mathbf{u}$ that has the same direction as the vector $\mathbf{v} = \langle 3, 4 \rangle$.

**SOLUTION**
First, let's determine the length of $\mathbf{v}$:

$$|\mathbf{v}| = \sqrt{3^2 + 4^2} = \sqrt{25} = 5$$

So we want a vector whose length is one-fifth that of $\mathbf{v}$ and whose direction is the same as that of $\mathbf{v}$. Such a vector is

$$\mathbf{u} = \frac{1}{5}\mathbf{v} = \frac{1}{5}\langle 3, 4 \rangle = \left\langle \frac{3}{5}, \frac{4}{5} \right\rangle$$

(You should check for yourself now that the length of this vector is 1.) *Note*: $-\mathbf{u} = \langle -\frac{3}{5}, -\frac{4}{5} \rangle$ is a unit vector that has the opposite direction $\mathbf{v}$. (You should check this for yourself as well.)

| EXAMPLE | 7 | Finding a unit vector given a direction |

The angle from the positive $x$-axis to the unit vector **u** is $\pi/3$, as indicated in Figure 13. Determine the components of **u**.

**SOLUTION**

Let $P$ denote the terminal point of **u**. Since $P$ lies on the unit circle, the coordinates of $P$ are by definition $(\cos \frac{\pi}{3}, \sin \frac{\pi}{3})$. We therefore have

$$\mathbf{u} = \left\langle \frac{1}{2}, \frac{\sqrt{3}}{2} \right\rangle$$

*Figure 13*

It was mentioned earlier that there are several ways in which vector addition resembles ordinary addition of real numbers. In the previous section, for example, we saw that vector addition is commutative. That is, for any two vectors **u** and **v**,

$$\mathbf{u} + \mathbf{v} = \mathbf{v} + \mathbf{u}$$

By using components, we can easily verify that this property holds. (In the previous section we used a geometric argument to establish this property.) We begin by letting $\mathbf{u} = \langle u_1, u_2 \rangle$ and $\mathbf{v} = \langle v_1, v_2 \rangle$. Then we have

$$\begin{aligned}
\mathbf{u} + \mathbf{v} &= \langle u_1, u_2 \rangle + \langle v_1, v_2 \rangle \\
&= \langle u_1 + v_1, u_2 + v_2 \rangle \\
&= \langle v_1 + u_1, v_2 + u_2 \rangle \qquad \text{Addition of real numbers is commutative.} \\
&= \langle v_1, v_2 \rangle + \langle u_1, u_2 \rangle \\
&= \mathbf{v} + \mathbf{u}
\end{aligned}$$

which is what we wanted to show.

There are a number of other properties of vector addition and scalar multiplication that can be proved in a similar fashion. In the following box we list a particular collection of these properties, known as the **vector space properties.** (Exercises 55–58 ask that you verify these properties by using components, just as we did for the commutative property.)

### Properties of Vector Addition and Scalar Multiplication

For all vectors **u**, **v**, and **w**, and for all scalars (real numbers) $a$ and $b$, the following properties hold.

1. $\mathbf{u} + (\mathbf{v} + \mathbf{w}) = (\mathbf{u} + \mathbf{v}) + \mathbf{w}$
2. $\mathbf{0} + \mathbf{v} = \mathbf{v} + \mathbf{0} = \mathbf{v}$
3. $\mathbf{v} + (-\mathbf{v}) = \mathbf{0}$
4. $\mathbf{u} + \mathbf{v} = \mathbf{v} + \mathbf{u}$
5. $a(\mathbf{u} + \mathbf{v}) = a\mathbf{u} + a\mathbf{v}$
6. $(a + b)\mathbf{v} = a\mathbf{v} + b\mathbf{v}$
7. $(ab)\mathbf{v} = a(b\mathbf{v})$
8. $1\mathbf{v} = \mathbf{v}$

# EXERCISE SET 9.3

**A**

*In Exercises 1–6, sketch each vector in an x-y coordinate system, and compute the length of the vector.*

**1.** $\langle 4, 3 \rangle$       **2.** $\langle 5, 12 \rangle$       **3.** $\langle -4, 2 \rangle$

**4.** $\langle -6, -6 \rangle$   **5.** $\langle \frac{3}{4}, -\frac{1}{2} \rangle$   **6.** $\langle -3, 0 \rangle$

*In Exercises 7–12 the coordinates of two points P and Q are given. In each case, determine the components of the vector $\overrightarrow{PQ}$. Write your answers in the form $\langle a, b \rangle$.*

**7.** $P(2, 3)$ and $Q(3, 7)$

**8.** $P(5, 1)$ and $Q(4, 9)$

**9.** $P(-2, -3)$ and $Q(-3, -2)$
**10.** $P(0, -4)$ and $Q(0, -8)$
**11.** $P(-5, 1)$ and $Q(3, -4)$
**12.** $P(1, 0)$ and $Q(0, 1)$

*In Exercises 13–32, assume that the vectors* **a, b, c,** *and* **d** *are defined as follows:*

$$\mathbf{a} = \langle 2, 3 \rangle \qquad \mathbf{b} = \langle 5, 4 \rangle \qquad \mathbf{c} = \langle 6, -1 \rangle \qquad \mathbf{d} = \langle -2, 0 \rangle$$

*Compute each of the indicated quantities.*

**13.** $\mathbf{a} + \mathbf{b}$

**14.** $\mathbf{c} + \mathbf{d}$

**15.** $2\mathbf{a} + 4\mathbf{b}$

**16.** $-2\mathbf{c} + 2\mathbf{d}$

**17.** $|\mathbf{b} + \mathbf{c}|$

**18.** $|5\mathbf{b} + 5\mathbf{c}|$

**19.** $|\mathbf{a} + \mathbf{c}| - |\mathbf{a}| - |\mathbf{c}|$

**20.** $1/|\mathbf{d}|$

**21.** $\mathbf{a} + (\mathbf{b} + \mathbf{c})$

**22.** $(\mathbf{a} + \mathbf{b}) + \mathbf{c}$

**23.** $3\mathbf{a} + 4\mathbf{a}$

**24.** $|4\mathbf{b} + 5\mathbf{b}|$

**25.** $\mathbf{a} - \mathbf{b}$

**26.** $\mathbf{b} - \mathbf{c}$

**27.** $3\mathbf{b} - 4\mathbf{d}$

**28.** $\dfrac{1}{|3\mathbf{b} - 4\mathbf{d}|}(3\mathbf{b} - 4\mathbf{a})$

**29.** $\mathbf{a} - (\mathbf{b} + \mathbf{c})$

**30.** $(\mathbf{a} - \mathbf{b}) - \mathbf{c}$

**31.** $|\mathbf{c} + \mathbf{d}|^2 - |\mathbf{c} - \mathbf{d}|^2$

**32.** $|\mathbf{a} + \mathbf{b}|^2 + |\mathbf{a} - \mathbf{b}|^2 - 2|\mathbf{a}|^2 - 2|\mathbf{b}|^2$

*In Exercises 33–38, express each vector in terms of the unit vectors* **i** *and* **j**.

**33.** $\langle 3, 8 \rangle$

**34.** $\langle 4, -2 \rangle$

**35.** $\langle -8, -6 \rangle$

**36.** $\langle -9, 0 \rangle$

**37.** $3\langle 5, 3 \rangle + 2\langle 2, 7 \rangle$

**38.** $|\langle 12, 5 \rangle|\langle 3, 4 \rangle + |\langle 3, 4 \rangle|\langle 12, 5 \rangle$

*In Exercises 39–42, express each vector in the form* $\langle a, b \rangle$.

**39.** $\mathbf{i} + \mathbf{j}$

**40.** $\mathbf{i} - 2\mathbf{j}$

**41.** $5\mathbf{i} - 4\mathbf{j}$

**42.** $\dfrac{1}{|\mathbf{i} + \mathbf{j}|}(\mathbf{i} + \mathbf{j})$

*In Exercises 43–48, find a unit vector having the same direction as the given vector.*

**43.** $\langle 4, 8 \rangle$

**44.** $\langle -3, 3 \rangle$

**45.** $\langle 6, -3 \rangle$

**46.** $\langle -12, 5 \rangle$

**47.** $8\mathbf{i} - 9\mathbf{j}$

**48.** $\langle 7, 3 \rangle - \mathbf{i} + \mathbf{j}$

*In Exercises 49–54, you are given an angle* $\theta$ *measured counterclockwise from the positive x-axis to a unit vector* $\mathbf{u} = \langle u_1, u_2 \rangle$. *In each case, determine the components* $u_1$ *and* $u_2$.

**49.** $\theta = \pi/6$

**50.** $\theta = \pi/4$

**51.** $\theta = 2\pi/3$

**52.** $\theta = 3\pi/4$

**53.** $\theta = 5\pi/6$

**54.** $\theta = 3\pi/2$

## B

*In Exercises 55–58, let* $\mathbf{u} = \langle u_1, u_2 \rangle$, $\mathbf{v} = \langle v_1, v_2 \rangle$, *and* $\mathbf{w} = \langle w_1, w_2 \rangle$. *Refer to the box on page 677.*

**55.** Verify Properties 1 and 2.

**56.** Verify Properties 3 and 4.

**57.** Verify Properties 5 and 6.

**58.** Verify Properties 7 and 8.

**59.** Verify that $\mathbf{v} + (\mathbf{u} - \mathbf{v}) = \mathbf{u}$.

**60.** Show that $|k\mathbf{v}| = |k||\mathbf{v}|$ for any real number $k$.

*In Exercises 61–77 we study the dot product of two vectors. Given two vectors* $\mathbf{A} = \langle x_1, y_1 \rangle$ *and* $\mathbf{B} = \langle x_2, y_2 \rangle$, *we define the* **dot product** $\mathbf{A} \cdot \mathbf{B}$ *as follows:*

$$\mathbf{A} \cdot \mathbf{B} = x_1 x_2 + y_1 y_2$$

*For example, if* $\mathbf{A} = \langle 3, 4 \rangle$ *and* $\mathbf{B} = \langle -2, 5 \rangle$, *then* $\mathbf{A} \cdot \mathbf{B} = (3)(-2) + (4)(5) = 14$. *Notice that the dot product of two vectors is a real number. For this reason, the dot product is also known as the* **scalar product.** *For Exercises 61–63 the vectors* **u, v,** *and* **w** *are defined as follows:*

$$\mathbf{u} = \langle -4, 5 \rangle \qquad \mathbf{v} = \langle 3, 4 \rangle \qquad \mathbf{w} = \langle 2, -5 \rangle$$

**61.** **(a)** Compute $\mathbf{u} \cdot \mathbf{v}$ and $\mathbf{v} \cdot \mathbf{u}$.
   **(b)** Compute $\mathbf{v} \cdot \mathbf{w}$ and $\mathbf{w} \cdot \mathbf{v}$.
   **(c)** Show that for any two vectors **A** and **B**, we have $\mathbf{A} \cdot \mathbf{B} = \mathbf{B} \cdot \mathbf{A}$. That is, show that the dot product is commutative. *Hint*: Let $\mathbf{A} = \langle x_1, y_1 \rangle$, and let $\mathbf{B} = \langle x_2, y_2 \rangle$.

**62.** **(a)** Compute $\mathbf{v} + \mathbf{w}$.
   **(b)** Compute $\mathbf{u} \cdot (\mathbf{v} + \mathbf{w})$.
   **(c)** Compute $\mathbf{u} \cdot \mathbf{v} + \mathbf{u} \cdot \mathbf{w}$.
   **(d)** Show that for any three vectors **A, B,** and **C** we have $\mathbf{A} \cdot (\mathbf{B} + \mathbf{C}) = \mathbf{A} \cdot \mathbf{B} + \mathbf{A} \cdot \mathbf{C}$.

**63.** **(a)** Compute $\mathbf{v} \cdot \mathbf{v}$ and $|\mathbf{v}|^2$.
   **(b)** Compute $\mathbf{w} \cdot \mathbf{w}$ and $|\mathbf{w}|^2$.

**64.** Show that for any vector **A** we always have $|\mathbf{A}|^2 = \mathbf{A} \cdot \mathbf{A}$. That is, the square of the length of a vector is equal to the dot product of the vector with itself. *Hint*: Let $\mathbf{A} = \langle x, y \rangle$.

*Let* $\theta$ *(where* $0 \le \theta \le \pi$*) denote the angle between the two nonzero vectors* **A** *and* **B**. *Then it can be shown that the cosine of* $\theta$ *is given by the formula*

$$\cos \theta = \frac{\mathbf{A} \cdot \mathbf{B}}{|\mathbf{A}||\mathbf{B}|}$$

*(See Exercise 77 for the derivation of this result.) In Exercises 65–70, sketch each pair of vectors as position vectors, then use this formula to find the cosine of the angle between the given pair of vectors. Also, in each case, use a calculator to compute the angle. Express the angle using degrees and using radians. Round the values to two decimal places.*

**65.** $\mathbf{A} = \langle 4, 1 \rangle$ and $\mathbf{B} = \langle 2, 6 \rangle$

**66.** $\mathbf{A} = \langle 3, -1 \rangle$ and $\mathbf{B} = \langle -2, 5 \rangle$

**67.** $\mathbf{A} = \langle 5, 6 \rangle$ and $\mathbf{B} = \langle -3, -7 \rangle$

**68.** $\mathbf{A} = \langle 3, 0 \rangle$ and $\mathbf{B} = \langle 1, 4 \rangle$

**69.** **(a)** $\mathbf{A} = \langle -8, 2 \rangle$ and $\mathbf{B} = \langle 1, -3 \rangle$
   **(b)** $\mathbf{A} = \langle -8, 2 \rangle$ and $\mathbf{B} = \langle -1, 3 \rangle$

**70.** **(a)** $\mathbf{A} = \langle 7, 12 \rangle$ and $\mathbf{B} = \langle 1, 2 \rangle$
   **(b)** $\mathbf{A} = \langle 7, 12 \rangle$ and $\mathbf{B} = \langle -1, -2 \rangle$

71. **(a)** Compute the cosine of the angle between the vectors $\langle 2, 5 \rangle$ and $\langle -5, 2 \rangle$.
    **(b)** What can you conclude from your answer in part (a)?
    **(c)** Draw a sketch to check your conclusion in part (b).
72. Follow Exercise 71, but use the vectors $\langle 6, -8 \rangle$ and $\langle -4, -3 \rangle$.
73. Let **A** and **B** be nonzero vectors.
    **(a)** If $\mathbf{A} \cdot \mathbf{B} = 0$, explain why **A** and **B** are perpendicular.
    **(b)** If **A** and **B** are perpendicular, explain why $\mathbf{A} \cdot \mathbf{B} = 0$.
    (a) and (b) together show that two nonzero vectors are perpendicular if and only if their dot product is zero.
74. Find a value for $t$ such that the vectors $\langle 15, -3 \rangle$ and $\langle -4, t \rangle$ are perpendicular.
75. Find a unit vector that is perpendicular to the vector $\langle -12, 5 \rangle$. (There are two answers.)

76. Suppose that **A** and **B** be nonzero vectors.
    **(a)** Show that $|\mathbf{A} + \mathbf{B}|^2 = |\mathbf{A}|^2 + 2\mathbf{A} \cdot \mathbf{B} + |\mathbf{B}|^2$
    *Hint:* Start with $|\mathbf{A} + \mathbf{B}|^2 = (\mathbf{A} + \mathbf{B}) \cdot (\mathbf{A} + \mathbf{B})$ and use Exercises 62(d), 64, and 61(c). *Alternatively,* let $\mathbf{A} = \langle x_1, y_1 \rangle$ and $\mathbf{B} = \langle x_2, y_2 \rangle$. Then separately compute each side of the equation in part (a).
    **(b)** Show that $|\mathbf{A} + \mathbf{B}|^2 = |\mathbf{A}|^2 + |\mathbf{B}|^2$ if and only if **A** and **B** are perpendicular. Draw a sketch with **A** and **B** joined "head to tail." This is a vector statement of the **Pythagorean theorem.**
77. Refer to the figure at the top of the next column. In this exercise we are going to derive the following formula for the cosine of the angle $\theta$ between two nonzero vectors **A** and **B**:

$$\cos \theta = \frac{\mathbf{A} \cdot \mathbf{B}}{|\mathbf{A}||\mathbf{B}|}$$

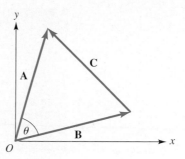

**(a)** Let **A** and **B** be nonzero vectors, and let $\mathbf{C} = \mathbf{A} - \mathbf{B}$. Show that

$$|\mathbf{C}|^2 = |\mathbf{A}|^2 + |\mathbf{B}|^2 - 2\mathbf{A} \cdot \mathbf{B}$$

*Hint:* Use the result or method of Exercise 76(a).

**(b)** According to the law of cosines, we have

$$|\mathbf{C}|^2 = |\mathbf{A}|^2 + |\mathbf{B}|^2 - 2|\mathbf{A}||\mathbf{B}| \cos \theta$$

Set this expression for $|\mathbf{C}|^2$ equal to the expression obtained in part (a), and then solve for $\cos \theta$ to obtain the required formula.

*Note:* The formula that we just derived can be written in the form

$$\mathbf{A} \cdot \mathbf{B} = |\mathbf{A}||\mathbf{B}| \cos \theta$$

This expresses the dot product in purely geometric terms: The dot product of two vectors is the product of the lengths of the two vectors and the cosine of their included angle. So the easy-to-compute algebraic expression in the components of **A** and **B** that is used to define the dot product on page 678 has important geometric applications. In particular, dot products can be used to compute lengths and angles and to determine whether two vectors are mutually perpendicular.

## PROJECT

### LINES, CIRCLES, AND RAY TRACING WITH VECTORS

In the $x$-$y$ plane, a line and its equations are uniquely determined by the line's slope (or undefined slope if the line is vertical) and the coordinates of one point on the line. We know an equation of the line with slope $m$ and $y$-intercept $b$ is $y = mx + b$.

Our first goal in this project is to find a vector equation for a line. Let $P_0$ be a point in the $x$-$y$ plane with **A** a nonzero vector. In Figure A we draw the position vector $\mathbf{P}_0$ from the origin to the point $P_0$ and the vector **A** with initial point $P_0$, and then draw the vectors $\mathbf{P}_0 + \mathbf{A}$, $\mathbf{P}_0 + 2\mathbf{A}$, $\mathbf{P}_0 + 3\mathbf{A}$, $\mathbf{P}_0 + (-1)\mathbf{A}$, and $\mathbf{P}_0 + (-2)\mathbf{A}$.

Figure A shows that each point $P$ on the line has a description of the form $\mathbf{P}_0 + t\mathbf{A}$ for *some* real number $t$. As $t$ varies over all real numbers we sweep out all points on the line. These observations give us a vector equation for the line

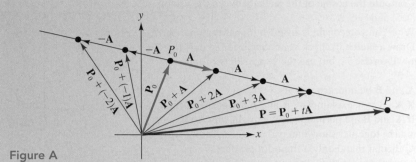

**Figure A**

through the point $P_0$ with **direction vector A**. (*Note*: A direction vector for a line is a nonzero vector that is parallel to the line.) Letting **P** denote the position vector from the origin to the arbitrary point $P$ on the line we have

$$\mathbf{P} = \mathbf{P}_0 + t\mathbf{A} \qquad \text{for } -\infty < t < \infty \tag{i}$$

---

**EXAMPLE**    A vector equation for a line

Consider the line in the *x-y* plane passing through the point $(-2, 1)$ with slope 2.
**(a)** Sketch the line and find its slope-intercept equation.
**(b)** Find a vector equation for the line.
**(c)** Find the points on the line corresponding to $t = -1, 0,$ and 2.

**SOLUTION**
**(a)** The line is sketched in Figure B. It has an equation of the form

$$y = mx + b$$

Here $m = 2$, so $y = 2x + b$. $(-2, 1)$ lies on the line, so

$$1 = 2(-2) + b$$
$$b = 5$$

Therefore $y = 2x + 5$.

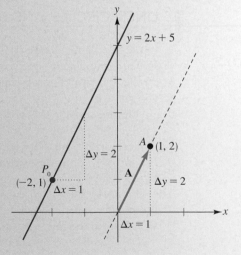

**Figure B**

**(b)** Let $P = (x, y)$ be any point on the line and let $P_0 = (-2, 1)$. So the position vectors from the origin to these points are $\mathbf{P} = \langle x, y \rangle$ and $\mathbf{P}_0 = \langle -2, 1 \rangle$. Given the slope 2, we can find the line's *direction* by drawing the line of slope 2 passing through the origin and picking a convenient point (different from the origin) on this line. See Figure B. Using the point $A = (1, 2)$, we see that the vector $\mathbf{A} = \langle 1, 2 \rangle$ is parallel to the line. So a vector equation for the line is

$$\mathbf{P} = \mathbf{P}_0 + t\mathbf{A} \qquad \text{for } -\infty < t < \infty$$

which in component form becomes

$$\langle x, y \rangle = \langle -2, 1 \rangle + t\langle 1, 2 \rangle \qquad \text{for } -\infty < t < \infty$$

**(c)** For $t = -1, \langle x, y \rangle = \langle -2, 1 \rangle + (-1)\langle 1, 2 \rangle = \langle -3, -1 \rangle$. So the vector $\langle -3, -1 \rangle$ goes from the origin to the point $P$ on the line, with $P = (-3, -1)$. Similarly, for $t = 0$ the point on the line is $P = (-2, 1)$ and for $t = 2$ the point is $P = (0, 5)$.

---

**EXERCISE 1**    Consider the line in the $x$-$y$ plane passing through the point $(1, -2)$ with slope 3.
**(a)** Sketch the line and find its slope-intercept equation.
**(b)** Find a vector equation for the line. Label three vectors on the line in part (a).
**(c)** Find the points on this line corresponding to $t = -2, -1, 0, 1$, and 2.

**EXERCISE 2**    Consider the line in the $x$-$y$ plane passing through the points $A = (-3, 1)$ and $B = (2, 4)$.
**(a)** Sketch the line and then find a vector equation for it.
**(b)** Find a vector equation for the line *segment* from $A$ to $B$. *Hint*: You need to restrict the $t$ values to a finite interval $k \le t \le l$ where $t = k$ corresponds to point $A$ and $t = l$ to point $B$.

We next look at an optical application of our vector equation for a line. Ray tracing techniques have been used in the design of camera lenses, microscopes, telescopes, and other optical devices for hundreds of years. More recently ray tracing has been used in computer graphics applications, particularly in the creation of realistic scenes for games and special effects for movies. In the last 40 years, computationally efficient vector ray tracing techniques have replaced older trigonometric methods. A basic problem in optical ray tracing is to find the point of intersection of a ray, determined by a point and a direction vector, with a spherical lens surface of known center and radius (see Figure C). (Of course it is possible that a given ray does not intersect a particular lens surface.)

In two dimensions, in the $x$-$y$ plane, the problem becomes as follows: Given two points $P_0$ and $C$, a nonzero vector $\mathbf{A}$, and a positive real number $r$, find the point $P$ of intersection of the line through $P_0$ in the direction of $\mathbf{A}$ with the circle of radius $r$ and center $C$. See Figure D, where we let $\mathbf{P}_0$, $\mathbf{P}$, and $\mathbf{C}$ denote the vectors from the origin to the points $P_0, P$, and $C$ respectively, and $\mathbf{P} - \mathbf{C}$ denotes the vector of length $r$ from the center of the circle to the point of intersection.

The point of intersection $P$ lies on the line through $P_0$ in the direction of $\mathbf{A}$ so

$$\mathbf{P} = \mathbf{P}_0 + t\mathbf{A} \qquad \text{for } \textit{some} \text{ real number } t \tag{ii}$$

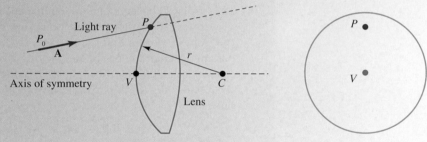

(i)  Schematic drawing of a cross-section
     of a rotationally symmetric lens

(ii)  Front view of lens

**Figure C**

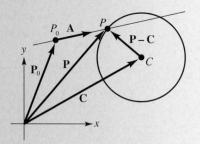

**Figure D**

The point $P$ also lies on the circle with center $C$ and radius $r$, so the distance from $C$ to $P$ is $r$. Using vectors, the length of the vector $\mathbf{P} - \mathbf{C}$ is $r$, that is

$$|\mathbf{P} - \mathbf{C}| = r \tag{iii}$$

We can solve the system of equations (ii) and (iii) for $t$ by substituting the expression for $\mathbf{P}$ from equation (ii) into equation (iii) and rearranging to get

$$|t\mathbf{A} + (\mathbf{P}_0 - \mathbf{C})| = r \tag{iv}$$

Squaring both sides of equation (iv) we get

$$|t\mathbf{A} + (\mathbf{P}_0 - \mathbf{C})|^2 = r^2 \tag{v}$$

Now (from Exercise 63 in Section 9.3) the squared magnitude of a vector is the dot product of the vector with itself. So

$$[t\mathbf{A} + (\mathbf{P}_0 - \mathbf{C})] \cdot [t\mathbf{A} + (\mathbf{P}_0 - \mathbf{C})] = r^2 \tag{vi}$$

Then [using Exercises 61(c) and 62(d) in Section 9.3] we have

$$t\mathbf{A} \cdot [t\mathbf{A} + (\mathbf{P}_0 - \mathbf{C})] + (\mathbf{P}_0 - \mathbf{C}) \cdot [t\mathbf{A} + (\mathbf{P}_0 - \mathbf{C})] = r^2 \tag{vii}$$

**EXERCISE 3**   Expand the left-hand side of equation (vii) and regroup the terms to obtain

$$(t\mathbf{A}) \cdot (t\mathbf{A}) + (t\mathbf{A}) \cdot (\mathbf{P}_0 - \mathbf{C}) + (\mathbf{P}_0 - \mathbf{C}) \cdot (t\mathbf{A}) + (\mathbf{P}_0 - \mathbf{C}) \cdot (\mathbf{P}_0 - \mathbf{C}) = r^2 \tag{viii}$$

**EXERCISE 4**
**(a)** Show that for any two vectors $\mathbf{A}$, $\mathbf{B}$, and real number $s$, $(s\mathbf{A}) \cdot \mathbf{B} = s(\mathbf{A} \cdot \mathbf{B}) = \mathbf{A} \cdot (s\mathbf{B})$.   *Hint*: Let $\mathbf{A} = \langle x_1, y_1 \rangle$ and $\mathbf{B} = \langle x_2, y_2 \rangle$.

**(b)** Use part (a) to put equation (viii) in the form of a quadratic equation in $t$ to obtain

$$(\mathbf{A} \cdot \mathbf{A})t^2 + [2\mathbf{A} \cdot (\mathbf{P}_0 - \mathbf{C})]t + [(\mathbf{P}_0 - \mathbf{C}) \cdot (\mathbf{P}_0 - \mathbf{C}) - r^2] = 0 \qquad \text{(ix)}$$

Then show that $t$ satisfies the quadratic equation

$$|\mathbf{A}|^2 t^2 + [2\mathbf{A} \cdot (\mathbf{P}_0 - \mathbf{C})]t + (|\mathbf{P}_0 - \mathbf{C}|^2 - r^2) = 0 \qquad \text{(x)}$$

Note that the coefficients in equation (ix) are written completely in terms of dot products, which is most convenient for computer computations. In equation (x) two of the coefficients look a little simpler in terms of lengths of vectors.

**EXERCISE 5**   Use the quadratic formula to solve equation (x) for $t$ and simplify to obtain

$$t = \frac{-\mathbf{A} \cdot (\mathbf{P}_0 - \mathbf{C}) \pm \sqrt{[\mathbf{A} \cdot (\mathbf{P}_0 - \mathbf{C})]^2 - |\mathbf{A}|^2(|\mathbf{P}_0 - \mathbf{C}|^2 - r^2)}}{|\mathbf{A}|^2} \qquad \text{(xi)}$$

Then explain the geometric significance of the numerical value of the expression $[\mathbf{A} \cdot (\mathbf{P}_0 - \mathbf{C})]^2 - |\mathbf{A}|^2(|\mathbf{P}_0 - \mathbf{C}|^2 - r^2)$ being positive, negative, or zero.

**EXERCISE 6**   In this exercise we will use formula (xi) to find the intersection of a light ray and a lens surface. In your own sketch of Figure C introduce a coordinate system such that the $x$-axis coincides with the axis of symmetry and the $y$-axis goes through the point $P_0$. Assume that $P_0$ is 1 cm above the $x$-axis, so its coordinates are $(0, 1)$, that the point $V$ is on the $x$-axis 13 cm to the right of the origin, that the radius of the first (spherical) surface of the lens is 5 cm, and that the center of the sphere is on the axis of symmetry. If $\mathbf{A} = \langle 7, 1 \rangle$ is a vector in the direction of the ray through $P_0$ and the top edge of the lens is 4 cm above the $x$-axis, find the point $P$ where the ray intersects the first surface of the lens.

*Hint*: From the given information and your figure conclude that $\mathbf{A} = \langle 7, 1 \rangle$, $\mathbf{P}_0 = \langle 0, 1 \rangle$, $r - 5$ and $\mathbf{C} = \langle 18, 0 \rangle$. Then find $\mathbf{P}_0 - \mathbf{C}$, and use formula (xi) to show that the two values for $t$ are $t = 2$ or 3. Then use equation (i) to find the points corresponding to the two values for $t$. Which, if any, is the point of intersection of the ray with the first surface? What is the geometric significance of the other point?

Real optical systems live in three-dimensional space, not in a two-dimensional plane, and not all rays in a rotationally symmetric system lie in a plane containing the axis of symmetry. It is surprising that our vector solution to the problem of finding the intersection of a line and a circle in the plane is, through the step-by-step derivation of equation (xi), exactly the same as the vector solution for the problem of the intersection of a line with a spherical surface in three-dimensional space. In three dimensions points have three coordinates and vectors have three components, but a line is still determined by a point it passes through and a vector in the direction of the line. So equation (i) is also the equation for a line in three dimensions. Every point on a spherical surface is the same distance from the center of the sphere so equation (iii) holds. The rest is vector algebra, which works the same in *any* dimension: This is a major advantage of a vector approach.

# 9.4 PARAMETRIC EQUATIONS

We will introduce the idea of parametric equations through a simple example. Suppose that we have a point $P(x, y)$ that moves in the $x$-$y$ plane and that the $x$- and $y$-coordinates of $P$ at time $t$ (in seconds) are given by the following pair of equations:

$$x = 2t \quad \text{and} \quad y = \frac{1}{2}t^2 \quad (t \geq 0)$$

This pair of *parametric equations* tells us the location of the point $P$ at any time $t$. For instance, when $t = 1$, we have

$$x = 2t = 2(1) = 2 \quad \text{and} \quad y = \frac{1}{2}t^2 = \frac{1}{2}(1)^2 = \frac{1}{2}$$

In other words, after 1 second, the coordinates of $P$ are $(2, \frac{1}{2})$. Let's see where $P$ is after 2 seconds. We have

$$x = 2t = 2(2) = 4 \quad \text{and} \quad y = \frac{1}{2}t^2 = \frac{1}{2}(2)^2 = 2$$

So, after 2 seconds, the location of the point $P$ is $(4, 2)$. In Table 1 we have computed the values of $x$ and $y$ (and hence the location of $P$) for integral values of $t$ running from 0 to 5. Figure 1(a) shows the points that are determined. (To avoid cluttering the figure, we have labeled only the points for $t = 2, \ldots, 5$.) In Figure 1(b) we have joined the points with a smooth curve. [If we were not certain of the pattern emerging in Figure 1(a), we could have computed additional points using fractional values for $t$.]

The curve in Figure 1(b) appears to be a portion of a parabola. We can confirm this as follows. From the equation $x = 2t$ we obtain $t = x/2$. Now we use this result to substitute for $t$ in the equation $y = \frac{1}{2}t^2$. This yields

$$y = \frac{1}{2}\left(\frac{x}{2}\right)^2 = \frac{1}{8}x^2$$

We conclude from this that the curve in Figure 1(b) is a portion of the parabola $y = \frac{1}{8}x^2$. The equations $x = 2t$ and $y = \frac{1}{2}t^2$ (with the restriction $t \geq 0$) are the **parametric equations** for the curve. The variable $t$ is called the **parameter.** In our initial example the parameter $t$ represented time. In other cases the parameter might have other interpretations, for example, as the slope of a certain line, as an angle, or as the length of a curve. See the project at the end of this section. In still other cases there may be no immediate interpretation for the parameter.

Before looking at additional examples, we point out two advantages in using parametric equations to describe curves. First, by restricting the values of the parameter (as we did in our initial example), we can focus on specific portions of a curve. Second, parametric equations let us think of a curve as a path traced out by a moving point; as the parameter $t$ increases, a definite direction of motion, called the **orientation** of the curve, is established.

In physics parametric equations are often used to describe the motion of an object. Suppose, for example, that a ball is thrown from a height of 6 feet, with an initial speed of 88 ft/sec and at an angle of 35° with the horizontal, as shown in Fig-

**TABLE 1**

| t | x | y |
|---|---|---|
| 0 | 0 | 0 |
| 1 | 2 | $\frac{1}{2}$ |
| 2 | 4 | 2 |
| 3 | 6 | $\frac{9}{2}$ |
| 4 | 8 | 8 |
| 5 | 10 | $\frac{25}{2}$ |

(a)

(b)

**Figure 1**
$x = 2t$, $y = \frac{1}{2}t^2$ $(t \geq 0)$.

**Figure 2**
The path of a ball thrown from a height of 6 ft, with an initial speed of 88 ft/s, at an angle of 35° with the horizontal

ure 2. Then (neglecting air resistance and spin), it can be shown that the parametric equations for the path of the ball are

$$x = (88 \cos 35°)t \tag{1}$$

$$y = 6 + (88 \sin 35°)t - 16t^2 \tag{2}$$

In these equations $x$ and $y$ are measured in feet and $t$ is in seconds, with $t = 0$ corresponding to the instant the ball is thrown.

With equations (1) and (2) we can calculate the location of the ball at any time $t$. For instance, to determine the location when $t = 1$ second, we substitute $t = 1$ in the equations to obtain

$$x = (88 \cos 35°)(1) \approx 72.1 \text{ ft}$$

and

$$y = 6 + (88 \sin 35°)(1) - 16(1)^2 \approx 40.5 \text{ ft}$$

So after one second the ball has traveled a horizontal distance of approximately 72.1 ft, and the height of the ball is approximately 40.5 ft. In Figure 3 we display this information along with the results for similar calculations corresponding to $t = 2$ and $t = 3$ seconds. [You should use equations (1) and (2) and your calculator to check the results in Figure 3 for yourself.]

**Figure 3**
The location of the ball after 1, 2, and 3 seconds

From Figure 3 we can see that the total horizontal distance traveled by the ball in flight is something between 220 ft and 240 ft. Using the parametric equations for the path of the ball, we can determine this distance exactly. We can also find out how long the ball is in the air. When the ball does hit the ground, its $y$-coordinate is zero. Replacing $y$ by zero in equation (2), we have

$$0 = 6 + (88 \sin 35°)t - 16\,t^2$$

This is a quadratic equation in the variable $t$. To solve for $t$, we use the quadratic formula

$$t = \frac{-b \pm \sqrt{b^2 - 4ac}}{2a}$$

with the following values for $a$, $b$, and $c$:

$$a = -16 \qquad b = 88 \sin 35° \qquad c = 6$$

As Exercise 19 asks you to check, the results are $t \approx 3.27$ and $t \approx -0.11$. We discard the negative root here because in equations (1) and (2) and in Figure 3, $t$ represents time, with $t = 0$ corresponding to the instant that the ball is thrown. Now, using $t = 3.27$, we can compute $x$:

$$x = (88 \cos 35°)t \approx (88 \cos 35°)(3.27) \approx 235.7 \text{ ft}$$

In summary, the ball is in the air for about 3.3 seconds, and the total horizontal distance is approximately 236 feet.

Just as in Figure 1, the curve in Figures 2 and 3 is a parabola. Exercise 22 asks you to verify this by solving equation (1) for $t$ in terms of $x$ and then substituting the result in equation (2). This process of obtaining an explicit equation relating $x$ and $y$ from the parametric equations is referred to as *eliminating the parameter.* The next example shows a technique that is often useful in this context. As background for this example, we point out that the graph of an equation of the form $\frac{x^2}{a^2} + \frac{y^2}{b^2} = 1$ is an *ellipse,* as is indicated in Figure 4. (We will study this curve in detail in Chapter 11.)

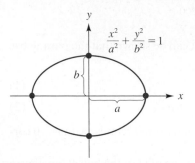

**Figure 4**
The ellipse $(x^2/a^2) + (y^2/b^2) = 1$ is symmetric about both coordinate axes. The intercepts of the ellipse are $x = \pm a$ and $y = \pm b$.

**EXAMPLE    1    Parametric equations for an ellipse**

The parametric equations of an ellipse are

$$x = 6 \cos t \qquad \text{and} \qquad y = 3 \sin t \quad (0 \le t \le 2\pi)$$

**(a)** Eliminate the parameter $t$ to obtain an $x$-$y$ equation for the curve.
**(b)** Graph the ellipse and indicate the points corresponding to $t = 0$, $\pi/2$, $\pi$, $3\pi/2$, and $2\pi$. As $t$ increases, what is the direction of travel along the curve?

**SOLUTION**
**(a)** So that we can apply the identity $\cos^2 t + \sin^2 t = 1$, we divide the first equation by 6 and the second by 3. This gives us

$$\frac{x}{6} = \cos t \qquad \text{and} \qquad \frac{y}{3} = \sin t$$

Squaring and then adding these two equations yields

$$\left(\frac{x}{6}\right)^2 + \left(\frac{y}{3}\right)^2 = \cos^2 t + \sin^2 t = 1$$

or

$$\frac{x^2}{6^2} + \frac{y^2}{3^2} = 1$$

This is the $x$-$y$ equation for the ellipse.
**(b)** Figure 5 shows the graph of the ellipse $(x^2/6^2) + (y^2/3^2) = 1$. When $t = 0$, the parametric equations yield

$$x = 6 \cos 0 = 6 \qquad \text{and} \qquad y = 3 \sin 0 = 0$$

Thus with $t = 0$ we obtain the point $(6, 0)$ on the ellipse, as is indicated in Figure 5. The points corresponding to $t = \pi/2$, $\pi$, $3\pi/2$, and $2\pi$ are ob-

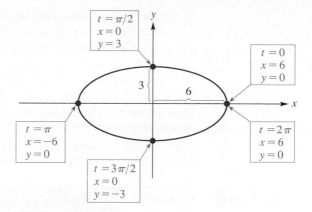

**Figure 5**
Parametric equations for this ellipse are $x = 6 \cos t$ and $y = 3 \sin t$. The $x$-$y$ equation is $(x^2/6^2) + (y^2/3^2) = 1$.

tained similarly. Note that as $t$ increases, the direction of travel around the ellipse is counterclockwise and that when $t = 2\pi$, we are back to the starting point, $(6, 0)$.

The parametric equations $x = 6 \cos t$ and $y = 3 \sin t$ that we graphed in Figure 5 are by no means the only parametric equations yielding that ellipse. Indeed, there are numerous parametric equations that give rise to the same ellipse. One such pair is

$$x = 6 \sin t \quad \text{and} \quad y = 3 \cos t \quad (0 \le t \le 2\pi)$$

As you can check for yourself, these equations lead to the same $x$-$y$ equation as before, namely, $(x^2/6^2) + (y^2/3^2) = 1$. The difference now is that in tracing out the curve from the parametric equations, we start (when $t = 0$) and end (when $t = 2\pi$) with the point $(0, 3)$ on the ellipse and we travel clockwise rather than counterclockwise. Similarly, the equations

$$x = 6 \sin 2t \quad \text{and} \quad y = 3 \cos 2t \quad (0 \le t \le 2\pi)$$

also produce the ellipse. In this case, as you can check for yourself, as $t$ runs from 0 to $2\pi$, we make two complete trips clockwise around the ellipse. If we think of $t$ as time, then the parametric equations $x = 6 \sin 2t$ and $y = 3 \cos 2t$ describe a point traveling around the ellipse $(x^2/6^2) + (y^2/3^2) = 1$ twice as fast as would be the case with the equations $x = 6 \sin t$ and $y = 3 \cos t$.

In Example 1 we saw that the parametric equations $x = 6 \cos t$ and $y = 3 \sin t$ represent an ellipse. The same method that we used in Example 1 can be used to establish the following general results.

## Parametric Equations for the Ellipse

Let $a$ and $b$ be positive constants. Then the parametric equations

$$x = a \cos t \quad \text{and} \quad y = b \sin t \quad (0 \le t \le 2\pi)$$

represent the ellipse shown in Figure 6. As $t$ increases, we move around the ellipse in a counterclockwise direction. The parametric equations

$$x = a \sin t \quad \text{and} \quad y = b \cos t \quad (0 \le t \le 2\pi)$$

also represent the ellipse in Figure 6. Here, the direction of motion is clockwise.

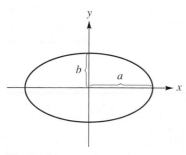

**Figure 6**
$x = a \cos t$ and $y = b \sin t$
or
$x = a \sin t$ and $y = b \cos t$,
both for $0 \le t \le 2\pi$

There is a particular case involving the parametric equations $x = a \cos t$ and $y = b \sin t$ that deserves mention. When $a$ and $b$ are equal, we have $x = a \cos t$ and $y = a \sin t$, from which we deduce that

$$x^2 + y^2 = a^2 \cos^2 t + a^2 \sin^2 t$$
$$= a^2(\cos^2 t + \sin^2 t) = a^2$$

Thus with $a = b$ the parametric equations describe a circle of radius $a$. And specializing further still, if $a = b = 1$, we obtain $x = \cos t$ and $y = \sin t$, for $0 \le t \le 2\pi$, as parametric equations for the unit circle. This agrees with our unit circle definitions for sine and cosine back in Section 7.3.

### EXAMPLE   2   Finding an x-y equation given parametric equations

The position of a point $P(x, y)$ at time $t$ is given by the parametric equations

$$x = 1 + 2t \quad \text{and} \quad y = 2 + 4t \quad (t \ge 0)$$

Find an $x$-$y$ equation for the path traced out by the point $P$.

**SOLUTION**
From the parametric equation for $x$ we obtain $t = (x - 1)/2$. Using this to substitute for $t$ in the second parametric equation, we have

$$y = 2 + 4\left(\frac{x-1}{2}\right) = 2 + 2(x - 1) = 2x$$

This tells us that the point $P$ moves along the line $y = 2x$. However, the entire line is not traced out, but only a portion of it. This is because of the original restriction $t \ge 0$. To see which portion of the line is described by the equations, we can successively let $t = 0, 1,$ and $2$ in the parametric equations. As you can check, the points obtained are $(1, 2)$, $(3, 6)$, and $(5, 10)$. So as $t$ increases, we move to the right along the line $y = 2x$, starting from the point $(1, 2)$; see Figure 7.

**Figure 7**
The parametric equations $x = 1 + 2t$ and $y = 2 + 4t$, with the restriction $t \ge 0$, describe the portion of the line $y = 2x$ to the right of and including the point $(1, 2)$.

One of the recurrent techniques that we have used for analyzing parametric equations in this section has been that of eliminating the parameter. It is important to note, however, that it is not always a simple matter to eliminate the parameter. Indeed, in most cases it is not even possible. When this occurs, we have several techniques available. We can set up a table with $t$, $x$, and $y$ and plot points; we can use the techniques of calculus; or we can use a graphing utility to obtain the graph. Even when we use a graphing utility, however, the techniques of calculus are helpful in understanding why the graph looks as it does.

## EXERCISE SET 9.4

### A

*In Exercises 1–6 you are given the parametric equations of a curve and a value for the parameter t. Find the coordinates of the point on the curve corresponding to the given value of t.*

1. $x = 2 - 4t, y = 3 - 5t; t = 0$
2. $x = 3 - t^2, y = 4 + t^3; t = -1$
3. $x = 5 \cos t, y = 2 \sin t; t = \pi/6$
4. $x = 4 \cos 2t, y = 6 \sin 2t; t = \pi/3$
5. $x = 3 \sin^3 t, y = 3 \cos^3 t; t = \pi/4$
6. $x = \sin t - \sin 2t, y = \cos t + \cos 2t; t = 2\pi/3$
7. Use the standard viewing rectangle for this exercise.
    (a) Graph the parametric equations $x = 2t, y = 0.5t^2$ with $t$-values running from 0 to 1; from 0 to 3; from 0 to 4. Compare the results (in a complete sentence or two).

**(b)** Graph the parametric equations given in part (a) using $t$-values running from $-5$ to $5$. Compare your picture to the graph shown in Figure 1(b) on page 684. What are the restrictions on $t$ in Figure 1(b)?

*In Exercises 8–17, graph the parametric equations after eliminating the parameter $t$. Specify the direction on the curve corresponding to increasing values of $t$. For Exercises 8–11, $t$ can be any real number; for Exercises 12–17, $0 \le t \le 2\pi$.*

**8.** $x = t + 1, y = t^2$
**9.** $x = 2t - 1, y = t^2 - 1$
**10.** $x = t^2 - 1, y = t + 1$
**11.** $x = t - 4, y = |t|$
**12.** $x = 5 \cos t, y = 2 \sin t$
**13.** $x = 2 \sin t, y = 3 \cos t$
**14.** $x = 4 \cos 2t, y = 6 \sin 2t$
**15.** $x = 2 \cos(t/2), y = \sin(t/2)$
**16.** **(a)** $x = 2 \cos t, y = 2 \sin t$
   **(b)** $x = 4 \cos t, y = 2 \sin t$
**17.** **(a)** $x = 3 \sin t, y = 3 \cos t$
   **(b)** $x = 5 \sin t, y = 3 \cos t$

Ⓖ **18.** **(a)** Graph the parametric equations $x = (88 \cos 35°)t$, $y = 6 + (88 \sin 35°)t - 16t^2$. Use settings that will give you a picture similar to Figure 3 on page 685.
   **(b)** Use the graphing utility to estimate the $x$-intercept of the graph. Check that your answer is consistent with the value determined in the text.

**19.** In the text we said that the solutions of the quadratic equation $0 = 6 + (88 \sin 35°)t - 16t^2$ are $t \approx 3.27$ and $t \approx -0.11$. Use the quadratic formula and your calculator to verify these results.

**20.** The following figure shows the parametric equations and the path for a ball thrown from a height of 5 ft, with an initial speed of 100 ft/sec and at an angle of 70° with the horizontal.

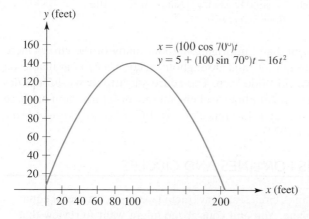

$$x = (100 \cos 70°)t$$
$$y = 5 + (100 \sin 70°)t - 16t^2$$

**(a)** Compute the $x$- and $y$-coordinates of the ball when $t = 1, 2,$ and $3$ seconds. (Round the answers to one decimal place.)
**(b)** How long is the ball in flight? (Round the answer to two decimal places.) What is the total horizontal distance traveled by the ball before it lands? (Round to the nearest foot.) Check that your answer is consistent with the figure.

**21.** The figure shows the parametric equations and the path for a ball thrown from a height of 5 ft, with an initial speed of 100 ft/s and at an angle of 45° with the horizontal. (So except for the initial angle, the data are the same as in Exercise 20.)

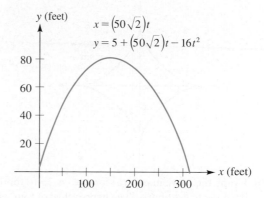

$$x = \left(50\sqrt{2}\right)t$$
$$y = 5 + \left(50\sqrt{2}\right)t - 16t^2$$

**(a)** Compute the $x$- and $y$-coordinates of the ball when $t = 1, 2,$ and $3$ seconds. (Round the answers to one decimal place.)
**(b)** How long is the ball in flight? (Round the answer to two decimal places.) What is the total horizontal distance traveled by the ball before it lands? (Round to the nearest foot.)

**22.** Refer to parametric equations (1) and (2) in the text. By eliminating the parameter $t$, show that the equations describe a parabola. (That is, show that the resulting $x$-$y$ equation has the form $y = ax^2 + bx + c$.)

*In Exercises 23–39, graph the parametric equations using the given range for the parameter $t$. In each case, begin with the standard viewing rectangle and then make adjustments, as necessary, so that the graph utilizes as much of the viewing screen as possible. For example, in graphing the circle given by $x = \cos t$ and $y = \sin t$, it would be natural to choose a viewing rectangle extending from $-1$ to $1$ in both the $x$- and $y$-directions.*

Ⓖ **23.** **(a)** $x = 3t + 2, y = 3t - 2, (-2 \le t \le 2)$
   **(b)** $x = 3t + 2, y = 3t - 2, (-3 \le t \le 3)$
Ⓖ **24.** $x = \ln(3t + 2), y = \ln(3t - 2)$ using:
   **(a)** $2/3 < t \le 1$
   **(b)** $2/3 < t \le 10$
   **(c)** $2/3 < t \le 100$
   **(d)** $2/3 < t \le 1000$
Ⓖ **25.** $x = 4 \cos t, y = 3 \sin t, 0 \le t \le 2\pi$ *(ellipse)*
Ⓖ **26.** $x = 4 \cos t, y = -3 \sin t, 0 \le t \le 2\pi$ (the same as the ellipse in Exercise 25 but traced out in the opposite direction)
Ⓖ **27.** $x = 4 \cos t, y = 3 \sin t, 0 \le t \le \pi/2$ (one-quarter of an ellipse)

**B**

**28.** **(a)** The curve in the accompanying figure is called an *astroid* (or a *hypocycloid of four cusps*). A pair of parametric equations for the curve is $x = \cos^3 t$, $y = \sin^3 t$. By eliminating the parameter $t$, find the $x$-$y$ equation for the curve.    *Hint*: In each equation, raise both sides to the two-thirds power.

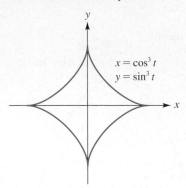

$x = \cos^3 t$
$y = \sin^3 t$

Ⓖ  **(b)**  Graph the curve in part (a) for $0 \le t \le 2\pi$ to reproduce the figure above. [The hypocycloid of four cusps was first studied by the Danish astronomer Olaf Roemer (1644–1710) and by the Swiss mathematician Jacob Bernoulli (1654–1705).]

Ⓖ  **29.**  $x = 2\cos t + \cos 2t,\ y = 2\sin t - \sin 2t,\quad 0 \le t \le 2\pi$ [This curve is the *deltoid*. It was first studied by the Swiss mathematician Leonhard Euler (1707–1783).]

Ⓖ  **30.**  $x = \dfrac{\cos t}{1 + \sin^2 t},\ y = \dfrac{\sin t \cos t}{1 + \sin^2 t},\quad 0 \le t \le 2\pi$
[This curve is the *lemniscate of Bernoulli*. The Swiss mathematician Jacob Bernoulli (1654–1705) studied the curve and took the name *lemniscate* from the Greek *lemniskos*, meaning "ribbon."]

Ⓖ  **31.**  $x = 2\tan t,\ y = 2\cos^2 t,\quad 0 \le t \le 2\pi$    *Remark*: If you eliminate the parameter $t$, you'll find that the Cartesian form of the curve is $y = 8/(x^2 + 4)$. (Verify this last state-

ment, first algebraically, then graphically.) The curve is known as the *witch of Agnesi*, named after the Italian mathematician and scientist Maria Gaetana Agnesi (1718–1799). The word "witch" in the name of the curve is the result of a mistranslation from Italian to English. In Agnesi's time, the curve was known as *la versiera*, an Italian name with a Latin root meaning "to turn." In translation, the word *versiera* was confused with another Italian word *avversiera*, which means "wife of the devil" or "witch."

Ⓖ  **32.**  $x = \dfrac{3t}{1 + t^3},\ y = \dfrac{3t^2}{1 + t^3},\quad -\infty < t < \infty$
*Hint*: Use $-10 \le t \le 10$. [This curve is the *folium of Descartes*. The word *folium* means "leaf." When Descartes drew the curve in 1638, he did not use negative values for coordinates. Thus he obtained only the first-quadrant portion of the curve, which resembles a leaf or loop. The complete graph of the curve was first given by the Dutch mathematician and scientist Christian Huygens in 1692. Huygens's graph is reproduced on page 108 in John Stillwell's *Mathematics and Its History*, Second Edition (New York: Springer Verlag, 2002).]

Ⓖ  **33.**  $x = 3t^2,\ y = 2t^3,\quad -2 \le t \le 2$ (*semicubical parabola*)

Ⓖ  **34.**  $x = \sec t,\ y = 2\tan t,\quad 0 \le t \le 2\pi$ (*hyperbola*)

Ⓖ  **35.**  $x = 3(t^2 - 3),\ y = t(t^2 - 3),\quad -3 \le t \le 3$
(*Tschirnhausen's cubic*)

Ⓖ  **36.**  $x = 8\cos t + 2\cos 4t,\ y = 8\sin t - 2\sin 4t,\quad 0 \le t \le 2\pi$
(*hypocycloid with five cusps*)

Ⓖ  **37.**  $x = 8\cos t + \cos 8t,\ y = 8\sin t - \sin 8t,\quad 0 \le t \le 2\pi$
(*hypocycloid with nine cusps*)

Ⓖ  **38.**  $x = \cos t + t\sin t,\ y = \sin t - t\cos t$ (*involute of a circle*)
   **(a)**  $-\pi \le t \le \pi$       **(c)**  $-4\pi \le t \le 4\pi$
   **(b)**  $-2\pi \le t \le 2\pi$

Ⓖ  **39.**  $x = \sin(0.8t + \pi),\ y = \sin t,\quad 0 \le t \le 10\pi$
(*Bowditch curve*)

NOTE    Historical background and information about many of the curves mentioned in Exercises 28 through 39 (and throughout Section 9.6) is available on the Internet through the World Wide Web. The address is http://www-groups.dcs .st-and.ac.uk/~history/Curves/. Another excellent source for information on these curves, and many others, is J. Dennis Lawrence's book *A Catalogue of Special Plane Curves* (Dover Publications, 1972).

# PROJECT

## PARAMETERIZATIONS FOR LINES AND CIRCLES

In the previous project on lines, circles, and ray tracing we derived a vector equation for a line in the $x$-$y$ plane. You and your group might want to review that derivation. In particular, let $P_0$ be a point in the $x$-$y$ plane, $\mathbf{P_0}$ be the position vector with endpoint $P_0$, and $\mathbf{A}$ be a nonzero vector. We showed that a vector equation for the line in the $x$-$y$ plane passing through the point $P_0$ with direction vector $\mathbf{A}$ is

$$\mathbf{P} = \mathbf{P_0} + t\mathbf{A} \qquad \text{for } -\infty < t < \infty \tag{i}$$

where $\mathbf{P}$ is the position vector of a point $P$ on the line (see Figure A).

**Figure A**

Using equation (i) and vector components we can derive two useful scalar equations for the same line. Let $P_0 = (x_0, y_0)$ be the given point on the line, $\mathbf{A} = \langle a, b \rangle \neq \langle 0, 0 \rangle$ be the nonzero direction vector of the line, and $P = (x, y)$ be an arbitrary point on the line. The corresponding position vectors for the points $P_0$ and $P$ are $\mathbf{P}_0 = \langle x_0, y_0 \rangle$ and $\mathbf{P} = \langle x, y \rangle$, respectively. Substituting into equation (i) we get

$$\mathbf{P} = \mathbf{P}_0 + t\mathbf{A} \qquad \text{for } -\infty < t < \infty$$
$$\langle x, y \rangle = \langle x_0, y_0 \rangle + t\langle a, b \rangle$$
$$\langle x, y \rangle = \langle x_0, y_0 \rangle + \langle ta, tb \rangle$$
$$\langle x, y \rangle = \langle x_0 + ta, y_0 + tb \rangle$$

So

$$\begin{cases} x = x_0 + ta \\ y = y_0 + tb \end{cases} \qquad \text{for } -\infty < t < \infty \qquad \text{(ii)}$$

Equations (ii) are called **parametric equations** for this line. If both $a$ and $b$ are nonzero then we can solve each equation in (ii) for $t$ to get

$$\frac{x - x_0}{a} = t = \frac{y - y_0}{b}$$

or more simply,

$$\frac{x - x_0}{a} = \frac{y - y_0}{b} \qquad \text{(iii)}$$

Equation (iii) is called the **symmetric equation** for this line. If either $a$ or $b$ is zero then the line has no symmetric equation.

Let's apply equations (i), (ii), and (iii) to find vector, parametric, and symmetric equations for the line in the $x$-$y$ plane passing through the point $P_0 = (-2, 1)$ with direction $\mathbf{A} = \langle 1, 2 \rangle$. See Figure B. (*Note*: This is a continuation of Example 1 from the previous project on lines, circles, and ray tracing.) A vector equation for this line is

$$\mathbf{P} = \mathbf{P}_0 + t\mathbf{A} \qquad \text{for } -\infty < t < \infty$$
$$\langle x, y \rangle = \langle -2, 1 \rangle + t\langle 1, 2 \rangle \qquad \text{for } -\infty < t < \infty$$

Then

$$\langle x, y \rangle = \langle -2 + t, 1 + 2t \rangle \qquad \text{for } -\infty < t < \infty$$

And we obtain parametric equations for the line

$$\begin{cases} x = -2 + t \\ y = 1 + 2t \end{cases} \qquad \text{for } -\infty < t < \infty$$

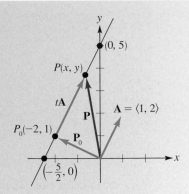

**Figure B**

Let's use the parametric equations to find the $x$ and $y$-intercepts of the line. For the $x$-intercept, $y = 0$ implies $1 + 2t = 0$ or $t = -1/2$. Then the $x$-intercept is $x = -2 - 1/2 = -5/2$. For the $y$-intercept, $x = 0$ implies $-2 + t = 0$ or $t = 2$. Then the $y$-intercept is $y = 1 + 2(2) = 5$. See Figure B. Finally, eliminating the parameter $t$ in the parametric equations gives us the symmetric equation for this line,

$$\frac{x + 2}{1} = \frac{y - 1}{2}$$

From the symmetric equation we have

$$x + 2 = \frac{y - 1}{2}$$
$$2(x + 2) = y - 1$$
$$y = 2x + 5$$

the slope-intercept equation for this line.

It is worth noting that all of our work with vector, parametric, and symmetric equations for lines generalizes in a natural way to three-dimensional and higher-dimensional Cartesian "spaces." We also note that there are other types of parametric equations for lines, but they do not concern us here.

Now we want to derive parametric equations for a circle in the $x$-$y$ plane. Let's start with the fundamental case of the circle of radius $a$ centered at the origin. Stand at the center of this circle and look along the positive $x$-axis to see the point $(a, 0)$ on the circle. Rotate your head (and body!) counterclockwise to view each point on the circle until your view returns to the point $(a, 0)$. Each point you see on the circle is at a distance $a$ from you. A convenient way to keep track of which point on the circle you are viewing is to use the angle $\theta$ of counterclockwise rotation from the positive $x$-axis to the point (see Figure C). As we know from basic trigonometry, each point $P$ on the circle has coordinates $(a \cos \theta, a \sin \theta)$ for some angle $\theta$, $0 \le \theta \le 2\pi$. So the $x$ and $y$-coordinates of $P$ are $a \cos \theta$ and $a \sin \theta$, respectively, and we have

$$\begin{cases} x = a \cos \theta \\ y = a \cos \theta \end{cases} \quad \text{for } 0 \le \theta \le 2\pi \qquad \text{(iv)}$$

Equations (iv) are called parametric equations for the circle in the $x$-$y$ plane centered at the origin with radius $a$.

As with lines, these are not the only parametric equations for this circle. We can use equations (iv) and a little geometry to derive more "intrinsic" paramet-

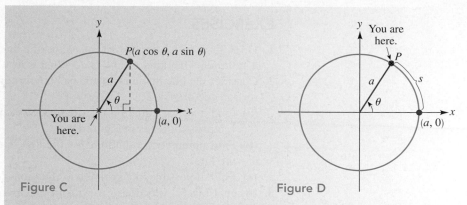

Figure C                                          Figure D

ric equations for this circle. Suppose, instead of being lucky enough to be standing at the center of the circle, we are standing at a point $P$ *on* the circle. Consider the arc-length $s$ from the point $(a, 0)$ to $P$. (See Figure D.) We know from geometry that $s = a\theta$, so $\theta = s/a$. Substituting into equations (iv) we obtain an **arc-length parameterization** for this circle.

$$\begin{cases} x = a\cos\left(\dfrac{s}{a}\right) \\ y = a\cos\left(\dfrac{s}{a}\right) \end{cases} \quad \text{for } 0 \le s \le 2\pi a \tag{v}$$

In Exercise 3 we ask you to explain why $s$ in equations (v) varies from 0 to $2\pi a$.

   Finally we mention another pair of parametric equations for the *unit* circle, that is, the circle in the $x$-$y$ plane centered at the origin with radius 1. Consider the line passing through the point $(-1, 0)$ on the unit circle with slope $m$. In Exercise 6 you will show that this line intersects the unit circle at the point $P\left(\dfrac{1 - m^2}{1 + m^2}, \dfrac{2m}{1 + m^2}\right)$. See Figure E. This construction is equivalent to the one discussed in the Writing Mathematics section at the end of Chapter 10, and can also be used to generate all Pythagorean triples. From this construction we obtain our third pair of parametric equations for the unit circle:

$$\begin{cases} x = \left(\dfrac{1 - m^2}{1 + m^2}\right) \\ y = \left(\dfrac{2m}{1 + m^2}\right) \end{cases} \quad \text{for } -\infty < m < \infty \tag{vi}$$

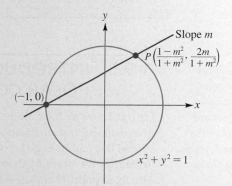

Figure E

## EXERCISES

1. Let $\mathbf{A} = \langle a, b \rangle \neq \mathbf{0}$ be a direction vector of a line through the point $(x_0, y_0)$. If $a = 0$ then what kind of line is it? What is its equation? What about $b = 0$?

2. Consider the line in the $x$-$y$ plane passing through the point $(2, -3)$ with a direction vector $\langle 4, -2 \rangle$.
   (a) Find a vector equation for the line. Sketch the line with Cartesian and vector notation as in Figure B.
   (b) Find parametric equations for the line. Find the $x$- and $y$-intercepts of the line.
   (c) Find, if possible, the symmetric equations for the line.

3. In equations (v) why does $s$ vary from 0 to $2\pi a$?

4. Consider the circle in the $x$-$y$ plane centered at the origin with radius 12.
   (a) Use equations (iv) to find parametric equations for this circle.
   (b) Find an arc-length parameterization for this circle.

5. Consider the circle in the $x$-$y$ plane centered at the point $(h, k)$ with radius $a$.
   (a) Use a fixed distance and a variable angle to find parametric equations for this circle. *Hint*: Modify Figure C and equations (iv) by "translation." Sketch this circle and label it as in Figure C.
   (b) Find an arc-length parameterization for this circle.

6. Show that the line with slope $m$ passing through the point $(-1, 0)$ intersects the unit circle at the point $P\left(\dfrac{1 - m^2}{1 + m^2}, \dfrac{2m}{1 + m^2}\right)$.

7. In Figure E let $A$ be the point $(1, 0)$, $P$ be the point $\left(\dfrac{1 - m^2}{1 + m^2}, \dfrac{2m}{1 + m^2}\right)$, and $O$ be the origin, and let angle $POA$ be $\theta$.
   (a) Explain why $\cos\theta = \dfrac{1 - m^2}{1 + m^2}$ and $\sin\theta = \dfrac{2m}{1 + m^2}$.
   (b) Prove: $\tan(\theta/2) = m$.
   (c) Let $Q$ be the point $(-1, 0)$ and explain why angle $PQA$ equals $\theta/2$.
   (d) Prove: $\cos\theta = \dfrac{1 - \tan^2(\theta/2)}{1 + \tan^2(\theta/2)}$ and $\sin\theta = \dfrac{2\tan(\theta/2)}{1 + \tan^2(\theta/2)}$.

   *Comment*: In the study of *techniques of integration* in calculus the results of this exercise are the basis for a substitution that transforms a rational expression in sines and cosines to a rational expression in a single variable $m$. Exercises 55 and 52 on page 596 and Exercise 101 on page 643 cover results related to those in Exercises 6 and 7 above.

[Jacob Bernoulli (1654–1705)] *was one of the first to use polar coordinates in a general manner, and not simply for spiral shaped curves.* —Florian Cajori in *A History of Mathematics,* 4th ed. (New York: Chelsea Publishing Company, 1985)

## 9.5   INTRODUCTION TO POLAR COORDINATES

Up until now, we have always specified the location of a point in the plane by means of a rectangular coordinate system. In this section we introduce another coordinate system that can be used to locate points in the plane. This is the system of **polar coordinates.** We begin by drawing a half-line or ray emanating from a fixed point $O$. The fixed point $O$ is called the **pole** or **origin,** and the half-line is called the **polar**

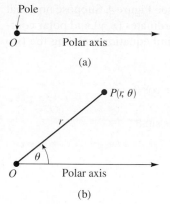

**Figure 1**

**axis.** The polar axis is usually depicted as being horizontal and extending to the right, as indicated in Figure 1(a). Now let $P$ be any point in the plane. As is indicated in Figure 1(b), we initially let $r$ denote the distance from $O$ to $P$, and we let $\theta$ denote the angle measured from the polar axis to $\overline{OP}$. (Just as in our earlier work with angles in standard position, we take the measure of $\theta$ to be positive if the rotation is counterclockwise and negative if it is clockwise.) Then the ordered pair $(r, \theta)$ serves to locate the point $P$ with respect to the pole and the polar axis. We refer to $r$ and $\theta$ as polar coordinates of $P$, and we write $P(r, \theta)$ to indicate that $P$ is the point with polar coordinates $(r, \theta)$.

Plotting points in polar coordinates is facilitated by the use of polar coordinate graph paper, such as that shown in Figure 2(a). Figure 2(b) shows the points with polar coordinates $A(2, \frac{\pi}{6})$, $B(3, \frac{2\pi}{3})$, and $C(4, 0)$.

**Figure 2**          (a)                              (b)

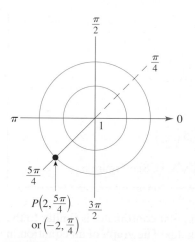

**Figure 3**

There is a minor complication that arises in using polar rather than rectangular coordinates. Consider, for example, the point $C(4, 0)$ in Figure 2(b). This point could just as well have been labeled with the coordinates $(4, 2\pi)$ or $(4, 2k\pi)$ for any integral value of $k$. Similarly, the coordinates $(r, \theta)$ and $(r, \theta + 2k\pi)$ represent the same point for all integral values of $k$. This is in marked contrast to the situation with rectangular coordinates, where the coordinate representation of each point is unique. Also, what polar coordinates should we assign to the origin? For if $r = 0$ in Figure 1(b), we cannot really define an angle $\theta$. To cover this case we agree on the convention that the coordinates $(0, \theta)$ denote the origin for all values of $\theta$. Finally, we point out that in working with polar coordinates, it is sometimes useful to let $r$ take on negative values. For example, consider the point $P(2, \frac{5\pi}{4})$ in Figure 3. The coordinates $(2, \frac{5\pi}{4})$ indicate that to reach $P$ from the origin, we go two units in the direction $5\pi/4$. Alternatively, we can describe this as $-2$ units in the $\pi/4$ direction. (Refer again to Figure 3.) For reasons such as this we will adhere to the convention that the polar coordinates $(r, \theta)$ and $(-r, \theta + \pi)$ represent the same point. (Since $r$ can now, in fact, be positive, negative, or zero, $r$ is referred to as a *directed distance*.)

It is often useful to consider both rectangular and polar coordinates simultaneously. To do this, we draw the two coordinate systems so that the origins coincide

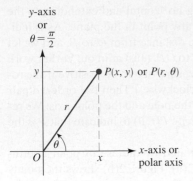

**Figure 4**

and the positive $x$-axis coincides with the polar axis; see Figure 4. Suppose now that a point $P$, other than the origin, has rectangular coordinates $(x, y)$ and polar coordinates $(r, \theta)$, as indicated in Figure 4. We wish to find equations relating the two sets of coordinates. From Figure 4 we see that

$$\cos \theta = \frac{x}{r} \qquad \text{so} \qquad x = r \cos \theta$$

$$\sin \theta = \frac{y}{r} \qquad \text{so} \qquad y = r \sin \theta$$

$$x^2 + y^2 = r^2$$

$$\tan \theta = \frac{y}{x}$$

Although Figure 4 displays the point $P$ in the first quadrant, it can be shown that these same equations hold when $P$ is in any quadrant. For reference we summarize these equations as follows.

**Relations Between Polar and Rectangular Coordinates**

$$x = r \cos \theta$$
$$y = r \sin \theta$$
$$x^2 + y^2 = r^2$$
$$\tan \theta = \frac{y}{x}$$

---

**EXAMPLE**  **1**  **Changing from polar to rectangular coordinates**

The polar coordinates of a point are $(5, \frac{\pi}{6})$. Find the rectangular coordinates.

**SOLUTION**
We are given that $r = 5$ and $\theta = \pi/6$. Thus

$$x = r \cos \theta = 5 \cos \frac{\pi}{6} = 5\left(\frac{\sqrt{3}}{2}\right)$$

and

$$y = r \sin \theta = 5 \sin \frac{\pi}{6} = 5\left(\frac{1}{2}\right)$$

The rectangular coordinates are therefore $(\frac{5}{2}\sqrt{3}, \frac{5}{2})$. See Figure 5.

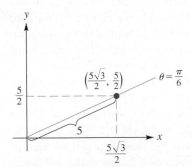

**Figure 5**

The definition of the graph of an equation in polar coordinates is similar to the corresponding definition for rectangular coordinates. The **graph** of an equation in polar coordinates is the set of all points $(r, \theta)$ with coordinates that satisfy the given equation. It is often the case that the equation of a curve is simpler in one coordinate system than in another. The next two examples show instances of this.

---

**EXAMPLE 2** **Converting a polar equation to rectangular form**

Convert each polar equation to rectangular form:

**(a)** $r = \cos \theta + 2 \sin \theta$;     **(b)** $r^2 = \sin 2\theta$.

**SOLUTION**

**(a)** In view of the transformation equations $x = r \cos \theta$ and $y = r \sin \theta$, we multiply both sides of the given equation by $r$, for $r \neq 0$, to obtain

$$r^2 = r \cos \theta + 2r \sin \theta$$

and therefore

$$x^2 + y^2 = x + 2y \qquad \text{or} \qquad x^2 - x + y^2 - 2y = 0$$

Before concluding that we have a rectangular form of the original equation, we need to check what happens when $r = 0$. This means checking that the origin is on (or not on) the graph of both the original and the transformed equation. Since $r = 0$ for $\theta = \arctan(-1/2)$, the origin is on the graph of the original equation. The origin is also on the graph of the equation $x^2 - x + y^2 - 2y = 0$, so it is a rectangular form of the given equation.
*Question for review*: What is the graph of this last equation?

**(b)** Using the double-angle formula for $\sin 2\theta$, we have

$$r^2 = 2 \sin \theta \cos \theta$$

Now, to obtain the expressions $r \sin \theta$ and $r \cos \theta$ on the right-hand side of the equation, we multiply both sides by $r^2$. This yields

$$r^4 = 2(r \sin \theta)(r \cos \theta)$$

and, consequently,

$$(x^2 + y^2)^2 = 2yx$$

or

$$x^4 + 2x^2 y^2 + y^4 - 2xy = 0$$

Since the origin lies on the graph of both the given equation and the last equation, this is a rectangular form of the given equation. Notice how much simpler the equation is in its polar coordinate form.

---

**EXAMPLE 3** **Converting a rectangular equation to polar form**

Convert the rectangular equation $x^2 + y^2 + ax = a\sqrt{x^2 + y^2}$ to polar form, expressing $r$ as a function of $\theta$. Assume that $a$ is a constant.

**SOLUTION**

Using the relations $x^2 + y^2 = r^2$ and $x = r \cos \theta$, we obtain

$$r^2 + ar \cos \theta = ar$$

Notice that this equation is satisfied by $r = 0$. In other words, the graph of this equation will pass through the origin. This is consistent with the fact that the original equation is satisfied when $x$ and $y$ are both zero. Now assume for the moment that $r \neq 0$. Then we can divide both sides of the last equation by $r$ to obtain

$$r + a \cos \theta = a \quad \text{or} \quad r = a - a \cos \theta$$

This expresses $r$ as a function of $\theta$, as required. Note that when $\theta = 0$, we obtain

$$r = a - a(1) = 0$$

That is, nothing has been lost in dividing through by $r$; the graph will still pass through the origin. Again, notice how much simpler the equation is in polar form.

Figure 6

When we work in an $x$-$y$ coordinate system, one of the basic tools is the formula for the distance between two points: $d = \sqrt{(x_2 - x_1)^2 + (y_2 - y_1)^2}$. There is a corresponding distance formula for use with polar coordinates. In Figure 6 we let $d$ denote the distance between the points with polar coordinates $(r_1, \theta_1)$ and $(r_2, \theta_2)$. Then, applying the law of cosines, we have $d^2 = r_1^2 + r_2^2 - 2r_1 r_2 \cos(\theta_2 - \theta_1)$. This is the distance formula in polar coordinates. For ease of reference we repeat this result in the box that follows.

## PROPERTY SUMMARY
### Distance Formula for Polar Coordinates

Let $d$ denote the distance between two points with polar coordinates $(r_1, \theta_1)$ and $(r_2, \theta_2)$. Then

$$d^2 = r_1^2 + r_2^2 - 2r_1 r_2 \cos(\theta_2 - \theta_1)$$

  **EXAMPLE 4** Finding the distance between points in polar coordinates

Compute the distance between the points with polar coordinates $(2, \frac{5\pi}{6})$ and $(4, \frac{\pi}{6})$.

**SOLUTION**
We use the distance formula, taking the points $(r_1, \theta_1)$ and $(r_2, \theta_2)$ to be $(2, \frac{5\pi}{6})$ and $(4, \frac{\pi}{6})$, respectively (see Figure 7). This yields

$$d^2 = r_1^2 + r_2^2 - 2r_1 r_2 \cos(\theta_2 - \theta_1)$$
$$= 2^2 + 4^2 - 2(2)(4)\cos\left(\frac{\pi}{6} - \frac{5\pi}{6}\right)$$
$$= 20 - 16 \cos\left(-\frac{2\pi}{3}\right) = 20 - 16\left(-\frac{1}{2}\right) = 28$$
$$d = \sqrt{28} = 2\sqrt{7}$$

You should check for yourself that the same result is obtained if we choose $(r_1, \theta_1)$ and $(r_2, \theta_2)$ to be $(4, \frac{\pi}{6})$ and $(2, \frac{5\pi}{6})$, respectively. This is because, in general, $\cos(\theta_2 - \theta_1) = \cos(\theta_1 - \theta_2)$. (Why?)

**Figure 7**

The distance formula can be used to find an equation for a circle. Suppose that the radius of the circle is $a$ and that the polar coordinates of the center are $(r_0, \theta_0)$. As is indicated in Figure 8, we let $(r, \theta)$ denote an arbitrary point on the circle. Then, since the distance between the points $(r, \theta)$ and $(r_0, \theta_0)$ is $a$, the radius of the circle, we have

$$r^2 + r_0^2 - 2rr_0 \cos(\theta - \theta_0) = a^2 \qquad (1)$$

This is the required equation. There is a special case of this equation that is worth noting. If the center of the circle is located at the origin, then $r_0 = 0$, and equation (1) becomes simply $r^2 = a^2$. Therefore

$$r = a \qquad \text{or} \qquad r = -a$$

The graph of each of these equations is a circle of radius $a$, with center at the origin.

**Figure 8**

### EXAMPLE 5    Finding a polar equation for a circle

Determine a polar equation for the circle satisfying the given conditions.
**(a)** The radius is 2, and the polar coordinates of the center are $(4, \frac{\pi}{5})$.
**(b)** The radius is 5, and the center is the origin.

**SOLUTION**
**(a)** Using equation (1), we have

$$r^2 + 4^2 - 2r(4)\cos\left(\theta - \frac{\pi}{5}\right) = 2^2$$

and therefore

$$r^2 - 8r \cos\left(\theta - \frac{\pi}{5}\right) = -12$$

**(b)** A polar equation for a circle of radius $a$ and with center at the origin is $r = a$. So if the radius is 5, the required equation is $r = 5$. (The equation $r = -5$ would yield the same graph.)

We conclude this section by discussing equation of lines in polar coordinates. There are two cases to consider: lines that pass through the origin and lines that do not pass through the origin. First, consider a line through the origin, and suppose that the line makes an angle $\theta_0$ with the positive $x$-axis; see Figure 9. The polar equation of this line is simply

$$\theta = \theta_0$$

Notice that this equation poses no restrictions on $r$. In other words, for every real number $r$, the point with polar coordinates $(r, \theta_0)$ lies on this line.

**Figure 9**

| EXAMPLE | 6 | Graphing a line through the pole |
|---|---|---|

Graph the line with polar equation $\theta = \pi/3$, and locate the points on this line for which $r = 1, 2,$ and $-1$.

**SOLUTION**
See Figure 10.

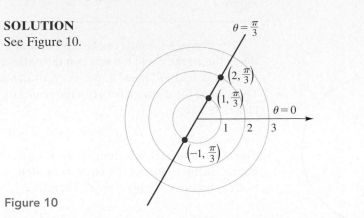

**Figure 10**

Now let us determine the polar equation for a line $\mathscr{L}$ that does not pass through the origin. As is indicated in Figure 11, we assume that the perpendicular distance from the origin to $\mathscr{L}$ is $d$ and that the polar coordinates of the point $N$ (in Figure 11) are $(d, \alpha)$. The point $P(r, \theta)$ in Figure 11 denotes an arbitrary point on line $\mathscr{L}$. We want to find an equation relating $r$ and $\theta$.

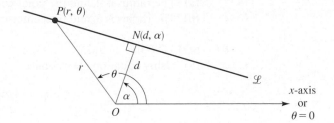

**Figure 11**

In right triangle $ONP$, note that $\angle PON = \theta - \alpha$, and therefore

$$\cos(\theta - \alpha) = \frac{d}{r} \qquad \text{or} \qquad r\cos(\theta - \alpha) = d$$

This is the polar equation of the line $\mathscr{L}$. (*Note*: Since cosine is an even function the equation is correct when the point $P$ is to "the right" of the point $N$.) For reference, we summarize our results about lines in the box that follows.

**▌ PROPERTY SUMMARY   Polar Equations for Lines**

1. *Line through the origin:* Suppose that a line passes through the origin and makes an angle $\theta_0$ with the positive $x$-axis (as indicated in Figure 9 on page 699). Then an equation for the line is $\theta = \theta_0$.
2. *Line not passing through the origin:* Suppose that the perpendicular distance from the origin to the line is $d$ and that the point $(d, \alpha)$ is the foot of the perpendicular from the origin to the line (as indicated in Figure 11). Then a polar equation for the line is $r\cos(\theta - \alpha) = d$.

## EXAMPLE 7  Finding a polar equation for a tangent line to a circle

**Figure 12**

Figure 12 shows a line tangent to the unit circle at the point $P$. The $x$-$y$ coordinates of $P$ are $(\frac{\sqrt{3}}{2}, \frac{1}{2})$.

**(a)** What are the polar coordinates of the point $P$?

**(b)** Find the polar equation for the tangent line.

**(c)** Use the polar equation to find the $x$- and $y$-intercepts of the tangent line.

**(d)** Find a rectangular equation for the line.

### SOLUTION

**(a)** Using the unit-circle definition for cosine, we have $\cos \alpha = \sqrt{3}/2$ and, consequently, $\alpha = \pi/6$. The polar coordinates of $P$ are therefore $(1, \frac{\pi}{6})$.

**(b)** In the general equation $r \cos(\theta - \alpha) = d$ we use the values $\alpha = \pi/6$ and $d = 1$ to obtain

$$r \cos\left(\theta - \frac{\pi}{6}\right) = 1 \tag{2}$$

This is the polar equation for the tangent line.

**(c)** The $x$-axis corresponds to $\theta = 0$. Substituting $\theta = 0$ in equation (2) gives us $r \cos\left(0 - \frac{\pi}{6}\right) = 1$, and therefore

$$r \cos \frac{\pi}{6} = 1 \quad \text{(Why?)}$$

$$r = \frac{1}{\sqrt{3}/2} = \frac{2}{\sqrt{3}} = \frac{2\sqrt{3}}{3}$$

This tells us that the tangent line meets the $x$-axis at the point with polar coordinates $(\frac{2\sqrt{3}}{3}, 0)$. So the $x$-intercept of the line is $2\sqrt{3}/3$. For the $y$-intercept we set $\theta = \pi/2$ in equation (2). As you should check for yourself, this yields $r = 2$. Thus the $y$-intercept of the tangent line is 2.

**(d)** From part (b),

$$r \cos\left(\theta - \frac{\pi}{6}\right) = 1$$

$$r\left(\cos \theta \cos \frac{\pi}{6} + \sin \theta \sin \frac{\pi}{6}\right) = 1$$

$$\frac{\sqrt{3}}{2} r \cos \theta + \frac{1}{2} r \sin \theta = 1$$

$$\frac{\sqrt{3}}{2} x + \frac{1}{2} y = 1 \quad \text{or} \quad \sqrt{3}x + y = 2$$

It is also instructive to find a rectangular equation for the line by using the point-slope formula for a line. We have a point $(\frac{\sqrt{3}}{2}, \frac{1}{2})$ on the line. The slope of the line is $\tan(\frac{\pi}{6} + \frac{\pi}{2})$. (Why?) Then the slope is

$$m = \tan\left(\frac{2\pi}{3}\right) = -\sqrt{3}$$

So the line has equation

$$y - \frac{1}{2} = -\sqrt{3}\left(x - \frac{\sqrt{3}}{2}\right)$$

which is equivalent to

$$\sqrt{3}x + y = 2$$

Finally, you can find the same equation by using the *x*- and *y*-intercepts from part (c).

# EXERCISE SET 9.5

## A

*In Exercises 1–3, graph each point in a polar coordinate system then convert the given polar coordinates to rectangular coordinates.*

1. **(a)** $(3, \frac{2\pi}{3})$ **(b)** $(4, \frac{11\pi}{6})$ **(c)** $(4, -\frac{\pi}{6})$
2. **(a)** $(5, \frac{\pi}{4})$ **(b)** $(-5, \frac{\pi}{4})$ **(c)** $(-5, -\frac{\pi}{4})$
3. **(a)** $(1, \frac{\pi}{2})$ **(b)** $(1, \frac{5\pi}{2})$ **(c)** $(-1, \frac{\pi}{8})$

*In Exercises 4–6, convert the given rectangular coordinates to polar coordinates. Express your answers in such a way that r is nonnegative and $0 \le \theta < 2\pi$.*

4. $(3, \sqrt{3})$   5. $(-1, -1)$   6. $(0, -2)$

*In Exercises 7–16, convert to rectangular form.*

7. $r = 2\cos\theta$
8. $2\sin\theta - 3\cos\theta = r$
9. $r = \tan\theta$
10. $r = 4$
11. $r = 3\cos 2\theta$
12. $r = 4\sin 2\theta$
13. $r^2 = 8/(2 - \sin^2\theta)$
14. $r^2 = 1/(3 + \cos^2\theta)$
15. $r\cos\left(\theta - \frac{\pi}{6}\right) = 2$
16. $r\sin\left(\theta + \frac{\pi}{4}\right) = 6$

*In Exercises 17–24, convert to polar form.*

17. $3x - 4y = 2$
18. $x^2 + y^2 = 25$
19. $y^2 = x^3$
20. $y = x^2$
21. $2xy = 1$
22. $x^2 + 4x + y^2 + 4y = 0$
23. $9x^2 + y^2 = 9$
24. $x^2(x^2 + y^2) = y^2$

*In Exercises 25–30 you are given a polar equation and its graph. Use the equation to determine polar coordinates of the points labeled with capital letters. (For the r-values, where necessary, use a calculator and round to two decimal places.)*

25. $r = \dfrac{4}{1 + \sin\theta}$

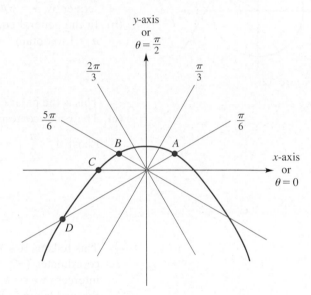

26. $r = \dfrac{2}{\cos\left(\theta - \dfrac{\pi}{3}\right)}$

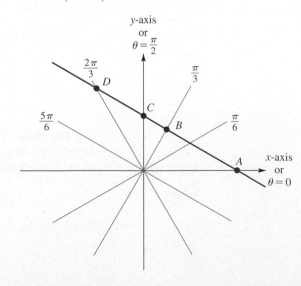

**27.** $r = 2\cos 2\theta$

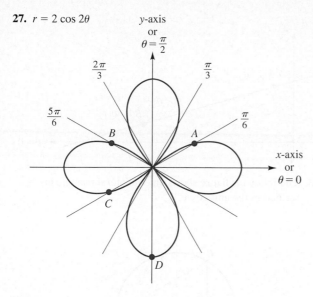

**28.** $r = -1 - \sin\theta$

**29.** $r = e^{\theta/6}$

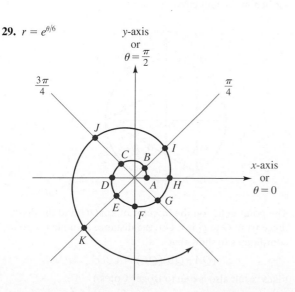

**30.** $r^2 = \cos 2\theta$

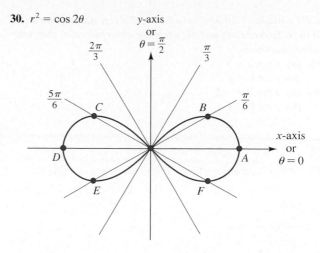

*In Exercises 31–34, compute the distance between the given points. (The coordinates are polar coordinates.)*

**31.** $(2, \frac{2\pi}{3})$ and $(4, \frac{\pi}{6})$      **32.** $(4, \pi)$ and $(3, \frac{7\pi}{3})$

**33.** $(4, \frac{4\pi}{3})$ and $(1, 0)$      **34.** $(3, \frac{5\pi}{6})$ and $(5, \frac{5\pi}{3})$

*In Exercises 35–38, determine a polar equation for the circle satisfying the given conditions.*

**35.** The radius is 2, and the polar coordinates for the center
are:   **(a)** $(4, 0)$      **(b)** $(4, \frac{2\pi}{3})$      **(c)** $(0, 0)$

**36.** The radius is $\sqrt{6}$, and the polar coordinates of the center
are:   **(a)** $(2, \pi)$      **(b)** $(2, \frac{3\pi}{4})$      **(c)** $(0, 0)$

**37.** The radius is 1, and the polar coordinates of the center
are:   **(a)** $(1, \frac{3\pi}{2})$      **(b)** $(1, \frac{\pi}{4})$

**38.** The radius is 6, and the polar coordinates of the center
are:   **(a)** $(-3, \frac{5\pi}{4})$      **(b)** $(-2, \frac{\pi}{4})$

*In Exercises 39–42 the polar equation of a line is given. In each case: **(a)** specify the perpendicular distance from the origin to the line; **(b)** determine the polar coordinates of the points on the line corresponding to $\theta = 0$ and $\theta = \pi/2$; **(c)** specify the polar coordinates of the foot of the perpendicular from the origin to the line; **(d)** use the results in parts (a), (b), and (c) to sketch the line; and **(e)** find a rectangular form for the equation of the line.*

**39.** $r\cos(\theta - \frac{\pi}{6}) = 2$      **40.** $r\cos(\theta - \frac{\pi}{4}) = 1$

**41.** $r\cos(\theta + \frac{2\pi}{3}) = 4$      **42.** $r\cos(\theta - \frac{\pi}{2}) = \sqrt{2}$

**43.** A line is tangent to the circle $x^2 + y^2 = 4$ at a point $P$ with
$x$-$y$ coordinates $(-\sqrt{3}, 1)$.
   **(a)** What are the polar coordinates of $P$?
   **(b)** Find a polar equation for the tangent line.
   **(c)** Use the polar equation to determine the $x$- and
      $y$-intercepts of the line.
   **(d)** Find a rectangular equation for the line.

**44.** Follow Exercise 43 using the circle $x^2 + y^2 = 36$ and the
point $P$ with $x$-$y$ coordinates $(-3, -3\sqrt{3})$.

*Notice that the rectangular form of the polar equation $r\cos\theta = a$ is $x = a$. Thus the graph of the polar equation $r\cos\theta = a$ is a vertical line with an $x$-intercept of $a$. Similarly, the graph of the* polar equation $r \sin \theta = b$ is a horizontal line with a y-intercept of b. In Exercises 45 and 46, use these observations to graph the polar equations.

**45.** (a)  $r \cos \theta = 3$
   (b)  $r \sin \theta = 3$
**46.** (a)  $r \cos \theta = -2$
   (b)  $r \sin \theta = 4$

# B

**47.** The accompanying figure shows the graph of a line $\mathcal{L}$.

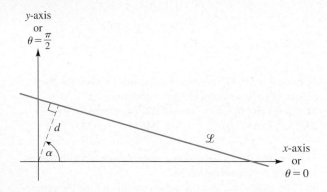

(a) According to the text, what is the polar equation for $\mathcal{L}$?
(b) By converting the equation in part (a) to rectangular form, show that the x-y equation for $\mathcal{L}$ is $x \cos \alpha + y \sin \alpha = d$. (This equation is called the **normal form** for a line.)   *Hint*: First use one of the addition formulas for cosine.

**48.** By converting the polar equation

$$r = a \cos \theta + b \sin \theta$$

to rectangular form, show that the graph is a circle, and find the center and the radius.

**49.** Show that the rectangular form of the equation $r = a \sin 3\theta$ is $(x^2 + y^2)^2 = ay(3x^2 - y^2)$.

**50.** Show that the rectangular form of the equation

$$r = \frac{ab}{(1 - a \cos \theta)} \qquad (a < 1)$$

is $(1 - a^2)x^2 + y^2 - 2a^2bx - a^2b^2 = 0$.

**51.** Show that the polar form of the equation $(x^2/a^2) - (y^2/b^2) = 1$ is

$$r^2 = \frac{a^2b^2}{b^2 \cos^2 \theta - a^2 \sin^2 \theta}.$$

**52.** Show that a polar equation for the line passing through the two points $A(r_1, \theta_1)$ and $B(r_2, \theta_2)$ is $rr_1 \sin(\theta - \theta_1) - rr_2 \sin(\theta - \theta_2) + r_1r_2 \sin(\theta_1 - \theta_2) = 0$. *Hint*: Use the following figure and the observation that

area $\triangle OAB$ = (area $\triangle OBP$) + (area $\triangle OPA$)

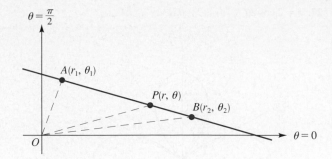

**53.** The following figure shows an equilateral triangle inscribed in the unit circle.

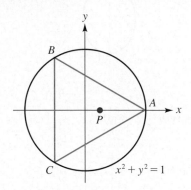

(a) Specify polar coordinates for the points $A$, $B$, and $C$.
(b) In the figure, $P$ denotes an arbitrary point between the origin and $A$ on the x-axis. Let the polar coordinates of $P$ be $(r, 0)$. Use the distance formula for polar coordinates to show that

$$(PA)(PB)(PC) = 1 - r^3$$

[This result is due to the English mathematician Roger Cotes (1682–1716).]

**54.** The following figure shows an equilateral triangle inscribed in the unit circle.

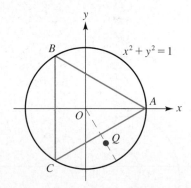

The point $Q$ lies on the bisector of $\angle AOC$, and the distance from $O$ to $Q$ is $r$. Use the distance formula for polar coordinates to show that

$$(QA)(QB)(QC) = 1 + r^3$$

(This result also is due to Roger Cotes.)

# 9.6 CURVES IN POLAR COORDINATES

In principle, the graph of any polar equation $r = f(\theta)$ can be obtained by setting up a table and plotting a sufficient number of points. Indeed, this is just the way a graphing calculator or a computer operates. Figure 1, for example, shows computer-generated graphs of the polar equations $r = (\sin 4\theta)^4 + \cos 3\theta$ and $r = \cos^2 5\theta + \sin 3\theta + 0.3$. In this section we'll concentrate on a few basic types of polar equations and their graphs. With the exception of Example 1 the polar equations that we consider involve trigonometric functions. To *understand* why the graphs look as they do, we will often use symmetry and the basic properties of the sine and cosine functions.

**Figure 1**
(a) A polar coordinate graph discovered by Henri Berger, a student in one of the author's mathematics classes at UCLA in Spring of 1988; (b) a polar coordinate graph discovered by Oscar Ramirez, a precalculus student at UCLA in Fall of 1991

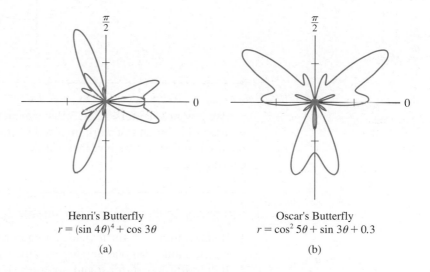

Henri's Butterfly
$r = (\sin 4\theta)^4 + \cos 3\theta$

(a)

Oscar's Butterfly
$r = \cos^2 5\theta + \sin 3\theta + 0.3$

(b)

**EXAMPLE 1  Graphing the spiral of Archimedes**

Graph the polar equation $r = \theta/\pi$ for $\theta \geq 0$.

**SOLUTION**
The equation shows that as $\theta$ increases, so does $r$. Geometrically, this means that as we plot points, moving counterclockwise with increasing $\theta$, the points will be farther and farther from the origin. In Table 1 we have computed values for $r$ corresponding to some convenient values of $\theta$. In Figure 2 we have plotted the points in the table and connected them with a smooth curve. The curve is known as the **spiral of Archimedes.**

**TABLE 1**

| $\theta$ | 0 | $\frac{\pi}{4}$ | $\frac{\pi}{2}$ | $\frac{3\pi}{4}$ | $\pi$ | $\frac{5\pi}{4}$ | $\frac{3\pi}{2}$ | $\frac{7\pi}{4}$ | $2\pi$ | $\frac{5\pi}{2}$ | $3\pi$ | $4\pi$ |
|---|---|---|---|---|---|---|---|---|---|---|---|---|
| $r$ | 0 | $\frac{1}{4}$ | $\frac{1}{2}$ | $\frac{3}{4}$ | 1 | $\frac{5}{4}$ | $\frac{3}{2}$ | $\frac{7}{4}$ | 2 | $\frac{5}{2}$ | 3 | 4 |

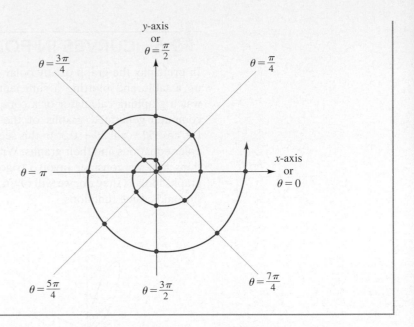

**Figure 2**

$r = \dfrac{\theta}{\pi} \quad (\theta \geq 0)$

We saw in Chapters 1 and 3 that symmetry considerations can often be used to lessen the amount of work involved in graphing equations. This is also true for polar equations. In the box that follows, we list four tests for symmetry in polar coordinates.

---

### Symmetry Tests in Polar Coordinates

1. If substituting $-\theta$ for $\theta$ yields an equivalent equation, then the graph is symmetric about the polar axis $\theta = 0$ (the $x$-axis).
2. If substituting $-\theta$ for $\theta$ and $-r$ for $r$ yields an equivalent equation, then the graph is symmetric about the line $\theta = \pi/2$ (the $y$-axis).
3. If substituting $\pi - \theta$ for $\theta$ yields an equivalent equation, then the graph is symmetric about the line $\theta = \pi/2$ (the $y$-axis).
4. If substituting $-r$ for $r$ yields an equivalent equation, then the graph is symmetric about the pole $r = 0$ (the origin).

CAUTION   As opposed to the case with the $x$-$y$ symmetry tests (in Chapter 2), if a polar equation fails a symmetry test, then it is still possible for the graph to possess the indicated symmetry. This is a consequence of the fact that the polar coordinates of a point are not unique. (For an example, see Example 3.)

---

The validity of the first test follows from the fact that the points $(r, \theta)$ and $(r, -\theta)$ are reflections of each other about the polar axis (the $x$-axis); see Figure 3. The validity of test 2 follows from the fact that the points $(r, \theta)$ and $(-r, -\theta)$ are reflections of each other about the line $\theta = \pi/2$ (the $y$-axis), as indicated in Figure 3. The other tests can be justified in a similar manner.

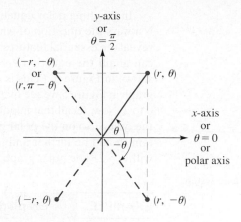

Figure 3

---

**EXAMPLE** **2**   **Graphing a cardioid**

Graph the polar equation $r = 1 - \cos \theta$.

**SOLUTION**

We know (from Section 7.3) that the cosine function satisfies the identity $\cos(-\theta) = \cos \theta$. So according to symmetry test 1, the graph of $r = 1 - \cos \theta$ will be symmetric about the line $\theta = 0$. In Figure 4(a) we have set up a table (using a calculator as necessary) with some convenient values of $\theta$ running from 0 to $\pi$. Plotting the points in the table leads to the curve shown in Figure 4(a). Reflecting this curve in the line $\theta = 0$, we obtain the graph in Figure 4(b). The fact that the period of the cosine function is $2\pi$ implies that we need not consider values of $\theta$ beyond $2\pi$. (Why?) Thus the curve in Figure 4(b) is the required graph of $r = 1 - \cos \theta$. The curve is a **cardioid.**

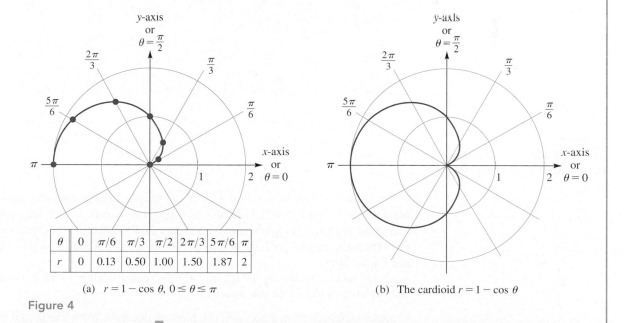

| $\theta$ | 0 | $\pi/6$ | $\pi/3$ | $\pi/2$ | $2\pi/3$ | $5\pi/6$ | $\pi$ |
|---|---|---|---|---|---|---|---|
| $r$ | 0 | 0.13 | 0.50 | 1.00 | 1.50 | 1.87 | 2 |

(a)   $r = 1 - \cos \theta,\ 0 \le \theta \le \pi$

(b)   The cardioid $r = 1 - \cos \theta$

Figure 4

**Figure 5**
The graph of $r = 1 - \cos \theta$ in a rectangular $\theta$-$r$ coordinate system

In graphing polar equations, just as in graphing Cartesian *x*-*y* equations, there is always the question of whether we have plotted a sufficient number of points to reveal the essential features of the graph. As a check on our work in Figure 4(a) we can graph the equation $r = 1 - \cos \theta$ in a *rectangular $\theta$-$r$ coordinate system*, as shown in Figure 5. (This is easy to do using reflection and translation.) From the graph in Figure 5 we see that as $\theta$ increases from 0 to $\pi$, the values of $r$ increase from 0 to 2. Now, recall that in polar coordinates, $r$ represents the directed distance from the origin. So on the polar graph, as we go from $\theta = 0$ to $\pi$, the points that we obtain should be farther and farther from the origin, starting with $r = 0$ and ending with $r = 2$. The polar graph in Figure 4(a) is consistent with these observations.

---

**EXAMPLE** | **3** | **Graphing a limaçon**

Graph the polar curve $r = 1 + 2 \sin \theta$.

**SOLUTION**
Using symmetry test 3, we replace $\theta$ by $\pi - \theta$ in the given equation:

$$r = 1 + 2 \sin(\pi - \theta) = 1 + 2(\sin \pi \cos \theta - \cos \pi \sin \theta)$$
$$= 1 + 2 \sin \theta \qquad \text{because } \sin \pi = 0 \text{ and } \cos \pi = -1$$

This shows that the graph is symmetric about the line $\theta = \pi/2$. (Note that symmetry test 2 fails for this equation, yet the graph is symmetric about the *y*-axis.)

Next, to see what to expect in polar coordinates, we first sketch the graph of the given equation in a rectangular $\theta$-$r$ coordinate system; see Figure 6. In Figure 6, notice that the maximum value of $|r|$ is 3. This implies that the required polar graph is contained within a circle of radius 3 about the origin. (We'll refer to this sketch several more times in the course of the solution.)

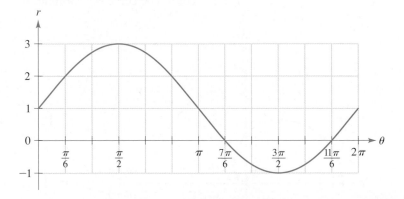

**Figure 6**
The graph of $r = 1 + 2 \sin \theta$ in a rectangular $\theta$-$r$ coordinate system

In Figure 7(a) we have set up a table and graphed the given polar equation for $\theta$ running from 0 to $\pi/2$. Note that as $\theta$ increases from 0 to $\pi/2$, the *r*-values increase from 1 to 3 (in agreement with Figure 6). By reflecting the curve in Figure 7(a) in the line $\theta = \pi/2$, we obtain the graph of $r = 1 + 2 \sin \theta$ for $0 \le \theta \le \pi$; see Figure 7(b).

Next, let's consider the values of $r$ as $\theta$ increases from $\pi$ to $3\pi/2$. Figure 6 tells us what to expect on this interval:

As $\theta$ increases from $\pi$ to $7\pi/6$, the *r*-values decrease from 1 to 0; as $\theta$ increases from $7\pi/6$ to $3\pi/2$, the *r*-values decrease from 0 to $-1$. However

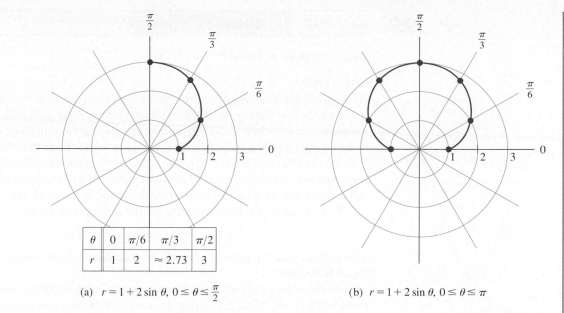

| $\theta$ | 0 | $\pi/6$ | $\pi/3$ | $\pi/2$ |
|---|---|---|---|---|
| $r$ | 1 | 2 | $\approx 2.73$ | 3 |

**Figure 7**   (a) $r = 1 + 2\sin\theta$, $0 \le \theta \le \dfrac{\pi}{2}$   (b) $r = 1 + 2\sin\theta$, $0 \le \theta \le \pi$

(in view of the convention regarding negative $r$-values), this will mean that the points on the polar graph are, in fact, moving farther and farther from the origin as $\theta$ increases from $7\pi/6$ to $3\pi/2$.

In Figure 8(a) we have set up a table for $\pi \le \theta \le 3\pi/2$ and added the corresponding points from Figure 7(b). Finally, again taking into account the symmetry to the line $\theta = \pi/2$, we sketch the graph for $0 \le \theta \le 2\pi$, as indicated in Figure 8(b). The curve in Figure 8(b) is a **limaçon.** (Not all limaçons have inner loops. See, for example, Exercises 29 and 30.)

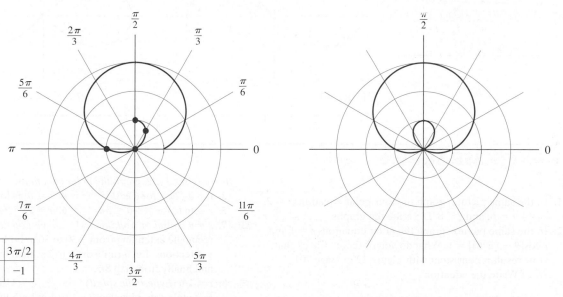

| $\pi$ | $7\pi/6$ | $4\pi/3$ | $3\pi/2$ |
|---|---|---|---|
| 1 | 0 | $\approx -0.73$ | $-1$ |

**Figure 8**   (a) $r = 1 + 2\sin\theta$, $0 \le \theta \le \dfrac{3\pi}{2}$   (b) The limaçon $r = 1 + 2\sin\theta$

**EXAMPLE** 4 **Graphing a lemniscate**

Graph the polar equation $r^2 = 4 \cos 2\theta$.

**SOLUTION**
As a guide for graphing the given polar equation, we first sketch the curve $y = 4 \cos 2\theta$ in a rectangular $\theta$-$y$ coordinate system. As is indicated in Figure 9, the period of $4 \cos 2\theta$ is $\pi$. So in graphing the given polar equation, it suffices to consider only the values of $\theta$ from 0 to $\pi$. Figure 9 also shows that $4 \cos 2\theta$ is negative on the interval $(\frac{\pi}{4} < \theta < \frac{3\pi}{4})$. The value of $r^2$, however, cannot be negative. Consequently, we do not need to consider values of $\theta$ in the open interval from $\pi/4$ to $3\pi/4$. Finally, Figure 9 shows that the absolute value of $4 \cos 2\theta$ is always less than or equal to 4. Consequently, for the polar graph we have

$$r^2 \le 4 \qquad \text{and therefore} \qquad |r| \le 2$$

This tells us that the polar graph will be contained within a circle of radius 2 about the origin.

For the polar graph we begin by computing a table of values with $\theta$ running from 0 to $\pi/4$; see Table 2. Plotting the points in Table 2 and joining them with a smooth curve leads to the graph shown in Figure 10(a). Then, rather than setting up another table with $\theta$ running from $3\pi/4$ to $\pi$, we rely on symmetry to complete the graph. According to the first two symmetry tests, the curve is symmetric about both the line $\theta = 0$ and the line $\theta = \pi/2$. Thus we obtain the graph shown in Figure 10(b). The curve is called a **lemniscate.**

**Figure 9**
$y = 4 \cos 2\theta$

**TABLE 2**

| $\theta$ | $r = \pm 2\sqrt{\cos 2\theta}$ |
|---|---|
| 0 | $\pm 2$ |
| $\frac{\pi}{12}$ | $\pm 1.86$ |
| $\frac{\pi}{8}$ | $\pm 1.68$ |
| $\frac{\pi}{6}$ | $\pm 1.41$ |
| $\frac{\pi}{4}$ | 0 |

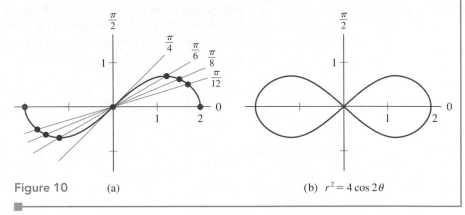

**Figure 10** (a)      (b) $r^2 = 4 \cos 2\theta$

# EXERCISE SET 9.6

**A**

**1.** In the same picture, graph the four polar equations $r = 2$, $r = 4$, $r = 6$, and $r = 8$. Describe the graphs.

G **2.** In the same picture, graph the polar equations $r = 1$ and $r \cos[\theta - (\pi/6)] = 1$. What do you observe? Check that your result is consistent with Figure 12 on page 701.
*Hint*: Write the equation

$$r \cos[\theta - (\pi/6)] = 1 \qquad \text{as} \qquad r = \frac{1}{\cos[\theta - (\pi/6)]}$$

*In Exercises 3–32, graph the polar equations.*

**3.** $r = \theta/(2\pi)$, for $\theta \ge 0$
**4.** $r = \theta/\pi$, for $-4\pi \le \theta \le 0$
**5.** $r = \ln \theta$, for $1 \le \theta \le 3\pi$
**6.** $r = e^{\theta/2\pi}$, for $0 \le \theta \le 2\pi$

G **7.** $r = \theta$ (*spiral of Archimedes*) *Suggestion*: Use a viewing rectangle extending from $-30$ to 30 in both the $x$- and $y$-directions. Let $\theta$ run from 0 to $2\pi$, then from 0 to $4\pi$, and finally from 0 to $8\pi$.

G **8.** $r = 1/\theta$ (*hyperbolic spiral*) *Suggestion*: Use a viewing rectangle extending from $-1$ to 1 in both the $x$- and $y$-directions. Let $\theta$ run from 0 to $2\pi$, then from 0 to $4\pi$, and finally from 0 to $8\pi$.

Ⓖ **9.** $r = 1/\sqrt{\theta}$ (*spiral of Cotes*, or *lituus*)   *Suggestion*: Use the guidelines in Exercise 8.

Ⓖ **10.** $r = \sqrt{\theta}$ (*spiral of Fermat*)   *Suggestion*: Use a viewing rectangle extending from $-5$ to $5$ in both the *x*- and *y*-directions. Let $\theta$ run from $\theta$ to $2\pi$, then from $0$ to $4\pi$, and finally from $0$ to $8\pi$.

Ⓖ **11.** $r = e^{-\theta/(2\pi)}$, for $0 \le \theta \le 2\pi$   Ⓖ **12.** $r = \sqrt{\theta}, 0 \le \theta \le 3\pi$

**13.** $r = 1 + \cos\theta$                           **14.** $r = 1 - \sin\theta$

**15.** $r = 2 - 2\sin\theta$                     **16.** $r = 3 + 3\cos\theta$

**17.** $r = 1 - 2\sin\theta$                     **18.** $r = 1 + 2\cos\theta$

**19.** $r = 2 + 4\cos\theta$                     **20.** $r = 2 - 4\sin\theta$

**21.** $r^2 = 4\sin 2\theta$                       **22.** $r^2 = 9\cos 2\theta$

**23.** $r^2 = \cos 4\theta$                         **24.** $r^2 = 3\sin 4\theta$

**25.** $r = \cos 2\theta$ (*four-leafed rose*)

**26.** $r = 2\sin 2\theta$ (*four-leafed rose*)

**27.** $r = \sin 3\theta$ (*three-leafed rose*)

**28.** $r = 2\cos 5\theta$ (*five-leafed rose*)

**29.** $r = 4 + 2\sin\theta$ (*limaçon with no inner loop*)

**30.** $r = 1.5 - \cos\theta$ (*limaçon with no inner loop*)

**31.** $r = 8\tan\theta$ (*kappa curve*)

**32.** $r = \csc\theta + 2$ (*conchoid of Nicomedes*)

Ⓖ **33. (a)** Use one of the polar symmetry tests to show that the graph of $r = \cos^2\theta - 2\cos\theta$ is symmetric about the *x*-axis.
  **(b)** Graph the equation given in part (a) and note that the curve is indeed symmetric about the *x*-axis.

Ⓖ **34.** As background for this exercise, read the caution note at the bottom of the box on page 706.
  **(a)** Graph the polar equation $r = \sin^2\theta - 2\sin\theta$. What type of symmetry do you observe?
  **(b)** Check (algebraically) that the equation $r = \sin^2\theta - 2\sin\theta$ satisfies symmetry test 3 on page 706, but not symmetry test 2.

*In Exercises 35–37, graph the polar equations.*

Ⓖ **35.** $r = \cos 3\theta$ (*three-leafed rose*)

Ⓖ **36.** $r = \sin 5\theta$

Ⓖ **37. (a)** $r = \cos 4\theta$ (*eight-leafed rose*)
  **(b)** $r = \sin 4\theta$

*In Exercises 38 and 39, match one of the graphs with each equation.*   *Hint: Compute the values of r when $\theta = 0$, $\pi/2$, $\pi$, and $3\pi/2$.*

**38. (a)** $r = 3 + 3\sin\theta$       **(c)** $r = 3 - 3\cos\theta$
  **(b)** $r = 3 - 3\sin\theta$       **(d)** $r = 3 + 3\cos\theta$

Graph A

Graph B

Graph C

Graph D

**39. (a)** $r = 3 + 2\cos\theta$       **(c)** $r = 2 - 3\cos\theta$
  **(b)** $r = 2 + 3\cos\theta$       **(d)** $r = 3 - 2\cos\theta$

Graph A

Graph B

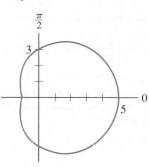

Graph C

Graph D

Ⓖ **40.** The *limaçon of Pascal* is defined by the equation $r = a\cos\theta + b$. [The curve is named after Étienne Pascal (1588–1640), the father of Blaise Pascal. According to mathematics historian Howard Eves, however, the curve is misnamed; it appears earlier, in the writings of Albrecht Dürer (1471–1528).] When $a = b$, the curve is a cardioid; when $a = 0$ the curve is a circle. Graph the following limaçons.
  **(a)** $r = 2\cos\theta + 1$       **(d)** $r = \cos\theta - 2$
  **(b)** $r = 2\cos\theta - 1$       **(e)** $r = 2\cos\theta + 2$
  **(c)** $r = \cos\theta + 2$         **(f)** $r = \cos\theta$

**B**

**41.** The figure on the next page shows a graph of the *logarithmic spiral* $\ln r = a\theta$ for $0 \le \theta \le 2\pi$. (In this equation, $a$ denotes a positive constant.)

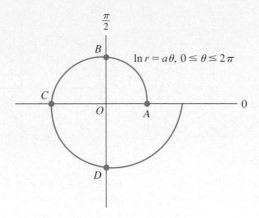

$\ln r = a\theta,\ 0 \le \theta \le 2\pi$

**(a)** Find the polar coordinates of the points $A$, $B$, $C$, and $D$, and then show that

$$\frac{OD}{OC} = \frac{OC}{OB} = \frac{OB}{OA} = e^{a\pi/2}$$

**(b)** Show that $\angle ABC$ and $\angle BCD$ are right angles.
*Hint:* Use rectangular coordinates to compute slopes.

**42. (a)** Graph the polar curves $r = 2 \cos \theta - 1$ and $r = 2 \cos \theta + 1$. What do you observe?

**(b)** Part (a) shows that algebraically nonequivalent polar equations may have identical graphs. (This is another consequence of the fact that the polar coordinates of a point are not unique.) Show that both equations in part (a) can be written $(x^2 - 2x + y^2)^2 - x^2 - y^2 = 0$.

**43. (a)** Graph the polar curves $r = \cos(\theta/2)$ and $r = \sin(\theta/2)$. What do you observe?

**(b)** Part (a) shows that algebraically nonequivalent polar equations may have identical graphs. (See Exercise 42 for another example.) Show that both polar equations can be written in the rectangular form

$$(x^2 + y^2)[2(x^2 + y^2) - 1]^2 - x^2 = 0$$

**44.** Let $k$ denote a positive constant, and let $F_1$ and $F_2$ denote the points with rectangular coordinates $(-k, 0)$ and $(k, 0)$, respectively. A curve known as the *lemniscate of Bernoulli* is defined as the set of points $P(x, y)$ such that $(F_1P) \times (F_2P) = k^2$.

**(a)** Show that the rectangular equation of the curve is
$(x^2 + y^2)^2 = 2k^2(x^2 - y^2)$.

**(b)** Show that the polar equation is $r^2 = 2k^2 \cos 2\theta$.

**(c)** Graph the equation $r^2 = 2k^2 \cos 2\theta$.

Ⓖ **45.** Graph the *lemniscate of Bernoulli* with polar equation $r^2 = 4 \cos 2\theta$. *Hint:* The equation is equivalent to the two equations $r = \pm 2\sqrt{\cos 2\theta}$. You'll find, however, that you need to consider only one of these.

Ⓖ **46.** Graph the *cissoid of Diocles*, $r = 10 \sin \theta \tan \theta$. [The Greek mathematician Diocles (ca. 180 B.C.) used the geometric properties of this curve to solve the problem of duplicating the cube. For an explanation of the problem and historical background, see the text by Howard Eves, *An Introduction to the History of Mathematics,* 6th ed., pp. 109–127 (Philadelphia: Saunders College Publishing, 1990).]

Ⓖ **47.** The polar curve $r = \cos^4 (\theta/4)$ has a property that is difficult to detect without the aid of a graphing utility. Graph the equation in the standard viewing rectangle. Note that the curve appears to have a simple inner loop to the left of the origin. Now zoom in on the origin. What do you observe?

*In Exercises 48–50, graph the polar curves.*

Ⓖ **48. (a)** $r = 2|\sin \theta|^{\sin \theta}$      **(b)** $r = 2|\sin \theta|^{\sin(\theta/2)}$

Ⓖ **49.** $r = (\sin \theta)/\theta, \quad 0 < \theta \le 4\pi$

Ⓖ **50.** Graph the polar curve

$$r = 1.5 \sin\left(\frac{30\theta}{17} + \frac{\pi}{30}\right) + 0.5$$

Use a viewing rectangle extending from $-2$ to $2$ in both the $x$- and $y$-directions. Let $\theta$ run from 0 to $34\pi$.

---

# Chapter 9  Summary of Principal Terms and Formulas

| Terms or formulas | Page reference | Comments |
|---|---|---|
| **1.** $\dfrac{\sin A}{a} = \dfrac{\sin B}{b} = \dfrac{\sin C}{c}$ <br> or $\dfrac{a}{\sin A} = \dfrac{b}{\sin B} = \dfrac{c}{\sin C}$ | 646 | This is the *law of sines.* In words, it states that in any triangle the ratio of the sine of an angle to the length of its opposite side is constant. We use it when we know one angle and its opposite side and one other side or angle. |
| **2.** $a^2 = b^2 + c^2 - 2bc \cos A$ <br> $b^2 = a^2 + c^2 - 2ac \cos B$ <br> $c^2 = a^2 + b^2 - 2ab \cos C$ | 648 | This is the *law of cosines.* We can use it to calculate the third side of a triangle when we are given two sides and the included angle. The formula can also be used to calculate the angles of a triangle when we know the three sides, as in Example 5 on page 650. |

| Terms or formulas | Page reference | Comments |
|---|---|---|
| **3.** Vector | 661 <br> 672 | Geometrically, a vector in the plane is a directed line segment. Vectors can be used to represent quantities that have both magnitude and direction, such as force and velocity. For examples, see Figures 1 and 2 in Section 9.2. Algebraically, a vector in the plane is an ordered pair of real numbers, denoted by $\langle x, y \rangle$; see Figure 3 in Section 9.3. The numbers $x$ and $y$ are called the *components* of the vector $\langle x, y \rangle$. |
| **4.** Vector equality | 662 <br> 672 | Geometrically, two vectors are said to be equal provided that they have the same length and the same direction. In terms of components, this means that two vectors are equal if and only if their corresponding components are equal. |
| **5.** Vector addition | 662 <br> 663 <br> 673 | Geometrically, two vectors can be added by using the parallelogram law, as in Figure 10 in Section 9.2. Algebraically, this is equivalent to the following componentwise formula for vector addition: $$\langle u_1, u_2 \rangle + \langle v_1, v_2 \rangle = \langle u_1 + v_1, u_2 + v_2 \rangle$$ |
| **6.** $\lvert \mathbf{v} \rvert = \sqrt{v_1^2 + v_2^2}$ | 661 <br> 672 | The expression on the left-hand side of the equation denotes the *length* or *magnitude* of the vector $\mathbf{v}$. The expression on the right-hand side of the equation tells us how to compute the length of $\mathbf{v}$ in terms of its respective $x$- and $y$-components $v_1$ and $v_2$. |
| **7.** $\overrightarrow{PQ} = \langle x_2 - x_1, y_2 - y_1 \rangle$ | 673 | This formula gives the components of the vector $\overrightarrow{PQ}$, where $P$ and $Q$ are the points $P(x_1, y_1)$ and $Q(x_2, y_2)$; see Figure 5 in Section 9.3 for a derivation of this formula. |
| **8.** The zero vector | 674 | The zero vector, denoted by $\mathbf{0}$, is the vector $\langle 0, 0 \rangle$. The zero vector plays the same role in vector addition as does the real number zero in addition of real numbers. For any vector $\mathbf{v}$ we have $$\mathbf{0} + \mathbf{v} = \mathbf{v} + \mathbf{0} = \mathbf{v}$$ |
| **9.** Scalar multiplication | 674 | For each real number $k$ and each vector $\mathbf{v} = \langle x, y \rangle$ the vector $k\mathbf{v}$ is defined by the equation $$k\mathbf{v} = \langle kx, ky \rangle$$ Geometrically, the length of $k\mathbf{v}$ is $\lvert k \rvert$ times the length of $\mathbf{v}$. The operation that forms the vector $k\mathbf{v}$ from the scalar $k$ and the vector $\mathbf{v}$ is called scalar multiplication. |
| **10.** The opposite of a vector | 675 | The opposite or negative of a vector $\mathbf{v}$, denoted $-\mathbf{v}$, is the vector defined by the equation $$-\mathbf{v} = (-1)\mathbf{v}$$ |
| **11.** Vector subtraction | 675 | The difference of two vectors $\mathbf{u}$ and $\mathbf{v}$, denoted $\mathbf{u} - \mathbf{v}$, is the vector defined by the equation $$\mathbf{u} - \mathbf{v} = \mathbf{u} + (-\mathbf{v})$$ |

| Terms or formulas | Page reference | Comments |
|---|---|---|
| **12.** $\mathbf{i} = \langle 1, 0 \rangle$ <br> $\mathbf{j} = \langle 0, 1 \rangle$ | 676 | These two equations define the *unit vectors* $\mathbf{i}$ and $\mathbf{j}$; see Figure 12 in Section 9.3. Any vector $\langle x, y \rangle$ can be expressed in terms of the unit vectors $\mathbf{i}$ and $\mathbf{j}$ as follows: $$\langle x, y \rangle = x\mathbf{i} + y\mathbf{j}$$ |
| **13.** Parametric equations | 684 | Suppose the $x$- and $y$-coordinates of the points on a curve are expressed as functions of another variable $t$: $$x = f(t) \qquad \text{and} \qquad y = g(t)$$ These equations are parametric equations of the curve, and $t$ is called a parameter. An example: A pair of parametric equations for the ellipse $(x^2/a^2) + (y^2/b^2) = 1$ is $x = a \cos t$ and $y = b \sin t$. |
| **14.** $x = r \cos \theta$ <br> $y = r \sin \theta$ <br> $x^2 + y^2 = r^2$ <br> $\tan \theta = y/x$ | 696 | These formulas relate the rectangular coordinates of a point $(x, y)$ to its polar coordinates $(r, \theta)$. See the boxed figure on page 696. |
| **15.** $d^2$ <br> $= r_1^2 + r_2^2 - 2r_1 r_2 \cos(\theta_2 - \theta_1)$ | 698 | This is the formula for the (square of the) distance $d$ between the points with polar coordinates $(r_1, \theta_1)$ and $(r_2, \theta_2)$. |
| **16.** $r^2 + r_0^2 - 2rr_0 \cos(\theta - \theta_0)$ <br> $\qquad\qquad = a^2$ | 699 | This is a polar equation for the circle with center $(r_0, \theta_0)$ and radius $a$. |
| **17.** $r \cos(\theta - \alpha) = d$ | 700 | This is a polar equation for a line not passing through the origin. In the equation, $d$ and $\alpha$ are constants; $d$ is the perpendicular distance from the origin to the line, and the (polar) point $(d, \alpha)$ is the foot of the perpendicular from the origin to the line. |

## Writing Mathematics

A regular feature in *Mathematics Magazine* is the "Proof Without Words" section. The idea is to present a proof of a well-known theorem in such a way that the entire proof is "obvious" from a well-chosen picture and at most several equations. Of course, what is obvious to a mathematician might not be so obvious to her or his students (as you well know).

The following clever proof without words for the law of cosines was developed by Professor Sidney H. Kung of Jacksonville University. (It was published in *Mathematics Magazine,* vol. 63, no. 5, December 1990.) Study the proof (or discuss it with friends) until you see how it works. Then, in a paragraph or two, write out the details of the proof as if you were explaining it to a classmate. (To facilitate your explanation, you will probably need to label some of the points in the given figure.)

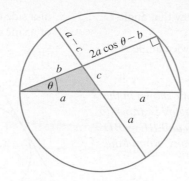

$(2a \cos \theta - b)b = (a - c)(a + c)$
$c^2 = a^2 + b^2 - 2ab \cos \theta$

Proof without words for the law of cosines, $\theta < 90°$ (by Professor Sidney H. Kung)

# Chapter 9     Review Exercises

*In Exercises 1–8 the lengths of the three sides of a triangle are denoted by a, b, and c; the angles opposite these sides are A, B, and C, respectively. In each exercise, use the given data to find the remaining sides and angles. Use a calculator, and round the final answers to one decimal place.*

**1.** $\angle A = 40°$, $\angle B = 85°$, $c = 16$ cm
**2.** $\angle C = 84°$, $\angle B = 16°$, $a = 9$ cm
**3.** **(a)** $a = 8$ cm, $b = 9$ cm, $\angle A = 52°$, $\angle B < 90°$
    **(b)** Use the data in part (a), but assume that $\angle B > 90°$.
**4.** **(a)** $a = 6.25$ cm, $b = 9.44$ cm, $\angle A = 12°$, $\angle B < 90°$
    **(b)** Use the data in part (a), but assume that $\angle B > 90°$.
**5.** $a = 18$ cm, $b = 14$ cm, $\angle C = 24°$
**6.** $a = 32.16$ cm, $b = 50.12$ cm, $\angle C = 156°$
**7.** $a = 4$ cm, $b = 7$ cm, $c = 9$ cm
**8.** $a = 12.61$ cm, $b = 19.01$ cm, $c = 14.14$ cm

*In Exercises 9–18, refer to the following figure. In each case, determine the indicated quantity. Use a calculator and round your result to two decimal places.*

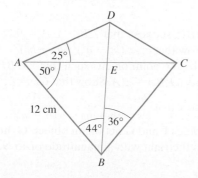

**9.** $BE$
**11.** area of $\triangle BCE$
**13.** area of $\triangle ABD$
**15.** $CD$
**17.** $AC$

**10.** $BC$
**12.** $BD$
**14.** $DE$
**16.** $AD$
**18.** area of $\triangle DEC$

*In Exercises 19 and 20, refer to the following figure, in which $\overline{BD}$ bisects $\angle ABC$.*

**19.** If $AB = 24$ cm, $BC = 40$ cm, and $AC = 56$ cm, find the length of the angle bisector $\overline{BD}$.
**20.** If $AB = 105$ cm, $BC = 120$ cm, and $AC = 195$ cm, find the length of the angle bisector $\overline{BD}$.

*In Exercises 21 and 22, refer to the following figure, in which $AD = DC$.*

**21.** If $AB = 12$ cm, $BC = 26$ cm, and $AD = DC = 17$ cm, find $BD$.
**22.** If $AB = 16$ cm, $BC = 22$ cm, and $AD = DC = 17$ cm, find $BD$.
**23.** In $\triangle ABC$, $a = 4$, $b = 5$, and $c = 6$.
    **(a)** Find $\cos A$ and $\cos C$.

*(continues)*

**(b)** Using the results in part (a), show that angle $C$ is twice angle $A$.

**24.** In $\triangle ABC$, suppose that angle $C$ is twice angle $A$. Show that $ab = c^2 - a^2$.

*In Exercises 25–30, refer to the framework shown in the accompanying figure. (Assume that the figure is drawn to scale.) In the figure, $\overline{AC}$ is parallel to $\overline{ED}$ and $BE = BD$. In each case, compute the indicated quantity. Round the final answers to two decimal places.*

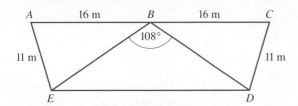

**25.** $\angle BED$      **26.** $\angle ABE$
**27.** $\angle AEB$      **28.** $\angle BAE$
**29.** $BE$          **30.** $DE$

**31.** The given figure shows a regular pentagon inscribed in a circle. The radius of the circle is 10 cm. Determine the following lengths, rounding the answers to two decimal places.
  **(a)** one side of the pentagon
  **(b)** $AC$

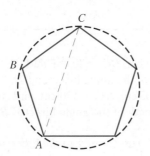

**32.** A pilot on a training flight is supposed to leave the airport and fly for 100 miles in the direction N40°E. Then he is supposed to turn around and fly directly back to the airport. By error, however, he makes the 100-mile return trip in the direction S25°W. How far is he now from the airport, and in what direction must he fly to get there? (Round the answers to one decimal place.)

**33.** The following figures show the same circle of diameter $D$ inscribed first in an equilateral triangle and then in a regular hexagon. Let $a$ denote the length of a side of the triangle, and let $b$ denote the length of a side of the hexagon. Show that $ab = D^2$.

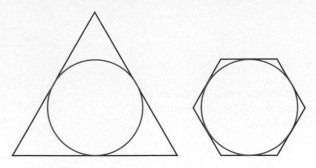

**34.** Suppose that $\triangle ABC$ is a right triangle with the right angle at $C$. Use the law of cosines to prove the following statements.
  **(a)** The square of the distance from $C$ to the midpoint of the hypotenuse is equal to one-fourth the square of the hypotenuse.
  **(b)** The sum of the squares of the distances from $C$ to the two points that trisect the hypotenuse is equal to five-ninths the square of the hypotenuse.
  **(c)** Let $P$, $Q$, and $R$ be points on the hypotenuse such that $AP = PQ = QR = RB$. Derive a result similar to your results in parts (a) and (b) for the sum of the squares of the distances from $C$ to $P$, $Q$, and $R$.

**35.** The perimeter and the area of the triangle in the figure are 20 cm and $10\sqrt{3}$ cm$^2$, respectively. Find $a$ and $b$. (Assume that $a < b$.)

**36.** In $\triangle ABC$, suppose that $\angle B - \angle A = 90°$.
  **(a)** Show that $c^2 = (b^2 - a^2)^2/(a^2 + b^2)$. *Hint:* Let $P$ be the point on $\overline{AC}$ such that $\angle CBP = 90°$ and $\angle PBA = \angle A$. Show that $CP = (a^2 + b^2)/2b$.
  **(b)** Show that $\dfrac{2}{c^2} = \dfrac{1}{(b+a)^2} + \dfrac{1}{(b-a)^2}$.

**37.** Two forces **F** and **G** act on an object, **G**, horizontally to the right with a magnitude of 15 N, and **F**

vertically upward with a magnitude of 20 N. Determine the magnitude and direction of the resultant force. (Use a calculator to determine the angle between the horizontal and the resultant; round the result to one decimal place.)

**38.** Determine the resultant of the two forces in the accompanying figure. (Use a calculator, and round the values you obtain for the magnitude and direction to one decimal place.)

**39.** Determine the horizontal and vertical components of the velocity vector **v** in the following figure. (Use a calculator, and round your answers to one decimal place.)

**40.** The heading and air speed of an airplane are 50° and 220 mph, respectively. If the wind is 60 mph from 140°, find the ground speed, the drift angle, and the course. (Use a calculator, and round your answers to one decimal place.)

**41.** A block rests on an inclined plane that makes an angle of 24° with the horizontal. The component of the weight parallel to the plane is 14.8 lb. Determine the weight of the block and the component of the weight perpendicular to the plane. (Use a calculator, and round your answers to one decimal place.)

**42.** Find the length of the vector $\langle 20, 99 \rangle$.

**43.** For which values of $b$ will the vectors $\langle 2, 6 \rangle$ and $\langle -5, b \rangle$ have the same length?

**44.** Given the points $A(2, 6)$ and $B(-7, 4)$, find the components of the following vectors. Write your answers in the form $\langle x, y \rangle$.

(a) $\overrightarrow{AB}$   (b) $\overrightarrow{BA}$   (c) $3\overrightarrow{AB}$   (d) $\dfrac{1}{|\overrightarrow{AB}|}\overrightarrow{AB}$

*In Exercises 45–56, compute each of the indicated quantities, given that the vectors* **a**, **b**, **c**, *and* **d** *are defined as follows:*

$$\mathbf{a} = \langle 3, 5 \rangle \qquad \mathbf{b} = \langle 7, 4 \rangle \qquad \mathbf{c} = \langle 2, -1 \rangle \qquad \mathbf{d} = \langle 0, 3 \rangle$$

**45.** $\mathbf{a} + \mathbf{b}$                    **46.** $\mathbf{b} - \mathbf{d}$

**47.** $3\mathbf{c} + 2\mathbf{a}$                **48.** $|\mathbf{a}|$

**49.** $|\mathbf{b} + \mathbf{d}|^2 - |\mathbf{b} - \mathbf{d}|^2$   **50.** $\mathbf{a} + (\mathbf{b} + \mathbf{c})$

**51.** $(\mathbf{a} + \mathbf{b}) + \mathbf{c}$        **52.** $\mathbf{a} - (\mathbf{b} - \mathbf{c})$

**53.** $(\mathbf{a} - \mathbf{b}) - \mathbf{c}$

**54.** $|\mathbf{a} + \mathbf{b}|^2 + |\mathbf{a} - \mathbf{b}|^2 - 2|\mathbf{a}|^2 - 2|\mathbf{b}|^2$

**55.** $4\mathbf{c} + 2\mathbf{a} - 3\mathbf{b}$       **56.** $|4\mathbf{c} + 2\mathbf{a} - 3\mathbf{b}|$

**57.** Express the vector $\langle 7, -6 \rangle$ in terms of the unit vectors **i** and **j**.

**58.** Express the vector $4\mathbf{i} - 6\mathbf{j}$ in the form $\langle a, b \rangle$.

**59.** Find a unit vector having the same direction as $\langle 6, 4 \rangle$.

**60.** Find two unit vectors that are perpendicular to $\langle \cos\theta, \sin\theta \rangle$. Simplify the components as much as possible.

*In Exercises 61 and 62, compute the distance between the points with the given polar coordinates. Use a calculator and round the final answers to two decimal places.*

**61.** $(3, \frac{\pi}{12})$ and $(2, \frac{17\pi}{18})$

**62.** $(1, 1)$ and $(3, 2)$

*In Exercises 63 and 64, determine a polar equation for the circle satisfying the given conditions.*

**63.** The radius is 3 and the polar coordinates of the center are $(5, \frac{\pi}{6})$.

**64.** The radius is 1 and the polar coordinates of the center are $(-3, \frac{\pi}{4})$.

*In Exercises 65 and 66, the polar equation of a line is given. In each case:* (a) *specify the perpendicular distance from the origin to the line;* (b) *determine the polar coordinates of the points on the line corresponding to* $\theta = 0$ *and* $\theta = \pi/2$; (c) *specify the polar coordinates of the foot of the perpendicular from the origin to the line;* (d) *sketch the line; and* (e) *find a rectangular form for the equation of the line.*

**65.** $r \cos(\theta - \frac{\pi}{3}) = 3$        **66.** $r \cos(\theta - 1) = \sqrt{5}$

*In Exercises 67–74, graph the polar equations.*

**67.** (a) $r = 2 - 2\cos\theta$        **68.** (a) $r^2 = 4\cos 2\theta$
      (b) $r = 2 - 2\sin\theta$              (b) $r^2 = 4\sin 2\theta$

**69.** (a) $r = 2\cos\theta - 1$        **70.** (a) $r = 2\cos\theta$
      (b) $r = 2\sin\theta - 1$              (b) $r = 2\cos\theta + 1$

**71. (a)** $r = 4 \sin 2\theta$
**(b)** $r = 4 \cos 2\theta$
**72. (a)** $r = 4 \sin 3\theta$
**(b)** $r = 4 \cos 3\theta$
**73. (a)** $r = 1 + 2 \sin(\theta/2)$
**(b)** $r = 1 - 2 \cos(\theta/2)$
**74. (a)** $r = (1.5)^\theta$ $(\theta \geq 0)$
**(b)** $r = (1.5)^\theta$ $(\theta \leq 0)$

*In Exercises 75–80, graph the curve (or line) determined by the parametric equations. Indicate the direction of travel along the curve as t increases. You may do this by plotting points or by eliminating the parameter (or both). Unless indicated, the domain is all real numbers.*

**75.** $x = 3 - 5t, y = 1 + t$
**76.** $x = t - 1, y = 3t$
**77.** $x = 3 \sin t, y = 6 \cos t$
**78.** $x = 2 \cos t, y = 2 \sin t$
**79.** $x = 4 \sec t, y = 3 \tan t$ for $0 \leq t \leq 2\pi$, except $t = \pi/2$ and $t = 3\pi/2$
**80.** $x = 1 + 3 \cos t, y = 2 + 4 \sin t$
**81.** In the accompanying figure, $P$ and $Q$ are two points on the polar curve $r = (\sin \theta)/\theta$ such that $\angle AOP = \angle POQ$. Follow steps (a) through (f) to prove that $\overline{PQ} \perp \overline{OQ}$.

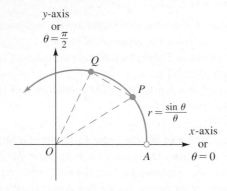

**(a)** Let $\alpha = \angle AOP = \angle POQ$. What are the polar coordinates of $P$ and $Q$ in terms of $\alpha$?
**(b)** What are the rectangular coordinates of $P$ and $Q$ in terms of $\alpha$?
**(c)** Using the coordinates determined in part (b), show that the slope of $\overline{OQ}$ is $\tan 2\alpha$.
**(d)** Using the coordinates determined in part (b), show that the slope of $\overline{PQ}$ is

$$\frac{\sin^2 2\alpha - 2 \sin^2 \alpha}{\sin 2\alpha \cos 2\alpha - 2 \sin \alpha \cos \alpha}$$

**(e)** Show that the expression in part (d) can be simplified to $-\cot 2\alpha$. *Hint:* In the numerator, replace $\sin^2 2\alpha$ by $1 - \cos^2 2\alpha$ and $\sin^2 \alpha$ by $\dfrac{1 - \cos 2\alpha}{2}$.

**(f)** Use the results in parts (c) and (e) to explain why $\overline{PQ} \perp \overline{OQ}$.

**82.** In this exercise you will use the following figure to derive the *Mollweide formula*:

$$\frac{a + b}{c} = \frac{\cos \frac{1}{2}(A - B)}{\sin \frac{1}{2}C}$$

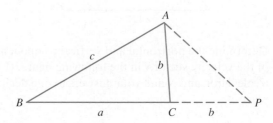

The figure is constructed as follows. Starting with $\triangle ABC$, extend side $\overline{BC}$ so that $CP = b$, as shown. Then draw line segment $\overline{AP}$.

**(a)** Show that $\angle APC = \angle PAC = \frac{1}{2}C$.
**(b)** Show that $\angle BAP = 90° + \frac{1}{2}(A - B)$. *Hint:* Start with the fact that $\angle BAP = A + \frac{1}{2}C$.
**(c)** Use the law of sines now in $\triangle ABP$ to show that

$$\frac{\sin[90° + \frac{1}{2}(A - B)]}{a + b} = \frac{\sin \frac{1}{2}C}{c}$$

**(d)** Use the result in part (c) to obtain the required identity.

**83.** In this exercise we use the law of sines to deduce the **law of tangents** for $\triangle ABC$:

$$\frac{a - b}{a + b} = \frac{\tan \frac{1}{2}(A - B)}{\tan \frac{1}{2}(A + B)}$$

This law was given by the Danish physician and mathematician Thomas Fink in his text *Geometria Rotundi*, published in Basel in 1583. (Our use of the terms "tangent" and "secant" is also due to Fink.)

**(a)** Suppose that $a, b, x,$ and $y$ are real numbers such that $\dfrac{a}{b} = \dfrac{x}{y}$. Verify that $\dfrac{a - b}{a + b} = \dfrac{x - y}{x + y}$.

**(b)** Use the law of sines and the result in part (a) to show that

$$\frac{a - b}{a + b} = \frac{\sin A - \sin B}{\sin A + \sin B}$$

**(c)** Use the result in part (a) and the sum-to-product formulas from Section 8.3 to complete the derivation of the law of tangents.

**84.** The following figure shows a sector of the unit circle $x^2 + y^2 = 1$. The central angle for the sector is $\alpha$ (a constant). The point $P(\cos \theta, \sin \theta)$ denotes an arbitrary point on the arc of the sector. From $P$, perpendiculars are drawn to the sides of the sector, meeting the sides at $Q$ and $R$, as shown. Show that the distance from $Q$ to $R$ does not depend on $\theta$.

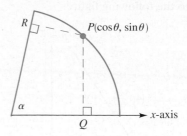

---

# Chapter 9      Test

1. In triangle $ABC$, let $A = 120°$, $b = 5$ cm, and $c = 3$ cm. Find $a$.

2. The sides of a triangle are 2 cm, 3 cm, and 4 cm. Determine the cosine of the angle opposite the longest side. On the basis of your answer, explain whether or not the angle opposite the longest side is an acute angle.

3. Two of the angles in a triangle are 30° and 45°. If the side opposite the 45° angle is $20\sqrt{2}$ cm, find the side opposite the 30° angle.

4. Each side of the square $STUV$ is 8 cm long. The point $P$ lies on diagonal $\overline{SU}$ such that $SP = 2$ cm. Find the distance from $P$ to $V$.

5. In $\triangle ABC$, $b = 5.8$ cm, $c = 3.2$ cm, and $A = 27°$. Find the remaining sides and angles of the triangle.

6. Two forces **F** and **G** act on an object. The force **G** acts horizontally with a magnitude of 2 N, and **F** acts vertically upward with a magnitude of 4 N.
   **(a)** Find the magnitude of the resultant.
   **(b)** Find $\tan \theta$, where $\theta$ is the angle between **G** and the resultant.

7. Two forces act on an object, as shown in the following figure.
   **(a)** Find the magnitude of the resultant. (Leave your answer in terms of radicals and the trigonometric functions.)
   **(b)** Find $\sin \theta$, where $\theta$ is the angle between the 12 N force and the resultant.

8. The heading and air speed of an airplane are 40° and 300 mph, respectively. If the wind is 50 mph from 130°, find the ground speed and the tangent of the drift angle. (Leave your answer in terms of radicals and the trigonometric functions.)

9. Let $\mathbf{A} = \langle 2, 4 \rangle$, $\mathbf{B} = \langle 3, -1 \rangle$, and $\mathbf{C} = \langle 4, -4 \rangle$.
   **(a)** Find $2\mathbf{A} + 3\mathbf{B}$.
   **(b)** Find $|2\mathbf{A} + 3\mathbf{B}|$.
   **(c)** Express $\mathbf{C} - \mathbf{B}$ in terms of **i** and **j**.

10. Let $P$ and $Q$ be the points $(4, 5)$ and $(-7, 2)$, respectively. Find a unit vector having the same direction as $\overrightarrow{PQ}$.

11. Convert the polar equation $r^2 = \cos 2\theta$ to rectangular form.

12. Graph the equation $r = 2(1 - \cos \theta)$.

13. Given the parametric equations $x = 4 \sin t$ and $y = 2 \cos t$, eliminate the parameter $t$ and sketch the graph.

14. Compute the distance between the two points with polar coordinates $(4, \frac{10\pi}{21}$ and $(1, \frac{\pi}{7})$.

**15.** Find a polar equation for the circle with center (in polar coordinates) $(5, \frac{\pi}{2})$ and with radius 2. Does the (polar) point $(2, \frac{\pi}{6})$ lie on this circle?

**16.** Refer to the following figure.

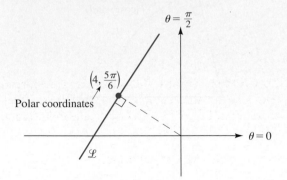

**(a)** Determine a polar equation for the line $\mathscr{L}$ in the figure.

**(b)** Use an addition formula to show that the polar equation of the line can be written $-r\sqrt{3}\cos\theta + r\sin\theta - 8 = 0$.

# A

# Appendix

## A.1   SIGNIFICANT DIGITS

Many of the numbers that we use in scientific work and in daily life are approximations. In some cases the approximations arise because the numbers are obtained through measurements or experiments. Consider, for example, the following statement from an astronomy textbook:

The diameter of the Moon is 3476 km.

We interpret this statement as meaning that the actual diameter $D$ is closer to 3476 km than it is to either 3475 km or 3477 km. In other words,

$$3475.5 \text{ km} \leq D \leq 3476.5 \text{ km}$$

The interval [3475.5, 3476.5] in this example provides information about the accuracy of the measurement. Another way to indicate accuracy in an approximation is by specifying the number of *significant digits* it contains. The measurement 3476 km has four significant digits. In general, the number of significant digits in a given number is found as follows.

---

### Significant Digits

The number of significant digits in a given number is determined by counting the digits from left to right, beginning with the leftmost nonzero digit.

EXAMPLES

| Number | Number of Significant Digits |
|--------|------------------------------|
| 1.43   | 3 |
| 0.52   | 2 |
| 0.05   | 1 |
| 4837   | 4 |
| 4837.0 | 5 |

---

Numbers obtained through measurements are not the only source of approximations in scientific work. For example, to five significant digits we have the following approximation for the irrational number $\pi$:

$$\pi \approx 3.1416$$

This statement tells us that $\pi$ is closer to 3.1416 than it is to either 3.1415 or 3.1417. In other words,

$$3.14155 \leq \pi \leq 3.14165$$

Table 1 provides some additional examples of the ideas we've introduced.

**TABLE 1**

| Number | Number of significant digits | Range of measurement |
|---|---|---|
| 37 | 2 | [36.5, 37.5] |
| 37.0 | 3 | [36.95, 37.05] |
| 268.1 | 4 | [268.05, 268.15] |
| 1.036 | 4 | [1.0355, 1.0365] |
| 0.036 | 2 | [0.0355, 0.0365] |

There is an ambiguity involving zero that can arise in counting significant digits. Suppose that someone measures the width $w$ of a rectangle and reports the result as 30 cm. How many significant digits are there? If the value 30 cm was obtained by measuring to the nearest 10 cm, then only the digit 3 is significant, and we can conclude only that the width $w$ lies in the range 25 cm $\leq w \leq$ 35 cm. On the other hand, if the 30 cm was obtained by measuring to the nearest 1 cm, then both the digits 3 and 0 are significant, and we have 29.5 cm $\leq w \leq$ 30.5 cm.

By using **scientific notation,** we can avoid the type of ambiguity discussed in the previous paragraph. A number written in the form

$$b \times 10^n \qquad \text{where } 1 \leq b < 10 \text{ and } n \text{ is an integer}$$

is said to be expressed in scientific notation. For the example in the previous paragraph, then, we would write

$$w = 3 \times 10^1 \text{ cm} \qquad \text{if the measurement is to the nearest 10 cm}$$

and

$$w = 3.0 \times 10^1 \text{ cm} \qquad \text{if the measurement is to the nearest 1 cm}$$

As the figures in Table 2 indicate, for a number $b \times 10^n$ in scientific notation the number of significant digits is just the number of digits in $b$. (This is one of the advantages in using scientific notation; the number of significant digits, and hence the accuracy of the measurement, is readily apparent.)

**TABLE 2**

| Measurement | Number of significant digits | Range of measurement |
|---|---|---|
| Mass of the Earth: | | |
| $6 \times 10^{27}$ g | 1 | [$5.5 \times 10^{27}$ g, $6.5 \times 10^{27}$ g] |
| $6.0 \times 10^{27}$ g | 2 | [$5.95 \times 10^{27}$ g, $6.05 \times 10^{27}$ g] |
| $5.974 \times 10^{27}$ g | 4 | [$5.9735 \times 10^{27}$ g, $5.9745 \times 10^{27}$ g] |
| Mass of a proton: | | |
| $1.67 \times 10^{-24}$ g | 3 | [$1.665 \times 10^{-24}$ g, $1.675 \times 10^{-24}$ g] |

Many of the numerical exercises in the text ask that you round the answers to a specified number of decimal places. Our rules for rounding are as follows.

**Rules for Rounding a Number (with more than *n* Decimal Places) to *n* Decimal Places**

1. If the digit in the $(n + 1)$st decimal place is greater than 5, increase the digit in the *n*th place by 1. If the digit in the $(n + 1)$st place is less than 5, leave the *n*th digit unchanged.
2. If the digit in the $(n + 1)$st decimal place is 5 and there is at least one nonzero digit to the right of this 5, increase the digit in the *n*th decimal place by 1.
3. If the digit in the $(n + 1)$st decimal place is 5 and there are no nonzero digits to the right of this 5, then increase the digit in the *n*th decimal place by 1 only if this results in an even digit.

The examples in Table 3 illustrate the use of these rules.

**▌ TABLE 3**

| Number | Rounded to one decimal place | Rounded to three decimal places |
|---|---|---|
| 4.3742 | 4.4 | 4.374 |
| 2.0515 | 2.1 | 2.052 |
| 2.9925 | 3.0 | 2.992 |

These same rules can be adapted for rounding a result to a specified number of significant digits. As examples of this, we have

2347    rounded to two significant digits is $2300 = 2.3 \times 10^3$

2347    rounded to three significant digits is $2350 = 2.35 \times 10^3$

975    rounded to two significant digits is $980 - 9.8 \times 10^2$

0.985    rounded to two significant digits is $0.98 = 9.8 \times 10^{-1}$

In calculator exercises that ask you to round your answers, it's important that you postpone rounding until the final calculation is carried out. For example, suppose that you are required to determine the hypotenuse *x* of the right triangle in Figure 1 to two significant digits. Using the Pythagorean theorem, we have

$$x = \sqrt{(1.36)^2 + (2.46)^2}$$

$$= 2.8 \qquad \text{using a calculator and rounding the}$$
$$\text{final result to two significant digits}$$

**Figure 1**

On the other hand, if we first round each of the given lengths to two significant digits, we obtain

$$x = \sqrt{(1.4)^2 + (2.5)^2}$$

$$= 2.9 \qquad \text{to two significant digits}$$

This last result is inappropriate, and we can see why as follows. As Table 4 shows, the maximum possible values for the sides are 1.365 and 2.465, respectively.

**▌ TABLE 4**

| Number | Range of measurement |
|---|---|
| 1.36 | [1.355, 1.365] |
| 2.46 | [2.455, 2.465] |

Thus the maximum possible value for the hypotenuse must be

$$\sqrt{(1.365)^2 + (2.465)^2} = 2.817\ldots \qquad \text{calculator display}$$
$$= 2.8 \qquad \text{to two significant digits}$$

This shows that the value 2.9 is indeed inappropriate, as we stated previously.

An error that is often made by people working with calculators and approximations is to report a final answer with a greater degree of accuracy than the data warrant. Consider, for example, the right triangle in Figure 2. Using the Pythagorean theorem and a calculator with an eight-digit display, we obtain

$$h = 3.6055513 \text{ cm}$$

This value for $h$ is inappropriate, because common sense tells us that the answer should be no more accurate than the data used to obtain that answer. In particular, since the given sides of the triangle apparently were measured only to the nearest tenth of a centimeter, we certainly should not expect any improvement in accuracy for the resulting value of the hypotenuse. An appropriate form for the value of $h$ here would be $h = 3.6$ cm. In general, for calculator exercises in this text that do not specify a required number of decimal places or significant digits in the final results, you should use the following guidelines.

**Figure 2**

---

### Guidelines for Computing with Approximations

1. *For adding and subtracting:* Round the final result so that it contains only as many decimal places as there are in the data with the fewest decimal places.
2. *For multiplying and dividing:* Round the final result so that it contains only as many significant digits as there are in the data with the fewest significant digits.
3. *For powers and roots:* In computing a power or a root of a real number $b$, round the result so that it contains as many significant digits as there are in $b$.

---

## A.2   PROPERTIES OF THE REAL NUMBERS

Today's familiar plus and minus signs were first used in 15th-century Germany as warehouse marks. They indicated when a container held something that weighed over or under a certain standard weight. —Martin Gardner in "Mathematical Games" (*Scientific American,* June 1977)

*I do not like $\times$ as a symbol for multiplication, as it is easily confounded with x; ... often I simply relate two quantities by an interposed dot. ... —G. W. Leibniz in a letter dated July 29, 1698*

In this section we will first list the basic properties for the real number system. Then we will use those properties to prove the familiar rules of algebra for working with signed numbers.

The set of real numbers is **closed** with respect to the operations of addition and multiplication. This means that when we add or multiply two real numbers, the result (that is, the **sum** or the **product**) is again a real number. Some of the other most basic properties and definitions for the real-number system are listed in the following box. In the box, the lowercase letters $a$, $b$, and $c$ denote arbitrary real numbers.

## PROPERTY SUMMARY Some Fundamental Properties of the Real Numbers

| | |
|---|---|
| Commutative properties | $a + b = b + a \qquad ab = ba$ |
| Associative properties | $a + (b + c) = (a + b) + c \qquad a(bc) = (ab)c$ |

Identity properties

1. There is a unique real number 0 (called **zero** or the **additive identity**) such that
$$a + 0 = a \qquad \text{and} \qquad 0 + a = a$$

2. There is a unique real number 1 (called **one** or the **multiplicative identity**) such that
$$a \cdot 1 = a \qquad \text{and} \qquad 1 \cdot a = a$$

Inverse properties

1. For each real number $a$ there is a real number $-a$ (called the **additive inverse** of $a$ or the **opposite** of $a$) such that
$$a + (-a) = 0 \qquad \text{and} \qquad (-a) + a = 0$$

2. For each real number $a \neq 0$ there is a real number denoted by $\dfrac{1}{a}$ (or $1/a$ or $a^{-1}$) and called the **multiplicative inverse** or **reciprocal** of $a$, such that
$$a \cdot \frac{1}{a} = 1 \qquad \text{and} \qquad \frac{1}{a} \cdot a = 1$$

| | |
|---|---|
| Distributive properties | $a(b + c) = ab + ac \qquad (b + c)a = ba + ca$ |

On reading this list of properties for the first time, many students ask the natural question, "Why do we even bother to list such obvious properties?" One reason is that all the other laws of arithmetic and algebra (including the not-so-obvious ones) can be derived from our rather short list. For example, the rule $0 \cdot a = 0$ can be proved by using the distributive property, as can the rule that the product of two negative numbers is a positive number. We now state and prove those properties and several others.

### THEOREM

Let $a$ and $b$ be real numbers. Then

(a) $a \cdot 0 = 0$  (c) $-(-a) = a$  (e) $(-a)(-b) = ab$
(b) $-a = (-1)a$  (d) $a(-b) = -ab$

### Proof of Part (a)

$$a \cdot 0 = a \cdot (0 + 0) \qquad \text{additive identity property}$$
$$a \cdot 0 = a \cdot 0 + a \cdot 0 \qquad \text{distributive property}$$

Now since $a \cdot 0$ is a real number, it has an additive inverse, $-(a \cdot 0)$. Adding this to both sides of the last equation, we obtain

$$a \cdot 0 + [-(a \cdot 0)] = (a \cdot 0 + a \cdot 0) + [-(a \cdot 0)]$$
$$a \cdot 0 + [-(a \cdot 0)] = a \cdot 0 + \{a \cdot 0 + [-(a \cdot 0)]\} \qquad \text{associative property of addition}$$
$$0 = a \cdot 0 + 0 \qquad \text{additive inverse property}$$
$$0 = a \cdot 0 \qquad \text{additive identity property}$$

Thus $a \cdot 0 = 0$, as we wished to show.

### Proof of Part (b)

$$0 = 0 \cdot a \qquad \text{using part (a) and the commutative of multiplication}$$
$$= [1 + (-1)]a \qquad \text{additive inverse property}$$
$$= 1 \cdot a + (-1)a \qquad \text{distributive property}$$
$$= a + (-1)a \qquad \text{multiplicative identity property}$$

Now, by adding $-a$ to both sides of this last equation, we obtain

$$-a + 0 = -a + [a + (-1)a]$$
$$-a = (-a + a) + (-1)a \qquad \text{additive identity property and associative property of addition}$$
$$-a = 0 + (-1)a \qquad \text{additive inverse property}$$
$$-a = (-1)a \qquad \text{additive identity property}$$

This last equation asserts that $-a = (-1)a$, as we wished to show.

### Proof of Part (c)

$$-(-a) + (-a) = 0 \qquad \text{additive inverse property}$$

By adding $a$ to both sides of this last equation, we obtain

$$[-(-a) + (-a)] + a = 0 + a$$
$$-(-a) + (-a + a) = a \qquad \text{associative property of addition and additive identity property}$$
$$-(-a) + 0 = a \qquad \text{additive inverse property}$$
$$-(-a) = a \qquad \text{additive identity property}$$

This last equation states that $-(-a) = a$, as we wished to show.

### Proof of Part (d)

$$a(-b) = a[(-1)b] \qquad \text{using part (b)}$$
$$= [a(-1)]b \qquad \text{associative property of multiplication}$$
$$= [(-1)a]b \qquad \text{commutative property of multiplication}$$
$$= (-1)(ab) \qquad \text{associative property of multiplication}$$
$$= -(ab) \qquad \text{using part (b)}$$

Thus $a(-b) = -ab$, as we wished to show.

### Proof of Part (e)

$$(-a)(-b) = -[(-a)b] \qquad \text{using part (d)}$$
$$= -[b(-a)] \qquad \text{commutative property of multiplication}$$
$$= -[-(ba)] \qquad \text{using part (d)}$$
$$= ba \qquad \text{using part (c)}$$
$$= ab \qquad \text{commutative property of multiplication}$$

We've now shown that $(-a)(-b) = ab$, as required.

# A.3   $\sqrt{2}$ IS IRRATIONAL

*The proof is by* reductio ad absurdum, *and* reductio ad absurdum,
*which Euclid loved so much, is one
of a mathematician's finest weapons.*
—G. H. Hardy (1877–1947)

We will use an *indirect proof* to show that the square root of 2 is an irrational number. The strategy is as follows:

1. We suppose that $\sqrt{2}$ is a rational number.
2. Using (1) and the usual rules of logic and algebra, we derive a contradiction.
3. On the basis of the contradiction in (2), we conclude that the supposition in (1) is untenable; that is, we conclude that $\sqrt{2}$ is irrational.

In carrying out the proof, we'll assume that the following three statements are known:

If $x$ is an even natural number, then $x = 2k$ for some natural number $k$.

Any rational number can be written in the form $a/b$, where the integers $a$ and $b$ have no common integral factors other than $\pm 1$. (In other words, any fraction can be reduced to lowest terms.)

If $x$ is a natural number and $x^2$ is even, then $x$ is even.

Our indirect proof now proceeds as follows. Suppose that $\sqrt{2}$ is a rational number. Then we can write

$$\sqrt{2} = \frac{a}{b} \qquad \text{where } a \text{ and } b \text{ are natural numbers with} \qquad (1)$$
$$\text{no common factor other than 1}$$

Since both sides of equation (1) are positive, we can square both sides to obtain the equation

$$2 = \frac{a^2}{b^2}$$

or

$$2b^2 = a^2 \qquad (2)$$

Since the left-hand side of equation (2) is an even number, the right-hand side must also be even. But if $a^2$ is even, then $a$ is even, and so

$$a = 2k \qquad \text{for some natural number } k$$

Using this last equation to substitute for $a$ in equation (2), we have

$$2b^2 = (2k)^2 = 4k^2$$

or

$$b^2 = 2k^2$$

Hence (reasoning as before) $b^2$ is even, and therefore $b$ is even. But then we have that both $b$ and $a$ are even, contrary to our hypothesis that $b$ and $a$ have no common factor other than 1. We conclude from this that equation (1) cannot hold; that is, there is no rational number $a/b$ such that $\sqrt{2} = a/b$. Thus $\sqrt{2}$ is irrational, as we wished to prove.

# B Appendix

## B.1 REVIEW OF INTEGER EXPONENTS

*I write $a^{-1}, a^{-2}, a^{-3}$, etc., for $\frac{1}{a}, \frac{1}{aa}, \frac{1}{aaa}$, etc.* —Isaac Newton (June 13, 1676)

In basic algebra you learned the exponential notation $a^n$, where $a$ is a real number and $n$ is a natural number. Because that definition is basic to all that follows in this and the next two sections of this appendix, we repeat it here.

---

### DEFINITION 1 | Base and Exponent

Given a real number $a$ and a natural number $n$, we define $a^n$ by

$$a^n = \underbrace{a \cdot a \cdot a \cdots a}_{n \text{ factors}}$$

In the expression $a^n$ the number $a$ is the **base,** and $n$ is the **exponent** or **power** to which the base is raised.

---

---

### EXAMPLE 1 | Using algebraic notation

Rewrite each expression using algebraic notation:
**(a)** $x$ to the fourth power, plus five;
**(b)** the fourth power of the quantity $x$ plus five;
**(c)** $x$ plus $y$, to the fourth power;
**(d)** $x$ plus $y$ to the fourth power.

**SOLUTION**
**(a)** $x^4 + 5$      **(b)** $(x + 5)^4$      **(c)** $(x + y)^4$      **(d)** $x + y^4$

---

CAUTION   Note that parts (c) and (d) of Example 1 differ only in the use of the comma. So for spoken purposes the idea in (c) would be more clearly conveyed by saying "the fourth power of the quantity $x$ plus $y$." In the case of (d), if you read it aloud to another student or your instructor, chances are you'll be asked, "Do you mean $x + y^4$ or do you mean $(x + y)^4$?"

MORAL   Algebra is a precise language; use it carefully. Learn to ask yourself whether what you've written will be interpreted in the manner you intended.

In basic algebra the four properties in the following box are developed for working with exponents that are natural numbers. Each of these properties is a direct consequence of the definition of $a^n$. For instance, according to the first property, we have $a^2a^3 = a^5$. To verify that this is indeed correct, we note that

$$a^2a^3 = (aa)(aaa) = a^5$$

## PROPERTY SUMMARY   Properties of Exponents

| Property | Examples |
|---|---|
| 1. $a^m a^n = a^{m+n}$ | $a^5 a^6 = a^{11}$; $(x + 1)(x + 1)^2 = (x + 1)^3$ |
| 2. $(a^m)^n = a^{mn}$ | $(2^3)^4 = 2^{12}$; $[(x + 1)^2]^3 = (x + 1)^6$ |
| 3. $\dfrac{a^m}{a^n} = \begin{cases} a^{m-n} & \text{if } m > n \\ \dfrac{1}{a^{n-m}} & \text{if } m < n \\ 1 & \text{if } m = n \end{cases}$ | $\dfrac{a^6}{a^2} = a^4$; $\dfrac{a^2}{a^6} = \dfrac{1}{a^4}$; $\dfrac{a^5}{a^5} = 1$ |
| 4. $(ab)^m = a^m b^m$; $\left(\dfrac{a}{b}\right)^m = \dfrac{a^m}{b^m}$ | $(2x^2)^3 = 2^3 \cdot (x^2)^3 = 8x^6$; $\left(\dfrac{x^2}{y^3}\right)^4 = \dfrac{x^8}{y^{12}}$ |

Of course, we assume that all of these expressions make sense; in particular, we assume that no denominator of a fraction is zero.

Now we want to extend our definition of $a^n$ to allow for exponents that are integers but not necessarily natural numbers. We begin by defining $a^0$.

---

**DEFINITION 2** | **Zero Exponent**

For any nonzero real number $a$,

$$a^0 = 1$$

($0^0$ is not defined.)

**EXAMPLES**

(a) $2^0 = 1$

(b) $(-\pi)^0 = 1$

(c) $\left(\dfrac{3}{1 + a^2 + b^2}\right)^n = 1$

---

It's easy to see the motivation for defining $a^0$ to be 1. Assuming that the exponent zero is to have the same properties as exponents that are natural numbers, we can write

$$a^0 a^n = a^{0+n}$$

That is,

$$a^0 a^n = a^n$$

Now we divide both sides of this last equation by $a^n$ to obtain $a^0 = 1$, which agrees with our definition.

Our next definition (see the box that follows) assigns a meaning to the expression $a^{-n}$ when $n$ is a natural number. Again, it's easy to see the motivation for this definition. We would like to have

$$a^n a^{-n} = a^{n+(-n)} = a^0 = 1$$

That is,

$$a^n a^{-n} = 1$$

Now we divide both sides of this last equation by $a^n$ to obtain $a^{-n} = 1/a^n$, in agreement with Definition 3.

---

**DEFINITION 3**  |  Negative Exponent

For any nonzero real number $a$ and natural number $n$,

$$a^{-n} = \frac{1}{a^n}$$

**EXAMPLES**

(a) $2^{-1} = \dfrac{1}{2^1} = \dfrac{1}{2}$

(b) $\left(\dfrac{1}{10}\right)^{-1} = \dfrac{1}{(\frac{1}{10})^1} = 10$

(c) $x^{-2} = \dfrac{1}{x^2}$

(d) $(a^2b)^{-3} = \dfrac{1}{(a^2b)^3} = \dfrac{1}{a^6b^3}$

(e) $\dfrac{1}{2^{-3}} = \dfrac{1}{1/2^3} = 2^3 = 8$

---

It can be shown that the four properties of exponents that we listed earlier continue to hold now for all integer exponents. We make use of this fact in the next three examples.

**EXAMPLE** 2  **Using properties of exponents**

Simplify the following expression. Write the answer in such a way that only positive exponents appear.

$$(a^2b^3)^2(a^5b)^{-1}$$

**SOLUTION**

FIRST METHOD

$$(a^2b^3)^2(a^5b)^{-1} = (a^2b^3)^2 \cdot \frac{1}{a^5b}$$

$$= \frac{a^4b^6}{a^5b} = \frac{b^{6-1}}{a^{5-4}} = \frac{b^5}{a}$$

ALTERNATIVE METHOD

$$(a^2b^3)^2(a^5b)^{-1} = (a^4b^6)(a^{-5}b^{-1})$$

$$= a^{4-5}b^{6-1} = a^{-1}b^5$$

$$= \frac{b^5}{a} \quad \text{as obtained} \atop \text{previously}$$

---

**EXAMPLE** 3  **Using properties of exponents**

Simplify the following expression, writing the answer so that negative exponents are not used.

$$\left(\frac{a^{-5}b^2c^0}{a^3b^{-1}}\right)^3$$

**SOLUTION**
We show two solutions. The first makes immediate use of the property $(a^m)^n = a^{mn}$. In the second solution we begin by working within the parentheses.

FIRST SOLUTION

$$\left(\frac{a^{-5}b^2c^0}{a^3b^{-1}}\right)^3 = \frac{a^{-15}b^6}{a^9b^{-3}}$$

$$= \frac{b^{6-(-3)}}{a^{9-(-15)}} = \frac{b^9}{a^{24}}$$

ALTERNATIVE SOLUTION

$$\left(\frac{a^{-5}b^2c^0}{a^3b^{-1}}\right)^3 = \left(\frac{b^3}{a^8}\right)^3$$

$$= \frac{b^9}{a^{24}}$$

 **EXAMPLE** 4 **Simplifying with variable exponents**

Simplify the following expressions, writing the answers so that negative exponents are not used. (Assume that $p$ and $q$ are natural numbers.)

(a) $\dfrac{a^{4p+q}}{a^{p-q}}$    (b) $(a^p b^q)^2 (a^{3p} b^{-q})^{-1}$

**SOLUTION**

(a) $\dfrac{a^{4p+q}}{a^{p-q}} = a^{4p+q-(p-q)}$

$$= a^{4p+q-p+q} = a^{3p+2q}$$

(b) $(a^p b^q)^2 (a^{3p} b^{-q})^{-1} = (a^{2p} b^{2q})(a^{-3p} b^q)$

$$= a^{-p} b^{3q}$$

$$= \frac{b^{3q}}{a^p}$$

 **EXAMPLE** 5 **Simplifying numerical quantities involving exponents**

Use the properties of exponents to compute the quantity $\dfrac{2^{10} \cdot 3^{13}}{27 \cdot 6^{12}}$.

**SOLUTION**

$$\frac{2^{10} \cdot 3^{13}}{27 \cdot 6^{12}} = \frac{2^{10} \cdot 3^{13}}{(3^3)(3 \cdot 2)^{12}}$$

$$= \frac{2^{10} \cdot 3^{13}}{3^3 \cdot 3^{12} \cdot 2^{12}} = \frac{2^{10} \cdot 3^{13}}{3^{15} \cdot 2^{12}}$$

$$= \frac{1}{(3^{15-13})(2^{12-10})} = \frac{1}{3^2 \cdot 2^2} = \frac{1}{36}$$

As an application of some of the ideas in this section, we briefly discuss **scientific notation,** which is a convenient form for writing very large or very small numbers. Such numbers occur often in the sciences. For instance, the speed of light in a vacuum is

$$29{,}979{,}000{,}000 \text{ cm/sec}$$

As written, this number would be awkward to work with in calculating. In fact, the number as written cannot even be displayed on some hand-held calculators, because there are too many digits. To write the number 29,979,000,000 (or any positive number) in scientific notation, we express it as a number between 1 and 10, multiplied by an appropriate power of 10. That is, we write it in the form

$$a \times 10^n \quad \text{where } 1 \le a < 10 \text{ and } n \text{ is an integer}$$

According to this convention, the number $4.03 \times 10^6$ is in scientific notation, but the same quantity written as $40.3 \times 10^5$ is not in scientific notation. To convert a given number into scientific notation, we'll rely on the following two-step procedure.

---

## To Express a Number Using Scientific Notation

1. First move the decimal point until it is to the immediate right of the first nonzero digit.
2. Then multiply by $10^n$ or $10^{-n}$, depending on whether the decimal point was moved $n$ places to the left or to the right, respectively.

---

For example, to express the number 29,979,000,000 in scientific notation, first we move the decimal point 10 places to the left so that it's located between the 2 and the 9, then we multiply by $10^{10}$. The result is

$$29{,}979{,}000{,}000 = 2.9979000000 \times 10^{10}$$

or, more simply,

$$29{,}979{,}000{,}000 = 2.9979 \times 10^{10}$$

As additional examples we list the following numbers expressed in both ordinary and scientific notation. For practice, you should verify each conversion for yourself using our two-step procedure.

$$55{,}708 = 5.5708 \times 10^4$$

$$0.000099 = 9.9 \times 10^{-5}$$

$$0.0000002 = 2 \times 10^{-7}$$

All scientific calculators have keys for entering numbers in scientific notation. (Indeed, many calculators will convert numbers into scientific notation for you.) If you have questions about how your own calculator operates with respect to scientific notation, you should consult the user's manual. We'll indicate only one example here, using a Texas Instruments graphing calculator. The keystrokes on other brands are quite similar. Consider the following number expressed in scientific notation: $3.159 \times 10^{20}$. (This gargantuan number is the diameter, in miles, of a galaxy at the center of a distant star cluster known as Abell 2029.) The sequence of keystrokes for entering this number on the Texas Instruments calculator is

$$3.519 \quad \boxed{\text{EE}} \quad 20$$

# EXERCISE SET B.1

## A

*In Exercises 1–4, evaluate each expression using the given value of x.*

**1.** $2x^3 - x + 4$; $x = -2$

**2.** $1 - x + 2x^2 - 3x^3$; $x = -1$

**3.** $\dfrac{1 - 2x^2}{1 + 2x^3}$; $x = -\dfrac{1}{2}$

**4.** $\dfrac{1 - (x - 1)^2}{1 + (x - 1)^2}$; $x = -1$

*In Exercises 5–16, use the properties of exponents to simplify each expression.*

**5.** (a) $a^3 a^{12}$
(b) $(a + 1)^3 (a + 1)^{12}$
(c) $(a + 1)^{12}(a + 1)^3$

**6.** (a) $(3^2)^3 - (2^3)^2$
(b) $(x^2)^3 - (x^3)^2$
(c) $(x^2)^a - (x^a)^2$

**7.** (a) $yy^2 y^8$
(b) $(y + 1)(y + 1)^2(y + 1)^8$
(c) $[(y + 1)(y + 1)^8]^2$

**8.** (a) $\dfrac{x^{12}}{x^{10}}$
(b) $\dfrac{x^{10}}{x^{12}}$
(c) $\dfrac{2^{10}}{2^{12}}$

**9.** (a) $\dfrac{(x^2 + 3)^{10}}{(x^2 + 3)^9}$
(b) $\dfrac{(x^2 + 3)^9}{(x^2 + 3)^{10}}$
(c) $\dfrac{12^{10}}{12^9}$

**10.** (a) $(y^2 y^3)^2$
(b) $y^2(y^3)^2$
(c) $2^m(2^n)^2$

**11.** (a) $\dfrac{t^{15}}{t^9}$
(b) $\dfrac{t^9}{t^{15}}$
(c) $\dfrac{(t^2 + 3)^{15}}{(t^2 + 3)^9}$

**12.** (a) $\dfrac{x^6}{x}$
(b) $\dfrac{x}{x^6}$
(c) $\dfrac{(x^2 + 3x - 2)^6}{x^2 + 3x - 2}$

**13.** (a) $\dfrac{x^6 y^{15}}{x^2 y^{20}}$
(b) $\dfrac{x^2 y^{20}}{x^6 y^{15}}$
(c) $\left(\dfrac{x^2 y^{20}}{x^6 y^{15}}\right)^2$

**14.** (a) $(x^2 y^3 z)^4$
(b) $2(x^2 y^3 z)^4$
(c) $(2x^2 y^3 z)^4$

**15.** (a) $4(x^3)^2$
(b) $(4x^3)^2$
(c) $\dfrac{(4x^2)^3}{(4x^3)^2}$

**16.** (a) $2(x - 1)^7 - (x - 1)^7$
(b) $[2(x - 1)]^7 - (x - 1)^7$
(c) $2(x - 1)^7 - [2(x - 1)]^7$

*For Exercises 17–38, simplify each expression. Write the answers in such a way that negative exponents do not appear. In Exercises 35–38, assume that the letters p and q represent natural numbers.*

**17.** (a) $64^0$
(b) $(64^3)^0$
(c) $(64^0)^3$

**18.** (a) $2^0 + 3^0$
(b) $(2^0 + 3^0)^3$
(c) $(2^3 + 3^3)^0$

**19.** (a) $10^{-1} + 10^{-2}$
(b) $(10^{-1} + 10^{-2})^{-1}$
(c) $[(10^{-1})(10^{-2})]^{-1}$

**20.** (a) $4^{-2} + 4^{-1}$
(b) $[(\tfrac{1}{4})^{-1} + (\tfrac{1}{4})^{-2}]^{-1}$
(c) $[(\tfrac{1}{4})^{-1}(\tfrac{1}{4})^{-2}]^{-1}$

**21.** $(\tfrac{1}{3})^{-1} + (\tfrac{1}{4})^{-1}$

**22.** $(\tfrac{1}{3} + \tfrac{1}{4})^{-1}$

**23.** (a) $5^{-2} + 10^{-2}$
(b) $(5 + 10)^{-2}$

**24.** (a) $(\tfrac{1}{4})^{-2} + (\tfrac{3}{4})^{-2}$
(b) $(\tfrac{1}{4} + \tfrac{3}{4})^{-2}$

**25.** $(a^2 bc^0)^{-3}$

**26.** $(a^3 b)^3(a^2 b^4)^{-1}$

**27.** $(a^{-2} b^{-1} c^3)^{-2}$

**28.** $(2^{-2} + 2^{-1} + 2^0)^{-2}$

**29.** $\left(\dfrac{x^3 y^{-2} z}{xy^2 z^{-3}}\right)^{-3}$

**30.** $\left(\dfrac{x^4 y^{-8} z^2}{xy^2 z^{-6}}\right)^2$

**31.** $\left(\dfrac{x^4 y^{-8} z^2}{xy^2 z^{-6}}\right)^{-2}$

**32.** $\left(\dfrac{a^3 b^{-9} c^2}{a^5 b^2 c^{-4}}\right)^0$

**33.** $\dfrac{x^2}{y^{-3}} \div \dfrac{x^2}{y^3}$

**34.** $(2x^2)^{-3} - 2(x^2)^{-3}$

**35.** $\dfrac{b^{p+1}}{b^p}$

**36.** $\dfrac{b^{p+2q}}{(b^2)^q}$

**37.** $(x^p)(x^p)$

**38.** $(2^{p-q})(2^{q-p+1})$

*In Exercises 39–42, use the properties of exponents in computing each quantity, as in Example 5. (The point here is to do as little arithmetic as possible.)*

**39.** $\dfrac{2^8 \cdot 3^{15}}{9 \cdot 3^{10} \cdot 12}$

**40.** $\dfrac{2^{12} \cdot 5^{13}}{10^{12}}$

**41.** $\dfrac{24^5}{32 \cdot 12^4}$

**42.** $\left(\dfrac{144 \cdot 125}{2^3 \cdot 3^2}\right)^{-1}$

*For Exercises 43–50, express each number in scientific notation.*

**43.** The average distance (in miles) from Earth to the Sun:

92,900,000

**44.** The average distance (in miles) from the planet Pluto to the Sun:

3,666,000,000

**45.** The average orbital speed (in miles per hour) of Earth:

66,800

**46.** The average orbital speed (in miles per hour) of the planet Mercury:

107,300

**47.** The average distance (in miles) from the Sun to the nearest star:

25,000,000,000,000,000,000

**48.** The equatorial diameter (in miles) of
(a) Mercury: 3031
(b) Earth: 7927
(c) Jupiter: 88,733
(d) the Sun: 865,000

**49.** The time (in seconds) for light to travel
   **(a)** one foot:

   0.000000001

   **(b)** across an atom:

   0.000000000000000001

   **(c)** across the nucleus of an atom:

   0.000000000000000000000001

**50.** The mass (in grams) of
   **(a)** a proton:

   0.00000000000000000000000167

   **(b)** an electron:

   0.000000000000000000000000000911

---

*Hindu mathematicians first recognized negative roots, and the two square roots of a positive number, . . . though they were suspicious also.* —David Wells in *The Penguin Dictionary of Curious and Interesting Numbers* (Harmondsworth, Middlesex, England: Penguin Books, Ltd., 1986)

## B.2  REVIEW OF *n*TH ROOTS

In this section we generalize the notion of square root that you studied in elementary algebra. The new idea is that of an *n*th root; the definition and some basic examples are given in the box that follows.

| **DEFINITION 1** | *n*th Roots |
| --- | --- |

Let *n* be a natural number. If *a* and *b* are real numbers and

$$a^n = b$$

then we say that *a* is an ***n*th root** of *b*. When $n = 2$ and when $n = 3$, we refer to the roots as **square roots** and **cube roots,** respectively.

**EXAMPLES**

Both 3 and −3 are square roots of 9 because $3^2 = 9$ and $(-3)^2 = 9$.

Both 2 and −2 are fourth roots of 16 because $2^4 = 16$ and $(-2)^4 = 16$.

2 is a cube root of 8 because $2^3 = 8$.

−3 is a fifth root of −243 because $(-3)^5 = -243$.

As the examples in the box suggest, square roots, fourth roots, and all *even* roots of positive numbers occur in pairs, one positive and one negative. In these cases we use the notation $\sqrt[n]{b}$ to denote the positive, or **principal,** *n*th root of *b*. As examples of this notation, we can write

$$\sqrt[4]{81} = 3 \qquad \text{(The principal fourth root of 81 is 3.)}$$

$$\sqrt[4]{81} \neq -3 \qquad \text{(The principal fourth root of 81 is not } -3.\text{)}$$

$$-\sqrt[4]{81} = -3 \qquad \text{(The negative of the principal fourth root of 81 is } -3.\text{)}$$

The symbol $\sqrt{\phantom{x}}$ is called a **radical sign,** and the number within the radical sign is the **radicand.** The natural number *n* used in the notation $\sqrt[n]{\phantom{x}}$ is called the **index** of the radical. For square roots, as you know from basic algebra, we suppress the index and simply write $\sqrt{\phantom{x}}$ rather than $\sqrt[2]{\phantom{x}}$. So, for example, $\sqrt{25} = 5$.

On the other hand, as we saw in the examples, cube roots, fifth roots, and in fact, all *odd* roots occur singly, not in pairs. In these cases, we again use the notation $\sqrt[n]{b}$ for the *n*th root. The definition and examples in the following box summarize our discussion up to this point.

| DEFINITION 2 | Principal *n*th Root |
|---|---|

1. Let $n$ be a natural number. If $a$ and $b$ are nonnegative real numbers, then

$$\sqrt[n]{b} = a \quad \text{if and only if} \quad b = a^n$$

The number $a$ is the **principal *n*th root** of $b$.

2. If $a$ and $b$ are negative and $n$ is an odd natural number, then

$$\sqrt[n]{b} = a \quad \text{if and only if} \quad b = a^n$$

**EXAMPLES**

$$\sqrt{25} = 5; \; \sqrt{25} \neq -5; \; -\sqrt{25} = -5$$

$$\sqrt[4]{\frac{1}{16}} = \frac{1}{2}; \; \sqrt[3]{8} = 2$$

$$\sqrt[5]{-\frac{1}{32}} = -\frac{1}{2}$$

There are five properties of $n$th roots that are frequently used in simplifying certain expressions. The first four are similar to the properties of square roots that are developed in elementary algebra. For reference we list these properties side by side in the following box. Property 5 is listed here only for the sake of completeness; we'll postpone discussing it until Appendix B.3.

**▌PROPERTY SUMMARY   Properties of *n*th Roots**

Suppose that $x$ and $y$ are real numbers and that $m$ and $n$ are natural numbers. Then each of the following properties holds, provided only that the expressions on both sides of the equation are defined (and so represent real numbers).

CORRESPONDING PROPERTIES FOR SQUARE ROOTS

1. $(\sqrt[n]{x})^n = x$    $(\sqrt{x})^2 = x$

2. $\sqrt[n]{xy} = \sqrt[n]{x}\sqrt[n]{y}$    $\sqrt{xy} = \sqrt{x}\sqrt{y}$

3. $\sqrt[n]{\dfrac{x}{y}} = \dfrac{\sqrt[n]{x}}{\sqrt[n]{y}}$    $\sqrt{\dfrac{x}{y}} = \dfrac{\sqrt{x}}{\sqrt{y}}$

4. $n$ even: $\sqrt[n]{x^n} = |x|$    $\sqrt{x^2} = |x|$

   $n$ odd: $\sqrt[n]{x^n} = x$

5. $\sqrt[m]{\sqrt[n]{x}} = \sqrt[mn]{x}$

Our immediate use for these properties will be in simplifying expressions involving $n$th roots. In general, we try to factor the expression under the radical so that one factor is the largest perfect $n$th power that we can find. Then we apply Property 2 or 3. For instance, the expression $\sqrt{72}$ is simplified as follows:

$$\sqrt{72} = \sqrt{(36)(2)} = \sqrt{36}\sqrt{2} = 6\sqrt{2}$$

In this procedure we began by factoring 72 as (36)(2). Note that 36 is the largest factor of 72 that is a perfect square. If we were to begin instead with a different factorization, for example, 72 = (9)(8), we could still arrive at the same answer, but it would take longer. (Check this for yourself.) As another example, let's simplify $\sqrt[3]{40}$. First, what (if any) is the largest perfect-cube factor of 40? The first few perfect cubes are

$$1^3 = 1 \qquad 2^3 = 8 \qquad 3^3 = 27 \qquad 4^3 = 64$$

so we see that 8 is a perfect-cube factor of 40, and we write

$$\sqrt[3]{40} = \sqrt[3]{(8)(5)} = \sqrt[3]{8}\sqrt[3]{5} = 2\sqrt[3]{5}$$

**EXAMPLE** 1    **Simplifying square roots**

Simplify:   **(a)** $\sqrt{12} + \sqrt{75}$;    **(b)** $\sqrt{\dfrac{162}{49}}$.

**SOLUTION**

**(a)** $\sqrt{12} + \sqrt{75} = \sqrt{(4)(3)} + \sqrt{(25)(3)}$

$\qquad\qquad\qquad = \sqrt{4}\sqrt{3} + \sqrt{25}\sqrt{3}$

$\qquad\qquad\qquad = 2\sqrt{3} + 5\sqrt{3} = (2 + 5)\sqrt{3}$

$\qquad\qquad\qquad = 7\sqrt{3}$

**(b)** $\sqrt{\dfrac{162}{49}} = \dfrac{\sqrt{162}}{\sqrt{49}} = \dfrac{\sqrt{81}\sqrt{2}}{7} = \dfrac{9\sqrt{2}}{7}$.

**EXAMPLE** 2    **Simplifying *n*th roots**

Simplify: $\sqrt[3]{16} + \sqrt[3]{250} - \sqrt[3]{128}$.

**SOLUTION**

$\sqrt[3]{16} + \sqrt[3]{250} - \sqrt[3]{128} = \sqrt[3]{8}\sqrt[3]{2} + \sqrt[3]{125}\sqrt[3]{2} - \sqrt[3]{64}\sqrt[3]{2}$

$\qquad\qquad\qquad\qquad\qquad = 2\sqrt[3]{2} + 5\sqrt[3]{2} - 4\sqrt[3]{2}$

$\qquad\qquad\qquad\qquad\qquad = 3\sqrt[3]{2}$

**EXAMPLE** 3    **Simplifying radicals containing variables**

Simplify each of the following expressions by removing the largest possible perfect-square or perfect-cube factor from within the radical:

**(a)** $\sqrt{8x^2}$;

**(b)** $\sqrt{8x^2}$, where $x \geq 0$;

**(c)** $\sqrt{18a^7}$, where $a \geq 0$;

**(d)** $\sqrt[3]{16y^5}$.

**SOLUTION**

**(a)** $\sqrt{8x^2} = \sqrt{(4)(2)(x^2)} = \sqrt{4}\sqrt{2}\sqrt{x^2} = 2\sqrt{2}|x|$

**(b)** $\sqrt{8x^2} = \sqrt{4}\sqrt{2}\sqrt{x^2}$

$\qquad\quad\; = 2\sqrt{2}x \qquad \sqrt{x^2} = x$ because $x \geq 0$

**(c)** $\sqrt{18a^7} = \sqrt{(9a^6)(2a)} = \sqrt{9a^6}\sqrt{2a}$

$\qquad\qquad\; = 3a^3\sqrt{2a}$

**(d)** $\sqrt[3]{16y^5} = \sqrt[3]{8y^3}\sqrt[3]{2y^2} = 2y\sqrt[3]{2y^2}$

| EXAMPLE | 4 | Simplifying *n*th roots containing variables |

Simplify each of the following, assuming that $a$, $b$, and $c$ are positive:

**(a)** $\sqrt{8ab^2c^5}$;   **(b)** $\sqrt[4]{\dfrac{32a^6b^5}{c^8}}$.

**SOLUTION**

**(a)** $\sqrt{8ab^2c^5} = \sqrt{(4b^2c^4)(2ac)} = \sqrt{4b^2c^4}\sqrt{2ac}$
$$= 2bc^2\sqrt{2ac}$$

**(b)** $\sqrt[4]{\dfrac{32a^6b^5}{c^8}} = \dfrac{\sqrt[4]{32a^6b^5}}{\sqrt[4]{c^8}}$

$$= \dfrac{\sqrt[4]{16a^4b^4}\sqrt[4]{2a^2b}}{c^2} = \dfrac{2ab\sqrt[4]{2a^2b}}{c^2}$$

In Examples 1 through 4 we used the definitions and properties of *n*th roots to simplify certain expressions. The box that follows shows some common errors to avoid in working with roots. Use the error box to test yourself: Cover up the columns labeled "Correction" and "Comment," and try to decide for yourself where the errors lie.

---

**ERRORS TO AVOID**

| Error | Correction | Comment |
|---|---|---|
| $\sqrt[4]{16} = \pm 2$ | $\sqrt[4]{16} = 2$ | Although $-2$ is one of the fourth roots of 16, it is not the *principal* fourth root. The notation $\sqrt[4]{16}$ is reserved for the principal fourth root. |
| $\sqrt{25} = -5$ | $\sqrt{25} = 5$ | Although $-5$ is one of the square roots of 25, it is not the *principal* square root. |
| $\sqrt{a+b} = \sqrt{a} + \sqrt{b}$ | The expression $\sqrt{a+b}$ cannot be simplified. | The properties of roots differ with respect to addition versus multiplication. For $\sqrt{ab}$ we do have the simplification $\sqrt{ab} = \sqrt{a}\sqrt{b}$ (assuming that $a$ and $b$ are nonnegative). |
| $\sqrt[3]{a+b} = \sqrt[3]{a} + \sqrt[3]{b}$ | The expression $\sqrt[3]{a+b}$ cannot be simplified. | For $\sqrt[3]{ab}$ we do have $\sqrt[3]{ab} = \sqrt[3]{a}\sqrt[3]{b}$. |

---

There are times when it is convenient to rewrite fractions involving radicals in alternative forms. Suppose, for example, that we want to rewrite the fraction $5/\sqrt{3}$ in an equivalent form that does not involve a radical in the denominator. This is called **rationalizing the denominator.** The procedure here is to multiply by 1 in this way:

$$\frac{5}{\sqrt{3}} = \frac{5}{\sqrt{3}}\cdot 1 = \frac{5}{\sqrt{3}}\cdot\frac{\sqrt{3}}{\sqrt{3}} = \frac{5\sqrt{3}}{3}$$

That is, $\dfrac{5}{\sqrt{3}} = \dfrac{5\sqrt{3}}{3}$, as required.

To rationalize a denominator of the form $a + \sqrt{b}$, we need to multiply the fraction not by $\sqrt{b}/\sqrt{b}$, but rather by $(a - \sqrt{b})/(a - \sqrt{b})\,(=1)$. To see why this is necessary, notice that

$$(a + \sqrt{b})\sqrt{b} = a\sqrt{b} + b$$

which still contains a radical, whereas

$$(a + \sqrt{b})(a - \sqrt{b}) = a^2 - a\sqrt{b} + a\sqrt{b} - b$$
$$= a^2 - b$$

which is free of radicals. Note that we multiply $a + \sqrt{b}$ by $a - \sqrt{b}$ to obtain an expression that is free of square roots by taking advantage of the form of a difference of two squares. Similarly, to rationalize a denominator of the form $a - \sqrt{b}$, we multiply the fraction by $(a + \sqrt{b})/(a + \sqrt{b})$. (The quantities $a + \sqrt{b}$ and $a - \sqrt{b}$ are said to be **conjugates** of each other.) The next two examples make use of these ideas.

| EXAMPLE | 5 | Rationalizing a square root denominator |

Simplify: $\dfrac{1}{\sqrt{2}} - 3\sqrt{50}$.

**SOLUTION**
First, we rationalize the denominator in the fraction $1/\sqrt{2}$:

$$\frac{1}{\sqrt{2}} = \frac{1}{\sqrt{2}} \cdot 1 = \frac{1}{\sqrt{2}} \cdot \frac{\sqrt{2}}{\sqrt{2}} = \frac{\sqrt{2}}{2}$$

Next, we simplify the expression $3\sqrt{50}$:

$$3\sqrt{50} = 3\sqrt{(25)(2)} = 3\sqrt{25}\sqrt{2} = (3)(5)\sqrt{2} = 15\sqrt{2}$$

Now, putting things together, we have

$$\frac{1}{\sqrt{2}} - 3\sqrt{50} = \frac{\sqrt{2}}{2} - 15\sqrt{2} = \frac{\sqrt{2}}{2} - \frac{30\sqrt{2}}{2}$$
$$= \frac{\sqrt{2} - 30\sqrt{2}}{2} = \frac{(1 - 30)\sqrt{2}}{2}$$
$$= \frac{-29\sqrt{2}}{2}$$

| EXAMPLE | 6 | Using the conjugate to rationalize a denominator |

Rationalize the denominator in the expression $\dfrac{4}{2 + \sqrt{3}}$.

**SOLUTION**
We multiply by 1, writing it as $\dfrac{2 - \sqrt{3}}{2 - \sqrt{3}}$.

$$\frac{4}{2 + \sqrt{3}} \cdot 1 = \frac{4}{2 + \sqrt{3}} \cdot \frac{2 - \sqrt{3}}{2 - \sqrt{3}}$$

$$= \frac{4(2 - \sqrt{3})}{4 - (\sqrt{3})^2} = \frac{4(2 - \sqrt{3})}{4 - 3} = \frac{8 - 4\sqrt{3}}{1}$$

$$= 8 - 4\sqrt{3}$$

*Note:* Check for yourself that multiplying the original fraction $\dfrac{2 + \sqrt{3}}{2 + \sqrt{3}}$ does *not* eliminate radicals in the denominator.

In the next example we are asked to rationalize the numerator rather than the denominator. This is useful at times in calculus.

---

**EXAMPLE  7    Rationalizing a numerator using the conjugate**

Rationalize the *numerator* of: $\dfrac{\sqrt{x} - \sqrt{3}}{x - 3}$, where $x \geq 0, x \neq 3$.

**SOLUTION**

$$\frac{\sqrt{x} - \sqrt{3}}{x - 3} \cdot 1 = \frac{\sqrt{x} - \sqrt{3}}{x - 3} \cdot \frac{\sqrt{x} + \sqrt{3}}{\sqrt{x} + \sqrt{3}}$$

$$= \frac{(\sqrt{x})^2 - (\sqrt{3})^2}{(x - 3)(\sqrt{x} + \sqrt{3})} = \frac{x - 3}{(x - 3)(\sqrt{x} + \sqrt{3})}$$

$$= \frac{1}{\sqrt{x} + \sqrt{3}}$$

---

The strategy for rationalizing numerators or denominators involving *n*th roots is similar to that used for square roots. To rationalize a numerator or a denominator involving an *n*th root, we multiply the numerator or denominator by a factor that yields a product that itself is a perfect *n*th power. The next example displays two instances of this.

**EXAMPLE  8    Rationalizing denominators containing *n*th roots**

**(a)**  Rationalize the denominator of: $\dfrac{6}{\sqrt[3]{7}}$.

**(b)**  Rationalize the denominator of: $\dfrac{ab}{\sqrt[4]{a^2b^3}}$, where $a > 0, b > 0$.

**SOLUTION**

**(a)**  $\dfrac{6}{\sqrt[3]{7}} \cdot 1 = \dfrac{6}{\sqrt[3]{7}} \cdot \dfrac{\sqrt[3]{7^2}}{\sqrt[3]{7^2}}$

$$= \frac{6\sqrt[3]{7^2}}{\sqrt[3]{7^3}}$$

$$= \frac{6\sqrt[3]{49}}{7} \qquad \text{as required}$$

**(b)** $\dfrac{ab}{\sqrt[4]{a^2b^3}} \cdot 1 = \dfrac{ab}{\sqrt[4]{a^2b^3}} \cdot \dfrac{\sqrt[4]{a^2b}}{\sqrt[4]{a^2b}}$

$\qquad = \dfrac{ab\sqrt[4]{a^2b}}{\sqrt[4]{a^4b^4}} = \dfrac{ab\sqrt[4]{a^2b}}{ab} = \sqrt[4]{a^2b}$

Finally, just as we used the difference of squares formula to motivate the method of rationalizing certain two-term denominators containing a square root term, we can use the difference or sum of cubes formula (see Appendix B.4) to rationalize a denominator involving a cube root term. In particular, in the sum of cubes formula $x^3 + y^3 = (x + y)(x^2 - xy + y^2)$, the expression $(x^2 - xy + y^2)$ is said to be the conjugate of the expression $x + y$.

**EXAMPLE 9** Using the conjugate to rationalize a denominator involving a cube root

Rationalize the denominator in the expression $\dfrac{1}{\sqrt[3]{a} + \sqrt[3]{b}}$.

**SOLUTION**
If we let $x = \sqrt[3]{a}$ and $y = \sqrt[3]{b}$, the conjugate of the denominator $x + y = \sqrt[3]{a} + \sqrt[3]{b}$ is

$$x^2 - xy + y^2 = (\sqrt[3]{a})^2 - \sqrt[3]{a}\sqrt[3]{b} + (\sqrt[3]{b})^2 = \sqrt[3]{a^2} - \sqrt[3]{ab} + \sqrt[3]{b^2}$$

where, for example, $(\sqrt[3]{a})^2 = \sqrt[3]{a}\sqrt[3]{a} = \sqrt[3]{a^2}$. Then

$$\dfrac{1}{\sqrt[3]{a} + \sqrt[3]{b}} = \dfrac{1}{\sqrt[3]{a} + \sqrt[3]{b}} \cdot \dfrac{\sqrt[3]{a^2} - \sqrt[3]{ab} + \sqrt[3]{b^2}}{\sqrt[3]{a^2} - \sqrt[3]{ab} + \sqrt[3]{b^2}}$$

$$= \dfrac{\sqrt[3]{a^2} - \sqrt[3]{ab} + \sqrt[3]{b^2}}{(\sqrt[3]{a})^3 + (\sqrt[3]{b})^3} = \dfrac{\sqrt[3]{a^2} - \sqrt[3]{ab} + \sqrt[3]{b^2}}{a + b}$$

# EXERCISE SET B.2

**A**

*In Exercises 1–8, determine whether each statement is TRUE or FALSE.*

**1.** $\sqrt{81} = -9$
**2.** $\sqrt{256} = 16$
**3.** $-\sqrt{100} = -10$
**4.** $\sqrt{49} = -7$
**5.** $\sqrt{4/3} = 2/\sqrt{3}$
**6.** $\sqrt{10 + 6} = \sqrt{10} + \sqrt{6}$
**7.** $(\sqrt[3]{10})^3 = 10$
**8.** $\sqrt{(-5)^2} = -5$

*For Exercises 9–18, evaluate each expression. If the expression is undefined (i.e., does not represent a real number), say so.*

**9. (a)** $\sqrt[3]{-64}$
　　**(b)** $\sqrt[4]{-64}$
**10. (a)** $\sqrt[5]{32}$
　　**(b)** $\sqrt[5]{-32}$
**11. (a)** $\sqrt[3]{8/125}$
　　**(b)** $\sqrt[3]{-8/125}$
**12. (a)** $\sqrt[3]{-1/1000}$
　　**(b)** $\sqrt[6]{-1/1000}$
**13. (a)** $\sqrt{-16}$
　　**(b)** $\sqrt[4]{-16}$
**14. (a)** $-\sqrt[4]{16}$
　　**(b)** $-\sqrt[4]{-16}$
**15. (a)** $\sqrt[4]{256/81}$
　　**(b)** $\sqrt[3]{-27/125}$
**16. (a)** $\sqrt[6]{64}$
　　**(b)** $\sqrt[6]{-64}$
**17. (a)** $\sqrt[5]{-32}$
　　**(b)** $-\sqrt[5]{-32}$
**18. (a)** $\sqrt[4]{(-10)^4}$
　　**(b)** $\sqrt[3]{(-10)^3}$

*In Exercises 19–44, simplify each expression. Unless otherwise specified, assume that all letters in Exercises 35–44 represent positive numbers.*

**19. (a)** $\sqrt{18}$
　　**(b)** $\sqrt[3]{54}$
**20. (a)** $\sqrt{150}$
　　**(b)** $\sqrt[3]{375}$
**21. (a)** $\sqrt{98}$
　　**(b)** $\sqrt[5]{-64}$
**22. (a)** $\sqrt{27}$
　　**(b)** $\sqrt[3]{-108}$

23. (a) $\sqrt{25/4}$
    (b) $\sqrt[4]{16/625}$
24. (a) $\sqrt{225/49}$
    (b) $\sqrt[5]{-256/243}$
25. (a) $\sqrt{2} + \sqrt{8}$
    (b) $\sqrt[3]{2} + \sqrt[3]{16}$
26. (a) $4\sqrt{3} - 2\sqrt{27}$
    (b) $2\sqrt[3]{81} + 3\sqrt[3]{24}$
27. (a) $4\sqrt{50} - 3\sqrt{128}$
    (b) $\sqrt[4]{32} + \sqrt[4]{162}$
28. (a) $\sqrt{3} - \sqrt{12} + \sqrt{48}$
    (b) $\sqrt[5]{-2} + \sqrt[5]{-64} - \sqrt[5]{486}$
29. (a) $\sqrt{0.09}$
    (b) $\sqrt[3]{0.008}$
30. (a) $\sqrt[3]{-2} + \sqrt[3]{2}$
    (b) $\sqrt{81/121} - \sqrt[3]{-8/1331}$
31. $4\sqrt{24} - 8\sqrt{54} + 2\sqrt{6}$
32. $\sqrt[3]{192} + \sqrt[3]{-81} + \sqrt{\sqrt[3]{9}}$
33. $\sqrt{\sqrt{64}}$
34. $\sqrt[3]{\sqrt{4096}}$
35. (a) $\sqrt{36x^2}$
    (b) $\sqrt{36y^2}$, where $y < 0$
36. (a) $\sqrt{225x^4y^3}$
    (b) $\sqrt[4]{16a^4}$, where $a < 0$
37. (a) $\sqrt{ab^2}\sqrt{a^2b}$
    (b) $\sqrt{ab^3}\sqrt{a^3b}$
38. (a) $\sqrt[3]{125x^6}$
    (b) $\sqrt[4]{64y^4}$, where $y < 0$
39. $\sqrt{72a^3b^4c^5}$
40. $\sqrt{(a+b)^5/(16a^2b^2)}$
41. $\sqrt[4]{16a^4b^5}$
42. $\sqrt[3]{8a^4b^6}$
43. $\sqrt[3]{16a^{12}b^2/c^9}$
44. $\sqrt[4]{ab^3}\sqrt[4]{a^3b}$

*In Exercises 45–70, rationalize the denominators and simplify where possible. (Assume that all letters represent positive quantities.)*

45. $4/\sqrt{7}$
46. $3/\sqrt{3}$
47. $1/\sqrt{8}$
48. $\sqrt{2}/\sqrt{3}$
49. $1/(1 + \sqrt{5})$
50. $\sqrt{2}/(1 - \sqrt{2})$
51. $(1 + \sqrt{3})/(1 - \sqrt{3})$
52. $(\sqrt{a} + \sqrt{b})/(\sqrt{a} - \sqrt{b})$
53. $(1/\sqrt{5}) + 4\sqrt{45}$
54. $(3/\sqrt{8}) - \sqrt{450}$
55. $1/\sqrt[3]{25}$
56. $4/\sqrt[3]{16}$
57. $3/\sqrt[4]{3}$
58. $\sqrt[3]{5}/\sqrt[3]{6}$
59. $3/\sqrt[5]{16a^4b^9}$
60. $3/\sqrt[4]{27a^5b^{11}}$
61. (a) $2/(\sqrt{3} + 1)$
    (b) $2/(\sqrt{3} - 1)$
62. (a) $1/(2\sqrt{5} + 1)$
    (b) $1/(2\sqrt{5} - 1)$
63. (a) $x/(\sqrt{x} - 2)$
    (b) $x/(\sqrt{x} - y)$
64. (a) $\sqrt{x}/(5 + \sqrt{x})$
    (b) $\sqrt{x}/(\sqrt{a} + \sqrt{x})$
65. (a) $(\sqrt{x} + \sqrt{2})/(\sqrt{x} - \sqrt{2})$
    (b) $(\sqrt{x} + \sqrt{a})/(\sqrt{x} - \sqrt{a})$
66. (a) $(\sqrt{3} + 2\sqrt{y})/(\sqrt{3} - 2\sqrt{y})$
    (b) $(\sqrt{x} - 2\sqrt{y})/(\sqrt{x} + 2\sqrt{y})$

67. $-2/(\sqrt{x + h} - \sqrt{x})$
68. $1/(\sqrt{x + h} - \sqrt{x - h})$
69. $1/(\sqrt[3]{a} - 1)$
70. $1/(\sqrt[3]{a} - \sqrt[3]{b})$

*In Exercises 71–76, rationalize the numerator.*

71. $(\sqrt{x} - \sqrt{5})/(x - 5)$
72. $(2\sqrt{y} + 3)/(4y - 9)$
73. $(\sqrt{2 + h} + \sqrt{2})/h$
74. $(\sqrt{1 + 2h} - 1)/(2h)$
75. $(\sqrt{x + h} - \sqrt{x})/h$
76. $(\sqrt{x + 2h} - \sqrt{x - 2h})/h$

*In Exercises 77–80, refer to the following table. The left-hand column of the table lists four errors to avoid in working with expressions containing radicals. In each case, give a numerical example showing that the expressions on each side of the equation are, in general, not equal. Use a calculator as necessary.*

| Errors to avoid | Numerical example showing that the formula is not, in general, valid |
|---|---|
| 77. $\sqrt{a + b} = \sqrt{a} + \sqrt{b}$ | |
| 78. $\sqrt{x^2 + y^2} = x + y$ | |
| 79. $\sqrt[3]{u + v} = \sqrt[3]{u} + \sqrt[3]{v}$ | |
| 80. $\sqrt[3]{p^3 + q^3} = p + q$ | |

**B**

81. (a) Use a calculator to evaluate $\sqrt{8 - 2\sqrt{7}}$ and $\sqrt{7} - 1$. What do you observe?
    (b) Prove that $\sqrt{8 - 2\sqrt{7}} = \sqrt{7} - 1$. *Hint:* In view of the definition of a principal square root, you need to check that $(\sqrt{7} - 1)^2 = 8 - 2\sqrt{7}$.

82. Use a calculator to provide empirical evidence indicating that both of the following equations may be correct:

$$\frac{2 - \sqrt{3}}{\sqrt{2} - \sqrt{2 - \sqrt{3}}} + \frac{2 + \sqrt{3}}{\sqrt{2} + \sqrt{2 + \sqrt{3}}} = \sqrt{2}$$

$$\sqrt{\sqrt{97.5 - (1/11)}} = \pi$$

The point of this exercise is to remind you that as useful as calculators may be, there is still the need for proofs in mathematics. In fact, it can be shown that the first equation is indeed correct, but the second is not.

# B.3 REVIEW OF RATIONAL EXPONENTS

*. . . Nicole Oresme, a bishop in Normandy (about 1323–1382), first conceived the notion of fractional powers, afterwards rediscovered by [Simon] Stevin [1548–1620] . . .* —Florian Cajori in *A History of Elementary Mathematics* (New York: Macmillan Co., 1917)

*If Descartes . . . had discarded the radical sign altogether and had introduced the notation for fractional as well as integral exponents, . . . it is conceivable that generations upon generations of pupils would have been saved the necessity of mastering the operations with two . . . notations when one alone (the exponential) would have answered all purposes.* —Florian Cajori, *A History of Mathematical Notations,* Vol. 1 (La Salle, Ill.: The Open Court Publishing Co., 1928)

We can use the concept of an $n$th root to give a meaning to fractional exponents that is useful and, at the same time, consistent with our earlier work. First, by way of motivation, suppose that we want to assign a value to $5^{1/3}$. Assuming that the usual properties of exponents continue to apply here, we can write

$$(5^{1/3})^3 = 5^1 = 5$$

That is,

$$(5^{1/3})^3 = 5$$

or

$$5^{1/3} = \sqrt[3]{5}$$

By replacing 5 and 3 with $b$ and $n$, respectively, we can see that we want to define $b^{1/n}$ to mean $\sqrt[n]{b}$. Also, by thinking of $b^{m/n}$ as $(b^{1/n})^m$, we see that the definition for $b^{m/n}$ ought to be $(\sqrt[n]{b})^m$. These definitions are formalized in the box that follows.

---

**DEFINITION** | **Rational Exponents**

1. Let $b$ denote a real number and $n$ a natural number. We define $b^{1/n}$ by

$$b^{1/n} = \sqrt[n]{b}$$

(If $n$ is even, we require that $b \geq 0$.)

2. Let $m/n$ be a rational number reduced to lowest terms. Assume that $n$ is positive and that $\sqrt[n]{b}$ exists. Then

$$b^{m/n} = (\sqrt[n]{b})^m$$

or, equivalently,

$$b^{m/n} = \sqrt[n]{b^m}$$

**EXAMPLES**

$4^{1/2} = \sqrt{4} = 2$

$(-8)^{1/3} = \sqrt[3]{-8} = -2$

$8^{2/3} = (\sqrt[3]{8})^2 = 2^2 = 4$

or, equivalently,

$8^{2/3} = \sqrt[3]{8^2} = \sqrt[3]{64} = 4$

---

It can be shown that the four properties of exponents that we listed in Appendix B.1 (on page A-9) continue to hold for rational exponents in general. In fact, we'll take this for granted rather than follow the lengthy argument needed for its verification. We will also assume that these properties apply to irrational exponents. For instance, we have

$$(2^{\sqrt{5}})^{\sqrt{5}} = 2^5 = 32$$

(The definition of irrational exponents is discussed in Section 5.1.) In the next three examples we display the basic techniques for working with rational exponents.

**EXAMPLE** | **1** | **Evaluating rational exponents**

Simplify each of the following quantities. Express the answers using positive exponents. If an expression does not represent a real number, say so.

**(a)** $49^{1/2}$     **(b)** $-49^{1/2}$     **(c)** $(-49)^{1/2}$     **(d)** $49^{-1/2}$

**SOLUTION**

**(a)** $49^{1/2} = \sqrt{49} = 7$

**(b)** $-49^{1/2} = -(49^{1/2}) = -\sqrt{49} = -7$

**(c)** The quantity $(-49)^{1/2}$ does not represent a real number because there is no real number $x$ such that $x^2 = -49$.

**(d)** $49^{-1/2} = \sqrt{49^{-1}} = \sqrt{1/49} = \dfrac{\sqrt{1}}{\sqrt{49}} = \dfrac{1}{7}$

Alternatively, we have

$$49^{-1/2} = (49^{1/2})^{-1} = 7^{-1} = \frac{1}{7}$$

**EXAMPLE** 2  **Simplifying expressions containing rational exponents**

Simplify each of the following. Write the answers using positive exponents. (Assume that $a > 0$.)

**(a)** $(5a^{2/3})(4a^{3/4})$ **(b)** $\sqrt[5]{\dfrac{16a^{1/3}}{a^{1/4}}}$ **(c)** $(x^2 + 1)^{1/5}(x^2 + 1)^{4/5}$

**SOLUTION**

**(a)** $(5a^{2/3})(4a^{3/4}) = 20a^{(2/3)+(3/4)}$

$\qquad\qquad\qquad\qquad = 20a^{17/12}$ $\qquad$ because $\frac{2}{3} + \frac{3}{4} = \frac{17}{12}$

**(b)** $\sqrt[5]{\dfrac{16a^{1/3}}{a^{1/4}}} = \left(\dfrac{16a^{1/3}}{a^{1/4}}\right)^{1/5}$

$\qquad\qquad\quad = (16a^{1/12})^{1/5}$ $\qquad$ because $\frac{1}{3} - \frac{1}{4} = \frac{1}{12}$

$\qquad\qquad\quad = 16^{1/5}a^{1/60}$

**(c)** $(x^2 + 1)^{1/5}(x^2 + 1)^{4/5} = (x^2 + 1)^1 = x^2 + 1$

**EXAMPLE** 3  **Evaluating rational exponents**

Simplify: **(a)** $32^{-2/5}$; **(b)** $(-8)^{4/3}$.

**SOLUTION**

**(a)** $32^{-2/5} = (\sqrt[5]{32})^{-2} = 2^{-2} = \dfrac{1}{2^2} = \dfrac{1}{4}$

Alternatively, we have

$$32^{-2/5} = (2^5)^{-2/5} = 2^{-2} = \frac{1}{2^2} = \frac{1}{4}$$

**(b)** $(-8)^{4/3} = (\sqrt[3]{-8})^4 = (-2)^4 = 16$

Alternatively, we can write

$$(-8)^{4/3} = [(-2)^3]^{4/3} = (-2)^4 = 16$$

Rational exponents can be used to simplify certain expressions containing radicals. For example, one of the properties of $n$th roots that we listed but did not discuss in Appendix B.2 is $\sqrt[m]{\sqrt[n]{x}} = \sqrt[mn]{x}$. Using exponents, it is easy to verify this property. We have

$$\sqrt[m]{\sqrt[n]{x}} = \left(x^{1/n}\right)^{1/m}$$
$$= x^{1/mm} = \sqrt[mm]{x} \qquad \text{as we wished to show}$$

---

**EXAMPLE** | **4** | **Using rational exponents to combine radicals**

Consider the expression $\sqrt{x}\sqrt[3]{y^2}$, where $x$ and $y$ are positive.
**(a)** Rewrite the expression using rational exponents.
**(b)** Rewrite the expression using only one radical sign.

**SOLUTION**
**(a)** $\sqrt{x}\sqrt[3]{y^2} = x^{1/2}y^{2/3}$

**(b)** $\sqrt{x}\sqrt[3]{y^2} = x^{1/2}y^{2/3}$           rewriting the fractions using
         $= x^{3/6}y^{4/6}$                  a common denominator
         $= \sqrt[6]{x^3}\sqrt[6]{y^4} = \sqrt[6]{x^3y^4}$

---

**EXAMPLE** | **5** | **Using rational exponents to simplify a radical expression**

Rewrite the following expression using rational exponents (assume that $x$, $y$, and $z$ are positive):

$$\sqrt{\dfrac{\sqrt[3]{x}\sqrt[4]{y^3}}{\sqrt[5]{z^4}}}$$

**SOLUTION**

$$\sqrt{\dfrac{\sqrt[3]{x}\sqrt[4]{y^3}}{\sqrt[5]{z^4}}} = \left(\dfrac{\sqrt[3]{x}\sqrt[4]{y^3}}{\sqrt[5]{z^4}}\right)^{1/2} = \left(\dfrac{x^{1/3}y^{3/4}}{z^{4/5}}\right)^{1/2}$$

$$= \dfrac{x^{1/6}y^{3/8}}{z^{2/5}} = x^{1/6}y^{3/8}z^{-2/5}$$

---

# EXERCISE SET B.3

**A**

*Exercises 1–14 are warm-up exercises to help you become familiar with the definition $b^{m/n} = \left(\sqrt[n]{b}\right)^m = \sqrt[n]{b^m}$. In Exercises 1–8, write the expression in the two equivalent forms $\left(\sqrt[n]{b}\right)^m$ and $\sqrt[n]{b^m}$. In Exercises 9–14, write the expression in the form $b^{m/n}$.*

**1.** $a^{3/5}$      **2.** $x^{3/7}$      **3.** $5^{2/3}$
**4.** $10^{4/5}$      **5.** $(x^2 + 1)^{3/4}$      **6.** $(a + b)^{7/10}$
**7.** $2^{xy/3}$      **8.** $2^{(a+1)/b}$      **9.** $\sqrt[3]{p^2}$
**10.** $\sqrt[5]{R^3}$      **11.** $\sqrt[7]{(1 + u)^4}$      **12.** $\sqrt[6]{(1 + u)^5}$
**13.** $\sqrt[p]{(a^2 + b^2)^3}$      **14.** $\sqrt[3p]{(a^2 + b^2)^{2p}}$

*In Exercises 15–50, evaluate or simplify each expression. Express the answers using positive exponents. If an expression is undefined (that is, does not represent a real number), say so. Assume that all letters represent positive numbers.*

**15.** $16^{1/2}$      **16.** $100^{1/2}$      **17.** $(1/36)^{1/2}$
**18.** $0.09^{1/2}$      **19.** $(-16)^{1/2}$      **20.** $(-1)^{1/2}$
**21.** $625^{1/4}$      **22.** $(1/81)^{1/4}$      **23.** $8^{1/3}$
**24.** $0.001^{1/3}$      **25.** $8^{2/3}$      **26.** $64^{2/3}$
**27.** $(-32)^{1/5}$      **28.** $(-1/125)^{1/3}$      **29.** $(-1000)^{1/3}$
**30.** $(-243)^{1/5}$      **31.** $49^{-1/2}$      **32.** $121^{-1/2}$
**33.** $(-49)^{-1/2}$      **34.** $(-64)^{-1/3}$      **35.** $36^{-3/2}$

**36.** $(-0.001)^{-2/3}$  **37.** $125^{2/3}$  **38.** $125^{-2/3}$

**39.** $(-1)^{3/5}$

**40.** $27^{4/3} + 27^{-4/3} + 27^0$

**41.** $32^{4/5} - 32^{-4/5}$

**42.** $64^{1/2} + 64^{-1/2} - 64^{4/3}$

**43.** $(9/16)^{-5/2} - (1000/27)^{4/3}$

**44.** $(256^{-3/4})^{4/3}$

**45.** $(2a^{1/3})(3a^{1/4})$

**46.** $\sqrt[5]{3a^4}$

**47.** $\sqrt[4]{64a^{2/3}/a^{1/3}}$

**48.** $(x^2 + 1)^{2/3}(x^2 + 1)^{4/3}$

**49.** $\dfrac{(x^2 + 1)^{3/4}}{(x^2 + 1)^{-1/4}}$

**50.** $\dfrac{(2x^2 + 1)^{-6/5}(2x^2 + 1)^{6/5}(x^2 + 1)^{-1/5}}{(x^2 + 1)^{9/5}}$

*For Exercises 51–58, follow Example 4 in the text to rewrite each expression in two ways:* **(a)** *using rational exponents and* **(b)** *using only one radical sign. (Assume that x, y, and z are positive.)*

**51.** $\sqrt{3}\sqrt[3]{6}$

**52.** $\sqrt{5}\sqrt[3]{7}$

**53.** $\sqrt[3]{6}\sqrt[4]{2}$

**54.** $\sqrt[3]{2}\sqrt[5]{2}$

**55.** $\sqrt[3]{x^2}\sqrt[5]{y^4}$

**56.** $\sqrt{x}\sqrt[3]{y}\sqrt[4]{z}$

**57.** $\sqrt[4]{x^a}\sqrt[3]{x^b}\sqrt{x^{a/6}}$

**58.** $\sqrt[3]{27\sqrt{64x}}$

*In Exercises 59–66, rewrite each expression using rational exponents rather than radicals. Assume that x, y, and z are positive.*

**59.** $\sqrt[3]{(x + 1)^2}$

**60.** $(1/\sqrt{x}) + \sqrt{x}$

**61.** $(\sqrt[5]{x + y})^2$

**62.** $\sqrt{\sqrt{x}}$

**63.** $\sqrt[3]{\sqrt{x}} + \sqrt{\sqrt[3]{x}}$

**64.** $\sqrt[3]{\sqrt{2}}$

**65.** $\sqrt{\sqrt[3]{x}\sqrt[4]{y}}$

**66.** $\sqrt[5]{\sqrt{x}\sqrt[3]{y}/\sqrt[4]{z^2}}$

**67.** Use a calculator to determine which is larger, $9^{10/9}$ or $10^{9/10}$.

**68.** Use a calculator to determine which number is closer to 3: $13^{3/7}$ or $6560^{1/8}$.

*In Exercises 69–74, refer to the following table. The left-hand column of the table lists six errors to avoid in working with expressions containing fractional exponents. In each case, give a numerical example showing that the expressions on each side of the equation are not equal. Use a calculator as necessary.*

| Errors to avoid | Numerical example showing that the formula is not, in general, valid |
|---|---|
| **69.** $(a + b)^{1/2} = a^{1/2} + b^{1/2}$ | |
| **70.** $(x^2 + y^2)^{1/2} = x + y$ | |
| **71.** $(u + v)^{1/3} = u^{1/3} + v^{1/3}$ | |
| **72.** $(p^3 + q^3)^{1/3} = p + q$ | |
| **73.** $x^{1/m} = \dfrac{1}{x^m}$ | |
| **74.** $x^{-1/2} - \dfrac{1}{x^2}$ | |

# B.4 REVIEW OF FACTORING

**fac·tor** (*fak'ter*), n. . . . . **2.** Math. *one of two or more numbers, algebraic expressions, or the like, that when multiplied together produce a given product;* . . . v.t. **10.** Math. *to express (a mathematical quantity) as a product of two or more quantities of like kind, as* $30 = 2 \cdot 3 \cdot 5$, *or* $x^2 - y^2 = (x + y)(x - y)$.—*The Random House Dictionary of the English Language*, 2nd ed. (New York: Random House, 1987)

There are many cases in algebra in which the process of *factoring* simplifies the work at hand. To **factor** a polynomial means to write it as a product of two or more nonconstant polynomials. For instance, a factorization of $x^2 - 9$ is given by

$$x^2 - 9 = (x - 3)(x + 3)$$

In this case, $x - 3$ and $x + 3$ are the **factors** of $x^2 - 9$.

There is one convention that we need to agree on at the outset. If the polynomial or expression that we wish to factor contains only integer coefficients, then the factors (if any) should involve only integer coefficients. For example, according to this convention, we will not consider the following type of factorization in this section:

$$x^2 - 2 = (x - \sqrt{2})(x + \sqrt{2})$$

because it involves coefficients that are irrational numbers. (We should point out, however, that factorizations such as this are useful at times, particularly in calculus.) As it happens, $x^2 - 2$ is an example of a polynomial that cannot be factored using integer coefficients. In such a case we say that the polynomial is **irreducible over the integers.**

If the coefficients of a polynomial are rational numbers, then we do allow factors with rational coefficients. For instance, the factorization of $y^2 - \frac{1}{4}$ over the rational numbers is given by

$$y^2 - \frac{1}{4} = \left(y - \frac{1}{2}\right)\left(y + \frac{1}{2}\right)$$

We'll consider five techniques for factoring in this section. These techniques will be applied in the next two sections and throughout the text. In Table 1 we sum-

## TABLE 1  Basic Factoring Techniques

| Technique | Example or formula | Remark |
|---|---|---|
| Common factor | $3x^4 + 6x^3 - 12x^2 = 3x^2(x^2 + 2x - 4)$ <br> $4(x^2 + 1) - x(x^2 + 1) = (x^2 + 1)(4 - x)$ | In any factoring problem, the first step always is to look for the common factor of highest degree. |
| Difference of squares | $x^2 - a^2 = (x - a)(x + a)$ | There is no corresponding formula for a sum of squares; $x^2 + a^2$ is irreducible over the integers. |
| Trial and error | $x^2 + 2x - 3 = (x + 3)(x - 1)$ | In this example the only possibilities, or trials, are <br> (a) $(x - 3)(x - 1)$     (c) $(x + 3)(x - 1)$ <br> (b) $(x - 3)(x + 1)$     (d) $(x + 3)(x + 1)$ <br> By inspection or by carrying out the indicated multiplications, we find that only case (c) checks. |
| Difference of cubes <br> Sum of cubes | $x^3 - a^3 = (x - a)(x^2 + ax + a^2)$ <br> $x^3 + a^3 = (x + a)(x^2 - ax + a^2)$ | Verify these formulas for yourself by carrying out the multiplications. Then memorize the formulas. |
| Grouping | $x^3 - x^2 + x - 1 = (x^3 - x^2) + (x - 1)$ <br> $= x^2(x - 1) + (x - 1) \cdot 1$ <br> $= (x - 1)(x^2 + 1)$ | This is actually an application of the common factor technique. |

marize these techniques. Notice that three of the formulas in the table are just restatements of Special Products formulas. Remember that it is the form or pattern in the formula that is important, not the specific choice of letters.

The idea in factoring is to use one or more of these techniques until each of the factors obtained is irreducible. The examples that follow show how this works in practice.

---

**EXAMPLE** | **1** | **Factoring using the difference-of-squares technique**

Factor:   **(a)** $x^2 - 49$;     **(b)** $(2a - 3b)^2 - 49$.

**SOLUTION**

**(a)** $x^2 - 49 = x^2 - 7^2$
$\qquad\qquad = (x - 7)(x + 7)$     difference of squares

**(b)** Notice that the pattern or form is the same as in part (a): It's a difference of squares. We have

$(2a - 3b)^2 - 49 = (2a - 3b)^2 - 7^2$
$\qquad\qquad\qquad = [(2a - 3b) - 7][(2a - 3b) + 7]$     difference of squares
$\qquad\qquad\qquad = (2a - 3b - 7)(2a - 3b + 7)$

---

   **EXAMPLE** | **2** | **Factoring using common factor and difference of squares**

Factor:   **(a)** $2x^3 - 50x$;     **(b)** $3x^5 - 3x$.

**SOLUTION**

**(a)** $2x^3 - 50x = 2x(x^2 - 25)$           common factor
$\qquad\qquad\quad = 2x(x - 5)(x + 5)$       difference of squares

**(b)** $3x^5 - 3x = 3x(x^4 - 1)$ ⠀⠀⠀⠀⠀⠀⠀⠀⠀⠀⠀⠀common factor

⠀⠀⠀⠀⠀⠀$= 3x[(x^2)^2 - 1^2]$

⠀⠀⠀⠀⠀⠀$= 3x(x^2 - 1)(x^2 + 1)$ ⠀⠀⠀⠀difference of squares

⠀⠀⠀⠀⠀⠀$= 3x(x - 1)(x + 1)(x^2 + 1)$ ⠀difference of squares, again

---

**EXAMPLE** ⠀**3**⠀⠀**Factoring by trial and error**

Factor: ⠀**(a)** $x^2 - 4x - 5$; ⠀⠀⠀⠀**(b)** $(a + b)^2 - 4(a + b) - 5$.

**SOLUTION**

**(a)** $x^2 - 4x - 5 = (x - 5)(x + 1)$ ⠀⠀⠀trial and error

**(b)** Note that the form of this expression is

$$(\ \ )^2 - 4(\ \ ) - 5$$

This is the same *form* as the expression in part (a), so we need only replace $x$ with the quantity $a + b$ in the solution for part (a). This yields

$$(a + b)^2 - 4(a + b) - 5 = [(a + b) - 5][(a + b) + 1]$$
$$= (a + b - 5)(a + b + 1)$$

---

**EXAMPLE** ⠀**4**⠀⠀**Factoring by trial and error**

Factor: $2z^4 + 9z^2 + 4$.

**SOLUTION**

We use trial and error to look for a factorization of the form $(2z^2 + ?)(z^2 + ?)$. There are three possibilities:

**(i)** $(2z^2 + 2)(z^2 + 2)$ ⠀⠀**(ii)** $(2z^2 + 1)(z^2 + 4)$ ⠀⠀**(iii)** $(2z^2 + 4)(z^2 + 1)$

Each of these yields the appropriate first term and last term, but (after checking) only possibility (ii) yields $9z^2$ for the middle term. The required factorization is then $2z^4 + 9z^2 + 4 = (2z^2 + 1)(z^2 + 4)$.

*Question*: Why didn't we consider any possibilities with subtraction signs in place of addition signs?

---

**EXAMPLE** ⠀**5**⠀⠀**Two irreducible expressions**

Factor: ⠀**(a)** $x^2 + 9$; ⠀⠀⠀⠀**(b)** $x^2 + 2x + 3$.

**SOLUTION**

**(a)** The expression $x^2 + 9$ is irreducible over the integers. (This can be discovered by trial and error.) If the given expression had instead been $x^2 - 9$, then it could have been factored as a difference of squares. Sums of squares, however, cannot in general be factored over the integers.

**(b)** The expression $x^2 + 2x + 3$ is irreducible over the integers. (Check this for yourself by trial and error.)

**EXAMPLE  6    Factoring using grouping and a special product**

Factor: $x^2 - y^2 + 10x + 25$.

**SOLUTION**
Familiarity with the special product $(a + b)^2 = a^2 + 2ab + b^2$ suggests that we try grouping the terms this way:

$$(x^2 + 10x + 25) - y^2$$

Then we have

$$
\begin{aligned}
x^2 - y^2 + 10x + 25 &= (x^2 + 10x + 25) - y^2 \\
&= (x + 5)^2 - y^2 \\
&= [(x + 5) - y][(x + 5) + y] \qquad \text{difference of squares} \\
&= (x - y + 5)(x + y + 5)
\end{aligned}
$$

  **EXAMPLE  7    Factoring using grouping**

Factor: $ax + ay^2 + bx + by^2$.

**SOLUTION**
We factor $a$ from the first two terms and $b$ from the second two to obtain

$$ax + ay^2 + bx + by^2 = a(x + y^2) + b(x + y^2)$$

We now recognize the quantity $x + y^2$ as a common expression that can be factored out. We then have

$$a(x + y^2) + b(x + y^2) = (x + y^2)(a + b)$$

The required factorization is therefore

$$ax + ay^2 + bx + by^2 = (x + y^2)(a + b)$$

Alternatively,

$$
\begin{aligned}
ax &+ ay^2 + bx + by^2 \\
&= (ax + bx) + (ay^2 + by^2) \\
&= x(a + b) + y^2(a + b) \\
&= (a + b)(x + y^2)
\end{aligned}
$$

  **EXAMPLE  8    Factoring sum and difference of cubes**

Factor:   **(a)** $t^3 - 125$;        **(b)** $8 + (a - 2)^3$.

**SOLUTION**
**(a)**
$$
\begin{aligned}
t^3 - 125 &= t^3 - 5^3 \\
&= (t - 5)(t^2 + 5t + 25) \qquad \text{difference of cubes}
\end{aligned}
$$
**(b)**
$$
\begin{aligned}
8 + (a - 2)^3 &= 2^3 + (a - 2)^3 \\
&= [2 + (a - 2)][2^2 - 2(a - 2) + (a - 2)^2] \qquad \text{sum of cubes}
\end{aligned}
$$

$$= a(4 - 2a + 4 + a^2 - 4a + 4)$$
$$= a(a^2 - 6a + 12)$$

As you can check now, the expression $a^2 - 6a + 12$ is irreducible over the integers. Therefore the required factorization is $a(a^2 - 6a + 12)$.

For some calculations (particularly in calculus) it's helpful to be able to factor an expression involving fractional exponents. For instance, suppose that we want to factor the expression

$$x(2x - 1)^{-1/2} + (2x - 1)^{3/2}$$

The common expression to factor out here is $(2x - 1)^{-1/2}$; the technique is to *choose the expression with the smaller exponent.*

---

**EXAMPLE** 9 **Factoring with rational exponents**

Factor: $x(2x - 1)^{-1/2} + (2x - 1)^{3/2}$.

**SOLUTION**

$$\begin{aligned} x(2x - 1)^{-1/2} + (2x - 1)^{3/2} &= (2x - 1)^{-1/2}[x + (2x - 1)^{3/2+1/2}] \\ &= (2x - 1)^{-1/2}[x + (2x - 1)^2] \\ &= (2x - 1)^{-1/2}(4x^2 - 3x + 1) \end{aligned}$$

---

We conclude this section with examples of four common errors to avoid in factoring. The first two errors in the box that follows are easy to detect; simply multiplying out the supposed factorizations shows that they do not check. The third error may result from a lack of familiarity with the basic factoring techniques listed on page A-26. The fourth error indicates a misunderstanding of what is required in factoring; the final quantity in a factorization must be expressed as a *product*, not a sum, of terms or expressions.

## ERRORS TO AVOID

| Error | Correction | Comment |
|---|---|---|
| $x^2 + 6x + 9 = (x - 3)^2$ | $x^2 + 6x + 9 = (x + 3)^2$ | Check the middle term. |
| $x^2 + 64 = (x + 8)(x + 8)$ | $x^2 + 64$ is irreducible over the integers. | A sum of squares is, in general, irreducible over the integers. (A difference of squares, however, can always be factored.) |
| $x^3 + 64$ is irreducible over the integers | $x^3 + 64 = (x + 4)(x^2 - 4x + 16)$ | Although a sum of squares is irreducible, a sum of cubes can be factored. |
| $x^2 - 2x + 3$ factors as $x(x - 2) + 3$ | $x^2 - 2x + 3$ is irreducible over the integers. | The polynomial $x^2 - 2x + 3$ is the *sum* of the expression $x(x - 2)$ and the constant 3. By definition, however, the factored form of a polynomial must be a *product* (of two or more nonconstant polynomials). |

# EXERCISE SET B.4

## A

*In Exercises 1–66, factor each polynomial or expression. If a polynomial is irreducible, state this. (In Exercises 1–6 the factoring techniques are specified.)*

1. (Common factor and difference of squares)
   (a) $x^2 - 64$
   (b) $7x^4 + 14x^2$
   (c) $121z - z^3$
   (d) $a^2b^2 - c^2$

2. (Common factor and difference of squares)
   (a) $1 - t^4$
   (b) $x^6 + x^5 + x^4$
   (c) $u^2v^2 - 225$
   (d) $81x^4 - x^2$

3. (Trial and error)
   (a) $x^2 + 2x - 3$
   (b) $x^2 - 2x - 3$
   (c) $x^2 - 2x + 3$
   (d) $-x^2 + 2x + 3$

4. (Trial and error)
   (a) $2x^2 - 7x - 4$
   (b) $2x^2 + 7x - 4$
   (c) $2x^2 + 7x + 4$
   (d) $-2x^2 - 7x + 4$

5. (Sum and difference of cubes)
   (a) $x^3 + 1$
   (b) $x^3 + 216$
   (c) $1000 - 8x^6$
   (d) $64a^3x^3 - 125$

6. (Grouping)
   (a) $x^4 - 2x^3 + 3x - 6$
   (b) $a^2x + bx - a^2z - bz$

7. (a) $144 - x^2$
   (b) $144 + x^2$
   (c) $144 - (y - 3)^2$

8. (a) $4a^2b^2 + 9c^2$
   (b) $4a^2b^2 - 9c^2$
   (c) $4a^2b^2 - 9(ab + c)^2$

9. (a) $h^3 - h^5$
   (b) $100h^3 - h^5$
   (c) $100(h + 1)^3 - (h + 1)^5$

10. (a) $x^4 - x^2$
    (b) $3x^4 - 48x^2$
    (c) $3(x + h)^4 - 48(x + h)^2$

11. (a) $x^2 - 13x + 40$
    (b) $x^2 - 13x - 40$

12. (a) $x^2 + 10x + 16$
    (b) $x^2 - 10x + 16$

13. (a) $x^2 + 5x - 36$
    (b) $x^2 - 13x + 36$

14. (a) $x^2 - x + 6$
    (b) $x^2 + x - 6$

15. (a) $3x^2 - 22x - 16$
    (b) $3x^2 - x - 16$

16. (a) $x^2 - 4x + 1$
    (b) $x^2 - 4x - 3$

17. (a) $6x^2 + 13x - 5$
    (b) $6x^2 - x - 5$

18. (a) $16x^2 + 18x - 9$
    (b) $16x^2 - 143x - 9$

19. (a) $t^4 + 2t^2 + 1$
    (b) $t^4 - 2t^2 + 1$
    (c) $t^4 - 2t^2 - 1$

20. (a) $t^4 - 9t^2 + 20$
    (b) $t^4 - 19t^2 + 20$
    (c) $t^4 - 19t^2 - 20$

21. (a) $4x^3 - 20x^2 - 25x$
    (b) $4x^3 - 20x^2 + 25x$

22. (a) $x^3 + x^2 + x$
    (b) $x^3 + 2x^2 + x$

23. (a) $ab - bc + a^2 - ac$
    (b) $(u + v)x - xy + (u + v)^2 - (u + v)y$

24. (a) $3(x + 5)^3 + 2(x + 5)^2$
    (b) $a(x + 5)^3 + b(x + 5)^2$

25. $x^2z^2 + xzt + xyz + yt$
26. $a^2t^2 + b^2t^2 - cb^2 - ca^2$
27. $a^4 - 4a^2b^2c^2 + 4b^4c^4$
28. $A^2 - B^2 + 16A + 64$
29. $A^2 + B^2$
30. $x^2 + 64$

31. $x^3 + 64$
32. $27 - (a - b)^3$
33. $(x + y)^3 - y^3$
34. $(a + b)^3 - 8c^3$
35. $x^3 - y^3 + x - y$
36. $8a^3 + 27b^3 + 2a + 3b$
37. (a) $p^4 - 1$
    (b) $p^8 - 1$
38. (a) $p^4 + 4$
    (b) $p^4 - 4$
39. $x^3 + 3x^2 + 3x + 1$
40. $-1 + 6x - 12x^2 + 8x^3$
41. $x^2 + 16y^2$
42. $4u^2 + 25v^2$
43. $\dfrac{25}{16} - c^2$
44. $\dfrac{81}{4} - y^2$
45. $z^4 - \dfrac{81}{16}$
46. $\dfrac{(a + b)^2}{4} - \dfrac{a^2b^2}{9}$
47. $\dfrac{125}{m^3n^3} - 1$
48. $\dfrac{x^3}{8} - \dfrac{512}{x^3}$
49. $\frac{1}{4}x^2 + xy + y^2$
50. $x^2 + x + 1$
51. $64(x - a)^3 - x + a$
52. $64(x - a)^4 - x + a$
53. $x^2 - a^2 + y^2 - 2xy$
54. $a^4 - (b + c)^4$
55. $21x^3 + 82x^2 - 39x$
56. $x^3a^2 - 8y^3a^2 - 4x^3b^2 + 32y^3b^2$
57. $12xy + 25 - 4x^2 - 9y^2$
58. $ax^2 + (1 + ab)xy + by^2$
59. $ax^2 + (a + b)x + b$
60. $(5a^2 - 11a + 10)^2 - (4a^2 - 15a + 6)^2$
61. $(x + 1)^{1/2} - (x + 1)^{3/2}$
62. $(x^2 + 1)^{3/2} + (x^2 + 1)^{7/2}$
63. $(x + 1)^{-1/2} - (x + 1)^{-3/2}$
64. $(x^2 + 1)^{-2/3} + (x^2 + 1)^{-5/3}$
65. $(2x + 3)^{1/2} - \frac{1}{3}(2x + 3)^{3/2}$
66. $(ax + b)^{-1/2} - \sqrt{ax + b}/b$

*In Exercises 67 and 68, evaluate the given expressions using factoring techniques. (The point here is to do as little actual arithmetic as possible.)*

67. (a) $100^2 - 99^2$
    (b) $8^3 - 6^3$
    (c) $1000^2 - 999^2$

68. (a) $10^3 - 9^3$
    (b) $50^2 - 49^2$
    (c) $\dfrac{15^3 - 10^3}{15^2 - 10^2}$

## B

*In Exercises 69–73, factor each expression.*

69. $A^3 + B^3 + 3AB(A + B)$
70. $p^3 - q^3 - p(p^2 - q^2) + q(p - q)^2$
71. $2x(a^2 + x^2)^{-1/2} - x^3(a^2 + x^2)^{-3/2}$
72. $\frac{1}{2}(x - a)^{-1/2}(x + a)^{-1/2} - \frac{1}{2}(x + a)^{1/2}(x - a)^{-3/2}$
73. $y^4 - (p + q)y^3 + (p^2q + pq^2)y - p^2q^2$
74. (a) Factor $x^4 + 2x^2y^2 + y^4$.
    (b) Factor $x^4 + x^2y^2 + y^4$.  *Hint:* Add and subtract a term. [Keep part (a) in mind.]
    (c) Factor $x^6 - y^6$ as a difference of squares.
    (d) Factor $x^6 - y^6$ as a difference of cubes. [Use the result in part (b) to obtain the same answer as in part (c).]

# B.5   REVIEW OF FRACTIONAL EXPRESSIONS

*But if you do use a rule involving mechanical calculation, be patient, accurate, and systematically neat in the working. It is well known to mathematical teachers that quite half the failures in algebraic exercises arise from arithmetical inaccuracy and slovenly arrangement.* — George Chrystal (1893)

The rules of basic arithmetic that you learned for working with simple fractions are also used for fractions involving algebraic expressions. In algebra, as in arithmetic, we say that a fraction is *reduced to lowest terms* or *simplified* when the numerator and denominator contain no common factors (other than 1 and −1). The factoring techniques that we reviewed in Appendix B.4 are used to reduce fractions. For example, to reduce the fraction $\dfrac{x^2 - 9}{x^2 + 3x}$, we write

$$\frac{x^2 - 9}{x^2 + 3x} = \frac{(x - 3)(x + 3)}{x(x + 3)} = \frac{x - 3}{x}$$

In the box that follows, we review two properties of negatives and fractions that will be useful in this section. Notice that Property 2 follows from Property 1 because

$$\frac{a - b}{b - a} = \frac{a - b}{-(a - b)} = -1$$

## PROPERTY SUMMARY   Negatives and Fractions

| Property | Example |
|---|---|
| 1. $b - a = -(a - b)$ | $2 - x = -(x - 2)$ |
| 2. $\dfrac{a - b}{b - a} = -1$ | $\dfrac{2x - 5}{5 - 2x} = -1$ |

## EXAMPLE  1   Using Property 2 to simplify a fractional expression

Simplify: $\dfrac{4 - 3x}{15x - 20}$.

**SOLUTION**

$$\frac{4 - 3x}{15x - 20} = \frac{4 - 3x}{5(3x - 4)}$$

$$= \frac{1}{5}\left(\frac{4 - 3x}{3x - 4}\right) = -\frac{1}{5} \qquad \text{using Property 2}$$

In Example 2 we display two more instances in which factoring is used to reduce a fraction. After that, Example 3 indicates how these skills are used to multiply and divide fractional expressions.

## EXAMPLE  2   Using factoring to simplify a fractional expression

Simplify:   **(a)** $\dfrac{x^3 - 8}{x^2 - 2x}$;   **(b)** $\dfrac{x^2 - 6x + 8}{a(x - 2) + b(x - 2)}$.

**SOLUTION**

(a) $\dfrac{x^3 - 8}{x^2 - 2x} = \dfrac{(x - 2)(x^2 + 2x + 4)}{x(x - 2)} = \dfrac{x^2 + 2x + 4}{x}$

(b) $\dfrac{x^2 - 6x + 8}{a(x - 2) + b(x - 2)} = \dfrac{(x - 2)(x - 4)}{(x - 2)(a + b)} = \dfrac{x - 4}{a + b}$

---

**EXAMPLE 3    Using factoring to simplify products and quotients**

Carry out the indicated operations and simplify:

(a) $\dfrac{x^3}{2x^2 + 3x} \cdot \dfrac{12x + 18}{4x^2 - 6x}$;    (b) $\dfrac{2x^2 - x - 6}{x^2 + x + 1} \cdot \dfrac{x^3 - 1}{4 - x^2}$;

(c) $\dfrac{x^2 - 144}{x^2 - 4} \div \dfrac{x + 12}{x + 2}$.

**SOLUTION**

(a) $\dfrac{x^3}{2x^2 + 3x} \cdot \dfrac{12x + 18}{4x^2 - 6x} = \dfrac{x^3}{x(2x + 3)} \cdot \dfrac{6(2x + 3)}{2x(2x - 3)}$

$\qquad = \dfrac{6x^3}{2x^2(2x - 3)} = \dfrac{3x}{2x - 3}$

(b) $\dfrac{2x^2 - x - 6}{x^2 + x + 1} \cdot \dfrac{x^3 - 1}{4 - x^2} = \dfrac{(2x + 3)(x - 2)}{(x^2 + x + 1)} \cdot \dfrac{(x - 1)(x^2 + x + 1)}{(2 - x)(2 + x)}$

$\qquad = \dfrac{-(2x + 3)(x - 1)}{2 + x}$    using the fact

$\qquad = \dfrac{-2x^2 - x + 3}{2 + x}$    that $\dfrac{x - 2}{2 - x} = -1$

(c) $\dfrac{x^2 - 144}{x^2 - 4} \div \dfrac{x + 12}{x + 2} = \dfrac{x^2 - 144}{x^2 - 4} \cdot \dfrac{x + 2}{x + 12}$

$\qquad = \dfrac{(x - 12)(x + 12)}{(x - 2)(x + 2)} \cdot \dfrac{x + 2}{x + 12} = \dfrac{x - 12}{x - 2}$

---

As in arithmetic, to combine two fractions by addition or subtraction, the fractions must have a common denominator, that is, the denominators must be the same. The rules in this case are

$$\frac{a}{b} + \frac{c}{b} = \frac{a + c}{b} \qquad \text{and} \qquad \frac{a}{b} - \frac{c}{b} = \frac{a - c}{b}$$

For example, we have

$$\frac{4x - 1}{x + 1} - \frac{2x - 1}{x + 1} = \frac{4x - 1 - (2x - 1)}{x + 1} = \frac{4x - 1 - 2x + 1}{x + 1} = \frac{2x}{x + 1}$$

Fractions with unlike denominators are added or subtracted by first converting to a common denominator. For instance, to add $9/a$ and $10/a^2$, we write

$$\frac{9}{a} + \frac{10}{a^2} = \frac{9}{a} \cdot \frac{a}{a} + \frac{10}{a^2}$$

$$= \frac{9a}{a^2} + \frac{10}{a^2} = \frac{9a + 10}{a^2}$$

Notice that the common denominator used was $a^2$. This is the **least common denominator.** In fact, other common denominators (such as $a^3$ or $a^4$) could be used here, but that would be less efficient. In general, the least common denominator for a given group of fractions is chosen as follows. Write down a product involving the irreducible factors from each denominator. The power of each factor should be equal to (but not greater than) the highest power of that factor appearing in any of the individual denominators. For example, the least common denominator for the two fractions $\dfrac{1}{(x+1)^2}$ and $\dfrac{1}{(x+1)(x+2)}$ is $(x+1)^2(x+2)$. In the example that follows, notice that the denominators must be in factored form before the least common denominator can be determined.

**EXAMPLE** **4**   **Using the least common denominator**

Combine into a single fraction and simplify:

**(a)** $\dfrac{3}{4x} + \dfrac{7x}{10y^2} - 2$;   **(b)** $\dfrac{x}{x^2-9} - \dfrac{1}{x+3}$;   **(c)** $\dfrac{15}{x^2+x-6} + \dfrac{x+1}{2-x}$.

**SOLUTION**

**(a)** Denominators: $2^2 \cdot x$; $2 \cdot 5 \cdot y^2$; $1$

Least common denominator; $2^2 \cdot 5xy^2 = 20xy^2$

$$\frac{3}{4x} + \frac{7x}{10y^2} - \frac{2}{1} = \frac{3}{4x}\cdot\frac{5y^2}{5y^2} + \frac{7x}{10y^2}\cdot\frac{2x}{2x} - \frac{2}{1}\cdot\frac{20xy^2}{20xy^2}$$

$$= \frac{15y^2 + 14x^2 - 40xy^2}{20xy^2}$$

*Note*: The final numerator is irreducible over the integers.

**(b)** Denominators: $x^2 - 9 = (x-3)(x+3)$; $x+3$

Least common denominator: $(x-3)(x+3)$

$$\frac{x}{x^2-9} - \frac{1}{x+3} = \frac{x}{(x-3)(x+3)} - \frac{1}{x+3}$$

$$= \frac{x}{(x-3)(x+3)} - \frac{1}{x+3}\cdot\frac{x-3}{x-3}$$

$$= \frac{x-(x-3)}{(x-3)(x+3)} = \frac{3}{(x-3)(x+3)}$$

**(c)** $\dfrac{15}{x^2+x-6} + \dfrac{x+1}{2-x} = \dfrac{15}{(x-2)(x+3)} - \dfrac{x+1}{x-2}$   using the fact that $2-x = -(x-2)$

$$= \frac{15}{(x-2)(x+3)} - \frac{x+1}{x-2}\cdot\frac{x+3}{x+3}$$

$$= \frac{15-(x^2+4x+3)}{(x-2)(x+3)} = \frac{-x^2-4x+12}{(x-2)(x+3)}$$

$$= \frac{(x-2)(-x-6)}{(x-2)(x+3)} = \frac{-x-6}{x+3} = -\frac{x+6}{x+3}$$

Notice in the last line that we were able to simplify the answer by factoring the numerator and reducing the fraction. (This is why we prefer to leave the least common denominator in factored form, rather than multiplying it out, in this type of problem.)

The next four examples illustrate using the least common denominator to simplify compound fractions, or complex fractions, which are fractions "within" fractions.

**EXAMPLE 5    Simplifying a compound fraction**

Simplify: $\dfrac{\dfrac{1}{3a} - \dfrac{1}{4b}}{\dfrac{5}{6a^2} + \dfrac{1}{b}}$.

**SOLUTION**

The least common denominator for the four individual denominators $3a$, $4b$, $6a^2$, and $b$ is $12a^2b$. Multiplying the given expression by $12a^2b/12a^2b$, which equals 1, yields

$$\frac{12a^2b}{12a^2b} \cdot \frac{\dfrac{1}{3a} - \dfrac{1}{4b}}{\dfrac{5}{6a^2} + \dfrac{1}{b}} = \frac{4ab - 3a^2}{10b + 12a^2}$$

**EXAMPLE 6    Simplifying a fraction containing negative exponents**

Simplify: $(x^{-1} + y^{-1})^{-1}$. (The answer is *not* $x + y$.)

**SOLUTION**

After applying the definition of negative exponent to rewrite the given expression, we'll use the method shown in Example 5.

$$(x^{-1} + y^{-1})^{-1} = \left(\frac{1}{x} + \frac{1}{y}\right)^{-1} = \frac{1}{\dfrac{1}{x} + \dfrac{1}{y}}$$

$$= \frac{xy}{xy} \cdot \frac{1}{\dfrac{1}{x} + \dfrac{1}{y}} = \frac{xy}{y + x} \qquad \text{multiplying by } 1 = \frac{xy}{xy}$$

**EXAMPLE 7    Simplifying a compound fraction**

Simplify: $\dfrac{\dfrac{1}{x + h} - \dfrac{1}{x}}{h}$. (This type of expression occurs in calculus.)

**SOLUTION**

$$\frac{\dfrac{1}{x + h} - \dfrac{1}{x}}{h} = \frac{(x + h)x}{(x + h)x} \cdot \frac{\dfrac{1}{x + h} - \dfrac{1}{x}}{h} \qquad \text{multiplying by } 1 = \frac{(x + h)x}{(x + h)x}$$

$$= \frac{x - (x + h)}{(x + h)xh} = \frac{-h}{(x + h)xh} = -\frac{1}{x(x + h)}$$

| EXAMPLE | 8 | Simplifying a compound fraction |

Simplify: $\dfrac{x - \dfrac{1}{x^2}}{\dfrac{1}{x^2} - 1}$.

**SOLUTION**

$$\frac{x - \dfrac{1}{x^2}}{\dfrac{1}{x^2} - 1} = \frac{x^2}{x^2} \cdot \frac{x - \dfrac{1}{x^2}}{\dfrac{1}{x^2} - 1} \qquad \text{multiplying by } 1 = \frac{x^2}{x^2}$$

$$= \frac{x^3 - 1}{1 - x^2} = -\frac{x^3 - 1}{x^2 - 1}$$

$$= -\frac{(x - 1)(x^2 + x + 1)}{(x - 1)(x + 1)} = -\frac{x^2 + x + 1}{x + 1}$$

# EXERCISE SET B.5

## A

*In Exercises 1–12, reduce the fractions to lowest terms.*

**1.** $\dfrac{x^2 - 9}{x + 3}$

**2.** $\dfrac{25 - x^2}{x - 5}$

**3.** $\dfrac{x + 2}{x^4 - 16}$

**4.** $\dfrac{x^2 - x - 20}{2x^2 + 7x + 4}$

**5.** $\dfrac{x^2 + 2x + 4}{x^3 - 8}$

**6.** $\dfrac{a + b}{ax^2 + bx^2}$

**7.** $\dfrac{9ab - 12b^2}{6a^2 - 8ab}$

**8.** $\dfrac{a^3 b^2 - 27b^5}{(ab - 3b^2)^2}$

**9.** $\dfrac{a^3 + a^2 + a + 1}{a^2 - 1}$

**10.** $\dfrac{(x - y)^2(a + b)}{(x^2 - y^2)(a^2 + 2ab + b^2)}$

**11.** $\dfrac{x^3 - y^3}{(x - y)^3}$

**12.** $\dfrac{x^4 - y^4}{(x^4 y + x^2 y^3 + x^3 y^2 + xy^4)(x - y)^2}$

*In Exercises 13–55, carry out the indicated operations and simplify where possible.*

**13.** $\dfrac{2}{x - 2} \cdot \dfrac{x^2 - 4}{x + 2}$

**14.** $\dfrac{ax + 3}{2a + 1} \div \dfrac{a^2 x^2 + 3ax}{4a^2 - 1}$

**15.** $\dfrac{x^2 - x - 2}{x^2 + x - 12} \cdot \dfrac{x^2 - 3x}{x^2 - 4x + 4}$

**16.** $(3t^2 + 4tx + x^2) \div \dfrac{3t^2 - 2tx - x^2}{t^2 - x^2}$

**17.** $\dfrac{x^3 + y^3}{x^2 - 4xy + 3y^2} \div \dfrac{(x + y)^3}{x^2 - 2xy - 3y^2}$

**18.** $\dfrac{a^2 - a - 42}{a^4 + 216a} \div \dfrac{a^2 - 49}{a^3 - 6a^2 + 36a}$

**19.** $\dfrac{4}{x} - \dfrac{2}{x^2}$

**20.** $\dfrac{1}{3x} + \dfrac{1}{5x^2} - \dfrac{1}{30x^3}$

**21.** $\dfrac{6}{a} - \dfrac{a}{6}$

**22.** $\dfrac{1}{a} + \dfrac{1}{b} + \dfrac{1}{c}$

**23.** $\dfrac{1}{x + 3} + \dfrac{3}{x + 2}$

**24.** $\dfrac{4}{x - 4} - \dfrac{4}{x + 1}$

**25.** $\dfrac{3x}{x - 2} - \dfrac{6}{x^2 - 4}$

**26.** $1 + \dfrac{1}{x} - \dfrac{1}{x^2}$

**27.** $\dfrac{a}{x - 1} + \dfrac{2ax}{(x - 1)^2} + \dfrac{3ax^2}{(x - 1)^3}$

**28.** $\dfrac{a^2 + 5a - 4}{a^2 - 16} - \dfrac{2a}{2a^2 + 8a}$

**29.** $\dfrac{4}{x - 5} - \dfrac{4}{5 - x}$

**30.** $\dfrac{x}{x + a} + \dfrac{a}{a - x}$

**31.** $\dfrac{a^2 + b^2}{a^2 - b^2} + \dfrac{a}{a + b} + \dfrac{b}{b - a}$

**32.** $\dfrac{3}{2x + 2} - \dfrac{5}{x^2 - 1} + \dfrac{1}{x + 1}$

**33.** $\dfrac{1}{x^2 + x - 20} - \dfrac{1}{x^2 - 8x + 16}$

**34.** $\dfrac{4}{6x^2 + 5x - 4} + \dfrac{1}{3x^2 + 4x} - \dfrac{1}{2x - 1}$

**35.** $\dfrac{2q + p}{2p^2 - 9pq - 5q^2} - \dfrac{p + q}{p^2 - 5pq}$

**36.** $\dfrac{1}{x - 1} + \dfrac{1}{x^2 - 1} + \dfrac{1}{x^3 - 1}$

**37.** $\dfrac{\dfrac{1}{x} + 1}{\dfrac{1}{x} - 1}$

**38.** $\dfrac{\dfrac{4}{a} - a}{\dfrac{2}{a} + 1}$

**39.** $\dfrac{\dfrac{1}{x} - \dfrac{1}{a}}{x - a}$

**40.** $\dfrac{\dfrac{1}{a} + \dfrac{1}{b}}{\dfrac{1}{a} - \dfrac{1}{b}}$

**41.** $\dfrac{a - \dfrac{1}{a}}{1 + \dfrac{1}{a}}$

**42.** $\dfrac{\dfrac{1}{x^2} - \dfrac{1}{y^2}}{\dfrac{1}{x} + \dfrac{1}{y}}$

**43.** $\dfrac{\dfrac{1}{2 + h} - \dfrac{1}{2}}{h}$

**44.** $\dfrac{\dfrac{3}{x^2 + h} - \dfrac{3}{x^2}}{h}$

**45.** $\dfrac{\dfrac{a}{x^2} + \dfrac{x}{a^2}}{a^2 - ax + x^2}$

**46.** $\dfrac{x + \dfrac{xy}{y - x}}{\dfrac{y^2}{x^2 - y^2} + 1}$

**47.** $(x^{-1} + 2)^{-1}$

**48.** $\dfrac{(x^{-2} + 2x)^{-1}}{x^2}$

**49.** $\left( \dfrac{1}{a^{-1}} + \dfrac{1}{a^{-2}} \right)^{-1}$

**50.** $(a^{-1} + a^{-2})^{-1}$

**51.** $x(x + y)^{-1} + y(x - y)^{-1}$

**52.** $x(2x - 2y)^{-1} + y(2y - 2x)^{-1}$

**B**

**53.** $\dfrac{\dfrac{a + b}{a - b} + \dfrac{a - b}{a + b}}{\dfrac{a - b}{a + b} - \dfrac{a + b}{a - b}} \cdot \dfrac{ab^3 - a^3b}{a^2 + b^2}$

**54.** $\dfrac{\sqrt{x + a}}{\sqrt{x - a}} - \dfrac{\sqrt{x - a}}{\sqrt{x + a}}$

**C**

**55.** $\dfrac{\left( a + \dfrac{1}{b} \right)^a \left( a - \dfrac{1}{b} \right)^b}{\left( b + \dfrac{1}{a} \right)^a \left( b - \dfrac{1}{a} \right)^b}$

**56.** Consider the three fractions

$$\frac{b - c}{1 + bc}, \qquad \frac{c - a}{1 + ca}, \qquad \text{and} \qquad \frac{a - b}{1 + ab}$$

**(a)** If $a = 1$, $b = 2$, and $c = 3$, find the sum of the three fractions. Also compute their product. What do you observe?

**(b)** Show that the sum and the product of the three given fractions are, in fact, always equal.

# Answers to Selected Exercises

## CHAPTER 1
### Exercise Set 1.1
**1. (a)** integer, rational number
**(b)** rational number   **3. (a)** natural number, integer, rational number
**(b)** rational number   **5. (a)** rational number   **(b)** rational number
**7.** irrational number   **9.** irrational number
**11.**

**13.**

**15.**

**17.**

**19.**

**21.**

**23.**

**25.**

**27.**

**29.**

**31.** False   **33.** True   **35.** False
**37.** False   **39.** True
**41.** $2 < x < 5$

**43.** $1 \le x \le 4$

**45.** $0 \le x < 3$

**47.** $-3 < x < \infty$

**49.** $-1 \le x < \infty$

**51.** $-\infty < x < 1$

**53.** $-\infty < x \le \pi$

**55. (a)** one decimal place   **(b)** two decimal places   **(c)** six decimal places
**(d)** nine decimal places
**57. (a)** $a = \sqrt{2}, b = \sqrt{8}$   **(b)** $a = \sqrt{2}, b = \sqrt{3}$   **59. (a)** $2^{1/2} = \sqrt{2}$
**(b)** $(\sqrt{2})^2 = 2$

### Exercise Set 1.2
**1.** 3   **3.** 6   **5.** 2   **7.** 0   **9.** 0   **11.** 17
**13.** 1   **15.** 0   **17.** 25   **19.** $-1$   **21.** 0
**23.** 3   **25.** $\sqrt{2} - 2$   **27.** $x - 3$
**29.** $t^2 + 1$   **31.** $\sqrt{3} + 4$   **33.** $-2x + 7$
**35.** 1   **37.** $3x + 11$   **39.** $|x - 1| - \frac{1}{2}$
**41.** $|x - 1| \ge \frac{1}{2}$   **43.** $|y + 4| < 1$
**45.** $|y| < 3$   **47.** $|x^2 - a^2| < M$
**49.**

**51.**

**53.**

**55.**

**57.**

**59.**

**61. (a)**

**(b)**

**(c)** The interval in part **(b)** does not include 2.

## Exercise Set 1.3
**1.** is a solution   **3.** not a solution
**5.** is a solution   **7.** $x = -1$   **9.** $m = 4$
**11.** $t = 14$   **13.** $y = -15$   **15.** $x = 3$
**17.** $x = 8$   **19.** no solution
**21.** $x = -\frac{16}{9}$   **23. (a)** $x = -\frac{5}{11}$
**(b)** $x = -\frac{2}{11}$   **(c)** no solution
**25.** $x = 3$ or $x = 2$   **27.** $t = -\frac{4}{3}$
or $t = -1$   **29.** $x = -8$ or $x = 5$
**31.** $x = -\frac{1}{3}$ or $x = 8$   **33.** $x = -\sqrt{5}$
**35.** $x = \dfrac{-3 \pm 3\sqrt{17}}{8} \approx -1.17, 1.92$
**37.** $x = \dfrac{-4 \pm \sqrt{10}}{3} \approx -2.39, -0.28$
**39.** $x = \sqrt{3} \pm \sqrt{2} \approx 0.32, 3.15$
**41.** $x = -\frac{5}{8}$ or $x = -\frac{1}{3}$   **43.** $y = \pm 5$
**45.** $x = \pm\sqrt[4]{5}$   **47. (a)** $x = -89$
or $x = -67$   **(b)** $y = -\frac{1}{6}$ or $y = \frac{13}{24}$
**49.** $x = \dfrac{b + 1}{a}$   **51.** $x = 1$
**53.** $x = \dfrac{1}{a + b}$   **55.** $x = \dfrac{2ab}{b + a}$
**57.** $x = 1$ or $x = -1$
**59.** $x = \dfrac{a^2 + ab + b^2}{a - b}$   **61.** $x = b$
**63.** $x = \dfrac{a + b}{2}$   **65.** $h = \dfrac{S - 2\pi r^2}{2\pi r}$
**67.** $r = \dfrac{d}{1 - dt}$   **69.** $x = \frac{5}{2}$ or $x = -4$
**71.** $x = \frac{1}{3}$ or $x = \frac{1}{2}$   **73.** no solution

## Exercise Set 1.4
**1.**

**3. (a)**

**(b)** 6 square units   **5. (a)** 5   **(b)** 13
**7. (a)** 10   **(b)** 9   **9.** 4   **11. (a)** $(4, \frac{1}{2})$
is farther from the origin   **(b)** $(-6, 7)$
is farther from the origin   **13. (a)** is a
right triangle   **(b)** is a right triangle
**(c)** not a right triangle   **15.** area $= 0$;
the three points are collinear
**17. (a)** $(6, 5)$   **(b)** $(\frac{1}{2}, -\frac{3}{2})$   **(c)** $(1, -4)$
**19. (a)** $(1, 1)$   **(b)** $\sqrt{34}$
**21. (a)**

**(b)** $1.8 million   **(c)** 45.5% error
**23. (a)**

| $t$ | 1995 | 1997 |
|---|---|---|
| $n$ | 14 | 30 |

22 million host computers
**(b)**

| $t$ | 1985 | 1987 |
|---|---|---|
| $n$ | 2 | 28 |

15 thousand host computers
**(c)** 1996: 0.83% error;
1986: 194.75% error
**25. (a)**

**(b)** both are $(0, \frac{7}{2})$   **(c)** The diagonals of a parallelogram bisect each other.
**27. (a)** $a = \sqrt{2}$; $b = \sqrt{3}$; $c = \sqrt{4} = 2$;
$d = \sqrt{5}$; $e = \sqrt{6}$; $f = \sqrt{7}$;
$g = \sqrt{8} = 2\sqrt{2}$
**29. (b)** both are $\left(\dfrac{a + b}{2}, \dfrac{c}{2}\right)$

## Exercise Set 1.5
**1.** does not lie on the graph
**3.** does not lie on the graph
**5.** lies on the graph
**7. (a)** $y = \frac{2}{3}x + 1$;

| $x$ | $-6$ | $-3$ | 0 | 3 | 6 |
|---|---|---|---|---|---|
| $y$ | $-3$ | $-1$ | 1 | 3 | 5 |

**(b)**

**9.** $x$-intercept: 4; $y$-intercept: 3

**11.** $x$-intercept: 2; $y$-intercept: $-4$

**13.** $x$-intercept: 1; $y$-intercept: 1

**15. (a)** $\text{Xmin} = -3, \text{Xmax} = 3,$
$\text{Xscl} = 1$ and $\text{Ymin} = -200,$
$\text{Ymax} = 200, \text{Yscl} = 100;$
$[-3, 3, 1]$ by $[-200, 200, 100]$
**(b)** $\text{Xmin} = -1, \text{Xmax} = 1.25,$
$\text{Xscl} = 0.25$ and $\text{Ymin} = -0.2,$
$\text{Ymax} = 0.1, \text{Yscl} = 0.1;$
$[-1, 1.25, 0.25]$ by $[-0.2, 0.1, 0.1]$
**17. (a)** $x$-intercepts: $-2, -1;$
$y$-intercept: 2    **(b)** no $x$-intercepts;
$y$-intercept: 3

**19. (a)** $x$-intercepts: $\dfrac{-1 \pm \sqrt{5}}{2}$;
$y$-intercept: $-1$
**(b)** no $x$-intercepts; $y$-intercept: 1
**21.** $x$-intercepts: $-1 \pm 2\sqrt{3} \approx -4.46,$
$2.46$; $y$-intercept: 0
**23.** $x$-intercept: $-\frac{8}{3}$;
$y$-intercepts: $-2, 6$
**25. (a)**

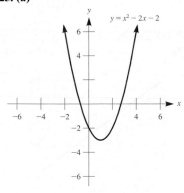

**(b)** $-0.7, 2.7$   **(c)** $1 \pm \sqrt{3} \approx -0.7, 2.7$

**27. (a)**

**(b)** $-1.6, 0, 1.6$
**(c)** $0, \pm\sqrt{5/2} \approx \pm1.6$
**29. (a)**

**(b)** $-1.7$   **(c)** $\sqrt[3]{-5} \approx -1.7$
**31.** $x$-intercepts: $-1.879, 0.347, 1.532$

**33.** $x$-intercepts: $-0.815, 0.875, 5.998$

**35. (a)** The $x$-intercept is between $-1$
and 0.

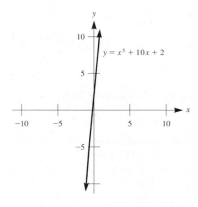

**(c)** $[0, 10]$   **(d)** Start with a large
viewing rectangle then zoom in near
the $x$-intercepts.   **37. (a)** $-20°$; this is
the $C$-intercept of the graph.
**(b)** $C = -17\frac{7}{9}$; this is the $F$-intercept
of the graph.   **39. (a)** $\sqrt{2} \approx 1.4$
**(b)** $\sqrt{3} \approx 1.7$   **(c)** $\sqrt{6} \approx 2.4$
**41. (a)** 500 bacteria   **(b)** 1.5 hours
**(c)** $t = 3.5$ hours   **(d)** between $t = 3$
and $t = 4$   **43.** $A$: $x = \frac{2}{5}\sqrt{5} \approx 0.894$;
$B$: $x = -\frac{1}{5}\sqrt{30} \approx -1.095$

## Exercise Set 1.6

**1. (a)** $-2$   **(b)** $3$   **(c)** $-\frac{7}{3}$   **(d)** $3$

**3. (a)** slope $= 1$

**(b)** slope $= 0$

**5. (a)** $\Delta x = 5$ sec; $\Delta y = 15$ ft;
$\dfrac{\Delta y}{\Delta x} = 3$ ft/sec
**(b)** $\Delta x = 15$ sec; $\Delta y = 45$ ft;
$\dfrac{\Delta y}{\Delta x} = 3$ ft/sec
**(c)** $\Delta x = 25$ sec; $\Delta y = 75$ ft;
$\dfrac{\Delta y}{\Delta x} = 3$ ft/sec
**7. (a)** $\Delta x = 10$ years;
$\Delta y = 25{,}000{,}000$ people
**(b)** $\Delta x = 20$ years;
$\Delta y = 50{,}000{,}000$ people
**(c)** $\Delta x = 10$ years;
$\Delta y = 25{,}000{,}000$ people
**9.** $\Delta t = 3$ years;
$\Delta N = -0.119$ trillion cigarettes
**11.** $m_3 < m_2 < m_4 < m_1$
**13.** not collinear   **15. (a)** $y = -5x - 9$
**(b)** $y = \frac{1}{3}x + \frac{4}{3}$   **17. (a)** $y = 2x$
**(b)** $y = -2x - 4$   **(c)** $y = \frac{1}{7}x - \frac{11}{7}$
**19. (a)** $x = -3$   **(b)** $y = 4$
**21.** $x = 0$   **23. (a)** $y = -4x + 7$
**(b)** $y = 2x + \frac{3}{2}$

**25. (a)** $y = 4x + 11$

**(b)** $y = \frac{1}{2}x - \frac{5}{4}$

**(c)** $y = -\frac{5}{6}x + 5$

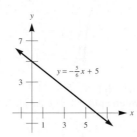

**(d)** $y = \frac{3}{4}x + \frac{3}{2}$

**(e)** $y = 4x - 2$

**27.** $y - 4 = 0$

**29. (a)** $x$-intercept: 5; $y$-intercept: 3;
area $= \frac{15}{2}$; perimeter $= 8 + \sqrt{34}$
**(b)** $x$-intercept: 5; $y$-intercept: $-3$;
area $= \frac{15}{2}$; perimeter $= 8 + \sqrt{34}$
**31. (a)** neither   **(b)** parallel
**(c)** perpendicular   **(d)** perpendicular
**33.** $y = \frac{2}{5}x + \frac{12}{5}$; $2x - 5y + 12 = 0$
**35.** $y = -\frac{4}{3}x + \frac{16}{3}$; $4x + 3y - 16 = 0$
**37.** They appear parallel for each
viewing rectangle.

**39. (a)** $y = \frac{4}{3}x$
**(b)**

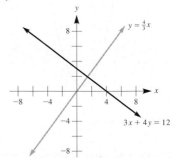

**41. (a)** $y = -\frac{2}{3}p + 410$   **(b)** 208 units
**(c)** \$183   **47.** 44.1 square units

**49. (a)**

**(b)** $y = -2x + 5$     **(c)** $(4, -3)$
**(d)** $3\sqrt{5}$

**51. (a)**

**(b)** point: $(-1, 2)$

**(c)** $y = \frac{3}{5}x + \frac{12}{5}$; $y = -\frac{3}{4}x + \frac{3}{2}$; $(-\frac{2}{3}, 2)$

## Exercise Set 1.7
**1. (a)**

**(b)**

**(c)**

**3. (a)**

**(b)**

**(c)**

**5. (a)**

**(b)**

**(c)**

**7.** $x$-intercepts: 2 and $-2$;
$y$-intercept: 4; symmetric about
the $y$-axis

**9.** no $x$- or $y$-intercepts; symmetric
about the origin

**11.** $x$- and $y$-intercepts: 0;
symmetric about the $y$-axis

**13.** no $x$- or $y$-intercepts;
symmetric about the origin

**15.** $x$- and $y$-intercepts: 0; symmetric
about the $y$-axis

**17.** $x$- and $y$-intercepts: 1;
no symmetry

**19.** $x$-intercept: 2; no $y$-intercept;
symmetric about the $x$-axis

**21.** $x$-intercepts:
$$\frac{-1 \pm \sqrt{33}}{4} \approx -1.69, 1.19;$$
$y$-intercept: $-4$; no symmetry

**23. (a)** $x$- and $y$-intercepts: 2;
no symmetry

**(b)** $x$-intercepts: $\pm 2$; $y$-intercept: 2;
symmetric about the $y$-axis

**25. (a)**

**(b)** no symmetry
**(c)**

**(d)** no symmetry
**27. (a)**

**(b)** no symmetry
**(c)**

**(d)** no symmetry
**29. (a)**

**(b)** no symmetry
**(c)**

**(d)** no symmetry
**31. (a)**

**(b)** $y$-axis symmetry
**(c)**

**(d)** no symmetry
**33. (a)**

**(b)** $y$-axis symmetry
**(c)**

**(d)** $y$-axis symmetry
**35. (a)**

**(b)** origin symmetry
**(c)**

**(d)** origin symmetry
**37. (a)**

**(b)** $y$-axis symmetry
**(c)**

**(d)** no symmetry  **39.** center: $(1, 5)$;
radius: 13; $(6, -7)$ lies on the circle
**41.** center: $(-8, 5)$; radius: $\sqrt{13}$;
$(-5, 2)$ does not lie on the circle
**43.** center: $(0, 0)$; radius: $\sqrt[4]{2}$;
$y$-intercepts: $\pm\sqrt[4]{2}$  **45.** center:
$(-4, 3)$; radius: 1; no $y$-intercepts
**47.** center: $(-3, \frac{1}{3})$; radius: $\sqrt{2}$;
no $y$-intercepts  **49. (a)** center:
$(2, -\frac{3}{2})$; radius: $\frac{13}{4}$
**(b)** $x$-intercepts: $-0.88$ and 4.88

**(c)** $x = \dfrac{8 + \sqrt{133}}{4} \approx -0.88,\ 4.88$

**51.**

**(c)**

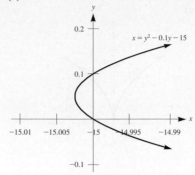

**55.** $3x - 4y = 0$    **57.** $x + y - 1 = 0$ and $x - 2y - 4 = 0$    **59.** $y$-axis symmetry    **61.** $y$-axis symmetry    **63.** $x$-axis symmetry    **65.** $x$-axis, $y$-axis, and origin symmetry    **67.** $x$-axis symmetry
**69.**

**71.**

## Chapter 1 Review Exercises
**1.** $|x - 6| = 2$    **3.** $|a - b| = 3$
**5.** $|x| > 10$    **7.** $\sqrt{6} - 2$
**9.** $x^4 + x^2 + 1$    **11. (a)** $-2x + 5$
**(b)** 1    **(c)** $2x - 5$
**13.** $3 < x < 5$

**15.** $-5 \leq x < 0$

**17.** $-1 \leq x$

**73.**

**53.** $(x - 3)^2 + (y - 2)^2 = 169$
**55.** $(x - 3)^2 + (y - 5)^2 = 9$
**57.** $y = 2 \pm \sqrt{19}$    **59. (a)** $x$-intercepts for each graph: $\frac{8}{3}$; $y$-intercept for $y = \frac{3}{4}x - 2$: $-2$; $y$-intercept for $y = |\frac{3}{4}x - 2|$: 2    **(b)** on the interval $[\frac{8}{3}, \infty)$    **(c)** The graph of $y = |\frac{3}{4}x - 2|$ can be obtained by reflecting $y = \frac{3}{4}x - 2$ about the $x$-axis for the interval $(-\infty, \frac{8}{3})$. For the interval $[\frac{8}{3}, \infty)$, no reflection is necessary.
**61. (b)**

**19.**

**21.**

**23. (a)**

**(b)**

**25.** $x = \frac{1}{3}$    **27.** $t = -\frac{37}{11}$    **29.** $t = -\frac{11}{3}$
**31.** $y = 8$    **33.** $x = \frac{1}{3}, -\frac{1}{2}$
**35.** $x = -6, 4$    **37.** $x = 10, -1$
**39.** $t = \dfrac{-1 \pm \sqrt{3}}{2}$    **41.** $y = -2x - 6$
**43.** $y = \frac{1}{4}x - \frac{5}{2}$    **45.** $y = 2x + 8$
**47.** $y = -2$    **49.** $y = x + 1$
**51.** $9x - 4y + 14 = 0$    **53.** $2x + y = 0$

**75. (a)**

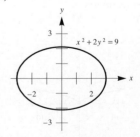

**(b)** intersect at $(-3, 0)$ and $(3, 0)$

**77. (a)**

**(b)**

**(c)** no intersection points

**79.**

**81. (a, b)**

**(c)**

**83.** $MA = MB = MC = \sqrt{c^2 + b^2}$;
all the same   **85. (a)** $\sqrt{130}$   **(b)** $-\frac{11}{3}$
**(c)** $(\frac{7}{2}, -\frac{1}{2})$   **87.** $\frac{49}{6}$ square units
**89. (a)** $(\frac{5}{3}, \frac{11}{3})$; they all intersect at the
same point.

**(b)** $\left(\dfrac{2a}{3} + \dfrac{2b}{3}, \dfrac{2c}{3}\right)$;

they all intersect at the same point.
**93. (a)**

**(b)**

**(c)**

**95.** $13\sqrt{5}/5$   **97.** $17\sqrt{13}/13$
**99. (a)** $(x - 1)^2 + (y - 1)^2 = 1$
**(b)** $\overline{AT}: y = \frac{9}{8}x$; $\overline{BU}: y = -\frac{1}{4}x + 1$;
$\overline{CS}: y = -3x + 3$   **(c)** $(\frac{8}{11}, \frac{9}{11})$;
they intersect in the same point.

## Chapter 1 Test
**1.** 1   **2. (a)** $(\frac{39}{10}, \frac{41}{10})$   **(b)** $[2, \infty)$
**3.** $x = 5$   **4.** $x = \frac{14}{11}, -1$
**5. (a)** $x = -5, 1$   **(b)** $x = -2 \pm \sqrt{5}$

**6.** $x = \dfrac{de - b}{a - ce}$   **7. (a)** $\Delta N = 777$

**(b)** $\dfrac{\Delta N}{\Delta t} \approx 194$ stations per year

**(c)** 11,759 stations
**8. (a)**

**(b)** 42.8 cm   **(c)** 18% error
**9.** $y = 5x - 7$   **10.** $y = \frac{6}{5}x - \frac{17}{5}$
**11.** $(3, 9)$   **12. (a)** origin symmetry
**(b)** $y$-axis symmetry
**(c)** no symmetry
**13.** $x$-intercept: 5; $y$-intercept: $-3$

**14.** $x$-intercepts: $1 \pm \sqrt{5}$;
$y$-intercepts: $-2 \pm 2\sqrt{2}$

**15. (a)**

**(b)** $x$-intercepts: $-2.2, 0, 4.2$
**(c)** $x$-intercepts: $0$,
$1 \pm \sqrt{10} \approx -2.2, 4.2$ **16.** yes
**17. (a)**

**(b)**

**(c)**

**18.** $\frac{121}{5}$ square units

# CHAPTER 2
## Exercise Set 2.1
**1.** $x = -4 \pm 3\sqrt{2} \approx -8.24, 0.24$
**3.** $x = -2 \pm \sqrt{3} \approx -3.73, -0.27$
**5.** $y = \dfrac{5 \pm \sqrt{41}}{4} \approx -0.35, 2.85$
**7.** no real roots **9.** $s = \frac{5}{2}$
**11.** $x = 4 \pm \sqrt{10} \approx 0.84, 7.16$
**13.** $x = \dfrac{1 \pm \sqrt{37}}{6} \approx -0.85, 1.18$
**15.** $y = -4 \pm \sqrt{15} \approx -7.87, -0.13$
**17.** no real roots **19. (a)** year 1917
**(b)** it is reasonable **21. (a)** year
1990; 3 years off **(b)** year 1997;
0 years off **23. (a)** $x$-intercepts:
0.268 and 3.732

**(b)** $x = 2 \pm \sqrt{3} \approx 0.2679, 3.7321$
**25. (a)** $x$-intercepts: $-16.367$ and $0.367$

**(b)** $x = -8 \pm \sqrt{70} \approx -16.3666$,
$0.3666$
**27. (a)** $x$-intercept: $-2.550$

**(b)** $x = -\sqrt{26}/2 \approx -2.5495$
**29.** sum: $-8$; product: $-20$
**31.** sum: 7; product: $\frac{9}{4}$
**33.** $x^2 - 14x + 33 = 0$

**35.** $x^2 - 2x - 1 = 0$
**37.** $4x^2 - 8x - 1 = 0$ **39.** $\sqrt{2}$ and $\sqrt{5}$
**41. (a)** 6 seconds **(b)** 1 second
(rising) 5 seconds (falling) **43.** two
real roots **45.** two real roots
**47.** one real root **49.** two real roots
**51.** $k = 36$ **53.** $k = \pm 2\sqrt{5}$
**55.** $r = \dfrac{-h \pm \sqrt{h^2 + 40}}{2}$
**57.** $t = 0$ or $t = \dfrac{v_0}{16}$
**59. (a)**

**(b)** $-4$ and 4; they are opposites
**(c)** $x = -4, 4$ **65.** $k = -\frac{10}{9}$ or $k = 2$
**69.** $x = 1$ or $x = \frac{1}{2}$
**71. (a)**

**(b)** $c = 9$ **(c)** one root: $x = 3$
**(d)** $c > 9$

## Exercise Set 2.2
**1.** $x = 4, 6$ **3.** $x = -\frac{11}{2}, -\frac{13}{2}$
**5.** $x = -\frac{10}{3}, 5$ **7.** $x = 5$ **9.** $x = 0, \frac{4}{5}$
**11. (a)**

**(b)** $x \approx 2.518$

**(c)** $x = \dfrac{2.2 + \sqrt{8.04}}{2} \approx 2.5177$

**13. (a)**

**(b)** $x \approx \pm 1.414$

**15.** $x = 0, 16$

**17.** $t = 5$   **19.** $x - 0, 2, -2$

**21.** $t = 0, -3, 1$   **23.** $x = 0, \frac{1}{4}, -6$

**25.** $x = \pm\sqrt{3}$   **27.** $y = -1, 1$

**29.** $t = \pm\sqrt{6}/3$

**31.** $x = 2 + \sqrt[3]{5} \approx 3.71$

**33.** $x = -4 - \sqrt[5]{16} \approx -5.74$

**35. (a)** $x = 3 + \sqrt[4]{30} \approx 5.34, 0.66$

**(b)** no solution

**37.** $x = 0, \pm\sqrt{6}, \pm 2$

**39.** $x = \pm\sqrt{\dfrac{-1 + \sqrt{5}}{2}}$

**41.** $x = \pm\sqrt{\dfrac{-3 + \sqrt{17}}{2}}$

**43.** $x = -2, 1$   **45.** $t = \frac{1}{3}, \frac{1}{4}$

**47.** $y = \frac{3}{5}, 4$   **49.** $x = \pm\frac{1}{3}$

**51.** $t = \pm 27$

**53.** $y = 1 + \sqrt[3]{7}$   **55.** $t = -4$

**57.** $x = \pm\frac{1}{27}, \pm 1$

**59.** $x = \pm\sqrt{1 + \sqrt{2}} \approx \pm 1.55$

**61.** $x = -1$   **63.** $x = 4$

**65.** $x = -1$   **67.** $x = -\frac{1}{2}$

**69.** $x = \pm 2, \pm 3$   **71.** $x = -4, -\frac{20}{9}$

**73.** no solutions   **75.** $y = 2$

**77. (a) (a)** $x \approx -1.65, -1.51, 1.51, 1.65$

**(b)** $x = -\sqrt{\dfrac{5 - \sqrt{0.2}}{2}} \approx -1.51,$

$\sqrt{\dfrac{5 - \sqrt{0.2}}{2}} \approx 1.51,$

$-\sqrt{\dfrac{5 + \sqrt{0.2}}{2}} \approx -1.65,$

$\sqrt{\dfrac{5 + \sqrt{0.2}}{2}} \approx 1.65$

**(b) (a)** no real roots

**(b)** no real roots

**79. (a)** $x \approx 0.49$ and $18.51$

**(b)** $x = \dfrac{19 \pm 5\sqrt{13}}{2} \approx 0.4861, 18.5139$

**81. (a)** $x \approx 19.94$

**(b)** $x = 11 + 4\sqrt{5} \approx 19.9443$

**83. (a)** $x \approx 2.78$

**(b)** $x = \frac{25}{9}$   **85. (a)** $x \approx -0.24$ and $4.24$

**(b)** $x = \left(\dfrac{1 \pm \sqrt{5}}{2}\right)^{3} \approx -0.2361,$
$4.2361$

**89.** $x = a + b$   **91.** $x = -\dfrac{a}{15}$

**Exercise Set 2.3**

**1.** $(-\infty, 9)$   **3.** $(-\infty, -\frac{9}{2})$   **5.** $(-\infty, \frac{5}{2})$

**7.** $(1, \infty)$   **9.** $[-\frac{1}{2}, 1]$

**11.** $(3.98, 3.998)$   **13.** $[-8, \frac{7}{5})$

**15. (a)** $[-\frac{1}{2}, \frac{1}{2}]$

**(b)** $(-\infty, -\frac{1}{2}) \cup (\frac{1}{2}, \infty)$

**17. (a)** $(-\infty, 0) \cup (0, \infty)$

**(b)** no solution   **19. (a)** $(-\infty, 3)$

**(b)** $(1, 3)$   **(c)** $(-\infty, 1) \cup (3, \infty)$

**21. (a)** $[-4, \infty)$   **(b)** $[-4, 6]$

**(c)** $(-\infty, -4) \cup (6, \infty)$

**23. (a)** $(a - c, \infty)$  **(b)** $(a - c, a + c)$
**(c)** $(-\infty, a - c] \cup [a + c, \infty)$
**25.** $(-10, 14)$  **27.** $(-11, 1)$
**29. (a)** $(-2h, h)$  **(b)** $(h, -2h)$
**31. (a)** $[a, \infty)$  **(b)** $a \approx 0.3$

**(c)** $[\frac{2}{7}, \infty)$  **33. (a)** $[a, b]$
**(b)** $a \approx 0.1, b \approx 0.6$

**(c)** $[\frac{1}{8}, \frac{5}{8}]$  **35.** $[-297°, 234°]$
**37.** $[-270°, 810°]$
**39.** $(-\infty, -\frac{7}{2}) \cup (\frac{5}{2}, \infty)$
**43. (a)** The positive slope tells us
that the sulfur dioxide emissions are
increasing.

**(b)** year 2008

**Exercise Set 2.4**
**1. (a)** $(-\infty, -1] \cup [4, \infty)$  **(b)** $[-1, 4]$
**3. (a)** no solution  **(b)** $(-\infty, \infty)$
**5. (a)** $[-1, 1] \cup [3, \infty)$
**(b)** $(-\infty, -1) \cup (1, 3)$  **7.** The curve
is positive on the set $(-1, 0) \cup (3, \infty)$,
which represents the solution set for
the inequality.

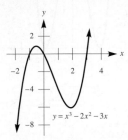

**9.** $(-3, 2)$  **11.** $(-\infty, 2) \cup (9, \infty)$
**13.** $(-\infty, 4] \cup [5, \infty)$
**15.** $(-\infty, -4] \cup [4, \infty)$
**17.** no solution
**19.** $(-7, -6) \cup (0, \infty)$  **21.** $(-\infty, \infty)$
**23.** $(-\infty, -\frac{3}{4}) \cup (-\frac{2}{3}, 0)$
**25.** $(-\infty, \frac{-1 - \sqrt{5}}{2}) \cup (\frac{-1 + \sqrt{5}}{2}, \infty)$
**27.** $[4 - \sqrt{14}, 4 + \sqrt{14}]$
**29.** $[-4, -3] \cup [1, \infty)$
**31.** $(-\infty, -6) \cup (-5, -4)$
**33.** $(-\infty, -\frac{1}{3}) \cup (\frac{1}{3}, 2) \cup (2, \infty)$
**35.** $(-\infty, -\frac{2}{3}) \cup \{3, -\frac{1}{3}\}$
**37.** $(-\infty, -\sqrt{5}] \cup [-2, 2] \cup [\sqrt{5}, \infty)$
**39.** $(-3, 3) \cup (4, \infty)$
**41.** $(-\sqrt{14}, -2\sqrt{2}) \cup (2\sqrt{2}, \sqrt{14})$
**43.** $(-1, 1]$  **45.** $(-\infty, \frac{3}{2}) \cup [2, \infty)$
**47.** $(-\infty, -1) \cup (0, 9)$
**49.** $(-\frac{7}{2}, -\frac{4}{3}) \cup (-1, 0) \cup (1, \infty)$
**51.** $(-\infty, -1)$  **53.** $(-1, 0)$
**55.** $[-1, 1) \cup (2, 4]$
**57.** $(-1, 2 - \sqrt{5}) \cup (1, 2 + \sqrt{5})$
**59.** $(-\infty, -1) \cup (1, 2) \cup (2, \infty)$
**61. (a)** $[0.697, 4.303]$

**(b)** $x = \dfrac{5 \pm \sqrt{13}}{2} \approx 0.697, 4.303$

**63. (a)** $(-0.329, 24.329)$

**(b)** $x = 12 \pm 2\sqrt{38} \approx -0.329, 24.329$
**65. (a)** $(-\infty, -1.554) \cup (1.554, \infty)$

**(b)** $x = \pm\sqrt{1 + \sqrt{2}} \approx \pm1.554$
**67. (a)** $[-2.236, 2.236]$

**(b)** $x = \pm\sqrt{5} \approx \pm2.236$
**69. (a)** $(-2.236, 2.236)$

**(b)** $x = \pm\sqrt{5} \approx \pm2.236$

**71.** $[-0.453, \infty)$

$y = x^3 + 2x + 1$

**73.** $(-\infty, 0.544) \cup (1, \infty)$

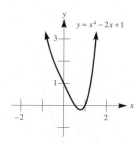

$y = x^4 - 2x + 1$

**75.** $(-3.079, 0) \cup (3.079, \infty)$

$y = x - \dfrac{x^3}{3!} + \dfrac{x^5}{5!} - \dfrac{x^7}{7!}$

**77. (a)** April through September
**(b)** January, October, November, December
**79.** $(-\infty, -2] \cup [2, \infty)$
**81.** $(-\infty, 0) \cup (\frac{1}{2}, \infty)$   **83.** $(\frac{1}{5}, \frac{4}{5})$
**85.** $c = 2$

## Chapter 2 Review Exercises
**1.** True   **3.** False   **5.** False
**7.** True   **9.** False   **11.** False
**13.** $x = \frac{1}{3}, -\frac{1}{2}$   **15.** $x = -6, 4$
**17.** $x = -1, 10$   **19.** $x = \frac{2}{3}, 3$
**21.** $t = \dfrac{-1 \pm \sqrt{3}}{2}$   **23.** $x = -6, -8$
**25.** $x = 256, 6561$   **27.** $x = \frac{1}{4}$
**29.** $x = 10$   **31.** $x = 2$   **33.** $x = \dfrac{1}{2y}$
**35.** $x = \dfrac{a + b}{ab}, -\dfrac{2}{a}$
**37.** $x = -a$ or $x = -b$

**39.** $(-2, 1)$   **41.** $[-\frac{1}{2}, \frac{1}{2}]$
**43.** $(-\infty, -2] \cup [3, \infty)$   **45.** $(-8, 5)$
**47.** $(3 - \sqrt{10}, 3 + \sqrt{10})$
**49.** $(-5, -3) \cup (3, 5)$   **51.** $(-2, \infty)$
**53.** $(-\frac{5}{2}, 4)$

**55.** $\left(-\infty, -\sqrt{\dfrac{3 + \sqrt{5}}{2}}\right) \cup$

$\left(-\sqrt{\dfrac{3 - \sqrt{5}}{2}}, 0\right) \cup$

$\left(0, \sqrt{\dfrac{3 - \sqrt{5}}{2}}\right) \cup \left(\sqrt{\dfrac{3 + \sqrt{5}}{2}}, \infty\right)$

**57.** $(-\infty, 3 - 2\sqrt{2}] \cup [3 + 2\sqrt{2}, \infty)$
**59.** $x^2 + 7x + 12 = 0$   **61.** 7 and 12
**63.** $-1 + \sqrt{2}$ cm
**65.** $(16 \text{ cm}, \infty)$   **67.** 21, 22, 23
**69.** $\dfrac{-(a + b) + \sqrt{a^2 + 6ab + b^2}}{4}$
**71.** The ball thrown from 100 ft.
**73.** $x = \sqrt{2}/2$   **75.** $\dfrac{r}{1 + \sqrt{2}}$

## Chapter 2 Test
**1. (a)** $x = -5, 1$   **(b)** $x = -2 \pm \sqrt{5}$
**2.** $x = \pm 2, \pm \sqrt{3}$   **3.** $x = -2, 2$
**4.** $x = -\frac{1}{3}, 1$   **5.** $-4$
**6.** $x^2 - 4x - 59 = 0$
**7.** $x = \pm\sqrt{\dfrac{3 + \sqrt{13}}{2}} \approx \pm 1.817$
**8. (a)** $x \approx -2.83, 2.83$

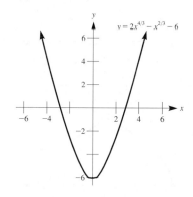

$y = 2x^{4/3} - x^{2/3} - 6$

**(b)** $x = \pm 2\sqrt{2} \approx \pm 2.83$   **9.** $(-\infty, 3]$
**10.** $(\frac{27}{10}, \frac{31}{10})$   **11.** $[\frac{7}{3}, 3]$   **12.** $[-8, \infty)$
**13.** $(-2, \frac{-3 - \sqrt{3}}{3}] \cup (-1, \frac{-3 + \sqrt{3}}{3}] \cup$
$(0, \infty)$   **14.** $[-\frac{3}{2}, \frac{3}{2}]$   **15.** $(-4, -7)$
**16.** $x = 6$ is a solution to the original equation. However, $x = -1$ results in the statement $\sqrt{4} = -2$, which is false. Thus $x = -1$ is an extraneous solution of the original equation, even though it

is a solution to the subsequent equation $x^2 - 5x - 6 = 0$.

## CHAPTER 3
### Exercise Set 3.1
**1. (a)** $g(1975) = \$2.00$
**(b)** $g(1995) - g(1975) = \$2.25$; The minimum wage increased \$2.25 from 1975 to 1995.   **3. (a)** range
**(b)** $h(\text{Mars}) = 2$   **(c)** $h(\text{Neptune})$; Neptune has more moons than does Pluto.   **5. (a)** $f$ and $g$   **(b)** range of $f$: $\{1, 2, 3\}$; range of $g$: $\{2, 3\}$   **7. (a)** $g$
**(b)** range of $g$: $\{i, j\}$   **9. (a)** $(-\infty, \infty)$
**(b)** $(-\infty, \frac{1}{5}) \cup (\frac{1}{5}, \infty)$   **(c)** $(-\infty, \frac{1}{5}]$
**(d)** $(-\infty, \infty)$   **11. (a)** $(-\infty, \infty)$
**(b)** $(-\infty, -3) \cup (-3, 3) \cup (3, \infty)$
**(c)** $(-\infty, -3) \cup [3, \infty)$   **(d)** $(-\infty, \infty)$
**13. (a)** $(-\infty, \infty)$
**(b)** $(-\infty, 3) \cup (3, 5) \cup (5, \infty)$
**(c)** $(-\infty, 3] \cup [5, \infty)$   **(d)** $(-\infty, \infty)$
**15. (a)** $(-\infty, -3) \cup (-3, \infty)$
**(b)** $(-\infty, -3) \cup [2, \infty)$
**(c)** $(-\infty, -3) \cup (-3, \infty)$
**17.** domain: $(-\infty, \infty)$; range: $(-\infty, \infty)$
**19.** domain: $(-\infty, \infty)$; range: $(-\infty, \infty)$
**21.** domain: $(-\infty, 6) \cup (6, \infty)$;
range: $(-\infty, \frac{4}{3}) \cup (\frac{4}{3}, \infty)$
**23. (a)** domain: $(-\infty, 5) \cup (5, \infty)$;
range: $(-\infty, 1) \cup (1, \infty)$
**(b)** domain: $(-\infty, \sqrt[3]{5}) \cup (\sqrt[3]{5}, \infty)$;
range: $(-\infty, 1) \cup (1, \infty)$
**25.** domain: $(-\infty, \infty)$; range: $[4, \infty)$
**27. (a)** $y = (x - 3)^2$   **(b)** $y = x^2 - 3$
**(c)** $y = (3x)^2$   **(d)** $y = 3x^2$
**29. (a)** $-1$   **(b)** $1$   **(c)** $5$   **(d)** $-\frac{3}{4}$
**(e)** $z^2 - 3z + 1$   **(f)** $x^2 - x - 1$
**(g)** $a^2 - a - 1$   **(h)** $x^2 + 3x + 1$
**(i)** $1$   **(j)** $4 - 3\sqrt{3}$   **(k)** $1 - \sqrt{2}$
**(l)** $2$   **31. (a)** $12x^2$   **(b)** $6x^2$   **(c)** $3x^4$
**(d)** $9x^4$   **(e)** $\frac{3}{4}x^2$   **(f)** $\frac{3}{2}x^2$   **33. (a)** $-3$
**(b)** $-\frac{7}{18}$   **(c)** $-2x^2 - 4x - 1$
**(d)** $1 - 2x^2 - 4xh - 2h^2$   **35. (a)** $2$
**(b)** $2$   **(c)** $2$   **37. (a)** $x = -2, 8$
**(b)** no real solutions   **(c)** $x = 3$
**39.** 1041 tee shirts per month
**41.** first model: 124 sales; second model: 100 sales   **43. (a)** $2x^2 + 5x + 2$
**(b)** $2x^2 - 11x + 14$   **(c)** $16x - 12$
**45.** $a = 1$ and $b = 2$   **47.** $a = 2$
**49. (a)** $f(a) = 0, f(2a) = \frac{1}{3}, f(3a) = \frac{1}{2}$:
No   **51.** $a = \frac{1}{2}$ and $b = -\frac{3}{2}$   **53.** $z$
**55.** $k = -1$   **57.** $c = 6$   **59.** $0$

**61.** *F* is a function, since each person has exactly one birth mother. *G* is not a function, since a person can have more than one aunt or no aunt.
**63.** $f(8) = 4; f(10) = 4; f(50) = 15$
**65. (a)** $G(10) = 5; G(14) = 9$
**(b)** $G(100) = 9; G(750) = 0;$
$G(1000) = 9$

## Exercise Set 3.2
**1.** $y = \sqrt{3} \approx 1.732$
**3.** $y = \sqrt{5}/5 \approx 0.447$  **5. (a)** yes
**(b)** no  **(c)** no  **(d)** yes
**7.** domain: $[-4, 2]$; range: $[-3, 3]$
**9.** domain: $[-3, 4]$; range: $[-2, 2]$
**11.** domain: $[-4, -1) \cup (-1, 4]$;
range: $[-2, 3)$  **13.** domain: $[-4, 3]$;
range: $\{2\}$  **15. (a)** 1  **(b)** $-3$  **(c)** no
**(d)** $x = 2$  **(e)** $-1$  **17. (a)** positive
**(b)** $f(-2) = 4; f(1) = 1; f(2) = 2;$
$f(3) = 0$  **(c)** $f(2)$  **(d)** $-3$  **(e)** 3
**(f)** domain: $[-2, 4]$; range: $[-2, 4]$
**19. (a)** $g(-2)$  **(b)** 5  **(c)** $f(2) - g(2)$
**(d)** $x = -2$ or $x = 3$  **(e)** range of $f$
**21. (a)**

**(b)**

**(c)**

**23.**

**25.**

**27. (a)**

**(b)**

**29. (a)**

**(b)**

**31. (a)**

**(b)**

**33.** $P(4, \sqrt[3]{4}) \approx P(4, 1.587)$,
$Q(\sqrt[3]{4}, \sqrt[3]{4}) \approx Q(1.587, 1.587)$,
$R(\sqrt[3]{4}, \sqrt[9]{4}) \approx R(1.587, 1.167)$
**35.** $P(\sqrt{2}, -\sqrt{2}) \approx P(1.414, -1.414)$,
$Q(-\sqrt{2}, -\sqrt{2}) \approx Q(-1.414, -1.414)$,
$R(-\sqrt{2}, \sqrt{2}) \approx R(-1.414, 1.414)$
**37. (a)**

**(b)** As the power on $x$ increases, the curve "hugs" the $x$-axis closer, before rising to the point $(1, 1)$.

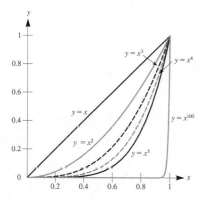

## Exercise Set 3.3

**1. (a)** A turning point is a point where the function changes from increasing to decreasing or from decreasing to increasing. For example, $y = |x|$, $y = x^2$, and $y = \sqrt{1 - x^2}$ all have turning points at $x = 0$. **(b)** A maximum value is a $y$-value corresponding to the highest point on the graph. For example, $y = 1$ is a maximum value for the function $y = \sqrt{1 - x^2}$ occurring at $x = 0$. **(c)** A minimum value is a $y$-value corresponding to the lowest point on the graph. For example, $y = 0$

is a minimum value for the functions $y = |x|$ and $y = x^2$. **(d)** A function $f$ is increasing on an interval if $f(x_1) < f(x_2)$ whenever $x_1 < x_2$ on the interval. For example, $y = |x|$ and $y = x^2$ are increasing on $[0, \infty)$, $y = x^3$ is increasing on $(-\infty, \infty)$, $y = \sqrt{x}$ is increasing on $[0, \infty)$, and $y = \sqrt{1 - x^2}$ is increasing on $[-1, 0]$. **(e)** A function $f$ is decreasing on an interval if $f(x_1) > f(x_2)$ whenever $x_1 < x_2$ on the interval. For example, $y = |x|$ and $y = x^2$ are decreasing on $(-\infty, 0]$, $y = 1/x$ is decreasing on either $(-\infty, 0)$ or $(0, \infty)$, and $y = \sqrt{1 - x^2}$ is decreasing on $[0, 1]$.
**3. (a)** $[-1, 1]$ **(b)** 1 (occurring at $x = 1$) **(c)** $-1$ (occurring at $x = 3$) **(d)** $[0, 1]$ and $[3, 4]$ **(e)** $[1, 3]$
**5. (a)** $[-3, 0]$
**(b)** 0 (occurring at $x = 0$ and $x = 4$) **(c)** $-3$ (occurring at $x = 2$) **(d)** $[2, 4]$ **(e)** $[0, 2]$ **7.** turning points: $(-1.15, 1.08)$ and $(1.15, -5.08)$; increasing: $(-\infty, -1.15] \cup [1.15, \infty)$; decreasing: $[-1.15, 1.15]$ **9.** 10 **11.** 0 **13.** 2 **15. (a)** $\frac{1}{3}$ °C/min
**(b)** $\frac{4}{3}$ °C/min **(c)** $\frac{1}{2}$ °C/min
**17. (a)** 1984–1990; 1978–1984: 1.8%/year; 1984–1990: 9.7%/year **(b)** 1978–1984: 1.7%/year; 1984–1990: 9.7%/year
**19. (a)** $\frac{1}{16} \approx 0.06$ million tons/year **(b)** 0.10 million tons/year
**21. (a)** $2x + 6$ **(b)** $2x + 2a$
**23. (a)** $4 + h$ **(b)** $2x + h$ **25. (a)** 8 **(b)** 8 **27. (a)** $x + a - 2$
**(b)** $2x + h - 2$ **29. (a)** $-\dfrac{1}{ax}$
**(b)** $-\dfrac{1}{x(x + h)}$
**31. (a)** $2x^2 + 2ax + 2a^2$
**(b)** $6x^2 + 6hx + 2h^2$
**33.** 48 feet/second
**35. (a)** $(64 + 16h)$ feet/second
**(b)**

| $h$(seconds) | 0.1 | 0.01 | 0.001 | 0.0001 | 0.00001 |
|---|---|---|---|---|---|
| Average velocity $\Delta s/\Delta t$ on interval $[2, 2 + h]$ | 65.6 | 64.16 | 64.016 | 64.0016 | 64.00016 |

**(c)** 64 feet/second
**37.** $0 \le x \le 100$: $-\frac{3}{25}$ dollars/item; $300 \le x \le 400$: $-\frac{3}{200}$ dollars/item. As more items are produced, the price should decrease.
**39.**

| Function | $|x|$ | $x^2$ | $x^3$ |
|---|---|---|---|
| Domain | $(-\infty, \infty)$ | $(-\infty, \infty)$ | $(-\infty, \infty)$ |
| Range | $[0, \infty)$ | $[0, \infty)$ | $(-\infty, \infty)$ |
| Turning point | $(0, 0)$ | $(0, 0)$ | none |
| Maximum value | none | none | none |
| Minimum value | 0 | 0 | none |
| Interval(s) where increasing | $(0, \infty)$ | $(0, \infty)$ | $(-\infty, \infty)$ |
| Interval(s) where decreasing | $(-\infty, 0)$ | $(-\infty, 0)$ | none |

**41.** $b = 5$ **45.** turning point: $(-0.1875, -0.0016)$; increase: $[-0.1875, \infty)$; decrease: $(-\infty, -0.1875]$

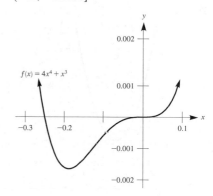

$f(x) = 4x^4 + x^3$

**47. (a)** They have the same graph.

$f(x) = g(x) = \dfrac{1}{\sqrt{x + \sqrt{2}}}$

**(b)** $x = 2$ is not in the domain of $f(x)$ but is in the domain of $g(x)$, so the equation doesn't hold for $x = 2$.

**Exercise Set 3.4**

**1. (a)** C  **(b)** F  **(c)** I  **(d)** A
**(e)** J  **(f)** K  **(g)** D  **(h)** B  **(i)** E
**(j)** H  **(k)** G

**3.**

**5.**

**7.**

**9.**

**11.**

**13.**

**15.**

**17.**

**19.**

**21.**

**23. (a)**

**(b)**

**(c)**

**25.**

**27.**

**29.**

**31.**

**33.**

**35.**

**37.**

**39.**

**41. (a)** $f(x)$ reflected across the $y$-axis

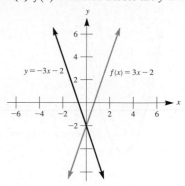

**(b)** $f(x)$ reflected across the $x$-axis

**43. (a)** $f(x)$ reflected across the $y$-axis

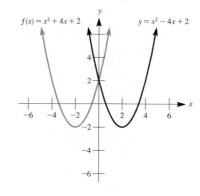

**(b)** $f(x)$ displaced down two units

**45. (a)** $f(x)$ reflected across the $y$-axis

**(b)** $f(x)$ reflected across the $x$-axis

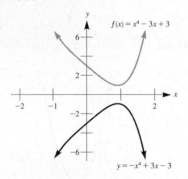

**(c)** $f(x)$ reflected across the $x$-axis, then displaced up three units

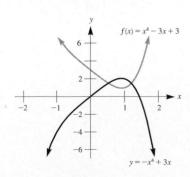

**47. (a)**

| x | $x^2$ | $x^2 - 1$ | $x^2 + 1$ |
|---|---|---|---|
| 0 | 0 | −1 | 1 |
| ±1 | 1 | 0 | 2 |
| ±2 | 4 | 3 | 5 |
| ±3 | 9 | 8 | 10 |

**(b)** $y = x^2 - 1$ is a vertical displacement down one unit from $y = x^2$, while $y = x^2 + 1$ is a vertical displacement up one unit (from $y = x^2$)

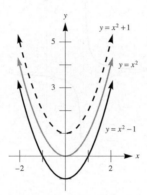

**49. (a)**

| x | $\sqrt{x}$ | $-\sqrt{x}$ |
|---|---|---|
| 0 | 0.0 | 0.0 |
| 1 | 1.0 | −1.0 |
| 2 | 1.4 | −1.4 |
| 3 | 1.7 | −1.7 |
| 4 | 2.0 | −2.0 |
| 5 | 2.2 | −2.2 |

**(b)** $y = -\sqrt{x}$ is a reflection of $y = \sqrt{x}$ across the $x$-axis

**51. (a)**

**(b)**

**53. (a)**

**(b)**

**55. (a)** $R(a + c, b + d)$
**(b)** $T(a + c, b + d)$
**(c)** The order of translations do not affect the final point.

**57. (a)**

$y = \dfrac{x}{x-1}$

**(c)** Translate to the right one unit and one unit up.    **59. (a)** $(-a, b + 2)$
**(b)** $(-a, -b + 2)$   **(c)** $(a + 3, -b)$
**(d)** $(a - 1, 1 - b)$   **(e)** $(-a + 1, b)$
**(f)** $(-a + 1, -b + 1)$

**Exercise Set 3.5**
**1. (a)** $x^2 - x - 7$
**(b)** $-x^2 + 5x + 5$   **(c)** $5$
**3. (a)** $x^2 - 2x - 8$   **(b)** $-x^2 + 2x + 8$
**5. (a)** $4x - 2$   **(b)** $4x - 2$   **(c)** $-4$
**7. (a)** $\dfrac{-x^4 + 22x^2 - 4x - 80}{2x^3 - x^2 - 18x + 9}$
**(b)** $-\frac{80}{9}$   **9. (a)** $-6x - 14$   **(b)** $-74$
**(c)** $-6x - 7$   **(d)** $-67$
**11. (a)** $(f \circ g)(x) = 9x^2 - 3x - 6$,
$(f \circ g)(-2) = 36$,
$(g \circ f)(x) = -3x^2 + 9x + 14$,
$(g \circ f)(-2) = -16$
**(b)** $(f \circ g)(x) = 2^{x^2+1}$,
$(f \circ g)(-2) = 32$, $(g \circ f)(x) = 2^{2x} + 1$,
$(g \circ f)(-2) = \frac{17}{16}$
**(c)** $(f \circ g)(x) = 3x^5 - 4x^2$,
$(f \circ g)(-2) = -112$,
$(g \circ f)(x) = 3x^5 - 4x^2$,
$(g \circ f)(-2) = -112$
**(d)** $(f \circ g)(x) = x$, $(f \circ g)(-2) = -2$,
$(g \circ f)(x) = x$, $(g \circ f)(-2) = -2$
**13. (a)** $\dfrac{-x + 7}{6x}$   **(b)** $\dfrac{-t + 7}{6t}$   **(c)** $\frac{5}{12}$
**(d)** $\dfrac{1 - 6x}{7}$   **(e)** $\dfrac{1 - 6y}{7}$   **(f)** $-\frac{11}{7}$
**15. (a)** $M(7) = \frac{13}{5}$, $M[M(7)] = 7$
**(b)** $(M \circ M)(x) = x$
**(c)** $(M \circ M)(7) = 7$

**17. (a)** $f[g(3)] = 1$   **(b)** $g[f(3)] = -3$
**(c)** $f[h(3)] = -1$   **(d)** $(h \circ g)(2) = 2$
**(e)** $h\{f[g(3)]\} = 2$
**(f)** $(g \circ f \circ h \circ f)(2) = -3$
**19.**

| $x$ | 0 | 1 | 2 | 3 | 4 |
|---|---|---|---|---|---|
| $(f \circ g)(x)$ | 1 | 3 | 2 | undef. | 2 |

| $x$ | −1 | 0 | 1 | 2 | 3 | 4 |
|---|---|---|---|---|---|---|
| $(g \circ f)(x)$ | 0 | 0 | 3 | 4 | 2 | undef. |

**21. (a)** $f \circ g$ is the graph of $f$ displaced 4 units to the left
**(b)**

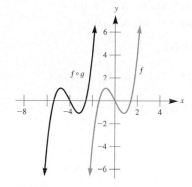

**23. (a)** domain: $[0, \infty)$; range: $[-3, \infty)$

$g(x) = \sqrt{x} - 3$

**(b)** domain: $(-\infty, \infty)$; range: $(-\infty, \infty)$

$f(x) = x - 1$

**(c)** $(f \circ g)(x) = \sqrt{x} - 4$; domain: $[0, \infty)$; range: $[-4, \infty)$

$(f \circ g)(x) = \sqrt{x} - 4$

**(d)** $g[f(x)] = \sqrt{x - 1} - 3$;
domain: $[1, \infty)$
**(e)**

$(g \circ f)(x) = \sqrt{x - 1} - 3$

**25. (a)**

| $t$ | $A$ | $t$ | $A$ |
|---|---|---|---|
| 0 | 707 | 3 | 1402 |
| 0.5 | 737 | 3.5 | 1648 |
| 1 | 804 | 4 | 1940 |
| 1.5 | 903 | 4.5 | 2284 |
| 2 | 1034 | 5 | 2685 |
| 2.5 | 1199 | | |

**(b)** $800$ m$^2$   **(c)** initially: $707$ m$^2$; after three hours this area has doubled
**(d)** 0 to 2.5: 196.8 m$^2$/hr; 2.5 to 5: 594.4 m$^2$/hr; faster over the interval from $t = 2.5$ to $t = 5$
**27. (a)** $(C \circ f)(t) = 100 + 450t - 25t^2$
**(b)** $\$1225$   **(c)** $\$1900$; no
**29. (a)** $f(x) = \sqrt[3]{x}$, $g(x) = 3x + 4$;
$F(x) = (f \circ g)(x)$   **(b)** $f(x) = |x|$,
$g(x) = 2x - 3$; $G(x) = (f \circ g)(x)$
**(c)** $f(x) = x^5$, $g(x) = ax + b$;
$H(x) = (f \circ g)(x)$   **(d)** $f(x) = \frac{1}{x}$,
$g(x) = \sqrt{x}$; $T(x) = (f \circ g)(x)$
**31. (a)** $f(x) = (b \circ c)(x)$
**(b)** $g(x) = (a \circ d)(x)$
**(c)** $h(x) = (c \circ d)(x)$
**(d)** $K(x) = (c \circ b)(x)$
**(e)** $l(x) = (c \circ a)(x)$
**(f)** $m(x) = (a \circ c)(x)$

**33. (b)**

**(c)** $0.44; (A \circ f)(6) = \dfrac{9\pi}{64} \approx 0.44$

**35. (a)** $x_1 = 2, x_2 = 4, x_3 = 8,$
$x_4 = 16, x_5 = 32, x_6 = 64$
**(b)** all six iterates are 0   **(c)** $x_1 = -2,$
$x_2 = -4, x_3 = -8, x_4 = -16, x_5 = -32,$
$x_6 = -64$   **37. (a)** $x_1 = -3, x_2 = -5,$
$x_3 = -9, x_4 = -17, x_5 = -33,$
$x_6 = -65$   **(b)** all six iterates are $-1$
**(c)** $x_1 = 3, x_2 = 7, x_3 = 15, x_4 = 31,$
$x_5 = 63, x_6 = 127$   **39. (a)** $x_1 = 0.81,$
$x_2 \approx 0.656, x_3 \approx 0.430, x_4 \approx 0.185,$
$x_5 \approx 0.034, x_6 \approx 0.001$
**(b)** all six iterates are 1
**(c)** $x_1 = 1.21, x_2 \approx 1.464, x_3 \approx 2.144,$
$x_4 \approx 4.595, x_5 \approx 21.114, x_6 \approx 445.792$
**41.** $x_1 \approx 0.316, x_2 \approx 0.562, x_3 \approx 0.750,$
$x_4 \approx 0.866$   **43. (a)** $f(1) = 4, f(2) = 1,$
$f(3) = 10, f(4) = 2, f(5) = 16, f(6) = 3$
**(b)** $f(1) = 4, f(4) = 2, f(2) = 1$
**(c)** $f(3) = 10, f(10) = 5, f(5) = 16,$
$f(16) = 8, f(8) = 4, f(4) = 2, f(2) = 1$
**(d)** $x_0 = 2: 2, 1$   $x_0 = 4: 4, 2, 1$
$x_0 = 5: 16, 8, 4, 2, 1$   $x_0 = 6: 6, 3, 10, 5,$
$16, 8, 4, 2, 1$   $x_0 = 7: 22, 11, 34, 17, 52,$
$26, 13, 40, 20, 10, 5, 16, 8, 4, 2, 1$

**45.** $f(x) = \dfrac{x + 6}{4}$

**47.** $a = -\frac{1}{2}$ and $b = \frac{1}{2}$
**49. (a)** $2x + 2a - 2$   **(b)** $4x + 4a - 4$
**51. (a)** $x_1 = 3, x_2 \approx 2.259259259,$
$x_3 \approx 1.963308018, x_4 \approx 1.914212754,$
$x_5 \approx 1.912932041, x_6 = \cdots = x_{10}$
$\approx 1.912931183$
The iterates converge to 1.912931183.
**(b)** $\sqrt[3]{7} \approx 1.912931183$; they are the
same   **(c)** fifth iterate; sixth iterate

## Exercise Set 3.6
**1. (a)** $h[k(x)] = x$ for every $x$ in the
domain of $k$.   **(b)** $k[h(x)] = x$ for
every $x$ in the domain of $h$.

**5. (a)**

**(b)** $f$ and $h$   **7.** 7   **9. (a)** 4
**(b)** $-1$   **(c)** $\sqrt{2}$   **(d)** $t + 1$
**11. (a)** $f^{-1}(x) = \dfrac{x - 1}{2}$
**(b)** $f^{-1}(5) = 2, \dfrac{1}{f(5)} = \dfrac{1}{11}$; no
**13. (a)** $f^{-1}(x) = \dfrac{x + 1}{3}$
**(c)**

**15. (a)** $f^{-1}(x) = x^2 + 1$ for $x \geq 0$
**(c)**

**17. (a)** domain: $(-\infty, 3) \cup (3, \infty)$;
range: $(-\infty, 1) \cup (1, \infty)$
**(b)** $f^{-1}(x) = \dfrac{3x + 2}{x - 1}$
**(c)** domain: $(-\infty, 1) \cup (1, \infty)$; range:
$(-\infty, 3) \cup (3, \infty)$; domain of $f$ = range
of $f^{-1}$, range of $f$ = domain of $f^{-1}$

**19.** $f^{-1}(x) = \sqrt[3]{\dfrac{x - 1}{2}}$
**21.** $f[f^{-1}(x)] = f^{-1}[f(x)] = x$
**23. (a)**

**(b)**

**(c)**

**(d)**

**25. (a)** $x = 7$   **(b)** $x = -3$
**27.** $t = \frac{9}{4}$   **29.** not one-to-one
**31.** not one-to-one   **33.** not
one-to-one   **35.** not one-to-one

**37.** not one-to-one

**39.** is one-to-one

**41. (a)**

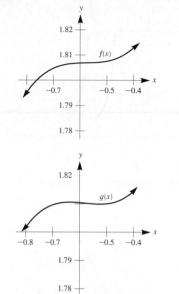

**(b)** $f$ is one-to-one, $g$ is not one-to-one
**43.** $A$: $(a, f(a))$; $B$: $(f(a), f(a))$;
$C$: $(f(f(a)), f(a))$; $D$: $(f(a), f(f(a)))$
**45. (a)** $-\frac{1}{8}$   **(b)** $f^{-1}(x) = \dfrac{x + 3}{x}$; $-8$;

they are reciprocals
**47. (a)** E   **(b)** C   **(c)** L   **(d)** A
**(e)** J   **(f)** G   **(g)** B   **(h)** M   **(i)** K
**(j)** D   **(k)** I   **(l)** H   **(m)** N   **(n)** F

**49. (a)** $-\dfrac{x + 2}{x + 1}$
**(b)** symmetry about the line $y = x$

## Chapter 3 Review Exercises
**1. (a)** $(-\infty, 3]$   **(b)** $(-\infty, \frac{1}{2}) \cup (\frac{1}{2}, \infty)$

**3.** yes   **5. (a)** $-\dfrac{1}{ax}$
**(b)** $1 - 4x - 2h$

**7. (a)** $g^{-1}(x) = \dfrac{1}{3x + 5}$

**9. (a)** $x$-intercepts: $-5$ and $1$;
$y$-intercept: $-1$

**(b)** $x$-intercept: $-1$; $y$-intercept: $-\frac{1}{2}$

**11. (a)** $5$   **(b)** $7 - 4\sqrt{2}$
**13.** $m(h) = 10 + h$
**15.**

**17. (a)** 2.5, 3.25, 3.625
**(b)** $A$: $f(1) = 2.5$; $B$: $f(2.5) = 3.25$;
$C$: $f(3.25) = 3.625$   **(c)** $y = 4$
**(d)** 3.813, 3.906, 3.953, 3.977, 3.988,
3.994, 3.997

**19.** no $x$-intercepts; $y$-intercept: 1

$$f(x) = \frac{1}{x+1}$$
$$x = -1$$

**21.** $x$-intercept: $-3$; $y$-intercept: 3

$$y = |x + 3|$$

**23.** $x$-intercepts: $\pm 1$; $y$-intercept: 1

$$h(x) = \sqrt{1 - x^2}$$

**25.** $x$-intercept: 0; $y$-intercept: 0

$$y = \left(\sqrt{x}\right)^2$$

**27.** $x$-intercept: 1; no $y$-intercept

$$(f \circ g)(x) = -\left(\sqrt{x - 1}\right)^2$$

**29.** no $x$- or $y$-intercepts

$$x = 1$$

**31.** $x$-intercept: $\frac{1}{2}$; $y$-intercept: $-1$

$$f^{-1}(x) = 2x - 1$$

**33.** $x$-intercept: 0; $y$-intercept: 0

$$\left(f \circ f^{-1}\right)(x) = x$$

**35.** $(-\infty, -3) \cup (-3, 3) \cup (3, \infty)$
**37.** $(-\infty, 4]$  **39.** $(-\infty, -1] \cup [3, \infty)$
**41.** $(-\infty, \frac{1}{3}) \cup (\frac{1}{3}, \infty)$
**43.** $(-\infty, \frac{2}{5}) \cup (\frac{2}{5}, \infty)$
**45.** $a(x) = (f \circ g)(x)$
**47.** $c(x) = (G \circ g)(x)$
**49.** $A(x) = (g \circ f \circ G)(x)$
**51.** $C(x) = (g \circ G \circ G)(x)$  **53.** 12
**55.** $-\frac{9}{19}$  **57.** $t^2 + t$  **59.** $x^2 - 5x + 6$
**61.** $x^4 - x^2$  **63.** $-2x^3 + 3x^2 - x$
**65.** $4x^2 - 2x$  **67.** $-2x^2 + 2x + 1$
**69.** $\dfrac{2x + 2}{2x - 5}$  **71.** $2x + h - 1$
**73.** $F^{-1}(x) = \dfrac{4x + 3}{1 - x}$  **75.** $x$
**77.** $\dfrac{1 + x}{2}$  **79.** $\frac{22}{7}$  **81.** negative

**83.** $-1$  **85.** $-1$  **87.** $(0, -2)$ and
$(5, 1)$  **89.** $[-6, 0]$ and $[5, 8]$
**91.** 0 at $x = 2$  **93.** no  **95.** $x = 4$
**97. (a)** $x = 10$  **(b)** $x = 0$  **99. (a)** 5
**(b)** $-3$  **(c)** 4  **(d)** $\frac{1}{4}$
**101.** $(f \circ f)(10)$  **103.** $[0, 4]$  **105.** 5
**107.** $(1, 3) \cup (6, 10)$  **109.** $(4, 7)$

## Chapter 3 Test

**1.** $(-\infty, -1] \cup [6, \infty)$
**2.** $(-\infty, \frac{2}{3}) \cup (\frac{2}{3}, \infty)$
**3. (a)** $2x^2 - 2x - 2$
**(b)** $2x^2 - 5x + 2$  **(c)** 54  **4.** $-\dfrac{2}{at}$
**5.** $4x + 2h - 5$  **6.** $g^{-1}(x) = -\dfrac{x}{6x + 4}$
**7.** $-\frac{8}{5}$  **8. (a)** $x$-intercepts: 4 and 2;
$y$-intercept: $-2$;

$$y = -|x - 3| + 1$$

**(b)** $x$-intercept: $-\frac{5}{2}$; $y$-intercept: $-\frac{5}{3}$

$$y = \frac{1}{x + 3} - 2$$
$$y = -2$$
$$x = -3$$

**9. (a)** $[-3, 1]$  **(b)** $(-2, 1)$
**(c)** $-3$ at $x = 2$  **(d)** 1 at $x = -2$
**(e)** $[-2, 2]$  **(f)** no  **10. (a)** $\frac{23}{4}$
**(b)** $12 - 7\sqrt{3}$  **11.** domain:
$(-\infty, -1) \cup (-1, \infty)$

$$y = F(x)$$

**12. (a)** 0.4, 0.8, 0.4, 0.8, 0.4, 0.8
**(b)** 0.4, 0.8, 0.4, 0.8, 0.4, 0.8
**13.**

**14.** $t = 1$   **15.** $b = 10$
**16. (a)** $\dfrac{\Delta F}{\Delta t} = 0.16a - 0.8$

**(b)** $-0.16\,°C/hour$

# CHAPTER 4
## Exercise Set 4.1
**1.** $f(x) = \frac{2}{3}x + \frac{2}{3}$   **3.** $g(x) = \sqrt{2}x$
**5.** $f(x) = x - \frac{7}{2}$   **7.** $f(x) = \frac{1}{2}x - 2$
**9.** yes   **11.** $V(t) = -2375t + 20000$
**13. (a)** $V(t) = -12000t + 60000$
**(b)**

| End of Year | Yearly Depreciation | Accumulated Depreciation | Value V |
|---|---|---|---|
| 0 | 0 | 0 | 60,000 |
| 1 | 12,000 | 12,000 | 48,000 |
| 2 | 12,000 | 24,000 | 36,000 |
| 3 | 12,000 | 36,000 | 24,000 |
| 4 | 12,000 | 48,000 | 12,000 |
| 5 | 12,000 | 60,000 | 0 |

**15. (a)** \$530   **(b)** \$538   **(c)** \$8/fan
**17. (a)**

**(b)** \$575   **(c)** \$575.50; the cost of
producing 151 units
**19. (a)** $B$ is traveling faster
**(b)** $A$ is farther to the right
**(c)** $t = 8$ sec
**21. (a)** $y = 362091.5x - 690,879,017.5$
**(b)** 33,304,000
**(c)** too low; 1.7% error
**23. (a)** $y = 3680x - 7,284,416$
**(b)** \$64,544 million

**(c)** 2.4% error
**25. (a)** $y = 4.92x - 35.55$
**(b)** 102.21 cm   **(c)** too high;
4.2% error   **(d)** 33.33 cm; too low;
8.3% error   **(e)** 377.73 cm; too high;
48.4% error
**27. (a)**

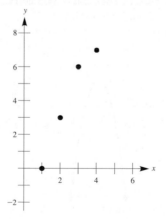

**(b)** slope: 2.5; $y$-intercept: $-2$

**(c)**

**29. (a)** 3,853,000; 0.8% error
**(b)** $f^{-1}(x) = \dfrac{x + 71238863.429}{37546.068}$
**(c)** year 2004
**31. (a)**

**(b)** 1809 million tons; 5.5% error
**(c)** 1954 million tons; 6.0% error
**33. (a)** 4,050,273   **(b)** no
**35. (a)** 3:57.6; too low; 0.17% error

**(b)** 4:11.3; too low; 1.61% error; This percent error is much larger, since 1911 is not in the data range.

**37. (a)** $A$ **(b)** $A^2$ **(c)** $AC$

**(d)** $AC$ **39. (a)** $\dfrac{1}{AC}$ **(b)** $\dfrac{1}{AC}$

**43.** $f(x) = 3x + 1$ **45.** $y = 2.4x - 2$

**47.** $y = 2.4x - 0.4$

**49.** $y = 0.084x + 37.241$

**51. (a)** $f(x) = \sqrt{2}x + (-1 + \sqrt{2})$ and $f(x) = -\sqrt{2}x + (-1 - \sqrt{2})$

**(b)** $f(x) = \sqrt[3]{2}x + (-1 + \sqrt[3]{2})$

**53.** $f(x) = x$

## Exercise Set 4.2

**1. (a)**

**(b)** 1990: linear $\approx 839.40$ billion; quadratic $\approx 1314.05$ billion
1998: linear $\approx 1030.03$ billion; quadratic $\approx 1861.32$ billion
**(c)** 1990: linear $\approx 26.8\%$ error; quadratic $\approx 14.7\%$ error.
1998: linear $\approx 35.0\%$ error; quadratic $\approx 17.4\%$ error.
The quadratic model produces the smaller percent error.

**3.**

| Projected U.S. Population (millions) | Actual U.S. Population (millions) | Projection Too High or Too Low? | % Error |
|---|---|---|---|
| 1970 | 191.12 | 203.30 | too low | 5.99% |
| 2000 | 258.35 | 275.60 | too low | 6.26% |

**5.** vertex: $(-2, 0)$; axis of symmetry: $x = -2$; minimum value: 0; $x$-intercept: $-2$; $y$-intercept: 4

**7.** vertex: $(-2, 0)$; axis of symmetry: $x = -2$; minimum value: 0; $x$-intercept: $-2$; $y$-intercept: 8

**9.** vertex: $(-2, 4)$; axis of symmetry: $x = -2$; maximum value: 4; $x$-intercepts: $-2 \pm \sqrt{2}$; $y$-intercept: $-4$

**11.** vertex: $(2, -4)$; axis of symmetry: $x = 2$; minimum value: $-4$; $x$-intercepts: 0 and 4; $y$-intercept: 0

**13.** vertex: $(0, 1)$; axis of symmetry: $x = 0$; maximum value: 1; $x$-intercepts: $\pm 1$; $y$-intercept: 1

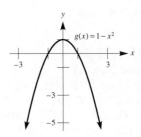

**15.** vertex: $(1, -4)$; axis of symmetry: $x = 1$; minimum value: $-4$; $x$-intercepts: 3 and $-1$; $y$-intercept: $-3$

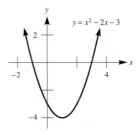

**17.** vertex: $(3, 11)$; axis of symmetry: $x = 3$; maximum value: 11; $x$-intercepts: $3 \pm \sqrt{11}$; $y$-intercept: 2

**19.** vertex: $(\frac{1}{6}, \frac{9}{4})$; axis of symmetry: $t = \frac{1}{6}$; maximum value: $\frac{9}{4}$; $t$-intercepts: $-\frac{1}{3}$ and $\frac{2}{3}$; $s$-intercept: 2

**21.** $x = 1$; minimum output
**23.** $x = \frac{3}{2}$; maximum output
**25.** $x = 0$; minimum output
**27.** minimum value: $-13$
**29.** maximum value: $\frac{25}{8}$
**31. (a)** minimum value
**(b)** minimum value: $-4.0$; $x_0 \approx 0.2$
**(c)** minimum value: $\frac{97}{24}$; $x_0 = \frac{1}{12}$
**33. (a)** maximum value
**(b)** maximum value: $-43.4$; $t_0 \approx 2.2$
**(c)** maximum value: $-\frac{391}{9}$; $t_0 = \frac{20}{9}$
**35.** 5 units    **37.** quadratic
**39.** neither    **41.** linear
**43. (a)** minimum value $= 8$ at $x = 3$
**(b)** minimum value $= 4$ at $x = 3$
**(c)** minimum value $= 64$ at $x = \pm\sqrt{3}$
**45. (a)** maximum value $= 4$
**(b)** maximum value $= 2\sqrt[3]{2} \approx 2.5$
**(c)** maximum value $= 16$
**47.** neither    **49.** quadratic
**51.** The graph of $y = 50x^2$ should be "narrower."

**53.** $x + a$    **55.** $x = \dfrac{a + b}{2}$
**57.** $y = -\frac{1}{2}(x - 2)^2 + 2$
**59.** $y = \frac{1}{4}(x - 3)^2 - 1$    **61.** $b = \pm 2$
**63. (a)**

| $x$ | $a$ | $a + h$ | $a + 2h$ |
|---|---|---|---|
| $f(x)$ | $ma + b$ | $ma + mh + b$ | $ma + 2mh + b$ |

**(b)** $mh$
**65. (a)** $y = 0.015089x^2 - 0.086075x + 3.364536$; 1989: 3.466 billion tons; 1996: 3.391 billion tons    **(b)** 1989: 1.70% error; 1996: 1.08% error
**(c)** 3.642 billion tons; 9.40% error

## Exercise Set 4.3

**1.** $x = 1$    **3.** no fixed points
**5.** $x = -1$ and $x = 5$    **7.** $t = 1$
**9.** $t = -3$ and $t = 4$    **11.** $x = 0$ and $x = \frac{4}{9}$    **13.** $u = -2$ and $u = 1$
**15.** $x = 10$    **17. (a)** one fixed point

**(b)** $x \approx -0.771$

**19. (a)** three fixed points

**(b)** $x \approx -1.206, -1.103, 2.309$
**21. (a)** two fixed points

**(b)** $x \approx -1.495, 0.798$    **23. (b)** fourth iterate    **(c)** twelfth iterate
**25. (a)**

| | From graph | From calculator |
|---|---|---|
| $x_1$ | 1.7 | 1.72 |
| $x_2$ | 0.8 | 0.796 |
| $x_3$ | 1.4 | 1.443 |
| $x_4$ | 1.0 | 0.990 |
| $x_5$ | 1.3 | 1.307 |
| $x_6$ | 1.1 | 1.085 |
| $x_7$ | 1.2 | 1.240 |
| $x_8$ | 1.1 | 1.132 |

**(b)** $x = \frac{20}{7} \approx 1.176$    **(c)** eighth iterate
**27.**

| | From graph | From calculator |
|---|---|---|
| $x_1$ | 0.36 | 0.36 |
| $x_2$ | 0.92 | 0.922 |
| $x_3$ | 0.29 | 0.289 |
| $x_4$ | 0.82 | 0.822 |
| $x_5$ | 0.58 | 0.585 |
| $x_6$ | 0.97 | 0.971 |
| $x_7$ | 0.11 | 0.113 |
| $x_8$ | 0.40 | 0.402 |
| $x_9$ | 0.96 | 0.962 |

**29. (a)** $x_{21} \approx 0.6632$, $x_{22} \approx 0.6477$, $x_{23} \approx 0.6617$, $x_{24} \approx 0.6492$, $x_{25} \approx 0.6605$
**(b)**

| $n$ | 20 | 21 | 22 | 23 | 24 | 25 |
|---|---|---|---|---|---|---|
| Number of fish after $n$ breeding seasons | 323 | 332 | 324 | 331 | 325 | 330 |

**(c)** $x_1 = 0.0675$, $x_2 \approx 0.04721$, $x_3 \approx 0.03373$, $x_4 \approx 0.02445$, $x_5 \approx 0.01789$. The iterates are approaching 0, which is a fixed point.
**31. (a)**

| $n$ | $x_n$ | Number of fish after $n$ breeding seasons |
|---|---|---|
| 0 | 0.1 | 50 |
| 1 | 0.279 | 140 |
| 2 | 0.6236 | 312 |
| 3 | 0.7276 | 364 |
| 4 | 0.6143 | 307 |
| 5 | 0.7345 | 367 |
| 6 | 0.6046 | 302 |
| 7 | 0.7411 | 371 |
| 8 | 0.5948 | 297 |
| 9 | 0.7471 | 374 |
| 10 | 0.5857 | 293 |

| $n$ | $x_n$ | Number of fish after $n$ breeding seasons |
|---|---|---|
| 21 | 0.7633 | 382 |
| 22 | 0.5601 | 280 |
| 23 | 0.7638 | 382 |
| 24 | 0.5592 | 280 |
| 25 | 0.7641 | 382 |
| 26 | 0.5587 | 279 |

**(b)** $x = \frac{21}{31} \approx 0.6774$
**(c)** $a \approx 0.7646$, $b \approx 0.5580$
**(d)** 382 fish, 279 fish
**33. (a)** $x_0 = c$: $x_1 = d$, $x_2 = c$, $x_3 = d$, $x_4 = c$, $x_5 = d$, $x_6 = c$; $x_0 = d$: $x_1 = c$, $x_2 = d$, $x_3 = c$, $x_4 = d$, $x_5 = c$, $x_6 = d$; With an initial input of either $c$ or $d$, the sequence of iterates alternates between $c$ and $d$.
**(b)** 0.8, 0.4, 0.8, 0.4, 0.8, 0.4
**(c)** $\{0.4, 0.8\}$  **(d)** $x_1 = 0.8$, $x_2 = 0.4$

**37. (a)** $a = \frac{6}{7}$, $b = \frac{3}{7}$
**(b)** $P(\frac{3}{7}, \frac{3}{7})$, $Q(\frac{3}{7}, \frac{6}{7})$, $R(\frac{6}{7}, \frac{6}{7})$, $S(\frac{6}{7}, \frac{3}{7})$

## Exercise Set 4.4
**1. (a)** $A(x) = 8x - x^2$; Dom $A = (0, 8)$
**(b)** $P(x) = 2x + \dfrac{170}{x}$; Dom $P = (0, \infty)$
**3. (a)** $D(x) = \sqrt{x^4 + 3x^2 + 1}$;
Dom $D = (-\infty, \infty)$
**(b)** $m(x) = \dfrac{x^2 + 1}{x}$;
Dom $m = (-\infty, 0) \cup (0, \infty)$
**5. (a)** $A(y) = \dfrac{\pi y^2}{4}$; Dom $A = (0, \infty)$
**(b)** $A(y) = \dfrac{\pi^2 y^2}{16}$; Dom $A = (0, \infty)$
**7. (a)** $P(x) = 16x - x^2$;
Dom $P = (-\infty, \infty)$
**(b)** $S(x) = 2x^2 - 32x + 256$;
Dom $S = (-\infty, \infty)$
**(c)** $D(x) = x^3 - (16 - x)^3$ or
$D(x) = (16 - x)^3 - x^3$;
Dom $D = (-\infty, \infty)$
**(d)** $A(x) = 8$; The average does not depend on what the two numbers are.
**9. (a)** Dom $P = [0, 20]$

**(b)** 8 units; $(8, 3)$   **(c)** $2$; $(12, 2)$
**(d)** $R(x) = 5x - \dfrac{x^2}{4}$; Dom $R = [0, 20]$

**(e)** $R(2) = \$8$; $R(8) = \$24$; $R(14) = \$21$
**(f)** $x = 10$; $\$25$; $p = \$2.50$

**11. (a)**

| $x$ | 1 | 2 | 3 | 4 | 5 | 6 | 7 |
|---|---|---|---|---|---|---|---|
| $P(x)$ | 17.88 | 19.49 | 20.83 | 21.86 | 22.49 | 22.58 | 21.75 |

**(b)** largest value: 22.58; $x = 6$
**(c)** 22.63
**13.** $A(x) = \dfrac{\sqrt{3}}{4}x^2$; Dom $A = [0, \infty)$
**15.** $R(V) = \sqrt[3]{V/2\pi}$; Dom $R = [0, \infty)$
**17.** $V(S) = \dfrac{S\sqrt{S\pi}}{6\pi}$; Dom $V = [0, \infty)$
**19.** $A(x) = \frac{1}{2}x\sqrt{400 - x^2}$;
Dom $A = (0, 20)$
**21.** $AB(x) = \dfrac{(x + 4)\sqrt{x^2 + 25}}{x}$;
Dom $AB = (0, \infty)$   **23. (a)** yes

**(b)** one turning point
**(c)** maximum value $= 625$; no minimum value   **25. (a)** no

**(b)** one turning point   **(c)** no maximum value; minimum value $\approx 0.87$   **27. (a)** no

**(b)** one turning point   **(c)** no maximum value; minimum value $\approx 25.69$   **29. (a) (a)** no

**(b)** one turning point   **(c)** no maximum value; minimum value $= 2$
**(b) (a)** no

**(b)** no turning points   **(c)** no maximum or minimum values

**31. (a)** $S(x) = x + \dfrac{\sqrt{11}}{x}$;

Dom $S = (0, \infty)$
minimum value $\approx 3.642$

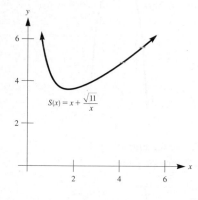

**(b)** $P(x) = -x^2 + \sqrt{11}x$;
Dom $P = (0, \sqrt{11})$
maximum value $= 2.75$

**33.** $A(x) = \frac{17}{144}x^2 - \frac{1}{3}x + \frac{1}{2}$;
Dom $A = (0, 3)$; yes

**35. (a)** $V(r) = \dfrac{\sqrt{3}}{3}\pi r^3$;
Dom $V = (0, \infty)$
**(b)** $S(r) = 2\pi r^2$; Dom $S = (0, \infty)$

**37. (a)** $r(h) = \dfrac{3h}{\sqrt{h^2 - 9}}$;
Dom $r = (3, \infty)$

**(b)** $h(r) = \dfrac{3r}{\sqrt{r^2 - 9}}$; Dom $h = (3, \infty)$

**39.** $A(x) = \dfrac{4x^2 + \pi(14 - x)^2}{16\pi}$;
Dom $A = (0, 14)$

**41.** $A(r) = \dfrac{r(1 - 4\pi r)}{4}$;
Dom $A = (0, \frac{1}{4\pi})$
**43.** $A(x) = \frac{\pi}{3}x^2$; Dom $A = (0, \infty)$
**45. (a)** $V(x) = 4x^3 - 28x^2 + 48x$;
Dom $V = (0, 3)$
**(b)**

| $x$ (in.) | 0 | 0.5 | 1.0 | 1.5 | 2.0 | 2.5 | 3.0 |
|---|---|---|---|---|---|---|---|
| volume (in.³) | 0 | 17.5 | 24 | 22.5 | 16 | 7.5 | 0 |

**(c)** $x = 1.0$
**(d)**

| $x$ (in.) | 0.8 | 0.9 | 1.0 | 1.1 | 1.2 | 1.3 | 1.4 |
|---|---|---|---|---|---|---|---|
| volume (in.³) | 22.5 | 23.4 | 24 | 24.2 | 24.2 | 23.9 | 23.3 |

**(e)** $x = 1.1$

**47. (a)** $A(r) = 32r - 2r^2 - \dfrac{\pi r^2}{2}$;
Dom $A = \left(0, \dfrac{32}{\pi + 2}\right)$
**(b)** downward; yes

**49. (a)** $y(s) = \dfrac{3s}{\sqrt{1 - s^2}}$;
Dom $y = (0, 1)$
**(b)** $s(y) = \dfrac{y}{\sqrt{y^2 + 9}}$; Dom $s = (0, \infty)$

**(c)** $z(s) = \dfrac{3}{\sqrt{1 - s^2}}$; Dom $z = (0, 1)$

**(d)** $s(z) = \dfrac{\sqrt{z^2 - 9}}{z}$; Dom $s = (3, \infty)$

**51. (a)** $m(a) = \dfrac{a^2 + 1}{a}$;
Dom $m = (-\infty, 0) \cup (0, \infty)$

**53.** $A(x) = \dfrac{8x - x^2}{4}$; Dom $A = (0, 8)$

**55.** $A(m) = \dfrac{2m^2 - 8m + 8}{m^2 - 4m}$;
Dom $m = (-\infty, 0)$

**57.** $A = \dfrac{(ma - b)^2}{-2m}$; Dom $A = (-\infty, 0)$

### Exercise Set 4.5
**1.** $\frac{25}{4}$   **3.** $\frac{1}{2}$   **5.** $\frac{25}{4}$ m by $\frac{25}{4}$ m
**7.** 1250 in.²   **9. (a)** 18   **(b)** $\frac{23}{4}$
**(c)** $\frac{47}{8}$   **(d)** $\frac{95}{16}$   **11. (a)** 16 feet; 12 feet
**(b)** 16 feet; 1 second
**(c)** $t = \frac{7}{4}$ sec or $t = \frac{1}{4}$ sec
**13.** $(\frac{7}{2}, \frac{2 + \sqrt{6}}{2})$; distance $= \sqrt{7}/2$
**15. (a)** $\frac{1}{2}$   **(b)** $\frac{1}{4}$   **17.** 125 ft by 250 ft
**19.** $x = 40$   **21.** $x = 60$;
maximum revenue $= \$900$; $p = \$15$
**23. (a)** $\frac{36}{13}$   **(b)** $6\sqrt{13}/13$; this is the square root.

**25. (a)**

**(b)** 1.5 miles   **(c)** $\frac{7}{4}$ miles   **27. (a)** $\frac{225}{2}$

**29.** $x = \sqrt{2}/2$; area $= \frac{1}{2}$   **31.** $\frac{49}{12}$

**35.** 100 yd by 150 yd

**39. (a)** $p(x) = -2x + 500$

**(b)** maximum revenue = \$31,250;
price = \$250   **41.** $t = \sqrt{3}$ or
$t = -\sqrt{3}$   **43. (a)** $(x - \frac{1}{2})^2 \geq 0$,
thus $(x - \frac{1}{2})^2 + \frac{3}{4} \geq \frac{3}{4} > 0$   **(b)** Since
$D = -3 < 0$, there are no $x$-intercepts.
Since the graph is a parabola opening
up, and there are no $x$-intercepts, the
$y$-values must be positive for all values
of $x$.

**45. (a)** $A(x) = \dfrac{4 + \pi}{16\pi}x^2 - 2x + 16$;

Dom $A = (0, 16)$   **(b)** $x = \dfrac{16\pi}{4 + \pi}$

**(c)** $\dfrac{\pi}{4}$   **47. (a)** $A = \pi r^2 + \dfrac{1000}{r}$

**(b)** height $\approx 5.42$ cm,
radius $\approx 5.42$ cm

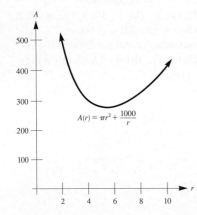

**49. (a)** $d = \sqrt{x^4 + x^2 - 6x + 9}$
**(b)** $(1, 1)$

**51. (a)** $S = 2\sqrt{9 + y^2} + 6 - y$
**(b)** $P(0, 1.73)$

**53. (a)**

**55.** 2   **59.** 2

## Exercise Set 4.6
**1.** (a) through (d)

**3. (a)**

**(b)** $[0, 1]$: $\dfrac{\Delta f}{\Delta x} = 1$, $\dfrac{\Delta g}{\Delta x} = 1$; $[0, \frac{1}{2}]$:
$\dfrac{\Delta f}{\Delta x} = \frac{1}{2}$, $\dfrac{\Delta g}{\Delta x} = \frac{1}{4}$   **5.** no $x$-intercepts;
$y$-intercept: 5

**7.** $x$-intercept: 1; $y$-intercept: $-1$

**9.** $x$-intercept: $4 + \sqrt[3]{2}$;
$y$-intercept: $-66$

**11.** $x$-intercept: $-5$; $y$-intercept: $-1250$

**13.** $x$-intercept: $-1$; $y$-intercept: $\frac{1}{2}$

**15.** $x$- and $y$-intercepts: 0

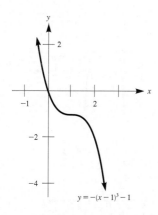

**17.** A polynomial function of degree 3 can have at most two turning points.
**19.** As $|x|$ gets very large, our function should be similar to $f(x) = a_3x^3$.
**21.** As $|x|$ gets very large with $x$ negative, then the graph should resemble $2x^5$.
**23.** This graph has a corner.

**25. (a)**

**(b)**

**27. (a)** $x$-intercepts: 2, 1, $-1$; $y$-intercept: 2

**(b)**

**29. (a)** $x$-intercepts: 0, 2, 1; $y$-intercept: 0

**31. (a)** $x$-intercepts: 0, 5, $-1$; $y$-intercept: 0

**(b)**

**33. (a)** $x$-intercepts: $-3$, $-2$, 2; $y$-intercept: $-12$

**(b)**

**35. (a)** $x$-intercepts: 0 and $-2$;
$y$-intercept: 0

**(b)**

**(c)**

**37. (a)** $x$-intercepts: 1, 4;
$y$-intercept: 128

**(b)**

**(c)**

**39. (a)** $x$-intercepts: $-1, 1, 3$;
$y$-intercept: 3

**(b)**

**(c)**

**41. (a)** $x$-intercepts: 0, 4, $-2$;
$y$-intercept: 0

**(b)**

**(c)**

**43. (a)** $x$-intercepts: 0, 2, $-2$;
$y$-intercept: 0

**(b)**

**(c)**

$$y = -4x(x - 2)^2(x + 2)^3$$

**47.** $x = 0, \dfrac{3 \pm \sqrt{29}}{2} \approx -1.193, 4.193$

**49.** $x = -6, \pm\sqrt{3} \approx \pm 1.732$

**51. (a)**

$$N(t) = t^7 + 8t^4 + 16t$$

**(b)** $t$-intercepts: 0.0, $-1.6$
**(c)** $t = 0, -\sqrt[3]{4} \approx -1.587$
**53.** From left to right: $f(x) = x$,
$g(x) = x^2, h(x) = x^3, F(x) = x^4$,
$G(x) = x^5, H(x) = x^6$   **55.** $[0, 0.68]$
**57.** no such value   **59. (a)** $(400, 1600)$
**(b)**

$$y = 4x$$
$$y = \dfrac{x^2}{100}$$

**61. (a)**

$$D(x) = x^2 - x^4$$

**(b)** $\left(\pm\frac{\sqrt{2}}{2}, \frac{1}{4}\right), (0, 0)$
**(c)** maximum vertical distance: $\frac{1}{4}$

$$y = x^2$$
$$y = x^4$$

**63. (a)** $A(x) = x(1 - x^4) = x - x^5$
**(b)** maximum area: 0.53 square units

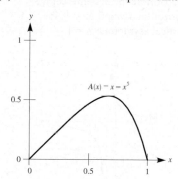

$$A(x) = x - x^5$$

**65. (b)** From part **(a)**, if $|x| < 1$, then
$x^n < x^m$, so the graph of $y = x^n$ lies
below the graph of $y = x^m$. If $|x| > 1$,
then $x^n > x^m$, so the graph of $y = x^n$
lies above the graph of $y = x^m$. These
are valid, since $m$ and $n$ are even, thus
ensuring that $x^m \geq 0$ and $x^n \geq 0$.
**(c)** If $m$ and $n$ are positive odd
integers, from part **(a)** the graph of
$y = x^m$ lies above the graph of $y = x^n$

for $0 < x < 1$, and it lies below the
graph of $y = x^n$ for $x > 1$.
If $-1 < x < 0$, however, $x^n > x^m$
(since $x$ is negative), and so the
graph of $y = x^n$ lies above the graph
of $y = x^m$. If $x < 1$, then $x^n < x^m$, so
the graph of $y = x^n$ lies below the
graph of $y = x^m$.

### Exercise Set 4.7
**1. (a)** domain: $(-\infty, 3) \cup (3, \infty)$;
$x$-intercept: $-5$; $y$-intercept: $-\frac{5}{4}$;
vertical asymptote: $x = 3$;
horizontal asymptote: $y = \frac{3}{4}$
**(b)**

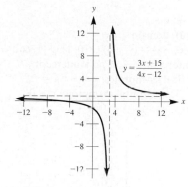

$$y = \dfrac{3x + 15}{4x - 12}$$

**3. (a)** domain: $(-\infty, 0) \cup (0, \infty)$;
$x$-intercepts: $\frac{1}{3}, \frac{1}{2}$; no $y$-intercept;
vertical asymptote: $x = 0$;
horizontal asymptote: $y = 3$
**(b)**

$$y = \dfrac{6x^2 - 5x + 1}{2x^2}$$

**5. (a)** domain:
$\left(-\infty, -\frac{1}{2}\right) \cup \left(-\frac{1}{2}, \frac{1}{2}\right) \cup \left(\frac{1}{2}, \infty\right)$;
$x$-intercepts: $\pm 3$; $y$-intercept: 9;
vertical asymptotes: $x = \frac{1}{2}$ and
$x = -\frac{1}{2}$; horizontal asymptote: $y = \frac{1}{4}$

**(b)**

**7. (a)** domain:
$(-\infty, -\frac{3}{2}) \cup (-\frac{3}{2}, 0) \cup (0, 1) \cup (1, \infty)$;
$x$-intercepts: $-\frac{4}{3}, 2$; no $y$-intercept;
vertical asymptotes: $x = -\frac{3}{2}, x = 0,$
$x = 1$; horizontal asymptote: $y = 0$
**(b)**

**9.** no $x$-intercept; $y$-intercept: $\frac{1}{4}$;
horizontal asymptote: $y = 0$;
vertical asymptote: $x = -4$

**11.** no $x$-intercept; $y$-intercept: $\frac{3}{2}$;
horizontal asymptote: $y = 0$;
vertical asymptote: $x = -2$

**13.** no $x$-intercept; $y$-intercept: $\frac{2}{3}$;
horizontal asymptote: $y = 0$;
vertical asymptote: $x = 3$

**15.** $x$-intercept: 3; $y$-intercept: 3;
horizontal asymptote: $y = 1$;
vertical asymptote: $x = 1$

**17.** $x$-intercept: $\frac{1}{2}$; $y$-intercept: $-2$;
horizontal asymptote: $y = 2$;
vertical asymptote: $x = -\frac{1}{2}$

**19.** no $x$-intercept; $y$-intercept: $\frac{1}{4}$;
horizontal asymptote: $y = 0$;
vertical asymptote: $x = 2$

**21.** no $x$-intercept; $y$-intercept: 3;
horizontal asymptote: $y = 0$;
vertical asymptote: $x = -1$

**23.** no $x$-intercept; $y$-intercept: $\frac{1}{8}$;
horizontal asymptote: $y = 0$;
vertical asymptote: $x = -2$

**25.** no $x$-intercept; $y$-intercept: $-\frac{4}{125}$;
horizontal asymptote: $y = 0$;
vertical asymptote: $x = -5$

**27.** $x$- and $y$-intercepts: 0;
horizontal asymptote: $y = 0$;
vertical asymptotes: $x = -2, x = 2$

**29. (a)** $x$-intercept: 0; $y$-intercept: 0;
horizontal asymptote: $y = 0$;
vertical asymptotes: $x = 1, x = -3$

**(b)** $x$-intercept: 0; $y$-intercept: 0;
horizontal asymptote: $y = 3$;
vertical asymptotes: $x = 1, x = -3$

**31.** $x$-intercepts: $-\frac{5}{4}, 1$; $y$-intercept: 1;
horizontal asymptote: $y = 2$;
vertical asymptotes: $x = \frac{5}{2}, x = -1$

**33. (a)** $x$-intercepts: 2, 4;
no $y$-intercept; horizontal asymptote:
$y = 1$; vertical asymptotes: $x = 0, x = 1$

**(b)** $x$-intercepts: 2, 4; no $y$-intercept;
horizontal asymptote: $y = 1$;
vertical asymptotes: $x = 0, x = 3$

**35. (a)** 500 bacteria
**(b)** 2500 bacteria

**37. (a)** $A(x) = 521 - \dfrac{1500}{x} - 7x$
**(b)**

**(c)** width $\approx 14.6$ inches,
length $\approx 34.2$ inches
**39.** crosses at $\left(\frac{11}{2}, 1\right)$

**41.** crosses at $\left(\frac{1}{3}, 1\right)$

**45. (a)**

**(b)**

$$y = \frac{x-2}{x+1}$$
$(x \neq 3)$

**(c)**

$$y = \frac{1}{x-4}$$
$(x \neq 1, 2, 3)$

$x = 4$

**47.** low point: $(-3, -\frac{1}{12})$

$$y = \frac{x}{(x-3)^2}$$

$x = 3$

**49. (b)**

| $x$ | $x + 4$ | $\dfrac{x^2 + x - 6}{x - 3}$ |
|---|---|---|
| 10 | 14 | 14.8571 |
| 100 | 104 | 104.0619 |
| 1000 | 1004 | 1004.0060 |
| $-10$ | $-6$ | $-6.4615$ |
| $-100$ | $-96$ | $-96.0583$ |
| $-1000$ | $-996$ | $-996.0600$ |

**(c)** vertical asymptote: $x = 3$;
$x$-intercepts: $-3, 2$; $y$-intercept: 2

**(d)**

$$y = \frac{x^2 + x - 6}{x - 3}$$
$y = x + 4$

$x = 3$

**(e)** $(3 + \sqrt{6}, 7 + 2\sqrt{6})$,
$(3 - \sqrt{6}, 7 - 2\sqrt{6})$

**51.**

$$y = \frac{-x^2 + 1}{x}$$
$y = -x$

**53. (a)**

$$f(x) = \frac{x^5 + 1}{x^2}$$

$$f(x) = \frac{x^5 + 1}{x^2}$$
$y = x^3$

**(b)**

$$f(x) = \frac{x^5 + 1}{x^2}$$
$y = x^3$

$$f(x) = \frac{x^5 + 1}{x^2}$$
$y = x^3$

Note that as $|x|$ increases, the curve $f(x)$ approaches the curve $y = x^3$.

$$f(x) = \frac{x^5 + 1}{x^2}$$
$y = x^3$

**(c)**

| $x$ | 5 | 10 | 50 | 100 | 500 |
|---|---|---|---|---|---|
| $d$ | 0.04 | 0.01 | 0.0004 | 0.0001 | 0.000004 |

| $x$ | $-5$ | $-10$ | $-50$ | $-100$ | $-500$ |
|---|---|---|---|---|---|
| $d$ | 0.04 | 0.01 | 0.0004 | 0.0001 | 0.000004 |

**(d)** As $|x|$ increases, the quantity $1/x^2$ approaches 0, and thus $f(x) \approx x^3$ when $|x|$ gets very large.

## Chapter 4 Review Exercises

**1.** $G(0) = -5$   **3.** $20,000

**5.**

$y = (x - 4)(x - 1)(x + 1)$

**7.** $V(t) = -180t + 1000$

**9.** $x$-intercept: $-\frac{5}{3}$; $y$-intercept: $\frac{5}{2}$;
horizontal asymptote: $y = 3$;
vertical asymptote: $x = -2$

$y = \dfrac{3x + 5}{x + 2}$

**11.**

$y = \dfrac{x}{(x + 2)(x - 4)}$

**13.** $P(w) = 2w + \dfrac{2\sqrt{144 - \pi^2 w^2}}{\pi}$

**15.** $f(x) = \frac{3}{8}x - \frac{5}{2}$

**17.** $f(x) = -\frac{3}{4}x + \frac{11}{4}$

**19.** vertex: $(-1, -4)$;
$x$-intercepts: $1, -3$; $y$-intercept: $-3$

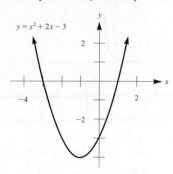

$y = x^2 + 2x - 3$

**21.** vertex: $(\frac{1}{2}, \frac{1}{2})$; no $x$-intercept;
$y$-intercept: 1

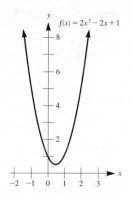

$f(x) = 2x^2 - 2x + 1$

**23.** 5   **25. (a)** maximum height: $\dfrac{v_0^2}{32}$ ft;
time. $t = \dfrac{v_0}{32}$ sec   **(b)** $t = \dfrac{v_0}{16}$ sec

**27.** $b = \frac{17}{3}, -11$   **29.** 1   **31.** $\frac{225}{4}$ cm$^2$

**33.** $a = 1$   **35.** $x = \frac{432}{59}$ cm $\approx 7.32$ cm

**39.** $x$-intercepts: $-4, 2$; $y$-intercept: $-8$

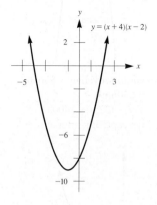

$y = (x + 4)(x - 2)$

**41.** $x$-intercepts: $-1, 0$; $y$-intercept: 0

$y = -x^2(x + 1)$

**43.** $x$-intercepts: $0, 2, -2$; $y$-intercept: 0

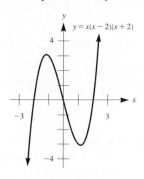

$y = x(x - 2)(x + 2)$

**45.** no $x$-intercept; $y$-intercept: $-1$;
horizontal asymptote: $y = 0$;
vertical asymptote: $x = 1$

$y = \dfrac{-1}{(x - 1)^2}$

**47.** $x$-intercept: 2; $y$-intercept: $\frac{2}{3}$;
horizontal asymptote: $y = 1$;
vertical asymptote: $x = 3$

$y = \dfrac{x - 2}{x - 3}$

**49.** $x$-intercept: 1; $y$-intercept: $\frac{1}{4}$; horizontal asymptote: $y = 1$; vertical asymptote: $x = 2$

**51.** $k = 6$
**53.** $(-\infty, 4 - 2\sqrt{3}] \cup [4 + 2\sqrt{3}, \infty)$
**55.** $A(m) = \dfrac{m}{2}$
**57.** $A(x) = (1 - x)\sqrt{1 - x^2}$

## Chapter 4 Test
**1.** $L(0) = -\frac{18}{7}$    **2. (a)** maximum value: 2; increasing: $(-\infty, 1)$
**(b)** $t = 0$    **3. (a)** $x$-intercepts: 3, $-4$; $y$-intercept: $-48$

**(b)**

**(c)**

**4. (a)**

**(b)**

**5.** turning point: $\left(\frac{7}{2}, \frac{73}{4}\right)$;
$x$-intercepts: $\dfrac{7 \pm \sqrt{73}}{2}$; $y$-intercept: 6;
axis of symmetry: $x = \frac{7}{2}$

**6.** maximum revenue = \$9600; price = \$40/unit
**7.** $V(t) = -1325t + 14000$
**8.** $x$-intercept: 3; $y$-intercept: $-\frac{27}{2}$

**9.** $x$-intercept: $\frac{3}{2}$; $y$-intercept: $-3$; vertical asymptote: $x = -1$; horizontal asymptote: $y = 2$

**10. (a)** $PQ(x) = \sqrt{10x^2 - 22x + 17}$
**(b)** $x = 1.1$    **11. (a)** vertical asymptotes: $x = 3, x = -3$; horizontal asymptote: $y = 1$
**(b)**

**(c)**

**(d)**

**12.** $A(w) = \frac{1}{2}w\sqrt{64 - w^2}$
**13. (a)** As $|x|$ increases in size for $x$ positive, $-x^3$ increases in the negative direction, which the pictured function does not.

**(b)** This graph has four turning points, and a polynominal function with highest degree term $-x^3$ can have at most two turning points.

**14. (a)** slope $\approx -9$ billion dollars/year

**(b)** $y = -8.84x + 316.74$; slope is close   **(c)** 1996: 263.7 billion dollars; 1999: 237.18 billion dollars; 1996: 0.8% error: 1999: 14.3% error

**15. (a)** $x = 0, \frac{1}{2}$   **(b)** no fixed points

**16. (a)**

|        | $x_1$ | $x_2$ | $x_3$ | $x_4$ | $x_5$ | $x_6$ |
|--------|-------|-------|-------|-------|-------|-------|
| From graph | 0.56 | 0.28 | 0.52 | 0.33 | 0.49 | 0.36 |
| From calculator | 0.56 | 0.286 | 0.518 | 0.332 | 0.490 | 0.360 |

**(b)** $x = \dfrac{-5 - \sqrt{85}}{10} \approx -1.4220$,

$x = \dfrac{-5 + \sqrt{85}}{10} \approx 0.4220$;

The iterates are approaching 0.4220.

**(c)** $x_1 = -0.4$, $x_2 = 0.44$, $x_3 = 0.4064$, $x_4 \approx 0.4348$, $x_5 \approx 0.4109$, $x_6 \approx 0.4311$. Yes, they are approaching the fixed point 0.4220.

# CHAPTER 5
## Exercise Set 5.1

**1. (a)** $10^9$   **(b)** $10^{15}$   **3.** 125   **5.** 16

**7.** 8   **9.** $5^{\sqrt{2}}$   **11. (a)** $x = 3$

**(b)** $t = \frac{3}{2}$   **(c)** $y = \frac{1}{4}$   **(d)** $z = \frac{5}{2}$

**13.** $(-\infty, \infty)$   **15.** $(-\infty, \infty)$

**17.**

**19.**

**21.**

**23.**

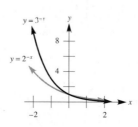

**25.** domain: $(-\infty, \infty)$; range: $(-\infty, 1)$; $x$- and $y$-intercepts: 0; asymptote: $y = 1$

**27.** domain: $(-\infty, \infty)$; range: $(1, \infty)$; no $x$-intercept; $y$-intercept: 2; asymptote: $y = 1$

**29.** domain: $(-\infty, \infty)$; range: $(0, \infty)$; no $x$-intercept; $y$-intercept: $\frac{1}{2}$; asymptote: $y = 0$

**31.** domain: $(-\infty, \infty)$; range: $(1, \infty)$; no $x$-intercept; $y$-intercept: 4; asymptote: $y = 1$

**33. (a)** no $x$-intercept; $y$-intercept: $-\frac{1}{9}$; asymptote: $y = 0$

**(b)**

**35. (a)** $x$-intercept: $-1$; $y$-intercept: $-3$;
asymptote: $y = -4$
**(b)**

**37. (a)** no $x$-intercept; $y$-intercept: $\frac{1}{10}$;
asymptote: $y = 0$
**(b)**

**39.** $x = -\frac{1}{3}$ **41.** $x = \frac{3}{2}, 1$

**43. (a)** $[0, 2]$: $\dfrac{\Delta f}{\Delta x} = 1.5$, $\dfrac{\Delta g}{\Delta x} = 1.5$;

$[2, 4]$: $\dfrac{\Delta f}{\Delta x} = 6$, $\dfrac{\Delta g}{\Delta x} = 6$

**(b)** $[4, 6]$: $\dfrac{\Delta f}{\Delta x} = 10.5$, $\dfrac{\Delta g}{\Delta x} = 24$;

$[6, 8]$: $\dfrac{\Delta f}{\Delta x} = 15$, $\dfrac{\Delta g}{\Delta x} = 96$

**(c)** $\dfrac{\Delta f}{\Delta x} = 24$, $\dfrac{\Delta g}{\Delta x} = 1536$

**47. (a)**

**(b)** domain: $(0, \infty)$; range: $(-\infty, \infty)$;
$x$-intercept: 1; no $y$-intercept;
asymptote: $x = 0$ **49. (a)** 1.4
**(b)** 1.41 **51. (a)** 1.5 **(b)** 1.52

**53. (a)** 1.7 **(b)** 1.73 **55. (a)** 1.6
**(b)** 1.62 **57.** $x \approx 0.3$ **59.** $x \approx 0.7$
**61. (a)**

**(b)**

**(c)**

**63. (a)**

**(b)** $(0.3, 2)$ is the point of intersection

## Exercise Set 5.2
**1.** False **3.** False **5.** True **7.** False
**9. (a)** two **(b)** two

**11.** domain: $(-\infty, \infty)$; range: $(0, \infty)$;
no $x$-intercept; $y$-intercept: 1;
asymptote: $y = 0$

**13.** domain: $(-\infty, \infty)$; range: $(-\infty, 0)$;
no $x$-intercept; $y$-intercept: $-1$;
asymptote: $y = 0$

**15.** domain: $(-\infty, \infty)$; range: $(1, \infty)$;
no $x$-intercept; $y$-intercept: 2;
asymptote: $y = 1$

**17.** domain: $(-\infty, \infty)$; range: $(1, \infty)$;
no $x$-intercept; $y$-intercept: $e + 1$;
asymptote: $y = 1$

**19.** domain: $(-\infty, \infty)$; range: $(-\infty, e)$; $x$-intercept: 1; $y$-intercept: $e - 1$; asymptote: $y = e$

**21. (a)** $y = e^x$ displaced to the left two units

**(b)** $y = e^x$ displaced to the left two units, then reflected across the $y$-axis

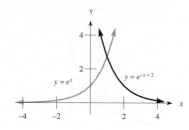

**23.** $\dfrac{\Delta f}{\Delta x} = 1$, $\dfrac{\Delta g}{\Delta x} = 1$, $\dfrac{\Delta h}{\Delta x} \approx 1.7$

**25. (a)**

**(b)**

**(c)**

**(d)** For $x < 0$, $2^{-x} < e^{-x} < 3^{-x}$ by (b), so $2^x > e^x > 3^x$ by taking reciprocals.

**27.** instantaneous rate of change = 6

| Interval | $\Delta f/\Delta x$ for $f(x) - x^2$ |
|---|---|
| [3, 3.1] | 6.1 |
| [3, 3.01] | 6.01 |
| [3, 3.001] | 6.001 |
| [3, 3.0001] | 6.0001 |
| [3, 3.00001] | 6.00001 |
| [2.9, 3] | 5.9 |
| [2.99, 3] | 5.99 |
| [2.999, 3] | 5.999 |
| [2.9999, 3] | 5.9999 |
| [2.99999, 3] | 5.99999 |

**29.**

| Interval | $\Delta f/\Delta x$ for $f(x) = e^x$ |
|---|---|
| [1.9, 2] | 7.031617 |
| [1.99, 2] | 7.352234 |
| [1.999, 2] | 7.385363 |
| [1.9999, 2] | 7.388687 |
| [1.99999, 2] | 7.389019 |
| [1.999999, 2] | 7.389053 |
| [1.9999999, 2] | 7.389056 |

**31. (a)** 255 bacteria per hour
**(b)** $t = 5$ hours: 148 bacteria per hour; $t = 5.5$ hours: 245 bacteria per hour
**33.** $P$: $e^{-1} \approx 0.37$; $Q$: 1; $R$: $e^{0.5} \approx 1.65$

**35.** A, D, E, G   **37.** B, D, E, G
**39.** A, D, F, G, H   **41.** A, D, F, G, H
**43.** graph: $e^{0.1} \approx 1.1$; calculator: $e^{0.1} \approx 1.105$   **45.** graph: $e^{-0.3} \approx 0.75$; calculator: $e^{-0.3} \approx 0.741$
**47.** graph: $e^{-1} \approx 0.35$; calculator: $e^{-1} \approx 0.368$

**49.** graph: $\dfrac{1}{\sqrt{e}} = e^{-0.5} \approx 0.6$;

calculator: $\dfrac{1}{\sqrt{e}} = e^{-0.5} \approx 0.607$

**51. (a)** $x \approx 0.4$   **(b)** $\ln 1.5 \approx 0.405$
**53. (a)** $x \approx 0.6$   **(b)** $\ln 1.8 \approx 0.588$
**55. (a)** $\cosh(0) = 1$, $\cosh(1) \approx 1.54$, $\cosh(-1) \approx 1.54$   **(b)** $(-\infty, \infty)$
**(c)** The graph is symmetric about the $y$-axis.
**(d)**

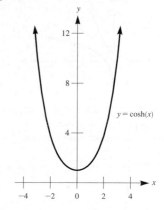

**57. (a)** $\sinh(0) = 0$, $\sinh(1) \approx 1.18$, $\sinh(-1) \approx -1.18$   **(b)** $(-\infty, \infty)$
**(c)** The graph is symmetric about the origin.
**(d)**

**(e)** three points

**59. (a)** $e^\pi$ is larger   **(b)** $e^\pi$ is larger
**61. (a)**

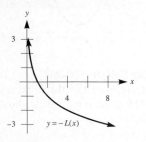

**(b)** domain: $(0, \infty)$; range: $(-\infty, \infty)$;
$x$-intercept: 1; asymptote: $x = 0$
**(c) (i)** $x$-intercept: 1; asymptote: $x = 0$

**(ii)** $x$-intercept: $-1$; asymptote: $x = 0$

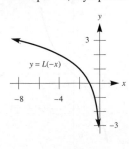

**(iii)** $x$-intercept: 2; asymptote: $x = 1$

**63. (a)** $[\cosh(x)]^2 - 2[\sinh(x)]^2 = 1$ is
not an identity; solution: $x = 0$

## Exercise Set 5.3
**1. (a)** $f[g(x)] = x$   **(b)** $g[f(x)] = x$; $f$
**3. (a)** $g(x) = \log_2 x$   **(b)** $2^{\log_2 x} = x$;
$\log_2(2^x) = x$   **(c)** $2^{\log_2 99} = 99$;
$\log_2(2^{-\pi}) = -\pi$   **5. (a)** is one-to-one
**(b)** not one-to-one   **(c)** is one-to-one
**7.** $f[f^{-1}(6)] = 6$   **9. (a)** $\log_3 9 = 2$
**(b)** $\log_{10} 1000 = 3$   **(c)** $\log_7 343 = 3$
**(d)** $\log_2 \sqrt{2} = \frac{1}{2}$   **11. (a)** $2^5 = 32$
**(b)** $10^0 = 1$   **(c)** $e^{1/2} = \sqrt{e}$
**(d)** $e^{-1} = \dfrac{1}{e}$
**13.**

| $x$ | 1 | 10 | $10^2$ | $10^3$ | $10^{-1}$ | $10^{-2}$ | $10^{-3}$ |
|---|---|---|---|---|---|---|---|
| $\log_{10} x$ | 0 | 1 | 2 | 3 | $-1$ | $-2$ | $-3$ |

**15. (a)** $\log_5 30$ is larger   **(b)** $\ln 17$ is
larger   **17. (a)** $\frac{3}{2}$   **(b)** $-\frac{5}{2}$   **(c)** $\frac{3}{2}$
**19. (a)** $x = \frac{1}{16}$   **(b)** $x = e^{-2} \approx 0.14$
**21. (a)** $(0, \infty)$   **(b)** $(-\infty, \frac{3}{4})$
**(c)** $(-\infty, 0) \cup (0, \infty)$   **(d)** $(0, \infty)$
**(e)** $(-\infty, -5) \cup (5, \infty)$   **23.** $A$: $(0, 1)$;
$B$: $(1, 0)$; $C$: $(4, 2)$; $D$: $(2, 4)$
**25. (a)** domain: $(0, \infty)$; range:
$(-\infty, \infty)$; $x$-intercept: 1; no $y$-intercept;
asymptote: $x = 0$

**(b)** domain: $(0, \infty)$; range: $(-\infty, \infty)$;
$x$-intercept: 1; no $y$-intercept;
asymptote: $x = 0$

**(c)** domain: $(-\infty, 0)$; range: $(-\infty, \infty)$;
$x$-intercept: $-1$; no $y$-intercept;
asymptote: $x = 0$

**(d)** domain: $(-\infty, 0)$; range: $(-\infty, \infty)$;
$x$-intercept: $-1$; no $y$-intercept;
asymptote: $x = 0$

**27.** domain: $(2, \infty)$; range: $(-\infty, \infty)$;
$x$-intercept: 5; no $y$-intercept;
asymptote: $x = 2$

**29.** domain: $(-e, \infty)$; range: $(-\infty, \infty)$; $x$-intercept: $-e + 1$; $y$-intercept: 1; asymptote: $x = -e$

**31. (a)** 4   **(b)** $-1$   **(c)** $\frac{1}{2}$
**33. (a)** $x \approx 1.4$   **(b)** $x \approx 1.398$
**35. (a)** $x \approx \pm 1.3$   **(b)** $x \approx \pm 1.266$
**37. (a)** $t \approx -0.3$   **(b)** $t \approx -0.349$
**39. (a)** $t \approx -0.4$   **(b)** $t \approx -0.380$
**41. (a)** $(0, 1)$

**(b)** $(1, \infty)$

**(c)** $(0, \infty)$

**(d)** $(-\infty, 0)$

**43.** The San Salvador quake was 1.6 times stronger.
**45.** The second quake is $10^d$ times stronger.   **47. (a)** $I = 10^{8/10} I_0$
**(b)** The power mower is $10^9$ times more intense.   **49. (a)** pH $\approx 3.5$; acid
**(b)** pH $= 0$   **51.** $[H^+] = 10^{-5.9}$
**53.** D, E, H   **55.** D, E, H
**57.** D, E, H   **59.** D, E, H
**61.** $f^{-1}(x) = -1 + \ln x$; $x$-intercept: $e$; asymptote: $x = 0$

**63.** $x \approx 10^{30}$

**65. (a)**

| Planet | $x$ | $y$ | $\ln x$ | $\ln y$ |
|---|---|---|---|---|
| Mercury | 0.387 | 0.241 | $-0.95$ | $-1.42$ |
| Venus | 0.723 | 0.615 | $-0.32$ | $-0.49$ |
| Earth | 1.000 | 1.000 | 0.00 | 0.00 |
| Mars | 1.523 | 1.881 | 0.42 | 0.63 |
| Jupiter | 5.202 | 11.820 | 1.65 | 2.47 |

**(b)** $\ln y = 1.50 \ln x$
**(d)**

| Planet | $x$ | $y$ (calculated) | $y$ (observed) |
|---|---|---|---|
| Saturn | 9.555 | 29.54 | 29.46 |
| Uranus | 19.22 | 84.26 | 84.01 |
| Neptune | 30.11 | 165.22 | 164.79 |
| Pluto | 39.44 | 247.69 | 248.50 |

**67. (a)** $y = -24.795459 + 7.453496 \ln x$

**(b)** $y = 0.1086x - 0.8890$
**(c)** logarithmic: 9.529 million; linear: 9.971 million   **(d)** logarithmic model is closer; logarithmic: 0.11% error; linear: 4.75% error
**69. (a)** $(1, \infty)$   **(b)** $f^{-1}(x) = e^{e^x}$
**71. (a)**

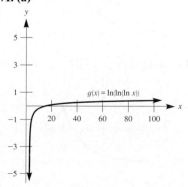

**(b)** $(-\infty, \infty)$   **(c)** no

## Exercise Set 5.4

**1.** 1    **3.** $\frac{1}{2}$    **5.** 4    **7.** 0    **9.** 4

**11.** $\log_{10} 60$    **13.** $\log_5 20$    **15. (a)** $\ln 6$

**(b)** $\ln\left(\frac{3}{16384}\right)$

**17.** $\log_b\left[\dfrac{4(1+x)^3}{(1-x)^{3/2}}\right]$

**19.** $\log_{10}\left[\dfrac{27\sqrt{x+1}}{(x^2+1)^6}\right]$

**21. (a)** $2\log_{10} x - \log_{10}(1+x^2)$
**(b)** $2\ln x - \frac{1}{2}\ln(1+x^2)$
**23. (a)** $\frac{1}{2}\log_{10}(3+x) + \frac{1}{2}\log_{10}(3-x)$
**(b)** $\frac{1}{2}\ln(2+x) + \frac{1}{2}\ln(2-x) -$
$\ln(x-1) - \frac{3}{2}\ln(x+1)$
**25. (a)** $\frac{1}{2}\log_b x - \frac{1}{2}$
**(b)** $\ln(1+x^2) + \ln(1+x^4) +$
$\ln(1+x^6)$    **27. (a)** $A + B$
**(b)** $-A - B$    **(c)** $3B$    **(d)** $-3B$
**29. (a)** $C - B$    **(b)** $B - C$
**(c)** $C - 2B$    **(d)** $C - 4A$
**31. (a)** $\dfrac{1}{B}$    **(b)** $\dfrac{A+C+1}{B}$

**33. (a)** $\dfrac{A}{B+1}$    **(b)** $\dfrac{B+C}{B+1}$

**35. (a)** 1    **(b)** 1    **37. (a)** $a + 2b + 3c$
**(b)** $1 + \frac{1}{2}a$    **(c)** $\frac{1}{2}(1 + a + b + c)$
**(d)** $1 + a - \frac{1}{2}b - \frac{1}{2}c$    **39. (a)** $1 + t$
**(b)** $u - t$    **(c)** $\frac{3}{2}t + \frac{1}{2}u - 1$
**(d)** $2 + t + \frac{1}{2}u$
**41. (a)** $x$-intercept: $x \approx 2.32$

**(b)** $x$-intercept: $x \approx 4.64$

**43.** $x = \dfrac{\ln 5 - \ln 2 + 1}{2}$

**45.** $x = \dfrac{\ln 13}{\ln 2}$

**47.** $x = \dfrac{1}{\ln 10}$

**49.** $x = \pm\sqrt{1 + \dfrac{\log_{10} 12}{\log_{10} 3}} \approx \pm 1.806$

**51.** $\dfrac{\log_{10} 5}{\log_{10} 2}$    **53.** $\dfrac{\log_{10} 3}{\log_{10} e}$    **55.** $\dfrac{\log_{10} 2}{\log_{10} b}$

**57.** $\dfrac{\ln 6}{\ln 10}$    **59.** $\dfrac{1}{\ln 10}$

**61.** $\dfrac{\ln(\ln x) - \ln(\ln 10)}{\ln 10}$

**63. (a)** true    **(b)** true    **(c)** true
**(d)** false    **(e)** true    **(f)** false
**(g)** true    **(h)** false    **(i)** true
**(j)** false    **(k)** false    **(l)** true
**(m)** true    **65. (f)** 2345.6
**(g)** 0.123456
**67.**

| $x$ | 0.1 | 0.05 | 0.005 | 0.0005 |
|---|---|---|---|---|
| $\ln(1+x)$ | 0.095310 | 0.048790 | 0.004987 | 0.000499 |

**69.** $a = 4, b = -\dfrac{\ln 243}{2.5}$

**71. (a)** $x = \dfrac{\log_{10} 3}{\log_{10} 2}$

**(b)** $\dfrac{\log_{10} 3}{\log_{10} 2} \approx 1.585$, $\dfrac{\ln 3}{\ln 2} \approx 1.585$

**75.** $x^3$
**79. (c)** $\log_\pi 2 + \dfrac{1}{\log_\pi 2}$ is larger

## Exercise Set 5.5

**1.** $x = \dfrac{\ln 3}{2\ln 3 - \ln 5} \approx 1.869$

**3.** $x = e^{e^{1.5}} \approx 88.384$    **5.** $x = \pm 8$

**7.** $x = \dfrac{3 - \sqrt{809}}{4} \approx -6.361$,

$x = \dfrac{3 + \sqrt{809}}{4} \approx 7.861$

**9.** $x = \log_{10} 2 \approx 0.301$    **11. (a)** true
for all $x > 0$
**(b)** $x = e^{-\sqrt{3}} \approx 0.177$, $x = e^{\sqrt{3}} \approx 5.652$
**13. (a)** true for all $x > 0$
**(b)** $x = 6^{1/5} \approx 1.431$
**15.** true for all $x > 0$
**17.** $x = \sqrt{3} \approx 1.732$    **19.** no real
solutions    **21.** no real solutions
**23.** $x = \frac{7}{3}$    **25. (a)** no real solutions
**(b)** $x = 0$    **(c)** $x = \ln 3 \approx 1.099$
**(d)** $x = \ln(1 + \sqrt{5}) \approx 1.174$

**27.** $x = \ln\left(\dfrac{1+\sqrt{5}}{2}\right) \approx 0.481$

**29.** $x = \dfrac{3\ln 5}{5\ln 2 - \ln 3 - \ln 5} \approx 6.372$

**31.** $x = 2$    **33.** $x = \frac{1}{2}$    **35.** $x = 3$
**37.** $x = \frac{203}{99}$    **39.** $x = 3$    **41.** $x = 7$

**43. (a)** $x = \dfrac{10^y}{3(10^y) - 1}$

**(b)** $x = \dfrac{1-y}{2}$    for $y < \dfrac{1}{3}$

**45. (a)** one solution    **(b)** $x \approx 0.57$

**47. (a)** one solution    **(b)** $x \approx 1.49$

**49. (a)** two solutions
**(b)** $x \approx 1.56$, $x \approx 3.15$

**51.** $x \le -1$    **53.** $x \ge \ln\frac{43}{4} \approx 2.375$

**55.** $x < \dfrac{2 - e^2}{5} \approx -1.078$

**57.** $x \ge \ln 100 - 2 \approx 2.605$
**59.** all real numbers    **61.** $-1 < x < \frac{1}{2}$
**63.** $x \le -1$ or $x \ge 5$    **65.** $0 < x < 1$

**67. (a)** $(4, \infty)$ **(b)** $4 < x \le 7$
**69.** $0 < x < 3$ **71.** $x = \frac{1}{2}, 2$
**73.** The graphs are identical

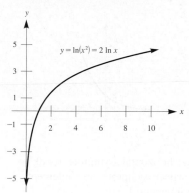

$y = \ln(x^2) = 2 \ln x$

**75.** $x = e^2$ or $x = e^{-4/3}$
**77.** $(0, 1) \cup (1, \infty)$ **79.** $x = \beta^{-1/\alpha}$
**81.** $x = \dfrac{1}{k} \ln \dfrac{y}{A}$
**83.** $x = -\dfrac{1}{k} \ln\left(\dfrac{a - y}{by}\right)$
**85. (a)** $x = e^{e^2}$ **(b)** $x \approx 1618.178$
**87. (a)** $x = \dfrac{\ln 1.5}{\ln 3}$ **(b)** $x \approx 0.369$
**89.** Since $e > 0, 2 - e < 2$, thus $\dfrac{2 - e}{3} < \dfrac{2}{3}$.
**91.** $(-3, -\sqrt{6}) \cup (\sqrt{6}, 3)$
**93.** $x = 1, x = 2$
**95.** $x = \dfrac{\ln(a - b)}{\ln(a + b)}$ **97.** $x = \dfrac{\pm b}{a + b}$

## Exercise Set 5.6
**1.** $1009.98 **3.** 8.45% **5.** $767.27
**7. (a)** $3869.68 **(b)** $4006.39
**9.** 13 quarters **11.** $3487.50
**13. (a)** 4.4 years **(b)** 4.43 years
**15.** 16 years **17.** $2610.23
**19.** 5.83% **21.** 6% investment
**23. (a)** 14 years **(b)** 13.86 years
**(c)** 1.01% **25.** $26.5 trillion
**27. (a)** 14 years
**(b)**

$A$ (dollars)

$A(t) = 7000e^{0.05t}$

56,000

28,000

$t$ (years)
14 28 42

## Exercise Set 5.7
**1. (a)** $k \approx 0.3209$ **(b)** 9951 bacteria
**(c)** 5.0 hours
**3.** $N_0 = 2000; k \approx 0.1769$
**5. (a)**

| Region | World | More dev. | Less dev. |
|---|---|---|---|
| 1995 population (billions) | 5.702 | 1.169 | 4.533 |
| Percent of population in 1995 | 100 | 20.5 | 79.5 |
| Relative growth rate (percent per year) | 1.5 | 0.2 | 1.9 |
| Year 2000 population (billions) | 6.146 | 1.181 | 4.985 |
| Percent of world population in 2000 | 100 | 19.22 | 81.11 |

**(b)** world: 1.3% error; more developed: 0.3% error; less developed: 2.1% error
**7. (a)** Chad: $N(t) = 8.0e^{0.033t}$; United Kingdom: $N(t) = 59.8e^{0.001t}$
**(b)** 60 years **9. (a)** Niger: 15.8 million; Portugal: 10.2 million
**(b)** 13 years; Portugal: 10.1 million
**11. (a)** 6.332 billion **(b)** higher; 4% error **13. (a)** 116 years
**(b)** 43 years **(c)** 27 years
**(d)** 19 years
**15. (a)**

| Year | 1998 ($t = 10$) | 2000 ($t = 12$) |
|---|---|---|
| Concentration of Carbon dioxide (ppm) | 365.6 | 368.6 |

**(b)** 1998: too low, 0.3% error; 2000: too high, 0.1% error
**17. (a)** New York: $N(t) = 18.976e^{0.006t}$; Arizona: $N(t) = 5.131e^{0.04t}$
**(b)** year 2040

**19. (a)**

| Region | 1990 population (millions) | Growth rate (%) | 2025 population |
|---|---|---|---|
| North America | 275.2 | 0.7 | 351.6 |
| Soviet Union | 291.3 | 0.7 | 372.2 |
| Europe | 499.5 | 0.2 | 535.7 |
| Nigeria | 113.3 | 3.1 | 335.3 |

**(b)** 222.0 million **(c)** North America: 76.4 mil; Soviet Union: 80.9 mil; Europe: 36.2 mil; combined: 193.5 mil **(d)** Our results support this projection.
**21.** By the end of the year 2000 the population of Mexico exceeded 100 million people.
**23. (a)**

| $t$ (seconds) | 0 | 550 | 1100 | 1650 | 2200 |
|---|---|---|---|---|---|
| $N$ (grams) | 8 | 4 | 2 | 1 | 0.5 |

**(b)**

| $t$ (years) | 0 | $4.9 \times 10^9$ | $9.8 \times 10^9$ | $14.7 \times 10^9$ | $19.6 \times 10^9$ |
|---|---|---|---|---|---|
| $N$ (grams) | 10 | 5 | 2.5 | 1.25 | 0.625 |

**25.** 0.55 gram **27. (a)** 4.29 grams
**(b)** 79 hours
**29. (a)**

$N$

$N_0$
$N_0/2$
$N_0/4$
$N_0/8$

3240 6480 9720
Time (years)

**(b)**

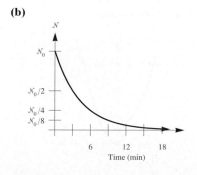

$N$

$N_0$
$N_0/2$
$N_0/4$
$N_0/8$

6 12 18
Time (min)

**31. (a)** 1.53 grams   **(b)** 43 years
**33. (a)** 73,000 years   **(b)** 10 half-lives
**(c)** 10 half-lives   **35. (a)** $k \approx -0.0248$
**(b)** 279 years   **(c)** 280 years
**37.** 0.02799997 ounces
**39. (a)** 8.5 billion; it is greater
**(b)** 0.934% per year
**41. (b)** $T \approx 32$ years; year 2004
**(c)** $y = 0.4606x + 24.0385$
**(d)** $T \approx 32$ years; year 2025
**43. (a)** $T \approx 34$ years; year 2033
**(b)** $T \approx 67$ years; year 2066
**(c)** $T \approx 52$ years; year 2051
**47.** 4.181 billion years old
**49.** 15,505 years old   **51.** 8,000 years
old; the site is older
**53.** years 10–5 B.C., which fit in the
historical range
**55. (a)**

| | $N(-1)$ | $N(0)$ | $N(1)$ | $N(4)$ | $N(5)$ |
|---|---|---|---|---|---|
| From graph | 0.25 | 0.5 | 1.0 | 3.5 | 3.75 |
| From calculator | 0.176 | 0.444 | 1.014 | 3.489 | 3.795 |

**(b)** $N(10) \approx 3.99854773$,
$N(15) \approx 3.99999021$,
$N(20) \approx 3.99999993$   **(c)** $t \approx 3$
**(d)** $t = \ln 24 \approx 3.178$
**57. (a)** $a = 4$   **(b)** $b = \ln \frac{8}{3} \approx 0.9808$
**59. (a)** $N(t) = \dfrac{162}{1 + 161e^{-0.50t}}$
**(b)** $N(4) \approx 7.1, N(8) \approx 41.0$,
$N(12) \approx 115.8, N(16) \approx 153.7$; $N(4)$
and $N(8)$ are lower; $N(12)$ and $N(16)$
**(c)** 10 days 4 hours
**61. (b)** If $k$ is close to 0, then
$e^k - 1 \approx (k + 1) - 1 = k$.

## Chapter 5 Review Exercises

**1.** $\log_5 126$   **3.** $\dfrac{4 \ln 1.5}{\ln 1.25}$ hours
**5.** $f$ is not one-to-one

**7.** $x = \dfrac{e + 1}{e - 1}$   **9.** $y = e^x$: domain:
$(-\infty, \infty)$, range: $(0, \infty)$; $y = \ln x$:
domain: $(0, \infty)$, range: $(-\infty, \infty)$

**11.** $-\frac{3}{2}$   **13.** $k \approx -0.05$
**15.** $x = 2 - \ln \frac{12}{5}$   **17.** year 2015
**19.** doubling time: 7 years

**21.** horizontal asymptote: $y = 0$;
no vertical asymptote; no $x$-intercept;
$y$-intercept: 1

**23.** no horizontal asymptote; vertical
asymptote: $x = 0$; $x$-intercept: 1;
no $y$-intercept

**25.** horizontal asymptote: $y = 1$;
no vertical asymptote; no $x$-intercept;
$y$-intercept: 3

**27.** horizontal asymptote: $y = 0$; no
vertical asymptote; no $x$-intercept;
$y$-intercept: 1

**29.** horizontal asymptote: $y = 1$;
no vertical asymptote; no $x$-intercept;
$y$-intercept: $e + 1$

**31.** no asymptotes; $x$- and
$y$-intercepts: 0

**33.** $x = 4$   **35.** $x = 3$   **37.** $x = \frac{2}{3}$
**39.** $x = \sqrt[3]{3}$   **41.** $x = \dfrac{1 - 2 \ln 3}{10}$

**43.** $x = \frac{200}{99}$  **45.** $x = 2$  **47.** all real numbers $x > 0$  **49.** $x = 1$  **51.** $\frac{1}{2}$
**53.** $\frac{1}{5}$  **55.** $-1$  **57.** 16  **59.** 4  **61.** 2
**63.** 2  **65.** $\frac{9}{14}$  **67.** $2a + 3b + \frac{c}{2}$
**69.** $8a + 4b$  **71.** between 2 and 3
**73.** between 2 and 3  **75.** $-3$ and $-2$
**77. (a)** third quadrant

**(b)** $x = \dfrac{-2e}{e+1} \approx -1.46$  **79.** $k = \dfrac{\ln \frac{1}{2}}{T}$

**81.** 6.25% remaining

**83.** $\dfrac{d \ln \frac{c}{b}}{\ln \frac{1}{2}}$ days  **85.** $\log_{10} 2$

**87.** $\ln 10$  **89.** $\ln x^a y^b$
**91.** $\frac{1}{2}\ln(x-3) + \frac{1}{2}\ln(x+4)$
**93.** $3\log_{10} x - \frac{1}{2}\log_{10}(1+x)$
**95.** $3\ln(1+2e) - 3\ln(1-2e)$

**97.** $\dfrac{\ln 2}{\ln(1 + \frac{R}{100})}$ years

**99.** 9.92%  **101.** $\dfrac{100 \ln 2}{R}$ years

**103. (a)** $7\frac{3}{4}$ years

**(b)** $\dfrac{\ln n}{\ln(1 + \frac{R}{400})}$ years

**105. (a)** $(0, \infty)$  **(b)** $[1, \infty)$
**107.** $(0, e^2) \cup (e^2, \infty)$

## Chapter 5 Test

**1.** domain: $(-\infty, \infty)$; range: $(-3, \infty)$;
$x$-intercept: $-\dfrac{\ln 3}{\ln 2}$; $y$-intercept: $-2$;
asymptote: $y = -3$

**2.** $\dfrac{\ln \frac{5}{3}}{\ln 1.033} \approx 16$ hours  **3.** $\log_2 17$

**4.** $\dfrac{\ln 15}{\ln 2}$  **5.** $10^{12}$  **6.** 4 years

**7. (a)** $(0, \infty)$
**(b)**

**8.** $3a - \frac{1}{2}b$  **9. (a)** $-\frac{1}{2}$  **(b)** $-1$
**10.** $x = 0, -2, 2$  **11. (a)** $k \approx -0.1733$

**(b)** 0.35 gram  **12.** $\ln \dfrac{x^2}{(x^2+1)^{1/3}}$

**13.** no solution
**14.** $g^{-1}(x) = 10^x + 1$; range: $(1, \infty)$
**15. (a)** 12 years
**(b)**

**16. (a)** $(0, \infty)$  **(b)** $x = 1, e^2$

**17. (a)** $\dfrac{1}{\ln \frac{4}{3}} \approx 3.48$  **(b)** 4

**18.** $x = 4$  **19.** $x = \ln \frac{3}{2} \approx 0.405$

**20. (a)** $x > \dfrac{\ln 1.6}{\ln 0.3} \approx -0.39$

**(b)** $(3, 4]$

# CHAPTER 6
## Exercise Set 6.1
**1. (a)** $\sin \theta = \frac{15}{17}$, $\cos \theta = \frac{8}{17}$, $\tan \theta = \frac{15}{8}$,
$\cot \theta = \frac{8}{15}$, $\sec \theta = \frac{17}{8}$, $\csc \theta = \frac{17}{15}$
**(b)** $\sin \beta = \frac{8}{17}$, $\cos \beta = \frac{15}{17}$, $\tan \beta = \frac{8}{15}$,
$\cot \beta = \frac{15}{8}$, $\sec \beta = \frac{17}{15}$, $\csc \beta = \frac{17}{8}$
**3. (a)** $\sin \theta = \sqrt{5}/5$, $\cos \theta = 2\sqrt{5}/5$,
$\tan \theta = \frac{1}{2}$, $\cot \theta = 2$, $\sec \theta = \sqrt{5}/2$,
$\csc \theta = \sqrt{5}$  **(b)** $\sin \beta = 2\sqrt{5}/5$,
$\cos \beta = \sqrt{5}/5$, $\tan \beta = 2$, $\cot \beta = \frac{1}{2}$,
$\sec \beta = \sqrt{5}$, $\csc \beta = \sqrt{5}/2$
**5. (a)** $\cos A = 3\sqrt{13}/13$,
$\sin A = 2\sqrt{13}/13$, $\tan A = \frac{2}{3}$

**(b)** $\sec B = \sqrt{13}/2$, $\csc B = \sqrt{13}/3$,
$\cot B = \frac{2}{3}$  **7.** $\sin B = \frac{12}{13}$, $\cos B = \frac{5}{13}$,
$\tan B = \frac{12}{5}$, $\cot B = \frac{5}{12}$, $\sec B = \frac{13}{5}$,
$\csc B = \frac{13}{12}$  **9. (a)** $\sin B = \frac{4}{5}$, $\cos A = \frac{4}{5}$
**(b)** $\sin A = \frac{3}{5}$, $\cos B = \frac{3}{5}$
**(c)** $(\tan A)(\tan B) = 1$
**11. (a)** $\cos A = \frac{24}{25}$, $\sin A = \frac{7}{25}$,
$\tan A = \frac{7}{24}$
**(b)** $\cos B = \frac{7}{25}$, $\sin B = \frac{24}{25}$, $\tan B = \frac{24}{7}$
**(c)** $(\tan A)(\tan B) = 1$
**13.** $\sin \theta \approx 0.906$, $\cos \theta \approx 0.423$,
$\tan \theta \approx 2.145$  **15.** $\sin \theta \approx 0.623$,
$\cos \theta \approx 0.783$, $\tan \theta \approx 0.795$
**17.** $\sin \theta \approx 0.985$, $\cos \theta \approx 0.173$,
$\tan \theta \approx 5.706$  **19.** $\sec \theta \approx 1.064$,
$\csc \theta \approx 2.924$, $\cot \theta \approx 2.747$
**21.** $\sec \theta \approx 1.049$, $\csc \theta \approx 3.326$,
$\cot \theta \approx 3.172$  **23.** $\sec \theta \approx 1.000$,
$\csc \theta < 57.299$, $\cot \theta \approx 57.290$
**37. (a)** $\cos 30° \approx 0.8660254038$,
$\cos 45° \approx 0.7071067812$
**(b)** $\cos 30° \approx 0.8660254038$,
$\cos 45° \approx 0.7071067812$
**39. (a)** Since $RC < QB < PA$, we have
$\sin 20° < \sin 40° < \sin 60°$.
**(b)** $\sin 20° \approx 0.3420$, $\sin 40° \approx 0.6428$,
$\sin 60° \approx 0.8660$  **41. (a)** $\cos \theta$
**(b)** $\sec \beta$  **45.** $\sin 3° \approx 0.0523359562$,
$\sin 6° \approx 0.1045284633$,
$\sin 9° \approx 0.1564344650$,
$\sin 12° \approx 0.2079116908$,
$\sin 15° \approx 0.2588190451$,
$\sin 18° \approx 0.3090169944$

## Exercise Set 6.2
**1. (a)** $11SC$  **(b)** $11 \sin \theta \cos \theta$
**3. (a)** $-8C^3S$  **(b)** $-8\cos^3 \theta \sin \theta$
**5. (a)** $1 + 2T + T^2$
**(b)** $1 + 2\tan \theta + \tan^2 \theta$
**7. (a)** $T^2 + T - 6$
**(b)** $\tan^2 \theta + \tan \theta - 6$
**9. (a)** $-1$  **(b)** $-1$  **11. (a)** $\dfrac{CS + 2}{S}$
**(b)** $\dfrac{\cos A \sin A + 2}{\sin A}$
**13. (a)** $(T - 1)(T + 9)$
**(b)** $(\tan \beta - 1)(\tan \beta + 9)$
**15. (a)** $(2C + 1)(2C - 1)$
**(b)** $(2\cos B + 1)(2\cos B - 1)$
**17. (a)** $3ST^2(3ST + 2)$
**(b)** $3\sec B \tan^2 B(3\sec B \tan B + 2)$
**19.** $\cos \theta = \sqrt{7}/4$, $\tan \theta = 3\sqrt{7}/7$,
$\cot \theta = \sqrt{7}/3$, $\sec \theta = 4\sqrt{7}/7$, $\csc \theta = \frac{4}{3}$
**21.** $\sin \beta = \sqrt{22}/5$, $\tan \beta = \sqrt{66}/3$,
$\cot \beta = \sqrt{66}/22$, $\sec \beta = 5\sqrt{3}/3$,
$\csc \beta = 5\sqrt{22}/22$

**23.** $\cos A = \frac{12}{13}$, $\tan A = \frac{5}{12}$, $\cot A = \frac{12}{5}$, $\sec A = \frac{13}{12}$, $\csc A = \frac{13}{5}$

**25.** $\sin B = \frac{4}{5}$, $\cos B = \frac{3}{5}$, $\cot B = \frac{3}{4}$, $\sec B = \frac{5}{3}$, $\csc B = \frac{5}{4}$

**27.** $\sin C = \sqrt{5}/3$, $\cos C = \frac{2}{3}$, $\tan C = \sqrt{5}/2$, $\cot C = 2\sqrt{5}/5$, $\csc C = 3\sqrt{5}/5$ **29.** $\sin \alpha = \sqrt{3}/2$, $\cos \alpha = \frac{1}{2}$, $\tan \alpha = \sqrt{3}$, $\sec \alpha = 2$, $\csc \alpha = 2\sqrt{3}/3$

**31.** $\sin \theta = 0.887$, $\tan \theta \approx 1.916$, $\cot \theta \approx 0.522$, $\sec \theta \approx 2.162$, $\csc \theta \approx 1.128$ **33.** $\sin \theta \approx 0.768$, $\cos \theta \approx 0.640$, $\cot \theta \approx 0.833$, $\sec \theta \approx 1.562$, $\csc \theta \approx 1.302$

**35.** $\sin A + \cos A$ **37.** $\csc \theta$
**39.** $\cos^2 B$ **41.** $\cos A + 4$
**43.** $2 \csc \theta$ **45.** $0$ **47.** $1$ **49.** $\tan \theta$
**51.** $-1$ **53.** $\sin^2 \theta$ **55.** $-2 \cos \theta - 1$

## Exercise Set 6.3

**1.** $BC = 30$ cm, $AC = 30\sqrt{3}$ cm

**3.** $AB = \dfrac{32\sqrt{3}}{3}$ cm, $BC = \dfrac{16\sqrt{3}}{3}$ cm

**5.** $AC \approx 11.5$ cm, $BC \approx 9.6$ cm
**7. (a)** 15.59 ft **(b)** 9 ft
**9.** 34 million miles **11.** 141.1 m
**13. (a)** $h \approx 27.3$ ft **(b)** 906.9 ft²
**15.** 1.5 in.²
**17.** $\frac{7}{2} \sin(360°/7) \approx 2.736$ square units
**19.** $\pi - 2\sqrt{2} \approx 0.313$ square units
**21.** $\sqrt{3} \approx 1.732$ square units
**25.** 10,660 ft **27.** 136 m
**29.** $BD = 18(\sqrt{3} - 1)$ cm
**31. (a)** $\angle BOA = 90° - \theta$, $\angle OAB = \theta$, $\angle BAP = 90° - \theta$, $\angle BPA = \theta$
**(b)** $AO = \sin \theta$, $AP = \cos \theta$, $OB = \sin^2 \theta$, $BP = \cos^2 \theta$

**33. (a)** $BC = \dfrac{5}{\sin \theta}$ **(b)** $AB = \dfrac{4}{\cos \theta}$

**(c)** $AC = 4 \sec \theta + 5 \csc \theta$
**35. (a)** $DE = \sin \theta$ **(b)** $OE = \cos \theta$
**(c)** $CF = \tan \theta$ **(d)** $OC = \sec \theta$
**(e)** $AB = \cot \theta$ **(f)** $OB = \csc \theta$
**37. (b)** 1080 miles
**39. (c)**

| $n$ | 5 | 10 | 50 | 100 |
|---|---|---|---|---|
| $A_n$ | 2.38 | 2.94 | 3.1333 | 3.1395 |

| $n$ | 1,000 | 5,000 | 10,000 |
|---|---|---|---|
| $A_n$ | 3.141572 | 3.1415918 | 3.1415924 |

**(d)** As $n$ gets larger, $A_n$ approaches the area of the circle, which is $\pi$.

## Exercise Set 6.4
**1. (a)** reference angle: 70°

**(b)** reference angle: 70°

**3. (a)** reference angle: 20°

**(b)** reference angle: 20°

**5. (a)** reference angle: 60°

**(b)** reference angle: 60°

**7. (a)** reference angle: 60°

**(b)** reference angle: 60°

**9.** $\cos 270° = 0$, $\sec 270°$ is undefined, $\sin 270° = -1$, $\csc 270° = -1$, $\tan 270°$ is undefined, $\cot 270° = 0$
**11.** $\cos(-270°) = 0$, $\sec(-270°)$ is undefined, $\sin(-270°) = 1$, $\csc(-270°) = 1$, $\tan(-270°)$ is undefined, $\cot(-270°) = 0$
**13.** $\cos 540° = -1$, $\sin 540° = 0$, $\tan 540° = 0$, $\sec 540° = -1$, $\csc 540°$ is undefined, $\cot 540°$ is undefined
**15.** $\sin 10° \approx 0.2$, $\sin(-10°) \approx -0.2$; $\sin 10° \approx 0.17$, $\sin(-10°) \approx -0.17$
**17.** $\cos 80° \approx 0.2$, $\cos(-80°) \approx 0.2$; $\cos 80° \approx 0.17$, $\cos(-80°) \approx 0.17$
**19.** $\sin 120° \approx 0.9$, $\sin(-120°) \approx -0.9$; $\sin 120° \approx 0.87$, $\sin(-120°) \approx -0.87$
**21.** $\sin 150° = 0.5$, $\sin(-150°) = -0.5$; $\sin 150° = 0.5$, $\sin(-150°) = -0.5$
**23.** $\cos 220° \approx -0.8$, $\cos(-220°) \approx -0.8$; $\cos 220° \approx -0.77$, $\cos(-220°) \approx -0.77$

**25.** $\cos 310° \approx 0.6$, $\cos(-310°) \approx 0.6$;
$\cos 310° \approx 0.64$, $\cos(-310°) \approx 0.64$
**27.** $\sin(40° + 360°) \approx 0.6$;
$\sin(40° + 360°) \approx 0.64$
**29.** $\sin 70°$ is larger; $\sin 70° \approx 0.94$,
$\cos 70° \approx 0.34$
**31.** $\cos 160°$ is larger;
$\cos 170° \approx -0.98$, $\cos 160° \approx -0.94$
**33.** $\cos 290°$ is larger; $\cos 280° \approx 0.17$,
$\cos 290° \approx 0.34$
**35.** $\sin 10°$ is larger; $\sin 10° \approx 0.17$,
$\sin(-10°) \approx -0.17$
**37.** $\sin 80°$ is larger; $\sin 80° \approx 0.98$,
$\sin 110° \approx 0.94$
**39.** $\cos(-110°)$ is larger;
$\sin(-80°) \approx -0.98$,
$\cos(-110°) \approx -0.34$
**41. (a)** $\cos 315° = \sqrt{2}/2$
**(b)** $\cos(-315°) = \sqrt{2}/2$
**(c)** $\sin 315° = -\sqrt{2}/2$
**(d)** $\sin(-315°) = \sqrt{2}/2$
**43. (a)** $\cos 300° = \frac{1}{2}$
**(b)** $\cos(-300°) = \frac{1}{2}$
**(c)** $\sin 300° = -\sqrt{3}/2$
**(d)** $\sin(-300°) = \sqrt{3}/2$
**45. (a)** $\cos 210° = -\sqrt{3}/2$
**(b)** $\cos(-210°) = -\sqrt{3}/2$
**(c)** $\sin 210° = -\frac{1}{2}$  **(d)** $\sin(-210°) = \frac{1}{2}$
**47. (a)** $\cos 390° = \sqrt{3}/2$
**(b)** $\cos(-390°) = \sqrt{3}/2$
**(c)** $\sin 390° = \frac{1}{2}$  **(d)** $\sin(-390°) = -\frac{1}{2}$
**49. (a)** $\sec 600° = -2$
**(b)** $\csc(-600°) = 2\sqrt{3}/3$
**(c)** $\tan 600° = \sqrt{3}$
**(d)** $\cot(-600°) = -\sqrt{3}/3$
**51.**

| $\theta$ | $\sin \theta$ | $\cos \theta$ | $\tan \theta$ |
|---|---|---|---|
| 0° | 0 | 1 | 0 |
| 30° | $\frac{1}{2}$ | $\sqrt{3}/2$ | $\sqrt{3}/3$ |
| 45° | $\sqrt{2}/2$ | $\sqrt{2}/2$ | 1 |
| 60° | $\sqrt{3}/2$ | $\frac{1}{2}$ | $\sqrt{3}$ |
| 90° | 1 | 0 | undefined |
| 120° | $\sqrt{3}/2$ | $-\frac{1}{2}$ | $-\sqrt{3}$ |
| 135° | $\sqrt{2}/2$ | $-\sqrt{2}/2$ | $-1$ |
| 150° | $\frac{1}{2}$ | $-\sqrt{3}/2$ | $-\sqrt{3}/3$ |
| 180° | 0 | $-1$ | 0 |

**53.** $\dfrac{35\sqrt{3}}{4}$ cm² **55.** 302.7 cm²
**57.** $108\sqrt{3} \approx 187.06$ cm²

**59. (a)**

| | Terminal side of angle $\theta$ lies in | | | |
|---|---|---|---|---|
| | Quadrant I | Quadrant II | Quadrant III | Quadrant IV |
| **$\cos \theta$** | positive | negative | negative | positive |
| **$\sin \theta$** | positive | positive | negative | negative |
| **$\tan \theta$** | positive | negative | positive | negative |

**61. (a)**

**(b)** $\theta$  **(c)** Because $180° - \theta$ lies in the second quadrant, where all $y$-coordinates are positive,
$\sin(180° - \theta) = \sin \theta$.  **63.** $A(\theta) = \sin \theta$
**65. (b)** $0° < \theta < 180°$
**67.** $(0°, 180°)$  **69. (c)** $(0°, 180°)$
**71. (d)** $\sin 75° = \dfrac{\sqrt{2} + \sqrt{6}}{4}$
**(f)** $\sin 105° = \frac{1}{4}(\sqrt{2} + \sqrt{6}) \approx 0.97$, but
$\sin 45° + \cos 45° = \frac{1}{2}\sqrt{2} + \frac{1}{2}\sqrt{3} \approx 1.57$

## Exercise Set 6.5
**1. (a)** $\cos \theta = 2\sqrt{6}/5$,
$\tan \theta = -\sqrt{6}/12$, $\cot \theta = -2\sqrt{6}$,
$\sec \theta = -5\sqrt{6}/12$, $\csc \theta = 5$
**(b)** $\cos \theta = -2\sqrt{6}/5$, $\tan \theta = \sqrt{6}/12$,
$\cot \theta = 2\sqrt{6}$, $\sec \theta = -5\sqrt{6}/12$,
$\csc \theta = -5$
**3. (a)** $\sin \theta = \frac{12}{13}$, $\tan \theta = \frac{12}{5}$, $\cot \theta = \frac{5}{12}$,
$\sec \theta = \frac{13}{5}$, $\csc \theta = \frac{13}{12}$
**(b)** $\sin \theta = -\frac{12}{13}$, $\tan \theta = \frac{12}{5}$, $\cot \theta = \frac{5}{12}$,
$\sec \theta = -\frac{13}{5}$, $\csc \theta = -\frac{13}{12}$
**5.** $\sin A = -\frac{1}{3}$, $\cos A = 2\sqrt{2}/3$,
$\tan A = -\sqrt{2}/4$, $\cot A = -2\sqrt{2}$,
$\sec A = 3\sqrt{2}/4$
**7.** $\cos B = -\frac{2}{3}$, $\sin B = -\sqrt{5}/3$,
$\tan B = \sqrt{5}/2$, $\cot B = 2\sqrt{5}/5$,
$\csc B = -3\sqrt{5}/5$
**9.** $\sin \theta = -\dfrac{\sqrt{9 - t^2}}{3}$,
$\tan \theta = -\dfrac{\sqrt{9 - t^2}}{t}$,

$\cot \theta = -\dfrac{t\sqrt{9 - t^2}}{9 - t^2}$, $\sec \theta = \dfrac{3}{t}$,
$\csc \theta = -\dfrac{3\sqrt{9 - t^2}}{9 - t^2}$
**11.** $\cos \theta = -\sqrt{1 - 9u^2}$,
$\tan \theta = \dfrac{3u\sqrt{1 - 9u^2}}{1 - 9u^2}$,
$\cot \theta = \dfrac{\sqrt{1 - 9u^2}}{3u}$,
$\sec \theta = -\dfrac{\sqrt{1 - 9u^2}}{1 - 9u^2}$, $\csc \theta = -\dfrac{1}{3u}$
**13.** $\sin \theta = \dfrac{\sqrt{9 - 3u^2}}{3}$,
$\tan \theta = \dfrac{\sqrt{3 - u^2}}{u}$,
$\cot \theta = \dfrac{u\sqrt{3 - u^2}}{3 - u^2}$, $\sec \theta = \dfrac{\sqrt{3}}{u}$,
$\csc \theta = \dfrac{\sqrt{9 - 3u^2}}{3 - u^2}$
**37. (a)** not an identity  **(b)** identity
**45. (a)** $(\cos \theta - \sin \theta)(1 + \cos \theta \sin \theta)$

## Chapter 6 Review Exercises
**1.** $\sqrt{2}/2$  **3.** $-\sqrt{3}$  **5.** $-2$  **7.** $-1$
**9.** $\sqrt{2}/2$  **11.** 1  **13.** $-2\sqrt{3}/3$
**15.** 2  **17.** 1  **19.** $a = \frac{1}{2}$, $c = \sqrt{3}/2$
**21.** $b = \frac{35}{2}$  **23.** $\sin A = \sqrt{55}/8$,
$\cot A = 3\sqrt{55}/55$  **25.** 5 square units
**27.** $\sin^2 A + \cos^2 B = \frac{1}{5}$
**29.** $a = 16\sqrt{3}/3$
**31.** $c = 9$; area $= 9\sqrt{19}/4$
**35.** $\cos \theta = \dfrac{p^4 - q^4}{p^4 + q^4}$, $\tan \theta = \dfrac{2p^2q^2}{p^4 - q^4}$
**37.** $\sin A \cos A$  **39.** $\sin^2 A$
**41.** $\cos A + \sin A$  **43.** $\sin A \cos A$
**45.** $2 \sin A \cos A$
**47.** $\cos 10° \approx 0.9848$
**49.** $\sin 10° \approx 0.1736$
**51.** $\sin \theta = \frac{4}{5}$, $\tan \theta = \frac{4}{3}$
**53.** $\tan \theta = -\frac{24}{7}$  **55.** $\cot \theta = \frac{5}{12}$
**57.** $\tan(90° - \theta) = \dfrac{5t\sqrt{1 - 25t^2}}{1 - 25t^2}$
**59.** $\sin \theta = \dfrac{2\sqrt{3} - \sqrt{6}}{6}$
**63.** $3600 \tan 35° \approx 2521$ cm²
**79. (a)** $PN = \sin \theta$  **(b)** $ON = \cos \theta$
**(c)** $PT = \tan \theta$  **(d)** $OT = \sec \theta$
**(e)** $NA = 1 - \cos \theta$
**(f)** $NT = \sin \theta \tan \theta$
**81.** $A(\theta) = \dfrac{(1 - \cos \theta)^2}{\sin \theta \cos \theta}$

## Chapter 6 Test
**1. (a)** $\sqrt{3}/3$ **(b)** $\sqrt{2}$ **(c)** 1 **(d)** 0
**2. (a)** negative **(b)** negative
**(c)** positive **3. (a)** 1 **(b)** −1 **(c)** 0
**4.** $(2\cot\theta + 3)(\cot\theta + 4)$ **5.** 18 cm$^2$
**6. (a)** $\sqrt{2}/2$ **(b)** $-\sqrt{3}/3$ **(c)** −2
**7.** $\cos\theta = -2\sqrt{5}/5$, $\tan\theta = \frac{1}{2}$
**8.** $\cos\theta = \dfrac{\sqrt{9-u^2}}{3}$,

$\cot\theta = -\dfrac{\sqrt{9-u^2}}{u}$
**9.** $-2\cos\theta - 1$
**10.** $\frac{81}{2}\sin 40° \approx 26.033$ m$^2$ **11.** 1
**12.** $CD = 50(\tan 55° - \tan 25°)$
**13. (a)** $\sin 85°$ is larger. **(b)** $\cos 5°$ is
larger. **(c)** $\tan 185°$ is larger.
**14. (a)** $AD = 2.75\cos 20°$,
$CD = 2.75\sin 20°$,
$DB = 3.25 - 2.75\cos 20°$
**(b)** $CB \approx 1.15$ cm

# CHAPTER 7
## Exercise Set 7.1
**1.** $\theta = 2.5$ radians **3.** $\theta = 2$ radians
**5. (a)** $\pi/4 \approx 0.79$ radians
**(b)** $\pi/2 \approx 1.57$ radians
**(c)** $3\pi/4 \approx 2.36$ radians
**7. (a)** 0 radians **(b)** $2\pi \approx 6.28$
radians **(c)** $5\pi/2 \approx 7.85$ radians
**9. (a)** 15° **(b)** 30° **(c)** 45°
**11. (a)** 60° **(b)** 300° **(c)** 720°
**13. (a)** 114.59° **(b)** 171.89°
**(c)** 565.49° **15.** smaller
**17.** $30° = \pi/6$ radians; $45° = \pi/4$
radians; $60° = \pi/3$ radians;
$120° = 2\pi/3$ radians; $135° = 3\pi/4$
radians; $150° = 5\pi/6$ radians
**19.**

| $\theta$ | $\sin\theta$ | $\cos\theta$ | $\tan\theta$ |
| --- | --- | --- | --- |
| 0 | 0 | 1 | 0 |
| $\pi/2$ | 1 | 0 | undefined |
| $\pi$ | 0 | −1 | 0 |
| $3\pi/2$ | −1 | 0 | undefined |
| $2\pi$ | 0 | 1 | 0 |

**21.** $0.5 < \cos 1 < 0.6$; $0.8 < \sin 1 < 0.9$;
$\cos 1 \approx 0.54$; $\sin 1 \approx 0.84$
**23.** $0.5 < \cos(-1) < 0.6$;
$-0.9 < \sin(-1) < -0.8$;
$\cos(-1) \approx 0.54$; $\sin(-1) \approx -0.84$
**25.** $-0.7 < \cos 4 < -0.6$;
$-0.8 < \sin 4 < -0.7$; $\cos 4 \approx -0.65$;
$\sin 4 \approx -0.76$

**27.** $-0.7 < \cos(-4) < -0.6$;
$0.7 < \sin(-4) < 0.8$; $\cos(-4) \approx -0.65$;
$\sin(-4) \approx 0.76$
**29.** $0.8 < \sin(1 + 2\pi) < 0.9$;
$\sin(1 + 2\pi) \approx 0.84$ **31. (a)** $\frac{1}{2}$ **(b)** $\frac{1}{2}$
**(c)** $\sqrt{3}/2$ **(d)** $-\sqrt{3}/2$ **33. (a)** $-\frac{1}{2}$
**(b)** $-\frac{1}{2}$ **(c)** $-\sqrt{3}/2$ **(d)** $\sqrt{3}/2$
**35. (a)** $-\sqrt{2}/2$ **(b)** $-\sqrt{2}/2$
**(c)** $-\sqrt{2}/2$ **(d)** $\sqrt{2}/2$ **37. (a)** −2
**(b)** $2\sqrt{3}/3$ **(c)** $\sqrt{3}$ **(d)** $-\sqrt{3}/3$
**39. (a)** $-2\sqrt{3}/3$ **(b)** −2
**(c)** $-\sqrt{3}/3$ **(d)** $\sqrt{3}$
**41.** 1 radian $\approx 57.30°$ **43.** $x = 0$

## Exercise Set 7.2
**1.** $s = 4\pi$ ft **3.** $s = \pi/2$ cm
**5. (a)** $A = 12\pi$ cm$^2 \approx 37.70$ cm$^2$
**(b)** $A = 50\pi/9$ m$^2 \approx 17.45$ m$^2$
**(c)** $A = 72\pi/5$ m$^2 \approx 45.24$ m$^2$
**(d)** $A = 1.296\pi$ cm$^2 \approx 4.07$ cm$^2$
**7.** $2\pi/5$ radians

**9. (a)** $\left(10 + \dfrac{5\pi}{6}\right)$ in. $\approx 12.62$ in.

**(b)** $25\pi/12$ in.$^2 \approx 6.54$ in.$^2$
**11.** $25.2$ cm$^2 - 18\sin 1.4$ cm$^2$
$\approx 7.46$ cm$^2$ **13. (a)** $12\pi$ radians/sec
**(b)** $144\pi$ cm/sec **(c)** $72\pi$ cm/sec
**15. (a)** $6\pi$ radians/sec
**(b)** $150\pi$ cm/sec **(c)** $75\pi$ cm/sec
**17. (a)** $50\pi/3$ radians/sec
**(b)** $750\pi$ cm/sec **(c)** $375\pi$ cm/sec
**19. (a)** 0.000073 radians/sec
**(b)** 1040 mph
**21. (a)** $200\pi$ radians/min
**(b)** $2000\pi$ cm/min
**(c)** $\frac{1000}{3}\pi$ radians/min **(d)** $\frac{500}{3}$ rpm
**23.** 4930 miles **25.** 1470 miles
**27.** 2690 miles

**29. (a)** $P = \left(\dfrac{2\pi}{3} + 1\right)s$

**(b)** $A = \left(\dfrac{\pi}{3} - \dfrac{\sqrt{3}}{4}\right)s^2$

**31. (a)** $A_{ABC} = \left(\dfrac{\pi}{3} - \dfrac{\sqrt{3}}{4}\right)s^2$;

$A_{ADF} = \left(\dfrac{\pi}{12} - \dfrac{\sqrt{3}}{16}\right)s^2$; $\dfrac{A_{ADF}}{A_{ABC}} = \dfrac{1}{4}$

**(b)** $A_{DBE} = \left(\dfrac{\pi}{8} - \dfrac{\sqrt{3}}{8}\right)s^2$

**(c)** $A_{DEF} = \left(\dfrac{\sqrt{3}}{4} - \dfrac{\pi}{8}\right)s^2$

**(d)** $A_{BEC} = \left(\dfrac{\pi}{12} - \dfrac{\sqrt{3}}{8}\right)s^2$

**33. (b)** $\frac{1}{2}(\pi - \sqrt{2}) \approx 0.86$
**35. (a)** $A(\cos\theta, \sin\theta)$

**37. (a)** $r(\theta) = \dfrac{12}{2+\theta}$

**(b)** $A(\theta) = \dfrac{72\theta}{(2+\theta)^2}$; no

**(c)** $\theta(r) = \dfrac{12}{r} - 2$ **(d)** $A(r) = 6r - r^2$;
yes **(e)** maximum = 9 cm$^2$ when
$r = 3$ cm, $\theta = 2$ radians

## Exercise Set 7.3
**1. (a)** $\sqrt{3}/2$ **(b)** $\sqrt{3}/2$ **(c)** $-\frac{1}{2}$
**(d)** $\frac{1}{2}$ **3. (a)** $\sqrt{3}/2$ **(b)** $\sqrt{3}/2$
**(c)** $\frac{1}{2}$ **(d)** $-\frac{1}{2}$ **5. (a)** $-\sqrt{2}/2$
**(b)** $-\sqrt{2}/2$ **(c)** $-\sqrt{2}/2$ **(d)** $\sqrt{2}/2$
**7. (a)** 2 **(b)** $2\sqrt{3}/3$ **(c)** $-\sqrt{3}$
**(d)** $\sqrt{3}/3$ **9. (a)** $t = \pi/2, 3\pi/2, 5\pi/2$,
and $7\pi/2$ (Other answers are possible.)
**(b)** $t = -\pi/2, -3\pi/2, -5\pi/2$, and
$-7\pi/2$ (Other answers are possible.)
**11. (a)** $\sin 2.06 \approx 0.88$;
$\cos 2.06 \approx -0.47$; $\tan 2.06 \approx -1.88$;
$\sec 2.06 \approx -2.13$; $\csc 2.06 \approx 1.13$;
$\cot 2.06 \approx -0.53$
**(b)** $\sin(-2.06) \approx -0.88$;
$\cos(-2.06) \approx -0.47$;
$\tan(-2.06) \approx 1.88$;
$\sec(-2.06) \approx -2.13$;
$\csc(-2.06) \approx -1.13$; $\cot(-2.06) \approx 0.53$
**13. (a)** $\sin(\pi/6) \approx 0.50$;
$\cos(\pi/6) \approx 0.87$; $\tan(\pi/6) \approx 1.73$;
$\sec(\pi/6) \approx 1.15$; $\csc(\pi/6) \approx 2.00$;
$\cot(\pi/6) \approx 0.58$
**(b)** $\sin(\frac{\pi}{6} + 2\pi) \approx 0.50$;
$\cos(\frac{\pi}{6} + 2\pi) \approx 0.87$;
$\tan(\frac{\pi}{6} + 2\pi) \approx 1.73$;
$\sec(\frac{\pi}{6} + 2\pi) \approx 1.15$;
$\csc(\frac{\pi}{6} + 2\pi) \approx 2.00$; $\cot(\frac{\pi}{6} + 2\pi) \approx 0.58$
**25.** $\cos t = -\frac{4}{5}$; $\tan t = \frac{3}{4}$
**27.** $\tan t = -\sqrt{39}/13$
**29.** $\sec\alpha = \frac{13}{5}$; $\cos\alpha = \frac{5}{13}$; $\sin\alpha = \frac{12}{13}$
**35.** $\dfrac{\sqrt{7}\cos\theta}{7}$ **37. (a)** $-\frac{2}{3}$ **(b)** $\frac{1}{4}$

**(c)** $\frac{1}{5}$ **(d)** $-\frac{1}{5}$ **39. (a)** $-\dfrac{1+2\sqrt{2}}{3}$

**(b)** 1 **41. (a)** $\sqrt{2}/2$ **(b)** $\sqrt{3}/2$
**(c)** 1 **43.** $\cos^2 t$ **45.** $\sin^2\theta$ **55.** $\frac{13}{31}$
**57.** Assuming that the radius of the
circle is 1, the coordinates of the point
labeled $(x, y)$ are $(\cos t, \sin t)$, and the
coordinates of the point labeled
$(-x, -y)$ are $(\cos(t + \pi), \sin(t + \pi))$.
So $y = \sin t$ and $-y = \sin(t + \pi)$,
from which it follows that

$\sin(t + \pi) = -\sin t$. Similarly, $-x = \cos(t + \pi)$ and $x = \cos t$, from which it follows that $\cos(t + \pi) = -\cos t$. Since $t - \pi$ results in the same intersection point with the unit circle as $t + \pi$, identities (ii) and (iv) follow in a similar manner.

**61. (a)**

| $t$ | 0.2 | 0.4 | 0.6 | 0.8 |
|---|---|---|---|---|
| $f(t)$ | 219.07 | 50.53 | 19.70 | 9.55 |

| $t$ | 1.0 | 1.2 | 1.4 |
|---|---|---|---|
| $f(t)$ | 6.14 | 7.98 | 33.88 |

**(b)** The smallest output is 6.14, which occurs at $t = 1.0$.
**(d)** $\tan^2 t + 9 \cot^2 t =$ $(\tan t - 3 \cot t)^2 + 6 \geq 0 + 6 \geq 6$
**(e)** The answer from part **(b)** is consistent with this result.
**63. (a)** Each side is 0.   **(b)** Each side is $(2 - \sqrt{2})/2$.   **(c)** no
**65. (a)**

| $t$ | $1 - \frac{1}{2}t^2$ | $\cos\theta$ |
|---|---|---|
| 0.02 | 0.998 | 0.999800 |
| 0.05 | 0.99875 | 0.998750 |
| 0.1 | 0.995 | 0.995004 |
| 0.2 | 0.980 | 0.980067 |
| 0.3 | 0.955 | 0.955336 |

**(b)**

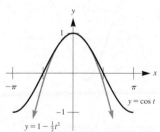

**67. (a)**

| $x$ | $\frac{1}{3}x^3 + x$ | $\frac{2}{15}x^5 + \frac{1}{3}x^3 + x$ | $\tan x$ |
|---|---|---|---|
| 0.1 | 0.100333 | 0.100335 | 0.100335 |
| 0.2 | 0.202667 | 0.202709 | 0.202710 |
| 0.3 | 0.309000 | 0.309324 | 0.309336 |
| 0.4 | 0.421333 | 0.422699 | 0.422793 |
| 0.5 | 0.541667 | 0.545833 | 0.546302 |

**(b)**

**69.** $P$: $\sin(\pi/12) \approx 0.259$; $Q$: $\frac{1}{2} = 0.5$; $R$: $\sqrt{2}/2 \approx 0.707$; $S$: $\sqrt{3}/2 \approx 0.866$; $T$: $\sin(5\pi/12) \approx 0.966$

## Exercise Set 7.4
**1.** period: 2; amplitude: 1
**3.** period: 4; amplitude: 6
**5.** period: 4; amplitude: 2
**7.** period: 6; amplitude: $\frac{3}{2}$
**9.** $(-\frac{7\pi}{2}, 1) \approx (-10.996, 1)$
**11.** $(\frac{5\pi}{2}, 1) \approx (7.854, 1)$
**13.** $(-4\pi, 0) \approx (-12.566, 0)$
**15.** $(-3\pi, 0) \approx (-9.425, 0)$
**17.** $(-\pi, 0) \approx (-3.142, 0)$
**19.** increasing   **21.** decreasing
**23.** $(\frac{9\pi}{2}, 0) \approx (14.137, 0)$
**25.** $(-4\pi, 1) \approx (-12.566, 1)$
**27.** $(\frac{\pi}{2}, 0) \approx (1.571, 0)$
**29.** $(4\pi, 1) \approx (12.566, 1)$
**31.** $(-\frac{5\pi}{2}, 0) \approx (-7.854, 0)$
**33.** decreasing   **35.** increasing
**37. (a)** $x$-intercept: $\pi$

**(b)** four turning points; $x$-coordinate: $\frac{\pi}{2}$

**(c)** five turning points: $x$-coordinate: $2\pi$

**(d)** $\frac{\pi}{2}$ units to the left
**(e)**

**39. (a)**

**(b)** In the vicinity of $x = 0$ the graphs of $y = \cos x$ and $y = 1 - 0.5x^2$ are very similar.

**(c)**

| $x$ | 1 | 0.5 | 0.1 |
|---|---|---|---|
| $\cos x$ | 0.54 | 0.8776 | 0.9950 |
| $1 - 0.5x^2$ | 0.50 | 0.8750 | 0.9950 |

| $x$ | 0.01 | 0.001 |
|---|---|---|
| $\cos x$ | 0.99995 | 0.9999995 |
| $1 - 0.5x^2$ | 0.99995 | 0.9999995 |

**41. (a)** 0.45  **(b)** 0.4510  **(c)** 5.8322
**(d)** 2.6906 and 3.5926  **43. (a)** 1.25
**(b)** 1.2661  **(c)** 5.0171  **(d)** 1.8755
and 4.4077  **45. (a)** 1.0  **(b)** 0.9884
**(c)** 5.2948  **(d)** 2.1532 and 4.1300
**47. (a)** 0.65  **(b)** 0.6435  **(c)** 2.4981
**(d)** 3.7851 and 5.6397  **49. (a)** 0.2
**(b)** 0.2014  **(c)** 2.9402  **(d)** 3.3430
and 6.0818  **51. (a)** 0.8  **(b)** 0.7754
**(c)** 2.3662  **(d)** 3.9170 and 5.5078
**53.** intersection points: $x \approx 2.498$ and
$x \approx 3.785$

**55. (a)** $x \approx 0.7574$; $x \approx 2.3842$

**(b)** $x \approx 3.8989$; $x \approx 5.5258$

**57. (a)** 0  **(b)** 0  **59.** $\left(\frac{\pi}{2}, \pi\right)$
**61. (a)**

| | $x_1$ | $x_2$ | $x_3$ |
|---|---|---|---|
| From graph | 1.0 | 0.55 | 0.85 |
| From calculator | 0.99500 | 0.54450 | 0.85539 |

| | $x_4$ | $x_5$ | $x_6$ |
|---|---|---|---|
| From graph | 0.65 | 0.80 | 0.70 |
| From calculator | 0.65593 | 0.79248 | 0.70208 |

| | $x_7$ |
|---|---|
| From graph | 0.75 |
| From Calculator | 0.76350 |

**(b)**

| $n$ | 0 | 1 | 2 | 3 |
|---|---|---|---|---|
| Number of fish after $n$ breeding seasons | 50 | 498 | 272 | 428 |

| $n$ | 4 | 5 | 6 | 7 |
|---|---|---|---|---|
| Number of fish after $n$ breeding seasons | 328 | 396 | 351 | 382 |

**(c)** 370 fish  **63. (a)** $C(\cos \theta, \sin \theta)$

## Exercise Set 7.5

**1. (a)** amplitude: 2; period: $2\pi$;
$x$-intercepts: 0, $\pi$, $2\pi$; increasing: $\left(0, \frac{\pi}{2}\right)$
and $\left(\frac{3\pi}{2}, 2\pi\right)$

**(b)** amplitude: 1; period: $\pi$;
$x$-intercepts: 0, $\frac{\pi}{2}$, $\pi$; increasing: $\left(\frac{\pi}{4}, \frac{3\pi}{4}\right)$

**3. (a)** amplitude: 1; period: $\pi$;
$x$-intercepts: $\frac{\pi}{4}$, $\frac{3\pi}{4}$; increasing: $\left(\frac{\pi}{2}, \pi\right)$

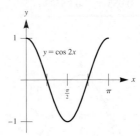

**(b)** amplitude: 2; period: $\pi$;
$x$-intercepts: $\frac{\pi}{4}$, $\frac{3\pi}{4}$; increasing: $\left(\frac{\pi}{2}, \pi\right)$

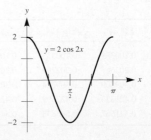

**5. (a)** amplitude: 3; period: 4; $x$-intercepts: $0, 2, 4$; increasing: $(0, 1)$ and $(3, 4)$

**(b)** amplitude: 3; period: 4; $x$-intercepts: $0, 2, 4$; increasing: $(1, 3)$

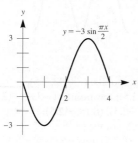

**7. (a)** amplitude: 1; period: 1; $x$-intercepts: $\frac{1}{4}, \frac{3}{4}$; increasing: $\left(\frac{1}{2}, 1\right)$

**(b)** amplitude: 4; period: 1; $x$-intercepts: $\frac{1}{4}, \frac{3}{4}$; increasing: $\left(0, \frac{1}{2}\right)$

**9.** $y = \sin x$: amplitude $= 1$, period $= 2\pi$; $y = 2 \sin x$: amplitude $= 2$, period $= 2\pi$; $y = 3 \sin x$: amplitude $= 3$, period $= 2\pi$; $y = 4 \sin x$: amplitude $= 4$, period $= 2\pi$

**11. (a)** $y = 2 \sin \pi x$: amplitude $= 2$, period $= 2$; $y = \sin 2\pi x$: amplitude $= 1$, period $= 1$
**(b)**

**13.** amplitude $= 1$; period $= 4\pi$; no $x$-intercepts; increasing on $(0, \pi)$ and $(3\pi, 4\pi)$

**15.** amplitude $= 2$; period $= \frac{2}{3}$; $x$-intercept $= \frac{1}{3}$; increasing on $\left(0, \frac{1}{3}\right)$

**17.** amplitude $= 1$; period $= 2\pi$; phase shift $= -\frac{\pi}{3}$; $x$-intercepts $= \frac{\pi}{6}, \frac{7\pi}{6}$; high points $= \left(-\frac{\pi}{3}, 1\right), \left(\frac{5\pi}{3}, 1\right)$; low point $= \left(\frac{2\pi}{3}, -1\right)$

**19.** amplitude $= 1$; period $= 2\pi$; phase shift $= -2$; $x$-intercepts $= -2, \pi - 2$, $2\pi - 2$; high point $= \left(\frac{3\pi}{2} - 2, 1\right)$; low point $= \left(\frac{\pi}{2} - 2, -1\right)$

**21.** amplitude = 1; period = $\frac{2\pi}{3}$;
phase shift = $-\frac{\pi}{6}$;
$x$-intercepts = $-\frac{\pi}{6}, \frac{\pi}{6}, \frac{\pi}{2}$;
high point = $(0, 1)$;
low point = $(\frac{\pi}{3}, -1)$

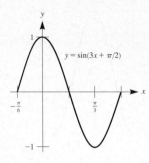

**23.** amplitude = 1; period = $2\pi$;
phase shift = $\frac{\pi}{2}$; $x$-intercepts = $\pi, 2\pi$;
high points = $(\frac{\pi}{2}, 1), (\frac{5\pi}{2}, 1)$
low point = $(\frac{3\pi}{2}, -1)$

**25.** amplitude = 2; period = 2; phase
shift = $-1$; $x$-intercepts = $-1, 0, 1$; high
point = $(\frac{1}{2}, 2)$; low point = $(-\frac{1}{2}, -2)$

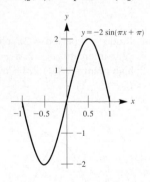

**27.** amplitude = 1; period = $2\pi$; phase
shift = $-1$; $x$-intercepts = $\frac{\pi}{2} - 1, \frac{3\pi}{2} - 1$;
high points = $(-1, 1), (2\pi - 1, 1)$;
low point = $(\pi - 1, -1)$

**29.** amplitude = 1; period = $\pi$;
phase shift = $\frac{\pi}{6}$; $x$-intercept = $\frac{2\pi}{3}$;
high points = $(\frac{\pi}{6}, 2), (\frac{7\pi}{6}, 2)$
low point = $(\frac{2\pi}{3}, 0)$

**31.** amplitude = 3; period = $3\pi$;
phase shift = $-\frac{\pi}{4}$; $x$-intercepts = $\frac{\pi}{2}, 2\pi$;
high points = $(-\frac{\pi}{4}, 3), (\frac{11\pi}{4}, 3)$;
low point = $(\frac{5\pi}{4}, -3)$

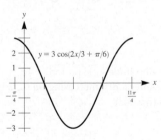

**33. (a)** amplitude: 2.5; period: $\frac{2}{3}$;
phase shift: $-\frac{4}{3\pi}$
**(b)**

**(c)** high points: $(-0.09, 2.5)$,
$(0.58, 2.5)$; low points: $(-0.42, -2.5)$,
$(0.24, -2.5)$, $(0.91, -2.5)$
**(d)** high points: $(-\frac{4}{3\pi} + \frac{1}{3}, 2.5)$,
$(-\frac{4}{3\pi} + 1, 2.5)$; low points: $(-\frac{4}{3\pi}, -2.5)$,
$(-\frac{4}{3\pi} + \frac{2}{3}, -2.5)$, $(-\frac{4}{3\pi} + \frac{4}{3}, -2.5)$
**35. (a)** amplitude: 2.5; period: 6; phase
shift: $-\frac{12}{\pi}$
**(b)**

**(c)** high points: $(-0.82, 2.5)$,
$(5.18, 2.5)$; low points: $(-3.82, -2.5)$,
$(2.18, -2.5)$, $(8.18, -2.5)$
**(d)** high points: $(-\frac{12}{\pi} + 3, 2.5)$,
$(-\frac{12}{\pi} + 9, 2.5)$; low points: $(-\frac{12}{\pi}, -2.5)$,
$(-\frac{12}{\pi} + 6, -2.5)$, $(-\frac{12}{\pi} + 12, -2.5)$
**37. (a)** amplitude: 1; period: $4\pi$;
phase shift: $-1.5$
**(b)**

**(c)** high points: $(1.64, 1), (14.21, 1)$;
low points: $(7.92, -1), (20.49, -1)$
**(d)** high points: $(-1.5 + \pi, 1)$,
$(-1.5 + 5\pi, 1)$; low points:
$(-1.5 + 3\pi, -1), (-1.5 + 7\pi, -1)$
**39. (a)** amplitude: 0.02; period: 200;
phase shift: 400

**(b)**

$y = 0.02 \cos(0.01 \pi x - 4\pi)$

**(c)** high points: $(400, 0.02)$, $(600, 0.02)$, $(800, 0.02)$; low points: $(500, -0.02)$, $(700, -0.02)$   **(d)** high points: $(400, 0.02)$, $(600, 0.02)$, $(800, 0.02)$; low points: $(500, -0.02)$, $(700, -0.02)$

**41.** $y = 1.5 \sin \frac{3}{2}x$   **43.** $y = \cos \frac{2\pi}{5}x$

**45.** $y = \pi \cos \frac{\pi}{4}x$

**47.** $y = 25.25 \sin(\frac{\pi}{6}t - \frac{2\pi}{3}) + 43.25$

**49.** $y = 6.3 \sin(\frac{\pi}{6}t + \frac{\pi}{4}) + 75.215$

**51.** $y = 25 \sin(\frac{\pi}{6}t - \frac{2\pi}{3}) + 90$

**53.**

$y = \cos^2 x$

**55.**

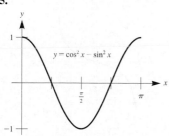

$y = \cos^2 x - \sin^2 x$

**57.** $G[F(x)]$ is the only one

**59. (a)**

$f(x) = e^{x/20}(\sin x)$

**(b)** The function is not periodic.

$f(x) = e^{x/20}(\sin x)$

**(c)** The graph of $y = e^{x/20}$ touches near the top of each cycle of the curve, while the graph of $y = -e^{x/20}$ touches near the bottom of each cycle.

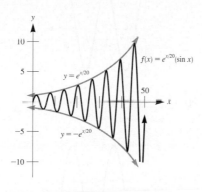

$f(x) = e^{x/20}(\sin x)$
$y = e^{x/20}$
$y = -e^{x/20}$

### Exercise Set 7.6

**1. (a)** $t = 0$: $s = 4$ cm; $t = 0.5$: $s \approx 2.83$ cm; $t = 1$: $s = 0$ cm; $t = 2$: $s = -4$ cm   **(b)** amplitude: 4 cm; period: 4 sec; frequency: $\frac{1}{4}$ cps

$s = 4 \cos \frac{\pi t}{2}$

**(c)** $t = 0, t = 2, t = 4, t = 6$, and $t = 8$ sec   **(d)** $t = 1, t = 3, t = 5$, and $t = 7$ sec   **(e)** $2 < t < 4$ and $6 < t < 8$

**3. (a)** amplitude: 3 ft; period: 6 sec; frequency: $\frac{1}{6}$ cps

$s = -3 \cos \frac{\pi t}{3}$

**(b)** $0 < t < 3$ and $6 < t < 9$
**(c)** $3 < t < 6$ and $9 < t < 12$
**(d)**

$v = \pi \sin \frac{\pi t}{3}$

**(e)** $t = 0, t = 3, t = 6, t = 9$, and $t = 12$ sec; the mass ($s$-coordinate) is at $-3, 3, -3, 3$, and $-3$ ft, respectively. **(f)** $t = 1.5$ and $t = 7.5$ sec; the mass is at 0 ft.   **(g)** $t = 4.5$ and $t = 10.5$ sec; the mass is at 0 ft
**(h)**

$v = \pi \sin \frac{\pi t}{3}$
$s = -3 \cos \frac{\pi t}{3}$

**5. (a)** amplitude: 170 volts; frequency: 60 cps
**(b)**

$v = 170 \cos(120\pi t)$

**(c)** $t = \frac{1}{60}$ sec and $t = \frac{1}{30}$ sec

**7. (a)**

| $t$ (sec) | 0 | 1 | 2 | 3 |
|---|---|---|---|---|
| $\theta$ (radians) | 0 | $\pi/3$ | $2\pi/3$ | $\pi$ |

| $t$ (sec) | 4 | 5 | 6 | 7 |
|---|---|---|---|---|
| $\theta$ (radians) | $4\pi/3$ | $5\pi/3$ | $2\pi$ | $7\pi/3$ |

**(b)** $1, \frac{1}{2}, -\frac{1}{2}, -1, -\frac{1}{2}, \frac{1}{2}, 1,$ and $\frac{1}{2}$

**(c)**

**(d)** $t = 2$ sec

$t = 3$ sec

$t = 4$ sec

**(e)** The $x$-coordinate of $Q$ is the same as the $x$-coordinate of $P$, which is $\cos\theta$.

**(f)** amplitude: 1; period: 6; frequency: $\frac{1}{6}$

**(g)**

**(h)** $t = 0, 3, 6, 9$ and $12$ sec; $x$-coordinates: $1, -1, 1, -1$ and $1$, respectively **(i)** $t = 4.5$ sec and $t = 10.5$ sec; $Q$ is located at the origin. **(j)** $t = 1.5$ sec and $t = 7.5$ sec; $Q$ is located at the origin.

**Exercise Set 7.7**

**1. (a)** $x$-intercept: $-\frac{\pi}{4}$; $y$-intercept: 1; asymptotes: $x = -\frac{3\pi}{4}$ and $x = \frac{\pi}{4}$

**(b)** $x$-intercept: $-\frac{\pi}{4}$; $y$-intercept: $-1$; asymptotes: $x = -\frac{3\pi}{4}$ and $x = \frac{\pi}{4}$

**3. (a)** $x$- and $y$-intercepts: 0; asymptotes: $x = -\frac{3\pi}{2}$ and $x = \frac{3\pi}{2}$

**(b)** $x$- and $y$-intercepts: 0; asymptotes: $x = -\frac{3\pi}{2}$ and $x = \frac{3\pi}{2}$

**5.** $x$- and $y$-intercepts: 0; asymptotes: $x = -1$ and $x = 1$

**7.** $x$-intercept: 1; no $y$-intercept; asymptotes: $x = 0$ and $x = 2$

**9.** $x$-intercept: $\frac{3\pi}{4}$; $y$-intercept: 1; asymptotes: $x = \frac{\pi}{4}$ and $x = \frac{5\pi}{4}$

**11.** $x$-intercept: $\frac{\pi}{4}$; no $y$-intercept; asymptotes: $x = 0$ and $x = \frac{\pi}{2}$

**13.** $x$-intercepts: $-\pi, 0, \pi$

**15. (a)**

**(b)**

**17. (a)**

**(b)**

**(c)**

**19. (a)**

**(b)**

**(c)**

**21.** no $x$-intercept; $y$-intercept: $-\sqrt{2}$;
asymptotes: $x = -\frac{3\pi}{4}$, $x = \frac{\pi}{4}$, and $x = \frac{5\pi}{4}$

**23.** no $x$- or $y$-intercepts; asymptotes:
$x = -2\pi$, $x = 0$, and $x = 2\pi$

**25.** no $x$- or $y$-intercepts; asymptotes:
$x = -1$, $x = 0$, and $x = 1$

**27.** no $x$-intercept; $y$-intercept: $-1$;
asymptotes: $x = -\frac{\pi}{2}$, $x = \frac{\pi}{2}$, and $x = \frac{3\pi}{2}$

**29.** no $x$-intercept; $y$-intercept: $-1$;
asymptotes: $x = \frac{\pi}{2}$, $x = \frac{3\pi}{2}$, and $x = \frac{5\pi}{2}$

**31.** no $x$-intercept; $y$-intercept: 3;
asymptotes: $x = -1$, $x = 1$, and $x = 3$

**33.** $\sin x = \csc x$ at odd multiples of $\frac{\pi}{2}$,
such as $-\frac{3\pi}{2}$, $-\frac{\pi}{2}$, $\frac{\pi}{2}$, and $\frac{3\pi}{2}$; there are no
points at which $\sin x = -\csc x$.

**35. (a)** $x$-intercepts: $-\frac{11}{18}$, $-\frac{5}{18}$, $\frac{1}{18}$, $\frac{7}{18}$ and
$\frac{13}{18}$; $y$-intercept: $-1$; no asymptotes

**(b)** no $x$-intercepts; $y$-intercept: $-4$;
asymptotes: $x = -\frac{11}{18}$, $x = -\frac{5}{18}$, $x = \frac{1}{18}$,
$x = \frac{7}{18}$, and $x = \frac{13}{18}$

**37. (a)** $x$-intercepts: $-\frac{5}{8}$, $-\frac{1}{8}$, $\frac{3}{8}$, and $\frac{7}{8}$;
$y$-intercept: $-3\sqrt{2}/2 \approx -2.12$; no
asymptotes

**(b)** no $x$-intercepts; $y$-intercept:
$-3\sqrt{2}$; asymptotes: $x = -\frac{5}{8}$, $x = -\frac{1}{8}$,
$x = \frac{3}{8}$, and $x = \frac{7}{8}$

**39.**

**45. (a)**

**51.**

(a) $y = x^3$  (b) $y = \tan x$  (c) $y = x^3$
**53.** $\cot^2 x = \csc^2 x - 1$ is an identity

**41.**

**(b)**

**43. (a)**

**47.**

**55. (a)**

(b) $x \approx 1$  (c) $x \approx 1.1071$  (d) yes
**57. (a)** Since $P$ and $Q$ are both points on the unit circle, the coordinates are $P(\cos s, \sin s)$ and $Q(\cos(s - \frac{\pi}{2}), \sin(s - \frac{\pi}{2}))$.
**(b)** Since $\triangle OAP$ is congruent to $\triangle OBQ$ (labeling the third vertex $B$), $OA = OB$ and $AP = BQ$. Because the $y$-coordinate at $Q$ is negative, we have concluded what was required.
**59. (b)** $\angle COD = \frac{\pi}{2} - s$, and $\angle AOD = \frac{\pi}{2} + s$

**(b)**

**49.**

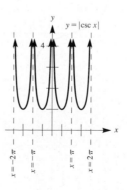

## Chapter 7 Review Exercises
**1. (a)** $-\sqrt{3}/2$ **(b)** $-\sqrt{3}$ **3.** $2 \sin t$
**5.**

**7.** amplitude: 1; period: $\pi$; phase shift: $\frac{\pi}{2}$

**9.** $-1$ **11.** $2\sqrt{3}/3$ **13.** $-\sqrt{3}/3$
**15.** $\frac{1}{2}$ **17.** 1 **19.** $-2$ **21.** 0.841
**23.** $-1$ **25.** 0.0123 **31.** $5 \cos \theta$
**33.** $10 \tan \theta$ **35.** $(\sqrt{5}/5)\cos \theta$
**37.** $-\frac{15}{8}$ **39.** $A(\theta) = \pi - \theta - \sin \theta$
**41.** $\frac{1}{2}(\pi - 2)$ cm$^2$ **43.** $y = 4 \sin x$
**45.** $y = -2 \cos 4x$ **47.** $x$-intercepts: $\frac{\pi}{8}$
and $\frac{3\pi}{8}$; high point: $(\frac{\pi}{4}, 3)$; low points:
$(0, -3)$ and $(\frac{\pi}{2}, -3)$

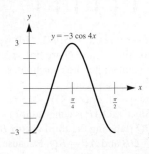

**49.** $x$-intercepts: $\frac{1}{2}, \frac{5}{2}$, and $\frac{9}{2}$; high point: $(\frac{3}{2}, 2)$; low point: $(\frac{7}{2}, -2)$

**51.** $x$-intercepts: $\frac{5}{2}$ and $\frac{11}{2}$; high points: $(1, 3)$, $(7, 3)$; low point: $(4, -3)$

**53. (a)**

**(b)**

**55. (a)**

**(b)**

**57. (a)** amplitude: 2.5 cm; period: 16 sec; frequency: $\frac{1}{16}$ cps

**(b)** $t = 0, t = 8, t = 16, t = 24$, and $t = 32$ sec **(c)** $t = 4, t = 12, t = 20$, and $t = 28$ sec

## Chapter 7 Test
**1. (a)** $-\frac{1}{2}$ **(b)** $-2$ **(c)** 1 **2.** $\frac{1}{4} \csc u$
**3.**

**4.** amplitude: 1; period: $\frac{2\pi}{3}$; phase shift: $\frac{\pi}{12}$

$$y = -\sin\left(3x - \frac{\pi}{4}\right)$$

**5.**

$$y = 3\tan\frac{\pi x}{4}$$

$x = 2$

**6. (a)** $\frac{35}{36}\pi$ radians  **(b)** $\dfrac{900}{\pi}$ degrees

**7. (a)** $\dfrac{25\pi}{12}$ cm  **(b)** $\dfrac{125\pi}{24}$ cm²

**8. (a)** $50\pi$ radians/sec
**(b)** $250\pi$ cm/sec
**10. (a)**

$$x = 10\cos\frac{\pi t}{3}$$

**(b)** passing through the origin: $t = 1.5$, $t = 4.5$, $t = 7.5$, and $t = 10.5$ sec; farthest from the origin: $t = 0$, $t = 3$, $t = 6$, $t = 9$, and $t = 12$ sec  **11. (a)** 1
**(b)** 0  **(c)** 0  **12. (a)** 1.1  **(b)** 1.1198
**(c)** 2.0218

## CHAPTER 8
### Exercise Set 8.1
**1.** $\sin 3\theta$  **3.** $\sin 2\theta$  **5.** $\cos 5u$
**7.** $\sqrt{3}/2$  **9.** $\sin B$  **11.** $\cos \theta$
**13.** $-\cos \theta$  **15.** $\sin t$
**17.** $\dfrac{\sqrt{6} - \sqrt{2}}{4}$  **19.** $\dfrac{\sqrt{6} + \sqrt{2}}{4}$

**21.** $\sqrt{2}\sin s$  **23.** $\sqrt{3}\sin \theta$
**25. (a)** $-\frac{16}{65}$  **(b)** $\frac{63}{65}$  **27. (a)** $-\frac{44}{125}$
**(b)** $-\frac{4}{5}$  **29. (a)** $2\sqrt{6}/5$  **(b)** $4\sqrt{6}/25$

**31.** $\sin(\theta + \beta) = \dfrac{2\sqrt{39} - 3\sqrt{13}}{26};$

$\cos(\beta - \theta) = \dfrac{2\sqrt{13} - 3\sqrt{39}}{26}$

**37.** $\tan(s + t) = -1$; $\tan(s - t) = -\frac{1}{7}$
**39.** $\tan(s + t) = \frac{5}{3}$; $\tan(s - t) = \frac{3}{5}$
**41.** $\tan 3t$  **43.** $\sqrt{3}$  **45.** $\tan x$
**47.** $-2 - \sqrt{3}$  **63. (b)** $\sqrt{a^2 + b^2}$
**65. (b)**

$$f(x) = \sqrt{2}\cos\left(x - \frac{\pi}{4}\right)$$

**71.** $\sqrt{3}/2$  **75. (a)** Using $\triangle ABH$, $\cos(\alpha + \beta) = AB/1$, so $\cos(\alpha + \beta) = AB$.  **(b)** Using $\triangle ACF$, $\cos \alpha = AC/AF = AC/\cos \beta$, so $AC = \cos \alpha \cos \beta$.  **(c)** Using $\triangle EFH$, $\sin(\angle EHF) = EF/HF$. But $\angle EHF = \alpha$, and $HF = \sin \beta$, so $\sin \alpha = EF/\sin \beta$, and thus $EF = \sin \alpha \sin \beta$.  **(d)** From part (a), $\cos(\alpha + \beta) = AB = AC - BC$. But $AC = \cos \alpha \cos \beta$ from part (b), and $BC = EF = \sin \alpha \sin \beta$ from part (c), so $\cos(\alpha + \beta) = \cos \alpha \cos \beta - \sin \alpha \sin \beta$.
**81. (a)**

| $t$ | 1 | 2 | 3 | 4 |
|-----|-----|-----|-----|-----|
| $f(t)$ | 1.5 | 1.5 | 1.5 | 1.5 |

**(b)** $f(t) = 1.5$.
**85. (a)** The two values are equal: $\tan A + \tan B + \tan C \approx -1.1918$; $\tan A \tan B \tan C \approx -1.1918$.
**(b)** $\tan \alpha + \tan \beta + \tan \gamma \approx -1.3764$; $\tan \alpha \tan \beta \tan \gamma \approx -1.3764$

### Exercise Set 8.2
**1. (a)** $\frac{336}{625}$  **(b)** $-\frac{527}{625}$  **(c)** $-\frac{336}{527}$
**3. (a)** $-\frac{8}{17}$  **(b)** $-\frac{15}{17}$  **(c)** $\frac{8}{15}$
**5. (a)** $\frac{1}{2}$  **(b)** $\sqrt{3}/2$  **(c)** $\sqrt{3}/3$
**7. (a)** $2\sqrt{2}/3$  **(b)** $\frac{1}{3}$  **(c)** $2\sqrt{2}$

**9. (a)** $-3\sqrt{7}/8$  **(b)** $-\frac{1}{8}$
**(c)** $\dfrac{\sqrt{8 + 2\sqrt{7}}}{4}$  **(d)** $\dfrac{\sqrt{8 - 2\sqrt{7}}}{4}$
**11. (a)** $4\sqrt{2}/9$  **(b)** $-\frac{7}{9}$  **(c)** $\sqrt{6}/3$
**(d)** $-\sqrt{3}/3$  **13. (a)** $\dfrac{\sqrt{2 - \sqrt{3}}}{2}$
**(b)** $\dfrac{\sqrt{2 + \sqrt{3}}}{2}$  **(c)** $2 - \sqrt{3}$
**15. (a)** $\dfrac{\sqrt{2 + \sqrt{3}}}{2}$  **(b)** $-\dfrac{\sqrt{2 - \sqrt{3}}}{2}$
**(c)** $-2 - \sqrt{3}$  **17. (a)** $\frac{24}{25}$  **(b)** $\frac{7}{25}$
**(c)** $\frac{24}{7}$  **19. (a)** $\frac{24}{25}$  **(b)** $-\frac{7}{25}$  **(c)** $-\frac{24}{7}$
**21. (a)** $\sqrt{10}/10$  **(b)** $3\sqrt{10}/10$  **(c)** $\frac{1}{3}$
**23. (a)** $\sqrt{5}/5$  **(b)** $2\sqrt{5}/5$  **(c)** $\frac{1}{2}$
**25.** $\sin 2\theta = \dfrac{2x\sqrt{25 - x^2}}{25};$

$\cos 2\theta = \dfrac{25 - 2x^2}{25}$

**27.** $\sin 2\theta = \dfrac{(x - 1)\sqrt{3 + 2x - x^2}}{2};$

$\cos 2\theta = \dfrac{1 + 2x - x^2}{2}$

**29.** $\sin^4 \theta = \dfrac{3 - 4\cos 2\theta + \cos 4\theta}{8}$

**31.** $\sin^4(\theta/2) = \dfrac{3 - 4\cos \theta + \cos 2\theta}{8}$

**51.** $\alpha + \beta = \pi/4$  **59. (a)** $-0.5$
**(c)** $\cos 108° \cos 36° = (-\cos 72°) \times (-\cos 144°) = \cos 72° \cos 144°$
**63. (b) (i)** This is true because of the double-angle formula for sine and the fact that $\cos 36° = \sin 54°$.  **(ii)** This is true because of the double-angle formula for sine and the fact that $\cos 18° = \sin 72°$.  **(iii)** Dividing each side by $4\sin 72°$ produces this result.

### Exercise Set 8.3
**1.** $\frac{1}{2}\cos 50°$  **3.** $\frac{1}{2}\cos 80°$
**5.** $\frac{1}{2}\sin 10° + \frac{1}{2}$  **7.** $\frac{1}{2}\cos(3\pi/5) - \frac{1}{2}$
**9.** $\frac{1}{2}\cos(3\pi/7) + \frac{1}{2}$  **11.** $\dfrac{1}{2} + \dfrac{\sqrt{3}}{4}$
**13.** $\frac{1}{2}\cos x - \frac{1}{2}\cos 7x$
**15.** $\frac{1}{2}\sin \theta + \frac{1}{2}\sin 11\theta$
**17.** $\frac{1}{2}\sin \theta + \frac{1}{2}\sin 2\theta$
**19.** $\frac{1}{2}\cos 2y - \frac{1}{2}\cos 4x$
**21.** $\frac{1}{2}\sin(3t - s) + \frac{1}{2}\sin(t + s)$
**23.** $\sqrt{2}\cos 10°$  **25.** $-\sqrt{2}\sin(\pi/20)$
**27.** $-2\sin 4\theta \sin \theta$  **29.** $\cos 5°$
**31.** $\sin 2\theta$  **33.** $\sqrt{3}$
**39.** $4\cos \theta \cos 4\theta \cos 2\theta$

**41. (a)** $2\cos(\frac{x}{2} - \frac{\pi}{4})$
**(b)** amplitude: 2; period: $4\pi$;
phase shift: $\frac{\pi}{2}$

**47.** 1
**51. (a)**
$\cos 30° + \cos 70° + \cos 80° \approx 1.38$;
$\cos 40° + \cos 25° + \cos 115° \approx 1.25$;
$\cos 55° + \cos 55° + \cos 70° \approx 1.49$
**(b)** $\frac{3}{2}$   **(c) (i)** This is the sum-to-
product formula for $\cos A + \cos B$.
**(ii)** This is true because
$\cos[(A - B)/2] \le 1$.   **(iii)** This is true
because $A + B = 180° - C$.
**(iv)** This is just division by 2.
**(v)** The identities used are
$\cos(90° - \theta) = \sin \theta$ and
$\cos \theta = 1 - 2\sin^2(\theta/2)$.
**(vi)** Multiplying this expression out
shows they are equal.   **(vii)** Since
$2[\sin(C/2) - \frac{1}{2}]^2 \ge 0$, the expression is
at most $3/2$.

## Exercise Set 8.4
**1.** yes   **3.** no   **5.** $\theta = (\pi/3) + 2\pi k$
or $\theta = (2\pi/3) + 2\pi k$, where $k$ is any
integer   **7.** $\theta = (7\pi/6) + 2\pi k$ or
$\theta = (11\pi/6) + 2\pi k$, where $k$ is any
integer   **9.** $\theta = \pi + 2\pi k$, where $k$ is
any integer   **11.** $\theta = (\pi/3) + \pi k$,
where $k$ is any integer
**13.** $x = \pi k$, where $k$ is any integer
**15.** $\theta = (\pi/2) + \pi k, \theta = (2\pi/3) + 2\pi k$
or $\theta = (4\pi/3) + 2\pi k$, where $k$ is any
integer   **17.** $t = \pi k$, where $k$ is any
integer   **19.** $x = (\pi/6) + 2\pi k$,
$x = (5\pi/6) + 2\pi k$ or
$x = (3\pi/2) + 2\pi k$, where $k$ is
any integer   **21.** $t = (\pi/4) + 2\pi k$
or $t = (3\pi/4) + 2\pi k$, where $k$ is any
integer

**23. (a)**

**(b)** $x \approx 6.28$   **(c)** $x = 2\pi$
**25.** $x \approx 1.39, 4.90$   **27.** $x \approx 0.46, 2.68$
**29.** $x \approx 1.41, 4.55$   **31.** $t \approx 1.37, 4.51$
**33.** $t \approx 1.11, 5.18$   **35.** $x \approx 1.25, 1.82,$
$4.39, 4.96$   **37.** $x \approx 0.85, 2.29$
**39.** $\theta \approx 14.5°, 165.5°$   **41.** $\theta \approx 53.1°,$
$126.9°, 233.1°, 306.9°$   **43.** $\theta \approx 128.2°,$
$231.8°$   **45.** $\theta = 0°, 120°, 240°$
**47.** $\theta = 75°, 105°, 195°, 225°, 315°, 345°$
**49.** $\theta = 90°, 270°$
**51.** $\theta = 30°, 120°, 210°, 300°$
**53.** $x \approx 0.898, 5.385$

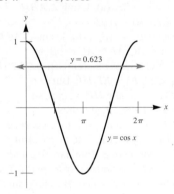

**55.** $x \approx 0.666, 2.475$

**57.** $x \approx 0.427, 2.715$

**59.** no solution

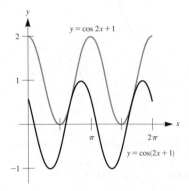

**61.** $x = 0, 1, x \approx 3.080, 4.080, 4.538,$
$5.538, 5.660$

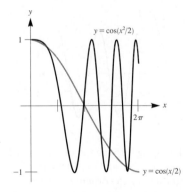

**63.** $x \approx 1.058, 3.739$

**65.** $x = 0, x \approx 0.695, 4.261$

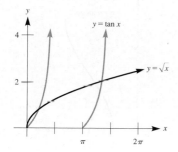

**67.** $x \approx 0.739, 3.881$

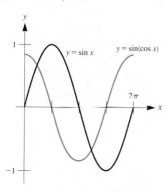

**69.** $x = 0, x \approx 4.493$

**71.** $x \approx 2.108, 5.746$

**73.** $x \approx 0.703$

**75.** $x = 0$ or $x = \pi$
**77.** $x = 2\pi/3$ or $x = \pi$
**79.** $\theta = (3\pi/16) + k\pi/4$, where $k$ is any integer   **81.** $\theta \approx 60.45°$
**85. (a)** $x \approx 1000.173$
**(b)** $x \approx 1001.022$
**87.** $P$: 0.315; $Q$: 0.685; $R$: 1.315
**89. (a)** $x = 2\cos 40°, 2\cos 160°,$
$2\cos 80°$
**(b)** $x = 4\sqrt{3}\cos 10°, 4\sqrt{3}\cos 130°,$
$4\sqrt{3}\cos 110°$   **(c)** $x = 2, -1 \pm \sqrt{3}$
**(d)** $x \approx -1.692, -1.357, 3.049$

## Exercise Set 8.5
**1.** $\pi/3$   **3.** $\pi/3$   **5.** $-\pi/6$   **7.** $\pi/4$
**9.** undefined   **11.** $\frac{1}{4}$   **13.** $\frac{3}{4}$
**15.** $-\pi/7$   **17.** $\pi/2$   **19.** $0$

**21. (a)** maximum value: 1.57
(when $x = 1$); minimum value: $-1.57$
(when $x = -1$)

**(b)** maximum value: $\frac{\pi}{2}$ (when $x = 1$);
minimum value: $-\frac{\pi}{2}$ (when $x = -1$)
**23. (a)**

**(b)** $y = -\pi/2, y = \pi/2$

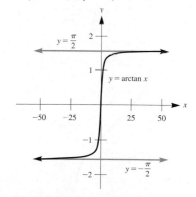

**25.** $3\sqrt{5}/7$   **27.** $-\sqrt{2}/2$   **29.** $\sqrt{5}/3$
**31.** $2\sqrt{2}/3$   **33.** $\frac{20}{21}$   **35.** $-2$
**37.** $\sqrt{3}/3$

**39.**

**(b)**

**51. (a)**

**41.**

**(c)**

**(b)**

**43.** $\dfrac{\theta}{4} - \sin 2\theta =$

$\dfrac{1}{4}\sin^{-1}\!\left(\dfrac{3x}{2}\right) - \dfrac{3x\sqrt{4-9x^2}}{2}$

**45.** $\theta - \cos\theta =$

$\tan^{-1}\!\left(\dfrac{x-1}{2}\right) - \dfrac{2}{\sqrt{5-2x+x^2}}$

**47. (a)**

**49. (a)**

**53. (a)**

**(b)**

**(b)**

**(c)**

**55.**

$f(x) = -\arctan(1 - x) - \dfrac{\pi}{2}$

$y = -\pi$

**57.** $\dfrac{8}{17}$    **59.** $31\sqrt{218}/1090$

**61. (a)** $-\dfrac{\pi}{2} \le \alpha \le \dfrac{\pi}{2}$ and $0 \le \beta \le \pi$, so $-\dfrac{\pi}{2} \le \alpha + \beta \le \dfrac{3\pi}{2}$    **63.** $t = \sqrt{2}/2$

**67.** $x = \pm\dfrac{1}{3}$    **69. (a)** $x = 0$ is not a solution, so $\cos^{-1} x > 0$. $\tan^{-1} x > 0$ only for $x > 0$.    **(c)** $(0.786, 0.666)$

**71.** $x \approx 0.74$

$y = \arccos x$

$y = x$

**73. (a)** $x \approx 0.96$

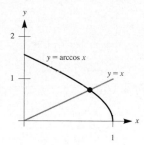

$y = \cos^{-1} x$

$y = 1.3\left(x - \dfrac{1}{2}\right)^2$

**(b)** $x \approx 0.96$

$y = \cos^{-1} x$

$y = 1.4\left(x - \dfrac{1}{2}\right)^2$

**75. (a)** $x \approx 0.24$

$y = 2\sin 3x$

$y = \arccos x$

**(b)** $x \approx 0.19$ and $x \approx 0.68$

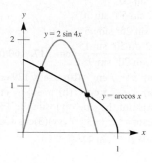

$y = 2\sin 4x$

$y = \arccos x$

**77. (a)** $x \approx 0.56$

$y = \left(\dfrac{1}{\tan^{-1} x + \sin^{-1} x}\right)$

$y = \sin 2x$

**(b)** $x \approx 0.51$ and $x \approx 0.84$

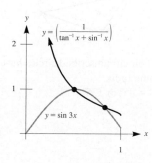

$y = \left(\dfrac{1}{\tan^{-1} x + \sin^{-1} x}\right)$

$y = \sin 3x$

**79.** $x \approx 0.71$

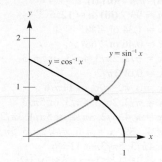

$y = \cos^{-1} x$

$y = \sin^{-1} x$

**81.** $x \approx 0.74$

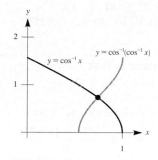

$y = \cos^{-1} x$

$y = \cos^{-1}(\cos^{-1} x)$

**83.** $x \approx 0.94$

$y = \dfrac{1}{\sin x}$

$y = \sin^{-1} x$

**85.** $x \approx 0.93$

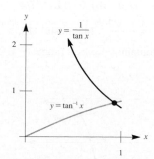

$y = \dfrac{1}{\tan x}$

$y = \tan^{-1} x$

**87. (b)** $DE = \sqrt{2}, CE = \sqrt{2}$, $BE = 3\sqrt{2}, AB = 3\sqrt{10}$, and $BD = \sqrt{10}$

## Chapter 8 Review Exercises

**43. (a)** $\pi/4$ **(b) (i)** $a \approx 14$
**(ii)** $a \approx 93$ **(iii)** $a \approx 1256$
**45.** $x \approx 1.34$ or $4.48$
**47.** $x \approx 0.46$ or $2.68$
**49.** $x = \pi/3, 2\pi/3, 4\pi/3,$ or $5\pi/3$
**51.** $x = 0$ or $3\pi/2$
**53.** $x = 0, \pi, 7\pi/6,$ or $11\pi/6$
**55.** $x = \pi/3, 2\pi/3, 4\pi/3,$ or $5\pi/3$
**57.** $x = \pi/4, \pi/2, 3\pi/4,$ or $5\pi/4, 3\pi/2,$
or $7\pi/4$ **59.** $x = \pi/6, \pi/3, 2\pi/3, 5\pi/6,$
$7\pi/6, 4\pi/3, 5\pi/3,$ or $11\pi/6$
**61.** $x = 3\pi/4$ or $7\pi/4$ **63.** $\sqrt{3}/2$
**65.** $\pi/6$ **67.** $\pi/6$ **69.** $\pi/3$ **71.** $2\pi/3$
**73.** $\frac{2}{7}$ **75.** $2\pi - 5$ **77.** $-\sqrt{2}/2$
**79.** $3\sqrt{2}/2$ **81.** $\frac{17}{7}$ **83.** $-\frac{4}{3}$
**85.** $3\sqrt{10}/10$ **95. (a)** $0.0625$

## Chapter 8 Test

**1.** $-\cos\theta$ **2.** $-\frac{3}{5}$ **3.** $-\frac{3}{2}$
**4.** $x \approx 1.25, 4.39$
**5.** $x = 7\pi/6, 11\pi/6$ **6.** $\sqrt{5}/5$
**7.** $x = 30°$ **8.** $\dfrac{\sqrt{18 + 12\sqrt{2}}}{6}$
**9.** restricted sine function: domain $=$
$[-\frac{\pi}{2}, \frac{\pi}{2}]$, range $= [-1, 1]$; $y = \sin^{-1} x$:
domain $= [-1, 1]$, range $= [-\frac{\pi}{2}, \frac{\pi}{2}]$

**10. (a)** $\pi/10$ **(b)** $0$ **11.** $\sqrt{7}/4$
**13.** $\dfrac{\sqrt{3} + \sqrt{2}}{4}$ **14.** $\tan 4\theta$ **15.** $x$
**16.** domain: $(-\infty, \infty)$; range: $(-\frac{\pi}{2}, \frac{\pi}{2})$

## CHAPTER 9
## Exercise Set 9.1

**1.** $4\sqrt{6}$ cm **3.** $20 \sin 50°$ cm
**5.** $a \approx 9.7$ cm; $c \approx 16.4$ cm
**7.** $A \approx 63.3°$; $C \approx 50.7°$; $c \approx 25.5$ cm
**9. (a)** $45°$ or $135°$ **(b)** $45°$
**(c)** $14.5°$ or $165.5°$ **(d)** $131.8°$
**11. (a)** $\sin B \approx 1.18 > 1$
**13. (b)** $\angle C = 105°$; $c \approx 1.93$
**(c)** $\angle C = 15°$; $c \approx 0.52$
**(d)** $A_1 \approx 0.68$; $A_2 \approx 0.18$
**15.** $a = \dfrac{2 \sin 110°}{\sin 20°}$ cm;
$b = \dfrac{2 \sin 50°}{\sin 20°}$ cm;
$c = \dfrac{2 \sin 50° \sin 70°}{\sin 20° \sin 95°}$ cm;
$d = \dfrac{2 \sin 50° \sin 15°}{\sin 20° \sin 95°}$ cm **17.** 160 ft
**19. (a)** $x = 7$ cm **(b)** $x = \sqrt{129}$ cm
**21. (a)** $x \approx 7.5$ cm **(b)** $x \approx 17.7$ cm
**23.** $x$ is not the side opposite the $130°$
angle; $6^2 = x^2 + 3^2 - 2(x)(3)\cos 130°$
**25.** $\cos A = \frac{113}{140}$; $\cos B = \frac{29}{40}$;
$\cos C = -\frac{5}{28}$
**27.** $A \approx 27.8°$; $B \approx 32.2°$; $C \approx 120°$
**29.** $A = 30°$; $B = 30°$; $C = 120°$
**31.** 5.9 units **33. (a)** $a \approx 4.2$ cm
**(b)** $C \approx 29.3°$ **(c)** $B \approx 110.7°$
**35.** approximately 31 miles
**37.** lighthouse $A$: 1.26 miles;
lighthouse $B$: 1.60 miles
**39.** $D \approx 860,000$ miles
**41. (b)** $a = 5, b = 3, c = 7$
(using $m = 2$ and $n = 1$) **43.** 2:40 P.M.
**47. (f)**

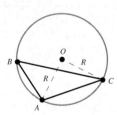

**(g)** Their circumscribed circles have
the same radii.
**51.** $C = 45°$ or $135°$

## Exercise Set 9.2

**1.** $|\overrightarrow{PQ}| = \sqrt{34}$

**3.** $|\overrightarrow{SQ}| = \sqrt{10}$

**5.** $|\overrightarrow{OP}| = \sqrt{10}$

**7.** $|\overrightarrow{PQ} + \overrightarrow{QS}| = 6\sqrt{2}$

**9.** $|\overrightarrow{OP} + \overrightarrow{PQ}| = 2\sqrt{13}$

**11.** $|\overrightarrow{OS} + \overrightarrow{SQ} + \overrightarrow{QP}| = \sqrt{10}$

**13.** $|\overrightarrow{OP} + \overrightarrow{QS}| = 6$

**15.** $|\overrightarrow{SR} + \overrightarrow{PO}| = 9$

**17.** $|\overrightarrow{OP} + \overrightarrow{RQ}| = \sqrt{37}$

**19.** $|\overrightarrow{SQ} + \overrightarrow{RO}| = \sqrt{61}$

**21.** $|\overrightarrow{OP} + \overrightarrow{OR}| = 3\sqrt{5}$

**23.** $|\overrightarrow{RP} + \overrightarrow{RS}| = 2\sqrt{13}$

**25.** $|\overrightarrow{SO} + \overrightarrow{SQ}| = 6\sqrt{5}$

**27.** $|\mathbf{F} + \mathbf{G}| = \sqrt{41}$ N; $\theta \approx 38.7°$
**29.** $|\mathbf{F} + \mathbf{G}| = 9\sqrt{2}$ N; $\theta = 45°$
**31.** $|\mathbf{F} + \mathbf{G}| \approx 7.90$ N; $\theta \approx 24.1°$
**33.** $|\mathbf{F} + \mathbf{G}| \approx 6.92$ N; $\theta \approx 34.67°$
**35.** $|\mathbf{F} + \mathbf{G}| \approx 39.20$ N; $\theta \approx 21.46°$
**37.** $|\mathbf{F} + \mathbf{G}| \approx 38.96$ N; $\theta \approx 29.44°$
**39.** $V_x \approx 13.86$ cm/sec; $V_y = 8$ cm/sec
**41.** $F_x \approx 3.62$ N; $F_y \approx 13.52$ N
**43.** $V_x \approx -0.71$ cm/sec;
$V_y \approx 0.71$ cm/sec
**45.** $F_x \approx -1.02$ N; $F_y \approx 0.72$ N
**47.** ground speed: 301.04 mph;
drift angle: 4.76°; course: 25.24°
**49.** ground speed: 293.47 mph;
drift angle: 8.82°; course: 91.18°
**51.** perpendicular: 9.83 lb; parallel:
6.88 lb   **53.** perpendicular: 11.82 lb;
parallel: 2.08 lb   **55. (a)** initial point:
$(-1, 2)$; terminal point: $(2, -3)$
**(b)** initial point: $(-1, 2)$;
terminal point: $(2, -3)$

**Exercise Set 9.3**
**1.** length = 5

**3.** length = $2\sqrt{5}$

**5.** length = $\sqrt{13}/4$

**7.** $\langle 1, 4 \rangle$   **9.** $\langle -1, 1 \rangle$   **11.** $\langle 8, -5 \rangle$
**13.** $\langle 7, 7 \rangle$   **15.** $\langle 24, 22 \rangle$   **17.** $\sqrt{130}$
**19.** $2\sqrt{17} - \sqrt{13} - \sqrt{37}$
**21.** $\langle 13, 6 \rangle$   **23.** $\langle 14, 21 \rangle$
**25.** $\langle -3, -1 \rangle$   **27.** $\langle 23, 12 \rangle$
**29.** $\langle -9, 0 \rangle$   **31.** $-48$   **33.** $3\mathbf{i} + 8\mathbf{j}$
**35.** $-8\mathbf{i} - 6\mathbf{j}$   **37.** $19\mathbf{i} + 23\mathbf{j}$
**39.** $\langle 1, 1 \rangle$   **41.** $\langle 5, -4 \rangle$
**43.** $\langle \frac{\sqrt{5}}{5}, \frac{2\sqrt{5}}{5} \rangle$
**45.** $\langle \frac{2\sqrt{5}}{5}, \frac{-\sqrt{5}}{5} \rangle$
**47.** $(8\sqrt{145}/145)\mathbf{i} - (9\sqrt{145}/145)\mathbf{j}$
**49.** $u_1 = \sqrt{3}/2$; $u_2 = \frac{1}{2}$
**51.** $u_1 = -\frac{1}{2}$; $u_2 = \sqrt{3}/2$
**53.** $u_1 = -\sqrt{3}/2$; $u_2 = \frac{1}{2}$

**61. (a)** $\mathbf{u} \cdot \mathbf{v} = 8$; $\mathbf{v} \cdot \mathbf{u} = 8$
**(b)** $\mathbf{v} \cdot \mathbf{w} = -14$; $\mathbf{w} \cdot \mathbf{v} = -14$
**63. (a)** $\mathbf{v} \cdot \mathbf{v} = 25$; $|\mathbf{v}|^2 = 25$
**(b)** $\mathbf{w} \cdot \mathbf{w} = 29$; $|\mathbf{w}|^2 = 29$

**65.** $\cos \theta = 7/\sqrt{170}$; $\theta \approx 57.53°$
or $\theta \approx 1.00$ radian

**67.** $\cos \theta = -57/\sqrt{3538}$; $\theta \approx 163.39°$
or $\theta \approx 2.85$ radians

**69. (a)** $\cos \theta = -7/\sqrt{170}$; $\theta \approx 122.47°$
or $\theta \approx 2.14$ radians

**(b)** $\cos \theta = 7/\sqrt{170}$; $\theta \approx 57.53°$ or
$\theta \approx 1.00$ radian

**71. (a)** $\cos \theta = 0$
**(b)** The vectors are perpendicular.
**(c)**

**73. (a)** $\mathbf{A} \cdot \mathbf{B} = 0$ implies $\cos \theta = 0$,
also $0 \le \theta < \pi$, and thus $\theta = \pi/2$.
So the vectors are perpendicular.
**(b)** If $\mathbf{A}$ and $\mathbf{B}$ are perpendicular, then
$\cos \theta = 0$, so $\mathbf{A} \cdot \mathbf{B} = 0$.
**75.** $\langle \frac{5}{13}, \frac{12}{13} \rangle$ and $\langle -\frac{5}{13}, -\frac{12}{13} \rangle$

## Exercise Set 9.4
**1.** $(2, 3)$  **3.** $(\frac{5\sqrt{3}}{2}, 1)$
**5.** $(\frac{3\sqrt{2}}{4}, \frac{3\sqrt{2}}{4})$
**7. (a)** $0 \le t \le 1$

$0 \le t \le 3$

$0 \le t \le 4$

As the interval for $t$ gets larger, the
curve resembles a parabola.
**(b)** $-5 \le t \le 5$

The restrictions on $t$ in Figure 1(b) are
$0 \le t \le 5$.
**9.**

**11.**

**13.**

**23. (a)**

**29.**

**31.**

**15.**

**(b)**

**25.**

**33.**

**17. (a)**

**(b)**

**27.**

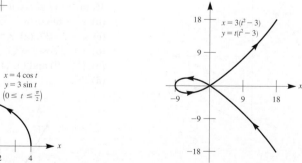

**35.**

**21. (a)**  $t = 1: x \approx 70.7, y \approx 59.7$
$t = 2: x \approx 141.4, y \approx 82.4$
$t = 3: x \approx 212.1, y \approx 73.1$
**(b)**  4.49 seconds; 317 feet

**37.**

$x = 8 \cos t + \cos 8t$
$y = 8 \sin t - \sin 8t$

**39.**

$x = \sin(0.8t + \pi)$
$y = \sin t$

**Exercise Set 9.5**
**1. (a)** $\left(-\frac{3}{2}, \frac{3\sqrt{3}}{2}\right)$
**(b)** $(2\sqrt{3}, -2)$

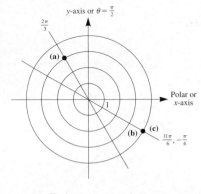

**(c)** $(2\sqrt{3}, -2)$

**3. (a)** $(0, 1)$
**(b)** $(0, 1)$

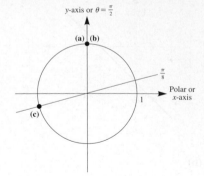

**(c)** $\left(-\dfrac{\sqrt{2 + \sqrt{2}}}{2}, -\dfrac{\sqrt{2 - \sqrt{2}}}{2}\right)$
**5.** $\left(\sqrt{2}, \frac{5\pi}{4}\right)$    **7.** $(x - 1)^2 + y^2 = 1$
**9.** $x^4 + x^2 y^2 - y^2 = 0$
**11.** $(x^2 + y^2)^3 = 9(x^2 - y^2)^2$
**13.** $\dfrac{x^2}{4} + \dfrac{y^2}{8} = 1$    **15.** $y = -\sqrt{3}x + 4$
**17.** $r = \dfrac{2}{3 \cos \theta - 4 \sin \theta}$
**19.** $r = \tan^2 \theta \sec \theta$    **21.** $r^2 = \csc 2\theta$
**23.** $r^2 = \dfrac{9}{9 \cos^2 \theta + \sin^2 \theta}$
**25.** $A\left(\frac{8}{3}, \frac{\pi}{6}\right), B\left(\frac{8}{3}, \frac{5\pi}{6}\right), C(4, \pi), D\left(8, \frac{7\pi}{6}\right)$
**27.** $A\left(1, \frac{\pi}{6}\right), B\left(1, \frac{5\pi}{6}\right), C\left(1, \frac{7\pi}{6}\right), D\left(-2, \frac{\pi}{2}\right)$
**29.** $A(1, 0), B\left(1.14, \frac{\pi}{4}\right), C\left(1.48, \frac{3\pi}{4}\right),$
$D(1.69, \pi), E\left(1.92, \frac{5\pi}{4}\right), F\left(2.19, \frac{3\pi}{2}\right),$
$G\left(2.50, \frac{7\pi}{4}\right), H(2.85, 2\pi), I\left(3.25, \frac{9\pi}{4}\right),$
$J\left(4.22, \frac{11\pi}{4}\right), K\left(5.48, \frac{13\pi}{4}\right)$
**31.** $2\sqrt{5}$    **33.** $\sqrt{21}$
**35. (a)** $r^2 - 8r \cos \theta = -12$
**(b)** $r^2 - 8r \cos\left(\theta - \frac{2\pi}{3}\right) = -12$
**(c)** $r = 2$    **37. (a)** $r = 2 \cos\left(\theta - \frac{3\pi}{2}\right)$
**(b)** $r = 2 \cos\left(\theta - \frac{\pi}{4}\right)$    **39. (a)** $2$
**(b)** $\left(\frac{4\sqrt{3}}{3}, 0\right)$ and $\left(4, \frac{\pi}{2}\right)$    **(c)** $\left(2, \frac{\pi}{6}\right)$
**(d)**

$r \cos(\theta - \pi/6) = 2$

**(e)** $\sqrt{3}x + y = 4$
**41. (a)** $4$    **(b)** $(-8, 0)$ and $\left(-\frac{8}{3}\sqrt{3}, \frac{\pi}{2}\right)$
**(c)** $\left(4, -\frac{2\pi}{3}\right)$

**(d)**

$r \cos(\theta + 2\pi/3) = 4$

**(e)** $-x - \sqrt{3}y = 8$
**43. (a)** $\left(2, \frac{5\pi}{6}\right)$
**(b)** $r \cos\left(\theta - \frac{5\pi}{6}\right) = 2$
**(c)** $x$-intercept: $-\frac{4\sqrt{3}}{3}$; $y$-intercept: $4$
**(d)** $-\sqrt{3}x + y = 4$
**45. (a)**

$x = 3$

**(b)**

$y = 3$

**47. (a)** $r \cos(\theta - \alpha) = d$
**53. (a)** $A(1, 0), B\left(1, \frac{2\pi}{3}\right), C\left(1, \frac{4\pi}{3}\right)$

**Exercise Set 9.6**
**1.** The graphs are four concentric circles with centers at the origin and radii 2, 4, 6, and 8.

**3.**

**5.**

**7.**

**9.**

**11.**

**13.**

**15.**

**17.**

**19.**

**21.**

**23.**

**25.**

**27.**

**29.**

**31.**

**33.**

**35.**

**37. (a)**

**(b)**

**39. (a)** $C$  **(b)** $D$  **(c)** $B$  **(d)** $A$
**41. (a)** $A(1, 0)$; $B(e^{a\pi/2}, \frac{\pi}{2})$; $C(e^{a\pi}, \pi)$; $D(e^{3a\pi/2}, \frac{3\pi}{2})$

**43. (a)** The curves are identical.

**45.**

**47.** The inner loop near the origin is not simple but rather a cardioid-type shape that passes through both the first and fourth quadrants.

**49.**

## Chapter 9 Review Exercises

**1.** $\angle C = 55°$, $a \approx 12.6$ cm, $b \approx 19.5$ cm
**3. (a)** $\angle B \approx 62.4°$, $\angle C \approx 65.6°$, $c \approx 9.2$ cm
**(b)** $\angle B \approx 117.6°$, $\angle C \approx 10.4°$, $c \approx 1.8$ cm  **5.** $c \approx 7.7$ cm, $\angle A \approx 108.5°$, $\angle B \approx 47.5°$
**7.** $\angle C \approx 106.6°$, $\angle B \approx 48.2°$, $\angle A \approx 25.2°$  **9.** 9.21 cm
**11.** 32.48 cm²  **13.** 55.23 cm²
**15.** 7.89 cm  **17.** 15.43 cm  **19.** 15 cm
**21.** 11 cm  **23. (a)** $\cos A = \frac{3}{4}$, $\cos C = \frac{1}{8}$  **25.** 36°  **27.** 58.76°
**29.** 18.65 m  **31. (a)** 11.76 cm
**(b)** 19.02 cm  **35.** $a = 5$, $b = 8$
**37.** $|\mathbf{R}| = 25$ N, $\theta \approx 53.1°$
**39.** $v_x \approx 41.0$ cm/sec, $v_y \approx 28.7$ cm/sec
**41.** $|\mathbf{W}| \approx 36.4$ lb, $|\mathbf{W}_p| \approx 33.2$ lb
**43.** $b = \pm\sqrt{15}$  **45.** $\langle 10, 9 \rangle$
**47.** $\langle 12, 7 \rangle$  **49.** 48  **51.** $\langle 12, 8 \rangle$
**53.** $\langle -6, 2 \rangle$  **55.** $\langle -7, -6 \rangle$  **57.** $7\mathbf{i} - 6\mathbf{j}$
**59.** $\langle 3\sqrt{13}/13, 2\sqrt{13}/13 \rangle$  **61.** 4.89
**63.** $r^2 - 10r\cos(\theta - \frac{\pi}{6}) = -16$
**65. (a)** 3  **(b)** $(6, 0), (2\sqrt{3}, \frac{\pi}{2})$
**(c)** $(3, \frac{\pi}{3})$
**(d)**

**(e)** $x + \sqrt{3}y = 6$
**67. (a)**

**(b)**

**73. (a)**

**81. (a)** $P\left(\dfrac{\sin \alpha}{\alpha}, \alpha\right), Q\left(\dfrac{\sin 2\alpha}{2\alpha}, 2\alpha\right)$

**(b)** $P\left(\dfrac{\sin \alpha \cos \alpha}{\alpha}, \dfrac{\sin^2 \alpha}{\alpha}\right),$

$Q\left(\dfrac{\sin 2\alpha \cos 2\alpha}{2\alpha}, \dfrac{\sin^2 2\alpha}{2\alpha}\right)$

**(f)** The product of the slopes of $\overline{PQ}$ and $\overline{OQ}$ is $-1$.

## Chapter 9 Test

**1.** $a = 7$ cm   **2.** If $\theta$ is the angle opposite the 4 cm side, then $\cos \theta = -\frac{1}{4} < 0$, so $\theta$ must be obtuse (not acute).   **3.** 20 cm

**4.** $2\sqrt{17 - 4\sqrt{2}}$ cm

**5.** $a \approx 3.3$ cm, $C \approx 26.2°$, $B \approx 126.8°$

**6. (a)** $2\sqrt{5}$ N   **(b)** $\tan \theta = 2$

**7. (a)** $4\sqrt{13 - 12 \cos 110°}$ N

**(b)** $\sin \theta = \dfrac{2 \sin 110°}{\sqrt{13 - 12 \cos 110°}}$

**8.** ground speed $= 50\sqrt{37}$ mph, $\tan \theta = \frac{1}{6}$

**9. (a)** $\langle 13, 5\rangle$   **(b)** $\sqrt{194}$   **(c)** $\mathbf{i} - 3\mathbf{j}$

**10.** $\langle \frac{-11\sqrt{130}}{130}, \frac{-3\sqrt{130}}{130}\rangle$

**11.** $(r^2 + y^2)^2 - x^2 - y^2$

**12.**

**69. (a)**

**(b)**

**(b)**

**75.**

**13.**

**14.** $\sqrt{13}$

**15.** $r^2 - 10r \cos(\theta - \frac{\pi}{2}) = -21$; no

**16. (a)** $r \cos(\theta - \frac{5\pi}{6}) = 4$

**71. (a)**

**77.**

**(b)**

**79.**

## CHAPTER 10
### Exercise Set 10.1

**1. (a)** yes   **(b)** no   **(c)** yes

**(d)** yes   **3.** yes   **5.** no

**7.** consistent (one solution)

**9.** inconsistent (no solution)

**11.** $(3, 5)$ **13.** $\left(-\frac{1}{28}, \frac{39}{28}\right)$

**15.** $\left(-\frac{34}{49}, -\frac{20}{49}\right)$ **17.** $\left(x, \frac{3 - 4x}{6}\right)$,

$x =$ any real number

**19. (a)** $(16.30, -24.5)$

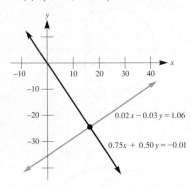

**(b)** $\left(\frac{5297}{325}, -\frac{7952}{325}\right) \approx (16.30, -24.47)$
**21.** $\left(-\frac{2}{9}, \frac{23}{27}\right)$ **23.** $\left(-\frac{283}{242}, -\frac{3}{121}\right)$
**25.** $\left(-\frac{226}{25}, -\frac{939}{50}\right)$ **27.** $\left(\frac{5}{8}, 0\right)$
**29.** $y = x^2 + 3x + 4$
**31.** $A = -28, B = -22$
**33. (a)** $p = \$6$: shortage of 6000 items;
$p = \$12$: shortage of 2400 items
**(b)** surplus of 2400 items
**(c)** equilibrium price: \$16; equilibrium
quantity: 3200 items **35.** 80 cc of
10% solution, 120 cc of 35% solution
**37.** 8 pounds of \$5.20 coffee, 8 pounds
of \$5.80 coffee

**39. (a)**

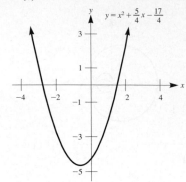

**41.** $a = 3, b = 2$
**43.** $\left(\frac{ab}{a + b}, \frac{ab}{a + b}\right); a \neq \pm b$
**45.** $\left(\frac{a + b}{ab}, \frac{-1}{ab}\right); a \neq 0$ and $b \neq 0$
**47.** $\left(-\frac{1}{11}, \frac{1}{9}\right)$ **49.** $(5, 2)$
**51.** $(e^{-2}, e^{-3}) \approx (0.14, 0.05)$
**53.** $(\ln 5, 0) \approx (1.61, 0)$
**55.** $(4, -8), (4, 2), (-1, -8), (-1, 2)$
**57.** 59 **59.** $\left(\frac{1}{b}, \frac{1}{a}\right)$
**61. (a)** $k = -\frac{29}{7}$ and 2

**(b)** $k = -\frac{29}{7}$:

$k = 2$:

**Exercise Set 10.2**
**1.** $(-3, -2, -1)$ **3.** $\left(-\frac{1}{60}, -\frac{2}{15}, \frac{3}{5}\right)$
**5.** $\left(\frac{25}{36}, \frac{5}{9}, -\frac{1}{3}\right)$ **7.** $\left(x, \frac{x}{8}, 0\right), x =$ any
real number **9.** $(-1, 0, 1, -5)$
**11.** $\left(\frac{11}{3}, \frac{8}{3}, \frac{17}{3}\right)$ **13.** $(1, 0, 1)$

**15.** $(2, 3, 1)$ **17.** inconsistent (no
solution) **19.** $\left(\frac{z + 1}{-7}, \frac{5(z + 1)}{7}, z\right)$,
$z =$ any real number
**21.** $\left(\frac{11 - 5z}{7}, \frac{-3z - 6}{7}, z\right)$,
$z =$ any real number **23.** $(4, 1, -3, 2)$
**25.** $\left(\frac{17 - 17z}{5}, \frac{8z - 3}{5}, z\right)$,
$z =$ any real number
**27.** $\left(\frac{12 + 10w}{11}, \frac{146 + 19w}{55}, \frac{61w + 159}{55}, w\right), w =$ any
real number
**29.** $\left(-\frac{5z}{12}, \frac{2z + 3}{3}, z\right), z =$ any real
number **31.** 6 Type I jets, 3 Type II
jets, 5 Type III jets
**33. (a)** $a + b + c = -2$
$a - b + c = 0$
$4a + 2b + c = 3$
**(b)** $a = 2, b = -1, c = -3$
**(c)**

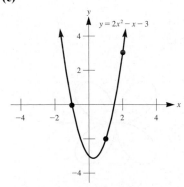

**(d)** $y = 2x^2 - x - 3$ **35.** 120 utility
chairs, 24 secretarial chairs,
10 managerial chairs
**37. (a)** $R(t) = -0.3t^2 + 3t + 1$
**(b)** December; \$850,000
**39.** $x = \ln a, y = \ln 2a, z = \ln \frac{a}{2}$
**41.** $T_1 = 42, T_2 = 43, T_3 = 40$
**43.** 60 miles

## Exercise Set 10.3

**1. (a)** two by three ($2 \times 3$)
**(b)** three by two ($3 \times 2$)
**3.** five by four ($5 \times 4$)
**5.** coefficient matrix is

$$\begin{pmatrix} 2 & 3 & 4 \\ 5 & 6 & 7 \\ 8 & 9 & 10 \end{pmatrix};$$ augmented matrix:

$$\begin{pmatrix} 2 & 3 & 4 & 10 \\ 5 & 6 & 7 & 9 \\ 8 & 9 & 10 & 8 \end{pmatrix}$$

**7.** coefficient matrix:

$$\begin{pmatrix} 1 & 0 & 1 & 1 \\ 1 & 1 & 0 & 2 \\ 0 & 1 & 1 & 1 \\ 2 & -1 & -1 & 0 \end{pmatrix};$$

augmented matrix:

$$\begin{pmatrix} 1 & 0 & 1 & 1 & -1 \\ 1 & 1 & 0 & 2 & 0 \\ 0 & 1 & 1 & 1 & 1 \\ 2 & -1 & -1 & 0 & 2 \end{pmatrix}$$

**9.** $(-1, -2, 3)$  **11.** $(-5, 1, 3)$
**13.** $(3, 0, -7)$  **15.** $(8, 9, -1)$
**17.** $\left( \dfrac{9z + 5}{19}, \dfrac{31z - 6}{19}, z \right),$
$z =$ any real number  **19.** $(2, -1, 0, 3)$
**21.** inconsistent (no solution)

**23.** $\begin{pmatrix} 3 & 2 \\ 2 & 4 \end{pmatrix}$  **25.** $\begin{pmatrix} 6 & 4 \\ 4 & 8 \end{pmatrix}$

**27.** $\begin{pmatrix} 11 & -2 \\ 11 & 1 \end{pmatrix}$  **29.** $\begin{pmatrix} 2 & 3 \\ -1 & 4 \end{pmatrix}$

**31.** not defined

**33.** $\begin{pmatrix} 10 & -2 \\ -8 & 0 \\ 4 & 6 \end{pmatrix}$

**35.** $\begin{pmatrix} 2 & 4 & 11 \\ -12 & 16 & 19 \\ 14 & 12 & 43 \end{pmatrix}$

**37.** $\begin{pmatrix} -9 & 10 & 10 \\ 4 & -8 & -12 \\ 10 & 4 & 21 \end{pmatrix}$

**39.** not defined

**41.** $\begin{pmatrix} 0 & 0 & 0 \\ 0 & 0 & 0 \\ 0 & 0 & 0 \end{pmatrix}$  **43.** $\begin{pmatrix} 4 & 2 \\ 2 & 5 \end{pmatrix}$

**45.** not defined

**47.** $\begin{pmatrix} 1 & 18 \\ -6 & 13 \end{pmatrix}$  **49.** $\begin{pmatrix} -16 & 75 \\ -25 & 34 \end{pmatrix}$

**51. (a)** $\begin{pmatrix} -13 & 1 & 40 \\ 43 & 17 & 0 \\ 89 & 61 & 60 \end{pmatrix}$

**(b)** $\begin{pmatrix} -13 & 1 & 40 \\ 43 & 17 & 0 \\ 89 & 61 & 60 \end{pmatrix}$

**(c)** $\begin{pmatrix} -52 & -82 & 61 \\ 87 & 141 & 0 \\ 216 & 318 & 165 \end{pmatrix}$

**(d)** $\begin{pmatrix} -52 & -82 & 61 \\ 87 & 141 & 0 \\ 216 & 318 & 165 \end{pmatrix}$

**53.** $\begin{pmatrix} -2474 & 1182 \\ 2358 & -144 \end{pmatrix}$

**55.** $\begin{pmatrix} 0.5 & 0 & 0 & 0 \\ 0 & 0.5 & 0 & 0 \\ 0 & 0 & 0.5 & 0 \\ 0 & 0 & 0 & 0.5 \end{pmatrix}$

**57. (a)** $\begin{pmatrix} 16 & 20 \\ 24 & 28 \end{pmatrix}$  **(b)** $\begin{pmatrix} 18 & 26 \\ 18 & 26 \end{pmatrix}$

**(c)** $\begin{pmatrix} 14 & 14 \\ 30 & 30 \end{pmatrix}$  **(d)** $\begin{pmatrix} 18 & 26 \\ 18 & 26 \end{pmatrix}$

**59. (a)** $\begin{pmatrix} x \\ -y \end{pmatrix}$  **(b)** $\begin{pmatrix} -x \\ y \end{pmatrix}$

**(c)** $\begin{pmatrix} -x \\ -y \end{pmatrix}$; this would represent a

reflection about the origin.

## Exercise Set 10.4

**5.** $\begin{pmatrix} -5 & 9 \\ 4 & -7 \end{pmatrix}$  **7.** $\begin{pmatrix} -\frac{6}{23} & \frac{1}{23} \\ \frac{5}{23} & \frac{3}{23} \end{pmatrix}$

**9.** no $A^{-1}$ exists  **11.** $\begin{pmatrix} 2 & -3 \\ 1 & 3 \end{pmatrix}$

**13.** $\begin{pmatrix} 2 & -1 \\ -3 & 2 \end{pmatrix}$  **15.** $\begin{pmatrix} \frac{6}{11} & 1 \\ -\frac{1}{11} & 0 \end{pmatrix}$

**17.** does not exist

**19.** $\begin{pmatrix} -1 & 2 & -3 \\ 2 & 1 & 0 \\ 4 & -2 & 5 \end{pmatrix}$

**21.** $\begin{pmatrix} 5 & -\frac{10}{3} & 1 \\ 0 & \frac{1}{3} & 0 \\ 4 & -\frac{8}{3} & 1 \end{pmatrix}$  **23.** $\begin{pmatrix} 2 & 1 & 4 \\ 3 & 2 & 5 \\ 0 & -1 & 1 \end{pmatrix}$

**25.** does not exist

**27.** $A^{-1} = \begin{pmatrix} -2.5 & 1.5 \\ 2 & -1 \end{pmatrix}$

**29.** $D^{-1}$ does not exist

**31.** $(DE)^{-1}$  **33. (a)** $x = -1$ and
$y = 1$  **(b)** $x = -132$ and $y = 48$
**35.** $x = 2, y = -1, z = 4$

**37. (a)** $\begin{pmatrix} -7 & 4 \\ 2 & -1 \end{pmatrix}$  **(b)** $(-1, 2)$

**39. (a)** $\begin{pmatrix} -1 & 0 & 2 \\ 3 & 1 & -6 \\ -2 & -1 & 5 \end{pmatrix}$

**(b)** $(21, -64, 55)$

**41. (a)** $\begin{pmatrix} \frac{31}{108} & \frac{2}{27} & \frac{7}{18} & -\frac{11}{108} \\ -\frac{53}{162} & \frac{1}{81} & -\frac{5}{27} & \frac{31}{162} \\ -\frac{55}{54} & -\frac{1}{27} & \frac{5}{9} & \frac{23}{54} \\ \frac{131}{54} & -\frac{4}{27} & -\frac{7}{9} & -\frac{43}{54} \end{pmatrix}$

**(b)** $\left( \frac{10}{9}, -\frac{22}{27}, -\frac{59}{9}, \frac{88}{9} \right)$

**45.** 324, 286, 225, 200, 241, 212
**47.** 41, 15, 38, 14, 28, 28, 38, $-23$, 15
**49.** SEE JOE  **51.** STUDY

**53.** $\begin{pmatrix} 4 & -6 & 4 & -1 \\ -6 & 14 & -11 & 3 \\ 4 & -11 & 10 & -3 \\ -1 & 3 & -3 & 1 \end{pmatrix}$

**55.** $A^{-1} = \begin{pmatrix} \dfrac{d}{ad - bc} & \dfrac{-b}{ad - bc} \\ \dfrac{-c}{ad - bc} & \dfrac{a}{ad - bc} \end{pmatrix}$

## Exercise Set 10.5

**1. (a)** 29  **(b)** $-29$  **3. (a)** 0
**(b)** 0  **5.** $-1$  **7.** 60  **9.** 9
**11. (a)** 314  **(b)** 674  **(c)** part (b)
**13. (a)** 0  **(b)** 0  **(c)** 0  **(d)** 0
**15.** 0  **17.** $-3$  **19.** 0  **21.** 570
**23.** 0  **25.** 12  **27. (a)** The right-hand
determinant should be 10 times the
left-hand determinant.
**(b)** det $A = 206$ and det $B = 2060$
**29. (a)** 20  **(b)** 20  **31. (a)** 174
**(b)** 174  **33.** $(y - x)(z - x)(z - y)$
**35.** $xy$  **39.** $(1, 1, 2)$
**41.** $(2, -3, -3)$  **43.** $(0, 0, 0)$
**45.** $(13 - \frac{11}{3}y, y, 13 - 4y)$, $y =$ any real
number  **47.** $(1, 0, -10, 2)$
**49.** $x = 4, -4, -1$

**63.** $\left( \dfrac{k(k - b)(k - c)}{a(a - b)(a - c)}, \right.$
$\dfrac{k(k - a)(k - c)}{b(b - a)(b - c)}, \left. \dfrac{k(k - a)(k - b)}{c(c - a)(c - b)} \right)$

**65.** $y = 2x + 5$  **69. (b)** $\begin{pmatrix} -\frac{9}{61} & \frac{7}{61} \\ \frac{1}{61} & \frac{6}{61} \end{pmatrix}$

## Exercise Set 10.6

**1.** $(0, 0), (3, 9)$

**3.** $(2\sqrt{6}, 1), (-2\sqrt{6}, 1)$

**5.** $(-1, -1)$    **7.** $(2, 3), (2, -3),$
$(-2, 3), (-2, -3)$    **9.** $(1, 0), (-1, 0)$

**11.** $\left(\dfrac{-1 + \sqrt{65}}{8}, \dfrac{1 + \sqrt{65}}{2}\right),$
$\left(\dfrac{-1 - \sqrt{65}}{8}, \dfrac{1 - \sqrt{65}}{2}\right)$

**13.** $(\frac{\sqrt{17}}{17}, 1), (\frac{\sqrt{17}}{17}, -1), (\frac{-\sqrt{17}}{17}, 1),$
$(\frac{-\sqrt{17}}{17}, -1)$

**15.** $(1, 0), (4, -\sqrt{3})$    **17.** $(2, 4)$

**19.** $(100, 1000), (100, \frac{1}{1000}), (\frac{1}{100}, 1000),$
$(\frac{1}{100}, \frac{1}{1000})$

**21.** $\left(\dfrac{2\ln 2 - 5\ln 3}{\ln 2 - \ln 3}, \dfrac{3\ln 2}{\ln 2 - \ln 3}\right)$

**23. (a)** $(2.19, -2.81), (-3.19, -8.19)$

**(b)** $\left(\dfrac{-1 + \sqrt{29}}{2}, \dfrac{-11 + \sqrt{29}}{2}\right)$
$\approx (2.193, -2.807),$
$\left(\dfrac{-1 - \sqrt{29}}{2}, \dfrac{-11 - \sqrt{29}}{2}\right)$
$\approx (-3.193, -8.193)$

**25. (a)** $(0.85, 2.36)$

**(b)** $\left(\dfrac{32 - 4\sqrt{37}}{9}, \dfrac{1 + \sqrt{37}}{3}\right)$
$\approx (0.852, 2.361)$

**27. (a)** $(0.60, 5.30)$

**(b)** $\left(\dfrac{\ln[(1 + \sqrt{13})/2]}{\ln 4}, \dfrac{7 + \sqrt{13}}{2}\right)$
$\approx (0.602, 5.303)$

**29.** $(-0.82, 0.67), (1.43, 2.04)$

**31.** $(1, 0), (12.34, 2.51)$

**33.** $(1.23, 1.86), (6.14, 230.95)$

**35. (b)** $u = 9, v = 8$    **37.** $\left(\dfrac{1}{a}, \dfrac{1}{b}\right)$

**39.** $(9, 14), (14, 9)$

**41.** $\dfrac{p - \sqrt{2d^2 - p^2}}{2}$ by
$\dfrac{p + \sqrt{2d^2 - p^2}}{2}$    **43. (a)** $N_0 = \frac{3}{2}$,
$k = \dfrac{\ln 8}{6}$    **(b)** $N_0 = 10^{-1/7}$,
$k = \frac{2}{7}\ln 10$    **45.** $\left(\dfrac{p^2}{A}, \dfrac{q^2}{A}, \dfrac{r^2}{A}\right)$ and
$\left(\dfrac{-p^2}{A}, \dfrac{-q^2}{A}, \dfrac{-r^2}{A}\right)$, where
$A = \sqrt{p^2 + q^2 + r^2}$

**47.** 9 cm and 40 cm

**49.** 3 cm by 20 cm

**51.** $(1, 2), (-1, -2), (2, 1), (-2, -1)$

**53.** $\left(\dfrac{1 + \sqrt{13}}{2}, \dfrac{-1 + \sqrt{13}}{2}\right),$
$\left(\dfrac{-1 + \sqrt{13}}{2}, \dfrac{1 + \sqrt{13}}{2}\right),$
$\left(\dfrac{1 - \sqrt{13}}{2}, \dfrac{-1 - \sqrt{13}}{2}\right),$
$\left(\dfrac{-1 - \sqrt{13}}{2}, \dfrac{1 - \sqrt{13}}{2}\right)$

**55.** $(2, 3), (-2, -3), (1, 2), (-1, -2)$

**57.** $(e^{9/2}, e^3)$

## Exercise Set 10.7

**1. (a)** no    **(b)** yes

**3.**

**5.**

**7.**

**9.**

**11.**

**13.**

**15.**

**17.**

**19.**

**21.**

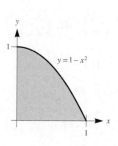

**23.** convex and bounded; vertices:
$(0, 0)$, $(7, 0)$, $(3, 8)$, $(0, 5)$

**25.** convex and bounded; vertices:
$(0, 0)$, $(0, 4)$, $(3, 5)$, $(8, 0)$

**27.** convex but not bounded; vertices:
$(2, 7)$, $(8, 5)$

**29.** convex but not bounded;
vertex: $(6, 0)$

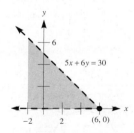

**31.** convex and bounded; vertices:
$(0, 0)$, $(0, 5)$, $(6, 0)$

**33.** convex and bounded; vertices:
$(5, 30), (10, 30), (20, 15), (20, 20)$

**35.** vertices: $(0, 1), (0, 2),$
$\left(\ln\dfrac{1 + \sqrt{5}}{2}, \dfrac{1 + \sqrt{5}}{2}\right)$

**37.**

**39.**

**41.**

## Chapter 10 Review Exercises

**1.** $(3, -5)$  **3.** $(-1, 4)$  **5.** $(-3, 15)$
**7.** $\left(-\frac{18}{5}, \frac{8}{5}\right)$  **9.** $\left(\frac{2}{3}, -\frac{1}{5}\right)$
**11.** $(-12, -8)$  **13.** $\left(\frac{1}{3}, -\frac{1}{4}\right)$
**15.** $\left(\dfrac{-1}{a^2 - 3a + 1}, \dfrac{1 - a}{a^2 - 3a + 1}\right)$;
$a \neq \dfrac{3 \pm \sqrt{5}}{2}$
**17.** $(a^2, 1 - a^2)$  **19.** $(a^2 - b^2, a^2 + b^2)$
**21.** $\left(\dfrac{pq(p + q)}{p^2 + q^2}, \dfrac{p^3 - q^3}{p^2 + q^2}\right)$; $p$ and $q$
not both zero  **23.** $(2, 3, 4)$
**25.** $(-1, -2, 0)$  **27.** $(x, 6 - 2x, -1)$,
$x = $ any real number
**29.** $\left(-\frac{1}{6}z, \frac{1}{2}z, z\right)$, $z = $ any real number
**31.** $(4, 3, -1, 2)$  **33.** $960$
**35.** $24$  **39.** $a = 2$ and $b = 1$
**43.** $\left(x + \dfrac{17}{6}\right)^2 + \left(y + \dfrac{8}{3}\right)^2 = \dfrac{245}{36}$
**45.** $\begin{pmatrix} 10 & -2 \\ 4 & 26 \end{pmatrix}$  **47.** $\begin{pmatrix} 8 & 4 \\ 4 & 32 \end{pmatrix}$
**49.** $\begin{pmatrix} 4 & -13 \\ 7 & 41 \end{pmatrix}$  **51.** $\begin{pmatrix} -3 & -14 \\ -4 & 3 \end{pmatrix}$
**53.** $\begin{pmatrix} 1 & 1 \\ 1 & 7 \end{pmatrix}$  **55.** $\begin{pmatrix} 1 & -11 \\ 6 & 36 \end{pmatrix}$
**57.** $\begin{pmatrix} 4 & 3 \\ 10 & 33 \end{pmatrix}$  **59.** $\begin{pmatrix} 4 & -1 \\ 2 & 12 \end{pmatrix}$
**61.** $\begin{pmatrix} -4 & 13 \\ -7 & -41 \end{pmatrix}$
**63.** $A^2 = \begin{pmatrix} 0 & 0 & 0 \\ 0 & 0 & 0 \\ ac & 0 & 0 \end{pmatrix}$;
$A^3 = \begin{pmatrix} 0 & 0 & 0 \\ 0 & 0 & 0 \\ 0 & 0 & 0 \end{pmatrix}$
**65. (a)** $\begin{pmatrix} 10 & -2 & 5 \\ 6 & -1 & 4 \\ 1 & 0 & 1 \end{pmatrix}$
**(b)** $(16, 15, 4)$  **67.** $\left(-\frac{3}{5}, -\frac{13}{20}, \frac{31}{20}\right)$

**69.** inconsistent (no solution)
**71.** $(-5 - 4y, y, -8 - 5y)$, $y = $ any
real number  **73.** $(4, 1, -1, 3)$
**75.** $(0, 0)$ and $(6, 36)$
**77.** $(3, 0)$ and $(-3, 0)$
**79.** $\left(\frac{5\sqrt{2}}{2}, \frac{\sqrt{14}}{2}\right), \left(-\frac{5\sqrt{2}}{2}, \frac{\sqrt{14}}{2}\right), \left(\frac{5\sqrt{2}}{2}, -\frac{\sqrt{14}}{2}\right),$
$\left(-\frac{5\sqrt{2}}{2}, -\frac{\sqrt{14}}{2}\right)$
**81.** $\left(\dfrac{-1 + \sqrt{5}}{2}, \dfrac{\sqrt{-2 + 2\sqrt{5}}}{2}\right)$
**83.** $(\sqrt{2}, 3\sqrt{2}), (-\sqrt{2}, -3\sqrt{2}),$
$\left(\frac{7\sqrt{22}}{33}, \frac{31\sqrt{22}}{33}\right), \left(\frac{-7\sqrt{22}}{33}, \frac{-31\sqrt{22}}{33}\right)$
**85.** $(5, 2), (5, -4), (1, 2), (1, -4)$
**87.** $\dfrac{as}{a + b}$ and $\dfrac{bs}{a + b}$
**89.** $24, 60, 120$
**91.** $\dfrac{\sqrt{n + 2m} + \sqrt{n - 2m}}{2}$ and
$\dfrac{\sqrt{n + 2m} - \sqrt{n - 2m}}{2}$,
$\dfrac{\sqrt{n - 2m} - \sqrt{n + 2m}}{2}$, and
$\dfrac{-\sqrt{n - 2m} - \sqrt{n + 2m}}{2}$
**93.** neither convex nor bounded

**95.** convex and bounded

## Chapter 10 Test
**1.** $(0, 3)$ and $\left(-\frac{11}{4}, \frac{81}{16}\right)$  **2.** $(3, -5)$
**3. (a)** $(1, -1, -3)$  **(b)** $(1, -1, -3)$
**4. (a)** $\begin{pmatrix} 2 & -10 \\ 3 & -5 \end{pmatrix}$  **(b)** $\begin{pmatrix} 8 & -4 \\ 7 & -6 \end{pmatrix}$

**5.** equilibrium price = $21; equilibrium quantity = 684 units

**6.** $\left(\frac{1}{116}, -\frac{1}{144}\right)$

**7.** coefficient matrix:

$$\begin{pmatrix} 1 & 1 & -1 \\ 2 & -1 & 2 \\ 1 & -2 & 1 \end{pmatrix}; \text{augmented}$$

matrix = $\begin{pmatrix} 1 & 1 & -1 & -1 \\ 2 & -1 & 2 & 11 \\ 1 & -2 & 1 & 10 \end{pmatrix}$

**8.** $(3, -3, 1)$

**9. (a)**
$$w + x + y + z = 40$$
$$-w + x + y - z = 0$$
$$4w - x - y - z = 0$$
$$-2w + 3x - 2y + 3z = 0$$

**(b)** $\begin{pmatrix} 1 & 1 & 1 & 1 \\ -1 & 1 & 1 & -1 \\ 4 & -1 & -1 & -1 \\ -2 & 3 & -2 & 3 \end{pmatrix}$

**(c)** inverse matrix:

$$\begin{pmatrix} 0.2 & 0 & 0.2 & 0 \\ 0.1 & 0.5 & 0.2 & 0.2 \\ 0.4 & 0 & -0.2 & -0.2 \\ 0.3 & -0.5 & -0.2 & 0 \end{pmatrix}$$

8 hours on math, 4 hours on English, 16 hours on chemistry, 12 hours on economics **10. (a)** 8
**(b)** $-8$  **11.** $-1120$

**12.** $\left(\frac{5 + \sqrt{5}}{2}, \frac{5 - \sqrt{5}}{2}\right)$,
$\left(\frac{5 - \sqrt{5}}{2}, \frac{5 + \sqrt{5}}{2}\right)$,
$\left(\frac{-5 + \sqrt{5}}{2}, \frac{-5 - \sqrt{5}}{2}\right)$,
$\left(\frac{-5 - \sqrt{5}}{2}, \frac{-5 + \sqrt{5}}{2}\right)$

**13.** $\left(1 - \frac{1}{5}C, -\frac{7}{5}C, C\right)$, $C$ = any real number

**14. (a)** $\begin{pmatrix} 1 & -2 & 3 \\ 2 & -5 & 10 \\ -1 & 2 & -2 \end{pmatrix}$

**(b)** $(12, 38, -9)$

**15.**

**16.** $P = -1$ and $Q = -4$
**17.** neither bounded nor convex

**18.** vertices: $(0, 0), (0, 7), (6, 10),$ $\left(\frac{261}{26}, \frac{225}{26}\right), (11, 0)$

**19.** $(e^{-19}, e^{-6}, e^{49})$

# CHAPTER 11
## Exercise Set 11.1
**1.** $\sqrt{89}$  **3.** $5x + 4y - 4 = 0$
**5.** $2x + 3y - 20 = 0$
**7.** $x$-intercepts: $6, -4$; $y$-intercepts: $\pm 2\sqrt{6}$  **9.** $13x - 7y - 35 = 0$
**11.** $12 + \sqrt{74}$  **13.** $\theta = \pi/3$ or $60°$
**15. (a)** $\theta = 1.37$ or $78.69°$
**(b)** $\theta = 1.77$ or $101.31°$
**17. (a)** $5\sqrt{2}/2$  **(b)** $5\sqrt{2}/2$
**19. (a)** $19\sqrt{41}/41$  **(b)** $19\sqrt{41}/41$
**21. (a)** $(x + 2)^2 + (y + 3)^2 = \frac{361}{13}$
**(b)** $\sqrt{5}$  **23.** $\frac{65}{2}$  **25.** $\frac{15 \pm 2\sqrt{30}}{5}$
**27.** $\frac{12}{5}$  **29.** $y = -3x + 12$
**31.** $y = \frac{1}{3}x + \frac{9}{2}$
**33. (a)** center: $(-5, 2)$; radius: $5\sqrt{2}$
**35.** $PQ = 5\sqrt{2}$
**39. (a)** $A: y = \frac{1}{3}x$;
$B: y = -x + 8$; $C: y = 2x - 10$
**(b)** $(6, 2)$

**43. (a)** slope: $-\dfrac{A}{B}$; $y$-intercept: $-\dfrac{C}{B}$

**47.** $\left(x - \dfrac{26}{11}\right)^2 + \left(y + \dfrac{25}{11}\right)^2 = \dfrac{4964}{121}$

**49.** $\left(x - 4 - \dfrac{10\sqrt{13}}{13}\right)^2 +$
$\left(y - 6 - \dfrac{15\sqrt{13}}{13}\right)^2 = 25;$
$\left(x - 4 + \dfrac{10\sqrt{13}}{13}\right)^2 +$
$\left(y - 6 + \dfrac{15\sqrt{13}}{13}\right)^2 = 25$

## Exercise Set 11.2
**1.** focus: $(0, 1)$; directrix: $y = -1$; focal width: 4

**3.** focus: $(-2, 0)$; directrix: $x = 2$; focal width: 8

**5.** focus: $(0, -5)$; directrix: $y = 5$; focal width: 20

**7.** focus: $(-7, 0)$; directrix: $x = 7$;
focal width: 28

**9.** focus: $(0, \frac{3}{2})$; directrix: $y = -\frac{3}{2}$;
focal width: 6

**11.** focus: $(0, \frac{7}{16})$; directrix: $y = -\frac{7}{16}$;
focal width: $\frac{7}{4}$

**13.** vertex: $(2, 3)$; focus: $(3, 3)$;
directrix: $x = 1$; focal width: 4

**15.** vertex: $(4, 2)$; focus: $(4, \frac{9}{4})$;
directrix: $y = \frac{7}{4}$; focal width: 1

**17.** vertex: $(0, -1)$; focus: $(\frac{1}{4}, -1)$;
directrix: $x = -\frac{1}{4}$; focal width: 1

**19.** vertex: $(3, 0)$; focus: $(3, \frac{1}{8})$;
directrix: $y = -\frac{1}{8}$; focal width: $\frac{1}{2}$

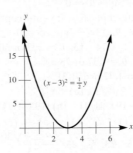

**21.** vertex: $(4, 1)$; focus: $(4, \frac{9}{8})$;
directrix: $y = \frac{7}{8}$; focal width: $\frac{1}{2}$

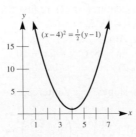

**23. (a)** 22.9 meters    **(b)** 0.3
**25. (a)** $x^2 = -\frac{80}{3}y$    **(b)** $14\frac{1}{16}$ feet
**27.** line of symmetry: $y = 1$

**29.** $x^2 = 12y$    **31.** $y^2 = 128x$
**33.** $y^2 = -9x$    **35. (a)** $y = \frac{9}{4}x - 1$
**(b)** $y = -\frac{9}{8}x - \frac{1}{4}$    **(c)** intersect at
$(\frac{2}{9}, -\frac{1}{2})$    **37. (a)** $(-\frac{1}{8}, \frac{1}{64})$
**(b)** $(\frac{15}{16}, \frac{257}{128})$    **(c)** $\overline{ST} = \frac{1}{2}$
**39.** side = $8\sqrt{3}p$ units,
area = $48\sqrt{3}p^2$ sq. units    **41. (a)** 6 m
**(b)** $5\frac{1}{3}$ m

## Exercise Set 11.3
**1.** $y = 4x - 4$

**3.** $y = x - 2$

**5.** $y = 6x + 9$

**7.** $y = x + 1$

**9.** $m = \frac{1}{4}$    **11.** $m = 12$

## Exercise Set 11.4

**1.** length of major axis: 6; length of minor axis: 4; foci: $(\pm\sqrt{5}, 0)$; eccentricity: $\sqrt{5}/3$

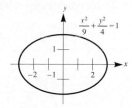

**3.** length of major axis: 8; length of minor axis: 2; foci: $(\pm\sqrt{15}, 0)$; eccentricity: $\sqrt{15}/4$

**5.** length of major axis: $2\sqrt{2}$; length of minor axis: 2; foci: $(\pm 1, 0)$; eccentricity: $\sqrt{2}/2$

**7.** length of major axis: 8; length of minor axis: 6; foci: $(0, \pm\sqrt{7})$; eccentricity: $\sqrt{7}/4$

**9.** length of major axis: $2\sqrt{15}/3$; length of minor axis: $2\sqrt{3}/3$; foci: $(0, \pm\frac{2\sqrt{3}}{3})$; eccentricity: $2\sqrt{5}/5$

**11.** length of major axis: 4; length of minor axis: $2\sqrt{2}$; foci: $(0, \pm\sqrt{2})$; eccentricity: $\sqrt{2}/2$

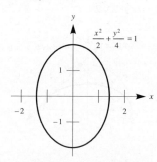

**13.** center: $(5, -1)$; length of major axis: 10; length of minor axis: 6; foci: $(9, -1)$ and $(1, -1)$; eccentricity: $\frac{4}{5}$

**15.** center: $(1, 2)$; length of major axis: 4; length of minor axis: 2; foci: $(1, 2 \pm \sqrt{3})$; eccentricity: $\sqrt{3}/2$

**17.** center: $(-3, 0)$; length of major axis: 6; length of minor axis: 2; foci: $(-3 \pm 2\sqrt{2}, 0)$; eccentricity: $2\sqrt{2}/3$

**19.** center: $(1, -2)$; length of major axis: 4; length of minor axis: $2\sqrt{3}$; foci: $(2, -2)$ and $(0, -2)$; eccentricity: $\frac{1}{2}$

**21.** center: $(4, 6)$; degenerate ellipse

**23.** no graph

**25.** $\dfrac{x^2}{25} + \dfrac{y^2}{16} = 1$ or $16x^2 + 25y^2 = 400$

**27.** $\dfrac{x^2}{16} + \dfrac{y^2}{15} = 1$ or $15x^2 + 16y^2 = 240$

**29.** $\dfrac{x^2}{21} + \dfrac{y^2}{25} = 1$ or $25x^2 + 21y^2 = 525$

**31.** $\dfrac{x^2}{9} + \dfrac{y^2}{9/4} = 1$ or $x^2 + 4y^2 = 9$

**33.** (a) $y = -\tfrac{4}{3}x + \tfrac{38}{3}$

(b) $y = \tfrac{7}{9}x + \tfrac{76}{9}$   (c) $y = \tfrac{1}{15}x - \tfrac{76}{15}$

**35.** (a) $y = -6x + 26$   (b) $\tfrac{169}{3}$

**37.** perihelion: 29.64 AU; aphelion: 49.24 AU   **39.** semimajor axis: 4.42 AU; eccentricity: 0.04

**41.** (c) $[-3, 3]$

(d)

| $x$ | 0 | 0.5 | 1.0 | 1.5 | 2.0 | 2.5 | 3.0 |
|---|---|---|---|---|---|---|---|
| $y$ | $\pm 2$ | $\pm 1.97$ | $\pm 1.89$ | $\pm 1.73$ | $\pm 1.49$ | $\pm 1.11$ | 0 |

(e)

**43.** circle: $(x - 1)^2 + y^2 = 1$;

ellipse: $\dfrac{(x - 4)^2}{16} + \dfrac{y^2}{7} = 1$

**49.** intersection points: $\left(\dfrac{ab}{A}, \dfrac{ab}{A}\right)$,

$\left(\dfrac{ab}{A}, -\dfrac{ab}{A}\right), \left(-\dfrac{ab}{A}, \dfrac{ab}{A}\right)$,

$\left(-\dfrac{ab}{A}, -\dfrac{ab}{A}\right)$,

where $A = \sqrt{a^2 + b^2}$

**53.** (b) $\left(-\tfrac{20}{7}, -\tfrac{18}{7}\right)$
**59.** (a)

(b) $a = 2\sqrt{3}, b = 2, c = 2\sqrt{2}$
(c) auxiliary circle: $x^2 + y^2 = 12$

(d) $x + y = 4$
(e)

(f) $y = x + 2\sqrt{2}$

## Exercise Set 11.5

**1.** vertices: $(\pm 2, 0)$; length of transverse axis: 4; length of conjugate axis: 2; asymptotes: $y = \pm\tfrac{1}{2}x$; foci: $(\pm\sqrt{5}, 0)$; eccentricity: $\sqrt{5}/2$

**3.** vertices: $(0, \pm 2)$; length of transverse axis: 4; length of conjugate axis: 2; asymptotes: $y = \pm 2x$; foci: $(0, \pm\sqrt{5})$; eccentricity: $\sqrt{5}/2$

**5.** vertices: $(\pm 5, 0)$; length of transverse axis: 10; length of conjugate axis: 8; asymptotes: $y = \pm\tfrac{4}{5}x$; foci: $(\pm\sqrt{41}, 0)$; eccentricity: $\sqrt{41}/5$

**7.** vertices: $(0, \pm\frac{\sqrt{2}}{2})$; length of transverse axis: $\sqrt{2}$; length of conjugate axis: $\frac{2\sqrt{3}}{3}$; asymptotes: $y = \pm\frac{\sqrt{6}}{2}x$; foci: $(0, \pm\frac{\sqrt{30}}{6})$; eccentricity: $\sqrt{15}/3$

$$\frac{y^2}{1/2} - \frac{x^2}{1/3} = 1$$

**9.** vertices: $(0, \pm 5)$; length of transverse axis: 10; length of conjugate axis: 4; asymptotes: $y = \pm\frac{5}{2}x$; foci: $(0, \pm\sqrt{29})$; eccentricity: $\sqrt{29}/5$

$$\frac{y^2}{25} - \frac{x^2}{4} = 1$$

**11.** center: $(5, -1)$; vertices: $(10, -1)$ and $(0, -1)$; length of transverse axis: 10; length of conjugate axis: 6; asymptotes: $y = \frac{3}{5}x - 4$ and $y = -\frac{3}{5}x + 2$; foci: $(5 \pm \sqrt{34}, -1)$; eccentricity: $\sqrt{34}/5$

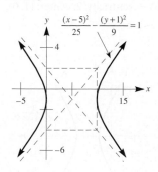

$$\frac{(x-5)^2}{25} - \frac{(y+1)^2}{9} = 1$$

**13.** center: $(1, 2)$; vertices: $(1, 4)$ and $(1, 0)$; length of transverse axis: 4; length of conjugate axis: 2; asymptotes: $y = 2x$ and $y = -2x + 4$; foci: $(1, 2 \pm \sqrt{5})$; eccentricity: $\sqrt{5}/2$

$$\frac{(y-2)^2}{4} - \frac{(x-1)^2}{1} = 1$$

**15.** center: $(-3, 4)$; vertices: $(1, 4)$ and $(-7, 4)$; length of transverse axis: 8; length of conjugate axis: 8; asymptotes: $y = x + 7$ and $y = -x + 1$; foci: $(-3 \pm 4\sqrt{2}, 4)$; eccentricity: $\sqrt{2}$

$$\frac{(x+3)^2}{16} - \frac{(y-4)^2}{16} = 1$$

**17.** center: $(0, 1)$; vertices: $(2, 1)$ and $(-2, 1)$; length of transverse axis: 4; length of conjugate axis: 4; asymptotes: $y = x + 1$ and $y = -x + 1$; foci: $(\pm 2\sqrt{2}, 1)$; eccentricity: $\sqrt{2}$

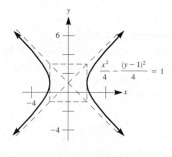

$$\frac{x^2}{4} - \frac{(y-1)^2}{4} = 1$$

**19.** center: $(2, 1)$; vertices: $(5, 1)$ and $(-1, 1)$; length of transverse axis: 6; length of conjugate axis: 6; asymptotes: $y = x - 1$ and $y = -x + 3$; foci: $(2 \pm 3\sqrt{2}, 1)$; eccentricity: $\sqrt{2}$

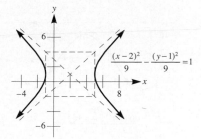

$$\frac{(x-2)^2}{9} - \frac{(y-1)^2}{9} = 1$$

**21.** center: $(0, -4)$; vertices: $(0, 1)$ and $(0, -9)$; length of transverse axis: 10; length of conjugate axis: 2; asymptotes: $y = 5x - 4$ and $y = -5x - 4$; foci: $(0, -4 \pm \sqrt{26})$; eccentricity: $\sqrt{26}/5$

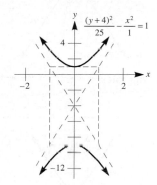

$$\frac{(y+4)^2}{25} - \frac{x^2}{1} = 1$$

**23.** degenerate hyperbola

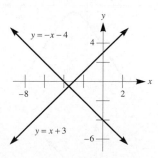

$$y = -x - 4$$
$$y = x + 3$$

**27.** $15x^2 - y^2 = 15$   **29.** $x^2 - 4y^2 = 4$
**31.** $2x^2 - 5y^2 = 10$
**33.** $y^2 - 32x^2 = 49$   **35.** $y^2 - 9x^2 = 9$
**39. (b)** $(0, \pm 6)$   **(c)** $F_1P = 5$, $F_2P = 13$

**41. (b)**

$$\frac{(y-3)^2}{25} - \frac{(x-4)^2}{9} = 1$$

$$\frac{(y-3)^2}{25} - \frac{(x-4)^2}{9} = 1$$

**(c)** asymptotes: $y = \pm\frac{5}{3}(x - 4) + 3$

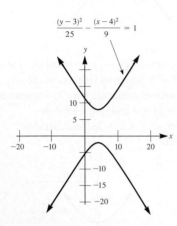

$$\frac{(y-3)^2}{25} - \frac{(x-4)^2}{9} = 1$$

**43.**

$$y = \frac{1}{4}x \pm \frac{1}{4}\sqrt{9x^2 - 8}$$

**51.** intersection point: $\left(\frac{51}{8}, \frac{15}{2}\right)$

$$y = \frac{4}{3}x - 1$$

$$\left(\frac{51}{8}, \frac{15}{2}\right)$$

$$16x^2 - 9y^2 = 144$$

**53.** $y = 2x - 2$

## Exercise Set 11.6

**1.** $F_1P = \dfrac{6\sqrt{19} - 8\sqrt{6}}{3}$,

$F_2P = \dfrac{6\sqrt{19} + 8\sqrt{6}}{3}$

**3.** $F_1P = 15 + 6\sqrt{2}, F_2P = 15 - 6\sqrt{2}$

**5. (a)** foci: $(\pm\sqrt{7}, 0)$; eccentricity: $\sqrt{7}/4$; directrices: $x = \pm 16\sqrt{7}/7$
**(b)** foci: $(\pm 5, 0)$; eccentricity: $\frac{5}{4}$; directrices: $x = \pm\frac{16}{5}$ **7. (a)** foci: $(\pm 1, 0)$; eccentricity: $\sqrt{13}/13$; directrices: $x = \pm 13$ **(b)** foci: $(\pm 5, 0)$; eccentricity: $5\sqrt{13}/13$; directrices: $x = \pm\frac{13}{5}$ **9. (a)** foci: $(\pm\sqrt{11}, 0)$; eccentricity: $\sqrt{11}/6$; directrices: $x = \pm 36\sqrt{11}/11$
**(b)** foci: $(\pm\sqrt{61}, 0)$; eccentricity: $\sqrt{61}/6$; directrices: $x = \pm 36\sqrt{61}/61$
**11.** $3x^2 + 4y^2 = 12$
**13.** $x^2 - y^2 = 2$

## Exercise Set 11.7

**1. (a)** eccentricity: $\frac{2}{3}$; center: $\left(-\frac{12}{5}, 0\right)$; endpoints of major axis: $\left(\frac{6}{5}, 0\right)$ and $(-6, 0)$; endpoints of minor axis: $\left(-\frac{12}{5}, \pm\frac{6\sqrt{5}}{5}\right)$

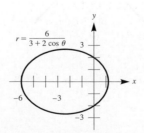

$$r = \frac{6}{3 + 2\cos\theta}$$

**(b)** eccentricity: $\frac{2}{3}$; center: $\left(\frac{12}{5}, 0\right)$; endpoints of major axis: $(6, 0)$ and $\left(-\frac{6}{5}, 0\right)$; endpoints of minor axis: $\left(\frac{12}{5}, \pm\frac{6\sqrt{5}}{5}\right)$

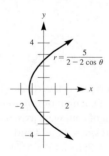

$$r = \frac{6}{3 - 2\cos\theta}$$

**3. (a)** vertex: $\left(\frac{5}{4}, 0\right)$; directrix: $x = \frac{5}{2}$

$$r = \frac{5}{2 + 2\cos\theta}$$

**(b)** vertex: $\left(-\frac{5}{4}, 0\right)$; directrix: $x = -\frac{5}{2}$

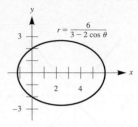

$$r = \frac{5}{2 - 2\cos\theta}$$

**5. (a)** eccentricity: 2; center: $(1, 0)$; $a = \frac{1}{2}; b = \frac{1}{2}\sqrt{3}; c = 1$

$$r = \frac{3}{2 + 4\cos\theta}$$

**(b)** eccentricity: 2; center: $(-1, 0)$; $a = \frac{1}{2}$; $b = \frac{1}{2}\sqrt{3}$; $c = 1$

$$r = \frac{3}{2 - 4\cos\theta}$$

**7.** center: $\left(-\frac{72}{5}, 0\right)$; eccentricity: $\frac{3}{2}$; length of traverse axis: $\frac{96}{5}$; length of conjugate axis: $\frac{48}{5}\sqrt{5}$

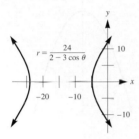

$$r = \frac{24}{2 - 3\cos\theta}$$

**9.** center: $\left(0, -\frac{3}{2}\right)$; eccentricity: $\frac{3}{5}$; length of major axis: 5; length of minor axis: 4

$$r = \frac{8}{5 + 3\sin\theta}$$

**11.** vertex: $\left(0, -\frac{6}{5}\right)$; directrix: $y = -\frac{12}{5}$

$$r = \frac{12}{5 - 5\sin\theta}$$

**13.** center: $\left(-\frac{5}{2}, 0\right)$; eccentricity: $\frac{5}{7}$; length of major axis: 7; length of minor axis: $2\sqrt{6}$

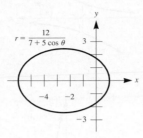

$$r = \frac{12}{7 + 5\cos\theta}$$

**15.** vertex: $\left(0, \frac{2}{5}\right)$; directrix: $y = \frac{4}{5}$

$$r = \frac{4}{5 + 5\sin\theta}$$

**17.** center: $(-6, 0)$; eccentricity: 2; length of transverse axis: 6; length of conjugate axis: $6\sqrt{3}$

$$r = \frac{9}{1 - 2\cos\theta}$$

**Exercise Set 11.8**

**1.** $\left(\frac{1}{2}, \frac{3\sqrt{3}}{2}\right)$   **3.** $(2, 0)$   **5.** $\left(-\frac{31}{13}, \frac{27}{13}\right)$
**7.** $\sin\theta = \frac{4}{5}$, $\cos\theta = \frac{3}{5}$
**9.** $\sin\theta = \frac{3}{5}$, $\cos\theta = \frac{4}{5}$
**11.** $\sin\theta = \frac{\sqrt{3}}{2}$, $\cos\theta = \frac{1}{2}$
**13.** $\sin\theta = \frac{7}{34}\sqrt{2}$, $\cos\theta = \frac{23}{34}\sqrt{2}$

**15.** $(x')^2 - (y')^2 = 9$

**17.**

$$\frac{(x')^2}{1/9} - \frac{(y')^2}{1} = 1$$

**19.**

$$y = -\frac{1}{2}x + \frac{1}{2}$$
$$y = -\frac{1}{2}x - \frac{1}{2}$$

**21.**

$$(y')^2 = 20x'$$

**23.**

$$\frac{(x'+2\sqrt{5}/5)^2}{1} - \frac{(y'+\sqrt{5}/5)^2}{4} = 1$$

**25.**

$$\frac{(x'-1)^2}{1} + \frac{(y'+1)^2}{1/2} = 1$$

**27.**

$(y'-\sqrt{2})^2 = 2\sqrt{2}(x'-11\sqrt{2}/2)$

**29.**

$$\frac{(x')^2}{1} + \frac{(y')^2}{7/2} = 1$$

**31.**

$$\frac{(x')^2}{16} + \frac{(y')^2}{4} = 1$$

**33.**

$$\frac{(y')^2}{4} - \frac{(x')^2}{36} = 1$$

**35.**

$(x')^2 = 4y'$

**37.**

$$\frac{(x')^2}{6} + \frac{(y')^2}{2/3} = 1$$

**39.** no graph
**41.** For $0° < \theta < 90°$, $0° < 2\theta < 180°$, which gives a full period of cot and Range cot $= (-\infty, \infty)$.
**43.** $x = x' \cos\theta - y' \sin\theta$;
$y = x' \sin\theta + y' \cos\theta$

## Chapter 11 Review Exercises
**17.** $146.3°$   **19.** $53\sqrt{61}/61$
**23. (a)** $y^2 = 16x$   **(b)** $x^2 = 16y$
**25.** $x^2 = 12y$   **27.** $15x^2 + 16y^2 = 960$
**29.** $25x^2 + 9y^2 = 900$
**31.** $3x^2 + 5y^2 = 30$
**33.** $5y^2 - 20x^2 = 36$
**35.** $36x^2 - 64y^2 = 81$

**37.** vertex: $(0, 0)$; focus: $(0, \frac{5}{2})$;
directrix: $y = -\frac{5}{2}$; focal width: 10

**39.** vertex: $(0, 3)$; focus: $(0, 0)$;
directrix: $y = 6$; focal width: 12

**41.** vertex: $(1, 1)$; focus: $(0, 1)$;
directrix: $x = 2$; focal width: 4

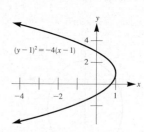

**43.** center: $(0, 0)$; length of major axis: 12; length of minor axis: 8; foci: $(\pm 2\sqrt{5}, 0)$; eccentricity: $\sqrt{5}/3$

**45.** center: $(0, 0)$; length of major axis: 6; length of minor axis: 2; foci: $(0, \pm 2\sqrt{2})$; eccentricity: $2\sqrt{2}/3$

$$\frac{x^2}{1} + \frac{y^2}{9} = 1$$

**47.** center: $(-3, 0)$; lengths of major and minor axes: 6; focus: $(-3, 0)$; eccentricity: 0

$$\frac{(x+3)^2}{9} + \frac{y^2}{9} = 1$$

**49.** center: $(0, 0)$; vertices: $(\pm 6, 0)$; asymptotes: $y = \pm \frac{2}{3}x$; foci: $(\pm 2\sqrt{13}, 0)$; eccentricity: $\sqrt{13}/3$

$$\frac{x^2}{36} - \frac{y^2}{16} = 1$$

**51.** center: $(0, 0)$; vertices: $(0, \pm 1)$; asymptotes: $y = \pm \frac{1}{3}x$; foci: $(0, \pm \sqrt{10})$; eccentricity: $\sqrt{10}$

$$\frac{y^2}{1} - \frac{x^2}{9} = 1$$

**53.** center: $(0, -3)$; vertices: $(0, 0)$ and $(0, -6)$; asymptotes: $y = x - 3$ and $y = -x - 3$; foci: $(0, -3 \pm 3\sqrt{2})$; eccentricity: $\sqrt{2}$

$$\frac{(y+3)^2}{9} - \frac{x^2}{9} = 1$$

**55.** parabola: vertex: $(4, 4)$; axis of symmetry: $y = 4$; focus: $(8, 4)$; directrix: $x = 0$

$$(y - 4)^2 = 16(x - 4)$$

**57.** ellipse: center: $(-2, 3)$; length of major axis: 8; length of minor axis: 6; foci: $(-2, 3 \pm \sqrt{7})$

$$\frac{(x+2)^2}{9} + \frac{(y-3)^2}{16} = 1$$

**59.** parabola: vertex: $(-3, 2)$; axis of symmetry: $x = -3$; focus: $(-3, 5)$; directrix: $y = -1$

$$(x + 3)^2 = 12(y - 2)$$

**61.** hyperbola: center: $(2, 1)$; vertices: $(5, 1)$ and $(-1, 1)$; asymptotes: $y = x - 1$ and $y = -x + 3$; foci: $(2 \pm 3\sqrt{2}, 1)$

$$\frac{(x-2)^2}{9} - \frac{(y-1)^2}{9} = 1$$

**63.** parabola: vertex: $(0, 6)$; axis of symmetry: $x = 0$; focus: $(0, \frac{11}{2})$; directrix: $y = \frac{13}{2}$

$$x^2 = 2(y - 6)$$

**65.** ellipse: center: $(0, 5)$; length of major axis: 8; length of minor axis: 2; foci: $(\pm \sqrt{15}, 5)$

$$\frac{x^2}{16} + \frac{(y-5)^2}{1} = 1$$

**67.** two lines: $4x - 5y = -2$ and $4x + 5y = 18$

## Chapter 11 Test

**1.** focus: $(-3, 0)$; directrix: $x = 3$

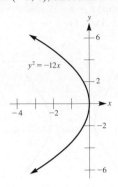

**2.** asymptotes: $y = \pm\frac{1}{2}x$;
foci: $(\pm\sqrt{5}, 0)$

**3.** $e = 0.001$; 19.078 AU
**4. (a)** $\theta = 60°$
**(b)**

**5.** $30°$  **6.** $\dfrac{x^2}{12} + \dfrac{y^2}{16} = 1$

**7.** $m = \pm\sqrt{15}/15$

**8.** $\sqrt{3}x - y - 2\sqrt{3} = 0$

**9.** $\dfrac{x^2}{3} - \dfrac{y^2}{1} = 1$  **10. (b)** 64

**11.** length of major axis: 10;
length of minor axis: 4; foci: $(\pm\sqrt{21}, 0)$

**12.** $3\sqrt{5}/5$

**13.**

**14.**

**15.** ellipse

**16.** focal width: 8; vertex: $(1, 2)$

**17. (a)** $x = \pm36\sqrt{11}/11$

**(b)** $F_1P = \dfrac{12 + \sqrt{11}}{2}$;

$F_2P = \dfrac{12 - \sqrt{11}}{2}$

**18.** $y = \frac{1}{6}x + \frac{13}{3}$  **19.** $y = 4x - 8$
**20.** focal length = 12.8 m;
focal ratio = 0.4

# CHAPTER 12
## Exercise Set 12.1

**1.**

| $i^2$ | $i^3$ | $i^4$ | $i^5$ | $i^6$ | $i^7$ | $i^8$ |
|---|---|---|---|---|---|---|
| $-1$ | $-i$ | $1$ | $i$ | $-1$ | $-i$ | $1$ |

**3. (a)** real part: 4; imaginary part: 5
**(b)** real part: 4; imaginary part: $-5$
**(c)** real part: $\frac{1}{2}$; imaginary part: $-1$
**(d)** real part: 0; imaginary part: 16
**5.** $c = 4, d = -3$  **7. (a)** $14 - 4i$
**(b)** $-4 - 8i$  **9. (a)** $19 - 17i$
**(b)** $19 - 17i$  **(c)** $\frac{11}{26} - \frac{23}{26}i$
**(d)** $\frac{11}{25} + \frac{23}{25}i$  **11. (a)** $11 - i$
**(b)** $11 - 7i$  **(c)** 4  **13.** $4 - 2i$
**15.** $30 + 19i$  **17.** 13
**19.** $-191 - 163i$  **21.** $19 - 4i$
**23.** $-70 + 84i$  **25.** $539 + 1140i$
**27.** $-46 + 9i$  **29.** $\frac{6}{97} + \frac{35}{97}i$
**31.** $\frac{6}{97} - \frac{35}{97}i$  **33.** $-\frac{5}{13} + \frac{12}{13}i$
**35.** $-4$  **37.** $\frac{1}{26} + \frac{5}{26}i$  **39.** $-i$
**41.** $i$  **43.** $-1$  **45.** $12i$
**47.** $-3\sqrt{5}i$  **49.** $-35$  **51.** $12\sqrt{2}i$
**53. (a)** $-3$  **(b)** $x = \dfrac{1}{2} \pm \dfrac{\sqrt{3}}{2}i$
**55. (a)** $-36$  **(b)** $z = -\frac{1}{5} \pm \frac{3}{5}i$
**57. (a)** $-23$  **(b)** $z = -\dfrac{3}{4} \pm \dfrac{\sqrt{23}}{4}i$
**59. (a)** $-\frac{29}{48}$  **(b)** $z = \dfrac{3}{4} \pm \dfrac{\sqrt{87}}{4}i$
**61. (a)** 0  **(b)** This verifies the
solution.
**63. (a)** $z + w = (a + c) + (b + d)i$
**(b)** $z - w = (a - c) + (b - d)i$
**(c)** $zw = (ac - bd) + (bc + ad)i$
**(d)** $\dfrac{z}{w} = \dfrac{ac + bd}{c^2 + d^2} + \dfrac{bc - ad}{c^2 + d^2}i$

**71.** $x = 3, \pm 2i$   **73.** $x = \pm 3,$
$\sqrt{2} \pm \sqrt{2}i, -\sqrt{2} \pm \sqrt{2}i$   **75.** real
part: $\dfrac{2a^2 - 2b^2}{a^2 + b^2}$; imaginary part: $0$
**77.** real part: $0$

## Exercise Set 12.2
**1.** quotient: $x - 5$; remainder: $-11$;
$x^2 - 8x + 4 = (x - 3)(x - 5) - 11$
**3.** quotient: $x - 11$; remainder: $53$;
$x^2 - 6x - 2 = (x + 5)(x - 11) + 53$
**5.** quotient: $3x^2 - \frac{3}{2}x - \frac{1}{4}$;
remainder: $\frac{13}{4}$; $6x^3 - 2x + 3 =$
$(2x + 1)(3x^2 - \frac{3}{2}x - \frac{1}{4}) + \frac{13}{4}$
**7.** quotient: $x^4 - 3x^3 + 9x^2 -$
$27x + 81$; remainder: $-241$;
$x^5 + 2 = (x + 3)(x^4 - 3x^3 +$
$9x^2 - 27x + 81) - 241$
**9.** quotient: $x^5 + 2x^4 + 4x^3 +$
$8x^2 + 16x + 32$; remainder: $0$;
$x^6 - 64 = (x - 2)(x^5 + 2x^4 +$
$4x^3 + 8x^2 + 16x + 32) + 0$
**11.** quotient: $5x^2 + 15x + 17$;
remainder: $-24x - 83$;
$5x^4 - 3x^2 + 2 = (x^2 - 3x + 5) \times$
$(5x^2 + 15x + 17) + (-24x - 83)$
**13.** quotient: $3y - 19$;
remainder: $89y + 35$;
$3y^3 - 4y^2 - 3 = (y^2 + 5y + 2) \times$
$(3y - 19) + (89y + 35)$
**15.** quotient: $t^2 - 2t - 4$;
remainder: $0$;
$t^4 - 4t^3 + 4t^2 - 16 = (t^2 - 2t + 4) \times$
$(t^2 - 2t - 4) + 0$
**17.** quotient: $z^4 + z^3 + z^2 + z + 1$;
remainder: $0$; $z^5 - 1 = (z - 1) \times$
$(z^4 + z^3 + z^2 + z + 1) + 0$
**19.** quotient: $ax + (b + ar)$;
remainder: $c + r(b + ar) =$
$ar^2 + br + c$; $ax^2 + bx + c = (x - r) \times$
$(ax + (b + ar)) + (ar^2 + br + c)$
**21.** quotient: $x - 1$; remainder: $-7$;
$x^2 - 6x - 2 = (x - 5)(x - 1) - 7$
**23.** quotient: $4x - 5$; remainder: $0$;
$4x^2 - x - 5 = (x + 1)(4x - 5) + 0$
**25.** quotient: $6x^2 + 19x + 78$;
remainder: $313$; $6x^3 - 5x^2 + 2x + 1 =$
$(x - 4)(6x^2 + 19x + 78) + 313$

**27.** quotient: $x^2 + 2x + 4$;
remainder: $7$; $x^3 - 1 = (x - 2) \times$
$(x^2 + 2x + 4) + 7$   **29.** quotient:
$x^4 - 2x^3 + 4x^2 - 8x + 16$;
remainder: $-33$; $x^5 - 1 = (x + 2) \times$
$(x^4 - 2x^3 + 4x^2 - 8x + 16) - 33$
**31.** quotient: $x^3 - 10x^2 + 40x - 160$;
remainder: $642$; $x^4 - 6x^3 + 2 =$
$(x + 4)(x^3 - 10x^2 + 40x - 160)$
$+ 642$   **33.** quotient: $x^2 + 6x + 57$;
remainder: $576$;
$x^3 - 4x^2 - 3x + 6 = (x - 10) \times$
$(x^2 + 6x + 57) + 576$
**35.** quotient: $x^2 - 6x + 30$;
remainder: $-150$; $x^3 - x^2 =$
$(x + 5)(x^2 - 6x + 30) - 150$
**37.** quotient: $54x^2 + 9x - 21$;
remainder: $0$;
$54x^3 - 27x^2 - 27x + 14 =$
$(x - \frac{2}{3})(54x^2 + 9x - 21) + 0$
**39.** quotient: $x^3 + 3x^2 + 12x + 36$;
remainder: $120$; $x^4 + 3x^2 + 12 =$
$(x - 3)(x^3 + 3x^2 + 12x + 36) + 120$
**41.** $(x - 2)(x^4 + 2x^3 + 4x^2 + 8x + 16)$
**43.** $(z - 3)(z^3 + 3z^2 + 9z + 27)$
**45.** quotient: $2x$; remainder: $1$
**47.** quotient: $3x^2 - \frac{3}{2}x + \frac{9}{4}$;
remainder: $\frac{1}{4}$   **49.** $k = 4$
**53.** quotient: $x + (-4 + i)$;
remainder: $-4i$   **55.** quotient:
$x + (-1 + i)$; remainder: $0$
**57.** $-6\sqrt{3} + 57$   **59.** $0$

## Exercise Set 12.3
**1.** yes   **3.** yes   **5.** yes   **7.** is a zero
**9.** is a zero   **11.** not a zero
**13. (a)** is a zero   **(b)** not a zero
**15.** $1, 2$ (multiplicity 3), $3$
**17. (a)** multiplicity at $-1$: $2$

$y = (x + 1)^2 (x + 2)$

**(b)** multiplicity at $-2$: $3$

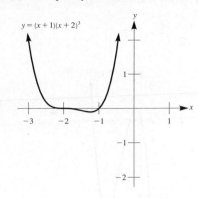
$y = (x + 1)(x + 2)^3$

**(c)** multiplicity at $-1$: $2$; multiplicity
at $-2$: $3$

$y = (x + 1)^2(x + 2)^3$

**19.** $f(-3) = -170$
**21.** $f(\frac{1}{2}) = -9$
**23.** $f(-\sqrt{2}) = -3\sqrt{2} - 2$
**25.** $x = -1, \dfrac{1 \pm i}{2}$   **27.** $x = \pm 3, 4$
**29.** $x = 1, -1 \pm \sqrt{6}$
**31.** $x = -2, \frac{2}{3}, 3$   **33.** $x = -\frac{3}{2}, \dfrac{1 \pm \sqrt{5}}{2}$
**35.** $x = 0, 5$   **37.** $x = -4, 3$
**39.** $x = -5, 2 - \sqrt{2} \approx 0.59,$
$2 + \sqrt{2} \approx 3.41$

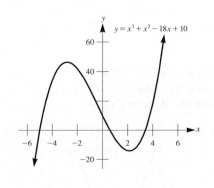
$y = x^3 + x^2 - 18x + 10$

**41.** $x = \frac{2}{3}, \frac{4 - \sqrt{14}}{2} \approx 0.13,$

$\frac{4 + \sqrt{14}}{2} \approx 3.87$

$y = 6x^3 - 28x^2 + 19x - 2$

**43.** $x = 1, -1, -\frac{1}{4}, 2$

$y = 4x^5 - 15x^4 + 8x^3 + 19x^2 - 12x - 4$

**45. (a)** 1.125    **(b)** $-0.046875$

**(c)** $t - 1$    **(d)** $t = 1, \dfrac{-1 \pm \sqrt{13}}{2}$

**47.** $x^3 - 4x^2 - 17x + 60 = 0$

**49.** $x^3 + 8x^2 + 13x + 6 = 0$

**51.** no such polynomial exists

**53. (a)** $g(r) = ar^3 + br^2 + cr + d$

**(b)** remainder: $ar^3 + br^2 + cr + d$

**55.** is a zero    **57.** $a = -1, b = -1$

**59.** $b = \pm 3\sqrt{2}/2$

**61.** $x = 2$ (multiplicity 2), $-4$

## Exercise Set 12.4

**1. (a)** yes    **(b)** yes    **(c)** yes

**(d)** no    **3.** no real roots

$f(x) = x^2 - 3x + 2.26$

**5.** three real roots

$f(x) = x^3 - 3x^2 + 3$

**7.** no real roots

$f(x) = x^4 + x^3 + x^2 + x + 1$

**9.** one real root

$f(x) = 0.2x^3 + 4.4x^2 - 109x - 1$

**11.** $[x - (-1)](x - 3)$

**13.** $4(x - \frac{1}{4})[x - (-6)]$

**15.** $[x - (-\sqrt{5})](x - \sqrt{5})$

**17.** $(x - 0)(x - (-3))(x - 3)$

$(x - (-\sqrt{2}i))(x - \sqrt{2}i)$

**19.** $f(x) = x^3 + x^2 - 5x + 3$

**21.** $f(x) = x^4 - 16$

**23.** $f(x) = x^6 + 10x^4 - 87x^2 + 144$

**25. (a)** $f(x) = x^4 - 4x^3 + 3x^2$

**(b)**

$f(x) = x^2(x - 1)(x - 3)$

**27. (a)** $f(x) = x(x - 1)^2(x - 3)^2$

$f(x) = x(x - 1)^2(x - 3)^2$

**29. (a)** $f(x) = x^2(x - 1)(x - 3)^3$

**(b)**

$f(x) = x^2(x - 1)(x - 3)^3$

**31.** $f(x) = -\frac{5}{42}x^2 + \frac{25}{42}x + \frac{30}{7}$

**33. (a)** $f(x) = \frac{1}{30}x^3 - \frac{19}{30}x + 1$

**(b)**

$f(x) = \frac{1}{30}(x^3 - 19x + 30)$

**35.** $x^2 + (i + \sqrt{3})x + i\sqrt{3} = 0$

**37.** $x^2 - 3x - 54 = 0$

**39.** $x^2 - 2x - 4 = 0$    **41.** $x^2 - 2ax + a^2 - b = 0$    **43. (a)** $x = 4$

**(b)**

$$y = x^3 + 3x - 76$$

**45.** $(x + 2 - 2i)(x + 2 + 2i) \times$
$(x - 2 - 2i)(x - 2 + 2i)$
**49.** $x = 5$ (multiplicity 2), $-10$
**51. (a)** $4x^2 + 2x - 1 = 0$

## Exercise Set 12.5

**1. (a)** see text **(b)** $\pm 1, \pm 11$
**3. (a)** The possible rational roots are
$\pm 1, \pm 5$, so there cannot be a rational
root larger than 5. No, 5 is not a root.
**(b)** The possible rational roots are $\pm 1$,
$\pm 5$, so 2 cannot be a root.
**(c)**

$$y = x^5 - 14x - 5$$

**5.** $\pm 1, \pm \frac{1}{2}, \pm \frac{1}{4}, \pm 3, \pm \frac{3}{2}, \pm \frac{3}{4}$
**7.** $\pm 1, \pm \frac{1}{2}, \pm \frac{1}{4}, \pm \frac{1}{8}, \pm 3, \pm \frac{3}{2}, \pm \frac{3}{4}, \pm \frac{3}{8}, \pm 9,$
$\pm \frac{9}{2}, \pm \frac{9}{4}, \pm \frac{9}{8}$
**9.** $\pm 1, \pm \frac{1}{2}, \pm 2, \pm 3, \pm \frac{3}{2}, \pm 6$
**17.** $x = 1, -1, -3$ **19.** $x = -\frac{1}{4}, \pm \sqrt{5}$
**21.** $x = -1, -\frac{2}{3}, -\frac{1}{3}$
**23.** $x = 1, -1, \dfrac{-1 \pm \sqrt{97}}{2}$
**25.** $x = 1$ (multiplicity 4)
**27.** $x = 1, -\frac{4}{3}, 6$ **29. (a)** 2 is an upper
bound, $-1$ is a lower bound
**(b)** 2 is an upper bound, $-1$ is a lower
bound **(c)** 6 is an upper bound, $-2$ is
a lower bound
**31.** between 0.68 and 0.69
**33.** between 2.88 and 2.89
**35.** between 4.31 and 4.32
**37. (a)** between $-3$ and $-2$
**(b)** between $-2.148$ and $-2.147$

**39. (a)** between $-6$ and $-5$
**(b)** between $-5.265$ and $-5.264$
**41. (b)** $A$ and $C$ have a common factor
of 5, so the result does not apply.
**(c)** $x = p/q$ is a root of the equation.
**43.** $x \approx 1.769$

$$y = 2x - 3$$
$$y = x^3 - 5$$

**45.** $x \approx 1.310$

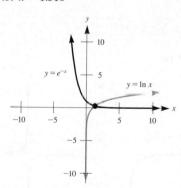

$$y = e^{-x}$$
$$y = \ln x$$

**47.** $x = \sqrt[3]{200} \approx 5.848$

$$y = x^5 + \tfrac{1}{2}x^3$$
$$y = x^5 + 100$$

**55.** $p = 3, x = 1$
**57. (a)** $x = \dfrac{-1 \pm i\sqrt{11}}{2}$ **59.** $b = 2$

## Exercise Set 12.6

**1.** $7 + 2i$ **3.** $5 - 2i, 3$ **5.** $-2 - i,$
$-3$ (multiplicity 2) **7.** $6 + 5i, -\frac{1}{4}$

**9.** $4 - \sqrt{2}i, \pm \frac{3i}{2}$ **11.** $10 - 2i, 1 \pm \sqrt{5}$
**13.** $\dfrac{1 - i\sqrt{2}}{3}, \frac{2}{5}$ **15.** $3 + 2i, -1 - i,$
$-1 \pm \sqrt{2}$ **17.** $x^2 - 2x - 5 = 0$
**19.** $x^2 - \frac{4}{3}x - \frac{2}{3} = 0$
**21. (c)** one positive real root

$$f(x) = 2x^4 - 3x^3 + 12x^2 + 22x - 60$$

**(d)** $-2, \frac{3}{2}$ **23. (b)** one negative
real root

$$f(x) = x^3 + 8x + 5$$

**(c)** $-0.5982$
**(d)** $x = \sqrt[3]{-2.5 + \sqrt{\frac{2723}{108}}} -$
$\sqrt[3]{2.5 + \sqrt{\frac{2723}{108}}} \approx -0.5982$
**25.** 2 complex roots and 1 negative
real root **27.** 4 complex roots and
1 negative real root **29.** 2 complex
roots, 1 positive real root and
1 negative real root **31.** either
1 positive real root and 2 negative real
roots, or 1 positive real root and
2 complex roots **33.** 1 positive real
root, 1 negative real root and
6 complex roots **35.** 1 positive real
root and 8 complex roots
**37.** 1 positive real root, 1 negative real
root and 6 complex roots
**39.** 1 positive real root, 1 negative real
root and 4 complex roots
**41.** 1 positive real root, 1 negative real
root and 2 complex roots
**43. (a)** $f(x) = x^4 + 2x^2 + 49$
**(b)** $-\sqrt{3} \pm 2i, \sqrt{3} - 2i$

## Exercise Set 12.7

**1. (a)** $A = 2, B = 5$ **(b)** $A = 2,$
$B = 5$ **3. (a)** $A = 4, B = -1$
**(b)** $A = 4, B = -1$
**5. (a)** $A = -\frac{1}{4}, B = \frac{3}{4}$
**(b)** $A = -\frac{1}{4}, B = \frac{3}{4}$
**7.** $A = 8, B = -21$
**9.** $A = -\frac{1}{5}, B = \frac{34}{5}$
**11.** $A = 4, B = -1, C = 6$
**13.** $A = \frac{2}{5}, B = \frac{3}{5}, C = -\frac{3}{5}$
**15.** $A = 1, B = -1, C = 1$
**17.** $A = \frac{10}{3}, B = \frac{1}{6}, C = -\frac{1}{2}$
**19.** $A = 4, B = 1, C = -5$
**21.** $A = 0, B = 1, C = 0, D = -4$
**23. (a)**

**(b)**

**(c)** $\dfrac{2x + 5}{(x - 4)(x + 3)} = \dfrac{13/7}{x - 4} + \dfrac{1/7}{x + 3}$
**25. (a)** $A = 3, B = 4, C = -1$
**(b)** $B = 4, C = -1$
**27. (a)** The possible rational roots
are $-1$ and $1$, neither of which
are roots.

**(b)**

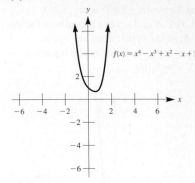

**(c)** $\left(x^2 + \dfrac{-1 + \sqrt{5}}{2}x + 1\right) \times$

$\left(x^2 + \dfrac{-1 - \sqrt{5}}{2}x + 1\right)$

**(d)** $x = \dfrac{1 - \sqrt{5} \pm i\sqrt{10 + 2\sqrt{5}}}{4},$

$\dfrac{1 + \sqrt{5} \pm i\sqrt{10 - 2\sqrt{5}}}{4}$

**29. (a)**

**(b)**

**(c)** $\dfrac{-1/48}{x + 2} + \dfrac{1/57}{x + 5} + \dfrac{1/304}{x - 14}$

## Exercise Set 12.8

**1. (a)** no **(b)** yes **3. (a)** no
**(b)** yes **5. (a)** $(x + 10)(x - 10)$
**(b)** $\dfrac{A}{x + 10} + \dfrac{B}{x - 10}$
**(c)** $\dfrac{4}{x + 10} + \dfrac{7}{x - 10}$

**7. (a)** $(x + \sqrt{5})(x - \sqrt{5})$
**(b)** $\dfrac{A}{x + \sqrt{5}} + \dfrac{B}{x - \sqrt{5}}$
**(c)** $\dfrac{5}{x + \sqrt{5}} + \dfrac{3}{x - \sqrt{5}}$
**9. (a)** $(x - 3)(x + 2)$
**(b)** $\dfrac{A}{x + 2} + \dfrac{B}{x - 3}$
**(c)** $\dfrac{-5}{x + 2} + \dfrac{12}{x - 3}$
**11. (a)** $(x - 3)(x - 2)(x + 2)$
**(b)** $\dfrac{A}{x - 3} + \dfrac{B}{x - 2} + \dfrac{C}{x + 2}$
**(c)** $\dfrac{8}{x - 3} + \dfrac{-2}{x - 2} + \dfrac{-3}{x + 2}$
**13. (a)** $x(x^2 + x + 1)$
**(b)** $\dfrac{A}{x} + \dfrac{Bx + C}{x^2 + x + 1}$
**(c)** $\dfrac{5}{x} + \dfrac{-3}{x^2 + x + 1}$
**15. (a)** $(x^2 + 1)^2$
**(b)** $\dfrac{Ax + B}{x^2 + 1} + \dfrac{Cx + D}{(x^2 + 1)^2}$
**(c)** $\dfrac{2x}{x^2 + 1} + \dfrac{3x - 4}{(x^2 + 1)^2}$
**17.** $\dfrac{\frac{19}{28}}{x - 6} + \dfrac{-\frac{3}{7}}{x + 1} + \dfrac{\frac{3}{4}}{x + 2}$
**19.** $\dfrac{10}{3x - 5} + \dfrac{-7}{2x - 3}$
**21.** $\dfrac{-1/5}{x} + \dfrac{(1 - 2\sqrt{5})/10}{x + \sqrt{5}} +$
$\dfrac{(1 + 2\sqrt{5}/10}{x - \sqrt{5}}$
**23.** $\dfrac{x}{x^2 + 4} + \dfrac{-4x + 2}{(x^2 + 4)^2}$
**25.** $\dfrac{\frac{3}{125}}{x} + \dfrac{\frac{122}{125}}{x - 5} + \dfrac{\frac{253}{25}}{(x - 5)^2} +$
$\dfrac{\frac{127}{5}}{(x - 5)^3}$
**27.** $\dfrac{\frac{1}{3}}{x - 1} + \dfrac{-\frac{1}{3}x - \frac{2}{3}}{x^2 + x + 1}$
**29.** $\dfrac{3}{x} + \dfrac{-2}{x^2} + \dfrac{4}{x + 1} + \dfrac{3}{(x + 1)^2}$
**31.** $\dfrac{\frac{8}{27}}{x + 3} + \dfrac{\frac{11}{54}}{x - 3} + \dfrac{\frac{1}{2}x + \frac{5}{18}}{x^2 + 9}$
**33.** $\dfrac{-x}{x^2 + 1} + \dfrac{x + 1}{x^2 + x + 1}$
**35.** $x = -3, -1, 2$
**37. (b)** $C = -2, D = 0$
**39.** $6x + 8 + \dfrac{2}{x - 3} + \dfrac{-1}{x - 1}$

**41.** $x - 4 + \dfrac{-\frac{1}{8}}{x} + \dfrac{\frac{1}{8}}{x-2} +$

$\dfrac{\frac{3}{4}}{(x-2)^2} + \dfrac{\frac{5}{2}}{(x-2)^3}$

**43.** $x^2 + 2x + 5 + \dfrac{-\frac{1}{4}}{x+1} +$

$\dfrac{\frac{1}{4}}{x-1} + \dfrac{-\frac{1}{2}}{x^2+1}$

**47.** $\dfrac{(pa+q)/(a-b)}{x-a} +$

$\dfrac{(pb+q)/(b-a)}{x-b}$

**49.** $\dfrac{(pa+q)/2a}{x-a} + \dfrac{(pa-q)/2a}{x+a}$

**51.**

$\dfrac{a^2}{(a-b)(a-c)} + \dfrac{b^2}{(b-a)(b-c)} +$
$\dfrac{1-ax}{\;} \qquad \dfrac{1-bx}{\;}$

$\dfrac{c^2}{(c-a)(c-b)} +$
$\dfrac{1-cx}{\;}$

**53.** $\dfrac{\frac{\sqrt{2}}{4}x + \frac{1}{2}}{x^2 + \sqrt{2}x + 1} + \dfrac{-\frac{\sqrt{2}}{4}x + \frac{1}{2}}{x^2 - \sqrt{2}x + 1}$

## Chapter 12 Review Exercises

**1.** $q(x) = x^3 + x^2 - 3x + 1$, $R(x) = -1$
**3.** quotient: $x^3 + 3x^2 + 7x + 21$;
remainder: 71
**5.** quotient: $2x^2 - 13x + 46$;
remainder: $-187$   **7.** quotient:
$5x - 20$; remainder: 0
**9.** $f(10) = 99{,}904$
**11.** $f(\frac{1}{10}) = -\frac{999}{1000}$
**13.** $f(a-1) = a^3$
**15. (a)** $f(-0.3) \approx -0.24$
**(b)** $f(-0.39) \approx -0.007$
**(c)** $f(-0.394) \approx 0.00003$
**17.** $a = -5$   **19.** $a = -1, -2$
**23.** $\pm 1, \pm 2, \pm 3, \pm 6, \pm 9, \pm 18$
**25.** $\pm 1, \pm\frac{1}{2}, \pm 2, \pm 4, \pm 8$   **27.** $\pm p, \pm 1$
**29.** $2, -\frac{3}{2}, -1$
**31.** $\frac{5}{2}, -1 \pm \sqrt{3}$   **33.** $\frac{2}{3}, \dfrac{-1 \pm i\sqrt{3}}{2}$
**35.** $-1, -\sqrt{7}$ (multiplicity 2),
$\sqrt{7}$ (multiplicity 2)
**37.** 2 (multiplicity 2), 5
**39.** see text

**41.** $6(x - \frac{4}{3})[x - (-\frac{5}{2})]$
**43.** $(x-4)(x - (-\sqrt[3]{5})) \times$

$\left(x - \dfrac{\sqrt[3]{5} + i\sqrt{3\sqrt[3]{25}}}{2}\right) \times$

$\left(x - \dfrac{\sqrt[3]{5} - i\sqrt{3\sqrt[3]{25}}}{2}\right)$

**45.** $2 \pm 3i, 3$   **47.** $1 \pm i\sqrt{2}, \pm\sqrt{7}$
**49.** 1 positive real root and 2 complex
roots   **51.** 1 negative real root and
2 complex roots   **53.** 1 positive real
root, 1 negative real root and
2 complex roots   **55. (c)** $-1, \pm i$
**57.** between 0.82 and 0.83
**59. (c)** between 6.93 and 6.94
**61.** $x^2 - 8x + 11 = 0$
**63.** $x^4 - 12x^3 + 35x^2 + 60x - 200 = 0$
**65.** $x^4 - 4x^3 - 4x^2 + 16x - 8 = 0$
**67.** zeros: $0, 3, -1$

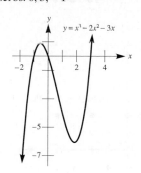

**69.** zeros: $0, -2, 2$

**71.** $5 + 6i$   **73.** 6   **75.** $\dfrac{1}{2} - \dfrac{\sqrt{3}}{2}i$
**77.** $3\sqrt{2} - 4\sqrt{2}i$   **81. (a)** $|6 + 2i| =$
$2\sqrt{10}, |6 - 2i| = 2\sqrt{10}$
**(b)** $|-3| = 3$
**87.** $\dfrac{-\frac{21}{20}}{10+x} + \dfrac{\frac{19}{20}}{10-x}$
**89.** $\dfrac{1}{x} + \dfrac{-1}{x+1} + \dfrac{-1}{(x+1)^2}$
**91.** $\dfrac{x}{x^2+3} + \dfrac{-3x+2}{(x^2+3)^2}$

**93. (a)** $(x^2 - x + 1)(x^2 - x - 1)$
**(b)** $\dfrac{\frac{1}{2}}{x^2 - x + 1} + \dfrac{x + \frac{1}{2}}{x^2 - x - 1}$

## Chapter 12 Test
**1.** $f(\frac{1}{2}) = -\frac{3}{2}$   **2.** $-3, 1 \pm \sqrt{6}$
**3.** $\pm 1, \pm\frac{1}{2}, \pm 2, \pm 3, \pm\frac{3}{2}, \pm 6$
**4.** $f(x) = 3x^2 + 21x - 24$
**5.** quotient: $4x^2 - 3x - 5$;
remainder: 8   **6.** see text
**7. (a)** 3 is an upper bound
**(b)** between 2.2 and 2.3   **8.** $1 \pm i$,
$3 \pm 2i, -2$   **9.** $q(x) = x^2 + 2x - 1$,
$R(x) = -3x + 7$
**10.** $2[x - (\frac{3}{2} + \frac{1}{2}i)][x - (\frac{3}{2} - \frac{1}{2}i)]$
**11. (a)** $\pm 1, \pm 2, \pm 3, \pm 4, \pm 6, \pm 8,$
$\pm 12, \pm 24$   **(c)** $x = 1$   **(d)** none
**12. (a)** $\frac{3}{2}$   **(b)** $\frac{3}{2}, \dfrac{-1 \pm i\sqrt{3}}{2}$
**13.** 1 positive real root, 1 negative real
root, and 2 complex roots
**14.** $x^3 + 6x + 20 = 0$
**15.** $f(x) = (x-2)(x - 3i)^3$
$[x - (1 + \sqrt{7})]^2$
**16.** $21 + (1 + \sqrt{3})i$   **17.** $-\frac{1}{17} + \frac{13}{17}i$
**18.** $\dfrac{\frac{16}{16}}{x} + \dfrac{-\frac{13}{32}}{x+4} + \dfrac{\frac{11}{32}}{x-4}$
**19.** $\dfrac{\frac{1}{4}}{x-1} + \dfrac{-\frac{1}{4}x - \frac{1}{4}}{x^2 + 3}$
**20.** $\dfrac{5}{x} + \dfrac{-1}{x-2} + \dfrac{3}{(x-2)^2}$

# CHAPTER 13
## Exercise Set 13.1
**27. (a)**

| $n$ | 1 | 2 | 3 | 4 | 5 |
|---|---|---|---|---|---|
| $f(n)$ | $\frac{1}{2}$ | $\frac{2}{3}$ | $\frac{3}{4}$ | $\frac{4}{5}$ | $\frac{5}{6}$ |

**(b)** $\frac{6}{7}$   **(c)** $f(n) = \dfrac{1}{1 \times 2} +$

$\dfrac{1}{2 \times 3} + \cdots + \dfrac{1}{n(n+1)} = \dfrac{n}{n+1}$

**29. (a)**

| $n$ | 1 | 2 | 3 | 4 | 5 |
|---|---|---|---|---|---|
| $f(n)$ | 1 | 4 | 9 | 16 | 25 |

**(b)** 36   **(c)** $f(n) = n^2$

## Exercise Set 13.2

**3.** 120 **5.** 105 **7. (a)** 10 **(b)** 5

**9.** $n^2 + 3n + 2$ **11.** 0

**13.** $a^9 + 9a^8b + 36a^7b^2 + 84a^6b^3 +$
$126a^5b^4 + 126a^4b^5 + 84a^3b^6 +$
$36a^2b^7 + 9ab^8 + b^9$

**15.** $8A^3 + 12A^2B + 6AB^2 + B^3$

**17.** $1 - 12x + 60x^2 - 160x^3 +$
$240x^4 - 192x^5 + 64x^6$

**19.** $x^2 + 4x\sqrt{xy} + 6xy + 4y\sqrt{xy} + y^2$

**21.** $x^{10} + 5x^8y^2 + 10x^6y^4 + 10x^4y^6 +$
$5x^2y^8 + y^{10}$

**23.** $1 - \dfrac{6}{x} + \dfrac{15}{x^2} - \dfrac{20}{x^3} + \dfrac{15}{x^4} - \dfrac{6}{x^5} + \dfrac{1}{x^6}$

**25.** $\dfrac{x^3}{8} - \dfrac{x^2y}{4} + \dfrac{xy^2}{6} - \dfrac{y^3}{27}$

**27.** $a^7b^{14} + 7a^6b^{12}c + 21a^5b^{10}c^2 +$
$35a^4b^8c^3 + 35a^3b^6c^4 + 21a^2b^4c^5 +$
$7ab^2c^6 + c^7$

**29.** $x^8 + 8\sqrt{2}x^7 + 56x^6 +$
$112\sqrt{2}x^5 + 280x^4 + 224\sqrt{2}x^3 +$
$224x^2 + 64\sqrt{2}x + 16$

**31.** $5\sqrt{2} - 7$ **33.** $89\sqrt{3} + 109\sqrt{2}$

**35.** $12 - 24\sqrt[3]{2} + 12\sqrt[3]{4}$

**37.** $x^{10} - 10x^9 + 35x^8 - 40x^7 -$
$30x^6 + 68x^5 + 30x^4 - 40x^3 -$
$35x^2 - 10x - 1$ **39.** $120a^2b^{14}$

**41.** $100x^{99}$ **43.** 45 **45.** 294912

**47.** 28 **49.** 40095

**53. (a)**

| $k$ | 0 | 1 | 2 | 3 | 4 | 5 | 6 | 7 | 8 |
|---|---|---|---|---|---|---|---|---|---|
| $\binom{8}{k}$ | 1 | 8 | 28 | 56 | 70 | 56 | 28 | 8 | 1 |

## Exercise Set 13.3

**1.** $\frac{1}{2}, \frac{2}{3}, \frac{3}{4}, \frac{4}{5}$ **3.** $-1, 1, -1, 1$

**5.** $\frac{1}{2}, \frac{1}{4}, \frac{1}{8}, \frac{1}{16}$ **7.** 3, 6, 9, 12,

**9.** $2, \frac{9}{4}, \frac{64}{27}, \frac{625}{256}$ **11.** $-1, 0, \frac{1}{3}, \frac{1}{2}$

**13.** $-2, 1, -\frac{8}{9}, 1$

**15.** 1, 4, 25, 676, 458329

**17.** 2, 2, 4, 8, 32 **19.** 1, 1, 2, 6, 24

**21.** 0, 1, 2, 4, 16

**23.**

**25.**

**27.**

**29.**

**31.**

**33.** 62 **35.** 40 **37.** $-\frac{19}{30}$ **39.** 903

**41.** 3 **43.** 41 **45.** $x + x^2 + x^3$

**47.** $\frac{25}{12}$ **49.** $-1$ **51.** $\frac{6}{7}$ **53.** $\sum\limits_{j=1}^{4} 5^j$

**55.** $\sum\limits_{j=1}^{6} x^j$ **57.** $\sum\limits_{k=1}^{12} \dfrac{1}{k}$

**59.** $\sum\limits_{j=1}^{5} (-1)^{j+1} 2^j$ **61.** $\sum\limits_{j=1}^{5} (-1)^{j+1} j$

**63. (a)**

| $t$ | 0 | 1 | 2 | 3 | 4 | 5 |
|---|---|---|---|---|---|---|
| $P_t$ | 300 | 1111 | 1829 | 1468 | 1691 | 1559 |

The population seems to be oscillating closer to a value near 1600.

**(b)**

| $t$ | $P_t$ | $t$ | $P_t$ |
|---|---|---|---|
| 0 | 300 | 11 | 1607 |
| 1 | 1111 | 12 | 1611 |
| 2 | 1829 | 13 | 1608 |
| 3 | 1468 | 14 | 1610 |
| 4 | 1691 | 15 | 1609 |
| 5 | 1559 | 16 | 1610 |
| 6 | 1640 | 17 | 1609 |
| 7 | 1591 | 18 | 1610 |
| 8 | 1621 | 19 | 1609 |
| 9 | 1602 | 20 | 1610 |
| 10 | 1614 | | |

**(c)** $P_{t-1} \approx 1609$
**65. (a)**

| $F_1$ | $F_2$ | $F_3$ | $F_4$ | $F_5$ | $F_6$ | $F_7$ | $F_8$ | $F_9$ | $F_{10}$ |
|---|---|---|---|---|---|---|---|---|---|
| 1 | 1 | 2 | 3 | 5 | 8 | 13 | 21 | 34 | 55 |

**(b)** $F_{22} = 17{,}711$; $F_{19} = 4181$
**(c)** $F_{30} = 832{,}040$   **71. (a)** $F_1 = 1$;
$F_2 = 1$   **(b)** $F_{24} = 46{,}368$; $F_{25} = 75{,}025$
**(c)** $F_{26} = 121{,}393$

## Exercise Set 13.4
**1. (a)** 2   **(b)** $-4$   **(c)** $\frac{1}{3}$   **(d)** $\sqrt{2}$
**3.** $a_{12} = 131$   **5.** $a_{100} = 501$
**7.** $a_{1000} = 998$   **9.** $d = \frac{11}{6}$; $a = -\frac{23}{2}$
**11.** $a = -190$   **13.** $d = -\frac{1}{8}$
**15.** $S_{1000} = 500{,}500$
**17.** $S_{13} = \dfrac{91\pi}{3}$   **19.** $a = \frac{1}{2}$
**21.** $S_{16} = -768$; $d = -\frac{104}{15}$
**23.** $d = \frac{6}{5}$; $a = -\frac{17}{5}$   **25.** 900
**27.** 2, 10, 18 or 18, 10, 2   **29.** $-1, 2,$
5 or 5, 2, $-1$   **31. (b)** $S_6 = -6 - 9\sqrt{2}$
**33.** $S_n = \dfrac{n}{2(1 - b)}[2 + (n - 3)\sqrt{b}]$

## Exercise Set 13.5
**1.** 6   **3.** 20; 100   **5.** $a_{100} = 1$
**7.** $a_8 = \frac{256}{6561}$   **9.** $r = \pm 4$
**11.** 7161   **13.** $63 + 31\sqrt{2}$   **15.** $\frac{1995}{64}$
**17.** $\frac{11111}{1000000} = 0.011111$   **19.** $\frac{2}{5}$
**21.** 101   **23.** $\frac{5}{9}$   **25.** $\frac{61}{495}$   **27.** $\frac{16}{37}$
**29.** $r = -\frac{1}{2}, -2$   **35.** 12 ft

## Exercise Set 13.6
**1.**

**3.**

**5.**

**7.**

**9.** $\sqrt{2} + \sqrt{2}i$   **11.** $-2\sqrt{3} + 2i$
**13.** $-1 - i$   **15.** $\sqrt{3}i$
**17.** $(\sqrt{6} - \sqrt{2}) + (\sqrt{6} + \sqrt{2})i$
**19.** $\cos(\pi/6) + i\sin(\pi/6)$
**21.** $2[\cos(2\pi/3) + i\sin(2\pi/3)]$
**23.** $4[\cos(7\pi/6) + i\sin(7\pi/6)]$
**25.** $6[\cos(3\pi/2) + i\sin(3\pi/2)]$
**27.** $\frac{1}{2}[\cos(11\pi/6) + i\sin(11\pi/6)]$
**29.** $3 + 3\sqrt{3}i$   **31.** $1 - \sqrt{3}i$
**33.** $3\sqrt{2}\cos(2\pi/7) + [3\sqrt{2}\sin(2\pi/7)]i$
**35.** $\dfrac{3\sqrt{2}}{2} + \dfrac{3\sqrt{2}}{2}i$   **37.** $\sqrt{3} + i$
**39.** 1   **41.** $\dfrac{243}{2} - \dfrac{243\sqrt{3}}{2}i$
**43.** $\dfrac{\sqrt{2}}{128} + \dfrac{\sqrt{2}}{128}i$   **45.** $-4i$
**47.** $-1 - i$   **49.** $\dfrac{1}{2} + \dfrac{\sqrt{3}}{2}i$
**51.** $128 + 128i$   **53.** $-128 + 128\sqrt{3}i$
**55.** $3i$, $-\frac{3}{2}\sqrt{3} - \frac{3}{2}i$, $\frac{3}{2}\sqrt{3} - \frac{3}{2}i$
**57.** $1, \frac{1}{2}\sqrt{2} + \frac{1}{2}\sqrt{2}i, i,$
$-\frac{1}{2}\sqrt{2} + \frac{1}{2}\sqrt{2}i, -1, -\frac{1}{2}\sqrt{2} - \frac{1}{2}\sqrt{2}i,$
$-i, \frac{1}{2}\sqrt{2} - \frac{1}{2}\sqrt{2}i$
**59.** $4, -2 + 2\sqrt{3}i, -2 - 2\sqrt{3}i$
**61.** $3, \frac{3}{2} + \frac{3}{2}\sqrt{3}i, -\frac{3}{2} + \frac{3}{2}\sqrt{3}i, -3,$
$-\frac{3}{2} - \frac{3}{2}\sqrt{3}i, \frac{3}{2} - \frac{3}{2}\sqrt{3}i$
**63.** 92,236,816
**65.** $0.95 + 0.31i, i, -0.95 + 0.31i,$
$-0.59 - 0.81i, 0.59 - 0.81i$
**67.** $\frac{1}{2}(\sqrt{6} - \sqrt{2}) + \frac{1}{2}(\sqrt{6} + \sqrt{2})i,$
$-\frac{1}{2}(\sqrt{6} + \sqrt{2}) + \frac{1}{2}(\sqrt{6} - \sqrt{2})i,$
$\frac{1}{2}(\sqrt{2} - \sqrt{6}) - \frac{1}{2}(\sqrt{2} + \sqrt{6})i$, and
$\frac{1}{2}(\sqrt{2} + \sqrt{6}) + \frac{1}{2}(\sqrt{2} - \sqrt{6})i$

**69. (a)** $1, -\frac{1}{2} + \frac{1}{2}\sqrt{3}i, -\frac{1}{2} - \frac{1}{2}\sqrt{3}i$
**71.** $-1$   **73.** 1

## Chapter 13 Review Exercises
**11.** $81a^4 + 108a^3b^2 +$
$54a^2b^4 + 12ab^6 + b^8$
**13.** $x^4 + 4x^3\sqrt{x} + 6x^3 + 4x^2\sqrt{x} + x^2$
**15.** $x^{10} - 10x^8y^2 + 40x^6y^4 - 80x^4y^6 +$
$80x^2y^8 - 32y^{10}$
**17.** $1 + \dfrac{5}{x} + \dfrac{10}{x^2} + \dfrac{10}{x^3} + \dfrac{5}{x^4} + \dfrac{1}{x^5}$
**19.** $a^4b^2 - 4a^3b^2\sqrt{ab} + 6a^3b^3 -$
$4a^2b^3\sqrt{ab} + a^2b^4$   **21.** $15xy^8$
**23.** 84   **25.** 28   **27.** Each side is 6.
**29.** Each side is 70.   **31.** Each side
is 8.   **33.** $1, \frac{4}{3}, \frac{3}{2}, \frac{8}{5}$

**35.** $-\frac{1}{2}, \frac{2}{3}, -\frac{3}{4}, \frac{4}{5}$

**37.** $-3, -12, -48, -192$
**39. (a)** $-5$   **(b)** $\frac{9}{10}$   **41.** $\displaystyle\sum_{k=1}^{5} \dfrac{5}{3k}$
**43.** $a_{18} = 73$   **45.** $a_{12} = \frac{5}{1024}$
**47.** $S_{12} = 177$
**49.** $S_{10} = 7{,}777{,}777{,}777$
**51.** $a_6 = -5\sqrt{10}$   **53.** $\frac{3}{4}$   **55.** $\frac{1}{10}$
**57.** $\frac{5}{11}$   **63. (a)** 42929   **(b)** 42925;
percent error: 0.00932%
**(c)** $6.48040 \times 10^{10}$
**(d)** $6.48027 \times 10^{10}$; percent error;
$2 \times 10^{-3}\%$
**65.** $r = \frac{1}{3}, 3, \dfrac{-8 \pm \sqrt{55}}{3}$

**73. (a)** 212993 **(b)** 103766 **(c)** $\frac{789}{512}$

**75.** $\frac{\sqrt{3}}{2} + \frac{1}{2}i$ **77.** $\frac{5\sqrt{2}}{2} - \frac{5\sqrt{2}}{2}i$

**79.** $3(\cos\frac{\pi}{2} + i\sin\frac{\pi}{2})$

**81.** $4(\cos\frac{11\pi}{6} + i\sin\frac{11\pi}{6})$

**83.** $6\sqrt{3} + 6i$ **85.** $\sqrt{6} + \sqrt{2}i$

**87.** $-16 + 16\sqrt{3}i$

**89.** $16384\sqrt{2} + 16384\sqrt{2}i$

**91.** $4i, -2\sqrt{3} - 2i, 2\sqrt{3} - 2i$

**93.** $\dfrac{\sqrt{2\sqrt{2}} + \sqrt{6\sqrt{2}}}{4} +$

$\dfrac{\sqrt{6\sqrt{2}} - \sqrt{2\sqrt{2}}}{4}i,$

$\dfrac{\sqrt{2\sqrt{2}} - \sqrt{6\sqrt{2}}}{4} +$

$\dfrac{\sqrt{6\sqrt{2}} + \sqrt{2\sqrt{2}}}{4}i,$

$\dfrac{-\sqrt{6\sqrt{2}} - \sqrt{2\sqrt{2}}}{4} +$

$\dfrac{\sqrt{2\sqrt{2}} - \sqrt{6\sqrt{2}}}{4}i,$

$\dfrac{\sqrt{6\sqrt{2}} - \sqrt{2\sqrt{2}}}{4} -$

$\dfrac{\sqrt{6\sqrt{2}} + \sqrt{2\sqrt{2}}}{4}i$

## Chapter 13 Test

**2. (a)** 27 **(b)** $-6$

**3. (a)** $S_n = \dfrac{a(1 - r^n)}{1 - r}$ **(b)** $\frac{174075}{1024}$

**4. (a)** 42240 **(b)** $5280a^7b^{12}$

**5.** $243x^{10} + 405x^8y^3 + 270x^6y^6 + 90x^4y^9 + 15x^2y^{12} + y^{15}$

**6.** 177 **7.** $\frac{7}{9}$ **8.** 5 and 27

**9.** $a_6 = -5\sqrt{10}$ **10.** 224

**11. (a)**

$a_n = \frac{1}{2}(n^2 - n)$

**(b)**

$b_1 = 1; b_n = (b_{n-1})^2 - nb_{n-1}$

**12.** $-1 + \sqrt{3}i$

**13.** $2[\cos(7\pi/4) + i\sin(7\pi/4)]$

**14.** $\frac{15}{2} + \frac{15}{2}\sqrt{3}i$ **15.** $2\sqrt{3} + 2i,$ $-2\sqrt{3} + 2i,$ and $-4i$

# APPENDIX B
## Exercise Set B.1

**1.** $-10$ **3.** $\frac{2}{3}$ **5. (a)** $a^{15}$

**(b)** $(a + 1)^{15}$ **(c)** $(a + 1)^{15}$

**7. (a)** $y^{11}$ **(b)** $(y + 1)^{11}$

**(c)** $(y + 1)^{18}$ **9. (a)** $x^2 + 3$

**(b)** $\dfrac{1}{x^2 + 3}$ **(c)** 12 **11. (a)** $t^6$ **(b)** $\dfrac{1}{t^6}$

**(c)** $(t^2 + 3)^6$ **13. (a)** $\dfrac{x^4}{y^5}$ **(b)** $\dfrac{y^5}{x^4}$

**(c)** $\dfrac{y^{10}}{x^8}$ **15. (a)** $4x^6$ **(b)** $16x^6$ **(c)** 4

**17. (a)** 1 **(b)** 1 **(c)** 1 **19. (a)** $\frac{11}{100}$

**(b)** $\frac{100}{11}$ **(c)** 1000 **21.** 7 **23. (a)** $\frac{1}{20}$

**(b)** $\frac{1}{225}$ **25.** $\dfrac{1}{a^6b^3}$ **27.** $\dfrac{a^4b^2}{c^6}$ **29.** $\dfrac{y^{12}}{x^6z^{12}}$

**31.** $\dfrac{y^{20}}{x^6z^{16}}$ **33.** $y^6$ **35.** $b$ **37.** $x^{2p}$

**39.** 576 **41.** 12 **43.** $9.29 \times 10^7$ miles

**45.** $6.68 \times 10^4$ mph

**47.** $2.5 \times 10^{19}$ miles

**49. (a)** $1.0 \times 10^{-9}$ seconds

**(b)** $1.0 \times 10^{-18}$ seconds

**(c)** $1.0 \times 10^{-24}$ seconds

## Exercise Set B.2

**1.** false **3.** true **5.** true **7.** true

**9. (a)** $-4$ **(b)** not a real number

**11. (a)** $\frac{2}{5}$ **(b)** $-\frac{2}{5}$ **13. (a)** not a real number **(b)** not a real number

**15. (a)** $\frac{4}{3}$ **(b)** $-\frac{3}{5}$ **17. (a)** $-2$

**(b)** 2 **19. (a)** $3\sqrt{2}$ **(b)** $3\sqrt[3]{2}$

**21. (a)** $7\sqrt{2}$ **(b)** $-2\sqrt[5]{2}$ **23. (a)** $\frac{5}{2}$

**(b)** $\frac{2}{5}$ **25. (a)** $3\sqrt{2}$ **(b)** $3\sqrt[3]{2}$

**27. (a)** $-4\sqrt{2}$ **(b)** $5\sqrt[4]{2}$

**29. (a)** 0.3 **(b)** 0.2 **31.** $-14\sqrt{6}$

**33.** $2\sqrt{2}$ **35. (a)** $6x$ **(b)** $-6y$

**37. (a)** $ab\sqrt{ab}$ **(b)** $a^2b^2$

**39.** $6ab^2c^2\sqrt{2ac}$ **41.** $2ab\sqrt[4]{b}$

**43.** $\dfrac{2a^4\sqrt[3]{2b^2}}{c^3}$ **45.** $\dfrac{4\sqrt{7}}{7}$ **47.** $\dfrac{\sqrt{2}}{4}$

**49.** $\dfrac{\sqrt{5} - 1}{4}$ **51.** $-2 - \sqrt{3}$

**53.** $\dfrac{61\sqrt{5}}{5}$ **55.** $\dfrac{\sqrt[3]{5}}{5}$ **57.** $\sqrt[4]{27}$

**59.** $\dfrac{3\sqrt[5]{2ab}}{2ab^2}$ **61. (a)** $\sqrt{3} - 1$

**(b)** $\sqrt{3} + 1$ **63. (a)** $\dfrac{x(\sqrt{x} + 2)}{x - 4}$

**(b)** $\dfrac{x(\sqrt{x} + y)}{x - y^2}$

**65. (a)** $\dfrac{x + 2\sqrt{2x} + 2}{x - 2}$

**(b)** $\dfrac{x + 2\sqrt{ax} + a}{x - a}$

**67.** $\dfrac{-2(\sqrt{x + h} + \sqrt{x})}{h}$

**69.** $\dfrac{\sqrt[3]{a^2} + \sqrt[3]{a} + 1}{a - 1}$ **71.** $\dfrac{1}{\sqrt{x} + \sqrt{5}}$

**73.** $\dfrac{1}{\sqrt{2 + h} - \sqrt{2}}$

**75.** $\dfrac{1}{\sqrt{x + h} + \sqrt{x}}$

**77.** $a = 9, b = 16$ **79.** $u = 1, v = 8$

**79. (a)** 1.645751

## Exercise Set B.3

**1.** $\sqrt[5]{a^3} = (\sqrt[5]{a})^3$ **3.** $\sqrt[3]{5^2} = (\sqrt[3]{5})^2$

**5.** $\sqrt[4]{(x^2 + 1)^3} = \sqrt[4]{(x^2 + 1)}^3$

**7.** $\sqrt[3]{2^{xy}} = (\sqrt[3]{2})^{xy}$ **9.** $p^{2/3}$

**11.** $(1 + u)^{4/7}$ **13.** $(a^2 + b^2)^{3/p}$

**15.** 4 **17.** $\frac{1}{6}$ **19.** not a real number

**21.** 5 **23.** 2 **25.** 4 **27.** $-2$

**29.** $-10$ **31.** $\frac{1}{7}$ **33.** not a real number **35.** $\frac{1}{216}$ **37.** 25 **39.** $-1$

**41.** $\frac{255}{16}$ **43.** $-\frac{28976}{243}$ **45.** $6a^{7/12}$

**47.** $2^{3/2}a^{1/12}$ **49.** $x^2 + 1$

**51. (a)** $2^{1/3}3^{5/6}$ **(b)** $\sqrt[6]{972}$

**53. (a)** $2^{7/12}\,3^{1/3}$   **(b)** $\sqrt[3]{10368}$
**55. (a)** $x^{2/3}\,y^{4/5}$   **(b)** $\sqrt[15]{x^{10}y^{12}}$
**57. (a)** $x^{(a+b)/3}$   **(b)** $\sqrt[3]{x^{a+b}}$
**59.** $(x+1)^{2/3}$   **(b)** $(x+y)^{2/5}$
**63.** $2x^{1/6}$   **65.** $x^{1/6}\,y^{1/8}$   **67.** $9^{10/9}$
**69.** $a=9,\,b=16$   **71.** $u=1,\,v=8$
**73.** $x=4,\,m=2$

## Exercise Set B.4

**1. (a)** $(x+8)(x-8)$   **(b)** $7x^2(x^2+2)$
**(c)** $z(11+z)(11-z)$
**(d)** $(ab+c)(ab-c)$
**3. (a)** $(x+3)(x-1)$
**(b)** $(x-3)(x+1)$   **(c)** irreducible
**(d)** $(-x+3)(x+1)$ or
$-(x-3)(x+1)$
**5. (a)** $(x+1)(x^2-x+1)$
**(b)** $(x+6)(x^2-6x+36)$
**(c)** $8(5-x^2)(25+5x^2+x^4)$
**(d)** $(4ax-5)(16a^2x^2+20ax+25)$
**7. (a)** $(12+x)(12-x)$
**(b)** irreducible   **(c)** $(9+y)(15-y)$
**9. (a)** $h^3(1+h)(1-h)$
**(b)** $h^3(10+h)(10-h)$
**(c)** $(h+1)^3(11+h)(9-h)$
**11. (a)** $(x-8)(x-5)$
**(b)** irreducible
**13. (a)** $(x+9)(x-4)$
**(b)** $(x-9)(x-4)$
**15. (a)** $(3x+2)(x-8)$
**(b)** irreducible
**17. (a)** $(3x-1)(2x+5)$
**(b)** $(6x+5)(x-1)$   **19. (a)** $(t^2+1)^2$
**(b)** $(t+1)^2(t-1)^2$   **(c)** irreducible

**21. (a)** $x(4x^2-20x-25)$
**(b)** $x(2x-5)^2$   **23. (a)** $(a-c)(b+a)$
**(b)** $(u+v-y)(x+u+v)$
**25.** $(xz+t)(xz+y)$   **27.** $(a^2-2b^2c^2)^2$
**29.** irreducible
**31.** $(x+4)(x^2-4x+16)$
**33.** $x(x^2+3xy+3y^2)$
**35.** $(x-y)(x^2+xy+y^2+1)$
**37. (a)** $(p^2+1)(p+1)(p-1)$
**(b)** $(p^4+1)(p^2+1)(p+1)(p-1)$
**39.** $(x+1)^3$   **41.** irreducible
**43.** $(\tfrac{5}{4}+c)(\tfrac{5}{4}-c)$
**45.** $(z^2+\tfrac{9}{4})(z+\tfrac{3}{2})(z-\tfrac{3}{2})$
**47.** $\left(\dfrac{5}{mn}-1\right)\left(\dfrac{25}{m^2n^2}+\dfrac{5}{mn}+1\right)$
**49.** $(\tfrac{1}{2}x+y)^2$
**51.** $(x-a)(8x-8a+1)\times$
$(8x-8a-1)$
**53.** $(x-y-a)(x-y+a)$
**55.** $x(7x-3)(3x+13)$
**57.** $(5-2x+3y)(5+2x-3y)$
**59.** $(ax+b)(x+1)$   **61.** $x(x+1)^{1/2}$
**63.** $x(x+1)^{-3/2}$   **65.** $-\tfrac{2}{3}x(2x+3)^{1/2}$
**67. (a)** $199$   **(b)** $296$   **(c)** $1999$
**69.** $(A+B)^3$
**71.** $x(a^2+x^2)^{-3/2}(2a^2+x^2)$
**73.** $(y^2-pq)(y-p)(y-q)$

## Exercise Set B.5

**1.** $x-3$   **3.** $\dfrac{1}{(x-2)(x^2+4)}$
**5.** $\dfrac{1}{x-2}$   **7.** $\dfrac{3b}{2a}$   **9.** $\dfrac{a^2+1}{a-1}$

**11.** $\dfrac{x^2+xy+y^2}{(x-y)^2}$   **13.** $2$
**15.** $\dfrac{x^2+x}{(x+4)(x-2)}$
**17.** $\dfrac{x^2-xy+y^2}{(x-y)(x+y)}$
**19.** $\dfrac{4x-2}{x^2}$   **21.** $\dfrac{36-a^2}{6a}$
**23.** $\dfrac{4x+11}{(x+3)(x+2)}$
**25.** $\dfrac{3x^2+6x-6}{(x-2)(x+2)}$
**27.** $\dfrac{6ax^2-4ax+a}{(x-1)^3}$   **29.** $\dfrac{8}{x-5}$
**31.** $\dfrac{2a}{a+b}$   **33.** $\dfrac{-9}{(x+5)(x-4)^2}$
**35.** $\dfrac{-p^2-pq-q^2}{p(2p+q)(p-5q)}$   **37.** $\dfrac{1+x}{1-x}$
**39.** $-\dfrac{1}{ax}$   **41.** $a-1$   **43.** $-\dfrac{1}{4+2h}$
**45.** $\dfrac{a+x}{a^2x^2}$   **47.** $\dfrac{x}{1+2x}$   **49.** $\dfrac{1}{a+a^2}$
**51.** $\dfrac{x^2+y^2}{x^2-y^2}$   **53.** $\dfrac{a^2-h^2}{2}$
**55.** $\left(\dfrac{a}{b}\right)^{a+b}$

# RESULTS FROM GEOMETRY

| | |
|---|---|
| **Triangle**<br>Area $= \frac{1}{2}bh$  | **Circle**<br>Area $= \pi r^2$<br>Circumference $= 2\pi r$  |
| **Trapezoid**<br>Area $= \frac{h}{2}(a + b)$  | **Parallelogram**<br>Area $= bh$  |
| **Rectangular Box**<br>Volume $= lwh$<br>Surface area $= 2wh + 2lh + 2wl$  | **Sphere**<br>Volume $= \frac{4}{3}\pi r^3$<br>Surface area $= 4\pi r^2$  |
| **Right Circular Cylinder**<br>Volume $= \pi r^2 h$<br>Lateral surface area $= 2\pi rh$  | **Right Circular Cone**<br>Volume $= \frac{1}{3}\pi r^2 h$<br>Lateral surface area $= \pi r\sqrt{r^2 + h^2}$  |

- The sum of the angles in a triangle is 180°.

- Two sides of a triangle are equal if and only if the angles opposite those sides are equal.

- In a 30°-60° right triangle, the length of the side opposite the 30° angle is half the length of the hypotenuse.

**THE PYTHAGOREAN THEOREM:** In a right triangle, the square of the length of the hypotenuse equals the sum of the squares of the lengths of the other two sides.

**HERON'S FORMULA:** If $a, b,$ and $c$ are the lengths of the sides of a triangle, then the area of the triangle is

$$\sqrt{s(s - a)(s - b)(s - c)}$$

where

$$s = \tfrac{1}{2}(a + b + c)$$

## THEOREMS FOR PROVING THAT TWO TRIANGLES ARE CONGRUENT:

1. If two sides and the included angle of one triangle are equal respectively to two sides and the included angle of another triangle, then the triangles are congruent.

2. If two angles and the included side of one triangle are equal respectively to two angles and the included side of another triangle, then the triangles are congruent.

3. If the three sides of one triangle are equal respectively to the three sides of another triangle, then the triangles are congruent.

## THEOREMS FOR PROVING THAT TWO TRIANGLES ARE SIMILAR:

1. If two angles of one triangle are equal respectively to two angles of another triangle, then the triangles are similar.

2. If the corresponding sides of two triangles are proportional, then the triangles are similar.

# GRAPHS

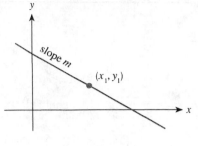

$$y - y_1 = m(x - x_1)$$

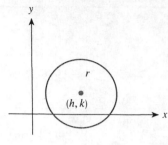

$$(x - h)^2 + (y - k)^2 = r^2$$

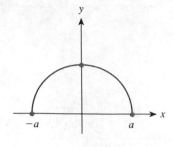

$$y = \sqrt{a^2 - x^2}$$

$$y = |x|$$

$$y = x^2$$

$$y = x^3$$

$$y = \sqrt{x}$$

$$y = \frac{1}{x}$$

$$y = [\![x]\!]$$

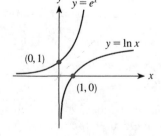

$$y = e^x \quad \text{and} \quad y = \ln x$$

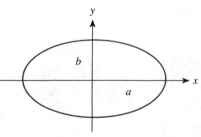

$$\frac{x^2}{a^2} + \frac{y^2}{b^2} = 1$$

$$\frac{x^2}{a^2} - \frac{y^2}{b^2} = 1$$

# FACTORING TECHNIQUES

| TECHNIQUE | EXAMPLE OR FORMULA |
|---|---|
| Common factor | $3x^4 + 6x^3 - 12x^2 = 3x^2(x^2 + 2x - 4)$ |
| | $4(x^2 + 1) - x(x^2 + 1) = (x^2 + 1)(4 - x)$ |
| Difference of squares | $x^2 - a^2 = (x - a)(x + a)$ |
| Trial and error | $x^2 + 2x - 3 = (x + 3)(x - 1)$ |
| Difference of cubes | $x^3 - a^3 = (x - a)(x^2 + ax + a^2)$ |
| Sum of cubes | $x^3 + a^3 = (x + a)(x^2 - ax + a^2)$ |
| Grouping | $\begin{aligned} x^3 - x^2 + x - 1 &= (x^3 - x^2) + (x - 1) \\ &= x^2(x - 1) + (x - 1) \\ &= (x - 1)(x^2 + 1) \end{aligned}$ |

# FORMULAS FROM COORDINATE GEOMETRY

1. The distance formula: $d = \sqrt{(x_2 - x_1)^2 + (y_2 - y_1)^2}$

2. The equation for a circle: $(x - h)^2 + (y - k)^2 = r^2$

3. The definition of slope: $m = \dfrac{y_2 - y_1}{x_2 - x_1}$

4. The point–slope formula: $y - y_1 = m(x - x_1)$

5. The slope–intercept formula: $y = mx + b$

6. The condition for two nonvertical lines to be parallel: $m_1 = m_2$

7. The condition for two nonvertical lines to be perpendicular: $m_1 m_2 = -1$

8. The midpoint formula: $\left( \dfrac{x_1 + x_2}{2}, \dfrac{y_1 + y_2}{2} \right)$

# PROPERTIES OF LOGARITHMS

In the following properties, $b$, $P$, and $Q$ are positive and $b \neq 1$.

1. (a) $\log_b b = 1$    (b) $\log_b 1 = 0$

2. $\log_b PQ = \log_b P + \log_b Q$

3. $\log_b (P/Q) = \log_b P - \log_b Q$

4. $\log_b P^n = n \log_b P$

5. $b^{\log_b P} = P$

6. $\log_b b^x = x$

# THE GREEK ALPHABET

| | | | | | |
|---|---|---|---|---|---|
| A | $\alpha$ | Alpha | H | $\eta$ | Eta |
| B | $\beta$ | Beta | $\Theta$ | $\theta$ | Theta |
| $\Gamma$ | $\gamma$ | Gamma | I | $\iota$ | Iota |
| $\Delta$ | $\delta$ | Delta | K | $\kappa$ | Kappa |
| E | $\varepsilon$ | Epsilon | $\Lambda$ | $\lambda$ | Lambda |
| Z | $\zeta$ | Zeta | M | $\mu$ | Mu |
| N | $\nu$ | Nu | T | $\tau$ | Tau |
| $\Xi$ | $\xi$ | Xi | Y | $\upsilon$ | Upsilon |
| O | $o$ | Omicron | $\Phi$ | $\phi, \varphi$ | Phi |
| P | $\rho$ | Rho | X | $\chi$ | Chi |
| $\Pi$ | $\pi$ | Pi | $\Psi$ | $\psi$ | Psi |
| $\Sigma$ | $\sigma$ | Sigma | $\Omega$ | $\omega$ | Omega |

# PRINCIPAL TRIGONOMETRIC IDENTITIES

## 1. CONSEQUENCES OF THE DEFINITIONS

**(a)** $\csc\theta = \dfrac{1}{\sin\theta}$
**(b)** $\sec\theta = \dfrac{1}{\cos\theta}$
**(c)** $\cot\theta = \dfrac{1}{\tan\theta}$
**(d)** $\tan\theta = \dfrac{\sin\theta}{\cos\theta}$
**(e)** $\cot\theta = \dfrac{\cos\theta}{\sin\theta}$

## 2. THE PYTHAGOREAN IDENTITIES

**(a)** $\sin^2\theta + \cos^2\theta = 1$
**(b)** $\tan^2\theta + 1 = \sec^2\theta$
**(c)** $\cot^2\theta + 1 = \csc^2\theta$

## 3. THE OPPOSITE-ANGLE FORMULAS

**(a)** $\sin(-\theta) = -\sin\theta$
**(b)** $\cos(-\theta) = \cos\theta$
**(c)** $\tan(-\theta) = -\tan\theta$

## 4. THE REDUCTION FORMULAS

**(a)** $\sin(\theta + 2\pi k) = \sin\theta$
**(b)** $\cos(\theta + 2\pi k) = \cos\theta$
**(c)** $\sin\left(\dfrac{\pi}{2} - \theta\right) = \cos\theta$

**(d)** $\cos\left(\dfrac{\pi}{2} - \theta\right) = \sin\theta$

## 5. THE ADDITION FORMULAS

**(a)** $\sin(s + t) = \sin s \cos t + \cos s \sin t$
**(b)** $\sin(s - t) = \sin s \cos t - \cos s \sin t$

**(c)** $\cos(s + t) = \cos s \cos t - \sin s \sin t$
**(d)** $\cos(s - t) = \cos s \cos t + \sin s \sin t$

**(e)** $\tan(s + t) = \dfrac{\tan s + \tan t}{1 - \tan s \tan t}$
**(f)** $\tan(s - t) = \dfrac{\tan s - \tan t}{1 + \tan s \tan t}$

## 6. THE DOUBLE-ANGLE FORMULAS

**(a)** $\sin 2\theta = 2 \sin\theta \cos\theta$
**(b)** $\cos 2\theta = \cos^2\theta - \sin^2\theta$
**(c)** $\tan 2\theta = \dfrac{2 \tan\theta}{1 - \tan^2\theta}$

## 7. THE HALF-ANGLE FORMULAS

**(a)** $\sin\dfrac{\theta}{2} = \pm\sqrt{\dfrac{1 - \cos\theta}{2}}$
**(b)** $\cos\dfrac{\theta}{2} = \pm\sqrt{\dfrac{1 + \cos\theta}{2}}$
**(c)** $\tan\dfrac{\theta}{2} = \dfrac{\sin\theta}{1 + \cos\theta}$

## 8. THE PRODUCT-TO-SUM FORMULAS

**(a)** $\sin A \sin B = \tfrac{1}{2}[\cos(A - B) - \cos(A + B)]$
**(b)** $\sin A \cos B = \tfrac{1}{2}[\sin(A + B) + \sin(A - B)]$

**(c)** $\cos A \cos B = \tfrac{1}{2}[\cos(A + B) + \cos(A - B)]$

## 9. THE SUM-TO-PRODUCT FORMULAS

**(a)** $\sin\alpha + \sin\beta = 2 \sin\dfrac{\alpha + \beta}{2} \cos\dfrac{\alpha - \beta}{2}$
**(b)** $\sin\alpha - \sin\beta = 2 \cos\dfrac{\alpha + \beta}{2} \sin\dfrac{\alpha - \beta}{2}$

**(c)** $\cos\alpha + \cos\beta = 2 \cos\dfrac{\alpha + \beta}{2} \cos\dfrac{\alpha - \beta}{2}$
**(d)** $\cos\alpha - \cos\beta = -2 \sin\dfrac{\alpha + \beta}{2} \sin\dfrac{\alpha - \beta}{2}$

# GRAPHS OF THE TRIGONOMETRIC FUNCTIONS

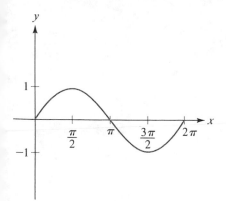

$y = \sin x$
Period: $2\pi$
Amplitude: 1

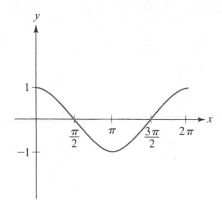

$y = \cos x$
Period: $2\pi$
Amplitude: 1

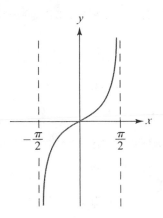

$y = \tan x$
Period: $\pi$

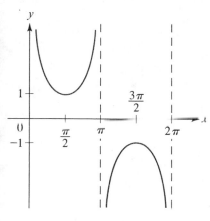

$y = \csc x$
Period: $2\pi$

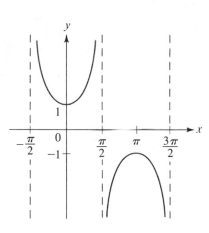

$y = \sec x$
Period: $2\pi$

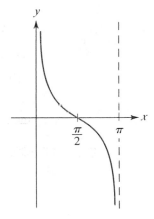

$y = \cot x$
Period: $\pi$

$y = \sin^{-1} x$

$y = \cos^{-1} x$

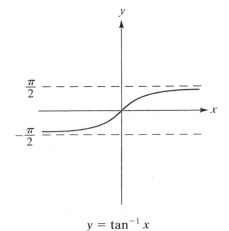

$y = \tan^{-1} x$

# Index